FIELDS OF READING

Motives for Writing

W9-BDN-118

EIGHTH EDITION

FIELDS OF READING

Motives for Writing

NANCY R. COMLEY
Queens College, CUNY

DAVID HAMILTON
University of Iowa

CARL H. KLAUS
University of Iowa

ROBERT SCHOLES
Brown University

NANCY SOMMERS
Harvard University

BEDFORD/ST. MARTIN'S   Boston ◆ New York

For Bedford/St. Martin's

Senior Developmental Editor: John Sullivan
Editorial Assistant: Jennifer Lyford
Senior Production Supervisor: Joe Ford
Marketing Manager: Karita dos Santos
Project Management: Books By Design, Inc.
Cover Design: Stephen Gleason Design
Cover Art: Cindy Lupi, *Blue Mountain*. By permission of Cindy Lupi, Marble Hill
  GA. *jli43559@aol.com*
Composition: Books By Design, Inc.
Printing and Binding: RR Donnelley & Sons, Inc.

President: Joan E. Feinberg
Editorial Director: Denise B. Wydra
Editor in Chief: Karen S. Henry
Director of Marketing: Karen Melton Soeltz
Director of Editing, Design, and Production: Marcia Cohen
Manager, Publishing Services: Emily Berleth

Library of Congress Control Number: 2006927526

Manufactured in the United States of America.

2 1 0 9 8 7
f e d c b a

For information, write: Bedford/St. Martin's, 75 Arlington Street, Boston, MA 02116
(617-399-4000)

ISBN-10: 0-312-44693-4
ISBN-13: 978-1-312-44693-2

Acknowledgments

Acknowledgments and copyrights appear at the back of the book on pages 810–814,
which constitute an extension of the copyright page.

Preface

The title *Fields of Reading: Motives for Writing* identifies our goal of providing students with tools to establish and develop their own motives for writing throughout their college years and professional lives. We believe that in order to become good writers, students must *read* good writing. Therefore, this eighth edition of *Fields of Reading* contains seventy-eight readings from a broad range of academic, professional, and literary writing. These readings come from a variety of sources. *Fields of Reading* draws on the major divisions of the curriculum—arts and humanities, social sciences and public affairs, and sciences and technologies—to present well-crafted and high-quality writing from these fields. It presents important readings by key voices in contemporary intellectual life—the kind of thought-provoking pieces one expects to encounter in college. In every field, students are exposed to key motives for writing. They see writers considering past experience (reflecting), conveying information (reporting), making sense of knowledge (explaining), and debating controversial ideas and issues (arguing).

Highlights of the Eighth Edition

Newly Organized by Academic Field. *Fields of Reading* has been reorganized into three academic fields—arts and humanities, social sciences and public affairs, and sciences and technologies—in order to highlight the cross-curricular nature of the book. In each of these three areas, we further divide the selections into four rhetorical categories—Reflecting, Reporting, Explaining, and Arguing—which represent essential kinds of reading and writing in virtually every academic or professional area. The unique dual organization by academic discipline and rhetorical purpose helps students to understand how subject, intent, and audience influence the form and style of their own writing.

New Reading Selections. Of the seventy-one prose selections, twenty-four are new to the eighth edition. These pieces represent a diverse array of well-known thinkers, critics, and scholars writing on timely and interesting topics. Selected because of their superior writing, the pieces represent a wide range of intellectual areas and include works by authors such as Monica M. Moore, Oliver Sacks, Jane van Lawick-Goodall, and Emily Martin. The collection encompasses a variety of genres and includes four documented essays. Also included among the selections are six new stories and one new poem that were chosen as models of rhetorical effectiveness and grouped under the same rhetorical and cross-curricular categories as their prose counterparts. In each unit, paired readings (newly marked in the table of contents) help students make thematic connections and see more than one side of an issue, giving them a richer perspective on important ideas.

Newly Revised Introduction. The introduction explains and illustrates the relationship between reading and writing. It now defines each of the four purposes for writing: Reflecting, Reporting, Explaining, and Arguing (which are illustrated by passages from the anthologized readings). It identifies and explains the rhetorical methods used to achieve each type of writing's aims, such as how description and narration are basic to reporting or how analogy, definition, and illustration are basic to explaining. We have included guidelines for acknowledging sources, including the broad issues of how to evaluate potential source materials and how to use them in a piece of writing. This section focuses particularly on sources drawn from the Web, because those sources pose the greatest pitfalls for students who might be uncertain of how to judge the relative worth of online material and incorporate it appropriately, with proper acknowledgment, in their own writing.

Extensive Critical Apparatus. Much of our critical apparatus focuses on the rhetorical concepts and techniques that apply to reading and writing across the curriculum as introduced in the prefatory note "For Students" (p. xxv). These materials, like the rest of the book, are meant to present reading and writing not in abstract terms, but through discussion and examples that vividly demonstrate what is actually involved in each activity. The headnote for each piece identifies and, wherever necessary, explains the professional fields of its author and the rhetorical context or source of its original publication. Similarly, the questions following each selection call for reading and writing that relate form and style to purpose, subject, and academic field. The Making Connections questions following selections also encourage students to explore relationships between and among readings.

Thematic Connections. For instructors who prefer to teach the selections by theme, we have grouped all of the selections by thematically related clusters. Any selection can be taught in terms of its themes or area of interest by using the updated Thematic Contents (p. xvii), which includes clusters on such topics as Cultures in Contact and Collision; Education; Race; and

Gender and Women's Experiences. As a result, students will have ample opportunity to read and consider different perspectives on a single issue or explore a particular issue in depth.

Rhetorical Index. For those instructors who wish to teach the selections using a traditional modes-based approach, the rhetorical index (p. 815) organizes the selections by such categories as analogy, comparison and contrast, definition, description, and narration.

Print and New Media Resources

Instructor's Manual. This manual, written by the editors, contains an introduction outlining four approaches to teaching with the book (curricular, thematic, rhetorical, and formalistic) and practical guidance for teaching each selection.

Companion Web site at bedfordstmartins.com/fields. The site includes TopLinks to help students further explore the issues in *Fields of Reading* and find out what other people have to say about those potential writing topics. It also includes a free, printable version of the instructor's manual.

Re:Writing Web site. Visit bedfordstmartins.com/rewriting for the best online collection of free, open, and easy-to-access resources for the writing class. Here you'll find plagiarism tutorials, model documents, style and grammar exercises, visual analysis activities, research guides, bibliography tools, and much more.

Interactive CD-ROMs available free when packaged with *Fields of Reading*. "I-Claim: Visualizing Argument" helps students see how argument works with six tutorials, an illustrated glossary, and more than seventy multimedia arguments. "I-Cite: Visualizing Sources" brings research to life through an animated introduction, four tutorials, and hands-on source practice.

Acknowledgments

For their detailed reactions to the seventh edition of *Fields of Reading* and suggestions for improving the book, we are grateful to the following reviewers: Valerie K. Anderson, York College; James Barilla, University of California, Davis; Cynthia Bates, University of California, Davis; Glenn Blalock, Texas Christian University; Mary Bly, University of California, Davis; Jeff Calkins, Tacoma Community College; Joe Campaña, University of Montana; Janice Cline, York College; Frances S. Davidson, Mercer County Community College; Helen Duclos, Arkansas State University; Mary Elfring, Elgin Community College; Jennifer Gandel, University of

Alabama; Don Gilliland, University of Alabama; Christine Herron-Pipitone, Raritan Valley Community College; Mike Jackson, Saint Bonaventure University; Mitchell Jackson, New York University School of Continuing and Professional Studies; Natalie Jones, University of Alabama; Megan King, University of Alabama; Tamara Kuzmenkov, Tacoma Community College; Todd Laufenberg, Waubonsee Community College; Susan Lonac, Whatcom Community College; Jeanne McDonald, Waubonsee Community College; Nancy B. McGowan, Boise State University; Eleanor Montero, Daytona Beach Community College; Gary Negin, California State University; Teri Pastore, Portland Community College/Rock Creek; Chris P. Pearce, Boston University; Barbara G. Pogue, Essex County College; Anna Purves, Lehman College; Kate Ryan, University of Montana; Robin Schore, Mercer County Community College; Kathleen Schroeder, California State University, San Bernardino; Ann Selby, Portland Community College; Ann Tabachnikov, Lehman College; John Weser, Santa Rosa Junior College; Angus Woodward, Our Lady of the Lake College; David Wright, Mt. Hood Community College; and Dennis Young, George Mason University.

Finally, we would like to thank our editor, John Sullivan, as well as the other staff members of Bedford/St. Martin's for their help and encouragement, in particular, Joan Feinberg, President; Denise Wydra, Editorial Director; Karen Henry, Editor in Chief, Boston; Steve Scipione, Executive Editor; Nancy Perry, Editor in Chief, New York; Karita dos Santos, Marketing Manager; Jennifer Lyford, Editorial Assistant; Marcia Cohen, Director/ Editing, Design and Manufacturing; Emily Berleth, Manager, Publishing Services; and Sandy Schechter, Permissions Manager. We are grateful to Terri Walton for updating and writing headnotes. We are also grateful to Alison Fields, production editor; Diane Kraut, text permissions editor; Linda McLatchie, copy editor; and Helane Probst, art permissions editor.

N. R. C.
D. H.
C. H. K.
R. S.
N. S.

Contents

ARTS AND HUMANITIES

REFLECTING IN THE Arts and Humanities   43

Maya Angelou, *Graduation*   43
  An eminent African American writer recalls her graduation from a racially segregated junior high school.

Alice Walker, *Beauty: When the Other Dancer Is the Self*   54
  A novelist and essayist recalls her changing reactions to a painful childhood injury.

Explaining in the Arts and Humanities 190

Arguing in the Arts and Humanities 268

SOCIAL SCIENCES AND PUBLIC AFFAIRS

SCIENCES AND TECHNOLOGIES

PAIRED READINGS

PAIRED READINGS

PAIRED READINGS

Thematic Contents

CULTURES IN CONTACT AND COLLISION

EDUCATION

ETHICS, VALUES, AND BELIEFS

FAMILY

HISTORY AND INTERPRETING THE PAST

HUMAN PORTRAITS

IDENTITY

VIOLENCE AND WAR

For Students

Fields of Reading: Motives for Writing, eighth edition, is intended to help you develop the abilities in reading and writing that you will need as you move from one course to another, one field of study to another, throughout your college career. In some senses, of course, all areas of study expect the same things of you—namely, close and careful reading as well as clear and exact writing, with an attentiveness above all to information and ideas. But the particular kinds of information, ideas, and concerns that distinguish each field of study also call for somewhat different reading and writing abilities. A book review for a literature course, for example, requires a different form and style from a lab report in physics. So we have tried to give you a sampling of the varied fields of writing you are likely to encounter in the academic world.

Most undergraduate schools are organized around some version of the traditional division of studies into "the humanities," "the social sciences," and "the sciences." The humanities generally include fields of learning that are thought of as having a cultural orientation, such as language, literature, history, philosophy, and religion. The social sciences, which include such fields as anthropology, economics, education, political science, psychology, and sociology, deal with social institutions and the behavior of their individual members. The sciences include fields of knowledge that are concerned with the natural and physical world, such as astronomy, botany, chemistry, physics, and zoology.

These traditional divisions of study are closely affiliated with applied areas of study and work that also exist in the professional world. The humanities, for example, are closely allied with the arts; the social sciences, with public affairs such as business and government; and the sciences, with technology. These divisions and clusterings of fields—Arts and Humanities, Social Sciences and Public Affairs, Sciences and Technologies—are so broadly applicable that we have used them as the major organizing principle in our table of contents.

Like any set of categories, these divisions are a convenient, but by no means foolproof, system of classification. Although the system can help you understand the academic world, it does not reflect the exact state of affairs in every specialized field at every college and university. Specialists in a particular field sometimes migrate from one area of learning to another, from the social sciences to the sciences, for example, according to the orientation of their research in a particular project. Or specialists from several fields may form an interdisciplinary area of research, such as environmental studies, which involves a wide range of academic disciplines—botany, chemistry, economics, philosophy, political science, and zoology. So the writing that results from these projects often can be categorized in more than one broad area of learning.

The writing we have collected in *Fields of Reading* can be understood not only in terms of the area of learning that it represents, but also in terms of the particular purpose it is meant to achieve. Every piece of writing, of course, is the product of an author's personal and professional motives, so in a sense the purposes for writing are as varied and ultimately mysterious as are authors themselves. But setting aside the mysteries of human nature, it is possible to identify and define a set of different purposes for writing, which we refer to as Reflecting, Reporting, Explaining, and Arguing, one or another of which predominates in most academic and professional writing. Therefore, we have used this set of purposes as the second organizing principle in our table of contents.

By Reflecting, we mean a kind of writing in which authors are concerned with recalling and thinking about their past experience, for personal experience is often an especially valuable source of knowledge and learning. By Reporting, we mean writing that is concerned primarily with conveying factual information about some particular aspect of the world, past or present. By Explaining, we mean writing that is concerned primarily with making sense of information or shedding light on a particular subject. By Arguing, we mean writing that is given to debating controversial explanations, values, or beliefs. Like our other categories, these are convenient, but not rigid, modes of classification. So they need to be used tactfully, with an awareness that to some degree they are bound to overlap. Most pieces of explanation, for example, will at some point involve reporting, if only to convey the information or subject to be explained. And most pieces of argument will call for some explanation, if only to make clear the issues that are at odds with one another. But generally you will find one or another of these purposes to be dominant in any particular piece of writing.

We think that an awareness of these basic purposes can be especially helpful both in the process of reading and in the process of writing, no matter what academic or professional field is involved. The introduction that follows provides an overview of Reflecting, Reporting, Explaining, and Arguing. In it you will find detailed definitions and examples of each purpose, as well as explanations and illustrations of how to carry it out in differing fields and situations. We also discuss various ways to read and understand the pieces in this book or any other material you might encounter in your studies. First, we discuss how to evaluate, incorporate, and document source materials and why such acknowledgment is important in every field of study. This introduction, like the headnotes and questions that accompany each essay, is meant to help you become a thoughtful and responsible reader and writer. The rest is up to your instructor, your classmates, and you.

FIELDS OF READING
Motives for Writing

Introduction

In assembling this book, we have sought out readings that engage us and that we hope will be of interest to you. Among them you will find many that discussion makes richer. You should also find several that provoke you to write. For no matter what your field of study, you will need to read and write. Often you will need to read critically, and your writing will prosper as it gains clarity, vigor, and argumentative force. This book brings together many readings with those goals in mind. Of course, a textbook is intended for the classroom and study, but should you carry it with you on vacation or keep it by your bed, we would not be shocked.

Writers become writers by reading writers who have gone before them. Writers take an active rather than a passive interest in the work of their predecessors. Such an interest leads to ideas of how to write as well as how to correct and extend earlier work, for in whatever discipline, writing lays down the record of our cultural advance. This reader invites you to enter that process, so we begin with a few observations about the relationship of reading and writing, and their importance in various academic fields.

From Reading to Writing

Reading precedes writing, and that has always been the case because writing is inconceivable without an idea of it derived from earlier writing. But there must have been a first instance, you say, and indeed that must be so. A curious experiment is to imagine that first writing, the very first instance, and to try to grasp the idea that first writer followed. Was he a hunter who had grown accustomed to reading tracks in sand and mud and who had discovered the advantage of being especially observant? Or was she a navigator who had grown familiar with informative patterns in the stars? Did the gash of lightning down a tree trunk suggest a mark a human might make? How long did it take for human observation — our earliest reading — to suggest runes, ideograms, hieroglyphs, and letters? Our era comes long after that moment, and so we write guided by an abundance of examples. It seems inconceivable, though, to imagine a first writer who awoke one day saying, simply, "I shall make writing," without any prior experience — indeed, sophisticated experience — of reading something, probably something in nature.

Writing as Conversation

But we come long after that primordial moment, and all our writing owes much to written texts that came before. This is especially true of professional and academic writing, subsets of which devote themselves to particular subjects and often to highly specialized methods of investigation. If you think of the relation of any one instance of such writing to that which preceded it, and to more that will follow, you can sense a conversation in which speakers respond to one another. Sometimes that conversation is a debate in which one writer confronts and argues with another. More often, later writers add to a conversation by extending and enlarging its subject.

"In form of speech is change," Geoffrey Chaucer wrote over six hundred years ago. "And words that once had value now wander into usage we find strange." We paraphrase from his long poem "Troilus and Criseyde," because his exact words in Middle English have themselves wandered off into territory somewhat foreign to modern readers. Centuries later, George Orwell entered that conversation with his essay "Politics and the English Language" and its concern for the degradation of language as propaganda — social, political, and commercial — bears witness to increasingly insidious ways of promoting doubtful versions of the truth. James Baldwin and Leslie Marmon Silko do not address Orwell's particular concerns, or Chaucer's, but their reflections on black English and Pueblo storytelling add to an ongoing conversation about the nature of language and its place in culture. We have recognized that conversation and have given some shape to it ourselves through the various editions of this reader by selecting Orwell's essay for an early edition, adding Baldwin later, and now bringing Silko into it as well as mentioning Chaucer.

We can think of Chaucer, Silko, Baldwin, and Orwell as taking part in a long-running conversation, and we can say that it takes place within the disciplinary framework of English studies or language and culture. The written conversations most of us enter into in college and professional life tend to occur within disciplinary structures such as economics or history or biology or political science. Consequently, writing has long been recognized as a subject that deserves close attention all across the university curriculum. English majors need to write, but so do majors in marketing, psychology, and physics. And while all that writing springs from a core facility with a language, in our case English, it also takes significantly diverging forms as writers specialize. This reader attempts to illustrate the core of usage that generates most of our writing as well as something of the paths toward specialization our writing can follow. So it is that we illustrate the activities of Reflecting, Reporting, Explaining, and Arguing in the broad subject areas of the Arts and Humanities, Social Sciences and Public Affairs, and the Sciences and Technologies.

Modes of Writing and Thinking

By conceiving our anthology in this way, we suggest that our first four categories are the constants, and the subject areas are the variables; that is, Reflecting and its companion terms describe mental acts — modes of writing we will call them — that take place within each different discipline. In other words, we can practice Reflecting or Reporting while engaging any particular discipline, but we may not so readily combine a movie review with laboratory science. It is not that each mode of writing is absolutely different from all the others. Obviously the lines between them blur, and most writing blends several ways of paying attention and of thinking. In fact, the set of them makes sense as a continuum in which one kind of writing leads naturally to another. Where to enter that continuum — where to begin — is itself an intriguing puzzle.

The Modes as a Continuum

In this anthology, we have always begun with Reflection. Literally, the word means "bending back," as in reversing the flow of a ray of light. And so we associate the practice with looking back on an event, or an idea, or a finding, after we have gained some distance from it. The word suggests that moment of tranquillity, after the storm, when we are better able to understand what all the bother was about. Thus we begin with a kind of paradox: the poised, backward-looking nature of Reflecting suggests the last and most sophisticated stage in a series of modes, not the introductory and the first stage.

Thinking about writing often leads into enigmas of this sort. Imagining that the first writer could not possibly have observed prior writing but must in some sense have known it is another such enigma. Indeed, reflective writing, our point of departure, is the mode generally associated with literature and so with what we are apt to think of as writing at its finest, such as the soliloquies of Hamlet. At the same time, it is the most intimate and personal of the four modes, and the evidence it offers for the conclusions it draws tends to be the most subjective. In that sense, Reflecting begins where we all begin, as writers summoning what resources we can from within ourselves.

We begin with Reflecting because it emphasizes our personal relation to writing, the vantage from which we set off. It may be the easiest mode of writing because we can all find something to say about experiences we have had. But rather than thinking of it as easy and introductory, let us imagine our continuum of modes as a spiral. Reflecting leads to Reporting, which leads to Explaining, which leads to Arguing, which leads back to Reflecting as we reconsider the reports, explanations, and arguments we have made. Seen this way, writing seems to demand a series of graduations as the stakes for the writer increase. You can learn to satisfy your readers with the full- ness and accuracy of your reports and with the clarity of your explanations. Now and then, if you work at it, you will even find that readers will agree that you have made your case and won an argument. However, as you come around to Reflecting again, assuming you have become absorbed in your work, no one — least of all you as the writer — can possibly say that you have ever reflected enough. But then you can always make a fuller re- port, explain in more detail, add nuance and subtlety to your arguments, and so we go around again. Let us slow down here and examine each mode of writing and thinking in more detail.

Reflecting

In the several "Reflecting" sections of this anthology, you will en- counter writing that touches on numerous topics: a high school graduation in Arkansas, a sacred landmark in Oklahoma, working at the factory where the Enola Gay was constructed, being a doctor confronting the AIDS epi- demic in Haiti, to name just a few. You will find that the writing in these sections relies heavily on personal experience, which, after all, is a basic source of our knowledge and understanding. If you think about someone you have known for a long time or about a long-remembered event in your life and then think about what you have learned from being with that per- son or going through that event, you will see that personal experience is, in- deed, a valuable source of knowledge. You will also notice that in thinking about that person or event you rely heavily on your remembrance of things past. Your memory, after all, is the storehouse of your personal knowledge, and whenever you look into this storehouse, you will invariably find an image or impression of your past experience. So you should not be sur- prised to find the authors in this section searching their own memories, for looking back is a hallmark of Reflection. We take pains to recall aspects of our experience in order to make sense of it for ourselves and for others.

This essential quality of reflective writing can be seen in the following passage from George Orwell's "Shooting an Elephant":

> One day something happened which in a roundabout way was enlightening. It was a tiny incident in itself, but it gave me a better glimpse than I had had before of the real nature of imperialism — the real motives for which despotic governments act. Early one morning the sub-inspector at a police station at the other end of the town rang me up on the phone and said that an elephant was rav- aging the bazaar. Would I please come and do something about it? I did not know what I could do, but I wanted to see what was hap- pening and I got on to a pony and started out.

This passage, which comes from the third paragraph of Orwell's essay, clearly presents him as being in a reflective frame of mind. In the opening sentence, he looks back to "one day" when "something happened" in Burma. In the midst of looking back, he also makes clear that this event is important to him because "in a roundabout way" it "was enlightening." Again, in the second sentence, he looks back not only to the event, "a tiny incident in itself," but also to the understanding that he gained from it — "a better glimpse than I had had before of the real nature of imperialism." Having announced the general significance of this event, he then returns to looking back at the event itself, to recalling the particular things that happened that day: the phone call informing him "that an elephant was ravaging the bazaar," the request that he "come and do something about it," and his decision to get "on to a pony" in order "to see what was happening."

   This alternation between recalling things and commenting on their significance is typical not only of Orwell's piece but of all the writing in this section. In some cases, however, the event reflected upon is less contained to a single time and place. It might involve a more general condition sustained over weeks or even years. Sometimes, too, the element of personal experience is crucial as the writer addresses a larger topic. So it is with Francine du Plessix Gray's essay, "The Work of Mourning."

   Gray's piece begins with a critique of contemporary self-help books that offer quick-fix ways of dealing with grief, but a third of the way through her essay, she focuses on her own personal experience of grief. "Until recently my own family has never been much good at mourning," she remarks, for "there is the case of my own father, the love of my early life, whose only daughter is as late a mourner as can be found." Suddenly her looking back becomes personal, her reflections an interpretation of what her father meant to her. Here too is an announcement of the guilt she carries because of having permitted the "disgrace" of insufficient mourning, for having been one of those who, in effect, turned her back on the ashes of a parent.

   The remainder of the essay concerns Gray's relation to her parents, their estrangement, her father's early death, her mother's remarriage, her mother's deflection of her tentative inquiries into the life of her father, and her own adoption of her mother's attitude so that she never visits his grave, not even when invited by the aunt and uncle who were closest to him.

   This portion of the essay is rich in its narration of her own experience, especially as she turns to her parents. But that narration is never distant from the chief work of Reflecting, which is her interpretation of that experience. A lifetime of reading and writing guides her interpretation, which has everything to do with paying for her "disgrace" toward her father and so learning how she must attend to her mother when her mother's time comes.

   The movement among different moments in time and between lessons found in reading and in lived experience will vary from writer to writer and from work to work, depending on the writer's reflective discoveries. Nevertheless, reflective writing usually contains several layers of memory, drawn from different times and places, and from different kinds of experience, all of it examined to discover just what makes it memorable. Most memorable experience sticks in our minds because it gives us, as Orwell says, "a better glimpse than [we] had had before of the real nature of" someone, something, or some aspect of the world. As a reader of reflective writing, you should always be attentive to the details of an author's recollected experience as well as to the "glimpse" that it gives the author, and you, into the "real nature" of things. And in your own reflective writing, you should make sure that you convey both dimensions of your experience — both what happened and what the events enabled you to see. Your account of what happened is in fact Reporting, which we will come to shortly; it is your interpretation of it, the value you give it, that places the work as a whole under the heading of Reflection.

The Range of Reflective Writing

The range of reflective writing is in one sense limitless, for it necessarily includes everything that makes up our own personal experience or anyone else's personal experience. Reflecting, in other words, may deal with anything that anyone has ever seen, heard, done, or thought about and considered memorable enough to motivate writing. Though the range of reflective writing is extraordinarily broad, the subject of any one piece is likely to be quite specific, and most pieces can be classified in terms of a few recurrent types of subject matter.

A single, memorable event is often the center of attention in reflective writing, as in Maya Angelou's "Graduation" or Orwell's "Shooting an Elephant." In reflecting on this kind of subject, the author usually provides a meticulous detailing of the event itself and some background information that serves as a context for making sense of it. In "Graduation," for example, Angelou tells about all the pregraduation excitement in her home, at school, and around town before turning to the graduation ceremony itself. And in "Shooting an Elephant," Orwell gives an overall description of his life as a colonial officer in Burma before he turns to his story of shooting the creature. That event, in turn, is of interest not only in itself but also for what it reveals to the author (and the reader) about some significant aspect of experience. Thus, for Angelou, graduation remains memorable because it helped her see how African American people have been "sustained" by "Black known and unknown poets"; for Orwell, the shooting remains memorable because it helped him see "the real nature of imperialism."

Another subject that often moves people to write reflectively is a notable person, as in N. Scott Momaday's "The Way to Rainy Mountain." When reflecting on a particular individual, writers seek to convey what they consider to be the most essential aspects of that person's character. They may review a number of memorable incidents or images from the person's life but always with the intention of locating behavior that seems central, that could be said to define that person. Momaday recalls the stories and legends that he heard from his grandmother, "the several postures that were peculiar to her," and her "long, rambling prayers."

❧Instead of concentrating on a particular person or event, reflective writing may center on a specific problem or significant issue in the author's past experience, as in Frederick Douglass's "Learning to Read and Write" or Martin Luther King Jr.'s "Pilgrimage to Nonviolence." A piece of this kind is likely to touch on a number of people and events and to encompass a substantial period of time in the process of recalling and reflecting on the problem with which it is concerned. Douglass covers seven years of his life as he tells about learning to read and write, and King recalls events and issues throughout his life that led him to espouse the principles of nonviolent resistance. Gray, similarly, draws on memories of each parent, of time with various members of her extended family, of college activities, and of her extensive and varied reading to come to grips with an emotional demand that is stronger than reason. In each case, the breadth of coverage serves to reveal the scope and complexity of the problem, as well as the author's special understanding of it.

As you can see from this brief survey of possibilities, reflective writing may deal with a single event, several events, or a whole lifetime of events. It may be as restricted in its attention as a close-up or as all-encompassing as a wide-angle shot. But no matter how little or how much experience it takes into account, reflective writing is always decisively focused through the author's persistent attempt to make sense of the past, to push memory to the point of understanding the significance of experience.

Methods of Reflecting

Your experience is unique, as is your memory, so in a sense you know the best methods to follow whenever you choose to reflect on something that interests you. But once you have recalled something in detail and made sense of it for yourself, you are still faced with the problem of how to present it to readers in a way that will also make sense to them. Given that your readers are probably not familiar with your experience, you must select and organize your material so that you provide a clear account of it. In your own mind you may summon that experience by a kind of shorthand, but leaving it that way would probably only confuse others. Besides, by filling out your account and submitting more and more detail to review by your own critical intelligence, you will give yourself the chance to uncover subtleties of understanding that you might otherwise have missed.

In the process of organizing your thoughts, your choice of subject often will suggest a corresponding method of presenting it clearly and meaningfully. If your reflections are focused on a single, circumscribed event, you will probably find it most appropriate to use a narrative presentation, telling your readers what happened in a relatively straightforward chronological order. Though you cover the event from beginning to end, your narrative should emphasize the details that you consider most striking and significant. In "Shooting an Elephant," Orwell devotes the largest segment in his piece to covering the brief instant when he finds himself on the verge of having to shoot the elephant despite his strong desire not to do so. In fact, he devotes one-third of the essay to those few moments of inner conflict because they bring about one of his major insights — "that when the white man turns tyrant it is his own freedom that he destroys." In telling about a memorable event of your own, you could make your story build toward some kind of climax or surprise or decisive incident, which leads to a moment of insight and upon which you would want to focus.

If your reflections center on a particular person, you might find it necessary to use both narrative and descriptive methods of presentation, telling about several events in order to reveal that person's character and thought. Though you rely heavily on narration, you will not be able to cover incidents in as much detail as if you were focusing on a single event. Instead, you should isolate the most striking details from each incident you choose to recall. Momaday relates his grandmother's background by way of the history of the Kiowa. But to describe her individual character, he isolates her postures, her manner of praying, and her dress — details that resonate with the "ancient awe" that he regards as central to her character. So, too, in writing about someone you have known, you could carefully select and arrange the details that you recall in order to convey a compelling impression of that person.

If your reflections are focused on a particular problem or issue, you may need to combine narrative, descriptive, and explanatory methods of presentation, bringing together your recollections of numerous events and persons to reveal the nature of the problem. You might survey the problem chronologically from beginning to end, or you might begin with a high point and circle around it, developing its context as you search for your understanding of that experience. Gray begins at an intellectual distance from her subject and sidles up to it. In "Pilgrimage to Nonviolence," by contrast, King immediately focuses on the "new and sometimes complex doctrinal lands" through which he traveled as he recalls the theological and philosophical ideas with which he struggled while formulating his convictions about nonviolence. Whe you write about a problem of your own, let your recollections guide you. There is no one right way to order them. You simply need to think carefully until you identify what is of central importance. Then you must decide on the best way to convey your understanding. In our selections so labeled, you will see a wide variety of writers finding their own singular ways of producing some very striking pieces of Reflection.

Reporting

In the "Reporting" sections of this text, you will find a naturalist describing the tool-using behavior of chimpanzees, a brain surgeon detailing the progress of a delicate operation, a historian telling about the plague that swept through medieval Europe, and a reporter describing the September 11, 2001, attacks on the World Trade Center and the Pentagon, among other pieces. Informative writing is basic to every field of endeavor, and the writers in these sections seek to fulfill that basic need by organizing and synthesizing material drawn from various sources: interviews, articles, books, public records, and firsthand observation. Working from such varied sources, these writers all provide detailed accounts of their subjects.

Though reporting depends on a careful gathering of information, it is by no means a mechanical and routine activity that consists simply of getting some facts and writing them down. Newspaper editors and criminal investigators often say that they want "just the facts," but they know that the facts are substantially shaped by the point of view of the person who is gathering and reporting them. By *point of view*, we mean both the physical and the mental standpoints from which a person observes or investigates something. Each of us, after all, stands at a particular point in space and time, as well as in thought and feeling, whenever we look at any subject. And where we stand in relation to the subject will determine the particular aspects of it that we perceive and bring out in our account.

The influence that differing points of view exert on reporting can be seen in the following passages from *The Diary of Anne Frank*. In the first one, Frank describes an extra assignment given to her in school as punishment for being a "chatterbox." That punishment, of course, comes from her teacher, whose point of view challenges her own; Mr. Keesing doesn't much care for chatterboxes.

> I thought and thought, and suddenly I had an idea. I wrote the three pages Mr. Keesing had assigned me and was satisfied. I argued that talking is a female trait and that I would do my best to keep it under control, but that I would never be able to break myself of the habit, since my mother talked as much as I did, if not more, and that there's not much you can do about inherited traits.

Clearly these two points of view are in conflict. From her teacher's point of view, Frank should keep still. She counters, however, with a defense of her behavior. Mr. Keesing seems to be a good sport. He had, Frank says, "a good laugh at my arguments" (paragraph 20), but soon her talking prompts him to assign a second essay to be entitled "An Incorrigible Chatterbox" and then a third one, "'Quack, Quack, Quack,' Said Mistress Chatterback":

> The class roared. I had to laugh too, though I'd nearly exhausted my ingenuity on the topic of chatterboxes. It was time to come up with something else, something original. My friend Sanne, who's good at poetry, offered to help me write the essay from beginning to end in verse. I jumped for joy. Keesing was trying to play a joke on me with this ridiculous subject, but I'd make sure the joke was on him.
>
> I finished my poem, and it was beautiful! It was about a mother duck and a father swan with three baby ducklings who were bitten

to death by the father because they quacked too much. Luckily, Keesing took the joke the right way. He read the poem to the class, adding his own comments, and to several other classes as well.

Keesing and Frank are in a kind of contest. Keesing sees his assignments as a way of correcting Frank's behavior. Frank takes them as a challenge and each one as an opportunity to turn the tables on Keesing.

Toward the end of this selection, in a short passage with an entirely different tone, and with those classroom pranks sadly in the past, Frank describes the morning on which she and her family set off for their hiding place. She is fully aware of how she looks, feels, and would look to others. She is aware, that is, of her own point of view while being fully able to anticipate the antagonistic point of view, not this time of a sympathetic teacher, but of someone who would betray her to Nazi officials:

> The four of us were wrapped in so many layers of clothes it looked as if we were going off to spend the night in a refrigerator, and all that just so we could take more clothes with us. No Jew in our situation would dare leave the house with a suitcase full of clothes. I was wearing two undershirts, three pairs of underpants, a dress, and over that a skirt, a jacket, a raincoat, two pairs of stockings, heavy shoes, a cap, a scarf and lots more.

The point of view that a writer takes will have an enormous effect on the writing. Sometimes point of view will be determined by where someone stands in space and time in relation to something else. Sometimes it will be determined by attitudes and feelings. It can be playful, as when Frank responds to discipline as if it were a contest. Just as quickly, point of view can turn solemn, as when she describes, briefly and evocatively, her first steps into hiding.

Among the most compelling aspects of point of view is that, by definition, it is intensely local: it belongs uniquely to the writer and is impossible for another writer to duplicate exactly. This distinctiveness of a writer's point of view is as apparent in Frank's report as it is in Harriet McBryde Johnson's "Unspeakable Conversations," which has a very different viewpoint.

> It's not that I'm ugly. It's more that most people don't know how to look at me. The sight of me is routinely discombobulating. The power wheelchair is enough to inspire gawking, but that's the least of it. Much more impressive is the impact on my body of more than four decades of a muscle-wasting disease. At this stage of my life, I'm Karen Carpenter thin, flesh mostly vanished, a jumble of bones in a floppy bag of skin.

Certainly it would be very hard to find another writer expressing the exact point of view of Harriet McBryde Johnson. Perhaps as rare is her striking ability to look so pointedly and unflinchingly at herself, and that becomes her strength as a writer. For even though she is so obviously different from all but a very few of her readers, we find ourselves, as readers, beginning to imagine the world from her physical and psychological point of view and empathizing with her. Similarly, through the good-humored combativeness of Anne Frank's behavior and then through the particularity of her ordeal in hiding, we come to feel for Anne Frank.

News reports, especially front-page lead stories, seek a very different point of view, one that is almost omniscient in its seemingly detached overview of a situation. Omniscience is of course impossible for us, but by synthesizing and summarizing diverse bits of information from several sources, a writer may seem to be, as we like to say, "on top of" the situation, as if everywhere all at once. So it is with Serge Schmemann's report, dated September 12, 2001, of the attacks of the day before. He was surely not in a position himself to witness all four planes or to observe their flight plans, their terrible conclusions in three different locations, the conditions on board any one of them, the subsequent collapse of the towers, the deaths of many rescue workers, and the movements of President George Bush throughout the day. Schmemann had to collect and organize this information and write from a point of view that seemed to see it all.

Once you imagine the various perspectives from which anything can be observed or investigated, you will see that no one person can possibly uncover everything there is to know about a subject. Schmemann's assignment was to come as close as possible to covering everything about September 11, 2001, but he certainly knew, as we all understand, that his report would be seen to be incomplete as soon as the following day. For this reason, as a reader, you need to identify the point of view from which an author gathered the information included in a piece so that you may judge for yourself its strengths and weaknesses. Then as a writer, you need to be as clear as possible about your own point of view and to understand its limitations. Once you begin to pay deliberate attention to point of view, you will come to see that by being open, direct, and accurate about it, by taking advantage of whatever vantage it offers but not claiming to see farther and more clearly than you possibly can, you will identify yourself, and be seen by others, as an honest writer.

The Range of Reportorial Writing

The purpose of reporting is in one sense straightforward and self-evident, particularly when it is defined in terms of its commonly accepted value to readers. Whether it involves a firsthand account of some recent happening or the documented record of a long-past sequence of events, reportorial writing informs readers about the various subjects that may interest them but that they cannot possibly observe or investigate on their own. You may never get to see chimpanzees in their native African habitats, but you can get a glimpse of their behavior through the firsthand account of Jane van Lawick-Goodall.

So, too, you may never have occasion to make your way through the many public records and personal reports of the bubonic plague that beset Europe in the mid-fourteenth century, but you can get a synoptic view of the plague from Barbara Tuchman's account, which is based on a thorough investigation of those sources. Reporting expands the range of its readers' perceptions and knowledge beyond the limits of their immediate experience. From the outlook of readers, then, the function of reporting does seem to be very clear-cut.

But if we shift our focus and look at reporting in terms of the writers' purposes, it often turns out to serve a more complex function than might at first be supposed. An example of this complexity can be seen in the following passage from van Lawick-Goodall's account:

> Suddenly I stopped, for I saw a slight movement in the long grass about sixty yards away. Quickly focusing my binoculars I saw that it was a single chimpanzee, and just then he turned in my direction. I recognized David Graybeard.
>
> Cautiously I moved around so that I could see what he was doing. He was squatting beside the red earth mound of a termite nest, and as I watched I saw him carefully push a long grass stem down into a hole in the mound. After a moment he withdrew it and picked something from the end with his mouth.

This passage seems on the whole to be a neutral bit of scientific reporting that details van Lawick-Goodall's observation of a particular chimpanzee probing for food in a termite nest. The only unusual aspect of the report is her naming the creature, which has the unscientific effect of personifying the animal. Otherwise, she is careful in the opening part of the description to establish the physical point of view from which she observed the chimpanzee. And at the end of the passage she is equally careful not to identify or even conjecture about what that "something" was that lay beyond her range of vision. As it turns out, however, this passage is a record not only of her observations but also of a pivotal moment in the story of how she came to make an important discovery about chimpanzees — that they are tool users — and thus how she came to regard their behavior as being much closer to that of human beings than had previously been supposed. So she climaxes her previous description of the chimpanzee with this sentence:

> I was too far away to make out what he was eating, but it was obvious that he was actually using a grass stem as a tool.

Van Lawick-Goodall evidently intends to be both informative and persuasive. To say a grass stem is a tool is to make an interpretive assertion about it. Choosing her words carefully, she prepares to make a case for her ideas about chimpanzee and human behavior. The use of tools had been seen to separate us from other animals; now she is ready to offer a very different argument.

As you can see from these selections, writers use reporting for a combination of purposes—(to provide information; to convey their attitudes, beliefs, or ideas about that information; and to influence the views of their readers) This joining of purposes is hardly surprising, given the factors involved in any decision to report on something. After all, whenever we make a report, we do so presumably because we believe that the subject of our report is important enough for others to be told about it. And presumably we believe the subject to be important because of what we have come to know and think. So when we are faced with deciding what information to report and how to report it, we inevitably base our decisions on these ideas. At every point in the process of planning and writing a report, we act on the basis of our particular priorities for conveying information about the subject. How could we do otherwise? How else could van Lawick-Goodall have decided what information to report out of all she must have observed during her first few months in Africa? Without specific purposes to control our reporting, our records of events would be as long as the events themselves and as unorganized as the day or days within which they occurred. Imagine reporting the whole of any single day—or hour for that matter—and you will see the problem.

Reporting, as you can see, necessarily serves a varied range of purposes—as varied as the writers and their subjects. Thus, whenever you read a piece of reportorial writing, you should try to discover what appear to be its guiding purposes by examining its point of view, structure, phrasing, and wording, much as we have in this discussion. Once you have identified the purpose, you should then consider how it has influenced the selection, arrangement, and weighting of information it presents. In your own writing, in turn, being aware of your purpose will help you organize your report to the best possible effect.

Methods of Reporting

Usually, you will find that the nature of your information suggests a corresponding method of presenting it clearly to your readers. If the information concerns a single event or covers a set of events spread over time, the most effective method is probably narration—that is, storytelling in a more or less chronological order. This is the basic form that van Lawick-Goodall uses, and it proves to be a persuasive way of unfolding her discovery about the behavior of chimpanzees. If the information concerns a particular place or scene or spectacle, your method may be more descriptive, presenting a verbal map of the area of action and so helping readers visualize the overall scene and its important details. If your assignment were to synthesize what is known, up to that moment, about a complex public event, as was the case with Schmemann's report on the 9/11 attacks, you would need to look at a wider series of events. You might begin, as he did, with the observable facts in New York and then introduce, as he did, other sources of information, such as flight schedules taken from the public record, Attorney General Ashcroft's announcements to reporters, the reported cell phone call from Barbara Olson (who was trapped on one of the flights), Mayor Giuliani's briefings to the press, White House announcements, and more. You would indicate the source of each piece of news and, by doing so, suggest the point of view from which it comes.

Once you have settled on a basic form, you should then devise a way of selecting, arranging, and proportioning your information to achieve your purposes effectively. You will need to review all the material you have gathered to determine what you consider to be the most important information to report. Some bits or kinds of information will strike you as more significant than others, and these are the ones that you should feature. Likewise, you will probably find that some information is simply not important enough to be mentioned. Van Lawick-Goodall, for example, produces a striking account of her first few months in Africa because she focuses primarily on her observation of chimpanzees, subordinating all the other material to her discoveries about their behavior. Thus, only on a couple of occasions does she include observations about the behavior of animals other than chimpanzees — in particular about the timidities of a bushbuck and a leopard. And she includes these observations only to point up by contrast the distinctively sociable behavior of chimpanzees. For the same reason, she proportions her coverage of several chimpanzee episodes to give the greatest amount of detail to the one that provides the most compelling indication of their advanced intelligence — namely, the final episode, which shows the chimpanzees' tool using and tool making, behaviors previously attributed only to human beings.

To help achieve your purposes, you should also give special thought to deciding on the perspective from which you present your information to the reader. Do you want to present the material in the first or the third person? Do you want to be present in the piece, as are van Lawick-Goodall and Anne Frank? Or do you want to be invisible, like Schmemann in his *New York Times* report? To some extent your answer to these questions will depend on whether you gathered the information through your own firsthand observations and want to convey your own reactions to these observations, as van Lawick-Goodall and Frank do in their pieces. But there are no hard-and-fast rules on this score. Look, for example, at "A Delicate Operation" by Roy C. Selby Jr. Although Selby must have written this piece on the basis of firsthand experience, he tells the story in the third person, removing himself almost completely from it except for such distant-sounding references to himself as "the surgeon." Selby is critically important to the information in this report, yet he evidently decided to deemphasize his presence so as to focus our attention on the operation itself.

As we have seen, not all reporting exists simply for its own sake. Sometimes a writer reports in order to set something else up. We have included two stories among our reports, not because reporting is the whole of their purpose, but because reporting bears decisively on their imagined action. Here, for example, in the opening paragraph of James Alan McPherson's story, "Problems of Art," we are invited to consider, through closely reported detail, the mind of the story's protagonist:

> Seated rigidly on the red, plastic-covered sofa, waiting for Mrs. Farragot to return from her errand, Corliss Milford decided he did not feel comfortable inside the woman's apartment. Why this was he could not tell. The living room itself, as far as he could see around, reflected the imprint of a mind as meticulous as his own. Every item seemed in place; every detail meshed into an overriding suggestion of order. This neatness did no damage to the image of Mrs. Farragot he had assembled, even before visiting her at home. Her first name was Mary, and she was thin and severe of manner. He recalled that her walnut-brown face betrayed few wrinkles; her large brown eyes were quick and direct without being forceful; her thin lips, during conversation, moved with precision and resolve. Even her blue summer dress, with pearl-white buttons up its front, advertised efficiency of character. The bare facts of her personal life, too, argued neatness and restraint; he had them down on paper, and the paper rested on his knee.

Throughout this passage our attention is torn between Mrs. Farragot and Mr. Milford, and that indeed has everything to do with the story.

Ultimately, then, the nature of a report is substantially determined not only by *what* a writer gathers from various sources but also by *how* a writer presents the information. In the "Reporting" sections of this text, you will have an opportunity to see various ways of presenting reported material in writing. In later sections, you will see how reporting combines with other kinds of writing — explaining and arguing.

Explaining

In the essays under "Explaining," you will find writings by specialists who seek to account for matters as various as the color of the sky, the origin of the universe, the content of urban legends, and the art of keeping a notebook. Explanation is an essential kind of writing in every academic field and profession. Facts, after all, do not speak for themselves, nor do figures add up on their own. To make sense of a subject, we need to see it in terms of something that is related to it — the color of the sky in terms of light waves from the sun, the content of urban legends in terms of the immediate circumstances in which they are told. To understand a subject, in other words, we must examine it in terms of some relevant context that will shed light on its origin and development, its nature and design, its elements and functions, its causes and effects, or its meaning and significance. For this reason, the writers in the "Explaining" sections draw on specific bodies of knowledge and systems of interpretation to explain the problems and subjects that they address.

This essential element of explaining can be seen in connection with the following passage from James Jeans's "Why the Sky Is Blue":

> We know that sunlight is a blend of lights of many colors — as we can prove for ourselves by passing it through a prism, or even through a jug of water, or as Nature demonstrates to us when she passes it through the raindrops of a summer shower and produces a rainbow. We also know that light consists of waves, and that the different colors of light are produced by waves of different lengths, red light by long waves and blue light by short waves. The mixture of waves which constitutes sunlight has to struggle through the obstacles it meets in the atmosphere, just as the mixture of waves at the seaside has to struggle past the columns of the pier. And these obstacles treat the light-waves much as the columns of the pier treat the sea-waves. The long waves which constitute red light are hardly affected, but the short waves which constitute blue light are scattered in all directions.
>
> Thus, the different constituents of sunlight are treated in different ways as they struggle through the earth's atmosphere. A wave of blue light may be scattered by a dust particle, and turned out of its course. After a time a second dust particle again turns it out of its course, and so on, until finally it enters our eyes by a path as zigzag as that of a flash of lightning. Consequently the blue waves of the sunlight enter our eyes from all directions. And that is why the sky looks blue.

Jeans's purpose here is to explain why the sky looks blue, and beginning in his opening sentence in this passage, he systematically establishes an explanatory context by setting forth relevant information about the nature and properties of sunlight, light, and light waves. That is, he approaches the explanatory problem in terms of knowledge drawn from his specialized fields of astronomy and physics. With this knowledge in hand, he then proceeds to show how "the different constituents of sunlight are treated in different ways as they struggle through the earth's atmosphere." In this way, he develops his explanation according to the analytic framework of an astronomer and physicist who is concerned with the interaction of the atmosphere and light waves. After formulating a cause-and-effect analysis that demonstrates that blue light is scattered "in all directions," Jeans is able to conclude that "the blue waves of the sunlight enter our eyes from all directions. And that is why the sky looks blue." Thus, the information that Jeans draws on from astronomy and physics allows him to offer a knowledgeable, systematic, and instructive explanation.

To appreciate how significant an explanatory context can be, consider how knowledge from other fields might influence an understanding of why the sky looks blue. A zoologist specializing in optics, for example, might note the importance of the retinal organs known as cones, which are thought to allow animals to receive and process color. Given this crucial bit of information, a zoologist might observe that the sky looks blue to human beings because their eyes are equipped with cones, whereas it does not look blue to animals such as guinea pigs, owls, and armadillos because their eyes lack cones. An anthropologist, in turn, might note that people living in coastal and island cultures tend to develop unusually rich vocabularies for describing how the sea looks and how the sky looks. Thus, an anthropologist might conclude that people who live in maritime environments are likely to be especially discerning about the colors of the sea and sky and therefore much more attuned to the nature and presence of blue.

Our hypothetical zoologist and anthropologist would both differ from Jeans in their explanatory approaches to the blue sky. Whereas Jeans sought to account for the source and prevalence of blue color, a zoologist and an anthropologist might take the color for granted and instead seek to account for the human ability to perceive the color or the propensity of some cultures to be especially discriminating in their perception of it. Their differing approaches would result from their differing fields of study. Each academic area, after all, involves a distinctive body of knowledge, a distinctive array of interests, and a distinctive set of methods for making sense of the subjects that its proponents study. Thus, each area is likely to approach problems from different angles and arrive at different kinds of explanations. No area can lay claim to the ultimate truth about things, but, as the case of the blue sky illustrates, each field does have a special angle on the truth, particularly about subjects that fall within its area of specialization. A zoologist and an anthropologist could be as enlightening in this case as is astronomer-physicist Jeans. In a broader sense, a particular subject or problem can be approached from one particular angle or from a combination of viewpoints, and each approach emerges from a corresponding body of knowledge that brings its own perspective to bear on an understanding of the subject. Relevant knowledge, quite simply, is the most essential element of explaining.

But knowledge alone is not sufficient to produce intelligible and effective explanation. Jeans's explanation, for example, depends not only on a body of information (about the properties and movement of light and light waves) but also on the form and style in which the information is presented. To develop your ability to explain, you will need to develop resourcefulness in putting your knowledge to use. One way to do this is to familiarize yourself with some of the many forms that explanatory writing can take in academic and professional situations.

The Range of Explanatory Writing

Explanatory writing serves a wide range of academic, professional, and public purposes. Rules and regulations, guidelines and instructions — these are familiar examples of explanation that tell people how to carry on many of the practical and public activities of their lives. Textbooks, such as the one you are reading right now, as well as simplified presentations of highly specialized research are common examples of explanatory writing that help people understand a particular body of information and ideas. Scholarly research papers, government documents, and other technical presentations of data and analysis, though less familiar to the general reader, are important kinds of explanation that advance knowledge and informed decision making.

To serve the differing needs of such varied purposes and audiences, explanatory writing incorporates various styles of presentation. Jeans's piece about the sky comes from a book he wrote as an introduction to astronomy. Thus, he uses a vocabulary that is accessible to most readers. And to make sure that beginners will understand the important concepts in his explanation, Jeans repeatedly illustrates his discussion with analogies and references to familiar experiences. In fact, if you look at the whole of Jeans's piece, you will see that he establishes his analogy of light waves to sea waves at the beginning of his discussion and then systematically uses it to organize and clarify the rest of his explanation.

For a variation in the format and style of explanatory writing, look at Oliver Sacks's "The Man Who Mistook His Wife for a Hat." Here Sacks, a neurologist, offers the results of a case study, which entails the close observation of an individual subject over time. Because the subject of a case study is by definition unique, the study cannot be replicated by other researchers. A case study therefore must be written in sufficient detail to document the observer's understanding of the subject and to enable other researchers to draw their own conclusions about what has been observed. You will find that Sacks provides a detailed description, history, and analysis of Dr. P.'s behavior. You will also find that Sacks writes on the whole in a standard rather than a specialized style, as befits an audience of generally educated readers.

Explanations can vary widely in their form, involving in every case a delicate mix of adjustments to the audience, purpose, specialized field, and subject matter. As a reader of explanations, you must be flexible in your approach, always willing to move through unfamiliar territory on the way to understanding the subject being discussed. As a writer of explanations, you must be equally flexible in choosing language and in selecting and arranging material to put your understanding in a form that satisfies you and fulfills the complex set of conditions that you are addressing at that moment.

Methods of Explaining

In planning a piece of explanatory writing, you should review your research materials with an eye to selecting an approach that is adjusted to the conditions of your explanatory situation. Some methods, you will find, are inescapable, no matter what your subject, audience, or purpose. Every piece of explanation requires that ideas be clarified and demonstrated through *illustration* — that is, through the citing of specific examples, as you can see from the earlier passage by Jeans and in the following excerpt from Sacks's essay on Dr. P., a musician and the man who mistook his wife for a hat:

> He saw all right, but what did he see? I opened out a copy of the *National Geographic* Magazine and asked him to describe some pictures in it.
>
> His responses here were very curious. His eyes would dart from one thing to another, picking up tiny features, individual features, as they had done with my face. A striking brightness, a color, a shape would arrest his attention and elicit comment — but in no case did he get the scene-as-a-whole. He failed to see the whole, seeing only details, which he spotted like blips on a radar screen. He never entered into relation with the picture as a whole — never faced, so to speak, *its* physiognomy. He had no sense whatever of a landscape or scene.
>
> I showed him the cover, an unbroken expanse of Sahara dunes.
>
> "What do you see here?" I asked.
>
> "I see a river," he said. "And a little guest-house with its terrace on the water. People are dining out on the terrace. I see colored parasols here and there." He was looking, if it was "looking," right off the cover into mid-air and confabulating nonexistent features, as if the absence of features in the actual picture had driven him to imagine the river and the terrace and the colored parasols.
>
> I must have looked aghast, but he seemed to think he had done rather well. There was a hint of a smile on his face. He also appeared to have decided that the examination was over and started to look around for his hat. He reached out his hand and took hold of his wife's head, tried to lift it off, to put it on. He had apparently mistaken his wife for a hat! His wife looked as if she was used to such things.

Sacks's obligation to illustrate and demonstrate Dr. P.'s unusual symptoms leads him here, as elsewhere in his piece, to report a detailed *narration* of Dr. P.'s actions. For reasons of clarity, reliability, and credibility, reporting constitutes an essential element of explaining. If an explanation cannot be illustrated or can be only weakly documented, it is likely to be unreliable and therefore not credible to readers. Notice however the interpretive sentences toward the end of each of the thicker paragraphs as Sacks seeks to explain, for himself and so for us, Dr. P's puzzling behavior.

An essay that depends on the use of special terms or concepts almost certainly will call for *definitions* to ensure that the reader understands the phrases as the writer intends them to be understood. In "Urban Legends: 'The Boyfriend's Death,'" Jan Harold Brunvand begins his study by defining urban legends as a subclass of folklore and by defining what is entailed in the study of folklore. In his essay about Dr. P., Sacks proceeds in a different way. He presents the case of Dr. P., who is suffering from visual agnosia, by trying to replicate for readers his own process of uncovering the mystery lying behind Dr. P.'s unusual behavior. He shows, through description and dialogue with Dr. P. and his wife, the remarkable things Dr. P. can do (his extraordinary musical ability, for example) and the ordinary things he cannot do (such as recognize the faces of his wife and friends). At the end of this descriptive section, Sacks reveals the pathological cause of Dr. P.'s condition. But that is an insufficient explanation for Sacks. First he asks how Dr. P.'s inability to make cognitive judgments should be interpreted. He talks about the limitations of neurological and psychological explanations of what appear to be neuropsychological disorders when those sciences overlook "the judgmental, the particular, the personal" and rely solely on the "abstract and computational." In so doing, Sacks defines the limits of cognitive neurology and psychology, suggesting that they, too, may suffer from "an agnosia essentially similar to Dr. P.'s." Definition, in other words, can be carried out in a variety of ways — by citing examples, by identifying essential qualities or characteristics, by offering synonyms, by making distinctions.

Other methods of explanation can be effective in a broad range of explanatory situations. If you are trying to explain the character, design, elements, or nature of something, you will often do best to *compare and contrast* it with something to which it is logically related. Comparison calls attention to similarities; contrast focuses on differences. Together, the methods work to clarify important points by playing related subjects against each other. In his study of urban legends, for example, Brunvand attempts to shed light on the complex circumstances that influence the content of such folktales by comparing and contrasting several versions of the same legendary story. This method enables him to show that popular urban legends, such as "The Boyfriend's Death," retain a basically unvarying plot as they travel from one storyteller and locale to another but that specific details are altered by individual storytellers to make them fit the circumstances of a particular audience. Like Brunvand's piece, some examples of comparison and contrast rely on a strategic balancing of similarities and differences. Other pieces depend largely on a sustained contrast. And still other pieces might work primarily in terms of comparison. Whenever you compare or contrast, your attention to similarities and differences will be adjusted to the needs of your explanatory situation.

A special form of comparison, *analogy*, can be useful in many explanatory situations. Analogies help readers understand difficult or unfamiliar ideas by putting them in tangible and familiar terms. In "Why the Sky Is Blue," Jeans's analogy of light waves to sea waves helps readers visualize a process that they could not otherwise see. As useful as analogies are, however, they rely on drawing resemblances between things that are otherwise unlike. Sea waves, after all, are not light waves, and the dimensions of the universe are not the same as anything within the range of ordinary human experience. The analogy works, but it goes, as we say, only so far. Whenever you develop an analogy as a tool of explanation, you have to become aware of its fitness and not try to force it beyond the limits of its use. In Sacks's essay quoted above, for example, we might wonder how far to take his analogy of a wife's head to a hat. What does Dr. P. do when he finds he cannot place her head easily on his own? Surely should he attempt some violence, that momentary and rather beguiling analogy would no longer suffice.

Some explanatory methods are especially suited to a particular kind of situation. If you are trying to show how to do something, how something works, or how something was done, you will use a method known as *process analysis*. In analyzing a process, your aim is to identify and describe each step in the process, showing how each one leads to the next, and explaining how the process as a whole leads to its final result. Jeans's piece, for example, analyzes the process by which light waves from the sun make their way through the earth's atmosphere and determine human perception of the color of the sky.

As you can tell, almost any piece of writing that aims to make sense of something combines several methods of explanation. This should come as no surprise if you stop to think about the way that people usually explain even the simplest things in their day-to-day conversations. The person will probably give you an overview of where the place is situated, a step-by-step set of movements to follow and places to look for, brief descriptions of prominent guideposts along the way, a review of the original directions, and possibly a remark or two about misleading spots to avoid. Similarly, when people try to explain something in writing, they want to help readers get from one place to another in a particular subject matter. Thus, in the midst of giving a process analysis or explaining by means of comparison and contrast, a writer might feel compelled to illustrate a point, define a term, or offer a telling analogy.

Another method of explanation, related to process analysis, is *causal analysis*. As the term suggests, this type of analysis seeks to explain the causes of things, particularly causes that are complex. Usually, a causal analysis begins with a complex outcome and then examines various explanations that might account for the situation. Sometimes, however, an analysis might begin with a particular cause and then examine the various effects that the cause has produced. Monica M. Moore follows this pattern of explanation in "Nonverbal Courtship Patterns in Women: Context and Consequences," in which she finds that the biological imperative of mating (the cause) produces a range of "flirting behaviors" as well as a range of "mate relevant" responses to them. By systematically identifying, observing, and enumerating those behaviors, she can defend her hypothesis about their cause. In this paragraph she begins to explain the methodology of her study, which, you could say, involves an analysis not only of *cause* but also of *process*:

> Subjects were covertly observed in one social context where opportunities for male–female interaction were available, a singles' bar. Subjects were observed for 30 minutes by two trained observers. Focal subjects were randomly selected from the pool of possible subjects at the start of the observation period. We observed a woman only if she was surrounded by at least 25 other people (generally there were more than 50 others present) and if she was not accompanied by a male. In order to record all instances of the relevant behaviors, observers kept a continuous narrative account of all behaviors exhibited by a single subject and the observable consequences of those actions (Altmann 1974). The following criteria were used for identifying behaviors: a nonverbal solicitation behavior was defined as a movement of body part(s) or whole body that resulted in male attention, operationally defined, within 15 seconds following the behavior. Male attention consisted of the male performing one of the following behaviors: approaching the subject, talking to her, leaning toward her or moving closer to her, asking the subject to dance, touching her, or kissing her. Field notes were transcribed from concealed audio tape recorders.

Because no two things can be identically accounted for, no set method exists for carrying out a causal analysis. Keep in mind, however, a few cautionary procedures. You should review other possible causes and other related circumstances before attempting to assert the priority of one cause or set of causes over another, and you should present enough evidence to demonstrate the reliability of your explanation. By doing so, you will avoid the temptation to oversimplify things. How would we respond, for example, if we were told that those flirting behaviors, so nicely defined and recorded, were staged by students who wanted to disturb Moore's experiment? Perhaps we would check out a few more singles' bars in a few more towns and cities to dispel our suspicions.

As with reporting, explaining too is a staple of fiction; so many things must be explained for the reader to comprehend the action. One story we have included, "Zeno and the Distance between Us," by Sharon Wahl, reads as if Wahl's protagonist had herself been one of Moore's "trained observers." Only this speaker is, we could say, somewhat more personally involved and interested.

How wide is the arm of a seat in a dark theater? The philosopher Zeno gave this paradox of motion: to reach him, I must cross half the distance between us. Then half the distance remaining; then half of that, and half again, and again, and again: I can only go halfway.

Proving, motion is impossible. . . .

Tonight we ran into each other checking videos from the library. We talked about an actress we both loved, who had a new movie. We both asked at the same time, Do you want to — ? That was easy. Now, for two hours, his hand will be in reach. His leg is in reach. My hand is on my thigh, like his, and my thigh is so close to his that moving the hand from mine to his, fitting my long thin fingers between his longer ones, would take less effort than shaking hands.

In the writings emphasizing explanation that you will find in this anthology, you will see how writers in different fields combine several different, identifiable methods. Then later we will see how explaining also contributes to arguing.

Arguing

In our sections on "Arguing," you will find authors taking positions on numerous controversial subjects — from the benefits of television to the status of African American English, from the reasons for a civilization's collapse to the problematic measurement of human intelligence. No matter what their academic fields or professions, these authors energetically defend their stands on the issues and questions they address. But this should come as no surprise. None of us, after all, holds lightly to our beliefs about what is true or beautiful or good. Indeed, most of us get especially fired up when our views are pitted against the beliefs of others. So you will find these authors vigorously engaged in the give and take of argument. As a consequence, you will repeatedly find yourself having to weigh the merits of competing positions in a debate about some controversial issue.

The distinctive quality of arguing can be seen in the following paragraphs from Martin Luther King Jr.'s "Letter from Birmingham Jail":

I think I should indicate why I am here in Birmingham, since you have been influenced by the view which argues against "outsiders coming in." I have the honor of serving as president of the Southern Christian Leadership Conference, an organization operating in every southern state, with headquarters in Atlanta, Georgia. We have some eighty-five affiliated organizations across the South, and one of them is the Alabama Christian Movement for Human Rights. Frequently we share staff, educational, and financial resources with our affiliates. Several months ago the affiliate here in Birmingham asked us to be on call to engage in a nonviolent direct-action program if such were deemed necessary. We readily consented, and when the hour came we lived up to our promise. So I, along with several members of my staff, am here because I was invited here. I am here because I have organizational ties here.

But more basically, I am in Birmingham because injustice is here. Just as the prophets of the eighth century B.C. left their villages and carried their "thus saith the Lord" far beyond the boundaries of their home towns, and just as the Apostle Paul left his village of Tarsus and carried the gospel of Jesus Christ to the far corners of the Greco-Roman world, so am I compelled to carry the gospel of freedom beyond my own home town. Like Paul, I must constantly respond to the Macedonian call for aid.

Moreover, I am cognizant of the interrelatedness of all communities and states. I cannot sit idly by in Atlanta and not be concerned about what happens in Birmingham. Injustice anywhere is a threat to justice everywhere. We are caught in an inescapable network of mutuality, tied in a single garment of destiny. Whatever affects one directly, affects all indirectly. Never again can we afford to live with the narrow, provincial "outside agitator" idea. Anyone who lives inside the United States can never be considered an outsider anywhere within its bounds.

These are the first few paragraphs of an argument that continues for several more pages. It is one of the finest statements of democratic values that our country has yet produced. Arguments usually place themselves against an opposing point of view. In this case, eight Alabama clergymen had published a statement calling King's actions "unwise and untimely." He was also accused of being an "outside agitator." King counters that accusation immediately by outlining his affiliations with the South, with Alabama, and even with Birmingham. He has ample reason, he argues, to be "here," a word he places unhesitatingly in the first sentence of the first paragraph quoted above and then three more times in the last two sentences of that paragraph.

From this point on, King's argument expands to include larger and larger ideas of appropriate affiliation and of justice. "I am in Birmingham because injustice is here," he says, opening his next paragraph by pivoting on "here," which by now has become thematic. Calling on biblical parallels to support his idea that the Christian is always "here," confronting need and injustice, King asserts first that all U.S. citizens have every right to converge on whatever "here" they identify as necessary. In the argument that follows, he expands on that idea. However local they may have been, the clergymen who had objected to his intervention had not been "here" at all — not with King, not on the side of justice. Nor had most white clergy or sympathetic white moderates been "here." Almost everyone had displaced King's "here" to some more distant "there," distant in time as much as in place, so much so that the "shallow understanding from people of good will" distressed King almost as much as had the overt antagonism of segregationist authorities.

The Range of Argumentative Writing

Argumentative writing so pervades our lives that we may not even recognize it as such in the many brochures and leaflets that come our way, urging us to vote for one candidate, or to support one cause rather than another. Argumentative writing also figures heavily in newspaper editorials, syndicated columns, and letters to the editor, which typically debate the pros and cons of some public issue, be it local taxes or national defense. Argument is fundamental in the judicial process, crucial in the legislative process, and serves the basic aims of the academic world, testing ideas and theories by pitting them against each other. Argument is an important activity in the advancement of knowledge and society.

The broad range of argumentative writing can be understood by considering the kinds of issues and questions that typically give rise to disagreement and debate. The most basic sources of controversy are questions of fact — the who, what, when, and where of things, as well as how much. Intense arguments over questions of fact can develop in any field, especially when the facts in question have a significant bearing on a subject. Stephen Jay Gould's essay "Women's Brains" is one such questioning of fact. An earlier scientist had argued that women were less intelligent than men, an assertion Gould challenges, and he does so by rereading the evidence the previous researcher had offered.

There is no disputing that Paul Broca had weighed more than 400 human brains and had found that male brains were, on average, noticeably weightier than the brains of women. But how to account for that difference is an open question, admitting of several possibilities; and even if those questions were to be settled, there is no verifiable correlation of brain size with intelligence. What size does correlate with reliably enough is height; taller persons have larger brains than do shorter prople. Men tend to be taller than women, and so their brains are larger. However, the average difference between the male and the female brain, Gould observes, "is exactly the average difference between a 5 foot 4 inch and a 6 foot 4 inch male in Broca's data. We would not (especially us short folks) want to ascribe greater intelligence to tall men."

Again and again in argumentative writing the reading and interpretation of data are at issue. "If Black English Isn't a Language, Then Tell Me, What Is?" is the title of a James Baldwin essay about the indivisibility of language and identity, the resistance of minority languages to being dismissed as "dialects," and the thorough infusion of American English with black experience. His knowledge of that infusion and his sensitivity to it lead to this assertion:

There was a moment, in time, and in this place, when my
brother, or my mother, or my father, or my sister, had to convey
to me, for example, the danger in which I was standing from the
white man standing just behind me, and to convey this with a
speed and in a language, that the white man could not possibly
understand. . . .

Now, if this passion, this skill, this (to quote Toni Morrison)
"sheer intelligence," this incredible music, the mighty achievement
of having brought a people utterly unknown to, or despised by
"history" — to have brought this people to their present, troubled,
troubling, and unassailable and unanswerable place — if this absolutely unprecedented journey does not indicate that black English is a language, I am curious to know what definition of languages is to be trusted.

Or in "A Designer Universe?" Steven Weinberg argues against reading into
whatever design we find in nature evidence of a "designer" that is "benevolent." A Nobel Prize winner in physics, Weinberg devotes most of his essay
to assessing the possibility of "design" from our limited point of view in "a
universe that is very large, and perhaps infinite." To a large extent, he observes, answers to this question are up to the individual. Speaking then as
one, he goes on to say,

My life has been remarkably happy, perhaps in the upper 99.99
percentile of human happiness, but even so, I have seen a mother
die painfully of cancer, a father's personality destroyed by Alzheimer's disease, and scores of second and third cousins murdered
in the Holocaust. Signs of a benevolent designer are pretty well
hidden.

And if that dry understatement isn't enough, he concludes, several paragraphs later, with this statement:

I learned that the aim of this conference is to have a constructive
dialogue between science and religion. I am all in favor of a dialogue between science and religion, but not a constructive dialogue. One of the great achievements of science has been, if not to
make it impossible for intelligent people to be religious, then at
least to make it possible for them not to be religious. We should
not retreat from this accomplishment.

Beliefs and values are almost always at issue in argumentative situations,
and they certainly are in these cases. Why should it be otherwise? What,
after all, is more worthy of argument? Insofar as there is any choice in the
matter at all, arguments over values are integral to the formation of society

and so determine much about how we live. Nothing illustrates that better than this well-known passage from the Declaration of Independence:

> We hold these truths to be self-evident, that all men are created equal, that they are endowed by their Creator with certain unalienable Rights, that among these are Life, Liberty and the pursuit of Happiness. That to secure these rights, Governments are instituted among Men, deriving their just powers from the consent of the governed. That whenever any Form of Government becomes destructive of these ends, it is the Right of the People to alter or to abolish it, and to institute new Government, laying its foundation on such principles and organizing its powers in such form, as to them shall seem most likely to effect their Safety and Happiness.

In this crucial passage, Thomas Jefferson and his congressional colleagues directly challenged several fundamental assumptions about the rights of people and the sources of governmental power that were held by the British king and by many British people and others throughout the world. Only in this way was it possible for them to make the compelling case for their ultimate claim that the colonies should be "FREE AND INDEPENDENT STATES . . . Absolved from all Allegiance to the British Crown."

Though Jefferson and his colleagues did not outline a new system of government in the Declaration itself, the document does enable us to see that conflicts over beliefs and values often come to have a decisive bearing on questions of policy and planning.

For another clear-cut example of conflict over beliefs, you can look at "Hiroshima" by John Berger. Berger, who began his career as a painter, describes a book called *Unforgettable Fire* that "consists of drawings and paintings made by people who were in Hiroshima on the day the bomb was dropped," August 6, 1945. None of the work was by professional artists, but Berger's familiarity with art traditions allowed him to identify the common denominator in what those artists saw. "These were images of hell," he observes, summarizing the effect of seeing so many images of skin falling off, of neighbors unable to recognize one another, of a child trying to bring water to her mother who is already dead; and, Berger adds, "I am not using the word as hyperbole."

Hyperbole it may not be, but Hell is unthinkable in a literal way, and so, Berger insists, the reality of it has been pushed aside in Western consciousness and suppressed. "Is it conceivable that the BBC would show these pictures on Channel One at a peak hour . . . ? I challenge them to do so." His argument is concerned with imposing his vision on our consciousness in just such a way and so bringing the fact of the bombs before us with a clear knowledge of the damage they caused. To do so, he must introduce a language for it that we will take literally, seriously, and not wave off as hyperbole. "It is possible today to arouse popular indignation or anger by speaking of the threat and immorality of terrorism," he begins, introducing a word that we are likely to find more urgent than "hell":

> What is able to shock people about terrorist acts is that often their targets are unselected and innocent — a crowd in a railroad station, people waiting for a bus to go home after work. The victims are chosen indiscriminately in the hope of producing a shock effect on political decision-making by their government.
>
> The two bombs dropped on Japan were terrorist actions. The calculation was terrorist. The indiscriminacy was terrorist.

And so he is able to conclude with an observation that he hopes will rouse us: "The small groups of terrorists operating today are, by comparison, humane killers."

Methods of Arguing

In any piece of argumentative writing, your primary purpose is to bring readers around to your point of view. Some readers, of course, will agree with you in advance, but others will disagree, and still others will be undecided. So in planning a piece of argumentative writing, you should begin by examining your material with an eye to discovering the issues that have to be addressed and the points that have to be made to present your case persuasively, especially to readers who oppose you or are undecided. This means that you will have to deal not only with issues that you consider relevant but also with matters that have been raised by your opponents. In other words, you will have to show readers that you have considered both sides of the controversy, as King did right from the start by confronting the issue of "outside agitators" rather than ignoring it. Gould does something similar by acknowledging that Broca did in fact measure a physical difference, and that there was a desire, on the part of many, to see that difference as a measure of intelligence. In fact, our general inclination to equate size with value works to Broca's advantage, and Gould has to give the matter serious thought to come up with a convincing argument.

After you have identified the crucial points to be addressed, you will then need to make a convincing case with respect to each of the points. Some methods for doing so are imperative no matter what point you are trying to prove. Every piece of argumentation requires that you offer readers evidence to support your position. Evidence in Berger's case includes in part the pictures he describes, but it has also, and crucially, to do with a definition of the word *terrorist*. If he can get us to accept his definition of that word, his case is largely made.

Sometimes this basic concern for providing readers with appropriate evidence will lead you into the activity of reporting. In his attempt to demonstrate the right of the colonies "to throw off such Government," Jefferson provides a lengthy and detailed list of "injuries" that the king of

Great Britain inflicted on the colonies. Reporting appropriate evidence constitutes the most basic means of making a persuasive case for any point under consideration. So any point for which evidence cannot be provided or for which only weak or limited evidence can be offered is likely to be much less convincing to readers than one that can be amply and vividly substantiated.

Often, too, a good deal of explaining must be done. Gould, for example, explains several possible reasons for the discrepancy of size between the male and female brain. Height is one possible reason. Another is the probable manner of death. Prolonged illness will wither a brain and reduce its size, and women, especially in the mid-nineteenth century when Broca worked, were more likely than men to die at advanced ages of lingering illness. Again and again in these arguments, the writer will introduce material that requires explanation.

But evidence alone will not be persuasive to readers unless it is brought to bear on a point in a reasonable and logical way. In one of its most familiar forms, induction, logic involves the process of moving from bits of evidence to a generalization or a conclusion that is based on that evidence. Berger, for example, moves from descriptions of individual paintings to his recognition that they represent Hell before taking up his reading of the bombing as a terrorist act. Similarly, Emily Martin, in "The Egg and the Sperm: How Science Has Constructed a Romance Based on Stereotypical Male-Female Roles," examines the imagery used in science textbooks and other discourse and finds metaphors based on the notion that men are active and women are passive. Though recent studies show that both the egg and the sperm are active in the process of fertilization, these stereotypes persist, as does a contradicting one of "woman as a dangerous and aggressive threat." This evidence allows Martin to generalize and make what is called an *inductive leap* to her hypothesis that our stereotyped understanding of cells lays the foundation for social control of the moment of fertilization. Berger makes a similar leap when he generalizes from the imagery of numerous paintings to the idea that what they represent, collectively, is Hell.

Deduction, a complementary form of logic, moves in the opposite direction, from general assumptions or premises to particular conclusions that can be derived from them. For example, having made the general claim that "a long train of abuses" entitles people "to throw off such Government" and having cited, in turn, a long list of abuses that Great Britain had inflicted on the colonies, Jefferson is able to reach the conclusion that the colonies "are Absolved from all Allegiance to the British Crown." Given his initial assumptions about "truths" that are "self-evident," his deduction seems to be a logical conclusion, as indeed it is. But as in any case of deductive logic, the conclusion is only as convincing as the premises on which it is based. Great Britain did not accept Jefferson's premises, so it did not accept his conclusions, logical though they were. Other countries of the time took a different view of the matter. So in developing an argument deductively, you need to keep in mind not only the logic of your case but also the appeal its premises are likely to have for those whom you are most interested in convincing. In fact, our most common, thoughtful reaction to an argument we dislike is to challenge the premises on which it is founded. No doubt several of the arguments gathered in these sections will offer you just such an opportunity.

One kind of argument of which we have not spoken is that which takes such an extreme position that it encourages the reader to adopt the opposite point of view. Sometimes this strategy is called *reductio ad absurdum*, which means "reducing" or carrying things to an absurd extreme, the evident absurdity of which, then, suggests the countering and quite sensible argument that is usually left unstated. Jonathan Swift's "Modest Proposal" to reduce the extreme poverty of Ireland and make its poor children less "a Burden to Their Parents or Country" by raising them to be slaughtered, like piglets or lambs, for the tables of the rich is the most famous argument of this kind, at least in English. Swift's "Proposal" has become so well known that every once in a while you will discover some other writer offering "a modest proposal," which will also and invariably be extreme. Imagine, for example, a proposal to reduce the poverty and overcrowding of many great cities by accelerating global warming until all the icebergs melt and those cities, often coastal, are flooded out of existence. Or one that would propose to solve an international epidemic, borne by birds, by felling all the forests of the world.

We assume that Swift's argument is ironic, that he means the opposite of what he says, and that is usually the intention of "modest proposals." The trouble with irony is that often the reader doesn't get it, in which case the writer seems a monster, and more than one has been attacked because of that belief. Irony can be dangerous. Daniel Defoe wrote a similarly ironic proposal, in his case to abolish Christianity, and he wound up in the stocks for so doing. Many a contemporary politician suffers several bad days with the press for saying something flippant, or ironic, that comes across as serious when taken out of context and quoted as a sound bite. Swift presses his point, and tips us off to his irony, by offering a series of positive proposals shortly before he concludes. These are so commonsensical, however, that they seem "immodest" proposals in the context he has developed. On the one hand, Swift is quite sure no one will adopt them; on the other hand, he knows, and most readers will feel, that they are exactly what is needed.

> [L]et no man talk to me of other expedients [other than raising children for food]: *Of taxing our absentees at five shillings a pound: Of using neither clothes, nor household furniture, except what is of our own growth and manufacture: Of utterly rejecting the materials and instruments that promote foreign luxury: Of curing the expensiveness of pride, vanity, idleness, and gaming in our women: Of introducing a vein of parsimony, prudence, and temperance: Of learning to love our country.*

And he adds twice as many more such suggestions, each wholly positive, but for all that quite unlikely to prove popular.

An ironic argument is something like the literary summit of the argumentative form and is unlikely to be your strategy often. But whatever combination of techniques you favor, when carrying out an argument, try to save a very telling point or bit of evidence or well-turned phrase for last. Effective storytellers and successful courtroom lawyers both know that a memorable detail, or a well-turned phrase, makes for a powerful climax, a kind of clincher. Swift's title is one such phrase for there is nothing modest about it, unless, of course, his readers were to adopt the sensible, temperate, somewhat boring strategies he lists toward the end. Moreover, Swift is able to conclude by offering as a clincher his own disinterest. He has nothing to gain personally from his proposal: "I have no children by which I can propose to get a single penny; the youngest being nine years old, and my wife past child-bearing."

In Swift's famous essay, in Jefferson and King's declarations of democratic principles, and in other selections in this anthology, you will see how different writers use the various resources of language to produce some very striking and compelling arguments.

Writing across the Curriculum

As we said earlier, modes of writing and thinking are the constants, given that they are always available as ways of proceeding in whatever discipline. The disciplines, however, in their most professional forms, use specialized modes of presentation that differ noticeably from each other. In this anthology, we have included several pieces that display that variation. We could have gone much further in doing so, but writing within disciplines, by its very nature, tends to sideline those who are not its practitioners. A researcher in medicine may well draft a legal brief, but not without first engaging in some serious legal study that moves away from medicine. Still less likely is a lawyer to turn out written reports of scientific research.

To a large extent, the observable differences between, say, writing up research in chemistry and writing philosophy or literary commentary have to do with the relation of writing to thought. Those of us who identify with literary study and with the humanities generally are more inclined to equate language-using with thinking. We think in words, or we think we think in words, and we tend to assume that without the words, there is no thought. No doubt there are many individuals within the humanities who would challenge that assertion, or who would say that though it may stand as a simplification, some manner of preverbal thought surely occurs. When we have said as much, however, we have already brought words to it, and that disguises our earlier mental labors.

Meanwhile, in other areas of endeavor, there are plenty of workers who feel they think in symbols or numbers, or in shapes, or in arrangements of elements visualized in a field, or in shades of black and white, or in sounds or colors. How did Beethoven think, we may ask, when he was composing symphonies? How did Einstein think as he pondered relativity? One does not have to be one of the few geniuses of the Western world to have sensed the power and reality of nonverbal thought in a practice in which one has acquired ability. As you play the piano, or basketball, or run down the sidewalk at night and adjust your step to leap smoothly over a puddle of water, thoughts come to you, and you act on them without consciously thinking about it. At the same time, it has become more necessary than ever for thinkers to write out or write up their thoughts in order to share them with others. Beethoven didn't just keep his music in his head. Einstein presented his theories as research papers.

There are, no doubt, a few exceptions to the need to bring one's work to the page. The only ones we remember, though, are very rare geniuses. Socrates and a few other towering intellects either did not write at all or preferred to lecture or just talk and so to demonstrate their thinking as a living process. Devoted students, however, cared enough about what they said to take good notes, to write very fast and remember strenuously. If they had not written it down, we would not have the record.

To bring all this back to the academic disciplines, we may observe that the marked differences in writing and in the presentation of research vary according to the degree of identification of thought with language. In the sciences, generally, the quest is for facts that are demonstrable through some kind of experimental research. Once they have been observed, they are felt to be significantly true apart from the language in which they will be presented, and so it makes sense for the facts to be discovered first and then written up. It won't matter whether the language is English, French, or Navajo. Clumsiness with the language may obscure the thought and increase the difficulty for both reader and writer, but the truth the writer attempts to convey won't change because of that.

In the humanities, however, the idea is less distinguishable from the sentence in and by which it is formed, so the research blends more with the writing. Imagine the ideas, the essential truths, of the Declaration of Independence being written today, by you, or by a committee from your class. Would the language be exactly the same? What would you change, if anything? Is it enough to say "all men are created equal"? Are "Life, Liberty and the pursuit of Happiness" sufficient goals? How much could change before your idea had changed and you found that you had changed everything?

There is a tendency too for explicit documentation to be a more exacting obligation in those areas of study in which the research can be thought to precede the writing. In your reading, note taking, and laboratory observations, you can identify the ideas, the procedures, and the findings of others; and so you can and should note clearly how you have used the work of others. This obligation follows all the way through the social sciences into the humanities of history, philosophical analysis, and literary study. There is another extreme, though, one we identify with literature, in which the display of indebtedness is rarely through footnotes but by allusion and echoing. Some hint is given, but it may be missed by less experienced readers. For example, people who have never heard of Jonathan Swift may be completely baffled and even angered by an op-ed piece in their local paper that urges citizens to make curbside sculptures from their trash rather than rely on what has proved to be inadequate garbage collection. They may consider the letter to be idiotic, even if it is entitled "My Modest Proposal."

Meanwhile, in your more usual writing for class assignments and beyond them, you must simply be aware that the rules of the game will vary somewhat, sometimes quite a lot from discipline to discipline. It is not the purpose of this text to illustrate all the possibilities. The most scientific of our selections, in that it is arranged like a laboratory report, is Monica M. Moore's account of observed flirtatious behavior. It will seem soft to a chemist or a physicist, and it reads, in fact, like a parody. The degree of parody is hard to gauge, at least for readers outside her field of study. Her subject and methodology must have been fun to conceive, and she probably had little trouble locating volunteer observers. However that may be, her report, with its careful separation of sections — the problem stated, the methods outlined and described, and then the results and discussion — is a model of writing in the sciences.

Rereading and Rewriting

We tend to believe that the books most worth reading are worth reading again, and that through rereading we get more out of them. Some people might read a favorite novel every year, or every few years, and find more and more in it each time. Teachers in all fields come to know their discipline better, more intimately, with more subtlety, as they teach and teach again, as they ponder its problems further, as they extend their study of it. It should be no surprise then that in this anthology, too, a second reading and often a third will bring you to understandings beyond what you first recognize. Everyday journalism is well known and quite properly appreciated for organization that puts the most important things first and that presents essential facts so that readers can pick them out at a glance. And so we read and dispose of the page and go on to the next day and its new information. But even so, we rarely take in all the facts at a glance; we often must reread, and if the journalist goes beyond the facts to offer some interpretation, we usually slow down to absorb both the information and its interpretation. Before venturing to offer our own, differing, view of the matter, we are well advised to reread a text thoroughly. If we neglect to do so, we often find, as someone else will happily remind us, that we have "gone off half-cocked."

Compared to our forebears, we are in an unusual position today, as our "Age of Information" envelops us in stream after stream of mediated presentation. We go from one thing to another; or one thing after another rushes at us and then passes us by. Turning back to reexperience a text often proves impossible. To some extent, "rereading" today becomes more a matter of pushing ahead and absorbing more and more examples until our sense of subtlety comes from a multiplicity of experiences as much as from reexperiencing any one of them. Still, we listen to CDs over and over and see movies again, especially our favorites. This allows us to become connoisseurs of detail and notice what we had not noticed before. It should be no surprise then that if you really want to know what is going on in one of the readings gathered here, you may need to reread it. You didn't become a discerning fan of your favorite band by just listening to a track or two. Similarly, you can't really come to know Momaday or Moore or Gould or Gray or any other writer on a single reading. And when it comes to writing — your writing — you write better by rewriting, which is to say, by rereading yourself.

Here again we confront the difficult and ultimately fruitless attempt to differentiate thought from writing. The academic paradigm has always been that first we do our research and then we write it up. In a broad sense, this is obviously true. You need to discover what you have to write about. You need a purpose and a sense of direction. All this implies making an outline first, and an outline is never a bad idea. However, a thoroughly perfected hierarchy of information, such as the one below, remains more an abstraction than a useful tool for most writers.

I.
  A.
    i.
    ii.
      a.
      b.
  B.
    i.
    ii.
      a.
      b.
II. . . .

A formal outline works occasionally, but the fact remains that each of those steps will become a sentence. Each sentence will introduce meaning that cannot be reduced to a simple letter or number. Those meanings, in turn, may lead you to altering your plan.

In practice, writing is a continuous interaction of attending to our thinking as it is just expressed and looking ahead. We can't get very far without an idea of where we want to go, and we often derail our attempts if we don't play close attention to what we have just said. Consequently, writing becomes a process of reading and rereading whatever we have written and then taking advantage of the leverage we have gained and pushing ahead. Often we find that we don't recognize our real subject until we have written pages and pages. Then suddenly we make a connection, or an imaginative leap, and we see where we are going. Berger, for example, may well have come to several other conclusions as to what those paintings represent before he thought of "Hsell." Perhaps he wrote of them first as representations of despair or as a more clinical documentation of disaster. But neither of those ideas quite satisfied him and he kept on thinking until his "eureka" moment occurred. At that point, he knew what to pare from his writing and how to develop what remained. The excitement of writing often ecomes in such moments of discovery, which, once made and recognized, dictate the organization of the work.

In a laboratory science, such a discovery is likely to be made before the writing begins. A researcher struggles with setting up the equipment, with determining how to measure a variable. Suddenly she sees something that rearranges everything and her problem is well on its way to resolution. In such a case, writing up a discovery afterward makes sense. This method works less well for a student attempting to write a term paper in history, even if she has recorded lots of research notes and found an order for them. It still may seem a muddle to her until, sticking with it, she makes a discovery and finds a powerful interpretive idea, perhaps after writing several pages. Her idea may never have come without all that preliminary writing, which then comes to seem more like fiddling with the experimental equipment in the lab and trying to figure out just how to set it up.

There is no one way to work out these problems. Today, furthermore, most writers use word processors. In a sense, revision has never been easier; we can run through our writing again and again, looking for that idea that will feel like a discovery and making changes along the way without retyping the whole piece. We write a bit, move back to the beginning, read through it all, and continue. Something in what we have written spurs the next thought. Whether we began with a list of topics, an outline, or just ideas in our head, as we write our writing makes its own suggestions. All good writers learn to be alert to them.

Even among poets, whom we might suppose to have the most complete identification of thought with writing, there are those who take notes constantly, who fill notebooks and journals with thinking. Is that research? Why not call it that? And there are those who sit in the dark, or lounge in a garden, or take long walks, thinking and thinking before taking up a pen. "What are you doing, Daddy?" Wallace Stevens's daughter asked when she came upon her father alone in a darkened study. "Thinking," he reportedly said. It remains for us to speculate how much that thinking changed as he put pen to paper.

Using and Acknowledging Sources

In most of the writing you will do, both during and after college, you will find yourself drawing on the ideas, information, and statements of others, interpreting this material, and combining it with your own experience, observation, and thought to generate new ideas of your own. Some of this material will come from your reading, some from lectures and class discussions, some from conversations and interviews. Our thinking does not take place in a vacuum but is shaped by a wide array of influences and sources.

To acknowledge your intellectual debts is by no means a confession that your work is unoriginal or without merit. In fact, original work in every field invariably builds on the prior work of researchers and thinkers. Most pieces you find in this book, except for those that deal entirely with personal experience, include some kind of acknowledgment or reference to the ideas, information, or statements of others. By acknowledging their sources, the writers of these pieces implicitly establish what is new or special in their own way of thinking. So you should always acknowledge the words and ideas that you borrow from others. Academic writing — the kind of writing you do in college and the kind of writing that most of your teachers do when they make contributions to their professional fields — depends on learning, on sources. Most of these sources are to be found in books and periodicals, but many are to be found in other places — especially on the Internet.

Taking Advantage of the Internet

The World Wide Web is an excellent resource for writers — if it is used properly. The Web is a vast network of information, much of which is not available in print or even on microfilm, and you can reach this material without moving from your chair. You can find online magazines and scholarly journals, groups discussing topics you are investigating, reports from organizations and institutions: words, pictures, music — it's all out there.

Even when the "same" text is available in a book, newspaper, or magazine, the Web version may offer advantages. The printed materials are easier to hold, carry, and read, but the Web materials are easier to find and search. If you don't take careful notes when you are reading a book, you may have great difficulty finding an important passage when you are writing about that book. With a digital text, however, whether on the Web or a disk, you can easily locate almost any passage you remember by using a search engine. Many search engines will bring back not just the word you are seeking but the whole context in which that word appears.

For example, one Web site, which your search engine can find, includes the text of all of Jane Austen's novels in digital form. If you go to that site and ask the search engine to find a particular word, such as *envy*, it will bring up every use of that word in all the novels, with the passage in which it occurs. If you are writing about Jane Austen, such a resource can be very helpful.

But if more information is available to you on the Web than in print, most Web resources have passed through less screening from editors and publishers than most books or magazine articles have. This means you have to be selective in what you use from the Web and cautious in how you use it.

Evaluating Web Sources   Many inexperienced users of the Web — including many students — do not use its resources effectively. They locate the name of an "expert," send the person an email, and ask for ideas they can use in writing papers or for a short summary of the person's knowledge that can be quoted in a paper to prove to a teacher that "research" has been done. But this is *not* research. Real experts seldom reply to such requests — they get too many — and false experts will lead a student astray. We know of a person who once had something he said about the 1962 Cuban missile crisis quoted on the Web. He has been getting emails ever since — asking him for his "expert" opinion — from students writing papers on that topic. But everything he knew, which was very little and wholly subjective, was in the material already quoted on the Web.

The Web is full of material that can be used in research. But none of that material will do your thinking for you. The value of a paper depends on the critical intelligence you bring to bear on the material you collect. Here are some things to look for in evaluating potential sources from the Web.

1. Is the creator or sponsor of the site identified? Does this information — or its absence — tell you anything about the purpose of the site? Does it reveal any possible biases?

2. Can you use links or a search engine to find out more about the site's creator or sponsor? Does this person or group seem knowledgeable? Trustworthy?

3. Is there an indication of when the site was created or last updated? Does the information seem current?

Using Web Information   Of course, you can take notes about material on the Web just as you can about print sources, but most Web sites also allow you to select and copy material that you can then paste directly into your own writing. In some cases, using the "Save As" command, you can save a whole page to your drive. Digital research tools also are available, and they allow you to drag and drop entire Web pages into research folders on your computer. In using material from the Web, here are a few rules you should follow.

1. If you use any material from a Web page in writing an academic paper, you must include a source citation in a list of works cited, in an endnote or a footnote, or in another location required by the documentation system you are using (see the next section, "Forms and Methods of Acknowledging Sources"). Web information is just like other information. You must give credit where credit is due.

2. Keep a record of the URL (Uniform Resource Locator) of the page from which you have taken the material, the date you accessed it, and any other information (such as the name of the site, its sponsor, or the author of the text) that might help someone locate the site again. Check the guidelines of your documentation system for what information is required.

3. If you paste another person's text into your own writing, you must indicate clearly that it is not your own material, either by putting it in quotation marks or by indenting it as you indent other long quotations. In either case, you need to cite your source. The Web makes it easy to cut and paste, so you need to take care in indicating where your material has come from.

4. Whether you just refer to information on the Web or actually copy it and paste it into your text, you must use it in your own argument. The bigger the item you paste, the more discussion and analysis you must develop. Don't fill your paper up with pasted material. Don't quote more than you need. And, remember, quoted material is most useful when you add something to or disagree with something in the quote. You are not looking for "answers" when you search the Web, but for material you can use in developing your *own* answers.

Forms and Methods of Acknowledging Sources

To get some idea of the various ways in which sources can be acknowledged, note the ways different writers in this book handle this task. The different methods are not just a question of differences among writers; different publications and disciplines have their own styles and standards. Within our collection, you will notice that some writers cite only the names of authors or interviewees or the titles of works from which they have gathered ideas or quoted statements. These citations are incorporated into the written discussion. You can see this technique used in Martin Luther King Jr.'s "Pilgrimage to Nonviolence." Other writers use footnotes or endnotes in which they provide the names of authors or interviewees, the titles of works, the dates of publication or of interviews, and specific page references, as you can see by looking at Theodore R. Sizer's "What High School Is" or Barbara Tuchman's "'This Is the End of the World': The Black Death." Finally, instead of using footnotes, some writers provide author and page references in the text of their discussion and include more detailed publication data, such as titles and dates of publication, in a complete list of works cited at the end, as Monica M. Moore does in her "Nonverbal Courtship Patterns in Women."

These various forms of acknowledgment are usually determined by the different audiences for which the pieces were written. Personal essays, newspaper reports, and magazine articles, which are written for a general audience, tend to rely on a more casual and shorthand form of acknowl-edgment, citing only the author or title of the source and placing that ac-knowledgment in the midst of the discussion. Work written for a more spe-cialized audience, such as academic research papers and scholarly articles or books, tends to rely on more detailed and systematic forms of acknowl-edgment, using either footnotes or a combination of references in the text and a complete list of works cited at the end. These specialized forms vary somewhat from one field to another, but papers in the arts and humanities tend to follow the guidelines set down by the Modern Language Associa-tion (MLA), and papers in the social sciences use the system of the Ameri-can Psychological Association (APA). In the sciences and technologies, each discipline tends to have its own system. For further reference, consult the *MLA Handbook for Writers of Research Papers*, 6th edition (New York: Modern Language Association of America, 2003), or the *Publication Man-ual of the American Psychological Association*, 5th edition (Washington, D.C.: American Psychological Association, 2001). The APA's guidelines can be found at the association's Web site, <http://www.apastyle.org/elecref .html>, which is being continually updated because, as they remind us, the requirements are changing, especially as we become more and more accus-tomed to using information on the Web as a resource.

As you can see, making proper acknowledgment of sources is both a matter of intellectual honesty and a social issue of many dimensions. Differ-ent groups agree on and enforce their own standards. That goes for your writing course as well. For the moment, your college or university or per-haps your writing class is the ultimate authority for you. Therefore, don't hesitate to look to your instructor for guidance. Most instructors have their specific preferences, but all will expect you to acknowledge your sources.

Documentation Models in MLA style

Because most of the writing courses in which *Fields of Reading* will be used require the Modern Language Association style, we provide examples of that style for several of the most commonly cited sources.

In the body of your paper, signal to your reader that you have used a source, and indicate, in parentheses, where the reader can find the source in your list of works cited. For instance, you might indicate the source of a quote this way:

> A recent biography starts out by claiming that Capote's father "might almost have been taken for a Yankee" (Clarke 3).

Include at the end of your essay a list of the sources you have cited. Al-phabetize the list by author's last name, and provide full publication infor-mation. Begin the first line of each entry flush left, and indent subsequent lines five spaces.

Book

Clarke, Gerald. Capote: A Biography. New York: Carroll & Graf, 2001.

Work in an Anthology

Didion, Joan. "On Keeping a Notebook." Fields of Reading: Motives for
    Writing. 8th ed. Ed. Nancy R. Comley, David Hamilton, Carl H.
    Klaus, Robert Scholes, and Nancy Sommers. Boston: Bedford/St. Mar-
    tin's, 2007. 328–34.

(Note that because you are citing Didion's essay, her name comes first and
is used to alphabetize this entry.)

Article in a Weekly Magazine

Goldstein, Patrick. "Yakety-Yak, Please Talk Back." Los Angeles Times
    Magazine 16 July 2005: 16+.

(The plus sign shows that the pages are not consecutive. If they are consecutive, show a page range, such as 16–18.)

Article in a Monthly Magazine

Smith, Gina. "Worlds without End." Buzz Sept. 2006: 46–48.

Web Site

National Council of Teachers of English. Jan. 2006. NCTE. 31 Mar. 2006
    <http://www.ncte.org>.

(Include the date of access for any online sources.)

E-Mail Message

Pyle, Kermia. "Re: Questions about French Fries." E-mail to the author. 31
    Mar. 2006.

Film or Video

The English Patient. Dir. Anthony Minghella. Perf. Willem Dafoe, Juliette
    Binoche, Ralph Fiennes, Kristin Scott Thomas. Miramax, 1996.

ARTS AND HUMANITIES

REFLECTING IN THE
Arts and Humanities

GRADUATION

Maya Angelou

In six volumes of autobiography, including her most recent, A
Song Flung Up to Heaven *(2002), Maya Angelou (b. 1928) has
written vividly of her struggles to achieve success as an actor, a
dancer, a songwriter, a teacher, and a poet. An active worker in the
civil rights movement of the 1960s, Angelou continues to focus
much of her writing on racial and cultural issues. She is Reynolds
Professor of American Studies at Wake Forest University in North
Carolina. The following selection is from* I Know Why the Caged
Bird Sings *(1969), in which she writes, "I speak to the Black experience, but I am always talking about the human condition."*

The children in Stamps[1] trembled visibly with anticipation. Some
adults were excited too, but to be certain the whole young population had
come down with graduation epidemic. Large classes were graduating
from both the grammar school and the high school. Even those who were
years removed from their own day of glorious release were anxious to
help with preparations as a kind of dry run. The junior students who
were moving into the vacating classes' chairs were tradition-bound to
show their talents for leadership and management. They strutted through
the school and around the campus exerting pressure on the lower grades.

---

[1]*Stamps*: A town in Arkansas. [Eds.]

Their authority was so new that occasionally if they pressed a little too hard it had to be overlooked. After all, next term was coming, and it never hurt a sixth grader to have a play sister in the eighth grade, or a tenth-year student to be able to call a twelfth grader Bubba. So all was endured in a spirit of shared understanding. But the graduating classes themselves were the nobility. Like travelers with exotic destinations on their minds, the graduates were remarkably forgetful. They came to school without their books, or tablets or even pencils. Volunteers fell over themselves to secure replacements for the missing equipment. When accepted, the willing workers might or might not be thanked, and it was of no importance to the pre-graduation rites. Even teachers were respectful of the now quiet and aging seniors, and tended to speak to them, if not as equals, as beings only slightly lower than themselves. After tests were returned and grades given, the student body, which acted like an extended family, knew who did well, who excelled, and what piteous ones had failed.

Unlike the white high school, Lafayette County Training School distinguished itself by having neither lawn, nor hedges, nor tennis court, nor climbing ivy. Its two buildings (main classrooms, the grade school and home economics) were set on a dirt hill with no fence to limit either its boundaries or those of bordering farms. There was a large expanse to the left of the school which was used alternately as a baseball diamond or basketball court. Rusty hoops on swaying poles represented the permanent recreational equipment, although bats and balls could be borrowed from the P.E. teacher if the borrower was qualified and if the diamond wasn't occupied.

Over this rocky area relieved by a few shady tall persimmon trees the graduating class walked. The girls often held hands and no longer bothered to speak to the lower students. There was a sadness about them, as if this old world was not their home and they were bound for higher ground. The boys, on the other hand, had become more friendly, more outgoing. A decided change from the closed attitude they projected while studying for finals. Now they seemed not ready to give up the old school, the familiar paths and classrooms. Only a small percentage would be continuing on to college — one of the South's A & M (agricultural and mechanical) schools, which trained Negro youths to be carpenters, farmers, handymen, masons, maids, cooks and baby nurses. Their future rode heavily on their shoulders, and blinded them to the collective joy that had pervaded the lives of the boys and girls in the grammar school graduating class.

Parents who could afford it had ordered new shoes and ready-made clothes for themselves from Sears and Roebuck or Montgomery Ward. They also engaged the best seamstresses to make the floating graduating dresses and to cut down secondhand pants which would be pressed to a military slickness for the important event.

Oh, it was important, all right. Whitefolks would attend the ceremony, and two or three would speak of God and home, and the Southern way of 5 life, and Mrs. Parsons, the principal's wife, would play the graduation march while the lower-grade graduates paraded down the aisles and took their seats below the platform. The high school seniors would wait in empty classrooms to make their dramatic entrance.

In the Store I was the person of the moment. The birthday girl. The center. Bailey[2] had graduated the year before, although to do so he had had to forfeit all pleasures to make up for his time lost in Baton Rouge.

My class was wearing butter-yellow piqué dresses, and Momma launched out on mine. She smocked the yoke into tiny crisscrossing puckers, then shirred the rest of the bodice. Her dark fingers ducked in and out of the lemony cloth as she embroidered raised daisies around the hem. Before she considered herself finished she had added a crocheted cuff on the puff sleeves, and a point crocheted collar.

I was going to be lovely. A walking model of all the various styles of fine hand sewing and it didn't worry me that I was only twelve years old and merely graduating from the eighth grade. Besides, many teachers in Arkansas Negro schools had only that diploma and were licensed to impart wisdom.

The days had become longer and more noticeable. The faded beige of former times had been replaced with strong and sure colors. I began to see my classmates' clothes, their skin tones, and the dust that waved off pussy willows. Clouds that lazed across the sky were objects of great concern to me. Their shiftier shapes might have held a message that in my new happiness and with a little bit of time I'd soon decipher. During that period I looked at the arch of heaven so religiously my neck kept a steady ache. I had taken to smiling more often, and my jaws hurt from the unaccustomed activity. Between the two physical sore spots, I suppose I could have been uncomfortable, but that was not the case. As a member of the winning team (the graduating class of 1940) I had outdistanced unpleasant sensations by miles. I was headed for the freedom of open fields.

Youth and social approval allied themselves with me and we trammeled memories of slights and insults. The wind of our swift passage remodeled my features. Lost tears were pounded to mud and then to dust. Years of withdrawal were brushed aside and left behind, as hanging ropes of parasitic moss. 10

My work alone had awarded me a top place and I was going to be one of the first called in the graduating ceremonies. On the classroom blackboard, as well as on the bulletin board in the auditorium, there were blue stars and white stars and red stars. No absences, no tardinesses, and my academic work was among the best of the year. I could say the preamble to the Constitution even faster than Bailey. We timed ourselves often: "WethepeopleoftheUnitedStatesinordertoformamoreperfectunion. . . ." I had memorized the Presidents of the United States from Washington to Roosevelt in chronological as well as alphabetical order.

---

[2]*Bailey*: The author's brother. [Eds.]

My hair pleased me too. Gradually the black mass had lengthened and thickened, so that it kept at last to its braided pattern, and I didn't have to yank my scalp off when I tried to comb it.

Louise and I had rehearsed the exercises until we tired out ourselves. Henry Reed was class valedictorian. He was a small, very black boy with hooded eyes, a long, broad nose and an oddly shaped head. I had admired him for years because each term he and I vied for the best grades in our class. Most often he bested me, but instead of being disappointed I was pleased that we shared top places between us. Like many Southern Black children, he lived with his grandmother, who was as strict as Momma and as kind as she knew how to be. He was courteous, respectful and soft-spoken to elders, but on the playground he chose to play the roughest games. I admired him. Anyone, I reckoned, sufficiently afraid or sufficiently dull could be polite. But to be able to operate at a top level with both adults and children was admirable.

His valedictory speech was entitled "To Be or Not to Be." The rigid tenth-grade teacher had helped him write it. He'd been working on the dramatic stresses for months.

The weeks until graduation were filled with heady activities. A group of small children were to be presented in a play about buttercups and daisies and bunny rabbits. They could be heard throughout the building practicing their hops and their little songs that sounded like silver bells. The older girls (nongraduates, of course) were assigned the task of making refreshments for the night's festivities. A tangy scent of ginger, cinnamon, nutmeg and chocolate wafted around the home economics building as the budding cooks made samples for themselves and their teachers. 15

In every corner of the workshop, axes and saws split fresh timber as the woodshop boys made sets and stage scenery. Only the graduates were left out of the general bustle. We were free to sit in the library at the back of the building or look in quite detachedly, naturally, on the measures being taken for our event.

Even the minister preached on graduation the Sunday before. His subject was, "Let your light so shine that men will see your good works and praise your Father, Who is in Heaven." Although the sermon was purported to be addressed to us, he used the occasion to speak to backsliders, gamblers and general ne'er-do-wells. But since he had called our names at the beginning of the service we were mollified.

Among Negroes the tradition was to give presents to children going only from one grade to another. How much more important this was when the person was graduating at the top of the class. Uncle Willie and Momma had sent away for a Mickey Mouse watch like Bailey's. Louise gave me four embroidered handkerchiefs. (I gave her crocheted doilies.) Mrs. Sneed, the minister's wife, made me an undershirt to wear for graduation, and nearly every customer gave me a nickel or maybe even a dime with the instruction "Keep on moving to higher ground," or some such encouragement.

Amazingly the great day finally dawned and I was out of bed before I knew it. I threw open the back door to see it more clearly, but Momma said, "Sister, come away from that door and put your robe on."

I hoped the memory of that morning would never leave me. Sunlight   20
was itself young, and the day had none of the insistence maturity would
bring it in a few hours. In my robe and barefoot in the backyard, under
cover of going to see about my new beans, I gave myself up to the gentle
warmth and thanked God that no matter what evil I had done in my life He
had allowed me to live to see this day. Somewhere in my fatalism I had expected to die, accidentally, and never have the chance to walk up the stairs
in the auditorium and gracefully receive my hard-earned diploma. Out of
God's merciful bosom I had won reprieve.

Bailey came out in his robe and gave me a box wrapped in Christmas
paper. He said he had saved his money for months to pay for it. It felt like a
box of chocolates, but I knew Bailey wouldn't save money to buy candy
when we had all we could want under our noses.

He was as proud of the gift as I. It was a soft-leather-bound copy of a
collection of poems by Edgar Allan Poe, or, as Bailey and I called him,
"Eap." I turned to "Annabel Lee" and we walked up and down the garden
rows, the cool dirt between our toes, reciting the beautifully sad lines.

Momma made a Sunday breakfast although it was only Friday. After
we finished the blessing, I opened my eyes to find the watch on my plate. It
was a dream of a day. Everything went smoothly and to my credit. I didn't
have to be reminded or scolded for anything. Near evening I was too jittery
to attend to chores, so Bailey volunteered to do all before his bath.

Days before, we had made a sign for the Store, and as we turned out
the lights Momma hung the cardboard over the doorknob. It read clearly:
CLOSED. GRADUATION.

My dress fitted perfectly and everyone said that I looked like a sun-   25
beam in it. On the hill, going toward the school, Bailey walked behind with
Uncle Willie, who muttered, "Go on, Ju." He wanted him to walk ahead
with us because it embarrassed him to have to walk so slowly. Bailey said
he'd let the ladies walk together, and the men would bring up the rear. We
all laughed, nicely.

Little children dashed by out of the dark like fireflies. Their crepe-paper
dresses and butterfly wings were not made for running and we heard more
than one rip, dryly, and the regretful "uh uh" that followed.

The school blazed without gaiety. The windows seemed cold and un-
friendly from the lower hill. A sense of ill-fated timing crept over me, and if
Momma hadn't reached for my hand I would have drifted back to Bailey
and Uncle Willie, and possibly beyond. She made a few slow jokes about
my feet getting cold, and tugged me along to the now-strange building.

Around the front steps, assurance came back. There were my fellow
"greats," the graduating class. Hair brushed back, legs oiled, new dresses
and pressed pleats, fresh pocket handkerchiefs and little handbags, all home-
sewn. Oh, we were up to snuff, all right. I joined my comrades and didn't
even see my family go in to find seats in the crowded auditorium.

The school band struck up a march and all classes filed in as had been
rehearsed. We stood in front of our seats, as assigned, and on a signal from
the choir director, we sat. No sooner had this been accomplished than the

band started to play the national anthem. We rose again and sang the song, after which we recited the pledge of allegiance. We remained standing for a brief minute before the choir director and the principal signaled to us, rather desperately I thought, to take our seats. The command was so unusual that our carefully rehearsed and smooth-running machine was thrown off. For a full minute we fumbled for our chairs and bumped into each other awkwardly. Habits change or solidify under pressure, so in our state of nervous tension we had been ready to follow our usual assembly pattern: the American national anthem, then the pledge of allegiance, then the song every Black person I knew called the Negro National Anthem. All done in the same key, with the same passion and most often standing on the same foot.

Finding my seat at last, I was overcome with a presentiment of worse   30
things to come. Something unrehearsed, unplanned, was going to happen, and we were going to be made to look bad. I distinctly remember being explicit in the choice of pronoun. It was "we," the graduating class, the unit, that concerned me then.

The principal welcomed "parents and friends" and asked the Baptist minister to lead us in prayer. His invocation was brief and punchy, and for a second I thought we were getting on the high road to right action. When the principal came back to the dais, however, his voice had changed. Sounds always affected me profoundly and the principal's voice was one of my favorites. During assembly it melted and lowed weakly into the audience. It had not been in my plan to listen to him, but my curiosity was piqued and I straightened up to give him my attention.

He was talking about Booker T. Washington, our "late great leader," who said we can be as close as the fingers on the hand, etc. . . . Then he said a few vague things about friendship and the friendship of kindly people to those less fortunate than themselves. With that his voice nearly faded, thin, away. Like a river diminishing to a stream and then to a trickle. But he cleared his throat and said, "Our speaker tonight, who is also our friend, came from Texarkana to deliver the commencement address, but due to the irregularity of the train schedule, he's going to, as they say, 'speak and run.'" He said that we understood and wanted the man to know that we were most grateful for the time he was able to give us and then something about how we were willing always to adjust to another's program, and without more ado — "I give you Mr. Edward Donleavy."

Not one but two white men came through the door off-stage. The shorter one walked to the speaker's platform, and the tall one moved to the center seat and sat down. But that was our principal's seat, and already occupied. The dislodged gentleman bounced around for a long breath or two before the Baptist minister gave him his chair, then with more dignity than the situation deserved, the minister walked off the stage.

Donleavy looked at the audience once (on reflection, I'm sure that he wanted only to reassure himself that we were really there), adjusted his glasses and began to read from a sheaf of papers.

He was glad "to be here and to see the work going on just as it was in 35
the other schools."

At the first "Amen" from the audience I willed the offender to immediate death by choking on the word. But Amens and Yes, sir's began to fall around the room like rain through a ragged umbrella.

He told us of the wonderful changes we children in Stamps had in store. The Central School (naturally, the white school was Central) had already been granted improvements that would be in use in the fall. A well-known artist was coming from Little Rock to teach art to them. They were going to have the newest microscopes and chemistry equipment for their laboratory. Mr. Donleavy didn't leave us long in the dark over who made these improvements available to Central High. Nor were we to be ignored in the general betterment scheme he had in mind.

He said that he had pointed out to people at a very high level that one of the first-line football tacklers at Arkansas Agricultural and Mechanical College had graduated from good old Lafayette County Training School. Here fewer Amen's were heard. Those few that did break through lay dully in the air with the heaviness of habit.

He went on to praise us. He went on to say how he had bragged that "one of the best basketball players at Fisk sank his first ball right here at Lafayette County Training School."

The white kids were going to have a chance to become Galileos and 40
Madame Curies and Edisons and Gauguins, and our boys (the girls weren't even in on it) would try to be Jesse Owenses and Joe Louises.

Owens and the Brown Bomber were great heroes in our world, but what school official in the white-goddom of Little Rock had the right to decide that those two men must be our only heroes? Who decided that for Henry Reed to become a scientist he had to work like George Washington Carver, as a bootblack, to buy a lousy microscope? Bailey was obviously always going to be too small to be an athlete, so which concrete angel glued to what county seat had decided that if my brother wanted to become a lawyer he had to first pay penance for his skin by picking cotton and hoeing corn and studying correspondence books at night for twenty years?

The man's dead words fell like bricks around the auditorium and too many settled in my belly. Constrained by hard-learned manners I couldn't look behind me, but to my left and right the proud graduating class of 1940 had dropped their heads. Every girl in my row had found something new to do with her handkerchief. Some folded the tiny squares into love knots, some into triangles, but most were wadding them, then pressing them flat on their yellow laps.

On the dais, the ancient tragedy was being replayed. Professor Parsons sat, a sculptor's reject, rigid. His large, heavy body seemed devoid of will or willingness, and his eyes said he was no longer with us. The other teachers examined the flag (which was draped stage right) or their notes, or the windows which opened on our now-famous playing diamond.

Graduation, the hush-hush magic time of frills and gifts and congratulations and diplomas, was finished for me before my name was called. The accomplishment was nothing. The meticulous maps, drawn in three colors of ink, learning and spelling decasyllabic words, memorizing the whole of *The Rape of Lucrece*[3] — it was for nothing. Donleavy had exposed us.

We were maids and farmers, handymen and washerwomen, and any-   45
thing higher that we aspired to was farcical and presumptuous.

Then I wished that Gabriel Prosser[4] and Nat Turner[5] had killed all white-folks in their beds and that Abraham Lincoln had been assassinated before the signing of the Emancipation Proclamation, and that Harriet Tubman[6] had been killed by that blow on her head and Christopher Columbus had drowned in the *Santa Maria.*

It was awful to be a Negro and have no control over my life. It was brutal to be young and already trained to sit quietly and listen to charges brought against my color with no chance of defense. We should all be dead. I thought I should like to see us all dead, one on top of the other. A pyramid of flesh with the whitefolks on the bottom, as the broad base, then the Indians with their silly tomahawks and teepees and wigwams and treaties, the Negroes with their mops and recipes and cotton sacks and spirituals sticking out of their mouths. The Dutch children should all stumble in their wooden shoes and break their necks. The French should choke to death on the Louisiana Purchase (1803) while silkworms ate all the Chinese with their stupid pigtails. As a species, we were an abomination. All of us.

Donleavy was running for election, and assured our parents that if he won we could count on having the only colored paved playing field in that part of Arkansas. Also — he never looked up to acknowledge the grunts of acceptance — also, we were bound to get some new equipment for the home economics building and the workshop.

He finished, and since there was no need to give any more than the most perfunctory thank-you's, he nodded to the men on the stage, and the tall white man who was never introduced joined him at the door. They left with the attitude that now they were off to something really important.

----

[3]*The Rape of Lucrece:* A 1,855-line narrative poem by William Shakespeare. [Eds.]

[4]*Gabriel Prosser* (c. 1775–1800): A leader of a thwarted slave rebellion in Virginia in 1800. [Eds.]

[5]*Nat Turner* (1800–1831): The leader of about sixty slaves who killed about fifty-five white Virginians in 1831. [Eds.]

[6]*Harriet Tubman* (c. 1820–1913): A Maryland slave who escaped to Pennsylvania in 1850 and who conducted approximately 300 persons to freedom on the Underground Railroad and worked as an abolitionist. [Eds.]

(The graduation ceremonies at Lafayette County Training School had been 50
a mere preliminary.)

The ugliness they left was palpable. An uninvited guest who wouldn't
leave. The choir was summoned and sang a modern arrangement of "Onward, Christian Soldiers," with new words pertaining to graduates seeking
their place in the world. But it didn't work. Elouise, the daughter of the
Baptist minister, recited "Invictus,"[7] and I could have cried at the imperti-
nence of "I am the master of my fate, I am the captain of my soul."

My name had lost its ring of familiarity and I had to be nudged to go
and receive my diploma. All my preparations had fled. I neither marched up
to the stage like a conquering Amazon, nor did I look in the audience for
Bailey's nod of approval. Marguerite Johnson, I heard the name again, my
honors were read, there were noises in the audience of appreciation, and I
took my place on the stage as rehearsed.

I thought about colors I hated: ecru, puce, lavender, beige and black.

There was shuffling and rustling around me, then Henry Reed was giving his valedictory address, "To Be or Not to Be." Hadn't he heard the
whitefolks? We couldn't *be,* so the question was a waste of time. Henry's
voice came out clear and strong. I feared to look at him. Hadn't he got the
message? There was no "nobler in the mind" for Negroes because the world
didn't think we had minds, and they let us know it. "Outrageous fortune"?
Now, that was a joke. When the ceremony was over I had to tell Henry Reed
some things. That is, if I still cared. Not "rub," Henry, "erase." "Ah, there's
the erase." Us.

Henry had been a good student in elocution. His voice rose on tides of
promise and fell on waves of warnings. The English teacher had helped him
to create a sermon winging through Hamlet's soliloquy. To be a man, a
doer, a builder, a leader, or to be a tool, an unfunny joke, a crusher of funky
toadstools. I marveled that Henry could go through with the speech as if we
had a choice.

I had been listening and silently rebutting each sentence with my eyes 55
closed; then there was a hush, which in an audience warns that something
unplanned is happening. I looked up and saw Henry Reed, the conservative, the proper, the A student, turn his back to the audience and turn to us
(the proud graduating class of 1940) and sing, nearly speaking,

> "Lift ev'ry voice and sing
> Till earth and heaven ring
> Ring with the harmonies of Liberty . . ."

---

[7]*"Invictus"*: A poem by the English poet William Ernest Henley (1849–1903).
Its inspirational conclusion is quoted here. [Eds.]

It was the poem written by James Weldon Johnson. It was the music composed by J. Rosamond Johnson. It was the Negro National Anthem. Out of habit we were singing it.

Our mothers and fathers stood in the dark hall and joined the hymn of encouragement. A kindergarten teacher led the small children onto the stage and the buttercups and daisies and bunny rabbits marked time and tried to follow:

> "Stony the road we trod
> Bitter the chastening rod
> Felt in the days when hope, unborn, had died.
> Yet with a steady beat
> Have not our weary feet
> Come to the place for which our fathers sighed?"

Each child I knew had learned that song with his ABC's and along with "Jesus Loves Me This I Know." But I personally had never heard it before. Never heard the words, despite the thousands of times I had sung them. Never thought they had anything to do with me.

On the other hand, the words of Patrick Henry had made such an impression on me that I had been able to stretch myself tall and trembling and say, "I know not what course others may take, but as for me, give me liberty or give me death."

And now I heard, really for the first time:

> "We have come over a way that with tears
> has been watered,
> We have come, treading our path through
> the blood of the slaughtered."

While echoes of the song shivered in the air, Henry Reed bowed his   60
head, said "Thank you," and returned to his place in the line. The tears that slipped down many faces were not wiped away in shame.

We were on top again. As always, again. We survived. The depths had been icy and dark, but now a bright sun spoke to our souls. I was no longer simply a member of the proud graduating class of 1940; I was a proud member of the wonderful, beautiful Negro race.

Oh, Black known and unknown poets, how often have your auctioned pains sustained us? Who will compute the only nights made less lonely by your songs, or the empty pots made less tragic by your tales?

If we were a people much given to revealing secrets, we might raise monuments and sacrifice to the memories of our poets, but slavery cured us of that weakness. It may be enough, however, to have it said that we survive in exact relationship to the dedication of our poets (include preachers, musicians and blues singers).

QUESTIONS

1. Why was grammar and high school graduation such an important event in Stamps, Arkansas? Note the rituals and preparations associated with this event. How do they compare with those that accompanied your own junior high or high school graduation?
2. At the beginning of the graduation ceremony, Angelou was "overcome with a presentiment of worse things to come. Something unrehearsed, unplanned, was going to happen" (paragraph 30). What "unrehearsed, unplanned" event does occur? How does Angelou convey to the reader the meaning of this event?
3. Toward the end of the essay we are told, "I was no longer simply a member of the proud graduating class of 1940; I was a proud member of the wonderful, beautiful Negro race" (paragraph 61). How did the experience of the graduation change Angelou's way of thinking about herself and her people?
4. Understanding the structure of this essay is important for understanding the meaning of the essay. How does Angelou organize her material, and how does this organization reflect her purpose? Why do you think Angelou changes her point of view from third person in the first five paragraphs to first person in the rest of the essay?
5. Think of an event in your life that didn't turn out as you expected. What were your expectations for this event? What was the reality? Write an essay in which you show the significance of this event by contrasting how you planned for the event with how it actually turned out.
6. We all have had experiences that have changed the directions of our lives. These experiences may be momentous, such as moving from one country to another or losing a parent, or they may be experiences that did not loom large at the time but that changed the way you thought about things, such as finding that your parents disapproved of your best friend because of her race. Recall such a turning point in your life, and give readers a sense of what your life was like before the event and how it changed after the event.

MAKING CONNECTIONS

1. Compare the points of view taken by Angelou and Alice Walker (p. 54). How does the "presence" of the valedictorian in Angelou's essay influence the point of view she takes?
2. Two things link this essay with George Orwell's "Shooting an Elephant" (p. 354): each essay turns on an unexpected event, and each event prompts reflections on political domination. The two essays are from dissimilar points of view, but both Orwell in the Indian village and Mr. Donleavy at the Stamps graduation ceremonies are outsiders. Write an essay in which you compare and contrast these two events.

BEAUTY:
When the Other Dancer Is the Self

Alice Walker

Born in Eatonton, Georgia, in 1944, Alice Walker is the youngest of eight children. Her father was a sharecropper, and her mother was a maid. A graduate of Sarah Lawrence College, Walker has been an active worker for civil rights. She has been a fellow of the Radcliffe Institute, a contributing and consulting editor for Ms. *magazine, and a teacher of literature and writing at a number of colleges and universities. She has published poetry, essays, short stories, and novels. Her novels, all dealing with the African American experience in the United States, include* The Third Life of Grange Copeland *(1970);* Meridian *(1976);* The Color Purple *(1982), for which she won both the Pulitzer Prize and the National Book Award;* The Temple of My Familiar *(1989);* Possessing the Secret of Joy *(1992);* By the Light of My Father's Smile *(1998); and* Now Is the Time to Open Your Heart *(2004). "Beauty: When the Other Dancer Is the Self" appeared first in* Ms. *magazine and later in a collection of essays,* In Search of Our Mothers' Gardens *(1983). When asked why she writes, Walker said, "I'm really paying homage to people I love, the people who are thought to be dumb and backward but who were the ones who first taught me to see beauty."*

It is a bright summer day in 1947. My father, a fat, funny man with beautiful eyes and a subversive wit, is trying to decide which of his eight children he will take with him to the county fair. My mother, of course, will not go. She is knocked out from getting most of us ready: I hold my neck stiff against the pressure of her knuckles as she hastily completes the braiding and then beribboning of my hair.

My father is the driver for the rich old white lady up the road. Her name is Miss Mey. She owns all the land for miles around, as well as the house in which we live. All I remember about her is that she once offered to pay my mother thirty-five cents for cleaning her house, raking up piles of her magnolia leaves, and washing her family's clothes, and that my mother — she of no money, eight children, and a chronic earache — refused it. But I do not think of this in 1947. I am two and a half years old. I want to go everywhere my daddy goes. I am excited at the prospect of riding in a car. Someone has told me fairs are fun. That there is room in the car for only three of us doesn't faze me at all. Whirling happily in my starchy frock, showing off my biscuit-polished patent-leather shoes and lavender socks, tossing my head in a way that makes my ribbons bounce, I stand, hands on hips, before my father. "Take me, Daddy," I say with assurance; "I'm the prettiest!"

Later, it does not surprise me to find myself in Miss Mey's shiny black car, sharing the back seat with the other lucky ones. Does not surprise me that I thoroughly enjoy the fair. At home that night I tell the unlucky ones all I can remember about the merry-go-round, the man who eats live chickens, and the teddy bears, until they say: that's enough, baby Alice. Shut up now, and go to sleep.

It is Easter Sunday, 1950. I am dressed in a green, flocked, scalloped-hem dress (handmade by my adoring sister, Ruth) that has its own smooth satin petticoat and tiny hot-pink roses tucked into each scallop. My shoes, new T-strap patent leather, again highly biscuit-polished. I am six years old and have learned one of the longest Easter speeches to be heard that day, totally unlike the speech I said when I was two: "Easter lilies / pure and white / blossom in / the morning light." When I rise to give my speech I do so on a great wave of love and pride and expectation. People in the church stop rustling their new crinolines. They seem to hold their breath. I can tell they admire my dress, but it is my spirit, bordering on sassiness (womanishness), they secretly applaud.

"That girl's a little *mess*," they whisper to each other, pleased.   5

Naturally I say my speech without stammer or pause, unlike those who stutter, stammer, or worst of all, forget. This is before the word "beautiful" exists in people's vocabulary, but "Oh, isn't she the *cutest* thing!" frequently floats my way. "And got so much sense!" they gratefully add . . . for which thoughtful addition I thank them to this day.

It was great fun being cute. But then, one day, it ended.

I am eight years old and a tomboy. I have a cowboy hat, cowboy boots, checkered shirt and pants, all red. My playmates are my brothers, two and four years older than I. Their colors are black and green, the only difference in the way we are dressed. On Saturday nights we all go to the picture show, even my mother; Westerns are her favorite kind of movie. Back home, "on the ranch," we pretend we are Tom Mix, Hopalong Cassidy, Lash LaRue (we've even named one of our dogs Lash LaRue); we chase each other for hours rustling cattle, being outlaws, delivering damsels from distress. Then my parents decide to buy my brothers guns. These are not "real" guns. They shoot "BBs," copper pellets my brothers say will kill birds. Because I am a girl, I do not get a gun. Instantly I am relegated to the position of Indian. Now there appears a great distance between us. They shoot and shoot at everything with their new guns. I try to keep up with my bow and arrows.

One day while I am standing on top of our makeshift "garage" — pieces of tin nailed across some poles — holding my bow and arrow and

looking out toward the fields, I feel an incredible blow in my right eye. I
look down just in time to see my brother lower his gun.

Both brothers rush to my side. My eye stings, and I cover it with my   10
hand. "If you tell," they say, "we will get a whipping. You don't want that to
happen, do you?" I do not. "Here is a piece of wire," says the older brother,
picking it up from the roof; "say you stepped on one end of it and the other
flew up and hit you." The pain is beginning to start. "Yes," I say. "Yes, I will
say that is what happened." If I do not say this is what happened, I know my
brothers will find ways to make me wish I had. But now I will say anything
that gets me to my mother.

Confronted by our parents we stick to the lie agreed upon. They place
me on a bench on the porch and I close my left eye while they examine
the right. There is a tree growing from underneath the porch that climbs
past the railing to the roof. It is the last thing my right eye sees. I watch as
its trunk, its branches, and then its leaves are blotted out by the rising
blood.

I am in shock. First there is intense fever, which my father tries to break
using lily leaves bound around my head. Then there are chills: my mother
tries to get me to eat soup. Eventually, I do not know how, my parents learn
what has happened. A week after the "accident" they take me to see a doctor. "Why did you wait so long to come?" he asks, looking into my eye and
shaking his head. "Eyes are sympathetic," he says. "If one is blind, the
other will likely become blind too."

This comment of the doctor's terrifies me. But it is really how I look
that bothers me most. Where the BB pellet struck there is a glob of whitish
scar tissue, a hideous cataract, on my eye. Now when I stare at people — a
favorite pastime, up to now — they will stare back. Not at the "cute" little
girl, but at her scar. For six years I do not stare at anyone, because I do not
raise my head.

Years later, in the throes of a mid-life crisis, I ask my mother and sister
whether I changed after the "accident." "No," they say, puzzled. "What do
you mean?"

What do I mean?   15

I am eight, and, for the first time, doing poorly in school, where I have
been something of a whiz since I was four. We have just moved to the place
where the "accident" occurred. We do not know any of the people around
us because this is a different county. The only time I see the friends I knew
is when we go back to our old church. The new school is the former state
penitentiary. It is a large stone building, cold and drafty, crammed to overflowing with boisterous, ill-disciplined children. On the third floor there is a
huge circular imprint of some partition that has been torn out.

"What used to be here?" I ask a sullen girl next to me on our way past
it to lunch.

"The electric chair," says she.

At night I have nightmares about the electric chair, and about all the people reputedly "fried" in it. I am afraid of the school, where all the students seem to be budding criminals.

"What's the matter with your eye?" they ask, critically.   20

When I don't answer (I cannot decide whether it was an "accident" or not), they shove me, insist on a fight.

My brother, the one who created the story about the wire, comes to my rescue. But then brags so much about "protecting" me, I become sick.

After months of torture at the school, my parents decide to send me back to our old community, to my old school. I live with my grandparents and the teacher they board. But there is no room for Phoebe, my cat. By the time my grandparents decide there *is* room, and I ask for my cat, she cannot be found. Miss Yarborough, the boarding teacher, takes me under her wing, and begins to teach me to play the piano. But soon she marries an African — a "prince," she says — and is whisked away to his continent.

At my old school there is at least one teacher who loves me. She is the teacher who "knew me before I was born" and bought my first baby clothes. It is she who makes life bearable. It is her presence that finally helps me turn on the one child at the school who continually calls me "one-eyed bitch." One day I simply grab him by his coat and beat him until I am satisfied. It is my teacher who tells me my mother is ill.

My mother is lying in bed in the middle of the day, something I have   25
never seen. She is in too much pain to speak. She has an abscess in her ear. I stand looking down on her, knowing that if she dies, I cannot live. She is being treated with warm oils and hot bricks held against her cheek. Finally a doctor comes. But I must go back to my grandparents' house. The weeks pass but I am hardly aware of it. All I know is that my mother might die, my father is not so jolly, my brothers still have their guns, and I am the one sent away from home.

"You did not change," they say.

Did I imagine the anguish of never looking up?

I am twelve. When relatives come to visit I hide in my room. My cousin Brenda, just my age, whose father works in the post office and whose mother is a nurse, comes to find me. "Hello," she says. And then she asks, looking at my recent school picture, which I did not want taken, and on which the "glob," as I think of it, is clearly visible, "You still can't see out of that eye?"

"No," I say, and flop back on the bed over my book.

That night, as I do almost every night, I abuse my eye. I rant and rave   30
at it, in front of the mirror. I plead with it to clear up before morning. I tell it I hate and despise it. I do not pray for sight. I pray for beauty.

"You did not change," they say.

I am fourteen and baby-sitting for my brother Bill, who lives in Boston. He is my favorite brother and there is a strong bond between us. Understanding my feelings of shame and ugliness he and his wife take me to a local hospital, where the "glob" is removed by a doctor named O. Henry. There is still a small bluish crater where scar tissue was, but the ugly white stuff is gone. Almost immediately I become a different person from the girl who does not raise her head. Or so I think. Now that I've raised my head I win the boyfriend of my dreams. Now that I've raised my head I have plenty of friends. Now that I've raised my head classwork comes from my lips faultlessly as Easter speeches did, and I leave high school as valedictorian, most popular student, and *queen*, hardly believing my luck. Ironically, the girl who was voted most beautiful in our class (and was) was later shot twice through the chest by a male companion, using a "real" gun, while she was pregnant. But that's another story in itself. Or is it?

"You did not change," they say.

It is now thirty years since the "accident." A beautiful journalist comes to visit and to interview me. She is going to write a cover story for her magazine that focuses on my latest book. "Decide how you want to look on the cover," she says. "Glamorous, whatever."

Never mind "glamorous," it is the "whatever" that I hear. Suddenly all   35
I can think of is whether I will get enough sleep the night before the photography session: if I don't, my eye will be tired and wander, as blind eyes will.

At night in bed with my lover I think up reasons why I should not appear on the cover of a magazine. "My meanest critics will say I've sold out," I say. "My family will now realize I write scandalous books."

"But what's the real reason you don't want to do this?" he asks.

"Because in all probability," I say in a rush, "my eye won't be straight."

"It will be straight enough," he says. Then, "Besides, I thought you'd made your peace with that."

And I suddenly remember that I have.   40

I remember:

I am talking to my brother Jimmy, asking if he remembers anything unusual about the day I was shot. He does not know I consider that day the last time my father, with his sweet home remedy of cool lily leaves, chose me, and that I suffered and raged inside because of this. "Well," he says, "all I remember is standing by the side of the highway with Daddy, trying to flag down a car. A white man stopped, but when Daddy said he needed somebody to take his little girl to the doctor, he drove off."

I remember:

I am in the desert for the first time. I fall totally in love with it. I am so overwhelmed by its beauty, I confront for the first time, consciously, the meaning of the doctor's words years ago: "Eyes are sympathetic. If one is blind, the other will likely become blind too." I realize I have dashed about the world madly, looking at this, looking at that, storing up images against the fading of the light. *But I might have missed seeing the desert!* The shock of that possibility — and gratitude for over twenty-five years of sight — sends me literally to my knees. Poem after poem comes — which is perhaps how poets pray.

ON SIGHT

I am so thankful I have seen
The Desert
And the creatures in the desert
And the desert Itself.

The desert has its own moon
Which I have seen
With my own eye.

There is no flag on it.

Trees of the desert have arms
All of which are always up
That is because the moon is up
The sun is up
Also the sky
The stars
Clouds
None with flags.

If there *were* flags, I doubt
the trees would point.
Would you?

But mostly, I remember this: 45

I am twenty-seven, and my baby daughter is almost three. Since her birth I have worried about her discovery that her mother's eyes are different from other people's. Will she be embarrassed? I think. What will she say? Every day she watches a television program called "Big Blue Marble." It begins with a picture of the earth as it appears from the moon. It is bluish, a little battered-looking, but full of light, with whitish clouds swirling around it. Every time I see it I weep with love, as if it is a picture of Grandma's house. One day when I am putting Rebecca down for her nap, she suddenly focuses on my eye. Something inside me cringes, gets ready to try to protect myself. All children are cruel about physical differences, I know from experience, and that they don't always mean to be is another matter. I assume Rebecca will be the same.

But no-o-o-o. She studies my face intently as we stand, her inside and me outside her crib. She even holds my face maternally between her dimpled little hands. Then, looking every bit as serious and lawyerlike as her father, she says, as if it may just possibly have slipped my attention: "Mommy, there's a *world* in your eye." (As in, "Don't be alarmed, or do anything crazy.") And then, gently, but with great interest: "Mommy, where did you *get* that world in your eye?"

For the most part, the pain left then. (So what, if my brothers grew up to buy even more powerful pellet guns for their sons and to carry real guns themselves. So what, if a young "Morehouse man"[1] once nearly fell off the steps of Trevor Arnett Library because he thought my eyes were blue.) Crying and laughing I ran to the bathroom, while Rebecca mumbled and sang herself off to sleep. Yes indeed, I realized, looking into the mirror. There *was* a world in my eye. And I saw that it was possible to love it: that in fact, for all it had taught me of shame and anger and inner vision, I *did* love it. Even to see it drifting out of orbit in boredom, or rolling up out of fatigue, not to mention floating back at attention in excitement (bearing witness, a friend has called it), deeply suitable to my personality, and even characteristic of me.

That night I dream I am dancing to Stevie Wonder's song "Always" (the name of the song is really "As," but I hear it as "Always"). As I dance, whirling and joyous, happier than I've ever been in my life, another bright-faced dancer joins me. We dance and kiss each other and hold each other through the night. The other dancer has obviously come through all right, as I have done. She is beautiful, whole and free. And she is also me.

QUESTIONS

1. Walker's essay moves forward in time through abrupt though steadily progressive descriptions of episodes. What effect on the reader does this structure produce? Why do you suppose Walker chose this form instead of providing transitions from one episode to the next?
2. Consider Walker's method of contrasting other people's memories with her own. What effect is created by the repetition of "You did not change"?
3. Consider Walker's choices of episodes or examples of beauty. How does each one work toward developing a definition of beauty?
4. In what ways does this essay play with the possible meanings of the familiar adage, "Beauty is in the eye of the beholder"?
5. One theme of this essay could be that of coming to terms with a disfigurement or with an imagined loss of physical beauty. Recall an event (or accident) in your own life that changed your perception of

---

[1]*Morehouse man*: A student at Morehouse College, a traditionally black college for men in Atlanta, Georgia. [Eds.]

yourself. Write a reflective narrative in which you use Walker's method of chronologically arranged episodes, including reflections on the time before the change, the change itself, and episodes following the change. Like Walker, you may want to contrast (or compare) your memories with those of others.

6. Recall a memorable event that occurred a year or more ago. It might be an event in your family's life or a public event at which you and your friends were present. Write down your memories of the event, and then interview your family or friends and write down their recollections. Compare the various memories of the event. Come to a conclusion about the differences or similarities you find and perhaps about the selectivity of memory.

MAKING CONNECTIONS

Walker's daughter's exclamation, "Mommy, there's a *world* in your eye" (paragraph 47), is a transcendent moment. It is also a metaphor. Other writers could also be said to have a world in their eye. For example, Carl Sagan's description of how insight depends on a degree of restriction (p. 620) is closely related to Walker's theme. Select another essay from one of the "Reflecting" sections, and show how Walker's reflections on her blind eye can help us understand the discoveries that the writer of the other essay is making.

MIRRORS

Lucy Grealy

Lucy Grealy (1963–2002), an award-winning poet, attended the Iowa Writer's Workshop and was a fellow at the Bunting Institute of Radcliffe. At the age of nine, Grealy had cancer of the jaw, and the right side of her jaw was removed. In the following essay, which first appeared in Harper's *and which received the National Magazine Award, Grealy writes about the thirty operations she had in twenty years to try to reconstruct her face. In both this selection and her book,* Autobiography of a Face *(1994), Grealy reflects on the obsessions and perceptions of physical beauty that dominate our culture. Her last book was the essay collection* As Seen on TV: Provocations *(2000). She died at the age of thirty-nine, an apparent suicide.*

There was a long period of time, almost a year, during which I never looked in a mirror. It wasn't easy; just as you only notice how often people eat on television when you yourself are on a diet, I'd never suspected just how omnipresent were our own images. I began as an amateur, avoiding merely mirrors, but by the end of the year I found myself with a professional knowledge of the reflected image, its numerous tricks and wiles, how it can spring up at any moment: a glass tabletop, a well-polished door handle, a darkened window, a pair of sunglasses, a restaurant's otherwise magnificent brass-plated coffee machine sitting innocently by the cash register.

I hadn't simply woken up one morning deciding not to look at myself as part of some personal experiment, as my friend Sally had attempted once before me: She'd lasted about three days before finally giving in to the need "to make sure I was still there." For Sally, not looking in the mirror meant enacting a conscious decision against a constant desire that, at the end of her three days, she still was at a loss to define as either solely habit or instinct. For me, however, the act of not looking was insidious. It was nihilistic, an insurgence too chaotic even to know if it was directed at the world or at myself.

At the time I was living alone in Scotland, surviving financially because of my eligibility for the dole, the vernacular for Britain's social security benefits. When I first arrived in Aberdeen I didn't know anyone, had no idea just how I was going to live, yet I went anyway because I'd met a plastic surgeon there who said he could help me. I had been living in London, working temp jobs. Before that I'd been in Berlin, and ostensibly had come to London only to earn money for a few weeks before returning to Germany. Exactly why I had this experience in London I don't know, but in my first week there I received more nasty comments about my face than I had in the past three years of living in Iowa, New York, and Germany. These comments, all from men and all odiously sexual, hurt and disoriented me so much I didn't think twice about a friendly suggestion to go see a plastic surgeon. I'd already had more than a dozen operations in the States, yet my insurance ran out and so did my hope that any real difference could be made. Here, however, was a surgeon who had some new techniques, and here was a government willing to foot the bill: I didn't feel I could pass up yet another chance to "fix" my face, which I confusedly thought concurrent with "fixing" my self, my soul, my life.

Sixteen years earlier, when I was nine and living in America, I came home from school one day with a toothache. Several weeks and misdiagnoses later surgeons removed most of the right side of my jaw as part of an attempt to prevent the cancer they found there from spreading. No one properly explained the operation to me and I awoke in a cocoon of pain that prevented me from moving or speaking. Tubes ran in and out of my body and because I couldn't ask, I made up my own explanations for their existence.

Up until this time I'd been having a great time in the hospital. For starters   5 it was in "The City," a place of traffic and noise and dangers and, best of all, elevators. Never having been in an elevator before, I thrilled not just at the ride itself, but also at the game of nonchalance played out in front of the other elevator-savvy children who stepped on and off without thought.

Second, I was free from school. In theory a school existed on the third floor for children well enough to attend, but my friend Derek and I quickly discovered that the volunteer who came each day after lunch to pick us up was a sucker for a few well-timed groans, and once we learned to play straight man for each other there was little trouble getting out of it. We made sure the nurses kept thinking we had gone off to school, leaving us free for a few brief hours to wander the mazelike halls of the ancient hospital. A favorite spot was the emergency waiting room; they had good magazines and sometimes you got to see someone covered in blood come through the door. Derek tried to convince me that a certain intersection in the subbasement was an ideal place to watch for bodies heading toward the morgue, but the one time we did actually see one get wheeled by beneath its clichéd white sheet, we silently allowed each other to save face by suddenly deciding it was so much more fun to steal get-well cards from the gift shop than hang out in a cold basement. Once we stole the cards we sent them out randomly to other kids on the ward, signing them "Love and Kisses, Michael Jackson." Our theory was to watch them open up what they would think was a card from a famous star, but no one ever actually fell for it; by then we were well pegged as troublemakers.

There was something else going on too, something I didn't know how to articulate. Adults treated me in a mysterious manner. They asked me to do things: lie still for X rays, not cry for needles, things that, although not easy, never seemed equal to the praise I received in return. Reinforced to me again and again was how I was "a brave girl" for not crying, "a good girl" for not complaining, and soon I began defining myself this way, equating strength with silence.

Then the chemotherapy began. In the early seventies chemo was even cruder than it is now, the basic premise of it to poison the patient right up until the very brink of their own death. Up until this point I almost never cried, almost always received some sort of praise and attention in return for this, got what I considered the better part of the deal. But now, now it was like a practical joke that had gotten out of hand. Chemotherapy was a nightmare and I wanted it to stop, I didn't want to be brave any more. Yet I had so grown used to defining myself as "brave," i.e., silent, that even more terrifying was the thought of losing this sense of myself, certain that if I broke down this would be seen as despicable in the eyes of both my parents and doctors.

Mostly the task of taking me into the city for the injections fell upon my mother, though sometimes my father had to take me. Overwhelmed by the sight of the vomiting and weeping, my father developed the routine of "going to get the car," meaning that he left the office before the actual injection on the premise that then he could have the car ready and waiting when it was all over. Ashamed of my suffering, I felt relief when he was finally out of the room. When my mother was with me she stayed in the room, yet this only made the distance even more tangible, an almost palpable distance built on the intensity of our desperate longing to be anywhere else, anywhere at all. She explained that it was wrong to cry before the needle went in; afterward was one thing, but before, that was mere fear, and hadn't I already demonstrated my bravery earlier? Every week, every Friday, or "d-day" as we called it, for two and a half years I climbed up onto that too-big doctor's table and told myself not to cry, and every week I failed. The injections were really two large syringes, filled with chemicals so caustic to the vein that each had to be administered only very slowly. The whole process took about four minutes; I had to remain very still throughout it. Dry retching began in the first fifteen seconds, then the throb behind my eyes gave everything a yellow-green aura, and the bone-deep pain of alternating extreme hot and cold flashes made me tremble, yet still I had to sit motionless and not move my arm. No one spoke to me, not the doctor who was a paradigm of the cold-fish physician, not the nurse who told my mother I reacted much more violently than many of the other children, and not my mother, who, surely overwhelmed by the sight of her child's suffering, thought the best thing to do was remind me to be brave, to try and not cry. All the while I hated myself for having wept before the needle went in, convinced that the nurse and my mother were right, that I was "overdoing it," that the throwing up was psychosomatic, that my mother was angry with me for not being good or brave enough. So involved with controlling my guilt and shame, the problem of physical pain seemed easy by comparison.

Yet each week, usually two or three days after the injection, there came the first flicker of feeling better, the always forgotten and gratefully rediscovered understanding that simply to be well in my body was the greatest thing I could ask for. I thought other people felt this gratitude, this appreciation and physical joy all the time, and I felt cheated because I only was able to feel it once a week.

When you are only ten, which is when the chemotherapy began, two and a half years seems like your whole life, yet it did finally end. I remember the last day of chemotherapy very clearly for two reasons: one, because it was the only day on which I succeeded in not crying, and because later, in private, I cried harder than I had in years; I thought now I would no longer be "special," that without the arena of chemotherapy in which to prove myself no one would ever love me, that I would fade unnoticed into the background. This idea about not being different didn't last very long. Before I thought people stared because I was bald. I wore a hat constantly, but this fooled no one, least of all myself.

During this time my mother worked in a nursing home in a Hasidic community. Hasidism dictates that married women cover their hair, and most commonly this is done with a wig. My mother's friends were all too willing to donate their discarded wigs, and soon the house filled with wigs. I never wore one of them, they frightened me even when my mother insisted I looked better in one of the few that actually fit, yet we didn't know how to say no to the women who kept graciously offering their wigs. The cats enjoyed sleeping on them and the dogs playing with them, and we grew used to having to pick a wig up off a chair we wanted to sit in. It never struck us as odd until one day a visitor commented wryly as he cleared a chair for himself, and suddenly a great wave of shame overcame me. I had nightmares about wigs, felt a flush if I even heard the word, and one night I put myself out of my misery by getting up after everyone was asleep, gathering all the wigs except for one the dogs were fond of and might miss, and which they had chewed anyway into something other than a wig. I hid all the rest in an old chest where they weren't found for almost a year.

But my hair eventually grew in, and it didn't take long before I understood that I looked different for other reasons. People stared at me in stores, other children made fun of me to the point where I came to expect it constantly, wherever I went. School became a battleground, and I came home at the end of each day exhausted with the effort of keeping my body so tense and hard that I was sure anything would bounce off of it.

I was living in an extreme situation, and because I did not particularly care for the world I was in, I lived in others, and because the world I did live in was a dangerous one, I incorporated this danger into my private life. I saw movies about and envied Indians, imagined myself one. Walking down the streets I walked down through the forest, my body ready for any opportunity to fight or flee one of the big cats I knew stalked the area. Vietnam and Cambodia were other places I walked through frequently, daily even as I made my way down the school hall, knowing a landmine or a sniper might give themselves away at any moment with the subtle, soft metal clicks I'd read about in the books I took from the library. When faced with a landmine, a mere insult about my face seemed a frivolous thing.

In the early years, when I was still on the chemo, I lived in worse places   15
than Cambodia. Because I knew it was somehow inappropriate, I read only
in secret Primo Levi,[1] Elie Wiesel,[2] every book by a survivor I could find by
myself without resorting to asking the librarian for. Auschwitz, Birkenau: I
felt the senseless blows of the Capos and somehow knew that because at
any moment we might be called upon to live for a week on one loaf of
bread and some water called soup, the peanut butter sandwich I found on
my plate was nothing less than a miracle, an utter and sheer miracle capable of making me literally weep with joy.

I decided I wanted to become a "deep" person. I wasn't exactly sure
what this would entail, but I believed that if I could just find the right philosophy, think the right thoughts, my suffering would end. To try to understand
the world I was in, I undertook to find out what was "real," and quickly
began seeing reality as existing in the lowest common denominator, that suffering was the one and only dependable thing. But rather than spend all of
my time despairing, though certainly I did plenty of that, I developed a form
of defensive egomania: I felt I was the only one walking about in the world
who understood what was really important. I looked upon people complaining about the most mundane things — nothing on TV, traffic jams, the price
of new clothes — and felt both joy because I knew how unimportant those
things really were and unenlightened feelings of superiority because other
people didn't. Because I lived a fantasy life in which I had to be thankful for
each cold, blanketless night I survived on the cramped wooden bunks,
chemotherapy — the nausea, pain, and deep despair it brought — was a
breeze, a stroll through the country in comparison. I was often miserable, but
I knew that to feel warm instead of cold was its own kind of joy, that to eat
was a reenactment of the grace of some god whom I could only dimly define,
and that simply to be alive was a rare, ephemeral miracle. It was like reliving
The Fall a dozen times a day: I was given these moments of grace and insight,
only to be invariably followed by a clumsy tumble into narcissism.

As I got older, as I became a teenager, I began to feel very isolated. My
nonidentical twin sister started going out with boys, and I started, my most
tragic mistake of all, to listen to and believe the taunts thrown at me daily by
the very boys she and the other girls were interested in. I was a dog, a monster, the ugliest girl they had ever seen. Of all the remarks the most damaging
wasn't even directed at me, but was really an insult to Jerry, a boy I never saw
because every day, between fourth and fifth periods when I was cornered by

---

[1]*Primo Levi* (1919–1987): An Italian chemist, novelist, poet, and memoirist.
He survived one year at Auschwitz and wrote about his war and postwar experiences. His death was an apparent suicide. [Eds.]

[2]*Elie Wiesel* (b. 1928): A Romanian-born American writer and scholar who survived over a year at various concentration camps, including Auschwitz. His writings
and work with persecuted groups earned him the Nobel Prize for Peace in 1986.
[Eds.]

this particular group, I was too ashamed to lift my eyes off the floor. "Hey, look, it's Jerry's girlfriend," they yelled when they saw me, and I felt such shame, knowing that this was the deepest insult they could throw at Jerry.

I became interested in horses and got a job at a run-down local stable. Having those horses to go to each day after school saved my life; I spent all of my time either with them or thinking about them. To keep myself thinking objectively I became an obsessive reader and an obsessive television watcher, anything to keep me away from the subjective. I convinced myself I was smarter than everyone else, that only I knew what mattered, what was important, but by the time I was sixteen this wasn't true, not by a long shot. Completely and utterly repressed, I was convinced that I never wanted a boyfriend, not ever, and wasn't it convenient for me, a blessing I even thought, that none would ever want me. I told myself I was free to concentrate on the "true reality" of life, whatever that was. My sister and her friends put on blue eye shadow, blow-dried their hair, and went to spend interminable hours in the local mall, and I looked down on them for this, knew they were misleading themselves and being overoccupied with the "mere surface" of living. I had thought like this when I was younger, but now it was different, now my philosophy was haunted by desires so frightening I was unable to even admit they existed.

It wasn't until I was in college that I finally allowed that maybe, just maybe, it might be nice to have a boyfriend. As a person I had, as they say, blossomed in college. I went to a small, liberal, predominantly female school and suddenly, after years of alienation in high school, discovered that there were other people I could enjoy talking to, people who thought me intelligent and talented. I was, however, still operating on the assumption that no one, not ever, would be physically attracted to me, and in a curious way this shaped my personality. I became forthright and honest and secure in the way only the truly self-confident are, those who do not expect to be rejected, and those like me, who do not even dare to ask and so also expect no rejection. I had come to know myself as a person, but it would be graduate school before I was literally, physically able to use my name and the word woman in the same sentence.

Throughout all of this I was undergoing reconstructive surgery in an attempt to rebuild my jaw. It started when I was fifteen, several years after the chemo ended. I had known for years I would have operations to fix my face, and sometimes at night I fantasized about how good my life would finally be then. One day I got a clue that maybe it would not be so easy. At fourteen I went first to an older plastic surgeon who explained the process of pedestals to me, and told me it would take ten years to fix my face. Ten years? Why even bother? I thought. I'll be ancient by then. I went to the library and looked up the pedestals he talked about. There were gruesome pictures of people with grotesque tubes of their own skin growing out of their bodies, tubes of skin that were harvested like some kind of crop and then rearranged in ways with results that did not look at all normal or acceptable to my eye. But then I met a younger surgeon, a man who was

20

working on a new way of grafting that did not involve pedestals, and I became more hopeful and once again began awaiting the fixing of my face, of the day when I would be whole, content, loved.

Long-term plastic surgery is not like the movies. There is no one single operation that will change everything, and there is certainly no slow unwrapping of the gauze in order to view the final product. There is always swelling, sometimes grotesque, there are often bruises, and always there are scars. After each operation, too scared to simply go look in the mirror, I developed an oblique method comprised of several stages. First, I tried to catch my reflection in an overhead lamp: The roundness of the metal distorted my image just enough to obscure details and give no true sense of size or proportion. Then I slowly worked my way up to looking at the reflection in someone's eyeglasses, and from there I went to walking as briskly as possible by a mirror, glancing only quickly. I repeated this as many times as it would take me, passing the mirror slightly more slowly each time until finally I was able to stand still and confront myself.

The theory behind most reconstructive surgery is to take large chunks of muscle, skin, and bone and slap them into the roughly appropriate place, then slowly begin to carve this mess into some sort of shape. It involves long, major operations, countless lesser ones, a lot of pain, and many, many years. And also, it does not always work. With my young surgeon in New York, who was becoming not so young with each passing year, I had two or three soft tissue grafts, two skin grafts, a bone graft, and some dozen other operations to "revise" my face, yet when I left graduate school at the age of twenty-five I was still more or less in the same position I had started in: a deep hole in the right side of my face and a rapidly shrinking left side and chin, a result of the radiation I'd had as a child and the stress placed upon it by the other operations. I was caught in a cycle of having a big operation, one that would force me to look monstrous from the swelling for many months, then have the subsequent revision operations that improved my looks tremendously, and then slowly, over the period of a few months or a year, watch the graft reabsorb back into my body, slowly shrink down and leave me with nothing but the scarred donor site the graft had originally come from.

I had little or no conception of how I appeared to other people. As a child, Halloween was my favorite holiday because I could put on a mask and walk among the blessed for a few brief, sweet hours. Such freedom I felt, walking down the street, my face hidden: Through the imperfect oval holes I could peer out at other faces, masked or painted or not, and see on those faces nothing but the normal faces of childhood looking back at me, faces I mistakenly thought were the faces everyone else but me saw all the time, faces that were simply curious and ready for fun, not the faces I usually braced myself for, the cruel, lonely, vicious ones I spent every day other than Halloween waiting to round each corner. As I breathed in the condensed, plastic air I somehow thought that I was breathing in normality, that this joy and weightlessness were what the world was comprised of, and it was only my face that kept me from it, my face that was my own mask, my own tangible barrier that kept me from knowing the true identity of the joy I was sure everyone but me lived with intimately. How could they not know it? Not know that to be free of the fear of taunts and the burden of knowing no one would ever love you was all anyone could ever ask for? I was a pauper walking for a short while in the clothes of the prince, and when the day ended, I gave up my disguise with dismay.

I also came to love winter, when I could wrap the lower half of my face up in a scarf: I could speak to people and they would have no idea of who and what they were really speaking to. I developed the bad habits of letting my long hair hang in my face, and of always covering my chin and mouth with my hand, hoping it might be seen as a thoughtful, accidental gesture. My one concession to this came in college, when I cut my hair short, very short, in an attempt to stop hiding behind it. It was also an attempt, though I didn't see it as such at the time, to desex myself. I had long, blond hair, and I also had a thin figure. Sometimes, from a distance, men would see the thin blonde and whistle, something I dreaded more than anything else because I knew as they got closer their tone would inevitably change, they would stare openly or, worse, turn away quickly, and by cutting my hair I felt I might possibly avoid this, clear up any misconception anyone, however briefly, might have about my being attractive.

Once in college my patient friends repeated for me endlessly that most of   25 it was in my mind, that, granted, I did not look like everyone else, but that didn't mean I looked bad. I am sure now that they were right some of the time. But with the constant surgery I was in a perpetual state of transfiguration. I rarely looked the same for more than six months at a time. So ashamed of my face, I was unable to even admit that this constant change affected me at all; I let everyone who wanted to know that it was only what was inside that mattered, that I had "grown used to" the surgery, that none of it bothered me at all. Just as I had done in childhood, I pretended nothing was wrong, and this was constantly mistaken by others for bravery. I spent a great deal of time looking in the mirror in private, positioning my head to show off my eyes and nose, which were not just normal, but quite pretty, as my still-patient friends told me often. But I could not bring myself to see them for more than a glimmer: I looked in the mirror and saw not the normal upper half of my face, but only the disfigured lower half. People still teased me. Not daily, not like when I was younger, but in ways that caused me more pain than ever before. Children stared at me and I learned to cross the street to avoid them; this bothered me but not as much as the insults I got from men. They weren't thrown at me because I was disfigured, they were thrown at me because I was a disfigured woman.

They came from boys, sometimes men, and almost always a group of them. Only two or three times have I ever been teased by a single person, and I can think of only one time when I was ever teased by a woman. Had I been a man, would I have had to walk down the street while a group of young women followed and denigrated my sexual worth?

Not surprisingly, I viewed sex as my salvation. I was sure that if only I could get someone to sleep with me it would mean I wasn't ugly, that I was an attractive person, a lovable person. It would not be hard to guess where this line of reasoning led me, which was into the beds of a few manipulative men who liked themselves even less than they liked me, and I in turn left each short-term affair hating myself, obscenely sure that if only I had been prettier it would have worked, he would have loved me and it would have been like those other love affairs I was certain "normal" women had all the time. Gradually I became unable to say "I'm depressed," but could only say "I'm ugly," because the two had become inextricably linked in my mind. Into that universal lie, that sad equation of "if only" which we are all prey to, I was sure that if only I had a normal face, then I would be happy.

What our brains know is one thing, yet what our hearts know is another matter entirely, and when I met this new surgeon in Scotland, I offhandedly explained to my friends back home "why not, it's free, isn't it?" unable to admit that I believed in the fixability of life all over again.

Originally, it was planned I would have something called a tissue expander, followed by a bone graft. A tissue expander is a small balloon placed under the skin and then slowly blown up over the course of several months, the object being to stretch out the skin and create room and cover for the new bone. It is a bizarre, nightmarish thing to do to your face, yet I was hopeful about the end results and I was also able to spend the three months the expansion took in the hospital. I've always felt safe in hospitals: It's the one place I feel justified, sure of myself, free from the need to explain the way I look. For this reason the first tissue expander was bearable, just, and the bone graft that followed it was a success, it did not melt away like the previous ones.

However, the stress put upon my original remaining jaw from the surgery instigated a period of deterioration of that bone, and it became apparent that I was going to need the same operation I'd just had on the right side done to the left. I remember my surgeon telling me this at an outpatient clinic. I planned to be traveling down to London that same night on an overnight train, and I barely made it to the station on time, I was in such a fumbling state of despair. I could not imagine doing it all over again, and just as I had done all my life, I was searching and searching through my intellect for a way to make it okay, make it bearable, for a way to do it. I lay awake all night on that train, feeling the tracks slip quickly and oddly erotic below me, when I remembered an afternoon from my three months in the hospital. Boredom was a big problem those long afternoons, the days punctuated and landmarked by meals and television programs. Waiting for the afternoon tea to come, wondering desperately how I could make time pass, it suddenly occurred to me I didn't have to make time pass, that it would do it of its own accord, that I simply had to relax and take no action. Lying on the train, remembering that, I realized I had no obligation to make my situation okay, that I didn't have to explain it, understand it, that I could invoke the idea of negative capability and just simply let it happen. By the time the train pulled into King's Cross Station, I felt able to bear it yet again, not entirely sure what other choice I had.

But there was an element I didn't yet know about. I returned to Scotland to set up a date to go in and have the tissue expander put in, and was told quite casually that I'd only be in the hospital three or four days. Wasn't I going to spend the whole expansion time in the hospital? I asked almost in a whisper. What's the point of that? You can just come in every day to the outpatient to have it expanded. Horrified by this, I was speechless. I would have to live and move about in the outside world with a giant balloon in my face? I can't remember what I did for the next few days before I went into the hospital, but I vaguely remember that these days involved a great deal of drinking alone in bars and at home.

I went in and had the operation and, just as they said, went home at the end of the week. The only thing I can truly say gave me any comfort during the months I lived with my tissue expander was my writing and Kafka. I started a novel and completely absorbed myself in it, writing for hours and hours every day. It was the only way I could walk down the street, to stand the stares I received, to think to myself "I'll bet none of them are writing a novel." It was that strange, old familiar form of egomania, directly related to my dismissive, conceited thoughts of adolescence. As for Kafka, who had always been one of my favorite writers even before the new fashion for him, he helped me in that I felt permission to feel alienated, and to have that alienation be okay, to make it bearable, noble even. In the way living in Cambodia helped me as a child, I walked the streets of my dark little Scottish city by the sea and knew without doubt that I was living in a story Kafka would have been proud to write.

This time period, however, was also the time I stopped looking in the mirror. I simply didn't want to know. Many times before in my life I have been repelled by the mirror, but the repulsion always took the form of a strange, obsessive attraction. Previously I spent many hours looking in the mirror, trying to see what it was that other people were seeing, a purpose I understand now was laughable, as I went to the mirror with an already clearly fixed, negative idea of what people saw. Once I even remember thinking how awful I looked in a mirror I was quickly passing in a shopping center, seeing perfectly all the flaws I knew were there, when I realized with a shock that I wasn't looking in a mirror, that I was looking through into a store at someone who had the same coat and haircut as me, someone who, when I looked closer, looked perfectly fine.

The one good thing about a tissue expander is that you look so bad with it in that no matter what you look like once it's finally removed, it has to be better. I had my bone graft and my fifth soft tissue graft and yes, even I had to admit I looked better. But I didn't look like me. Something was wrong: Was this the face I had waited through twenty years and almost thirty operations for? I somehow just couldn't make what I saw in the mirror correspond to the person I thought It was. It wasn't just that I felt ugly, I simply could not associate the image as belonging to me. My own image was the image of a stranger, and rather than try to understand this, I simply ignored it. I reverted quickly back to my tissue expander mode of not looking in the mirror, and quickly improved it to include not looking at any image of myself. I perfected the technique of brushing my teeth without a

mirror, grew my hair in such a way that it would require only a quick simple brush, and wore clothes that were simply and easily put on, no complex
layers or lines that might require even the most minor of visual adjustments.

On one level I understood that the image of my face was merely that,   35
an image, a surface that was not directly related to any true, deep definition
of the self. But I also knew that it is only through image that we experience
and make decisions about the everyday world, and I was not always able
to gather the strength to prefer the deeper world over the shallower one.
I looked for ways to relate the two, to find a bridge that would allow
me access to both, anything no matter how tenuous, rather than ride
out the constant swings between peace and anguish. The only direction I
had to go in to achieve this was simply to strive for a state of awareness and
self-honesty that sometimes, to this day, rewards me and sometimes ex-
hausts me.

Our whole lives are dominated, though it is not always so clearly trans-
latable, with the question "How do I look?" Take all the many nouns in our
lives: car; house; job; family; love; friends; and substitute the personal pronoun — it is not that we are all so self-obsessed, it is that all things eventually
relate back to ourselves, and it is our own sense of how we appear to the
world by which we chart our lives, how we navigate our personalities that
would otherwise be adrift in the ocean of other peoples' obsessions.

One particular afternoon I remember very lucidly, an afternoon, toward the end of my yearlong separation from the mirror. I was talking to
someone, an attractive man as it happened, and we were having a wonderful, engaging conversation. For some reason it flickered across my
mind to wonder what I looked like to him. What was he seeing when he
saw me? So many times I've asked this of myself, and always the answer
was a bad one, an ugly one. A warm, smart woman, yes, but still, an unattractive one. I sat there in the café and asked myself this old question
and, startlingly, for the first time in my life I had no answer readily prepared. I had literally not looked in a mirror for so long that I quite simply had no clue as to what I looked like. I looked at the man as he spoke;
my entire life I had been giving my negative image to people, handing it
to them and watching the negative way it was reflected back to me. But
now, because I had no idea what I was giving him, the only thing I had
to judge by was what he was giving me, which, as reluctant as I was to
admit it, was positive.

That afternoon in that café I had a moment of the freedom I had been
practicing for behind my Halloween mask as a child. But where as a child
I expected it to come as a result of gaining something, a new face, it came
to me then as the result of shedding something, of shedding my image. I
once thought that truth was an eternal, that once you understood something it was with you forever. I know now that this isn't so, that most
truths are inherently unretainable, that we have to work hard all our lives
to remember the most basic things. Society is no help; the images it gives
us again and again want us only to believe that we can most be ourselves

by looking like someone else, leaving our own faces behind to turn into ghosts that will inevitably resent us and haunt us. It is no mistake that in movies and literature the dead sometimes know they are dead only after they can no longer see themselves in the mirror. As I sat there feeling the warmth of the cup against my palm this small observation seemed like a great revelation to me, and I wanted to tell the man I was with about it, but he was involved in his own topic and I did not want to interrupt him, so instead I looked with curiosity over to the window behind him, its night-darkened glass reflecting the whole café, to see if I could recognize myself.

QUESTIONS

1. What did Grealy learn about herself from her "yearlong separation from the mirror"?
2. Why did Grealy think that "fixing" her face would "fix" herself, her soul, her life? What is the significance of the word *fix*?
3. One of the features of this essay that makes it so compelling is Grealy's command of details. Locate details that you believe are effective, and think about their function. Try to rewrite some of Grealy's sentences to remove the details. What is lost? How do details link the author and the reader?
4. Grealy tells us, "Most truths are inherently unretainable," and "we have to work hard all our lives to remember the most basic things" (paragraph 38). What truths does Grealy refer to?
5. How does Grealy use her personal experience as evidence so that her essay becomes a larger story with greater relevance to others?
6. Grealy writes about the freedom she feels as a result of accepting the truth about her face. Such freedom, as Grealy shows, is never easily achieved. Reflect on a struggle or conflict in your own life, and write a brief essay on the "truths" that have emerged from your struggle.

MAKING CONNECTIONS

1. Both Alice Walker (p. 54) and Grealy struggle to accept their bodies and their appearance. In what ways are their struggles similar? In what ways are they different? What does this struggle achieve for each writer?
2. Do you agree with the observation that Alice Walker loses sight in order to gain sight and that Grealy loses face in order to gain face?

LEARNING TO READ AND WRITE

Frederick Douglass

Frederick Augustus Washington Bailey (1817–1895) was born to a slave mother on the Eastern Shore of Maryland. His father was a white man. After his escape from the South in 1838, he adopted the name of Douglass and worked to free other slaves and later (after the Civil War) to protect the rights of freed slaves. He was a newspaper editor, a lecturer, the United States minister to Haiti, and the author of several books about his life and times. The Narrative of the Life of Frederick Douglass: An American Slave *(1841), from which the following selection has been taken, is his best-known work.*

I lived in Master Hugh's family about seven years. During this time, I succeeded in learning to read and write. In accomplishing this, I was compelled to resort to various stratagems. I had no regular teacher. My mistress, who had kindly commenced to instruct me, had, in compliance with the advice and direction of her husband, not only ceased to instruct, but had set her face against my being instructed by any one else. It is due, however, to my mistress to say of her, that she did not adopt this course of treatment immediately. She at first lacked the depravity indispensable to shutting me up in mental darkness. It was at least necessary for her to have some training in the exercise of irresponsible power, to make her equal to the task of treating me as though I were a brute.

My mistress was, as I have said, a kind and tender-hearted woman; and in the simplicity of her soul she commenced, when I first went to live with her, to treat me as she supposed one human being ought to treat another. In entering upon the duties of a slaveholder, she did not seem to perceive that I sustained to her the relation of a mere chattel, and that for her to treat me as a human being was not only wrong, but dangerously so. Slavery proved as injurious to her as it did to me. When I went there, she was a pious, warm, and tender-hearted woman. There was no sorrow or suffering for which she had not a tear. She had bread for the hungry, clothes for the naked, and comfort for every mourner that came within her reach. Slavery soon proved its ability to divest her of these heavenly qualities. Under its influence, the tender heart became stone, and the lamblike disposition gave way to one of tiger-like fierceness. The first step in her downward course was in her ceasing to instruct me. She now commenced to practise her husband's precepts. She finally became even more violent in her opposition than her husband himself. She was not satisfied with simply doing as well as he had commanded; she seemed anxious to do better. Nothing seemed to make her more angry than to see me with a newspaper. She seemed to think that here lay the danger. I have had her rush at me with a face made all up of fury, and snatch from me a newspaper, in a manner that fully revealed her apprehension. She was an apt woman; and a little experience soon demonstrated, to her satisfaction, that education and slavery were incompatible with each other.

From this time I was most narrowly watched. If I was in a separate room any considerable length of time, I was sure to be suspected of having a book, and was at once called to give an account of myself. All this, however, was too late. The first step had been taken. Mistress, in teaching me the alphabet, had given me the *inch,* and no precaution could prevent me from taking the *ell.*[1]

The plan which I adopted, and the one by which I was most successful, was that of making friends of all the little white boys whom I met in the street. As many of these as I could, I converted into teachers. With their kindly aid, obtained at different times and in different places, I finally succeeded in learning to read. When I was sent on errands, I always took my book with me, and by doing one part of my errand quickly, I found time to get a lesson before my return. I used also to carry bread with me, enough of which was always in the house, and to which I was always welcome; for I was much better off in this regard than many of the poor white children in our neighborhood. This bread I used to bestow upon the hungry little urchins, who, in return, would give me that more valuable bread of knowledge. I am strongly tempted to give the names of two or three of those little boys, as a testimonial of the gratitude and affection I bear them; but prudence forbids; — not that it would injure me, but it might embarrass them; for it is almost an unpardonable offence to teach slaves to read in this Christian country. It is enough to say of the dear little fellows, that they lived on Philpot Street, very near Durgin and Bailey's ship-yard. I used to talk this matter of slavery over with them. I would sometimes say to them, I wished I could be as free as they would be when they got to be men. "You will be free as soon as you are twenty-one, *but I am a slave for life!* Have not I as good a right to be free as you have?" These words used to trouble them; they would express for me the liveliest sympathy, and console me with the hope that something would occur by which I might be free.

I was now about twelve years old, and the thought of being *a slave for*   5
life began to bear heavily upon my heart. Just about this time, I got hold of a book entitled "The Columbian Orator."[2] Every opportunity I got, I used to read this book. Among much of other interesting matter, I found in it a

---

    [1]*ell*: A unit of measurement, no longer used, equal to 45 inches. [Eds.]
    [2]*The Columbian Orator*: A collection of speeches widely used in early-nineteenth-century schools to teach argument and rhetoric. [Eds.]

dialogue between a master and his slave. The slave was represented as having run away from his master three times. The dialogue represented the conversation which took place between them, when the slave was retaken the third time. In this dialogue, the whole argument in behalf of slavery was brought forward by the master, all of which was disposed of by the slave. The slave was made to say some very smart as well as impressive things in reply to his master — things which had the desired though unexpected effect; for the conversation resulted in the voluntary emancipation of the slave on the part of the master.

In the same book, I met with one of Sheridan's mighty speeches on and in behalf of Catholic emancipation.[3] These were choice documents to me. I read them over and over again with unabated interest. They gave tongue to interesting thoughts of my own soul, which had frequently flashed through my mind, and died away for want of utterance. The moral which I gained from the dialogue was the power of truth over the conscience of even a slaveholder. What I got from Sheridan was a bold denunciation of slavery, and a powerful vindication of human rights. The reading of these documents enabled me to utter my thoughts, and to meet the arguments brought forward to sustain slavery; but while they relieved me of one difficulty, they brought on another even more painful than the one of which I was relieved. The more I read, the more I was led to abhor and detest my enslavers. I could regard them in no other light than a band of successful robbers, who had left their homes, and gone to Africa, and stolen us from our homes, and in a strange land reduced us to slavery. I loathed them as being the meanest as well as the most wicked of men. As I read and contemplated the subject, behold! that very discontentment which Master Hugh had predicted would follow my learning to read had already come, to torment and sting my soul to unutterable anguish. As I writhed under it, I would at times feel that learning to read had been a curse rather than a blessing. It had given me a view of my wretched condition, without the remedy. It opened my eyes to the horrible pit, but to no ladder upon which to get out. In moments of agony, I envied my fellow-slaves for their stupidity. I have often wished myself a beast. I preferred the condition of the meanest reptile to my own. Any thing, no matter what, to get rid of thinking! It was this everlasting thinking of my condition that tormented me. There was no getting rid of it. It was pressed upon me by every object within sight or hearing, animate or inanimate. The silver trump of freedom had roused my soul to eternal wakefulness. Freedom now appeared, to disappear no more forever. It was heard in every sound, and seen in every thing. It was ever present to torment me with a sense of my wretched condition. I saw nothing without seeing it, I heard nothing without hearing it, and felt nothing without feel-

---

[3]*Richard Brinsley Sheridan* (1751–1816): A British dramatist, orator, and politician. Roman Catholics were not allowed to vote in England until 1829. [Eds.]

ing it. It looked from every star, it smiled in every calm, breathed in every wind, and moved in every storm.

I often found myself regretting my own existence, and wishing myself dead; and but for the hope of being free, I have no doubt but that I should have killed myself, or done something for which I should have been killed. While in this state of mind, I was eager to hear any one speak of slavery. I was a ready listener. Every little while, I could hear something about the abolitionists. It was some time before I found what the word meant. It was always used in such connections as to make it an interesting word to me. If a slave ran away and succeeded in getting clear, or if a slave killed his master, set fire to a barn, or did any thing very wrong in the mind of a slave-holder, it was spoken of as the fruit of *abolition*. Hearing the word in this connection very often, I set about learning what it meant. The dictionary afforded me little or no help. I found it was "the act of abolishing"; but then I did not know what was to be abolished. Here I was perplexed. I did not dare to ask any one about its meaning, for I was satisfied that it was something they wanted me to know very little about. After a patient waiting, I got one of our city papers, containing an account of the number of petitions from the north, praying for the abolition of slavery in the District of Columbia, and of the slave trade between the States. From this time I understood the words *abolition* and *abolitionist*, and always drew near when that word was spoken, expecting to hear something of importance to myself and fellow-slaves. The light broke in upon me by degrees. I went one day down on the wharf of Mr. Waters; and seeing two Irishmen unloading a scow of stone, I went, unasked, and helped them. When we had finished, one of them came to me and asked me if I were a slave. I told him I was. He asked, "Are ye a slave for life?" I told him that I was. The good Irishman seemed to be deeply affected by the statement. He said to the other that it was a pity so fine a little fellow as myself should be a slave for life. He said it was a shame to hold me. They both advised me to run away to the north; that I should find friends there, and that I should be free. I pretended not to be interested in what they said, and treated them as if I did not understand them; for I feared they might be treacherous. White men have been known to encourage slaves to escape, and then, to get the reward, catch them and return them to their masters. I was afraid that these seemingly good men might use me so; but I nevertheless remembered their advice, and from that time I resolved to run away. I looked forward to a time at which it would be safe for me to escape. I was too young to think of doing so immediately; besides, I wished to learn how to write, as I might have occasion to write my own pass. I consoled myself with the hope that I should one day find a good chance. Meanwhile, I would learn to write.

The idea as to how I might learn to write was suggested to me by being in Durgin and Bailey's ship-yard, and frequently seeing the ship carpenters, after hewing, and getting a piece of timber ready for use, write on the timber the name of that part of the ship for which it was intended. When a piece of timber was intended for the larboard side, it would be marked thus — "L." When a piece was for the starboard side, it would be marked thus — "S." A piece for the larboard side forward, would be marked thus — "L. F." When a piece was for starboard side forward, it would be marked thus — "S. F." For larboard aft, it would be marked thus — "L. A." For starboard aft, it would be marked thus — "S. A." I soon learned the names of these letters, and for what they were intended when placed upon a piece of timber in the ship-yard. I immediately commenced copying them, and in a short time was able to make the four letters named. After that, when I met with any boy who I knew could write, I would tell him I could write as well as he. The next word would be, "I don't believe you. Let me see you try it." I would then make the letters which I had been so fortunate as to learn, and ask him to beat that. In this way I got a good many lessons in writing, which it is quite possible I should never have gotten in any other way. During this time, my copy-book was the board fence, brick wall, and pavement; my pen and ink was a lump of chalk. With these, I learned mainly how to write. I then commenced and continued copying the Italics in Webster's Spelling Book, until I could make them all without looking on the book. By this time, my little Master Thomas had gone to school, and learned how to write, and had written over a number of copy-books. These had been brought home, and shown to some of our near neighbors, and then laid aside. My mistress used to go to class meeting at the Wilk Street meetinghouse every Monday afternoon, and leave me to take care of the house. When left thus, I used to spend the time in writing in the spaces left in Master Thomas's copy-book, copying what he had written. I continued to do this until I could write a hand very similar to that of Master Thomas. Thus, after a long, tedious effort for years, I finally succeeded in learning how to write.

QUESTIONS

1. As its title proclaims, Douglass's book is a narrative, the story of his life. So, too, is this selection a narrative, the story of his learning to read and write. Identify the main events of this story, and list them in chronological order.

2. Douglass is documenting some of the events in his life in this selection, but certain events are not simply reported. Instead, they are described so that we may see, hear, and feel what was experienced by the people who were present during each event. Which events are described most fully in this narrative? How does Douglass seek to engage our interest and direct our feelings through such scenes?

3. In this selection from his memoir and in the entire book, Douglass is engaged in evaluating an institution — slavery — and arguing a case against it. Can you locate the points in the text where reflecting gives way to argumentation? How does Douglass support his argument against slavery? What contributes to his persuasiveness?

4. The situation of Roman Catholics and by inference the Irish is a subtheme in this essay. You can trace it by locating every mention of Catholicism and the Irish in the text. How does this theme relate to African American slavery? Locate *The Columbian Orator* in your library, or find out more about Sheridan and why he argued on behalf of "Catholic emancipation" (paragraph 6).

5. A subnarrative in this text tells the story of Master Hugh's wife, the "mistress" of the household in which Douglass learned to read and write. Retell *her* story in your own words. Consider how her story relates to Douglass's own story and how it relates to Douglass's larger argument about slavery.

6. Put yourself in the place of Master Hugh's wife, and retell all events in her words and from her point of view. To do so, you will have to decide both what she might have come to know about all these events and how she would feel about them. You will also have to decide when she is writing. Is she keeping a diary during this time (the early 1830s), or is she looking back from the perspective of later years? Has she been moved to write by reading Douglass's own book, which appeared in 1841? If so, how old would she be then, and what would she think about these past events? Would she be angry, bitter, repentant, embarrassed, indulgent, scornful, or what?

MAKING CONNECTIONS

1. What are the most common themes of the African American writers in this section — Maya Angelou (p. 43), Alice Walker (p. 54), and Douglass? On what issues, when they write about writing, do they have the most in common with the authors represented here who are white?

2. For Maya Angelou (p. 43), Alice Walker (p. 54), and Frederick Douglass, events of childhood and youth are particularly important. Compare how at least two of these writers viewed events when they were young, how they present their younger selves or viewpoints, and how they connect childhood experience to adult knowledge.

MOTHER TONGUE

Amy Tan

Born in 1952 in Oakland, California, Amy Tan is the daughter of immigrants who fled China's Communist revolution in the late 1940s. Her Chinese name, An-Mei, means "blessing from America." Tan has remarked that she once tried to distance herself from her ethnicity, but writing her first novel, The Joy Luck Club *(1989), helped her discover "how very Chinese I was." Known as a gifted storyteller, Tan has written four other novels,* The Kitchen God's Wife *(1991),* The Hundred Secret Senses *(1995),* The Bonesetter's Daughter *(2001), and* Saving Fish from Drowning *(2005), as well as a collection of essays,* The Opposite of Fate: Memories of a Writing Life *(2004), and two children's books. The following essay, in which Tan reflects on her experience as a bilingual child speaking both Chinese and English, was originally published in* The Threepenny Review *in 1990.*

I am not a scholar of English or literature. I cannot give you much more than personal opinions on the English language and its variations in this country or others.

I am a writer. And by that definition, I am someone who has always loved language. I am fascinated by language in daily life. I spend a great deal of my time thinking about the power of language — the way it can evoke an emotion, a visual image, a complex idea, or a simple truth. Language is the tool of my trade. And I use them all — all the Englishes I grew up with.

Recently, I was made keenly aware of the different Englishes I do use. I was giving a talk to a large group of people, the same talk I had already given to half a dozen other groups. The nature of the talk was about my writing, my life, and my book *The Joy Luck Club.* The talk was going along well enough, until I remembered one major difference that made the whole talk sound wrong. My mother was in the room. And it was perhaps the first time she had heard me give a lengthy speech, using the kind of English I have never used with her. I was saying things like "The intersection of memory upon imagination" and "There is an aspect of my fiction that relates to thus-and-thus" — a speech filled with carefully wrought grammatical phrases, burdened, it suddenly seemed to me, with nominalized forms, past perfect tenses, conditional phrases, all the forms of standard English that I had learned in school and through books, the forms of English I did not use at home with my mother.

Just last week, I was walking down the street with my mother, and I again found myself conscious of the English I was using, the English I do use with her. We were talking about the price of new and used furniture and I heard myself saying this: "Not waste money that way." My husband was with us as well, and he didn't notice any switch in my English. And then I realized why. It's because over the twenty years we've been together I've often used that same kind of English with him, and sometimes he even uses it with me. It has become our language of intimacy, a different sort of English that relates to family talk, the language I grew up with.

So you'll have some idea of what this family talk I heard sounds like,   5
I'll quote what my mother said during a recent conversation which I video-taped and then transcribed. During this conversation, my mother was talking about a political gangster in Shanghai who had the same last name as her family's, Du, and how the gangster in his early years wanted to be adopted by her family, which was rich by comparison. Later, the gangster became more powerful, far richer than my mother's family, and one day showed up at my mother's wedding to pay his respects. Here's what she said in part:

"Du Yusong having business like fruit stand. Like off the street kind. He is Du like Du Zong—but not Tsung-ming Island people. The local people call putong, the river east side, he belong to that side local people. That man want to ask Du Zong father take him in like become own family. Du Zong father wasn't look down on him, but didn't take seriously, until that man big like become a mafia. Now important person, very hard to inviting him. Chinese way, came only to show respect, don't stay for dinner. Respect for making big celebration, he shows up. Mean gives lots of re-spect. Chinese custom. Chinese social life that way. If too important won't have to stay too long. He come to my wedding. I didn't see, I heard it. I gone to boy's side, they have YMCA dinner. Chinese age I was nineteen."

You should know that my mother's expressive command of English be-lies how much she actually understands. She reads the *Forbes* report, listens to *Wall Street Week*, converses daily with her stockbroker, reads all of Shirley MacLaine's[1] books with ease — all kinds of things I can't begin to understand. Yet some of my friends tell me they understand 50 percent of what my mother says. Some say they understand 80 to 90 percent. Some say they understand none of it, as if she were speaking pure Chinese. But to me, my mother's English is perfectly clear, perfectly natural. It's my mother tongue. Her language, as I hear it, is vivid, direct, full of observation and imagery. That was the language that helped shape the way I saw things, ex-pressed things, made sense of the world.

---

[1]*Shirley MacLaine* (b. 1934): An American actor, dancer, and writer. She has written her memoirs and several books on spirituality and self-help.

Lately, I've been giving more thought to the kind of English my mother speaks. Like others, I have described it to people as "broken" or "fractured" English. But I wince when I say that. It has always bothered me that I can think of no way to describe it other than "broken," as if it were damaged and needed to be fixed, as if it lacked a certain wholeness and soundness. I've heard other terms used, "limited English," for example. But they seem just as bad, as if everything is limited, including people's perceptions of the limited English speaker.

I know this for a fact, because when I was growing up, my mother's "limited" English limited *my* perception of her. I was ashamed of her English. I believed that her English reflected the quality of what she had to say. That is, because she expressed them imperfectly her thoughts were imperfect. And I had plenty of empirical evidence to support me: the fact that people in department stores, at banks, and at restaurants did not take her seriously, did not give her good service, pretended not to understand her, or even acted as if they did not hear her.

My mother has long realized the limitations of her English as well. When I was fifteen, she used to have me call people on the phone to pretend I was she. In this guise, I was forced to ask for information or even to complain and yell at people who had been rude to her. One time it was a call to her stockbroker in New York. She had cashed out her small portfolio and it just so happened we were going to go to New York the next week, our very first trip outside California. I had to get on the phone and say in an adolescent voice that was not very convincing, "This is Mrs. Tan."

And my mother was standing in the back whispering loudly, "Why he don't send me check, already two weeks late. So mad he lie to me, losing me money."

And then I said in perfect English, "Yes, I'm getting rather concerned. You had agreed to send the check two weeks ago, but it hasn't arrived."

Then she began to talk more loudly. "What he want, I come to New York tell him front of his boss, you cheating me?" And I was trying to calm her down, make her be quiet, while telling the stockbroker, "I can't tolerate any more excuses. If I don't receive the check immediately, I am going to have to speak to your manager when I'm in New York next week." And sure enough, the following week there we were in front of this astonished stockbroker, and I was sitting there red-faced and quiet, and my mother, the real Mrs. Tan, was shouting at his boss in her impeccable broken English.

We used a similar routine just five days ago, for a situation that was far less humorous. My mother had gone to the hospital for an appointment, to find out about a benign brain tumor a CAT scan had revealed a month ago. She said she had spoken very good English, her best English, no mistakes. Still, she said, the hospital did not apologize when they said they had lost the CAT scan and she had come for nothing. She said they did not seem to

10

have any sympathy when she told them she was anxious to know the exact diagnosis, since her husband and son had both died of brain tumors. She said they would not give her any more information until the next time and she would have to make another appointment for that. So she said she would not leave until the doctor called her daughter. She wouldn't budge. And when the doctor finally called her daughter, me, who spoke in perfect English — lo and behold — we had assurances the CAT scan would be found, promises that a conference call on Monday would be held, and apologies for any suffering my mother had gone through for a most regrettable mistake.

I think my mother's English almost had an effect on limiting my possibilities in life as well. Sociologists and linguists probably will tell you that a person's developing language skills are more influenced by peers. But I do think that the language spoken in the family, especially in immigrant families which are more insular, plays a large role in shaping the language of the child. And I believe that it affected my results on achievement tests, IQ tests, and the SAT. While my English skills were never judged as poor, compared to math, English could not be considered my strong suit. In grade school I did moderately well, getting perhaps B's, sometimes B-pluses, in English and scoring perhaps in the sixtieth or seventieth percentile on achievement tests. But those scores were not good enough to override the opinion that my true abilities lay in math and science, because in those areas I achieved A's and scored in the ninetieth percentile or higher.

This was understandable. Math is precise; there is only one correct answer. Whereas, for me at least, the answers on English tests were always a judgment call, a matter of opinion and personal experience. Those tests were constructed around items like fill-in-the-blank sentence completion, such as "Even though Tom was _____ , Mary thought he was _____ ." And the correct answer always seemed to be the most bland combinations of thoughts, for example, "Even though Tom was shy, Mary thought he was charming," with the grammatical structure "even though" limiting the correct answer to some sort of semantic opposites, so you wouldn't get answers like "Even though Tom was foolish, Mary thought he was ridiculous." Well, according to my mother, there were very few limitations as to what Tom could have been and what Mary might have thought of him. So I never did well on tests like that.

The same was true with word analogies, pairs of words in which you were supposed to find some sort of logical, semantic relationship — for example, "*Sunset* is to *nightfall* as _____ is to _____ ." And here you would be presented with a list of four possible pairs, one of which showed the same kind of relationship: *red* is to *stoplight*, *bus* is to *arrival*, *chills* is to *fever*, *yawn* is to *boring*. Well, I could never think that way. I knew what the tests were asking, but I could not block out of my mind the images already created by the first pair, "*sunset* is to *nightfall*" — and I would see a burst

15

of colors against a darkening sky, the moon rising, the lowering of a curtain of stars. And all the other pairs of words — *red, bus, stoplight, boring* — just threw up a mass of confusing images, making it impossible for me to sort out something as logical as saying: "A sunset precedes nightfall" is the same as "a chill precedes a fever." The only way I would have gotten that answer right would have been to imagine an associative situation, for example, my being disobedient and staying out past sunset, catching a chill at night, which turns into feverish pneumonia as punishment, which indeed did happen to me.

I have been thinking about all this lately, about my mother's English, about achievement tests. Because lately I've been asked, as a writer, why there are not more Asian Americans represented in American literature. Why are there few Asian Americans enrolled in creative writing programs? Why do so many Chinese students go into engineering? Well, these are broad sociological questions I can't begin to answer. But I have noticed in surveys — in fact, just last week — that Asian students, as a whole, always do significantly better on math achievement tests than in English. And this makes me think that there are other Asian American students whose English spoken in the home might also be described as "broken" or "limited." And perhaps they also have teachers who are steering them away from writing and into math and science, which is what happened to me.

Fortunately, I happen to be rebellious in nature and enjoy the challenge of disproving assumptions made about me. I became an English major my first year in college, after being enrolled as premed. I started writing nonfiction as a freelancer the week after I was told by my former boss that writing was my worst skill and I should hone my talents toward account management.

But it wasn't until 1985 that I finally began to write fiction. And at first   20
I wrote using what I thought to be wittily crafted sentences, sentences that would finally prove I had mastery over the English language. Here's an example from the first draft of a story that later made its way into *The Joy Luck Club*, but without this line: "That was my mental quandary in its nascent state." A terrible line, which I can barely pronounce.

Fortunately, for reasons I won't get into today, I later decided I should envision a reader for the stories I would write. And the reader I decided upon was my mother, because these were stories about mothers. So with this reader in mind — and in fact she did read my early drafts — I began to write stories using all the Englishes I grew up with: the English I spoke to my mother, which for lack of a better term might be described as "simple"; the English she used with me, which for lack of a better term might be described as "broken"; my translation of her Chinese, which could certainly be described as "watered down"; and what I imagined to be her translation of her Chinese if she could speak in perfect English, her internal language, and for that I sought to preserve the essence, but neither an English nor a Chinese structure. I wanted to capture what language ability tests can never reveal: her intent, her passion, her imagery, the rhythms of her speech and the nature of her thoughts.

Apart from what any critic had to say about my writing, I knew I had succeeded where it counted when my mother finished reading my book and gave me her verdict: "So easy to read."

QUESTIONS

1. Why does Tan begin her essay with the disclaimer, "I am not a scholar of English or literature. I cannot give you much more than personal opinions on the English language and its variations in this country or others"? What advantage does this disclaimer offer Tan?
2. What are the different "Englishes" with which Tan grew up? Find an example of each "English." What did Tan need to learn about each?
3. Tan tells us that, as a writer, she cares about the way language "can evoke an emotion, a visual image, a complex idea, or a simple truth" (paragraph 2). Look closely at Tan's language. Find passages in her essay where her language is evocative. Where does Tan surprise you with her choice of words or her ability to use language to evoke emotion or imagery?
4. What did Tan learn about her "mother tongue"?
5. Think about your own mother tongue. In what ways does it reflect how you see and make sense of the world? What have you had to understand, accept, or reject about your mother tongue?
6. Tan writes that "the language spoken in the family, especially in immigrant families . . . , plays a large role in shaping the language of the child" (paragraph 15). Write an essay in which you reflect on the role of language in your family.

MAKING CONNECTIONS

What kind of conversation can you imagine between Tan and George Orwell, author of "Politics and the English Language" (p. 280)? How, for instance, would Tan respond to Orwell's claim that thought can corrupt language as much as language can corrupt thought?

UNSPEAKABLE CONVERSATIONS

Harriet McBryde Johnson

Harriet McBryde Johnson (b. 1957) is an attorney and disability rights activist in Charleston, South Carolina. She has published nonfiction articles in New Mobility, Mouth, South Carolina Lawyer, *and the* New York Times Magazine *and has won many awards both for her activism and for her writing, such as* New Mobility's *Person of the Year (2003) and the South Carolina Fiction Project award (1999 and 2003). Johnson says that the oral storytelling tradition in which she was raised greatly influences her style. "My professional and political life is all about using words to influence behavior," she says. "Persuading people requires conveying information, surely, but also eliciting emotions." She has written a memoir,* Too Late to Die Young: Nearly True Tales from a Life *(2005), and a young adult novel,* Accidents of Nature *(2006). "Unspeakable Conversations" appeared in the* New York Times Magazine.

He insists he doesn't want to kill me. He simply thinks it would have been better, all things considered, to have given my parents the option of killing the baby I once was, and to let other parents kill similar babies as they come along and thereby avoid the suffering that comes with lives like mine and satisfy the reasonable preferences of parents for a different kind of child. It has nothing to do with me. I should not feel threatened.

Whenever I try to wrap my head around his tight string of syllogisms,[1] my brain gets so fried it's . . . almost fun. Mercy! It's like "Alice in Wonderland."

It is a chilly Monday in late March, just less than a year ago. I am at Princeton University. My host is Prof. Peter Singer, often called — and not just by his book publicist — the most influential philosopher of our time. He is the man who wants me dead. No, that's not at all fair. He wants to legalize the killing of certain babies who might come to be like me if allowed to live. He also says he believes that it should be lawful under some circumstances to kill, at any age, individuals with cognitive impairments so severe that he doesn't consider them "persons." What does it take to be a person? Awareness of your own existence in time. The capacity to harbor preferences as to the future, including the preference for continuing to live.

---

[1]*syllogism*: Deductive reasoning using a major premise, a minor premise, and a conclusion. Reasoning from general to specific. [Eds.]

86

The author in Charleston, S.C.

At this stage of my life, he says, I am a person. However, as an infant, I wasn't. I, like all humans, was born without self-awareness. And eventually, assuming my brain finally gets so fried that I fall into that wonderland where self and other and present and past and future blur into one boundless, formless all or nothing, then I'll lose my personhood and therefore my right to life. Then, he says, my family and doctors might put me out of my misery, or out of my bliss or oblivion, and no one count it murder.

I have agreed to two speaking engagements. In the morning, I talk to 150 undergraduates on selective infanticide. In the evening, it is a convivial discussion, over dinner, of assisted suicide. I am the token cripple with an opposing view.

I had several reasons for accepting Singer's invitation, some grounded in my involvement in the disability rights movement, others entirely personal. For the movement, it seemed an unusual opportunity to experiment with modes of discourse that might work with very tough audiences and bridge the divide between our perceptions and theirs. I didn't expect to straighten out Singer's head, but maybe I could reach a student or two. Among the personal reasons: I was sure it would make a great story, first for telling and then for writing down.

By now I've told it to family and friends and colleagues, over lunches and dinners, on long car trips, in scads of e-mail messages and a couple of formal speeches. But it seems to be a story that just won't settle down. After all these tellings, it still lacks a coherent structure; I'm miles away from a rational argument. I keep getting interrupted by questions — like these:

Q: Was he totally grossed out by your physical appearance?

A: He gave no sign of it. None whatsoever.

Q: How did he handle having to interact with someone like you?   10

A: He behaved in every way appropriately, treated me as a respected professional acquaintance and was a gracious and accommodating host.

Q: Was it emotionally difficult for you to take part in a public discussion of whether your life should have happened?

A: It was very difficult. And horribly easy.

Q: Did he get that job at Princeton because they like his ideas on killing disabled babies?

A: It apparently didn't hurt, but he's most famous for animal rights.   15
He's the author of "Animal Liberation."

Q: How can he put so much value on animal life and so little value on human life?

That last question is the only one I avoid. I used to say I don't know; it doesn't make sense. But now I've read some of Singer's writing, and I admit it does make sense — within the conceptual world of Peter Singer. But I don't want to go there. Or at least not for long.

So I will start from those other questions and see where the story goes this time.

That first question, about my physical appearance, needs some explaining.

It's not that I'm ugly. It's more that most people don't know how to   20
look at me. The sight of me is routinely discombobulating.[2] The power wheelchair is enough to inspire gawking, but that's the least of it. Much more impressive is the impact on my body of more than four decades of a muscle-wasting disease. At this stage of my life, I'm Karen Carpenter thin, flesh mostly vanished, a jumble of bones in a floppy bag of skin. When, in childhood my muscles got too weak to hold up my spine, I tried a brace for a while, but fortunately a skittish anesthesiologist said no to fusion, plates and pins — all the apparatus that might have kept me straight. At 15, I threw away the back brace and let my spine reshape itself into a deep twisty S-curve. Now my right side is two deep canyons. To keep myself upright, I lean forward, rest my rib cage on my lap, plant my elbows beside my knees.

---

[2]*discombobulating*: Confusing or disconcerting, upsetting. [Eds.]

Since my backbone found its own natural shape, I've been entirely comfortable in my skin.

I am in the first generation to survive to such decrepitude. Because antibiotics were available, we didn't die from the childhood pneumonias that often come with weakened respiratory systems. I guess it is natural enough that most people don't know what to make of us.

Two or three times in my life — I recall particularly one largely crip, largely lesbian cookout halfway across the continent — I have been looked at as a rare kind of beauty. There is also the bizarre fact that where I live, Charleston, S.C., some people call me Good Luck Lady: they consider it propitious to cross my path when a hurricane is coming and to kiss my head just before voting day. But most often the reactions are decidedly negative. Strangers on the street are moved to comment:

> I admire you for being out; most people would give up.
> God bless you! I'll pray for you.
> You don't let the pain hold you back, do you?
> If I had to live like you, I think I'd kill myself.

I used to try to explain that in fact I enjoy my life, that it's a great sensual pleasure to zoom by power chair on these delicious muggy streets, that I have no more reason to kill myself than most people. But it gets tedious. God didn't put me on this street to provide disability awareness training to the likes of them. In fact, no god put anyone anywhere for any reason, if you want to know.

But they don't want to know. They think they know everything there is to know, just by looking at me. That's how stereotypes work. They don't know that they're confused, that they're really expressing the discombobulation that comes in my wake.

So. What stands out when I recall first meeting Peter Singer in the   25
spring of 2001 is his apparent immunity to my looks, his apparent lack of discombobulation, his immediate ability to deal with me as a person with a particular point of view.

Then, 2001. Singer has been invited to the College of Charleston, not two blocks from my house. He is to lecture on "Rethinking Life and Death." I have been dispatched by Not Dead Yet, the national organization leading the disability-rights opposition to legalized assisted suicide and disability-based killing. I am to put out a leaflet and do something during the Q. and A.

On arriving almost an hour early to reconnoiter, I find the scene almost entirely peaceful; even the boisterous display of South Carolina spring is muted by gray wisps of Spanish moss and mottled oak bark.

I roll around the corner of the building and am confronted with the unnerving sight of two people I know sitting on a park bench eating veggie pitas with Singer. Sharon is a veteran activist for human rights. Herb is South Carolina's most famous atheist. Good people, I've always thought — now sharing veggie pitas and conversation with a proponent of genocide. I try to beat a retreat, but Herb and Sharon have seen me. Sharon tosses her trash and comes over. After we exchange the usual courtesies, she asks, "Would you like to meet Professor Singer?"

She doesn't have a clue. She probably likes his book on animal rights. "I'll just talk to him in the Q. and A."

But Herb, with Singer at his side, is fast approaching. They are looking   30
at me, and Herb is talking, no doubt saying nice things about me. He'll be saying that I'm a disability rights lawyer and that I gave a talk against assisted suicide at his secular humanist group a while back. He didn't agree with everything I said, he'll say, but I was brilliant. Singer appears interested, engaged. I sit where I'm parked. Herb makes an introduction. Singer extends his hand.

I hesitate: I shouldn't shake hands with the Evil One. But he is Herb's guest, and I simply can't snub Herb's guest at the college where Herb teaches. Hereabouts the rule is that if you're not prepared to shoot on sight, you have to be prepared to shake hands. I give Singer the three fingers on my right hand that still work. "Good afternoon, Mr. Singer. I'm here for Not Dead Yet." I want to think he flinches just a little. Not Dead Yet did everything possible to disrupt his first week at Princeton. I sent a check to the fund for the 14 arrestees, who included comrades in power chairs. But if Singer flinches, he instantly recovers. He answers my questions about the lecture format. When he says he looks forward to an interesting exchange, he seems entirely sincere.

It *is* an interesting exchange. In the lecture hall that afternoon, Singer lays it all out. The "illogic" of allowing abortion but not infanticide, of allowing withdrawal of life support but not active killing. Applying the basic assumptions of preference utilitarianism, he spins out his bone-chilling argument for letting parents kill disabled babies and replace them with nondisabled babies who have a greater chance at happiness. It is all about allowing as many individuals as possible to fulfill as many of their preferences as possible.

As soon as he's done, I get the microphone and say I'd like to discuss selective infanticide. As a lawyer, I disagree with his jurisprudential assumptions. Logical inconsistency is not a sufficient reason to change the law. As an atheist, I object to his using religious terms ("the doctrine of the sanctity of human life") to characterize his critics. Singer takes a note pad out of his pocket and jots down my points, apparently eager to take them on, and I proceed to the heart of my argument: that the presence or absence of a disability doesn't predict quality of life. I question his replacement-baby theory, with its assumption of "other things equal," arguing that people are not fungible.[3] I draw out a comparison of myself and my nondisabled

---

[3]*fungible*: A legal term usually referring to goods as being of a kind to be freely exchangeable for another of like kind. [Eds.]

Members of Not Dead Yet protesting Singer's appointment at Princeton in September 1999.

brother Mac (the next-born after me), each of us with a combination of gifts and flaws so peculiar that we can't be measured on the same scale.

He responds to each point with clear and lucid counterarguments. He proceeds with the assumption that I am one of the people who might rightly have been killed at birth. He sticks to his guns, conceding just enough to show himself open-minded and flexible. We go back and forth for 10 long minutes. Even as I am horrified by what he says, and by the fact that I have been sucked into a civil discussion of whether I ought to exist, I can't help being dazzled by his verbal facility. He is so respectful, so free of condescension, so focused on the argument, that by the time the show is over, I'm not exactly angry with him. Yes, I am shaking, furious, enraged — but it's for the big room, 200 of my fellow Charlestonians who have listened with polite interest, when in decency they should have run him out of town on a rail.

My encounter with Peter Singer merits a mention in my annual canned letter that December. I decide to send Singer a copy. In response, he sends me the nicest possible e-mail message. Dear Harriet (if he may) . . . Just back from Australia, where he's from. Agrees with my comments on the world situation. Supports my work against institutionalization. And then some pointed questions to clarify my views on selective infanticide. 35

I reply. Fine, call me Harriet, and I'll reciprocate in the interest of equality, though I'm accustomed to more formality. Skipping agreeable preambles, I answer his questions on disability-based infanticide and pose some of my own. Answers and more questions come back. Back and forth over several weeks it proceeds, an engaging discussion of baby killing, disability prejudice and related points of law and philosophy. Dear Harriet. Dear Peter.

Singer seems curious to learn how someone who is as good an atheist as he is could disagree with his entirely reasonable views. At the same time, I am trying to plumb his theories. What has him so convinced it would be best to allow parents to kill babies with severe disabilities, and not other kinds of babies, if no infant is a "person" with a right to life? I learn it is partly that both biological and adoptive parents prefer healthy babies. But I have trouble with basing life-and-death decisions on market considerations when the market is structured by prejudice. I offer a hypothetical comparison: "What about mixed-race babies, especially when the combination is entirely nonwhite, who I believe are just about as unadoptable as babies with disabilities?" Wouldn't a law allowing the killing of these undervalued babies validate race prejudice? Singer agrees there is a problem. "It would be horrible," he says, "to see mixed-race babies being killed because they can't be adopted, whereas white ones could be." What's the difference? Preferences based on race are unreasonable. Preferences based on ability are not. Why? To Singer, it's pretty simple: disability makes a person "worse off."

Are we "worse off"? I don't think so. Not in any meaningful sense. There are too many variables. For those of us with congenital conditions, disability shapes all we are. Those disabled later in life adapt. We take constraints that no one would choose and build rich and satisfying lives within them. We enjoy pleasures other people enjoy, and pleasures peculiarly our own. We have something the world needs.

Pressing me to admit a negative correlation between disability and happiness, Singer presents a situation: imagine a disabled child on the beach, watching the other children play.

It's right out of the telethon. I expected something more sophisticated   40 from a professional thinker. I respond: "As a little girl playing on the beach, I was already aware that some people felt sorry for me, that I wasn't frolicking with the same level of frenzy as other children. This annoyed me, and still does." I take the time to write a detailed description of how I, in fact, had fun playing on the beach without the need of standing, walking or running. But, really, I've had enough. I suggest to Singer that we have exhausted our topic, and I'll be back in touch when I get around to writing about him.

He responds by inviting me to Princeton. I fire off an immediate maybe.

Of course, I'm flattered. Mama will be impressed.

But there are things to consider. Not Dead Yet says — and I completely agree — that we should not legitimate Singer's views by giving them a forum. We should not make disabled lives subject to debate. Moreover, any spokesman chosen by the opposition is by definition a token. But even if

I'm a token, I won't have to act like one. And anyway, I'm kind of stuck. If I decline, Singer can make some hay: "I offered them a platform, but they refuse rational discussion." It's an old trick, and I've laid myself wide open.

My invitation is to have an exchange of views with Singer during his undergraduate course. He also proposes a second "exchange" open to the whole university, later in the day. This sounds a lot like debating my life — and on my opponent's turf, with my opponent moderating to boot. I offer a counterproposal, to which Singer proves amenable. I will open the class with some comments on infanticide and related issues and then let Singer grill me as hard as he likes before we open it up for the students. Later in the day, I might take part in a discussion of some other disability issue in a neutral forum. Singer suggests a faculty-student discussion group sponsored by his department but with cross-departmental membership. The topic I select is "Assisted Suicide, Disability Discrimination and the Illusion of Choice: A Disability Rights Perspective." I inform a few movement colleagues of this turn of events, and advice starts rolling in. I decide to go with the advisers who counsel me to do the gig, lie low and get out of Dodge.

I ask Singer to refer me to the person who arranges travel at Princeton. 45 I imagine some capable and unflappable woman like my sister, Beth, whose varied job description at a North Carolina university includes handling visiting artists. Singer refers me to his own assistant, who certainly seems capable and unflappable enough. However, almost immediately Singer jumps back in via e-mail. It seems the nearest hotel has only one wheelchair-accessible suite, available with two rooms for $600 per night. What to do? I know I shouldn't be so accommodating, but I say I can make do with an inaccessible room if it has certain features. Other logistical issues come up. We go back and forth. Questions and answers. Do I really need a lift-equipped vehicle at the airport? Can't my assistant assist me into a conventional car? How wide is my wheelchair?

By the time we're done, Singer knows that I am 28 inches wide. I have trouble controlling my wheelchair if my hand gets cold. I am accustomed to driving on rough, irregular surfaces, but I get nervous turning on steep slopes. Even one step is too many. I can swallow purees, soft bread and grapes. I use a bedpan, not a toilet. None of this is a secret; none of it cause for angst. But I do wonder whether Singer is jotting down my specs in his little note pad as evidence of how "bad off" people like me really are.

I realize I must put one more issue on the table: etiquette. I was criticized within the movement when I confessed to shaking Singer's hand in Charleston, and some are appalled that I have agreed to break bread with him in Princeton. I think they have a very good point, but, again, I'm stuck. I'm engaged for a day of discussion, not a picket line. It is not in my power to marginalize Singer at Princeton; nothing would be accomplished by displays of personal disrespect. However, chumminess is clearly inappropriate. I tell Singer that in the lecture hall it can't be Harriet and Peter; it must be Ms. Johnson and Mr. Singer.

He seems genuinely nettled. Shouldn't it be Ms. Johnson and Professor Singer, if I want to be formal? To counter, I invoke the ceremonial low-country usage, Attorney Johnson and Professor Singer, but point out that Mr./Ms. is the custom in American political debates and might seem more normal in New Jersey. All right, he says. Ms./Mr. it will be.

I describe this awkward social situation to the lawyer in my office who has served as my default lunch partner for the past 14 years. He gives forth a full-body shudder.

"That poor, sorry son of a bitch! He has no idea what he's in for."   50

Being a disability rights lawyer lecturing at Princeton does confer some cachet at the Newark airport. I need all the cachet I can get. Delta Airlines has torn up my power chair. It is a fairly frequent occurrence for any air traveler on wheels.

When they inform me of the damage in Atlanta, I throw a monumental fit and tell them to have a repair person meet me in Newark with new batteries to replace the ones inexplicably destroyed. Then I am told no new batteries can be had until the morning. It's Sunday night. On arrival in Newark, I'm told of a plan to put me up there for the night and get me repaired and driven to Princeton by 10 a.m.

"That won't work. I'm lecturing at 10. I need to get there tonight, go to sleep and be in my right mind tomorrow."

"What? You're lecturing? They told us it was a conference. We need to get you fixed tonight!"

Carla, the gate agent, relieves me of the need to throw any further fits   55
by undertaking on my behalf the fit of all fits.

Carmen, the personal assistant with whom I'm traveling, pushes me in my disabled chair around the airport in search of a place to use the bedpan. However, instead of diaper-changing tables, which are functional though far from private, we find a flip-down plastic shelf that doesn't took like it would hold my 70 pounds of body weight. It's no big deal; I've restricted my fluids. But Carmen is a little freaked. It is her first adventure in power-chair air travel. I thought I prepared her for the trip, but I guess I neglected to warn her about the probability of wheelchair destruction. I keep forgetting that even people who know me well don't know much about my world.

We reach the hotel at 10:15 p.m., four hours late.

I wake up tired. I slept better than I would have slept in Newark with an unrepaired chair, but any hotel bed is a near guarantee of morning crankiness. I tell Carmen to leave the TV off. I don't want to hear the temperature.

I do the morning stretch. Medical people call it passive movement, but it's not really passive. Carmen's hands move my limbs, following my precise instructions, her strength giving effect to my will. Carmen knows the routine, so it is in near silence that we begin easing slowly into the day. I let myself be propped up to eat oatmeal and drink tea. Then there's the bedpan and then bathing and dressing, still in bed. As the caffeine kicks in, silence gives way to conversation about practical things. Carmen lifts me into my chair and straps a rolled towel under my ribs for comfort and stability. She tugs at my clothes to remove wrinkles that could cause pressure sores. She switches on my motors and gives me the means of moving without anyone's help. They don't call it a power chair for nothing.

I drive to the mirror. I do my hair in one long braid. Even this primal   60
hairdo requires, at this stage of my life, joint effort. I undo yesterday's braid, fix the part and comb the hair in front. Carmen combs where I can't reach. I divide the mass into three long hanks and start the braid just behind my left ear. Section by section, I hand it over to her, and her unimpaired young fingers pull tight, crisscross, until the braid is fully formed.

A big polyester scarf completes my costume. Carmen lays it over my back. I tie it the way I want it, but Carmen starts fussing with it, trying to tuck it down in the back. I tell her that it's fine, and she stops.

On top of the scarf, she wraps the two big shawls that I hope will substitute for an overcoat. I don't own any real winter clothes. I just stay out of the cold, such cold as we get in Charleston.

We review her instructions for the day. Keep me in view and earshot. Be instantly available but not intrusive. Be polite but don't answer any questions about me. I am glad that she has agreed to come. She's strong, smart, adaptable and very loyal. But now she is digging under the shawls, fussing with that scarf again. "Carmen. "What are you doing?"

"I thought I could hide this furry thing you sit on."   65

"Leave it. Singer knows lots of people eat meat. Now he'll know some crips sit on sheepskin."

The walk is cold but mercifully short. The hotel is just across the street from Princeton's wrought-iron gate and a few short blocks from the building where Singer's assistant shows us to the elevator. The elevator doubles as the janitor's closet — the cart with the big trash can and all the accouterments is rolled aside so I can get in. Evidently there aren't a lot of wheelchair people using this building.

We ride the broom closet down to the basement and are led down a long passageway to a big lecture hall. As the students drift in, I engage in light badinage with the sound technician. He is squeamish about touching me, but I insist that the cordless lavaliere is my mike of choice. I invite him to clip it to the big polyester scarf.

The students enter from the rear door, way up at ground level, and walk down stairs to their seats. I feel like an animal in the zoo. I hadn't reckoned on the architecture, those tiers of steps that separate me from a human wall of apparent physical and mental perfection, that keep me confined down here in my pit.

It is 5 before 10. Singer is loping down the stairs. I feel like signaling to   70
Carmen to open the door, summon the broom closet and get me out of

here. But Singer greets me pleasantly and hands me Princeton's check for $500, the fee he offered with apologies for its inadequacy.

So. On with the show.

My talk to the students is pretty Southern. I've decided to pound them with heart, hammer them with narrative and say "y'all" and "folks." I play with the emotional tone, giving them little peaks and valleys, modulating three times in one 45-second patch. I talk about justice. Even beauty and love. I figure they haven't been getting much of that from Singer.

Of course, I give them some argument too. I mean to honor my contractual obligations, I lead with the hypothetical about mixed-race, non-white babies and build the ending around the question of who should have the burden of proof as to the quality of disabled lives. And woven throughout the talk is the presentation of myself as a representative of a minority group that has been rendered invisible by prejudice and oppression, a participant in a discussion that would not occur in a just world.

I let it go a little longer than I should. Their faces show they're going where I'm leading, and I don't look forward to letting them go. But the clock on the wall reminds me of promises I mean to keep, and I stop talking and submit myself to examination and inquiry.

Singer's response is surprisingly soft. Maybe after hearing that this discussion is insulting and painful to me, he doesn't want to exacerbate my discomfort. His refraining of the issues is almost pro forma, abstract, entirely impersonal. Likewise, the students' inquiries are abstract and fairly predictable: anencephaly,[4] permanent unconsciousness, eugenic abortion. I respond to some of them with stories, but mostly I give answers I could have e-mailed in. I call on a young man near the top of the room.

"Do you eat meat?"

"Yes. I do."

"Then how do you justify ——"

"I haven't made any study of animal rights, so anything I could say on the subJect wouldn't be worth everyone's time."

The next student wants to work the comparison of disability and race, and Singer joins the discussion until he elicits a comment from me that he can characterize as racist. He scores a point, but that's all right. I've never claimed to be free of prejudice, just struggling with it.

Singer proposes taking me on a walk around campus, unless I think it would be too cold. What the hell? "It's probably warmed up some. Let's go out and see how I do."

He doesn't know how to get out of the building without using the stairs, so this time it is my assistant leading the way. Carmen has learned of another elevator, which arrives empty. When we get out of the building, she falls behind a couple of paces, like a respectful chaperone.

---

[4]*anencephaly*: Congenital absence of a part or all of the brain. [Eds.]

In the classroom there was a question about keeping alive the unconscious. In response, I told a story about a family I knew as a child, which
took loving care of a nonresponsive teenage girl, acting out their unconditional commitment to each other, making all the other children, and me as
their visitor, feel safe. This doesn't satisfy Singer. "Let's assume we can
prove, absolutely, that the individual is totally unconscious and that we can
know, absolutely, that the individaul will never regain consciousness."

I see no need to state an objection, with no stenographer present to   85
record it; I'll play the game and let him continue.

"Assuming all that," he says, "don't you think continuing to take care
of that individual would be a bit — weird?"

"No. Done right, it could be profoundly beautiful."

"But what about the caregiver, a woman typically, who is forced to
provide all this service to a family member, unable to work, unable to have
a life of her own?"

"That's not the way it should be. Not the way it has to be. As a society,
we should pay workers to provide that care, in the home. In some places,
it's been done that way for years. That woman shouldn't be forced to do it,
any more than my family should be forced to do my care.

Singer takes me around the architectural smorgasbord that is Princeton   90
University by a route that includes not one step, unramped curb or turn on
a slope. Within the strange limits of this strange assignment, it seems Singer
is doing all he can to make me comfortable.

He asks what I thought of the students' questions.

"They were fine, about what I expected. I was a little surprised by the
question about meat eating."

"I apologize for that. That was out of left field. But — I think what he
wanted to know is how you can have such high respect for human life and
so little respect for animal life."

"People have lately been asking me the converse, how you can have so
much respect for animal life and so little respect for human life."

"And what do you answer?"   95

"I say I don't know. It doesn't make a lot of sense to me."

"Well, in my view ——"

"Look. I have lived in blissful ignorance all these years, and I'm not
prepared to give that up today."

"Fair enough," he says and proceeds to recount bits of Princeton history. He stops. "This will be of particular interest to you, I think. This is
where your colleagues with Not Dead Yet set up their blockade." I'm grateful for the reminder. My brothers and sisters were here before me and behaved far more appropriately than I am doing.

A van delivers Carmen and me early for the evening forum. Singer says   100
he hopes I had a pleasant afternoon.

Yes, indeed. I report a pleasant lunch and a very pleasant nap, and I tell
him about the Christopher Reeve Suite in the hotel, which has been remodeled to accommodate Reeve, who has family in the area.

"Do you suppose that's the $600 accessible suite they told me about?"

"Without doubt. And if I'd known it was the Christopher Reeve Suite, I would have held out for it."

"Of course you would have!" Singer laughs. "And we'd have had no choice, would we?"

We talk about the disability rights critique of Reeve and various other   105 topics. Singer is easy to talk to, good company. Too bad he sees lives like mine as avoidable mistakes.

I'm looking forward to the soft vegetarian meal that has been arranged; I'm hungry. Assisted suicide, as difficult as it is, doesn't cause the agony I felt discussing disability-based infanticide. In this one, I understand, and to some degree can sympathize with, the opposing point of view — misguided though it is.

My opening sticks to the five-minute time limit. I introduce the issue as framed by academic articles Not Dead Yet recommended for my use. Andrew Batavia argues for assisted suicide based on autonomy, a principle generally held high in the disability rights movement. In general, he says, the movement fights for our right to control our own lives; when we need assistance to effect our choices, assistance should be available to us as a matter of right. If the choice is to end our lives, he says, we should have assistance then as well. But Carol Gill says that it is differential treatment — disability discrimination — to try to prevent most suicides while facilitating the suicides of ill and disabled people. The social-science literature suggests that the public in general, and physicians in particular, tend to underestimate the quality of life of disabled people, compared with our own assessments of our lives. The case for assisted suicide rests on stereotypes that our lives are inherently so bad that it is entirely rational if we want to die.

I side with Gill. What worries me most about the proposals for legalized assisted suicide is their veneer of beneficence — the medical determination that for a given individual, suicide is reasonable or right. It is not about autonomy but about nondisabled people telling us what's good for us.

In the discussion that follows, I argue that choice is illusory in a context of pervasive inequality. Choices are structured by oppression. We shouldn't offer assistance with suicide until we all have the assistance we need to get out of bed in the morning and live a good life. Common causes of suicidality — dependence, institutional confinement, being a burden —are entirely curable. Singer, seated on my right, participates in the discussion but doesn't dominate it. During the meal, I occasionally ask him to put things within my reach, and he competently complies.

I feel as if I'm getting to a few of them, when a student asks me a ques-   110 tion. The words are all familiar, but they're strung together in a way so meaningless that I can't even retain them — it's like a long sentence in Tagalog. I can only admit my limitations. "That question's too abstract for me to deal with. Can you rephrase it?"

He indicates that it is as clear as he can make it, so I move on.

A little while later, my right elbow slips out from under me. This is awkward. Normally I get whoever is on my right to do this sort of thing. Why not now? I gesture to Singer. He leans over, and I whisper, "Grasp this wrist and pull forward one inch, without lifting." He follows my instructions to the letter. He sees that now I can again reach my food with my fork. And he may now understand what I was saying a minute ago, that most of the assistance disabled people need does not demand medical training.

A philosophy professor says, "It appears that your objections to assisted suicide are essentially tactical."

"Excuse me?"

"By that I mean they are grounded in current conditions of political, 115 social and economic inequality. What if we assume that such conditions do not exist?"

"Why would we want to do that?"

"I want to get to the real basis for the position you take."

I feel as if I'm losing caste. It is suddenly very clear that I'm not a philosopher. I'm like one of those old practitioners who used to visit my law school, full of bluster about life in the real world. Such a bore! A once-sharp mind gone muddy! And I'm only 44 — not all that old.

The forum is ended, and I've been able to eat very little of my puréed food. I ask Carmen to find the caterer and get me a container. Singer jumps up to take care of it. He returns with a box and obligingly packs my food to go.

When I get home, people are clamoring for the story. The lawyers want 120 the blow-by-blow of my forensic triumph over the formidable foe; when I tell them it wasn't like that, they insist that it was. Within the disability rights community, there is less confidence. It is generally assumed that I handled the substantive discussion well, but people worry that my civility may have given Singer a new kind of legitimacy. I hear from Laura, a beloved movement sister. She is appalled that I let Singer provide even minor assistance at the dinner. "Where was your assistant?" she wants to know. How could I put myself in a relationship with Singer that made him appear so human, even kind?

I struggle to explain. I didn't feel disempowered; quite the contrary, it seemed a good thing to make him do some useful work. And then, the hard part: I've come to believe that Singer actually is human, even kind in his way. There ensues a discussion of good and evil and personal assistance and power and philosophy and tactics for which I'm profoundly grateful.

I e-mail Laura again. This time I inform her that I've changed my will. She will inherit a book that Singer gave me, a collection of his writings with a weirdly appropriate inscription: To Harriet Johnson, So that you will have a better answer to questions about animals. And thanks for coming to Princeton. Peter Singer. March 25, 2002." She responds that she is changing her will, too. I'll get the autographed photo of Jerry Lewis she received as an M.D.A. poster child. We joke that each of us has given the other a "reason to live."

I have had a nice e-mail message from Singer, hoping Carmen and I and the chair got home without injury, relaying positive feedback from my audiences—and taking me to task for a statement that isn't supported by a relevant legal authority, which he looked up. I report that we got home exhausted but unharmed and concede that he has caught me in a generalization that should have been qualified. It's clear that the conversation will continue.

I am soon sucked into the daily demands of law practice, family, community and politics. In the closing days of the state legislative session, I help get a bill passed that I hope will move us one small step toward a world in which killing won't be such an appealing solution to the "problem" of disability. It is good to focus on this kind of work. But the conversations with and about Singer continue. Unable to muster the appropriate moral judgments, I ask myself a tough question: am I in fact a silly little lady whose head is easily turned by a man who gives her a kind of attention she enjoys? I hope not, but I confess that I've never been able to sustain righteous anger for more than about 30 minutes at a time. My view of life tends more toward tragedy.

The tragic view comes closest to describing how I now look at Peter   125
Singer. He is a man of unusual gifts, reaching for the heights. He writes that he is trying to create a system of ethics derived from fact and reason, that largely throw off the perspectives of religion, place, family, tribe, community and maybe even species—to "take the point of view of the universe." His is a grand, heroic undertaking.

But like the protagonist in a classical drama, Singer has his flaw. It is his unexamined assumption that disabled people are inherently "worse off," that we "suffer," that we have lesser "prospects of a happy life." Because of this all-too-common prejudice, and his rare courage in taking it to its logical conclusion, catastrophe looms. Here in the midpoint of the play, I can't look at him without fellow-feeling.

I am regularly confronted by people who tell me that Singer doesn't deserve my human sympathy. I should make him an object of implacable wrath, to be cut off, silenced, destroyed absolutely. And I find myself lacking a logical argument to the contrary.

I am talking to my sister Beth on the phone. "You kind of like the monster, don't you?" she says.

I find myself unable to evade, certainly unwilling to lie. "Yeah, in a way. And he's not exactly a monster."

"You know, Harriet, there were some very pleasant Nazis. They say the   130
SS guards went home and played on the floor with their children every night."

She can tell that I'm chastened; she changes the topic, lets me off the hook. Her harshness has come as a surprise, She isn't inclined to moralizing; in our family, I'm the one who sets people straight.

When I put the phone down, my argumentative nature feels frustrated. In my mind, I replay the conversation, but this time defend my position.

"He's not exactly a monster. He just has some strange ways of looking at things."

"He's advocating genocide."

"That's the thing. In his mind, he isn't. He's only giving parents a 135 choice. He thinks the humans he is talking about aren't people, aren't 'persons.'"

"But that's the way it always works, isn't it? They're always animals or vermin or chattel goods. Objects, not persons. He's repackaging some old ideas. Making them acceptable."

"I think his ideas are new, in a way. It's not old-fashioned hate. It's a twisted, misinformed, warped kind of beneficence. His motive is to do good."

"What do you care about motives?" she asks, "Doesn't this beneficent killing make disabled brothers and sisters just as dead?"

"But he isn't killing anyone. It's just talk."

"Just talk? It's talk with an agenda, talk aimed at forming policy. Talk 140 that's getting a receptive audience. You of all people know the power of that kind of talk."

"Well, sure, but——"

"If talk didn't matter, would you make it your life's work?"

"But," I say, "his talk won't matter in the end. He won't succeed in re-inventing morality. He stirs the pot, brings things out into the open. But ultimately we'll make a world that's fit to live in, a society that has room for all its flawed creatures. History will remember Singer as a curious example of the bizarre things that can happen when paradigms collide."

"What if you're wrong? What if he convinces people that there's no morally significant difference between a fetus and a newborn, and just as disabled fetuses are routinely aborted now, so disabled babies are routinely killed? Might some future generation take it further than Singer wants to go? Might some say there's no morally significant line between a newborn and a 3-year-old?"

"Sure. Singer concedes that a bright line cannot be drawn. But he doesn't 145 propose killing anyone who prefers to live."

"That overarching respect for the individual's preference for life— might some say it's a fiction, a fetish, a quasi-religious belief?"

"Yes," I say. "That's pretty close to what I think. As an atheist, I think all preferences are moot once you kill someone. The injury is entirely to the surviving community."

"So what if that view wins out, but you can't break disability prejudice? What if you wind up in a world where the disabled person's 'irrational' preference to live must yield to society's 'rational' interest in reducing the incidence of disability? Doesn't horror kick in somewhere? Maybe as you watch the door close behind whoever has wheeled you into the gas chamber?"

"That's not going to happen."

"Do you have empirical evidence?" she asks. "A logical argument?"   150

"Of course not. And I know it's happened before, in what was considered the most progressive medical community in the world. But it won't happen. I have to believe that."

Belief. Is that what it comes down to? Am I a person of faith after all? Or am I clinging to foolish hope that the tragic protagonist, this one time, will shift course before it's too late?

I don't think so. It's less about belief, less about hope, than about a practical need for definitions I can live with.

If I define Singer's kind of disability prejudice as an ultimate evil, and him as a monster, then I must so define all who believe disabled lives are inherently worse off or that a life without a certain kind of consciousness lacks value. That definition would make monsters of many of the people with whom I move on the sidewalks, do business, break bread, swap stories and share the grunt work of local politics. It would reach some of my family and most of my nondisabled friends, people who show me personal kindness and who sometimes manage to love me through their ignorance. I can't live with a definition of ultimate evil that encompasses all of them. I can't refuse the monster-majority basic respect and human sympathy. It's not in my heart to deny every single one of them, categorically, my affection and my love.

The peculiar drama of my life has placed me in a world that by and   155 large thinks it would be better if people like me did not exist. My fight has been for accommodation, the world to me and me to the world.

As a disability pariah, I must struggle for a place, for kinship, for community, for connection. Because I am still seeking acceptance of my humanity, Singer's call to get past species seems a luxury way beyond my reach. My goal isn't to shed the perspective that comes from my particular experience, but to give voice to it. I want to be engaged in the tribal fury that rages when opposing perspectives are let loose.

As a shield from the terrible purity of Singer's vision, I'll look to the corruption that comes from interconnectedness. To justify my hopes that Singer's theoretical world — and its entirely logical extensions — won't become real, I'll invoke the muck and mess and undeniable reality of disabled lives well lived. That's the best I can do.

QUESTIONS

1. Johnson's reasons for accepting Singer's Princeton invitation are political and personal. For political purposes, this would be the "opportunity to work with very tough audiences." Her personal reason is that "I was sure it would make a great story." In what ways does Johnson's opening paragraph prepare the reader for her story?

2. In paragraphs 8–16, Johnson lists questions that bother her. Does she ever come close to answering any of them? What are some of the modes of discourse she uses to tell her story?

3. When Johnson disagrees with Singer's statement that "disability makes a person 'worse off'" (paragraph 37), she says, "Not in any meaningful sense. . . . We have something the world needs" (paragraph 38). Discuss what she means by that.

4. In paragraph 156, Johnson says, "My goal isn't to shed the perspective that comes from my particular experience, but to give voice to it." How does she do this in her story?

5. In this story, Johnson brings reality to the abstract world of Princeton, but with mixed results, as demonstrated in her exchange with the philosophy professor (paragraphs 113–118). What does Johnson mean by "I feel as if I'm losing caste?"

6. In paragraphs 131–152, what is Johnson's purpose in "replay[ing] the conversation" with her sister Beth, who has chided her for liking "the monster" (Singer). How does this exchange function in relation to her conclusion, or closing argument, in paragraphs 153–157?

MAKING CONNECTIONS

Compare Johnson's description of her physical self (paragraph 20) and her attitude toward her disability with those of Lucy Grealy (p. 62) and Alice Walker (p. 54).

THE WORK OF MOURNING

Francine du Plessix Gray

Francine du Plessix Gray was born in 1930 in France. Her father was a French diplomat, and her mother was a Russian émigré to France. After her father's death, she emigrated with her mother to New York and learned to speak English when she was twelve. Her mother, a haute couture milliner, and stepfather, an important figure in the Condé Nast publishing empire, were a powerful couple in New York society. Gray is a regular contributor to The New Yorker *and the author of numerous essays and books, including the novels* Lovers and Tyrants *(1976) and* World without End *(1981); non-fiction* Adam and Eve and the City *(1987) and* Soviet Women: Walking the Tightrope *(1990), biographies* Simone Weil *(2001) and the Pulitzer Prize finalist* At Home with the Marquis de Sade: A Life *(1998); and a memoir of her mother and stepfather,* Them: A Memoir of Parents *(2005). She has been decorated by the French government as Chevalier de l'Ordre des Arts et des Lettres and is a member of the American Academy of Arts and Letters. Of* Them, *Gray has said, "All writers are hunters, and parents are the most available prey." The following piece was published in* American Scholar *in 2000.*

. . . Mourning, Freud constantly reminds us, is hard, slow, patient *work*, a meticulous process that must be carried out "bit by bit" (that phrase is repeated a half-dozen times), over a far vaster amount of time than twentieth-century society has allotted to any ritual of grief. Crucial to this toil, he tells us, is our careful examination, "piecemeal," as he puts it, of each association, each place, each belonging once shared with the departed (*don't* sell the house the first year, *don't* hasten to put the clothes away, continue to polish his/her silver). Equally essential are those traditional gestures of ritualized grief (memorial services, visits to a grave or commemorative site) that confirm the absence of the dead one. In this slow, long-drawn-out, and gradual work of severance, Freud writes, "each single one of the memories and situations of expectancy which demonstrate the libido's attachment to the lost object is met by the verdict of reality that the object no longer exists. . . . When this work has been accomplished the ego will have succeeded in freeing its libido from the lost object."

What happens if the work of mourning does not proceed on this detailed and stately course, if the enormous energy available for the labor of grief does not find its proper tools or associations? It can become what Freud calls "pathological mourning." Like those spirits of the dead in

Greek literature who, if improperly mourned, return to cause malevolent mischief—devastating crops, destroying whole towns—the psychic energies of mourning, if repressed, can wreak grievous harm. They can turn inward into a dangerous process of self-devouring (as when we "eat our hearts out"). They can metamorphose into what we now call depression, a condition for which Freud preferred the more resonant, tradition-laden term *melancholia*. And, most tragically, they can give rise to self-hatred and self-destruction. "The patient represents his ego to us as worthless, incapable of any achievement and morally despicable, he reproaches himself, vilifies himself and expects to be cast out and punished. . . . This . . . delusion of mainly moral inferiority is completed by sleeplessness and refusal to take nourishment, and by an overcoming of the instinct which compels every living thing to cling to life."

It is not traditional, but very useful, to read Freud and Homer simultaneously. What is most striking in both texts is the sheer energy civilized folk have devoted to rituals of mourning. Here I am in books 5, 6, and 7 of *The Iliad*, looking in on the clamorous terror of Homeric battle. Lances are being driven clear through eye sockets, livers, and genitals, brains pour out of mouths and severed heads, limbless torsos spin like marbles about the black-blooded earth, men catch their gushing bowels in their hands, crashing "thunderously as towering oaks" onto the blood-soaked ground, and throughout this mayhem there remains on both sides one obsession, one concern: to call an occasional truce that will let each side bury its dead properly. So onto this field of carnage warriors ride, carrying the olive branch, announcing a respite that will enable each camp to carry out its funeral rites. By mutual consent, and for this purpose only, all fighting stops. And on both sides the night is spent in lamentations, in washing and anointing the treasured corpses, in adorning funeral pyres with flowers and drenching them with wine, in honoring with cleansing fire the bones that will eventually be carried back to the warriors' homes. Quite as high and treasurable as wealth and fame, Homer intimates throughout this epic, is the honor of a proper funeral, and life's principal terror is the disgrace of being insufficiently mourned and inadequately buried.

Juxtaposing Freud and Homer over the years, I've come to understand that rituals not only express feelings but mold them and tame them; that mourning rites serve in great part to protect survivors from the excesses of their pain; and that agnosticism does not excuse us from respecting these institutions. For the less a society believes in the existence of a "soul" or "spirit," the more it may need to seek reassurance in specific funeral rites. In the view of some extreme materialists, in fact, whatever "spirit" we possess might rely all the more on a proper handling of our only dead-sure reality—the body. Think of the care lavished for decades on Lenin's embalmed remains in the belief that his psyche would continue to guide the nation as long as his body avoided corruption! Communism may never recover from Vladimir Ilyich's prosaic, unceremonious interment.

Mind you, until recently my own family has never been much good at   5
mourning. There is the case of my stepfather, who bade me get rid of my
mother's clothes within a week of her death, sold the house they'd lived
in for forty-nine years within the month, and promptly had his second,
near-fatal heart attack. There is the case of my husband's aunt, eighty-six-
year-old Rosalind, who, after the death of her second husband, committed
suicide while staying at a summer hotel with her baby sister, my eighty-
four-year-old mother-in-law. "Just send her ashes parcel post!" her sons
bellowed on the telephone from New York when queried about funeral
arrangements. And there is the case of my own father, the love of my early
life, whose only daughter is as late a mourner as can be found.

II

When my father, an officer in the Free French Air Force, was shot down
over the Mediterranean in the first summer of World War II — I was nine
years old — the news of his death was hidden from me for well over a year.
My parents' marriage had been an unhappy one. I had always been under
my father's supervision, idolizing my distant mother, a seductive, formidably
ambitious woman, alternating warmth and glacial narcissism, with whom I
had seldom even shared a meal until I came into her charge. She continued to
hide his death from me after we came to America, leading me to believe that
he was still alive, "somewhere in the Resistance." The news would be broken to me only by a family acquaintance. I wept solidly for months, and for
years to come would follow strangers down the streets for hours under the
delusion that my father was still alive, carrying out secret missions. There
were precise geographic obstacles to my performing any of those gestures of
ritualized grief needed, as Freud puts it, "to confirm the absence of the dead
one." The burial site — a vast military cemetery on Gibraltar — lay thousands of miles across the ocean, and was made further unreachable by war.

My mother had been in love for years with a friend of her youth, and
remarried soon after my father's death. The suddenness of the wedding, to
which I was not invited, may have made my bereavement all the more complex. "The funeral baked meats did coldly furnish forth the marriage tables," says the quintessentially melancholic griever, Hamlet, upon his
mother's remarriage. As my new parents banqueted on their long-awaited
happiness, I was shunted out of their lives for weeks at a time to stay with
various friends, warmhearted exiles as impecunious as we, whose only
guest facilities were a living room couch. On these makeshift beds I often
woke throughout the night shaking with tears, and was barely able to stay
awake during the school day that ensued. I remember weeping with particular violence every time one of my birthdays came around, terrified that I
was *getting very old*. "I am *decaying* with time" — such was the anxiety
that plagued me as I turned twelve, thirteen, fourteen — "I'm getting so old
that I can die at any time now." (It's worth noting that it was the theme of

"Suicide and Children" — leitmotiv of a psychoanalytic conference held in Vienna in 1912 — that first inspired Freud to write "Mourning and Melancholia.") There was no one to whom I could communicate my anxiety; such confessions would have singled me out as "weird" among my peers, and my relationship with my mother was dictated by one delicate strategy — my attempts to win her love by being the cheerfully successful, "attractive" teenager, while constantly reminding her, as an extra bargaining chip, that I could not forgive her earlier neglect.

So in the following American years, my blissfully remarried mother would continue to evade every mention of my father, wipe away every trace of the warrior lying in his military grave thousands of miles across the ocean. Like my stepfather, she geared all activity to goals of social advancement and career, worked prodigiously hard, gambled, laughed, dined and entertained the years away as she sought out the company of the powerful, talented, and wealthy. (The dead are none of these; snobs are seldom good at mourning.) And within a year or two, I began to play her game, I began to forget with her, for it was by far the easier and lazier path. Gorgeous, fabulously successful, renowned for her scathing wit, she had survived the upheavals and famines of the Russian Revolution, a serious case of tuberculosis, an unhappy first marriage, the turmoil of our exodus from occupied France. Throughout this she had avoided all soul-searching and conversation, all mention of and confrontations with the past, and I wanted a piece of her action — her might, her power over others. We were the newly minted family in the new country off to a phenomenal new start. I joined my new parents in their memory-destroying dance, I collaborated like a traitor, I soon transferred to my charming, generous stepfather the affection I had borne for the dead warrior. I came to know the euphoria of burying the ancestral past rather than burying the dead. As for the terrors of my nightly awakenings, by late adolescence they were efficiently repressed, waning apace with most memories of my father, with most conscious interest in his life or death.

III

It is 1948 and I am a freshman at Bryn Mawr, playing the role of Ismene in a college production of Jean Anouilh's *Antigone*. According to what I've just learned in Western Civ, Antigone, custodian of primeval ritual observances, preserver of tribal memory, confronts her uncle Creon, the archetypal male technocrat who, in his obsession with political expediency, is ready to violate any divine law that stands in his way. Against the advice of her accommodating sister, Ismene, she safeguards her dead brother, a rebel against Creon's state, from suffering the greatest dishonor in Greek society — being left "unburied, food for the wild dogs and wheeling vultures." Following the dictates of her conscience and of the Greek religion, she offers her brother the burial rites forbidden him by Creon and suffers the consequences, going to her grave "unsung, unwed." Male *polis* versus female hearth: I have quite grasped these essentials and here I am, a proto-Marxist and militantly secular eighteen-year-old, sympathizing totally with the docile, pragmatic, panicky Ismene, even enjoying moments of approval for the tyrant Creon. Prosperity and survival above all! The orderly society must continue! The forces of progress must prevail! Antigone, in my eyes, is an unintelligibly *archaic* creature, morbid and freakish in her addiction to rites that I find *antiquated*, *meaningless* (I remember thinking those very words). How I disdain Antigone when she tells me, "You've chosen to live, and I to die." How I relish the moments when I chide my sister for venturing on "hopeless quests," for being "much possessed by death."

Only decades later did I grasp the link between Ismene's limp obedience to Creon and my own cowardice about the rites and rights of a dead one lost in war. Only recently have I realized that the role of Ismene, "that beauteous measure of the ordinary," as Kierkegaard describes her, was the one my mother and I had played together for some years. And I would continue to play it for decades to come. A few months after my rendering of Ismene, I received an unsettling letter from a beloved aunt and uncle, my father's favorite cousins, whom I had revisited briefly since the war. They were informing me that my father's body was about to be repatriated, that his remains were due back at the ancestral vault in Brittany the following July, that our family was gathering for the final burial, that everyone, of course, expected me to come. It was a few years after the war's end; I was eighteen years old. I remember a sense of being assaulted, of being threatened in some very private space that I now realize was the site of an inchoate, deeply sunken grief: how dare they order me to cross the ocean and appear on such and such a day for an abstract and tedious family duty! I was my mother's child; I remember thinking those very words: *tedious, abstract.*

So even though I fully planned to be in France that summer, I wrote back to my aunt telling her not to expect me; I crassly lied and said I could not leave the States that year. "Thank you for letting me know, there's no way I can make it, I'm so glad you'll be there." By which I meant, thanks for minding my business, just take care of it without me. Don't bother me with Memory, I was also saying, echoing my mother. I, too, was burying a parent through the slothful route of a postal service.

IV

Unlike Freud, who assigns to the work of mourning an evenly calibrated, methodical, almost industrial pace, Elisabeth Kübler-Ross divides the process of accepting death, which can be applied as well to the course of grief, into five often tumultuous stages: (1) denial ("No, not me"), (2) rage and anger ("Why me?"), (3) bargaining ("Yes, me, but . . ."), (4) depression ("Yes, me"), (5) acceptance of death ("It's okay, my own time is close"). Kübler-Ross's schema is not that different from the Judaic view of the mourning process, which recognizes the following four phases: (1) three days of deep grief, often ritualized through the *kriyah* or rending of clothes, symbol of the rage and internal tearing asunder that survivors often feel upon their loss; (2) seven days of mourning — "sitting *shivah*" — during which relatives and acquaintances visit the mourners, who are thus able to retell and relive their memories of the deceased and share their emotions; (3) thirty days of gradual readjustment; (4) eleven months of remembrance and healing.

According to these approaches, I seem to have been one of those pathological Hamletian mourners who spend decades in a folly of stage 1. For a few years in my twenties I was settled in Paris, with a job as a journalist. I knew only too well the exact site of my father's tomb at his family's vault in Brittany, but did not once return to visit it. I saw my father's closest friend and confidant, Pierre F, one of the dearest persons of my childhood, and changed the subject whenever he began to speak of his dead comrade. I turned away from the charming, accomplished woman who I knew had been my father's lover for several prewar years, and I never called either one of his companions during the several visits I made to France in the following fifteen years. When visiting with my aunt and uncle, subtle, prescient beings who had grasped the nature of my reticence and knew never to press me on the issue of my father, I prattled on about politics, my Paris men and jobs, and later my marriage, my two children.

But many of us are thrust out of that first stage of rage and denial by the approach of middle age, that often cataclysmic time of reassessment which can readily unclench a flood of new emotions about memory and grief. In the spring of 1970, almost thirty years after my father's death, I suddenly felt an urgent, unprecedented need to learn all there was to know about him, craved every shred of information about his character, his idiosyncrasies, the nature of his fate. When I went to Paris that year, I asked my uncle to help me look up both of my father's only surviving friends. The beautiful woman had just died the previous year. Pierre F was suffering from terminal cancer, and a month after I'd returned to the United States I received a note from my uncle telling me that Pierre had died. I'd arrived at the treasures — the repositories of much of the information I was seeking — a few months too late.

In the following years, my regret and guilt, my long-repressed tender-   15
ness for these two links to my childhood, turned into a new wave of rage and self-hatred, as did every aspect of my long cowardice concerning my father's memory. If I followed Kübler-Ross, I would say that, like other grievers disadvantaged by history or circumstance, I jumbled the three middle stages of mourning — anger, bargaining, depression — into one dangerously turbulent phase. The plight of such survivors is described in a recently published volume of my Bereavement Lit collection, *Ambiguous Loss: Learning to Live with Unresolved Grief*, which deals with the perilous belated syndromes caused by the loss of loved ones "not known to be alive or dead," "missing in action, lost due to immigration or adoption." Such mourners can relive the self-reproaching depression they suffered in their youth, such as those fits of anxiety I knew as a child when I had woken, weeping, in near-strangers living rooms. ("Ambiguous loss," I read in the book just cited, "is unique in that the trauma goes on and on . . . [and] alternates between

hope and hopelessness.") Much of life's meaning can be threatened. There can be impulses to self-destruction. "My heart was utterly darkened," Saint Augustine wrote as he relived the death of a boyhood friend. "I became a great riddle to myself, and asked my soul, *why she was so sad, and why she disquieted me sorely*; but she knew not what to answer me."

I sought help. It was suggested that I should, at long last, visit my father's grave.

During an extended stay with my aunt, whom I finally encouraged, indeed constantly exhorted, to share every crucial and trivial detail she remembered about our mutual lost love — be it his generosity, his expertise in tennis and Oriental art, or his heroism in war — I finally acquired the courage to return to the ancestral vault where he is buried. There is a passage in my novel *Lovers and Tyrants* in which I describe the first visit of my protagonist, Stephanie, to her (my) father's tomb:

> I kneel down on the sealing stone which stands between me and the dead, that separates his body from mine. . . . And then suddenly my liberation comes. I am free now, kneeling on the stone, suddenly free and shaking, my head resting against the rusty metal handle that could be lifted for our reunion. I weep, I shake, I pound at the floor with my head, I kick it, I beat it with my hands. . . . He is there, he is there, he is there. Above all else he is now allowed to live in my memory, totally restored and whole now, as if resurrected, the reality of his death accepted, faced.

I may have been a bit optimistic in that passage. But I do know that I've rejected Ismene and come close to embracing Antigone. I've come to understand that Creon's refusal to accept an equipoise between the rights of the living and those of the dead — a balance essential to our psychic survival — is what brings on his own destruction.

I've also come to know that healthy mourning has to do with relearning reality; that we must cease to desire the loved ones' return and must recreate a new psychic space in which we continue to love them in absence and separation. Above all, I now realize that we can only continue to propagate their values, their lives' meanings, by some dynamic interaction with the story of their lives, that information is our most valuable treasure, that we may have to learn those life narratives before we can begin the proper work of grief.

So go for it! I say to my students when they inform me that they want to tape the recollections of a grandmother, a great-granduncle, their own guardians of tribal memory. Go for it now, or you may get there too late, as I did. Do it for me.

V

It is June 2000, and there's so much to do at Mother's grave! I must   20
prune the rhododendrons, give them a particularly good feeding after this

arduous winter, perhaps put in some new evergreens on either side of the tombstone that surmounts her ashes and bears her name and dates — Tatiana Iakovleva du Plessix Liberman, 1906–1991. She lies half a mile from my house as the bird flies, less than a mile on foot. In the proper weather I can even walk a few hundred yards down my road and cut across a wide swath of fields, and there she is under a bed of myrtle, at the northwest end of my village cemetery. My husband and I chose this plot for our entire family a few decades ago. I have been easy, familiar with death ever since my near breakdown at my father's tomb. Mother had gone in first, waiting for us, and now, as of the past winter, my cherished stepfather's name and dates are engraved below hers. After I've pruned and fed the rhodies I must weed the myrtle, a hellish task to get at the lawn grass without breaking the delicate roots — I am possessive, tidy if not narcissistic about Mother's grave, as she was with her own appearance in life. I feel guilty, for instance, about the current sparseness of the foliage on the rhodies; I failed to wrap them in burlap last fall, as I had in previous years, to shelter them from our icy winters. It had been a hellish November, with my dearest friend, Ethel C, dying just four days before my stepfather, and as I moved from mourning to mourning I kept forgetting the burlap each time I went to visit Mother. . . . Beyond my frequent horticultural checks, and birthdays and Christmases, I come to see her on every important occasion of the year — before taking a trip abroad, for instance, as if to get her blessing, and when a new grandchild is born, to share the joy, and upon crises, to glean counsel. . . . I suppose that having her near me, visitable upon a moment's whim, is a way of taming her, of having her under my control. For by the time I reached adulthood she had tried to make up for the past with invasive possessiveness, generosity. I had fought back, guarding my frontiers at every step, deviously continuing to charm her while reminding her that I'd never quite forgiven her theft and botching of my father's memory. A decade ago, when she started shuttling back and forth to the hospital and I knew she had no great time left, I started visiting her obsessively, regretting — too late, of course, it is always too late — that I had not started earlier to give and to forgive. She was deeply pleased, but continued to take pleasure in plying her sarcasm. "You know, everyone loves me except you," she once announced, sitting up from her pillows as if she were serving for the match. "You," she said, pointing her long clawed finger, "are merely *afraid* of me." She fell back on her bed. "Just teasing," she added with a grin of sadistic satisfaction. Take that. She died a few weeks later. I sat with her in the intensive care unit a few hours before her end, pressing my face upon hers, begging her forgiveness and outpouring mine, for whatever it was worth. What a model you have been, after all, I told her. What force and shrewdness and power of survival you passed on to me, despite your cowardice. Thank you, my love, I'll never cease to thank you. What pride I took, following her death, in doing all that my stepfather's own illness disabled him from doing — funeral home, newspapers, church and flowers, hosting a wake for hundreds of guests. I had gone through every stage of filial struggle with her — wrath, rebellion, reconciliation, acceptance — and now at last I knew the luxury of properly mourning a parent. As my family and I passed by her open coffin at the Russian Orthodox church service, I felt — beyond my immense sorrow, that brutal sense of physical severance most deeply suffered by daughters — something that resembled a kind of triumph: dear God, I've survived her. And now that her grave is totally under my control, she is my docile little girl, sandstone-soft, every memory of her to be sculpted and honed according to my whims. I can erase the sites of darkness and retain only the very best of her — the scathing intelligence, the rage to live, the acts of extravagant kindness. There's nothing like a grave, particularly if your life was almost botched for lack of one. Now the guardians are all gone, I reflect as I drastically prune the rhododendrons back in hopes that they'll regrow, they're all gone, and I'm the sole custodian, the weight of memory and information is all on me, to share or to withhold, I'm finally in charge.

QUESTIONS

1. Note that the title of Gray's essay is taken from the direct translation of the German title (*Traüer Arbeit*) for Freud's "Mourning and Melancholia." Why is "The Work of Mourning" an appropriate title for this essay?

2. Discuss Gray's closing statement: "I'm the sole custodian, the weight of memory and information is all on me, to share or to withhold, I'm finally in charge." Why is that so important to her?

3. Go to a large bookstore and jot down the titles of the latest in "Bereavement Lit," as Gray calls it (paragraph 15). What appear to be the latest trends in mourning?

4. At the end of Part IV, Gray challenges her students to tape the recollections of "their own guardians of tribal memory." Take up her challenge, and ask an older relative about an ancestor you never knew much about. Transcribe this story, and then analyze the types of remembrances this person has.

5. Write about a wake, funeral, or memorial service that you felt honored the memory of the deceased through specific remembrances and actions, or one that was disappointing. In either case, explain why you felt as you did.

MAKING CONNECTIONS

In Gray's account, compare Freud's method of mourning with Kübler-Ross's "On the Fear of Death" (p. 479). How does Gray make use of Freud and Kübler-Ross in her essay?

DON YSIDRO

Bruce Holland Rogers

*Bruce Holland Rogers was born in Tucson, Arizona, grew up in
Colorado, and currently lives in Eugene, Oregon. He has taught
creative writing at the University of Colorado and the University of
Illinois and is a motivational speaker who provides training in cre-
ativity and problem solving. Rogers has written a nonfiction book,*
Word Work: Surviving and Thriving as a Writer *(2002), and many
articles, essays, poems, and short stories. The genres of his work
have been described as literary, fantasy, science fiction, mystery, and
experimental fiction. Rogers has won the 1999 Pushcart Prize and
Bram Stoker Award for "The Dead Boy at Your Window," the
Nebula Award for Best Short Story of 1998 for "Thirteen Ways to
Water," and the Nebula Award for Best Novelette of 1996, for
"Lifeboat on a Burning Sea," among other awards. Rogers started
a subscription service in which he sends subscribers three short-
short stories a month for a five-dollar yearly fee. His story "Don
Ysidro," one of his subscription stories, won the 2004 World Fan-
tasy Award for the best short fiction work of fantasy published in
the English language.*

On that last morning, anyone who came to visit me could see that I was
dying. I knew it myself. As if I had cotton in my ears, I heard the voice of
don Leandro saying to my wife, "Doña Susana, I think it is time to fetch the
priest," and I thought, yes, it's time. We don't have our own priest, or even
our own church, so someone has to drive in a pickup truck to get the priest
from El Puentecito. But don't be fooled by what you may hear in Malpasa
or in Palpan de Baranda. Here we remain Catholic. Yes, we make pots in
the old way. That's why tourists come here. And it's true, as is sometimes
whispered, that we have restored certain other practices from the past. But
not as they were done back then. Those were bloody and terrible times, the
times of the Mejica.[1] They say that the sacrificial blood covered the sun
pyramids from top to bottom. Thank the Virgin, we don't do anything like
that.

A little after the priest came and went, I died. Word spread. People
came to our house. My family asked first for things of mine that they
wanted. Then the other neighbors. Don Francisco stood near my body and

[1]*Mejica*: Ancient Mexican tribe. [Eds.]

113

said, "Don Ysidro, may I have your shovel? I need one, and your sons-in-law can dig new clay for Susana."

I said, "Take it with my blessing."

Susana said, "He says for you to take it."

Next was doña Eustacia. She asked for one of my *seguetas*[2] for scrap-   5
ing pots.

I said, "Of course. Go with my blessing," and Susana said, "He says for you to take it."

When don Tomás came, he asked for my boots, the ones of red leather with the roosters in the stitching.

I said, "Tomás, you thieving rascal! I know very well that you took two of my chickens that night seven years ago to feed to your whore from Puebla. And here you come asking not for a segueta or some wire, but for my good boots!"

And Susana said, "He says for you to take them." Because, of course, she couldn't hear me. In any case, I would have let Tomás have the boots. I only wanted to see him blush just one time.

They came and asked for everything that Susana would not need. They   10
asked even for things for which it was not necessary to ask. They asked for things I had already promised to them. They even asked for permission to dig white clay from the place where I liked to find it. They asked, and I said yes, with my blessings. We are nothing if not polite.

Last of all, they asked for a few of my hairs to make brushes for painting pots. They cut what locks there were with scissors. They asked for my hands and cut them off with a knife for butchering goats. They said, "Don Ysidro, we want your face." I agreed, and they flayed off the skin very carefully and tenderly. They put my hands in a metal drum and burned them. They dried my face in the sun. Meanwhile, they wrapped the rest of my body in a shroud and buried it in the churchyard according to the customs of the Church.

For a time after that, I was in an emptiness, a nowhere place. I didn't see. I didn't hear. I couldn't speak. I wasn't anywhere, not in my house, not in the coffin in the ground. Nowhere. But that would change.

All my life, I had taught the other people of my village to make pots as I made them. That was nothing special. We all did this. I made my own don Ysidro pots, except when doña Isabela showed me how to make her little tiny ones, or don Marcos demonstrated how he painted his. Then for a while, I would make little tiny pots just like doña Isabela or pots painted in the style of don Marcos. When doña Jenífera had gone to the capital to see the birds and animals on ancient pots, she imitated those decorations, showed us, and soon we all knew how to do it. The rest of the time, I made pots in my own manner, though sometimes with a little touch of Isabela or Marcos or Jenífera that I had learned from them and made my own.

---

[2]*segueta*: A small hacksaw. [Eds.]

Now for the week after I had died, everyone in the village would be making pots as I had made them. Even the children, if they were old enough to make pots of their own. They dug white clay from my favorite place, soaked it, filtered it, let it settle, and poured off the clear water from the slurry. When the clay was dry enough, they mixed in the ashes of my hands. Then they made clay tortillas and pressed them into big plaster molds for the base, just like the ones I used. Sometimes they used my very own molds. They made snakes of clay, attached them to the bases, wound them around from the bottom up. My pots didn't have necks. Neither did these. The people — my family and all the rest of the town — scraped these pots smooth, rubbed them to a shine, and painted them with black paint, using brushes of my own hair and in designs I would have used: lizards and rabbits with checkered backs, or else just checkers that started big around the middle of the pot and became intricate at the lip. Those were pots in the don Ysidro style. They fired them. The ones that the fire didn't break, they brought to my house. Susana put pots all around the front room, and even in the bed where I had lain.

But I didn't see this. I only knew it was happening.   15

These pots in my house sat undisturbed. The people burned the brushes made from my hair.

On the third day, there was a feast at my house. Probably there were all kinds of tamales, some with olives and meat, some with seeds and beans. Men and women drank *pulque*,[3] and there was perhaps melon water for the children. The sun went down. Candles were lit. A fire burned in my fireplace.

At midnight, don Leandro opened a box and took out the mask made of my own skin. He put my face over his face, and I opened our eyes. I came from the place that was nowhere. I was in the room. I looked at the faces, at the wide eyes of the living, at Susana holding her hand over her mouth. I saw my grandchildren, Carlos and Jalea, Ana and Quinito. And for the first time, I could see the pots in the living room. They glowed in the candlelight. Together, don Leandro and I went into the bedroom and I saw the pots there on the bed. We returned to the living room, and I said with our mouth, "I see that I am not dead after all!"

"No, no, don Ysidro," they assured me. "You are not dead!"

I laughed. That's what you feel like doing when you see that you aren't   20
dead.

Then don Leandro threw the mask into the fire, and I wasn't in the mask any more. I was in the pots. In all those round pots made by the hands of my friends, my rivals, my family, my neighbors. I was there, in each one. The people took me away from my house, pot by pot, and I entered their houses with them. In my former home, they left only the pot that Susana had made in my style.

---

[3]*pulque*: An alcoholic drink made from fermented cactus juice. [Eds.]

From that night forward, I was all over the village. People stored corn in me, or rice, or beans. They used me to carry water. And I spread out from there, for if tourists came to buy pots and happened to admire me, the potter would say, "Oh, that's don Ysidro." And the tourist would nod and perhaps buy the pot that he thought was merely *made* by don Ysidro.

I am still in my little village, but I am in Stockholm, too, and Seattle. I am in Toronto and Buenos Aires. Some of me is in Mexico, the capital, though I am mostly still at home here in the village where I grew up, grew old, and died. I sit on Susana's shelf where I can watch her make ordinary tortillas for her breakfast or clay tortillas for her pots. She is old, but her hands are still quick as birds. Sometimes she knows that I am watching her, and she looks over her shoulder and laughs. Whether she can hear it or not, my answering laughter is deep and full and round like a great big pot in the manner of don Ysidro.

QUESTIONS

1. Why do you suppose that Rogers made Don Ysidro the narrator of the story? What expectations does the opening paragraph set up for the reader?
2. The narrator says, "And it's true, as is sometimes whispered, that we have restored certain other practices from the past" (paragraph 1). What are these practices?
3. Judging from the actions of the community, how would you describe Don Ysidro's standing in it? Is this story also a portrait of an artist?
4. If Susana, Don Ysidro's wife, were asked to contribute to the "Bereavement Lit," (Gray, paragraph 15), what might be her advice to new widows?
5. Are there pots or other artifacts in your house that arouse positive or negative memories of a relative or friend who is deceased? Explain.

MAKING CONNECTIONS

How would you describe the work of mourning in Don Ysidro's community? Does it resemble, if not actually, then theoretically, any of the practices described in Gray's essay (p. 104)?

REPORTING IN THE
Arts and Humanities

AT HOME, AT SCHOOL, IN HIDING

Anne Frank

Anne Frank (1929–1945) was born in Germany and lived there until 1933, when her family moved to Holland to avoid the anti-Jewish laws and other anti-Jewish conditions that were then taking hold in Nazi Germany. But the oppressiveness of those conditions spread to Holland after the Nazi occupation in the summer of 1940, as Frank reports in the following excerpt from her diary. She started her diary on June 12, 1942, and continued keeping it until August 1, 1944. Three days after the last entry, the Frank family and a few employees who had been hiding with them from the Nazis since July 1942 were arrested and taken to a concentration camp in Auschwitz, Poland. In October 1944, Anne and her sister, Margot, were moved to a concentration camp at Bergen-Belsen, Germany, where Anne died of typhoid fever in late February or early March 1945, a month or so before the camp was liberated by British troops. Her father, Otto Frank, was the only member of the family to survive the Holocaust, and in 1947 he produced a condensed version of the diary, which had been hidden for safekeeping by two of his secretaries. The following excerpt is from the "Definitive Edition," published in 1995, which includes all of the material that Anne Frank had imagined herself using in "a novel" or some other kind of account about "how we lived, what we ate and what we talked about as Jews in hiding." Her thoughts about making her story known came to mind after she heard a radio broadcast in March 1944 about a planned postwar collection of diaries and letters dealing with the war.

SATURDAY, JUNE 20, 1942

Writing in a diary is a really strange experience for someone like me. Not only because I've never written anything before, but also because it seems to me that later on neither I nor anyone else will be interested in the musings of a thirteen-year-old schoolgirl. Oh well, it doesn't matter. I feel like writing, and I have an even greater need to get all kinds of things off my chest.

"Paper has more patience than people." I thought of this saying on one of those days when I was feeling a little depressed and was sitting at home with my chin in my hands, bored and listless, wondering whether to stay in or go out. I finally stayed where I was, brooding. Yes, paper *does* have more patience, and since I'm not planning to let anyone else read this stiff-backed notebook grandly referred to as a "diary," unless I should ever find a real friend, it probably won't make a bit of difference.

Now I'm back to the point that prompted me to keep a diary in the first place: I don't have a friend.

Let me put it more clearly, since no one will believe that a thirteen-year-old girl is completely alone in the world. And I'm not. I have loving parents and a sixteen-year-old sister, and there are about thirty people I can call friends. I have a throng of admirers who can't keep their adoring eyes off me and who sometimes have to resort to using a broken pocket mirror to try and catch a glimpse of me in the classroom. I have a family, loving aunts and a good home. No, on the surface I seem to have everything, except my one true friend. All I think about when I'm with friends is having a good time. I can't bring myself to talk about anything but ordinary everyday things. We don't seem to be able to get any closer, and that's the problem. Maybe it's my fault that we don't confide in each other. In any case, that's just how things are, and unfortunately they're not liable to change. This is why I've started the diary.

To enhance the image of this long-awaited friend in my imagination, I   5
don't want to jot down the facts in this diary the way most people would do, but I want the diary to be my friend, and I'm going to call this friend *Kitty*.

Since no one would understand a word of my stories to Kitty if I were to plunge right in, I'd better provide a brief sketch of my life, much as I dislike doing so.

My father, the most adorable father I've ever seen, didn't marry my mother until he was thirty-six and she was twenty-five. My sister Margot was born in Frankfurt am Main in Germany in 1926. I was born on June 12, 1929. I lived in Frankfurt until I was four. Because we're Jewish, my father immigrated to Holland in 1933, when he became the Managing Director of the Dutch Opekta Company, which manufactures products used in making jam. My mother, Edith Holländer Frank, went with him to Holland in September, while Margot and I were sent to Aachen to stay with our grandmother. Margot went to Holland in December, and I followed in February, when I was plunked down on the table as a birthday present for Margot.

I started right away at the Montessori nursery school. I stayed there until I was six, at which time I started first grade. In sixth grade my teacher was Mrs. Kuperus, the principal. At the end of the year we were both in tears as we said a heartbreaking farewell, because I'd been accepted at the Jewish Lyceum, where Margot also went to school.

Our lives were not without anxiety, since our relatives in Germany were suffering under Hitler's anti-Jewish laws. After the pogroms[1] in 1938 my two uncles (my mother's brothers) fled Germany, finding safe refuge in North America. My elderly grandmother came to live with us. She was seventy-three years old at the time.

After May 1940 the good times were few and far between: first there was the war, then the capitulation and then the arrival of the Germans, which is when the trouble started for the Jews. Our freedom was severely restricted by a series of anti-Jewish decrees: Jews were required to wear a yellow star; Jews were required to turn in their bicycles; Jews were forbidden to use streetcars; Jews were forbidden to ride in cars, even their own; Jews were required to do their shopping between 3 and 5 p.m.; Jews were required to frequent only Jewish-owned barbershops and beauty parlors; Jews were forbidden to be out on the streets between 8 p.m. and 6 a.m.; Jews were forbidden to attend theaters, movies or any other forms of entertainment; Jews were forbidden to use swimming pools, tennis courts, hockey fields or any other athletic fields; Jews were forbidden to go rowing; Jews were forbidden to take part in any athletic activity in public; Jews were forbidden to sit in their gardens or those of their friends after 8 p.m.; Jews were forbidden to visit Christians in their homes; Jews were required to attend Jewish schools, etc. You couldn't do this and you couldn't do that, but life went on. Jacque always said to me, "I don't dare do anything anymore, 'cause I'm afraid it's not allowed."

In the summer of 1941 Grandma got sick and had to have an operation, so my birthday passed with little celebration. In the summer of 1940 we didn't do much for my birthday either, since the fighting had just ended in Holland. Grandma died in January 1942. No one knows how often *I* think of her and still love her. This birthday celebration in 1942 was intended to make up for the others, and Grandma's candle was lit along with the rest.

The four of us are still doing well, and that brings me to the present date of June 20, 1942, and the solemn dedication of my diary.

SATURDAY, JUNE 20, 1942

Dearest Kitty!

Let me get started right away; it's nice and quiet now. Father and Mother are out and Margot has gone to play Ping-Pong with some other young people at her friend Trees's. I've been playing a lot of Ping-Pong myself lately. So much that five of us girls have formed a club. It's called "The Little Dipper Minus Two." A really silly name, but it's based on a mistake. We wanted to give our club a special name; and because there were five of us, we came up

---

[1]*pogroms*: Violence against Jews and Jewish homes, businesses, and synagogues. [Eds.]

with the idea of the Little Dipper. We thought it consisted of five stars, but we turned out to be wrong. It has seven, like the Big Dipper, which explains the "Minus Two." Ilse Wagner has a Ping-Pong set, and the Wagners let us play in their big dining room whenever we want. Since we five Ping-Pong players like ice cream, especially in the summer, and since you get hot playing Ping-Pong, our games usually end with a visit to the nearest ice-cream parlor that allows Jews: either Oasis or Delphi. We've long since stopped hunting around for our purses or money — most of the time it's so busy in Oasis that we manage to find a few generous young men of our acquaintance or an admirer to offer us more ice cream than we could eat in a week.

You're probably a little surprised to hear me talking about admirers at such a tender age. Unfortunately, or not, as the case may be, this vice seems to be rampant at our school. As soon as a boy asks if he can bicycle home with me and we get to talking, nine times out of ten I can be sure he'll become enamored on the spot and won't let me out of his sight for a second. His ardor eventually cools, especially since I ignore his passionate glances and pedal blithely on my way. If it gets so bad that they start rambling on about "asking Father's permission," I swerve slightly on my bike, my schoolbag falls, and the young man feels obliged to get off his bike and hand me the bag, by which time I've switched the conversation to another topic. These are the most innocent types. Of course, there are those who blow you kisses or try to take hold of your arm, but they're definitely knocking on the wrong door. I get off my bike and either refuse to make further use of their company or act as if I'm insulted and tell them in no uncertain terms to go on home without me.

There you are. We've now laid the basis for our friendship. Until   15
tomorrow.

Yours, Anne

SUNDAY, JUNE 21, 1942

Dearest Kitty,

Our entire class is quaking in its boots. The reason, of course, is the upcoming meeting in which the teachers decide who'll be promoted to the next grade and who'll be kept back. Half the class is making bets. G. Z. and I laugh ourselves sick at the two boys behind us, C. N. and Jacques Kocernoot, who have staked their entire vacation savings on their bet. From morning to night, it's "You're going to pass," "No, I'm not," "Yes, you are," "No, I'm not." Even G.'s pleading glances and my angry outbursts can't calm them down. If you ask me, there are so many dummies that about a quarter of the class should be kept back, but teachers are the most unpredictable creatures on earth. Maybe this time they'll be unpredictable in the right direction for a change.

I'm not so worried about my girlfriends and myself. We'll make it. The only subject I'm not sure about is math. Anyway, all we can do is wait. Until then, we keep telling each other not to lose heart.

I get along pretty well with all my teachers. There are nine of them, seven men and two women. Mr. Keesing, the old fogey who teaches math, was mad at me for the longest time because I talked so much. After several warnings, he assigned me extra homework. An essay on the subject "A Chatterbox." A chatterbox, what can you write about that? I'd worry about that later, I decided. I jotted down the assignment in my notebook, tucked it in my bag and tried to keep quiet.

That evening, after I'd finished the rest of my homework, the note about the essay caught my eye. I began thinking about the subject while chewing the tip of my fountain pen. Anyone could ramble on and leave big spaces between the words, but the trick was to come up with convincing arguments to prove the necessity of talking. I thought and thought, and suddenly I had an idea. I wrote the three pages Mr. Keesing had assigned me and was satisfied. I argued that talking is a female trait and that I would do my best to keep it under control, but that I would never be able to break myself of the habit, since my mother talked as much as I did, if not more, and that there's not much you can do about inherited traits.

Mr. Keesing had a good laugh at my arguments, but when I proceeded   20
to talk my way through the next class, he assigned me a second essay. This time it was supposed to be on "An Incorrigible Chatterbox." I handed it in, and Mr. Keesing had nothing to complain about for two whole classes. However, during the third class he'd finally had enough. "Anne Frank, as punishment for talking in class, write an essay entitled '"Quack, Quack, Quack," Said Mistress Chatterback.'"

The class roared. I had to laugh too, though I'd nearly exhausted my ingenuity on the topic of chatterboxes. It was time to come up with something else, something original. My friend Sanne, who's good at poetry, offered to help me write the essay from beginning to end in verse. I jumped for joy. Keesing was trying to play a joke on me with this ridiculous subject, but I'd make sure the joke was on him.

I finished my poem, and it was beautiful! It was about a mother duck and a father swan with three baby ducklings who were bitten to death by the father because they quacked too much. Luckily, Keesing took the joke the right way. He read the poem to the class, adding his own comments, and to several other classes as well. Since then I've been allowed to talk and haven't been assigned any extra homework. On the contrary, Keesing's always making jokes these days.

Yours, Anne

WEDNESDAY, JULY 1, 1942

Dearest Kitty,

Until today I honestly couldn't find the time to write you. I was with friends all day Thursday, we had company on Friday, and that's how it went until today.

Hello and I have gotten to know each other very well this past week, and he's told me a lot about his life. He comes from Gelsenkirchen and is living with his grandparents. His parents are in Belgium, but there's no way he can get there. Hello used to have a girlfriend named Ursul. I know her too. She's perfectly sweet and perfectly boring. Ever since he met me, Hello has realized that he's been falling asleep at Ursul's side. So I'm kind of a pep tonic. You never know what you're good for!

Jacque spent Saturday night here. Sunday afternoon she was at Han-   25
neli's, and I was bored stiff.

Hello was supposed to come over that evening, but he called around six. I answered the phone, and he said, "This is Helmuth Silberberg. May I please speak to Anne?"

"Oh, Hello. This is Anne."

"Oh, hi, Anne. How are you?"

"Fine, thanks."

"I just wanted to say I'm sorry but I can't come tonight, though I   30
would like to have a word with you. Is it all right if I come by and pick you up in about ten minutes?"

"Yes, that's fine. Bye-bye!"

"Okay, I'll be right over. Bye-bye!"

I hung up, quickly changed my clothes and fixed my hair. I was so nervous I leaned out the window to watch for him. He finally showed up. Miracle of miracles, I didn't rush down the stairs, but waited quietly until he rang the bell. I went down to open the door, and he got right to the point.

"Anne, my grandmother thinks you're too young for me to be seeing you on a regular basis. She says I should be going to the Lowenbachs', but you probably know that I'm not going out with Ursul anymore."

"No, I didn't know. What happened? Did you two have a fight?"   35

"No, nothing like that. I told Ursul that we weren't suited to each other and so it was better for us not to go together anymore, but that she was welcome at my house and I hoped I would be welcome at hers. Actually, I thought Ursul was hanging around with another boy, and I treated her as if she were. But that wasn't true. And then my uncle said I should apologize to her, but of course I didn't feel like it, and that's why I broke up with her. But that was just one of the reasons.

"Now my grandmother wants me to see Ursul and not you, but I don't agree and I'm not going to. Sometimes old people have really old-fashioned ideas, but that doesn't mean I have to go along with them. I need my grandparents, but in a certain sense they need me too. From now on I'll be free on Wednesday evenings. You see, my grandparents made me sign up for a wood-carving class, but actually I go to a club organized by the Zionists.[2] My grandparents don't want me to go, because they're anti-Zionists. I'm not a fanatic Zionist, but it interests me. Anyway, it's been such a mess lately that I'm planning to quit. So next Wednesday will be my last meeting. That

---

[2]*Zionists:* Followers of an international movement to segregate the Jewish people as a state and to establish a Jewish state in Palestine, modern-day Israel. [Eds.]

means I can see you Wednesday evening, Saturday afternoon, Saturday evening, Sunday afternoon and maybe even more."

"But if your grandparents don't want you to, you shouldn't go behind their backs."

"All's fair in love and war."

Just then we passed Blankevoort's Bookstore and there was Peter Schiff 40 with two other boys; it was the first time he'd said hello to me in ages, and it really made me feel good.

Monday evening Hello came over to meet Father and Mother. I had bought a cake and some candy, and we had tea and cookies, the works, but neither Hello nor I felt like sitting stiffly on our chairs. So we went out for a walk, and he didn't deliver me to my door until ten past eight. Father was furious. He said it was very wrong of me not to get home on time. I had to promise to be home by ten to eight in the future. I've been asked to Hello's on Saturday.

Wilma told me that one night when Hello was at her house, she asked him, "Who do you like best, Ursul or Anne?"

He said, "It's none of your business."

But as he was leaving (they hadn't talked to each other the rest of the evening), he said, "Well, I like Anne better, but don't tell anyone. Bye!" And whoosh . . . he was out the door.

In everything he says or does, I can see that Hello is in love with me, and 45 it's kind of nice for a change. Margot would say that Hello is eminently suitable. I think so too, but he's more than that. Mother is also full of praise: "A good-looking boy. Nice and polite." I'm glad he's so popular with everyone. Except with my girlfriends. He thinks they're very childish, and he's right about that. Jacque still teases me about him, but I'm not in love with him. Not really. It's all right for me to have boys as friends. Nobody minds.

Mother is always asking me who I'm going to marry when I grow up, but I bet she'll never guess it's Peter, because I talked her out of that idea myself, without batting an eyelash. I love Peter as I've never loved anyone, and I tell myself he's only going around with all those other girls to hide his feelings for me. Maybe he thinks Hello and I are in love with each other, which we're not. He's just a friend, or as Mother puts it, a beau.

Yours, Anne

WEDNESDAY, JULY 8, 1942

Dearest Kitty,

It seems like years since Sunday morning. So much has happened it's as if the whole world had suddenly turned upside down. But as you can see, Kitty, I'm still alive, and that's the main thing, Father says. I'm alive all right, but don't ask where or how. You probably don't understand a word I'm saying today, so I'll begin by telling you what happened Sunday afternoon.

At three o'clock (Hello had left but was supposed to come back later), the doorbell rang. I didn't hear it, since I was out on the balcony, lazily reading in the sun. A little while later Margot appeared in the kitchen doorway looking very agitated. "Father has received a call-up notice from the SS,"[3] she whispered. "Mother has gone to see Mr. van Daan" (Mr. van Daan is Father's business partner and a good friend.)

I was stunned. A call-up: everyone knows what that means. Visions of concentration camps and lonely cells raced through my head. How could we let Father go to such a fate? "Of course he's not going," declared Margot as we waited for Mother in the living room. "Mother's gone to Mr. van Daan to ask whether we can move to our hiding place tomorrow. The van Daans are going with us. There will be seven of us altogether." Silence. We couldn't speak. The thought of Father off visiting someone in the Jewish Hospital and completely unaware of what was happening, the long wait for Mother, the heat, the suspense — all this reduced us to silence.

Suddenly the doorbell rang again. "That's Hello," I said.   50

"Don't open the door!" exclaimed Margot to stop me. But it wasn't necessary, since we heard Mother and Mr. van Daan downstairs talking to Hello, and then the two of them came inside and shut the door behind them. Every time the bell rang, either Margot or I had to tiptoe downstairs to see if it was Father, and we didn't let anyone else in. Margot and I were sent from the room, as Mr. van Daan wanted to talk to Mother alone.

When she and I were sitting in our bedroom, Margot told me that the call-up was not for Father, but for her. At this second shock, I began to cry. Margot is sixteen — apparently they want to send girls her age away on their own. But thank goodness she won't be going; Mother had said so herself, which must be what Father had meant when he talked to me about our going into hiding. Hiding . . . where would we hide? In the city? In the country? In a house? In a shack? When, where, how . . . ? These were questions I wasn't allowed to ask, but they still kept running through my mind.

Margot and I started packing our most important belongings into a schoolbag. The first thing I stuck in was this diary, and then curlers, handkerchiefs, schoolbooks, a comb and some old letters. Preoccupied by the thought of going into hiding, I stuck the craziest things in the bag, but I'm not sorry. Memories mean more to me than dresses.

Father finally came home around five o'clock, and we called Mr. Kleiman to ask if he could come by that evening. Mr. van Daan left and went to get Miep. Miep arrived and promised to return later that night, taking with her a bag full of shoes, dresses, jackets, underwear and stockings. After that it was quiet in our apartment; none of us felt like eating. It was still hot, and everything was very strange.

We had rented our big upstairs room to a Mr. Goldschmidt, a divorced   55 man in his thirties, who apparently had nothing to do that evening, since despite all our polite hints he hung around until ten o'clock.

---

[3]*SS*: The Schutzstaffel (German). By 1942, the SS, under the leadership of Heinrich Himmler, was the principal instrument of internal rule in Germany. Some SS units were put in charge of Germany's concentration camps. [Eds.]

Miep and Jan Gies came at eleven. Miep, who's worked for Father's company since 1933, has become a close friend, and so has her husband Jan. Once again, shoes, stockings, books and underwear disappeared into Miep's bag and Jan's deep pockets. At eleven-thirty they too disappeared.

I was exhausted, and even though I knew it'd be my last night in my own bed, I fell asleep right away and didn't wake up until Mother called me at five-thirty the next morning. Fortunately, it wasn't as hot as Sunday; a warm rain fell throughout the day. The four of us were wrapped in so many layers of clothes it looked as if we were going off to spend the night in a refrigerator, and all that just so we could take more clothes with us. No Jew in our situation would dare leave the house with a suitcase full of clothes. I was wearing two undershirts, three pairs of underpants, a dress, and over that a skirt, a jacket, a raincoat, two pairs of stockings, heavy shoes, a cap, a scarf and lots more. I was suffocating even before we left the house, but no one bothered to ask me how I felt.

Margot stuffed her schoolbag with schoolbooks, went to get her bicycle and, with Miep leading the way, rode off into the great unknown. At any rate, that's how I thought of it, since I still didn't know where our hiding place was.

At seven-thirty we too closed the door behind us; Moortje, my cat, was the only living creature I said good-bye to. According to a note we left for Mr. Goldschmidt, she was to be taken to the neighbors, who would give her a good home.

The stripped beds, the breakfast things on the table, the pound of meat   60
for the cat in the kitchen — all of these created the impression that we'd left in a hurry. But we weren't interested in impressions. We just wanted to get out of there, to get away and reach our destination in safety. Nothing else mattered.

More tomorrow.

Yours, Anne

QUESTIONS

1. In the first entry for June 20, Frank writes at length about wanting her diary to be a very special kind of friend. What kind of friend does she have in mind? How would you characterize Frank's friendship with Kitty as it develops over the several entries included in this excerpt?

2. How are your impressions of the friendship (and of Frank) affected by the fact that she sometimes goes several days without writing anything in her diary?

3. What kind of person does Frank appear to be from the information she reports and the stories she tells about her family? About anti-Jewish decrees? About her boyfriends? About her experiences at school?

4. What kind of person does Frank appear to be from the thoughts and feelings she expresses about these different aspects of her life? Does she

come across differently (or similarly) when she is writing about these different aspects of her life?

5. In what respects does Frank's life as a thirteen-year-old seem most different from yours when you were thirteen? In what respects does it seem most similar to yours when you were that age? In what ways do you identify with Frank? In what ways do you find her experience so different as to greatly distance you from her?

6. Given what you discover about Frank's day-to-day life with her friends and at school, what do you consider to be the most important similarities and differences between young adolescent life then and now?

7. Compare and contrast the anti-Jewish decrees that Frank reports with racist decrees that you have read about in South Africa, the United States, and other countries around the world.

8. Keep a diary for several weeks in which you try to make a detailed report of the different aspects of your life in a form that you might be willing to share with a close friend (real or imaginary) as well as with a large body of readers.

MAKING CONNECTIONS

What similarities do you find between the lives of the women that Amanda Coyne describes in "The Long Good-bye: Mother's Day in Federal Prison" (p. 141) or the women in the San Francisco County Jail described by Christina Boufis (p. 150) and Frank's reaction to her own imprisonment?

A NEW KIND OF WAR

Ernest Hemingway

Ernest Hemingway (1899–1961) was born in Oak Park, Illinois. In 1918, during World War I, Hemingway served as an ambulance driver and was seriously wounded on the Italian front. After the war, he worked as a reporter for the Toronto Star *and lived in Paris, where he became a member of a lively and productive expatriate community characterized by Gertrude Stein as "a lost generation." His first novel,* The Sun Also Rises *(1926), brought him immediate recognition as a spokesman for the "lost generation" of Americans living abroad after the war. Hemingway's writing also stood out for its uniquely sparse and direct literary style. Along with several short story collections, Hemingway's works include* A Farewell to Arms *(1929),* For Whom the Bell Tolls *(1940), and* The Old Man and the Sea *(1952), for which he was awarded the Pulitzer Prize. Hemingway worked as a correspondent during the Spanish civil war and during World War II, traveling with American troops in France and Germany. He received the Nobel Prize in literature in 1954. Though known for his adventurous and active lifestyle — he was an avid fisherman and big-game hunter — Hemingway became plagued with medical problems later in life. He was hospitalized in 1960 after moving to Idaho. In 1961, unable to write because treatment for mental instability affected his memory, he killed himself with the shotgun he had so often used as a hunter. "A New Kind of War" is one of his early dispatches from the Spanish civil war and is collected in* By-line, Ernest Hemingway: Selected Articles and Dispatches of Four Decades *(1967).*

Madrid. — The window of the hotel is open and, as you lie in bed, you hear the firing in the front line seventeen blocks away. There is a rifle fire all night long. The rifles go tacrong, capong, craang, tacrong, and then a machine gun opens up. It has a bigger calibre and is much louder, rong, cararong, rong, rong. Then there is the incoming boom of a trench mortar shell and a burst of machine gun fire. You lie and listen to it and it is a great thing to be in bed with your feet stretched out gradually warming the cold foot of the bed and not out there in University City or Carabanchel. A man is singing hard-voiced in the street below and three drunks are arguing when you fall asleep.

In the morning, before your call comes from the desk, the roaring burst of a high explosive shell wakes you and you go to the window and look out to see a man, his head down, his coat collar up, sprinting desperately across the paved square. There is the acrid smell of high explosive you hoped you'd never smell again, and, in a bathrobe and bedroom slippers, you hurry down the marble stairs and almost into a middle-aged woman, wounded in the abdomen, who is being helped into the hotel entrance by two men in blue workmen's smocks. She has her two hands crossed below her big, old-style Spanish bosom and from between her fingers the blood is spurting in a thin stream. On the corner, twenty yards away, is a heap of rubble, smashed cement and thrown up dirt, a single dead man, his torn clothes dusty, and a great hole in the sidewalk from which the gas from a broken main is rising, looking like a heat mirage in the cold morning air.

"How many dead?" you ask a policeman.

"Only one," he says. "It went through the sidewalk and burst below. If it would have burst on the solid stone of the road there might have been fifty."

A policeman covers the top of the trunk, from which the head is miss-   5
ing; they send for someone to repair the gas main and you go in to breakfast. A charwoman, her eyes red, is scrubbing the blood off the marble floor
of the corridor. The dead man wasn't you nor anyone you know and everyone is very hungry in the morning after a cold night and a long day the day
before up at the Guadalajara front.

"Did you see him?" asked someone else at breakfast.

"Sure," you say.

"That's where we pass a dozen times a day. Right on that corner." Someone makes a joke about missing teeth and someone else says not to make that joke. And everyone has the feeling that characterizes war. It wasn't me, see? It wasn't me.

The Italian dead up on the Guadalajara front weren't you, although Italian dead, because of where you had spent your boyhood, always seemed, still, like our dead. No. You went to the front early in the morning in a miserable little car with a more miserable little chauffeur who suffered visibly the closer he came to the fighting. But at night, sometimes late, with-out lights, with the big trucks roaring past, you came on back to sleep in a bed with sheets in a good hotel, paying a dollar a day for the best rooms on the front. The smaller rooms in the back, on the side away from the shelling, were considerably more expensive. After the shell that lit on the sidewalk in front of the hotel you got a beautiful double corner room on that side, twice the size of the one you had had, for less than a dollar. It wasn't me they killed. See? No. Not me. It wasn't me anymore.

Then, in a hospital given by the American Friends of Spanish Democ-   10
racy, located out behind the Morata front along the road to Valencia, they
said, "Raven[1] wants to see you."

"Do I know him?"

"I don't think so," they said, "but he wants to see you."

"Where is he?"

---

[1] J. Robert Raven.

"Upstairs."

In the room upstairs they are giving a blood transfusion to a man with   15
a very gray face who lay on a cot with his arm out, looking away from the
gurgling bottle and moaning in a very impersonal way. He moaned mechanically and at regular intervals and it did not seem to be him that made
the sound. His lips did not move.

"Where's Raven?" I asked.

"I'm here," said Raven.

The voice came from a high mound covered by a shoddy gray blanket.
There were two arms crossed on the top of the mound and at one end there
was something that had been a face, but now was a yellow scabby area
with a wide bandage cross where the eyes had been.

"Who is it?" asked Raven. He didn't have lips, but he talked pretty
well without them and with a pleasant voice.

"Hemingway," I said. "I came up to see how you were doing."   20

"My face was pretty bad," he said. "It got sort of burned from the
grenade, but it's peeled a couple of times and it's doing better."

"It looks swell," I said. "It's doing fine."

I wasn't looking at it when I spoke.

"How are things in America?" he asked "What do they think of us
over there?"

"Sentiment's changed a lot," I said. "They're beginning to realize the   25
government is going to win this war."

"Do you think so?"

"Sure," I said.

"I'm awfully glad," he said. "You know, I wouldn't mind any of this if I
could just watch what was going on. I don't mind the pain, you know. It
never seemed important really. But I was always awfully interested in things
and I really wouldn't mind the pain at all if I could just sort of follow things
intelligently. I could even be some use. You know, I didn't mind the war at
all. I did all right in the war. I got hit once before and I was back and rejoined
the battalion in two weeks. I couldn't stand to be away. Then I got this."

He had put his hand in mine. It was not a worker's hand. There were
no callouses and the nails on the long, spatulate fingers were smooth and
rounded.

"How did you get it?" I asked.   30

"Well, there were some troops that were routed and we went over to
sort of reform them and we did and then we had quite a fight with the fascists and we beat them. It was quite a bad fight, you know, but we beat
them and then someone threw this grenade at me."

Holding his hand and hearing him tell it, I did not believe a word of it.
What was left of him did not sound like the wreckage of a soldier somehow. I did not know how he had been wounded, but the story did not
sound right. It was the sort of way everyone would like to have been
wounded. But I wanted him to think I believed it.

"Where did you come from?" I asked.

"From Pittsburgh. I went to the University there."

"What did you do before you joined up here?"   35

"I was a social worker," he said. Then I knew it couldn't be true and I wondered how he had really been so frightfully wounded and I didn't care. In the war that I had known, men often lied about the manner of their wounding. Not at first; but later. I'd lied a little myself in my time. Especially late in the evening. But I was glad he thought I believed it, and we talked about books, he wanted to be a writer, and I told him about what happened north of Guadalajara and promised to bring some things from Madrid next time we got out that way. I hoped maybe I could get a radio.

"They tell me Dos Passos and Sinclair Lewis[2] are coming over, too," he said.

"Yes," I said. "And when they come I'll bring them up to see you."

"Gee, that will be great," he said. "You don't know what that will mean to me."

"I'll bring them," I said.   40

"Will they be here pretty soon?"

"Just as soon as they come I'll bring them."

"Good boy, Ernest," he said. "You don't mind if I call you Ernest do you?"

The voice came very clear and gentle from that face that looked like some hill that had been fought over in muddy weather and then baked in the sun.

"Hell, no," I said. "Please. Listen, old-timer, you're going to be fine.   45
You'll be a lot of good, you know. You can talk on the radio."

"Maybe," he said. "You'll be back?"

"Sure," I said. "Absolutely."

"Goodbye, Ernest," he said.

"Goodbye," I told him.

Downstairs they told me he'd lost both eyes as well as his face and was   50
also badly wounded all through the legs and in the feet.

"He's lost some toes, too," the doctor said, "but he doesn't know that."

"I wonder if he'll ever know it."

"Oh, sure he will," the doctor said, "He's going to get well."

And it still isn't you that gets hit but it is your countryman now. Your countryman from Pennsylvania, where once we fought at Gettysburg.

Then, walking along the road, with his left arm in an airplane splint,   55
walking with the gamecock walk of the professional British soldier that neither ten years of militant party work nor the projecting metal wings of the splint could destroy, I met Raven's commanding officer, Jock Cunningham, who had three fresh rifle wounds through his upper left arm (I looked at

---

[2]*John Dos Passos* (1896–1970): American novelist.

Sinclair Lewis (1885–1951): American novelist, playwright, and journalist; 1930 Nobel Prize winner. [Eds.]

them, one was septic) and another rifle bullet under his shoulder blade that had entered his left chest, passed through, and lodged there. He told me, in military terms, the history of the attempt to rally retiring troops on his battalion's right flank, of his bombing raid down a trench which was held at one end by the fascists and at the other end by the government troops, of the taking of this trench and, with six men and a Lewis gun, cutting off a group of some eighty fascists from their own lines, and of the final desperate defense of their impossible position his six men put up until the government troops came up and, attacking, straightened out the line again. He told it clearly, completely convincingly, and with a strong Glasgow accent. He had deep, piercing eyes sheltered like an eagle's, and, hearing him talk, you could tell the sort of soldier he was. For what he had done he would have had a V.C.[3] in the last war. In this war there are no decorations. Wounds are the only decorations and they do not award wound stripes.

"Raven was in the same show," he said. "I didn't know he'd been hit. Ay, he's a good mon. He got his after I got mine. The fascists we'd cut off were very good troops. They never fired a useless shot when we were in that bad spot. They waited in the dark there until they had us located and then opened with volley fire. That's how I got four in the same place."

We talked for a while and he told me many things. They were all important, but nothing was as important as what Jay Raven, the social worker from Pittsburgh with no military training, had told me was true. This is a strange new kind of war where you learn just as much as you are able to believe.

April 14, 1937

QUESTIONS

1. The Spanish civil war is often seen as " the opening battle of World War II . . . [and] was the culmination of a prolonged period of national unrest." If you know very little about this war, find out more. The quotation above is from Cary Nelson, "The Spanish Civil War: An Overview," which contains a concise description of the Spanish civil war as well as a useful bibliography of sources; it is available at <http://www.english.uiuc.edu/maps/scw/overview.htm>. What was the state of the war in mid-April 1937?

2. Describe Hemingway's narrative stance in the piece. What effect does he wish to achieve through the use of direct address: "the window is open and, as you lie in bed . . ."?

---

[3] *V.C.*: Victoria Cross. British medal awarded for conspicuous bravery in battle. [Eds.]

3. What is "new" about the Spanish civil war? What does the very first sentence suggest: "The window is open and, as you lie in bed, you hear the firing in the front line seventeen blocks away"?

4. Much of this dispatch is about Jay Raven, a badly wounded social worker from Pittsburgh who is a member of the International Brigade. Hemingway doesn't believe Raven's story of his wounding: "men often lied about the manner of their wounding" (paragraph 36). How does he set himself up to be chastened for his disbelief?

5. Writing about a war is challenging. How would you describe Hemingway's approach to his subject? He cannot describe the entire war but instead must choose some aspect of it that will inform his audience in more than a simple reportorial way. Though this piece was categorized as a dispatch because it was wired to the news service NANA, it carried Hemingway's byline. How would you describe his method? Compare Hemingway's piece with a bylined piece from Iraq or Afghanistan, and write about similarities and differences in style and approach.

MAKING CONNECTIONS

The deliberate targeting of civilians was new in 1937; a few years later it would be common. A few days after Hemingway wrote his dispatch, Fascist planes strafed civilians and leveled the town of Guernica. This should have been a warning to the international community as to what lay ahead for them unless they came to the aid of the Spanish loyalists. Strafing and bombing civilians became a feature of World War II and culminated in atomic bombs' wiping out thousands of people in the conflagrations of Hiroshima and Nagasaki. Compare John Berger's approach to his subject in "Hiroshima" (p. 268) and Serge Schmemann's reporting of the attack on the World Trade Center (p. 415) with Hemingway's approach.

HATSUYO NAKAMURA

John Hersey

John Hersey (1914–1993) was born in Tientsin, China, where his father was a YMCA administrator and his mother a missionary. After graduating from Yale in 1936, Hersey was a war correspondent in China and Japan. When the United States entered World War II, Hersey covered the war in the South Pacific, the Mediterranean, and Moscow. In 1945, he won the Pulitzer Prize for his novel A Bell for Adano. *In 1946,* Hiroshima, *a book about the effects of the atomic bomb on the lives of six people, was widely acclaimed. Almost forty years later, Hersey returned to Japan to find out what the lives of those six people had been like. Their stories form the final chapter of the 1985 edition of* Hiroshima. *The selection presented here first appeared in* The New Yorker, *as did the first edition of* Hiroshima. *A prolific writer of fiction and nonfiction, Hersey believed that "journalism allows its readers to witness history; fiction gives its readers an opportunity to live it."*

In August, 1946, a year after the bombing of Hiroshima, Hatsuyo Nakamura was weak and destitute. Her husband, a tailor, had been taken into the Army and had been killed at Singapore on the day of the city's capture, February 15, 1942. She lost her mother, a brother, and a sister to the atomic bomb. Her son and two daughters — ten, eight, and five years old — were buried in rubble when the blast of the bomb flung her house down. In a frenzy, she dug them out alive. A month after the bombing, she came down with radiation sickness; she lost most of her hair and lay in bed for weeks with a high fever in the house of her sister-in-law in the suburb of Kabe, worrying all the time about how to support her children. She was too poor to go to a doctor. Gradually, the worst of the symptoms abated, but she remained feeble; the slightest exertion wore her out.

She was near the end of her resources. Fleeing from her house through the fires on the day of the bombing, she had saved nothing but a rucksack of emergency clothing, a blanket, an umbrella, and a suitcase of things she had stored in her air-raid shelter; she had much earlier evacuated a few kimonos to Kabe in fear of a bombing. Around the time her hair started to grow in again, her brother-in-law went back to the ruins of her house and recovered her late husband's Sankoku sewing machine, which needed repairs. And though she had lost the certificates of a few bonds and other meager wartime savings, she had luckily copied off their numbers before the bombing and taken the record to Kabe, so she was eventually able to cash them in. This money enabled her to rent for fifty yen a month — the equivalent then of less

133

than fifteen cents — a small wooden shack built by a carpenter in the Nobori-cho neighborhood, near the site of her former home. In this way, she could free herself from the charity of her in-laws and begin a courageous struggle, which would last for many years, to keep her children and herself alive.

The hut had a dirt floor and was dark inside, but it was a home of sorts. Raking back some rubble next to it, she planted a garden. From the debris of collapsed houses she scavenged cooking utensils and a few dishes. She had the Sankoku fixed and began to take in some sewing, and from time to time she did cleaning and laundry and washed dishes for neighbors who were somewhat better off than she was. But she got so tired that she had to take two days' rest for every three days she worked, and if she was obliged for some reason to work for a whole week she then had to rest for three or four days. She soon ran through her savings and was forced to sell her best kimono.

At that precarious time, she fell ill. Her belly began to swell up, and she had diarrhea and so much pain she could no longer work at all. A doctor who lived nearby came to see her and told her she had roundworm, and he said, incorrectly, "If it bites your intestine, you'll die." In those days, there was a shortage of chemical fertilizers in Japan, so farmers were using night soil, and as a consequence many people began to harbor parasites, which were not fatal in themselves but were seriously debilitating to those who had had radiation sickness. The doctor treated Nakamura-san (as he would have addressed her) with santonin, a somewhat dangerous medicine derived from certain varieties of artemisia.[1] To pay the doctor, she was forced to sell her last valuable possession, her husband's sewing machine. She came to think of that as marking the lowest and saddest moment of her whole life.

In referring to those who went through the Hiroshima and Nagasaki   5
bombings, the Japanese tended to shy away from the term "survivors," because in its focus on being alive it might suggest some slight to the sacred dead. The class of people to which Nakamura-san belonged came, therefore, to be called by a more neutral name, "hibakusha" — literally, "explosion-affected persons." For more than a decade after the bombings, the hibakusha lived in an economic limbo, apparently because the Japanese government did not want to find itself saddled with anything like moral responsibility for heinous acts of the victorious United States. Although it soon became clear that many hibakusha suffered consequences of their exposure to the bombs which were quite different in nature and degree from those of survivors even of the ghastly fire bombings in Tokyo and elsewhere, the government made no special provision for their relief — until, ironically, after the storm of rage that swept across Japan when the twenty-three crewmen of a fishing vessel, the Lucky Dragon No. 5, and its cargo of tuna were irradiated by the American test of a hydrogen bomb at Bikini in 1954. It took three years even then for a relief law for the hibakusha to pass the Diet.

---

[1]*artemisia*: A genus of herbs and shrubs, including sagebrush and wormwood, distinguished by strong-smelling foliage. [Eds.]

Though Nakamura-san could not know it, she thus had a bleak period ahead of her. In Hiroshima, the early postwar years were, besides, a time, especially painful for poor people like her, of disorder, hunger, greed, thievery, black markets. Non-hibakusha employers developed a prejudice against the survivors as word got around that they were prone to all sorts of ailments, and that even those like Nakamura-san, who were not cruelly maimed and had not developed any serious overt symptoms, were unreliable workers, since most of them seemed to suffer, as she did, from the mysterious but real malaise that came to be known as one kind of lasting "A-bomb sickness": a nagging weakness and weariness, dizziness now and then, digestive troubles, all aggravated by a feeling of oppression, a sense of doom, for it was said that unspeakable diseases might at any time plant nasty flowers in their bodies, and even in those of their descendants.

As Nakamura-san struggled to get from day to day, she had no time for attitudinizing about the bomb or anything else. She was sustained, curiously, by a kind of passivity, summed up in a phrase she herself sometimes used — "*Shikata ga-nai,*" meaning, loosely, "It can't be helped." She was not religious, but she lived in a culture long colored by the Buddhist belief that resignation might lead to clear vision; she had shared with other citizens a deep feeling of powerlessness in the face of a state authority that had been divinely strong ever since the Meiji Restoration,[2] in 1868; and the hell she had witnessed and the terrible aftermath unfolding around her reached so far beyond human understanding that it was impossible to think of them as the work of resentable human beings, such as the pilot of the *Enola Gay,*[3] or President Truman,[4] or the scientists who had made the bomb — or even, nearer at hand, the Japanese militarists who had helped to bring on the war. The bombing almost seemed a natural disaster — one that it had simply been her bad luck, her fate (which must be accepted), to suffer.

When she had been wormed and felt slightly better, she made an arrangement to deliver bread for a baker named Takahashi, whose bakery was in Nobori-cho. On days when she had the strength to do it, she would take orders for bread from retail shops in her neighborhood, and the next morning she would pick up the requisite number of loaves and carry them in baskets and boxes through the streets to the stores. It was exhausting work, for which she earned the equivalent of about fifty cents a day. She had to take frequent rest days.

After some time, when she was feeling a bit stronger, she took up another kind of peddling. She would get up in the dark and trundle a borrowed two-wheeled pushcart for two hours across the city to a section called Eba, at the

---

[2]*Meiji Restoration*: A revolution in Japan that restored imperial rule in 1868 under young Emperor Meiji and transformed the country from a feudal state into a modern state. [Eds.]

[3]*Enola Gay*: The U.S. Army Air Force's B-29 bomber that dropped an atomic bomb on Hiroshima. [Eds.]

[4]*Harry S Truman* (1884–1972): The president of the United States who gave the order to use the atomic bomb in Japan. [Eds.]

mouth of one of the seven estuarial rivers that branch from the Ota River
through Hiroshima. There, at daylight, fishermen would cast their leaded
skirt-like nets for sardines, and she would help them to gather up the catch
when they hauled it in. Then she would push the cart back to Nobori-cho
and sell the fish for them from door to door. She earned just enough for food.

A couple of years later, she found work that was better suited to her need   10
for occasional rest, because within certain limits she could do it on her own
time. This was a job of collecting money for deliveries of the Hiroshima
paper, the *Chugoku Shimbun*, which most people in the city read. She had to
cover a big territory, and often her clients were not at home or pleaded that
they couldn't pay just then, so she would have to go back again and again.
She earned the equivalent of about twenty dollars a month at this job. Every
day, her will power and her weariness seemed to fight to an uneasy draw.

In 1951, after years of this drudgery, it was Nakamura-san's good luck,
her fate (which must be accepted), to become eligible to move into a better
house. Two years earlier, a Quaker professor of dendrology from the University of Washington named Floyd W. Schmoe, driven, apparently, by deep
urges for expiation and reconciliation, had come to Hiroshima, assembled a
team of carpenters, and, with his own hands and theirs, begun building a series of Japanese-style houses for victims of the bomb; in all, his team eventually built twenty-one. It was to one of these houses that Nakamura-san had
the good fortune to be assigned. The Japanese measure their houses by multi-
ples of the area of the floor-covering *tsubo* mat, a little less than four square
yards, and the Dr. Shum-o houses, as the Hiroshimans called them, had two
rooms of six mats each. This was a big step up for the Nakamuras. This
home was redolent of new wood and clean matting. The rent, payable to the
city government, was the equivalent of about a dollar a month.

Despite the family's poverty, the children seemed to be growing normally. Yaeko and Myeko, the two daughters, were anemic, but all three had
so far escaped any of the more serious complications that so many young hibakusha were suffering. Yaeko, now fourteen, and Myeko, eleven, were in
middle school. The boy, Toshio, ready to enter high school, was going to
have to earn money to attend it, so he took up delivering papers to the places
from which his mother was collecting. These were some distance from their
Dr. Shum-o house, and they had to commute at odd hours by streetcar.

The old hut in Nobori-cho stood empty for a time, and, while continuing
with her newspaper collections, Nakamura-san converted it into a small street
shop for children, selling sweet potatoes, which she roasted, and *dagashi*, or little candies and rice cakes, and cheap toys, which she bought from a wholesaler.

All along, she had been collecting for papers from a small company,
Suyama Chemical, that made mothballs sold under the trade name Paragen.
A friend of hers worked there, and one day she suggested to Nakamura-san
that she join the company, helping wrap the product in its packages. The
owner, Nakamura-san learned, was a compassionate man, who did not
share the bias of many employers against hibakusha; he had several on his

staff of twenty women wrappers. Nakamura-san objected that she couldn't work more than a few days at a time; the friend persuaded her that Suyama would understand that.

So she began. Dressed in company uniforms, the women stood, some- 15 what bent over, on either side of a couple of conveyor belts, working as fast as possible to wrap two kinds of Paragen in cellophane. Paragen had a dizzying odor, and at first it made one's eyes smart. Its substance, powdered paradichlorobenzene, had been compressed into lozenge-shaped mothballs and into larger spheres, the size of small oranges, to be hung in Japanese-style toilets, where their rank pseudomedicinal smell would offset the unpleasantness of non-flushing facilities.

Nakamura-san was paid, as a beginner, a hundred and seventy yen — then less than fifty cents — a day. At first, the work was confusing, terribly tiring, and a bit sickening. Her boss worried about her paleness. She had to take many days off. But little by little she became used to the factory. She made friends. There was a family atmosphere. She got raises. In the two ten-minute breaks, morning and afternoon, when the moving belt stopped, there was a birdsong of gossip and laughter, in which she joined. It appeared that all along there had been, deep in her temperament, a core of cheerfulness, which must have fueled her long fight against A-bomb lassitude, something warmer and more vivifying than mere submission, than saying "*Shikata ga-nai.*" The other women took to her; she was constantly doing them small favors. They began calling her, affectionately, *Oba-san* — roughly, "Auntie."

She worked at Suyama for thirteen years. Though her energy still paid its dues, from time to time, to the A-bomb syndrome, the searing experiences of that day in 1945 seemed gradually to be receding from the front of her mind.

The Lucky Dragon No. 5 episode took place the year after Nakamura-san started working for Suyama Chemical. In the ensuing fever of outrage in the country, the provision of adequate medical care for the victims of the Hiroshima and Nagasaki bombs finally became a political issue. Almost every year since 1946, on the anniversary of the Hiroshima bombing, a Peace Memorial Meeting had been held in a park that the city planners had set aside, during the city's rebuilding, as a center of remembrance, and on August 6, 1955, delegates from all over the world gathered there for the first World Conference Against Atomic and Hydrogen Bombs. On its second day, a number of hibakusha tearfully testified to the government's neglect of their plight. Japanese political parties took up the cause, and in 1957 the Diet at last passed the A-Bomb Victims Medical Care Law. This law and its subsequent modifications defined four classes of people who would be eligible for support: those who had been in the city limits on the day of the bombing; those who had entered an area within two kilometers of the hypocenter in the first fourteen days after it; those who had come into physical contact with bomb victims, in administering first aid or in disposing of their bodies; and those who had been embryos in the wombs of women in any of the first three categories. These hibakusha were entitled to receive so-called health books, which would entitle them to free medical treatment. Later revisions of the law provided for monthly allowances to victims suffering from various aftereffects.

Like a great many hibakusha, Nakamura-san had kept away from all the agitation, and, in fact, also like many other survivors, she did not even bother to get a health book for a couple of years after they were issued. She had been too poor to keep going to doctors, so she had got into the habit of coping alone, as best she could, with her physical difficulties. Besides, she shared with some other survivors a suspicion of ulterior motives on the part of the political-minded people who took part in the annual ceremonies and conferences.

Nakamura-san's son, Toshio, right after his graduation from high school, went to work for the bus division of the Japanese National Railways. He was in the administrative offices, working first on timetables, later in accounting. When he was in his midtwenties, a marriage was arranged for him, through a relative who knew the bride's family. He built an addition to the Dr. Shum-o house, moved in, and began to contribute to his mother's support. He made her a present of a new sewing machine.   20

Yaeko, the older daughter, left Hiroshima when she was fifteen, right after graduating from middle school, to help an ailing aunt who ran a *ryo-kan*, a Japanese-style inn. There, in due course, she fell in love with a man who ate at the inn's restaurant, and she made a love marriage.

After graduating from high school, Myeko, the most susceptible of the three children to the A-bomb syndrome, eventually became an expert typist and took up instructing at typing schools. In time, a marriage was arranged for her.

Like their mother, all three children avoided pro-hibakusha and antinuclear agitation.

In 1966, Nakamura-san, having reached the age of fifty-five, retired from Suyama Chemical. At the end, she was being paid thirty thousand yen, or about eighty-five dollars, a month. Her children were no longer dependent on her, and Toshio was ready to take on a son's responsibility for his aging mother. She felt at home in her body now; she rested when she needed to, and she had no worries about the cost of medical care, for she had finally picked up Health Book No. 1023993. It was time for her to enjoy life. For her pleasure in being able to give gifts, she took up embroidery and the dressing of traditional *kimekomi* dolls, which are supposed to bring good luck. Wearing a bright kimono, she went once a week to dance at the Study Group of Japanese Folk Music. In set movements, with expressive gestures, her hands now and then tucking up the long folds of the kimono sleeves, and with head held high, she danced, moving as if floating, with thirty agreeable women to a song of celebration of entrance into a house:

> May your family flourish
> For a thousand generations,
> For eight thousand generations.

A year or so after Nakamura-san retired, she was invited by an organi-   25
zation called the Bereaved Families' Association to take a train trip with
about a hundred other war widows to visit the Yasukuni Shrine, in Tokyo.
This holy place, established in 1869, was dedicated to the spirits of all the
Japanese who had died in wars against foreign powers, and could be thought
roughly analogous, in terms of its symbolism for the nation, to the Arlington
National Cemetery—with the difference that souls, not bodies, were hal-
lowed there. The shrine was considered by many Japanese to be a focus of a
still smoldering Japanese militarism, but Nakamura-san, who had never seen
her husband's ashes and had held on to a belief that he would return to her
someday, was oblivious of all that. She found the visit baffling. Besides the
Hiroshima hundred, there were huge crowds of women from other cities on
the shrine grounds. It was impossible for her to summon up a sense of her
dead husband's presence, and she returned home in an uneasy state of mind.

Japan was booming. Things were still rather tight for the Nakamuras,
and Toshio had to work very long hours, but the old days of bitter struggle
began to seem remote. In 1975, one of the laws providing support to the
hibakusha was revised, and Nakamura-san began to receive a so-called
health-protection allowance of six thousand yen, then about twenty dollars, a
month; this would gradually be increased to more than twice that amount.
She also received a pension, toward which she had contributed at Suyama,
of twenty thousand yen, or about sixty-five dollars, a month; and for several years she had been receiving a war widow's pension of another twenty
thousand yen a month. With the economic upswing, prices had, of course,
risen steeply (in a few years Tokyo would become the most expensive city in
the world), but Toshio managed to buy a small Mitsubishi car, and occasionally he got up before dawn and rode a train for two hours to play golf
with business associates. Yaeko's husband ran a shop for sales and service
of air-conditioners and heaters, and Myeko's husband ran a newsstand and
candy shop near the railroad station.

In May each year, around the time of the Emperor's birthday, when the
trees along broad Peace Boulevard were at their feathery best and banked
azaleas were everywhere in bloom, Hiroshima celebrated a flower festival.
Entertainment booths lined the boulevard, and there were long parades,
with floats and bands and thousands of marchers. This year, Nakamura-san
danced with the women of the folk-dance association, six dancers in each
of sixty rows. They danced to "Oiwai-Ondo," a song of happiness, lifting
their arms in gestures of joy and clapping in rhythms of threes:

> Green pine trees, cranes and turtles . . .
> You must tell a story of your hard times
> And laugh twice.

The bombing had been four decades ago. How far away it seemed!
The sun blazed that day. The measured steps and the constant lifting of
the arms for hours at a time were tiring. In midafternoon, Nakamura-san

suddenly felt woozy. The next thing she knew, she was being lifted, to her great embarrassment and in spite of begging to be let alone, into an ambulance. At the hospital, she said she was fine; all she wanted was to go home. She was allowed to leave.

QUESTIONS

1. What does Hatsuyo Nakamura's story tell us about the larger group of atomic-bomb survivors?
2. Why do you think Hersey chose Hatsuyo Nakamura as a subject to report on? How is she presented to us? How are we meant to feel about her?
3. In composing his article, Hersey presumably interviewed Hatsuyo Nakamura and reports from her point of view. At what points does he augment her story? For example, look at paragraph 5. What material in the article probably comes from Nakamura? What material probably comes from other sources?
4. How has Hersey arranged his material? He has covered forty years of Hatsuyo Nakamura's life in twenty-nine paragraphs. Make a list of the events he chose to report. At what points does he condense large blocks of time?
5. Interview a relative or someone else who participated in World War II or in some other war, such as Vietnam. How did the war change that person's life? What events does he or she consider most important in the intervening years?
6. Most Americans of certain ages remember days of critical national events — the attack on Pearl Harbor, the Kennedy and King assassinations, the space shuttle disasters, and so on. Interview several people about one such day, finding out where they were when they first learned of the event, how they reacted, what long-term impact they felt, and how they view that day now. Use the information from your interviews to write a report.

MAKING CONNECTIONS

1. Imagine an encounter between Nakamura and either Zoë Tracy Hardy ("What Did You Do in the War, Grandma? A Flashback to August 1945," p. 366), or William L. Laurence ("Atomic Bombing of Nagasaki Told by Flight Member," p. 387). What might these people say to each other? Write the dialogue for a possible conversation between them.
2. One characteristic of reports is to be tentative or even oblique in drawing conclusions. Compare Hersey's report to one by Richard Selzer (p. 605), or Roy C. Selby Jr. (p. 634), and assess their differing methods of coming to a conclusion. What would you say are the points of the two reports you chose to compare?

THE LONG GOOD-BYE:
Mother's Day in Federal Prison

Amanda Coyne

Amanda Coyne (b. 1966) was born in Colorado and subsequently migrated with her family from Alaska to ten other states as her father's "relentless pursuit of better employment" led him to hold such titles as fry cook, janitor, librarian, college professor, magazine editor, and presidential speechwriter. Coyne describes her own life as having thus far been "similarly kinetic and varied." "Between traveling, experimenting with religion, countercultural lifestyles, and writing," she has been employed as a waitress, nursing home assistant, teacher, public relations associate, and public policy analyst. A graduate of the University of Iowa, Coyne is currently a staff writer with the Anchorage Press *in Alaska. Her work has been published in the* New York Times Magazine, Harper's, Bust *magazine,* Jane *magazine, and she has read her pieces on National Public Radio's* All Things Considered *and Public Radio International's* This American Life. *The following essay, which appeared in* Harper's *(May 1997), was her first publication.*

You can spot the convict-moms here in the visiting room by the way they hold and touch their children and by the single flower that is perched in front of them — a rose, a tulip, a daffodil. Many of these mothers have untied the bow that attaches the flower to its silver-and-red cellophane wrapper and are using one of the many empty soda cans at hand as a vase. They sit proudly before their flower-in-a-Coke-can, amid Hershey bar wrappers, half-eaten Ding Dongs, and empty paper coffee cups. Occasionally, a mother will pick up her present and bring it to her nose when one of the bearers of the single flower — her child — asks if she likes it. And the mother will respond the way that mothers always have and always will respond when presented with a gift on this day. "Oh, I just love it. It's perfect. I'll put it in the middle of my Bible." Or, "I'll put it on my desk, right next to your school picture." And always: "It's the best one here."

But most of what is being smelled today is the children themselves. While the other adults are plunking coins into the vending machines, the mothers take deep whiffs from the backs of their children's necks, or kiss and smell the backs of their knees, or take off their shoes and tickle their feet and then pull them close to their noses. They hold them tight and take in their own second scent — the scent assuring them that these are still their children and that they still belong to them.

141

Jennifer, Prisoner number 07235-029.

The visitors are allowed to bring in pockets full of coins, and today that Mother's Day flower, and I know from previous visits to my older sister here at the Federal Prison Camp for women in Pekin, Illinois, that there is always an aberrant urge to gather immediately around the vending machines. The sandwiches are stale, the coffee weak, the candy bars the ones we always pass up in a convenience store. But after we hand the children over to their mothers, we gravitate toward those machines. Like milling in the kitchen at a party. We all do it, and nobody knows why. Polite conversation ensues around the microwave while the popcorn is popping and the processed-chicken sandwiches are being heated. We ask one another where we are from, how long a drive we had. An occasional whistle through the teeth, a shake of the head. "My, my, long way from home, huh?" "Staying at the Super 8 right up the road. Not a bad place." "Stayed at the Econo Lodge last time. Wasn't a good place at all." Never asking the questions we really want to ask: "What's she in for?" "How much time's she got left?" You never ask in the waiting room of a doctor's office either. Eventually, all of us — fathers, mothers, sisters, brothers, a few boyfriends, and very few husbands — return to the queen of the day, sitting at a fold-out table loaded with snacks, prepared for five or so hours of attempted normal conversation.

Most of the inmates are elaborately dressed, many in prison-crafted dresses and sweaters in bright blues and pinks. They wear meticulously applied makeup in corresponding hues, and their hair is replete with loops and curls — hair that only women with the time have the time for. Some of the better seamstresses have crocheted vests and purses to match their outfits. Although the world outside would never accuse these women of making haute-couture fashion statements, the fathers and the sons and the boyfriends and the very few husbands think they look beautiful, and they tell them so repeatedly. And I can imagine the hours spent preparing for this visit — hours of needles and hooks clicking over brightly colored yards of yarn. The hours of discussing, dissecting, and bragging about these visitors — especially the men. Hours spent in the other world behind the door where we're not allowed, sharing lipsticks and mascaras, and unraveling the occasional hair-tangled hot roller, and the brushing out and lifting and teasing . . . and the giggles that abruptly change into tears without warning — things that define any female-only world. Even, or especially, if that world is a female federal prison camp.

While my sister Jennifer is with her son in the playroom, an inmate's   5 mother comes over to introduce herself to my younger sister, Charity, my brother, John, and me. She tells us about visiting her daughter in a higher-security prison before she was transferred here. The woman looks old and tired, and her shoulders sag under the weight of her recently acquired bitterness.

"Pit of fire," she says, shaking her head. "Like a pit of fire straight from hell. Never seen anything like it. Like something out of an old movie about prisons." Her voice is getting louder and she looks at each of us with pleading eyes. "My *daughter* was there. Don't even get me started on that place. Women die there."

John and Charity and I silently exchange glances.

"My daughter would come to the visiting room with a black eye and I'd think, 'All she did was sit in the car while her boyfriend ran into the house.' She didn't even touch the stuff. Never even handled it."

She continues to stare at us, each in turn. "Ten years. That boyfriend talked and he got three years. She didn't know anything. Had nothing to tell them. They gave her ten years. They called it conspiracy. Conspiracy? Aren't there real criminals out there?" She asks this with hands outstretched, waiting for an answer that none of us can give her.

The woman's daughter, the conspirator, is chasing her son through the   10 maze of chairs and tables and through the other children. She's a twenty-four-year-old blonde, whom I'll call Stephanie, with Dorothy Hamill[1] hair and matching dimples. She looks like any girl you might see in any shopping mall in middle America. She catches her chocolate-brown son and tickles him, and they laugh and trip and fall together onto the floor and laugh harder.

Had it not been for that wait in the car, this scene would be taking place at home, in a duplex Stephanie would rent while trying to finish her two-year degree in dental hygiene or respiratory therapy at the local community college. The duplex would be spotless, with a blown-up picture of her and her son over the couch and ceramic unicorns and horses occupying

---

[1]*Dorothy Hamill*: The 1976 Olympic gold medal–winning figure skater whose "wedge" haircut became wildly popular in the United States. [Eds.]

the shelves of the entertainment center. She would make sure that her son went to school every day with stylishly floppy pants, scrubbed teeth, and a good breakfast in his belly. Because of their difference in skin color, there would be occasional tension — caused by the strange looks from strangers, teachers, other mothers, and the bullies on the playground, who would chant after they knocked him down, "Your Momma's white, your Momma's white." But if she were home, their weekends and evenings would be spent together transcending those looks and healing those bruises. Now, however, their time is spent eating visiting-room junk food and his school days are spent fighting the boys in the playground who chant, "Your Momma's in prison, your Momma's in prison."

He will be ten when his mother is released, the same age my nephew will be when his mother is let out. But Jennifer, my sister, was able to spend the first five years of Toby's life with him. Stephanie had Ellie after she was incarcerated. They let her hold him for eighteen hours, then sent her back to prison. She has done the "tour," and her son is a well-traveled six-year-old. He has spent weekends visiting his mother in prisons in Kentucky, Texas, Connecticut (the Pit of Fire), and now at last here, the camp — minimum security, Pekin, Illinois.

Ellie looks older than his age. But his shoulders do not droop like his grandmother's. On the contrary, his bitterness lifts them and his chin higher than a child's should be, and the childlike, wide-eyed curiosity has been replaced by defiance. You can see his emerging hostility as he and his mother play together. She tells him to pick up the toy that he threw, say, or to put the deck of cards away. His face turns sullen, but she persists. She takes him by the shoulders and looks him in the eye, and he uses one of his hands to swat at her. She grabs the hand and he swats with the other. Eventually, she pulls him toward her and smells the top of his head, and she picks up the cards or the toy herself. After all, it is Mother's Day and she sees him so rarely. But her acquiescence makes him angrier, and he stalks out of the playroom with his shoulders thrown back.

Toby, my brother and sister and I assure one another, will not have these resentments. He is better taken care of than most. He is living with relatives in Wisconsin. Good, solid, middle-class, churchgoing relatives. And when he visits us, his aunts and his uncle, we take him out for adventures where we walk down the alley of a city and pretend that we are being chased by the "bad guys." We buy him fast food, and his uncle, John, keeps him up well past his bedtime enthralling him with stories of the monkeys he met in India. A perfect mix, we try to convince one another. Until we take him to see his mother and on the drive back he asks the question that most confuses him, and no doubt all the other children who spend much of their lives in prison visiting rooms: "Is my Mommy a bad guy?" It is the question that most seriously disorders his five-year-old need to clearly separate right from wrong. And because our own need is perhaps just as great, it is the question that haunts us as well.

Now, however, the answer is relatively simple. In a few years, it won't   15
be. In a few years we will have to explain mandatory minimums, and the war on drugs, and the murky conspiracy laws, and the enormous amount

of money and time that federal agents pump into imprisoning low-level drug dealers and those who happen to be their friends and their lovers. In a few years he might have the reasoning skills to ask why so many armed robbers and rapists and child-molesters and, indeed, murderers are punished less severely than his mother. When he is older, we will somehow have to explain to him the difference between federal crimes, which don't allow for parole, and state crimes, which do. We will have to explain that his mother was taken from him for five years not because she was a drug dealer but because she made four phone calls for someone she loved.

But we also know it is vitally important that we explain all this without betraying our bitterness. We understand the danger of abstract anger, of being disillusioned with your country, and, most of all, we do not want him to inherit that legacy. We would still like him to be raised as we were, with the idea that we live in the best country in the world with the best legal system in the world — a legal system carefully designed to be immune to political mood swings and public hysteria; a system that promises to fit the punishment to the crime. We want him to be a good citizen. We want him to have absolute faith that he lives in a fair country, a country that watches over and protects its most vulnerable citizens: its women and children.

So for now we simply say, "Toby, your mother isn't bad, she just did a bad thing. Like when you put rocks in the lawn mower's gas tank. You weren't bad then, you just did a bad thing."

Once, after being given this weak explanation, he said, "I wish I could have done something really bad, like my Mommy. So I could go to prison too and be with her."

We notice a circle forming on one side of the visiting room. A little boy stands in its center. He is perhaps nine years old, sporting a burnt-orange three-piece suit and pompadour hair. He stands with his legs slightly apart, eyes half-shut, and sways back and forth, flashing his cuffs and snapping his fingers while singing:

> . . . *Doesn't like crap games with barons and earls.*
> *Won't go to Harlem in ermine and pearls.*
> *Won't dish the dirt with the rest of the girls.*
> *That's why the lady is a tramp.*

He has a beautiful voice and it sounds vaguely familiar. One of the visitors informs me excitedly that the boy is the youngest Frank Sinatra impersonator and that he has been on television even. The boy finishes his performance and the room breaks into applause. He takes a sweeping bow, claps his miniature hands together, and points both little index fingers at the audience. "More. Later. Folks." He spins on his heels and returns to the table where his mother awaits him, proudly glowing. "Don't mess with the hair, Mom," we overhear. "That little boy's slick," my brother says with true admiration.

Sitting a few tables down from the youngest Frank Sinatra is a table of Mexican-Americans. The young ones are in white dresses or button-down oxfords with matching ties. They form a strange formal contrast to the rest of the rowdy group. They sit silently, solemnly listening to the white-haired woman, who holds one of the table's two roses. I walk past and listen to the grandmother lecture her family. She speaks of values, of getting up early every day, of going to work. She looks at one of the young boys and points a finger at him. "School is the most important thing. *Nada más importante.*[2] You get up and you go to school and you study, and you can make lots of money. You can be big. You can be huge. Study, study, study."

The young boy nods his head. "Yes, *abuelita.*[3] Yes, *abuelita,*" he says.

The owner of the other flower is holding one of the group's three infants. She has him spread before her. She coos and kisses his toes and nuzzles his stomach.

When I ask Jennifer about them, she tells me that it is a "mother and daughter combo." There are a few of them here, these combos, and I notice that they have the largest number of visitors and that the older inmate, the grandmother, inevitably sits at the head of the table. Even here, it seems, the hierarchical family structure remains intact. One could take a picture, replace the fast-food wrappers with chicken and potatoes, and these families could be at any restaurant in the country, could be sitting at any dining room table, paying homage on this day to the one who brought them into the world.

Back at our table, a black-haired, Middle Eastern woman dressed in   25 loose cottons and cloth shoes is whispering to my brother with a sense of urgency that makes me look toward my sister Charity with questioning eyes and a tilt of my head. Charity simply shrugs and resumes her conversation with a nineteen-year-old ex–New York University student — another conspirator. Eight years.

Prison, it seems, has done little to squelch the teenager's rebellious nature. She has recently been released from solitary confinement. She wears new retro-bellbottom jeans and black shoes with big clunky heels. Her hair is short, clipped perfectly ragged and dyed white — all except the roots, which are a stylish black. She has beautiful pale skin and beautiful red lips. She looks like any midwestern coed trying to escape her origins by claiming New York's East Village as home. She steals the bleach from the laundry room, I learn later, in order to maintain that fashionable white hue. But stealing the bleach is not what landed her in the hole. She committed the inexcusable act of defacing federal property. She took one of her government-issue T-shirts and wrote in permanent black magic marker, "I have been in your system. I have examined your system." And when she turned around it read, "I find it very much in need of repair."

But Charity has more important things to discuss with the girl than rebelling against the system. They are talking fashion. They talk prints versus plains, spring shoes, and spring dresses. Charity informs the girl that sling-back, high-heeled sandals and pastels are all the rage. She makes

---

[2]*Nada más importante:* Nothing more important (Spanish). [Eds.]
[3]*abuelita:* Grandma (Spanish). [Eds.]

a disgusted face and says, "Damn! Pinks and blues wash me out. I hate pastels. I don't *have* any pastels."

This fashion blip seems to be putting the girl into a deep depression. And so Charity, attempting to lighten up the conversation, puts her nose toward the girl's neck.

"New Armani scent, Gio," my sister announces.

The girl perks up. She nods her head. She calls one of the other inmates   30 over.

Charity performs the same ritual: "Coco Chanel." And again: "Paris, Yves St. Laurent."

The line gets longer, and the girls talk excitedly to one another. It seems that Charity's uncanny talent for divining brand-name perfumes is perhaps nowhere on earth more appreciated than here with these sensory-starved inmates.

As Charity continues to smell necks and call out names, I turn back to my brother and find that the woman who was speaking to him so intensely has gone. He stares pensively at the concrete wall ahead of him.

"What did she want?" I ask.

"She heard I was a sculptor. She wants me to make a bust, presented in   35 her name, for Qaddafi."

"A bust of what?"

"Of Qaddafi. She's from Libya. She was a freedom fighter. Her kids are farmed out to strangers here — foster homes. It's Qaddafi's twenty-eighth anniversary as dictator in September. She knows him. He's mad at her now, but she thinks that he'll get over it and get her kids back to Libya if she gives him a present."

"Obsession. Calvin Klein," I hear my sister pronounce. The girls cheer in unison.

I get up and search for the girl. I want to ask her about her crime. I look in the book room only to find the four-foot Frank Sinatra crooning "Somewhere over the Rainbow" to a group of spellbound children.

I ask Ponytail, one of the female guards, where the woman went.   40 "Rule," she informs me. "Cannot be in the visiting room if no visitor is present. Should not have been here. Had to go back to unit one." I have spoken to Ponytail a few times while visiting my sister and have yet to hear her use a possessive pronoun, a contraction, or a conjunction.

According to Jennifer, Ponytail has wanted to be a prison guard since she was a little girl. She is one of the few female guards here and she has been here the longest, mainly because the male guards are continuously being fired for "indiscretions" with the inmates. But Ponytail doesn't mess around. She is also the toughest guard here, particularly in regard to the federal rules governing exposed skin. She is disgusted by any portion of the leg showing above the required eight-inch shorts length. In summer, they say, she is constantly whipping out her measuring tape and writing up those who are even a fraction of an inch off.

Last summer posed a particular problem for Ponytail, though. It seems that the shorts sold in the commissary were only seven inches from crotch to seam. And because they were commissary-issued, Ponytail couldn't censor them. So, of course, all the women put away their own shorts in favor of the commissary's. This disturbed Ponytail — a condition that eventually, according to one of the girls, developed into a low-grade depression. "She walked around with that sad old tape in her hands all summer, throwing it from one hand to the other and looking at our legs. After a while, not one of us could get her even to crack a smile — not that she's a big smiler, but you can get those corners to turn sometimes. Then she started looking downright sad, you know real depressed like."

Ponytail makes sure that the girls get proper medical care. Also none of the male guards will mess with them when she's around. But even if those things weren't true, the girls would be fond of Ponytail. She is in a way just another woman in the system, and perhaps no other group of women realizes the absolute necessity for female solidarity. These inmates know with absolute certainty what women on the outside only suspect — that men still hold ultimate power over their bodies, their property, and their freedom.

So as a token of this solidarity, they all agreed to slip off their federal shorts and put on their own. Ponytail perked up, the measuring tape appeared again with a vengeance, and quite a few of the shorts owners spent much of their free time that summer cleaning out toilet bowls and wiping the scuffs off the gym floor.

It's now 3:00. Visiting ends at 3:30. The kids are getting cranky, and the   45
adults are both exhausted and wired from too many hours of conversation, too much coffee and candy. The fathers, mothers, sisters, brothers, and the few boyfriends, and the very few husbands are beginning to show signs of gathering the trash. The mothers of the infants are giving their heads one last whiff before tucking them and their paraphernalia into their respective carrying cases. The visitors meander toward the door, leaving the older children with their mothers for one last word. But the mothers never say what they want to say to their children. They say things like, "Do well in school," "Be nice to your sister," "Be good for Aunt Betty, or Grandma." They don't say, "I'm sorry I'm sorry I'm sorry. I love you more than anything else in the world and I think about you every minute and I worry about you with a pain that shoots straight to my heart, a pain so great I think I will just burst when I think of you alone, without me. I'm sorry."

We are standing in front of the double glass doors that lead to the outside world. My older sister holds her son, rocking him gently. They are both crying. We give her a look and she puts him down. Charity and I grasp each of his small hands, and the four of us walk through the doors. As we're walking out, my brother sings one of his banana songs to Toby.

"Take me out to the —" and Toby yells out, "Banana store!"

"Buy me some —"

"Bananas!!"

"I don't care if I ever come back. For it's root, root, root for the —"   50

"Monkey team!"

I turn back and see a line of women standing behind the glass wall. Some of them are crying, but many simply stare with dazed eyes. Stephanie is holding both of her son's hands in hers and speaking urgently to him. He is struggling, and his head is twisting violently back and forth. He frees one of his hands from her grasp, balls up his fist, and punches her in the face. Then he walks with purpose through the glass doors and out the exit. I look back at her. She is still in a crouched position. She stares, unblinking, through those doors. Her hands have left her face and are hanging on either side of her. I look away, but before I do, I see drops of blood drip from her nose, down her chin, and onto the shiny marble floor.

QUESTIONS

1. How would you describe Coyne's point of view in this piece? Detached or involved? Insider or outsider? How does her point of view affect your perception of the federal prison for women that she writes about in this piece?

2. Why do you think that Coyne focuses on Mother's Day at the prison? What kinds of details is she able to report that might not be observable on most other days at the prison? What kinds of details are likely to be missing (or obscured) on such a day as this?

3. Coyne has come to visit her sister Jennifer, but why do you suppose she tells so little about Jennifer compared to what she reports about the other prisoners, particularly Stephanie and the nineteen-year-old former New York University student? Why do you suppose that Coyne tells so much about Stephanie's child, Ellie, and the young Frank Sinatra impersonator but so little about Jennifer's child, Toby?

4. What do you infer from the special attention that Coyne gives to reporting on the actions of her sister Charity and the guard Ponytail?

5. Given the selection and arrangement of descriptive details about the people who figure in this account, what do you consider to be Coyne's major purposes in writing this piece?

6. Compare and contrast Coyne's piece on women's prisons and female prisoners to one or two other stories that you find on this subject in newspapers, in magazines, or on the Internet.

7. Spend a few hours investigating a prison in your community, and write a report highlighting the details that you think are most important in revealing the quality of life in that prison.

MAKING CONNECTIONS

Compare and contrast the way that worlds collide in the visiting room of the women's prison with the cultural collisions that Judith Ortiz Cofer describes in "The Story of My Body" (p. 336).

TEACHING LITERATURE AT THE COUNTY JAIL

Christina Boufis

*Christina Boufis (b. 1961) grew up on Long Island and is a gradu-
ate of Barnard College. She received an M.A. in English language
and literature from the University of Virginia and a Ph.D. in
English literature and a certificate in Women's Studies from the
Graduate Center of the City University of New York. She is currently a visiting faculty member in the Liberal Arts Department
at the San Francisco Art Institute. She has also taught writing at
Stanford, the University of California at Berkeley, and the San
Francisco County Jail. She is the coeditor of* On the Market:
Surviving the Academic Job Search *(1997), and her work has
appeared in many popular and academic journals. She has said
that the following essay "was written out of necessity: teaching
at the jail was so overwhelming at first that I absolutely had to
write about it to get some distance from my students' painful
experiences and be able to go back the next day." This essay first
appeared in* The Common Review *(Fall 2001).*

There is no money for books, so I am photocopying Toni Morrison's
Sula[1] chapter by chapter. This is in defiance of all copyright laws, but I think
if she knew, Morrison would understand. Sometimes I even imagine her
walking into our classroom, and I wonder how she would react to what she
saw: twenty-five women dressed in fluorescent orange, reading her works out
loud. It's been almost four years since I began teaching at the San Francisco
County Jail, and I barely notice the bright orange uniforms anymore, or that
my class is far from the traditional university setting in which I once imagined myself. Instead, I see only the women and their individual faces.

I arrived in San Francisco in 1994, as a new county jail was being built.
That year also marked a turning point in California's history: it was the
first time the state's corrections budget exceeded that of the entire University of California system. I didn't know this then; I knew only that I wanted
to live and work in the city of my choice rather than follow the vagaries of
a bleak academic job market. When I heard that a substitute teaching position in high-school equivalency was available at the jail, I didn't hesitate.
Although I knew next to nothing about the subject, I had spent the last sev-

---

[1]*Toni Morrison* (b. 1931): The winner of the 1993 Nobel Prize for literature.
Sula (1973) is one of her novels. [Eds.]

eral years in graduate school reading about women in literature. I was eager to work with real ones.

Other than telling me that many women inmates have difficulty reading (most are at a fourth- to seventh-grade reading level, I later discovered) and that I should perhaps start with simple math exercises, my predecessor prepared me for little. He was in a great hurry, offered the class for as long as I would have it, and took off for Tahoe[2] without waiting for my answer. Obviously, he'd had enough.

But he gave me a parting gift: a copy of Alice Walker's *The Color Purple*,[3] stored in the top drawer of the classroom filing cabinet. "Sometimes, at the end of class, if they're quiet, I read it out loud to them," he explained. Though the class was held at San Francisco's newest county jail (nicknamed the "glamour slammer" for its seemingly posh facility), the building's school-like appearance belied the fact that the Sheriff's Department spent not a single cent on any of the educational or rehabilitative programs that went on inside. Thus there was no money for more copies of Walker's novel or anyone else's. The class I was teaching was funded by the local community college, which provided only GED[4] books.

I forgot all about *The Color Purple* my first harried, difficult day at the   5
jail. My shock at seeing the women, who appeared as a blur of orange, turned to alienation, then anger, as the class wore on. "Man, we're going to eat you alive," one woman repeatedly uttered. Others told me they didn't have to do any work and weren't going to. A few more crumpled up the math exercises I'd photocopied and told me they didn't know their multiplication tables.

But toward the end of class, one woman seemed to take pity on me and asked for "the book."

"What book?" I replied a little too eagerly.

"The book, the book," others chimed in as if it were obvious.

Another student pointed to the filing cabinet, and I remembered Walker's novel. There was some disagreement about where the previous instructor had left off, but the last ten minutes of class were spent in relative silence as I read and they listened. I wasn't happy with this as a pedagogical strategy — I'd much rather the students read for themselves — but I was thankful that it worked. The women nodded sympathetically to Celie's painful story and thanked me when they left for the day.

"Miss B, Miss B," calls Tanya, a woman who looks and acts much   10
younger than her nineteen years. It has been several months since the other instructor was let go and I was hired; my nickname is a sign of acceptance.

---

[2]*Tahoe*: Lake Tahoe, the largest alpine lake in North America. It is surrounded by the Sierra Nevadas on the California-Nevada border. [Eds.]

[3]*Alice Walker* (b. 1944): The best-selling writer of the Pulitzer Prize–winning novel *The Color Purple* (1982). [Eds.]

[4]*GED*: General equivalency diploma. [Eds.]

Tanya sits up front — the better to get my attention — and soon her pleas take on added urgency. "I need a pencil. I need some more paper." When she finishes with one demand, she moves on to the next. When she gets bored, which happens fairly quickly, she calls repeatedly for *Sula* as if she were a great personal friend. "Where's *Sula*? When do we get to *Sula*?"

I have kept up the practice that my predecessor initiated, spending the last half hour of class reading novels or plays aloud, but with a difference: the students do the reading. The women have come to depend on this promise. The strategy also helps with continuity in what I found to be an almost impossible teaching situation. Turnover is extremely high at county jails and likewise in my classroom. I can have from six to sixteen new students a day and I never know how long any of them will stay. Most serve sentences of less than a year, yet jail is a liminal time during which many wait indeterminately to be sentenced on to prison or parole. Release dates can come and go mysteriously without the promised freedom and no explanation for the delay. Life is thus more volatile in county jails than in prisons and the future more uncertain. Not surprisingly, jails are one of the least studied and understood institutions in the criminal justice system.

Such unsettledness can make anyone edgy, if not downright crazy. Although Tanya has difficulty keeping up with the novel, it doesn't seem to matter. What is important to her is the routine we have established in class, my assurance that we will read the work each day. From what I know of my students' backgrounds, even this modicum of stability was often missing from their lives. Many were homeless before incarceration; few had support from parents, friends, or partners. For Tanya and some of the others, *Sula* has become a talisman of security, something they can rely on in a constantly shifting world.

Tanya has difficulty understanding some of the language and following the plot, but many of the other women do not. They are quick to spot the fact that when Sula's brother, Plum, returns from the war he is a drug addict, though Morrison never states this directly. They can tell by several clues: Plum's weight loss and antisocial behavior, his sugary diet, and the "bent spoon black from steady cooking" found in his bedroom.

The following semester, I teach this same novel in my college writing seminar at the University of California, Berkeley. My Berkeley students don't pick up on the drug connection. Most of them think that Plum uses the spoon to cook soup in his room, and they look at me with disbelief when I tell them otherwise.

My jail students seem able to spot danger everywhere, practically in the way an author uses a semicolon. Reading an O. Henry short story, they immediately inferred that one character was a prostitute, just from the author's description of an abandoned shoe. And if my Berkeley students are frustrated with Morrison for not providing explanations (for Sula's mother's missing leg, or Sula's role in a murder), the women at the jail shrug off such ambiguities. They assume that a character can do an evil act, such as not rescuing someone from drowning, and not be evil herself. My

Berkeley students want to know what I think the work ultimately means, and they are frustrated with Morrison for being evasive. My jail students seem to rest more easily in uncertainty, knowing that life itself does not provide answers.

I can sympathize with both sets of student reactions (I clearly remember being an undergraduate eager to understand the depths of literature), yet the more I discover about my students at the jail, both individually and statistically, the more I appreciate their acute and emotionally sensitive readings. Studies vary, but several show that as many as 90 percent of incarcerated women have been sexually, emotionally, or physically abused. Like their imprisoned sisters elsewhere, most of my students are mothers, women of color, and the sole supporters of young children. They are also most likely in jail on drug charges, primarily for possessing minor amounts of crack cocaine. Before the 1980s "war on drugs" legislation mandated jail time for possessing crack cocaine — but none for possessing the same amount of its more expensive cousin, powder cocaine (a drug used predominantly by whites) — these women would have had rehabilitation or community-based programs as options. Not anymore.

The longer I worked at the jail, the more my curiosity was piqued by what I learned and the more I wanted to help. Years of reading Victorian novels had left me with a strong sense of social reform; I believed I could make a difference teaching at the jail, more so than at other places. And I still believe this despite the fact that I have seen hundreds of women get released from jail and come back again — often the same ones, and often more times than I can count.

Tanya is released before we finish reading *Sula*, and I promise to send the remaining chapters to the address she's given. She tells me that when she gets out, she is going to get her son back, get a job, and turn her life around. I am surprised when she mentions her baby; she looks so much like a child and in need of mothering herself.

We finish Morrison's novel, but it is anticlimactic. No one seems particularly interested in discussing the themes, nor is anyone as thrilled as I hoped they'd be when I announce that our next novel will be Zora Neale Hurston's *Their Eyes Were Watching God*.[5] The class seems subdued and sad. Perhaps this is due to Tanya's absence: although so many students come and go, Tanya has been a steady presence, and her noisy but good-natured complaints have punctuated our days.   20

I try to get one new student to do some work. She is much older, perhaps around fifty-five, and near toothless. "My mind is on burying my son, not on this schoolwork," she tells me, shaking her head. "It ain't right that

---

[5]*Zora Neale Hurston* (1891–1960): A writer and folklorist. *Their Eyes Were Watching God* (1937) is her most popular novel. [Eds.]

they should put me in here when I ain't been in a classroom for thirty years. And I just buried my son. It don't make no sense."

I don't know what to say. Educational programs are mandatory at this jail, but the policy makes little sense to me, too, at times.

The next day, the women are livelier, and we begin reading *Their Eyes*. They quickly pick up on the dialect, something I feared would be prohibitive. "That's country," says one woman. Instead of finding Hurston's phonetic spellings a hindrance to understanding, the women seem to relish sounding out the dialogue and laugh when they trip over words. One fairly new student, a white woman whose face is pockmarked with what looks like deep cigarette burns, stands up to give Hurston's novel a try. The other students are encouraging, telling her to go on when she stumbles, and even yelling at me when I correct a mispronunciation. "Let her do it, Miss B! She's getting it."

As the novel continues, the women become hooked on the story and wonder what will happen next. They recognize Joe Starks for the smooth talker he is and think that the main character, Janie, should have stayed with her first husband, Logan, instead of running off with the slick Joe. "Logan wasn't so bad," says one student who has been in and out of jail several times — this despite the fact that Logan had wanted to buy Janie a mule to plow the field, and the protagonist remarks that she cannot love her first husband. "Besides, he was trying to teach her an important lesson — how to work."

When we get to the part where Janie meets her true love, Tea Cake, who   25
takes her to a new world in the Florida Everglades, my students are quick to note that "he turned her out." I ask about the phrase and am told that it means to be introduced to new people and places, a whole new way of life.

"Is it a bad thing?"

"It doesn't have to be," one woman explains, "but it usually is. You're turned on to the life." That is, a life of drug use or prostitution.

I ask them to write essays about this, and I get back many that explain how they were turned out to drugs: on first dates, with boyfriends, cousins, even mothers.

When we get to the same scene in my Berkeley class, I say something about Tea Cake turning Janie out. My Cal students stare at me as if I've said something incredibly dumb. Some of them have heard the term before, but it doesn't resonate with meaning. We move on.

Tanya, I have heard, is back in jail. Out for less than a week before get-   30
ting rearrested, she likely did not get the photocopies I sent her. She was apparently caught selling drugs to an undercover cop on the same street corner where she was arrested before. I ask the program's administrator about the rumor I heard, and she confirms it. Tanya said she needed money for clothes and that's why she was selling. "It didn't occur to her to get a job," the administrator states. Yet, knowing her educational level, I wonder how easy it would have been for her to get one.

When Tanya comes back into class, she hugs me and asks me not to be mad at her. I'm not and I tell her so. I am always happy to see my former students again, even in jail; at least I know that they are alive and safe. But the rest of the class is unruly. It's a Monday, the day after visiting hours when the women are allowed a two-hour personal contact with their children. The aftermath of these visits is a palpable feeling of malaise. The women often can't concentrate, nor do they feel like doing anything but talking and complaining.

There are four new students, one of whom tells me she is going to prison in a few days and won't bother doing anything. "That crack took away my brain," says another. One young woman who always sits sullenly in the back spits out, "Why don't you take a day off? All the other classes are canceled today. How come ours isn't?"

I'm frustrated and tired of coercing them to work. So I pull out a passage from *Their Eyes*, where Janie talks about feeling like a rut in a road, beaten down, with the life all beneath the surface, and I tell them to respond in writing.

After much cajoling, they begin to write. One woman details the years she spent with a husband who, like Janie's Joe, always put her down. A new student calls me over and tells me she felt trampled this way when she was homeless. "I need more than one sheet of paper to tell this," she states. I agree.

My best student, Linnea, writes quickly, then hands me her essay to   35
read. "I felt I was in a rut when I found myself homeless, hooked on drugs and losing some of my hope," she writes. "I found myself doing things (sexually) that I never thought I would do for drugs. I would have sex in an alleyway, the back seat of an abandoned vehicle, and even out in the open park in front of crowds of people. I would eat out of trash cans. I would go days without bathing, or changing my clothes. . . . I would even try to sell drugs on a very, very small scale. I felt my life was becoming meaningless. . . . I now have a chance to regain my life by being here."

As painful as these stories often are, the women always want to share them by reading them out loud. They clap after each one and make supportive comments. "All you need now is Jesus," or "You're gonna make it, girl. I know it." I correct their punctuation ("Oh yeah, I forget how to use periods," says one student) but am often at a loss for words on the content.

From their essays and comments in class, I can piece together the world that many of my students come from. It's a world of broken promises — mothers who abandon them, boyfriends and fathers who rape them, partners who beat them — and one where home and school are fractured places at best. But despite some of the horrific experiences these women have had, there's a strong element of hope in their writing, a survivor's instinct that things can get better and life will turn around.

We are reading Toni Morrison's *The Bluest Eye*, a somber book about a girl, Pecola, who has internalized white standards of beauty and believes she would be loved if only she had blue eyes. One day, I tell my students that I sometimes feel self-conscious about my position: I'm a white woman teaching mostly African American literature to women of color. "Damn, Miss B, you worry too much," says one student. "Yeah," says another, "you think too hard." As unbelievable as it may sound, there is no racial tension among the women in the jail. Drugs, abuse, and poverty are the great levelers here, at least from what I've seen. It is these elements that transcend division by race, uniting my students with one another and the literature we read.

Similarly, Pecola's life is one of repeated rejection and abuse: she is raped by her father, neglected by her mother. This is by far my students' favorite work, and I suggest they write letters to the author. I vow to someday send them to Toni Morrison and apologize for photocopying her novels.

"Dear Toni," one woman writes, "I can really apperciate your book   40
cuz it gives without a doubt insight. . . . Also men abusing women it is a strong issue and your book brought strength to me as a woman of abuse." Despite the bleak outcome of the novel, the women find positive messages. "Dear Professor Morrison," writes another, "this book made me think about how we put off the beauty of are black people an put on the ugly, but I see the light now an when I leave jail I will keep my Lord with me black women like you makes me proud."

"To Toni Morrison," writes another, "I love the slang that you use it was kind of difficult getting it together but it was real. I love real stuff. . . . you are a dream come true."

"Dear Ms. Morrison. I really enjoyed reading 'The Bluest Eye.' . . . Even tho the cover states that the story is fiction, I truly believe that some little girl may have gone through this. It was a common thing. And Im sorry to say, that it still happens. . . . P.S. If you can please send me an autograph book I would really enjoy it. Thank you."

QUESTIONS

1. Boufis teaches in two different worlds. In each world, her students have their own kinds of knowledge, and for each audience, Boufis must shift her mode of teaching. What does she learn about teaching from her students in the county jail?
2. What does Boufis criticize about the criminal justice system in California? What do you think needs to be changed?
3. Boufis chooses to read books by African American women writers with her county jail students. If you are familiar with the books she mentions in this essay, what was your experience reading them? Why would you or would you not consider them good choices for these students?

4. Boufis starts teaching at the county jail as a substitute teacher, but she stays on as a regular teacher there. What reasons does she give for continuing to teach there?
5. What programs are available for prisoners in your local county jail? If there aren't any, what reasons are given for this lack? Write a report on what you learn.

MAKING CONNECTIONS

Compare Boufis's and Amanda Coyne's (p. 141) criticisms of harsh penalties for low-level drug dealing. Do some further research on this issue, and write a report of your findings.

LABOR DAY HURRICANE, 1935

Douglas Trevor

Douglas Trevor was born in Pasadena in 1969 and grew up in Denver, Colorado, and Key West, Florida. He is currently an associate professor of English at the University of Iowa. He received his undergraduate degree in comparative literature from Princeton University and his doctorate from Harvard University in English renaissance literature. Trevor has published short fiction in The Paris Review, Glimmer Train, Epoch, New England Review, *and other publications. He wrote* The Poetics of Melancholy in Early Modern England *(2004), and his first collection of stories,* The Thin Tear in the Fabric of Space *(2005), won the 2005 Iowa Short Fiction Award. His work has also been anthologized in* The Best American Nonrequired Reading 2005 *and* The O. Henry Prize Stories 2006. *"Labor Day Hurricane, 1935" appeared in* The Thin Tear in the Fabric of Space.

I'll tell you everything I remember from those days although surely I have rearranged certain details, or forgotten others altogether. What I do remember I feel as if I can reach out and touch, but what I can't recall has slipped away from me for good. That's the greatest effect that aging has had on me: not that I forget things, but that what I remember I *really* remember. The memories that haven't dissolved have hardened and calcified inside of me, like so many of my body's infirmities.

I remember very little about the hurricane itself, in part because it hit the Middle Keys, not the Lower, so we were spared the brunt of its power. Unlike others, even others in my family, I was not surprised when the storm arrived because my Uncle Archibald had predicted its appearance early Sunday afternoon, almost exactly twenty-four hours in advance. Uncle Archibald had a barometer on his front porch that he checked with religious regularity during the summer and early fall. When the barometer's mercury went down, however slightly, he would relate the news to one of my three brothers. They, especially Jerry and Jack, were almost always out front, either doing yard work or chatting with friends. I was not privy to Uncle Archibald's summonings, as I was usually inside, doing the housework with my mother, sewing, reading, or helping Frederick with his piano scales. As a young girl I had spent hours every day playing in our lush, overgrown yard — chasing lizards with Jerry and Jack, or playing hide-and-seek with Frederick once he was old enough — but in 1935 I was sixteen and young women did not play outside with their brothers back then. Rather, they helped their mothers keep house, or minded their younger siblings.

I adored all of my brothers, each for slightly different reasons. Like our father, Jerry and Jack were lean and tall, with fair, ruddy complexions, and thin, sandy hair. While we had always been close growing up, by that summer it was clear that they inhabited a new world of which I could only sneak glimpses; now there were moments when they lowered their voices when I entered the room, or shared a laugh over an unspecified adventure in which I had played no part. Jerry was the oldest, at nineteen, but it was Jack, two years younger, who was the most serious and — I suppose — most like our father, although he tempered his naturally stern expression with a wry smile you had to be looking for to catch. Frederick, only eleven, was already of a stockier build than his brothers, with dark hair like our mother's and dazzling, green eyes. He was liable to do anything, from dragging a half-dead water rat into the house to throwing coconuts onto our tin roof from the palm tree in back, convincing my mother that we were being attacked by the German soldiers who were rumored to be setting up camps in Mexico. Frederick was incorrigible but also sweet, and we all awaited his adolescence and young adulthood with a mix of excitement and dread.

Perhaps because I was given relatively few opportunities to stare into its glass up close, I believed fully in the talismanic powers of Uncle Archibald's barometer. He had ordered the device out of the Sears Roebuck Catalogue four years before and had paid a princely sum for it to be shipped, in a crate packed with straw, down to Key West. Its glass tube was set in a thick iron stand that stood to the immediate right of his front door, where others on the island placed umbrella holders. Its prominent positioning had rankled my mother when it was first unveiled. "Is it absolutely necessary," she had asked my father at dinner, "for your brother to adorn the front of his home with scientific experiments?" This was in 1931, when Mother still spoke at dinner. My father did not bother to answer her and she never brought it up again.

That Sunday, just minutes after our lunch was concluded, Uncle Archibald had been so bold as to come over and speak to my father directly, telling him through the open window on the front porch that a hurricane of ferocious proportions was brewing in the Florida Straits.   5

"I know of its ferocity," he added, his fingers flicking the ends of his moustache, "because of the precipitous drop of the mercury in the barometer. You see, rather than flutter as it has in the past, atmospheric pressure is now falling steadily. It's already below twenty-eight, a very bad sign indeed."

But my father dismissed the dire warning, as he always did, with a wave of his hand, and Uncle Archibald doffed his straw hat and shuffled back to his house without another word. Like the rest of us, he was accustomed to our father's grim, ruthless ways, but Uncle Archibald seemed scarcely perturbed by it, or anything else, save the readings he made of barometric pressure in our vicinity.

In the late summer and early fall. Uncle Archibald announced the annihilation of Key West on a daily basis. It was never the case that a storm might graze the tip of the island, or churn up the water on the Atlantic side. Rather, Uncle Archibald interpreted every fluctuation in his barometer with hopeful fatalism as a sign that we were soon going to be left floating in Garrison Bight, holding onto the thick, slatted shutters of our homes. Uncle Archibald was obsessed with instruments of measurement in general. In the dark wood sitting room of his home was a wicker rocking chair, dozens of milk crates filled with bicycle parts, piles of botany and horticultural books, several antique thermometers, a thermoscope handcrafted in Italy, supposedly according to designs left by Galileo, a large ship compass said to have been retrieved from the USS *Maine*, and a mammoth portrait of Theodore Roosevelt. Uncle Archibald adored the former president, although, like my father, he cared little for the current one, FDR. In fact. Uncle Archibald went so far as to model his handlebar moustache loosely on the Rough Rider's facial hair, refusing to cut it off even after it had been out of style for more than a decade. He even tried to add sizable girth to his frame, but no one in our family, save Uncle Edwin, seemed capable of putting on any weight and so Uncle Archibald remained his gaunt self. He always had a freshly cut hibiscus in the lapel of his faded seersucker jacket, or some other flower that had often been grafted with another species of plant, so that the petals were curiously shaped and the color otherworldly. The right pocket of his jacket seemed to fill on its own with saltwater taffy that could otherwise only be purchased in Miami for an outrageous sum, so that when any of us children greeted him we usually dipped our hand into the pocket ourselves, unless our father was nearby, as he disapproved of such behavior.

More generally, my father disapproved of Uncle Archibald. In the early evenings, he would usually offer his meteorological hunches and my father would wipe them away with the back of his hand. Then he would retire to our back porch for his glass of scotch and a cigar. Uncle Archibald never joined him because he was never invited to, although he made a point of taking a drink and having a smoke on the back porch of *his* house, which was separated from ours by about five feet, at the exact same time. There the two of them would sit, their heads encircled by their respective plumes of cigar smoke, and say nothing. Uncle Archibald might shift loudly in his chair, clear his throat, or slap at a mosquito on his neck or arm while exclaiming for effect, but my father would respond to none of his gesticulations, and the few times that I heard Uncle Archibald dare to ask his older brother a question it went unanswered. While the front porches of our homes, which faced the busy Division Street, required civility, our backyards were enclosed, private, and therefore unencumbered by social niceties.

The source of the tension between the two men was traceable to our   10 family business, Columbia Laundry Service, which my father ran with the aid of his youngest brother, Edwin. Uncle Edwin lived on the other side of the island, considered less fashionable because of the salt ponds and the Catholic churches whose congregations were comprised of the Cubans who had worked in the cigar and pineapple canning factories on Duval Street before the Great Depression came along and wiped them out. Now the men stood in small groups downtown during the day, sharing spirits cloaked in brown bags and occasionally getting in fights. The Atlantic side of Key West was supposedly cooler than the Gulf side due to the trade winds, although neither I nor any of my brothers had ever felt their effects. These winds were supposed to bring some relief to my Aunt Grace, who suffered from asthma and rheumatism, and perhaps they did, but nothing could change the fact that she was married to Uncle Edwin, who was preternaturally irritable and a disturbingly voracious eater of stone crab, which he procured in bulk from a fisherman up on Big Pine Key.

Up until 1929, Uncle Archibald had run the laundry service with Uncle Edwin and my father, but that year, a disagreement ensued that rearranged our family for good. I learned of its particulars only by chance. I was doing the dishes in the kitchen by myself one night because Frederick had fallen out of the ficus tree in back while attempting to imitate one of the neighborhood cats and had required hot compresses that my mother could apply only if Jerry and Jack held down his arms and legs. Exactly what I overheard spoken between Uncle Archibald and Father on our back porch has long since escaped me. The gist was an accusation on Uncle Archibald's part that Uncle Edwin's receipts did not accurately reflect the income of Columbia Laundry Service. While Uncle Archibald, a certified public accountant balanced the books, it was Edwin who worked the storefront and managed the employees while my father met with, and tried to solicit, commercial clients for our services. Faced with the choice of regarding either his youngest brother as a thief or his middle brother as a liar, my father opted for the latter, relieving Uncle Archibald of his responsibilities at the store. The consequences of his accusation were probably fully anticipated by Uncle Archibald, who had long ago become too restless to "account" for more than a few hours a day and could usually be found either at the docks downtown, asking fishermen questions about clouds and swells that made their eyebrows wrinkle in confusion, or at the automotive repair shop on Simonton, picking through tires and metal frames that might be used in the construction of a water bicycle he was designing that would make it possible for a single person, with adequate leg strength, to pedal from Key West to Havana.

It was not long after his departure from the family business that it became clear even to us children that Uncle Archibald was up to something more entrepreneurial than the construction of a water bike. First he purchased a new boat: a diesel-powered Tony Jensen, the precise dimensions of which I cannot recall but it must have been at least thirty feet from bow to stern. Uncle Archibald had the wooden hull painted red and named the boat the *Edith Kermit* after Teddy Roosevelt's second wife, implying that he too was starting over again. Why Uncle Archibald needed a boat of such size was a mystery to all of us, until he began to wear so-called Cuban shirts, short-sleeved knits with wide collars and pronounced hems, and smoke Monte Cristos rather than cigars from Tampa. I don't know how we all came to learn that he was using his new vessel to run rum in from Havana, but it was even easier to intuit that his venture was only a partial success. Prohibition ended officially in 1933, but unofficially in Key West sometime before that. There was, quite clearly, more competition in offering spirits on the island than laundering services, and it was not long before Uncle Archibald returned to more conventional dress, although never to Columbia Laundry Service.

Regardless of the situation at the family business, Uncle Archibald was hardly banished from our lives; on the contrary, the more distance created between him and our father, the more appealing he became to me and my brothers. Unlike our father, whose relationship with his middle brother was distanced but still a relationship. Uncle Edwin stopped speaking to Uncle Archibald altogether. Meanwhile, the Great Depression continued to take away our customers, so that by 1935 our paying clients were reduced to two; the Casa Marina Hotel, which needed fewer and fewer sheets and towels to be washed since vacationers in the Keys had slowed to a trickle, and the Florida East Coast Railway. Father had secured this last client in the early 1920s by agreeing to buy all of the linens, towels, napkins, and tablecloths for one of the two trains that would run from Miami to Key West and then leasing their use to the railway on a month-to-month basis. He had borrowed heavily to make the investment but without the outlay we would have never secured the contract and by 1935 it was this contract that kept our laundry service, and by extension our family, afloat when so many businesses and people around us were losing everything.

But I am forgetting the hurricane. Sunday afternoons were solemn times around our house. We would sit together in the living room, dressed in our church clothes, pursuing the silent diversions we were permitted on the Sabbath. Mom usually sat with an open Bible on her lap while Jerry and Jack played a version of checkers that only they understood. I would usually take Frederick under my wing, either to work a puzzle with him or read a book, although that day I cannot recall how he occupied himself. I was sitting on the couch next to Mother, that I do remember, rereading my favorite novel. *Look Homeward, Angel*, when the phone let out a shrill ring.

I'm not sure that our phone had ever rung before on a Sunday, and the occurrence was so odd that my father seemed for the first time that I could remember genuinely unsure what to do. This terrified us all, since that meant he might very well lose his temper and scold us roundly for somehow being responsible for the interruption, which would have reduced our mother to tears. She had been diagnosed as "nervous" just three months before, when she began to cry one afternoon and could not stop, requiring Dr. Moore to come by and prescribe a tablespoon of Dover's powder to be taken with a half glass of brandy before bed each night. A visit to a sanatorium was also proposed, but in the midst of the Depression it was an expense our family could not afford. So it was, I think, in light of her condition that, rather than rage, my father walked over to the kitchen doorway, lifted up the earpiece, and calmly — although sternly — identified himself.

15

He turned his back to us promptly and spoke for several minutes, much longer than he normally would have, issuing *Yes, sirs* and *Yes, of courses* that were so out of character we all watched with mute fascination. When he hung up he stepped toward us, his hands linked behind his back, and leaned out over his patent-leather shoes, which he stared down at intensely. He was the tallest of his brothers, although by today's standards I suppose his height would be barely average, and he wore his thin, red hair in a severe part that began just above his left ear and veered sharply back over his head. The pink pouches of skin beneath his eyes puckered out above his cheekbones but otherwise his was a body and face filled with sharp edges and straight lines.

"That was Mr. Pinder from the Railway Office in Miami," he said. "The Associated Press has issued a bulletin predicting that a storm, perhaps of hurricane strength, will hit Havana and then pass out into the Gulf sometime tomorrow."

My first impulse was to smile at the news, since it vindicated Uncle Archibald's prediction, at least partly, but I restrained myself.

"To err on the side of caution, however," Father continued, "a rescue train is being sent down to Lower Matecumbe to fetch the men working on the Overseas Highway. It is the train that carries our goods on it, which means that we will have a full load to wash come Tuesday, when regular train service begins again."

None of us said anything. We knew of the workers who were building   20
the highway; they had been Bonus Marchers, World War I veterans who had descended on Washington demanding to be compensated for their service. Franklin Roosevelt had put them to work in the Keys, building a highway that was to run mostly alongside the railway, so that motorists could drive from Miami to Key West without having to take any ferries. Father was opposed to the project, as it would presumably decrease railway traffic and thus our laundry business, and his opposition grew once the highway workers began to flock to Key West on the weekends after their paydays, to drink their wages at the saloons downtown. Jerry, Jack, and their friends had been accosted by these men more than once; they were, in my father's words, a debauched and licentious crew, and the WPA that paid their wages — indeed the whole New Deal — was, according to him, the sign of the end of free enterprise in America.

"Mr. Pinder emphasized," Father continued, "that we should take all due precautions, as this storm might easily veer off its projected path. We shall therefore prepare ourselves for the possible eventuality of being visited directly by this hurricane. Jerry, you and Jack must change into your work clothes, withdraw the storm boards from beneath the front porch, and begin to cover up the windows. Frederick, you may assist them, but only if you promise to be helpful and do as they say." Frederick nodded his head seriously. Father turned to me. "Mary, you and your mother should prepare the interior of the house: take the china out of the cupboards in the kitchen and fill the large pitcher with water from the cistern. We shall ride out the storm in the pantry. I shall go this minute and fetch Uncle Edwin and Aunt Grace, who should not be left alone on the far side of the island when the threat of a serious storm is in the vicinity."

He turned to leave out the back porch but quickly spun around, his thumb hooking into the lower right pocket of his vest, just beneath the chain of his gold watch, as if to thwart his momentum in the other direction. "When you're done with our house, boys," he added, "see to it that Uncle Archibald has his home secured as well. And make it known to him, Jerry, that he is welcome in our home, as I am sure his own pantry is too cluttered to permit him safe refuge. I am also of the opinion, you may convey to him, that there is some safety in numbers."

The boys had already hopped to their feet with excitement, having been spared hours of listless boredom with the prospect of an outdoor activity that our father wouldn't dare interrupt until it was completed. Mother's reaction to our father's speech was more subdued. She placed her open Bible against her chest, closed her eyes for a moment, and placed her hand across the bridge of her nose. She was of slight build and small, almost birdlike, with remarkably pale skin and very thin, black hair that she kept pinned in a bun and, whenever she ventured outside, tucked beneath either one of her feathered hats or a bonnet. Finally she rose to her feet and, without a word, motioned to me. I felt my spirits dip. Since her nervous episode Mother had barely spoken at all, and her eyes, which were big and black and seemed to occupy a disproportionate amount of her face, shifted nervously, avoiding the gaze of others. Being alone with her, rather than outside with my brothers, was torture, but of course I had no choice in the matter and so I followed her into the kitchen.

We did not learn that the hurricane's path had shifted until later that afternoon, when Mr. Pinder phoned again, this time to report that the storm might hit anywhere between Key West and Key Largo the following day. That evening, we enjoyed a crystal clear sky, a steady, pleasant breeze, and a beautiful sunset. Aunt Grace and Uncle Edwin spent the night in Jerry and Jack's room, which meant that my older brothers slept downstairs: Jack on the daybed in the living room and Jerry on the front porch. There had been little contact between us children and our uncle and aunt, just a dinner marked by the soft clank of silverware against plates and the satisfied grunts of Uncle Edwin. In the morning, we had a small breakfast of Cuban bread and grapefruit. With no chores to do. Jerry, Jack, Frederick, and I were allowed to linger in front of our boarded-up house, in part because my parents were eager to create some distance between us and Aunt Grace, whose lungs were taxed by loud noises and anything else having to do with young people. She had instructed Uncle Edwin to place a chair in the back room behind the kitchen and sat there in seclusion, occasionally calling out to my mother for a fresh glass of limeade.

The four of us stood outside, with strict instructions to stay nearby, and waited for some sign of impending doom. We were all frightened. Key West 25 seemed quieter than usual, even quieter than it typically was on a holiday. No automobiles passed in front of our house, which like the other homes on our street looked alien and bleak. All of the residences were encased in boards and, in some cases, old sails and strips of newspaper, anything to dampen the effect of the expected winds. Bayview Park, which our front porch faced, was utterly deserted, but neither that nor the lack of people about fully explained the calm. It was Jack who noticed that there were no birds on the island; they had all flown away in anticipation of the storm.

Then we saw the band of dark clouds, and felt the first bit of rain, thick drops that fell first haphazardly and then, only a moment later, in sheets. It was just a little after one in the afternoon. Perhaps my memory has played tricks on me, but I seem to recall the entire sky turning black in seconds. My father called to us and as we scurried around to the back of the house I distinctly remember a gust of wind knocking Frederick to his knees. Uncle Archibald rushed over from his back porch just as we rounded the corner of our house, his barometer held awkwardly in his hands, his straw hat pinched under his arm. He had not wanted to venture inside without us, I felt quite sure, and so I gave him a smile meant to be supportive. He responded by wiggling his moustache slightly, wrinkling his eyebrows, and — once we were inside — removing the red royal poinciana blossom from the lapel of his worn, white suit and placing it very gently in my hair above my ear.

Mother and I had set blankets and pillows from the upstairs bedrooms on the floor in the pantry, and the nine of us sat down, with father securing the door behind us. Aunt Grace and Uncle Edwin established themselves at the far end of the cramped room, which was lit by the candelabra from the dining room table. Like our mother, Aunt Grace was dressed in a black satin dress, although she wore a black bonnet low over her face. All of us children huddled, instinctively, in the opposite corner from our aunt, while I was fortunate to have Uncle Archibald to my immediate left, with Mother and Father next to him.

For some time none of us spoke. We could hear the rain coming down, and the hum of the wind, but it sounded very distant. I felt scared but less so than when I had been outside. In my heart I believed that the pantry protected us, since it was so small I assumed that no storm would have the patience to probe for its precise location. Frederick broke the silence. "Father," he asked, "what if we need to . . ." and he glanced down at his dark blue knickers, which were uncharacteristically clean.

"There's a chamber pot," Father pointed at the long shelf several feet above his head that ran the length of the small room, on which Mother and I had placed our china, which sat wrapped in bath towels and dish rags. "If need be we shall draw a blanket —"

Aunt Grace interrupted him by exclaiming briefly, only keeping her taut   30 mouth closed so that the wail seemed to come from behind her head. She and Uncle Edwin had brought in a picnic basket they must have packed the day before, which he opened, removing a dishcloth over which he carefully dribbled a smattering of water from the large pitcher to his right before dabbing at her forehead while she fanned herself with her hand.

With Aunt Grace clearly on the verge of delirium, we all knew to be quiet and sat there glumly, listening to the storm. For several minutes even Uncle Archibald was still, and in my mind I wondered who would begin to fidget first, he or my brother Frederick. It ended up being my uncle. I had forgotten to take note of his barometer, which he had placed against the wall on his left side, in between him and my mother, but after what must have seemed to him to be an excruciatingly long time, he stood up and, crouching sharply — since the pantry was located under the stairwell of our home and our end of the room was beneath the lowest part of the stairs — pulled the barometer out so that it loomed in front of him. Then he sat back down, but not before withdrawing a handkerchief from his back pocket, which he used to wipe down the glass. He slowly rocked the barometer very gently on its iron base so that it inched toward him. Then he leaned forward, withdrawing his monocle from his vest pocket, and stared intently at the mercury level in the glass.

"Yes, still falling, still falling," he said softly. Jerry and Jack leaned across my lap, trying to get a better look, but I scooted forward to preserve my vantage point, I could see the line of yellow liquid in the tube perfectly, and could even count the marks between the numbers etched on the side of the glass. It was, I felt, somehow right that at long last I could enjoy studying this mysterious instrument of measurement up close, and I thrilled at the thought that perhaps Uncle Archibald had subtly arranged our single-file entrance into the pantry so that I would be seated next to him.

"Yes, well below twenty-eight, well below." His whiskers trembled as he exhaled. "This shall be a truly ferocious storm. Absolutely ferocious."

Uncle Archibald's breath condensed on the glass and, as if summoned by his assessment, the storm did seem suddenly to pick up strength. We could hear the raindrops pounding against the roof and the boarded-up windows, their tone deeper and more serious than when — during other storms — they merely plucked against thin glass, and above and beneath this noise rose the sound of the wind, which had begun to scream and hiss. I nestled close to my uncle, who — a few minutes later — conducted another reading, at which point my father, the recipient of a withering stare from Aunt Grace and a look of absolute horror from my mother, asked his brother to desist from such outbursts. Uncle Archibald nodded glumly and gently rocked the barometer back against the wall. Not content that it sit there so brazenly, however, my father took off his jacket and draped it over the iron stand, hiding the instrument from our view.

We all sat still for what seemed like years, listening to the storm, which   35 continued to rage but did not seem to be increasing in strength, I had noticed Uncle Edwin some time before, looking uncomfortable, and first I attributed it to the storm before realizing, as he gently opened the lid of his picnic basket, that of course he was hungry. He withdrew a tin, wrapped in a piece of newspaper, that he opened, withdrawing a piece of stone crab that had already been removed from its shell. He placed the piece in his mouth before holding out the tin in our direction. "Please," he mumbled, making a point of looking at me, since he knew I would be the least likely to accept his offer, as eating shellfish produced a red rash on my neck. My brothers declined as well, and Uncle Edwin licked his fingers before eating another claw.

"Odd, that we are to remain ignorant of a means of measuring the storm's power," Uncle Archibald spoke in a rush, his voice higher than his brothers' and far more fluttery, "whilst we indulge in food that can do nothing save make our dwelling place smell like Morgan Bartlum's bait shop."

Uncle Edwin snickered in response, permitting himself one more piece before putting the tin back in the picnic basket. I confess to having smelled nothing disagreeable at all, just the wax from the candles, Uncle Archibald's worn suit, and a hint of rum that always hung about him faintly, like a halo. We sat in silence for the next hour or so, save for Aunt Grace, from whose mouth an exasperated sigh would occasionally escape. Along with Archibald, I had expected Frederick to put up resistance to such close quarters, but instead he fell asleep shortly after Edwin's next sampling of stone crab. When he awoke a short time later, it was because he needed to empty his bladder, which required my father to pull the chamber pot down from the shelf and then look around the room with dread. "I do think, Jeremiah," Uncle Archibald said coolly, "that it would not be unsafe for young Frederick to relieve himself on the other side of the door." Father agreed, and after Frederick was done Jack and Jerry soon followed his example.

As the hours passed, my brothers nodded off while the storm pounded our home, occasionally causing the frame to shift but otherwise carrying on less obtrusively than I would have thought. I was no longer frightened so much as bored. I could not sleep and wanted to fetch my book, which was just a few feet away in the living room, but to have asked permission, I knew, would have riled my father, so I kept silent and passed the time sneaking glances at my older relatives. Mother stared blankly at the floor for one hour, and then another, her expression remaining unchanged, only her nostrils thinning whenever she inhaled. Father shifted uncomfortably again and again, his fingers drumming his forearm impatiently, the heel of his leather shoe occasionally tapping the tile beneath us. I could not determine whether or not Aunt Grace slept, as her bonnet was pulled tight around her face, but I suspected that she did, since she displayed no reaction to Uncle Edwin's systematic emptying of the contents of the picnic basket into his mouth: first the remaining bits of stone crab, then sugar cookies, a banana, half a loaf of Cuban bread, and finally a healthy slab of cured beef. Although Uncle Archibald was largely silent, he did pass me several pieces of taffy, and apologized more than once for his right hand, which had begun, after several hours, to quiver slightly, and then finally shake more or less constantly, knocking into the sleeve of my dress over and over again.

A tremendous crash roused all of us. It seemed to have come from the front of the house and presented Uncle Archibald the opportunity to check his timepiece. He showed me its face and barely managed a thin smile. It was eight o'clock in the evening. We had been sequestered together for more than seven hours, and the night had barely begun. Perhaps sensing this, or feeling — I think now, with the benefit of hindsight — desperate for a drink but afraid to produce his flask in front of us, lest my father admonish him, Uncle Archibald stood up abruptly, knocking his head against the low ceiling.

"I daresay," he rubbed his crown furiously, the thin strands of his hair   40
standing on end, "I must excuse myself, tempest be damned!" And he placed his straw hat on his head, unlatched the door, and walked out of the pantry. We all waited breathlessly for his return. The minutes went by, more than seemed appropriate. I thought of him never returning; of course I did not think of him dead, I did not understand yet what death was, but I thought of his barometer sitting there in the pantry where he had left it, gathering dust, its powers dissipated since no one else could interpret its signs.

The door opened abruptly and again we all started. Without saying anything, Uncle Archibald walked over to his instrument and pulled it into the center of the pantry. Then he held his monocle up again to his left eye and reexamined the glass tube. "We have," he announced, "passed through the greatest threat posed by this storm. The winds, from my observation, are not hurricane force, and barometric pressure has begun to rise. Indeed, I see no reason for us to remain in these narrow confines. You have, Jeremiah, lost the large banyan tree in front, and a good many branches and leaves, but the exterior of the house appears to have made it through quite well."

We sat still, and looked over at Father for permission to move. He rose slowly to his feet, on the one hand surely loath to trust his brother on the subject of the storm, but on the other hand as desperate as all of us to move out of the pantry, the walls of which seemed to be tightening by the minute. Uncle Edwin assured our release by lumbering to his feet and then uncharacteristically yanking his wife to hers.

"So that is all you have to say for your mighty hurricane, Archie? One tree!" he bellowed.

"It was a bad one," Uncle Archibald smoothed down his whiskers. He seemed not the least bit rattled by the fact that his youngest brother was addressing him directly for the first time in six years. "Perhaps not here, but wherever the eye passed was very bad. It was a concentrated demon, yes, but a demon nonetheless."

Edwin waved his hand at him, then picked up his picnic basket and   45
walked by him gruffly, out into the dining room. "You give voice to delusions," he grumbled as he passed through the doorway. "You always have."

Aunt Grace nodded her head in agreement as she followed behind him. "Delusions!" she snickered, unfastening her bonnet, presumably because we were no longer threatened by the weather.

Their dramatic exit was diminished by the fact that, even if we were not in the eye of the hurricane, we were in the midst of a significant storm, which meant that our father could not drive them home. So Aunt Grace and Uncle Edwin marched out of the pantry and, after a brief pause, into our dark living room. While Father surveyed the outside with Uncle Archibald and Jerry, Mother and I brought out some pork from the icebox and made the best sandwiches we could.

The rest of the evening I can barely recall; just a quick meal, with the sound of branches breaking outside and the rain pattering madly, and a sense of relief when Father sent us off to bed. Frederick asked permission to sleep with me, since he didn't want to be alone, and we hugged each other under the sheets as the storm raged on. Before drifting into sleep more easily than I would have ever imagined, I remember making a deal with the God in which I only vaguely believed: if he permitted us safe passage through the storm, I would no longer bemoan the tiny island on which I lived, a place where nothing seemed to happen save the occasional tropical and great depression.

The next morning, work around our home began early. Father helped the boys take down the boards from the windows, saw the banyan tree into removable pieces, and mend our fence, several slats of which had been broken by the tree. According to my brothers, Uncle Edwin watched them work from alongside the house, until he spied Curtis Anderson passing by in his truck. Uncle Edwin waved him down in the hopes that he might be driving over to the Atlantic side of the island, where his mother, Mrs. Anderson, the town librarian, lived, and indeed he was. Mr. Anderson offered Uncle Edwin and Aunt Grace a ride home and they were gone in a flash, bidding us all goodbye with hurried, stiff waves. By that time, Mother and I had finished restoring our china to the kitchen, and I was given permission to remain on the front steps of our porch. That was where I was perched when a boy rode up on a bicycle and asked for my father. He was from the East Coast Railway Office downtown, he explained, handing him an envelope before tipping his blue hat and hiking off hurriedly. The phone lines were down, so it was impossible to place any calls, but nonetheless, the delivery of a letter seemed serious, even ominous, and Jerry and Jack set down their saws in order to watch our father's reaction. He read the correspondence slowly, and when he placed the letter back in the envelope I knew something was wrong because he called out his brother's name in an urgent, nearly hysterical way. "Archie! Archie!" he cried. And Frederick, who had been piling branches on the sidewalk, stopped in his tracks.

It turned out the eye of the hurricane had passed over Upper Mate-   50
cumbe Key,[1] striking the train that had been sent down to rescue the highway workers. It was overturned, that was all the letter said about the train, and that forty miles of track between Marathon and Tavernier had been

---

[1]*Upper Matecumbe Key*: Island in the Florida Keys devastated by the Labor Day storm. Most of the dead were Works Progress Administration workers helping to build a bridge. The estimated loss of life in 1935 was 600 dead and 400 missing.

wiped out. There would be no train service from Miami for some time, we didn't know for how long.

"We must," Father was pacing in front of the house, the corduroy pants he wore when he worked outside streaked with dirt and brown stains from the fallen leaves, "we must fetch our assets. Today, before they are picked over."

Uncle Archibald had rushed over when my father called for him, and his suspenders still hung around his waist. He was wearing one of his old Cuban shirts, the collar of which brimmed with shaving cream. He shook his head in disagreement. "I'm not sure I'll be able to get the *Edith Kermit* running; it might have been damaged in the storm."

"You must get it running. We have no choice, Archie, otherwise we're ruined."

"Even if we can make it up the Keys, Jeremiah, I doubt the linens will have come through the storm very well."

"It's all we have. In the current situation . . ." He shook his head. The   55
matter was grave enough that he couldn't be bothered to shield us from the discussion. "No, we must recoup our goods. There is nothing else we can do." He looked around the yard furtively, as if he might find a solution to our problem in the shrubs and hedges that seemed to have made it through the storm quite well. Then he addressed us directly. "Children, we are making a trip up the Keys today, to Islamorada —"

"Jeremiah!" I had not noticed the appearance of my mother in the doorway, or heard her raise her voice above a whisper in many months, and the shock of her booming voice made me rise to my feet. "Jeremiah, I do not want the children going up the Keys, not after a storm. Can't you and Edwin round up some workers from the store?"

"My dear Martha, if we cannot salvage our goods, we will have no way of paying the workers for the day's labor. We must go together, all of us, save Edwin and Grace, whose constitutions would not bear such a day. We will need as many hands as possible."

"A young woman, retrieving sheets . . ." Mother beckoned toward me and I burned suddenly with fear at the thought of being left at home. I had been north of Marathon Key only a few times before, and in Miami just once, so any trip was to be treasured, regardless of the circumstances. Plus, the thought of hearing of the adventure secondhand from my brothers, none of whom could tell a tale straight from beginning to end, meant that I would never know what exactly had transpired. I began to plot how I might somehow hide myself aboard the *Edith Kermit*, only that ended up being unnecessary.

"You and Mary may remain in the boat, Martha," my father said by way of reply, "I'm afraid we will need you both in order to fold the sheets. Besides, I cannot leave you here alone, and I will need Archie's help with the boat." He paused. "It will be good for the children to see what supports our family, Martha. We have far more than most."

Mother said nothing; she just motioned to me so that I would follow her   60
inside, which I gladly did, excited by the prospect that our work in the

kitchen would be in the service of a voyage to Upper Matecumbe Key. We put what little food we had remaining in our own picnic basket, and filled two pitchers of water from the overflowing cistern in back. Then I was permitted to put on my recreational clothes: a coarse cloth dress that fit easily over my swimming suit, which Mother suggested I wear in case I got wet, and a light shawl. She elected not to change out of her black satin dress, although she added a plain, yellow bonnet that seemed, in my view, not quite to match.

By this time the boys were also ready for the voyage, having put on their swimming trunks, plus long-sleeved, linen shirts to minimize mosquito bites. Our car, a Model A sedan, would have never been able to pass through the streets, filled as they were with rainwater and broken branches, so we walked to the *Edith Kermit*, which was only a block away, anchored on the near side of Garrison Bight. Uncle Archibald met us there, having walked directly over to see if he could get his boat running. None of the vessels in the bight appeared to have been damaged, although a few had been loosed from their moorings and were floating in the middle of the inlet, while the palm trees that lined the water along what would become Roosevelt Boulevard had been stripped of their coconuts and canopies. We loaded the craft, placing the picnic basket and pitchers of water in the small aft cabin, and the various tools gathered by the boys in the metal container in the bow, previously half filled with a few life preservers and fishing tackle, while Uncle Archibald cursed and coaxed the diesel engine to life. When it finally turned over, spewing black and then finally gray smoke into the air, he was able to verify that we had enough fuel for the trip up to Islamorada, but not enough to return.

"And there will be no petroleum available in all of the Keys that lie before us?" my father asked him. Uncle Archibald shrugged. "I cannot predict the situation that we will encounter," was his simple reply. He still believed that the atmospheric dip recorded by his barometer had exacted a terrible blow somewhere in our world, although none of us did. Not even I, his most faithful follower, was willing to dismiss what I saw around me: the expected aftereffects of a serious storm, but nothing more.

Uncle Archibald let Frederick unloop the ropes that kept the *Edith Kermit* tied to the dock and soon we had passed out of the bight and through Cow Key Channel. The water was like glass and once we had passed the reef and were in the Atlantic Uncle Archibald opened up the engine. Jerry, Jack, Frederick, and I quickly moved to the bow and tasted the froth of the salt foam on our lips as we skimmed over waves and skirted the coral fingers surrounding Pelican Shoal.

How long the trip took I cannot recall, as I have never in my long life had reason to do it again. At least several hours, long enough for the light to change markedly. Although we made good time for most of the voyage, when it came time to turn toward Islamorada, Uncle Archibald became confused by his map. Upper Matecumbe did not seem to line up where it was supposed to, at least not at first. Our boat slowed to a crawl, taking the current as it circled around the key right in the bow, so that the waves and splashes sent us scurrying into the stern, where Mother sat alone on the back bench of the boat, her hands gripping her forearms, her feet pressed up against a coil of rope.

In fact, Uncle Archibald had not misread his map; the banks of Upper Matecumbe were just unrecognizable, having been shorn of all foliage and stripped of the few wooden shacks and homes that had sat undisturbed for years. Boats were now all around us, many with men at their sides, pulling and tugging large pieces of driftwood aboard. We slowed even more, the *Edith Kermit* now bobbing up and down as much as moving forward, so that the mosquitoes began to flicker around our faces.   65

It was right then, or at least in my mind's recollection, as I swatted at an insect, that the images around me slowed and crystallized. We were now within shouting distance of the first vessel and I saw that it was not driftwood these men were pulling and yanking at but bodies, the limbs yellow and stiffened, their clothing torn and drooping on their frames. And then I saw, in the water on our right, the bloated face of a young girl, the eyes glazed open, her neck swollen and black, her naked body translucent under the water, and heard my mother scream and felt myself grabbed and pushed into the aft cabin by Uncle Archibald. Father brought Mother and Frederick down after me, ordering the three of us to stay seated, only Mother had not stopped screaming, and now Frederick was crying and pressing his hands to his ears. The smell of rum, once stashed beneath the bench on which we sat, was thick in the stale air and I remember not quite being able to catch my breath and shaking my head, trying to shed the image I had of the dead girl in the water, the face that would haunt my dreams for years and years to come.

So I ended up being there, in the aftermath of the Labor Day Hurricane, but only somewhat. Yes, I was in the boat with my brothers, but I didn't see all that they did, and they never told me what I missed, not that I asked. We spoke of that day only with our eyes, never our mouths. I do recall clearly what transpired next. A vessel approached ours, cutting through the water cleanly, and after its engine cut off a voice identified itself loudly as that of a Coast Guard captain.

"We are directing the relief boats to the other side," he yelled out.

"We have not come to offer relief," my father shouted back. "We have come to reclaim our linens and towels from the derailed cars of the East Coast Railway."

"Sir, those cars are filled with the dead," came the reply. "You have brought your boat into hell, my dear man. You are in hell."   70

My mother exclaimed once more, before wailing in a high-pitched moan, and then fell silent. I had placed my arms around Frederick and squeezed him tight.

"I speak of goods which we own and lease to the Railway . . ." My father was not himself either. He had always thought he could control the world around him, and we were all witnessing that day proof to the contrary.

"Do you hear me, sir?" the captain continued. "We have dozens of dead on this key. There are bodies everywhere: in the surf, in the few trees that survived the winds, and in your precious railway cars. If you cannot help us assist the suffering then you must leave. Forget your goods, sir, and thank God for your life."

The engine of the cutter kicked in and the boat sped away, its wake rocking our vessel. Now there were other noises, other engines, shouts, even cries. We were closer to shore and I heard Jack of all people, my level-headed and unflappable brother, exclaim, Papa, no! Please, Papa!" And then there was Uncle Archibald, cursing like a man possessed, and our boat suddenly turning sharply to the left side (is that port?), picking up speed, and then several minutes of silence as the engine hummed, before the door opened and Father — his hair disheveled, his shirt untucked — asked me to hold my mother's arms while he meted out an inordinate dose of her Dover's powder, which I did not know was an opiate until years and years later, when I saw it described as such in a Victorian medical book I thought to purchase at a yard sale because I liked its binding. And then no noises for a while, except the diesel engine, or at least none that I remember.

We made it back only so far as Lower Matecumbe, staying close to land so that we could make it ashore as soon as we ran out of fuel. When the engine cut out we sat, the three of us, in the aft cabin, Frederick's whimpers now audible with the engine noise subsided, my mother, the powder dissolved fully in her bloodstream, looking out at nothing, her mouth pinched in a ghostly half smile. Uncle Archibald and the boys had to call to the shore for several minutes before a rowboat could be scrounged up. Then my father descended again. "You must go ashore here, Mary," he said to me. "Jerry will go with you and Frederick, then Jack and Mother. You must all take the ferry to No Name Key, Archibald and I shall stay with the boat."

I struggled to my feet, the weight of my young brother heavy on my chest. I thought of the dead girl in the water: her fair hair fanning out, the eyes so savage and dumb.

"Do not look about you," my father said, steadying me with his hand. His face was drained of its color and he looked very old. "This is where the camps were for the highway workers so it might be very bad. Promise me you shall not look about."

I nodded. Frederick was pried from me, screaming, while I stepped down into the rowboat before a young man, his eyes blazing, who sat at the oars. He wore overalls with nothing underneath them and his arms were thin as wires. They handed Frederick back to me and, together with Jack, we were rowed ashore.

The mind adapts to anything; it is quite astounding. From the brief time we left the *Edith Kermit* to our disembarkment on Lower Matecumbe, for the space of maybe one hundred yards, the mind adjusted to the sight of the floating dead, the dismembered dead, the decapitated dead, and then, once we were ashore, the half-buried dead, the naked dead, covered with blowflies (their hums filling the dark air), the dead with their faces somehow melted off, the dead that looked almost as if they were living. Farther up the beach, some of the bodies had been placed in wooden coffins, while others were piled together and wrapped in sheets, their feet pointing up in the air. In a tight circle, the three of us waited for Mother and Jerry, then joined the crowd at the dock and boarded the last ferry of the day: a boat filled with refugees from the storm we had missed, but not entirely.

At No Name Key, Jerry recognized a classmate whose boat could hold   80 three more for Key West; otherwise, Frederick, Mother, and I would have had to wait on the docks with the others who had no one to pick them up. We traveled home slowly. The seas were choppy and our vessel was small and overloaded. Jerry and Jack did not return until late the next day, and Uncle Archibald and Father two days after that. Stubble and grime had overtaken Uncle Archibald's fine moustache, which would disappear for good when he shaved the next day, while my father's own face was sunburned and cracked. He carried, in the crook of his arm, a handful of badly soiled sheets, and while we all wondered what they had encountered when they had finally made it to the train, none of us asked; the small bundle of worthless goods said enough.

The Florida East Coast Railway declared bankruptcy a few days later, and Columbia Laundry Service closed its doors at the end of that month. As a favor, father was given a job at the Casa Marina Hotel, but he was inappropriately dispositioned for the hospitality industry, which had ground to a halt anyway, and he quit before he could be relieved of his post. Satisfactory employment would elude him for more than a decade but he never stopped working and managed, somehow, to feed us. It helped that Jerry and then Jack got work with the Florida State Highway Department, and were on the crew that finished the Overseas Highway, although Jack would have his fibula shattered by an iron support beam on Big Pine Key and would never walk without pain again.

They never restored train service to Key West. With our business closed, Aunt Grace and Uncle Edwin moved up to Saint Augustine, where her family was from. It was to be a temporary arrangement, but like most residents who moved away at that time, they never returned to the island. A year later, desperate for money, we were forced to sell Uncle Archibald's house and dispose of his bicycle parts and tires and metal frames. He moved in with us, into the back room behind the kitchen, but he could not stand being in our home with nothing to do. There seemed, in the face of such punishing bleakness, little reason to think of fantastic contrivances such as water bikes, and by the time I was twenty Uncle Archibald spent his days and nights on Caroline Street with the other town drunks. The lilt in his speech, the dart in his eye, and the beautiful flowers in his lapel were by then just a memory. Until he died, many years later, I could not reclaim his image as my dapper uncle; in fact, I hated him for the way he smelled of rainwater and fried plantains and for how he tripped over his consonants.

My mother was institutionalized in 1939. We saw her each Christmas for five years following but by 1944 the opium had drained her memory entirely, turning her skin the color and texture of flour, and we stopped visiting. She died a year later, as did Frederick on Okinawa, fighting the Japanese.

I'll tell you what I think and you may take it or leave it as you wish. I think that most families are very fragile. Those impressive genealogies we have all seen, say in the inside covers of books, give false hope. Most families are like the torchwood and palms that somehow grow on hard coral and limestone, and then one day encounter unanticipated wind and rain and are wiped clean away. And that we who somehow survive remember so little, and pass on even less, is a merciful and melancholic thing—more merciful than melancholic, but only just.

QUESTIONS

1. In the first paragraph, we learn that the narrator is elderly. What is she telling you about aging, and why? How does this information affect your reading of the story?
2. For the narrator, Uncle Archibald's barometer possesses "talismanic powers" (paragraph 4), but her father pays no attention to Archibald's warnings. Why is this so? How is Uncle Archibald presented by the narrator?
3. The narrator's family is thrown together by the storm, stuck in a small pantry for seven hours. What do you learn about their relationships during that time? Does the coming of the storm validate Uncle Archibald's predictions?
4. The narrator concludes her story with this thought: "I think that most families are very fragile. . . . Most families are like the torchwood and palms that somehow grow on hard coral and limestone, and then one day encounter unanticipated wind and rain and are wiped clean away." Unpack this simile and discuss its application to the narrator's family.
5. Consider the very last sentence, and read it back into the story. Compare it with the opening of the story and its statement on remembering and memory (paragraph 1).
6. For a research project, find out what type of hurricane tracking was in use in 1935. One Web site you can visit for a Weather Bureau report on the 1935 storm is <http://aoml.noaa.gov/Storm_pages/labor_day/labor_article.html>. There's a chart containing barometric readings for September 2, 1935, collected by a Weather Bureau observer who the next morning found himself in a coconut tree. How do his readings compare with Uncle Archibald's?

MAKING CONNECTIONS

How might the narrator of Susan Choi's "Memorywork" (p. 198) respond to the comments of the narrator of "Labor Day Hurricane, 1935" on memory and remembering?

PROBLEMS OF ART

James Alan McPherson

*James Alan McPherson was born in Savannah, Georgia, in 1943.
He earned degrees from Morris Brown College and Harvard
University, and in 1969 he earned an M.F.A. from the University
of Iowa, where he has been a professor of English since 1981.
McPherson received first prize in the* Atlantic Monthly *short story
contest in 1965, and in 1969 his first collection of short stories,*
Hue and Cry, *was published. His writing has been published
in many periodicals, including the* New York Times Magazine,
Esquire, Reader's Digest, Newsday, Ploughshares, The Iowa
Review, *and* Callaloo, *and he was an editor of* DoubleTake *magazine. McPherson is noted for his portrayals of working-class people coping with the vagaries of everyday life. Explaining his
approach to the characters in his stories, McPherson has said,
"Certain of these people [my characters] happen to be black, and
certain of them happen to be white; but I have tried to keep the
color part of most of them far in the background, where these
things should rightly be kept." Most recently he has written* Crab-
cakes: A Memoir *(1998) and* A Region Not Home: Reflections
from Exile *(2000). His many honors include the literature award
of the National Institute of Arts and Letters (1970), a Guggenheim Fellowship (1972–73), a MacArthur fellowship (1981), and
a Pushcart Prize (1995). He received a Pulitzer Prize in 1978 for
his second collection of short stories,* Elbow Room *(1977), in
which "Problems of Art" appeared.*

Seated rigidly on the red, plastic-covered sofa, waiting for Mrs. Farragot to return from her errand, Corliss Milford decided he did not feel
comfortable inside the woman's apartment. Why this was he could not tell.
The living room itself, as far as he could see around, reflected the imprint of
a mind as meticulous as his own. Every item seemed in place; every detail
meshed into an overriding suggestion of order. This neatness did no damage
to the image of Mrs. Farragot he had assembled, even before visiting her at
home. Her first name was Mary, and she was thin and severe of manner. He
recalled that her walnut-brown face betrayed few wrinkles; her large brown
eyes were quick and direct without being forceful; her thin lips, during conversation, moved with precision and resolve. Even her blue summer dress,
with pearl-white buttons up its front, advertised efficiency of character. The
bare facts of her personal life, too, argued neatness and restraint; he had

them down on paper, and the paper rested on his knee. Milford juggled his knee; the paper shifted, but did not fall. That too, he thought. It was part of why he felt uneasy. For a few seconds, he entertained the notion that the living room was no more than a sound stage on a movie lot. Somehow, it seemed too calculated.

Milford's suspicion of an undisclosed reality was heightened by the figure in the painting on the wall across the room. It was the portrait of a sad-eyed Jesus. Immaculate in white and blue robes, the figure held a pink hand just above the red, valentine-shaped heart painted at the center of its chest. Bright drops of red blood dripped from the valentine. Such pictures as this Milford had seen before in dimestores. Though it had a certain poignancy, he thought, it was . . . cheap. It conveyed a poverty of the artist's imagination and tended to undermine the sophistication of those who purchased such dimensionless renditions. Did not the Latin poor build great cathedrals? Even country Baptists wheeled their preachers about in Cadillacs. Why then, Milford asked himself, would a poor black woman compound an already bleak existence by worshiping before a dimestore rendition of a mystery? He recalled having heard someplace something about the function of such images, but could not recall exactly what he had heard. The plastic crinkled as he shifted on the sofa to review Mrs. Farragot's papers. She had been born in Virginia, but had lived for many years in Los Angeles. She was a widow, but received no compensation from her husband's social security. She had been arrested for driving under the influence of alcohol, although she insisted that she was a teetotaler. About the only consistent factual evidence about her that Milford knew was her insistence, over a period of two weeks, that no one but a white lawyer could represent her at the license revocation hearing. For her firm stand on this, she was now notorious in all the cubbyhole offices of Project Gratis. Milford looked again at the portrait. Perhaps that explains it, he thought. Then he thought, perhaps it does not.

He leaned back on the sofa, impatient now for Mrs. Farragot to return. According to his watch it was 11:45 a.m. The hearing was scheduled for 1:30 p.m. The day was already humid and muggy, and would probably grow warmer as events developed in the afternoon. But Milford was used to it. For want of a better rationalization, he liked to call such occasions invigorating. Now he sighed and glanced again about the room, wondering just who would return with her to act as witness and corroborator. Since his mind was trained to focus on those areas where random facts formed a confluence of palpable reality, he became restless for easy details. His eyes swept over the brown coffee table; above the red, plastic-covered armchair across the room; past the tall glass china closet packed with jade-green and brandy-red and sunset-orange cut-glass ashtrays and knickknacks whose scalelike patterns sparkled in the late morning sunlight streaming lazily through the open window on bright particles of dust; beyond the china closet to the yellow-white door leading into the quiet, smell-less kitchen from which sounded the hum of a refrigerator; past the doorframe, quickly, and to the sofa's edge on his right to where a group of pictures in cheap aluminum frames stood grouped on a brown plywood end table. These he examined more closely. The larger one was of Mrs. Mary Farragot. It was a close-up of her face as it must have looked ten years ago. There were fewer wrinkles and no strains of gray in her ebony black hair. She was smiling contentedly. This, Milford thought, was not the face of an alcoholic. It reflected strength and motherly concern. Next to this picture was a small color print of two children. Both were smiling. One, a blond boy seated in a blue high chair, grinned with his spoon raised above a yellow dish of cereal, as if about to strike. The little girl with dark brown hair, posed extravagantly beside the chair, her skinny right arm raised in anticipation of the falling spoon. The picture was inscribed: "To Aunt Mary, Love, Tracy and Ken." Corliss Milford did not pause to examine their faces. Instead, his eyes were drawn to the third picture. This was a faded black and white enlargement of a very weak print. Behind the glass stood a robust black man in army uniform, saluting majestically. His grin was mischievous and arrogant; his nostrils flared. The thumb of his raised hand stood prominently from his temple; a few inches above the hand the edge of an army private's cap hung casually over his forehead like an enlarged widow's peak.

This is a good picture, Milford decided. He picked it up and examined its details more closely. The man stood in what was obviously an exaggeration of attention. He saw that the man's left brogan was hooked nonchalantly around his right ankle. In the background a flagpole whistled up some six or eight feet above the man's head. The flag was snapping briskly in what might have been the morning breeze, although the faded condition of the print obscured the true direction of the sun. Milford counted the number of stars in the flag. Then he peered deeper into the background, beyond the pole, and saw what might have been palm trees, and beyond these mountains. His eyes moved from the mountains back to the flagpole and down the pole past the saluting soldier to the bottom of the picture, where the grass was smooth as a billiard table. His eyes fastened on a detail he had missed before: a bugle stood upright on its mouth just at the soldier's feet; in fact, the man's left brogan was pointing slyly at the bugle. This was why the man was grinning. Near the bugle, at an angle, someone, probably the soldier, had written: "To Mary Dear, Lots of Love, 'Sweet Willie,'" There was a flowing line just below this inscription, as if the signer had taken sudden inspiration.

Corliss Milford shifted his eyes to the papers on the sofa beside him.   5
Mrs. Farragot had reported that she was a widow. He had written that down. But now he recalled she had actually said "grass widow," which meant that Sweet Willie was still around. It also explained why she was not drawing social security. Perhaps, he thought, it also justified her frustration if indeed she had been drunk when arrested. There was no doubt that it accounted completely for the bitterness which had compelled her to request specifically the services of a white lawyer. From his picture, Milford concluded, Willie Farragot seemed to reek of irresponsibility. Perhaps all the

men she knew were like him. This would account for the difficulty she seemed to be having in getting a witness to corroborate her story that she had not been drunk or driving when arrested.

Now he shifted his eyes to the print on the wall, but this time with more understanding. He had re-entered the living room on another level, and now he could sympathize. Still, he did not like the painting. A disturbing absence of nuance undermined the face: the small brown eyes were dimensionless, as if even they did not believe the message they had been calculated to convey. The pigeon nose had no special prominence, no irregularity suggestive of regality; even the lips, wafer-thin and pink, suggested only a glisten of determination. In the entire face, from forehead to chin, there was not the slightest hint of tragedy or transcendence. To appreciate it, Milford concluded, required of one an act of faith. The robes, though enamel white and royal blue, drooped without majesty from shoulders that were round and ordinary. And the larger-than-life valentine heart seemed to have been merely positioned at the center of the figure's chest. The entire image suffered badly from a lack of calculation. It did not draw one into it. Its total effect did no more than suggest that the image, at the complete mercy of a commercial artist, had resigned itself to being painted. The face reflected a nonchalant resignation to this fate. If the mouth was a little sad it was not from the weight of this world's sins but rather from an inability to comprehend the nature of sin itself.

Milford was beginning to draw contrasts between the figure and the picture of Sweet Willie when Mrs. Mary Farragot opened the door and stepped quickly into the room. A heavy-set brown-skinned man followed behind her. "May Francis Cripps wouldn't come," she announced in a quiet, matter-of voice, "but Clarence was there too. He seen it all. Clarence Winfield, this here's Mr. Milford from that free law office round there."

Milford stepped to the center of the room and extended his hand.

"How do?" the man, named Winfield, boomed. He grasped Milford's hand and squeezed it firmly. "Everything Miss Mary told you, she told you the truth. I was there and I seen it all. Them cops had no call to arrest her. She warn't drunk, she warn't driving, and I know damn well she warn't going nowheres in that car." While saying this Winfield ran the thumb of his left hand around the inside of his belt, tucking his shirt more neatly into his trousers. "Like I say," he continued, dropping Milford's hand, "I was there and I seen the whole thing."

Corliss Milford stepped back and considered the man. He wore a light brown seersucker suit and a red shirt. A red silk handkerchief flowered from the pocket of his jacket. A red silk tie dangled in his left hand. He had obviously just finished shaving because the pungent scent of a cheap cologne wafted from his body each time he moved. There was something familiar about the cologne, Milford thought; he imagined he had smelled it before, but could not remember when or where. He turned and sat on the plastic-covered sofa, crossing his leg. "I'm from Project Gratis," Milford announced. "Did Mrs. Farragot tell you about my interest in her case?"

   10

Clarence Winfield nodded. "When Miss Mary told me what happen I put on my business clothes and rush right on over here. I told her" — and here he threw a comforting glance at Mrs. Farragot, who stood several feet behind him — "I told her, I say, 'Miss Mary, you don't have to beg May Francis and Big Boy and them to testify for you.' Anyway, that nigger Big Boy couldn't hit a crooked lick with a straight stick."

"Speak good English now, Clarence, for the Lord's sakes," Mrs. Farragot called. "We got to go downtown. And there's one thing I learnt about white people: if they don't understand what you saying they just ain't gonna hear it." She looked conspiratorially at Milford.

The lawyer did not say anything.

Clarence Winfield glanced again at Mrs. Farragot. "I knows good English," he said. "Don't you forget, I worked round white folks too. They hears what they wants to hear." Then he looked at Milford and said, "No offense intended."

The lawyer studied the two of them. Over Winfield's broad shoulder he   15
saw Mrs. Farragot leaning against the chair, directly under the painting. With both hands placed firmly on her hips, she stood surveying the two men with something close to despair playing over her face. Milford noticed her high brown cheeks twitch slightly. Her lips were drawn and thin. She seemed about to say something to Winfield, but no words came from her mouth. The big, middle-aged black man remained standing in the middle of the room as if waiting for something to happen. The longer Milford studied him, the more he became convinced that it was not the smell of the cologne but something else, possibly something about his carriage, which made him seem so familiar. The man seemed eager to be in motion. He seemed self-conscious and awkward standing at attention. Corliss Milford took up the papers from the sofa. He flipped a page to the statement of facts he had typed before leaving the office. "Now Mr. Winfield," he said, "please tell me what you saw the night of August 7 of this year."

Clarence Winfield cleared his throat several times, then glanced once more at Mrs. Farragot. "That there's a night I remember well," he began slowly. "It was hot as a sonofabitch, I was setting on my porch with May Francis Cripps and Buster Williams. It warn't no more than eight-thirty 'cause the sun had just gone down and the sky up the street was settling in from pink to purple to black. I remember it well. We had us some beer and was shooting the shit and the only sound was crickets scraping and a few kids up the block raising hell when all at once there come this loud honking. I look 'cross the street and seen Miss Mary here come running out her door and down the stairs. I knowed it was her 'cause she left the door open and the light from in here come out through the screen and spotlight her porch like a stage. Yeah, come to think of it, just like a stage. See, there was this car right behind hers that was park so close the headlights was burning right into Miss Mary's tail end, and right up close behind *him* was another car. Well, the guy was trap and couldn't get out. I don't know who was in that car, but that guy kept honking his horn 'cause he couldn't move without scratching against Miss Mary's car. I never found out who that guy was, but man, he played Dixie on that horn. See, he couldn't back back either 'cause that car behind had him squeezed in like a Maine sardine. That's the way it is round here in summertime. There's so many big cars park end to end it look like some big-time I-talian gangsters was having a convention. For folks poor as these round here, I don't know where in the *hell* all these here cars come from. Me, I drive . . ."

"You see what I mean, Clarence?" Mrs. Farragot interrupted. She walked toward Winfield, her hands still on her hips. "The man didn't ask about no *gangsters*! All he want is the *facts*!" Then she threw up her hands, cast a look of exasperation at Milford, and dropped into the plastic-covered arm-chair beneath the painting.

"It's all right," Milford told the two of them. He set down his notes and watched Mrs. Farragot. She was sprawled in the armchair; her arms were folded, her legs were crossed, and there was great impatience in her face. Milford attempted to communicate to her, with a slight movement of his pencil, that he had no objection to the mode of Winfield's presentation.

For his own part, Clarence Winfield grinned bashfully. Then he said, "'Scuse me, Miss Mary; you right." Then he swallowed again and proceeded, this time pausing tentatively before each sentence. "Well, me and May Francis and Buster listen to all this racket and we seen Miss Mary here, plain as day, open up her car and start it up and cut on the headlights. Now *her* car was lighting up the taillights of the car in front of her, and it reflect back on her behind the wheel. I seen that. And I heard this guy steady honking on his horn. Well, just about then who should drive up the street in his new Buick but Big Boy Ralston. He lives up the block there, 'bout five houses down from me. Big Boy a security guard down to the bank and I guess he just naturally take his work serious. I mean he bring it home when he come. Anyway, he drives up just about even with this guy that's honking and he stops and calls out, 'Who that making all that motherfucking racket?' Well, this makes the other guy mad and then he *really* tore into that horn. By this time the street is all lit up like a department store. All three of 'em got they headlights and brakelights on so the street's all white and yellow and red and Big Boy car is fire engine red and the sky is black and purple now, with just a little bit of pink way over West yonder where the sun done gone down. But this guy is still playing Chopsticks on that horn. Big Boy holler, 'If you don't quit that racket I'ma put my foot up your ass as far as your nose!' Well, that there just shell old Buster's peanuts. He scream out, 'Stomp on his ass, Big Boy!' Big Boy lean out the window and look over at us setting on the porch. He holler, 'That go for you too, Buster. I'm tired of this shit every night. Ain't y'all got nothing else to do but set on them motherfucking steps selling wolf tickets?' But this guy is honking hard and strong now, and he don't pay Big Boy no mind. So Big Boy scream, 'You blowing your own funeral music, chump!' And he jerk open the door of his Buick. But right about then I seen Miss Mary pull out of her spot and go *fa*ward about three feet. I seen that, 'cause my eyes got

pulled in that direction when her brakelight went off and the red in the
back of her car went all yellow and white. Well, Big Boy leaves his motor
running and he jumps out his car and slam the door. Old Buster laugh and
say to me and May Francis, 'Watch old Big Boy *bogart* this motherfucker. I
ain't seen a Friday go by yet he don't floor somebody.' I think old Buster
was right. When Big Boy round his car his shoulders was hunched like he
was fixing to clean house. The light was shining on his brown uniform and
that red Buick and I tell you the truth, you couldn't hardly tell the steel in
that Buick from the steel in him. He moved round that car like six feet and
three hundred pounds of mad nigger in a *po*-lice uniform fixing to clean
him somebody's *plow*!"

Here Winfield paused to chuckle. "Lawd," he said, not looking at any-   20
one in particular, "that there was a *night*! We just set and watch and drunk
our beer. People run out they houses. Some look out they windows. Some
of them bad kids round here commence to sic Big Boy on. Well, this guy in
the car warn't no fool. He must of knowed he didn't have a snowball's
chance in hell against Big Boy. He cut his wheels fast and scrunch out of
that space like a flash. Fact is, he just miss swatting Big Boy as he wheeled
round that Buick. Well, old Big Boy rush back round his front end to get in
his car and go after the guy. But just then, who should I see but Miss Mary
here come back backing up real slow-like into her old parking space. Well,
just then *four* things happen, all at the same time. Them wild kids yell; Miss
Mary's brakelights come on fast and red; there was a real loud *scrruunch*!;
and Big Boy scream, 'Mother-*fuck*!' See, Miss Mary here done back-back
right into the side of his red Buick."

Milford sat transfixed. He leaned forward on the sofa, oblivious to
anything but the big man in the brown seersucker suit standing quietly in
the center of the room. He did not notice Mrs. Mary Farragot, seated in the
armchair beneath the picture of Jesus, draw her crossed arms tighter about
her breasts.

"*Now*," Clarence Winfield continued, wetting his lips slowly, "now we
come to the part *you* interested in. See, when Big Boy mad he don't have no
respect for *nobody*! He run over to Miss Mary's car, pull open the door, and
commence to give her hell. Buster Williams spit on the sidewalk and said to
us, 'Oh shit! Now they go'n be some *real* trouble. The one thing *nobody*
can do is mess with Big Boy Buick. Me, I seen the time he near kilt a guy for
putting a dent in his *bumper*, so you know they's hell to pay now with the
side all smash in. Somebody better run and call up the *po*-lice!' He nudge
May Francis and she taken and run up to her place to call up the law. And
just in time too. I heard Big Boy tell Miss Mary here, 'Woman, what the
fuck you mean backing into my car that way? If you was a man I'd kick
your ass to kingdom come!' Lawd, he cuss this poor woman here something awful . . ."

"Please; Clarence," Mrs. Farragot called from behind him, "Just get
the thing told." She looked at Milford while saying this. "This man ain't
got all day."

Corliss Milford said nothing. Nor did he allow his eyes to respond to Mrs. Farragot's searching expression. Instead, he kept his face turned toward the big man standing before him and touched his pencil to the paper on his lap.

Clarence Winfield smiled, as if the gesture had reassured him. "Okay," 25 he said, to no one in particular. "Me and Buster run on over before Big Boy could swing on Miss Mary here. Like I say. Big Boy don't much care *who* he swing on when he gets mad. Poor Miss Mary here just standing there in her peejays crying and carrying on, she so excited, and there was dogs barking and them wild kids was running round whooping and hollering in the floodlights of them two cars, and by this time the sky was all black and purple with no pink. I tell you, man, it was a sight. Buster, he run down the corner for more beer and Miss Bessie Mayfair, up the block, lean out her window and scream, '*Fish sandwiches! Hot fresh fish sandwiches*, just out the *pan*! Don't *rush*, they's *plenty. Fifty cents!*' Miss Bessie don't miss a chance to make a dollar. Anyway, long about then a squad car come screaming up with red and white lights flashing and it screech to a stop right longside Big Boy's red Buick and this white cop lean out the passenger window and holler, 'Stand back! Don't nobody touch the body. The law is here to take *charge!*' Big Boy push me away from him and look at that cop. He stare him dead in the face and say, 'Drop dead yourself, creampuff!' Hot damn! That's what I heard him say. That street was all lit up like a department store with red and white lights flashing on all them people in blue and brown and pink clothes. Lawd, it was a sight! But even in all them lights I saw this white cop turn red in the face; his own strobe lights made his face look like it was bleeding. I seen that. I seen the driver get out of the car. It was a colored fellow and he walk like he was was ready to do somebody in. He walk up real close to Big Boy and look him dead in the eye. He say, real cool-like, 'What it is, feller?' and Big Boy say, 'Plenty! This here woman done *ruin* my new Buick Electra with *push*-button drive and *black leather* bucket seats! There ain't a worser thing that could of happen to me.' So the colored cop begin to question Miss Mary. She was so mad and angry and crying so much I guess he thought she was drunk, 'cause he ask her to walk the line. He just walk over to the sidewalk and point the toe of his shoe to a crack. Well, Miss Mary here look at him and say; 'No. No, *sah*. N.O. *Naw!*' That's what I recollect she said. Then I heard him tell her the law was writ so that if she refuse she was bound to lose her license. Well, by this time there was so much commotion going on till I suspect Miss Mary here was too embarrassed to even *think* about walking no line. Folks was laughing, drinking beer, grabbing for fish sandwiches, and raising so much hell till I reckon a private person like Miss Mary here would rather lose her license than walk the line in her peejays. So she refuse. Well, them two cops put her in the car and taken her off to jail. Like I said, I seen it all, and I done told you the truth of all I seen. And I'm ready anytime to go down and tell the same thing to the judge."

Corliss Milford completed his notes. He had scribbled sporadically during the recitation. Now he looked up at Clarence Winfield, who shifted impatiently as though confirming his eagerness to be on his way down-town. Then he looked at Mrs. Mary Farragot, still seated in the armchair behind Winfield, her arms locked tightly across her breasts. "His story corroborates yours in all essential details," Milford called to her.

"Of course it do," Mrs. Farragot answered. "That ain't the problem." She shrugged. "The problem is how in the *hell* can I tell a white judge something like all that Clarence just said without being thrown out of court?" She paused and sighed, raising her head so that her hair almost touched the edge of the picture frame. "What I wanted me in the first place," Mrs. Farragot added slowly, "was a white boy that could make some *logic* out of all that."

Now both she and Winfield looked imploringly at Corliss Milford.

At 1:45 p.m. the three of them sat waiting outside the hearing room of the Department of Motor Vehicles. During the drive downtown, Milford had attempted to think through the dimensions of the situation; now he decided that Mrs. Farragot had been right all along. Since this was not a jury case, there was no way a judge would allow Clarence Winfield to tell his version of the story. As Mrs. Farragot had anticipated, any defense she offered would have to be confined to the facts. Milford cast a sidewise glance at the woman, seated on the bench beside him, with new appreciation of her relative sophistication. In the car she had disclosed that she did domestic work for a suburban stockbroker; from listening in on conversations between the broker and his wife, she must have discerned how a bureaucracy, and the people who made it function, must of necessity be restricted to the facts. And as colorful as were the circumstances of her case, there was not the slightest possibility that any responsible lawyer could include them in her defense.

A pity, too, Milford thought, turning his gaze to Clarence Winfield. Despite the imprecision of his language, the man possessed a certain rough style. He watched Winfield pacing the waxed tile floor of the corridor. The black man had put on his tie now, but because of the excessive heat allowed it to hang loosely about his collar. At one point, with Milford looking on, Winfield lifted his right foot and polished the pointed toe of his shoe against the cloth of his left trouser leg. When he saw Milford watching, Winfield grinned. A pity, the lawyer concluded. Now he would have to restrict the man's statement to yes or no answers to specific questions. He motioned for Winfield to come over to the bench. "Now listen," Milford said, "when you talk to the hearing officer, restrict your statement to the *last* part of your story, the part about her *not* being drunk when she was arrested. You understand?"

30

Clarence Winfield nodded slyly.

"And don't volunteer anything, please. I'll ask all the questions."

Winfield nodded again.

"Do like he tell you now Clarence, hear?" Mrs. Farragot said leaning sideways on the bench. "Don't mess up things for me in front of that man in there." Then she said to Milford, "Clarence one of them from down-home. He tend to talk around a point."

"Ah hell!" Winfield said, and was about to say more when the door to 35 the hearing room opened and a voice called, "Mary Farragot?"

It was a woman's voice.

Corliss Milford stood. "I'm representing Mrs. Farragot," he said. "I'm with Brown and Barlow's Project Gratis."

"Well, we're ready," the woman called, and she stepped out into the corridor. She was short and plump, but not unattractive in a dark green pantsuit. Her silver blond hair was cut short. Dark eyelashes, painted, Milford suspected, accentuated her pink face. "I'm Hearing Officer Harriet Wilson," she announced.

As she stood holding open the door, Milford noticed Mrs. Farragot staring intently at Hearing Officer Harriet Wilson. The expression on her face was one he had not seen before. Suddenly he remembered the photograph of Mrs. Farragot on her plywood end table, and the expression became more familiar. He touched her shoulder and whispered, "Let's go on in." They filed into the hearing room, Mrs. Farragot leading and Clarence Winfield bringing up the rear. Over his shoulder, Milford saw the hearing officer sniffing the air as she shut the door. The room was humid. Over on the window sill a single electric fan rotated wearily, blowing more humid air into the small room. They seated themselves in metal chairs around a dark brown hardwood table. Only Hearing Officer Harriet Wilson remained standing.

"Now," Hearing Officer Wilson said, "we're ready to begin." She smiled 40 round the table pleasantly, her eyes coming to rest on the red silk handkerchief flowering out of Clarence Winfield's coat pocket. It seemed to fascinate her. "Now," she said again, moving her eyes slowly away from the handkerchief, "I'll get the complaining officer and we'll begin." She moved toward a glass door at the back of the room.

"Lawyer Milford," Mrs. Farragot whispered as the glass door opened and shut. She tugged his coat. "Lawyer Milford, I thought it was men that handled these hearings."

Milford shrugged. "Times change," he answered.

Mrs. Farragot considered this. She glanced at the glass door, then at Winfield seated on her right. "Tell you what, Lawyer Milford," she said suddenly. "Actually, Clarence don't do too bad when he talk. Maybe you ought to let him tell his story after all."

"I thought we had already agreed on procedure," the lawyer muttered. He found himself irritated by the mysterious look which had again appeared in Mrs. Farragot's eyes. She looked vaguely amused. "We can't change now," he told her.

"Miss Mary," Winfield volunteered, "I can't tell it exactly like I did 45 before."

"Clarence, that don't matter, long as you hit on the facts. Ain't that right?" she asked Milford.

He had no choice but to nod agreement.

"Good," Mrs. Farragot said. She straightened in her chair and brushed her hand lightly across her sweating forehead.

It seemed to Milford she was smiling openly now.

Hearing Officer Harriet Wilson re-entered the room. Behind her, carry-   50
ing a bulky tape recorder, stepped the arresting officer. He was a tall, olive-
brown-skinned man who moved intently in a light gray summer suit. Cool
dignity flashed in his dark brown eyes; his broad nose twitched, seeming to
sniff the air. He placed the recorder on the table near Hearing Officer Wilson's chair, then seated himself at the head of the table. He crossed his leg
casually. Then he gazed at the three seated on his right and said, "Officer
Otis S. Smothers."

"How do you do?" Winfield called across the table.

Milford nodded curtly.

Mrs. Farragot said nothing. Her eyes were fixed on the tape recorder.

Hearing Officer Harriet Wilson noticed her staring and said, "This is
not a jury matter, dear. At this hearing all we do is tape all relevant testimony and forward it on to the central officer at the state capital. The boys
up there make the final decision."

Milford felt a knee press against his under the table. "I should of   55
knowed," Mrs. Farragot whispered beside him. "Won't be long they gonna
just give you a lie detector and railroad you that way."

Milford shushed her into silence.

From the head of the table Officer Smothers seemed to be studying
them, quiet amusement tugging at the corners of his plump lips.

Officer Wilson placed a finger on the record button and looked round
the table. Milford felt Mrs. Farragot tense beside him. A desperate warmth
seemed to exude from her body. Officer Wilson smiled cheerily at Clarence
Winfield, but sobered considerably as her eyes came to rest on Officer
Smothers. She pressed the record button. After reciting the date and case
record into the microphone, she swore in the parties. Then she motioned for
Officer Smothers to make his statement. It seemed to Milford that Smothers, while taking his oath, had raised his right hand a bit higher than Mrs.
Farragot and Winfield. Now he told his version of the story, presenting a
minor masterpiece of exactness and economy. His vocabulary was precise,
his delivery flawless. When he reached the part of his testimony concerning
the sobriety test, he pulled a sheet of paper from his coat pocket and recited,
". . . suspect was informed of her legal obligation to submit to the test. Suspect's reply was . . ." and he touched a lean brown finger to the page ". . . 'I
ain't go'n do *nothin*'!'" These words, delivered in comic imitation of a
whine, stung Milford's ears. Even Mrs. Farragot, he noticed, winced at the
sound. And Clarence Winfield, slouching in his chair, looked sheepish and
threatened. To Milford the action seemed especially cruel when Smothers
looked over at Hearing Officer Wilson and said in crisp, perfect English,
"That's all I have to say," as though he intended to end the recital of facts
without some account of his own response to the refusal. Milford watched
Smothers as he leaned back in his chair, looking just a bit self-righteous.

"If you have no questions," Hearing Officer Harriet Wilson said to
Milford. Her finger was already on the off button of the recorder.

"You *did* offer her a test, then?" Milford asked, stalling for time to re-   60
consider his position.

"Of course," Smothers replied, his fingers meshed, his hands resting professionally on his knee.

"And you had already concluded there was probable cause to believe she was drunk?"

"Certainly"

"How?"

"Her breath, her heavy breathing, and her slurred speech."   65

"Could you have mistaken a Southern accent for slurred speech?"

"No, I couldn't have," Smothers answered nonchalantly. "I'm from the South myself."

Across the table Hearing Officer Harriet Wilson smiled to herself, her finger tapping the metal casing just above the off button on the recorder.

"Let me say something here," Clarence interrupted. "I was there. I seen the whole thing. It warn't like that at all."

Hearing Officer Wilson looked at Winfield out of the corner of her eye.   70
"Do you want this witness to testify now?" she asked Milford.

But before the lawyer could answer he felt the pressure of Mrs. Farragot's hand on his shoulder. Looking up, he saw her standing over him. "Nome, thank you," he heard her say in a voice very much unlike her own. She was facing Hearing Officer Wilson but looking directly at the recorder. Her face expressionless. Only her voice betrayed emotion. "I'm innocent," Mrs. Farragot began. "But who go'n believe me, who go'n take my word against the word of that officer? Both of us black, but he ain't bothering his self with that and I ain't concerning myself with it either. But I do say I'm innocent of the charges he done level against me. The night this thing happen I was inside my house in my pajamas minding my own business. I wasn't even *fixing* to drive no car . . ."

She told her side of the story.

While she talked, in a slow, precise tone, Milford watched the two officers. It was obvious that Hearing Officer Harriet Wilson was deeply moved; she kept her eyes lowered to the machine. But Officer Smothers seemed impervious to the woman's pleadings. His meshed fingers remained propped on his knee; his eyes wandered coolly about the room. At one point he lifted his left hand to rub the side of his nose.

When Mrs. Farragot had finished speaking she eased down into her chair. No one spoke for almost a minute; the only sounds in the room were the soft buzz of the recorder and the hum of the window fan. Then Clarence Winfield cleared his throat noisily. Officer Harriet Wilson jumped.

"Tell me something, Officer Smothers?" Milford said. "If you did offer   75
a test, which one was it?"

"I asked her to walk the line, as both of us have already testified," Smothers answered.

"That was the only test you offered?"

"That's right," Smothers said in a tired voice.

"But doesn't the statute provide that a suspect has the right to choose one of *three* tests: *either* the breathalyzer, the blood, or the urine? As I read the statute, there's nothing about walking the line."

"I suppose that's right," Officer Smothers said.   80

"Are you authorized to choose, arbitrarily, a test of your own devising?"

"My choice was *not* arbitrary!" Smothers protested. "The policy is to use that one on the scene. Usually, the others are used down at the station."

Now Milford relaxed. He smiled teasingly at the olive-skinned officer. "*Was* this lady offered one of the other tests down at the station before being booked?"

"I don't really know," the officer answered. "I didn't stay around after filing the report."

Milford turned to Mrs. Farragot, new confidence cooling his words.   85
"*Were* you offered any other tests?"

"No, suh," she said quietly, her voice almost breaking. "They didn't offer me nothing in front of my house and they didn't offer me nothing down to the jail. They just taken me in a cell in my pajamas."

"We've had enough," Hearing Officer Harriet Wilson said. Her pink face seemed both sad and amused. She pressed the off button. "You'll hear from the board within thirty days," she called across the table to Mrs. Farragot. "In the meantime you can retain your license."

They all stood abruptly. Milford smiled openly at Officer Smothers, noting with considerable pleasure the man's hostile glare. Milford offered his hand. They barely touched palms. Then the lawyer took Mrs. Farragot's arm and steered her toward the door. Clarence Winfield came behind, tearing off his tie. Just before Winfield closed the door, Hearing Officer Harriet Wilson's voice came floating after them on the moist heat of the room: "Otis, tell the boys that in the future . . ."

Milford and Clarence Winfield waited by the bench while Mrs. Farragot rushed down the corridor toward the ladies' room. Winfield walked around, adjusting his trousers. Milford felt pleased with himself. He had taken command of a chaotic situation and forced it to a logical outcome. Absently, he followed Clarence Winfield over to the water fountain and waited while Winfield refreshed himself. "This meant a lot to her," Milford observed.

Winfield kept a stiff thumb on the metal button. The cold water splashed   90
the side of his face as he turned his face upward and nodded agreement.

"All this sweat over one freak accident," Milford observed.

"Yeah," Winfield said. He straightened and wiped his face with the red silk handkerchief. "Many's the time I've told Miss Mary about that drinking."

"What's a beer on a hot night," Milford said, bending to drink.

Clarence Winfield chuckled. "Man, Miss Mary don't drink no *beer*!" He leaned close to Milford's ear. "She don't drink nothing but Maker's Mark." He laughed again. "I thought you *knowed* that."

Turning his head, Milford saw Mrs. Farragot coming up the hall. Her   95
blue dress swished gaily. It seemed to him that she was strutting. He observed for certain that she was smiling broadly, not unlike the picture of her next to Sweet Willie on the coffee table in her home.

Clarence Winfield nudged him, causing the cold water to splash into his eyes. "Don't you pay it no mind," Winfield was saying. "Between the two of us, why we ought to be able to straighten her out."

QUESTIONS

1. What are the "problems of art"? What kinds of art are represented in the story?
2. What is the relevance of the Jesus picture and the photographs in Mrs. Farragot's living room? Why is Milford's "suspicion of an undisclosed reality" heightened by the "portrait of a sad-eyed Jesus" (paragraph 2)? What sort of a lawyer is Corliss Milford? We are told in paragraph 3: "Since his mind was trained to focus on those areas where random facts formed a confluence of palpable reality, he became restless for easy details." What kind of details does he get from Mrs. Farragot?
3. Why does Clarence Winfield "seem so familiar" (paragraph 15) to Corliss Milford?
4. Milford considers Winfield's description of the facts an effective one, while Mrs. Farragot does not. Why not? Analyze Winfield's narrative of events. What elements of storytelling does he use?
5. What is Mrs. Farragot reading into the courtroom situation? Why is she "smiling openly"? (paragraph 49). What makes her decide to testify? Compare her version of events with that of Winfield's with an eye to their rhetorical strategies.
6. How does Officer Smothers undermine his recitation of the "facts"? How does Mrs. Farragot's narrative of events further undermine Smothers's report?
7. After winning the case, Milford observes that Mrs. Farragot was "strutting" and "smiling broadly, not unlike the picture of her next to Sweet Willie on the coffee table" (paragraph 95). What does this imply? Why does Winfield suggest that the two of them "ought to be able to straighten her out" (paragraph 96)? Do you believe him? Why or why not?

MAKING CONNECTIONS

One of the interesting challenges in interpreting "Problems of Art is determining who is telling the story; that is, from what (or whose) point of view is the story told? Consider this issue in other fiction such as Rogers, "Don Ysidro" (p. 113) or Trevor, "Labor Day Hurricane, 1935." Compare the authors' choices with McPherson's, and write a short paper in which you consider why these writers choose the points of view that they do.

EXPLAINING IN THE
Arts and Humanities

ON KEEPING A NOTEBOOK

Joan Didion

*Joan Didion was born in Sacramento, California, in 1934 and
graduated from the University of California at Berkeley in 1956.
Until the publication of her first novel,* Run River, *in 1963, she
worked as an editor for* Vogue *magazine. Since then, she has
written four more novels, including* Play It as It Lays *(1971) and*
The Last Thing He Wanted *(1996); six books of essays, most
notably* Slouching towards Bethlehem *(1968) and* The White
Album *(1979); and, in collaboration with her husband, John
Gregory Dunne, a number of successful screenplays. As both
novelist and essayist, Didion has shown herself to be a trenchant
observer and interpreter of American society and culture. Many
of her essays also explore her own private life in intimate detail.
Her recent book,* The Year of Magical Thinking *(2005), has been
described as a memoir of grief. In 2003, Didion's husband of
thirty-nine years died suddenly of a heart attack as he sat down
to dinner. Eighteen months later, her thirty-nine-year-old daughter
died of acute pancreatitis. After her daughter's death, Didion
decided not to alter* The Year of Magical Thinking, *which was
already completed. Her latest book,* We Tell Ourselves Stories in
Order to Live: Collected Nonfiction, *will be published in 2006.
The following piece appeared in* Holiday *magazine in 1966 and
was collected in* Slouching towards Bethlehem.

"'That woman Estelle,'" the note reads, "'is partly the reason why George Sharp and I are separated today.' *Dirty crepe-de-Chine wrapper, hotel bar, Wilmington RR, 9:45 a.m. August Monday morning.*"

Since the note is in my notebook, it presumably has some meaning to me. I study it for a long while. At first I have only the most general notion of what I was doing on an August Monday morning in the bar of the hotel across from the Pennsylvania Railroad station in Wilmington, Delaware (waiting for a train? missing one? 1960? 1961? why Wilmington?), but I do remember being there. The woman in the dirty crepe-de-Chine wrapper had come down from her room for a beer, and the bartender had heard before the reason why George Sharp and she were separated today. "Sure," he said, and went on mopping the floor. "You told me." At the other end of the bar is a girl. She is talking, pointedly, not to the man beside her but to a cat lying in the triangle of sunlight cast through the open door. She is wearing a plaid silk dress from Peck & Peck, and the hem is coming down.

Here is what it is: the girl has been on the Eastern Shore, and now she is going back to the city, leaving the man beside her, and all she can see ahead are the viscous summer sidewalks and the 3 a.m. long-distance calls that will make her lie awake and then sleep drugged through all the steaming mornings left in August (1960? 1961?). Because she must go directly from the train to lunch in New York, she wishes that she had a safety pin for the hem of the plaid silk dress, and she also wishes that she could forget about the hem and the lunch and stay in the cool bar that smells of disinfectant and malt and make friends with the woman in the crepe-de-Chine wrapper. She is afflicted by a little self-pity, and she wants to compare Estelles. That is what that was all about.

Why did I write it down? In order to remember, of course, but exactly what was it I wanted to remember? How much of it actually happened? Did any of it? Why do I keep a notebook at all? It is easy to deceive oneself on all those scores. The impulse to write things down is a peculiarly compulsive one, inexplicable to those who do not share it, useful only accidentally, only secondarily, in the way that any compulsion tries to justify itself. I suppose that it begins or does not begin in the cradle. Although I have felt compelled to write things down since I was five years old, I doubt that my daughter ever will, for she is a singularly blessed and accepting child, delighted with life exactly as life presents itself to her, unafraid to go to sleep and unafraid to wake up. Keepers of private notebooks are a different breed altogether, lonely and resistant rearrangers of things, anxious malcontents, children afflicted apparently at birth with some presentiment of loss.

My first notebook was a Big Five tablet, given to me by my mother with   5
the sensible suggestion that I stop whining and learn to amuse myself by writing down my thoughts. She returned the tablet to me a few years ago; the first entry is an account of a woman who believed herself to be freezing to death in the Arctic night, only to find, when day broke, that she had stumbled onto the Sahara Desert, where she would die of the heat before

lunch. I have no idea what turn of a five-year-old's mind could have prompted so insistently "ironic" and exotic a story, but it does reveal a certain predilection for the extreme which has dogged me into adult life; perhaps if I were analytically inclined I would find it a truer story than any I might have told about Donald Johnson's birthday party or the day my cousin Brenda put Kitty Litter in the aquarium.

So the point of my keeping a notebook has never been, nor is it now, to have an accurate factual record of what I have been doing or thinking. That would be a different impulse entirely, an instinct for reality which I sometimes envy but do not possess. At no point have I ever been able successfully to keep a diary; my approach to daily life ranges from the grossly negligent to the merely absent, and on those few occasions when I have tried dutifully to record a day's events, boredom has so overcome me that the results are mysterious at best. What is this business about "shopping, typing piece, dinner with E, depressed"? Shopping for what? Typing what piece? Who is E? Was this "E" depressed, or was I depressed? Who cares?

In fact I have abandoned altogether that kind of pointless entry; instead I tell what some would call lies. "That's simply not true," the members of my family frequently tell me when they come up against my memory of a shared event. "The party was *not* for you, the spider was *not* a black widow, *it wasn't that way at all*." Very likely they are right, for not only have I always had trouble distinguishing between what happened and what merely might have happened, but I remain unconvinced that the distinction, for my purposes, matters. The cracked crab that I recall having for lunch the day my father came home from Detroit in 1945 must certainly be embroidery, worked into the day's pattern to lend verisimilitude; I was ten years old and would not now remember the cracked crab. The day's events did not turn on cracked crab. And yet it is precisely that fictitious crab that makes me see the afternoon all over again, a home movie run all too often, the father bearing gifts, the child weeping, an exercise in family love and guilt. Or that is what it was to me. Similarly, perhaps it never did snow that August in Vermont; perhaps there never were flurries in the night wind, and maybe no one else felt the ground hardening and summer already dead even as we pretended to bask in it, but that was how it felt to me, and it might as well have snowed, could have snowed, did snow.

How it felt to me: that is getting closer to the truth about a notebook. I sometimes delude myself about why I keep a notebook, imagine that some thrifty virtue derives from preserving everything observed. See enough and write it down, I tell myself, and then some morning when the world seems drained of wonder, some day when I am only going through the motions of doing what I am supposed to do, which is write — on that bankrupt morning I will simply open my notebook and there it will all be, a forgotten account with accumulated interest, paid passage back to the world out there: dialogue overheard in hotels and elevators and at the hat-check counter in

Pavillon (one middle-aged man shows his hat check to another and says, "That's my old football number"); impressions of Bettina Aptheker and Benjamin Sonnenberg and Teddy ("Mr. Acapulco") Stauffer; careful *aperçus* about tennis bums and failed fashion models and Greek shipping heiresses, one of whom taught me a significant lesson (a lesson I could have learned from F. Scott Fitzgerald, but perhaps we all must meet the very rich for ourselves) by asking, when I arrived to interview her in her orchid-filled sitting room on the second day of a paralyzing New York blizzard, whether it was snowing outside.

I imagine, in other words, that the notebook is about other people. But of course it is not. I have no real business with what one stranger said to another at the hat-check counter in Pavillon; in fact I suspect that the line "That's my old football number" touched not my own imagination at all, but merely some memory of something once read, probably "The Eighty-Yard Run." Nor is my concern with a woman in a dirty crepe-de-Chine wrapper in a Wilmington bar. My stake is always, of course, in the unmentioned girl in the plaid silk dress. *Remember what it was to be me*: that is always the point.

It is a difficult point to admit. We are brought up in the ethic that others, any others, all others, are by definition more interesting than ourselves; taught to be diffident, just this side of self-effacing. ("You're the least important person in the room and don't forget it," Jessica Mitford's governess would hiss in her ear on the advent of any social occasion; I copied that into my notebook because it is only recently that I have been able to enter a room without hearing some such phrase in my inner ear.) Only the very young and the very old may recount their dreams at breakfast, dwell upon self, interrupt with memories of beach picnics and favorite Liberty lawn dresses and the rainbow trout in a creek near Colorado Springs. The rest of us are expected, rightly, to affect absorption in other people's favorite dresses, other people's trout.

And so we do. But our notebooks give us away, for however dutifully we record what we see around us, the common denominator of all we see is always, transparently, shamelessly, the implacable "I." We are not talking here about the kind of notebook that is patently for public consumption, a structural conceit for binding together a series of graceful *pensées*; we are talking about something private, about bits of the mind's string too short to use, an indiscriminate and erratic assemblage with meaning only for its maker.

And sometimes even the maker has difficulty with the meaning. There does not seem to be, for example, any point in my knowing for the rest of my life that, during 1964, 720 tons of soot fell on every square mile of New York City, yet there it is in my notebook, labeled "FACT." Nor do I really need to remember that Ambrose Bierce liked to spell Leland Stanford's name "£eland $tanford" or that "smart women almost always wear black in Cuba," a fashion hint without much potential for practical application. And does not the relevance of these notes seem marginal at best?:

10

In the basement museum of the Inyo County Courthouse in Independence, California, sign pinned to a mandarin coat: "This MANDARIN COAT was often worn by Mrs. Minnie S. Brooks when giving lectures on her TEAPOT COLLECTION."

Redhead getting out of car in front of Beverly Wilshire Hotel, chinchilla stole, Vuitton bags with tags reading:

MRS LOU FOX
HOTEL SAHARA
VEGAS

Well, perhaps not entirely marginal. As a matter of fact, Mrs. Minnie S. Brooks and her MANDARIN COAT pull me back into my own childhood, for although I never knew Mrs. Brooks and did not visit Inyo County until I was thirty, I grew up in just such a world, in houses cluttered with Indian relics and bits of gold ore and ambergris and the souvenirs my Aunt Mercy Farnsworth brought back from the Orient. It is a long way from that world to Mrs. Lou Fox's world, where we all live now, and is it not just as well to remember that? Might not Mrs. Minnie S. Brooks help me to remember what I am? Might not Mrs. Lou Fox help me to remember what I am not?

But sometimes the point is harder to discern. What exactly did I have in mind when I noted down that it cost the father of someone I know $650 a month to light the place on the Hudson in which he lived before the Crash? What use was I planning to make of this line by Jimmy Hoffa: "I may have my faults, but being wrong ain't one of them"? And although I think it interesting to know where the girls who travel with the Syndicate have their hair done when they find themselves on the West Coast, will I ever make suitable use of it? Might I not be better off just passing it on to John O'Hara? What is a recipe for sauerkraut doing in my notebook? What kind of magpie keeps this notebook? "*He was born the night the Titanic went down.*" That seems a nice enough line, and I even recall who said it, but is it not really a better line in life than it could ever be in fiction?

But of course that is exactly it: not that I should ever use the line, but that   15
I should remember the woman who said it and the afternoon I heard it. We were on her terrace by the sea, and we were finishing the wine left from lunch, trying to get what sun there was, a California winter sun. The woman whose husband was born the night the *Titanic* went down wanted to rent her house, wanted to go back to her children in Paris. I remember wishing that I could afford the house, which cost $1,000 a month. "Someday you will," she said lazily. "Someday it all comes." There in the sun on her terrace it seemed easy to believe in someday, but later I had a low-grade afternoon hangover and ran over a black snake on the way to the supermarket and was flooded with inexplicable fear when I heard the checkout clerk explaining to the man ahead of me why she was finally divorcing her husband. "He left me no choice," she

said over and over as she punched the register. "He has a little seven-month-old baby by her, he left me no choice." I would like to believe that my dread then was for the human condition, but of course it was for me, because I wanted a baby and did not then have one and because I wanted to own the house that cost $1,000 a month to rent and because I had a hangover.

It all comes back. Perhaps it is difficult to see the value in having one's self back in that kind of mood, but I do see it; I think we are well advised to keep on nodding terms with the people we used to be, whether we find them attractive company or not. Otherwise they turn up unannounced and surprise us, come hammering on the mind's door at 4 a.m. of a bad night and demand to know who deserted them, who betrayed them, who is going to make amends. We forget all too soon the things we thought we could never forget. We forget the loves and the betrayals alike, forget what we whispered and what we screamed, forget who we were. I have already lost touch with a couple of people I used to be; one of them, a seventeen-year-old, presents little threat, although it would be of some interest to me to know again what it feels like to sit on a river levee drinking vodka-and-orange-juice and listening to Les Paul and Mary Ford and their echoes sing "How High the Moon" on the car radio. (You see I still have the scenes, but I no longer perceive myself among those present, no longer could even improvise the dialogue.) The other one, a twenty-three-year-old, bothers me more. She was always a good deal of trouble, and I suspect she will reappear when I least want to see her, skirts too long, shy to the point of aggravation, always the injured party, full of recriminations and little hurts and stories I do not want to hear again, at once saddening me and angering me with her vulnerability and ignorance, an apparition all the more insistent for being so long banished.

It is a good idea, then, to keep in touch, and I suppose that keeping in touch is what notebooks are all about. And we are all on our own when it comes to keeping those lines open to ourselves: your notebook will never help me, nor mine you. *"So what's new in the whiskey business?"* What could that possibly mean to you? To me it means a blonde in a Pucci bathing suit sitting with a couple of fat men by the pool at the Beverly Hills Hotel. Another man approaches, and they all regard one another in silence for a while. "So what's new in the whiskey business?" one of the fat men finally says by way of welcome, and the blonde stands up, arches one foot and dips it in the pool, looking all the while at the cabaña where Baby Pignatari is talking on the telephone. That is all there is to that, except that several years later I saw the blonde coming out of Saks Fifth Avenue in New York with her California complexion and a voluminous mink coat. In the harsh wind that day she looked old and irrevocably tired to me, and even the skins in the mink coat were not worked the way they were doing them that year, not the way she would have wanted them done, and there is the point of the story. For a while after that I did not like to look in the mirror, and my eyes would skim the newspapers and pick out only the deaths, the cancer victims, the premature coronaries, the suicides, and I stopped riding the Lexington Avenue IRT because I noticed for the first time that all the strangers I had seen for years—the man with the seeing-eye dog, the spinster who read the classified pages every day, the fat girl who always got off with me at Grand Central—looked older than they once had.

It all comes back. Even that recipe for sauerkraut: even that brings it back. I was on Fire Island when I first made that sauerkraut, and it was raining, and we drank a lot of bourbon and ate the sauerkraut and went to bed at ten, and I listened to the rain and the Atlantic and felt safe. I made the sauerkraut again last night and it did not make me feel any safer, but that is, as they say, another story.

QUESTIONS

1. The first paragraphs of Didion's essay present a pattern that she replicates throughout the remainder of the piece—the transcription of a passage from her notebook, an elaboration, and an attempt to explain her original motives for taking note of this observation. She thereby reproduces her own curiosity about her writing. How many times does she quote from her notebook, and how do her responses differ (in length, emphasis, quality)? How do the responses evolve as the essay progresses?

2. Didion offers a number of tentative answers to her main question, "Why do I keep a notebook at all?" (paragraph 4). Make a list of these responses and their revisions throughout the essay. Why doesn't she simply explain at the beginning "what notebooks are all about" (paragraph 17) rather than waiting until the last paragraphs? Do you find this way of explaining to be effective? Explain why or why not.

3. Consider the title of the essay, "On Keeping a Notebook." Select a phrase from the essay that you think would serve as a better title—for example, "How it felt to me," or "the truth about a notebook" (paragraph 8)—or make up your own. How does the title of an essay (yours included) create expectations about what will be explained in the body of the text?

4. How does Didion distinguish between a diary and a notebook? Does that distinction affect her sense of the difference "between what happened and what merely might have happened" (paragraph 7)? Is Didion concerned with truth in her notebook writing?

5. Didion's style feels somewhat like a conversation with herself. Note how she begins some sentences informally with words like *so, or, and,* and *well.* In effect, she's working through a dialogue between her present and her past. Write an essay in which you quote your own writing from a different period (a notebook, journal, or even writing assignment from a previous year), and then reflect on why this was important to you at the time. What does it teach you about keeping in touch with your past selves?

6. What is the point of notebooks for you? Begin an essay with a statement from Didion with which you disagree, and then proceed to discuss what you suggest as an alternative reason for writing.

MAKING CONNECTIONS

Didion writes, "I think we are well advised to keep on nodding terms with the people we used to be, whether we find them attractive company or not" (paragraph 16). Compare how Didion, Maya Angelou in "Graduation" (p. 43) and Alice Walker in "Beauty: When the Other Dancer Is the Self" (p. 54) view events from their youth and how they connect their youthful experiences to adult knowledge.

MEMORYWORK

Susan Choi

*Susan Choi was born in 1969 in Indiana and grew up in Texas.
She received her undergraduate degree in literature from Yale
University and an M.F.A. from Cornell University. Several of her
works of short fiction have been published in such journals as* Iowa
Review *and* Epoch. *Her first novel,* The Foreign Student (1998),
*is set in Sewanee, Tennessee, in the 1950s and won the Asian-
American Literary Award for Fiction. Her second novel,* American
Woman (2003), *is a portrait of a young antiwar radical in the
1970s and was a Pulitzer Prize finalist. On her reaction to being
called a "Southern writer," Choi declared, "I was tickled and flattered. It put me in good company. The South takes literature really
seriously, perhaps more so than in other parts of the country. It
seems to me that more people read, and that people are interested
in examining their history in a clear-eyed way. I met more people
who are interested in examining racial issues than anywhere else.
They are interested in their own history and don't try to white-
wash." Choi has been a Guggenheim Fellow and a lecturer at
Cornell University, and she currently lives in New York City.
"Memorywork," which portrays a mother forced by her growing
daughter to confront her own aversion to remembering her past,
first appeared in the summer 1993 edition of* The Iowa Review.

In 1963 I was in Ann Arbor. I remember the usual things, like a blouse
that I wore as often as I thought I could get away with it, and where I was
the day they shot Kennedy. I think everyone must remember things like
that. The blouse was thin and white, with no sleeves and a peter pan collar.
Small buttons the milky color of imitation pearl. It was a flirtatious little
blouse. Because I remember it so well I will always confuse myself in memory, thinking that it was a warm summer day when JFK died.

I was walking through the quad before I knew what had happened.
The eeriest feeling of my life: something palpably malicious hung in the air,
like a sharply drawn breath held trapped in the lungs for too long. There
was something else strange, wrong, that gave me the thought of summer. It
was biting cold yet the quad was peppered with small knots of people who
stood absolutely still, shoulder to shoulder their heads almost touching.
Like tiny football huddles, engaged in silent prayer. At the heart of each
group was a transistor radio, stuttering that terribly lonely, distant radio
sound. I passed one group and heard a soft noise of choking, and later I
knew it was weeping.

Kennedy had been to Ann Arbor the year before, to unveil the Peace Corps. I met Jay at the speech, and that is the source of another snag in my memory. I will always associate Jay with JFK, and this has me convinced that I cried the day that JFK was shot. I was in love, and my love threw an umbrella of tremulous, precarious emotion over everything. I felt dangerously alive, in pain, on the very brink of disaster all the time. I have never been happier than I was then. I am always happy to feel on the verge of death.

But the truth is that I didn't cry when JFK was shot. I reported for work, as a secretary's helper in the economics department. When they waved me away, I was glad to go. I went home, flipped on the news, and fell asleep. Years later I had to admit to Bettina that I slept through most of the sixties. I wore that peter pan collared blouse straight through for another decade, until the day it fell apart in the wash.

When I married Jay I agreed with him that we couldn't have any children until the dissertation was done. It would be impossible, he said. First things first: the dissertation, the degree, the job. Could I wait that long? It was funny, because we both knew that I was only acting disappointed for him. I didn't want children, ever. My pretending to yearn and to pine was a lie. He knew, but it wasn't until much later that he hated me for it. We would giggle together about Macready, fishing the first draft of his dissertation out of a sewer grating with a bent-out coat hanger. Macready was Irish, Catholic, married since his undergraduate years. His five children had fed the dissertation between the rusted teeth of the sewer grating, a page at a time. The only copy. Children! We giggled, made love, smoked fiercely.

I proofed Jay's dissertation for what seemed like ten years, but it must have only been four. I kept my job as a secretary's helper, and when the secretary was fired for being pregnant, I was promoted to full secretary. Jay wondered why I didn't take advantage of staff privileges, audit a class or two. It was another lie we shared. I pretended to be simple, and content with the helpful things I did. I corrected his spelling. I balanced our checkbook. "A Jew," he would confirm, with a tone of finality that strangely sickened me. Then, I always laughed.

There are some pictures of us, from that time when were happy. Just a few stacks, taken three different days, maybe three years apart. All that time, and only this remains. It's strange to think that you buy a camera, and suddenly there's another form of selective memory, rivaling your own. The pictures are bent and fused together, cardboardy to the touch. They are edged with a border of white. When Bettina pulls them apart, the fronts cling to the backs and carry a papery fuzz away that cannot be removed. Strange, linty clouds float over our faces, obscuring our expressions.

Bettina is aggrieved. She is almost twelve, old enough to drag herself out of my enforced amnesia and insist upon having a past. She hauls old shoeboxes out of my closet, upending their contents onto the floor. Carbon copies of old letters, in no apparent order. Medical bills. Half the manuscript of a story that begins. *She stood by the window, day after day, watching the rain . . .*

"Bettina!" I bark. From my bed I snatch at the air.

"Where are they?" She is on her hands and knees, pushing stubbornly   10
through the slum of yellowed paper.

"Where are what?"

"The pictures."

"You have the pictures right there in front of you."

These are all the same day." She peers at them with irritation, pulling
carefully. She winces when they part with the tearing sound that means they
will be forever marred by fuzz. "There's no date on these," she complains.
She is flabbergasted by my disregard for the past, for what she thinks is her
past. She is angry that I haven't kept it in better shape for her.

I half-crane for a better view, half-cringe. I don't really want to see   15
those pictures. "1963," I declare. There is the blouse. I am smiling as if I
would break. That fantastic, sweet pain. It must have been early on.

"Where are the pictures of me? The pictures of me, when Dad was
here?" Bettina is deliberately emotionless, businesslike. She is only cleaning,
cleaning up this lousy mess I've made of our lives.

"I don't know," I tell her. "Now clean up that mess."

"*Are* there pictures of me?"

I waver between telling her No, telling her I don't remember, telling her
Yes, somewhere. I don't want to say Yes. I don't want her to keep rooting
around. I abruptly remember something I have been fighting hard to forget,
a day I found Bettina shrieking in her room, a rare moment of hysteria.
Even as a baby, she was usually sullen, glowering, silent. This day she wept
until I appeared in the door, and then she hurled something at me. It might
have been a lamp. Later I found the carbon, under her bed, of a letter I
wrote to my sister that year, the year Bettina was eight. *When will I grow
into this?* I had written. *When will it start? Everyone says I will learn to
love her sometime . . . in answer to your question, No, she doesn't do a
damn thing to help me. She's a kid. She doesn't do a damn thing.*

"I'll look for them," I tell her. For a moment, staring at the small, dark,   20
truculent crown of her head, I am overwhelmed. She is a little foreigner, a little Martian. Sometimes, like this time, I love her. More often it is a struggle.

"Don't knock yourself out," she murmurs. She scoops the tattered
salad of paper back into the boxes and leaves the room. A few minutes later
I hear her music, the rock and roll that strikes a vaguely familiar chord in
me whenever she plays it. If she is safely in her room, I will dance a little. I
think it is the music from when I was young. I think I remember it.

Bettina is being taught a healthy respect for the past. It seems to be her
classroom theme this year, the final year of elementary school. Next year she
will be sent off to begin the harrowing career of a middle-schooler; maybe
this is why the teacher working feverishly, self-righteously, to instill the kids
with a sense of history and worth. I went storming to the school in an indignant rage when Bettina told me the latest project. I had complied, even gone
out of my way, for the other projects. I thought I was paying my taxes so

that I could leave these things to trained professionals, but I did them. I taught her to bake bread for Know the Pioneers week. Another girl did hand-churned butter; Bettina's bread, unlike Bettina, was assimilated into the classroom scene with great success. Then I called my older sister for a crash course on the life of our mother, who had never bothered to know me, for Grand-parentstory Week. I began to suspect that this unknown woman, this teacher, was using my child to teach me an un-flattering lesson about myself, but I pretended great delight. I masqueraded as a normal, interested parent, until The Way They Were. When Bettina told me she needed a picture of her parents as young lovers, taken before she was born, I'd had enough. I would not have my child taught that every family was a Robert Redford love story. It seemed indecent, and insulting.

The classroom was in a temporary shack on blocks. When I opened the door I felt the need to duck, the door seemed so small, and I nearly fell into the room. I was fiercely blushing. I'd done myself up to be fearful but I knew I'd overshot and ended up pathetic. I was packed into a one-piece suit from my secretarial days, and it was too tight. The skirt crept up off the hips and bunched fretfully around my waist. I was teetering in heels. I stood uncertainly on the threshold, flushed and mortified. It had been so long since I'd made myself up, I was checking my rouge every other second in the rearview the whole way over. Now I was convinced all over again that it was much too bright.

The teacher was older than I had expected, perhaps even older than I was. Her hair was blonde but so abundant and fibrous that it could have been fake. Her face wore a matronly expression that defied any attempt to place her age. She had no wedding band, which surprised me.

"I'm Bettina's mother," I managed. I ventured unsteadily into the room 25 and tried to look inquisitive. The large bulletin board was decorated with an elaborate racetrack, scattered across with cardboard cutouts of horses in flight. Each horse was slightly different, in color or in posture, and the lines were precise and delicate. I paused, admiring the care. They were emblazoned with names, the names proudly arcing across their flanks. I located Bettina near the lead. The board proclaimed: Attendance Winners!

It was true that she hardly missed a day. She never wanted to stay home.

"I'm Miss Shank," the teacher said, smiling broadly. The smile seemed to acknowledge the gracelessness of her name. "Bettina's right up there," she added. "It's a very close race this year."

"It's pretty." I nodded at the board.

"Oh." She waved a hand dismissively. "Horses are my great passion," she said. She said it as though it were an admission. "I'm really thrilled to meet you at last," she continued quickly. "I was sorry you couldn't make Open House, but it looks like you're feeling better."

I registered this rapidly. Bettina never told me about an Open House, 30 but this was the sort of omission she committed without forethought. I was surprised she'd said I was sick. Out of last minute embarrassment, or malice.

"I was very ill," I agreed, smiling.

Miss Shank dragged an adult-sized chair out of one corner and gestured to it. "They're big kids," she laughed, "but we're bigger, right?"

I nodded, numbly. I had imagined the visit as a flouncing through the door, a flinging of words, a quick exit. Now I was embarrassed and at a loss. She seemed so personable, so personal. I flirted briefly with suspicion, tried to suspect she was taking me in. I reminded myself of Grandparentstory Week and how much it had hurt me. My oldest sister played mother to me because our own mother was too old, too tired, too uninterested to care by the time I was born. So I was also an unwanted child, I know it's unfair. Then I thought of Know the Pioneers Week. I had to practice the bread secretly, two afternoons in a row, while Bettina was at school. I was always a lousy cook and it made me ashamed. It was another thing Jay had used to humiliate me, again and again, until he finally left.

"It's about The Way They Were," I began, and stopped abruptly. My hands worked anxiously around the edges of my purse. It was a tiny purse, a purse I never used. My real purse was huge, stained, hideous.

She nodded wisely. "Bettina was concerned. She explained that most of   35
your old pictures were lost in the fire."

I absorbed this news without betraying shock. Of course: the fire.

She paused, eyeing me with a reserved empathy. "It's not really the pictures themselves that are important. The point is to teach the children a lesson they often learn too late, that their parents were once young, beautiful, excited about the future." She laughed. "Not to say that now all of you parents are old, ugly, and resigned."

I couldn't help it. I burst out laughing also, and she smiled, appreciatively.

"It's just so hard for children to see beyond themselves, at this age. When they realize there was a time before they were born, a time when their parents actually existed without them, it teaches them something they may not show for a long time, but—" she held up a finger of warning— "it will come out one day. Children have to learn to esteem their parents as people, not just old windbags, disciplinarians, handservants. It's very hard." She sat back, a little breathless.

"Do you have children?" I ventured. I already knew what the answer   40
was.

"No," she blurted out. After a slight pause she said again, "No, I don't."

I nodded carefully. I was cautious, afraid of appearing judgmental. Now I saw us as allies, as strategists. She seemed suddenly embarrassed.

"I know what you're thinking," she claimed.

"No, I think it's wonderful." My heart sank, unworthy of her project. "I really do."

She twisted one strange lock of hair, angrily. "You know, I lost my par-   45
ents a few years ago, both of them. They weren't so old. It was an accident. I'd never imagined they would be gone one day, without warning." She nodded, without looking at me. "I'd always assumed there would be an interval, between knowing they would die, and death."

"Time at the deathbed," I offered. "A chance to say things."

"Yes." She caught my eye again, a little fiercely. She was not smiling anymore. "It's an old story, right? 'I never had a chance to say,' et cetera.

"I lost my mother when I was very young," I assured her. "I was angry, for years. Just sort of, I don't know, angry."

She nodded. We both looked away, at other parts of the room. In one corner I thought I could see an essay, tacked to the wall, in Bettina's hand. Her unexpectedly childish, cringing, disastrous cursive. I tried to look at my watch. I was always afraid when I left Bettina alone. Not afraid of what she was doing, but afraid of what she might find. I thought of the pictures, the letters, the furious disarray of my files. And Bettina picking through them with single-minded determination, and her unacknowledged fear of what she would find, what she would confirm about us both.

Miss Shank spoke up again, with formal caution. "Would I be too bold to assume . . . that there was never a fire?"   50

I smiled wanly. "Bettina thinks I'm sloppy. Maybe it seems like a fire to her." I wondered what made me find excuses for her. "There are some pictures of her parents, before we divorced. I haven't taken a whole lot of care with them." Briefly remembering my initial rage, I added, "It hasn't been a picture book life."

"I'm sorry," Miss Shank murmured. "It was an intrusion, a really thoughtless intrusion, and I'm sorry." She shrugged helplessly. My stomach became an anxious fist, unhappily aware that I was in the wrong. I didn't want her to surrender an apology to me, it made me stunned with shame. I wanted her to be severe with me, to be scolding, to exclaim that she had expected better. I realized I hadn't spoken.

"I feel so stupid," she added uneasily. "I guess I'm still stuck an angry child. I've never got to be an angry parent."

I stood up quickly, embarrassed. I wanted to say something that would dissipate our conversation like so much courteous hot air. "Bettina likes you very much," I offered. Bettina never spoke about her teachers at all, but when I said this I thought it was true.

Miss Shank took the cue, and stood also. "Bettina is very bright," she   55
said mechanically. "Excellent in her reading, excellent in her memorywork. I'm enjoying having her."

I backed unevenly to the door. "Thank you," I said. It was a catastrophe, because I liked her. My incompetence infuriated me. I actually liked her.

"Thank *you*" she said stiffly.

Bettina's choice lies in a small envelope on the table. It couldn't be called a choice: it was the only one we found. A wedding picture. Suddenly, I remember a day at the height of summer — 1965? 1964? — when Jay and I were renting a broken-down house in the country. I could put three things together and have the date exact, but I will not put three things together. Jay was teaching in the summer session at Eastern Michigan. Our porch had a trellis, choked with roses. I said, "They only grow if you don't care either way." We put bright green butterfly chairs in the yard, and took two pictures. One of Jay reclining in his chair, a pipe clamped between his teeth, a look of incredible audacity on his face. One of me stretched out in my chair, my eyes tensely closed, my body pale as a corpse.

I couldn't tell Bettina that it was always that way: he and I, alone. I couldn't tell her the truth: that our love never did endure company, and that we three would not have endured at all. She believes I cheated her out of a father, and her father believes the same. But what I want to ask is, If the child was so important, why am I the one who has her? If the child was the reason, how could he have gone without her? I want to ask this, but there is no decent way to do it. There is no decent woman who would say it.

So, there were always two of us. Never a third, to hold the camera and   60 click. And the only picture of Jay and me together is on our wedding day.

Bettina was skeptical. I don't seem to do anything but give her fuel for her skepticism. "You didn't have any friends?" she demanded. "Any at all?"

"I guess we never had a friend and a camera at the same time."

Bettina shook her head, annoying me with her childish doubt. She peered closely at the wedding picture. It is a snapshot; there was no official photographer. Someone must have mailed it to us. It is a terrible picture, taken in the lounge of the University Chapel, a low room muffled by dun-colored drapes. The furniture is all orange and avocado, kitchen colors. Jutting into the frame at the left, the end of a folding table showing its metal legs beneath a white cloth. Stumbling out of the frame at the right, my sister. She appears to be my mother, both because she is old enough to have been my mother and because she is visibly disgusted. Jay and I stand in the middle, dressed only slightly better than the most casual guest. He is eating cake with his hand, staring off to one side. I face the camera flashing that explosive, murderous smile.

"I'm sorry," I told Bettina. I was, terribly, sorry.

"It's alright," she said. She regarded the picture with sudden, quiet un-   65 derstanding. As though the truth of it was what pleased her.

"Ain't no fairy tale, kid." I fought the urge to put my hand in her tangled hair and really mess it up. I kept still, looking over her shoulder.

"Mom," she said, leaning forward with an exaggerated air of secrecy. "*Truth is —*"

She made mocking eyebrows, letting the sentence dangle like an idiot question.

I waited for her to finish.

"Truth is, I've known it all along."   70

Today is the day that I have to get rid of it. I watch Bettina eat her breakfast, chewing every bite with a methodical fixity that amuses me. She is turning into a real person, this kid. She read somewhere that chewing every bite one hundred times could lead to weight loss, fooling the brain into filling the stomach with less. Now, in retrospect, she has proclaimed she has a weight problem.

I used to kill myself to love her. Now, without trying, I find myself liking her. More and more.

"Don't forget the picture," I tell her. The bus is blaring impatiently, but she is unflustered. She snatches up the envelope, throwing me a sly grin on her way out the door.

After she is gone I sit at the table a long time, willing myself to do it. I have to get rid of it because keeping it means hiding it, and hiding the ugly things about yourself gains nothing and loses so much time. It is only Bettina growing larger, angrier, increasingly articulate and demanding that forces my head out of the sand and commands me to do something. I remember passing a long window and being shocked by my own reflection: a squat little fireplug on legs. One moment of awareness in ten years. Later I told Bettina I wished I'd had a full-length mirror all my life. I always refused to own one, out of righteous indignation, or false pride. Now, I regretted it acutely. If I'd had one, maybe things would have been different. Maybe I would have paid better attention to what I looked like, and ended up a better person in the end.

"You can't be serious," she'd sneered. "You think your whole life 75 would've turned out differently, if you had a bigger *mirror?*"

I go into my bedroom and pull the spare blankets out of a dresser drawer. Aside from what is discarded in the closet there are the things I'd truly hoped to lose. I empty the drawer and carefully slide my hand beneath the paper liner. There is only more paper, the sheets pressed carefully between the liner and the bed of the drawer like cherished leaves: a letter from Jay that made me vomit the first time I read it, and the carbon Bettina found, four years ago. Also, a very large photograph, an X-ray, in livid black and white. She does not know anything about it, but this is the picture Bettina is always looking for, a picture that offers some proof.

In it, the fetus is featureless and budlike, a lumpen blaze of light. At sixteen weeks everything is there, in grotesque proportion: the bulbous head, the delicate hinge of a leg, a hint of an arm. It is a poor X-ray, and the details are blurred. Still, you can see that something must accentuate the curl of that tiny body. The body is not simply shaped like a curl, it really *is* curling, clutching and clinging at something with inconceivable determination. Bent on being alive. The wisp of a thread betrays the prize in its fist, a prize it snatched like the brass ring off a merry-go-round. You may not be able to see it, but it's there. Impossibly, almost hilariously there. The baby is brandishing an IUD, and earning a place in Michigan medical history for us both.

I take the X-ray into the kitchen and set it on fire. It makes a rank smell from the developing chemicals and the gloss, but it burns. The corners cringe together, furling and swiftly blackening. When it is done I sweep the ashes together and throw them all over the yard. Then I make a tall glass of lemonade and play like it's summer.

Truth is, Bettina is right to be suspicious; I remember more than I admit. I remember that in 1967 we were in Ypsilanti, and preparing to leave. The prelude was complete: dissertation, degree, a job near the ocean.

Jay and I shared the twin sense that the beginning had finally arrived, but our expectations were not the same. Jay had turned his unswerving attention to the accomplishment of children. For him children had always been the fourth term in the series, the next logical step. And it's true, I had always known this. But I was depending on a romantic change of scenery: we would walk near the sea and be battered by wind until our differences left us. Jay would realize it was just too soon for children, and then everything could start. I would pull myself together and do something of my own.

I'd started putting the Ypsilanti house into boxes months ahead of   80
time. Those days were gigantic, emptied of everything but waiting. I was always alone. An eventless year is easiest to remember, in all its tiresome detail: the whirr of the electric clock, the morning light thick with dust. My flaking gold barrette and my plushy flowered housecoat. Always looking ahead, I lost track of the time. Summer seemed perpetual.

When I realized I hadn't been bleeding, I didn't know how many months I had skipped. There were no other symptoms. I knew the absence was a sure sign, but it was flatly impossible. After Jay banned birth control I had barely hesitated before visiting a doctor. I justified it as a necessary deceit, the only way to buy myself some time, and I was confident I could bring Jay around without his ever having to know. The thing would hang within me like a small pendant, a wire scrawl, undetectable. Jay and I would just happen to be unlucky, for six months or maybe a year, and soon it would cease to matter. It never occurred to me that the thing wouldn't work.

When the extraordinary circumstances of the pregnancy were explained to Jay, he was very quiet. The packing, abruptly suspended, had left the house with a vaguely exploded look. For days we picked carefully through the rooms, staring mostly at the floor. Our eyes met once over a teetering pile of books, once through the spidery stack of the butterfly chairs. I think he was grateful for the obstacles between us. When I finally sought him out, in his study, the X-ray lay on the desk between his hands. I stood at his back and felt the motionless rage there, hanging off him like a cape. I wanted to yank it away and be done with it. Things had changed and we had to let them change.

"Tricky thief." He could not see me nod at the picture.

"Like its mother," he said.

I was silent. It was already scripted, anything I could have said, and his   85
response. If I'd wanted to wait: we'd waited. If I never wanted children: I'd lied. "Jay," I said. "Please turn around."

"I can't," he said.

Bettina will demonstrate her memorywork. I am very honored. She does not normally come to me with these things, but this time I asked. I wanted to know what it was. "I hear you're real good at it," I tell her. "Miss Shank said you were excellent." I pause over "excellent," and swell a little with pleasure. "*Excellent.*"

Bettina frowns darkly. "Miss Shank told you? What'd you do, go and embarrass me?"

"Me? Embarrass you?" I wave her away with a grand gesture. "Go on. I was just trying to find out why you're doing so well. I thought you had some unholy arrangement with this woman."

Bettina turns very solemn. She puts on that you're-not-gonna-believe- 90 this look again. "Mom," she says mournfully. "Truth is, I'm *real smart.*"

She's a hell of a thief. I never wanted to admit how much of Jay she got away with, but lately I can see him standing in her place, and I can be captivated by it. I don't have to hate her for it.

"I know, kid. And I'm sorry."

Bettina grimaces and bolts out of her chair. She takes a place in the middle of the kitchen and tries to look resigned. "Well," she chants, "memorywork is both a means to an end and an end in itself. It fills the mind with well-known treasures and trains it to acquire even more. It is a skill!" Bettina flings with an arm and sighs with false passion. Her impersonation of Miss Shank is dead-on, and I have to laugh.

Bettina clears her throat severely. "I have a stunning repertoire. What would you like to hear?"

"What have you got?" I ask her. "Speeches? Poems?" 95

She gazes away, biting her tongue thoughtfully. "I have 'Four Score and Twenty Years Ago.' I have 'Two Roads Submerged.' I have a lot of weird political stuff, but only excerpts. 'King's Dream.' 'Kennedy's New Frontier.'"

I worry about making a good choice. I feel a little stupid. "A poem of your choice," I tell her. "Anything but that one about the roads."

"All right." Bettina looks anxious, but confident. "I have one that I kind of like."

"I'm ready," I tell her. I sit back and search for an attentive face, praying I won't be bored. I am almost always bored. But when Bettina starts to speak, straining her voice to be louder, I know she'll never bore me. Her poem is beautiful. Really, it is fantastic.

QUESTIONS

1. How well does the title, "Memorywork," represent this story?
2. What does the narrator mean when she notes, "It's strange to think that you buy a camera, and suddenly there's another form of selective memory, rivaling your own" (paragraph 7)?
3. Bettina's search for her past, through her own curiosity and encouraged by her school project, is upsetting to her mother when the request comes for "a picture of her parents as young lovers" (paragraph 22). Why is this so?
4. What is the importance of the mother's meeting with Miss Shank?

5. Bettina finds the picture of her young parents and one of their wedding day. How does her mother respond to them? How do they contribute to the story of the marriage?

6. What does the X-ray of Bettina as a fetus predict about her?

7. Find a family photograph of your parents when they were young. What associations can you make between their young selves and your own? According to John Berger, "[W]e are always looking at the relation between things and ourselves" (*Ways of Seeing*, 9). In a sense, you are trying to recreate a past in which you were not present. Note how your parents present themselves to the camera, what the setting is, and other details that would contribute to your description.

MAKING CONNECTIONS

In "Memoria ex Machina" (p. 626), Marshall Jon Fisher opens with the memories generated by a silver Seiko watch he owned as a thirteen-year-old. With relation to memories of the past, he quotes Proust: "The past is hidden somewhere outside the realm, beyond the reach of intellect, in some material object (in the sensation which that material object will give us) which we do not suspect" (paragraph 6). How does the narrator in "Memorywork" confront her past through the old photographs? How would she comment on Fisher's statement that "[o]nly machines — tape recorders, cameras, video cameras — can accurately preserve the details of our former selves, of our loved ones' younger faces, of our long-gone possessions" (paragraph 13)?

URBAN LEGENDS:
"The Boyfriend's Death"

Jan Harold Brunvand

Trained in the study of folklore, Jan Harold Brunvand (b. 1933) has become a leading collector and interpreter of contemporary legends. These "urban legends" are stories told around campfires and in college dormitories, often as true experiences that happened to somebody other than the teller of the tale. For many years a professor at the University of Utah, Brunvand has been the editor of the Journal of American Folklore *and* American Folklore: An Encyclopedia *(1996), and is the author of the standard introduction to the field,* The Study of American Folklore: An Introduction, *fourth edition (1997). The following selection is taken from the first of his several collections of urban legends,* The Vanishing Hitchhiker: American Urban Legends and Their Meanings *(1981). Here Brunvand defines* urban legend, *gives one striking example, and offers some explanations about how and why such stories flourish even in the midst of a highly technologized society. The selection as reprinted is complete, except for the deletion of a few brief references to other discussions elsewhere in Brunvand's book.*

We are not aware of our own folklore any more than we are of the grammatical rules of our language. When we follow the ancient practice of informally transmitting "lore" — wisdom, knowledge, or accepted modes of behavior — by word of mouth and customary example from person to person, we do not concentrate on the form or content of our folklore; instead, we simply listen to information that others tell us and then pass it on — more or less accurately — to other listeners. In this stream of unselfconscious oral tradition the information that acquires a clear story line is called *narrative folklore*, and those stories alleged to be true are *legends*. This, in broad summary, is the typical process of legend formation and transmission as it has existed from time immemorial and continues to operate today. It works about the same way whether the legendary plot concerns a dragon in a cave or a mouse in a Coke bottle.

It might seem unlikely that legends — *urban* legends at that — would continue to be created in an age of widespread literacy, rapid mass communications, and restless travel. While our pioneer ancestors may have had to rely heavily on oral traditions to pass the news along about changing events and frontier dangers, surely we no longer need mere "folk" reports of what's happening, with all their tendencies to distort the facts. A moment's

reflection, however, reminds us of the many weird, fascinating, but unverified rumors and tales that so frequently come to our ears — killers and
madmen on the loose, shocking or funny personal experiences, unsafe manufactured products, and many other unexplained mysteries of daily life.
Sometimes we encounter different oral versions of such stories, and on occasion we may read about similar events in newspapers or magazines; but
seldom do we find, or even seek after, reliable documentation. The lack of
verification in no way diminishes the appeal urban legends have for us. We
enjoy them merely as stories, and we tend at least to half-believe them as
possibly accurate reports. And the legends we tell, as with any folklore, reflect many of the hopes, fears, and anxieties of our time. In short, legends
are definitely part of our modern folklore — legends which are as traditional, variable, and functional as those of the past.

Folklore study consists of collecting, classifying, and interpreting in
their full cultural context the many products of everyday human interaction
that have acquired a somewhat stable underlying form and that are passed
traditionally from person to person, group to group, and generation to generation. Legend study is a most revealing area of such research because the
stories that people believe to be true hold an important place in their worldview. "If it's true, it's important" is an axiom to be trusted, whether or not
the lore really *is* true or not. Simply becoming aware of this modern folklore which we all possess to some degree is a revelation in itself, but going
beyond this to compare the tales, isolate their consistent themes, and relate
them to the rest of the culture can yield rich insights into the state of our
current civilization. . . .

Urban Legends as Folklore

Folklore subsists on oral tradition, but not all oral communication is
folklore. The vast amounts of human interchange, from casual daily conversations to formal discussions in business or industry, law, or teaching,
rarely constitute straight oral folklore. However, all such "communicative
events" (as scholars dub them) are punctuated routinely by various units
of traditional material that are memorable, repeatable, and that fit recurring social situations well enough to serve in place of original remarks.
"Tradition" is the key idea that links together such utterances as nick-
names, proverbs, greeting and leave-taking formulas, wisecracks, anec-
dotes, and jokes as "folklore"; indeed, these are a few of the best known
"conversational genres" of American folklore. Longer and more complex
folk forms — fairy tales, epics, myths, legends, or ballads, for example —
may thrive only in certain special situations of oral transmission. All true
folklore ultimately depends upon continued oral dissemination, usually
within fairly homogeneous "folk groups," and upon the retention through
time of internal patterns and motifs that become traditional in the oral exchanges. The corollary of this rule of stability in oral tradition is that all

items of folklore, while retaining a fixed central core, are constantly changing as they are transmitted, so as to create countless "variants" differing in length, detail, style, and performance technique. Folklore, in short, consists of oral tradition in variants.

Urban legends belong to the subclass of folk narratives, legends, 5 that — unlike fairy tales — are believed, or at least believable, and that — unlike myths — are set in the recent past and involve normal human beings rather than ancient gods or demigods. Legends are folk history, or rather quasi-history. As with any folk legends, urban legends gain credibility from specific details of time and place or from references to source authorities. For instance, a popular western pioneer legend often begins something like, "My great-grandmother had this strange experience when she was a young girl on a wagon train going through Wyoming when an Indian chief wanted to adopt her. . . ." Even though hundreds of different great-grandmothers are supposed to have had the same doubtful experience (being desired by the chief because of her beautiful long blond hair), the fact seldom reaches legend-tellers; if it does, they assume that the family lore has indeed spread far and wide. This particular popular tradition, known as "Goldilocks on the Oregon Trail," interests folklorists because of the racist implications of a dark Indian savage coveting a fair young civilized woman — this legend is familiar in the *white* folklore only — and it is of little concern that the story seems to be entirely apocryphal.

In the world of modern urban legends there is usually no geographical or generational gap between teller and event. The story is *true*; it really occurred, and recently, and always to someone else who is quite close to the narrator, or at least "a friend of a friend." Urban legends are told both in the course of casual conversations and in such special situations as campfires, slumber parties, and college dormitory bull sessions. The legends' physical settings are often close by, real, and sometimes even locally renowned for other such happenings. Though the characters in the stories are usually nameless, they are true-to-life examples of the kind of people the narrators and their audience know firsthand.

One of the great mysteries of folklore research is where oral traditions originate and who invents them. One might expect that at least in modern folklore we could come up with answers to such questions, but this is seldom, if ever, the case. . . .

The Performance of Legends

Whatever the origins of urban legends, their dissemination is no mystery. The tales have traveled far and wide, and have been told and retold from person to person in the same manner that myths, fairy tales, or ballads spread in earlier cultures, with the important difference that today's legends are also disseminated by the mass media. Groups of age-mates, especially adolescents, are one important American legend channel, but other paths of transmission are among office workers and club members, as well as among religious, recreational, and regional groups. Some individuals make a point of learning every recent rumor or tale, and they can enliven any coffee break, party, or trip with the latest supposed "news." The telling of one story inspires other people to share what they have read or heard, and in a short time a lively exchange of details occurs and perhaps new variants are created.

Tellers of these legends, of course, are seldom aware of their roles as "performers of folklore." The conscious purpose of this kind of storytelling is to convey a true event, and only incidentally to entertain an audience. Nevertheless, the speaker's demeanor is carefully orchestrated, and his or her delivery is low-key and soft-sell. With subtle gestures, eye movements, and vocal inflections the stories are made dramatic, pointed, and suspenseful. But, just as with jokes, some can tell them and some can't. Passive tellers of urban legends may just report them as odd rumors, but the more active legend tellers re-create them as dramatic stories of suspense and, perhaps, humor.

"The Boyfriend's Death"

With all these points in mind — folklore's subject-matter, style, and oral 10
performance — consider this typical version of a well-known urban legend that folklorists have named "The Boyfriend's Death," collected in 1964 (the earliest documented instance of the story) by folklorist Daniel R. Barnes from an eighteen-year-old freshman at the University of Kansas. The usual tellers of the story are adolescents, and the normal setting for the narration is a college dormitory room with fellow students sprawled on the furniture and floors.

> This happened just a few years ago out on the road that turns off highway 59 by the Holiday Inn. This couple were parked under a tree out on this road. Well, it got to be time for the girl to be back at the dorm, so she told her boyfriend that they should start back. But the car wouldn't start, so he told her to lock herself in the car and he would go down to the Holiday Inn and call for help. Well, he didn't come back and he didn't come back, and pretty soon she started hearing a scratching noise on the roof of the car. "Scratch, scratch . . . scratch, scratch." She got scareder and scareder, but he didn't come back. Finally, when it was almost daylight, some people came along and stopped and helped her out of the car, and she looked up and there was her boyfriend hanging from the tree, and his feet were scraping against the roof of the car. This is why the road is called "Hangman's Road."

Here is a story that has traveled rapidly to reach nationwide oral circulation, in the process becoming structured in the typical manner of folk narratives. The traditional and fairly stable elements are the parked couple, the abandoned girl, the mysterious scratching (sometimes joined by a dripping sound and ghostly shadows on the windshield), the daybreak rescue, and the horrible climax. Variable traits are the precise location, the reason for her abandonment, the nature of the rescuers, murder details, and the concluding placename explanation. While "The Boyfriend's Death" seems to have captured teenagers' imaginations as a separate legend only since the early 1960s, it is clearly related to at least two older yarns, "The Hook" and "The Roommate's Death." All three legends have been widely collected by American folklorists, although only scattered examples have been published, mostly in professional journals. Examination of some of these variations helps to make clear the status of the story as folklore and its possible meanings.

At Indiana University, a leading American center of folklore research, folk-narrative specialist Linda Dégh and her students have gathered voluminous data on urban legends, especially those popular with adolescents. Dégh's preliminary published report on "The Boyfriend's Death" concerned nineteen texts collected from IU students from 1964 to 1968. Several storytellers had heard it in high school, often at parties; others had picked it up in college dormitories or elsewhere on campus. Several students expressed some belief in the legend, supposing either that it had happened in their own hometowns, or possibly in other states, once as far distant as "a remote part of Alabama." One informant reported that "she had been sworn to that the incident actually happened," but another, who had heard some variations of the tale, felt that "it seemed too horrible to be true." Some versions had incorporated motifs from other popular teenage horror legends or local ghost stories. . . .

One of the Indiana texts, told in the state of Washington, localizes the story there near Moses Lake, "in the country on a road that leads to a dead-end right under a big weeping willow tree . . . about four or five miles from town." As in most American versions of the story, these specific local touches make believable what is essentially a traveling legend. In a detail familiar from other variants of "The Boyfriend's Death," the body — now decapitated — is left hanging upside down from a branch of the willow tree with the fingernails scraping the top of the car. Another version studied by the Indiana researcher is somewhat aberrant, perhaps because the student was told the story by a friend's parents who claimed that "it happened a long time ago, probably thirty or forty years." Here a murderer is introduced, a "crazy old lady" on whose property the couple has parked. The victim this time is skinned rather than decapitated, and his head scrapes the car as the corpse swings to and fro in the breezy night.

A developing motif in "The Boyfriend's Death" is the character and role of the rescuers, who in the 1964 Kansas version are merely "some people." The standard identification later becomes "the police," authority figures whose presence lends further credence to the story. They are either called by the missing teenagers' parents, or simply appear on the scene in the morning to check the car. In a 1969 variant from Leonardtown, Maryland, the police give a warning, "Miss, please get out of the car and walk to the police car with us, but don't look back." . . . In a version from Texas collected in 1971, set "at this lake somewhere way out in nowhere," a policeman gets an even longer line: "Young lady, we want you to get out of the car and come with us. Whatever you do, don't turn, don't turn around, just keep walking, just keep going straight and don't look back at the car." The more detailed the police instructions are, the more plausible the tale seems to become. Of course the standard rule of folk-narrative plot development now applies: the taboo must be broken (or the "interdiction violated" as some scholars put it). The girl always *does* look back, like Orpheus in the underworld, and in a number of versions her hair turns white from the shock of what she sees, as in a dozen other American legends.

In a Canadian version of "The Boyfriend's Death," told by a fourteen-   15
year-old boy from Willowdale, Ontario, in 1973, the words of the police-men are merely summarized, but the opening scene of the legend is developed more fully, with several special details, including . . . a warning heard on the car radio. The girl's behavior when left behind is also described in more detail.

> A guy and his girlfriend are on the way to a party when their car starts to give them some trouble. At that same time they catch a news flash on the radio warning all people in the area that a lunatic killer has escaped from a local criminal asylum. The girl becomes very upset and at that point the car stalls completely on the highway. The boyfriend gets out and tinkers around with the engine but can't get the car to start again. He decides that he is going to have to walk on up the road to a gas station and get a tow truck but wants his girlfriend to stay behind in the car. She is frightened and pleads with him to take her, but he says that she'll be safe on the floor of the car covered with a blanket so that anyone passing will think it is an abandoned car and not bother her. Besides he can sprint along the road and get back more quickly than if she comes with him in her high-heeled shoes and evening dress. She finally agrees and he tells her not to come out unless she hears his signal of three knocks on the window. . . .

She does hear knocks on the car, but they continue eerily beyond three; the sound is later explained as the shoes of the boyfriend's corpse bumping the car as the body swings from a limb above the car.

The style in which oral narratives are told deserves attention, for the live telling that is dramatic, fluid, and often quite gripping in actual folk performance before a sympathetic audience may seem stiff, repetitious, and awkward on the printed page. Lacking in all our examples of "The Boy-friend's Death" is the essential ingredient of immediate context — the setting of the legend-telling, the storyteller's vocal and facial expression and gestures, the audience's reaction, and the texts of other similar tales narrated at the same session. Several of the informants explained that the story was told to them in spooky situations, late at night, near a cemetery, out camping, or even "while on a hayride or out parked," occasionally near the site of the supposed murder. Some students refer to such macabre legends, therefore, as "scary stories," "screamers," or "horrors."

A widely-distributed folk legend of this kind as it travels in oral tradition acquires a good deal of its credibility and effect from the localized details inserted by individual tellers. The highway and motel identification in the Kansas text are good examples of this, and in a New Orleans version, "The Boyfriend's Death" is absorbed into a local teenage tradition about "The Grunch" — a half-sheep, half-human monster that haunts specific local sites. One teenager there reported, "A man and lady went out by the lake and in the morning they found 'em hanging upside down on a tree and they said grunches did it." Finally, rumors or news stories about missing persons or violent crimes (as mentioned in the Canadian version) can merge with urban legends, helping to support their air of truth, or giving them renewed circulation after a period of less frequent occurrence.

Even the bare printed texts retain some earmarks of effective oral tradition. Witness in the Kansas text the artful use of repetition (typical of folk narrative style): "Well, he didn't come back and he didn't come back . . . but he didn't come back." The repeated use of "well" and the building of lengthy sentences with "and" are other hallmarks of oral style which give the narrator complete control over his performance, tending to squeeze out interruptions or prevent lapses in attention among the listeners. The scene that is set for the incident — lonely road, night, a tree looming over the car, out of gas — and the sound effects — scratches or bumps on the car — contribute to the style, as does the dramatic part played by the policeman and the abrupt ending line: "She looked back, and she saw. . . !" Since the typical narrators and auditors of "The Boyfriend's Death" themselves like to "park" and may have been alarmed by rumors, strange sights and noises, or automobile emergencies (all intensified in their effects by the audience's knowing other parking legends), the abrupt, unresolved ending leaves open the possibilities of what "really happened."

Urban Legends as Cultural Symbols

Legends can survive in our culture as living narrative folklore if they contain three essential elements: a strong basic story-appeal, a foundation in actual belief, and a meaningful message or "moral." That is, popular stories like "The Boyfriend's Death" are not only engrossing tales, but also "true," or at least so people think, and they teach valuable lessons. Jokes are a living part of oral tradition, despite being fictional and often silly, because of their humor, brevity, and snappy punch lines, but legends are by nature longer, slower, and more serious. Since more effort is needed to tell

and appreciate a legend than a joke, it needs more than just verbal art to
carry it along. Jokes have significant "messages" too, but these tend to be
disguised or implied. People tell jokes primarily for amusement, and they
seldom sense their underlying themes. In legends the primary messages are
quite clear and straightforward; often they take the form of explicit warnings or good examples of "poetic justice." Secondary messages in urban
legends tend to be suggested metaphorically or symbolically; these may
provide deeper criticisms of human behavior or social condition.

People still tell legends, therefore, and other folk take time to listen to   20
them, not only because of their inherent plot interest but because they seem
to convey true, worthwhile, and relevant information, albeit partly in a
subconscious mode. In other words, such stories are "news" presented to
us in an attractive way, with hints of larger meanings. Without this multiple
appeal few legends would get a hearing in the modern world, so filled with
other distractions. Legends survive by being as lively and "factual" as the
television evening news, and, like the daily news broadcasts, they tend to
concern deaths, injuries, kidnappings, tragedies, and scandals. Apparently
the basic human need for meaningful personal contact cannot be entirely
replaced by the mass media and popular culture. A portion of our interest
in what is occurring in the world must be filled by some face-to-face reports
from other human beings.

On a literal level a story like "The Boyfriend's Death" simply warns
young people to avoid situations in which they may be endangered, but at a
more symbolic level the story reveals society's broader fears of people, especially women and the young, being alone and among strangers in the darkened world outside the security of their own home or car. Note that the
young woman in the story (characterized by "her high-heeled shoes and
evening dress") is shown as especially helpless and passive, cowering under
the blanket in the car until she is rescued by men. Such themes recur in various forms in many other urban legends. . . .

In order to be retained in a culture, any form of folklore must fill some
genuine need, whether this be the need for an entertaining escape from reality, or a desire to validate by anecdotal examples some of the culture's ideals
and institutions. For legends in general, a major function has always been
the attempt to explain unusual and supernatural happenings in the natural
world. To some degree this remains a purpose for urban legends, but their
more common role nowadays seems to be to show that the prosaic contemporary scene is capable of producing shocking or amazing occurrences
which may actually have happened to friends or to near-acquaintances but
which are nevertheless explainable in some reasonably logical terms. On
the one hand we want our factual lore to inspire awe, and at the same time
we wish to have the most fantastic tales include at least the hint of a rational explanation and perhaps even a conclusion. Thus an escaped lunatic,
a possibly *real* character, not a fantastic invader from outer space or
Frankenstein's monster, is said to be responsible for the atrocities committed in the gruesome tales that teenagers tell. As sometimes happens in real

life, the car radio gives warning, and the police get the situation back under control. (The policemen's role, in fact, becomes larger and more commanding as the story grows in oral tradition.) Only when the young lovers are still alone and scared are they vulnerable, but society's adults and guardians come to their rescue presently.

In common with brief unverified reports ("rumors"), to which they are often closely related, urban legends gratify our desire to know about and to try to understand bizarre, frightening, and potentially dangerous or embarrassing events that *may* have happened. (In rumors and legends there is always some element of doubt concerning where and when these things *did* occur.) These floating stories appeal to our morbid curiosity and satisfy our sensation-seeking minds that demand gratification through frequent infusions of new information, "sanitized" somewhat by the positive messages. Informal rumors and stories fill in the gaps left by professional news reporting, and these marvelous, though generally false, "true" tales may be said to be carrying the folk-news — along with some editorial matter — from person to person even in today's technological world.

QUESTIONS

1. In your own words, define *urban legend*.
2. Had you ever heard the story of "The Boyfriend's Death" before you read it here? Did you believe it was true? Can you remember the circumstances in which you first heard this legend (or a similar one)? Describe your first encounter with the tale. How does your experience compare with those described by Brunvand?
3. Below is a list of other tales collected by Brunvand. Do you know any stories that might correspond to these titles?

    The Vanishing Hitchhiker
    The Mexican Pet
    The Baby-Sitter and the Man Upstairs
    The Microwaved Pet
    The Toothbrush Story
    Alligators in the Sewers
    The Nude in the RV
    The Kidney Heist

    Briefly describe the stories you have heard. Compare the various versions produced by members of the class. What are the variables in the tale, and what seem to be the common features?
4. Do you know a story that sounds like an urban legend but is true? Can you prove it?
5. Select an urban legend that you have recently heard. Write down the best version of it that you can, and analyze what you have written as an urban legend. That is, explain the features that mark it as an urban legend, and discuss the elements that make it interesting or appealing to you.

6. Can you remember someone who told you something as a "true" story that you now recognize is an urban legend? Write an essay in which you describe that person, report on the legend that he or she told you, and explain to that person that the story he or she told is not true but is an urban legend. If you think that your explanation would not convince the person in question, try to explain why this is so. Describe the resistance you might encounter, and indicate how you might modify your explanation to make it more persuasive.

MAKING CONNECTIONS

1. Compare Brunvand's account of urban legend formation with Edmund O. Wilson's account of narrative formation in "Life Is a Narrative" (p. 736). Describe their similarities and differences.
2. Brunvand writes "And the legends we tell, as with any folklore, reflect many of the hopes, fears, and anxieties of our time" (p. 210). Surely those fears and anxieties today include terrorism. Search the Internet for controversial theories or alternatives to the official narratives about the events of September 11, 2001. Compare one of these alternative versions to the report from the *New York Times* by Serge Schmemann (p. 415). First, describe the major differences between these accounts. Then, perform a reading of the alternative narrative in the way that Brunvand reads urban legends. That is, on a symbolic level, how might you account for the existence of the alternative narrative you have found for the events of September 11? How might you account for its details as it deviates from the account as given by Schmemann?

WHAT HIGH SCHOOL IS

Theodore R. Sizer

*Born in New Haven, Connecticut, in 1932, and educated at Yale
and Harvard, Theodore R. Sizer has been headmaster at Phillips
Academy in Andover, Massachusetts, dean of the Graduate School
of Education at Harvard, and chair of the Education Department
at Brown. He is the author of several influential books on educational reform and American secondary schools, including* Horace's
Hope: What Works for the American High School *(1996),* The Students Are Watching: Schools and the Moral Contract *(1999, with
Nancy Faust Sizer), and, most recently,* The Red Pencil: Convictions from Experience in Education *(2004) and* Keeping School:
Letters to Families from Principals of Two Small Schools *(2004).
The following selection is a chapter from an earlier book,* Horace's
Compromise: The Dilemma of the American High School *(1984),
which reports the results of a study of American high schools
sponsored by the National Association of Independent Schools.*

Mark, sixteen and a genial eleventh-grader, rides a bus to Franklin
High School, arriving at 7:25. It is an Assembly Day, so the schedule is
adapted to allow for a meeting of the entire school. He hangs out with his
friends, first outside school and then inside, by his locker. He carries a pile
of textbooks and notebooks; in all, it weighs eight and a half pounds.

From 7:30 to 8:19, with nineteen other students, he is in Room 304 for
English class. The Shakespeare play being read this year by the eleventh
grade is *Romeo and Juliet*. The teacher, Ms. Viola, has various students in
turn take parts and read out loud. Periodically, she interrupts the (usually
halting) recitations to ask whether the thread of the conversation in the
play is clear. Mark is entertained by the stumbling readings of some of his
classmates. He hopes he will not be asked to be Romeo, particularly if his
current steady, Sally, is Juliet. There is a good deal of giggling in class, and
much attention paid to who may be called on next. Ms. Viola reminds the
class of a test on this part of the play to be given next week.

The bell rings at 8:19. Mark goes to the boys' room, where he sees a
classmate who he thinks is a wimp but who constantly tries to be a buddy.
Mark avoids the leech by rushing off. On the way, he notices two boys engaged in some sort of transaction, probably over marijuana. He pays them
no attention. 8:24. Typing class. The rows of desks that embrace big office
machines are almost filled before the bell. Mark is uncomfortable here: typing class is girl country. The teacher constantly threatens what to Mark is a
humiliatingly female future: "Your employer won't like these erasures."

The minutes during the period are spent copying a letter from a handbook onto business stationery. Mark struggles to keep from looking at his work; the teacher wants him to watch only the material from which he is copying. Mark is frustrated, uncomfortable, and scared that he will not complete his letter by the class's end, which would be embarrassing.

Nine tenths of the students present at school that day are assembled in the auditorium by the 9:18 bell. The dilatory tenth still stumble in, running down aisles. Annoyed class deans try to get the mob settled. The curtains part; the program is a concert by a student rock group. Their electronic gear flashes under the lights, and the five boys and one girl in the group work hard at being casual. Their movements on stage are studiously at three-quarter time, and they chat with one another as though the tumultuous screaming of their schoolmates were totally inaudible. The girl balances on a stool; the boys crank up the music. It is very soft rock, the sanitized lyrics surely cleared with the assistant principal. The girl sings, holding the mike close to her mouth, but can scarcely be heard. Her light voice is tentative, and the lyrics indecipherable. The guitars, amplified, are tuneful, however, and the drums are played with energy.

The students around Mark — all juniors, since they are seated by   5
class — alternately slouch in their upholstered, hinged seats, talking to one another, or sit forward, leaning on the chair backs in front of them, watching the band. A boy near Mark shouts noisily at the microphone-fondling singer, "Bite it . . . ohhh," and the area around Mark explodes in vulgar male laughter, but quickly subsides. A teacher walks down the aisle. Songs continue, to great applause. Assembly is over at 9:46, two minutes early.

9:53 and biology class. Mark was at a different high school last year and did not take this course there as a tenth-grader. He is in it now, and all but one of his classmates are a year younger than he. He sits on the side, not taking part in the chatter that goes on after the bell. At 9:57, the public address system goes on, with the announcements of the day. After a few words from the principal ("Here's today's cheers and jeers . . ." with a cheer for the winning basketball team and a jeer for the spectators who made a ruckus at the gymnasium), the task is taken over by officers of ASB (Associated Student Bodies). There is an appeal for "bat bunnies." Carnations are for sale by the Girls' League. Miss Indian American is coming. Students are auctioning off their services (background catcalls are heard) to earn money for the prom. Nominees are needed for the ballot for school bachelor and school bachelorette. The announcements end with a "thought for the day. When you throw a little mud, you lose a little ground."

At 10:04 the biology class finally turns to science. The teacher, Mr. Robbins, has placed one of several labeled laboratory specimens — some are pinned in frames, others swim in formaldehyde — on each of the classroom's eight laboratory tables. The three or so students whose chairs circle each of these benches are to study the specimen and make notes about it or drawings of it. After a few minutes each group of three will move to another table. The teacher points out that these specimens are of organisms already studied in previous classes. He says that the period-long test set for the following day will involve observing some of these specimens — then to be without labels — and writing an identifying paragraph on each. Mr. Robbins points out that some of the printed labels ascribe the specimens names different from those given in the textbook. He explains that biologists often give several names to the same organism.

The class now falls to peering, writing, and quiet talking. Mr. Robbins comes over to Mark, and in whispered words asks him to carry a requisition form for science department materials to the business office. Mark, because of his "older" status, is usually chosen by Robbins for this kind of errand. Robbins gives Mark the form and a green hall pass to show to any teacher who might challenge him, on his way to the office, for being out of a classroom. The errand takes Mark four minutes. Meanwhile Mark's group is hard at work but gets to only three of the specimens before the bell rings at 10:42. As the students surge out, Robbins shouts a reminder about a "double" laboratory period on Thursday.

Between classes one of the seniors asks Mark whether he plans to be a candidate for schoolwide office next year. Mark says no. He starts to explain. The 10:47 bell rings, meaning that he is late for French class.

There are fifteen students in Monsieur Bates's language class. He hands   10
out tests taken the day before: "*C'est bien fait, Etienne . . . c'est mieux, Marie . . . Tch, tch, Robert . . .*" Mark notes his C+ and peeks at the A− in front of Susanna, next to him. The class has been assigned seats by M. Bates; Mark resents sitting next to prissy, brainy Susanna. Bates starts by asking a student to read a question and give the correct answer. "*James, question un.*" James haltingly reads the question and gives the answer that Bates, now speaking English, says is incomplete. In due course: "*Mark, question cinq.*" Mark does his bit, and the sequence goes on, the eight quiz questions and answers filling about twenty minutes of time.

"Turn to page forty-nine. *Maintenant, lisez après moi . . .*" and Bates reads a sentence and has the class echo it. Mark is embarrassed by this and mumbles with a barely audible sound. Others, like Susanna, keep the decibel count up, so Mark can hide. This I-say-you-repeat drill is interrupted once by the public address system, with an announcement about a meeting for the cheerleaders. Bates finishes the class, almost precisely at the bell, with a homework assignment. The students are to review these sentences for a brief quiz the following day. Mark takes note of the assignment, because he knows that tomorrow will be a day of busy-work in French class. Much though he dislikes oral drills, they are better than the workbook stuff that Bates hands out. Write, write, write, for Bates to throw away, Mark thinks.

11:36. Down to the cafeteria, talking noisily, hanging, munching. Getting to room 104 by 12:17: U.S. history. The teacher is sitting cross-legged on his desk when Mark comes in, heatedly arguing with three students over the fracas that had followed the previous night's basketball game. The teacher, Mr. Suslovic, while agreeing that the spectators from their school certainly were provoked, argues that they should neither have been so obviously obscene in yelling at the opposing cheerleaders nor have allowed Coke cans to be rolled out on the floor. The three students keep saying that "it isn't fair." Apparently they and some others had been assigned "Saturday mornings" (detentions) by the principal for the ruckus.

At 12:34, the argument appears to subside. The uninvolved students, including Mark, are in their seats, chatting amiably. Mr. Suslovic climbs off his desk and starts talking: "We've almost finished this unit, chapters nine and ten . . ." The students stop chattering among themselves and turn toward Suslovic. Several slouch down in their chairs. Some open notebooks. Most have the five-pound textbook on their desks.

Suslovic lectures on the cattle drives, from north Texas to railroads west of St. Louis. He breaks up this narrative with questions ("Why were the railroad lines laid largely east to west?"), directed at nobody in particular and eventually answered by Suslovic himself. Some students take notes. Mark doesn't. A student walks in the open door, hands Mr. Suslovic a list, and starts whispering with him. Suslovic turns from the class and hears out this messenger. He then asks, "Does anyone know where Maggie Sharp is?" Someone answers, "Sick at home"; someone else says, "I thought I saw her at lunch." Genial consternation. Finally Suslovic tells the messenger, "Sorry, we can't help you," and returns to the class: "Now, where were we?" He goes on for some minutes. The bell rings. Suslovic forgets to give the homework assignment.

1:11 and Algebra II. There is a commotion in the hallway: someone's   15
locker is rumored to have been opened by the assistant principal and a narcotics agent. In the five-minute passing time, Mark hears the story three times and three ways. A locker had been broken into by another student. It was Mr. Gregory and a narc. It was the cops, and they did it without Gregory's knowing. Mrs. Ames, the mathematics teacher, has not heard anything about it. Several of the nineteen students try to tell her and start arguing among themselves. "O.K., that's enough." She hands out the day's problem, one sheet to each student. Mark sees with dismay that it is a single, complicated "word" problem about some train that, while traveling at 84 mph, due west, passes a car that was going due east at 55 mph. Mark struggles: Is it $d = rt$ or $t = rd$? The class becomes quiet, writing, while Mrs. Ames writes some additional, short problems on the blackboard. "Time's up." A sigh; most students still writing. A muffled "Shit." Mrs. Ames frowns. "Come on, now." She collects papers, but it takes four minutes for her to corral them all.

"Copy down the problems from the board." A minute passes. "William, try number one." William suggests an approach. Mrs. Ames corrects and cajoles, and William finally gets it right. Mark watches two kids to his right passing notes; he tries to read them, but the handwriting is illegible from his distance. He hopes he is not called on, and he isn't. Only three students are asked to puzzle out an answer. The bell rings at 2:00. Mrs. Ames shouts a homework assignment over the resulting hubbub.

Mark leaves his books in his locker. He remembers that he has homework, but figures that he can do it during English class the next day. He knows that there will be an in-class presentation of one of the *Romeo and Juliet* scenes and that he will not be in it. The teacher will not notice his homework writing, or won't do anything about it if she does.

Mark passes various friends heading toward the gym, members of the basketball teams. Like most students, Mark isn't an active school athlete. However, he is associated with the yearbook staff. Although he is not taking "Yearbook" for credit as an English course, he is contributing photographs. Mark takes twenty minutes checking into the yearbook staff's headquarters (the classroom of its faculty adviser) and getting some assignments of pictures from his boss, the senior who is the photography editor. Mark knows that if he pleases his boss and the faculty adviser, he'll take that editor's post for the next year. He'll get English credit for his work then.

After gossiping a bit with the yearbook staff, Mark will leave school by 2:35 and go home. His grocery market bagger's job is from 4:45 to 8:00, the rush hour for the store. He'll have a snack at 4:30, and his mother will save him some supper to eat at 8:30. She will ask whether he has any homework, and he'll tell her no. Tomorrow, and virtually every other tomorrow, will be the same for Mark, save for the lack of the assembly: each period then will be five minutes longer.

Most Americans have an uncomplicated vision of what secondary education should be. Their conception of high school is remarkably uniform across the country, a striking fact, given the size and diversity of the United States and the politically decentralized character of the schools. This uniformity is of several generations' standing. It has, however, two appearances, each quite different from the other, one of words and the other of practice, a world of political rhetoric and Mark's world.   20

A California high school's general goals, set out in 1979, could serve equally well most of America's high schools, public and private. This school had as its ends:

- Fundamental scholastic achievement . . . to acquire knowledge and share in the traditionally academic fundamentals . . . to develop the ability to make decisions, to solve problems, to reason independently, and to accept responsibility for self-evaluation and continuing self-improvement.
- Career and economic competence . . .
- Citizenship and civil responsibility . . .
- Competence in human and social relations . . .
- Moral and ethical values . . .
- Self-realization and mental and physical health . . .

- Aesthetic awareness . . .
- Cultural diversity . . .[1]

In addition to its optimistic rhetoric, what distinguishes this list is its comprehensiveness. The high school is to touch most aspects of an adolescent's existence — mind, body, morals, values, career. No one of these areas is given especial prominence. School people arrogate to themselves an obligation to all.

An example of the wide acceptability of these goals is found in the courts. Forced to present a detailed definition of "thorough and efficient education," elementary as well as secondary, a West Virginia judge sampled the best of conventional wisdom and concluded that

> there are eight general elements of a thorough and efficient system of education: (a) Literacy, (b) The ability to add, subtract, multiply, and divide numbers, (c) Knowledge of government to the extent the child will be equipped as a citizen to make informed choices among persons and issues that affect his own governance, (d) Self-knowledge and knowledge of his or her total environment to allow the child to intelligently choose life work — to know his or her options, (e) Work-training and advanced academic training as the child may intelligently choose, (f) Recreational pursuits, (g) Interests in all creative arts such as music, theater, literature, and the visual arts, and (h) Social ethics, both behavioral and abstract, to facilitate compatibility with others in this society.[2]

That these eight — now powerfully part of the debate over the purpose and practice of education in West Virginia — are reminiscent of the influential list, "The Seven Cardinal Principles of Secondary Education," promulgated in 1918 by the National Education Association, is no surprise.[3] The rhetoric of high school purpose has been uniform and consistent for decades. Americans agree on the goals for their high schools.

---

[1]Shasta High School, Redding, California. An eloquent and analogous statement, "The Essentials of Education," one stressing explicitly the "interdependence of skills and content" that is implicit in the Shasta High School statement, was issued in 1980 by a coalition of educational associations, Organizations for the Essentials of Education (Urbana, Illinois).

[2]Judge Arthur M. Recht, in his order resulting from *Pauley v. Kelly*, 1979, as reprinted in *Education Week*, May 26, 1982, p. 10. See also, in *Education Week*, January 16, 1983, pp. 21, 24, Jonathan P. Sher, "The Struggle to Fulfill a Judicial Mandate: How Not to 'Reconstruct' Education in W. Va."

[3]Bureau of Education, Department of the Interior, "Cardinal Principles of Secondary Education: A Report of the Commission on the Reorganization of Secondary Education, appointed by the National Education Association," *Bulletin*, no. 35 (Washington: U.S. Government Printing Office, 1918).

That agreement is convenient, but it masks the fact that virtually all the words in these goal statements beg definition. Some schools have labored long to identify specific criteria beyond them; the result has been lists of daunting pseudospecificity and numbing earnestness. However, most leave the words undefined and let the momentum of traditional practice speak for itself. That is why analyzing how Mark spends his time is important: from watching him one uncovers the important purposes of education, the ones that shape practice. Mark's day is similar to that of other high school students across the country, as similar as the rhetoric of one goal statement to others'. Of course, there are variations, but the extent of consistency in the shape of school routine for a large and diverse adolescent population is extraordinary, indicating more graphically than any rhetoric the measure of agreement in America about what one does in high school, and, by implication, what it is for.

The basic organizing structures in schools are familiar. Above all, students are grouped by age (that is, freshman, sophomore, junior, senior), and all are expected to take precisely the same time — around 720 school days over four years, to be precise — to meet the requirements for a diploma. When one is out of his grade level, he can feel odd, as Mark did in his biology class. The goals are the same for all, and the means to achieve them are also similar.

Young males and females are treated remarkably alike; the schools'   25
goals are the same for each gender. In execution, there are differences, as those pressing sex discrimination suits have made educators intensely aware. The students in metalworking classes are mostly male; those in home economics, mostly female. But it is revealing how much less sex discrimination there is in high schools than in other American institutions. For many young women, the most liberated hours of their week are in school.

School is to be like a job: you start in the morning and end in the afternoon, five days a week. You don't get much of a lunch hour, so you go home early, unless you are an athlete or are involved in some special school or extracurricular activity. School is conceived of as the children's workplace, and it takes young people off parents' hands and out of the labor market during prime-time work hours. Not surprisingly, many students see going to school as little more than a dogged necessity. They perceive the day-to-day routine, a Minnesota study reports, as one of "boredom and lethargy." One of the students summarizes: School is "boring, restless, tiresome, puts ya to sleep, tedious, monotonous, pain in the neck."[4]

The school schedule is a series of units of time: the clock is king. The base time block is about fifty minutes in length. Some schools, on what they call modular scheduling, split that fifty-minute block into two or even three

---

[4]Diane Hedin, Paula Simon, and Michael Robin, *Minnesota Youth Poll: Youth's Views on School and School Discipline*, Minnesota Report 184 (1983), Agricultural Experiment Station, University of Minnesota, p. 13.

pieces. Most schools have double periods for laboratory work, especially in the sciences, or four-hour units for the small numbers of students involved in intensive vocational or other work-study programs. The flow of all school activity arises from or is blocked by these time units. "How much time do I have with my kids" is the teacher's key question.

Because there are many claims for those fifty-minute blocks, there is little time set aside for rest between them, usually no more than three to ten minutes, depending on how big the school is and, consequently, how far students and teachers have to walk from class to class. As a result, there is a frenetic quality to the school day, a sense of sustained restlessness. For the adolescents, there are frequent changes of room and fellow students, each change giving tempting opportunities for distraction, which are stoutly resisted by teachers. Some schools play soft music during these "passing times," to quiet the multitude, one principal told me.

Many teachers have a chance for a coffee break. Few students do. In some city schools where security is a problem, students must be in class for seven consecutive periods, interrupted by a heavily monitored twenty-minute lunch period for small groups, starting as early as 10:30 a.m. and running to after 1:00 p.m. A high premium is placed on punctuality and on "being where you're supposed to be." Obviously, a low premium is placed on reflection and repose. The students rush from class to class to collect knowledge. Savoring it, it is implied, is not to be done much in school, nor is such meditation really much admired. The picture that these familiar patterns yield is that of an academic supermarket. The purpose of going to school is to pick things up, in an organized and predictable way, the faster the better.

What is supposed to be picked up is remarkably consistent among all sorts of high schools. Most schools specifically mandate three out of every five courses a student selects. Nearly all of these mandates fall into five areas — English, social studies, mathematics, science, and physical education. On the average, English is required to be taken each year, social studies and physical education three out of the four high school years, and mathematics and science one or two years. Trends indicate that in the mid-eighties there is likely to be an increase in the time allocated to these last two subjects. Most students take classes in these four major academic areas beyond the minimum requirements, sometimes in such special areas as journalism and "yearbook," offshoots of English departments.[5]

Press most adults about what high school is for, and you hear these subjects listed. *High school? That's where you learn English and math and*

30

---

[5]I am indebted to Harold F. Sizer and Lyde E. Sizer for a survey of the diploma requirements of fifty representative secondary schools, completed for *A Study of High Schools*.

that sort of thing. Ask students, and you get the same answer. High school is to "teach" these "subjects."

What is often absent is any definition of these subjects or any rationale for them. They are just there, labels. Under those labels lie a multitude of things. A great deal of material is supposed to be "covered"; most of these courses are surveys, great sweeps of the stuff of their parent disciplines.

While there is often a sequence *within* subjects — algebra before trigonometry, "first-year" French before "second-year" French — there is rarely a coherent relationship or sequence *across* subjects. Even the most logically related matters — reading ability as a precondition for the reading of history books, and certain mathematical concepts or skills before the study of some of physics — are only loosely coordinated, if at all. There is little demand for a synthesis of it all; English, mathematics, and the rest are discrete items, to be picked up individually. The incentive for picking them up is largely through tests and, with success at these, in credits earned.

Coverage within subjects is the key priority. If some imaginative teacher makes a proposal to force the marriage of, say, mathematics and physics or to require some culminating challenges to students to use several objects in the solution of a complex problem, and if this proposal will take "time" away from other things, opposition is usually phrased in terms of what may be thus forgone. If we do that, we'll have to give up colonial history. We won't be able to get to programming. We'll not be able to read *Death of a Salesman.* There isn't time. The protesters usually win out.

The subjects come at a student like Mark in random order, a kaleidoscope of worlds: algebraic formulae to poetry to French verbs to Ping-Pong to the War of the Spanish Succession, all before lunch. Pupils are to pick up these things. Tests measure whether the picking up has been successful. 35

The lack of connection between stated goals, such as those of the California high school cited earlier, and the goals inherent in school practice is obvious and, curiously, tolerated. Most striking is the gap between statements about "self-realization and mental and physical growth" or "moral and ethical values" — common rhetoric in school documents — and practice. Most physical education programs have neither the time nor the focus really to ensure fitness. Mental health is rarely defined. Neither are ethical values, save at the negative extremes, such as opposition to assault or dishonesty. Nothing in the regimen of a day like Mark's signals direct or implicit teaching in this area. The "school boy code" (not ratting on a fellow student) protects the marijuana pusher, and a leechlike associate is shrugged off without concern. The issue of the locker search was pushed aside, as not appropriate for class time.

Most students, like Mark, go to class in groups of twenty to twenty-seven students. The expected attendance in some schools, particularly those in low-income areas, is usually higher, often thirty-five students per class, but high absentee rates push the actual numbers down. About twenty-five per class is an average figure for expected attendance, and the actual numbers are somewhat lower. There are remarkably few students who go to class in groups much larger or smaller than twenty-five.[6]

A student such as Mark sees five or six teachers per day; their differing styles and expectations are part of his kaleidoscope. High school staffs are highly specialized: guidance counselors rarely teach mathematics, mathematics teachers rarely teach English, principals rarely do any classroom instruction. Mark, then, is known a little bit by a number of people, each of whom sees him in one specialized situation. No one may know him as a "whole person" — unless he becomes a special problem or has special needs.

Save in extracurricular or coaching situations, such as in athletics, drama, or shop classes, there is little opportunity for sustained conversation between student and teacher. The mode is a one-sentence or two-sentence exchange: *Mark, when was Grover Cleveland president?* Let's see, was 1890 . . . or something . . . wasn't he the one . . . he was elected twice, wasn't he . . . Yes . . . *Gloria, can you get the dates right?* Dialogue is strikingly absent, and as a result the opportunity of teachers to challenge students' ideas in a systematic and logical way is limited. Given the rushed, full quality of the school day, it can seldom happen. One must infer that careful probing of students' thinking is not a high priority. How one gains (to quote the California school's statement of goals again) "the ability to make decisions, to solve problems, to reason independently, and to accept responsibility for self-evaluation and continuing self-improvement" without being challenged is difficult to imagine. One certainly doesn't learn these things merely from lectures and textbooks.

Most schools are nice places. Mark and his friends enjoy being in   40
theirs. The adults who work in schools generally like adolescents. The academic pressures are limited, and the accommodations to students are substantial. For example, if many members of an English class have jobs after school, the English teacher's expectations for them are adjusted, downward. In a word, school is sensitively accommodating, as long as students are punctual, where they are supposed to be, and minimally dutiful about picking things up from the clutch of courses in which they enroll.

This characterization is not pretty, but it is accurate, and it serves to describe the vast majority of American secondary schools. "Taking subjects" in a systematized, conveyer-belt way is what one does in high school. That this process is, in substantial respects, not related to the rhetorical purposes of education is tolerated by most people, perhaps because they do not really either believe in those ill-defined goals or, in their heart of hearts, believe that schools can or should even try to achieve them. The students are happy taking subjects. The parents are happy, because that's what they did in high

---

[6]Education Research Service, Inc., *Class Size: A Summary of Research* (Arlington, Virginia, 1978); and *Class Size Research: A Critique of Recent Meta-Analyses* (Arlington, Virginia, 1980).

school. The rituals, the most important of which is graduation, remain intact. The adolescents are supervised safely and constructively most of the time, during the morning and afternoon hours, and they are off the labor market. That is what high school is all about.

Questions

1. The first nineteen paragraphs of this essay are a report. What do you think of this report? Given your own experience, how accurate is it? What attitude does the report convey, or is it objective?
2. Paragraph 19 is the conclusion of the report. It ends the story of Mark's day. Does it draw or imply any conclusions from the events reported?
3. How is the explanatory section of the essay (paragraphs 20–41) organized? The first subtopic discussed is the goals of high school. What are the other subtopics?
4. What is the major conclusion of this explanation? To what extent do you agree with the last sentence of the essay and what it implies?
5. How does the report (paragraphs 1–19) function in the explanation that follows? What would be lost if the report were omitted? In considering how the two sections of the essay relate, note especially places where the explanation specifically refers to the report.
6. Your view of high school might be different than Sizer's, or perhaps your high school was different than the one he describes. Write an essay that is organized like Sizer's but that presents your own report and explanation of what school is.
7. Using the basic outline of Sizer's essay, write your own explanation of the workings of some institution — store, family, religious group, club, team, or whatever else you know well. Think of your project in terms of Sizer's title: "What X Is."

Making Connections

How do you suppose Sizer got this information about Mark and "what high school is"? Compare his approach to those of Jane van Lawick-Goodall (p. 395) and Monica M. Moore (p. 486). Which one of these writers comes closest, do you think, to Sizer's method for researching his essay? Explain the resemblances and differences.

YOUR FACE IN LIGHTS:
The Secrets of Cinematography

Alec Wilkinson

*Alec Wilkinson (b. 1952) graduated from Bennington College
with a degree in music. He currently lives in New York City and is
a staff writer for* The New Yorker. *Wilkinson has written seven
books:* Midnights: A Year with the Wellfleet Police *(1982), about a
year he spent as a police officer in a small Cape Cod town;* Moon-
shine: A Life in Pursuit of White Liquor *(1985);* Big Sugar: Seasons in the Cane Fields of Florida *(1989);* The Riverkeeper *(1991);*
A Violent Act *(1993), about a widow who struggles to raise her
two sons after her husband is murdered;* My Mentor: A Young
Writer's Friendship with William Maxwell *(2002), which recalls
Wilkinson's friendship with the novelist and short story writer
William Maxwell, who for forty years was a fiction editor at* The
New Yorker; *and* Mr. Apology and Other Essays *(2003), a collection of profiles, essays, and reporting. Wilkinson has received a
Guggenheim Fellowship, a Robert F. Kennedy Book Award, and
a Lyndhurst Prize. Wilkinson often writes about interesting characters and their relationship to their work. The following essay,
which appeared in* The New Yorker, *describes the lighting expertise of British cinematographer Roger Pratt.*

Movies intently depict the play of emotion on the human face. "Unless
you're simply destroying things, eighty per cent of what we do is close-ups
or medium shots of the human face," a cameraman told me. Movie cameras customarily record their subjects at an angle. An object filmed from
straight in front appears to be flat. A cube from straight on is a square. A
movement to the left or right reveals a second side. A shift up or down
shows another. No angle can include more than three sides. Absent the effect of light, the vantage that shows the greatest complexity is typically the
most flattering.

Light is to movies what perspective is to paintings — the device that
persuades the eye that a flat and vertical surface is also deep. A face filmed
from directly in front will also seem to be flat, especially if the light falls on
it evenly. This circumstance is usually favorable for an older actress, because it obscures imperfections; the cheeks become smooth. To be filmed indoors sympathetically, a face needs to be lit by more than one light. A cameraman will often place a small light called a catch light close to the
camera's lens. The catch light will be reflected in the actress's eyes. A face

with no light in the eyes will seem remote, abstracted, the face of someone it is difficult to feel a connection with.

Cameramen provide tension by means of the angle at which they light a character. We absorb images from left to right, the same way we read. Looking at a face that is lit from the left side is "restful," another camera-man told me. Lighting against the grain—from the right, that is—intro-duces a discordance. Light from below distorts a face: unnatural shadows appear; horror films and monster movies often have bottom lighting. Light from the top makes a face appear gaunt. The eyes go dark. The actor will look like a figure in a mental institution or maybe as if he were dangerous. To make Marlon Brando appear threatening and enigmatic in "The Godfa-ther," the cameraman lit him from above. Among the other specialty lights specific to the face are kick lights and hair lights. Kick lights are used from behind an actor to show the grain and shape of the face. They are com-monly used in he-man movies, to illuminate sweat on an actor's cheeks; Sylvester Stallone uses kick lights a lot. A cameraman who is filming an actor with dark hair against a dark background and who doesn't want to see only the actor's face can use a hair light to make his hair stand out. In the studio days, cameramen used to light the faces of stars with more inten-sity than anyone else's. If there was a hundred-watt bulb on one actor, there would be a hundred-and-ten-watt bulb on the star.

To observe the effect of light on an actress's face, one might note in "The End of the Affair" the difference between Julianne Moore's appear-ance in the grip of sexual excitement and as a pallid figure on her deathbed. The cameraman was a British cinematographer named Roger Pratt. Pratt is admired for his perhaps unexampled ability to light the faces of women and photograph them to their best advantage.

"A large part of cinema is photographing women," David Hare told me, "and yet there are plenty of cameramen who can't do it." Hare and Pratt worked together, in 1987, on Hare's film "Paris by Night." "In 'Paris by Night,' we had Charlotte Rampling, about whom it is said that it is im-possible to take an unflattering picture," Hare went on. "Well, it *is* possible to take an unflattering picture of her. Roger playing with the light on her face was like a child completely engaged."

Chuck Finch, the gaffer whom Pratt works with most often, says, "When Roger lights a woman, he looks to see if she has any imperfections, and he corrects them by using lights. We've lit some really top-looking women, and he always does a really good job."

Pratt was at work last summer—in Malta, England, and Mexico—on "Troy," which stars Brad Pitt and is based mostly on the Iliad. It is being directed by Wolfgang Petersen. When I asked Petersen about Pratt's ability to light faces, he said, "So much goes through the eyes. Roger takes care of that, especially with Diane Kruger, who plays Helen. To light her in a way so that she comes across not only as beautiful but also as soulful is essen-tial for this picture. You can take fifty thousand soldiers and hundreds of

5

ships, but if you are not really moved by what the actors do it doesn't succeed."

Before lighting an actress's face, Pratt asks which side of her profile she prefers to have filmed. A producer on his first movie told him, "Light the women well, and you'll have a long career."

What I know about cinematography comes mostly from talking with cameramen such as Emmanuel Lubezki, Allen Daviau, John Bailey, Roger Deakins, and John Toll; from reading "Painting with Light," by the cameraman John Alton; and from spending eight days in Mexico with Pratt.

"Troy" was filmed outside Cabo San Lucas, at the southern end of Baja   10 California. From the hotels by the ocean where the cast and crew stayed, you drove through the town, past car washes and gas stations and cantinas and stores and empty lots with wrecked cars, along the coast several miles to a rutty dirt road through a shacky neighborhood of tin-roofed cinder-block houses, some with red-and-black shawls for doors, past dirt yards scuffed to the texture of a floor, past scrawny dogs, and children with coal-black hair, past a little barbed-wire gate with a skinny young man who looked proud of his policeman's hat and baggy guard's uniform, then through a landscape of cactus and lizards and snakes to the set. Pratt would arrive at the set each morning except Sunday at seven and have breakfast. Work began at seven-thirty and lasted until the light failed. To be on schedule, it was necessary that each day produce three or four minutes of useful film.

The Trojan Wall, a few hundred feet across, with huge doors in the center, had been built on gently sloping ground about a mile back from the ocean, and the Temple of Apollo had been built on the beach. Bulldozers swept the beach clear of footprints. The Trojan Wall was held up from behind by scaffolding. In front of the wall were the actors and the cameras and tents for makeup and wardrobe and first aid and catering and taking care of the actors' spears and shields. Behind the wall were huge tents for the cafeteria and more wardrobe and makeup and the actors' trailers and the parking lot.

The cast included a thousand Mexicans dressed as soldiers, who were filmed at some distance, and two hundred and fifty-two men from a sports club in Bulgaria, who were employed for closer engagements. The Bulgarians were taller than the Mexicans and more imposing. Everyone liked to be finished with his routine at the hotel health club before the Bulgarians arrived. By the time all the soldiers were in costume and had had their watches removed, it was usually around eleven. Much of the soldiers' day was spent standing in ranks, about fifty across. To fill out the ranks, dummies were placed among them. Mexican men had been hired to supply the soldiers with water. The men carried water cans on their backs, stacks of plastic cups in their hands, and black trash bags attached to their belts. When there was a water break, they sprinted toward the soldiers and travelled along the ranks. The soldiers called out, "Water, water!" On longer breaks, the soldiers sat down in the sun, their eyes turned to slits, and sometimes they slept. At lunchtime, they left their spears and helmets and breastplates in the field, as if they had fled in disarray.

When the picture is finished, thousands of soldiers will appear on the screen, the bulk of them animated. Each time Pratt had the camera pointed at a section of the set that was unoccupied by soldiers, he and Wolfgang Petersen would confer with Nick Davis, the man in charge of special digital effects, about the difficulty and expense of filling the empty part of the screen. Occasionally, Pratt and Petersen would shoot a scene, study it on video monitors, and decide to shoot it again. Pratt would ask Petersen, "Same thing?" and Petersen would say, "Same thing, only more expensive," meaning that the shot would be wider, including more space that would have to be filled.

Pratt usually stood beside the cameras and the actors, and Petersen stood or sat in a tent fifteen or twenty feet away, watching the video screens that showed each camera's shots. "This video business is fantastic," Pratt told me one day. "It's altered the way things are done. The director used to stand by the actors and have eye contact. Now some directors just shout from the tent, 'Act better!'"

The tents were grouped together, like a bazaar. Waiting to be called, the actors stood beneath them, occasionally brushed and stroked and fussed over like show dogs. To prepare a scene, a sword-fight, say, a crew would bring a camera from the tents, paying cable across the field like fishing line. The stunt doubles would take the place of the actors so that the cameras could frame them. Then two men would carry over the principal camera, setting it down on a piece of fabric, like a portable altar, and Pratt would lean forward and look into the lens.

Pratt is fifty-six. He was born in Leicester, in the Midlands. His father was a vicar, who taught himself Greek and Latin, and showed religious films in his church during Lent. To Pratt's mother, the honorable professions were teaching, the law, medicine, and social work. Pratt was not a disappointment to her, but she always hoped that eventually he would find a proper job. Since 1980, he has made thirty-two movies, including "Brazil," "Mona Lisa," "Batman," "The Fisher King," "Shadowlands," "Twelve Monkeys," "Iris," and "Harry Potter and the Chamber of Secrets."

Lynda Obst produced "The Fisher King," in 1991, which was directed by Terry Gilliam. "In the late eighties and early nineties, you had the camera operator as star," she told me. "There were lots of dazzling cinematographers. You could always see their work, you could see the camera move. Wow, look at the camera move! There were also the star lighting cameramen—they'll relight the sky. They'll light for hours and hours to make everything look like the magic hour. What I saw with Roger is that he could give you the same dazzling effects, and the same perspectives, without the extra time and without showing the moves. He will give to an hour-and-a-half lighting setup the same magic quality that takes others all day to deliver, and he has tricks up his sleeve to give compelling magical effects in a minute. He can get all the beauty without having been the one who's running the set.

"Some of these techniques he's sidestepping are really expensive," she went on. "Roger is like Mr. Science. He's innovative, and he doesn't try to make himself look like a genius. A lot of guys don't like him for doing this, because he demystifies the craft, but he doesn't care about that. The mystery is within him."

Pratt has an oval face, like an upside-down egg, and a fringe of reddish-brown hair. He has a thin beard. His skin is pale. Under the Mexican sun, his face had turned red, as if he had been climbing stairs. At the corners of his eyes are spiky creases that remained white — they looked like war paint. His carriage is so erect that it is as if his arms had been pinned back. Around the set, he wore shorts and a short-sleeved shirt with a floppy hat and a red bandanna around his neck. When he had to speak to a person some distance from where he was, he unfurled a small black umbrella. Standing beside the person, he held the umbrella over both of them. When we talked, he would usually sit at an angle to me, and look at me askance, which gave the impression of a bird or an animal leaving open a path for escape. He wasn't evasive. He simply seemed perplexed that anyone was interested. Terry Gilliam told me, "Roger finds it embarrassing to talk about what he does. The big names make quite a deal of it, but that's not like him. He stays just under the radar. He does his work. If he's anything, he's too self-deprecating."

"The job is such a practical one, really," Pratt told me. "That's always   20
been most in my mind. It's such an expensive hobby, making films, an expensive hobby and full of very strong egos all around the line, so the idea of living like a painter who could struggle in a garret and do exactly what you want if you could live off a dollar a day goes out the window. Pictures run on the iron rails, everybody serves the beast. They have stopped films in the first couple of weeks, but it's highly unusual. It's typically an unstoppable machine that every director is striving to ride. All the pressures and interests are at stake. Unlike writing a novel or painting a picture, this work has nothing self-motivated and controlling about it. I'm just trying to ease off from the idea that I could turn up on a set and control the way things look, according to my personal aesthetic."

Pratt is fond of lighting techniques used in black-and-white movies — the employment, that is, of light to convey mood and to separate objects from each other. In a black-and-white movie, a man in a dark suit against a dark background would be lost. To be seen, he would have to be lit from behind, so that light appears as a border on his shoulders and arms. In a color movie, a cameraman would probably light the suit, making it brighter than what was behind the man. "All it's about is that it's a two-dimensional medium, isn't it, film?" Pratt said. "To make it three-dimensional, there are tricks of lighting and lenses and where you photograph from. Picking out objects one against another would seem to be easy, but I would rather do it by tonal separation. The black-and-white sky has tones of gray from white to black — that's all you have to play with. Black-and-white photography got to such heights and then color came in, and it's as if people forgot all they had learned."

Black-and-white lighting techniques were abandoned because color film initially needed so much more light to register an image than black-and-white film did. In early color films, in "Singin' in the Rain," for example, there are so many lights being used that when several characters come together in the center of the image there are shadows all over the place. The most unnatural film lighting is employed by television comedies. The set is usually so thoroughly lit that there are no shadows at all. It is impossible to tell where the light is coming from. Along with many other cameramen, Pratt likes having one source of light and one shadow, the way the sun and the full moon work. His idea of perfect light is the kind in the painting by Georges de La Tour, the seventeenth-century French painter, that depicts a man sitting at a table with a candle on it. "The light comes from the center of the picture and falls off toward the edges," Pratt told me, "All the references are absolutely right. The candle as La Tour painted it would do its own work — he could observe its effects and copy them. For us, it's not so easy; it means a big lamp belting from somewhere up near the ceiling. If you use candlelight, you get a flame, a hugely underexposed candle, and a fairly underexposed image of the people around it.

"The trouble with the eye is it's fixed to the brain," he went on. "It's very sophisticated in terms of focus and what it's reading. When an eye looks at a face, it has a brain reference for the tone and color it should have. If you were standing in a supermarket with fluorescent lights above you, your eye would compare what it sees with all the other images of the kind it has seen before and is familiar with. If you put a camera in there, everyone you photographed would be green, because of the nature of fluorescent light. A camera is a much blunter instrument, without an inventory of references."

According to Pratt, moonlight is the most challenging fabrication that appears commonly in movies. "It's so difficult to achieve that cameramen are sometimes judged by their ability to simulate it," he says. One reason moonlight is difficult is that it involves creating a circumstance that is contrary to fact. In a room in a movie where moonlight comes through a window, we see dark shadows and soft colors. The light must be dark enough to suggest night but also contain sufficient illumination so that what needs to be seen can be seen. In a real room lit by the moon, we see mostly in black-and-white. On a huge landscape, the light, to be convincing, must fall with the same intensity on an actor in the foreground as it does on the trees or the hills or the sand dunes in the background. Unless intercepted by clouds, actual moonlight is uniform.

Moonlight cannot easily be slipped into a movie. It can't be subtle or peripheral. It pervades the frame. It insists that we take note of it. Because we have seen the approximations of it often enough, the conclusion we arrive at is not "That's moonlight" but "That's moonlight in a movie." Perhaps by the equator the full moon glows resonantly enough so that one could use it to film, but it doesn't anywhere else. Movie moonlight is usually a blue light that is intentionally cold and uniform — that is, not filled in — and with the shadows left as shadows instead of being lit for definition. In the least artfully lit rooms, someone turns off the lights and the room becomes brighter than it was when the lights were on.

Moonlight in a movie requires more equipment than any other conventional effect. It is most often created using enormous lights on cranes some distance from the set, perhaps a hundred yards. When the area to be lit is capacious, the lights are sometimes a quarter mile away from the far reaches of the set. The lights most widely used to replicate moonlight are called Musco lights. Musco lights were invented to light stadiums and car racetracks that had no permanent illumination.

Twenty-five years ago, it was very difficult to duplicate moonlight mechanically. It had to be done in the laboratory. Moonlight scenes in old Westerns, for example, would be shot during the day and underexposed. The process is called "day for night." Day for night is still used occasionally, to save money or for some other practical reason. A practical reason to use day for night might be to film a big landscape that would require too many lights or a moonlit scene on the ocean. You can't really put a crane and Musco lights out on the ocean, not cheaply, anyway. Filming day for night involves using enormous amounts of light to overcome the effect of the sun on the actors' faces, to make the light appear even, that is. Sometimes so much light is pumped onto the actors' faces to compensate that it becomes painful. They wear contact lenses that have been darkened to resemble sunglasses.

The other nighttime effect that Pratt often replicates is firelight. "Troy" has a lot of torchlit scenes, which, along with the moonlit scenes, were filmed in Malta. "Harry Potter and the Chamber of Secrets" also has a lot of torchlit scenes. Pratt describes it as "a very flambeaux movie." He and his crew produce the twitchy quality of firelight by means of a device they call a flame box, a strobe light operated according to a computer program written by Pratt and Chuck Finch with the help of an assistant. Pratt told me that Finch understood more of the technical elements of the flame box. When I asked Finch how it worked, he looked at me as if I were simple and said, "I can't tell you that, can I. Then everyone would know."

Cameramen have traditionally been tinkerers, gadget guys, back-yard rocket scientists. They like refining ideas — "What if you take this light and put it on the back of a truck, or make it hydraulic, or fix a camera on a crane and work it with remote controls?" They like savoring a problem that requires a novel technical solution. When one of them stumbles on a new procedure or device, they all notice. Pretty much every cameraman who saw "Rocky" in the theatre noted the long shot in which Sylvester Stallone climbs the steps of the museum and turns and looks back at where he came from. No camera they were aware of could manage such a shot. A camera on a crane or a dolly could follow Stallone up the steps, but once he turned around the track would show, and no cameraman running alongside Stallone with a handheld camera could keep the camera level. The shot had been made with a Steadicam, which was invented in Philadelphia by a cameraman named Garrett Brown. Brown was determined to find a way to walk around with a camera and make it as stable as a camera on a dolly.

Cameramen also appreciate accidental discoveries. Filming Robert Blake 30 during "In Cold Blood," Conrad Hall moved lights around while Blake rehearsed a scene in which, the night before his execution, he recalls his father to a priest. Blake, in shackles, is standing beside a window. It is raining. Hall was trying to find the best means of lighting the rain against the window when he noticed that the shadows of the water running down the windowpane appeared on Blake's cheek and made Blake look as if he were weeping. One of the many cameramen who called Hall to ask how he had managed the effect was Allen Daviau. Years later, Daviau, filming "The Color Purple," had a scene in which Whoopi Goldberg's character was sweeping the floor while engaged in a melancholy reverie about another character. "It's day, not night," Daviau told me, "and we're filming in color, not black-and-white, but I used the reflection of the water on her face. It just felt right to quote him."

Unless a scene includes a crowd, there are almost always more people behind the camera than on the screen. It is also a peculiarity of the movies that even the simplest effect usually requires a great deal of equipment to bring it about. Early in "The Grapes of Wrath," Henry Fonda walks through the door of an abandoned house at night. He lights a match. The match appears to be the source of light that illuminates his face and the spooky room as he examines it. In the estimation of the cameraman who described the scene to me, the effect involved perhaps "twenty electricians and twenty grips and about a dozen things happening in about a second and a half — switches being thrown, dimmers applied, lights being turned on and off, and some kind of flame."

The way the cameraman lights and films an actor conveys to the audience an impression of the character. One cameraman described this to me as underscoring an actor's performance by giving him "a hallmark look. You can then introduce him later in a picture and the audience will immediately know who he is." He said that he gives a signature look to a character by observing how the actor moves and by, so far as is possible, lighting him with a consistency, perhaps even placing him often in the same part of the frame: in the foreground if he is an aggressive figure, or perhaps in the middle distance, with space around him, if he is passive, or from slightly below if he is meant to be a looming and threatening presence. By using a consistent light on a character and then changing it, a cameraman can imply that something has changed in the character's mind, that he has perhaps reached a decision and means to behave differently. Has he always been lit from the right side, and is he now lit from the left? Has he always appeared on the right side of the frame and is he now on the left? Did he always appear to be in brighter light and therefore less mysterious? Even an astute observer is not likely to register the change for what it is, a technical matter, but the effect it conveys will still be felt by the audience.

Any choice a cameraman makes must work within the context of the picture, otherwise the labor will show. If the frame is overdone, is too lush or too pointed in its references, the film will advance slowly. A movie's unfolding also has something to do with the way the frame is occupied. A cameraman "has a responsibility to use all parts of the screen, to give the eye a rhythm of change," one of them told me. Too little variation and the movie will seem static.

One night, I had dinner with Pratt at a French restaurant in the hills above Cabo San Lucas. I asked about the films in his father's church.

"'Fact and Faith' films, they were called," he said. "Made in the States,   35
I think. Miracles. They were quite frightening, really. They had a kind of scientific bent — 'If the world is like this, and contains this and this, then that would mean having a God.' Some were medical — 'Isn't it wonderful the body is so complicated, it could only be so because of God.' Very expensively produced, might have been Mormon. The most amazing were ones about the life of Christ. Seeing a man rise from the dead, that was awe-inspiring, really.

"What impressed me most of all is that a mechanical piece of equipment would turn up in the church, along with a piece of film in a tin, and when they were put together, and the lights were turned off, they came to life. How could one add up to the other? How does that series of images translate into something you have an emotion for, especially those films which were upsetting, with people dying and rising again?"

Pratt ordered a Mexican beer, and it sounded really good, so I asked for one, too. "My mother always thought that an hour-and-a-half film took an hour and a half to make," he said. "Till her dying day, she could never figure out what I did with the rest of it."

A waiter took our orders. "My father was a bit of a showman himself," Pratt went on. "I can't think of any other vicars who had films in their church. He was popular and filled a church regularly, which was good, then not so good, because that meant they sent him on to another church, which needed to be resurrected. We had to move from a bucolic village to an inner city. My nought to eight was spent in a country parsonage with a garden and chickens and next door a farmer who plowed with horses. We moved to a very spooky Victorian vicarage in the middle of a bad area, which was a huge blow.

"I went to church as a child, but it wasn't that I was interested in church so much as I identified it as a family effort. It was like you might go help out your father in his job if he was a carpenter, carry him tools on the ladder. School was six days a week, and Sunday was get up and help Dad in the choir or wherever you were needed.

"I was about twenty-one when he died. He had what you call demen-   40
tia. He was still in his job, and he'd always been very good at preaching; he just used notes, he always could recite the services, and then he started faltering and that's what gave Mother a clue.

"He had really fought hard and long to educate himself, so education was everything to him, and anything less than excellence was unacceptable. In comparison to my brothers, I wasn't a good student. My elder brother, who was a linguist, was a very good pianist as well; there was talk of his pursuing it on the stage. What I was good at is the sciences, but somehow or other the artistic life took hold of me."

I asked Pratt what an objective description of his abilities might be. He thought for a moment. "It's in the area — it could be good, it could be bad — of trying to get the best out of the film for the director," he said. Then he shook his head. "That's too vague," he went on. "There's some D.P.s who embody their aesthetic on whatever film they work on. Sets have to be redesigned, colors changed, costumes changed, schedules changed. When I worked with Terry Gilliam, I had so much faith in what he wanted to do that I struggled to find what he wanted; I wished to fulfill the dream he had, because I knew it was a good dream, as quick as possible."

Pratt shrugged. "People do have the most flowery language to talk about cinematography, the art of it," he said, "but for me there are many problems on a film that have nothing to do with theories of color or highfalutin aesthetics. Because my job is concerned with big lumps of lights and metal cameras and laboratories, it's something that makes half of me very pragmatic; it's the opposite of artistic. I look at myself as a technician. A lot of my time is spent in a chemical factory. That's what a photographic lab is, if you've ever been in one. In England, I would go to the lab early in the morning, before we shoot, to see what the film looks like. It's all dripping chemicals and mixers and trays and tubes everywhere. Photography relies on science. Photography is science, isn't it? Photographs, they're really just chemicals in labs, aren't they? Lights on paper. Images in silver halide. Celluloid. But they turn into live things, like the projector in my father's church, which was inert but had such an effect to convey."

The waiter put the beer on the table, and Pratt sat forward. "Lazarus rising from the dead," he said. "That left a frightening impression."

QUESTIONS

1. A film theorist would say that Roger Pratt was manipulating "cinematic apparatus which participates in the psychic and social construction of spectators whose subjectivity is then reconfirmed by belief in the image."[1] How would Pratt describe what he does? (And what is his opinion of cinema theory?)

---

[1]Philip Rosen, *Narrative Apparatus, Ideology* (New York: Columbia UP, 1986), p. 283.

2. In paragraphs 17–18, Lynda Obst, producer of *The Fisher King*, describes how Pratt is able "to give compelling magical effects in a minute.
   . . . Roger is like Mr. Science. He's innovative, and he doesn't try to
   make himself look like a genius. A lot of guys don't like him for doing
   this, because he demystifies the craft, but he doesn't care about that. The
   mystery is within him." How would you describe "the mystery" that
   Obst praises? You might first think about your reactions as a spectator
   of a film you especially liked, and why. How might Pratt describe his
   "mystery"?

3. Consider Wilkinson's arrangement of his material. How does he introduce Roger Pratt, his subject? What purpose does the section on shooting *Troy* serve? How much does he learn from Pratt, who, according to
   Terry Gilliam, "finds it embarrassing to talk about what he does" (paragraph 19)? Why does Wilkinson place Pratt's description of his boyhood
   and the effect of his father's showing of "Fact and Faith" films at the end?

4. Describe the effect that those "Faith and Fact" films had on Pratt's
   choice of a career.

5. After having absorbed the "secrets of cinematography" presented here,
   go see a film and look for some of the effects described. For example,
   how is the hero or heroine given "a hallmark look" (paragraph 32)?
   Make notes as you watch, and write up a description of the effects you
   noticed.

MAKING CONNECTIONS

In his essay "Metapsychological Approaches to the Impression of Reality in
the Cinema," film scholar Jean-Louis Baudry uses the parable of Plato's
Cave (see "The Cave," p. 241) to make "it reveal, from a considerable historic distance, the approximate construct of the cinematographic apparatus. In other words, a same apparatus was responsible for the invention of
the cinema." Consider Plato as cameraman. How would you describe his
lighting effects and their purpose in Roger Pratt's terms?

THE CAVE

Plato

*Plato (c. 427–347 BCE), the student of Socrates and teacher of
Aristotle, is the most revered thinker in Western civilization. As
Alfred North Whitehead stated, "All of Western philosophy is but
a footnote to Plato. . . . [H]is shadow falls over all of Western
thought." Most of the historically significant issues with which
philosophy has been concerned — the nature of being, the question of how we know things, the purposes of right action, the
structure of an ordered society, the meaning of love and beauty —
were issues that he raised. Plato's signature work was his concept
of idealism — the doctrine of a permanent realm of eternal Forms
that shape our mutable, material world. Idealism developed in
reaction to the Sophists, who claimed their science of language
could lead to the truth. Plato, however, thought it dangerous to
suppose that the highest realities — Truth, Goodness, Beauty —
could have the flickering impermanence of human words. Plato
believed that language, even matter, could be shaped to cheat
and deceive. Because he mistrusted writing, Plato's own famous
works, namely* The Republic *and* Ion, *are written not as treatises
but as dialogues with Socrates. This has, however, led to problems
of interpretation and consistency. Nonetheless, these two works
have held up as two of the most important and engaging works in
philosophical thinking.*

*"The Cave," perhaps the best-known of Plato's allegories, is pre-
sented as a story and then interpreted by the questioner. It appears
at the start of Book VII of* The Republic. *The following version was
translated by Paul Shorey and published in 1961.*

Next, said I, compare our nature in respect of education and its lack to
such an experience as this. Picture men dwelling in a sort of subterranean
cavern with a long entrance open to the light on its entire width. Conceive
them as having their legs and necks fettered from childhood, so that they
remain in the same spot, able to look forward only, and prevented by the
fetters from turning their heads. Picture further the light from a fire burning
higher up and at a distance behind them, and between the fire and the prisoners and above them a road along which a low wall has been built, as the
exhibitors of puppet shows have partitions before the men themselves,
above which they show the puppets.

All that I see, he said.

See also, then, men carrying past the wall implements of all kinds that rise above the wall, and human images and shapes of animals as well, wrought in stone and wood and every material, some of these bearers presumably speaking and others silent.

A strange image you speak, of, he said, and strange prisoners.

Like to us, I said. For, to begin with, tell me do you think that these   5
men would have seen anything of themselves or of one another except the shadows cast from the fire on the wall of the cave that fronted them?

How could they, he said, if they were compelled to hold their heads unmoved through life?

And again, would not the same be true of the objects carried past them?

Surely.

If then they were able to talk to one another, do you not think that they would suppose that in naming the things that they saw they were naming the passing objects?

Necessarily.   10

And if their prison had an echo from the wall opposite them, when one of the passers-by uttered a sound, do you think that they would suppose anything else than the passing shadow to be the speaker?

By Zeus, I do not, said he.

Then in every way such prisoners would deem reality to be nothing else than the shadows of the artificial objects.

Quite inevitably, he said.

Consider, then, what would be the manner of the release and healing   15
from these bonds and this folly if in the course of nature something of this sort should happen to them. When one was freed from his fetters and compelled to stand up suddenly and turn his head around and walk and to lift up his eyes to the light, and in doing all this felt pain and, because of the dazzle and glitter of the light, was unable to discern the objects whose shadows he formerly saw, what do you suppose would be his answer if someone told him that what he had seen before was all a cheat and an illusion, but that now, being nearer to reality and turned toward more real things, he saw more truly? And if also one should point out to him each of the passing objects and constrain him by questions to say what it is, do you not think that he would be at a loss and that he would regard what he formerly saw as more real than the things now pointed out to him?

Far more real, he said.

And if he were compelled to look at the light itself, would not that pain his eyes, and would he not turn away and flee to those things which he is able to discern and regard them as in very deed more clear and exact than the objects pointed out?

It is so, he said.

And if, said I, someone should drag him thence by force up the ascent which is rough and steep, and not let him go before he had drawn him out into the light of the sun, do you not think that he would find it painful to be

THE CAVE

so haled along, and would chafe at it, and when he came out into the light, that his eyes would be filled with its beams so that he would not be able to see even one of the things that we call real?

Why, no, not immediately, he said.   20

Then there would be need of habituation, I take it, to enable him to see the things higher up. And at first he would most easily discern the shadows and, after that, the likenesses or reflections in water of men and other things, and later, the things themselves, and from these he would go on to contemplate the appearances in the heavens and heaven itself, more easily by night, looking at the light of the stars and the moon, than by day the sun and the sun's light.

Of course.

And so, finally, I suppose, he would be able to look upon the sun itself and see its true nature, not by reflections in water or phantasms of it in an alien setting, but in and by itself in its own place.

Necessarily, he said.

And at this point he would infer and conclude that this it is that pro-   25
vides the seasons and the courses of the year and presides over all things in the visible region, and is in some sort the cause of all these things that they had seen.

Obviously, he said, that would be the next step.

Well then, if he recalled to mind his first habitation and what passed for wisdom there, and his fellow bondsmen, do you not think that he would count himself happy in the change and pity them?

He would indeed.

And if there had been honors and commendations among them which they bestowed on one another and prizes for the man who is quickest to make out the shadows as they pass and best able to remember their customary precedences, sequences, and coexistences, and so most successful in guessing at what was to come, do you think he would be very keen about such rewards, and that he would envy and emulate those who were honored by these prisoners and lorded it among them, or that he would feel with Homer and greatly prefer while living on earth to be serf of another, a landless man, and endure anything rather than opine with them and live that life?

Yes, he said, I think that he would choose to endure anything rather than such a life.   30

And consider this also, said I. If such a one should go down again and take his old place would he not get his eyes full of darkness, thus suddenly coming out of the sunlight?

He would indeed.

Now if he should be required to contend with these perpetual prisoners in "evaluating" these shadows while his vision was still dim and before his eyes were accustomed to the dark — and this time required for habituation would not be very short — would he not provoke laughter, and would it not be said of him that he had returned from his journey aloft with his eyes ruined and that it was not worth while even to attempt the ascent? And if it were possible to lay hands on and to kill the man who tried to release them and lead them up, would they not kill him?

They certainly would, he said.

This image then, dear Glaucon, we must apply as a whole to all that   35
has been said, likening the region revealed through sight to the habitation of the prison, and the light of the fire in it to the power of the sun. And if you assume that the ascent and the contemplation of the things above is the soul's ascension to the intelligible region, you will not miss my surmise, since that is what you desire to hear. But God knows whether it is true. But, at any rate, my dream as it appears to me is that in the region of the known the last thing to be seen and hardly seen is the idea of good, and that when seen it must needs point us to the conclusion that this is indeed the cause for all things of all that is right and beautiful, giving birth in the visible world to light, and the author of light and itself in the intelligible world being the authentic source of truth and reason, and that anyone who is to act wisely in private or public must have caught sight of this.

I concur, he said, so far as I am able.

Come then, I said, and join me in this further thought, and do not be surprised that those who have attained to this height are not willing to occupy themselves with the affairs of men, but their souls ever feel the upward urge and the yearning for that sojourn above. For this, I take it, is likely if in this point too the likeness of our image holds.

Yes, it is likely.

And again, do you think it at all strange, said I, if a man returning from divine contemplations to the petty miseries of men cuts a sorry figure and appears most ridiculous, if, while still blinking through the gloom, and before he has become sufficiently accustomed to the environing darkness, he is compelled, in courtrooms or elsewhere to contend about the shadows of justice or the images that cast the shadows and to wrangle in debate about the notions of these things in the minds of those who have never seen justice itself?

It would be by no means strange, he said.   40

But a sensible man, I said, would remember that there are two distinct disturbances of the eyes arising from two causes, according as the shift is from light to darkness or from darkness to light, and, believing that the same thing happens to the soul too, whenever he saw a soul perturbed and unable to discern something, he would not laugh unthinkingly, but would observe whether coming from a brighter life its vision was obscured by the unfamiliar darkness, or whether the passage from the deeper dark of ignorance into a more luminous world and the greater brightness had dazzled its vision. And so he would deem the one happy in its experience and way of life and pity the other, and if it pleased him to laugh at it, his laughter would be less laughable than that at the expense of the soul that had come down from the light above.

That is a very fair statement, he said.

Then, if this is true, our view of these matters must be this, that education is not in reality what some people proclaim it to be in their professions. What they aver is that they can put true knowledge into a soul that does not possess it, as if they were inserting vision into blind eyes.

They do indeed, he said.

But our present argument indicates, said I, that the true analogy for this   45 indwelling power in the soul and the instrument whereby each of us apprehends is that of an eye that could not be converted to the light from the darkness except by turning the whole body. Even so this organ of knowledge must be turned around from the world of becoming together with the entire soul, like the scene-shifting periactus in the theater, until the soul is able to endure the contemplation of essence and the brightest region of being. And this, we say, is the good, do we not?

QUESTIONS

1. In this well-known passage from Plato's *Republic*, Socrates uses an extended analogy to explain his fundamental ideas concerning the illusory nature of human experience versus the truth to be found through "the soul's ascension to the intelligible region." To help yourself visualize the analogy, examine the illustration that is included with the text, and see how closely it squares with your understanding of the scene. Are there any details in Plato that are missing or misrepresented in the drawing?

2. In what ways are human beings like chained prisoners in a cave, able to see only the shadows of carved images of things? Why is their delusion not remediable by simply releasing them from the chains that impede their accurate perception of things?

3. Given that Socrates puts so much emphasis on the accurate versus inaccurate perception of things, how do you account for his statement "likening the region revealed through sight to the habitation of the prison"? How, one might ask, are we imprisoned by our eyes, by our visual perceptions? What, after all, could be more liberating than to see things clearly with our own eyes?

4. Compare and contrast life in the cave with the situation of spectators in a movie house, in a room watching TV, at a desk surfing the Internet, or at a computer playing a video game. Assuming that Socrates would probably consider all these media even more illusory than life in the cave — images of shadows of images! — how would you respond to his charges?

5. Think of a time when the scales, as they say, fell away from your eyes and you perceived someone or something in a completely new light. What did you see, what did you realize, that you hadn't perceived or understood before? Write an essay in which you tell the story, using images and ideas from Socrates' allegory to explain and illustrate your own situation before, during, and after the moment of coming into the light.

MAKING CONNECTIONS

Imagine how Socrates would criticize Steven Johnson's "Watching TV Makes You Smarter" (p. 301), and how Johnson in turn would defend himself against Socrates' attack. Then write an imaginary dialogue between the two.

BLOCKED

Joan Acocella

Joan Acocella was born in 1945 in San Francisco. She received her undergraduate degree in English from the University of California at Berkeley and a doctorate in comparative literature from Rutgers University. She has coauthored and coedited many books, and her writing appears in such publications as New York Times Book Review, Art in America, Times Literary Supplement, London Review of Books, *and* New York Review of Books. *Currently a fellow of the New York Institute for the Humanities, Acocella has a number of disparate interests. She has written about psychology, including* Abnormal Psychology: Current Perspectives *(1977), which she coauthored, and* Creating Hysteria: Women and Multiple Personality Disorder *(1999). Her most recent book is* Willa Cather and the Politics of Criticism *(2000). However, she is probably best known for her writing about dance. Acocella is currently dance critic for* The New Yorker, *and she wrote the biography* Mark Morris *(1993) and edited both* The Diary of Vaslav Nijinsky: Unexpurgated Edition *(1999) and* Andre Levinson on Dance *(1991). Her writing is known for conveying a sophisticated appreciation of performance in a relaxed, inviting style. "Blocked" appeared in* The New Yorker *and describes historical and current conceptions of writer's block.*

"Yesterday was my Birth Day," Coleridge wrote in his notebook in 1804, when he was thirty-two. "So completely has a whole year passed, with scarcely the fruits of a *month.* — O Sorrow and Shame. . . . I have done nothing!" It was true. Most of the poems for which he is remembered were written when he was in his mid-twenties. After that, any ambitious writing project inspired in him what he called "an indefinite indescribable Terror," and he wasted much of the rest of his life on opium addiction. How could he have done this? Why didn't he pull himself together? A friend asked him the same question. "You bid me rouse myself," he replied. "Go, bid a man paralytic in both arms rub them briskly together, and that will cure him. Alas! (he would reply) that I cannot move my arms is my complaint."

Coleridge is one of the first known cases of what we call writer's block. Sometimes, "block" means complete shutdown: the writer stops writing, or stops producing anything that seems to him worth publishing. In other cases, he simply stops writing what he wants to write. He may manage other kinds of writing, but not the kind he sees as his vocation. (Coleridge turned out a great deal of journalism and literary criticism in his later years, but he still saw himself as disabled, because he wasn't writing serious poetry.)

Writer's block is a modem notion. Writers have probably suffered over their work ever since they first started signing it, but it was not until the early nineteenth century that creative inhibition became an actual issue in literature, something people took into account when they talked about the art. That was partly because, around this time, the conception of the art changed. Before, writers regarded what *they* did as a rational, purposeful activity, which they controlled. By contrast, the early Romantics came to see poetry as something externally, and magically, conferred. In Shelley's words, "A man cannot say, 'I will compose poetry.'" Poetry was the product of "some invisible influence, like an inconstant wind," which more or less blew the material into the poet, and he just had to wait for this to happen. In terms of getting up in the morning and sitting down to work, a crueller theory can hardly be imagined, and a number of the major Romantic poets showed its effects. Wordsworth, like Coleridge, produced his best poetry early on, in about ten years. Poets, in their youth, "begin in gladness," he wrote, when he was in his thirties, in "Resolution and Independence." "But thereof come in the end despondency and madness."

After the English Romantics, the next group of writers known for not writing were the French Symbolists. Mallarmé, "the Hamlet of writing," as Roland Barthes called him, published some sixty poems in thirty-six years. Rimbaud, notoriously, gave up poetry at the age of nineteen. In the next generation, Paul Valéry wrote some poetry and prose in his early twenties and then took twenty years off, to study his mental processes. Under prodding from friends, he finally returned to publishing verse and in six years produced the three thin volumes that secured his fame. Then he gave up again. These fastidious Frenchmen, when they described the difficulties of writing, did not talk, like Wordsworth and Coleridge, about a metaphysical problem, or even a psychological problem. To them, the problem was with language: how to get past its vague, cliche-crammed character and arrive at the actual nature of experience. They needed a scalpel, they felt, and they were given a mallet.

It is curious to see this writing inhibition arise in the nineteenth century, for many of the writers of that century, or at least the novelists, were monsters of productivity. Scott, Balzac, Hugo, Dickens, Trollope: these men published as if they couldn't stop, and they were proud of it. Every day for years, Trollope reported in his "Autobiography," he woke in darkness and wrote from 5:30 a.m. to 8:30 a.m., with his watch in front of him. He required of himself two hundred and fifty words every quarter of an hour. If he finished one novel before eight-thirty, he took out a fresh piece of paper and started the next. The writing session was followed, for a long stretch of time, by a day job with the postal service. Plus, he said, he always hunted at least twice a week. Under this regimen, he produced forty-nine novels in thirty-five years. Having prospered so well, he urged his method on all writers: "Let their work be to them as is his common work to the common laborer. No gigantic efforts will then be necessary. He need tie no wet towels round his brow, nor sit for thirty hours at his desk without moving, — as men have sat, or said that they have sat."

Had this advice been given in 1850, it might have been gratefully accepted. But Trollope's autobiography was published in 1883, the year after his death. By that time, romantic notions about writing had filtered down to the public. Many readers now believed that literature was something produced by fine-minded, unhappy people who did not hunt, and to this audience Trollope's recommendations seemed clear evidence of shallowness. According to Michael Sadleir, who wrote the introduction to the Oxford World's Classics edition of the "Autobiography," the book "extinguished its author's good name for a quarter of a century." Trollope was later rehabilitated, but still today there is a prejudice against prolific writers. Joyce Carol Oates, who has published thirty-eight novels, twenty-one story collections, nine books of poetry, and twelve essay collections, and who also teaches full time at Princeton, has had to answer rude questions about her rate of production. "Is there a compulsive element in all this activity?" one interviewer asked her.

In the United States, the golden age of artistic inhibition was probably the period immediately following the Second World War, which saw the convergence of two forces. One was a sudden rise in the prestige of psychoanalysis. The second was a tremendous surge in ambition on the part of American artists — a lot of talk about the Great American Novel and hitting the ball out of the park. Some of those hopes were fulfilled. The fifties were a thrilling decade in American literature (Norman Mailer, Saul Bellow, Ralph Ellison, Eugene O'Neill, Tennessee Williams). But, as the bar rose, so did everyone's anxiety, and the doctor was called. Many, many writers went into psychoanalysis in those years, and they began writing about the relationship of art and neurosis. Early on, in 1941, came Edmund Wilson's book "The Wound and the Bow," which reinvoked the ancient Greek formula of the mad genius. After discussing the psychological harm suffered in childhood by Dickens, Kipling, and others, Wilson concluded that "genius and disease, like strength and mutilation, may be inextricably bound up together." In 1945, Wilson made the point again, by publishing, under the title "The Crack-Up," a collection of the later writings of his friend F. Scott Fitzgerald. Famous at twenty-three, washed up at forty, dead at forty-four, Fitzgerald was already everyone's favorite example of artistic flameout, but this posthumous volume, with Fitzgerald's own description of his situation ("No choice, no road, no hope"), helped plant the idea that his early exit was somehow a normal pattern, at least for American writers. As he famously put it, "There are no second acts in American lives." In 1947, *Partisan Review* printed an essay, "Writers and Madness," by one of its editors, William Barrett, claiming that the modern writer was by definition an "estranged neurotic," because the difficulty of being authentic in a false-faced world forced him to go deeper and deeper into the unconscious, thus pushing him toward madness: "The game is to go as close as possible without crossing over." Many did cross over, he added darkly.

Not everyone agreed that writers were mental cases, but a number of psychoanalysts did, and their loudest spokesman was Edmund Bergler, a Viennese émigré who in the forties and fifties put forth what is probably the most confident theory of writer's block ever advanced. First of all, he coined the term. (Formerly, people had spoken of "creative inhibition" or the like.) Second, he proclaimed its cause: oral masochism, entrapment in rage over the milk-denying pre-Oedipal mother. Starved before, the writer chose to become starved again — that is, blocked. Bergler claimed to have treated more than forty writers, with a hundred-percent success rate. That didn't mean that the writers became like other people. "I have never seen a 'normal' writer," Bergler reported. Even if their work was going well, this was often "entirely surrounded by neuroticism in private life" — squalid love affairs, homosexuality, etc. They had recompense, however: "*the megalomaniac pleasure of creation . . . produces a type of elation which cannot be compared with that experienced by other mortals*" (italics his).

In today's psychology of writer's block, as in today's psychology in general, the focus is less on the unconscious than on brain chemistry. Blocked writers are now being treated with antidepressants such as Prozac, though some report that the drugs tend to eliminate their desire to write together with their regret over not doing so. Others are being given Ritalin and other stimulants, on the theory that their problems may be due to the now fashionable condition of attention deficit disorder.

We are even getting biological theories of literary creativity and its stoppage. In a 1993 book called "Touched with Fire: Manic-Depressive Illness and the Artistic Temperament," the psychologist Kay Redfield Jamison argued that manic-depressive illness was the source of much of the best poetry produced from the eighteenth century to the twentieth. This year, we were offered a follow-up hypothesis, in "The Midnight Disease: The Drive to Write, Writer's Block, and the Creative Brain," by Alice W. Flaherty, who teaches neurology at Harvard Medical School. Like Jamison, Flaherty thinks that mood disorders may jump-start the literary imagination. (Also like Jamison, she has suffered from a mood disorder, and she feels that she owes her writing career to her manic phases.) But she goes further, speculating at length on which parts of the brain are responsible for literary creativity and its interruption. She believes that writing is generated along the pathways that connect the limbic system — a structure deep in the brain, the source of emotion and drive — with the temporal lobe, which controls our ability to grasp linguistic and philosophical meaning. As for block, she thinks the main problem may lie in the frontal lobe, because block shares some characteristics with disorders arising from frontal-lobe damage, such as Broca's aphasia, which destroys the ability to produce normal language.

Flaherty understands that these biological theories may shock people   10
who still cherish the idea that art comes from something other than the action of neurotransmitters, and she spends many intelligent pages trying to

shepherd us through the difficulty of accepting that the mind is actually the brain, a physical organ. She thinks we can concede this without discarding the more exalted concepts of inspiration, the "inner voice," and so on. She, too, believes in those things. Nevertheless, she is a brain scientist, and she can't help offering a few Frankensteinian suggestions. For example, she describes a new technique called transcranial magnetic stimulation, in which brain activity is controlled via the manipulation of magnetic fields. "It may soon be possible," she speculates, "to ward off depression and at least some types of writer's block by holding a magnetic wand over a precise location on our skulls."

In talk therapy, the trend these days is cognitive-behavioral therapy, which teaches you to revise your thoughts and preconceptions in order to change the behavior that issues from them. Apart from one-on-one treatment, there are a number of cognitive-behavioral books for blocked writers — for example, "Break Writer's Block Now!," by Jerrold Mundis, a novelist. Mundis also has a set of four audiocassettes that, for seventy-seven dollars, will talk you through his technique. I've listened to the tapes. The idea is to remove your fear of writing by combatting your negative thoughts with self-affirmations ("I am a richly talented writer"), by controlling in your mind the size of your project (don't start fantasizing about selling your novel to Hollywood), by thinking of what you're writing as just a draft (don't revise as you write), and, above all, by carefully scheduling your work and quitting the minute your assigned daily writing session is over (use a timer). Mundis's manner is very cheerleadery, in the way of motivational training, and his Web site, www.unblock.org, where you can order the tapes, reads like a subway ad for a baldness cure. Still, some of his advice is good, at least for beginning writers.

Many of these theorists regard block as a thing in itself, a mental condition that one can be stricken with. Is it? Like most of today's recognized psychological disorders, it is a concept that other cultures, other times, have done fine without. Not only did the notion of block not appear until the nineteenth century, in Europe, but many Europeans today don't seem to know what it is. According to Zachary Leader's 1991 "Writer's Block," the best book on the subject (much of my historical information comes from it), the French and the Germans have no term for writer's block. Even in England, where the idea is supposed to have been born, modern writers tend to sniff at it. "I don't get writing blocks except from the stationer," Anthony Burgess told an interviewer. "I can't understand the American literary block . . . unless it means that the blocked man isn't forced economically to write (as the English writer, lacking campuses and grants, usually is) and hence can afford the luxury of fearing the critics' pounce on a new work not as good as the last." Burgess may be correct that writer's block, by now, is largely an American idea, a product of American overreaching. Particularly in its mid-century version, with Bergler's talk of megalomania and elation, the concept is suspiciously glamorous — Faustian, *poète maudit*.

The term itself is grandiose, with its implication that writers contain within them great wells of creativity to which their access is merely impeded.

But the fact remains that some writers do stop writing, long before they want to. Why? Scientists have a rule that you don't explain things by remote and elaborate causes when simpler, more immediate causes offer themselves. In tales of block, certain circumstances turn up again and again. They are by no means sufficient causes — as we know, a condition that defeats one person may toughen up, even encourage, another — but they are probably contributing factors. One, paradoxically, is great praise. A story that haunts the halls of *The New Yorker* is that of Joseph Mitchell, who came on staff in 1938, wrote many brilliant pieces, and then, after the publication of his greatest piece, "Joe Gould's Secret," in 1964, came to the office almost every day for the next thirty-two years without filing another word. In a series of tributes published in *The New Yorker* upon Mitchell's death, in 1996, Calvin Trillin recalled hearing once that Mitchell was "writing away at a normal pace until some professor called him the greatest living master of the English declarative sentence and stopped him cold."

There are many other theories about Mitchell. (For one thing, "Joe Gould's Secret" was about a blocked writer.) It is nevertheless the case that, however much artists may want attention, getting it can put them off their feed, particularly when it comes at the beginning of their careers. That may have been the case with Dashiell Hammett. Hammett wrote his first four novels in three years, while he was in his thirties, and they made him famous. Then he went to Hollywood, where he made piles of money and spent much of it in bars. In 1934, when he was thirty-nine, his fifth novel, "The Thin Man," came out, and that was the end, though he lived for almost three more decades. In his later life, he said that he stopped publishing because he felt he was repeating himself: "It is the beginning of the end when you discover that you have a style." He tried to alter his style. He wanted to go mainstream, leave the detective novel behind. He wrote and wrote, but he never accomplished anything that satisfied him.

Again, however, Scott Fitzgerald's is the paradigmatic story of early success, early failure, and not just because his talent was so great but because he saw what was happening to him and wrote about it. In 1937, he published an essay, "Early Success" — it is included in "The Crack-Up" — in which he said that "premature success gives one an almost mystical conception of destiny as opposed to will power. . . . The man who arrives young believes that he exercises his will because his star is shining," a conviction that leaves him little to fall back on when the star isn't shining. That same year, Fitzgerald, finished (in his opinion) as a novelist — and also, by this time, seriously alcoholic — moved to Hollywood in order to make some money as a screenwriter. At the studios, he tried to stay on the wagon, but he repeatedly went on weeklong benders, which, when his friends finally located him, left him in need of round-the-clock nursing and tubal feeding. He soon found himself out of work as a result. To fill in financially, he wrote a series of stories for *Esquire* about a fictional screenwriter, Pat

15

Hobby, whose life was an antic version of his own. Hobby used to get two thousand dollars a week from the studios; now he gets three hundred and fifty. (In 1929, Fitzgerald was being paid four thousand dollars per story by *The Saturday Evening Post*. For the Hobby stories, *Esquire* seems to have paid him a hundred and fifty dollars apiece.) Formerly, Hobby was one of the men in Hollywood who "had wives and Filipinos and swimming pools." Now, in order to eat, he has to steal food from movie sets. The Hobby stories are a self-loathing comedy. Like Coleridge's notebooks, they make you want to scream. Why couldn't this lavishly gifted artist straighten himself out? He tried. In 1939, he began a novel — another wonderful one. "The Last Tycoon," about Hollywood — but six chapters into it he dropped dead of a heart attack. Five years later, a Fitzgerald revival began, and he soon became what he is to us now, an American classic. But, as far as he knew when he died, he was a forgotten man.

Fitzgerald's and Hammett's histories are not the only ones in which writing problems are complicated by alcoholism. From the nineteen-twenties at least through the fifties, American literature was awash in alcohol. Tom Dardis begins his book "The Thirsty Muse: Alcohol and the American Writer" (1989) by noting that of the seven native-born Americans awarded the Nobel Prize for Literature five were alcoholics: Sinclair Lewis, Eugene O'Neill, William Faulkner, Ernest Hemingway, and John Steinbeck. As for problem drinkers who didn't get the Nobel Prize, Dardis assembles an impressive list, including Edna St. Vincent Millay, Hart Crane, Thomas Wolfe, Dorothy Parker, Ring Lardner, Djuna Bames, John O'Hara, Tennessee Williams, John Berryman, Carson McCullers, James Jones, John Cheever, Jean Stafford, Truman Capote, Raymond Carver, and James Agee. A number of these careers ended early, and badly.

When an alcoholic writer stops writing, do we call this block or just alcoholism? (Or something else: Hemingway suffered serious depressions.) Such cases lack the bleak dignity generally associated with block. Instead of the lonely writer, at his desk, staring at the blank page, we get a disorderly drunk, being hauled off to detox. The relationship between writing and alcohol is a knotty problem, but it clearly involves a circular process. Many writers use alcohol to help themselves write — to calm their anxieties, lift their inhibitions. This may work for a while (Faulkner wrote all his best novels while drinking whiskey, continually, at his desk), but eventually the writing suffers. The unhappy writer then drinks more; the writing then suffers more, and so on. In my observation, American writers today drink much less than their predecessors. I asked a psychoanalyst what they do instead, to take the edge off. "Exercise," he said.

"Whom the gods wish to destroy," Cyril Connolly once said, "they first call promising." A subdivision of the early-success problem is second-novel syndrome. The writer produces a first novel, and it is a hit; then he sits down to write a second novel, and finds his brain clenched. Jeffrey Eugenides' first novel, "The Virgin Suicides" (1993), was an enormous critical success. It

also sold very well, and was made into a movie. His second novel, "Middlesex," was published two years ago, and won the Pulitzer Prize. But between
those two books lie nine years. I asked Eugenides why. One reason, he said,
was that "Middlesex" was far more ambitious than "The Virgin Suicides."
(It is a sweeping family chronicle, more than five hundred pages long and
full of Greek and American history.) But another reason was the circumstances surrounding a second novel:

> No one is waiting for you to write your first book. No one cares if
> you finish it. But after your first, if it goes well, everyone seems to
> be waiting. You're suddenly considered to be a professional writer,
> a fiction machine, but you know very well that you're just getting
> going. You go from having nothing to lose to having everything to
> lose, and that's what creates the panic. . . . In my own case, I de-
> cided to give myself the time to learn the things I needed to know
> in order to write my second book, rather than just writing it in a
> rush because there were now people eager to read it. Finally, of
> course, I had to leave the country. In Berlin I regained the blessed
> anonymity I'd had while writing "The Virgin Suicides." I got back
> to thinking only about the book. . . . Now [since "Middlesex"] I've
> lost the anonymity I had in Berlin and so am moving to Chicago. If
> things continue to go well, I will end up living in Elko, Nevada.

Eugenides survived second-novel syndrome, and so do most novelists,
but some are felled by it. "To Kill a Mockingbird" (1960), Harper Lee's
first novel, published when she was thirty-four, was an immediate best-
seller. It won the Pulitzer Prize. It was made into a hit movie. And then
came nothing. In 1961, Lee told an interviewer that she was working on
her second novel, but that she wrote very slowly, producing only a page or
two a day. Maybe we will hear from her yet, but she is now seventy-eight.

We will not hear from Ralph Ellison. Ellison's first novel, "Invisible   20
Man" (1952), was also a best-seller, and more than that. It was an "art"
novel, a modernist novel, and it was by a black writer. It therefore raised
hopes that literary segregation might be breachable. In its style the book
combined the arts of black culture — above all, jazz — with white influences:
Dostoyevsky, Joyce, Faulkner. Its message was likewise integrationist —
good news in the nineteen-fifties, at the beginning of the civil-rights movement. "Invisible Man" became a fixture of American-literature curricula.
Ellison was awarded the Presidential Medal of Freedom. He was not just a
writer; he was a hero. And everyone had great hopes for his second novel.

So did he. It was to be a "symphonic" novel, combining voices from all
parts of the culture. It grew and grew. Eventually, he thought it might require three volumes. He worked on it for forty years, until he died in 1994,
at the age of eighty, leaving behind more than two thousand pages of manuscript and notes. His literary executor, John F. Callahan, tried at first to assemble the projected symphonic work. Finally, he threw up his hands and

carved a simpler, one-volume novel out of the material. This book, entitled "Juneteenth," was published in 1999. Some reviewers praised it; others cold-shouldered it, as not-Ellison.

Ellison's was probably the most commented upon case of block in the history of American literature, and it was a tremendous sorrow to him. He had other griefs, too. While his integrationist message was welcomed in the nineteen-fifties, by the seventies it looked to many people, particularly black writers, like Uncle Tomism, and this dignified man was booed and heckled when he spoke at public events. In discussions of writer's block, it is sometimes said that a writer can be stopped when he outlives the world he was writing about, and for. That may have been true, in part, for Ellison.

Long before the nineteen-fifties — indeed, starting with Freud's 1910 book on Leonardo da Vinci — psychoanalysts were pondering creative block, and what they saw there, as elsewhere, was unconscious conflict. According to this line of thought, the artist trawls his unconscious for his material, but every now and then, in that dark estuary, he encounters something so frightening to him that he simply comes to a halt, and no one ever knows why. Maybe so, but sometimes the conflict is conscious: the artist knows why. Such may have been the case with E. M. Forster, who published five successful novels and then, to the dismay of his readers, gave up fiction at the age of forty-five. According to some commentators, part of the problem was that Forster finally figured out, in his thirties, that he was homosexual, at which point he felt he could no longer write about heterosexual love and marriage, which had been the substance of his fiction. Nor could he publish a novel about homosexuals; such a thing could not be printed in England in his time. He did write a homosexual novel, "Maurice," which he finished in 1914, but he had to put it in a drawer. After a ten-year gap, he produced one final novel, his greatest, "A Passage to India" — again heterosexual, but with a newly dark view of sex — and then, for the remaining forty-six years of his life, he confined himself to nonfiction. It should be added that he expressed no regret over this, a fact that may place him outside the category of the blocked. Presumably, a blocked writer feels guilty, feels like a failure — the Coleridge pattern.

A purer and more colorful example is that of Henry Roth. Roth's first novel, "Call It Sleep," a highly autobiographical narrative of Jewish immigrant life in New York, was published in 1934, when he was twenty-eight. It did not make much of a splash at first, but when it was reprinted in paperback, in 1964, it became a sensation. At the time of the reprint, Roth was living in complete obscurity on a duck farm in Maine. Apart from a few stories soon after "Call It Sleep," he hadn't published anything in thirty years. Nor did his belated triumph rouse him quickly, though the royalties from the paperback allowed him to sell the duck farm and buy a mobile home in Albuquerque. But in 1979, at the age of seventy-three, he embarked on a new novel, which eventually swelled to four volumes, under the general title "Mercy of a Rude Stream." The first volume appeared in

1994, and it was well received. In 1995 came the second volume, "A Diving Rock on the Hudson," and this was greeted with even more interest, for in it the protagonist, Ira — who Roth gave readers every reason to believe was based on himself — begins an affair at age fifteen with his twelve-year-old sister, Minnie. The sex scenes are very raw. Ira and Minnie go to it every Sunday morning when their mother leaves to do her shopping.

Prior to the publication of "A Diving Rock," Roth's editor, Robert   25
Weil, then of St. Martin's, persuaded him to alert his sister, Rose Broder, to the contents of the book. "How can you do this to me?" she wrote back, and she reminded him that she was the one who had believed in him as a writer, and who had typed "Call It Sleep." Roth responded by prefacing "A Diving Rock" with a statement that none of it was autobiographical — which many people took as further indication that it was autobiographical. Once the book came out, interviewers called Broder, and she denied the whole thing. "This is not pleasant for me," she told *The Jewish Week.* "I'm a very old lady." Soon afterward, she entered into an agreement with Roth whereby, in return for immunity from legal action, he paid her ten thousand dollars and promised that in future volumes there would be no more sex between Ira and Minnie. Roth told Weil — his narrator also says it in "A Diving Rock" — that the incest story was a major reason that the novel was delayed for so many years.

Beneath this drama, however, there may lie another tale. When Roth wrote "Call It Sleep," he was living with Eda Lou Walton, a well-known critic, twelve years older than he, who, he said, became "a mistress and a mother" to him. Walton later claimed that she did a huge amount of editorial work on "Call It Sleep." When Roth returned to fiction, he had another helper at his elbow. In 1989, a seventeen-year-old high-school student, Felicia Steele, went to work for Roth as his typist, and she soon graduated from typing to editing. For a year, she and her boyfriend even moved in with Roth. Day by day, she worked on his manuscript, cutting and shaping it under Weil's direction. Steele, now an English professor at the College of New Jersey, says that she was grateful to have this task: "I got a whole second education from Henry." Weil, too, says he felt honored to serve Roth's gift. For both of them, however, it was a herculean labor, requiring five years' work on thousands of pages of manuscript. So while Roth's sixty-year dry period may have been due to his feelings about his relationship with his sister, he may also, during those years, have had another, less sensational problem: that he couldn't produce a finished manuscript without a full-time editor.

These are among the most famous writer's block stories in modern literature — the supposed spine-tinglers — and all of them, when you look at them, come to seem unremarkable. Maybe the English are right: block is just a hocus-pocus covering life's regular, humbling facts. People made too much fuss over you, or expected too much of you. Or you just got tired. When I put the question of block to Elizabeth Hardwick, who was part of New York's high-pressure literary world in the postwar years, she seemed to believe that a major problem was just the passing of youth. "I don't think getting older is good for the creative process," she said. "Writing is so hard. It's the only time in your life when you have to think." But loss of energy is only one problem. Some people use up their material. There has been much puzzlement among literary historians over the petering out of Melville's career as a novelist after he published "Moby-Dick," at the age of thirty-two, and various theories have been advanced: that he was permanently embittered by the reviews of "Moby-Dick," that he felt his fiction revealed too much about his latent homosexuality, and so forth. But John Updike, in an essay on this question, says that basically Melville exhausted his artistic capital — his seafaring years — in "Typee," "Omoo," and "Moby-Dick." If, after those books, he wrote a couple of mediocre novels and then gave up the trade, it is no surprise.

With so many ordinary facts lurking behind its impressive name, writer's block may come to seem just that, a name, and names can be dangerous. The philosopher Ian Hacking has written about the problem of "dynamic nominalism," meaning that once you invent a category — as, for example, the category of "homosexual" seems to have been invented in the late nineteenth century — people will sort themselves into it, behave according to the description, and thus contrive new ways of being. Possibly, some writers become blocked simply because the concept exists, and invoking it is easier for them than writing. Some may also find it a more interesting complaint to bring to a psychoanalyst than garden-variety inertia. (One analyst, Donald Kaplan, has written that analysis may in fact not be good for blocked writers. They use it, he says, as a further ground for procrastination. First I'll finish the analysis, they say, then I'll tackle the book.) But for most writers the danger of "block" is that it gives them something to scare themselves with. They are a superstitious lot anyway. Alice Flaherty, in "The Midnight Disease," tells the story of a novelist who, at a literary dinner party, brought up the subject of block. Later, she got angry phone calls from several of the other guests, telling her that her thoughtless remark left them unable to write for days.

They have reason to be jumpy, though. Writing is a nerve-flaying job. First of all, what the Symbolists said is true: cliches come to the mind much more readily than anything fresh or exact. To hack one's way past them requires a huge, bleeding effort. (For anyone who wonders why seasoned writers tend to write for only about three or four hours a day, that's the answer.) In the same interview in which Anthony Burgess sneered at crybaby Americans, he concluded by saying that a writer can never be happy: "The anxiety involved is intolerable. And . . . the financial rewards just don't make up for the expenditure of energy, the damage to health caused by stimulants and narcotics, the fear that one's work isn't good enough. I think, if I had enough money, I'd give up writing tomorrow."

Apart from the effort, there is the self-exposure. The American reading 30
public knows more about Philip Roth than they know about some of their
first-degree relatives, and though Roth may have had some pleasure in that
unbaring, it is probably no accident that he now lives in the country, where
people are less likely to meet him on the street and tell him what they think
of him. (J. D. Salinger also retreated to the woods, shortly after the publication of "The Catcher in the Rye," in 1951. Reportedly, he has gone on writing — there are tales of a room-sized safe filled with manuscripts — but he
hasn't published anything in forty years. "Publishing is a terrible invasion
of my privacy," he said in a rare interview in 1974.) I can say from experience that even if you are not a novelist, even if you are a reviewer of dance
and books, total strangers will come up to you and say that they know how
you feel, and not just about dance and books. They are right. You told
them how you felt.

Anxiety over self-revelation was probably not as common in the old
days, when the exposure was channelled through conventional forms (ode,
sonnet) that masked the writer's identity to some extent. In former times,
too, art forthrightly answered the audience's emotional needs: tell me a
story, sing me a song. Modernism, in refusing to do that duty, may have a
lot to answer for in the development of artistic neurosis. If art wasn't going
to address the audience's basic needs, then presumably it was doing something finer, more mysterious — something, in other words, that could put
the artist into a sweat. As long as art remained, in some measure, artisanal —
with, for example, the young Leonardo da Vinci arriving in the morning at
Verrocchio's studio and being told to paint in the angel's wing — it must
have fostered steadier minds. Still, I wonder whether the artist's task was
ever easy. Leonardo's contemporaries reported that his hand shook as he
plied the brush. And he left many works unfinished. Freud hypothesized
that Leonardo's problems stemmed from the Oedipus complex. (He was
born illegitimate; his abandoned mother kissed him too much.) But could
they have been due to a less sexy cause — sheer ambition? Competition
among Italian artists of the Renaissance was intense. In his later life,
Leonardo quit painting for long periods.

Art-making should be a nice job, yet somehow, for many people, it's
not. And they don't know why and would rather not think about it. Once,
in an unintentionally comic essay, the analyst Donald Kaplan, who was
very interested in art, reported ruefully that his artist patients rarely discussed their work with him. If they even mentioned it, they used it only as a
chronological marker ("'It was around the time I was doing those brown
paintings'"). All they wanted to talk about was the circumstances around
their work: noisy children, obtuse reviewers. And, once Kaplan helped
them deal with these matters, they quit treatment. They didn't know and
didn't care what underlay their creative function. They just wanted to get
back to it, as long as it lasted.

QUESTIONS

1. In your own words, define "writer's block." How does your definition differ from Acocella's? How is it similar to hers?
2. Make a list of all the theories that Acocella discusses concerning the origin of writer's block. Which of these theories do you consider most plausible, which most outlandish, and why?
3. List all the remedies for writer's block that Acocella discusses. As in question 2, which ones do you think are the most plausible, and which ones do you feel are the most outlandish?
4. Acocella's essay is concerned exclusively with the blocks of professional writers. Suppose you were writing an essay about the blocks of student writers. What are some causes that you would add to her list, and what are some additional remedies?
5. Had you ever heard about writer's block before you read about it here? Have you ever known anyone (including yourself) who suffered from writer's block? Based on your prior knowledge or experience, what did you consider to be the major cause of writer's block?
6. Before reading Acocella's essay, what did you consider to be the best remedy for writer's block?
7. Write an essay about the most frustrating writer's block (or writing difficulty) that you ever experienced. What were the major causes of your problem? How did you overcome it? What did you learn from the experience that helped you prevent or overcome similar problems?

MAKING CONNECTIONS

Writer's block is just one of the many ways that psychological disturbance can manifest itself, as you can see by looking at the pieces by Bruno Bettelheim (p. 657) and Oliver Sacks (p. 711). Compare and contrast the narrative techniques that each of these writers uses to explain the origin, development, and treatment of the problems that interest them. Which of the pieces do you find most informative and illuminating — and why?

LANGUAGE AND LITERATURE FROM A PUEBLO INDIAN PERSPECTIVE

Leslie Marmon Silko

Leslie Marmon Silko (b. 1948), a poet and fiction writer, was born in Albuquerque, New Mexico, and grew up on the Laguna Pueblo reservation. She graduated from the University of New Mexico in 1969, the same year she published her first short story, "Tony's Story," in Thunderbird, *the student literary magazine. Her first book of poems,* Laguna Women, *appeared in 1974, and her first novel,* Ceremony, *in 1977. Silko's work reflects her belief in the importance of preserving Native American traditions and ways of life. In her second novel,* Storyteller *(1981), Silko uses Native American stories, in the form of prose and poetry, to retell her own family's story. Her most recent works include* Yellow Woman and A Beauty of the Spirit: Essays on Native American Life Today *(1996) and the novel* Gardens in the Dunes *(1999). She has taught at the University of New Mexico and the University of Arizona, Tucson. The following piece was first published in* English Literature: Opening Up the Canon *(1979), edited by Leslie A. Fiedler and Houston A. Baker Jr.*

Where I come from, the words most highly valued are those spoken from the heart, unpremeditated and unrehearsed. Among the Pueblo people, a written speech or statement is highly suspect because the true feelings of the speaker remain hidden as she reads words that are detached from the occasion and the audience. I have intentionally not written a formal paper because I want you to *hear* and to experience English in a structure that follows patterns from the oral tradition. For those of you accustomed to being taken from point A to point B to point C, this presentation may be somewhat difficult to follow. Pueblo expression resembles something like a spider's web — with many little threads radiating from the center, crisscrossing one another. As with the web, the structure emerges as it is made, and you must simply listen and trust, as the Pueblo people do, that meaning will be made.

My task is a formidable one: I ask you to set aside a number of basic approaches that you have been using and probably will continue to use, and, instead, to approach language from the Pueblo perspective, one that embraces the whole of creation and the whole of history and time.

What changes would Pueblo writers make to English as a language for literature? I have some examples of stories in English that I will use to address this question. At the same time, I would like to explain the importance of storytelling and how it relates to a Pueblo theory of language.

So I will begin, appropriately enough, with the Pueblo Creation story, an all-inclusive story of how life began. In this story, Tse'itsi'nako, Thought Woman, by thinking other sisters, and together with her sisters, thought of everything that is. In this way, the world was created. Everything in this world was a part of the original Creation; the people at home understood that far away there were other human beings, also a part of this world. The Creation story even includes a prophecy that describes the origin of European and African peoples and also refers to Asians.

This story, I think, suggests something about why the Pueblo people   5
are more concerned with story and communication and less concerned with a particular language. There are at least six, possibly seven, distinct languages among the twenty pueblos of the southwestern United States, for example, Zuñi and Hopi. And from mesa to mesa there are subtle differences in language. But the particular language being spoken isn't as important as what a speaker is trying to say, and this emphasis on the story itself stems, I believe, from a view of narrative particular to the Pueblo and other Native American peoples — that is, that language *is* story.

I will try to clarify this statement. At Laguna Pueblo, for example, many individual words have their own stories. So when one is telling a story and one is using words to tell the story, each word that one is speaking has a story of its own, too. Often the speakers, or tellers, will go into these word stories, creating an elaborate structure of stories within stories. This structure, which becomes very apparent in the actual telling of a story, informs contemporary Pueblo writing and storytelling as well as the traditional narratives. This perspective on narrative — of story within story, the idea that one story is only the beginning of many stories and the sense that stories never truly end — represents an important contribution of Native American cultures to the English language.

Many people think of storytelling as something that is done at bedtime, that it is something done for small children. But when I use the term *storytelling*, I'm talking about something much bigger than that. I'm talking about something that comes out of an experience and an understanding of that original view of Creation — that we are all part of a whole; we do not differentiate or fragment stories and experiences. In the beginning, Tse'itsi'nako, Thought Woman, thought of all things, and all of these things are held together as one holds many things together in a single thought.

So in the telling (and you will hear a few of the dimensions of this telling), first of all, as mentioned earlier, the storytelling always includes the audience, the listeners. In fact, a great deal of the story is believed to be inside the listener; the storyteller's role is to draw the story out of the listeners. The storytelling continues from generation to generation.

Basically, the origin story constructs our identity — with this story, we know who we are. We are the Lagunas. This is where we come from. We came this way. We came by this place. And so from the time we are very young, we hear these stories, so that when we go out into the world, when one asks who we are or where we are from, we immediately know: we are the people who came from the north. We are the people of these stories.

In the Creation story, Antelope says that he will help knock a hole in the Earth so that the people can come up, out into the next world. Antelope tries and tries; he uses his hooves but is unable to break through. It is then that Badger says, "Let me help you." And Badger very patiently uses his claws and digs a way through, bringing the people into the world. When the Badger clan people think of themselves, or when the Antelope people think of themselves, it is as people who are of *this* story, and this is *our* place, and we fit into the very beginning when the people first came, before we began our journey south.

Within the clans there are stories that identify the clan. One moves, then, from the idea of one's identity as a tribal person into clan identity, then to one's identity as a member of an extended family. And it is the notion of extended family that has produced a kind of story that some distinguish from other Pueblo stories, though Pueblo people do not. Anthropologists and ethnologists have, for a long time, differentiated the types of stories the Pueblos tell. They tended to elevate the old, sacred, and traditional stories and to brush aside family stories, the family's account of itself. But in Pueblo culture, these family stories are given equal recognition. There is no definite, preset pattern for the way one will hear the stories of one's own family, but it is a very critical part of one's childhood, and the storytelling continues throughout one's life. One will hear stories of importance to the family — sometimes wonderful stories — stories about the time a maternal uncle got the biggest deer that was ever seen and brought it back from the mountains. And so an individual's identity will extend from the identity constructed around the family — "I am from the family of my uncle who brought in this wonderful deer, and it was a wonderful hunt."

Family accounts include negative stories, too; perhaps an uncle did something unacceptable. It is very important that one keep track of all these stories — both positive and not so positive — about one's own family and other families. Because even when there is no way around it — old Uncle Pete *did* do a terrible thing — by knowing the stories that originate in other families, one is able to deal with terrible sorts of things that might happen within one's own family. If a member of the family does something that cannot be excused, one always knows stories about similarly inexcusable things done by a member of another family. But this knowledge is not communicated for malicious reasons. It is very important to understand this. Keeping track of all the stories within the community gives us all a certain distance, a useful perspective, that brings incidents down to a level we can deal with. If others have done it before, it cannot be so terrible. If others have endured, so can we.

The stories are always bringing us together, keeping this whole together, keeping this family together, keeping this clan together. "Don't go away, don't isolate yourself, but come here, because we have all had these kinds of experiences." And so there is this constant pulling together to resist the tendency to run or hide or separate oneself during a traumatic emotional experience. This separation not only endangers the group but the individual as well — one does not recover by oneself.

Because storytelling lies at the heart of Pueblo culture, it is absurd to attempt to fix the stories in time. "When did they tell the stories?" or "What time of day does the storytelling take place?" — these questions are nonsensical from a Pueblo perspective, because our storytelling goes on constantly: as some old grandmother puts on the shoes of a child and tells her the story of a little girl who didn't wear her shoes, for instance, or someone comes into the house for coffee to talk with a teenage boy who has just been in a lot of trouble, to reassure him that someone else's son has been in that kind of trouble, too. Storytelling is an ongoing process, working on many different levels.

Here's one story that is often told at a time of individual crisis (and I   15
want to remind you that we make no distinctions between types of story — historical, sacred, plain gossip — because these distinctions are not useful when discussing the Pueblo *experience* of language). There was a young man who, when he came back from the war in Vietnam, had saved up his army pay and bought a beautiful red Volkswagen. He was very proud of it. One night he drove up to a place called the King's Bar, right across the reservation line. The bar is notorious for many reasons, particularly for the deep arroyo located behind it. The young man ran in to pick up a cold six-pack, but he forgot to put on his emergency brake. And his little red Volkswagen rolled back into the arroyo and was all smashed up. He felt very bad about it, but within a few days everybody had come to him with stories about other people who had lost cars and family members to that arroyo, for instance, George Day's station wagon, with his mother-in-law and kids inside. So everybody was saying, "Well, at least your mother-in-law and kids weren't in the car when it rolled in," and one can't argue with that kind of story. The story of the young man and his smashed-up Volkswagen was now joined with all the other stories of cars that fell into that arroyo.

Now I want to tell you a very beautiful little story. It is a very old story that is sometimes told to people who suffer great family or personal loss. This story was told by my Aunt Susie. She is one of the first generation of people at Laguna who began experimenting with English — who began working to make English speak for us, that is, to speak from the heart. (I come from a family intent on getting the stories told.) As you read the story, I think you will hear that. And here and there, I think, you will also hear the influence of the Indian school at Carlisle, Pennsylvania, where my Aunt Susie was sent (like being sent to prison) for six years.

This scene is set partly in Acoma, partly in Laguna. Waithea was a little girl living in Acoma and one day she said, "Mother, I would like to have some *yashtoah* to eat." *Yashtoah* is the hardened crust of corn mush that curls up. *Yashtoah* literally means "curled up." She said, "I would like to have some *yashtoah*," and her mother said, "My dear little girl. I can't make you any *yashtoah* because we haven't any wood, but if you will go down off the mesa, down below, and pick up some pieces of wood and bring them home, I will make you some *yashtoah*." So Waithea was glad and ran down the precipitous cliff of Acoma mesa. Down below, just as her mother had told her, there were pieces of wood, some curled, some crooked in shape, that she was to pick up and take home. She found just such wood as these.

She brought them home in a little wicker basket. First she called to her mother as she got home, "*Nayah, deeni!* Mother, upstairs!" The Pueblo people always called "upstairs" because long ago their homes were two, three stories, and they entered from the top. She said, "*Deeni! Upstairs!*" and her mother came. The little girl said, "I have brought the wood you wanted me to bring." And she opened her little wicker basket to lay out the pieces of wood, but here they were snakes. They were snakes instead of the crooked sticks of wood. And her mother said, "Oh my dear child, you have brought snakes instead!" She said, "Go take them back and put them back just where you got them." And the little girl ran down the mesa again, down below to the flats. And she put those snakes back just where she got them. They were snakes instead, and she was very hurt about this, and so she said, "I'm not going home. I'm going to Kawaik, the beautiful lake place Kawaik, and drown myself in that lake, *byn'yah'nah* [the 'west lake']. I will go there and drown myself."

So she started off, and as she passed by the Enchanted Mesa near Acoma, she met an old man, very aged, and he saw her running, and he said, "My dear child, where are you going?" "I'm going to Kawaik and jump into the lake there."

"Why?" "Well, because," she said, "my mother didn't want to make any   20
yashtoah for me." The old man said, "Oh, no! You must not go, my child. Come with me and I will take you home." He tried to catch her, but she was very light and skipped along. And every time he would try to grab her she would skip faster away from him.

The old man was coming home with some wood strapped to his back and tied with yucca. He just let that strap go and let the wood drop. He went as fast as he could up the cliff to the little girl's home. When he got to the place where she lived, he called to her mother. "*Deeni!*" "Come on up!" And he said, "I can't. I just came to bring you a message. Your little daughter is running away. She is going to Kawaik to drown herself in the lake there." "Oh my dear little girl!" the mother said. So she busied herself with making the *yashtoah* her little girl liked so much. Corn mush curled at the top. (She must have found enough wood to boil the corn meal and make the *yashtoah*.)

While the mush was cooling off, she got the little girl's clothing, her *manta* dress and buckskin moccasins and all her other garments, and put them in a bundle — probably a yucca bag. And she started down as fast as she could on the east side of Acoma. (There used to be a trail there, you know. It's gone now, but it was accessible in those days.) She saw her daughter way at a distance and she kept calling: "Stsamaku! My daughter! Come back! I've got your yashtoah for you." But the little girl would not turn. She kept on ahead and she cried: "My mother, my mother, she didn't want me to have any *yashtoah*. So now I'm going to Kawaik and drown myself." Her mother heard her cry and said, "My little daughter, come back here!" "No," and she kept a distance away from her. And they came nearer and nearer to the lake. And she could see her daughter now, very plain. "Come back, my daughter! I have your *yashtoah*." But no, she kept on, and finally she reached the lake and she stood on the edge.

She had tied a little feather in her hair, which is traditional (in death they tie this feather on the head). She carried a feather, the little girl did, and she tied it in her hair with a piece of string; right on top of her head she put the feather. Just as her mother was about to reach her, she jumped into the lake. The little feather was whirling around and around in the depths below. Of course the mother was very sad. She went, grieved, back to Acoma and climbed her mesa home. She stood on the edge of the mesa and scattered her daughter's clothing, the little moccasins, the *yashtoah*. She scattered them to the east, to the west, to the north, to the south. And the pieces of clothing and the moccasins and *yashtoah* all turned into butterflies. And today they say that Acoma has more beautiful butterflies: red ones, white ones, blue ones, yellow ones. They came from this little girl's clothing.

Now this is a story anthropologists would consider very old. The version I have given you is just as Aunt Susie tells it. You can occasionally hear some English she picked up at Carlisle — words like *precipitous*. You will also notice that there is a great deal of repetition, and a little reminder about *yashtoah* and how it is made. There is a remark about the cliff trail at Acoma — that it was once there but is there no longer. This story may be told at a time of sadness or loss, but within this story many other elements are brought together. Things are not separated out and categorized; all things are brought together, so that the reminder about the *yashtoah* is valuable information that is repeated — a recipe, if you will. The information about the old trail at Acoma reveals that stories are, in a sense, maps, since even to this day there is little information or material about trails that is passed around with writing. In the structure of this story the repetitions are, of course, designed to help you remember. It is repeated again and again, and then it moves on.

There are a great many parallels between Pueblo experiences and those 25
of African and Caribbean peoples — one is that we have all had the conqueror's language imposed on us. But our experience with English has been somewhat different in that the Bureau of Indian Affairs schools were not interested in teaching us the canon of Western classics. For instance, we never heard of Shakespeare. We were given Dick and Jane, and I can re-

member reading that the robins were heading south for the winter. It took me a long time to figure out what was going on. I worried for quite a while about our robins in Laguna because they didn't leave in the winter, until I finally realized that all the big textbook companies are up in Boston and *their* robins do go south in the winter. But in a way, this dreadful formal education freed us by encouraging us to maintain our narratives. Whatever literature we were exposed to at school (which was damn little), at home the storytelling, the special regard for telling and bringing together through the telling, was going on constantly.

And as the old people say, "If you can remember the stories, you will be all right. Just remember the stories." When I returned to Laguna Pueblo after attending college, I wondered how the storytelling was continuing (anthropologists say that Laguna Pueblo is one of the more acculturated pueblos), so I visited an English class at Laguna-Acoma High School. I knew the students had cassette tape recorders in their lockers and stereos at home, and that they listened to Kiss and Led Zeppelin and were well informed about culture in general. I had with me an anthology of short stories by Native American writers, *The Man to Send Rain Clouds*. One story in the book is about the killing of a state policeman in New Mexico by three Acoma Pueblo men in the early 1950s. I asked the students how many had heard this story and steeled myself for the possibility that the anthropologists were right, that the old traditions were indeed dying out and the students would be ignorant of the story. But instead, all but one or two raised their hands — they had heard the story, just as I had heard it when I was young, some in English, some in Laguna.

One of the other advantages that we Pueblos have enjoyed is that we have always been able to stay with the land. Our stories cannot be separated from their geographical locations, from actual physical places on the land. We were not relocated like so many Native American groups who were torn away from their ancestral land. And our stories are so much a part of these places that it is almost impossible for future generations to lose them — there is a story connected with every place, every object in the landscape.

Dennis Brutus has talked about the "yet unborn" as well as "those from the past," and how we are still *all* in *this* place, and language — the storytelling — is our way of passing through or being with them, of being together again. When Aunt Susie told her stories, she would tell a younger child to go open the door so that our esteemed predecessors might bring their gifts to us. "They are out there," Aunt Susie would say. "Let them come in. They're here, they're here with us *within* the stories."

A few years ago, when Aunt Susie was 106, I paid her a visit, and while I was there she said, "Well, I'll be leaving here soon. I think I'll be leaving here next week, and I will be going over to the Cliff House." She said, "It's going to be real good to get back over there." I was listening, and I was thinking that she must be talking about her house at Paguate village, just north of Laguna. And she went on, "Well, my mother's sister [and she gave her Indian name] will be there. She has been living there. She will be there and we will be over there, and I will get a chance to write down these stories I've been telling you." Now you must understand, of course, that Aunt Susie's mother's sister, a great storyteller herself, has long since passed over into the land of the dead. But then I realized, too, that Aunt Susie wasn't talking about death the way most of us do. She was talking about "going over" as a journey, a journey that perhaps we can only begin to understand through an appreciation for the boundless capacity of language that, through storytelling, brings us together, despite great distances between cultures, despite great distances in time.

QUESTIONS

1. In paragraph 1, Silko compares "Pueblo expression" to "a spider's web — with many little threads radiating from the center, crisscrossing one another." Assuming that her piece is like a web, what is its center, what are the threads that radiate from its center, and in what sense do they "crisscross" one another?

2. Quite apart from Silko's metaphor of the web, how would you describe or characterize the organization or structure of her piece? What do you consider to be its chief characteristics? In your own words, how would you distinguish it from a standard piece of writing in English?

3. What are the main purposes of Pueblo storytelling, according to Silko? What do you consider to be the main purposes of storytelling in English?

4. What are the main characteristics of Pueblo storytelling, according to Silko, and how are those characteristics related to their audience and purpose?

5. Write an analysis of the story that Silko tells in paragraphs 17–23, and indicate how it exemplifies the characteristics of Pueblo storytelling.

6. Think of a story that has been passed down to you from your ancestors. Write an essay in which you tell the story and reflect on its significance for you and other members of your family.

MAKING CONNECTIONS

Compare and contrast Silko's view of language and literature from a Pueblo Indian perspective with Amy Tan's account of language and writing from her Asian American perspective (p. 80) and/or James Baldwin's view from an African American perspective (p. 276). In what respects, if any, do they overlap? In what significant ways do they differ?

ARGUING IN THE
Arts and Humanities

HIROSHIMA

John Berger

After beginning his career as a painter and drawing instructor, John Berger (b. 1926) became one of Britain's most influential art critics. He has achieved recognition as a screenwriter, novelist, and documentary writer. As a Marxist, he is concerned with the ideological and technological conditioning of our ways of seeing both art and the world. In Ways of Seeing *(1972), he explores the interrelation between words and images, between verbal and visual meaning. "Hiroshima" first appeared in 1981 in the journal* New Society *and later in a collection of essays,* The Sense of Sight *(1985). Berger examines how the facts of nuclear holocaust have been hidden through "a systematic, slow and thorough process of suppression and elimination . . . within the reality of politics." Images, rather than words, Berger asserts, can help us see through the "mask of innocence" that evil wears.*

The whole incredible problem begins with the need to reinsert those events of 6 August 1945 back into living consciousness.

I was shown a book last year at the Frankfurt Book Fair. The editor asked me some question about what I thought of its format. I glanced at it quickly and gave some reply. Three months ago I was sent a finished copy of the book. It lay on my desk unopened. Occasionally its title and cover picture caught my eye, but I did not respond. I didn't consider the book urgent, for I believed that I already knew about what I would find within it.

Did I not clearly remember the day — I was in the army in Belfast — when we first heard the news of the bomb dropped on Hiroshima? At how many meetings during the first nuclear disarmament movement had I and others not recalled the meaning of that bomb?

And then, one morning last week, I received a letter from America, accompanying an article written by a friend. This friend is a doctor of philosophy and a Marxist. Furthermore, she is a very generous and warm-hearted woman. The article was about the possibilities of a third world war. Vis-à-vis the Soviet Union she took, I was surprised to read, a position very close to Reagan's. She concluded by evoking the likely scale of destruction which would be caused by nuclear weapons, and then welcomed the positive possibilities that this would offer the socialist revolution in the United States.

It was on that morning that I opened and read the book on my desk. It   5
is called *Unforgettable Fire*.[1]

The book consists of drawings and paintings made by people who were in Hiroshima on the day that the bomb was dropped, thirty-six years ago today. Often the pictures are accompanied by a verbal record of what the image represents. None of them is by a professional artist. In 1974, an old man went to the television center in Hiroshima to show to whomever was interested a picture he had painted, entitled "At about 4 pm, 6th August 1945, near Yurozuyo bridge."

This prompted an idea of launching a television appeal to other survivors of that day to paint or draw their memories of it. Nearly a thousand pictures were sent in, and these were made into an exhibition. The appeal was worded: "Let us leave for posterity pictures about the atomic bomb, drawn by citizens."

Clearly, my interest in these pictures cannot be an art-critical one. One does not musically analyze screams. But after repeatedly looking at them, what began as an impression became a certainty. These were images of hell.

I am not using the word as hyperbole. Between these paintings by women and men who have never painted anything else since leaving school, and who have surely, for the most part, never traveled outside Japan, between these traced memories which had to be exorcised, and the numerous representations of hell in European medieval art, there is a very close affinity.

This affinity is both stylistic and fundamental. And fundamentally it is   10
to do with the situations depicted. The affinity lies in the degree of the multiplication of pain, in the lack of appeal or aid, in the pitilessness, in the equality of wretchedness, and in the disappearance of time.

I am 78 years old. I was living at Midorimachi on the day of the A-bomb blast. Around 9 am that morning, when I looked out of my window, I saw several women coming along the street one after another towards the Hiroshima prefectural hospital. I realized for the first time, as it is sometimes said, that when people are very much frightened hair really does stand on end. The women's hair was, in fact, standing straight up and the skin of their arms was peeled off. I suppose they were around 30 years old.

Time and again, the sober eyewitness accounts recall the surprise and horror of Dante's verses about the Inferno. The temperature at the center of the Hiroshima fireball was 300,000 degrees centigrade. The survivors are called in Japanese *hibakuska* — "those who have seen hell."

Suddenly, one man who was stark naked came up to me and said in a quavering voice, "Please help me!" He was burned and swollen all over from the effects of the A-bomb. Since I did not recognize him as my neighbor, I asked who he was. He answered that he was Mr. Sasaki, the son of Mr. Ennosuke Sasaki, who had a lumber shop in Funairi town. That morning he had been doing volunteer labor service, evacuating the houses near the prefectural office in Kato town. He had been burned black all over and had started back to his home in Funairi. He looked miserable — burned and sore, and naked with only pieces of his gaiters trailing behind as he walked. Only the part of his hair covered by his soldier's hat was left, as if he was wearing a bowl. When I touched him, his burned

How survivors saw it. A painting by Kazuhiro Ishizu, aged 68.

At the Aioi bridge, by Sawami Katagiri, aged 76.

skin slipped off. I did not know what to do, so I asked a passing driver to take him to Eba hospital.

Does not this evocation of hell make it easier to forget that these scenes belonged to life? Is there not something conveniently unreal about hell? The whole history of the twentieth century proves otherwise.

Very systematically in Europe the conditions of hells have been constructed. It is not even necessary to list the sites. It is not even necessary to repeat the calculations of the organizers. We know this, and we choose to forget it.

We find it ridiculous or shocking that most of the pages concerning, for example, Trotsky were torn out of official Soviet history. What has been torn out of our history are the pages concerning the experience of the two atom bombs dropped on Japan.

Of course, the facts are there in the textbooks. It may even be that school children learn the dates. But what these facts mean — and originally their meaning was so clear, so monstrously vivid, that every commentator in the world was shocked, and every politician was obliged to say (whilst planning differently), "Never again" — what these facts mean has now been torn out. It has been a systematic, slow and thorough process of suppression and elimination. This process has been hidden within the reality of politics. 15

Do not misunderstand me. I am not here using the word "reality" ironically, I am not politically naïve. I have the greatest respect for political reality, and I believe that the innocence of political idealists is often very dangerous. What we are considering is how in this case in the West — not in Japan for obvious reasons and not in the Soviet Union for different reasons — political and military realities have eliminated another reality.

The eliminated reality is both physical —

Yokogawa bridge above Tenma river, 6th August 1945, 8:30 am.
    People crying and moaning were running towards the city. I did
not know why. Steam engines were burning at Yokogawa station.
    Skin of cow tied to wire.
    Skin of girl's hip was hanging down.
    "My baby is dead, isn't she?"

and moral.

    The political and military arguments have concerned such issues as de-
terrence, defense systems, relative strike parity, tactical nuclear weapons
and — pathetically — so-called civil defense. Any movement for nuclear disarmament today has to contend with those considerations and dispute their
false interpretation. To lose sight of them is to become as apocalyptic as the
Bomb and all utopias. (The construction of hells on earth was accompanied
in Europe by plans for heavens on earth.)

    What has to be redeemed, reinserted, disclosed and never be allowed to
be forgotten, is the other reality. Most of the mass means of communication
are close to what has been suppressed.

    These paintings were shown on Japanese television. Is it conceivable that   20
the BBC would show these pictures on Channel One at a peak hour? Without
any reference to "political" and "military" realities, under the straight title,
This Is How It Was, 6th August 1945? I challenge them to do so.

    What happened on that day was, of course, neither the beginning nor the
end of the act. It began months, years before, with the planning of the action,
and the eventual final decision to drop two bombs on Japan. However much
the world was shocked and surprised by the bomb dropped on Hiroshima, it
has to be emphasized that it was not a miscalculation, an error, or the result
(as can happen in war) of a situation deteriorating so rapidly that it gets out
of hand. What happened was consciously and precisely planned. Small scenes
like this were part of the plan:

    I was walking along the Hihiyama bridge about 3 pm on 7th Au-
    gust. A woman, who looked like an expectant mother, was dead.
    At her side, a girl of about three years of age brought some water
    in an empty can she had found. She was trying to let her mother
    drink from it.
        As soon as I saw this miserable scene with the pitiful child, I em-
    braced the girl close to me and cried with her, telling her that her
    mother was dead.

    There was a preparation. And there was an aftermath. The latter included
long, lingering deaths, radiation sickness, many fatal illnesses which developed
later as a result of exposure to the bomb, and tragic genetical effects on generations yet to be born.

I refrain from giving the statistics: how many hundreds of thousands of dead, how many injured, how many deformed children. Just as I refrain from pointing out how comparatively "small" were the atomic bombs dropped on Japan. Such statistics tend to distract. We consider numbers instead of pain. We calculate instead of judging. We relativize instead of refusing.

It is possible today to arouse popular indignation or anger by speaking of the threat and immorality of terrorism. Indeed, this appears to be the central plank of the rhetoric of the new American foreign policy ("Moscow is the world-base of all terrorism") and of British policy towards Ireland. What is able to shock people about terrorist acts is that often their targets are unselected and innocent — a crowd in a railway station, people waiting for a bus to go home after work. The victims are chosen indiscriminately in the hope of producing a shock effect on political decision-making by their government.

The two bombs dropped on Japan were terrorist actions. The calculation 25 was terrorist. The indiscriminacy was terrorist. The small groups of terrorists operating today are, by comparison, humane killers.

Another comparison needs to be made. Today terrorist groups mostly represent small nations or groupings, who are disputing large powers in a position of strength. Whereas Hiroshima was perpetrated by the most powerful alliance in the world against an enemy who was already prepared to negotiate, and was admitting defeat.

To apply the epithet "terrorist" to the acts of bombing Hiroshima and Nagasaki is logically justifiable, and I do so because it may help to reinsert that act into living consciousness today. Yet the word changes nothing in itself.

The first-hand evidence of the victims, the reading of the pages which have been torn out, provokes a sense of outrage. This outrage has two natural faces. One is a sense of horror and pity at what happened; the other face is self-defensive and declares: *this should not happen again (here)*. For some the *here* is in brackets, for others it is not.

The face of horror, the reaction which has now been mostly suppressed, forces us to comprehend the reality of what happened. The second reaction, unfortunately, distances us from that reality. Although it begins as a straight declaration, it quickly leads into the labyrinth of defense policies, military arguments and global strategies. Finally it leads to the sordid commercial absurdity of private fall-out shelters.

This split of the sense of outrage into, on one hand, horror, and, on the 30 other hand, expediency occurs because the concept of evil has been abandoned. Every culture, except our own in recent times, has had such a concept.

That its religious or philosophical bases vary is unimportant. The concept of evil implies a force or forces which have to be continually struggled against so that they do not triumph over life and destroy it. One of the very first written texts from Mesopotamia, 1,500 years before Homer, speaks of this struggle, which was the first condition of human life. In public thinking nowadays, the concept of evil has been reduced to a little adjective to support an opinion or hypothesis (abortions, terrorism, ayatollahs).

Nobody can confront the reality of 6th August 1945 without being forced to acknowledge that what happened was evil. It is not a question of opinion or interpretation, but of events.

The memory of these events should be continually before our eyes. This is why the thousand citizens of Hiroshima started to draw on their little scraps of paper. We need to show their drawings everywhere. These terrible images can now release an energy for opposing evil and for the lifelong struggle of that opposition.

And from this a very old lesson may be drawn. My friend in the United States is, in a sense, innocent. She looks beyond a nuclear holocaust without considering its reality. This reality includes not only its victims but also its planners and those who support them. Evil from time immemorial has often worn a mask of innocence. One of evil's principal modes of being is *looking beyond* (with indifference) that which is before the eyes.

> August 9th: On the west embankment of a military training field was a young boy four or five years old. He was burned black, lying on his back, with his arms pointing towards heaven.

Only by looking beyond or away can one come to believe that such evil is relative, and therefore under certain conditions justifiable. In reality — the reality to which the survivors and the dead bear witness — it can never be justified.

Note

1. Edited by Japan Broadcasting Corporation, London, Wildwood House, 1981; New York, Pantheon, 1981.

QUESTIONS

1. Berger begins his essay with this powerful sentence: "The whole incredible problem begins with the need to reinsert those events of 6 August 1945 back into living consciousness." What is "the whole incredible problem" as Berger describes and defines it?
2. Berger argues that what happened on August 6, 1945, was "consciously and precisely planned" (paragraph 21). What evidence does he present to support this claim? How does this argument advance his larger purpose?
3. Berger tells his readers that he refrains from giving statistics because "statistics tend to distract" (paragraph 23). What do statistics distance us from understanding about Hiroshima?
4. The content in Berger's essay ranges from thoughts about Hiroshima, to images of hell, to political realities, to terrorist actions, to concepts of

evil. How does he connect these various subjects? What is the chain of reasoning?

5. Berger offers various images from the book *Unforgettable Fire*, such as "August 9th: On the west embankment of a military training field was a young boy four or five years old. He was burned black, lying on his back, with his arms pointing towards heaven" (paragraph 34). Look at the various places in the essay where Berger presents such images from *Unforgettable Fire*. What effect does this evidence have on you? How does this evidence strengthen Berger's argument?

6. Spend some time looking at and thinking about the paintings by the survivors, Kazuhiro Ishizu and Sawami Katagiri, reprinted on pages 270 and 271. What do you *see* in these paintings? What do these images represent to you?

MAKING CONNECTIONS

Zoë Tracy Hardy's essay "What Did You Do in the War, Grandma?" (p. 366) reports on Hiroshima from the other side of that experience. How different are Berger's and Hardy's essays in their conclusions about the meaning of the event? Do the two essays contradict one another or reinforce one another?

IF BLACK ENGLISH ISN'T A LANGUAGE, THEN TELL ME, WHAT IS?

James Baldwin

James Baldwin (1924–1987) was born in Harlem and followed his father's vocation, becoming a preacher at the age of fourteen. At seventeen, he left the ministry and devoted himself to writing. Baldwin's most frequent subject was the relationship between blacks and whites, about which he wrote, "The color of my skin made me automatically an expert." Baldwin himself might also have added that his life's work lay in defining and legitimizing the black voice; like George Orwell, Baldwin argued that language is "a political instrument, means, and proof of power." He wrote five novels, a book of stories, one play, and several collections of essays. The following essay on language and legitimacy first appeared in 1979 in the New York Times *and later was included in* The Price of the Ticket: Collected Nonfiction, 1948–1985 *(1985).*

The argument concerning the use, or the status, or the reality, of black English is rooted in American history and has absolutely nothing to do with the question the argument supposes itself to be posing. The argument has nothing to do with language itself but with the role of language. Language, incontestably, reveals the speaker. Language, also, far more dubiously, is meant to define the other — and, in this case, the other is refusing to be defined by a language that has never been able to recognize him.

People evolve a language in order to describe and thus control their circumstances or in order not to be submerged by a situation that they cannot articulate. (And if they cannot articulate it, they are submerged.) A Frenchman living in Paris speaks a subtly and crucially different language from that of the man living in Marseilles; neither sounds very much like a man living in Quebec; and they would all have great difficulty in apprehending what the man from Guadeloupe, or Martinique, is saying, to say nothing of the man from Senegal — although the "common" language of all these areas is French. But each has paid, and is paying, a different price for this "common" language, in which, as it turns out, they are not saying, and cannot be saying, the same things: They each have very different realities to articulate, or control.

What joins all languages, and all men, is the necessity to confront life, in order, not inconceivably, to outwit death: The price for this is the acceptance, and achievement, of one's temporal identity. So that, for example, though it is not taught in the schools (and this has the potential of becoming a political issue) the south of France still clings to its ancient and musical Provençal, which resists being described as a "dialect." And much of the tension in the Basque countries, and in Wales, is due to the Basque and Welsh determination not to allow their languages to be destroyed. This determination also feeds the flames in Ireland for among the many indignities the Irish have been forced to undergo at English hands is the English contempt for their language.

It goes without saying, then, that language is also a political instrument, means, and proof of power. It is the most vivid and crucial key to identity: It reveals the private identity, and connects one with, or divorces one from, the larger, public, or communal identity. There have been, and are, times and places, when to speak a certain language could be dangerous, even fatal. Or, one may speak the same language, but in such a way that one's antecedents are revealed, or (one hopes) hidden. This is true in France, and is absolutely true in England: The range (and reign) of accents on that damp little island make England coherent for the English and totally incomprehensible for everyone else. To open your mouth in England is (if I may use black English) to "put your business in the street." You have confessed your parents, your youth, your school, your salary, your self-esteem, and, alas, your future.

Now, I do not know what white Americans would sound like if there had   5
never been any black people in the United States, but they would not sound the way they sound. *Jazz*, for example, is a very specific sexual term, as in *jazz me, baby*, but white people purified it into the Jazz Age. *Sock it to me*, which means, roughly, the same thing, has been adopted by Nathaniel Hawthorne's descendants with no qualms or hesitations at all, along with *let it all hang out* and *right on! Beat to his socks*, which was once the black's most total and despairing image of poverty, was transformed into a thing called the Beat Generation, which phenomenon was, largely, composed of *uptight*, middle-class white people, imitating poverty, trying to *get down*, to *get with it*, doing their *thing*, doing their despairing best to be *funky*, which we, the blacks, never dreamed of doing — we were funky, baby, like *funk* was going out of style.

Now, no one can eat his cake, and have it, too, and it is late in the day to attempt to penalize black people for having created a language that permits the nation its only glimpse of reality, a language without which the nation would be even more *whipped* than it is.

I say that the present skirmish is rooted in American history, and it is. Black English is the creation of the black diaspora. Blacks came to the United States chained to each other, but from different tribes. Neither could speak the other's language. If two black people, at that bitter hour of the world's history, had been able to speak to each other, the institution of chattel slavery could never have lasted as long as it did. Subsequently, the slave was given, under the eye, and the gun, of his master, Congo Square, and the Bible — or, in other words, and under those conditions, the slave began the formation of the black church, and it is within this unprecedented tabernacle that black English began to be formed. This was not, merely, as in the European example, the adoption of a foreign tongue, but an alchemy that transformed ancient elements into a new language: *A language comes into existence by means of brutal necessity, and the rules of the language are dictated by what the language must convey.*

There was a moment, in time, and in this place, when my brother, or my mother, or my father, or my sister, had to convey to me, for example, the danger in which I was standing from the white man standing just behind me, and to convey this with a speed and in a language, that the white man could not possibly understand, and that, indeed, he cannot understand, until today. He cannot afford to understand it. This understanding would reveal to him too much about himself and smash that mirror before which he has been frozen for so long.

Now, if this passion, this skill, this (to quote Toni Morrison) "sheer intelligence," this incredible music, the mighty achievement of having brought a people utterly unknown to, or despised by "history" — to have brought this people to their present, troubled, troubling, and unassailable and unanswerable place — if this absolutely unprecedented journey does not indicate that black English is a language, I am curious to know what definition of languages is to be trusted.

A people at the center of the western world, and in the midst of so hostile a population, has not endured and transcended by means of what is patronizingly called a "dialect." We, the blacks, are in trouble, certainly, but we are not inarticulate because we are not compelled to defend a morality that we know to be a lie.   10

The brutal truth is that the bulk of the white people in America never had any interest in educating black people, except as this could serve white purposes. It is not the black child's language that is despised. It is his experience. A child cannot be taught by anyone who despises him, and a child cannot afford to be fooled. A child cannot be taught by anyone whose demand, essentially, is that the child repudiate his experience, and all that gives him sustenance, and enter a limbo in which he will no longer be black, and in which he knows that he can never become white. Black people have lost too many black children that way.

And, after all, finally, in a country with standards so untrustworthy, a country that makes heroes of so many criminal mediocrities, a country unable to face why so many of the nonwhite are in prison, or on the needle, or standing, futureless, in the streets — it may very well be that both the child, and his elder, have concluded that they have nothing whatever to learn from the people of a country that has managed to learn so little.

QUESTIONS

1. Baldwin begins his essay by challenging the standard argument concerning black English: "The argument has nothing to do with language itself

but with the role of language" (paragraph 1). What distinctions does Baldwin note between "language itself" and "the role of language"? Why is this distinction central to his argument?

2. Baldwin's position on black English is at odds with those who would like to deny black English status as a language. Summarize Baldwin's position. Summarize the position of Baldwin's opponents.

3. In paragraph 4, Baldwin writes, "It goes without saying, then, that language is also a political instrument, means, and proof of power." How, according to Baldwin, does language connect or divide one from "public, or communal identity"? What evidence does he provide to support this claim that language is a political instrument?

4. Baldwin asks his readers, "What is language?" and thus leads them to define for themselves "what definition of languages is to be trusted" (paragraph 9). Do you find that Baldwin's definition and position are persuasive? Explain.

5. Reread Baldwin's memorable conclusion. How does he prepare you for this conclusion? What are you left to contemplate?

6. How has Baldwin's essay made you think about your own use of language and the role language plays in your identity? Baldwin makes an important distinction between *dialect* and *language*. Write an essay in which you take a position on the role of language in shaping your identity.

7. Select a dialect with which you are familiar. Analyze the features of this dialect. Write an essay in which you develop a position showing how this dialect reflects the richness of its culture.

Making Connections

1. Both Baldwin and George Orwell (p. 280) are interested in understanding language as a political instrument. Write an essay in which you examine their views on the politics of language, pointing out their similarities and differences.

2. Both Baldwin and Martin Luther King Jr. (p. 346) make strong arguments about racial questions. Both of these writers are considered to be exceptional masters of English prose. What color is their English? Write an essay in which you consider them as argumentative writers. Are their styles of argument different? Do they use the same vocabulary? How would you characterize each of them as a writer? Do you prefer one style over the other? Do you find that one of their arguments is more effective than the other? Present your opinions, and make your case.

POLITICS AND THE ENGLISH LANGUAGE

George Orwell

The rise of totalitarianism in Europe led George Orwell (1903–1950) to write about its causes in his most famous novels, Animal Farm *(1945) and* 1984 *(1949), and in essays like "Politics and the English Language." In this essay, written in 1946, Orwell tells his readers that "in our time, political speech and writing are largely the defense of the indefensible." He attacks language that consists "largely of euphemism, question begging, and sheer cloudy vagueness." Orwell, like John Berger earlier in this section, is concerned with the ways in which language is often used to conceal unpleasant and horrifying realities.*

Most people who bother with the matter at all would admit that the English language is in a bad way, but it is generally assumed that we cannot by conscious action do anything about it. Our civilization is decadent and our language — so the argument runs — must inevitably share in the general collapse. It follows that any struggle against the abuse of language is a sentimental archaism, like preferring candles to electric light or hansom cabs to aeroplanes. Underneath this lies the half-conscious belief that language is a natural growth and not an instrument which we shape for our own purposes.

Now, it is clear that the decline of a language must ultimately have political and economic causes: it is not due simply to the bad influence of this or that individual writer. But an effect can become a cause, reinforcing the original cause and producing the same effect in an intensified form, and so on indefinitely. A man may take to drink because he feels himself to be a failure, and then fail all the more completely because he drinks. It is rather the same thing that is happening to the English language. It becomes ugly and inaccurate because our thoughts are foolish, but the slovenliness of our language makes it easier for us to have foolish thoughts. The point is that the process is reversible. Modern English, especially written English, is full of bad habits which spread by imitation and which can be avoided if one is willing to take the necessary trouble. If one gets rid of these habits one can think more clearly, and to think clearly is a necessary first step towards political regeneration: so that the fight against bad English is not frivolous and is not the exclusive concern of professional writers. I will come back to this presently, and I hope that by that time the meaning of what I have said here will have become clearer. Meanwhile, here are five specimens of the English language as it is now habitually written.

These five passages have not been picked out because they are especially bad—I could have quoted far worse if I had chosen—but because they illustrate various of the mental vices from which we now suffer. They are a little below the average, but are fairly representative samples. I number them so that I can refer back to them when necessary:

"(1) I am not, indeed, sure whether it is not true to say that the Milton who once seemed not unlike a seventeenth-century Shelley had not become, out of an experience ever more bitter in each year, more alien [*sic*] to the founder of that Jesuit sect which nothing could induce him to tolerate."

Professor Harold Laski (Essay in *Freedom of Expression*)

"(2) Above all, we cannot play ducks and drakes with a native battery of idioms which prescribes such egregious collocations of vocables as the basic *put up with* for *tolerate* or *put at a loss* for *bewilder*."

Professor Lancelot Hogben (*Interglossa*)

"(3) On the one side we have the free personality: by definition it is not neurotic, for it has neither conflict nor dream. Its desires, such as they are, are transparent, for they are just what institutional approval keeps in the forefront of consciousness; another institutional pattern would alter their number and intensity; there is little in them that is natural, irreducible, or culturally dangerous. But *on the other* side, the social bond itself is nothing but the mutual reflection of these self-secure integrities. Recall the definition of love. Is not this the very picture of a small academic? Where is there a place in this hall of mirrors for either personality or fraternity?"

Essay on psychology in *Politics* (New York)

"(4) All the 'best people' from the gentlemen's clubs, and all the frantic fascist captains, united in common hatred of Socialism and bestial horror of the rising tide of the mass revolutionary movement, have turned to acts of provocation, to foul incendiarism, to medieval legends of poisoned wells, to legalize their own destruction of proletarian organizations, and rouse the agitated petty-bourgeoisie to chauvinistic fervour on behalf of the fight against the revolutionary way out of the crisis."

Communist pamphlet

"(5) If a new spirit *is* to be infused into this old country, there is one thorny and contentious reform which must be tackled, and that is the humanization and galvanization of the B.B.C. Timidity here will bespeak cancer and atrophy of the soul. The heart of Britain may be sound and of strong beat, for instance, but the British lion's roar at present is like that of Bottom in Shakespeare's *Midsummer Night's*

Dream — as gentle as any sucking dove. A virile new Britain cannot continue indefinitely to be traduced in the eyes or rather ears, of the world by the effete languors of Langham Place, brazenly masquerading as 'standard English.' When the Voice of Britain is heard at nine o'clock, better far and infinitely less ludicrous to hear aitches honestly dropped than the present priggish, inflated, inhibited, schoolma'amish arch braying of blameless bashful mewing maidens!"

Letter in Tribune

Each of these passages has faults of its own, but, quite apart from avoidable ugliness, two qualities are common to all of them. The first is staleness of imagery: the other is lack of precision. The writer either has a meaning and cannot express it, or he inadvertently says something else, or he is almost indifferent as to whether his words mean anything or not. This mixture of vagueness and sheer incompetence is the most marked characteristic of modern English prose, and especially of any kind of political writing. As soon as certain topics are raised, the concrete melts into the abstract and no one seems able to think of turns of speech that are not hackneyed: prose consists less and less of *words* chosen for the sake of their meaning, and more and more of *phrases* tacked together like the sections of a prefabricated hen-house. I list below, with notes and examples, various of the tricks by means of which the work of prose-construction is habitually dodged:

Dying Metaphors.   A newly invented metaphor assists thought by evoking   5
a visual image, while on the other hand a metaphor which is technically "dead" (e.g. *iron resolution*) has in effect reverted to being an ordinary word and can generally be used without loss of vividness. But in between these two classes there is a huge dump of worn-out metaphors which have lost all evocative power and are merely used because they save people the trouble of inventing phrases for themselves. Examples are: *Ring the changes on, take up the cudgels for, toe the line, ride roughshod over, stand shoulder to shoulder with, play into the hands of, no axe to grind, grist to the mill, fishing in troubled waters, on the order of the day, Achilles' heel, swan song, hotbed.* Many of these are used without knowledge of their meaning (what is a "rift," for instance?), and incompatible metaphors are frequently mixed, a sure sign that the writer is not interested in what he is saying. Some metaphors now current have been twisted out of their original meaning without those who use them even being aware of the fact. For example, *toe the line* is sometimes written *tow the line.* Another example is *the hammer and the anvil,* now always used with the implication that the anvil gets the worst of it. In real life it is always the anvil that breaks the hammer, never the other way about: a writer who stopped to think what he was saying would be aware of this, and would avoid perverting the original phrase.

Operators or Verbal False Limbs.   These save the trouble of picking out appropriate verbs and nouns, and at the same time pad each sentence with extra syllables which give it an appearance of symmetry. Characteristic phrases are: *render inoperative, militate against, make contact with, be subjected to, give rise to, give grounds for, have the effect of, play a leading part (role) in, make itself felt, take effect, exhibit a tendency to, serve the purpose of, etc., etc.* The keynote is the elimination of simple verbs. Instead of being a single word, such as *break, stop, spoil, mend, kill,* a verb becomes a *phrase,* made up of a noun or adjective tacked on to some general-purposes verb such as *prove, serve, form, play, render.* In addition, the passive voice is wherever possible used in preference to the active, and noun constructions are used instead of gerunds (*by examination of* instead of *by examining*). The range of verbs is further cut down by means of the *-ize* and *de-* formation, and the banal statements are given an appearance of profundity by means of the *not un-* formation. Simple conjunctions and prepositions are replaced by such phrases as *with respect to, having regard to, the fact that, by dint of, in view of, in the interests of, on the hypothesis that;* and the ends of sentences are saved from anticlimax by such resounding commonplaces as *greatly to be desired, cannot be left out of account, a development to be expected in the near future, deserving of serious consideration, brought to a satisfactory conclusion,* and so on and so forth.

Pretentious Diction. Words like *phenomenon, element, individual* (as noun), *objective, categorical, effective, virtual, basic, primary, promote, constitute, exhibit, exploit, utilize, eliminate, liquidate,* are used to dress up simple statements and give an air of scientific impartiality to biased judgments. Adjectives like *epoch-making, epic, historic, unforgettable, triumphant, age-old, inevitable, inexorable, veritable,* are used to dignify the sordid processes of international politics, while writing that aims at glorifying war usually takes on an archaic color, its characteristic words being: *realm, throne, chariot, mailed fist, trident, sword, shield, buckler, banner, jackboot, clarion.* Foreign words and expressions such as *cul de sac, ancien régime, deus ex machina, mutatis mutandis, status quo, gleichschaltung, weltanschauung,* are used to give an air of culture and elegance. Except for the useful abbreviations *i.e., e.g.,* and *etc.,* there is no real need for any of the hundreds of foreign phrases now current in English. Bad writers, and especially scientific, political and sociological writers, are nearly always haunted by the notion that Latin or Greek words are grander than Saxon ones, and unnecessary words like *expedite, ameliorate, predict, extraneous, deracinated, clandestine, subaqueous* and hundreds of others constantly gain ground from their Anglo-Saxon opposite numbers.[1] The jargon peculiar to Marxist writing (*hyena, hangman,*

---

[1]An interesting illustration of this is the way in which the English flower names which were in use till very recently are being ousted by Greek ones, *snapdragon* becoming *antirrhinum, forget-me-not* becoming *myosotis,* etc. It is hard to see any practical reason for this change of fashion: it is probably due to an instinctive turning-away from the more homely word and a vague feeling that the Greek word is scientific.

cannibal, petty bourgeois, these gentry, lackey, flunky, mad dog, White Guard, etc.) consists largely of words and phrases translated from Russian, German or French; but the normal way of coining a new word is to use a Latin or Greek root with the appropriate affix and, where necessary, the -ize formation. It is often easier to make up words of this kind (deregionalize, impermissible, extramarital, nonfragmentatory and so forth) than to think up the English words that will cover one's meaning. The result, in general, is an increase in slovenliness and vagueness.

Meaningless Words.   In certain kinds of writing, particularly in art criticism and literary criticism, it is normal to come across long passages which are almost completely lacking in meaning.[2] Words like romantic, plastic, values, human, dead, sentimental, natural, vitality, as used in art criticism, are strictly meaningless in the sense that they not only do not point to any discoverable object, but are hardly ever expected to do so by the reader. When one critic writes, "The outstanding feature of Mr. X's work is its living quality," while another writes, "The immediately striking thing about Mr. X's work is its peculiar deadness," the reader accepts this as a simple difference of opinion. If words like black and white were involved, instead of the jargon words dead and living, he would see at once that language was being used in an improper way. Many political words are similarly abused. The word Fascism has now no meaning except in so far as it signifies "something not desirable." The words democracy, socialism, freedom, patriotic, realistic, justice, have each of them several different meanings which cannot be reconciled with one another. In the case of a word like democracy, not only is there no agreed definition, but the attempt to make one is resisted from all sides. It is almost universally felt that when we call a country democratic we are praising it: consequently the defenders of every kind of régime claim that it is a democracy, and fear that they might have to stop using the word if it were tied down to any one meaning. Words of this kind are often used in a consciously dishonest way. That is, the person who uses them has his own private definition, but allows his hearer to think he means something quite different. Statements like Marshal Pétain was a true patriot, The Soviet Press is the freest in the world, The Catholic Church is opposed to persecution, are almost always made with intent to deceive. Other words used in variable meanings, in most cases more or less dishonestly, are: class, totalitarian, science, progressive, reactionary, bourgeois, equality.

---

[2]Example: "Comfort's catholicity of perception and image, strangely Whitmanesque in range, almost the exact opposite in aesthetic compulsion, continues to evoke that trembling atmospheric accumulative hinting at a cruel, an inexorably serene timelessness . . . Wrey Gardiner scores by aiming at simple bull's-eyes with precision. Only they are not so simple, and through this contented sadness runs more than the surface bittersweet of resignation" (Poetry Quarterly).

Now that I have made this catalog of swindles and perversions, let me give another example of the kind of writing that they lead to. This time it must of its nature be an imaginary one. I am going to translate a passage of good English into modern English of the worst sort. Here is a well-known verse from *Ecclesiastes*:

> "I returned and saw under the sun, that the race is not to the swift, nor the battle to the strong, neither yet bread to the wise, nor yet riches to men of understanding, nor yet favor to men of skill; but time and chance happeneth to them all."

Here it is in modern English: 10

> "Objective consideration of contemporary phenomena compels the conclusion that success or failure in competitive activities exhibits no tendency to be commensurate with innate capacity, but that a considerable element of the unpredictable must invariably be taken into account."

This is a parody, but not a very gross one. Exhibit (3), above, for instance, contains several patches of the same kind of English. It will be seen that I have not made a full translation. The beginning and ending of the sentence follow the original meaning fairly closely, but in the middle the concrete illustrations — race, battle, bread — dissolve into the vague phrase "success or failure in competitive activities." This had to be so, because no modern writer of the kind I am discussing — no one capable of using phrases like "objective consideration of contemporary phenomena" — would ever tabulate his thoughts in that precise and detailed way. The whole tendency of modern prose is away from concreteness. Now analyse these two sentences a little more closely. The first contains forty-nine words but only sixty syllables, and all its words are those of everyday life. The second contains thirty-eight words of ninety syllables: eighteen of its words are from Latin roots, and one from Greek. The first sentence contains six vivid images, and only one phrase ("time and chance") that could be called vague. The second contains not a single fresh, arresting phrase, and in spite of its ninety syllables it gives only a shortened version of the meaning contained in the first. Yet without a doubt it is the second kind of sentence that is gaining ground in modern English. I do not want to exaggerate. This kind of writing is not yet universal, and outcrops of simplicity will occur here and there in the worst-written page. Still, if you or I were told to write a few lines on the uncertainty of human fortunes, we should probably come much nearer to my imaginary sentence than to the one from *Ecclesiastes*.

As I have tried to show, modern writing at its worst does not consist in picking out words for the sake of their meaning and inventing images in order to make the meaning clearer. It consists in gumming together long strips of words which have already been set in order by someone else, and making the results presentable by sheer humbug. The attraction of this way of writing is that it is easy. It is easier — even quicker, once you have the habit — to say *In my opinion it is a not unjustifiable assumption that* than to say *I think*. If you use ready-made phrases, you not only don't have to hunt about for words; you also don't have to bother with the rhythms of your sentences, since these phrases are generally so arranged as to be more or less euphonious. When you are composing in a hurry — when you are dictating to a stenographer, for instance, or making a public speech — it is natural to fall into a pretentious, Latinized style. Tags like *a consideration which we should do well to bear in mind* or *a conclusion to which all of us would readily assent* will save many a sentence from coming down with a bump. By using stale metaphors, similes and idioms, you save much mental effort, at the cost of leaving your meaning vague, not only for your reader but for yourself. This is the significance of mixed metaphors. The sole aim of a metaphor is to call up a visual image. When these images clash — as in *The Fascist octopus has sung its swan song, the jackboot is thrown into the melting pot* — it can be taken as certain that the writer is not seeing a mental image of the objects he is naming; in other words he is not really thinking. Look again at the examples I gave at the beginning of this essay. Professor Laski (1) uses five negatives in fifty-three words. One of these is superfluous, making nonsense of the whole passage, and in addition there is the slip *alien* for akin, making further nonsense, and several avoidable pieces of clumsiness which increase the general vagueness. Professor Hogben (2) plays ducks and drakes with a battery which is able to write prescriptions, and, while disapproving of the everyday phrase *put up with*, is unwilling to look *egregious* up in the dictionary and see what it means. (3), if one takes an uncharitable attitude towards it, is simply meaningless: probably one could work out its intended meaning by reading the whole of the article in which it occurs. In (4), the writer knows more or less what he wants to say, but an accumulation of stale phrases chokes him like tea leaves blocking a sink. In (5), words and meaning have almost parted company. People who write in this manner usually have a general emotional meaning — they dislike one thing and want to express solidarity with another — but they are not interested in the detail of what they are saying. A scrupulous writer, in every sentence that he writes, will ask himself at least four questions, thus: What am I trying to say? What words will express it? What image or idiom will make it clearer? Is this image fresh enough to have an effect? And he will probably ask himself two more: Could I put it more shortly? Have I said anything that is avoidably ugly? But you are not obliged to go to all this trouble. You can shirk it by simply throwing your mind open and letting the ready-made phrases come crowding in. They will construct your sentences for you — even think your thoughts for you, to a certain extent — and at need they will perform the important service of partially concealing your meaning even from yourself. It is at this point that the special connection between politics and the debasement of language becomes clear.

In our time it is broadly true that political writing is bad writing. Where it is not true, it will generally be found that the writer is some kind of rebel, expressing his private opinions and not a "party line." Orthodoxy, of whatever color, seems to demand a lifeless, imitative style. The political dialects to be found in pamphlets, leading articles, manifestos, White Papers and the speeches of under-secretaries do, of course, vary from party to party, but they are all alike in that one almost never finds in them a fresh, vivid, home-made turn of speech. When one watches some tired hack on the platform mechanically repeating the familiar phrases — *bestial atrocities, iron heel, bloodstained tyranny, free peoples of the world, stand shoulder to shoulder* — one often has a curious feeling that one is not watching a live human being but some kind of dummy: a feeling which suddenly becomes stronger at moments when the light catches the speaker's spectacles and turns them into blank discs which seem to have no eyes behind them. And this is not altogether fanciful. A speaker who uses that kind of phraseology has gone some distance towards turning himself into a machine. The appropriate noises are coming out of his larynx, but his brain is not involved as it would be if he were choosing his words for himself. If the speech he is making is one that he is accustomed to make over and over again, he may be almost unconscious of what he is saying, as one is when one utters the responses in church. And this reduced state of consciousness, if not indispensable, is at any rate favorable to political conformity.

In our time, political speech and writing are largely the defense of the indefensible. Things like the continuance of British rule in India, the Russian purges and deportations, the dropping of the atom bombs on Japan, can indeed be defended, but only by arguments which are too brutal for most people to face, and which do not square with the professed aims of political parties. Thus political language has to consist largely of euphemism, question-begging and sheer cloudy vagueness. Defenseless villages are bombarded from the air, the inhabitants driven out into the countryside, the cattle machine-gunned, the huts set on fire with incendiary bullets: this is called *pacification*. Millions of peasants are robbed of their farms and sent trudging along the roads with no more than they can carry: this is called *transfer of population* or *rectification of frontiers*. People are imprisoned for years without trial, or shot in the back of the neck or sent to die of scurvy in Arctic lumber camps: this is called *elimination of unreliable elements*. Such phraseology is needed if one wants to name things without calling up mental pictures of them. Consider for instance some comfortable English professor defending Russian totalitarianism. He cannot say outright, "I believe in killing off your opponents when you can get good results by doing so." Probably, therefore, he will say something like this:

"While freely conceding that the Soviet régime exhibits certain features 15 which the humanitarian may be inclined to deplore, we must, I think, agree that a certain curtailment of the right to political opposition is an unavoidable concomitant of transitional periods, and that the rigors which the

Russian people have been called upon to undergo have been amply justified in the sphere of concrete achievement."

The inflated style is itself a kind of euphemism. A mass of Latin words falls upon the facts like soft snow, blurring the outlines and covering up all the details. The great enemy of clear language is insincerity. When there is a gap between one's real and one's declared aims, one turns as it were instinctively to long words and exhausted idioms, like a cuttlefish squirting out ink. In our age there is no such thing as "keeping out of politics." All issues are political issues, and politics itself is a mass of lies, evasions, folly, hatred and schizophrenia. When the general atmosphere is bad, language must suffer. I should expect to find — this is a guess which I have not sufficient knowledge to verify — that the German, Russian and Italian languages have all deteriorated in the last ten or fifteen years, as a result of dictatorship.

But if thought corrupts language, language can also corrupt thought. A bad usage can spread by tradition and imitation, even among people who should and do know better. The debased language that I have been discussing is in some ways very convenient. Phrases like *a not unjustifiable assumption, leaves much to be desired, would serve no good purpose, a consideration which we should do well to bear in mind*, are a continuous temptation, a packet of aspirins always at one's elbow. Look back through this essay, and for certain you will find that I have again and again committed the very faults I am protesting against. By this morning's post I have received a pamphlet dealing with conditions in Germany. The author tells me that he "felt impelled" to write it. I open it at random, and here is almost the first sentence that I see: "(The Allies) have an opportunity not only of achieving a radical transformation of Germany's social and political structure in such a way as to avoid a nationalistic reaction in Germany itself, but at the same time of laying the foundations of a cooperative and unified Europe." You see, he "feels impelled" to write — feels, presumably, that he has something new to say — and yet his words, like cavalry horses answering the bugle, group themselves automatically into the familiar dreary pattern. This invasion of one's mind by ready-made phrases (*lay the foundations, achieve a radical transformation*) can only be prevented if one is constantly on guard against them, and every such phrase anaesthetizes a portion of one's brain.

I said earlier that the decadence of our language is probably curable. Those who deny this would argue, if they produced an argument at all, that language merely reflects existing social conditions, and that we cannot influence its development by any direct tinkering with words and constructions. So far as the general tone or spirit of a language goes, this may be true, but it is not true in detail. Silly words and expressions have often disappeared, not through any evolutionary process but owing to the conscious action of a minority. Two recent examples were *explore every avenue* and *leave no stone unturned*, which were killed by the jeers of a few journalists. There is a long list of flyblown metaphors which could similarly be got rid of if enough people would interest themselves in the job; and it should also be possible to laugh the *not un-* formation out of existence,[3] to reduce the amount of Latin and Greek in the average sentence, to drive out foreign phrases and strayed scientific words, and, in general, to make pretentiousness unfashionable. But all these are minor points. The defense of the English language implies more than this, and perhaps it is best to start by saying what it does not imply.

To begin with it has nothing to do with archaism, with the salvaging of obsolete words and turns of speech, or with the setting up of a "standard English" which must never be departed from. On the contrary, it is especially concerned with the scrapping of every word or idiom which has outworn its usefulness. It has nothing to do with correct grammar and syntax, which are of no importance so long as one makes one's meaning clear, or with the avoidance of Americanisms, or with having what is called a "good prose style." On the other hand it is not concerned with fake simplicity and the attempt to make written English colloquial. Nor does it even imply in every case preferring the Saxon word to the Latin one, though it does imply using the fewest and shortest words that will cover one's meaning. What is above all needed is to let the meaning choose the word, and not the other way about. In prose, the worst thing one can do with words is to surrender to them. When you think of a concrete object, you think wordlessly, and then, if you want to describe the thing you have been visualizing you probably hunt about till you find the exact words that seem to fit. When you think of something abstract you are more inclined to use words from the start, and unless you make a conscious effort to prevent it, the existing dialect will come rushing in and do the job for you, at the expense of blurring or even changing your meaning. Probably it is better to put off using words as long as possible and get one's meaning as clear as one can through pictures or sensations. Afterwards one can choose—not simply *accept*—the phrases that will best cover the meaning, and then switch round and decide what impression one's words are likely to make on another person. This last effort of the mind cuts out all stale or mixed images, all prefabricated phrases, needless repetitions, and humbug and vagueness generally. But one can often be in doubt about the effect of a word or a phrase, and one needs rules that one can rely on when instinct fails. I think the following rules will cover most cases:

(i) Never use a metaphor, simile or other figure of speech which you are used to seeing in print.

(ii) Never use a long word where a short one will do.

(iii) If it is possible to cut a word out, always cut it out.

(iv) Never use the passive where you can use the active.

---

[3]One can cure oneself of the *not un-* formation by memorizing this sentence: *A not unblack dog was chasing a not unsmall rabbit across a not ungreen field.*

(v) Never use a foreign phrase, a scientific word or a jargon word if you can think of an everyday English equivalent.

(vi) Break any of these rules sooner than say anything outright barbarous.

These rules sound elementary, and so they are, but they demand a deep   20
change of attitude in anyone who has grown used to writing in the style now fashionable. One could keep all of them and still write bad English, but one could not write the kind of stuff that I quoted in those five specimens at the beginning of this article.

I have not here been considering the literary use of language, but merely language as an instrument for expressing and not for concealing or preventing thought. Stuart Chase and others have come near to claiming that all abstract words are meaningless, and have used this as a pretext for advocating a kind of political quietism. Since you don't know what Fascism is, how can you struggle against Fascism? One need not swallow such absurdities as this, but one ought to recognize that the present political chaos is connected with the decay of language, and that one can probably bring about some improvement by starting at the verbal end. If you simplify your English, you are freed from the worst follies of orthodoxy. You cannot speak any of the necessary dialects, and when you make a stupid remark its stupidity will be obvious, even to yourself. Political language — and with variations this is true of all political parties, from Conservatives to Anarchists — is designed to make lies sound truthful and murder respectable, and to give an appearance of solidity to pure wind. One cannot change this all in a moment, but one can at least change one's own habits, and from time to time one can even, if one jeers loudly enough, send some worn-out and useless phrase — some *jackboot, Achilles' heel, hotbed, melting pot, acid test, veritable inferno* or other lump of verbal refuse — into the dustbin where it belongs.

QUESTIONS

1. What is Orwell's position on the ways that modern writers are destroying the English language?
2. Orwell argues that "thought corrupts language," but he also argues that "language can also corrupt thought" (paragraph 17). What argument is he making? How does language corrupt thought?
3. Orwell writes in paragraph 17, "Look back through this essay, and for certain you will find that I have again and again committed the very faults I am protesting against." Does Orwell, in fact, break his own rules? If so, what might his purpose be in doing so?
4. What sense of himself does Orwell present to his readers? How would you describe his persona, his character?
5. Why do people write badly, according to Orwell? What causes does he identify in his essay? Do you agree with him? Explain.

6. Orwell presents guidelines for good writing in paragraph 19. Take one of your recent essays, and analyze how your writing measures up to Orwell's standards.
7. Spend one week developing a list of examples of bad writing from newspapers and popular magazines. Use this material as the basis for an essay in which you develop a thesis to argue your position on politics and language.
8. Written sixty years ago, this is probably the best known of all of Orwell's essays. How insightful and current do you find it today? Take five examples from your reading, as Orwell takes from his, and use them as evidence in an argument of your own about the state of contemporary written English. Take your examples from anything you like, including this book — even this question — if you wish. Be careful to choose recent pieces of writing.

MAKING CONNECTIONS

1. Given Orwell's concern with the language of political writing, consider how he might judge his own political writing in "Shooting an Elephant" (p. 354) or Hemingway's piece of political reportage in "A New Kind of War" (p. 127). Use Orwell's six rules as a standard for assessing each piece, and state which one you think is more in keeping with his standards for political writing.
2. John Berger (p. 268) and James Baldwin (p. 276), as represented by their essays in this section, are two writers who probably were influenced by Orwell's essay "Politics and the English Language." Choose either Berger's or Baldwin's essay, and write an essay of your own explaining the connections that you find between Orwell and either Berger or Baldwin.

WHY WE HATE TEACHERS

Garret Keizer

*A graduate of the University of Vermont, Garret Keizer (b. 1954)
worked as a high school English teacher for fifteen years, an experience that provided the basis for his first book,* No Place but Here:
A Teacher's Vocation in a Rural Community *(1988). He went on
to become an Episcopal minister, a transition he chronicled in*
A Dresser of Sycamore Trees: The Finding of a Ministry *(1991).
A prolific essayist, Keizer has also published* Help: The Original
Human Dilemma *(2004) and a young adult novel,* God of Beer
(2002). The following essay appeared in a 2001 issue of Harper's
magazine devoted to contemporary American education.

> Glory, glory, alleluia.
> Teacher hit me with a ruler.
> I knocked her on the bean
> With a rotten tangerine,
> And she ain't gonna teach no more.
> — "Mine Eyes Have Seen
>   the Glory of the
>   Burning of the School"
>   (Traditional)

As soon as I entered first grade, I began throwing up my breakfast
every day, Monday through Friday, usually two or three minutes before the
school bus came. I do not recall having what are nowadays referred to as
"academic difficulties." In fact, I was already the good student I would continue to be right through graduate school. Nor do I recall being picked on
in any particular way; that would come later. What I recall is being struck
at about the same time as my mother handed me my lunch with an irre-
sistible urge to vomit my breakfast—that, and the sight of my mother on
her knees again, wiping up my mess.

I have long since marveled at the way in which my parents, without benefit of formal courses in psychology or any thought of sending me to a psychologist (this was 1959), set about trying to cure me by a psychological
stratagem at once desperate, risky, and ingenious. It amounted to the con-
trivance of an epiphany. One evening they announced that the next day I
would not be going to school. Instead, my mother and I would be taking a
trip "up country" to see Aunt Em and have a picnic. Aunt Em and her husband were caretakers of a sprawling rural cemetery in which I delighted to
play and explore. They lived in a house "as old as George Washington."
Propped against one of their porch pillars was an enormous Chiclet-shaped

rock, an object of great fascination for me, which they claimed was a petrified dinosaur tooth. There were few places on earth I would rather have gone.

The next morning arrived like an early Christmas. I watched impatiently as my mother packed a lunch for our adventure. Then, just at the time when the school bus would have picked me up, she turned to me and in a tone of poignant resignation said, "Now, you see, Gary, there is nothing wrong with your stomach. You get sick because you don't want to go to school." She handed me my lunch and told me that we were not going to Aunt Em's that day. I did not throw up. I forget whether or not I cried. But, for the most part, I was cured.

I say for the most part because even now, at the age of forty-eight, I am rarely able to walk into any school without feeling something of the same duodenal ominousness that haunted my first days as a student. I doubt I am unique in this, though it does seem like an odd symptom for someone who went to school for almost twenty years, who taught high school for fifteen years after that, who saw his wife through graduate school after she had done the same for him, and who will be in his mid-fifties by the time he has seen his daughter through college. I have spent most of my life "in school," doing homework or correcting it, which means that for much of my life I have either skipped breakfast or eaten it as an act of faith.

And I still catch myself thinking of that aborted trip to Aunt Em's. I picture myself running over the mown graves, past generations of polished monuments, with a cool breeze at my back and the clouds unfolding like angel wings above me. It amounts to a waking dream, with a dream's psychic symbolism, and what I think it means is that I have reconciled myself to death by imagining it as the most sublime form of hooky: the blessed stage at which no one will ever again, in any form whatsoever, make me go to school.

I do not have frightful memories of my first-grade teacher, though my parents have told me she was "stern." I remember her punishing a boy who'd meandered into the girls' bathroom by forcing him to wear a cardboard sign that read I AM A GIRL TODAY. I remember another boy, a budding Leonardo da Vinci, whose crammed, cluttered desk she would from time to time dump over onto the floor, like an unfaithful wife's wardrobe tossed onto the street. I can still see him kneeling among his precocious drawings and playground-excavated fossils, straightening things up as best as he could, while the rest of us looked on with the dumbstruck fascination of smaller-brained primates. I can see these things clearly, but I do not remember the teacher herself as an ogre. As for the memories of my two classmates, the first of whom would eventually become an outlaw biker and the second of whom probably went on through a long progression of larger and even messier desks, I am not so sure.

Such stories of cruel and unusual punishment probably account at least partially for that hideous strain of American folk humor, with a pedigree that runs from Washington Irving to Garrison Keillor: the Tale of the Teacher We Drove Nuts. I used to know a man who would tell me, in the tone of someone bragging about his first sexual experience, how he and his friends had driven a nun at his Catholic school to a nervous breakdown. "Let's put it this way: She didn't come back the next year." It so happens that I was working as a teacher when I first heard the story. So was the man who told it to me.

It's hard to imagine a parallel from another profession, perhaps some folksy yarn about an undertaker driven to tears by a repeated switcheroo of his embalming fluid and his coffee, a cashier who fell down foaming at the mouth after making change for one too many ten-pound bags of dimes. It's simplistic to say that we see these tales as innocuous because their protagonists are only children. We also see them as innocuous because their victims are only teachers (and usually women). We like to tell these stories, I think, because they requite some primal — as in "primary" school — pain within us.

For many children, going to school amounts to a fall from grace. I have long sensed a mystical connection between the iconic apple on the teacher's desk and the apple Adam ate from the forbidden tree; I am tempted to take them for the same apple. Perhaps the New England Puritans who taught their children the alphabet starting with the A in "Adam's Fall" were playing with the same idea. Although teachers may figure variously in the myth as Eve, the Serpent, or God, they are almost always the flaming cherubim who bar our return to the innocence of early childhood. For better or for worse, a teacher was our first surrogate mother. The wicked stepmother and the fairy godmother are *mothers*, after all, and in the fairy tales of personal history they both tend to have teaching licenses. In other words, the story of our first encounter with school is either the tale of how we betrayed our mothers for a princess or the tale of how they abandoned us to a witch.

And the last chapter mirrors the first: the teacher who took us from our   10
mothers appears in another guise to take our children from us later on. The teacher who is a boy's first crush is also his mother's first rival. Furthermore, in an era when mothers frequently work outside the home, a teacher with the benefit of a shorter day and a longer summer vacation not only spends the best hours of the day with our children; she spends the brightest days of the year with her own. I believe this accounts for much of the disdain for teachers, particularly in working-class communities like mine. If someone gave me the power and the money to make one change that might improve the public perception of teachers, I would give working parents more time with their kids. At the very least, that would remind them to be grateful for the hours their kids are in school.

There are, of course, other ways in which schools represent a psychic fall; and teachers, the guardian angels of its trajectory. Although schools in a democracy purport to exist for the creation of "a level playing field," it does not take us long to discover that level playing fields exist mainly to sort out winners from losers. Unless we came from a large family with parents who went out of their way to play favorites, school was our first introduction to the idea of relative merit. It is not an idea with as much application to the so-called real world as we might think. Neither are any number of schoolhouse rigors justified in that name. Certainly we encounter relative merit in the world. My work as an adult is evaluated and rewarded, and I must face the fact that others are going to be better at it than I am.

But that oppressive sense of minute gradation, of success not as a mansion of many rooms but as a ladder of infinite rungs — where does that exist but in a classroom, or in the imagination of the adult who still sits there? To be a kid again, I must walk to my assigned place in a room ranked with little desks, each occupied by a writer my age, or as he was at my age. And the Updike kid always has his hand up first, and the teacher can't seem to get enough of his stories about rabbits, whereas my poems about turtles always seem to lag behind in her esteem. "Taking your degree" is the most precise phrase in all of education: that is what we take from our first day in kindergarten, our *degree* of relative worth. The educational apple of Adam's Fall, by which the first American primer said "we sinned all," did not give us the knowledge of good and evil but of good, better, and best, world without end.

Another way in which our teachers took us out of the Garden was by taking us out of the moment. It was in school that the future first began its incessant bullying of the present and the past. The watchword was "preparation," and, considered only by the criterion of effective pedagogy, the watchword could hardly be called progressive. Ask a random sample of parents if and when school began to grow sour for their kids, and they will usually say "sometime around fourth or fifth grade"; that is, when teachers began working with a more intentional zeal to "get kids ready for high school," a process that might be likened to getting Sir John Gielgud ready to do a Pepsi commercial. Diminishment follows diminishment, until we reach graduate school, where the ability and certainly the desire to teach are not only rare but generally held in contempt. Few can go that far without developing grave suspicions about the future — perhaps one reason why so many people end up stalled in graduate school. The Serpent promised that we would become "as gods," though it seems that what he really meant is that with the right amount of training and gumption we could become as serpents.

For some of us that meant we could become teachers. We could bring the process of preparation full circle, like the myth of the serpent that devours its own tail. That is, admittedly, a paradoxical image. To be a teacher in America is to embody any number of seeming contradictions, some peculiar to the profession and others intrinsic to the nature of democracy itself.

For one thing, teachers can find themselves an embarrassing exception to the first article of their own creed: that education prepares one to be privileged and prosperous. Of the professional classes, theirs is probably one of the least esteemed; it is certainly one of the least paid. Teaching has traditionally been a port of entry, the Ellis Island by which the children of blue-collar workers entered the professional classes. I seldom see a first-year teacher with her tote bag or briefcase without conjuring up the image of an immigrant and his duffel bag of worldly belongings — so full of faith, so free of cynicism, so ripe for exploitation. And such an easy target for prejudice. 15

Occupying a no-man's-land between the union hall and the reserved parking space, able in some cases to take a sabbatical but in many cases unable to get to a toilet, teachers sometimes find themselves caught in a crossfire of contradictory resentments. On the one hand, the public expects teachers to have some of the same expertise and even some of the same polish as physicians, though no teacher of my acquaintance has ever had the opportunity of hiring his own nurse in the form of a classroom aide — assuming he even had one. On the other hand, those who see teachers as no more than a highly specialized class of clock-punchers are prone to ask what truck driver ever had a nine-week vacation, or what waitress ever had a pension fund.

It almost goes without saying that a teacher's perceived status will vary with the status of the perceiver. So to the svelte mom in the Volvo, Ms. Hart is an air-headed twit without a creative bone in her body, who probably had to write crib notes all over her chubby little hand just to get through Hohum State College with a C. To the burly dad in the rusty pickup truck, Ms. Hart is a book-addled flake without a practical bone in her body but with plenty of good teeth in her head thanks to a dental plan that comes out of said dad's property taxes. In Shakespeare's *King Henry VI*, a common rebel known as Dick the Butcher says, "The first thing we do, let's kill all the lawyers," but to honor the sentiments inside as well as outside the palace Ms. Hart has to die first.

Of course there are any number of parents, in Volvos, old Fords, and on Harley-Davidsons, who will see Ms. Hart as an angel. And of those who see otherwise, might at least a few be responding to her pedagogical competence rather than to her professional status? Undoubtedly so. Teachers probably provide some of the most and least inspiring examples we have of human beings in the act of work. A friend of mine remarked to me recently, "No one, not even a farmer, works harder than a hardworking teacher. But there is nothing on this earth lazier than a lazy teacher." Having taught school for a good part of my adult life, I tend to agree. I wouldn't say that extremes of this kind are unique to teachers, however. I would propose that the same extremes can be found in any occupation that shares the following characteristics: a notable degree of specialized training, a mission to help other human beings, a duty to help them irrespective of their ability to pay, and a measure of authority that comes from all of the above. In short, the extremes of character and performance that exist among teachers also exist among doctors and police. But most of us, even if we grow up to be invalids or criminals, will have spent more time with teachers than with either of their counterparts.

What also sets teachers apart is the milder consequences of their extremes. Doctors and cops can kill somebody or save her life; teachers at their worst or best can usually do no more than to ruin or to improve it. Because the extremes of benefit and detriment are less, the mystique may be less also. But because those extremes do exist and are so noticeable, the mediocre quality of the mediocre teacher tends to be noticeable as well. An average guy seldom looks more average than in front of a classroom.

In a society that touts both "excellence" and "equality," teachers are perhaps our best example of the complex interplay of those two values — both   20 in the evaluative nature of their work and in their own status as workers. We put them down in the clichés of populist rhetoric and we put them up in the titanium shrines of space shuttles, but the truth is, taken as a whole, they're probably more representative of "ordinary Americans" than any single occupational group. If I were Arthur Miller, I would not have made Willy Loman a salesman; I would have made him a teacher. In the lines in which Willy calls the Chevrolet "the greatest car ever built" and then, several pages later, says, "That goddamn Chevrolet, they ought to prohibit the manufacture of that car!" I would have him talking about the American public school.

Yet another way in which the conflicting currents of our democracy affect our resentment of teachers has to do with how we conceive of service, which is not much different from how Süleyman the Magnificent conceived of service. In aristocratic societies, service is the butler who appears when the master pulls the velvet bell rope. In a society like ours, service is the desk clerk who's supposed to come running (with a smile) whenever any tourist slaps the bell. Our version may be the more "democratic," but like the Greeks, whose democracies preceded our own, we always seem to need a few slaves in order to feel truly emancipated.

It would be foolish to suggest that teachers are a kind of slave. It would be equally foolish to forget that not so long ago they were virtually a kind of indentured servant. That they have advanced beyond servitude is not always regarded as a cause for celebration. Add teachers to that list of groups and persons who eventually "got so uppity" that they threatened to diminish the status that came of having them under our thumbs. Here again I must be careful not to overstate my case. One of my favorite school stories has to do with a principal who told a friend of mine that although he understood his frustration when his son's teacher consistently failed to return his phone calls, he should understand that "returning calls has never been Mrs. Van Winkle's strength."

Still, even when one allows for the maddening imperviousness — and equally maddening impunity — of certain teachers, one is still struck from time to time by the popular assumption that public schools, like Third World bazaars and Atlantic City casinos, ought to be places where the almighty spender can throw his weight around like Almighty God. Whenever one hears that dearly beloved phrase "local control," and one hears it in my corner of New England about once a day, the accent is usually on *control*; and the control, firmly on the teachers. Of course this is also true beyond the local level, most recently in proposals to fingerprint teachers in order to "protect children." What politician as keen on protecting his or her career as on protecting children would ever propose fingerprinting clergy, orthodontists, or live-in boyfriends? Not to forget every legislator employing a page.

For the most part, though, I do not hear teachers criticized for having slipped their leashes so much as for having dropped their halos. "Teachers are not supposed to be in it for the money; they're supposed to be in it for the children" — a sentiment that sounds reasonable enough until we remember that even the most altruistic teachers have been known to produce children,

and that teachers' children have been known to eat. Still, one can almost hear
the aggrieved tones of unrequited love in the voices of those who wistfully recall the days "when a teacher was respected" and wouldn't have known what
to do with anything so crass as a dollar bill, not if you taped it to her nose.

Once again there's a contradiction lurking under the rhetoric, which re-   25
veals a cultural contradiction as well. Teachers are also resented *for* their altruism, and one does not have to look too far for examples of the resentment.
I remember sitting next to a father at Town Meeting who in his litany of
grievances against teachers closed with this: "They teach kids not to work."
It was a hardworking man who said this. What I think he meant was: "They
teach kids that there are other things in life *besides* work, that is, besides
work done for money." I recall another father, also hardworking but with the
added perspective of being a teacher's husband, who gave as his explanation
for the bitter controversy surrounding a guidance counselor at his school: "I
think people resent her goodness."

It was a remark that struck home, in part because home for me is a hard-
scrabble place where many people have led very hard lives. In their eyes,
teachers make children unfit to live in a world where survival belongs to the
toughest. Special education, cooperative learning, second chances — even art
and music — are "fine for some," but what have such things to do with real
life as these people have known it? And if all this coddling is indeed valuable,
does that mean that a hard life is not? I'm told there's a Sicilian proverb that
says, "It's a foolish man who educates his children so they can despise him."
It's a foolish man who doesn't see that fear at the root of nearly everything
we might call reactionary.

People are said to hate change, even though in our society political
change, at least, is supposed to come about by the will of the people. I imagine that for many of them hating teachers comes down to the same thing.
Whenever our society changes, or wishes to change, or pretends that it wishes
to change, schools and teachers are enlisted in the cause. If we decide that cy-
berspace is the place to go, we start by sending the second grade. If we come
to fear that morality is going to hell in a handbasket, we draw up a curriculum of "values-based" education. No teacher can hear the phrase "launching
a new initiative" without knowing that the launching pad is going to be located on top of his desk.

If we oppose a given change, we may be inclined to disdain the teacher
who carries it forward, though in many cases this amounts to hearing bad
news and killing the messenger. Our chagrin can come not only from the
change itself but from the sense of having to subsidize our own obsolescence.
We shall never require a sign outside a school building that reads YOUR TAX
DOLLARS AT WORK: people feel them at work, no less than the workings of
their own bowels, which is why, in times of unsettling social change and political insecurity, citizens will sometimes descend with merciless indignation on a
school budget. The first thing we do, let's kill all the special programs. I have
even heard people say, "It's the one thing left that I have some control over."

But schools have not only been placed in the vanguard of change; they have in many ways been used to contain and minimize change. So if, for instance, we want to continue to practice de facto racial segregation, we can pretend otherwise by busing children between racially homogeneous schools. If we are content to see the gap between rich and poor grow wider every year, but wish to seem more "compassionate," we can try to establish some semblance of equity in the funding of public education. Ostensibly, our guiding principle here is that the first step in changing society for the better is changing schools.

That is a fairly sound guiding principle — provided that the *first* step 30 doesn't wind up being the *only* step. Schools can indeed be better places than the communities that sustain them, but never much better, and never better for long. In the end, we can only change the world by changing the world. When something happens in a schoolyard to remind us of this, something awful and sad, we lash out at "the teachers" and "the schools." They were supposed to be making the world a better place, or at least maintaining the illusion that we wanted them to.

Public schools embody our democratic principles and contradictions better than any other institution we know. In schools we behold our own spitting image as a people who value equality but crave excellence, who live for the moment but bet on the future, who espouse altruism but esteem self-reliance, who sincerely believe in change but just as sincerely doubt that change will do them any good. Whether we call these contradictions schizophrenia or creative tension, beauty or ugliness, will depend on the eye of the beholder. Public-school teachers themselves are no less an embodiment of the same contradictions, just as in the broadest sense all teachers embody the subjects that they teach. At least the more memorable ones do. Think of it sometime: lean Mr. Silverstein didn't teach you math; he *was* math, fleshed out in its angular glory. All of this is to say that the best teaching is incarnational. Teaching is the *word* — the music, the formula, and even the Constitution of the United States — made flesh and dwelling among us.

The forty-odd years that I have spent in school are not unlike the forty-eight years I have spent in my body, a mix of pain and pleasure in which the pain has perhaps been more intense but the pleasure more constant, more influential, and, in some way I can't entirely explain, more true. At some level it was most fitting that my mother sent me off to school that morning, and every morning, by handing me my lunch, as if to say that the part of me that learns is one with the part that eats, even if on certain mornings it was also one with the part that pukes. In contrast, the daydream of the boy I was at six, playing among the tombstones when he ought to have been at school, amounts to a wish for disembodiment. It is the vision of a gnostic heaven, in which the emancipated spirits of the elect rise from the complications of the flesh, not in a new body but in no body at all.

The same can be said for many of the present initiatives to diminish radically the scope of public education in America, if not to abolish it altogether.

The utopian school, the cyber-school, the voucher-subsidized school, the school of "school choice," all reduce to a fantasy of social and political transcendence—an attempt to sidestep the contradictions of democracy, the cruel jokes of genetics, the crueler jokes of class, and the darker side of diversity. If we can but find the right gnosis, you see, the secret path to educational enlightenment, we shall at last be able to shed the blemished, prickly skin of the body politic and live as unencumbered spirits with harps and cornets or whichever golden instrument best accompanies the appropriate lifestyle choice. It may sound like a return to Eden, like the miraculous reversal of some irreversible fall, but make no mistake; it is the equivalent of a wish for death.

QUESTIONS

1. This essay is about teachers and includes an explanation of why we feel emotionally about them, but it is finally an argument about schools and what we should and shouldn't expect of them. Summarize this argument.
2. Consider Keizer's explanation of why we feel strongly about teachers, particularly the comparison to the wicked stepmothers and fairy godmothers of folk tales. How persuasive are these and similar explanatory passages in this essay? That is, do they work for you? Why or why not?
3. One element of argument is establishing the authority of the speaker for the statements that he or she makes. How does Keizer attempt to do this?
4. A good argument presents counterarguments and deals with them. Can you find examples of this process in Keizer's essay?
5. Long essays, like this one, need to repeat ideas, phrases, and images throughout the text. Can you find examples of this kind of repetition in Keizer's essay?
6. This essay mixes personal experiences with a generalized argument. Consider some examples of Keizer's use of personal experiences. How effectively does he move from the personal level to a general level?
7. You know a lot about schools and teachers. Take Keizer's title (or a variant on it), and produce an essay of your own on that topic.

MAKING CONNECTIONS

Look at other essays in this collection that deal with teaching and learning — by Theodore R. Sizer (p. 219), Frederick Douglass (p. 74), and Patrik Jonsson (p. 424)—and consider their descriptions of teaching and learning, as well as their ideas of how education should be improved. Drawing on these essays and your own experience, make an argument about how teaching and learning might be improved in a specific academic course or field of study with which you are familiar.

WATCHING TV MAKES YOU SMARTER

Steven Johnson

Steven Johnson (b. 1968) is a writer, computer expert, cultural critic, and cofounder of the online magazine Feed. *His articles have been published in periodicals such as* Harper's, The New Yorker, the Wall Street Journal, *and the* New York Times. *His four books concern the intersections of science, technology, and culture, particularly popular culture.* Interface Culture: How New Technology Transforms the Way We Create and Communicate *(1997) explores how information technology, especially the Internet, fundamentally changes our experience of communicating and interacting with one another. In* Emergence: The Connected Lives of Ants, Brains, Cities, and Software *(2001), Johnson defines emergence as "the movement from low-level rules to high-level sophistication." Emergent systems are not organized around centralized authority; rather, the emergent system organizes itself. In* Mind Wide Open: Your Brain and the Neuroscience of Everyday Life *(2004), Johnson describes the current state of research into the science of the brain by subjecting himself to a battery of neurological tests and sharing the results, and at the same time describing what he sees as the influence of this knowledge on our own conception of our minds and ourselves. The following piece appeared in the* New York Times Magazine *and was adapted from Johnson's book* Everything Bad Is Good for You: How Today's Popular Culture Is Actually Making Us Smarter *(2005).*

The Sleeper Curve

SCIENTIST A: Has he asked for anything special?
SCIENTIST B: Yes, this morning for breakfast . . . he requested something called "wheat germ, organic honey and tiger's milk."
SCIENTIST A: Oh, yes. Those were the charmed substances that some years ago were felt to contain life-preserving properties.
SCIENTIST B: You mean there was no deep fat? No steak or cream pies or . . . hot fudge?
SCIENTIST A: Those were thought to be unhealthy.
— FROM WOODY ALLEN'S "SLEEPER"

On Jan. 24, the Fox network showed an episode of its hit drama "24," the real-time thriller known for its cliffhanger tension and often-gruesome violence. Over the preceding weeks, a number of public controversies had erupted around "24," mostly focused on its portrait of Muslim terrorists and its penchant for torture scenes. The episode that was shown on the 24th only fanned the flames higher: in one scene, a terrorist enlists a hit man to kill his child for not fully supporting the jihadist cause; in another scene, the secretary of defense authorizes the torture of his son to uncover evidence of a terrorist plot.

But the explicit violence and the post-9/11 terrorist anxiety are not the only elements of "24" that would have been unthinkable on prime-time network television 20 years ago. Alongside the notable change in content lies an equally notable change in form. During its 44 minutes—a real-time hour, minus 16 minutes for commercials—the episode connects the lives of 21 distinct characters, each with a clearly defined "story arc," as the Hollywood jargon has it: a defined personality with motivations and obstacles and specific relationships with other characters. Nine primary narrative threads wind their way through those 44 minutes, each drawing extensively upon events and information revealed in earlier episodes. Draw a map of all those intersecting plots and personalities, and you get structure that— where formal complexity is concerned—more closely resembles "Middlemarch" than a hit TV drama of years past like "Bonanza."

For decades, we've worked under the assumption that mass culture follows a path declining steadily toward lowest-common-denominator standards, presumably because the "masses" want dumb, simple pleasures and big media companies try to give the masses what they want. But as that "24" episode suggests, the exact opposite is happening: the culture is getting more cognitively demanding, not less. To make sense of an episode of "24," you have to integrate far more information than you would have a few decades ago watching a comparable show. Beneath the violence and the ethnic stereotypes, another trend appears: to keep up with entertainment like "24," you have to pay attention, make inferences, track shifting social relationships. This is what I call the Sleeper Curve: the most debased forms of mass diversion—video games and violent television dramas and juvenile sitcoms—turn out to be nutritional after all.

I believe that the Sleeper Curve is the single most important new force altering the mental development of young people today, and I believe it is largely a force for good: enhancing our cognitive faculties, not dumbing them down. And yet you almost never hear this story in popular accounts of today's media. Instead, you hear dire tales of addiction, violence, mindless escapism. It's assumed that shows that promote smoking or gratuitous violence are bad for us. While those that thunder against teen pregnancy or intolerance have a positive role in society. Judged by that morality-play standard, the story of popular culture over the past 50 years—if not 500— is a story of decline: the morals of the stories have grown darker and more ambiguous, and the antiheroes have multiplied.

The usual counterargument here is that what media have lost in moral   5
clarity, they have gained in realism. The real world doesn't come in nicely
packaged public-service announcements, and we're better off with entertainment like "The Sopranos" that reflects our fallen state with all its ethical ambiguity. I happen to be sympathetic to that argument, but it's not the
one I want to make here. I think there is another way to assess the social
virtue of pop culture, one that looks at media as a kind of cognitive workout, not as a series of life lessons. There may indeed be more "negative messages" in the mediasphere today. But that's not the only way to evaluate
whether our television shows or video games are having a positive impact.
Just as important — if not more important — is the kind of thinking you
have to do to make sense of a cultural experience. That is where the Sleeper
Curve becomes visible.

Televised Intelligence

Consider the cognitive demands that televised narratives place on their
viewers. With many shows that we associate with "quality" entertainment —
"The Mary Tyler Moore Show," "Murphy Brown," "Frasier" — the intelligence arrives fully formed in the words and actions of the characters on-
screen. They say witty things to one another and avoid lapsing into tired
sitcom clichés, and we smile along in our living rooms, enjoying the company of these smart people. But assuming we're bright enough to understand the sentences they're saying, there's no intellectual labor involved in
enjoying the show as a viewer. You no more challenge your mind by watching these intelligent shows than you challenge your body watching "Monday Night Football." The intellectual work is happening on-screen, not off.

But another kind of televised intelligence is on the rise. Think of the
cognitive benefits conventionally ascribed to reading: attention, patience,
retention, the parsing of narrative threads. Over the last half-century, programming on TV has increased the demands it places on precisely these
mental faculties. This growing complexity involves three primary elements:
multiple threading, flashing arrows, and social networks.

According to television lore, the age of multiple threads began with the
arrival in 1981 of "Hill Street Blues," the Steven Bochco police drama invariably praised for its "gritty realism." Watch an episode of "Hill Street
Blues" side by side with any major drama from the preceding decades —
"Starsky and Hutch," for instance, or "Dragnet" — and the structural
transformation will jump out at you. The earlier shows follow one or two
lead characters, adhere to a single dominant plot, and reach a decisive conclusion at the end of the episode. Draw an outline of the narrative threads
in almost every "Dragnet" episode, and it will be a single line: from the initial crime scene, through the investigation, to the eventual cracking of the
case. A typical "Starsky and Hutch" episode offers only the slightest variation on this linear formula: the introduction of a comic subplot that usually

appears only at the tail ends of the episode, creating a structure that looks like the graph below. The vertical axis represents the number of individual threads, and the horizontal axis is time.

"Starsky and Hutch" (any episode)

A "Hill Street Blues" episode complicates the picture in a number of profound ways. The narrative weaves together a collection of distinct strands — sometimes as many as 10, though at least half of the threads involve only a few quick scenes scattered through the episode. The number of primary characters — and not just bit parts — swells significantly. And the episode has fuzzy borders: picking up one or two threads from previous episodes at the outset and leaving one or two threads open at the end. Charted graphically, an average episode looks like this:

"Hill Street Blues" (episode 85)

Critics generally cite "Hill Street Blues" as the beginning of "serious   10
drama" narrative in the television medium — differentiating the series from the single-episode dramatic programs from the 50's, which were Broadway plays performed in front of a camera. But the "Hill Street" innovations weren't all that original; they'd long played a defining role in popular television, just not during the evening hours. The structure of a "Hill Street" episode — and indeed of all the critically acclaimed dramas that followed, from "thirtysomething" to "Six Feet Under" — is the structure of a soap opera. "Hill Street Blues" might have sparked a new golden age of television drama during its seven-year run, but it did so by using a few crucial tricks that "Guiding Light" and "General Hospital" mastered long before.

Bochco's genius with "Hill Street" was to marry complex narrative structure with complex subject matter. "Dallas" had already shown that the extended, interwoven threads of the soap-opera genre could survive the weeklong interruptions of a prime-time show, but the actual content of "Dallas" was fluff. (The most probing issue it addressed was the question, now folkloric, of who shot J.R.) "All in the Family" and "Rhoda" showed that you could tackle complex social issues, but they did their tackling in the comfort of the sitcom living room. "Hill Street" had richly drawn characters confronting difficult social issues and a narrative structure to match.

Since "Hill Street" appeared, the multi-threaded drama has become the most widespread fictional genre on prime time: "St. Elsewhere," "L.A. Law," "thirtysomething," "Twin Peaks," "N.Y.P.D. Blue," "E.R.," "The West Wing," "Alias," "Lost." (The only prominent holdouts in drama are shows like "Law and Order" that have essentially updated the venerable "Drag-net" format and thus remained anchored to a single narrative line.) Since the early 80's, however, there has been a noticeable increase in narrative complexity in these dramas. The most ambitious show on TV to date, "The Sopranos," routinely follows up to a dozen distinct threads over the course of an episode, with more than 20 recurring characters. An episode from late in the first season looks like this:

"The Sopranos" (episode 8)

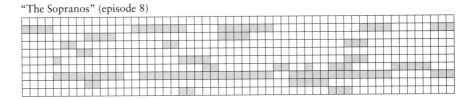

The total number of active threads equals the multiple plots of "Hill Street," but here each thread is more substantial. The show doesn't offer a clear distinction between dominant and minor plots; each story line carries its weight in the mix. The episode also displays a chordal mode of story-telling entirely absent from "Hill Street": a single scene in "The Sopranos" will often connect to three different threads at the same time, layering one plot atop another. And every single thread in this "Sopranos" episode builds on events from previous episodes, and continues on through the rest of the season and beyond.

Put those charts together, and you have a portrait of the Sleeper Curve rising over the past 30 years of popular television. In a sense, this is as much a map of cognitive changes in the popular mind as it is a map of on-screen developments, as if the media titans decided to condition our brains to follow ever-larger numbers of simultaneous threads. Before "Hill Street," the conventional wisdom among television execs was that audiences wouldn't be comfortable following more than three plots in a single episode, and in-deed, the "Hill Street" pilot, which was shown in January 1981, brought complaints from viewers that the show was too complicated. Fast-forward two decades, and shows like "The Sopranos" engage their audiences with narratives that make "Hill Street" look like "Three's Company." Audiences happily embrace that complexity because they've been trained by two decades of multi-threaded dramas.

Multi-threading is the most celebrated structural feature of the modern   15
television drama, and it certainly deserves some of the honor that has been doled out to it. And yet multi-threading is only part of the story.

The Case for Confusion

Shortly after the arrival of the first-generation slasher movies — "Hal-loween," "Friday the 13th" — Paramount released a mock-slasher flick called "Student Bodies," parodying the genre just as the "Scream" series would do 15 years later. In one scene, the obligatory nubile teenage baby sitter hears a noise outside a suburban house; she opens the door to investigate, finds nothing and then goes back inside. As the door shuts behind her, the camera swoops in on the doorknob, and we see that she has left the door unlocked. The camera pulls back and then swoops down again for emphasis. And then a flashing arrow appears on the screen, with text that helpfully explains: "Unlocked!"

That flashing arrow is parody, of course, but it's merely an exaggerated version of a device popular stories use all the time. When a sci-fi script inserts into some advanced lab a nonscientist who keeps asking the science geeks to explain what they're doing with that particle accelerator, that's a flashing arrow that gives the audience precisely the information it needs in order to make sense of the ensuing plot. ("Whatever you do, don't spill water on it, or you'll set off a massive explosion!") These hints serve as a kind of narrative hand-holding. Implicitly, they say to the audience, "We realize you have no idea what a particle accelerator is, but here's the deal: all you need to know is that it's a big fancy thing that explodes when wet." They focus the mind on relevant details: "Don't worry about whether the baby sitter is going to break up with her boyfriend. Worry about that guy lurking in the bushes." They reduce the amount of analytic work you need to do to make sense of a story. All you have to do is follow the arrows.

By this standard, popular television has never been harder to follow. If narrative threads have experienced a population explosion over the past 20 years, flashing arrows have grown correspondingly scarce. Watching our pinnacle of early 80's TV drama, "Hill Street Blues," we find there's an informational wholeness to each scene that differs markedly from what you see on shows like "The West Wing" or "The Sopranos" or "Alias" or "E.R."

"Hill Street" has ambiguities about future events: will a convicted killer be executed? Will Furillo marry Joyce Davenport? Will Renko find it in himself to bust a favorite singer for cocaine possession? But the present-tense of each scene explains itself to the viewer with little ambiguity. There's an open question or a mystery driving each of these stories — how will it turn out? — but there's no mystery about the immediate activity on the screen. A contemporary drama like "The West Wing," on the other hand, constantly embeds mysteries into the present-tense events: you see characters performing actions or discussing events about which crucial information has been deliberately withheld. Anyone who has watched more than a handful of "The West Wing" episodes closely will know the feeling: scene after scene refers to some clearly crucial but unexplained piece of information, and after the sixth reference, you'll find yourself wishing you could rewind the tape to figure out what they're talking about, assuming you've missed something. And then you realize that you're supposed to be confused. The open question posed by these sequences is not "How will this turn out in the end?" The question is "What's happening right now?"

The deliberate lack of hand-holding extends down to the microlevel of   20
dialogue as well. Popular entertainment that addresses technical issues —
whether they are the intricacies of passing legislation, or of performing
a heart bypass, or of operating a particle accelerator — conventionally
switches between two modes of information in dialogue: texture and substance. Texture is all the arcane verbiage provided to convince the viewer
that they're watching Actual Doctors at Work; substance is the material
planted amid the background texture that the viewer needs to make sense
of the plot.

Conventionally, narratives demarcate the line between texture and substance by inserting cues that flag or translate the important data. There's
an unintentionally comical moment in the 2004 blockbuster "The Day
After Tomorrow" in which the beleaguered climatologist (played by Dennis
Quaid) announces his theory about the imminent arrival of a new ice age to
a gathering of government officials. In his speech, he warns that "we have
hit a critical desalinization point!" At this moment, the writer-director
Roland Emmerich — a master of brazen arrow-flashing — has an official
follow with the obliging remark: "It would explain what's driving this extreme weather." They might as well have had a flashing "Unlocked!" arrow
on the screen.

The dialogue on shows like "The West Wing" and "E.R.," on the other
hand, doesn't talk down to its audiences. It rushes by, the words accelerating in sync with the high-speed tracking shots that glide through the corridors and operating rooms. The characters talk faster in these shows, but
the truly remarkable thing about the dialogue is not purely a matter of
speed; it's the willingness to immerse the audience in information that most
viewers won't understand. Here's a typical scene from "E.R.":

[WEAVER *and* WRIGHT *push a gurney containing a 16-year-old girl.*
   Her parents, JANNA *and* FRANK MIKAMI, *follow close behind.*
   CARTER *and* LUCY *fall in.*]
WEAVER: 16-year-old, unconscious, history of biliary atresia.
CARTER: Hepatic coma?
WEAVER: Looks like it.
MR. MIKAMI: She was doing fine until six months ago.
CARTER: What medication is she on?
MRS. MIKAMI: Ampicillin, tobramycin, vitamins A, D, and K.
LUCY: Skin's jaundiced.
WEAVER: Same with the sclera. Breath smells sweet.
CARTER: Fetor hepaticus?
WEAVER: Yep.
LUCY: What's that?
WEAVER: Her liver's shut down. Let's dip a urine. [*To* CARTER]
   Guys, it's getting a little crowded in here, why don't you deal with the
   parents? Start lactulose, 30 cc's per NG.
CARTER: We're giving medicine to clean her blood.

WEAVER: Blood in the urine, two-plus.
CARTER: The liver failure is causing her blood not to clot.
MRS. MIKAMI: Oh, God. . . .
CARTER: Is she on the transplant list?
MR. MIKAMI: She's been Status 2a for six months, but they haven't been able to find her a match.
CARTER: Why? What's her blood type?
MR. MIKAMI: AB.
[*This hits* CARTER *like a lightning bolt.* LUCY *gets it, too. They share a look.*]

There are flashing arrows here, of course — "The liver failure is causing her blood not to clot" — but the ratio of medical jargon to layperson translation is remarkably high. From a purely narrative point of view, the decisive line arrives at the very end: "AB." The 16-year-old's blood type connects her to an earlier plot line, involving a cerebral-hemorrhage victim who — after being dramatically revived in one of the opening scenes — ends up brain-dead. Far earlier, before the liver-failure scene above, Carter briefly discusses harvesting the hemorrhage victim's organs for transplants, and another doctor makes a passing reference to his blood type being the rare AB (thus making him an unlikely donor). The twist here revolves around a statistically unlikely event happening at the E.R. — an otherwise perfect liver donor showing up just in time to donate his liver to a recipient with the same rare blood type. But the show reveals this twist with remarkable subtlety. To make sense of that last "AB" line — and the look of disbelief on Carter's and Lucy's faces — you have to recall a passing remark uttered earlier regarding a character who belongs to a completely different thread. Shows like "E.R." may have more blood and guts than popular TV had a generation ago, but when it comes to storytelling, they possess a quality that can only be described as subtlety and discretion.

Even Bad TV Is Better

Skeptics might argue that I have stacked the deck here by focusing on relatively highbrow titles like "The Sopranos" or "The West Wing," when in fact the most significant change in the last five years of narrative entertainment involves reality TV. Does the contemporary pop cultural landscape look quite as promising if the representative show is "Joe Millionaire" instead of "The West Wing"?

I think it does, but to answer that question properly, you have to avoid   25
the tendency to sentimentalize the past. When people talk about the golden age of television in the early 70's — invoking shows like "The Mary Tyler Moore Show" and "All in the Family" — they forget to mention how awful most television programming was during much of that decade. If you're going to look at pop-culture trends, you have to compare apples to apples,

or in this case, lemons to lemons. The relevant comparison is not between "Joe Millionaire" and "MASH"; it's between "Joe Millionaire" and "The Newlywed Game," or between "Survivor" and "The Love Boat."

What you see when you make these head-to-head comparisons is that a rising tide of complexity has been lifting programming at the bottom of the quality spectrum and at the top. "The Sopranos" is several times more demanding of its audiences than "Hill Street" was, and "Joe Millionaire" has made comparable advances over "Battle of the Network Stars." This is the ultimate test of the Sleeper Curve theory: even the junk has improved.

If early television took its cues from the stage, today's reality programming is reliably structured like a video game: a series of competitive tests, growing more challenging over time. Many reality shows borrow a subtler device from gaming culture as well: the rules aren't fully established at the outset. You learn as you play.

On a show like "Survivor" or "The Apprentice," the participants — and the audience — know the general objective of the series, but each episode involves new challenges that haven't been ordained in advance. The final round of the first season of "The Apprentice," for instance, threw a monkey wrench into the strategy that governed the play up to that point, when Trump announced that the two remaining apprentices would have to assemble and manage a team of subordinates who had already been fired in earlier episodes of the show. All of a sudden the overarching objective of the game — do anything to avoid being fired — presented a potential conflict to the remaining two contenders: the structure of the final round favored the survivor who had maintained the best relationships with his comrades. Suddenly, it wasn't enough just to have clawed your way to the top; you had to have made friends while clawing. The original "Joe Millionaire" went so far as to undermine the most fundamental convention of all — that the show's creators don't openly lie to the contestants about the prizes — by inducing a construction worker to pose as a man of means while 20 women competed for his attention.

Reality programming borrowed another key ingredient from games; the intellectual labor of probing the system's rules for weak spots and opportunities. As each show discloses its conventions, and each participant reveals his or her personality traits and background, the intrigue in watching comes from figuring out how the participants should best navigate the environment that has been created for them. The pleasure in these shows comes not from watching other people being humiliated on national television; it comes from depositing other people in a complex, high-pressure environment where no established strategies exist and watching them find their bearings. That's why the water-cooler conversation about these shows invariably tracks in on the strategy displayed on the previous night's episode: why did Kwame pick Omarosa in that final round? What devious strategy is Richard Hatch concocting now?

When we watch these shows, the part of our brain that monitors the 30 emotional lives of the people around us — the part that tracks subtle shifts in intonation and gesture and facial expression — scrutinizes the action on the screen, looking for clues. We trust certain characters implicitly and vote others off the island in a heartbeat. Traditional narrative shows also trigger emotional connections to the characters, but those connections don't have the same participatory effect, because traditional narratives aren't explicitly about strategy. The phrase "Monday-morning quarterbacking" describes the engaged feeling that spectators have in relation to games as opposed to stories. We absorb stories, but we second-guess games. Reality programming has brought that second-guessing to prime time, only the game in question revolves around social dexterity rather than the physical kind.

The Rewards of Smart Culture

The quickest way to appreciate the Sleeper Curve's cognitive training is to sit down and watch a few hours of hit programming from the late 70's on Nick at Nite or the SOAPnet channel or on DVD. The modern viewer who watches a show like "Dallas" today will be bored by the content — not just because the show is less salacious than today's soap operas (which it is by a small margin) but also because the show contains far less information in each scene, despite the fact that its soap-opera structure made it one of the most complicated narratives on television in its prime. With "Dallas," the modern viewer doesn't have to think to make sense of what's going on, and not having to think is boring. Many recent hit shows — "24," "Survivor," "The Sopranos," "Alias," "Lost," "The Simpsons," "E.R." — take the opposite approach, layering each scene with a thick network of affiliations. You have to focus to follow the plot, and in focusing you're exercising the parts of your brain that map social networks, that fill in missing information, that connect multiple narrative threads.

Of course, the entertainment industry isn't increasing the cognitive complexity of its products for charitable reasons. The Sleeper Curve exists because there's money to be made by making culture smarter. The economics of television syndication and DVD sales mean that there's a tremendous financial pressure to make programs that can be watched multiple times, revealing new nuances and shadings on the third viewing. Meanwhile, the Web has created a forum for annotation and commentary that allows more complicated shows to prosper, thanks to the fan sites where each episode of shows like "Lost" or "Alias" is dissected with an intensity usually reserved for Talmud scholars. Finally, interactive games have trained a new generation of media consumers to probe complex environments and to think on their feet, and that gamer audience has now come to expect the same challenges from their television shows. In the end, the Sleeper Curve tells us something about the human mind. It may be drawn toward the sensational where content is concerned — sex does sell, after all. But the mind also likes to be challenged; there's real pleasure to be found in solving puzzles, detecting patterns, or unpacking a complex narrative system.

In pointing out some of the ways that popular culture has improved our minds, I am not arguing that parents should stop paying attention to the way their children amuse themselves. What I am arguing for is a change in the criteria we use to determine what really is cognitive junk food and what is genuinely nourishing. Instead of a show's violent or tawdry content, instead of wardrobe malfunctions or the F-word, the true test should be whether a given show engages or sedates the mind. Is it a single thread strung together with predictable punch lines every 30 seconds? Or does it map a complex social network? Is your on-screen character running around shooting everything in sight, or is she trying to solve problems and manage resources? If your kids want to watch reality TV, encourage them to watch "Survivor" over "Fear Factor." If they want to watch a mystery show, encourage "24" over "Law and Order." If they want to play a violent game, encourage Grand Theft Auto over Quake. Indeed, it might be just as helpful to have a rating system that used mental labor and not obscenity and violence as its classification scheme for the world of mass culture.

Kids and grown-ups each can learn from their increasingly shared obsessions. Too often we imagine the blurring of kid and grown-up cultures as a series of violations: the 9-year-olds who have to have nipple broaches explained to them thanks to Janet Jackson; the middle-aged guy who can't wait to get home to his Xbox. But this demographic blur has a commendable side that we don't acknowledge enough. The kids are forced to think like grown-ups: analyzing complex social networks, managing resources, tracking subtle narrative intertwinings, recognizing long-term patterns. The grown-ups, in turn, get to learn from the kids: decoding each new technological wave, parsing the interfaces and discovering the intellectual rewards of play. Parents should see this as an opportunity, not a crisis. Smart culture is no longer something you force your kids to ingest, like green vegetables. It's something you share.

QUESTIONS

1. Johnson's title makes a very broad claim; he clearly doesn't think that any and all TV programs will make one smarter. What specific kinds of programs does he have in mind? Given the kinds of programs that he endorses and his reasons for doing so, what kinds of programs do you suppose he would criticize as likely to make one dumber?

2. "Smarter" is such a broad term that it could refer to several different mental abilities. Based on your reading of Johnson, in what specific sense(s) do you think TV is likely to make one smarter? In what specific sense(s) is it not likely to make one smarter? What exactly do you think he means when he says that watching TV is a "kind of cognitive workout" (paragraph 5)? How does Johnson's idea of smartness compare or contrast with your own?

3. Johnson's thesis essentially involves a cause-and-effect claim about watching TV. What kinds of evidence does he offer to support his claim that TV has such an effect? What kinds of evidence might help to strengthen his argument?

4. The drift of Johnson's observations suggests that he favors programs that tend to be as complex, unpredictable, and uncued as life itself. That being the case, why not pay more attention to life than a TV version of it? In what ways does watching TV serials or "reality" TV provide better cognitive workouts than paying close attention to unmediated life? In what respects might closely observing life make one smarter than watching TV?

5. Use Johnson's graphing method to analyze an episode from your favorite TV serial. For each strand in your graph, write a brief phrase to identify the characters and/or problem that it involves. How many distinct "threads" did you note in the episode? How many different characters were involved? How thick or thin was the treatment of each thread? What insights about the episode did you gain from this analysis? What features of the episode might be overlooked by Johnson's kind of analysis?

6. After considering the five preceding sets of questions, write an essay evaluating Johnson's argument. Indicate what you consider to be its strengths and weaknesses, taking into account the quality of its logic and evidence, as well as your own personal experience of TV.

MAKING CONNECTIONS

Just as Johnson thinks that certain kinds of TV will make one smarter, Christina Boufis (p. 150) believes that certain kinds of reading will make one smarter. Compare and contrast their ideas of smartness, and consider which one is likely to be more academically helpful, more professionally helpful, and more existentially helpful.

SOMETHING BORROWED

Malcolm Gladwell

English-born Malcolm Gladwell (b. 1963) grew up in Canada and received an undergraduate degree in history from the University of Toronto in 1984. From 1987 to 1996, he was a reporter for the Washington Post, *first as a science writer and then as New York City bureau chief. Since 1996, he has been a staff writer for* The New Yorker, *for which he has researched and written about topics as diverse as the relationship between intelligence and achievement, SAT preparation courses, paper filing systems, disposable diapers, and the history of caffeine. His first book,* The Tipping Point: How Little Things Make a Big Difference *(2000), focused on the idea that major societal trends can be initiated by seemingly minor circumstances. His second book,* Blink: The Power of Thinking without Thinking *(2005), is about what Gladwell calls "rapid cognition . . . the kind of thinking that happens in a blink of an eye." He distinguishes this kind of thinking from the term* intuition, *which he says connotes emotional reaction rather than rational, albeit almost instantaneous, thought. In 2005, Gladwell was named one of* Time *magazine's 100 Most Influential People. The following article appeared in* The New Yorker. *Other articles by Gladwell and information about him and his work can be accessed at <http://www.gladwell.com>.*

One day this spring, a psychiatrist named Dorothy Lewis got a call from her friend Betty, who works in New York City. Betty had just seen a Broadway play called "Frozen," written by the British playwright Bryony Lavery. "She said, 'Somehow it reminded me of you. You really ought to see it,'" Lewis recalled. Lewis asked Betty what the play was about, and Betty said that one of the characters was a psychiatrist who studied serial killers. "And I told her, 'I need to see that as much as I need to go to the moon.'"

Lewis has studied serial killers for the past twenty-five years. With her collaborator, the neurologist Jonathan Pincus, she has published a great many research papers, showing that serial killers tend to suffer from predictable patterns of psychological, physical, and neurological dysfunction: that they were almost all the victims of harrowing physical and sexual abuse as children, and that almost all of them have suffered some kind of brain injury or mental illness. In 1998, she published a memoir of her life and work entitled "Guilty by Reason of Insanity." She was the last person to visit Ted Bundy before he went to the electric chair. Few people in the world have spent as much time thinking about serial killers as Dorothy Lewis, so when her friend Betty told her that she needed to see "Frozen" it struck her as a busman's holiday.

But the calls kept coming. "Frozen" was winning raves on Broadway, and it had been nominated for a Tony. Whenever someone who knew Dorothy Lewis saw it, they would tell her that she really ought to see it, too. In June, she got a call from a woman at the theatre where "Frozen" was playing. "She said she'd heard that I work in this field, and that I see murderers, and she was wondering if I would do a talk-back after the show," Lewis said. "I had done that once before, and it was a delight, so I said sure. And I said, would you please send me the script, because I wanted to read the play."

The script came, and Lewis sat down to read it. Early in the play, something caught her eye, a phrase: "it was one of those days." One of the murderers Lewis had written about in her book had used that same expression. But she thought it was just a coincidence. "Then, there's a scene of a woman on an airplane, typing away to her friend. Her name is Agnetha Gottmundsdottir. I read that she's writing to her colleague, a neurologist called David Nabkus. And with that I realized that more was going on, and I realized as well why all these people had been telling me to see the play."

Lewis began underlining line after line. She had worked at New York   5
University School of Medicine. The psychiatrist in "Frozen" worked at New York School of Medicine. Lewis and Pincus did a study of brain injuries among fifteen death-row inmates. Gottmundsdottir and Nabkus did a study of brain injuries among fifteen death-row inmates. Once, while Lewis was examining the serial killer Joseph Franklin, he sniffed her, in a grotesque, sexual way. Gottmundsdottir is sniffed by the play's serial killer, Ralph. Once, while Lewis was examining Ted Bundy, she kissed him on the cheek. Gottmundsdottir, in some productions of "Frozen," kisses Ralph. "The whole thing was right there," Lewis went on. "I was sitting at home reading the play, and I realized that it was I. I felt robbed and violated in some peculiar way. It was as if someone had stolen — I don't believe in the soul, but, if there was such a thing, it was as if someone had stolen my essence."

Lewis never did the talk-back. She hired a lawyer. And she came down from New Haven to see "Frozen." "In my book," she said, "I talk about where I rush out of the house with my black carry-on, and I have two black pocket-books, and the play opens with her" — Agnetha — "with one big black bag and a carry-on, rushing out to do a lecture." Lewis had written about biting her sister on the stomach as a child. Onstage, Agnetha fantasized out loud about attacking a stewardess on an airplane and "biting out her throat." After the play was over, the cast came onstage and took questions from the audience. "Somebody in the audience said, 'Where did Bryony Lavery get the idea for the psychiatrist?'" Lewis recounted. "And one of the cast members, the male lead, said, 'Oh, she said that she read it in an

English medical magazine.'" Lewis is a tiny woman, with enormous, child-like eyes, and they were wide open now with the memory. "I wouldn't have cared if she did a play about a shrink who's interested in the frontal lobe and the limbic system. That's out there to do. I see things week after week on television, on 'Law & Order' or 'C.S.I.,' and I see that they are using material that Jonathan and I brought to light. And it's wonderful. That would have been acceptable. But she did more than that. She took things about my own life, and that is the part that made me feel violated."

At the request of her lawyer, Lewis sat down and made up a chart detailing what she felt were the questionable parts of Lavery's play. The chart was fifteen pages long. The first part was devoted to thematic similarities between "Frozen" and Lewis's book "Guilty by Reason of Insanity." The other, more damning section listed twelve instances of almost verbatim similarities — totalling perhaps six hundred and seventy-five words — between passages from "Frozen" and passages from a 1997 magazine profile of Lewis. The profile was called "Damaged." It appeared in the February 24, 1997, issue of *The New Yorker*. It was written by me.

Words belong to the person who wrote them. There are few simpler ethical notions than this one, particularly as society directs more and more energy and resources toward the creation of intellectual property. In the past thirty years, copyright laws have been strengthened. Courts have become more willing to grant intellectual-property protections. Fighting piracy has become an obsession with Hollywood and the recording industry, and, in the worlds of academia and publishing, plagiarism has gone from being bad literary manners to something much closer to a crime. When, two years ago, Doris Kearns Goodwin was found to have lifted passages from several other historians, she was asked to resign from the board of the Pulitzer Prize committee. And why not? If she had robbed a bank, she would have been fired the next day.

I'd worked on "Damaged" through the fall of 1996. I would visit Dorothy Lewis in her office at Bellevue Hospital, and watch the videotapes of her interviews with serial killers. At one point, I met up with her in Missouri. Lewis was testifying at the trial of Joseph Franklin, who claims responsibility for shooting, among others, the civil-rights leader Vernon Jordan and the pornographer Larry Flynt. In the trial, a videotape was shown of an interview that Franklin once gave to a television station. He was asked whether he felt any remorse. I wrote:

> "I can't say that I do," he said. He paused again, then added, "The only thing I'm sorry about is that it's not legal."
> "What's not legal?"
> Franklin answered as if he'd been asked the time of day: "Killing Jews."

That exchange, almost to the word, was reproduced in "Frozen."

Lewis, the article continued, didn't feel that Franklin was fully respon-   10
sible for his actions. She viewed him as a victim of neurological dysfunction
and childhood physical abuse. "The difference between a crime of evil and
a crime of illness," I wrote, "is the difference between a sin and a symptom." That line was in "Frozen," too — not once but twice. I faxed Bryony
Lavery a letter:

> I am happy to be the source of inspiration for other writers, and
> had you asked for my permission to quote — even liberally — from
> my piece, I would have been delighted to oblige, But to lift mate-
> rial, without my approval, is theft.

Almost as soon as I'd sent the letter, though, I began to have second
thoughts. The truth was that, although I said I'd been robbed, I didn't feel
that way. Nor did I feel particularly angry. One of the first things I had said
to a friend after hearing about the echoes of my article in "Frozen" was
that this was the only way I was ever going to get to Broadway — and I was
only half joking. On some level, I considered Lavery's borrowing to be a
compliment. A savvier writer would have changed all those references to
Lewis, and rewritten the quotes from me, so that their origin was no longer
recognizable. But how would I have been better off if Lavery had disguised
the source of her inspiration?
      Dorothy Lewis, for her part, was understandably upset. She was consid-
ering a lawsuit. And, to increase her odds of success, she asked me to assign
her the copyright to my article. I agreed, but then I changed my mind. Lewis
had told me that she "wanted her life back." Yet in order to get her life back,
it appeared, she first had to acquire it from me. That seemed a little strange.
      Then I got a copy of the script for "Frozen." I found it breathtaking, I
realize that this isn't supposed to be a relevant consideration. And yet it was:
instead of feeling that my words had been taken from me, I felt that they had
become part of some grander cause. In late September the story broke. The
Times, the *Observer* in England, and the Associated Press all ran stories
about Lavery's alleged plagiarism, and the articles were picked up by newspapers around the world. Bryony Lavery had seen one of my articles, responded to what she read, and used it as she constructed a work of art. And
now her reputation was in tatters. Something about that didn't seem right.

      In 1992, the Beastie Boys released a song called "Pass the Mic," which
begins with a six-second sample taken from the 1976 composition "Choir,"
by the jazz flutist James Newton. The sample was an exercise in what is
called multiphonics, where the flutist "overblows" into the instrument while
simultaneously singing in a falsetto. In the case of "Choir," Newton played a
C on the flute, then sang C, D-flat, C — and the distortion of the overblown
C, combined with his vocalizing, created a surprisingly complex and haunt-
ing sound. In "Pass the Mic," the Beastie Boys repeated the Newton sample
more than forty times. The effect was riveting.

In the world of music, copyrighted works fall into two categories — the   15
recorded performance and the composition underlying that performance. If
you write a rap song, and want to sample the chorus from Billy Joel's
"Piano Man," you first have to get permission from the record label to use
the "Piano Man" recording, and then get permission from Billy Joel (or
whoever owns his music) to use the underlying composition. In the case
of "Pass the Mic," the Beastie Boys got the first kind of permission — the
rights to use the recording of "Choir" — but not the second. Newton sued,
and he lost — and the reason he lost serves as a useful introduction to how
to think about intellectual property.

At issue in the case wasn't the distinctiveness of Newton's performance.
The Beastie Boys, everyone agreed, had properly licensed Newton's performance when they paid the copyright recording fee. And there was no
question about whether they had copied the underlying music to the sample. At issue was simply whether the Beastie Boys were required to ask for
that secondary permission: was the composition underneath those six seconds so distinctive and original that Newton could be said to own it? The
court said that it wasn't.

The chief expert witness for the Beastie Boys in the "Choir" case was
Lawrence Ferrara, who is a professor of music at New York University, and
when I asked him to explain the court's ruling he walked over to the piano
in the corner of his office and played those three notes: C, D-flat, C. "That's
it!" he shouted. "There ain't nothing else! That's what was used. You know
what this is? It's no more than a mordent, a turn. It's been done thousands
upon thousands of times. No one can say they own that."

Ferrara then played the most famous four-note sequence in classical
music, the opening of Beethoven's Fifth: G, G, G, E-flat. This was unmis-
takably Beethoven. But was it original? "That's a harder case," Ferrara
said. "Actually, though, other composers wrote that. Beethoven himself
wrote that in a piano sonata, and you can find figures like that in composers who predate Beethoven. It's one thing if you're talking about *da-da-
da dummm, da-da-da dummm* — those notes, with those durations. But
just the four pitches, G, G, G, E-flat? Nobody owns those."

Ferrara once served as an expert witness for Andrew Lloyd Webber,
who was being sued by Ray Repp, a composer of Catholic folk music. Repp
said that the opening few bars of Lloyd Webber's 1984 "Phantom Song,"
from "The Phantom of the Opera," bore an overwhelming resemblance to
his composition "Till You," written six years earlier, in 1978. As Ferrara
told the story, he sat down at the piano again and played the beginning of
both songs, one after the other; sure enough, they sounded strikingly similar. "Here's Lloyd Webber," he said, calling out each note as he played it.
"Here's Repp. Same sequence. The only difference is that Andrew writes a
perfect fourth and Repp writes a sixth."

But Ferrara wasn't quite finished. "I said, let me have everything An-   20
drew Lloyd Webber wrote prior to 1978 — 'Jesus Christ Superstar,' 'Joseph,'
'Evita.'" He combed through every score, and in "Joseph and the Amazing

Technicolor Dreamcoat" he found what he was looking for. "It's the song 'Benjamin Calypso.'" Ferrara started playing it. It was immediately familiar. "It's the first phrase of 'Phantom Song.' It's even using the same notes. But wait—it gets better. Here's 'Close Every Door,' from a 1969 concert performance of 'Joseph.'" Ferrara is a dapper, animated man, with a thin, well-manicured mustache, and thinking about the Lloyd Webber case was almost enough to make him jump up and down. He began to play again. It was the second phrase of "Phantom." "The first half of 'Phantom' is in 'Benjamin Calypso.' The second half is in 'Close Every Door.' They are identical. On the button. In the case of the first theme, in fact, 'Benjamin Calypso' is closer to the first half of the theme at issue than the plaintiff's song. Lloyd Webber writes something in 1984, and he borrows from himself."

In the "Choir" case, the Beastie Boys' copying didn't amount to theft because it was too trivial. In the "Phantom" case, what Lloyd Webber was alleged to have copied didn't amount to theft because the material in question wasn't original to his accuser. Under copyright law, what matters is not that you copied someone else's work. What matters is *what* you copied, and *how much* you copied. Intellectual-property doctrine isn't a straightforward application of the ethical principle "Thou shalt not steal." At its core is the notion that there are certain situations where you *can* steal. The protections of copyright, for instance, are time-limited; once something passes into the public domain, anyone can copy it without restriction. Or suppose that you invented a cure for breast cancer in your basement lab. Any patent you received would protect your intellectual property for twenty years, but after that anyone could take your invention. You get an initial monopoly on your creation because we want to provide economic incentives for people to invent things like cancer drugs. But everyone gets to steal your breast-cancer cure—after a decent interval—because it is also in society's interest to let as many people as possible copy your invention; only then can others learn from it, and build on it, and come up with better and cheaper alternatives. This balance between the protecting and the limiting of intellectual property is, in fact, enshrined in the Constitution: "Congress shall have the power to promote the Progress of Science and useful Arts, by securing for limited"—note that specification, *limited*—"Times to Authors and Inventors the exclusive Right to their respective Writings and Discoveries."

So is it true that words belong to the person who wrote them, just as other kinds of property belong to their owners? Actually, no. As the Stanford law professor Lawrence Lessig argues in his new book "Free Culture":

> In ordinary language, to call a copyright a "property" right is a bit misleading, for the property of copyright is an odd kind of property. . . . I understand what I am taking when I take the picnic table you put in your backyard. I am taking a thing, the picnic table, and after I take it, you don't have it. But what am I taking when I take the good idea you had to put a picnic table in the backyard—by,

for example, going to Sears, buying a table, and putting it in my backyard? What is the thing that I am taking then?

The point is not just about the thingness of picnic tables versus ideas, though that is an important difference. The point instead is that in the ordinary case — indeed, in practically every case except for a narrow range of exceptions — ideas released to the world are free. I don't take anything from you when I copy the way you dress — though I might seem weird if I do it every day. . . . Instead, as Thomas Jefferson said (and this is especially true when I copy the way someone dresses), "He who receives an idea from me, receives instruction himself without lessening mine; as he who lights his taper at mine, receives light without darkening me."

Lessig argues that, when it comes to drawing this line between private interests and public interests in intellectual property, the courts and Congress have, in recent years, swung much too far in the direction of private interests. He writes, for instance, about the fight by some developing countries to get access to inexpensive versions of Western drugs through what is called "parallel importation" — buying drugs from another developing country that has been licensed to produce patented medicines. The move would save countless lives. But it has been opposed by the United States not on the ground that it would cut into the profits of Western pharmaceutical companies (they don't sell that many patented drugs in developing countries anyway) but on the ground that it violates the sanctity of intellectual property. "We as a culture have lost this sense of balance," Lessig writes. "A certain property fundamentalism, having no connection to our tradition, now reigns in this culture."

Even what Lessig decries as intellectual-property extremism, however, acknowledges that intellectual property has its limits. The United States didn't say that developing countries could never get access to cheap versions of American drugs. It said only that they would have to wait until the patents on those drugs expired. The arguments that Lessig has with the hard-core proponents of intellectual property are almost all arguments about *where* and *when* the line should be drawn between the right to copy and the right to protection from copying, not *whether* a line should be drawn.

But plagiarism is different, and that's what's so strange about it. The ethical rules that govern when it's acceptable for one writer to copy another are even more extreme than the most extreme position of the intellectual-property crowd: when it comes to literature, we have somehow decided that copying is *never* acceptable. Not long ago, the Harvard law professor Laurence Tribe was accused of lifting material from the historian Henry Abraham for his 1985 book, "God Save This Honorable Court." What did the charge amount to? In an exposé that appeared in the conservative publication *The Weekly Standard*, Joseph Bottum produced a number of examples of close paraphrasing, but his smoking gun was this one borrowed sentence: "Taft publicly pronounced Pitney to be a 'weak member' of the Court to whom he could not assign cases." That's it. Nineteen words.

Not long after I learned about "Frozen," I went to see a friend of mine who works in the music industry. We sat in his living room on the Upper East Side, facing each other in easy chairs, as he worked his way through a mountain of CDs. He played "Angel," by the reggae singer Shaggy, and then "The Joker," by the Steve Miller Band, and told me to listen very carefully to the similarity in bass lines. He played Led Zeppelin's "Whole Lotta Love" and then Muddy Waters's "You Need Love," to show the extent to which Led Zeppelin had mined the blues for inspiration. He played "Twice My Age," by Shabba Ranks and Krystal, and then the saccharine seventies pop standard "Seasons in the Sun," until I could hear the echoes of the second song in the first. He played "Last Christmas," by Wham!, followed by Barry Manilow's "Can't Smile Without You" to explain why Manilow might have been startled when he first heard that song, and then "Joanna," by Kool and the Gang, because, in a different way, "Last Christmas" was an homage to Kool and the Gang as well. "That sound you hear in Nirvana," my friend said at one point, "that soft and then loud, kind of exploding thing, a lot of that was inspired by the Pixies. Yet Kurt Cobain" — Nirvanas lead singer and songwriter — "was such a genius that he managed to make it his own. And 'Smells Like Teen Spirit'?" — here he was referring to perhaps the best-known Nirvana song. "That's Boston's 'More Than a Feeling.'" He began to hum the riff of the Boston hit, and said, "The first time I heard 'Teen Spirit,' I said, 'That guitar lick is from "More Than a Feeling."'" But it was different — it was urgent and brilliant and new."

He played another CD. It was Rod Stewart's "Do Ya Think I'm Sexy," a huge hit from the nineteen-seventies. The chorus has a distinctive, catchy hook — the kind of tune that millions of Americans probably hummed in the shower the year it came out. Then he put on "Taj Mahal," by the Brazilian artist Jorge Ben Jor, which was recorded several years before the Rod Stewart song. In his twenties, my friend was a d.j. at various downtown clubs, and at some point he'd become interested in world music. "I caught it back then," he said. A small, sly smile spread across his face. The opening bars of "Taj Mahal" were very South American, a world away from what we had just listened to. And then I heard it. It was so obvious and unambiguous that I laughed out loud; virtually note for note, it was the hook from "Do Ya Think I'm Sexy." It was possible that Rod Stewart had independently come up with that riff, because resemblance is not proof of influence. It was also possible that he'd been in Brazil, listened to some local music, and liked what he heard.

My friend had hundreds of these examples. We could have sat in his living room playing at musical genealogy for hours. Did the examples upset him? Of course not, because he knew enough about music to know that these patterns of influence — cribbing, tweaking, transforming — were at the very heart of the creative process. True, copying could go too far. There were tunes when one artist was simply replicating the work of another, and to let that pass inhibited true creativity. But it was equally dangerous to be overly vigilant in policing creative expression, because if Led Zeppelin hadn't been free to mine the blues for inspiration we wouldn't have got "Whole Lotta Love," and if Kurt Cobain couldn't listen to "More Than a Feeling" and pick out and transform the part he really liked we wouldn't have "Smells Like Teen Spirit" — and, in the evolution of rock, "Smells Like Teen Spirit" was a real step forward from "More Than a Feeling." A successful music executive has to understand the distinction between borrowing that is transformative and borrowing that is merely derivative, and that distinction, I realized, was what was missing from the discussion of Bryony Lavery's borrowings. Yes, she had copied my work. But no one was asking why she had copied it, or what she had copied, or whether her copying served some larger purpose.

Bryony Lavery came to see me in early October. It was a beautiful Saturday afternoon, and we met at my apartment. She is in her fifties, with short tousled blond hair and pale-blue eyes, and was wearing jeans and a loose green shirt and clogs. There was something rugged and raw about her. In the *Times* the previous day, the theatre critic Ben Brantley had not been kind to her new play, "Last Easter." This was supposed to be her moment of triumph. "Frozen" had been nominated for a Tony. "Last Easter" had opened Off Broadway. And now? She sat down heavily at my kitchen table. "I've had the absolute gamut of emotions," she said, playing nervously with her hands as she spoke, as if she needed a cigarette. "I think when one's working, one works between absolute confidence and absolute doubt, and I got a huge dollop of each. I was terribly confident that I could write well after 'Frozen,' and then this opened a chasm of doubt." She looked up at me. "I'm terribly sorry," she said.

Lavery began to explain: "What happens when I write is that I find that I'm somehow zoning on a number of things. I find that I've cut things out of newspapers because the story or something in them is interesting to me, and seems to me to have a place onstage. Then it starts coagulating. It's like the soup starts thickening. And then a story, which is also a structure, starts emerging. I'd been reading thrillers like 'The Silence of the Lambs,' about fiendishly clever serial killers. I'd also seen a documentary of the victims of the Yorkshire killers, Myra Hindley and Ian Brady, who were called the Moors Murderers. They spirited away several children. It seemed to me that killing somehow wasn't fiendishly clever. It was the opposite of clever. It was as banal and stupid and destructive as it could be. There are these interviews with the survivors, and what struck me was that they appeared to be frozen in time. And one of them said, 'If that man was out now, I'm a forgiving man but I couldn't forgive him. I'd kill him.' That's in 'Frozen.' I was thinking about that. Then my mother went into hospital for a very simple operation, and the surgeon punctured her womb, and therefore her intestine, and she got peritonitis and died." 30

When Lavery started talking about her mother, she stopped, and had to collect herself. "She was seventy-four, and what occurred to me is that I utterly forgave him. I thought it was an honest mistake. I'm very sorry it

happened to my mother, but it's an honest mistake." Lavery's feelings confused her, though, because she could think of people in her own life whom
she had held grudges against for years, for the most trivial of reasons. "In a
lot of ways, 'Frozen' was an attempt to understand the nature of forgiveness," she said.

Lavery settled, in the end, on a play with three characters. The first is a
serial killer named Ralph, who kidnaps and murders a young girl. The second is the murdered girl's mother, Nancy. The third is a psychiatrist from
New York, Agnetha, who goes to England to examine Ralph. In the course
of the play, the three lives slowly intersect — and the characters gradually
change and become "unfrozen" as they come to terms with the idea of forgiveness. For the character of Ralph, Lavery says that she drew on a book
about a serial killer titled "The Murder of Childhood," by Ray Wyre and
Tim Tate. For the character of Nancy, she drew on an article written in the
Guardian by a woman named Marian Partington, whose sister had been
murdered by the serial killers Frederick and Rosemary West. And, for the
character of Agnetha, Lavery drew on a reprint of my article that she had
read in a British publication. "I wanted a scientist who would understand,"
Lavery said — a scientist who could explain how it was possible to forgive a
man who had killed your daughter, who could explain that a serial killing
was not a crime of evil but a crime of illness. "I wanted it to be *accurate*,"
she added.

So why didn't she credit me and Lewis? How could she have been so
meticulous about accuracy but not about attribution? Lavery didn't have
an answer. "I thought it was O.K. to use it," she said with an embarrassed
shrug. "It never occurred to me to ask you. I thought it was *news*."

She was aware of how hopelessly inadequate that sounded, and when
she went on to say that my article had been in a big folder of source material that she had used in the writing of the play, and that the folder had got
lost during the play's initial run, in Birmingham, she was aware of how inadequate that sounded, too.

But then Lavery began to talk about Marian Partington, her other im-   35
portant inspiration, and her story became more complicated. While she was
writing "Frozen," Lavery said, she wrote to Partington to inform her of how
much she was relying on Partington's experiences. And when "Frozen"
opened in London she and Partington met and talked. In reading through
articles on Lavery in the British press, I found this, from the *Guardian* two
years ago, long before the accusations of plagiarism surfaced:

> Lavery is aware of the debt she owes to Partington's writing and is
> eager to acknowledge it.
> "I always mention it, because I am aware of the enormous debt
> that I owe to the generosity of Marian Partington's piece. . . . You
> have to be hugely careful when writing something like this, because
> it touches on people's shattered lives and you wouldn't want them
> to come across it unawares."

Lavery wasn't indifferent to other people's intellectual property, then; she was just indifferent to my intellectual property. That's because, in her eyes, what she took from me was different. It was, as she put it, "news." She copied my description of Dorothy Lewis's collaborator, Jonathan Pincus, conducting a neurological examination. She copied the description of the disruptive neurological effects of prolonged periods of high stress. She copied my transcription of the television interview with Franklin. She reproduced a quote that I had taken from a study of abused children, and she copied a quotation from Lewis on the nature of evil. She didn't copy my musings, or conclusions, or structure. She lifted sentences like "It is the function of the cortex — and, in particular, those parts of the cortex beneath the forehead, known as the frontal lobes — to modify the impulses that surge up from within the brain, to provide judgment, to organize behavior and decision-making, to learn and adhere to rules of everyday life." It is difficult to have pride of authorship in a sentence like that. My guess is that it's a reworked version of something I read in a textbook. Lavery knew that failing to credit Partington would have been wrong. Borrowing the personal story of a woman whose sister was murdered by a serial killer matters because that story has real emotional value to its owner. As Lavery put it, it touches on someone's shattered life. Are boilerplate descriptions of physiological functions in the same league?

It also matters *how* Lavery chose to use my words. Borrowing crosses the line when it is used for a derivative work. It's one thing if you're writing a history of the Kennedys, like Doris Kearns Goodwin, and borrow, without attribution, from another history of the Kennedys. But Lavery wasn't writing another profile of Dorothy Lewis. She was writing a play about something entirely new — about what would happen if a mother met the man who killed her daughter. And she used my descriptions of Lewis's work and the outline of Lewis's life as a building block in making that confrontation plausible. Isn't that the way creativity is supposed to work? Old words in the service of a new idea aren't the problem. What inhibits creativity is new words in the service of an old idea.

And this is the second problem with plagiarism. It is not merely extremist. It has also become disconnected from the broader question of what does and does not inhibit creativity. We accept the right of one writer to engage in a full-scale knockoff of another — think how many serial-killer novels have been cloned from "The Silence of the Lambs." Yet, when Kathy Acker incorporated parts of a Harold Robbins sex scene verbatim in a satiric novel, she was denounced as a plagiarist (and threatened with a lawsuit). When I worked at a newspaper, we were routinely dispatched to "match" a story from the *Times*: to do a new version of someone else's idea. But had we "matched" any of the *Times*' words — even the most banal of phrases — it could have been a firing offense. The ethics of plagiarism have turned into the narcissism of small differences: because journalism cannot own up to its heavily derivative nature, it must enforce originality on the level of the sentence.

Dorothy Lewis says that one of the things that hurt her most about "Frozen" was that Agnetha turns out to have had an affair with her collaborator, David Nabkus. Lewis feared that people would think she had had an affair with her collaborator, Jonathan Pincus. "That's slander," Lewis told me. "I'm recognizable in that. Enough people have called me and said, 'Dorothy, its about you,' and if everything up to that point is true, then the affair becomes true in the mind. So that is another reason that I feel violated. If you are going to take the life of somebody, and make them absolutely identifiable, you don't create an affair, and you certainly don't have that as a climax of the play."

It is easy to understand how shocking it must have been for Lewis to sit   40
in the audience and see her "character" admit to that indiscretion. But the truth is that Lavery has every right to create an affair for Agnetha, because Agnetha is not Dorothy Lewis. She is a fictional character, drawn from Lewis's life but endowed with a completely imaginary set of circumstances and actions. In real life, Lewis kissed Ted Bundy on the cheek, and in some versions of "Frozen" Agnetha kisses Ralph. But Lewis kissed Bundy only because he kissed her first, and there's a big difference between responding to a kiss from a killer and initiating one. When we first see Agnetha, she's rushing out of the house and thinking murderous thoughts on the airplane. Dorothy Lewis also charges out of her house and thinks murderous thoughts. But the dramatic function of that scene is to make us think, in that moment, that Agnetha is crazy. And the one inescapable fact about Lewis is that she is not crazy: she has helped get people to rethink their notions of criminality because of her unshakable command of herself and her work. Lewis is upset not just about how Lavery copied her life story, in other words, but about how Lavery *changed* her life story. She's not merely upset about plagiarism. She's upset about art — about the use of old words in the service of a new idea — and her feelings are perfectly understandable, because the alterations of art can be every bit as unsettling and hurtful as the thievery of plagiarism. It's just that art is not a breach of ethics.

When I read the original reviews of "Frozen," I noticed that time and again critics would use, without attribution, some version of the sentence "The difference between a crime of evil and a crime of illness is the difference between a sin and a symptom." That's my phrase, of course. I wrote it. Lavery borrowed it from me, and now the critics were borrowing it from her. The plagiarist was being plagiarized. In this case, there is no "art" defense: nothing new was being done with that line. And this was not "news." Yet do I really own "sins and symptoms"? There is a quote by Gandhi, it turns out, using the same two words, and I'm sure that if I were to plow through the body of English literature I would find the path littered with crimes of evil and crimes of illness. The central fact about the "Phantom" case is that Ray Repp, if he was borrowing from Andrew Lloyd Webber, certainly didn't realize it, and Andrew Lloyd Webber didn't realize that he was borrowing from himself. Creative property, Lessig reminds us, has many lives — the newspaper arrives at our door, it becomes part of the archive of human knowledge, then it wraps fish. And, by the time ideas pass into their third and fourth lives, we lose track of where they came from, and we lose control of where they are going. The final dishonesty of the plagiarism fundamentalists is to encourage us to pretend that these chains of influence and evolution do not exist, and that a writer's words have a virgin birth and an eternal life. I suppose that I could get upset about what happened to my words. I could also simply acknowledge that I had a good, long ride with that line — and let it go.

"It's been absolutely bloody, really, because it attacks my own notion of my character," Lavery said, sitting at my kitchen table. A bouquet of flowers she had brought were on the counter behind her. "It feels absolutely terrible. I've had to go through the pain for being careless. I'd like to repair what happened, and I don't know how to do that. I just didn't think I was doing the wrong thing . . . and then the article comes out in the *New York Times* and every continent in the world." There was a long silence. She was heartbroken. But, more than that, she was confused, because she didn't understand how six hundred and seventy-five rather ordinary words could bring the walls tumbling down. "It's been horrible and bloody." She began to cry. "I'm still composting what happened. It will be for a purpose . . . whatever that purpose is."

QUESTIONS

1. Gladwell's title is taken from a well-known expression, "Something old, something new, something borrowed, something blue." Consult an online reference source to find out the origin and meaning of the expression, and consider its relevance to the present context.
2. In paragraph 8, Gladwell asserts that "[w]ords belong to the person who wrote them. There are few simpler ethical notions than this one." And in that same paragraph, he compares Doris Kearns Goodwin's lifting of passages to robbing a bank. But in paragraph 41, when discussing how others had lifted a sentence of his own, Gladwell says, "I suppose that I could get upset about what happened to my words. I could also simply acknowledge that I had a good, long ride with that line — and let it go." Given such an apparent contradiction, where exactly does Gladwell stand on the matter of plagiarism?
3. In paragraph 41, Gladwell says, "The final dishonesty of the plagiarism fundamentalists is to encourage us to pretend that these chains of influence and evolution do not exist, and that a writer's words have a virgin birth and an eternal life." What does he mean by "plagiarism fundamentalists," and what are the other dishonesties that he attributes to them?
4. During the course of his article, Gladwell discusses borrowings that have taken place in playwriting, history writing, musical composition, musical performance, medical research, and journalism. In what respects

are intellectual property rights the same from field to field? In what respects do they differ?

5. Given what Gladwell says about "*where* and *when* the line should be drawn between the right to copy and the right to protection from copying" (paragraph 24), how do you suppose he would draw the line with respect to copying in the visual arts? Consider, for example, the artwork on the front cover of this book, for which we had to request permission and pay a fee in order to reproduce it. Under what circumstances do you suppose we would be legally free to borrow from this picture without requesting permission or paying a fee?

6. In paragraphs 36–38, Gladwell appears to sanction the copying of whole sentences and passages, if they are used to create "something entirely new," rather than to produce a "derivative work" (paragraph 37). How does he rationalize copying from something old in a work that is entirely new?

7. When and how did you first become aware of the problems connected with borrowing or copying material produced by others? What problems, if any, have you had in using the words or ideas of others? Write an essay telling about your most problematic experience in using someone else's work. What were the problems you encountered, how did you solve them, and what did you learn from the experience?

MAKING CONNECTIONS

Compare and contrast Gladwell's view of copying with your instructor's view of it, with the introductory section in this text on "Using and Acknowledging Sources," and with the academic regulations of your college. Which of these views is the strictest? Which is the most relaxed? Which one seems most reasonable to you — and why?

SOCIAL
SCIENCES
AND PUBLIC
AFFAIRS

REFLECTING IN THE

Social Sciences and Public Affairs

THE WAY TO RAINY MOUNTAIN

N. Scott Momaday

N. Scott Momaday was born in Lawton, Oklahoma, in 1934. His father was a Kiowa, and his mother part Cherokee. After attending schools on Navajo, Apache, and Pueblo reservations, Momaday graduated from the University of New Mexico and earned his doctorate at Stanford University. His works include two poetry collections, Angle of Geese and Other Poems *(1974) and* The Gourd Dancer *(1976); a memoir,* The Names *(1976); an essay compilation,* A Man Made of Words *(1997); and two mixed-media works,* In the Presence of the Sun *(1992), a collection of poems and drawings, and* In the Bear's House *(1999), a collection of paintings, a dialogue, poetry, and prose. In 1969, his novel* House Made of Dawn *won the Pulitzer Prize. When asked about his writing, Momaday said, "When I was growing up on the reservations of the Southwest, I saw people who were deeply involved in their traditional life, in the memories of their blood. They had, as far as I can see, a certain strength and beauty that I find missing in the modern world. I like to celebrate that involvement in my writing." The following essay appeared first in the* Reporter *magazine in 1967 and later as the introduction to* The Way to Rainy Mountain *(1969), a collection of Kiowa legends.*

A single knoll rises out of the plain in Oklahoma, north and west of the Wichita range. For my people, the Kiowas, it is an old landmark, and they gave it the name Rainy Mountain. The hardest weather in the world is there. Winter brings blizzards, hot tornadic winds arise in the spring, and in summer the prairie is an anvil's edge. The grass turns brittle and brown, and it cracks beneath your feet. There are green belts along the rivers and creeks, linear groves of hickory and pecan, willow and witch hazel. At a distance in July or August the steaming foliage seems almost to writhe in fire. Great green and yellow grasshoppers are everywhere in the tall grass, popping up like corn to sting the flesh, and tortoises crawl about on the red earth, going nowhere in the plenty of time. Loneliness is an aspect of the land. All things in the plain are isolate; there is no confusion of objects in the eye, but *one* hill or *one* tree or *one* man. To look upon that landscape in the early morning, with the sun at your back, is to lose the sense of proportion. Your imagination comes to life, and this, you think, is where Creation was begun.

I returned to Rainy Mountain in July. My grandmother had died in the spring, and I wanted to be at her grave. She had lived to be very old and at last infirm. Her only living daughter was with her when she died, and I was told that in death her face was that of a child.

I like to think of her as a child. When she was born, the Kiowas were living the last great moment of their history. For more than a hundred years they had controlled the open range from the Smoky Hill River to the Red, from the headwaters of the Canadian to the fork of the Arkansas and Cimarron. In alliance with the Comanches, they had ruled the whole of the Southern Plains. War was their sacred business, and they were the finest horsemen the world has ever known. But warfare for the Kiowas was pre-eminently a matter of disposition rather than of survival, and they never understood the grim, unrelenting advance of the U.S. Cavalry. When at last, divided and ill provisioned, they were driven onto the Staked Plains in the cold of autumn, they fell into panic. In Palo Duro Canyon they abandoned their crucial stores to pillage and had nothing then but their lives. In order to save themselves, they surrendered to the soldiers at Fort Sill and were imprisoned in the old stone corral that now stands as a military museum. My grandmother was spared the humiliation of those high gray walls by eight or ten years, but she must have known from birth the affliction of defeat, the dark brooding of old warriors.

Her name was Aho, and she belonged to the last culture to evolve in North America. Her forebears came down from the high country in western Montana nearly three centuries ago. They were a mountain people, a mysterious tribe of hunters whose language has never been classified in any major group. In the late seventeenth century they began a long migration to the south and east. It was a journey toward the dawn, and it led to a golden age. Along the way the Kiowas were befriended by the Crows, who gave them the culture and religion of the Plains. They acquired horses, and their ancient nomadic spirit was suddenly free of the ground. They acquired Tai-me, the sacred sun-dance doll, from that moment the object and symbol of their worship, and so shared in the divinity of the sun. Not least, they acquired the sense of destiny, therefore courage and pride. When they entered upon the Southern Plains they had been transformed. No longer were they slaves to the simple necessity of survival; they were a lordly and dangerous society of fighters and thieves, hunters and priests of the sun. According to their origin myth, they entered the world through a hollow log. From one point of view, their migration was the fruit of an old prophecy, for indeed they emerged from a sunless world.

Though my grandmother lived out her long life in the shadow of Rainy   5
Mountain, the immense landscape of the continental interior lay like memory in her blood. She could tell of the Crows, whom she had never seen, and of the Black Hills, where she had never been. I wanted to see in reality what she had seen more perfectly in the mind's eye, and drove fifteen hundred miles to begin my pilgrimage.

A dark mist lay over the Black Hills, and the land was like iron. At the top of a ridge I caught sight of Devil's Tower upthrust against the gray sky as if in the birth of time the core of the earth had broken through its crust and the motion of the world was begun. There are things in nature that engender an awful quiet in the heart of man; Devil's Tower is one of them. Two centuries ago, because of their need to explain it, the Kiowas made a legend at the base of the rock. My grandmother said:

"Eight children were there at play, seven sisters and their brother. Suddenly the boy was struck dumb; he trembled and began to run upon his hands and feet. His fingers became claws, and his body was covered with fur. There was a bear where the boy had been. The sisters were terrified; they ran, and the bear after them. They came to the stump of a great tree, and the tree spoke to them. It bade them climb upon it, and as they did so, it began to rise into the air. The bear came to kill them, but they were just beyond its reach. It reared against the tree and scored the bark all around with its claws. The seven sisters were borne into the sky, and they became the stars of the Big Dipper." From that moment, and so long as the legend lives, the Kiowas have kinsmen in the night sky. Whatever they were in the mountains, they could be no more. However tenuous their well-being, however much they had suffered and would suffer again, they had found a way out of the wilderness.

My grandmother had a reverence for the sun, a holy regard that now is all but gone out of mankind. There was a wariness in her, and an ancient awe. She was a Christian in her later years, but she had come a long way about, and she never forgot her birthright. As a child she had been to the sun dances; she had taken part in that annual rite, and by it she had learned the restoration of her people in the presence of Tai-me. She was about seven when the last Kiowa sun dance was held in 1887 on the Washita River above Rainy Mountain Creek. The buffalo were gone. In order to consummate the ancient sacrifice — to impale the head of a buffalo bull upon the Tai-me tree — a delegation of old men journeyed into Texas, there to beg and barter for an animal from the Goodnight herd. She was ten when the Kiowas came together for the last time as a living sun-dance culture. They

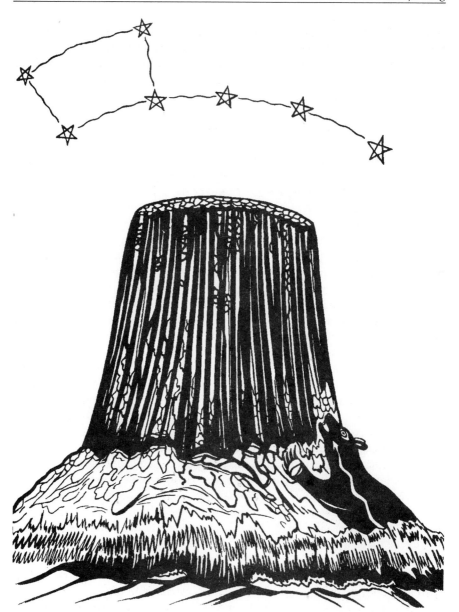

Illustration of Devil's Tower by Alfred Momaday for his son's memoir, *The Way to Rainy Mountain*. Copyright © 1969 by the University of New Mexico Press. All rights reserved.

could find no buffalo; they had to hang an old hide from the sacred tree. Before the dance could begin, a company of soldiers rode out from Fort Sill under orders to disperse the tribe. Forbidden without cause the essential act of their faith, having seen the wild herds slaughtered and left to rot upon the ground, the Kiowas backed away forever from the tree. That was July 20, 1890, at the great bend of the Washita. My grandmother was there. Without bitterness, and for as long as she lived, she bore a vision of deicide.[1]

Now that I can have her only in memory, I see my grandmother in the several postures that were peculiar to her: standing at the wood stove on a winter morning and turning meat in a great iron skillet; sitting at the south window, bent above her beadwork, and afterwards, when her vision failed, looking down for a long time into the fold of her hands; going out upon a cane, very slowly as she did when the weight of age came upon her; praying. I remember her most often at prayer. She made long, rambling prayers out of suffering and hope, having seen many things. I was never sure that I had the right to hear, so exclusive were they of all mere custom and company. The last time I saw her she prayed standing by the side of the bed at night, naked to the waist, the light of a kerosene lamp moving upon her dark skin. Her long black hair, always drawn and braided in the day, lay upon her shoulders and against her breasts like a shawl. I do not speak Kiowa, and I never understood her prayers, but there was something inherently sad in the sound, some merest hesitation upon the syllables of sorrow. She began in a high and descending pitch, exhausting her breath to silence; then again and again — and always the same intensity of effort, of something that is, and is not, like urgency in the human voice. Transported so in the dancing light among the shadows of her room, she seemed beyond the reach of time. But that was illusion; I think I knew then that I should not see her again.

Houses are like sentinels in the plain, old keepers of the weather watch.   10
There, in a very little while, wood takes on the appearance of great age. All colors wear soon away in the wind and rain, and then the wood is burned gray and the grain appears and the nails turn red with rust. The window panes are black and opaque; you imagine there is nothing within, and indeed there are many ghosts, bones given up to the land. They stand here and there against the sky, and you approach them for a longer time than you expect. They belong in the distance; it is their domain.

Once there was a lot of sound in my grandmother's house, a lot of coming and going, feasting and talk. The summers there were full of excitement and reunion. The Kiowas are a summer people; they abide the cold and keep to themselves, but when the season turns and the land becomes warm and vital they cannot hold still; an old love of going returns upon them. The aged visitors who came to my grandmother's house when I was a child were made of lean and leather, and they bore themselves upright. They wore great black

---

[1]*deicide*: The killing of a deity or god. [Eds.]

hats and bright ample shirts that shook in the wind. They rubbed fat upon their hair and wound their braids with strips of colored cloth. Some of them painted their faces and carried the scars of old and cherished enmities. They were an old council of warlords, come to remind and be reminded of who they were. Their wives and daughters served them well. The women might indulge themselves; gossip was at once the mark and compensation of their servitude. They made loud and elaborate talk among themselves, full of jest and gesture, fright and false alarm. They went abroad in fringed and flowered shawls, bright beadwork and German silver. They were at home in the kitchen, and they prepared meals that were banquets.

There were frequent prayer meetings, and nocturnal feasts. When I was a child I played with my cousins outside, where the lamplight fell upon the ground and the singing of the old people rose up around us and carried away into the darkness. There were a lot of good things to eat, a lot of laughter and surprise. And afterwards, when the quiet returned, I lay down with my grandmother and could hear the frogs away by the river and feel the motion of the air.

Now there is a funereal silence in the rooms, the endless wake of some final word. The walls have closed in upon my grandmother's house. When I returned to it in mourning, I saw for the first time in my life how small it was. It was late at night, and there was a white moon, nearly full. I sat for a long time on the stone steps by the kitchen door. From there I could see out across the land; I could see the long row of trees by the creek, the low light upon the rolling plains, and the stars of the Big Dipper. Once I looked at the moon and caught sight of a strange thing. A cricket had perched upon the handrail, only a few inches away. My line of vision was such that the creature filled the moon like a fossil. It had gone there, I thought, to live and die, for there, of all places, was its small definition made whole and eternal. A warm wind rose up and purled like the longing within me.

The next morning, I awoke at dawn and went out on the dirt road to Rainy Mountain. It was already hot, and the grasshoppers began to fill the air. Still, it was early in the morning, and birds sang out of the shadows. The long yellow grass on the mountain shone in the bright light, and a scissortail hied above the land. There, where it ought to be, at the end of a long and legendary way, was my grandmother's grave. She had at last succeeded to that holy ground. Here and there on the dark stones were ancestral names. Looking back once, I saw the mountain and came away.

QUESTIONS

1. What is this essay about? Explain whether it is a history of the Kiowas, a biography of Momaday's grandmother, or a narrative of his journey.
2. Trace the movement in time in this essay. How much takes place in the present, the recent past, the distant past, or legendary time? What effect does such movement create?

3. How much of the essay reports events, and how much of the essay represents a sense of place or of people through description of what Momaday sees and feels? Trace the pattern of reporting and representing, and consider Momaday's purpose in such an approach to his subject.
4. The first paragraph ends by drawing the reader into the writer's point of view: "Your imagination comes to life, and this, you think, is where Creation was begun." Given the description of the Oklahoma landscape that precedes this in the paragraph, how do you react to Momaday's summarizing statement? Why? What other passages in the essay evoke a sense of place?
5. Visit a place that has historical significance. It may be a place where you or members of your family lived in the past, or it may be a place of local or national historical significance. Describe the place as it appears now, and report on events that took place there in the past. What, if any, evidence do you find in the present of those events that took place in the past?
6. If you have a grandparent or an older friend living nearby, ask this person about his or her history. What does this person remember about the past that is no longer in the present? Are there objects — pictures, clothing, medals, and so on — that can speak to you of your subject's past life? Reflect on the person's present life as well as on those events from the past that seem most memorable. Write an essay in which you represent your subject's life by concentrating on the place where he or she lives and the surrounding objects that help you to understand the past and present life.

MAKING CONNECTIONS

1. Compare Momaday's essay to Alice Walker's (p. 54), focusing on the way each essay moves through time. How do these essayists differ in their conception and representation of time, and how do those differences relate to their individual purposes as writers?
2. Compare the Kiowa legend that Momaday's grandmother told him with the Pueblo creation story and other tales that Leslie Marmon Silko (p. 260) tells in her article on the nature and significance of storytelling in Pueblo culture. What similarities and what differences in narrative technique and purpose do you notice in these two stories from Native American tribes?

THE STORY OF MY BODY

Judith Ortiz Cofer

Born in rural Puerto Rico, Judith Ortiz Cofer (b. 1952) moved to the United States in 1954 and spent most of her girlhood in Paterson, New Jersey. She took frequent trips to her native island to visit with family there. A graduate of Augusta College with a master's degree from Florida Atlantic University, she joined the faculty of the University of Georgia in 1984 and is now Franklin Professor of English and Creative Writing there. Her first book was a poetry collection, Perigrina *(1986), and it was followed by her first novel,* The Line of the Sun *(1989), a Pulitzer Prize nominee;* Silent Dancing: A Partial Remembrance of a Puerto Rican Childhood *(1990);* The Latin Deli *(1993);* An Island Like You: Stories of the Barrio *(1998);* The Year of Our Revolution: Selected and New Prose and Poetry *(1998); and* Woman in Front of the Sun: On Becoming a Writer *(2000), among others. She once recalled, "Writing began for me as fascination with a language I was not born into. I first perceived of language, especially the English language, as a barrier, a challenge to be met with the same kind of closed-eye bravado that prompted me to jump into the deep end of the pool before taking my first swimming lesson. . . . I managed to surface and breathe the air of the real world, just as I took in words my first year in America—breathlessly, and yes, almost desperately, for I needed to be able to communicate almost as much as I needed to breathe."*

Migration is the story of my body.
— VÍCTOR HERNÁNDEZ CRUZ

Skin

I was born a white girl in Puerto Rico but became a brown girl when I came to live in the United States. My Puerto Rican relatives called me tall; at the American school, some of my rougher classmates called me Skinny Bones, and the Shrimp because I was the smallest member of my classes all through grammer school until high school, when the midget Gladys was given the honorary post of front row center for class pictures and scorekeeper, bench warmer, in P.E. I reached my full stature of five feet in sixth grade.

I started out life as a pretty baby and learned to be a pretty girl from a pretty mother. Then at ten years of age I suffered one of the worst cases of chicken pox I have ever heard of. My entire body, including the inside of my ears and in between my toes, was covered with pustules which in a fit of panic at my appearance I scratched off my face, leaving permanent scars. A cruel school nurse told me I would always have them—tiny cuts that looked as if a mad cat had plunged its claws deep into my skin. I grew my hair long and hid behind it for the first years of my adolescence. This was when I learned to be invisible.

Color

In the animal world it indicates danger: the most colorful creatures are often the most poisonous. Color is also a way to attract and seduce a mate. In the human world color triggers many more complex and often deadly re-actions. As a Puerto Rican girl born of "white" parents, I spent the first years of my life hearing people refer to me as *blanca*, white. My mother in-sisted that I protect myself from the intense island sun because I was more prone to sunburn than some of my darker, *trigueño* playmates. People were always commenting within my hearing about how my black hair contrasted so nicely with my "pale" skin. I did not think of the color of my skin con-sciously except when I heard the adults talking about complexion. It seems to me that the subject is much more common in the conversation of mixed-race peoples than in mainstream United States society, where it is a touchy and sometimes even embarrassing topic to discuss, except in a political con-text. In Puerto Rico I heard many conversations about skin color. A preg-nant woman could say, "I hope my baby doesn't turn out *prieto*" (slang for "dark" or "black") "like my husband's grandmother, although she was a good-looking *negra* in her time." I am a combination of both, being olive-skinned—lighter than my mother yet darker than my fair-skinned father. In America, I am a person of color, obviously a Latina. On the Island I have been called everything from a *paloma blanca*, after the song (by a black suitor), to *la gringa*.

My first experience of color prejudice occurred in a supermarket in Pa-terson, New Jersey. It was Chrismastime, and I was eight or nine years old. There was a display of toys in the store where I went two or three times a day to buy things for my mother, who never made lists but sent for milk, cigarettes, a can of this or that, as she remembered from hour to hour. I en-joyed being trusted with money and walking half a city block to the new, modern grocery store. It was owned by three good-looking Italian brothers. I liked the younger one with the crew-cut blond hair. The two older ones watched me and the other Puerto Rican kids as if they thought we were going to steal something. The oldest one would sometimes even try to hurry me with my purchases, although part of my pleasure in these expeditions came from looking at everything in the well-stocked aisles. I was also teaching myself to read English by sounding out the labels in packages: L&M cigarettes, Borden's homogenized milk, Red Devil potted ham, Nestle's chocolate mix, Quaker oats, Bustelo coffee, Wonder bread, Colgate toothpaste, Ivory soap, and Goya (makers of products used in Puerto Rican dishes) everything — these are some of the brand names that taught me nouns. Several times this man had come up to me, wearing his blood-stained butcher's apron, and towering over me had asked in a harsh voice whether there was something he could help me find. On the way out I would glance at the younger brother who ran one of the registers and he would often smile and wink at me.

It was the mean brother who first referred to me as "colored." It was a   5 few days before Christmas, and my parents had already told my brother and me that since we were in Los Estados now, we would get our presents on December 25 instead of Los Reyes, Three Kings Day, when gifts are exchanged in Puerto Rico. We were to give them a wish list that they would take to Santa Claus, who apparently lived in the Macy's store downtown — at least that's where we had caught a glimpse of him when we went shopping. Since my parents were timid about entering the fancy store, we did not approach the huge man in the red suit. I was not interested in sitting on a stranger's lap anyway. But I did covet Susie, the talking schoolteacher doll that was displayed in the center aisle of the Italian brothers' supermarket. She talked when you pulled a string on her back. Susie had a limited repertoire of three sentences: I think she could say: "Hello, I'm Susie Schoolteacher," "Two plus two is four," and one other thing I cannot remember. The day the older brother chased me away, I was reaching to touch Susie's blonde curls. I had been told many times, as most children have, not to touch anything in a store that I was not buying. But I had been looking at Susie for weeks. In my mind, she was my doll. After all, I had put her on my Christmas wish list. The moment is frozen in my mind as if there were a photograph of it on file. It was not a turning point, a disaster, or an earth-shaking revelation. It was simply the first time I considered — if naively — the meaning of skin color in human relations.

I reached to touch Susie's hair. It seems to me that I had to get on tiptoe, since the toys were stacked on a table and she sat like a princess on top of the fancy box she came in. Then I heard the booming "Hey, kid, what do you think you're doing!" spoken very loudly from the meat counter. I felt caught, although I knew I was not doing anything criminal. I remember not looking at the man, but standing there, feeling humiliated because I knew everyone in the store must have heard him yell at me. I felt him approach, and when I knew he was behind me, I turned around to face the bloody butcher's apron. His large chest was at my eye level. He blocked my way. I started to run out of the place, but even as I reached the door I heard him shout after me: "Don't come in here unless you gonna buy something. You PR kids put your dirty hands on stuff. You always look dirty. But maybe dirty brown is your natural color." I heard him laugh and someone else too in the back. Outside in the sunlight I looked at my hands. My nails needed a little cleaning as they always did, since I liked to paint with watercolors, but I took a bath every night. I thought the man was dirtier than I was in his stained apron. He was also always sweaty — it showed in big yellow circles under his shirtsleeves. I sat on the front steps of the apartment building where we lived and looked closely at my hands, which showed the only skin I could see, since it was bitter cold and I was wearing my quilted play coat, dungarees, and a knitted navy cap of my father's. I was not pink like my friend Charlene and her sister Kathy, who had blue eyes and light brown hair. My skin is the color of the coffee my grandmother made, which was half milk, *leche con café* rather than *café con leche*. My mother is the opposite mix. She has a lot of café in her color. I could not understand how my skin looked like dirt to the supermarket man.

I went in and washed my hands thoroughly with soap and hot water, and borrowing my mother's nail file, I cleaned the crusted watercolors from underneath my nails. I was pleased with the results. My skin was the same color as before, but I knew I was clean. Clean enough to run my fingers through Susie's fine gold hair when she came home to me.

Size

My mother is barely four feet eleven inches in height, which is average for women in her family. When I grew to five feet by age twelve, she was amazed and began to use the word tall to describe me, as in "Since you are tall, this dress will look good on you." As with the color of my skin, I didn't consciously think about my height or size until other people made an issue of it. It is around the preadolescent years that in America the games childen play for fun become fierce competitions where everyone is out to "prove" they are better than others. It was in the playground and sports fields that my size-related problems began. No matter how familiar the story is, every child who is the last chosen for a team knows the torment of waiting to be called up. At the Paterson, New Jersey, public schools that I attended, the volleyball or softball game was the metaphor for the battlefield of life to the inner city kids — the black kids versus the Puerto Rican kids, the whites versus the blacks versus the Puerto Rican kids; and I was 4F, skinny, short, bespectacled, and apparently impervious to the blood thirst that drove many of my classmates to play ball as if their lives depended on it. Perhaps they did. I would rather be reading a book than sweating, grunting, and running the risk of pain and injury. I simply did not see the point in competitive sports. My main form of exercise then was walking to the library, many city blocks away from my barrio.

Still, I wanted to be wanted. I wanted to be chosen for the teams. Physical education was compulsory, a class where you were actually given a grade. On my mainly all A report card, the C for compassion I always received from the P.E. teachers shamed me the same as a bad grade in a real class. Invariably, my father would say: "How can you make a low grade for *playing games?*" He did not understand. Even if I had managed to make a hit (it never happened) or get the ball over that ridiculously high net, I already had a reputation as a "shrimp," a hopeless nonathlete. It was an area where the girls who didn't like me for one reason or another — mainly because I did better than they on academic subjects — could lord it over me; the playing field was the place where even the smallest girl could make me feel powerless and inferior. I instinctively understood the politics even then; how the *not* choosing me until the teacher forced one of the team captains to call my name was a coup of sorts — there, you little show-off, tomorrow you can beat us in spelling and geography, but this afternoon you are the loser. Or perhaps those were only my own bitter thoughts as I sat or stood in the sidelines while the big girls were grabbed like fish and I, the little brown tadpole, was ignored until Teacher looked over in my general direction and shouted, "Call Ortiz," or, worse, "Somebody's *got* to take her."

No wonder I read Wonder Woman comics and had Legion of Super   10 Heroes daydreams. Although I wanted to think of myself as "intellectual," my body was demanding that I notice it. I saw the little swelling around my once-flat nipples, the fine hairs growing in secret places; but my knees were still bigger than my thighs, and I always wore long- or half-sleeve blouses to hide my bony upper arms. I wanted flesh on my bones — a thick layer of it. I saw a new product advertised on TV. Wate-On. They showed skinny men and women before and after taking the stuff, and it was a transformation like the ninety-seven-pound-weakling-turned-into-Charles-Atlas ads that I saw on the back covers of my comic books. The Wate-On was very expensive. I tried to explain my need for it in Spanish to my mother, but it didn't translate very well, even to my ears — and she said with a tone of finality, eat more of my good food and you'll get fat — anybody can get fat. Right. Except me. I was going to have to join a circus someday as Skinny Bones, the woman without flesh.

Wonder Woman was stacked. She had a cleavage framed by the spread wings of a golden eagle and a muscular body that has become fashionable with women only recently. But since I wanted a body that would serve me in P.E., hers was my ideal. The breasts were an indulgence I allowed myself. Perhaps the daydreams of bigger girls were more glamorous, since our ambitions are filtered through our needs, but I wanted first a powerful body. I daydreamed of leaping up above the gray landscape of the city to where the sky was clear and blue, and in anger and self-pity, I fantasized about scooping my enemies up by their hair from the playing fields and dumping them on a barren asteroid. I would put the P.E. teachers each on their own rock in space too, where they would be the loneliest people in the universe, since I knew they had no "inner resources," no imagination, and in outer space, there would be no air for them to fill their deflated volleyballs with. In my mind all P.E. teachers have blended into one large spiky-haired woman with a whistle on a string around her neck and a volleyball under one arm. My

Wonder Woman fantasies of revenge were a source of comfort to me in my early career as a shrimp.

I was saved from more years of P.E. torment by the fact that in my sophomore year of high school I transferred to a school where the midget, Gladys, was the focal point of interest for the people who must rank according to size. Because her height was considered a handicap, there was an unspoken rule about mentioning size around Gladys, but of course, there was no need to say anything. Gladys knew her place: front row center in class photographs. I gladly moved to the left or to the right of her, as far as I could without leaving the picture completely.

Looks

Many photographs were taken of me as a baby by my mother to send to my father, who was stationed overseas during the first two years of my life. With the army in Panama when I was born, he later traveled often on tours of duty with the navy. I was a healthy, pretty baby. Recently, I read that people are drawn to big-eyed round-faced creatures, like puppies, kittens, and certain other mammals and marsupials, koalas, for example, and, of course, infants. I was all eyes, since my head and body, even as I grew older, remained thin and small-boned. As a young child I got a lot of attention from my relatives and many other people we met in our barrio. My mother's beauty may have had something to do with how much attention we got from strangers in stores and on the street. I can imagine it. In the pictures I have seen of us together, she is a stunning young woman by Latino standards: long, curly black hair, and round curves in a compact frame. From her I learned how to move, smile, and talk like an attractive woman. I remember going into a bodega for our groceries and being given candy by the proprietor as a reward for being *bonita*, pretty.

I can see in the photographs, and I also remember, that I was dressed in the pretty clothes, the stiff, frilly dresses, with layers of crinolines underneath, the glossy patent leather shoes, and, on special occasions, the skull-hugging little hats and the white gloves that were popular in the late fifties and early sixties. My mother was proud of my looks, although I was a bit too thin. She could dress me up like a doll and take me by the hand to visit relatives, or go to the Spanish mass at the Catholic church, and show me off. How was I to know that she and the others who called me "pretty" were representatives of an aesthetic that would not apply when I went out into the mainstream world of school?

In my Paterson, New Jersey, public schools there were still quite a few   15
white children, although the demographics of the city were changing rapidly. The original waves of Italian and Irish immigrants, silk-mill workers, and laborers in the cloth industries had been "assimilated." Their children were now the middle-class parents of my peers. Many of them moved their children to the Catholic schools that proliferated enough to have leagues of

basketball teams. The names I recall hearing still ring in my ears: Don Bosco High versus St. Mary's High, St. Joseph's versus St. John's. Later I too would be transferred to the safer environment of a Catholic school. But I started school at Public School Number 11. I came there from Puerto Rico, thinking myself a pretty girl, and found that the hierarchy for popularity was as follows: pretty white girl, pretty Jewish girl, pretty Puerto Rican girl, pretty black girl. Drop the last two categories; teachers were too busy to have more than one favorite per class, and it was simply understood that if there was a big part in the school play, or any competition where the main qualification was "presentability" (such as escorting a school visitor to or from the principal's office), the classroom's public address speaker would be requesting the pretty and/or nice-looking white boy or girl. By the time I was in the sixth grade, I was sometimes called by the principal to represent my class because I dressed neatly (I knew this from a progress report sent to my mother, which I translated to her) and because all the "presentable" white girls had moved to the Catholic schools (I later surmised this part). But I was still not one of the popular girls with the boys. I remember one incident where I stepped out into the playground in my baggy gym shorts and one Puerto Rican boy said to the other: "What do you think?" The other one answered: "Her face is OK, but look at the toothpick legs." The next best thing to a compliment I got was when my favorite male teacher, while handing out the class pictures, commented that with my long neck and delicate features I resembled the movie star Audrey Hepburn. But the Puerto Rican boys had learned to respond to a fuller figure: long necks and a perfect little nose were not what they looked for in a girl. That is when I decided I was a "brain." I did not settle into the role easily. I was nearly devastated by what the chicken pox episode had done to my self-image. But I looked into the mirror less often after I was told that I would always have scars on my face, and I hid behind my long black hair and my books.

After the problems at the public school got to the point where even nonconfrontational little me got beaten up several times, my parents enrolled me at St. Joseph's High School. I was then a minority of one among the Italian and Irish kids. But I found several good friends there — other girls who took their studies seriously. We did our homework together and talked about the Jackies. The Jackies were two popular girls, one blonde and the other red-haired, who had women's bodies. Their curves showed even in the blue jumper uniforms with straps that we all wore. The blonde Jackie would often let one of the straps fall off her shoulder, and although she, like all of us, wore a white blouse underneath, all the boys stared at her arm. My friends and I talked about this and practiced letting our straps fall off our shoulders. But it wasn't the same without breasts or hips.

My final two and a half years of high school were spent in Augusta, Georgia, where my parents moved our family in search of a more peaceful environment. There we became part of a little community of our army-connected relatives and friends. School was yet another matter. I was enrolled in a huge school of nearly two thousand students that had just that year been forced to integrate. There were two black girls and there was me. I did extremely well academically. As to my social life, it was, for the most part, uneventful — yet it is in my memory blighted by one incident. In my junior year, I became wildly infatuated with a pretty white boy. I'll call him Ted. Oh, he was pretty: yellow hair that fell over his forehead, a smile to die for — and he was a great dancer. I watched him at Teen Town, the youth center at the base where all the military brats gathered on Saturday nights. My father had retired from the navy, and we had all our base privileges — one other reason we had moved to Augusta. Ted looked like an angel to me. I worked on him for a year before he asked me out. This meant maneuvering to be within the periphery of his vision at every possible occasion. I took the long way to my classes in school just to pass by his locker, I went to football games, which I detested, and I danced (I too was a good dancer) in front of him at Teen Town — this took some fancy footwork, since it involved subtly moving my partner toward the right spot on the dance floor. When Ted finally approached me, "A Million to One" was playing on the jukebox, and when he took me into his arms, the odds suddenly turned in my favor. He asked me to go to a school dance the following Saturday. I said yes, breathlessly. I said yes, but there were obstacles to surmount at home. My father did not allow me to date casually. I was allowed to go to major events like a prom or a concert with a boy who had been properly screened. There was such a boy in my life, a neighbor who wanted to be a Baptist missionary and was practicing his anthropological skills on my family. If I was desperate to go somewhere and needed a date, I'd resort to Gary. This is the type of religious nut that Gary was: when the school bus did not show up one day, he put his hands over his face and prayed to Christ to get us a way to get to school. Within ten minutes a mother in a station wagon, on her way to town, stopped to ask why we weren't in school. Gary informed her that the Lord had sent her just in time to find us a way to get there in time for roll call. He assumed that I was impressed. Gary was even good-looking in a bland sort of way, but he kissed me with his lips tightly pressed together. I think Gary probably ended up marrying a native woman from wherever he may have gone to preach the Gospel according to Paul. She probably believes that all white men pray to God for transportation and kiss with their mouths closed. But it was Ted's mouth, his whole beautiful self, that concerned me in those days. I knew my father would say no to our date, but I planned to run away from home if necessary. I told my mother how important this date was. I cajoled and pleaded with her from Sunday to Wednesday. She listened to my arguments and must have heard the note of desperation in my voice. She said very gently to me: "You better be ready for disappointment." I did not ask what she meant. I did not want her fears for me to taint my happiness. I asked her to tell my father about my date. Thursday at breakfast my father looked at me across the table with his eyebrows together. My mother looked at him with her mouth set in a straight line. I looked down at my bowl of cereal. Nobody said anything. Friday I tried on every dress in my closet. Ted would be picking me up at six on Saturday: dinner and then the sock hop at school. Friday night I was in my room doing my nails or something else in preparation for Saturday (I know I groomed myself nonstop all week) when the telephone rang. I ran to get it. It was Ted. His voice sounded funny when he said my name, so funny that I felt compelled to ask: "Is something wrong?" Ted blurted it all out without a preamble. His father had asked who he was going out with. Ted had told him my name. "Ortiz? That's Spanish, isn't it?" the father had asked. Ted had told him yes, then shown him my picture in the yearbook. Ted's father had shaken his head. No. Ted would not be taking me out. Ted's father had known Puerto Ricans in the army. He had lived in New York City while studying architecture and had seen how the spics lived. Like rats. Ted repeated his father's words to me as if I should understand *his* predicament when I heard why he was breaking our date. I don't remember what I said before hanging up. I do recall the darkness of my room that sleepless night and the heaviness of my blanket in which I wrapped myself like a shroud. And I remember my parents' respect for my pain and their gentleness toward me that weekend. My mother did not say "I warned you," and I was grateful for her understanding silence.

In college, I suddenly became an "exotic" woman to the men who had survived the popularity wars in high school, who were now practicing to be worldly: they had to act liberal in their politics, in their lifestyles, and in the women they went out with. I dated heavily for a while, then married young. I had discovered that I needed stability more than social life. I had brains for sure and some talent in writing. These facts were a constant in my life. My skin color, my size, and my appearance were variables — things that were judged according to my current self-image, the aesthetic values of the times, the places I was in, and the people I met. My studies, later my writing, the respect of people who saw me as an individual person they cared about, these were the criteria for my sense of self-worth that I would concentrate on in my adult life.

QUESTIONS

1. According to its title, this piece purportedly tells a story, but it is divided into subtitled sections ("Skin," "Color," "Size," "Looks") like an article or essay. In what sense(s) does it tell a story, and how would you define the plot of that story? Does it have a clear beginning, middle, and end? In what ways might it be considered an essay?
2. Consider the significance of the epigraph that Cofer chose for her essay. In what ways is "migration" equivalent to the story of her body? How does the act of migration or the idea of migration pertain to the story of her body? How does it contribute to the meaning of her story?
3. Though the title of this piece implies that it will tell a single story, Cofer actually tells several stories in these reflections. In what ways do these

multiple stories add up to a single story? What is the overarching theme of that story?

4. Cofer devotes separate sections to "Skin," "Color," "Size," and "Looks," even though they are concerned with overlapping, perhaps even synonymous aspects of her appearance. What is the distinctive slant of each section that accounts for its title and its separateness? Why do you suppose she begins with "Skin" and ends with "Looks"? Why "Color" before "Size" rather than vice versa?

5. Adapting Cofer's organizational approach to your own situation, write a piece about the story of your body. Feel free to use her categories (in whatever order you wish), or invent categories of your own. You might also try to find (or create) a suitable epigraph for your piece or adapt hers to suit your story.

MAKING CONNECTIONS

Compare Cofer's story of her body to Lucy Grealy's story of her disfigured face (p. 62) and/or Alice Walker's story of her damaged eye (p. 54). In considering each of their stories, take note of how they use various narrative techniques to highlight the causes and the painful details of their maladies, as well as their adjustment to those problems.

PILGRIMAGE TO NONVIOLENCE

Martin Luther King Jr.

The son of a minister, Martin Luther King Jr. (1929–1968) was ordained a Baptist minister in his father's church in Atlanta, Georgia, at the age of eighteen. He sprang into prominence in 1955 when he called a citywide boycott of the segregated bus system in Montgomery, Alabama, and he continued to be the most prominent civil rights activist in America until his assassination on April 4, 1968. During those tumultuous years, he was jailed at least fourteen times and endured countless threats against his life, but he persevered in his fight against racial discrimination, using a synthesis of the nonviolent philosophy of Mahatma Gandhi and Jesus's Sermon on the Mount. The 1964 Nobel Peace Prize was only one of the many awards he received, and his several books are characterized as much by their eloquent prose style as by their moral fervor. "Pilgrimage to Nonviolence" originally appeared in the magazine Christian Century *and was revised and updated for a collection of his sermons,* Strength to Love *(1963), the source of the following text.*

In my senior year in theological seminary, I engaged in the exciting reading of various theological theories. Having been raised in a rather strict fundamentalist tradition, I was occasionally shocked when my intellectual journey carried me through new and sometimes complex doctrinal lands, but the pilgrimage was always stimulating, gave me a new appreciation for objective appraisal and critical analysis, and knocked me out of my dogmatic slumber.

Liberalism provided me with an intellectual satisfaction that I had never found in fundamentalism. I became so enamored of the insights of liberalism that I almost fell into the trap of accepting uncritically everything it encompassed. I was absolutely convinced of the natural goodness of man and the natural power of human reason.

I

A basic change in my thinking came when I began to question some of the theories that had been associated with so-called liberal theology. Of course, there are aspects of liberalism that I hope to cherish always: its devotion to the search for truth, its insistence on an open and analytical mind, and its refusal to abandon the best lights of reason. The contribution of liberalism to the philosophical-historical criticism of biblical literature has been of immeasurable value and should be defended with religious and scientific passion.

But I began to question the liberal doctrine of man. The more I observed the tragedies of history and man's shameful inclination to choose the low road, the more I came to see the depths and strength of sin. My reading of the works of Reinhold Niebuhr made me aware of the complexity of human motives and the reality of sin on every level of man's existence.[1] Moreover, I came to recognize the complexity of man's social involvement and the glaring reality of collective evil. I realized that liberalism had been all too sentimental concerning human nature and that it leaned toward a false idealism.

I also came to see the superficial optimism of liberalism concerning human nature overlooked the fact that reason is darkened by sin. The more I thought about human nature, the more I saw how our tragic inclination for sin encourages us to rationalize our actions. Liberalism failed to show that reason by itself is little more than an instrument to justify man's defensive ways of thinking. Reason, devoid of the purifying power of faith, can never free itself from distortions and rationalizations.   5

Although I rejected some aspects of liberalism, I never came to an all-out acceptance of neo-orthodoxy. While I saw neo-orthodoxy as a helpful corrective for a sentimental liberalism, I felt that it did not provide an adequate answer to basic questions. If liberalism was too optimistic concerning human nature, neo-orthodoxy was too pessimistic. Not only on the question of man, but also on other vital issues, the revolt of neo-orthodoxy went too far. In its attempt to preserve the transcendence of God, which had been neglected by an overstress of his immanence in liberalism, neo-orthodoxy went to the extreme of stressing a God who was hidden, unknown, and "wholly other." In its revolt against overemphasis on the power of reason in liberalism, neo-orthodoxy fell into a mood of antirationalism and semifundamentalism, stressing a narrow uncritical biblicism. This approach, I felt, was inadequate both for the church and for personal life.

So although liberalism left me unsatisfied on the question of the nature of man, I found no refuge in neo-orthodoxy. I am now convinced that the truth about man is found neither in liberalism nor in neo-orthodoxy. Each represents a partial truth. A large segment of Protestant liberalism defined man only in terms of his essential nature, his capacity for good; neo-orthodoxy tended to define man only in terms of his existential nature, his capacity for evil. An adequate understanding of man is found neither in the thesis of liberalism nor in the antithesis of neo-orthodoxy, but in a synthesis which reconciles the truths of both.

---

[1]*Reinhold Niebuhr* (1892–1971): An American theologian, social activist, and noted writer on social and religious issues. [Eds.]

During the intervening years I have gained a new appreciation for the philosophy of existentialism. My first contact with the philosophy came through my reading of Kierkegaard and Nietzsche.[2] Later I turned to a study of Jaspers, Heidegger, and Sartre.[3] These thinkers stimulated my thinking; while questioning each, I nevertheless learned a great deal through a study of them. When I finally engaged in a serious study of the writings of Paul Tillich,[4] I became convinced that existentialism, in spite of the fact that it had become all too fashionable, had grasped certain basic truths about man and his condition that could not be permanently overlooked.

An understanding of the "finite freedom" of man is one of the permanent contributions of existentialism, and its perception of the anxiety and conflict produced in man's personal and social life by the perilous and ambiguous structure of existence is especially meaningful for our time. A common denominator in atheistic or theistic existentialism is that man's existential situation is estranged from his essential nature. In their revolt against Hegel's essentialism,[5] all existentialists contend that the world is fragmented. History is a series of unreconciled conflicts, and man's existence is filled with anxiety and threatened with meaninglessness. While the ultimate Christian answer is not found in any of these existential assertions, there is much here by which the theologian may describe the true state of man's existence.

Although most of my formal study has been in systematic theology and   10
philosophy, I have become more and more interested in social ethics. During my early teens I was deeply concerned by the problem of racial injustice. I considered segregation both rationally inexplicable and morally unjustifiable. I could never accept my having to sit in the back of a bus or in the segregated section of a train. The first time that I was seated behind a curtain in a dining car I felt as though the curtain had been dropped on my selfhood. I also learned that the inseparable twin of racial injustice is economic injustice. I saw how the systems of segregation exploited both the Negro and the poor whites. These early experiences made me deeply conscious of the varieties of injustice in our society.

---

[2]*Søren Kierkegaard* (1813–1855): A Danish religious and aesthetic philosopher, concerned especially with the role of the individual. *Friedrich Nietzsche* (1844–1900): A German philosopher and moralist who sought a heroic, creative rejuvenation for a Western civilization that he considered decadent. [Eds.]

[3]*Karl Jaspers* (1883–1969): A German philosopher. *Martin Heidegger* (1889–1976): A German philosopher. *Jean-Paul Sartre* (1905–1980): A French philosopher and novelist. All three were existentialists, concerned with the existence and responsibility of the individual in an unknowable universe. [Eds.]

[4]*Paul Tillich* (1886–1965): A German-born American philosopher and theologian whose writings drew on psychology and existentialism. [Eds.]

[5]*Georg Friedrich Hegel* (1770–1831): A German philosopher best known for his theory of the dialectic (thesis versus antithesis produces synthesis). [Eds.]

II

Not until I entered theological seminary, however, did I begin a serious intellectual quest for a method that would eliminate social evil. I was immediately influenced by the social gospel. In the early 1950s I read Walter Rauschenbusch's *Christianity and the Social Crisis*, a book which left an indelible imprint on my thinking. Of course, there were points at which I differed with Rauschenbusch. I felt that he was a victim of the nineteenth-century "cult of inevitable progress," which led him to an unwarranted optimism concerning human nature. Moreover, he came perilously close to identifying the Kingdom of God with a particular social and economic system, a temptation to which the church must never surrender. But in spite of these shortcomings, Rauschenbusch gave to American Protestantism a sense of social responsibility that it should never lose. The gospel at its best deals with the whole man, not only his soul but also his body, not only his spiritual well-being but also his material well-being. A religion that professes a concern for the souls of men and is not equally concerned about the slums that damn them, the economic conditions that strangle them, and the social conditions that cripple them, is a spiritually moribund religion.

After reading Rauschenbusch, I turned to a serious study of the social and ethical theories of the great philosophers. During this period I had almost despaired of the power of love to solve social problems. The turn-the-other-cheek and the love-your-enemies philosophies are valid, I felt, only when individuals are in conflict with other individuals; when racial groups and nations are in conflict, a more realistic approach is necessary.

Then I was introduced to the life and teachings of Mahatma Gandhi.[6] As I read his works I became deeply fascinated by his campaigns of nonviolent resistance. The whole Gandhian concept of *satyagraha* (*satya* is truth which equals love and *graha* is force; *satyagraha* thus means truth-force or love-force) was profoundly significant to me. As I delved deeper into the philosophy of Gandhi, my skepticism concerning the power of love gradually diminished, and I came to see for the first time that the Christian doctrine of love, operating through the Gandhian method of nonviolence, is one of the most potent weapons available to an oppressed people in their struggle for freedom. At that time, however, I acquired only an intellectual understanding and appreciation of the position, and I had no firm determination to organize it in a socially effective situation.

When I went to Montgomery, Alabama, as a pastor in 1954, I had not the slightest idea that I would later become involved in a crisis in which nonviolent resistance would be applicable. After I had lived in the community about a year, the bus boycott began. The Negro people of Montgomery, exhausted by the humiliating experience that they had constantly faced on the buses, expressed in a massive act of noncooperation their determination to

---

[6]*Mahatma Gandhi* (1869–1948): A Hindu nationalist and spiritual leader. [Eds.]

be free. They came to see that it was ultimately more honorable to walk the streets in dignity than to ride the buses in humiliation. At the beginning of the protest, the people called on me to serve as their spokesman. In accepting this responsibility, my mind, consciously or unconsciously, was driven back to the Sermon on the Mount and the Gandhian method of nonviolent resistance. This principle became the guiding light of our movement. Christ furnished the spirit and motivation and Gandhi furnished the method.

The experience in Montgomery did more to clarify my thinking in regard to the question of nonviolence than all of the books that I had read. As the days unfolded, I became more and more convinced of the power of nonviolence. Nonviolence became more than a method to which I gave intellectual assent; it became a commitment to a way of life. Many issues I had not cleared up intellectually concerning nonviolence were now resolved within the sphere of practical action.

My privilege of traveling to India had a great impact on me personally, for it was invigorating to see firsthand the amazing results of a nonviolent struggle to achieve independence. The aftermath of hatred and bitterness that usually follows a violent campaign was found nowhere in India, and a mutual friendship, based on complete equality, existed between the Indian and British people within the Commonwealth.

I would not wish to give the impression that nonviolence will accomplish miracles overnight. Men are not easily moved from their mental ruts or purged of their prejudiced and irrational feelings. When the underprivileged demand freedom, the privileged at first react with bitterness and resistance. Even when the demands are couched in nonviolent terms, the initial response is substantially the same. I am sure that many of our white brothers in Montgomery and throughout the South are still bitter toward the Negro leaders, even though these leaders have sought to follow a way of love and nonviolence. But the nonviolent approach does something to the hearts and souls of those committed to it. It gives them new self-respect. It calls up resources of strength and courage that they did not know they had. Finally, it so stirs the conscience of the opponent that reconciliation becomes a reality.

III

More recently I have come to see the need for the method of nonviolence in international relations. Although I was not yet convinced of its efficacy in conflicts between nations, I felt that while war could never be a positive good, it could serve as a negative good by preventing the spread and growth of an evil force. War, horrible as it is, might be preferable to surrender to a totalitarian system. But I now believe that the potential destructiveness of modern weapons totally rules out the possibility of war ever again achieving a negative good. If we assume that mankind has a right to survive, then we must find an alternative to war and destruction. In our day of space vehicles and guided ballistic missiles, the choice is either nonviolence or nonexistence.

I am no doctrinaire pacifist, but I have tried to embrace a realistic pacifism which finds the pacifist position as the lesser evil in the circumstances. I do not claim to be free from the moral dilemmas that the Christian non-pacifist confronts, but I am convinced that the church cannot be silent while mankind faces the threat of nuclear annihilation. If the church is true to her mission, she must call for an end to the arms race.

Some of my personal sufferings over the last few years have also served to shape my thinking. I always hesitate to mention these experiences for fear of conveying the wrong impression. A person who constantly calls attention to his trials and sufferings is in danger of developing a martyr complex and impressing others that he is consciously seeking sympathy. It is possible for one to be self-centered in his self-sacrifice. So I am always reluctant to refer to my personal sacrifices. But I feel somewhat justified in mentioning them in this essay because of the influence they have had upon my thought.

20

Due to my involvement in the struggle for the freedom of my people, I have known very few quiet days in the last few years. I have been imprisoned in Alabama and Georgia jails twelve times. My home has been bombed twice. A day seldom passes that my family and I are not the recipients of threats of death. I have been the victim of a near-fatal stabbing. So in a real sense I have been battered by the storms of persecution. I must admit that at times I have felt that I could no longer bear such a heavy burden, and have been tempted to retreat to a more quiet and serene life. But every time such a temptation appeared, something came to strengthen and sustain my determination. I have learned now that the Master's burden is light precisely when we take his yoke upon us.

My personal trials have also taught me the value of unmerited suffering. As my sufferings mounted I soon realized that there were two ways in which I could respond to my situation — either to react with bitterness or seek to transform the suffering into a creative force. I decided to follow the latter course. Recognizing the necessity for suffering, I have tried to make of it a virtue, if only to save myself from bitterness. I have attempted to see my personal ordeals as an opportunity to transfigure myself and heal the people involved in the tragic situation which now obtains. I have lived these last few years with the conviction that unearned suffering is redemptive. There are some who still find the Cross a stumbling block, others consider it foolishness, but I am more convinced than ever before that it is the power of God unto social and individual salvation. So like the Apostle Paul I can now humbly, yet proudly, say, "I bear in my body the marks of the Lord Jesus."

The agonizing moments through which I have passed during the last few years have also drawn me closer to God. More than ever before I am convinced of the reality of a personal God. True, I have always believed in the personality of God. But in the past the idea of a personal God was little more than a metaphysical category that I found theologically and philosophically satisfying. Now it is a living reality that has been validated in the experiences of everyday life. God has been profoundly real to me in recent years. In the midst of outer dangers I have felt an inner calm. In the midst of lonely days and dreary nights I have heard an inner voice saying, "Lo, I will be with you." When the chains of fear and the manacles of frustration have all but stymied my efforts, I have felt the power of God transforming the fatigue of despair into the buoyancy of hope. I am convinced that the universe is under the control of a loving purpose, and that in the struggle for righteousness man has cosmic companionship. Behind the harsh appearances of the world there is a benign power. To say that this God is personal is not to make him a finite object beside other objects or attribute to him the limitations of human personality; it is to take what is finest and noblest in our consciousness and affirm its perfect existence in him. It is certainly true that human personality is limited, but personality as such involves no necessary limitations. It means simply self-consciousness and self-direction. So in the truest sense of the word, God is a living God. In him there is feeling and will, responsive to the deepest yearnings of the human heart: *this* God both evokes and answers prayer.

The past decade has been a most exciting one. In spite of the tensions and uncertainties of this period something profoundly meaningful is taking place. Old systems of exploitation and oppression are passing away; new systems of justice and equality are being born. In a real sense this is a great time to be alive. Therefore, I am not yet discouraged about the future. Granted that the easygoing optimism of yesterday is impossible. Granted that we face a world crisis which leaves us standing so often amid the surging murmur of life's restless sea. But every crisis has both its dangers and its opportunities. It can spell either salvation or doom. In a dark, confused world the Kingdom of God may yet reign in the hearts of men.

QUESTIONS

1. King found the extremes of liberalism on one hand and neo-orthodoxy on the other unsatisfactory. Why?
2. Existentialism (paragraph 8) and Walter Rauschenbusch's social gospel (paragraph 11) proved more useful to King than liberalism or neo-orthodoxy. How did these concepts help shape his outlook?
3. King is interested in religious and philosophical theories not for their own sake but for their usefulness in the social world. How do Mahatma Gandhi's example (paragraphs 13 and 16) and King's own experience in Montgomery (paragraphs 14, 15, and 17) illustrate this concern?
4. How did King's personal faith in God aid in his struggles and sufferings? Is his dream of a better society totally dependent on the existence of this "benign power" (paragraph 23)?
5. King's intellectual development is described as a pilgrimage from a simple fundamentalist attitude through conflicting theological and philo-

sophical concepts to an intensified belief in a benign God and a commitment to international nonviolence. How is his final set of beliefs superior to his original one? Has he convinced you of the validity of his beliefs?

6. King writes for a general audience rather than one with theological and philosophical training. How successful is King at clarifying religious and philosophical concepts for the general reader? Point out examples that show how he treats such concepts.

7. Again and again King employs the classical rhetorical strategy of concession: the opposition's viewpoint is stated and partially accepted before King gives his own viewpoint. Locate two or three instances of this strategy, and explain how it aids a reader's understanding (if not acceptance) of King's views.

8. King's essay reflects on how he came to accept the method of nonviolence. Have you, over time, changed your thoughts or methods of approaching an issue or problem? Has someone you know well done this? If so, write an essay reflecting on the events central to this change and their significance.

9. King's hopes for a better world were expressed in the early 1960s. Based on your knowledge of history since then, write an essay in which you justify or disqualify King's guarded optimism.

MAKING CONNECTIONS

1. Like several other writers in this book, King reflects on a turning point in his life. Consider his essay in relation to two or three others, such as those by Maya Angelou (p. 43), Alice Walker (p. 54), George Orwell (p. 354), or Zoë Tracy Hardy (p. 366). Compare and contrast the ways these writers present their turning points. How does each present the crucial moment or event, and how does each show its meaning?

2. One way a writer convinces us is by the authority we sense in the person as he or she writes. What details in King's essay contribute to our sense of him as an authoritative person, a writer we are inclined to believe? What do you find of similar persuasiveness in the essays of Maya Angelou (p. 43), Judith Ortiz Cofer (p. 336), George Orwell (p. 354), or Zoë Tracy Hardy (p. 366)?

SHOOTING AN ELEPHANT

George Orwell

George Orwell (1903–1950) was the pen name of Eric Blair, the son of a British customs officer serving in Bengal, India. As a boy he was sent home to prestigious English schools, where he learned to dislike the rich and powerful. After finishing preparatory school at Eton College, he returned to Asia to serve as an officer of the British police in India and Burma, where he became disillusioned with imperialism. He later studied conditions among the urban poor and the coal miners of Wigan, a city in northwestern England, which strengthened his socialist beliefs. He was wounded in the Spanish civil war, defending the lost cause of the left against the fascists. Under the name Orwell, he wrote accounts of all of these experiences as well as the anti-Stalinist fable Animal Farm *(1945) and the novel* 1984 *(1949). In the following essay, first published in 1936, Orwell attacks the politics of imperialism.*

In Moulmein, in Lower Burma, I was hated by large numbers of people—the only time in my life that I have been important enough for this to happen to me. I was sub-divisional police officer of the town, and in an aimless, petty kind of way anti-European feeling was very bitter. No one had the guts to raise a riot, but if a European woman went through the bazaars alone somebody would probably spit betel juice over her dress. As a police officer I was an obvious target and was baited whenever it seemed safe to do so. When a nimble Burman tripped me up on the football field and the referee (another Burman) looked the other way, the crowd yelled with hideous laughter. This happened more than once. In the end the sneering yellow faces of young men that met me everywhere, the insults hooted after me when I was at a safe distance, got badly on my nerves. The young Buddhist priests were the worst of all. There were several thousands of them in the town and none of them seemed to have anything to do except stand on street corners and jeer at Europeans.

All this was perplexing and upsetting. For at that time I had already made up my mind that imperialism was an evil thing and the sooner I chucked up my job and got out of it the better. Theoretically—and secretly, of course—I was all for the Burmese and all against their oppressors, the British. As for the job I was doing, I hated it more bitterly than I can perhaps make clear. In a job like that you see the dirty work of Empire at close quarters. The wretched prisoners huddling in the stinking cages of the lock-ups, the grey, cowed faces of the long-term convicts, the scarred buttocks of the men who had been flogged with bamboos — all these oppressed me with an intolerable sense of guilt. But I could get nothing into perspective. I was young and ill-educated and I had had to think out my problems in the utter silence that is imposed on every Englishman in the East. I did not even know that the British Empire is dying, still less did I know that it is a great deal better than the younger empires that are going to supplant it. All I knew was that I was stuck between my hatred of the empire I served and my rage against the evil-spirited little beasts who tried to make my job impossible. With one part of my mind I thought of the British Raj[1] as an unbreakable tyranny, as something clamped down, in *saecula saeculorum*,[2] upon the will of prostrate peoples; with another part I thought that the greatest joy in the world would be to drive a bayonet into a Buddhist priest's guts. Feelings like these are the normal by-product of imperialism; ask any Anglo-Indian official, if you can catch him off duty.

One day something happened which in a roundabout way was enlightening. It was a tiny incident in itself, but it gave me a better glimpse than I had had before of the real nature of imperialism — the real motives for which despotic governments act. Early one morning the sub-inspector at a police station at the other end of the town rang me up on the phone and said that an elephant was ravaging the bazaar. Would I please come and do something about it? I did not know what I could do, but I wanted to see what was happening and I got on to a pony and started out. I took my rifle, an old .44 Winchester and much too small to kill an elephant, but I thought the noise might be useful *in terrorem*.[3] Various Burmans stopped me on the way and told me about the elephant's doings. It was not, of course, a wild elephant, but a tame one which had gone "must."[4] It had been chained up, as tame elephants always are when their attack of "must" is due, but on the previous night it had broken its chain and escaped. Its mahout,[5] the only person who could manage it when it was in that state, had set out in pursuit, but had taken the wrong direction and was now twelve hours' journey away, and in the morning the elephant had suddenly reappeared in town. The Burmese population had no weapons and were quite helpless against it. It had already destroyed somebody's bamboo hut, killed a cow and raided some fruit-stalls and devoured the stock; also it had met the municipal rubbish van and, when the driver jumped out and took to his heels, had turned the van over and inflicted violences upon it.

The Burmese sub-inspector and some Indian constables were waiting for me in the quarter where the elephant had been seen. It was a very poor

---

[1]*British Raj*: British rule in India and Burma. [Eds.]
[2]*saecula saeculorum*: Forever and ever. [Eds.]
[3]*in terrorem*: For fright. [Eds.]
[4]*"must"*: The frenzied state of the bull elephant in sexual excitement. [Eds.]
[5]*mahout*: An elephant's keeper. [Eds.]

quarter, a labyrinth of squalid bamboo huts, thatched with palm-leaf, winding all over a steep hillside. I remember that it was a cloudy, stuffy morning at the beginning of the rains. We began questioning the people as to where the elephant had gone and, as usual, failed to get any definite information. That is invariably the case in the East; a story always sounds clear enough at a distance, but the nearer you get to the scene of events the vaguer it becomes. Some of the people said that the elephant had gone in one direction, some said that he had gone in another, some professed not even to have heard of any elephant. I had almost made up my mind that the whole story was a pack of lies, when we heard yells a little distance away. There was a loud, scandalized cry of "Go away, child! Go away this instant!" and an old woman with a switch in her hand came round the corner of a hut, violently shooing away a crowd of naked children. Some more women followed, clicking their tongues and exclaiming; evidently there was something that the children ought not to have seen. I rounded the hut and saw a man's dead body sprawling in the mud. He was an Indian, a black Dravidian coolie,[6] almost naked, and he could not have been dead many minutes. The people said that the elephant had come suddenly upon him round the corner of the hut, caught him with its trunk, put its foot on his back and ground him into the earth. This was the rainy season and the ground was soft, and his face had scored a trench a foot deep and a couple of yards long. He was lying on his belly with arms crucified and head sharply twisted to one side. His face was coated with mud, the eyes wide open, the teeth bared and grinning with an expression of unendurable agony. (Never tell me, by the way, that the dead look peaceful. Most of the corpses I have seen looked devilish.) The friction of the great beast's foot had stripped the skin from his back as neatly as one skins a rabbit. As soon as I saw the dead man I sent an orderly to a friend's house nearby to borrow an elephant rifle. I had already sent back the pony, not wanting it to go mad with fright and throw me if it smelt the elephant.

The orderly came back in a few minutes with a rifle and five cartridges, and meanwhile some Burmans had arrived and told us that the elephant was in the paddy fields below, only a few hundred yards away. As I started forward practically the whole population of the quarter flocked out of the houses and followed me. They had seen the rifle and were all shouting excitedly that I was going to shoot the elephant. They had not shown much interest in the elephant when he was merely ravaging their homes, but it was different now that he was to be shot. It was a bit of fun to them, as it would be to an English crowd; besides they wanted the meat. It made me vaguely uneasy. I had no intention of shooting the elephant — I had merely sent for the rifle to defend myself if necessary — and it is always unnerving to have a crowd following you. I marched down the hill, looking and feel-

5

---

[6]*Dravidian coolie*: *Dravidian* refers to a large ethnic group from south and central India. A *coolie* is an unskilled laborer. [Eds.]

ing a fool, with the rifle over my shoulder and an ever-growing army of people jostling at my heels. At the bottom, when you got away from the huts, there was a metalled road and beyond that a miry waste of paddy fields a thousand yards across, not yet ploughed but soggy from the first rains and dotted with coarse grass. The elephant was standing eight yards from the road, his left side towards us. He took not the slightest notice of the crowd's approach. He was tearing up bunches of grass, beating them against his knees to clean them and stuffing them into his mouth.

I had halted on the road. As soon as I saw the elephant I knew with perfect certainty that I ought not to shoot him. It is a serious matter to shoot a working elephant — it is comparable to destroying a huge and costly piece of machinery — and obviously one ought not to do it if it can possibly be avoided. And at that distance, peacefully eating, the elephant looked no more dangerous than a cow. I thought then and I think now that his attack of "must" was already passing off; in which case he would merely wander harmlessly about until the mahout came back and caught him. Moreover, I did not in the least want to shoot him. I decided that I would watch him for a little while to make sure that he did not turn savage again, and then go home.

But at that moment I glanced around at the crowd that had followed me. It was an immense crowd, two thousand at the least and growing every minute. It blocked the road for a long distance on either side. I looked at the sea of yellow faces above the garish clothes — faces all happy and excited all over this bit of fun, all certain that the elephant was going to be shot. They were watching me as they would watch a conjurer about to perform a trick. They did not like me, but with the magical rifle in my hands I was momentarily worth watching. And suddenly I realized that I should have to shoot the elephant after all. The people expected it of me and I had got to do it; I could feel their two thousand wills pressing me forward, irresistibly. And it was at this moment, as I stood there with the rifle in my hands, that I first grasped the hollowness, the futility of the white man's dominion in the East. Here was I, the white man with his gun, standing in front of the unarmed native crowd — seemingly the leading actor of the piece; but in reality I was only an absurd puppet pushed to and fro by the will of those yellow faces behind. I perceived in this moment that when the white man turns tyrant it is his own freedom that he destroys. He becomes a sort of hollow, posing dummy, the conventionalized figure of a sahib. For it is the condition of his rule that he shall spend his life in trying to impress the "natives," and so in every crisis he has got to do what the "natives" expect of him. He wears a mask, and his face grows to fit it. I had got to shoot the elephant. I had committed myself to doing it when I sent for the rifle. A sahib has got to act like a sahib; he has got to appear resolute, to know his own mind and do definite things. To come all that way, rifle in hand, with two thousand people marching at my heels, and then to trail feebly away, having done nothing — no, that was impossible. The crowd would laugh at me. And my whole life, every white man's life in the East, was one long struggle not to be laughed at.

But I did not want to shoot the elephant. I watched him beating his bunch of grass against his knees, with that preoccupied grandmotherly air that elephants have. It seemed to me that it would be murder to shoot him. At that age I was not squeamish about killing animals, but I had never shot an elephant and never wanted to. (Somehow it always seems worse to kill a *large* animal.) Besides, there was the beast's owner to be considered. Alive, the elephant was worth at least a hundred pounds; dead, he would only be worth the value of his tusks, five pounds, possibly. But I had got to act quickly. I turned to some experienced-looking Burmans who had been there when we arrived, and asked them how the elephant had been behaving. They all said the same thing: he took no notice of you if you left him alone, but he might charge if you went too close to him.

It was perfectly clear to me what I ought to do. I ought to walk up to within, say, twenty-five yards of the elephant and test his behavior. If he charged, I could shoot; if he took no notice of me, it would be safe to leave him until the mahout came back. But also I knew that I was going to do no such thing. I was a poor shot with a rifle and the ground was soft mud into which one would sink at every step. If the elephant charged and I missed him, I should have about as much chance as a toad under a steam-roller. But even then I was not thinking particularly of my own skin, only of the watchful yellow faces behind. For at the moment, with the crowd watching me, I was not afraid in the ordinary sense, as I would have been if I had been alone. A white man mustn't be frightened in front of "natives"; and so, in general, he isn't frightened. The sole thought in my mind was that if anything went wrong those two thousand Burmans would see me pursued, caught, trampled on and reduced to a grinning corpse like that Indian up the hill. And if that happened it was quite probable that some of them would laugh. That would never do. There was only one alternative. I shoved the cartridges into the magazine and lay down on the road to get a better aim.

The crowd grew very still, and a deep, low, happy sigh, as of people 10
who see the theatre curtain go up at last, breathed from innumerable throats. They were going to have their bit of fun after all. The rifle was a beautiful German thing with cross-hair sights. I did not then know that in shooting an elephant one would shoot to cut an imaginary bar running from ear-hole to ear-hole. I ought, therefore, as the elephant was sideways on, to have aimed straight at his ear-hole; actually I aimed several inches in front of this, thinking the brain would be further forward.

When I pulled the trigger I did not hear the bang or feel the kick — one never does when a shot goes home — but I heard the devilish roar of glee that went up from the crowd. In that instant, in too short a time, one would have thought, even for the bullet to get there, a mysterious, terrible change had come over the elephant. He neither stirred nor fell, but every line of his body had altered. He looked suddenly stricken, shrunken, immensely old, as though the frightful impact of the bullet had paralyzed him without knocking him down. At last, after what seemed a long time — it might have been five seconds, I dare say — he sagged flabbily to his knees. His mouth slobbered. An enormous senility seemed to have settled upon him. One could have imagined him thousands of years old. I fired again into the same spot. At the second shot he did not collapse but climbed with desperate slowness to his feet and stood weakly upright, with legs sagging and head drooping. I fired a third time. That was the shot that did for him. You could see the agony of it jolt his whole body and knock the last remnant of strength from his legs. But in falling he seemed for a moment to rise, for as his hind legs collapsed beneath him he seemed to tower upward like a huge rock toppling, his trunk reaching skywards like a tree. He trumpeted, for the first and only time. And then down he came, his belly towards me, with a crash that seemed to shake the ground even where I lay.

I got up. The Burmans were already racing past me across the mud. It was obvious that the elephant would never rise again, but he was not dead. He was breathing very rhythmically with long rattling gasps, his great mound of a side painfully rising and falling. His mouth was wide open — I could see far down into caverns of pale pink throat. I waited for a long time for him to die, but his breathing did not weaken. Finally I fired my two remaining shots into the spot where I thought his heart must be. The thick blood welled out of him like red velvet, but still he did not die. His body did not even jerk when the shots hit him, the tortured breathing continued without a pause. He was dying, very slowly and in great agony, but in some world remote from me where not even a bullet could damage him further. I felt that I had got to put an end to that dreadful noise. It seemed dreadful to see the great beast lying there, powerless to move and yet powerless to die, and not even to be able to finish him. I sent back for my small rifle and poured shot after shot into his heart and down his throat. They seemed to make no impression. The tortured gasps continued as steadily as the ticking of a clock.

In the end I could not stand it any longer and went away. I heard later that it took him half an hour to die. Burmans were bringing dahs[7] and baskets even before I left, and I was told they had stripped his body almost to the bones by the afternoon.

Afterwards, of course, there were endless discussions about the shooting of the elephant. The owner was furious, but he was only an Indian and could do nothing. Besides, legally I had done the right thing, for a mad elephant has to be killed, like a mad dog, if its owner fails to control it. Among the Europeans opinion was divided. The older men said I was right, the younger men said it was a damn shame to shoot an elephant for killing a coolie, because an elephant was worth more than any damn Coringhee coolie. And afterwards I was very glad that the coolie had been killed; it put me legally in the right and it gave me a sufficient pretext for shooting the elephant. I often wondered whether any of the others grasped that I had done it solely to avoid looking a fool.

----

[7]*dahs*: Large knives. [Eds.]

QUESTIONS

1. Describe Orwell's mixed feelings about serving as a police officer in Burma.
2. How do the natives "force" Orwell to shoot the elephant against his better judgment? How does he relate this personal episode to the larger problems of British imperialism?
3. What is Orwell's final reaction to his deed? How literally can we take his statement that he "was very glad that the coolie had been killed" (paragraph 14)?
4. From the opening sentence Orwell displays a remarkable candor concerning his feelings. How does this personal, candid tone add to or detract from the strength of the essay?
5. Orwell's recollection of shooting the elephant is shaped to support a specific point or thesis. Where does Orwell state this thesis? Is this placement effective?
6. In what ways does this essay read more like a short story than an expository essay? How effective is Orwell's use of narrative and personal experience?
7. Orwell often wrote with a political purpose, with a "desire to push the world in a certain direction, to alter other people's idea of the kind of society that they should strive after," as he said in his essay "Why I Write." To what extent does the "tiny incident" in this essay illuminate "the real nature of imperialism" (paragraph 3)? Does Orwell succeed in altering your idea of imperialism?
8. Using Orwell's essay as a model, write a reflection in which the narration of "a tiny incident" illuminates a larger social or political problem.

MAKING CONNECTIONS

Orwell and Ernest Hemingway (p. 127) both tell stories that climax in moments of heightened awareness. Compare and contrast the way these two writers present their moments of recognition. Consider, for example, the pacing and timing of their discoveries within their stories as a whole, and try to account for the distinctive way that each author handles his moment of discovery.

TOOLS OF TORTURE:
An Essay on Beauty and Pain

Phyllis Rose

*Born in 1942 in New York City, Phyllis Rose holds degrees from
Radcliffe College, Yale University, and Harvard University. She is
the author of* A Woman of Letters: A Life of Virginia Woolf *(1978),*
Never Say Goodbye: Essays *(1991), and* The Year of Reading Proust
(1997), as well as the editor of The Norton Book of Women's Lives
(1993). Rose contributes frequently to periodicals such as The Atlantic Monthly *and* The New York Review of Books, *and she also
serves on the editorial board of* The American Scholar. *Rose has
said, "I love the essay form because I very often don't know when
I start on a subject where I'm going to end up. I find out what I
think." This essay was first published in* The Atlantic Monthly *in
October 1986.*

In a gallery off the rue Dauphine, near the *parfumerie* where I get my
massage, I happened upon an exhibit of medieval torture instruments. It
made me think that pain must be as great a challenge to the human imagination as pleasure. Otherwise there's no accounting for the number of torture
instruments. One would be quite enough. The simple pincer, let's say, which
rips out flesh. Or the head crusher, which breaks first your tooth sockets,
then your skull. But in addition I saw tongs, thumbscrews, a rack, a ladder,
ropes and pulleys, a grill, a garrote, a Spanish horse, a Judas cradle, an iron
maiden, a cage, a gag, a strappado, a stretching table, a saw, a wheel, a
twisting stork, an inquisitor's chair, a breast breaker, and a scourge. You
don't need complicated machinery to cause incredible pain. If you want to
saw your victim down the middle, for example, all you need is a slightly bigger than usual saw. If you hold the victim upside down so the blood stays in
his head, hold his legs apart, and start sawing at the groin, you can get as far
as the navel before he loses consciousness.

Even in the Middle Ages, before electricity, there were many things you
could do to torment a person. You could tie him up in an iron belt that held
the arms and legs up to the chest and left no point of rest, so that all his muscles went into spasm within minutes and he was driven mad within hours.
This was the twisting stork, a benign-looking object. You could stretch him
out backward over a thin piece of wood so that his whole body weight
rested on his spine, which pressed against the sharp wood. Then you could
stop up his nostrils and force water into his stomach through his mouth.

Then, if you wanted to finish him off, you and your helper could jump on his stomach, causing internal hemorrhage. This torture was called the rack. If you wanted to burn someone to death without hearing him scream, you could use a tongue lock, a metal rod between the jaw and collarbone that prevented him from opening his mouth. You could put a person in a chair with spikes on the seat and arms, tie him down against the spikes, and beat him, so that every time he flinched from the beating he drove his own flesh deeper onto the spikes. This was the inquisitor's chair. If you wanted to make it worse, you could heat the spikes. You could suspend a person over a pointed wooden pyramid and whenever he started to fall asleep, you could drop him onto the point. If you were Ippolito Marsili, the inventor of this torture, known as the Judas Cradle, you could tell yourself you had invented something humane, a torture that worked without burning flesh or breaking bones. For the torture here was supposed to be sleep deprivation.

The secret of torture, like the secret of French cuisine, is that nothing is unthinkable. The human body is like a foodstuff, to be grilled, pounded, filleted. Every opening exists to be stuffed, all flesh to be carved off the bone. You take an ordinary wheel, a heavy wooden wheel with spokes. You lay the victim on the ground with blocks of wood at strategic points under his shoulders, legs, and arms. You use the wheel to break every bone in his body. Next you tie his body onto the wheel. With all its bones broken, it will be pliable. However, the victim will not be dead. If you want to kill him, you hoist the wheel aloft on the end of a pole and leave him to starve. Who would have thought to do this with a man and a wheel? But, then, who would have thought to take the disgusting snail, force it to render its ooze, stuff it in its own shell with garlic butter, bake it, and eat it?

Not long ago I had a facial—only in part because I thought I needed one. It was research into the nature and function of pleasure. In a dark booth at the back of the beauty salon, the aesthetician put me on a table and applied a series of ointments to my face, some cool, some warmed. After a while she put something into my hand, cold and metallic. "Don't be afraid, madame," she said. "It is an electrode. It will not hurt you. The other end is attached to two metal cylinders, which I roll over your face. They break down the electricity barrier on your skin and allow the moisturizers to penetrate deeply." I didn't believe this hocus-pocus. I didn't believe in the electricity barrier or in the ability of these rollers to break it down. But it all felt very good. The cold metal on my face was a pleasant change from the soft warmth of the aesthetician's fingers. Still, since Algeria it's hard to hear the word "electrode" without fear. So when she left me for a few minutes with a moist, refreshing cheesecloth over my face, I thought, What if the goal of her expertise had been pain, not moisture? What if the electrodes had been electrodes in the Algerian sense? What if the cheesecloth mask were dipped in acid?

In Paris, where the body is so pampered, torture seems particularly sinister, not because it's hard to understand but because—as the dark side   5 of sensuality—it seems so easy. Beauty care is among the glories of Paris. *Soins esthétiques*[1] include makeup, facials, massages (both relaxing and reducing), depilations (partial and complete), manicures, pedicures, and tanning, in addition to the usual run of *soins* for the hair: cutting, brushing, setting, waving, styling, blowing, coloring, and streaking. In Paris the state of your skin, hair, and nerves is taken seriously, and there is little of the puritanical thinking that tries to pursuade us that beauty comes from within. Nor do the French think, as Americans do, that beauty should be offhand and low-maintenance. Spending time and money on *soins esthétiques* is appropriate and necessary, not self-indulgent. Should that loving attention to the body turn malevolent, you have torture. You have the procedure—the aesthetic, as it were—of torture, the explanation for the rich diversity of torture instruments, but you do not have the cause.

Historically torture has been a tool of legal systems, used to get information needed for a trial or, more directly, to determine guilt or innocence. In the Middle Ages confession was considered the best of all proofs, and torture was the way to produce a confession. In other words, torture didn't come into existence to give vent to human sadism. It is not always private and perverse but sometimes social and institutional, vetted by the government and, of course, the Church. (There have been few bigger fans of torture than Christianity and Islam.) Righteousness, as much as viciousness, produces torture. There aren't squads of sadists beating down the doors to the torture chambers begging for jobs. Rather, as a recent book on torture by Edward Peters says, the institution of torture creates sadists; the weight of a culture, Peters suggests, is necessary to recruit torturers. You have to convince people that they are working for a great goal in order to get them to overcome their repugnance to the task of causing physical pain to another person. Usually the great goal is the preservation of society, and the victim is presented to the torturer as being in some way out to destroy it.

From another point of view, what's horrifying is how easily you can persuade someone that he is working for the common good. Perhaps the most appalling psychological experiment of modern times, by Stanley Milgram, showed that ordinary, decent people in New Haven, Connecticut, could be brought to the point of inflicting (as they thought) severe electric shocks on other people in obedience to an authority and in pursuit of a goal, the advancement of knowledge, of which they approved. Milgram used—some would say abused—the prestige of science and the university to make his point, but his point is chilling nonetheless. We can cluck over torture, but the evidence at least suggests that with intelligent handling most of us could be brought to do it ourselves.

In the Middle Ages, Milgram's experiment would have had no point. It would have shocked no one that people were capable of cruelty in the interest

---

[1]*Soins esthétiques*: Literally, "beauty cares"; that is, beauty treatments or cosmetic aids. [Eds.]

of something they believed in. That was as it should be. Only recently in the history of human thought has the avoidance of cruelty moved to the forefront of ethics. "Putting cruelty first," as Judith Shklar says in *Ordinary Vices*, is comparatively new. The belief that the "pursuit of happiness" is one of man's inalienable rights, the idea that "cruel and unusual punishment" is an evil in itself, the Benthamite[2] notion that behavior should be guided by what will produce the greatest happiness for the greatest number — all these principles are only two centuries old. They were born with the eighteenth-century democratic revolutions. And in two hundred years they have not been universally accepted. Wherever people believe strongly in some cause, they will justify torture — not just the Nazis, but the French in Algeria.

Many people who wouldn't hurt a fly have annexed to fashion the imagery of torture — the thongs and spikes and metal studs — hence reducing it to the frivolous and transitory. Because torture has been in the mainstream and not on the margins of history, nothing could be healthier. For torture to be merely kinky would be a big advance. Exhibitions like the one I saw in Paris, which presented itself as educational, may be guilty of pandering to the tastes they deplore. Solemnity may be the wrong tone. If taking one's goals too seriously is the danger, the best discouragement of torture may be a radical hedonism that denies that any goal is worth the means, that refuses to allow the nobly abstract to seduce us from the sweetness of the concrete. Give people a good croissant and a good cup of coffee in the morning. Give them an occasional facial and a plate of escargots. Marie Antoinette picked a bad moment to say "Let them eat cake," but I've often thought she was on the right track.

All of which brings me back to Paris, for Paris exists in the imagination   10
of much of the world as the capital of pleasure — of fun, food, art, folly, seduction, gallantry, and beauty. Paris is civilization's reminder to itself that nothing leads you less wrong than your awareness of your own pleasure and a genial desire to spread it around. In that sense the myth of Paris constitutes a moral touchstone, standing for the selfish frivolity that helps keep priorities straight.

QUESTIONS

1. In the first two paragraphs of her essay, Rose lists more than thirty different tools of torture, and as she moves further into her list, she explains how each tool works and what kinds of torture it produces. Why do you think she goes into such elaborate detail? Why doesn't she confine herself

---

[2]*Benthamite*: One who believes in the social policies of the nineteenth-century English philosopher Jeremy Bentham, who propounded the idea of the greatest good for the greatest number of people. [Eds.]

to the tools she discusses in the first paragraph? How did you feel as you read these two paragraphs?

2. When Rose considers some tools of pleasure at the beauty salon, she also devotes two paragraphs (4 and 5) to her discussion, but the list of things she considers is shorter than her list of torture devices. Why do you suppose she is less detailed about pleasure?

3. Rose's reflections seem to be based in part on a supposition that tools of beauty (or pleasure) and tools of torture are the flip side of each other. What evidence and reasoning does she offer for this idea? In paragraph 9, she also seems to suggest that a widespread love of pleasure might be sufficient to put an end to torture. What evidence and reasoning does she offer for this idea?

4. In paragraphs 6 through 8, Rose is primarily concerned with exploring the origins and motivations for torture. What key points does she make in each paragraph, and what evidence does she offer in each case?

5. In paragraph 1, Rose names several tools of torture without explaining how they work. Research two or three of these tools, and then write an essay that compares and contrasts their origin, design, and effectiveness.

6. Though Rose focuses on medieval tools of torture, such tools also have been used more recently. Investigate two or three tools used in the twentieth century, and write an essay comparing and contrasting them to medieval tools of torture.

MAKING CONNECTIONS

How do Rose's ideas about the causes of sadistic behavior compare with those of Stanley Milgram (p. 453), whom she discusses in her essay?

WHAT DID YOU DO IN THE WAR, GRANDMA?
A Flashback to August 1945

Zoë Tracy Hardy

Born in 1926 and raised in the Midwest, Zoë Tracy Hardy was one of millions of young women who worked in defense plants during World War II. Considered at first to be surrogates for male workers, these women — sometimes called "Rosie the Riveters" — soon were building bombers that their supervisors declared "equal in the construction [to] those turned out by experienced workmen in the plant's other departments," as a news feature at the time stated. After the eventful summer described in the following essay, Hardy finished college, married, and began teaching college English in Arizona, Guam, and Colorado. This essay first appeared in the August 1985 issue of Ms. *magazine — exactly forty years after the end of World War II.*

It was unseasonably cool that day in May, 1945, when I left my mother and father and kid brother in eastern Iowa and took the bus all the way to Omaha to help finish the war. I was 18, and had just completed my first year at the University of Iowa without distinction. The war in Europe had ended in April; the war against the Japanese still raged. I wanted to go where something *real* was being done to end this bitter war that had always been part of my adolescence.

I arrived in Omaha at midnight. The YWCA, where I promised my family I would get a room, was closed until 7 a.m., so I curled up in a cracked maroon leather chair in the crowded, smoky waiting room of the bus station.

In the morning I set off on foot for the YWCA, dragging a heavy suitcase and carrying my favorite hat trimmed in daisies in a large round hatbox. An hour of lugging and resting brought me to the Y, a great Victorian house of dark brick, where I paid two weeks in advance (most of my money) for board and a single room next to a bathroom that I would share with eight other girls. I surrendered my red and blue food-ration stamp books and my sugar coupons to the cook who would keep them as long as I stayed there.

I had eaten nothing but a wartime candy bar since breakfast at home the day before, but breakfast at the Y was already over. So, queasy and light-headed, I went back out into the cold spring day to find my job. I set out for the downtown office of the Glenn L. Martin Company. It was at their plant south of the city that thousands of workers, in around-the-clock shifts, built the famous B-29 bombers, the great Superfortresses, which the papers said would end the war.

I filled out an application and thought about the women welders and riveters and those who operated machine presses to help put the Superfortresses together. I grew shakier by the minute, more and more certain I was unqualified for any job here.

My interview was short. The personnel man was unconcerned about my total lack of skills. If I passed the physical, I could have a job in the Reproduction Department, where the blueprints were handled.

Upstairs in a gold-walled banquet room furnished with examination tables and hospital screens, a nurse sat me on a stool to draw a blood sample from my arm. I watched my blood rolling slowly into the needle. The gold walls wilted in the distance, and I slumped forward in a dead faint.

A grandfatherly doctor waved ammonia under my nose, and said if I would go to a café down the street and eat the complete 50-cent breakfast, I had the job.

The first week in the Reproduction Department, I learned to cut and fold enormous blueprints as they rolled from a machine that looked like a giant washing machine wringer. Then I was moved to a tall, metal contraption with a lurid light glowing from its interior. An ammonia guzzler, it spewed out smelly copies of specifications so hot my finger-tips burned when I touched them. I called it the dragon, and when I filled it with ammonia, the fumes reminded me of gold walls dissolving before my eyes. I took all my breaks outdoors, even when it was raining.

My boss, Mr. Johnson,[1] was a sandy-haired man of about 40, who spoke pleasantly when he came around to say hello and to check our work. Elsie, his secretary, a cool redhead, seldom spoke to any of us and spent most of her time in the darkroom developing negatives and reproducing photographs.

One of my coworkers in Reproduction was Mildred, a tall dishwater blond with a horsey, intelligent face. She was the first woman I'd ever met with an earthy unbridled tongue.

When I first arrived, Mildred warned me always to knock on the darkroom door before going in because Mr. Johnson and Elsie did a lot of screwing in there. I didn't believe her, I thought we were supposed to knock to give Elsie time to protect her negatives from the sudden light. "Besides," I said, "there isn't room to lie down in there." Mildred laughed until tears squeezed from the corners of her eyes. "You poor kid," she said. "Don't you *know* you don't have to lie down?"

---

[1]All names but the author's have been changed.

I was stunned. "But it's easier if you do," I protested, defensive about my sex education. My mother, somewhat ahead of her time, had always been explicit in her explanations, and I had read "Lecture 14," an idyllic description of lovemaking being passed around among freshman girls in every dormitory in the country.

"Sitting, standing, any quick way you can in time of war," Mildred winked wickedly. She was as virginal as I, but what she said reminded us of the steady dearth of any day-to-day presence of young men in our lives.

We were convinced that the war would be over by autumn. We were   15
stepping up the napalm and incendiary bombing of the Japanese islands, the British were now coming to our aid in the Pacific, and the Japanese Navy was being reduced to nothing in some of the most spectacular sea battles in history.

Sometimes, after lunch, I went into the assembly areas to see how the skeletons of the B-29s were growing from our blueprints. At first there were enormous stark ribs surrounded by scaffolding two and three stories high. A few days later there was aluminum flesh over the ribs and wings sprouting from stubs on the fuselage. Women in overalls and turbans, safety glasses, and steel-toed shoes scrambled around the wings with riveting guns and welding torches, fitting fuel tanks in place. Instructions were shouted at them by hoarse, paunchy old men in hard hats. I cheered myself by thinking how we were pouring it on, a multitude of us together creating this great bird to end the war.

Away from the plant, however, optimism sometimes failed me. My room at the Y was bleak. I wrote letters to my unofficial fiancé and to other young men in the service who had been friends and classmates. Once in a while I attempted to study, thinking I would redeem my mediocre year at the university.

During those moments when I sensed real homesickness lying in wait, I would plan something to do with Betty and Celia, friends from high school, who had moved to Omaha "for the duration" and had jobs as secretaries for a large moving and storage company. Their small apartment was upstairs in an old frame house in Benson, a northwest suburb. Celia and Betty and I cooked, exchanged news from servicemen we all knew and talked about plans for the end of the war. Betty was engaged to her high school sweetheart, a soldier who had been wounded in Germany and who might be coming home soon. We guessed she would be the first one of us to be married, and we speculated, in the careful euphemisms of "well-brought-up girls," about her impending introduction to sex.

By the first of July, work and the pace of life had lost momentum. The war news seemed to repeat itself without advancing, as day after day battles were fought around jungly Pacific islands that all seemed identical and unreal.

At the plant, I was moved from the dragon to a desk job, a promotion   20
of sorts. I sat on a high stool in a cubicle of pigeonholed cabinets and filed

blueprints, specs, and deviations in the proper holes. While I was working, I saw no one and couldn't talk to anybody.

In mid-July Betty got married. Counsel from our elders was always to wait — wait until things settle down after the war. Harold, still recuperating from shrapnel wounds, asked Betty not to wait.

Celia and I attended the ceremony on a sizzling afternoon in a musty Presbyterian church. Harold was very serious, gaunt-faced and thin in his loose-hanging Army uniform. Betty, a fair-skinned, blue-eyed brunet in a white street dress, looked pale and solemn. After the short ceremony, they left the church in a borrowed car. Someone had given them enough gasoline stamps for a honeymoon trip to a far-off cabin on the shore of a piney Minnesota lake.

Celia and I speculated on Betty's introduction to lovemaking. I had "Lecture 14" in mind and hoped she would like lovemaking, especially way off in Minnesota, far from the sweltering city and the war. Celia thought it didn't matter much whether a girl liked it or not, as long as other important parts of marriage got off to a good start.

That weekend Celia and I took a walk in a park and watched a grandfather carefully pump a seesaw up and down for his small grandson. We saw a short, middle-aged sailor walking with a sad-faced young woman who towered over him. "A whore," Celia said. "Probably one of those from the Hotel Bianca." Celia had been in Omaha longer than I and knew more of its secrets.

I wanted, right then, to see someone young and male and healthy cross　25 the grass under the trees, someone without wounds and without a cap, someone with thick disheveled hair that hadn't been militarily peeled down to the green skin on the back of his skull. Someone wearing tennis shorts to show strong, hair-matted legs, and a shirt with an open neck and short sleeves revealing smooth, hard muscles and tanned skin. Someone who would pull me out of this gloom with a wide spontaneous smile as he passed.

In the next few days, the tempo of the summer changed subtly. From friends stationed in the Pacific, I began to get letters free from rectangular holes where military censors had snipped out "sensitive" words. Our Navy was getting ready to surround the Japanese islands with a starvation blockade, and our B-29s had bombed the industrial heart of the country. We were dropping leaflets warning the Japanese people that we would incinerate hundreds of thousands of them by firebombing 11 of their major cities. Rumors rippled through the plant back in Omaha. The Japanese Empire would collapse in a matter of weeks, at most.

One Friday night, with Celia's help, I moved out of the Y to Celia's apartment in Benson. We moved by streetcar. Celia carried my towels and my full laundry bag in big rolls, one under each arm, and wore my straw picture hat with the daisies, which bobbled wildly on top of her head. My hatbox was crammed with extra underwear and the war letters I was determined to save. When we climbed aboard the front end of the streetcar, I dropped the hatbox, spilled an armload of books down the aisle, and banged my suitcase into the knees of an elderly man who was trying to help me retrieve them.

We began to laugh, at everything, at nothing, and were still laughing when we hauled everything off the car and down one block to the apartment, the daisies all the while wheeling recklessly on Celia's head.

It was a good move. Summer nights were cooler near the country, and so quiet I could hear the crickets. The other upstairs apartment was occupied by Celia's older sister, Andrea, and her husband, Bob, who hadn't been drafted.

Late in July, an unusual thing happened at the plant. Mr. Johnson asked us to work double shifts for a few days. The situation was urgent, he said, and he wanted 100 percent cooperation from the Reproduction Department, even if it meant coming to work when we felt sick or postponing something that was personally important to us. 30

The next morning no one from the day shift was missing, and the place was full of people from the graveyard shift. Some of the time I worked in my cubicle counting out special blueprints and deviations. The rest of the time I helped the crews sweating over the blueprint machine cut out prints that contained odd lines and numbers that I had never seen before. Their shapes were different, too, and there was no place for them in the numbered pigeonholes of my cubicle. Some prints were small, about four inches square. Mildred said they were so cute she might tuck one in her shoe and smuggle it home as a souvenir even if it meant going to the federal pen if she got caught.

During those days I learned to nap on streetcars. I had to get up at 4:30, bolt down breakfast, and catch the first car to rumble out of the darkness at 5:15. The double shift wasn't over until 11:30, so I got home about one in the morning.

The frenzy at the plant ended as suddenly as it had begun. Dazed with fatigue, I slept through most of a weekend and hoped we had pushed ourselves to some limit that would lift us over the last hump of the war.

On Monday the familiar single shift was not quite the same. We didn't know what we had done, but an undercurrent of anticipation ran through the department because of those double shifts — and the news. The papers told of factories that were already gearing up to turn out refrigerators, radios, and automobiles instead of bombs and planes.

In Reproduction, the pace began to slacken. Five hundred thirty-six B-29s, planes we had put together on the Nebraska prairie, had firebombed the principal islands of the Japanese Empire: Hokkaido, Honshu, Kyushu, Shikoku. We had reduced to ashes more than 15 square miles of the heart of Tokyo. The battered and burned Japanese were so near defeat that there couldn't be much left for us to do. With surprising enthusiasm, I began to plan for my return to college. 35

Going home on the streetcar the first Tuesday afternoon in August, I heard about a puzzling new weapon. Some excited people at the end of the car were jabbering about it, saying the Japanese would be forced to surrender in a matter of hours.

When I got home, Andrea, her round bespectacled face flushed, met me at the head of the stairs. "Oh, come and listen to the radio — it's a new bomb — it's almost over!"

I sat down in her living room and listened. There was news, then music, then expanded news. Over and over the newscaster reported that the United States had unlocked a secret of the universe and unleashed a cosmic force — from splitting atoms of uranium — on the industrial seaport of Hiroshima. Most of the city had been leveled to the ground, and many of its inhabitants disintegrated to dust in an instant by a single bomb. "Our scientists have changed the history of the world," the newscaster said. He sounded as if he could not believe it himself.

We ate dinner from our laps and continued to listen as the news pounded on for an hour, then two, then three. I tried, at last, to *think* about it. In high school physics we had already learned that scientists were close to splitting an atom. We imagined that a cupful of the tremendous energy from such a phenomenon might run a car back and forth across the entire country dozens of times. I could visualize that. But I could not imagine how such energy put into a small bomb would cause the kind of destruction described on the radio.

About nine, I walked over to McCollum's grocery store to buy an   40
evening paper. The headline said we had harnessed atomic power. I skimmed through a front page story. Science had ushered us into a strange new world, and President Truman had made two things clear: the bomb had created a monster that could wipe out civilization; and some protection against this monster would have to be found before its secret could be given to the world.

Back out in the dark street, I hesitated. For the first time I could remember, I felt a rush of terror at being out in the night alone.

When I got back to the apartment, I made a pot of coffee and sat down at the kitchen table to read the rest of the paper. President Truman had said: "The force from which the sun draws its power has been loosed against those who brought war to the Far East. . . . If they do not now accept our terms they may expect a rain of ruin from the air the like of which has never been seen on this earth." New and more powerful bombs were now being developed.

I read everything, looking for some speculation from someone about how we were going to live in this new world. There was nothing. About midnight Andrea knocked on my open door to get my attention. She stood there a moment in her nightgown and curlers looking at me rather oddly. She asked if I was all right.

I said yes, just trying to soak it all in.

Gently she told me I had better go to bed and think about how soon the   45
war would be over.

The next day Reproduction was nearly demolished by the spirit of celebration. The *Enola Gay*, the plane that had dropped the bomb, was one of ours. By Thursday morning the United States had dropped a second atomic bomb, an even bigger one, on an industrial city, Nagasaki, and the Russians had declared war on Japan.

At the end of the day, Mr. Johnson asked us to listen to the radio for announcements about when to return to work, then shook hands all around.
"You've all done more than you know to help win the war," he said.

We said tentative good-byes. I went home and over to McCollum's for
an evening paper. An Army Strategic Air Forces expert said that there was
no comparison between the fire caused by the atomic bomb and that of a
normal conflagration. And there were other stories about radiation, like
X-rays, that might cripple and poison living things for hours, weeks, maybe
years, until they died.

I went to bed late and had nightmares full of flames and strange dry
gale winds. The next noon I got up, exhausted, and called Mildred. She said
they were still saying not to report to work until further notice. "It's gonna
bore our tails off," she moaned. "I don't know how long we can sit around
here just playing hearts." I could hear girls laughing in the background.

"Mildred," I blurted anxiously, "do you think we should have done this   50
thing?"

"Why not? Better us than somebody else, kid."

I reminded her that we knew the Japanese were finished weeks ago and
asked her if it wasn't sort of like kicking a dead horse — brutally.

"Look," she said. "The war is really over even if the bigwigs haven't
said so yet. What more do you want?"

The evening paper finally offered a glimmer of relief. One large headline said that serious questions about the morality of *Americans* using such
a weapon were being raised by some civilians of note and some churchmen.
I went to bed early and lay listening to the crickets and thinking about
everyone coming home — unofficial fiancés, husbands, fathers, brothers —
all filling the empty spaces between kids and women and old men, putting a
balance in our lives we hadn't known in years.

Yet the bomb haunted me. I was still awake when the windowpanes   55
lightened up at daybreak.

It was all over on August 14, 1945. Unconditional surrender.

For hours at a time, the bomb's importance receded in the excitement
of that day. Streetcar bells clanged up and down the streets; we heard
sirens, whistles, church bells. A newscaster described downtown Omaha as
a free-for-all. Perfect strangers were hugging each other in the streets; some
were dancing. Churches had thrown open their doors, and people were
streaming in and out, offering prayers of thanksgiving. Taverns were giving
away free drinks.

Andrew wanted us to have a little whiskey, even though we were under
age, because there would never be another day like this as long as we lived.
I hated the first taste of it, but as we chattered away, inventing wild, gratifying futures, I welcomed the muffler it wrapped around the ugliness of the
bomb.

In the morning Mildred called to say our jobs were over and that we
should report to the plant to turn in our badges and get final paychecks. She

had just talked to Mr. Johnson, who told her that those funny blueprints we had made during double shift had something to do with the bomb.

"Well, honey," she said, "I don't understand atomic energy, but old jazzy Johnson said we had to work like that to get the *Enola Gay* and the *thing* to go together." 60

I held my breath, waiting for Mildred to say she was kidding, as usual. Ordinary 19- and 20-year-old girls were not, not in the United States of America, required to work night and day to help launch scientific monsters that would catapult us all into a precarious "strange new world" — forever. But I knew in my bones that Mildred, forthright arrow-straight Mildred, was only telling me what I had already, unwillingly, guessed.

After a long silence she said, "Well, kid, give me your address in Iowa, and I'll send you a Christmas card for auld lang syne."

I wanted to cry as we exchanged addresses. I liked Mildred. I hated the gap that I now sensed would always be between me and people like her.

"It's been nice talking dirty to you all summer," she said.

"Thanks." I hung up, slipped down the stairs, and walked past the streetcar line out into the country. 65

The whole countryside was sundrenched, fragrant with sweet clover and newly mown alfalfa. I leaned against a fence post and tried to think.

The President had said we had unleashed the great secret of the universe in this way, to shorten the war and save American lives. Our commitment to defeat the Japanese was always clear to me. They had attacked us first. But we had already firebombed much of the Japanese Empire to char. That seemed decisive enough, and terrible enough.

If he had asked me whether I would work very hard to help bring this horror into being, knowing it would shorten the war but put the world into jeopardy for all time, how would I have answered?

I would have said, "No. With all due respect, Sir, how could such a thing make a just end to our just cause?"

But the question had never been asked of us. And I stood now, in the warm sun, gripping a splintery fence post, outraged by our final insignificance — all of us who had worked together in absolute trust to end the war. 70

An old cow stood near the fence switching her tail. I looked at her great, uncomprehending brown eyes and began to sob.

After a while I walked back to the apartment, mentally packing my suitcase and tying up my hatbox of war letters. I knew it was going to be very hard, from now on, for the whole world to take care of itself.

I wanted very much to go home.

QUESTIONS

1. How does Hardy's attitude toward the war change in this essay? What event causes her to reevaluate her attitude?
2. Describe Hardy's feelings about the introduction of atomic power into her world. Are they optimistic or pessimistic?

3. "You've all done more than you know to help win the war," Hardy's boss tells her (paragraph 47). How does she react to the fact that she was not informed of the purpose of her work? How does her reaction differ from that of her coworker, Mildred?

4. As Hardy's attitude toward war changes, her attitude toward sex changes as well. Trace this change in attitude. What connection, if any, do you see between the two?

5. Is this essay merely a personal reminiscence, or does the author have a larger purpose? Explain what you think her purpose is.

6. This essay was published over twenty years ago and more than forty years after the events it describes. Are Hardy's fears and speculations (on atomic power, on the authority of the government, on sex) dated in any way, or are they still relevant today? Explain your answer.

7. Have you, like Hardy, ever wondered about the larger social implications of any job that you've held or that a friend or parent holds? Write an essay like Hardy's reflecting on that job and describing how your attitude changed as you placed the job in a larger context.

Making Connections

Could Hardy's essay be described as a "pilgrimage" to a particular intellectual or political position, somewhat like Martin Luther King Jr.'s "Pilgrimage to Nonviolence" (p. 346)? How fair would that retitling be to Hardy's essay? What aspects of pilgrimage do you find in it?

R EPORTING IN THE

Social Sciences and Public Affairs

"THIS IS THE END OF THE WORLD": The Black Death

Barbara Tuchman

Barbara Wertheim Tuchman (1912–1989) wrote books on histori-
cal subjects ranging over six centuries — from the Middle Ages to
the Vietnam War. Her careful research and lively writing in books
like The Guns of August *(1962),* A Distant Mirror *(1978),* The
March of Folly: From Troy to Vietnam *(1984), and* The First
Salute *(1988) pleased not only the general public but many profes-*
sional historians as well. She twice won the Pulitzer Prize. A Dis-
tant Mirror, *from which the following selection has been taken,*
was on the New York Times *best-seller list for more than nine*
months.

In October 1347, two months after the fall of Calais, Genoese trading
ships put into the harbor of Messina in Sicily with dead and dying men at
the oars. The ships had come from the Black Sea port of Caffa (now Feo-
dosiya) in the Crimea, where the Genoese maintained a trading post. The
diseased sailors showed strange black swellings about the size of an egg or
an apple in the armpits and groin. The swellings oozed blood and pus and
were followed by spreading boils and black blotches on the skin from internal bleeding. The sick suffered severe pain and died quickly within five days
of the first symptoms. As the disease spread, other symptoms of continuous

fever and spitting of blood appeared instead of the swellings or buboes. These victims coughed and sweated heavily and died even more quickly, within three days or less, sometimes in 24 hours. In both types everything that issued from the body — breath, sweat, blood from the buboes and lungs, bloody urine, and blood-blackened excrement — smelled foul. Depression and despair accompanied the physical symptoms, and before the end "death is seen seated on the face."

The disease was bubonic plague, present in two forms: one that infected the bloodstream, causing the buboes and internal bleeding, and was spread by contact; and a second, more virulent pneumonic type that infected the lungs and was spread by respiratory infection. The presence of both at once caused the high mortality and speed of contagion. So lethal was the disease that cases were known of persons going to bed well and dying before they woke, of doctors catching the illness at a bedside and dying before the patient. So rapidly did it spread from one to another that to a French physician, Simon de Covino, it seemed as if one sick person "could infect the whole world." The malignity of the pestilence appeared more terrible because its victims knew no prevention and no remedy.

The physical suffering of the disease and its aspects of evil mystery were expressed in a strange Welsh lament which saw "death coming into our midst like black smoke, a plague which cuts off the young, a rootless phantom which has no mercy for fair countenance. Woe is me of the shilling in the armpit! It is seething, terrible . . . a head that gives pain and causes a loud cry . . . a painful angry knob . . . Great is its seething like a burning cinder . . . a grievous thing of ashy color." Its eruption is ugly like the "seeds of black peas, broken fragments of brittle sea-coal . . . the early ornaments of black death, cinders of the peelings of the cockle weed, a mixed multitude, a black plague like halfpence, like berries. . . ."

Rumors of a terrible plague supposedly arising in China and spreading through Tartary (Central Asia) to India and Persia, Mesopotamia, Syria, Egypt, and all of Asia Minor had reached Europe in 1346. They told of a death toll so devastating that all of India was said to be depopulated, whole territories covered by dead bodies, other areas with no one left alive. As added up by Pope Clement VI at Avignon, the total of reported dead reached 23,840,000. In the absence of a concept of contagion, no serious alarm was felt in Europe until the trading ships brought their black burden of pestilence into Messina while other infected ships from the Levant carried it to Genoa and Venice.

By January 1348 it penetrated France via Marseille, and North Africa   5 via Tunis. Shipborne along coasts and navigable rivers, it spread westward from Marseille through the ports of Languedoc to Spain and northward up the Rhône to Avignon, where it arrived in March. It reached Narbonne, Montpellier, Carcassonne, and Toulouse between February and May, and at the same time in Italy spread to Rome and Florence and their hinterlands. Between June and August it reached Bordeaux, Lyon, and Paris, spread to Burgundy and Normandy, and crossed the Channel from Normandy into

A detail from *The Triumph of Death*, a fresco by Francesco Traini in the Camposanto, Pisa, Italy, c. 1350.

southern England. From Italy during the same summer it crossed the Alps into Switzerland and reached eastward to Hungary.

In a given area the plague accomplished its kill within four to six months and then faded, except in the larger cities, where, rooting into the close-quartered population, it abated during the winter, only to reappear in spring and rage for another six months.

In 1349 it resumed in Paris, spread to Picardy, Flanders, and the Low Countries, and from England to Scotland and Ireland as well as to Norway, where a ghost ship with a cargo of wool and a dead crew drifted offshore until it ran aground near Bergen. From there the plague passed into Sweden, Denmark, Prussia, Iceland, and as far as Greenland. Leaving a strange pocket of immunity in Bohemia, and Russia unattacked until 1351, it had passed from most of Europe by mid-1350. Although the mortality rate was erratic, ranging from one fifth in some places to nine tenths or almost total elimination in others, the overall estimate of modern demographers has settled — for the area extending from India to Iceland — around the same figure expressed in Froissart's casual words: "a third of the world died." His estimate, the common one at the time, was not an inspired guess but a borrowing of St. John's figure for mortality from plague in Revelation, the favorite guide to human affairs of the Middle Ages.

A third of Europe would have meant about 20 million deaths. No one knows in truth how many died. Contemporary reports were an awed impression, not an accurate count. In crowded Avignon, it was said, 400 died daily;

7,000 houses emptied by death were shut up; a single graveyard received 11,000 corpses in six weeks; half the city's inhabitants reportedly died, including 9 cardinals or one third of the total, and 70 lesser prelates. Watching the endlessly passing death carts, chroniclers let normal exaggeration take wings and put the Avignon death toll at 62,000 and even at 120,000, although the city's total population was probably less than 50,000.

When graveyards filled up, bodies at Avignon were thrown into the Rhône until mass burial pits were dug for dumping the corpses. In London in such pits corpses piled up in layers until they overflowed. Everywhere reports speak of the sick dying too fast for the living to bury. Corpses were dragged out of homes and left in front of doorways. Morning light revealed new piles of bodies. In Florence the dead were gathered up by the Compagnia della Misericordia — founded in 1244 to care for the sick — whose members wore red robes and hoods masking the face except for the eyes. When their efforts failed, the dead lay putrid in the streets for days at a time. When no coffins were to be had, the bodies were laid on boards, two or three at once, to be carried to graveyards or common pits. Families dumped their own relatives into the pits, or buried them so hastily and thinly "that dogs dragged them forth and devoured their bodies."

Amid accumulating death and fear of contagion, people died without   10
last rites and were buried without prayers, a prospect that terrified the last hours of the stricken. A bishop in England gave permission to laymen to make confession to each other as was done by the Apostles, "or if no man is present then even to a woman," and if no priest could be found to administer extreme unction, "then faith must suffice." Clement VI found it necessary to grant remissions of sin to all who died of the plague because so many were unattended by priests. "And no bells tolled," wrote a chronicler of Siena, "and nobody wept no matter what his loss because almost everyone expected death. . . . And people said and believed, 'This is the end of the world.'"

In Paris, where the plague lasted through 1349, the reported death rate was 800 a day, in Pisa 500, in Vienna 500 to 600. The total dead in Paris numbered 50,000 or half the population. Florence, weakened by the famine of 1347, lost three to four fifths of its citizens, Venice two thirds, Hamburg and Bremen, though smaller in size, about the same proportion. Cities, as centers of transportation, were more likely to be affected than villages, although once a village was infected, its death rate was equally high. At Givry, a prosperous village in Burgundy of 1,200 to 1,500 people, the parish register records 615 deaths in the space of fourteen weeks, compared to an average of thirty deaths a year in the previous decade. In three villages of Cambridgeshire, manorial records show a death rate of 47 percent, 57 percent, and in one case 70 percent. When the last survivors, too few to carry on, moved away, a deserted village sank back into the wilderness and disappeared from the map altogether, leaving only a grass-covered ghostly outline to show where mortals once had lived.

In enclosed places such as monasteries and prisons, the infection of one person usually meant that of all, as happened in the Franciscan convents of

Burial of plague victims, from *Annales de Gilles li Muisis* (The Annals of Gilles li Muisis, c. 1272–1352).

Carcassonne and Marseille, where every inmate without exception died. Of the 140 Dominicans at Montpellier only seven survived. Petrarch's brother Gherardo, member of a Carthusian monastery, buried the prior and 34 fellow monks one by one, sometimes three a day, until he was left alone with his dog and fled to look for a place that would take him in. Watching every comrade die, men in such places could not but wonder whether the strange peril that filled the air had not been sent to exterminate the human race. In Kilkenny, Ireland, Brother John Clyn of the Friars Minor, another monk left alone among dead men, kept a record of what had happened lest "things which should be remembered perish with time and vanish from the memory of those who come after us." Sensing "the whole world, as it were, placed within the grasp of the Evil One," and waiting for death to visit him too, he wrote, "I leave parchment to continue this work, if perchance any man survive and any of the race of Adam escape this pestilence and carry on the work which I have begun." Brother John, as noted by another hand, died of the pestilence, but he foiled oblivion.

The largest cities of Europe, with populations of about 100,000, were Paris and Florence, Venice and Genoa. At the next level, with more than 50,000, were Ghent and Bruges in Flanders, Milan, Bologna, Rome, Naples, and Palermo, and Cologne. London hovered below 50,000, the only city in England except York with more than 10,000. At the level of 20,000 to 50,000 were Bordeaux, Toulouse, Montpellier, Marseille, and Lyon in France, Barcelona, Seville, and Toledo in Spain, Siena, Pisa, and other secondary cities in Italy, and the Hanseatic trading cities of the Empire. The plague raged through them all, killing anywhere from one third to two thirds of their inhabitants. Italy, with a total population of 10 to 11 million, probably suffered the heaviest toll. Following the Florentine bankruptcies, the crop failures and workers' riots of 1346–47, the revolt of Cola di Rienzi that plunged Rome into anarchy, the plague came as the peak of successive calamities. As if the world were indeed in the grasp of the Evil One, its first appearance on the European mainland in January 1348 coincided with a fearsome earthquake that carved a path of wreckage from Naples up to Venice. Houses collapsed, church towers toppled, villages were crushed, and the destruction reached as far as Germany and Greece. Emotional response, dulled by horrors, underwent a kind of atrophy epitomized by the chronicler who wrote, "And in these days was burying without sorrowe and wedding without friendschippe."

In Siena, where more than half the inhabitants died of the plague, work was abandoned on the great cathedral, planned to be the largest in the world, and never resumed, owing to loss of workers and master masons and "the melancholy and grief" of the survivors. The cathedral's truncated transept still stands in permanent witness to the sweep of death's scythe. Agnolo di Tura, a chronicler of Siena, recorded the fear of contagion that froze every other instinct. "Father abandoned child, wife husband, one brother another," he wrote, "for this plague seemed to strike through the breath and sight. And so they died. And no one could be found to bury the dead for money or friendship. . . . And I, Agnolo di Tura, called the Fat, buried my five children with my own hands, and so did many others likewise."

There were many to echo his account of inhumanity and few to balance   15
it, for the plague was not the kind of calamity that inspired mutual help. Its loathsomeness and deadliness did not herd people together in mutual distress, but only prompted their desire to escape each other. "Magistrates and notaries refused to come and make the wills of the dying," reported a Franciscan friar of Piazza in Sicily; what was worse, "even the priests did not come to hear their confessions." A clerk of the Archbishop of Canterbury reported the same of English priests who "turned away from the care of their benefices from fear of death." Cases of parents deserting children and children their parents were reported across Europe from Scotland to Russia. The calamity chilled the hearts of men, wrote Boccaccio in his famous account of the plague in Florence that serves as introduction to the *Decameron*. "One man shunned another . . . kinsfolk held aloof, brother was forsaken by brother, oftentimes husband by wife; nay, what is more, and scarcely to be believed, fathers and mothers were found to abandon their own children to their fate, untended, unvisited as if they had been strangers." Exaggeration and literary pessimism were common in the 14th century, but the Pope's physician, Guy de Chauliac, was a sober, careful observer who reported the same phenomenon: "A father did not visit his son, nor the son his father. Charity was dead."

Yet not entirely. In Paris, according to the chronicler Jean de Venette, the nuns of the Hotel Dieu or municipal hospital, "having no fear of death, tended the sick with all sweetness and humility." New nuns repeatedly took the places of those who died, until the majority "many times renewed by death now rest in peace with Christ as we may piously believe."

When the plague entered northern France in July 1348, it settled first in Normandy and, checked by winter, gave Picardy a deceptive interim until the next summer. Either in mourning or warning, black flags were flown from church towers of the worst-stricken villages of Normandy. "And in that time," wrote a monk of the abbey of Fourcarment, "the mortality was so great among the people of Normandy that those of Picardy mocked them." The same unneighborly reaction was reported of the Scots, separated by a winter's immunity from the English. Delighted to hear of the disease that was scourging the "southrons," they gathered forces for an invasion, "laughing at their enemies." Before they could move, the savage mortality fell upon them too, scattering some in death and the rest in panic to spread the infection as they fled.

In Picardy in the summer of 1349 the pestilence penetrated the castle of Coucy to kill Enguerrand's[1] mother, Catherine, and her new husband. Whether her nine-year-old son escaped by chance or was perhaps living elsewhere with one of his guardians is unrecorded. In nearby Amiens, tannery workers, responding quickly to losses in the labor force, combined to bargain for higher wages. In another place villagers were seen dancing to drums and trumpets, and on being asked the reason, answered that, seeing their neighbors die day by day while their village remained immune, they believed that they could keep the plague from entering "by the jollity that is in us. That is why we dance." Further north in Tournai on the border of Flanders, Gilles li Muisis, Abbot of St. Martin's, kept one of the epidemic's most vivid accounts. The passing bells rang all day and all night, he recorded, because sextons were anxious to obtain their fees while they could. Filled with the sound of mourning, the city became oppressed by fear, so that the authorities forbade the tolling of bells and the wearing of black and restricted funeral services to two mourners. The silencing of funeral bells and of criers' announcements of deaths was ordained by most cities. Siena imposed a fine on the wearing of mourning clothes by all except widows.

Flight was the chief recourse of those who could afford it or arrange it. The rich fled to their country places like Boccaccio's young patricians of Florence, who settled in a pastoral palace "removed on every side from the roads" with "wells of cool water and vaults of rare wines." The urban poor died in their burrows, "and only the stench of their bodies informed neighbors of their deaths." That the poor were more heavily afflicted than the rich was clearly remarked at the time, in the north as in the south. A Scottish chronicler, John of Fordun, stated flatly that the pest "attacked especially the meaner sort and common people — seldom the magnates." Simon de Covino of Montpellier made the same observation. He ascribed it to the misery and want and hard lives that made the poor more susceptible, which was half the

---

[1]*Enguerrand de Coucy*: A French nobleman. Tuchman follows his life as a way of unifying her study of the fourteenth century. [Eds.]

truth. Close contact and lack of sanitation was the unrecognized other half. It was noticed too that the young died in greater proportion than the old; Simon de Covino compared the disappearance of youth to the withering of flowers in the fields.

In the countryside peasants dropped dead on the roads, in the fields, in   20
their houses. Survivors in growing helplessness fell into apathy, leaving ripe wheat uncut and livestock untended. Oxen and asses, sheep and goats, pigs and chickens ran wild and they too, according to local reports, succumbed to the pest. English sheep, bearers of the precious wool, died throughout the country. The chronicler Henry Knighton, canon of Leicester Abbey, reported 5,000 dead in one field alone, "their bodies so corrupted by the plague that neither beast nor bird would touch them," and spreading an appalling stench. In the Austrian Alps wolves came down to prey upon sheep and then, "as if alarmed by some invisible warning, turned and fled back into the wilderness." In remote Dalmatia bolder wolves descended upon a plague-stricken city and attacked human survivors. For want of herdsmen, cattle strayed from place to place and died in hedgerows and ditches. Dogs and cats fell like the rest.

The dearth of labor held a fearful prospect because the 14th century lived close to the annual harvest both for food and for next year's seed. "So few servants and laborers were left," wrote Knighton, "that no one knew where to turn for help." The sense of a vanishing future created a kind of dementia of despair. A Bavarian chronicler of Neuberg on the Danube recorded that "Men and women . . . wandered around as if mad" and let their cattle stray "because no one had any inclination to concern themselves about the future." Fields went uncultivated, spring seed unsown. Second growth with nature's awful energy crept back over cleared land, dikes crumbled, salt water reinvaded and soured the lowlands. With so few hands remaining to restore the work of centuries, people felt, in Walsingham's words, that "the world could never again regain its former prosperity."

Though the death rate was higher among the anonymous poor, the known and the great died too. King Alfonso XI of Castile was the only reigning monarch killed by the pest, but his neighbor King Pedro of Aragon lost his wife, Queen Leonora, his daughter Marie, and a niece in the space of six months. John Cantacuzene, Emperor of Byzantium, lost his son. In France the lame Queen Jeanne and her daughter-in-law Bonne de Luxemburg, wife of the Dauphin, both died in 1349 in the same phase that took the life of Enguerrand's mother. Jeanne, Queen of Navarre, daughter of Louis X, was another victim. Edward III's second daughter, Joanna, who was on her way to marry Pedro, the heir of Castile, died in Bordeaux. Women appear to have been more vulnerable than men, perhaps because, being more housebound, they were more exposed to fleas. Boccaccio's mistress Fiammetta, illegitimate daughter of the King of Naples, died, as did Laura, the beloved — whether real or fictional — of Petrarch. Reaching out to us in the future, Petrarch cried, "Oh happy posterity who will not experience such abysmal woe and will look upon our testimony as a fable."

In Florence Giovanni Villani, the great historian of his time, died at 68 in the midst of an unfinished sentence: " . . . *e dure questo pistolenza fino a . . .* (in the midst of this pestilence there came to an end . . .)." Siena's master painters, the brothers Ambrogio and Pietro Lorenzetti, whose names never appear after 1348, presumably perished in the plague, as did Andrea Pisano, architect and sculptor of Florence. William of Ockham and the English mystic Richard Rolle of Hampole both disappear from mention after 1349. Francisco Datini, merchant of Prato, lost both his parents and two siblings. Curious sweeps of mortality afflicted certain bodies of merchants in London. All eight wardens of the Company of Cutters, all six wardens of the Hatters, and four wardens of the Goldsmiths died before July 1350. Sir John Pulteney, master draper and four times Mayor of London, was a victim, likewise Sir John Montgomery, Governor of Calais.

Among the clergy and doctors the mortality was naturally high because of the nature of their professions. Out of 24 physicians in Venice, 20 were said to have lost their lives in the plague, although, according to another account, some were believed to have fled or to have shut themselves up in their houses. At Montpellier, site of the leading medieval medical school, the physician Simon de Covino reported that, despite the great number of doctors, "hardly one of them escaped." In Avignon, Guy de Chauliac confessed that he performed his medical visits only because he dared not stay away for fear of infamy, but "I was in continual fear." He claimed to have contracted the disease but to have cured himself by his own treatment; if so, he was one of the few who recovered.

Clerical mortality varied with rank. Although the one-third toll of cardinals reflects the same proportion as the whole, this was probably due to their concentration in Avignon. In England, in strange and almost sinister procession, the Archbishop of Canterbury, John Stratford, died in August 1348, his appointed successor died in May 1349, and the next appointee three months later, all three within a year. Despite such weird vagaries, prelates in general managed to sustain a higher survival rate than the lesser clergy. Among bishops the deaths have been estimated at about one in twenty. The loss of priests, even if many avoided their fearful duty of attending the dying, was about the same as among the population as a whole.

Government officials, whose loss contributed to the general chaos, found, on the whole, no special shelter. In Siena four of the nine members of the governing oligarchy died, in France one third of the royal notaries, in Bristol 15 out of the 52 members of the Town Council or almost one third. Tax-collecting obviously suffered, with the result that Philip VI was unable to collect more than a fraction of the subsidy granted him by the Estates in the winter of 1347–48.

Lawlessness and debauchery accompanied the plague as they had during the great plague of Athens of 430 B.C., when according to Thucydides, men grew bold in the indulgence of pleasure: "For seeing how the rich died in a moment and those who had nothing immediately inherited their property, they reflected that life and riches were alike transitory and they resolved to enjoy themselves while they could." Human behavior is timeless. When St. John had his vision of plague in Revelation, he knew from some experience or race memory that those who survived "repented not of the work of their hands. . . . Neither repented they of their murders, nor of their sorceries, nor of their fornication, nor of their thefts."

Notes

Although Tuchman's notes are labeled by page number, the numbers in this Notes section refer to the paragraphs in which the sources are mentioned. Tuchman does not use numbered footnotes. At the end of her book, she numbers her notes by page number and provides a source for each quotation and citation. Following her notes, she provides a bibliography that provides the full citation for every reference given in her notes.

1. "death is seen seated": Simon de Covino, q. Campbell, 80.

2. "could infect the whole world": q. Gasquet, 41.

3. Welsh lament: q. Ziegler, 190.

9. "dogs dragged them forth": Agnolo di Tura, q. Ziegler, 58.

10. "or if no man is present": Bishop of Bath and Wells, q. Ziegler, 125. "No bells tolled": Agnolo di Tura, q. Schevill, Siena, 211. The same observation was made by Gabriel de Muisis, notary of Piacenza, q. Crawfurd, 113.

11. Givry parish register: Renouard, 111. three villages of Cambridgeshire: Saltmarsh.

12. Petrarch's brother: Bishop, 273. Brother John Clyn: q. Ziegler, 195.

13. "And in these days": q. Deaux, 143, citing only "an old northern chronicle."

14. Agnolo Di Tura, "Father abandoned child": q. Ziegler, 58.

15. "Magistrates and notaries": q. Deaux, 49. English priests turned away: Ziegler, 261. Parents deserting children: Hecker, 30. Guy De Chauliac, "A father": q. Gasquet, 50–51.

16. nuns of the Hotel Dieu: *Chron. Jean de Venette*, 49.

17. Picards and Scots mock mortality of neighbors: Gasquet, 53, and Ziegler, 198.

18. Catherine de Coucy: *L'Art de vérifier*, 237. Amiens tanners: Gasquet, 57. "By the jollity that is in us": *Grandes Chrôns.*, VI, 486–87.

19. John of Fordun: q. Ziegler, 199. Simon de Covino on the poor: Gasquet, 42. on youth: Cazelles, *Peste*.

20. Knighton on sheep: q. Ziegler, 175. Wolves of Austria and Dalmatia: ibid., 84, 111. dogs and cats: Muisis, q. Gasquet, 44, 61.

21. Bavarian chronicler of Neuberg: q. Ziegler, 84. Walsingham, "the world could never": Denifle, 273.

22. "Oh happy posterity": q. Ziegler, 45.

23. Giovanni Villani, "*e dure questo*": q. Snell, 334.

24. physicians of Venice: Campbell, 98. Simon de Covino: ibid., 31. Guy de Chauliac, "I was in continual fear": q. Thompson *Ec. and Soc.*, 379.

27. Thucydides: q. Crawfurd, 30–31.

Bibliography

L'Art de vérifier les dates des faits historiques, par un Religieux de la Congregation de St.-Maur, vol. XII. Paris, 1818.

Bishop, Morris. *Petrarch and His World.* Indiana University Press, 1963.

Campbell, Anna M. *The Black Death and Men of Learning.* Columbia University Press, 1931.

Cazelles, Raymond. *"La Peste de 1348–49 en Langue d'oil: épidémie prolitarienne et enfantine."* Bull philologique et historique, 1962, pp. 293–305.

Chronicle of Jean de Venette. Trans. Jean Birdsall. Ed. Richard A. Newhall. Columbia University Press, 1853.

Crawfurd, Raymond. *Plague and Pestilence in Literature and Art.* Oxford, 1914.

Deaux, George. *The Black Death, 1347.* London, 1969.

Denifle, Henri. *La Désolation des églises, monastères et hôpitaux en France pendant la guerre de cent ans,* vol. I. Paris, 1899.

Gasquet, Francis Aidan, Abbot. *The Black Death of 1348 and 1349,* 2nd ed. London, 1908.

Grandes Chroniques de France, vol. VI (to 1380). Ed. Paulin Paris. Paris, 1838.

Hecker, J. F. C. *The Epidemics of the Middle Ages.* London, 1844.

Renouard, Yves. *"La Peste noire de 1348–50."* Rev. de Paris, March, 1950.

Saltmarsh, John. "Plague and Economic Decline in England in the Later Middle Ages." *Cambridge Historical Journal,* vol. VII, no. 1, 1941.

Schevill, Ferdinand. *Siena: The History of a Medieval Commune.* New York, 1909.

Snell, Frederick. *The Fourteenth Century.* Edinburgh, 1899.

Thompson, James Westfall. *Economic and Social History of Europe in the Later Middle Ages.* New York, 1931.

Ziegler, Philip. *The Black Death.* New York, 1969. (The best modern study.)

QUESTIONS

1. Try to imagine yourself in Tuchman's position. If you were assigned the task of reporting on the Black Plague in Europe, how would you go about it? What problems would you expect to encounter in the research and in the composition of your report?

2. The notes and bibliography reveal a broad scholarly base: Tuchman's research was clearly prodigious. But so were the problems of organization after the research had been done. Tuchman had to present her information to readers in a way that would be clear and interesting. How has she solved her problem? What overall patterns of organization do you find in this selection? Mark off subsections with topics of their own.

3. How does Tuchman organize her paragraphs? Consider paragraph 20, for example. What is the topic? What are the subtopics? Why does the paragraph begin and end as it does? Consider paragraph 22. How does the first sentence serve as a transition from the previous paragraph? How is the rest of the paragraph ordered? Does the next paragraph start a new topic or continue developing the topic announced at the beginning of paragraph 22?

4. Many paragraphs end with direct quotations. Examine some of these. What do they have in common? Why do you think Tuchman closes so many paragraphs in this way?

5. Much of this essay is devoted to the reporting of facts and figures. This could be very tedious, but Tuchman is an expert at avoiding dullness. How does she help the reader see and feel the awfulness of the plague? Locate specific examples in the text, and discuss their effectiveness.
6. Examine Tuchman's list of sources, and explain how she has used them. Does she quote directly from each source, or does she paraphrase it? Does she use a source to illustrate a point, as evidence for argument, or in some other way?
7. Taking Tuchman as a model, write a report on some other catastrophe, blending factual reporting with description of what it was like to be there. This will require both careful research and artful selection and arrangement of the fruits of that research.
8. Using Tuchman's notes to *A Distant Mirror* as a reference guide, find out more about some specific place or event mentioned by Tuchman. Write a report of your findings.

Making Connections

1. Compare this account of the Black Death to the writing by William L. Laurence (p. 387) or Jane van Lawick-Goodall (p. 395) included in this section. Make your comparison in terms of the points of view established and sustained in the reports you compare. What is Tuchman's point of view toward her subject?
2. Compare this account of the Black Death to Abraham Verghese's report of Hurricane Katrina (p. 616). In considering these two reports of extraordinary disaster, compare how they narrate the development and course of the disaster, how they describe and highlight the details of human suffering, and how they analyze various attempts to deal with the disaster.

ATOMIC BOMBING OF NAGASAKI TOLD BY FLIGHT MEMBER

William L. Laurence

William L. Laurence (1888–1977) was born in Lithuania and came to the United States in 1905. He studied at Harvard and the Boston University Law School. His main interest, however, was always science, and after working at the New York World *for five years, Laurence went to the* New York Times *as a science reporter. During World War II, Laurence was the only reporter who knew about the top-secret testing of the atomic bomb. On August 9, 1945, he was permitted to fly with the mission to drop the second atomic bomb on Nagasaki. Three days earlier, more than one hundred thousand people had been killed in the Hiroshima bombing. Laurence won the Pulitzer Prize for this account of the bombing of Nagasaki. The article appeared in the* New York Times *on September 9, 1945.*

With the atomic-bomb mission to Japan, August 9 (Delayed) — We are on our way to bomb the mainland of Japan. Our flying contingent consists of three specially designed B-29 Superforts, and two of these carry no bombs. But our lead plane is on its way with another atomic bomb, the second in three days, concentrating in its active substance an explosive energy equivalent to twenty thousand and, under favorable conditions, forty thousand tons of TNT.

We have several chosen targets. One of these is the great industrial and shipping center of Nagasaki, on the western shore of Kyushu, one of the main islands of the Japanese homeland.

I watched the assembly of this man-made meteor during the past two days and was among the small group of scientists and Army and Navy representatives privileged to be present at the ritual of its loading in the Superfort last night, against a background of threatening black skies torn open at intervals by great lightning flashes.

It is a thing of beauty to behold, this "gadget." Into its design went millions of man-hours of what is without doubt the most concentrated intellectual effort in history. Never before had so much brain power been focused on a single problem.

This atomic bomb is different from the bomb used three days ago with such devastating results on Hiroshima.

I saw the atomic substance before it was placed inside the bomb. By itself it is not at all dangerous to handle. It is only under certain conditions, produced in the bomb assembly, that it can be made to yield up its energy,

5

and even then it gives only a small fraction of its total contents — a fraction, however, large enough to produce the greatest explosion on earth.

The briefing at midnight revealed the extreme care and the tremendous amount of preparation that had been made to take care of every detail of the mission, to make certain that the atomic bomb fully served the purpose for which it was intended. Each target in turn was shown in detailed maps and in aerial photographs. Every detail of the course was rehearsed — navigation, altitude, weather, where to land in emergencies. It came out that the Navy had rescue craft, known as Dumbos and Superdumbos, stationed at various strategic points in the vicinity of the targets, ready to rescue the fliers in case they were forced to bail out.

The briefing period ended with a moving prayer by the chaplain. We then proceeded to the mess hall for the traditional early-morning breakfast before departure on a bombing mission.

A convoy of trucks took us to the supply building for the special equipment carried on combat missions. This included the Mae West,[1] a parachute, a lifeboat, an oxygen mask, a flak suit, and a survival vest. We still had a few hours before take-off time, but we all went to the flying field and stood around in little groups or sat in jeeps talking rather casually about our mission to the Empire, as the Japanese home islands are known hereabouts.

In command of our mission is Major Charles W. Sweeney, twenty-five,   10
of 124 Hamilton Avenue, North Quincy, Massachusetts. His flagship, carrying the atomic bomb, is named *The Great Artiste*, but the name does not appear on the body of the great silver ship, with its unusually long, four-bladed, orange-tipped propellers. Instead, it carries the number 77, and someone remarks that it was "Red" Grange's winning number on the gridiron.

We took off at 3:50 this morning and headed northwest on a straight line for the Empire. The night was cloudy and threatening, with only a few stars here and there breaking through the overcast. The weather report had predicted storms ahead part of the way but clear sailing for the final and climactic stages of our odyssey.

We were about an hour away from our base when the storm broke. Our great ship took some heavy dips through the abysmal darkness around us, but it took these dips much more gracefully than a large commercial air liner, producing a sensation more in the nature of a glide than a "bump," like a great ocean liner riding the waves except that in this case the air waves were much higher and the rhythmic tempo of the glide was much faster.

I noticed a strange eerie light coming through the window high above the navigator's cabin, and as I peered through the dark all around us I saw a startling phenomenon. The whirling giant propellers had somehow become

---

[1]*Mae West*: A personal flotation device or life jacket. Sailors named the device after the well-known film star. [Eds.]

great luminous disks of blue flame. The same luminous blue flame appeared on the plexiglass windows in the nose of the ship, and on the tips of the giant wings. It looked as though we were riding the whirlwind through space on a chariot of blue fire.

It was, I surmised, a surcharge of static electricity that had accumulated on the tips of the propellers and on the di-electric material of the plastic windows. One's thoughts dwelt anxiously on the precious cargo in the invisible ship ahead of us. Was there any likelihood of danger that this heavy electric tension in the atmosphere all about us might set it off?

I expressed my fears to Captain Bock, who seems nonchalant and unperturbed at the controls. He quickly reassured me.   15

"It is a familiar phenomenon seen often on ships. I have seen it many times on bombing missions. It is known as St. Elmo's fire."

On we went through the night. We soon rode out the storm and our ship was once again sailing on a smooth course straight ahead, on a direct line to the Empire.

Our altimeter showed that we were traveling through space at a height of seventeen thousand feet. The thermometer registered an outside temperature of thirty-three degrees below zero Centigrade, about thirty below Fahrenheit. Inside our pressurized cabin the temperature was that of a comfortable air-conditioned room and a pressure corresponding to an altitude of eight thousand feet. Captain Bock cautioned me, however, to keep my oxygen mask handy in case of emergency. This, he explained, might mean either something going wrong with the pressure equipment inside the ship or a hole through the cabin by flak.

The first signs of dawn came shortly after five o'clock. Sergeant Curry, of Hoopeston, Illinois, who had been listening steadily on his earphones for radio reports, while maintaining a strict radio silence himself, greeted it by rising to his feet and gazing out the window.

"It's good to see the day," he told me. "I get a feeling of claustrophobia   20
hemmed in this cabin at night."

He is a typical American youth, looking even younger than his twenty years. It takes no mind reader to read his thoughts.

"It's a long way from Hoopeston," I find myself remarking.

"Yep," he replies, as he busies himself decoding a message from outer space.

"Think this atomic bomb will end the war?" he asks hopefully.

"There is a very good chance that this one may do the trick," I assured   25
him, "but if not, then the next one or two surely will. Its power is such that no nation can stand up against it very long." This was not my own view. I had heard it expressed all around a few hours earlier, before we took off. To anyone who had seen this man-made fireball in action, as I had less than a month ago in the desert of New Mexico, this view did not sound overoptimistic.

By 5:50 it was really light outside. We had lost our lead ship, but Lieutenant Godfrey, our navigator, informs me that we had arranged for that contingency. We have an assembly point in the sky above the little island of

Yakushima, southeast of Kyushu, at 9:10. We are to circle there and wait for the rest of our formation.

Our genial bombardier, Lieutenant Levy, comes over to invite me to take his front-row seat in the transparent nose of the ship, and I accept eagerly. From that vantage point in space, seventeen thousand feet above the Pacific, one gets a view of hundreds of miles on all sides, horizontally and vertically. At that height the vast ocean below and the sky above seem to merge into one great sphere.

I was on the inside of that firmament, riding above the giant mountains of white cumulus clouds, letting myself be suspended in infinite space. One hears the whirl of the motors behind one, but it soon becomes insignificant against the immensity all around and is before long swallowed by it. There comes a point where space also swallows time and one lives through eternal moments filled with an oppressive loneliness, as though all life had suddenly vanished from the earth and you are the only one left, a lone survivor traveling endlessly through interplanetary space.

My mind soon returns to the mission I am on. Somewhere beyond these vast mountains of white clouds ahead of me there lies Japan, the land of our enemy. In about four hours from now one of its cities, making weapons of war for use against us, will be wiped off the map by the greatest weapon ever made by man: In one tenth of a millionth of a second, a fraction of time immeasurable by any clock, a whirlwind from the skies will pulverize thousands of its buildings and tens of thousands of its inhabitants.

But at this moment no one yet knows which one of the several cities   30
chosen as targets is to be annihilated. The final choice lies with destiny. The winds over Japan will make the decision. If they carry heavy clouds over our primary target, the city will be saved, at least for the time being. None of its inhabitants will ever know that the wind of a benevolent destiny had passed over their heads. But that same wind will doom another city.

Our weather planes ahead of us are on their way to find out where the wind blows. Half an hour before target time we will know what the winds have decided.

Does one feel any pity or compassion for the poor devils about to die? Not when one thinks of Pearl Harbor[2] and of the Death March on Bataan.[3]

Captain Bock informs me that we are about to start our climb to bombing altitude.

---

[2]*Pearl Harbor*: The U.S. Navy base on the island of Oahu, Hawaii, that was attacked by the Japanese Imperial Navy on December 7, 1941. The surprise attack caused the death of 1,177 people and prompted the United States to enter World War II. [Eds.]

[3]*Death March on Bataan*: The forced march of American and Filipino defenders of the Bataan peninsula in the Philippines. The men were forced by their Japanese captors to march more than sixty miles with almost no food or water to a prisoner-of-war camp in Manila. Between 5,000 and 11,000 died before reaching the camp. [Eds.]

He manipulates a few knobs on his control panel to the right of him, and I alternately watch the white clouds and ocean below me and the altimeter on the bombardier's panel. We reached our altitude at nine o'clock. We were then over Japanese waters, close to their mainland. Lieutenant Godfrey motioned to me to look through his radar scope. Before me was the outline of our assembly point. We shall soon meet our lead ship and proceed to the final stage of our journey.

We reached Yakushima at 9:12 and there, about four thousand feet ahead of us, was *The Great Artiste* with its precious load. I saw Lieutenant Godfrey and Sergeant Curry strap on their parachutes and I decided to do likewise.

We started circling. We saw little towns on the coastline, heedless of our presence. We kept on circling, waiting for the third ship in our formation.

It was 9:56 when we began heading for the coastline. Our weather scouts had sent us code messages, deciphered by Sergeant Curry, informing us that both the primary target as well as the secondary were clearly visible.

The winds of destiny seemed to favor certain Japanese cities that must remain nameless. We circled about them again and again and found no opening in the thick umbrella of clouds that covered them. Destiny chose Nagasaki as the ultimate target.

We had been circling for some time when we noticed black puffs of smoke coming through the white clouds directly at us. There were fifteen bursts of flak in rapid succession, all too low. Captain Bock changed his course. There soon followed eight more bursts of flak, right up to our altitude, but by this time they were too far to the left.

We flew southward down the channel and at 11:33 crossed the coastline and headed straight for Nagasaki, about one hundred miles to the west. Here again we circled until we found an opening in the clouds. It was 12:01 and the goal of our mission had arrived.

We heard the prearranged signal on our radio, put on our arc welder's glasses, and watched tensely the maneuverings of the strike ship about half a mile in front of us.

"There she goes!" someone said.

Out of the belly of *The Great Artiste* what looked like a black object went downward.

Captain Bock swung to get out of range; but even though we were turning away in the opposite direction, and despite the fact that it was broad daylight in our cabin, all of us became aware of a giant flash that broke through the dark barrier of our arc welder's lenses and flooded our cabin with intense light.

We removed our glasses after the first flash, but the light still lingered on, a bluish-green light that illuminated the entire sky all around. A tremendous blast wave struck our ship and made it tremble from nose to tail. This was followed by four more blasts in rapid succession, each resounding like the boom of cannon fire hitting our plane from all directions.

Observers in the tail of our ship saw a giant ball of fire rise as though from the bowels of the earth, belching forth enormous white smoke rings.

Next they saw a giant pillar of purple fire, ten thousand feet high, shooting skyward with enormous speed.

By the time our ship had made another turn in the direction of the atomic explosion the pillar of purple fire had reached the level of our altitude. Only about forty-five seconds had passed. Awe-struck, we watched it shoot upward like a meteor coming from the earth instead of from outer space, becoming ever more alive as it climbed skyward through the white clouds. It was no longer smoke, or dust, or even a cloud of fire. It was a living thing, a new species of being, born right before our incredulous eyes.

At one stage of its evolution, covering millions of years in terms of seconds, the entity assumed the form of a giant square totem pole, with its base about three miles long, tapering off to about a mile at the top. Its bottom was brown, its center was amber, its top white. But it was a living totem pole, carved with many grotesque masks grimacing at the earth.

Then, just when it appeared as though the thing had settled down into a state of permanence, there came shooting out of the top a giant mushroom that increased the height of the pillar to a total of forty-five thousand feet. The mushroom top was even more alive than the pillar, seething and

Nagasaki: Damage wrought on second city to be hit by missile. Large factory, right, is a mass of torn steel and rubble. Bridges over canal at left are either demolished or unusable.

boiling in a white fury of creamy foam, sizzling upward and then descending earthward, a thousand Old Faithful geysers rolled into one.

It kept struggling in an elemental fury, like a creature in the act of break-   50
ing the bonds that held it down. In a few seconds it had freed itself from its gigantic stem and floated upward with tremendous speed, its momentum carrying it into the stratosphere to a height of about sixty thousand feet.

But no sooner did this happen when another mushroom, smaller in size than the first one, began emerging out of the pillar. It was as though the decapitated monster was growing a new head.

As the first mushroom floated off into the blue it changed its shape into a flowerlike form, its giant petals curving downward, creamy white outside, rose-colored inside. It still retained that shape when we last gazed at it from a distance of about two hundred miles. The boiling pillar of many colors could also be seen at that distance, a giant mountain of jumbled rainbows, in travail. Much living substance had gone into those rainbows. The quivering top of the pillar was protruding to a great height through the white clouds, giving the appearance of a monstrous prehistoric creature with a ruff around its neck, a fleecy ruff extending in all directions, as far as the eye could see.

QUESTIONS

1. What do we learn from this article about the crew members on the mission? Why has Laurence bothered to tell us about them?
2. Laurence's description of the bomb as "a thing of beauty" (paragraph 4) suggests that this eyewitness report is not wholly objective. What is Laurence's moral stance on this mission?
3. Consider Laurence's arrangement of time in his narrative. What effect do you think he wishes to create by switching back and forth between past tense and present tense?
4. Consider Laurence's description of the blast and its resulting cloud (paragraphs 44–52). His challenge as a reporter is to help his newspaper readers see this strange and awesome thing. What familiar images does he use to represent this unfamiliar sight? What do those images say — especially the last one — about Laurence's feelings as he watched the cloud transform itself?
5. Write an eyewitness report about an event that you participated in and that you consider important. Present the preparations or actions that led up to the event, and include information about the people who were involved. What imagery can you use to describe the glorious, funny, or chaotic event itself?
6. For a report on the basis for Laurence's attitude toward the bombings of Hiroshima and Nagasaki, look at as many newspapers as you can for August 6 through 10 in 1945. Be sure to look at the editorial pages as well as the front pages. If possible, also interview relatives and friends

who are old enough to remember the war or who might have fought in it. What attitudes toward the bomb and its use were expressed then? How do these compare or contrast with Laurence's attitude?

MAKING CONNECTIONS

1. Describe the differences in point of view taken toward this cataclysmic event by Laurence, John Hersey (p. 133), and Zoë Tracy Hardy (p. 366). How does each writer respond to this unparalleled story? Which responses do you find most unusual, most believable, most sympathetic? Why?
2. Imagine a meeting today between Laurence and Hatsuyo Nakamura from John Hersey's piece (p. 133). What might they say to each other? How might Laurence reflect today on his feelings more than sixty years ago? Imagine this meeting, and write a report of it. If you prefer, substitute Zoë Tracy Hardy (p. 366) for Hatsuyo Nakamura.

FIRST OBSERVATIONS

Jane van Lawick-Goodall

Jane van Lawick-Goodall (b. 1934), the British student of animal behavior, began her work as an assistant to Louis Leakey, an anthropologist and paleontologist whose studies focused on human origins. In 1960, with his help, she settled in Tanzania, East Africa, in the Gombe Stream Game Reserve to investigate the behavior of chimpanzees in their natural habitat. Her discoveries have been widely published in professional journals and in a number of books for more general audiences, including Through a Window: My Thirty Years with the Chimpanzees of Gombe *(1990),* Reason for Hope: A Spiritual Journey *(1999), and two autobiographies in letters, published in 2000 and 2001.* The Chimpanzees of Gombe: Patterns of Behavior *(1986) is recognized as the definitive work on chimpanzees. In 1977, van Lawick-Goodall founded the Jane Goodall Institute, a nonprofit organization for wildlife research, education, and conservation. She has been granted many honorary degrees and awards, including an honorary foreign membership in the American Academy of Arts and Sciences. The selection reprinted here is taken from* In the Shadow of Man *(1971), a popular work in which she is careful to report her own behavior as well as that of her chimpanzee subjects.*

For about a month I spent most of each day either on the Peak or overlooking Mlinda Valley where the chimps, before or after stuffing themselves with figs, ate large quantities of small purple fruits that tasted, like so many of their foods, as bitter and astringent as sloes or crab apples. Piece by piece, I began to form my first somewhat crude picture of chimpanzee life.

The impression that I had gained when I watched the chimps at the msulula tree of temporary, constantly changing associations of individuals within the community was substantiated. Most often I saw small groups of four to eight moving about together. Sometimes I saw one or two chimpanzees leave such a group and wander off on their own or join up with a different association. On other occasions I watched two or three small groups joining to form a larger one.

Often, as one group crossed the grassy ridge separating the Kasekela Valley from the fig trees on the home valley, the male chimpanzee, or chimpanzees, of the party would break into a run, sometimes moving in an upright position, sometimes dragging a fallen branch, sometimes stamping or slapping the hard earth. These charging displays were always accompanied by loud pant-hoots and afterward the chimpanzee frequently would swing

My best place on the Peak offered one of the best vantage points
in the area.

up into a tree overlooking the valley he was about to enter and sit quietly,
peering down and obviously listening for a response from below. If there
were chimps feeding in the fig trees they nearly always hooted back, as
though in answer. Then the new arrivals would hurry down the steep slope
and, with more calling and screaming, the two groups would meet in the fig
trees. When groups of females and youngsters with no males present joined
other feeding chimpanzees, usually there was none of this excitement; the
newcomers merely climbed up into the trees, greeted some of those already
there, and began to stuff themselves with figs.

While many details of their social behavior were hidden from me by the foliage, I did get occasional fascinating glimpses. I saw one female, newly arrived in a group, hurry up to a big male and hold her hand toward him. Almost regally he reached out, clasped her hand in his, drew it toward him, and kissed it with his lips. I saw two adult males embrace each other in greeting. I saw youngsters having wild games through the treetops, chasing around after each other or jumping again and again, one after the other, from a branch to a springy bough below. I watched small infants dangling happily by themselves for minutes on end, patting at their toes with one hand, rotating gently from side to side. Once two tiny infants pulled on opposite ends of a twig in a gentle tug-of-war. Often, during the heat of midday or after a long spell of feeding, I saw two or more adults grooming each other, carefully looking through the hair of their companions.

At that time of year the chimps usually went to bed late, making their 5
nests when it was too dark to see properly through binoculars, but sometimes they nested earlier and I could watch them from the Peak. I found that every individual, except for infants who slept with their mothers, made his own nest each night. Generally this took about three minutes: the chimp chose a firm foundation such as an upright fork or crotch, or two horizontal branches. Then he reached out and bent over smaller branches onto this foundation, keeping each one in place with his feet. Finally he tucked in the small leafy twigs growing around the rim of his nest and lay down. Quite often a chimp sat up after a few minutes and picked a handful of leafy twigs, which he put under his head or some other part of his body before

Chimpanzees make nests to sleep in.

settling down again for the night. One young female I watched went on and on bending down branches until she had constructed a huge mound of greenery on which she finally curled up.

I climbed up into some of the nests after the chimpanzees had left them. Most of them were built in trees that for me were almost impossible to climb. I found that there was quite complicated interweaving of the branches in some of them. I found, too, that the nests were fouled with dung; and later, when I was able to get closer to the chimps, I saw how they were always careful to defecate and urinate over the edge of their nests, even in the middle of the night.

During that month I really came to know the country well, for I often went on expeditions from the Peak, sometimes to examine nests, more frequently to collect specimens of the chimpanzees' food plants, which Bernard Verdcourt had kindly offered to identify for me. Soon I could find my way around the sheer ravines and up and down the steep slopes of three valleys — the home valley, the Pocket, and Mlinda Valley — as well as a taxi driver finds his way about in the main streets and byways of London. It is a period I remember vividly, not only because I was beginning to accomplish something at last, but also because of the delight I felt in being completely by myself. For those who love to be alone with nature I need add nothing further; for those who do not, no words of mine could ever convey, even in part, the almost mystical awareness of beauty and eternity that accompanies certain treasured moments. And, though the beauty was always there, those moments came upon me unaware: when I was watching the pale flush preceding dawn; or looking up through the rustling leaves of some giant forest tree into the greens and browns and black shadows that occasionally ensnared a bright fleck of the blue sky; or when I stood, as darkness fell, with one hand on the still-warm trunk of a tree and looked at the sparkling of an early moon on the never still, sighing water of the lake.

One day, when I was sitting by the trickle of water in Buffalo Wood, pausing for a moment in the coolness before returning from a scramble in Mlinda Valley, I saw a female bushbuck moving slowly along the nearly dry streambed. Occasionally she paused to pick off some plant and crunch it. I kept absolutely still, and she was not aware of my presence until she was little more than ten yards away. Suddenly she tensed and stood staring at me, one small forefoot raised. Because I did not move, she did not know what I was — only that my outline was somehow strange. I saw her velvet nostrils dilate as she sniffed the air, but I was downwind and her nose gave her no answer. Slowly she came closer, and closer — one step at a time, her neck craned forward — always poised for instant flight. I can still scarcely believe that her nose actually touched my knee; yet if I close my eyes I can feel again, in imagination, the warmth of her breath and the silken impact of her skin. Unexpectedly I blinked and she was gone in a flash, bounding away with loud barks of alarm until the vegetation hid her completely from my view.

It was rather different when, as I was sitting on the Peak, I saw a leopard coming toward me, his tail held up straight. He was at a slightly lower level than I, and obviously had no idea I was there. Ever since arrival in Africa I had had an ingrained, illogical fear of leopards. Already, while working at the Gombe, I had several times nearly turned back when, crawling through some thick undergrowth, I had suddenly smelled the rank smell of cat. I had forced myself on, telling myself that my fear was foolish, that only wounded leopards charged humans with savage ferocity.

On this occasion, though, the leopard went out of sight as it started to climb up the hill—the hill on the peak of which I sat. I quickly hastened to climb a tree, but halfway there I realized that leopards can climb trees. So I uttered a sort of halfhearted squawk. The leopard, my logical mind told me, would be just as frightened of me if he knew I was there. Sure enough, there was a thudding of startled feet and then silence. I returned to the Peak, but the feeling of unseen eyes watching me was too much. I decided to watch for the chimps in Mlinda Valley. And, when I returned to the Peak several hours later, there, on the very rock which had been my seat, was a neat pile of leopard dung. He must have watched me go and then, very carefully, examined the place where such a frightening creature had been and tried to exterminate my alien scent with his own.

As the weeks went by the chimpanzees became less and less afraid. Quite often when I was on one of my food-collecting expeditions I came across chimpanzees unexpectedly, and after a time I found that some of them would tolerate my presence provided they were in fairly thick forest and I sat still and did not try to move closer than sixty to eighty yards. And so, during my second month of watching from the Peak, when I saw a group settle down to feed I sometimes moved closer and was thus able to make more detailed observations.

It was at this time that I began to recognize a number of different individuals. As soon as I was sure of knowing a chimpanzee if I saw it again, I named it. Some scientists feel that animals should be labeled by numbers—that to name them is anthropomorphic—but I have always been interested in the *differences* between individuals, and a name is not only more individual than a number but also far easier to remember. Most names were simply those which, for some reason or other, seemed to suit the individuals to whom I attached them. A few chimps were named because some facial expression or mannerism reminded me of human acquaintances.

The easiest individual to recognize was old Mr. McGregor. The crown of his head, his neck, and his shoulders were almost entirely devoid of hair, but a slight frill remained around his head rather like a monk's tonsure. He was an old male—perhaps between thirty and forty years of age (the longevity record of a captive chimp is forty-seven years). During the early months of my acquaintance with him, Mr. McGregor was somewhat belligerent. If I accidentally came across him at close quarters he would threaten me with an upward and backward jerk of his head and a shaking of branches before climbing down and vanishing from my sight. He reminded me, for some reason, of Beatrix Potter's old gardener in *The Tale of Peter Rabbit*.

Ancient Flo with her deformed, bulbous nose and ragged ears was equally easy to recognize. Her youngest offspring at that time were two-year-old Fifi, who still rode everywhere on her mother's back, and her juvenile son, Figan, who was always to be seen wandering around with his mother and little sister. He was then about six years old; it was approximately a year before he would attain puberty. Flo often traveled with another old mother, Olly. Olly's long face was also distinctive; the fluff of hair on the back of her head — though no other feature — reminded me of my aunt, Olwen. Olly, like Flo, was accompanied by two children, a daughter younger than Fifi, and an adolescent son about a year older than Figan.

Then there was William, who, I am certain, must have been Olly's   15 blood brother. I never saw any special signs of friendship between them, but their faces were amazingly alike. They both had long upper lips that wobbled when they suddenly turned their heads. William had the added distinction of several thin, deeply etched scar marks running down his upper lip from his nose.

Two of the other chimpanzees I knew well by sight at that time were David Graybeard and Goliath. Like David and Goliath in the Bible, these two individuals were closely associated in my mind because they were very often together. Goliath, even in those days of his prime, was not a giant, but he had a splendid physique and the springy movements of an athlete. He probably weighed about one hundred pounds. David Graybeard was less afraid of me from the start than were any of the other chimps. I was always pleased when I picked out his handsome face and well-marked silvery beard in a chimpanzee group, for with David to calm the others, I had a better chance of approaching to observe them more closely.

Before the end of my trial period in the field I made two really exciting discoveries — discoveries that made the previous months of frustration well worth while. And for both of them I had David Graybeard to thank.

One day I arrived on the Peak and found a small group of chimps just below me in the upper branches of a thick tree. As I watched I saw that one of them was holding a pink-looking object from which he was from time to time pulling pieces with his teeth. There was a female and a youngster and they were both reaching out toward the male, their hands actually touching his mouth. Presently the female picked up a piece of the pink thing and put it to her mouth: it was at this moment that I realized the chimps were eating meat.

After each bite of meat the male picked off some leaves with his lips and chewed them with the flesh. Often, when he had chewed for several minutes on this leafy wad, he spat out the remains into the waiting hands of the female. Suddenly he dropped a small piece of meat, and like a flash the youngster swung after it to the ground. Even as he reached to pick it up the undergrowth exploded and an adult bushpig charged toward him. Screaming, the juvenile leaped back into the tree. The pig remained in the open, snorting and moving backward and forward. Soon I made out the shapes of three small striped piglets. Obviously the chimps were eating a baby pig.

The size was right and later, when I realized that the male was David Graybeard, I moved closer and saw that he was indeed eating piglet.

For three hours I watched the chimps feeding. David occasionally let   20
the female bite pieces from the carcass and once he actually detached a small piece of flesh and placed it in her outstretched hand. When he finally climbed down there was still meat left on the carcass; he carried it away in one hand, followed by the others.

Of course I was not sure, then, that David Graybeard had caught the pig for himself, but even so, it was tremendously exciting to know that these chimpanzees actually ate meat. Previously scientists had believed that although these apes might occasionally supplement their diet with a few insects or small rodents and the like they were primarily vegetarians and fruit eaters. No one had suspected that they might hunt larger mammals.

It was within two weeks of this observation that I saw something that excited me even more. By then it was October and the short rains had begun. The blackened slopes were softened by feathery new grass shoots and in some places the ground was carpeted by a variety of flowers. The Chimpanzees' Spring, I called it. I had had a frustrating morning, tramping up and down three valleys with never a sign or sound of a chimpanzee. Hauling myself up the steep slope of Mlinda Valley I headed for the Peak, not only weary but soaking wet from crawling through dense undergrowth. Suddenly I stopped, for I saw a slight movement in the long grass about sixty yards away. Quickly focusing my binoculars I saw that it was a single chimpanzee, and just then he turned in my direction. I recognized David Graybeard.

Cautiously I moved around so that I could see what he was doing. He was squatting beside the red earth mound of a termite nest, and as I watched I saw him carefully push a long grass stem down into a hole in the mound. After a moment he withdrew it and picked something from the end with his mouth. I was too far away to make out what he was eating, but it was obvious that he was actually using a grass stem as a tool.

I knew that on two occasions casual observers in West Africa had seen chimpanzees using objects as tools: one had broken open palm-nut kernels by using a rock as a hammer, and a group of chimps had been observed pushing sticks into an underground bees' nest and licking off the honey. Somehow I had never dreamed of seeing anything so exciting myself.

For an hour David feasted at the termite mound and then he wandered   25
slowly away. When I was sure he had gone I went over to examine the mound. I found a few crushed insects strewn about, and a swarm of worker termites sealing the entrances of the nest passages into which David had obviously been poking his stems. I picked up one of his discarded tools and carefully pushed it into a hole myself. Immediately I felt the pull of several termites as they seized the grass, and when I pulled it out there were a number of worker termites and a few soldiers, with big red heads, clinging on with their mandibles. There they remained, sticking out at right angles to the stem with their legs waving in the air.

Before I left I trampled down some of the tall dry grass and constructed a rough hide — just a few palm fonds leaned up against the low branch of a tree and tied together at the top. I planned to wait there the next day. But it was another week before I was able to watch a chimpanzee "fishing" for termites again. Twice chimps arrived, but each time they saw me and moved off immediately. Once a swarm of fertile winged termites — the princes and princesses, as they are called — flew off on their nuptial flight, their huge white wings fluttering frantically as they carried the insects higher and higher. Later I realized that it is at this time of year, during the short rains, when the worker termites extend the passages of the nest to the surface, preparing for these emigrations. Several such swarms emerge between October and January. It is principally during these months that the chimpanzees feed on termites.

On the eighth day of my watch David Graybeard arrived again, together with Goliath, and the pair worked there for two hours. I could see much better: I observed how they scratched open the sealed-over passage entrances with a thumb or forefinger. I watched how they bit the end off their tools when they became bent, or used the other end, or discarded them in favor of new ones. Goliath once moved at least fifteen yards from the heap to select a firm-looking piece of vine, and both males often picked three or four stems while they were collecting tools, and put the spares beside them on the ground until they wanted them.

Tool*making* — leaves are stripped from a stem to make a tool suitable for termite-fishing. In addition, the edges of a wide blade of grass may be stripped off in order to make an appropriate tool.

Most exciting of all, on several occasions they picked small leafy twigs and prepared them for use by stripping off the leaves. This was the first recorded example of a wild animal not merely *using* an object as a tool, but actually modifying an object and thus showing the crude beginnings of tool*making*.

Previously man had been regarded as the only toolmaking animal. Indeed, one of the clauses commonly accepted in the definition of man was that he was a creature who "made tools to a regular and set pattern." The chimpanzees, obviously, had not made tools to any set pattern. Nevertheless, my early observations of their primitive toolmaking abilities convinced a number of scientists that it was necessary to redefine man in a more complex manner than before. Or else, as Louis Leakey put it, we should by definition have to accept the chimpanzee as Man.

QUESTIONS

1. This essay is principally an example of reporting; that is, it is a gathering of facts by a clearheaded, unbiased observer. Identify passages in the essay in which this kind of reporting takes place.
2. Although van Lawick-Goodall is a mostly neutral observer of chimpanzee behavior, neutrality is impossible in any absolute sense. For example, she writes with an eye always on comparisons of chimpanzee and human behaviors. Make a list of words from paragraphs 3 and 4 that reveal that particular bias.
3. Describe how van Lawick-Goodall's comparisons of chimpanzee and human behaviors become increasingly prominent as her essay continues.
4. Paraphrase the last discovery van Lawick-Goodall reports toward the end of her essay. What exactly was her contribution to science in this instance? What other activities, described earlier in the piece, make that discovery understandable, perhaps even unsurprising once we come to it?
5. What do you make of the choice outlined in paragraph 29? Which choice do you suppose the scientists made? Why?
6. Van Lawick-Goodall's scientific work resembles that of an anthropologist in that she goes into the field to observe the behavior of a social group. Even from this short piece we can learn a good deal about the practices and the way of life of such a worker in the field. Describe van Lawick-Goodall's life in the field, making whatever inferences you can from this single essay.
7. Amplify the description of van Lawick-Goodall's life in the field that you created for question 6 by reading articles about her and her work.
8. Place yourself somewhere, and observe behavior more or less as van Lawick-Goodall does. You might observe wildlife — pigeons, sparrows, crows, squirrels, or whatever is available — or you might observe some aspect of human behavior. If you choose the latter, look for behavior that is unfamiliar to you, such as that of children at play, workers on a

job, or members of a social group very different from your own. Write a report detailing your observations.

9. After you have completed question 8, write a second, shorter report in which you comment on the nature of your task as an observer. Was it difficult to watch? Was it difficult to decide what was meaningful behavior? Did you influence what you saw so that you could not be confident that the behavior was representative? Can you propose any improvement in your methodology?

10. One of the tools that van Lawick-Goodall lacks in her research is the ability to interview relevant parties. Imagine her interviewing Mr. McGregor, Goliath, and David Graybeard. What questions would she be likely to ask? What would you like to know about one of those individuals if you were able to interview him? Write out the interview that you can imagine.

Making Connections

1. Both van Lawick-Goodall and John Yarbrough in Malcolm Gladwell's "The Naked Face" (p. 519) study a specific kind of animal in its natural habitat. How are their procedures similar? How are they different? What kinds of refinement do they venture in their studies as they proceed? How do their procedures influence both their findings and their presentation of those findings?

2. Compare and contrast van Lawick-Goodall's account of observing the chimpanzees with Amanda Coyne's observations of convict moms at the federal prison camp (p. 141). To what extent are both writers ethnographers, studying and describing behavior in a specific society?

THE NATURE FAKER

Richard Harding Davis

Richard Harding Davis (1864–1916) is not a generally recognized figure today, but he was the most widely known reporter of his time, as well as a popular novelist and playwright. He was born in Philadelphia. After studying at Lehigh University and Johns Hopkins University, Davis began his newspaper career in 1886. By the 1890s, having written for the New York Sun *and been managing editor for* Harper's Weekly, *his name had become well recognized. In 1896, Davis, along with illustrator Frederic Remington, was commissioned by newspaper magnate William Randolph Hearst to cover the rebellion in Cuba to overthrow Spanish rule. When Hearst changed the facts of one of the articles to make it more sensational, Davis was outraged and refused to continue to work for Hearst. Davis witnessed the bombing of the Cuban province of Matanzas from a U.S. Navy flagship. After this incident, the navy prohibited reporters on any U.S. ships for the rest of the conflict. Throughout his journalistic career, Davis traveled widely and reported on six wars for newspapers in London and New York. He published seven volumes of war reporting, which led to his being called the first modern war correspondent. Davis was also successful as a popular novelist. In 1890, he published a short story, "Gallegher," in* Scribner's Magazine, *which attracted wide attention. He published seven popular novels, some of them best sellers, including* Soldiers of Fortune *(1897),* The Bar Sinister *(1903), and* Vera the Medium *(1908), and eleven collections of his stories, including* Van Bibber and Others *(1892),* The Lion and the Unicorn *(1899),* The Scarlet Car *(1907), and* The Boy Scout *(1917). Davis also wrote more than twenty-five plays, and at one time, three of his plays were running simultaneously on Broadway. On writing, Davis said, "The secret of good writing is to say an old thing in a new way or to say a new thing in an old way." After his death at home from a heart attack at age fifty-one, Teddy Roosevelt wrote of Davis, "He was as good an American as ever lived." The following story was published in the collection* The Man Who Could Not Lose *(1918).*

Richard Herrick was a young man with a gentle disposition, much money, and no sense of humor. His object in life was to marry Miss Catherweight. For three years she had tried to persuade him this could not be, and finally, in order to convince him, married some one else. When the woman he loves marries another man, the rejected one is popularly supposed to take to drink or to foreign travel. Statistics show that, instead, he instantly falls in love with the best friend of the girl who refused him. But, as Herrick truly loved Miss Catherweight, he could not worship any other woman, and so he became a lover of nature. Nature, he assured his men friends, does not disappoint you. The more thought, care, affection you give to nature, the more she gives you in return, and while, so he admitted, in wooing nature there are no great moments, there are no heart-aches. Jackson, one of the men friends, and of a frivolous disposition, said that he also could admire a landscape, but he would rather look at the beautiful eyes of a girl he knew than at the Lakes of Killarney, with a full moon, a setting sun, and the aurora borealis for a background. Herrick suggested that, while the beautiful eyes might seek those of another man, the Lakes of Killarney would always remain where you could find them. Herrick pursued his new love in Connecticut on an abandoned farm which he converted into a "model" one. On it he established model dairies and model incubators. He laid out old-fashioned gardens, sunken gardens, Italian gardens, landscape gardens, and a game preserve.

The game preserve was his own especial care and pleasure. It consisted of two hundred acres of dense forest and hills and ridges of rock. It was filled with mysterious caves, deep chasms, tiny gurgling streams, nestling springs, and wild laurel. It was barricaded with fallen tree-trunks and moss-covered rocks that had never felt the foot of man since that foot had worn a moccasin. Around the preserve was a high fence stout enough to keep poachers on the outside and to persuade the wild animals that inhabited it to linger on the inside. These wild animals were squirrels, rabbits, and raccoons. Every day, in sunshine or in rain, entering through a private gate, Herrick would explore this holy of holies. For such vermin as would destroy the gentler animals he carried a gun. But it was turned only on those that preyed upon his favorites. For hours he would climb through this wilderness, or, seated on a rock, watch a bluebird building her nest or a squirrel laying in rations against the coming of the snow. In time he grew to think he knew and understood the inhabitants of this wild place of which he was the overlord. He looked upon them not as his tenants but as his guests. And when they fled from him in terror to caves and hollow tree-trunks, he wished he might call them back and explain he was their friend, that it was due to him they lived in peace. He was glad they were happy. He was glad it was through him that, undisturbed, they could live the simple life.

His fall came through ambition. Herrick himself attributed it to his too great devotion to nature and nature's children. Jackson, he of the frivolous mind, attributed it to the fact that any man is sure to come to grief who turns from the worship of God's noblest handiwork, by which Jackson meant woman, to worship chipmunks and Plymouth Rock hens. One night Jackson lured Herrick into New York to a dinner and a music hall. He invited also one Kelly, a mutual friend of a cynical and combative disposition. Jackson liked to hear him and Herrick abuse each other, and always introduced subjects he knew would cause each to lose his temper.

But, on this night, Herrick needed no goading. He was in an ungrateful mood. Accustomed to food fresh from the soil and the farmyard, he sneered at hothouse asparagus, hothouse grapes, and cold-storage quail. At the music hall he was even more difficult. In front of him sat a stout lady who when she shook with laughter shed patchouli and a man who smoked American cigarettes. At these and the steam heat, the nostrils of Herrick, trained to the odor of balsam and the smoke of open wood fires, took offense. He refused to be amused. The monologue artist, in whom Jackson found delight, caused Herrick only to groan; the knockabout comedians he hoped would break their collar-bones; the lady who danced Salome, and who fascinated Kelly, Herrick prayed would catch pneumonia and die of it. And when the drop rose upon the Countess Zichy's bears, his dissatisfaction reached a climax.

There were three bears — a large papa bear, a mamma bear, and the baby bear. On the programme they were described as Bruno, Clara, and Ikey. They were of a dusty brown, with long, curling noses tipped with white, and fat, tan-colored bellies. When father Bruno, on his hind legs and bare feet, waddled down the stage, he resembled a . . . gentleman in a brown bathing suit who had lost his waist-line. As he tripped doubtfully forward, with mincing steps, he continually and mournfully wagged his head. He seemed to be saying: "This water is much too cold for me." The mamma bear was dressed in a poke bonnet and white apron, and resembled the wolf who frightened Little Red Riding-Hood, and Ikey, the baby bear, wore rakishly over one eye the pointed cap of a clown. To those who knew their vaudeville, this was indisputable evidence that Ikey would furnish the comic relief. Nor did Ikey disappoint them. He was a wayward son. When his parents were laboriously engaged in a boxing-match, or dancing to the "Merry Widow Waltz," or balancing on step-ladders, Ikey, on all fours, would scamper to the foot-lights and, leaning over, make a swift grab at the head of the first trombone. And when the Countess Zichy, apprised by the shouts of the audience of Ikey's misconduct, waved a toy whip, Ikey would gallop back to his pedestal and howl at her. To every one, except Herrick and the first trombone, this playfulness on the part of Ikey furnished great delight.

The performances of the bears ended with Bruno and Clara dancing heavily to the refrain of the "Merry Widow Waltz," while Ikey pretended to conduct the music of the orchestra. On the final call, Madame Zichy threw to each of the animals a beer bottle filled with milk; and the gusto with which the savage-looking beasts uncorked the bottles and drank from them greatly amused the audience. Ikey, standing on his hind legs, his head thrown back, with both paws clasping the base of the bottle, shoved the neck far down his throat, and then, hurling it from him, and cocking his clown's hat over his eyes, gave a masterful imitation of a very intoxicated bear.

"That," exclaimed Herrick hotly, "is a degrading spectacle. It degrades the bear and degrades me and you."

"No, it bores me," said Kelly.

"If you understood nature," retorted Herrick, "and nature's children, it would infuriate you."

"I don't go to a music hall to get infuriated," said Kelly.

"Trained dogs I don't mind," exclaimed Herrick. "Dogs are not wild   10 animals. The things they're trained to do are of *use*. They can guard the house, or herd sheep. But a bear is a wild beast. Always will be a wild beast. You can't train him to be of use. It's degrading to make him ride a bicycle. I hate it! If I'd known there were to be performing bears to-night, I wouldn't have come!"

"And if I'd known you were to be here to-night, I wouldn't have come!" said Kelly. "Where do we go to next?"

They went next to a restaurant in a gayly decorated cellar. Into this young men like themselves and beautiful ladies were so anxious to hurl themselves that to restrain them a rope was swung across the entrance and page boys stood on guard. When a young man became too anxious to spend his money, the page boys pushed in his shirt front. After they had fought their way to a table, Herrick ungraciously remarked he would prefer to sup in a subway station. The people, he pointed out, would be more human, the decorations were much of the same Turkish-bath school of art, and the air was no worse.

"Cheer up, Clarence!" begged Jackson, "you'll soon be dead. To-morrow you'll be back among your tree-toads and sunsets. And, let us hope," he sighed, "no one will try to stop you!"

"What worries me is this," explained Herrick. "I can't help thinking   15 that, if one night of this artificial life is so hard upon me, what must it be to those bears!"

Kelly exclaimed, with exasperation: "Confound the bears!" he cried. "If you must spoil my supper weeping over animals, weep over cart-horses. They work. Those bears are loafers. They're as well fed as pet canaries. They're aristocrats."

"But it's not a free life!" protested Herrick. "It's not the life they love."

"It's a darned sight better," declared Kelly, "than sleeping in a damp wood, eating raw blackberries ——"

"The more you say," retorted Herrick, "the more you show you know nothing whatsoever of nature's children and their habits."

"And all you know of them," returned Kelly, "is that a cat has nine   20 lives, and a barking dog won't bite. You're a nature faker." Herrick refused to be diverted.

"It hurt me," he said. "They were so big, and good-natured, and help-less. I'll bet that woman beats them! I kept thinking of them as they were in the woods, tramping over the clean pine needles, eating nuts, and — and honey, and ——"

"Buns!" suggested Jackson.

"I can't forget them," said Herrick. "It's going to haunt me, tomor-row, when I'm back in the woods; I'll think of those poor beasts capering in a hot theatre, when they ought to be out in the open as God meant they ——"

"Well, then," protested Kelly, "take 'em to the open. And turn 'em loose! And I hope they bite you!"

At this Herrick frowned so deeply that Kelly feared he had gone too far. 25 Inwardly, he reproved himself for not remembering that his friend lacked a sense of humor. But Herrick undeceived him.

"You are right" he exclaimed. "To-morrow I will buy those bears, take them to the farm, and turn them loose!"

No objections his friend could offer could divert him from his purpose. When they urged that to spend so much money in such a manner was criminally wasteful, he pointed out that he was sufficiently rich to indulge any extravagant fancy, whether in polo ponies or bears; when they warned him that if he did not look out the bears would catch him alone in the woods, and eat him, he retorted that the bears were now educated to a different diet; when they said he should consider the peace of mind of his neighbors, he assured them the fence around his game preserve would restrain an elephant.

"Besides," protested Kelly, "what you propose to do is not only impracticable, but it's cruelty to animals. A domesticated animal can't return to a state of nature, and live."

"Can't it?" jeered Herrick. "Did you ever read 'The Call of the Wild'?"

"Did you ever read," retorted Kelly, "what happened at the siege of La- 30 dysmith when the oats ran low and they drove the artillery horses out to grass? They starved, that's all. And if you don't feed your bears on milk out of a bottle they'll starve too."

"That's what will happen," cried Jackson; "those bears have forgotten what a pine forest smells like. Maybe it's a pity, but it's the fact. I'll bet if you could ask them whether they'd rather sleep in a cave on your farm or be headliners in vaudeville, they'd tell you they were 'devoted to their art.'"

"Why!" exclaimed Kelly, "they're so far from nature that if they didn't have that colored boy to comb and brush them twice a day they'd be ashamed to look each other in the eyes."

"And another thing," continued Jackson, "trained animals love to 'show off.' They're children. Those bears *enjoy* doing those tricks. They *enjoy* the applause. They enjoy dancing to the 'Merry Widow Waltz.' And if you lock them up in your jungle, they'll get so homesick that they'll give a performance twice a day to the squirrels and woodpeckers."

"It's just as hard to unlearn a thing as to learn it," said Kelly sententiously. "You can't make a man who has learned to wear shoes enjoy going around in his bare feet."

"Rot!" cried Herrick. "Look at me. Didn't I love New York? I loved it 35 so I never went to bed for fear I'd miss something. But when I went 'Back to the Land,' did it take me long to fall in love with the forests and the green fields? It took me a week. I go to bed now the same day I get up, and I've passed on my high hat and frock coat to a scarecrow. And I bet you when those bears once scent the wild woods they'll stampede for them like Croker going to a third alarm."

"And I repeat," cried Kelly, "you are a nature faker. And I leave it to the bears to prove it.

"We have done our best," sighed Jackson. "We have tried to save him money and trouble. And now all he can do for us in return is to give us seats for the opening performance."

What the bears cost Herrick he never told. But it was a very large sum. As the Countess Zichy pointed out, bears as bears, in a state of nature, are cheap. If it were just a bear he wanted, he himself could go to Pike County, Pennsylvania, and trap one. What he was paying for, she explained, was the time she had spent in educating the Bruno family, and added to that the time during which she must now remain idle while she educated another family.

Herrick knew for what he was paying. It was the pleasure of rescuing unwilling slaves from bondage. As to their expensive education, if they returned to a state of ignorance as rapidly as did most college graduates he knew, he would be satisfied. Two days later, when her engagement at the music hall closed, Madame Zichy reluctantly turned over her pets to their new manager. With Ikey she was especially loath to part.

"I'll never get one like him," she said. "Ikey is the funniest four-legged   40
clown in America. He's a natural-born comedian. Folks think I learn him those tricks, but it's all his own stuff. Only last week we was playing Paoli's in Bridgeport, and when I was putting Bruno through the hoops, Ikey runs to the stage-box and grabs a pound of caramels out of a girls lap and swallows the box. And in St. Paul, if the trombone hadn't worn a wig, Ikey would have scalped him. Say, it was a scream! When the audience see the trombone snatched bald-headed, and him trying to get back his wig, and Ikey chewing it, they went crazy. You can't learn a bear tricks like that. It's just genius. Some folks think I taught him to act like he was intoxicated, but he picked that up, too, all by himself, through watching my husband. And Ikey's very fond of beer on his own account. If I don't stop them, the stage hands would be always slipping him drinks. I hope you won't give him none."

"I will not!" said Herrick.

The bears, Ikey in one cage and Bruno and Clara in another, travelled by express to the station nearest the Herrick estate. There they were transferred to a farm wagon, and grumbling and growling, and with Ikey howling like an unspanked child, they were conveyed to the game preserve. At the only gate that entered it, Kelly and Jackson and a specially invited house party of youths and maidens were gathered to receive them. At a greater distance stood all of the servants and farm hands, and as the wagon backed against the gate, with the door of Ikey's cage opening against it, the entire audience, with one accord, moved solidly to the rear. Herrick, with a pleased but somewhat nervous smile, mounted the wagon. But before he could unlock the cage Kelly demanded to be heard. He insisted that, following the custom of all great artists, the bears should give a farewell performance.

He begged that Bruno and Clara might be permitted to dance together. He pointed out that this would be the last time they could listen to the strains of the "Merry Widow Waltz." He called upon everybody present to whistle it.

The suggestion of an open-air performance was received coldly. At the moment no one seemed able to pucker his lips into a whistle, and some even explained that with that famous waltz they were unfamiliar.

One girl attained an instant popularity by pointing out that the bears   45
could waltz just as well on one side of the fence as the other. Kelly, cheated of
his free performance, then begged that before Herrick condemned the bears to
starve on acorns, he should give them a farewell drink, and Herrick, who was
slightly rattled, replied excitedly that he had not ransomed the animals only to
degrade them. The argument was interrupted by the French chef falling out of
a tree. He had climbed it, he explained, in order to obtain a better view.

When, in turn, it was explained to him that a bear also could climb a
tree, he remembered he had left his oven door open. His departure reminded
other servants of duties they had neglected, and one of the guests, also, on remembering he had put in a long-distance call, hastened to the house. Jackson
suggested that perhaps they had better all return with him, as the presence of
so many people might frighten the bears. At the moment he spoke, Ikey emitted a hideous howl, whether of joy or rage no one knew, and few remained
to find out. It was not until Herrick had investigated and reported that Ikey
was still behind the bars that the house party cautiously returned. The house
party then filed a vigorous protest. Its members, with Jackson as spokesman,
complained that Herrick was relying entirely too much on his supposition
that the bears would be anxious to enter the forest. Jackson pointed out that,
should they not care to do so, there was nothing to prevent them from doubling back under the wagon; in which case the house party and all of the
United States lay before them. It was not until a lawn-tennis net and much
chicken wire was stretched in intricate thicknesses across the lower half of
the gate that Herrick was allowed to proceed. Unassisted, he slid back the
cage door, and without a moment's hesitation Ikey leaped from the wagon
through the gate and into the preserve. For an instant, dazed by the sudden
sunlight, he remained motionless, and then, after sniffing delightedly at the
air, stuck his nose deep into the autumn leaves. Turning on his back, he luxu-
riously and joyfully kicked his legs, and rolled from side to side.

Herrick gave a shout of joy and triumph. "What did I tell you!" he
called. "See how he loves it! See how happy he is."

"Not at all," protested Kelly. "He thought you gave him the sign to
'roll over.' Tell him to 'play dead,' and he'll do that." "Tell *all* the bears to
'play dead,'" begged Jackson, "until I'm back in the billiard-room."

Flushed with happiness, Herrick tossed Ikey's cage out of the wagon,
and opened the door of the one that held Bruno and Clara. On their part,
there was a moment of doubt. As though suspecting a trap, they moved to
the edge of the cage, and gazed critically at the screen of trees and tangled
vines that rose before them.

"They think it's a new backdrop," explained Kelly.   50

But the delight with which Ikey was enjoying his bath in the autumn
leaves was not lost upon his parents. Slowly and clumsily they dropped to
the ground. As though they expected to be recalled, each turned to look
at the group of people who had now run to peer through the wire meshes of
the fence. But, as no one spoke and no one signalled, the three bears, in single file, started toward the edge of the forest. They had of cleared space to
cover only a little distance, and at each step, as though fearful they would

be stopped and punished, one or the other turned his head. But no one halted them. With quickening footsteps the bears, now almost at a gallop, plunged forward. The next instant they were lost to sight, and only the crackling of the underbrush told that they had come into their own.

Herrick dropped to the ground and locked himself inside the preserve.

"I'm going after them," he called, "to see what they'll do."

There was a frantic chorus of entreaties.

"Don't be an ass!" begged Jackson. "They'll eat you." Herrick waved   55
his hand reassuringly.

"They won't even see me," he explained. "I can find my way about this place better than they can. And I'll keep to windward of them, and watch them. Go to the house," he commanded. "I'll be with you in an hour, and report."

It was with real relief that, on assembling for dinner, the house party found Herrick, in high spirits, with the usual number of limbs, and awaiting them. The experiment had proved a great success. He told how, unheeded by the bears, he had, without difficulty, followed in their tracks. For an hour he had watched them. No happy school-children, let loose at recess, could have embraced their freedom with more obvious delight. They drank from the running streams, for honey they explored the hollow tree-trunks, they sharpened their claws on moss-grown rocks, and among the fallen oak leaves scratched violently for acorns. So satisfied was Herrick with what he had seen, with the success of his experiment, and so genuine and unselfish was he in the thought of the happiness he had brought to the beasts of the forests, that for him no dinner ever passed more pleasantly. Miss Waring, who sat next to her host, thought she had seldom met a man with so kind and simple a nature. She rather resented the fact, and she was inwardly indignant that so much right feeling and affection could be wasted on farmyard fowls, and four-footed animals. She felt sure that some nice girl, seated at the other end of the table, smiling through the light of the wax candles upon Herrick, would soon make him forget his love of "Nature and Nature's children." She even saw herself there, and this may have made her exhibit more interest in Herrick's experiment than she really felt. In any event, Herrick found her most sympathetic, and when dinner was over carried her off to a corner of the terrace. It was a warm night in early October, and the great woods of the game preserve that stretched below them were lit with a full moon.

On his way to the lake for a moonlight row with one of the house party who belonged to that sex that does not row, but looks well in the moonlight, Kelly halted, and jeered mockingly.

"How can you sit there," he demanded, "while those poor beasts are freezing in a cave, with not even a silk coverlet or a pillow-sham. You and your valet ought to be down there now carrying them pajamas."

"Kelly," declared Herrick, unruffled in his moment of triumph, "I hate   60
to say, 'I told you so,' but you force me. Go away," he commanded. "You have neither imagination nor soul."

"And that's true," he assured Miss Waring, as Kelly and his companion left them. "Now, I see nothing in what I accomplished that is ridiculous. Had you watched those bears as I did, you would have felt that sympathy that exists between all who love the out-of-door life. A dog loves to see his master pick up his stick and his hat to take him for a walk, and the man enjoys seeing the dog leaping and quartering the fields before him. They are both the happier. At least I am happier to-night, knowing those bears are at peace and at home, than I would be if I thought of them being whipped through their tricks in a dirty theatre." Herrick pointed to the great forest trees of the preserve, their tops showing dimly in the mist of moonlight. "Somewhere, down in that valley," he murmured, "are three happy animals. They are no longer slaves and puppets — they are their own masters. For the rest of their lives they can sleep on pine needles and dine on nuts and honey. No one shall molest them, no one shall force them through degrading tricks. Hereafter they can choose their life, and their own home among the rocks, and the ——" Herrick's words were frozen on his tongue. From the other end of the terrace came a scream so fierce, so long, so full of human suffering, that at the sound the blood of all that heard it turned to water. It was so appalling that for an instant no one moved, and then from every part of the house, along the garden walks, from the servants' quarters, came the sound of pounding feet. Herrick, with Miss Waring clutching at his sleeve, raced toward the other end of the terrace. They had not far to go. Directly in front of them they saw what had dragged from the very soul of the woman the scream of terror.

The drawing-room opened upon the terrace, and, seated at the piano, Jackson had been playing for those in the room to dance. The windows to the terrace were open. The terrace itself was flooded with moon-light. Seeking the fresh air, one of the dancers stepped from the drawing-room to the flags outside. She had then raised the cry of terror and fallen in a faint. What she had seen, Herrick a moment later also saw. On the terrace in the moonlight, Bruno and Clara, on their hind legs, were solemnly waltzing. Neither the scream nor the cessation of the music disturbed them. Contentedly, proudly, they continued to revolve in hops and leaps. From their happy expression, it was evident they not only were enjoying themselves, but that they felt they were greatly affording immeasurable delight to others. Sick at heart, furious, bitterly hurt, with roars of mocking laughter in his ears, Herrick ran toward the stables for help. At the farther end of the terrace the butler had placed a tray of liqueurs, whiskeys, and soda bottles. His back had been turned for only a few moments, but the time had sufficed.

Lolling with his legs out, stretched in a wicker chair, Herrick beheld the form of lkey. Between his uplifted paws he held aloof the base of a decanter; between his teeth, and well jammed down his throat, was the long neck of the bottle. From it issued the sound of gentle gurgling. Herrick seized the decanter and hurled it crashing upon the terrace. With difficulty Ikey rose. Swaying and shaking his head reproachfully, he gave Herrick a perfectly accurate imitation of an intoxicated bear.

QUESTIONS

1. This story takes its title from the scornful name that Kelly applies to Herrick in paragraphs 20 and 36. That phrase was created by the early-twentieth century naturalist John Burroughs to deride the work of popular writers who portrayed animals as being endowed with the rational and sentient capacities of human beings. Considered in this light, to what extent is Herrick a "nature faker"? In what sense might he be described simply as a "nature lover"? Think of a two- or three-word phrase that you believe would characterize Herrick more accurately.

2. Herrick's argument with Kelly and Jackson clearly involves two opposing views about the nature, needs, and training of animals. What are the main points of their disagreement? To what extent might their disagreement boil down to the question of whether nature or nurture is more influential in the shaping of animal needs and desires? To what extent might their disagreement center on the question of whether animals are purely instinctual?

3. Whose side did you favor when the argument first arose? Whose side did you favor when the bears first took up residence in Herrick's game preserve? Whose side did you favor after the bears' performance at Herrick's dinner party?

4. How were your opinions influenced by the differing temperaments and behavior of the three characters? How were your opinions influenced by the plot of the story?

5. Although we have included this story in the section on "Reporting in the Social Sciences and Public Affairs," what would you think if it were anthologized as an example of "Arguing in the Social Sciences and Public Affairs"? In what respects does the story seem designed to make a case about the nature and treatment of domesticated animals? In what respects does it seem to be an informative story without any ax to grind?

6. Given your firsthand knowledge of domesticated animals, write a narrative essay or short story that implicitly makes a case for what you believe to be the nature and proper treatment of such creatures.

MAKING CONNECTIONS

Consider how the two main characters in this story, Herrick and Kelly, would respond to van Lawick-Goodall's piece about the behavior and abilities of chimpanzees (p. 395). Then consider how van Lawick-Goodall would respond to each of them. Do you suppose that they would agree on anything about the nature of animals or the proper treatment of animals? Or would there be disagreement all around?

U.S. ATTACKED:
Hijacked Jets Destroy Twin Towers and Hit Pentagon in Day of Terror

Serge Schmemann

Serge Schmemann (b. 1945) spent his youth in Paris before attending Harvard University, where he received his bachelor's degree, and Columbia University, where he earned a master's degree in journalism. He then worked as a correspondent for the Associated Press wire service and later as a reporter for the New York Times, *serving as bureau chief in Bonn, Jerusalem, and Moscow. Currently editorial page editor for the* International Herald Tribune, *Schmemann was awarded a Pulitzer Prize in 1991 for coverage of the reunification of East and West Germany. In 1997, he published* Echos of a Native Land: Two Centuries of a Village, *about life in rural Russia. Schmemann has also written a children's book,* When the Wall Came Down: The Berlin Wall and the Fall of Soviet Communism *(2006). The following originally appeared in the* New York Times *on September 12, 2001.*

Hijackers rammed jetliners into each of New York's World Trade Center towers yesterday, toppling both in a hellish storm of ash, glass, smoke, and leaping victims, while a third jetliner crashed into the Pentagon in Virginia. There was no official count, but President Bush said thousands had perished, and in the immediate aftermath the calamity was already being ranked the worst and most audacious terror attack in American history.

The attacks seemed carefully coordinated. The hijacked planes were all en route to California, and therefore gorged with fuel, and their departures were spaced within an hour and 40 minutes. The first, American Airlines Flight 11, a Boeing 767 out of Boston for Los Angeles, crashed into the north tower at 8:48 a.m. Eighteen minutes later, United Airlines Flight 175, also headed from Boston to Los Angeles, plowed into the south tower.

Then an American Airlines Boeing 757, Flight 77, left Washington's Dulles International Airport bound for Los Angeles, but instead hit the western part of the Pentagon, the military headquarters where 24,000 people work, at 9:40 a.m. Finally, United Airlines Flight 93, a Boeing 757 flying from Newark to San Francisco, crashed near Pittsburgh, raising the possibility that its hijackers had failed in whatever their mission was.

There were indications that the hijackers on at least two of the planes were armed with knives. Attorney General John Ashcroft told reporters in

The New York Times

"All the News That's Fit to Print"

Late Edition
New York: Today, sunny, a few afternoon clouds. High 77. Tonight, slightly more humid. Low 65. Tomorrow, sun then clouds. High 81. Yesterday, high 81, low 83. Weather map, Page C19.

VOL. CL . . No. 51,874   Copyright © 2001 The New York Times   NEW YORK, WEDNESDAY, SEPTEMBER 12, 2001   Et beyond the greater New York metropolitan area   75 CENTS

U.S. ATTACKED

HIJACKED JETS DESTROY TWIN TOWERS AND HIT PENTAGON IN DAY OF TERROR

A CREEPING HORROR

Buildings Burn and Fall as Onlookers Search for Elusive Safety

By N. R. KLEINFIELD

It kept getting worse.

The horror arrived in episodic bursts of chilling disbelief, signified first by trembling floors, sharp eruptions, cracked windows. There was the actual unfathomable realization of a gaping, flaming hole in a first one of the tall towers, and then the same hang all over again in its twin. Then was the merciless sight of bodies helplessly tumbling out, some of them in flames.

Finally, the mighty towers themselves were reduced to nothing. Dense plumes of smoke raced through the downtown avenues, coursing between the buildings, shaped like tornadoes on their sides.

Every sound was cause for alarm. A plane appeared overhead. Was another one coming? No, it was a fighter jet. But was it friend or enemy? People scrambled for their lives, but they didn't know where to go. Should they go north, south, east, west? Stay astride, go indoors? People hid behind cars and each other. Some contemplated jumping into the river.

For those trying to flee the very epicenter of the collapsing World Trade Center towers, the most horrid thought of all finally dawned on them: nowhere was safe.

For several panic-stricken hours yesterday morning, people in Lower Manhattan witnessed the inexpressible, the incomprehensible, the unthinkable. "I don't know what the gates of hell look like, but it's got to be like this," said John Maloney, a security director for an American firm in the trade center. "I'm a combat veteran, Vietnam, and I never saw anything like this."

The first warnings were small ones. Blocks away, Jim Farmer, a film composer, was having breakfast at a small restaurant on West Broadway. He heard the sound of a jet. An odd sound — too loud, it seemed, to be

Continued on Page A7

A Somber Bush Says Terrorism Cannot Prevail

By ELISABETH BUMILLER with DAVID E. SANGER

WASHINGTON, Sept. 11 — President Bush vowed tonight to retaliate against those responsible for today's attacks on New York and Washington, declaring that he would "make no distinction between the terrorists who committed these acts and those who harbor them."

"These acts of mass murder were intended to frighten our nation into chaos and retreat, but they have failed," the president said in his first speech to the nation from the Oval Office. "Our country is strong. Terrorist acts can shake the foundation of our biggest buildings, but they cannot touch the foundation of America."

His speech came after a day of trauma that seems destined to define his presidency. Seeking to at once calm the nation and declare his determination to exact retribution, he told a country numbed by repeated scenes of carnage that "these acts shattered steel, but they cannot dent the steel of American resolve."

Mr. Bush spoke only hours after returning from a zigzag course across the country, as his Secret Service and military security teams moved him from Florida, where he woke up this morning expecting to tout his education bill, to command posts in Louisiana and Nebraska before it was determined the attacks had probably ended and he could safely return to the capital.

It was a sign of the catastrophic

Continued on Page A4

AMERICAN TARGETS A ball of fire exploded outward after the second of two jetliners slammed into the World Trade Center; less than two hours later, both of the 110-story towers were gone. Hijackers crashed a third airliner into the Pentagon, setting off a huge explosion and fire.

President Vows to Exact Punishment for 'Evil'

By SERGE SCHMEMANN

Hijackers rammed jetliners into each of New York's World Trade Center towers yesterday, toppling both in a hellish storm of ash, glass, smoke and leaping victims, while a third jetliner crashed into the Pentagon in Virginia. There was no official count, but President Bush said thousands had perished, and in the immediate aftermath the calamity was already being ranked the worst and most audacious terror attack in American history.

The attacks seemed carefully coordinated. The hijacked planes were all en route to California, and therefore gorged with fuel, and their departures were spaced within an hour and 40 minutes. The first, American Airlines Flight 11, a Boeing 767 out of Boston for Los Angeles, crashed into the north tower at 8:48 a.m. Eighteen minutes later, United Airlines Flight 175, also headed from Boston to Los Angeles, plowed into the south tower.

Then an American Airlines Boeing 757, Flight 77, left Washington's Dulles International Airport bound for Los Angeles, but instead hit the western part of the Pentagon, the military headquarters where 24,000 people work, at 9:40 a.m. Finally, United Airlines Flight 93, a Boeing 757 flying from Newark to San Francisco, crashed near Pittsburgh, raising the possibility that its hijackers had failed in whatever their mission was.

There were indications that the hijackers on at least two of the planes were armed with knives. Attorney General John Ashcroft told reporters in the evening that the suspects on Flight 11 were armed that way. And Barbara Olson, a television commentator who was traveling on American Flight 77, managed to reach her husband, Solicitor General Theodore Olson, by cell phone and to tell him that the hijackers were armed with knives and a box cutter.

In all, 266 people perished in the four planes and several score more were known dead elsewhere. Numerous firefighters, police officers and other rescue workers who responded to the initial disaster in Lower Manhattan were killed or injured when the buildings collapsed. Hundreds were treated for cuts, broken bones, burns and smoke inhalation.

But the real carnage was concealed for now by the twisted, smoking, ash-choked carcasses of the twin towers, in which thousands of people used to work on a weekday. The collapse of the towers caused another World Trade Center building to fall 7 hours later, and several

Continued on Page A14

SECOND PLANE United Airlines Flight 175 nearing the trade center's south tower.

Awaiting the Aftershocks

Washington and Nation Plunge Into Fight With Enemy Hard to Identify and Punish

By R. W. APPLE Jr.

WASHINGTON, Sept. 11 — Today's devastating and astonishingly well-coordinated attacks on the World Trade Center towers in New York and on the Pentagon outside of Washington plunged the nation into a warlike struggle against an enemy that will be hard to identify with certainty and hard to punish with precision.

The whole nation — to a degree the whole world — shook as hijacked airliners plunged into buildings that symbolize the financial and military might of the United States. The sense of security and self-confidence that Americans take as their birthright suffered a grievous blow, from which recovery will be slow. The aftershocks will be nearly as bad, as hundreds and possibly thousands of people discover that friends or relatives died awful, fiery deaths.

Scenes of chaos and destruction evocative of the nightmare world of Hieronymus Bosch, with smoke and debris blotting out the sun, were carried by television into homes and workplaces across the nation. Echoing Franklin D. Roosevelt's description of the attack on Pearl Harbor as an event "which will live in infamy," Gov. George E. Pataki of New York, a Republican, spoke of "an incredible outrage" and Senator Charles E. Schumer of New York, a Democrat, spoke of "a dastardly attack."

But mere words seem inadequate to describe the sense of shock and horror that people felt. As Washington struggled to regain a sense of equilibrium, with warplanes and heavily armed helicopters crossing overhead, and present national security officials earnestly debated the possibility of a Congressional declaration of war — not against precisely whom, and in what exact circumstances? Warships were maneuvering to protect New York and Washington. The North American Air Defense Command, which had seemed to many a relic of the cold war, adopted a pos-

Continued on Page A24

MORE ON THE ATTACKS

RESCUERS BECOME VICTIMS Firefighters who rushed to the trade center were killed.   PAGE A1

SEARCH FOR SURVIVORS Some people trapped in the rubble for hours were rescued.   PAGE A1

OFFICIALS SUSPECT BIN LADEN Eavesdropping intercepts after the attacks were cited.   PAGE A21

TERRORISTS EXPLOIT WEAKNESS Investigators had criticized precautions against hijacking.   PAGE A17

CASUALTIES IN WASHINGTON An unknown number of people were killed at the Pentagon.   PAGE A1

FOR HOME DELIVERY CALL 1-800-NYTIMES

U.S. Attacked.

the evening that the suspects on Flight 11 were armed that way. And Barbara Olson, a television commentator who was traveling on American Flight 77, managed to reach her husband, Solicitor General Theodore Olson, by cell phone and to tell him that the hijackers were armed with knives and a box cutter.

In all, 266 people perished in the four planes and several score more were known dead elsewhere. Numerous firefighters, police officers, and other rescue workers who responded to the initial disaster in Lower Manhattan were killed or injured when the buildings collapsed. Hundreds were treated for cuts, broken bones, burns, and smoke inhalation.

But the real carnage was concealed for now by the twisted, smoking, ash-choked carcasses of the twin towers, in which thousands of people used to work on a weekday. The collapse of the towers caused another World Trade Center building to fall seven hours later, and several other buildings in the area were damaged or aflame.

"I have a sense it's a horrendous number of lives lost," said Mayor Rudolph W. Giuliani. "Right now we have to focus on saving as many lives as possible." The mayor warned that "the numbers are going to be very, very high." He added that the medical examiner's office will be ready "to deal with thousands and thousands of bodies if they have to."

For hours after the attacks, rescuers were stymied by other buildings that threatened to topple. But by 11 p.m., rescuers had been able to begin serious efforts to locate and remove survivors. Mr. Giuliani said two Port Authority police officers had been pulled from the ruins, and he said hope existed that more people could be saved. Earlier, police officer volunteers using dogs had found four bodies in the smoldering, stories-high pile of rubble where the towers had once stood and had taken them to a makeshift morgue in the lobby of an office building at Vesey and West Streets.

Within an hour of the attacks, the United States was on a war footing. The military was put on the highest state of alert, National Guard units were called out in Washington and New York, and two aircraft carriers were dispatched to New York harbor. President Bush remained aloft in Air Force One, following a secretive route and making only brief stopovers at Air Force bases in Louisiana and Nebraska before finally setting down in Washington at 7 p.m. His wife and daughters were evacuated to a secure, unidentified location. The White House, the Pentagon and the Capitol were evacuated, except for the Situation Room in the White House where Vice President Cheney remained in charge, giving the eerie impression of a national capital virtually stripped of its key institutions.

Nobody immediately claimed responsibility for the attacks. But the scale and sophistication of the operation, the extraordinary planning required for concerted hijackings by terrorists who had to be familiar with modern jetliners, and the history of major attacks on American targets in recent years led many officials and experts to point to Osama bin Laden, the Islamic militant believed to operate out of Afghanistan. Afghanistan's hard-line Taliban rulers rejected such suggestions, but officials took that as a defensive measure. Senator Orrin Hatch, Republican of Utah, told reporters that the United States had some evidence that people associated with Mr. bin Laden had sent out messages "actually saying over the airwaves, private airwaves at that, that they had hit two targets." In the evening, explosions were reported in Kabul, the Afghan capital. But officials at the Pentagon denied that the United States had attacked that city.

President Bush, facing his first major crisis in office, vowed that the United States would hunt down and punish those responsible for the "evil, despicable acts of terror," which, he said, took thousands of American lives. He said the United States would make no distinction between those who carried out the hijackings and those who harbored and supported them.

"These acts of mass murder were intended to frighten our nation into chaos and retreat, but they have failed," a somber president told the nation in an address from the Oval office shortly after 8:30 p.m. "The search is under way for those who are behind these evil acts," Mr. Bush said. "We will make no distinction between the terrorists who committed these acts and those who harbor them."

The repercussions of the attack swiftly spread across the nation. Air traffic across the United States was halted at least until today and international flights were diverted to Canada. Borders with Canada and Mexico were closed. Most federal buildings across the country were shut down. Major skyscrapers and a variety of other sites, ranging from Disney theme parks to the Golden Gate Bridge and United Nations headquarters in New York, were evacuated.

But it was in New York that the calamity achieved levels of horror and destruction known only in war. The largest city in the United States, the financial capital of the world, was virtually closed down. Transportation into Manhattan was halted, as was much of public transport within the city. Parts of Lower Manhattan were left without power, compelling Mayor Giuliani to order Battery Park City to be evacuated. Major stock exchanges closed. Primary elections for mayor and other city offices were cancelled. Thousands of workers, released from their offices in Lower Manhattan but with no way to get home except by foot, set off in vast streams, down the avenues and across the bridges under a beautiful, clear sky, accompanied by the unceasing serenade of sirens.

While doctors and nurses at hospitals across the city tended to hundreds of damaged people, a disquieting sense grew throughout the day at other triage centers and emergency rooms that there would, actually, be less work: the morgues were going to be busiest.   15

A sense of shock, grief, and solidarity spread rapidly through the city. There was the expectation that friends and relatives would be revealed among the victims. Schools prepared to let students stay overnight if they could not get home or if it emerged that there was no one to go home to. There was also the fear that it was not over: stores reported a run on basic goods. And there was the urge to help. Thousands of New Yorkers lined up outside hospitals to donate blood.

As in great crises past, people exchanged stories of where they were when they heard the news. "There is a controlled professionalism, but also a sense of shock," said Mark G. Ackerman, an official at the St. Vincent Medical Center. "Obviously New York and all of us have experienced a trauma that is unparalleled." "I invite New Yorkers to join in prayer," said Cardinal Edward M. Egan as he emerged from the emergency room of St. Vincent's in blue hospital garb. "This is a tragedy that this great city can handle. I am amazed at the goodness of our police and our firefighters and our hospital people."

All communications creaked under the load of the sudden emergency. Mobile phones became all but useless, intercity lines were clogged and major Internet servers reported overloads.

The area around the World Trade Center resembled a desert after a terrible sandstorm. Parts of buildings, crushed vehicles, and the shoes, purses, umbrellas, and baby carriages of those who fled lay covered with thick, gray ash, through which weeping people wandered in search of safety, each with a story of pure horror.

Imez Graham, 40, and Dee Howard, 37, both of whom worked on the 20 61st floor of the north tower, were walking up Chambers Street, covered in soot to their gracefully woven dreadlocks caked in soot, barefoot. They had spent an hour walking down the stairs after the first explosion. They were taken to an ambulance, when the building collapsed. They jumped out and began to walk home. "They need me; I've got to get home," Ms. Howard said. Where was that? "As far away from here as possible." In Chinatown, a woman offered them a pair of dainty Chinese sandals. Nearby, construction workers offered to hose the soot off passing people.

The twin pillars of the World Trade Center were among the best-known landmarks in New York, 110-floor unadorned blocks that dominated any approach to Manhattan. It is probably that renown, and the thousands of people who normally work there each weekday, that led Islamic militants to target the towers for destruction already in 1993, then by parking vans loaded with explosives in the basement.

There is no way to know how many people were at work shortly before 9 a.m. when the first jetliners sliced into the north tower, also known as One World Trade Center. CNN and other television networks were quick to focus their cameras on the disaster, enabling untold numbers of viewers to witness the second jetliner as it banked into the south tower 18 minutes later, blowing a cloud of flame and debris out the other side.

Even more viewers were tuned in by 9:50 a.m. when the south tower suddenly vanished in swirling billows of ash, collapsing in on itself. Then at 10:29 a.m. the north tower followed. A choking grey cloud billowed out, blocking out the bright sunshine and chasing thousands of panicked workers through the canyons of Lower Manhattan. Plumes continued to rise high over the city late into the night.

"The screaming was just horrendous," recalled Carol Webster, an official of the Nyack College Alliance Seminary who had just emerged from the

PATH trains when the carnage began. "Every time there would be another explosion, people would start screaming and thronging again."

The scenes of horror were indelible; people who left from the broken   25
towers, people who fought for pay phones, people white with soot and red with blood. "We saw people jumping from the tower as the fire was going on," said Steve Baker, 27. "The sky went black, all this stuff came onto us, we ran."

The timing was murderous for the armada of rescue vehicles that gathered after the planes crashed, and were caught under the collapsing buildings. Many rescue workers were reported killed or injured, and the anticipation that Building Seven would soon follow led to a suspension of operations. The firefighters union said that at least 200 of its members had died. Mayor Giuliani, along with the police and fire commissioners and the director of emergency management, was forced to abandon a temporary command center at 75 Barclay Street, a block from the World Trade Center, and the mayor emerged with his gray suit covered with ash.

In the evening, officials reported that Buildings Five and Seven of the World Trade Center had also collapsed, and buildings all around the complex had their windows blown out. The Rector Street subway station collapsed, and the walkway at West Street was gone.

World leaders hastened to condemn the attacks, including Palestinian leader Yasir Arafat and Libya's Muammar el-Qaddafi. European leaders began quiet discussions last night about how they might assist the United States in striking back, and Russia's president, Vladimir Putin, joined in expressing support for a retaliatory strike. But in the West Bank city of Nablus, rejoicing Palestinians, who have been locked in a bitter struggle with Israel for almost a year, went into the streets to chant, "God is great!" and to distribute candies to celebrate the attacks.

Many governments took their own precautions against attack. Israel evacuated many of its embassies abroad, and nonessential staffers at NATO headquarters in Brussels were ordered home. In Afghanistan, the ruling Taliban argued that Mr. bin Laden could not have been responsible for the attacks. "What happened in the United States was not a job of ordinary people," an official, Abdul Hai Mutmaen, told Reuters. "It could have been the work of governments. Osama bin Lader cannot do this work."

Apart from the major question of who was responsible, a host of other   30
questions were certain to be at the forefront in coming days and weeks. One was the timing — why September 11? The date seemed to have no obvious meaning. One of the men convicted in the bombing of the United States Embassy in Nairobi in 1998, in which 213 were killed, was originally scheduled for sentencing on September 12. But the sentencing of the man, Mohamed Rasheed Daoud al-'Owhali, had been put off to mid-October. It was possible that Mr. Al-'Owhali and the others convicted with him were close witnesses to the bombings, since terror suspects typically await sentencing at the Metropolitan Correctional Center in Lower Manhattan. Officials have not confirmed that the convicted Nairobi bombers are there.

Many questions would also be raised about how hijackers managed to seize four jets with all the modern safeguards in place. Initial information was sketchy, although a passenger on the United Airlines jetliner that crashed in Pennsylvania managed to make a cellular phone call from the toilet. "We are being hijacked, we are being hijacked," the man shouted at 9:58 a.m. As he was speaking, the plane crashed about eight miles east of Jennerstown, killing all 45 aboard.

For all the questions, what was clear was that the World Trade Center would take its place among the great calamities of American history, a day of infamy like Pearl Harbor, Oklahoma City, Lockerbie. The very absence of the towers would become a symbol after their domination of the New York skyline for 25 years. Though initial reviews were mixed when the towers were dedicated in 1976, they came into their own as landmarks with passing years. King Kong climbed one tower in a remake of the movie classic. In April, the Port Authority of New York and New Jersey, which ran the World Trade Center through its first 30 years, leased the complex for $3.2 billion to a group led by Larry A. Silverstein, a developer, and Westfield America Inc. In recent years, the complex has filled up with tenants and revenues have increased. In addition to the towers — designed by the architect Minoru Yamasaki, each 1,350 feet tall — the complex included four other buildings, two of which were also gone, for a total of 12 million square feet of rentable office space.

Morning of Mayhem

By 8 a.m. yesterday morning, a chain of events had been set in motion that, two hours later, would erase the World Trade Center towers from the New York City skyline, rip open the west wall of the Pentagon, drop four planes from the sky and kill an uncounted number of people. Following is a look at how events unfolded.

7:55 a.m.　　American Airlines Flight 11 leaves Boston bound for Los Angeles.

8:00 a.m.　　United Airlines Flight 93 leaves Newark bound for San Francisco.

8:10 a.m.　　American Airlines Flight 77 departs Washington bound for Los Angeles.

8:15 a.m.　　United Airlines Flight 175 departs Boston bound for Los Angeles.

8:48 a.m.　　Flight 11 hits the north tower of the World Trade Center.

9:00 a.m.　　President Bush, who is in Sarasota, Fla., is informed of the attacks.

9:06 a.m.	Flight 175 strikes the south tower of the World Trade Center.
9:15 a.m.	President Bush makes statement condemning terrorist attacks.
9:18 a.m.	The F.A.A. shuts down all New York City airports.
9:21 a.m.	All bridges and tunnels into Manhattan are closed.
9:40 a.m.	Flight 77 hits the Pentagon.
	The F.A.A. grounds all flights.
9:50 a.m.	South tower of the World Trade Center collapses.
10:00 a.m.	President Bush leaves Sarasota. The White House is evacuated.
10:10 a.m.	Flight 93 crashes in Somerset County, 80 miles southeast of Pittsburgh. A portion of the Pentagon collapses.
10:28 a.m.	North tower of the World Trade Center collapses.
11:05 a.m.	U.N. headquarters in New York is fully evacuated.
12:04 p.m.	Los Angeles International airport is closed and evacuated.
12:15 p.m.	San Francisco International Airport is closed and evacuated.
1:05 p.m.	President Bush speaks from Barksdale Air Force Base in Louisiana.
1:45 p.m.	Pentagon announces that warships and aircraft carriers will take up positions in the New York and Washington areas.

QUESTIONS

1. There were four separate articles on page 1 of the *New York Times* on September 12, 2001. Schmemann's, the lead article, gave an overview of the events of September 11. How does he arrange his story? Does he rely on a chronological arrangement, or does he make other choices? If so, describe them.
2. How many sources does the writer draw on for this piece? What kinds of sources are they? Why do Imez Graham and Dee Howard appear in this article (paragraph 20)?
3. Reporters are supposed to be objective. How well does Schmemann meet this criterion? What examples of evaluative language can you find? For example, he refers to the wrecked towers as "carcasses" (paragraph 6). What is the effect of such language?
4. Look at the first pages of other newspapers printed on September 12, 2001, in the United States or other countries. Do they simply reprint Schmemann's story from the *Times*, or do they use other material? How do these other writers present the events?

5. Look at the front page of a newspaper from December 8, 1941, the day after the Japanese attack on Pearl Harbor, Hawaii. How does the presentation of that disaster compare with this lead article from September 12, 2001?
6. Many books and articles appeared after the events of September 11. Examine at least six, and write a report on one that you think is the most effective, giving the reasons for your choice.

MAKING CONNECTIONS

Compare Schmemann's report with that of another disaster, William L. Laurence's "Atomic Bombing of Nagasaki Told by Flight Member" (p. 387), which also appeared in the *New York Times*. Both writers witnessed an event, though one was a more active participant.

EDGY FIRST COLLEGE ASSIGNMENT:
Study the Koran

Patrik Jonsson

Born in Sweden in 1969, Patrik Jonsson immigrated to the United States with his family when he was eight, living first in Georgia and later in New Hampshire. He got his first newspaper job after graduating from high school and has worked for the Portsmouth (N.H.) Press, *the* Portsmouth Herald, *and the* Deming (N.M.) Headlight. *Currently a staff reporter for the* Christian Science Monitor, *he is based in Raleigh, North Carolina, and covers the southern region. He has also contributed to the* Boston Globe. *Of the following piece, written for the* Monitor *in the summer of 2002, Jonsson said, "The Koran piece was one of the most interesting I've done. The debate really seemed to strike at the heart of some hard-to-untangle emotions Americans are experiencing after 9/11, while trying to figure out just exactly how to deal with the often-ambiguous duality of what the Koran teaches."*

Brynn Hardman was all set to sit back and glide through some Danielle Steel on Atlantic Beach this summer. Just graduated from high school in Raleigh, North Carolina, she was looking forward to a bit of light fare before hitting the heavy tomes of freshman year. Instead, the tanned teen is immersed in the curlicue phrasings of what would have been her personal last choice for beachside reading: the Koran.[1]

Ms. Hardman and 3,500 other soon-to-be freshmen at the University of North Carolina in Chapel Hill have a controversial assignment: to delve into excerpts of a text invoked by the September 11 terrorists. Only two pages into *Approaching the Qur'an*, by Michael Sells, Hardman says the book is "an awful choice."

For the past three years, UNC freshmen have been handed summer reading tasks on topics such as the growth of Civil War reenactments and the Vietnam War. But this year's choice raises a question other campuses are likely to face as the United States wages its war on terrorism: How far should a public school go in educating students about religion when the

---

[1]*Koran (or Qur'an):* The sacred book of Islam. Muslims believe it contains the actual word of God (Allah) as transmitted by the angel Gabriel to the prophet Mohammad.

424

faith in question sits at the center of present-day conflicts — and is closely linked in many students' minds to terror?

"The timing couldn't be worse," says Jody Hardman, a public school teacher who's on campus with her daughter for an orientation session. "At a time when we're told we can't say 'under God' during the pledge, here's a public school assigning the Koran." Last week, three students and a conservative Christian organization took their discontent a step further and filed a lawsuit.

UNC officials say they have not only the prerogative but the responsibility to open students' eyes to the Muslim religion and culture. Indeed, pundits here on campus say UNC's experiment should be a call to other institutions to follow suit — for the good of the country. But critics say this bulwark of liberal thought — a campus where antiwar signs went up even before bombs had begun falling over Afghanistan — has crossed the line by forcing students to read the book. The controversy simply fuels UNC's reputation of chief gadfly here, smack in the heart of Baptist country. People with religious objections can opt out by writing an essay explaining why, but they still must attend a group discussion when they arrive in mid-August.

"The question is, what's the big role of the university here?" says Carl Ernst, the religious-studies professor who recommended the book to a selection committee of faculty, staff, and students. "[Critics] assume the choice represents advocacy, but we just want to advance knowledge," he says. "This will not explain the terrorist attacks of last September, but this will be a first step toward understanding something important about Islamic spirituality and to see its adherents as human beings."

So far, no other university has gone so far as to mandate the reading of the Koran, although many schools have seen renewed interest in religious and international studies after September 11.

No Proselytizing Here

For many people, a quick perusal of *Approaching the Qur'an* would dispel the idea that this assignment is a scheme to proselytize. Instead, the book about the "early revelations," which includes a CD of sung prayer, delves into the mystery and poetry of the spoken Koran. It explores how the text has wended its way into the hearts of 1 billion people and deep into the framework of politics and culture in the East. "The purpose of this book is neither to refute nor to promote the Qur'anic message," Mr. Sells writes. "Rather, the goal is to allow those who do not have access to the Qur'an in its recited, Arabic form to encounter one of the most influential texts in human history in a manner that is accessible."

For the parents of freshman Jennifer DeCurtis of Asheville, North Carolina, the choice of a book that focuses on a major world religion is appropriate — even during a war with religious overtones. "I think it will open their thinking up to what Islam is really all about," says dad David DeCurtis. "And

I think that's an appropriate role for a school like UNC." Some parents, on the other hand, have refused to let their children attend because of the assignment. Other parents and alumni have called the chancellor to complain.

What's more, the ACLU[2] has vowed to oversee some of the discussion   10 groups, which will be led by about 180 faculty volunteers who were trained this summer. School officials say the program will "pass the smell test." But they won't comment on the lawsuit, which was filed by three freshmen of various religious backgrounds and the Virginia-based Family Policy Network.

John Sanders, a fellow at the conservative John Locke Foundation in Raleigh, North Carolina, which has long questioned a variety of university actions, says he wouldn't have a problem if the school was merely urging teenagers to read the text before they come to school. It's the requirement that rubs. "We're at war, after all," says Mr. Sanders. "This isn't akin to teaching the Bible. We do need to understand them, yes, but it's not the best thing to cram this down people's throats right now."

Still, Fred Eckel, faculty adviser for the Campus Crusade for Christ, says that studying a variety of religious texts may not be a bad idea, especially since the school already has an energetic religious-studies department. "As a person who supports prayer in schools, it makes no sense to object to the use of other religious texts in the classroom, as long as the discussions are appropriate," Professor Eckel says. "It's a positive thing to discuss issues in the Koran, and it may also further discussions that need to be going on within the Christian community."

For Professor Ernst, the choice to bring the Koran to Baptist country isn't so revolutionary. He points to the narrative of Omar Ibin Sayyid, a Muslim brought here as a slave from Africa in the eighteenth century and the subject of an exhibit soon to go up at the Ackland Museum on campus. "Studies suggest that about 15 percent of slaves were indeed Muslims," he says.

What's more, many of North Carolina's cities — which have attracted Middle Easterners seeking jobs and education — are now dotted with mosques. One local Muslim was arrested during the post-September 11 investigations last fall, and a national newsweekly recently documented that at least one "American Al Qaeda" made his home in the region before departing for the Middle East.

Offering Insights

At its heart, however, the assignment is meant to give insight into why   15 the Koran has such a strong hold on its adherents, UNC officials say. They point out that the book also makes clear that the Koran condemns using

---

[2]*ACLU:* American Civil Liberties Union, a nonpartisan organization whose mission is to preserve the individual rights guaranteed by the Constitution and laws of the United States.

the term *jihad*, or struggle, as a justification for politically based battles—
one of the main differences of opinion between the September 11 terrorists
and many other Muslims.

As author Sells writes: "At the day of reckoning . . . meaning and justice are brought together. The Qur'an warns those who reject the day of
reckoning and who are entrenched in lives of acquisition and injustice that
an accounting awaits them. Yet these warnings are not more dire or grim
than the warnings the biblical Jesus gives in the parables about burning and
gnashing of teeth. And in Qur'anic recitation, all Qur'anic passages on
alienation between humankind and God are dominated by a tone, not of
anger or wrath, but of sadness."

Such messages are important, UNC faculty and administrators say, to
counter the hate-filled rhetoric put forth by Osama bin Laden and other Islamic radicals who see themselves at war with the Western world. "If
Americans don't want to learn about them because of the attacks last September, we are missing an opportunity to advance ourselves and learn
about who we are, as well," Ernst says. "After all, there are more Muslims
in the United States than Jews."

UNC Chancellor James Moeser, who approved the committee's book
choice, says, "This is Chapel Hill being Chapel Hill. People are proud of us
for doing this. I had a representative from a Jewish group here tell me,
'Here I am, a Jew teaching about the Koran to Southern Baptists.' The
point is, this is the front door to an exciting experience and a sample of
what they will be getting at Chapel Hill."

Predictably, perhaps, students who were on campus this summer for an
orientation largely criticized the assignment. Ford Williams doesn't mind
being forced to study during his last official summer of childhood. His objection is more personal. A soccer standout at Broughton, he and his team
were in Trinidad and Tobago on September 11. While the tourney went on,
armed guards kept the team under close watch. The players found it almost
impossible to concentrate. "I don't really care about learning about [Mus-
lims] right now," he says. "I'm not in an enlightened state of mind. If anything, I want to worry about ourselves and turn to our own religion."
Kevin Silva from Bedford, Massachusetts, agrees: "I feel kind of forced to
do something I wouldn't normally do."

But their new friend Jon Van Assen from South River, New Jersey,   20
takes a more pragmatic view of the assignment: "It's provocative, but that's
what gets people thinking," he says.

Mr. Williams adds a final assessment: "It's not like reading 'Tom
Sawyer,' that's for sure."

QUESTIONS

1. This news story appeared in September 2002. What objections does it
   raise to requiring students to read the Koran? Who is quoted? How
   would you have reacted to this assignment? Explain.

2. Carl Ernst, a University of North Carolina religious studies professor, says "The question is, what's the big role of the university here?" (paragraph 6). How does he answer this question? Do you agree with him? Would his answer apply to your college or university?
3. If you have been in a class where an assigned reading was considered offensive or too controversial by one or more students who objected to reading it, how did the instructor handle the situation? What was your view of the matter?
4. Do some research into the controversy over reading the Koran at the University of North Carolina at Chapel Hill. Did the lawsuit filed by "three freshmen . . . and the Virginia-based Family Policy Network" (paragraph 10) ever come to trial, or was it dropped? Write a report of your findings.

MAKING CONNECTIONS

Read Bernard Lewis's "I'm Right, You're Wrong, Go to Hell" (p. 536), and write an essay in which you discuss religious values and attitudes, drawing upon both Lewis and Jonsson for examples. You may wish to reflect, explain, or argue about these matters, but try to make it clear which you are doing — wondering about something, answering a question, or making a point.

NICKEL AND DIMED:
On (Not) Getting By in America

Barbara Ehrenreich

A native of Butte, Montana, Barbara Ehrenreich (b. 1941) is one of the country's most outspoken social critics. After graduating from Reed College, Ehrenreich earned her Ph.D. in biology from Roosevelt University in Chicago. Instead of becoming a research scientist, though, she decided to pursue liberal political activism. As she began working on leaflets and newsletters, she has said, writing "crept up on" her. She was soon a regular contributor to Ms. *magazine and has since written for* The New Republic, Mother Jones, *and* Time, *among many other periodicals. Ehrenreich's books include* Complaints and Disorders: The Sexual Politics of Sickness *(1973),* Fear of Falling: The Inner Life of the Middle Class *(1989),* The Worst Years of Our Lives: Irreverent Notes from the Decade of Greed *(1990),* The Snarling Citizen: Collected Essays *(1995),* Blood Rites: Origins and History of the Passions of War *(1997), and* Bait and Switch: The (Futile) Pursuit of the American Dream *(2005). The recipient of a Guggenheim Fellowship and a MacArthur grant, Ehrenreich contributed the following essay, which provided the basis for her 2001 book of the same title, to* The Atlantic *in 1999. As she later told an interviewer, it began in a meeting with the editor of the magazine when "the conversation drifted to talking about welfare reform and the assumption that these single moms could just get out there in the workforce and get a job and then everything would be okay. They'd be lifted out of poverty. We were both agreeing that nobody seems to see that the math doesn't work. That's when I made this, perhaps disastrous, suggestion that somebody should go out there and do the old-fashioned kind of journalism, just try it for themselves and write about it. I did not expect him to say, 'Yeah, great idea. It should be you.'"*

At the beginning of June 1998 I leave behind everything that normally soothes the ego and sustains the body—home, career, companion, reputation, ATM card—for a plunge into the low-wage workforce. There, I become another, occupationally much diminished "Barbara Ehrenreich"—depicted on job-application forms as a divorced homemaker whose sole work experience consists of housekeeping in a few private homes. I am terrified, at the beginning, of being unmasked for what I am: a middle-class journalist setting out to explore the world that welfare mothers are entering, at the rate of approximately 50,000 a month, as welfare reform kicks in. Happily, though, my fears turn out to be entirely unwarranted: during a month of poverty and toil, my name goes unnoticed and for the most part unuttered. In this parallel universe where my father never got out of the mines and I never got through college, I am "baby," "honey," "blondie," and, most commonly, "girl."

My first task is to find a place to live. I figure that if I can earn $7 an hour — which, from the want ads, seems doable — I can afford to spend $500 on rent, or maybe, with severe economies, $600. In the Key West area, where I live, this pretty much confines me to flophouses and trailer homes — like the one, a pleasing fifteen-minute drive from town, that has no aircondi- tioning, no screens, no fans, no television, and, by way of diversion, only the challenge of evading the landlord's Doberman pinscher. The big problem with this place, though, is the rent, which at $675 a month is well beyond my reach. All right, Key West is expensive. But so is New York City, or the Bay Area, or Jackson Hole, or Telluride, or Boston, or any other place where tourists and the wealthy compete for living space with the people who clean their toilets and fry their hash browns.[1] Still, it is a shock to realize that "trailer trash" has become, for me, a demographic category to aspire to.

So I decide to make the common trade-off between affordability and convenience, and go for a $500-a-month efficiency thirty miles up a twolane highway from the employment opportunities of Key West, meaning forty- five minutes if there's no road construction and I don't get caught behind some sun-dazed Canadian tourists. I hate the drive, along a roadside stud- ded with white crosses commemorating the more effective head-on colli- sions, but it's a sweet little place — a cabin, more or less, set in the swampy back yard of the converted mobile home where my landlord, an affable TV repairman, lives with his bartender girlfriend. Anthropologically speaking, a bustling trailer park would be preferable, but here I have a gleaming white floor and a firm mattress, and the few resident bugs are easily vanquished.

Besides, I am not doing this for the anthropology. My aim is nothing so mistily subjective as to "experience poverty" or find out how it "really feels" to be a long-term low-wage worker. I've had enough unchosen en- counters with poverty and the world of low-wage work to know it's not a place you want to visit for touristic purposes; it just smells too much like fear. And with all my real-life assets — bank account, IRA, health insur- ance, multiroom home — waiting indulgently in the background, I am, of course, thoroughly insulated from the terrors that afflict the genuinely poor.

---

[1]According to the Department of Housing and Urban Development, the "fair- market rent" for an efficiency is $551 here in Monroe County, Florida. A compara- ble rent in the five boroughs of New York City is $704; in San Francisco, $713; and in the heart of Silicon Valley, $808. The fair-market rent for an area is defined as the amount that would be needed to pay rent plus utilities for "privately owned, decent, safe, and sanitary rental housing of a modest (non-luxury) nature with suitable amenities."

No, this is a purely objective, scientific sort of mission. The humanitarian rationale for welfare reform—as opposed to the more punitive and stingy impulses that may actually have motivated it—is that work will lift poor women out of poverty while simultaneously inflating their self-esteem and hence their future value in the labor market. Thus, whatever the hassles involved in finding child care, transportation, etc., the transition from welfare to work will end happily, in greater prosperity for all. Now there are many problems with this comforting prediction, such as the fact that the economy will inevitably undergo a downturn, eliminating many jobs. Even without a downturn, the influx of a million former welfare recipients into the low-wage labor market could depress wages by as much as 11.9 percent, according to the Economic Policy Institute (EPI) in Washington, D.C.

But is it really possible to make a living on the kinds of jobs currently available to unskilled people? Mathematically, the answer is no, as can be shown by taking $6 to $7 an hour, perhaps subtracting a dollar or two an hour for child care, multiplying by 160 hours a month, and comparing the result to the prevailing rents. According to the National Coalition for the Homeless, for example, in 1998 it took, on average nationwide, an hourly wage of $8.89 to afford a one-bedroom apartment, and the Preamble Center for Public Policy estimates that the odds against a typical welfare recipient's landing a job at such a "living wage" are about 97 to 1. If these numbers are right, low-wage work is not a solution to poverty and possibly not even to homelessness.

It may seem excessive to put this proposition to an experimental test. As certain family members keep unhelpfully reminding me, the viability of low-wage work could be tested, after a fashion, without ever leaving my study. I could just pay myself $7 an hour for eight hours a day, charge myself for room and board, and total up the numbers after a month. Why leave the people and work that I love? But I am an experimental scientist by training. In that business, you don't just sit at a desk and theorize; you plunge into the everyday chaos of nature, where surprises lurk in the most mundane measurements. Maybe, when I got into it, I would discover some hidden economies in the world of the low-wage worker. After all, if 30 percent of the workforce toils for less than $8 an hour, according to the EPI, they may have found some tricks as yet unknown to me. Maybe—who knows?—I would even be able to detect in myself the bracing psychological effects of getting out of the house, as promised by the welfare wonks at places like the Heritage Foundation. Or, on the other hand, maybe there would be unexpected costs—physical, mental, or financial—to throw off all my calculations. Ideally, I should do this with two small children in tow, that being the welfare average, but mine are grown and no one is willing to lend me theirs for a month-long vacation in penury. So this is not the perfect experiment, just a test of the best possible case: an unencumbered woman, smart and even strong, attempting to live more or less off the land.

On the morning of my first full day of job searching, I take a red pen to the want ads, which are auspiciously numerous. Everyone in Key West's booming "hospitality industry" seems to be looking for someone like me — trainable, flexible, and with suitably humble expectations as to pay. I know I possess certain traits that might be advantageous — I'm white and, I like to think, well-spoken and poised — but I decide on two rules: One, I cannot use any skills derived from my education or usual work — not that there are a lot of want ads for satirical essayists anyway. Two, I have to take the best-paid job that is offered me and of course do my best to hold it; no Marxist rants or sneaking off to read novels in the ladies' room. In addition, I rule out various occupations for one reason or another: Hotel front-desk clerk, for example, which to my surprise is regarded as unskilled and pays around $7 an hour, gets eliminated because it involves standing in one spot for eight hours a day. Waitressing is similarly something I'd like to avoid, because I remember it leaving me bone tired when I was eighteen, and I'm decades of varicosities and back pain beyond that now. Telemarketing, one of the first refuges of the suddenly indigent, can be dismissed on grounds of personality. This leaves certain supermarket jobs, such as deli clerk, or housekeeping in Key West's thousands of hotel and guest rooms. House-keeping is especially appealing, for reasons both atavistic and practical: it's what my mother did before I came along, and it can't be too different from what I've been doing part-time, in my own home, all my life.

So I put on what I take to be a respectful-looking outfit of ironed Bermuda shorts and scooped-neck T-shirt and set out for a tour of the local hotels and supermarkets. Best Western, Econo Lodge, and HoJo's all let me fill out application forms, and these are, to my relief, interested in little more than whether I am a legal resident of the United States and have committed any felonies. My next stop is Winn-Dixie, the supermarket, which turns out to have a particularly onerous application process, featuring a fifteen-minute "interview" by computer since, apparently, no human on the premises is deemed capable of representing the corporate point of view. I am conducted to a large room decorated with posters illustrating how to look "professional" (it helps to be white and, if female, permed) and warning of the slick promises that union organizers might try to tempt me with. The interview is multiple choice: Do I have anything, such as childcare problems, that might make it hard for me to get to work on time? Do I think safety on the job is the responsibility of management? Then, popping up cunningly out of the blue: How many dollars' worth of stolen goods have I purchased in the last year? Would I turn in a fellow employee if I caught him stealing? Finally, "Are you an honest person?"

Apparently, I ace the interview, because I am told that all I have to do   10
is show up in some doctor's office tomorrow for a urine test. This seems to be a fairly general rule: if you want to stack Cheerio boxes or vacuum hotel rooms in chemically fascist America, you have to be willing to squat down and pee in front of some health worker (who has no doubt had to do the same thing herself). The wages Winn-Dixie is offering — $6 and a cou-

ple of dimes to start with — are not enough, I decide, to compensate for this indignity.[2]

I lunch at Wendy's, where $4.99 gets you unlimited refills at the Mexican part of the Super-bar, a comforting surfeit of refried beans and "cheese sauce." A teenage employee, seeing me studying the want ads, kindly offers me an application form, which I fill out, though here, too, the pay is just $6 and change an hour. Then it's off for a round of the locally owned inns and guesthouses. At "The Palms," let's call it, a bouncy manager actually takes me around to see the rooms and meet the existing housekeepers, who, I note with satisfaction, look pretty much like me — faded ex-hippie types in shorts with long hair pulled back in braids. Mostly, though, no one speaks to me or even looks at me except to proffer an application form. At my last stop, a palatial B&B, I wait twenty minutes to meet "Max," only to be told that there are no jobs now but there should be one soon, since "nobody lasts more than a couple weeks." (Because none of the people I talked to knew I was a reporter, I have changed their names to protect their privacy and, in some cases perhaps, their jobs.)

Three days go by like this, and, to my chagrin, no one out of the approximately twenty places I've applied calls me for an interview. I had been vain enough to worry about coming across as too educated for the jobs I sought, but no one even seems interested in finding out how overqualified I am. Only later will I realize that the want ads are not a reliable measure of the actual jobs available at any particular time. They are, as I should have guessed from Max's comment, the employers' insurance policy against the relentless turnover of the low-wage workforce. Most of the big hotels run ads almost continually, just to build a supply of applicants to replace the current workers as they drift away or are fired, so finding a job is just a matter of being at the right place at the right time and flexible enough to take whatever is being offered that day. This finally happens to me at one of the big discount hotel chains, where I go, as usual, for housekeeping and am sent, instead, to try out as a waitress at the attached "family restaurant," a dismal spot with a counter and about thirty tables that looks out on a parking garage and features such tempting fare as "Pollish [sic] sausage and BBQ sauce" on 95-degree days. Phillip, the dapper young West Indian who introduces himself as the manager, interviews me with about as

---

[2]According to the *Monthly Labor Review* (November 1996), 28 percent of work sites surveyed in the service industry conduct drug tests (corporate workplaces have much higher rates), and the incidence of testing has risen markedly since the Eighties. The rate of testing is highest in the South (56 percent of work sites polled), with the Midwest in second place (50 percent). The drug most likely to be detected — marijuana, which can be detected in urine for weeks — is also the most innocuous, while heroin and cocaine are generally undetectable three days after use. Prospective employees sometimes try to cheat the tests by consuming excessive amounts of liquids and taking diuretics and even masking substances available through the Internet.

much enthusiasm as if he were a clerk processing me for Medicare, the principal questions being what shifts can I work and when can I start. I mutter something about being woefully out of practice as a waitress, but he's already on to the uniform: I'm to show up tomorrow wearing black slacks and black shoes; he'll provide the rust-colored polo shirt with HEARTHSIDE embroidered on it, though I might want to wear my own shirt to get to work, ha ha. At the word "tomorrow," something between fear and indignation rises in my chest. I want to say, "Thank you for your time, sir, but this is just an experiment, you know, not my actual life."

So begins my career at the Hearthside, I shall call it, one small profit center within a global discount hotel chain, where for two weeks I work from 2:00 till 10:00 p.m. for $2.43 an hour plus tips.[3] In some futile bid for gentility, the management has barred employees from using the front door, so my first day I enter through the kitchen, where a red-faced man with shoulder-length blond hair is throwing frozen steaks against the wall and yelling, "Fuck this shit!" "That's just Jack," explains Gail, the wiry middleaged waitress who is assigned to train me. "He's on the rag again" — a condition occasioned, in this instance, by the fact that the cook on the morning shift had forgotten to thaw out the steaks. For the next eight hours, I run after the agile Gail, absorbing bits of instruction along with fragments of personal tragedy. All food must be trayed, and the reason she's so tired today is that she woke up in a cold sweat thinking of her boyfriend, who killed himself recently in an upstate prison. No refills on lemonade. And the reason he was in prison is that a few DUIs caught up with him, that's all, could have happened to anyone. Carry the creamers to the table in a monkey bowl, never in your hand. And after he was gone she spent several months living in her truck, peeing in a plastic pee bottle and reading by candlelight at night, but you can't live in a truck in the summer, since you need to have the windows down, which means anything can get in, from mosquitoes on up.

At least Gail puts to rest any fears I had of appearing overqualified. From the first day on, I find that of all the things I have left behind, such as home and identity, what I miss the most is competence. Not that I have ever felt utterly competent in the writing business, in which one day's success augurs nothing at all for the next. But in my writing life, I at least have some notion of procedure: do the research, make the outline, rough out a draft, etc. As a server, though, I am beset by requests like bees: more iced tea here, ketchup over there, a to-go box for table fourteen, and where are the high chairs, anyway? Of the twenty-seven tables, up to six are usually mine at

[3]According to the Fair Labor Standards Act, employers are not required to pay "tipped employees," such as restaurant servers, more than $2.13 an hour in direct wages. However, if the sum of tips plus $2.13 an hour falls below the minimum wage, or $5.15 an hour, the employer is required to make up the difference. This fact was not mentioned by managers or otherwise publicized at either of the restaurants where I worked.

any time, though on slow afternoons or if Gail is off, I sometimes have the whole place to myself. There is the touch-screen computer-ordering system to master, which is, I suppose, meant to minimize server-cook contact, but in practice requires constant verbal fine-tuning: "That's gravy on the mashed, okay? None on the meatloaf," and so forth — while the cook scowls as if I were inventing these refinements just to torment him. Plus, something I had forgotten in the years since I was eighteen: about a third of a server's job is "side work" that's invisible to customers — sweeping, scrubbing, slicing, re-filling, and restocking. If it isn't all done, every little bit of it, you're going to face the 6:00 p.m. dinner rush defenseless and probably go down in flames. I screw up dozens of times at the beginning, sustained in my shame entirely by Gail's support — "It's okay, baby, everyone does that sometime" — because, to my total surprise and despite the scientific detachment I am doing my best to maintain, I care.

The whole thing would be a lot easier if I could just skate through it as 15 Lily Tomlin in one of her waitress skits, but I was raised by the absurd Booker T. Washingtonian precept that says: If you're going to do something, do it well. In fact, "well" isn't good enough by half. Do it better than anyone has ever done it before. Or so said my father, who must have known what he was talking about because he managed to pull himself, and us with him, up from the mile-deep copper mines of Butte to the leafy suburbs of the Northeast, ascending from boilermakers to martinis before booze beat out ambition. As in most endeavors I have encountered in my life, doing it "better than anyone" is not a reasonable goal. Still, when I wake up at 4:00 a.m. in my own cold sweat, I am not thinking about the writing deadlines I'm neglecting; I'm thinking about the table whose order I screwed up so that one of the boys didn't get his kiddie meal until the rest of the family had moved on to their Key Lime pies. That's the other powerful motivation I hadn't expected — the customers, or "patients," as I can't help thinking of them on account of the mysterious vulnerability that seems to have left them temporarily unable to feed themselves. After a few days at the Hearthside, I feel the service ethic kick in like a shot of oxytocin, the nurturance hormone. The plurality of my customers are hard-working locals — truck drivers, construction workers, even house-keepers from the attached hotel — and I want them to have the closest to a "fine dining" experience that the grubby circumstances will allow. No "you guys" for me; everyone over twelve is "sir" or "ma'am." I ply them with iced tea and coffee refills; I return, mid-meal, to inquire how everything is; I doll up their salads with chopped raw mushrooms, summer squash slices, or whatever bits of produce I can find that have survived their sojourn in the cold-storage room mold-free.

There is Benny, for example, a short, tight-muscled sewer repairman, who cannot even think of eating until he has absorbed a half hour of air-conditioning and ice water. We chat about hyperthermia and electrolytes until he is ready to order some finicky combination like soup of the day, garden salad, and a side of grits. There are the German tourists who are so touched by my pidgin "Willkommen" and "Ist alles gut?" that they actually tip. (Europeans, spoiled by their trade-union-ridden, high-wage welfare states, generally do not know that they are supposed to tip. Some restaurants, the Hearthside included, allow servers to "grat" their foreign customers, or add a tip to the bill. Since this amount is added before the customers have a chance to tip or not tip, the practice amounts to an automatic penalty for imperfect English.) There are the two dirt-smudged lesbians, just off their construction shift, who are impressed enough by my suave handling of the fly in the piña colada that they take the time to praise me to Stu, the assistant manager. There's Sam, the kindly retired cop, who has to plug up his tracheotomy hole with one finger in order to force the cigarette smoke into his lungs.   *ew!*

Sometimes I play with the fantasy that I am a princess who, in penance for some tiny transgression, has undertaken to feed each of her subjects by hand. But the non-princesses working with me are just as indulgent, even when this means flouting management rules—concerning, for example, the number of croutons that can go on a salad (six). "Put on all you want," Gail whispers, "as long as Stu isn't looking." She dips into her own tip money to buy biscuits and gravy for an out-of-work mechanic who's used up all his money on dental surgery, inspiring me to pick up the tab for his milk and pie. Maybe the same high levels of agape can be found throughout the "hospitality industry." I remember the poster decorating one of the apartments I looked at, which said "If you seek happiness for yourself you will never find it. Only when you seek happiness for others will it come to you," or words to that effect—an odd sentiment, it seemed to me at the time, to find in the dank one-room basement apartment of a bellhop at the Best Western. At the Hearthside, we utilize whatever bits of autonomy we have to ply our customers with the illicit calories that signal our love. It is our job as servers to assemble the salads and desserts, pouring the dressings and squirting the whipped cream. We also control the number of butter patties our customers get and the amount of sour cream on their baked potatoes. So if you wonder why Americans are so obese, consider the fact that waitresses both express their humanity and earn their tips through the covert distribution of fats.

Ten days into it, this is beginning to look like a livable lifestyle. I like Gail, who is "looking at fifty" but moves so fast she can alight in one place and then another without apparently being anywhere between them. I clown around with Lionel, the teenage Haitian busboy, and catch a few fragments of conversation with Joan, the svelte fortyish hostess and militant feminist who is the only one of us who dares to tell Jack to shut the fuck up. I even warm up to Jack when, on a slow night and to make up for a particularly unwarranted attack on my abilities, or so I imagine, he tells me about his glory days as a young man at "coronary school"—or do you say "culinary"?—in Brooklyn, where he dated a knock-out Puerto Rican chick and learned everything there is to know about food. I finish up at 10:00 or 10:30, depending on how much side work I've been able to get done during the shift, and cruise home to the tapes I snatched up at random when I left my real home—Marianne Faithfull, Tracy Chapman, Enigma,

King Sunny Ade, the Violent Femmes — just drained enough for the music to set my cranium resonating but hardly dead. Midnight snack is Wheat Thins and Monterey Jack, accompanied by cheap white wine on ice and whatever AMC has to offer. To bed by 1:30 or 2:00, up at 9:00 or 10:00, read for an hour while my uniform whirls around in the landlord's washing machine, and then it's another eight hours spent following Mao's central instruction, as laid out in the Little Red Book, which was: Serve the people.

I could drift along like this, in some dreamy proletarian idyll, except for two things. One is management. If I have kept this subject on the margins thus far it is because I still flinch to think that I spent all those weeks under the surveillance of men (and later women) whose job it was to monitor my behavior for signs of sloth, theft, drug abuse, or worse. Not that managers and especially "assistant managers" in low-wage settings like this are exactly the class enemy. In the restaurant business, they are mostly former cooks or servers, still capable of pinch-hitting in the kitchen or on the floor, just as in hotels they are likely to be former clerks, and paid a salary of only about $400 a week. But everyone knows they have crossed over to the other side, which is, crudely put, corporate as opposed to human. Cooks want to prepare tasty meals; servers want to serve them graciously; but managers are there for only one reason — to make sure that money is made for some theoretical entity that exists far away in Chicago or New York, if a corporation can be said to have a physical existence at all. Reflecting on her career, Gail tells me ruefully that she had sworn, years ago, never to work for a corporation again. "They don't cut you no slack. You give and you give, and they take."

Managers can sit — for hours at a time if they want — but it's their job   20
to see that no one else ever does, even when there's nothing to do, and this is why, for servers, slow times can be as exhausting as rushes. You start dragging out each little chore, because if the manager on duty catches you in an idle moment, he will give you something far nastier to do. So I wipe, I clean, I consolidate ketchup bottles and recheck the cheesecake supply, even tour the tables to make sure the customer evaluation forms are all standing perkily in their places — wondering all the time how many calories I burn in these strictly theatrical exercises. When, on a particularly dead afternoon, Stu finds me glancing at a *USA Today* a customer has left behind, he assigns me to vacuum the entire floor with the broken vacuum cleaner that has a handle only two feet long, and the only way to do that without incurring orthopedic damage is to proceed from spot to spot on your knees.

On my first Friday at the Hearthside there is a "mandatory meeting for all restaurant employees," which I attend, eager for insight into our overall marketing strategy and the niche (your basic Ohio cuisine with a tropical twist?) we aim to inhabit. But there is no "we" at this meeting. Phillip, our top manager except for an occasional "consultant" sent out by corporate headquarters, opens it with a sneer: "The break room — it's disgusting. Butts in the ashtrays, newspapers lying around, crumbs." This windowless little room, which also houses the time clock for the entire hotel, is where we stash our bags and civilian clothes and take our half-hour meal breaks. But a break room is not a right, he tells us. It can be taken away. We should also know that the lockers in the break room and whatever is in them can be searched at any time. Then comes gossip; there has been gossip; gossip (which seems to mean employees talking among themselves) must stop. Off-duty employees are henceforth barred from eating at the restaurant, because "other servers gather around them and gossip." When Phillip has exhausted his agenda of rebukes, Joan complains about the condition of the ladies' room and I throw in my two bits about the vacuum cleaner. But I don't see any backup coming from my fellow servers, each of whom has subsided into her own personal funk; Gail, my role model, stares sorrowfully at a point six inches from her nose. The meeting ends when Andy, one of the cooks, gets up, muttering about breaking up his day off for this almighty bullshit.

Just four days later we are suddenly summoned into the kitchen at 3:30 p.m., even though there are live tables on the floor. We all—about ten of us—stand around Phillip, who announces grimly that there has been a report of some "drug activity" on the night shift and that, as a result, we are now to be a "drug-free" workplace, meaning that all new hires will be tested, as will possibly current employees on a random basis. I am glad that this part of the kitchen is so dark, because I find myself blushing as hard as if I had been caught toking up in the ladies' room myself: I haven't been treated this way—lined up in the corridor, threatened with locker searches, peppered with carelessly aimed accusations—since junior high school. Back on the floor, Joan cracks, "Next they'll be telling us we can't have sex on the job." When I ask Stu what happened to inspire the crackdown, he just mutters about "management decisions" and takes the opportunity to up-braid Gail and me for being too generous with the rolls. From now on there's to be only one per customer, and it goes out with the dinner, not with the salad. He's also been riding the cooks, prompting Andy to come out of the kitchen and observe—with the serenity of a man whose customary implement is a butcher knife—that "Stu has a death wish today."

Later in the evening, the gossip crystallizes around the theory that Stu is himself the drug culprit, that he uses the restaurant phone to order up marijuana and sends one of the late servers out to fetch it for him. The server was caught, and she may have ratted Stu out or at least said enough to cast some suspicion on him, thus accounting for his pissy behavior. Who knows? Lionel, the busboy, entertains us for the rest of the shift by standing just behind Stu's back and sucking deliriously on an imaginary joint.

The other problem, in addition to the less-than-nurturing management style, is that this job shows no sign of being financially viable. You might imagine, from a comfortable distance, that people who live, year in and year out, on $6 to $10 an hour have discovered some survival stratagems unknown to the middle class. But no. It's not hard to get my co-workers to talk about their living situations, because housing, in almost every case, is the principal source of disruption in their lives, the first thing they fill you in on when they arrive for their shifts. After a week, I have compiled the following survey:

- Gail is sharing a room in a well-known downtown flophouse for which she and a roommate pay about $250 a week. Her roommate, a male friend, has begun hitting on her, driving her nuts, but the rent would be impossible alone.

- Claude, the Haitian cook, is desperate to get out of the two-room apartment he shares with his girlfriend and two other, unrelated, people. As far as I can determine, the other Haitian men (most of whom only speak Creole) live in similarly crowded situations.

- Annette, a twenty-year-old server who is six months pregnant and has been abandoned by her boyfriend, lives with her mother, a postal clerk.

- Marianne and her boyfriend are paying $170 a week for a one-person trailer.

- Jack, who is, at $10 an hour, the wealthiest of us, lives in the trailer he owns, paying only the $400-a-month lot fee.

- The other white cook, Andy, lives on his dry-docked boat, which, as far as I can tell from his loving descriptions, can't be more than twenty feet long. He offers to take me out on it, once it's repaired, but the offer comes with inquiries as to my marital status, so I do not follow up on it.

- Tina and her husband are paying $60 a night for a double room in a Days Inn. This is because they have no car and the Days Inn is within walking distance of the Hearthside. When Marianne, one of the breakfast servers, is tossed out of her trailer for subletting (which is against the trailer-park rules), she leaves her boyfriend and moves in with Tina and her husband.

- Joan, who had fooled me with her numerous and tasteful outfits (hostesses wear their own clothes), lives in a van she parks behind a shopping center at night and showers in Tina's motel room. The clothes are from thrift shops.[4]

It strikes me, in my middle-class solipsism, that there is gross improvidence in some of these arrangements. When Gail and I are wrapping silverware in napkins—the only task for which we are permitted to sit—she tells me she is thinking of escaping from her roommate by moving into the

---

[4]I could find no statistics on the number of employed people living in cars or vans, but according to the National Coalition for the Homeless's 1997 report "Myths and Facts About Homelessness," nearly one in five homeless people (in twenty-nine cities across the nation) is employed in a full- or part-time job.

Days Inn herself. I am astounded: How can she even think of paying between $40 and $60 a day? But if I was afraid of sounding like a social worker, I come out just sounding like a fool. She squints at me in disbelief, "And where am I supposed to get a month's rent and a month's deposit for an apartment?" I'd been feeling pretty smug about my $500 efficiency, but of course it was made possible only by the $1,300 I had allotted myself for start-up costs when I began my low-wage life: $1,000 for the first month's rent and deposit, $100 for initial groceries and cash in my pocket, $200 stuffed away for emergencies. In poverty, as in certain propositions in physics, starting conditions are everything.

There are no secret economies that nourish the poor; on the contrary, there are a host of special costs. If you can't put up the two months' rent you need to secure an apartment, you end up paying through the nose for a room by the week. If you have only a room, with a hot plate at best, you can't save by cooking up huge lentil stews that can be frozen for the week ahead. You eat fast food, or the hot dogs and styrofoam cups of soup that can be microwaved in a convenience store. If you have no money for health insurance—and the Hearthside's niggardly plan kicks in only after three months—you go without routine care or prescription drugs and end up paying the price. Gail, for example, was fine until she ran out of money for estrogen pills. She is supposed to be on the company plan by now, but they claim to have lost her application form and need to begin the paperwork all over again. So she spends $9 per migraine pill to control the headaches she wouldn't have, she insists, if her estrogen supplements were covered. Similarly, Marianne's boyfriend lost his job as a roofer because he missed so much time after getting a cut on his foot for which he couldn't afford the prescribed antibiotic.

My own situation, when I sit down to assess it after two weeks of work, would not be much better if this were my actual life. The seductive thing about waitressing is that you don't have to wait for payday to feel a few bills in your pocket, and my tips usually cover meals and gas, plus something left over to stuff into the kitchen drawer I use as a bank. But as the tourist business slows in the summer heat, I sometimes leave work with only $20 in tips (the gross is higher, but servers share about 15 percent of their tips with the busboys and bartenders). With wages included, this amounts to about the minimum wage of $5.15 an hour. Although the sum in the drawer is piling up, at the present rate of accumulation it will be more than a hundred dollars short of my rent when the end of the month comes around. Nor can I see any expenses to cut. True, I haven't gone the lentil-stew route yet, but that's because I don't have a large cooking pot, pot holders, or a ladle to stir with (which cost about $30 at Kmart, less at thrift stores), not to mention onions, carrots, and the indispensable bay leaf. I do make my lunch almost every day—usually some slow-burning, high-protein combo like frozen chicken patties with melted cheese on top and canned pinto beans on the side. Dinner is at the Hearthside, which offers its employees a choice of BLT, fish sandwich, or hamburger for only $2. The burger lasts longest, especially if it's heaped with gut-puckering jalapeños, but my midnight my stomach is growling again. . . .

When I moved out of the trailer park, I gave the key to number 46 to Gail and arranged for my deposit to be transferred to her. She told me that Joan is still living in her van and that Stu had been fired from the Hearthside. . . .

In one month, I had earned approximately $1,040 and spent $517 on food, gas, toiletries, laundry, phone, and utilities. If I had remained in my $500 efficiency, I would have been able to pay the rent and have $22 left over (which is $78 less than the cash I had in my pocket at the start of the month). During this time I bought no clothing except for the required slacks and no prescription drugs or medical care (I did finally buy some vitamin B to compensate for the lack of vegetables in my diet). Perhaps I could have saved a little on food if I had gotten to a supermarket more often, instead of convenience stores, but it should be noted that I lost almost four pounds in four weeks, on a diet weighted heavily toward burgers and fries.

How former welfare recipients and single mothers will (and do) survive   30
in the low-wage workforce, I cannot imagine. Maybe they will figure out how to condense their lives — including child-raising, laundry, romance, and meals — into the couple of hours between full-time jobs. Maybe they will take up residence in their vehicles, if they have one. All I know is that I couldn't hold two jobs and I couldn't make enough money to live on with one. And I had advantages unthinkable to many of the long-term poor — health, stamina, a working car, and no children to care for and support. Certainly nothing in my experience contradicts the conclusion of Kathryn Edin and Laura Lein, in their recent book *Making Ends Meet: How Single Mothers Survive Welfare and Low-Wage Work*, that low-wage work actually involves more hardship and deprivation than life at the mercy of the welfare state. In the coming months and years, economic conditions for the working poor are bound to worsen, even without the almost inevitable recession. As mentioned earlier, the influx of former welfare recipients into the low-skilled workforce will have a depressing effect on both wages and the number of jobs available. A general economic downturn will only enhance these effects, and the working poor will of course be facing it without the slight, but nonetheless often saving, protection of welfare as a backup.

The thinking behind welfare reform was that even the humblest jobs are morally uplifting and psychologically buoying. In reality they are likely to be fraught with insult and stress. But I did discover one redeeming feature of the most abject low-wage work—the camaraderie of people who are, in almost all cases, far too smart and funny and caring for the work they do and the wages they're paid. The hope, of course, is that someday these people will come to know what they're worth, and take appropriate action.

Questions

1. Ehrenreich tells us in the first paragraph who she is and what she wants to uncover: "I am . . . a middle-class journalist setting out to explore the world that welfare mothers are entering, at the rate of approximately 50,000 a month, as welfare reform kicks in." What questions does Ehrenreich ask about this world? How does she make you, her reader, care about these questions?
2. According to Ehrenreich, what is the rationale for welfare reform? Why does she distrust this rationale?
3. Ehrenreich plunges us into the middle of her work life at the Hearthside. Identify the details and images that you find most compelling and memorable. How do these details help her to establish her credibility?
4. Ehrenreich tells us that she spent "weeks under the surveillance of men (and later women) whose job it was to monitor my behavior for signs of sloth, theft, drug abuse, or worse" (paragraph 19). What role do these supervisors play in Ehrenreich's work life?
5. Ehrenreich points to housing as "the principal source of disruption" (paragraph 24) in her coworkers' lives. Look at her survey of where and how her coworkers live. What does this survey suggest about the difficulties of "(not) getting by in America"?
6. At the end of the essay, Ehrenreich calculates how much money she earned and how much she spent during her month as a waitress. What conclusions does she draw from her budget?
7. What questions are you asking about work? Keep a journal in which you ask yourself questions about your current job or former jobs.
8. Go to the library, and research the federal Welfare Reform Act of 1996. What main arguments did members of Congress offer for and against welfare reform during the debates that preceded their vote on the act? Research the consequences of welfare reform within your region or state.

Making Connections

This text contains an argument, about work and its rewards, but a lot more is going on here. Compare the use of personal experience and feelings in this piece with their use in one or more of the other texts in this book. You might consider Jonathan Franzen's "Sifting the Ashes" (p. 574).

Explaining in the
Social Sciences and Public Affairs

The Futile Pursuit
of Happiness

Jon Gertner

Jon Gertner is a contributing writer to the New York Times Magazine. *He has worked as a senior editor at* American Lawyer *and*
Money *magazines, and his articles have appeared in* Inc., Money,
*and other periodicals. Among other subjects, he has written about
the significance of DVDs for the film industry, the claims of health
benefits from eating chocolate, marketers who specialize in marketing to children, and various business and finance matters. The following article appeared in the* New York Times Magazine *and was
the most frequently emailed article of 2003, according to the* New
York Times *Web site. It was reprinted in* The Best American Nonrequired Reading *(2004), edited by Dave Eggers.*

If Daniel Gilbert is right, then you are wrong. That is to say, if Daniel
Gilbert is right, then you are wrong to believe that a new car will make you
as happy as you imagine. You are wrong to believe that a new kitchen will
make you happy for as long as you imagine. You are wrong to think that
you will be more unhappy with a big single setback (a broken wrist, a broken heart) than with a lesser chronic one (a trick knee, a tense marriage).
You are wrong to assume that job failure will be crushing. You are wrong
to expect that a death in the family will leave you bereft for year upon year,
forever and ever. You are even wrong to reckon that a cheeseburger you

order in a restaurant—this week, next week, a year from now, it doesn't really matter when—will definitely hit the spot That's because when it comes to predicting exactly how you will feel in the future, you are most likely wrong.

A professor in Harvard's department of psychology, Gilbert likes to tell people that he studies happiness. But it would be more precise to say that Gilbert—along with the psychologist Tim Wilson of the University of Virginia, the economist George Loewenstein of Carnegie Mellon, and the psychologist (and Nobel laureate in economics) Daniel Kahneman of Princeton—has taken the lead in studying a specific type of emotional and behavioral prediction. In the past few years, these four men have begun to question the decision-making process that shapes our sense of well-being: How do we predict what will make us happy or unhappy—and then how do we feel after the actual experience? For example, how do we suppose we will feel if our favorite college football team wins or loses, and then how do we really feel a few days after the game? How do we predict we'll feel about purchasing jewelry, having children, buying a big house, or being rich? And then how do we regard the outcomes? According to this small corps of academics, almost all actions—the decision to buy jewelry, have kids, buy the big house, or work exhaustively for a fatter paycheck—are based upon our predictions of the emotional consequences of these events.

Until recently, this was uncharted territory. How we forecast our feelings, and whether those predictions match our future emotional states, had never been the stuff of laboratory research. But in scores of experiments, Gilbert, Wilson, Kahneman, and Loewenstein have made a slew of observations and conclusions that undermine a number of fundamental assumptions: namely, that we humans understand what we want and are adept at improving our well-being—that we are good at maximizing our utility, in the jargon of traditional economics. Further, their work on prediction raises some unsettling and somewhat more personal questions. To understand affective forecasting, as Gilbert has termed these studies, is to wonder if everything you have ever thought about life choices, and about happiness, has been at the least somewhat naive and, at worst, greatly mistaken.

The problem, as Gilbert and company have come to discover, is that we falter when it comes to imagining how we will feel about something in the future. It isn't that we get the big things wrong. We know we will experience visits to Le Cirque and to the periodontist differently; we can accurately predict that we'd rather be stuck in Montauk than in a Midtown elevator. What Gilbert has found, however, is that we overestimate the intensity and the duration of our emotional reactions—our "affect" to future events. In other words, we might believe that a new BMW will make life perfect. But it will almost certainly be less exciting than we anticipated; nor will it excite us for as long as predicted. The vast majority of Gilbert's test participants through the years have consistently made just these sorts of errors both in the laboratory and in real-life situations. And whether Gilbert's subjects were trying to predict how they would feel in the future about a plate of spaghetti with meat sauce, the defeat of a preferred politi-cal candidate, or romantic rejection seemed not to matter. On average, bad events proved less intense and more transient than test participants pre-dicted. Good events proved less intense and briefer as well.

Gilbert and his collaborator Tim Wilson call the gap between what we predict and what we ultimately experience the "impact bias" — "impact" meaning the errors we make in estimating both the intensity and duration of our emotions and "bias" our tendency to err. The phrase characterizes how we experience the dimming excitement over not just a BMW but also over any object or event that we presume will make us happy. Would a 20 percent raise or winning the lottery result in a contented life? You may pre-dict it will, but almost surely it won't turn out that way. And a new plasma television? You may have high hopes, but the impact bias suggests that it will almost certainly be less cool, and in a shorter time, than you imagine. Worse, Gilbert has noted that these mistakes of expectation can lead di-rectly to mistakes in choosing what we think will give us pleasure. He calls this "miswanting."

"The average person says, 'I know I'll be happier with a Porsche than a Chevy,'" Gilbert explains. "'Or with Linda rather than Rosalyn. Or as a doctor rather than as a plumber.' That seems very clear to people. The problem is, I can't get into medical school or afford the Porsche. So for the average person, the obstacle between them and happiness is actually getting the futures that they desire. But what our research shows — not just ours, but Loewenstein's and Kahneman's — is that the real problem is figuring out which of those futures is going to have the high payoff and is really going to make you happy.

"You know, the Stones said, 'You can't always get what you want,'" Gilbert adds. "I don't think that's the problem. The problem is you can't al-ways know what you want."

Gilbert's papers on affective forecasting began to appear in the late 1990s, but the idea to study happiness and emotional prediction actually came to him on a sunny afternoon in 1992, just as he and his friend Jonathan Jay Koehler sat down for lunch outside the psychology building at the University of Texas at Austin, where both men were teaching at the time. Gilbert was uninspired about his studies and says he felt despair about his failing marriage. And as he launched into a discussion of his per-sonal life, he swerved to ask why economists focus on the financial aspects of decision making rather than the emotional ones. Koehler recalls, "Gilbert said something like: 'It all seems so small. It isn't really about money; it's about happiness. Isn't that what everybody wants to know when we make a decision?'" For a moment, Gilbert forgot his troubles, and two more questions came to him. Do we even know what makes us happy? And if it's difficult to figure out what makes us happy in the moment, how can we predict what will make us happy in the future?

In the early 1990s, for an up-and-coming psychology professor like Gilbert to switch his field of inquiry from how we perceive one another to happiness, as he did that day, was just a hairsbreadth short of bizarre. But Gilbert has always liked questions that lead him somewhere new. Now forty-five, Gilbert dropped out of high school at fifteen, hooking into what he calls "the tail end of the hippie movement" and hitchhiking aimlessly from town to town with his guitar. He met his wife on the road; she was hitching in the other direction. They married at seventeen, had a son at eighteen, and settled down in Denver. "I pulled weeds, I sold rebar, I sold carpet, I installed carpet, I spent a lot of time as a phone solicitor," he recalls. During this period he spent several years turning out science-fiction stories for magazines like Amazing Stories. Thus, in addition to being "one of the most gifted social psychologists of our age," as the psychology writer and professor David G. Myers describes him to me, Gilbert is the author of "The Essence of Grunk," a story about an encounter with a creature made of egg salad that jets around the galaxy in a rocket-powered refrigerator.

Psychology was a matter of happenstance. In the midst of his sci-fi career Gilbert tried to sign up for a writing course at the local community college, but the class was full; he figured that psych, still accepting registrants, would help him with character development in his fiction. It led instead to an undergraduate degree at the University of Colorado at Denver, then a Ph.D. at Princeton, then an appointment at the University of Texas, then the appointment at Harvard. "People ask why I study happiness," Gilbert says, "and I say, 'Why study anything else?' It's the holy grail. We're studying the thing that all human action is directed toward." 10

One experiment of Gilbert's had students in a photography class at Harvard choose two favorite pictures from among those they had just taken and then relinquish one to the teacher. Some students were told their choices were permanent; others were told they could exchange their prints after several days. As it turned out, those who had time to change their minds were less pleased with their decisions than those whose choices were irrevocable.

Much of Gilbert's research is in this vein. Another recent study asked whether transit riders in Boston who narrowly missed their trains experienced the self-blame that people tend to predict they'll feel in this situation. (They did not.) And a paper waiting to be published, "The Peculiar Longevity of Things Not So Bad," examines why we expect that bigger problems will always dwarf minor annoyances, "When really bad things happen to us, we defend against them," Gilbert explains. "People, of course, predict the exact opposite. If you ask, 'What would you rather have, a broken leg or a trick knee?' they'd probably say, 'Trick knee.' And yet, if your goal is to accumulate maximum happiness over your lifetime, you just made the wrong choice. A trick knee is a bad thing to have."

All of these studies establish the links between prediction, decision making, and well-being. The photography experiment challenges our common assumption that we would be happier with the option to change our minds when in fact we're happier with closure. The transit experiment demonstrates that we tend to err in estimating our regret over missed opportunities. The "things not so bad" work shows our failure to imagine how grievously irritations compromise our satisfaction. Our emotional defenses snap into action when it comes to a divorce or a disease but not for lesser problems. We fix the leaky roof on our house, but over the long haul, the broken screen door we never mend adds up to more frustration.

Gilbert does not believe all forecasting mistakes lead to similar results; a death in the family, a new gym membership, and a new husband are not the same, but in how they affect our well-being they are similar. "Our research simply says that whether it's the thing that matters; or the thing that doesn't, both of them matter less than you think they will," he says. Things that happen to you or that you buy or own — as much as you think they make a difference to your happiness, you're wrong by a certain amount. You're overestimating how much of a difference they make. None of them makes the difference you think. And that's true of positive and negative events."

Much of the work of Kahneman, Loewenstein, Gilbert, and Wilson 15 takes its cue from the concept of adaptation, a term psychologists have used since at least the 1950s to refer to how we acclimate to changing circumstances. George Loewenstein sums up this human capacity as follows: "Happiness is a signal that our brains use to motivate us to do certain things. And in the same way that our eye adapts to different levels of illumination, we're designed to kind of go back to the happiness set point. Our brains are not trying to be happy. Our brains are trying to regulate us." In this respect, the tendency toward adaptation suggests why the impact bias is so pervasive. As Tim Wilson says: "We don't realize how quickly we will adapt to a pleasurable event and make it the backdrop of our lives. When any event occurs to us, we make it ordinary. And through becoming ordinary, we lose our pleasure."

It is easy to overlook something new and crucial in what Wilson is saying. Not that we invariably lose interest in bright and shiny things over time — this is a long-known trait — but that we're generally unable to recognize that we adapt to new circumstances and therefore fail to incorporate this fact into our decisions. So, yes, we will adapt to the BMW and the plasma TV, since we adapt to virtually everything. But Wilson and Gilbert and others have shown that we seem unable to predict that we will adapt. Thus, when we find the pleasure derived from a thing diminishing, we move on to the next thing or event and almost certainly make another error of prediction, and then another, ad infinitum.

As Gilbert points out, this glitch is also significant when it comes to negative events like losing a job or the death of someone we love, in response to which we project a permanently inconsolable future. "The thing I'm most interested in, that I've spent the most time studying, is our failure to recognize how powerful psychological defenses are once they're activated," Gilbert says. "We've used the metaphor of the 'psychological immune system' — it's just a metaphor, but not a bad one for that system of defenses that helps you feel better when bad things happen. Observers of the human condition since Aristotle have known that people have these defenses. Freud spent his life, and his daughter Anna spent her life, worrying about these defenses. What's surprising is that people don't seem to recognize that they have these defenses, and that these defenses will be triggered by negative events." During the course of my interviews with Gilbert, a close friend of his died. "I am like everyone in thinking, I'll never get over this and life will never be good again," he wrote to me in an e-mail message as he planned a trip to Texas for the funeral. "But because of my work, there is always a voice in the back of my head — a voice that wears a lab coat and has a lot of data tucked under its arm — that says, 'Yes, you will, and yes, it will.' And I know that voice is right."

Still, the argument that we imperfectly imagine what we want and how we will cope is nevertheless disorienting. On the one hand, it can cast a shadow of regret on some life decisions. Why did I decide that working one hundred hours a week to earn more would make me happy? Why did I think that retiring to Sun City, Arizona, would please me? On the other hand, it can be enlightening. No wonder this teak patio set hasn't made me as happy as I expected. Even if she dumps me, I'll be okay. Either way, predicting how things will feel to us over the long term is mystifying. A large body of research on well-being seems to suggest that wealth above middle-class comfort makes little difference to our happiness, for example, or that having children does nothing to improve well-being — even as it drives marital satisfaction dramatically down. We often yearn for a roomy, isolated home (a thing we easily adapt to), when, in fact, it will probably compromise our happiness by distancing us from neighbors. (Social interaction and friendships have been shown to give lasting pleasure.) The big isolated home is what Loewenstein, forty-eight, himself bought. "I fell into a trap I never should have fallen into," he told me.

Loewenstein's office is up a narrow stairway in a hidden corner of an enormous, worn brick building on the edge of the Carnegie Mellon campus in Pittsburgh. He and Gilbert make for an interesting contrast. Gilbert is garrulous, theatrical, dazzling in his speech and writing; he fills a room. Loewenstein is soft-spoken, given to abstraction, and lithe in the way of a hard-core athlete; he seems to float around a room. Both men profess tremendous admiration for the other, and their different disciplines — psychology and economics — have made their overlapping interests in affective forecasting more complementary than fraught. While Gilbert's most notable contribution to affective forecasting is the impact bias, Loewenstein's is something called the "empathy gap."

Here's how it expresses itself. In a recent experiment, Loewenstein tried   20
to find out how likely people might be to dance alone to Rick James's "Super Freak" in front of a large audience. Many agreed to do so for a certain amount of money a week in advance, only to renege when the day came to take the stage. This sounds like a goof, but it gets at the fundamental difference between how we behave in "hot" states (those of anxiety, courage, fear, drug craving, sexual excitation, and the like) and "cold" states of rational calm. This empathy gap in thought and behavior — we

cannot seem to predict how we we'll behave in a hot state when we are in a cold state — affects happiness in an important but somewhat less consistent way than the impact bias. "So much of our lives involves making decisions that have consequences for the future," Loewenstein says. "And if our decision making is influenced by these transient emotional and psychological states, then we know we're not making decisions with an eye toward future consequences." This may be as simple as an unfortunate proclamation of love in a moment of lust, Loewenstein explains, or something darker, like an act of road rage or of suicide.

Among other things, this line of inquiry has led Loewenstein to collaborate with health experts looking into why people engage in unprotected sex when they would never agree to do so in moments of cool calculation. Data from tests in which volunteers are asked how they would behave in various "heat of the moment" situations — whether they would have sex with a minor, for instance, or act forcefully with a partner who asks them to stop — have consistently shown that different states of arousal can alter answers by astonishing margins. "These kinds of states have the ability to change us so profoundly that we're more different from ourselves in different states than we are from another person," Loewenstein says.

Part of Loewenstein's curiosity about hot and cold states comes from situations in which his emotions have been pitted against his intellect. When he's not teaching, he treks around the world, making sure to get to Alaska to hike or kayak at least once a year. A scholar of mountaineering literature, he once wrote a paper that examined why climbers have a poor memory for pain and usually ignore turn-back times at great peril. But he has done the same thing himself many times. He almost died in a whitewater canoeing accident and vowed afterward that he never wanted to see his runaway canoe again. A couple of hours later, he went looking for it. The same goes for his climbing pursuits, "You establish your turn-back time, and then you find yourself still far from the peak," he says. "So you push on. You haven't brought enough food or clothes, and then as a result, you're stuck at thirteen thousand feet, and you have to just sit there and shiver all night without a sleeping bag or warm clothes. When the sun comes up, you're half-frozen, and you say, 'Never again.' Then you get back and immediately start craving getting out again." He pushes the point: "I have tried to train my emotions." But he admits that he may make the same mistakes on his next trip.

Would a world without forecasting errors be a better world? Would a life lived without forecasting errors be a richer life? Among the academics who study affective forecasting, there seems little doubt that these sorts of questions will ultimately jump from the academy to the real world. "If people do not know what is going to make them better off or give them pleasure," Daniel Kahneman says, "then the idea that you can trust people to do what will give them pleasure becomes questionable." To Kahneman, who did some of the first experiments in the area in the early 1990s, affective forecasting could greatly influence retirement planning, for example, where mistakes in prediction (how much we save, how much we spend, how we choose a community we think we'll enjoy) can prove irreversible. He sees a role for affective forecasting in consumer spending, where a "cooling off" period might remedy buyer's remorse. Most important, he sees vital applications in health care, especially when it comes to informed consent. "We consider people capable of giving informed consent once they are told of the objective effects of a treatment," Kahneman says. "But can people anticipate how they and other people will react to a colostomy or to the removal of their vocal cords? The research on affective forecasting suggests that people may have little ability to anticipate their adaptation beyond the early stages." Loewenstein, along with his collaborator Dr. Peter Ubel, has done a great deal of work showing that nonpatients overestimate the displeasure of living with the loss of a limb, for instance, or paraplegia. To use affective forecasting to prove that people adapt to serious physical challenges far better and will be happier than they imagine, Loewenstein says, could prove invaluable.

There are downsides to making public policy in light of this research, too. While walking in Pittsburgh one afternoon, Loewenstein tells me that he doesn't see how anybody could study happiness and not find himself leaning left politically; the data make it all too clear that boosting the living standards of those already comfortable, such as through lower taxes, does little to improve their levels of well-being, whereas raising the living standards of the impoverished makes an enormous difference. Nevertheless, he and Gilbert (who once declared in an academic paper, "Windfalls are better than pratfalls, A's are better than C's, December 25 is better than April 15, and everything is better than a Republican administration") seem to lean libertarian in regard to pushing any kind of prescriptive agenda. "We're very, very nervous about overapplying the research," Loewenstein says, "Just because we figure out that X makes people happy and they're choosing Y, we don't want to impose X on them. I have a discomfort with paternalism and with using the results coming out of our field to impose decisions on people."

Still, Gilbert and Loewenstein can't contain the personal and philo-   25
sophical questions raised by their work. After talking with both men, I found it hard not to wonder about my own predictions at every turn. At times it seemed like knowing the secret to some parlor trick that was nonetheless very difficult to pull off — when I ogled a new car at the Honda dealership as I waited for a new muffler on my '92 Accord, for instance, or as my daughter's fever spiked one evening and I imagined something terrible, and then something more terrible thereafter. With some difficulty, I could observe my mind overshooting the mark, zooming past accuracy toward the sublime or the tragic. It was tempting to want to try to think about the future more moderately. But it seemed nearly impossible as well.

To Loewenstein, who is especially attendant to the friction between his emotional and deliberative processes, a life without forecasting errors would most likely be a better, happier life. "If you had a deep understanding of the impact bias and you acted on it, which is not always that easy to do, you would tend to invest your resources in the things that would make you happy," he says. This might mean taking more time with friends instead of more time for making money. He also adds that a better understanding of the empathy gap — those hot and cold states we all find ourselves in on frequent occasions — could save people from making regrettable decisions in moments of courage or craving.

Gilbert seems optimistic about using the work in terms of improving "institutional judgment" — how we spend health care dollars, for example — but less sanguine about using it to improve our personal judgment. He admits that he has taken some of his research to heart; for instance, his work on what he calls the psychological immune system has led him to believe that he would be able to adapt to even the worst turn of events. In addition, he says that he now takes more chances in life, a fact corroborated in at least one aspect by his research partner Tim Wilson, who says that driving with Gilbert in Boston is a terrifying, white-knuckle experience. "But I should have learned many more lessons from my research than I actually have," Gilbert admits. I'm getting married in the spring because this woman is going to make me happy forever, and I know it." At this, Gilbert laughs, a sudden, booming laugh that fills his Cambridge office. He seems to find it funny not because it's untrue, but because nothing could be more true. This is how he feels. "I don't think I want to give up all these motivations," he says, "that belief that there's the good and there's the bad and that this is a contest to try to get one and avoid the other. I don't think I want to learn too much from my research in that sense."

Even so, Gilbert is currently working on a complex experiment in which he has made affective forecasting errors "go away." In this test, Gilbert's team asks members of Group A to estimate how they'll feel if they receive negative personality feedback. The impact bias kicks in, of course, and they mostly predict they'll feel terrible, when in fact they end up feeling okay. But if Gilbert shows Group B that others have gotten the same feedback and felt okay afterward, then its members predict they'll feel okay as well. The impact bias disappears, and the participants in Group B make accurate predictions.

This is exciting to Gilbert. But at the same time, its not a technique he wants to shape into a self-help book, or one that he even imagines could be practically implemented, "Hope and fear are enduring features of the human experience," he says, "and it is unlikely that people are going to abandon them anytime soon just because some psychologist told them they should." In fact, in his recent writings, he has wondered whether forecasting errors might somehow serve a larger functional purpose he doesn't yet understand. If he could wave a wand tomorrow and eliminate all affective-forecasting errors, I ask, would he? "The benefits of not making this error would seem to be that you get a little more happiness," he says. "When choosing between two jobs, you wouldn't sweat as much because you'd say: 'You know, I'll be happy in both. I'll adapt to either circumstance pretty well, so there's no use in killing myself for the next week.' But maybe our caricatures of the future — these overinflated assessments of how good or bad things will be — maybe it's these illusory assessments that keep us moving in one direction over the other. Maybe we don't want a society of people who shrug and say, 'It won't really make a difference.'

"Maybe its important for there to be carrots and sticks in the world,   30 even if they are illusions," he adds. "They keep us moving towards carrots and away from sticks."

QUESTIONS

1. Explanations can be dull things. How does Gertner guard against reader apathy in the beginning of his article?
2. This explanation has a simple point — that happiness is unpredictable — and a more complex one, which involves the mechanisms and processes of anticipation and realization. Try to sum up, in your own words, the more complex explanation contained in this essay.
3. Gertner is actually reporting on the work of other people, whose explanations he is presenting to us, but focuses mainly on Daniel Gilbert and George Loewenstein. He pays some attention to their personal qualities, both physical and mental. Why do you suppose he does this?
4. Gertner actually moves back and forth between Gilbert and Loewenstein in the course of his essay. This is particularly noticeable at the end, when they are represented as concluding two different things about the possible results of their research. How would you describe this difference? Can you tell what Gertner's own position is?
5. Write an essay in which you develop your own response to the conclusion of Gertner's article. You may wish to agree or disagree with either Gilbert or Loewenstein, but present your own view, using material drawn from your own experience of anticipation and realization of pleasant and painful things.

MAKING CONNECTIONS

Gertner's title alludes to an important phrase from the Declaration of Independence (p. 554). How do you suppose Thomas Jefferson would respond to Gertner's suggestion that the pursuit of happiness is futile? Is Gertner mocking that Jeffersonian ideal?

SOME CONDITIONS OF OBEDIENCE AND DISOBEDIENCE TO AUTHORITY

Stanley Milgram

Stanley Milgram (1933–1984) was born in New York, went to Queens College and Harvard University, and was a professor of social psychology at the Graduate Center of the City University of New York. The following explanation of Milgram's obedience experiment first appeared in the professional journal Human Relations *in 1965 and made him famous, causing a storm of controversy over his method of experimentation and the results of his experiment. Milgram once said of his work, "As a social psychologist, I look at the world not to master it in any practical sense, but to understand it and to communicate that understanding to others."*

The situation in which one agent commands another to hurt a third turns up time and again as a significant theme in human relations.[1] It is powerfully expressed in the story of Abraham, who is commanded by God to kill his son. It is no accident that Kierkegaard,[2] seeking to orient his thought to the central themes of human experience, chose Abraham's conflict as the springboard to his philosophy.

War too moves forward on the triad of an authority which commands a person to destroy the enemy, and perhaps all organized hostility may be viewed as a theme and variation on the three elements of authority, executant,

[1]This research was supported by two grants from the National Science Foundation: NSF G-7916 and NSF G-24152. Exploratory studies carried out in 1960 were financed by a grant from the Higgins Funds of Yale University. I am grateful to John T. Williams, James J. McDonough, and Emil Elges for the important part they played in the project. Thanks are due also to Alan Elms, James Miller, Taketo Murata, and Stephen Stier for their aid as graduate assistants. My wife, Sasha, performed many valuable services. Finally, I owe a profound debt to the many persons in New Haven and Bridgeport who served as subjects.

[2]*Søren Kierkegaard* (1813–1855): Danish philosopher and theologian. [Eds.]

and victim.[3] We describe an experimental program, recently concluded at Yale University, in which a particular expression of this conflict is studied by experimental means.

In its most general form the problem may be defined thus: if *X* tells *Y* to hurt *Z*, under what conditions will *Y* carry out the command of *X* and under what conditions will he refuse? In the more limited form possible in laboratory research, the question becomes: If an experimenter tells a subject to hurt another person, under what conditions will the subject go along with this instruction, and under what conditions will he refuse to obey? The laboratory problem is not so much a dilution of the general statement as one concrete expression of the many particular forms this question may assume.

One aim of the research was to study behavior in a strong situation of deep consequence to the participants, for the psychological forces operative in powerful and lifelike forms of the conflict may not be brought into play under diluted conditions.

This approach meant, first, that we had a special obligation to protect the welfare and dignity of the persons who took part in the study; subjects were, of necessity, placed in a difficult predicament, and steps had to be taken to ensure their well-being before they were discharged from the laboratory. Toward this end, a careful, post-experimental treatment was devised and has been carried through for subjects in all conditions.[4]

5

---

[3]Consider, for example, J. P. Scott's analysis of war in his monograph on aggression:

> . . . while the actions of key individuals in a war may be explained in terms of direct stimulation to aggression, vast numbers of other people are involved simply by being part of an organized society.
>
> . . . For example, at the beginning of World War I an Austrian archduke was assassinated in Sarajevo. A few days later soldiers from all over Europe were marching toward each other, not because they were stimulated by the archduke's misfortune, but because they had been trained to obey orders. (Slightly rearranged from Scott (1958), *Aggression*, p. 103.)

[4]It consisted of an extended discussion with the experimenter and, of equal importance, a friendly reconciliation with the victim. It is made clear that the victim did *not* receive painful electric shocks. After the completion of the experimental series, subjects were sent a detailed report of the results and full purposes of the experimental program. A formal assessment of this procedure points to its overall effectiveness. Of the subjects, 83.7 percent indicated that they were glad to have taken part in the study; 15.1 percent reported neutral feelings; and 1.3 percent stated that they were sorry to have participated. A large number of subjects spontaneously requested that they be used in further experimentation. Four-fifths of the subjects felt that more experiments of this sort should be carried out, and 74 percent indicated that they had learned something of personal importance as a result of being in the study. Furthermore, a university psychiatrist, experienced in outpatient treatment, interviewed a sample of experimental subjects with the aim of uncovering possible injurious effects resulting from participation. No such effects were in evidence. Indeed, subjects typically felt that their participation was instructive and enriching. A more detailed discussion of this question can be found in Milgram (1964).

Terminology

If *Y* follows the command of *X* we shall say that he has obeyed *X*; if he fails to carry out the command of *X*, we shall say that he has disobeyed *X*. The terms to *obey* and to *disobey*, as used here, refer to the subject's overt action only, and carry no implication for the motive or experiential states accompanying the action.[5]

To be sure, the everyday use of the word *obedience* is not entirely free from complexities. It refers to action within varying situations, and connotes diverse motives within those situations: a child's obedience differs from a soldier's obedience, or the love, honor, and *obey* of the marriage vow. However, a consistent behavioral relationship is indicated in most uses of the term: in the act of obeying, a person does what another person tells him to do. *Y* obeys *X* if he carries out the prescription for action which *X* has addressed to him; the term suggests, moreover, that some form of dominance-subordination, or hierarchical element, is part of the situation in which the transaction between *X* and *Y* occurs.

A subject who complies with the entire series of experimental commands will be termed an *obedient* subject; one who at any point in the

---

[5]To *obey* and to *disobey* are not the only terms one could use in describing the critical action of *Y*. One could say that *Y* is cooperating with *X*, or displays conformity with regard to *X*'s commands. However, *cooperation* suggests that *X* agrees with *Y*'s ends, and understands the relationship between his own behavior and the attainment of those ends. (But the experimental procedure, and, in particular, the experimenter's command that the subject shock the victim even in the absence of a response from the victim, preclude such understanding.) Moreover, cooperation implies status parity for the co-acting agents, and neglects the asymmetrical, dominance-subordination element prominent in the laboratory relationship between experimenter and subject. *Conformity* has been used in other important contexts in social psychology, and most frequently refers to imitating the judgments or actions of others when no explicit requirement for imitation has been made. Furthermore, in the present study there are two sources of social pressure; pressure from the experimenter issuing the commands, and pressure from the victim to stop the punishment. It is the pitting of a common man (the victim) against an authority (the experimenter) that is the distinctive feature of the conflict. At a point in the experiment the victim demands that he be let free. The experimenter insists that the subject continue to administer shocks. Which act of the subject can be interpreted as conformity? The subject may conform to the wishes of his peer or to the wishes of the experimenter, and conformity in one direction means the absence of conformity in the other. Thus the word has no useful reference in this setting, for the dual and conflicting social pressures cancel out its meaning.

In the final analysis, the linguistic symbol representing the subject's action must take its meaning from the concrete context in which that action occurs; and there is probably no word in everyday language that covers the experimental situation exactly, without omissions or irrelevant connotations. It is partly for convenience, therefore, that the terms *obey* and *disobey* are used to describe the subject's actions. At the same time, our use of the words is highly congruent with dictionary meaning.

command series defies the experimenter will be called a *disobedient* or *defiant* subject. As used in this report the terms refer only to the subject's performance in the experiment, and do not necessarily imply a general personality disposition to submit to or reject authority.

Subject Population

The subjects used in all experimental conditions were male adults, residing in the greater New Haven and Bridgeport areas, aged 20 to 50 years, and engaged in a wide variety of occupations. Each experimental condition described in this report employed 40 fresh subjects and was carefully balanced for age and occupational types. The occupational composition for each experiment was: workers, skilled and unskilled: 40 percent; white collar, sales, business: 40 percent; professionals: 20 percent. The occupations were intersected with three age categories (subjects in 20's, 30's, and 40's, assigned to each condition in the proportions of 20, 40, and 40 percent, respectively).

The General Laboratory Procedure[6]

The focus of the study concerns the amount of electric shock a subject   10
is willing to administer to another person when ordered by an experimenter to give the "victim" increasingly more severe punishment. The act of administering shock is set in the context of a learning experiment, ostensibly designed to study the effect of punishment on memory. Aside from the experimenter, one naïve subject and one accomplice perform in each session. On arrival each subject is paid $4.50. After a general talk by the experimenter, telling how little scientists know about the effect of punishment on memory, subjects are informed that one member of the pair will serve as teacher and one as learner. A rigged drawing is held so that the naïve subject is always the teacher, and the accomplice becomes the learner. The learner is taken to an adjacent room and strapped into an "electric chair."

The naïve subject is told that it is his task to teach the learner a list of paired associates, to test him on the list, and to administer punishment whenever the learner errs in the test. Punishment takes the form of electric shock, delivered to the learner by means of a shock generator controlled by the naïve subject. The teacher is instructed to increase the intensity of elec-

---

[6]A more detailed account of the laboratory procedure can be found in Milgram (1963). A similar and independently evolved experimental procedure, employing a shock generator, victim, and learning task, was reported by Buss (1961). Buss used the technique for studying aggression, not obedience, and did not make use of the fundamental measure employed in the present study: breakoff points.

tric shock one step on the generator on each error. The learner, according to plan, provides many wrong answers, so that before long the naïve subject must give him the strongest shock on the generator. Increases in shock level are met by increasingly insistent demands from the learner that the experiment be stopped because of the growing discomfort to him. However, in clear terms the experimenter orders the teacher to continue with the procedure in disregard of the learner's protests. *Thus, the naïve subject must resolve a conflict between two mutually incompatible demands from the social field. He may continue to follow the orders of the experimenter and shock the learner with increasing severity, or he may refuse to follow the orders of the experimenter and heed the learner's pleas. The experimenter's authority operates not in a free field, but against ever-mounting countervailing pressure from the person being punished.*

A few technical points need to be considered before the findings of the study are described. For the purpose of delivering shock, a simulated shock generator is used, with 30 clearly marked voltage levels that range from 15 to 450 volts. (Each level is activated by one of 30 individual lever switches set in a horizontal line.) The naïve subject is given a sample shock of 45 volts to convince him of the authenticity of the instrument. The generator bears verbal designations that range from "Slight Shock" to "Danger: Severe Shock."

The responses of the victim are standardized on tape, and each protest is coordinated to a particular voltage level on the shock generator. Starting with 75 volts the learner begins to grunt and moan. At 150 volts he demands to be let out of the experiment. At 180 volts he cries out that he can no longer stand the pain. At 300 volts he refuses to provide any more answers to the memory test, insisting that he is no longer a participant in the experiment and must be freed. In response to this last tactic, the experimenter instructs the naïve subject to treat the absence of an answer as equivalent to a wrong answer, and to follow the usual shock procedure. The experimenter reinforces his demand with the statement: "You have no other choice, you must go on!" (This imperative is used whenever the naïve subject tries to break off the experiment.) If the subject refuses to give the next higher level of shock, the experiment is considered at an end. A quantitative value is assigned to the subject's performance based on the maximum-intensity shock he administered before breaking off. Thus any subject's score may range from zero (for a subject unwilling to administer the first shock level) to 30 (for a subject who proceeds to the highest voltage level on the board). For any particular subject and for any particular experimental condition, the degree to which participants have followed the experimenter's orders may be specified with a numerical value, corresponding to the metric on the shock generator.

This laboratory situation gives us a framework in which to study the subject's reactions to the principal conflict of the experiment. Again, this conflict is between the experimenter's demands that he continue to administer the electric shock, and the learner's demands, which become increasingly more insistent, that the experiment be stopped. The crux of the study is to vary systematically the factors believed to alter the degree of obedience to the experimental commands, to learn under what conditions submission to authority is most probable and under what conditions defiance is brought to the fore.

Pilot Studies

Pilot studies for the present research were completed in the winter of 1960; they differed from the regular experiments in a few details: for one, the victim was placed behind a silvered glass, with the light balance on the glass such that the victim could be dimly perceived by the subject (Milgram, 1961).   15

Though essentially qualitative in treatment, these studies pointed to several significant features of the experimental situation. At first no vocal feedback was used from the victim. It was thought that the verbal and voltage designations on the control panel would create sufficient pressure to curtail the subject's obedience. However, this was not the case. In the absence of protests from the learner, virtually all subjects, once commanded, went blithely to the end of the board, seemingly indifferent to the verbal designations ("Extreme Shock" and "Danger: Severe Shock"). This deprived us of an adequate basis for scaling obedient tendencies. A force had to be introduced that would strengthen the subject's resistance to the experimenter's commands, and reveal individual differences in terms of a distribution of break-off points.

This force took the form of protests from the victim. Initially, mild protests were used, but proved inadequate. Subsequently, more vehement protests were inserted into the experimental procedure. To our consternation, even the strongest protests from the victim did not prevent all subjects from administering the harshest punishment ordered by the experimenter; but the protests did lower the mean maximum shock somewhat and created some spread in the subject's performance; therefore, the victim's cries were standardized on tape and incorporated into the regular experimental procedure.

The situation did more than highlight the technical difficulties of finding a workable experimental procedure: It indicated that subjects would obey authority to a greater extent than we had supposed. It also pointed to the importance of feedback from the victim in controlling the subject's behavior.

One further aspect of the pilot study was that subjects frequently averted their eyes from the person they were shocking, often turning their heads in an awkward and conspicuous manner. One subject explained: "I didn't want to see the consequences of what I had done." Observers wrote:

> . . . subjects showed a reluctance to look at the victim, whom they could see through the glass in front of them. When this fact was

brought to their attention they indicated that it caused them discomfort to see the victim in agony. We note, however, that although the subject refuses to look at the victim, he continues to administer shocks.

This suggested that the salience of the victim may have, in some degree, 20 regulated the subject's performance. If, in obeying the experimenter, the subject found it necessary to avoid scrutiny of the victim, would the converse be true? If the victim were rendered increasingly more salient to the subject, would obedience diminish? The first set of regular experiments was designed to answer this question.

Immediacy of the Victim

This series consisted of four experimental conditions. In each condition the victim was brought "psychologically" closer to the subject giving him shocks.

In the first condition (Remote Feedback) the victim was placed in another room and could not be heard or seen by the subject, except that, at 300 volts, he pounded on the wall in protest. After 315 volts he no longer answered or was heard from.

The second condition (Voice Feedback) was identical to the first except that voice protests were introduced. As in the first condition the victim was placed in an adjacent room, but his complaints could be heard clearly through a door left slightly ajar and through the walls of the laboratory.[7]

The third experimental condition (Proximity) was similar to the second, except that the victim was now placed in the same room as the subject,

---

[7]It is difficult to convey on the printed page the full tenor of the victim's responses, for we have no adequate notation for vocal intensity, timing, and general qualities of delivery. Yet these features are crucial to producing the effect of an increasingly severe reaction to mounting voltage levels. (They can be communicated fully only by sending interested parties the recorded tapes.) In general terms, however, the victim indicates no discomfort until the 75-volt shock is administered, at which time there is a light grunt in response to the punishment. Similar reactions follow the 90- and 105-volt shocks, and at 120 volts the victim shouts to the experimenter that the shocks are becoming painful. Painful groans are heard on administration of the 135-volt shock, and at 150 volts the victim cries out, "Experimenter, get me out of here! I won't be in the experiment any more! I refuse to go on!" Cries of this type continue with generally rising intensity, so that at 180 volts the victim cries out, "I can't stand the pain," and by 270 volts his response to the shock is definitely an agonized scream. Throughout, he insists that he be let out of the experiment. At 300 volts the victim shouts in desperation that he will no longer provide answers to the memory test; and at 315 volts, after a violent scream, he reaffirms with vehemence that he is no longer a participant. From this point on, he provides

and 1⅜ feet from him. Thus he was visible as well as audible, and voice cues were provided.

The fourth, and final, condition of this series (Touch-Proximity) was   25
identical to the third, with this exception: The victim received a shock only when his hand rested on a shockplate. At the 150-volt level the victim again demanded to be let free and, in this condition, refused to place his hand on the shockplate. The experimenter ordered the naïve subject to force the victim's hand onto the plate. Thus obedience in this condition required that the subject have physical contact with the victim in order to give him punishment beyond the 150-volt level.

Forty adult subjects were studied in each condition. The data revealed that obedience was significantly reduced as the victim was rendered more immediate to the subject. The mean maximum shock for the conditions is shown in Figure 1.

Expressed in terms of the proportion of obedient to defiant subjects, the findings are that 34 percent of the subjects defied the experimenter in the Remote condition, 37.5 percent in Voice Feedback, 60 percent in Proximity, and 70 percent in Touch-Proximity.

How are we to account for this effect? A first conjecture might be that as the victim was brought closer the subject became more aware of the intensity of his suffering and regulated his behavior accordingly. This makes sense, but our evidence does not support the interpretation. There are no consistent differences in the attributed level of pain across the four conditions (i.e., the amount of pain experienced by the victim as estimated by the subject and expressed on a 14-point scale). But it is easy to speculate about alternative mechanisms:

> *Empathic cues.* In the Remote and to a lesser extent the Voice Feedback conditions, the victim's suffering possesses an abstract, remote quality for the subject. He is aware, but only in a conceptual sense, that his actions

---

no answers, but shrieks in agony whenever a shock is administered; this continues through 450 volts. Of course, many subjects will have broken off before this point.

A revised and stronger set of protests was used in all experiments outside the Proximity series. Naturally, new baseline measures were established for all comparisons using the new set of protests.

There is overwhelming evidence that the great majority of subjects, both obedient and defiant, accepted the victims' reactions as genuine. The evidence takes the form of: (a) tension created in the subjects (see discussion of tension); (b) scores on "estimated-pain" scales filled out by subjects immediately after the experiment; (c) subjects' accounts of their feelings in post-experimental interviews; and (d) quantifiable responses to questionnaires distributed to subjects several months after their participation in the experiments. This matter will be treated fully in a forthcoming monograph.

(The procedure in all experimental conditions was to have the naïve subject announce the voltage level before administering each shock, so that — independently of the victim's responses — he was continually reminded of delivering punishment of ever-increasing severity.)

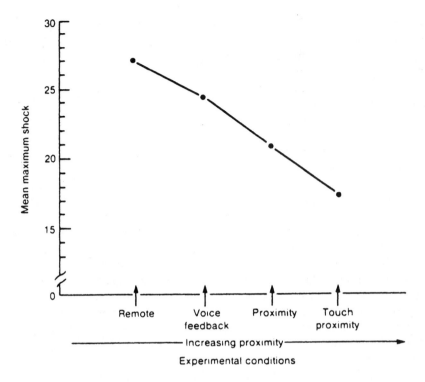

FIGURE 1 Mean maxima in proximity series.

cause pain to another person; the fact is apprehended, but not felt. The phenomenon is common enough. The bombardier can reasonably suppose that his weapons will inflict suffering and death, yet this knowledge is divested of affect and does not move him to a felt, emotional response to the suffering resulting from his actions. Similar observations have been made in wartime. It is possible that the visual cues associated with the victim's suffering trigger empathic responses in the subject and provide him with a more complete grasp of the victim's experience. Or it is possible that the empathic responses are themselves unpleasant, possessing drive properties which cause the subject to terminate the arousal situation. Diminishing obedience, then, would be explained by the enrichment of empathic cues in the successive experimental conditions.

Denial and narrowing of the cognitive field. The Remote condition allows   30
a narrowing of the cognitive field so that the victim is put out of mind. The subject no longer considers the act of depressing a lever relevant to moral judgment, for it is no longer associated with the victim's suffering. When the victim is close it is more difficult to exclude him phenomenologically. He necessarily intrudes on the subject's awareness since he is continuously visible. In the Remote condition his existence and reactions are made known only after the shock has been administered. The auditory

feedback is sporadic and discontinuous. In the Proximity conditions his inclusion in the immediate visual field renders him a continuously salient element for the subject. The mechanism of denial can no longer be brought into play. One subject in the Remote condition said: "It's funny how you really begin to forget that there's a guy out there, even though you can hear him. For a long time I just concentrated on pressing the switches and reading the words."

Reciprocal fields. If in the Proximity condition the subject is in an improved position to observe the victim, the reverse is also true. The actions of the subject now come under proximal scrutiny by the victim. Possibly, it is easier to harm a person when he is unable to observe our actions than when he can see what we are doing. His surveillance of the action directed against him may give rise to shame, or guilt, which may then serve to curtail the action. Many expressions of language refer to the discomfort or inhibitions that arise in face-to-face confrontation. It is often said that it is easier to criticize a man "behind his back" than to "attack him to his face." If we are in the process of lying to a person it is reputedly difficult to "stare him in the eye." We "turn away from others in shame" or in "embarrassment" and this action serves to reduce our discomfort. The manifest function of allowing the victim of a firing squad to be blindfolded is to make the occasion less stressful for him, but it may also serve a latent function of reducing the stress of the executioner. In short, in the Proximity conditions, the subject may sense that he has become more salient in the victim's field of awareness. Possibly he becomes more self-conscious, embarrassed, and inhibited in his punishment of the victim.

Phenomenal unity of act. In the Remote condition it is more difficult for the subject to gain a sense of *relatedness* between his own actions and the consequences of these actions for the victim. There is a physical and spatial separation of the act and its consequences. The subject depresses a lever in one room, and protests and cries are heard from another. The two events are in correlation, yet they lack a compelling phenomenological unity. The structure of a meaningful act — *I am hurting a man* — breaks down because of the spatial arrangements, in a manner somewhat analogous to the disappearance of phi phenomena[8] when the blinking lights are spaced too far apart. The unity is more fully achieved in the Proximity condition as the victim is brought closer to the action that causes him pain. It is rendered complete in Touch-Proximity.

---

[8]*phi phenomena*: Optical illusions of motion. The phi phenomenon is an illusion of apparent motion that is generated when similar stationary objects are presented one after another at a certain time interval. [Eds.]

Incipient group formation. Placing the victim in another room not only takes him further from the subject, but the subject and the experimenter are drawn relatively closer. There is incipient group formation between the experimenter and the subject, from which the victim is excluded. The wall between the victim and the others deprives him of an intimacy which the experimenter and subject feel. In the Remote condition, the victim is truly an outsider, who stands alone, physically and psychologically.

When the victim is placed close to the subject, it becomes easier to form an alliance with him against the experimenter. Subjects no longer have to face the experimenter alone. They have an ally who is close at hand and eager to collaborate in a revolt against the experimenter. Thus, the changing set of spatial relations leads to a potentially shifting set of alliances over the several experimental conditions.

Acquired behavior dispositions. It is commonly observed that labora-   35
tory mice will rarely fight with their litter mates. Scott (1958) explains this in terms of passive inhibition. He writes: "By doing nothing under . . . circumstances [the animal] learns to do nothing, and this may be spoken of as passive inhibition . . . this principle has great importance in teaching an individual to be peaceful, for it means that he can learn not to fight simply by not fighting." Similarly, we may learn not to harm others simply by not harming them in everyday life. Yet this learning occurs in a context of proximal relations with others, and may not be generalized to that situation in which the person is physically removed from us. Or possibly, in the past, aggressive actions against others who were physically close resulted in retaliatory punishment which extinguished the original form of response. In contrast, aggression against others at a distance may have only sporadically led to retaliation. Thus the organism learns that it is safer to be aggressive toward others at a distance, and precarious to be so when the parties are within arm's reach. Through a pattern of rewards and punishments, he acquires a disposition to avoid aggression at close quarters, a disposition which does not extend to harming others at a distance. And this may account for experimental findings in the remote and proximal experiments.

Proximity as a variable in psychological research has received far less attention than it deserves. If men were sessile[9] it would be easy to understand this neglect. But we move about; our spatial relations shift from one situation to the next, and the fact that we are near or remote may have a powerful effect on the psychological processes that mediate our behavior toward others. In the present situation, as the victim is brought closer to the subject ordered to give him shocks, increasing numbers of subjects break off the experiment,

---

[9]*sessile*: Permanently attached, not moving freely. [Eds.]

refusing to obey. The concrete, visible, and proximal presence of the victim acts in an important way to counteract the experimenter's power to generate disobedience.[10]

Closeness of Authority

If the spatial relationship of the subject and victim is relevant to the degree of obedience, would not the relationship of subject to experimenter also play a part?

There are reasons to feel that, on arrival, the subject is oriented primarily to the experimenter rather than to the victim. He has come to the laboratory to fit into the structure that the experimenter — not the victim — would provide. He has come less to understand his behavior than to *reveal* that behavior to a competent scientist, and he is willing to display himself as the scientist's purposes require. Most subjects seem quite concerned about the appearance they are making before the experimenter, and one could argue that this preoccupation in a relatively new and strange setting makes the subject somewhat insensitive to the triadic nature of the social situation. In other words, the subject is so concerned about the show he is putting on for the experimenter that influences from other parts of the social field do not receive as much weight as they ordinarily would. This overdetermined orientation to the experimenter would account for the relative insensitivity of the subject to the victim, and would also lead us to believe that alterations in the relationship between subject and experimenter would have important consequences for obedience.

In a series of experiments we varied the physical closeness and degree of surveillance of the experimenter. In one condition the experimenter sat just a few feet away from the subject. In a second condition, after giving initial instructions, the experimenter left the laboratory and gave his orders by telephone. In still a third condition the experimenter was never seen, providing instructions by means of a tape recording activated when the subjects entered the laboratory.

Obedience dropped sharply as the experimenter was physically removed from the laboratory. The number of obedient subjects in the first   40

---

[10]Admittedly, the terms *proximity*, *immediacy*, *closeness*, and *salience-of-the-victim* are used in a loose sense, and the experiments themselves represent a very coarse treatment of the variable. Further experiments are needed to refine the notion and tease out such diverse factors as spatial distance, visibility, audibility, barrier interposition, etc.

The Proximity and Touch-Proximity experiments were the only conditions where we were unable to use taped feedback from the victim. Instead, the victim was trained to respond in these conditions as he had in Experiment 2 (which employed taped feedback). Some improvement is possible here, for it should be technically feasible to do a proximity series using taped feedback.

condition (Experimenter Present) was almost three times as great as in the second, where the experimenter gave his orders by telephone. Twenty-six subjects were fully obedient in the first condition, and only nine in the second (Chi square obedient vs. defiant in the two conditions, df = 14.7; $p < 0.001$). Subjects seemed able to take a far stronger stand against the experimenter when they did not have to encounter him face to face, and the experimenter's power over the subject was severely curtailed.[11]

Moreover, when the experimenter was absent, subjects displayed an interesting form of behavior that had not occurred under his surveillance. Though continuing with the experiment, several subjects administered lower shocks than were required and never informed the experimenter of their deviation from the correct procedure. (Unknown to the subjects, shock levels were automatically recorded by an Esterline-Angus event recorder wired directly into the shock generator; the instrument provided us with an objective record of the subjects' performance.) Indeed, in telephone conversations some subjects specifically assured the experimenter that they were raising the shock level according to instruction, whereas in fact they were repeatedly using the lowest shock on the board. This form of behavior is particularly interesting: although these subjects acted in a way that clearly undermined the avowed purposes of the experiment, they found it easier to handle the conflict in this manner than to precipitate an open break with authority.

Other conditions were completed in which the experimenter was absent during the first segment of the experiment, but reappeared at the point that the subject definitely refused to give higher shocks when commanded by telephone. Although he had exhausted his power via telephone, the experimenter could frequently force further obedience when he reappeared in the laboratory.

Experiments in this series show that the *physical presence* of an authority is an important force contributing to the subject's obedience or defiance. Taken together with the first experimental series on the proximity of the victim, it would appear that something akin to fields of force, diminishing in effectiveness with increasing psychological distance from their source, have a controlling effect on the subject's performance. As the victim is brought closer, the subject finds it harder to administer shocks to him. When the victim's position is held constant relative to the subject, and the authority is made more remote, the subject finds it easier to break off the experiment. This effect is substantial in both cases, but manipulation of the experimenter's position yielded the more powerful results. Obedience to destructive commands is highly dependent on the proximal relations between authority and subject.

---

[11]The third condition also led to significantly lower obedience than this first situation in which the experimenter was present, but it contains technical difficulties that require extensive discussion.

Tensions

The description of final scores does not fully convey the character of the subjects' performance, and it would be useful to interrupt our reporting of quantitative relationships to remark on the subjects' general reaction to the situation.

One might suppose that a subject would simply break off or continue   45 as his conscience and temperament dictated. Yet this is very far from what happened. There were powerful reactions of tension and emotional strain in a substantial proportion of the participants. Persons were observed to sweat, tremble, stutter, bite their lips, and groan as they found themselves increasingly implicated in the experimental conflict. Some sense of the subjects' mood can be found in a transcript of their remarks at break-off point. Here are the remarks of two defiant subjects:

> Is he banging? . . . Is he hurt out there? Well, I don't want to be responsible for anything that happens to him. No, I can't go on with it. I don't know whether he's all right or not. I mean he may have a heart condition or something; I wouldn't feel right doing it. He's banging for help. He's evidently in trouble or he wouldn't bang . . . I don't see any sense to this — to knocking him out or something. I just can't see it.
>   [*Subject refuses to administer shocks*]   [*Subject 0108*]

> The man is banging. He wants to get out . . . I'm sorry. If the man wants to get out I'd just as soon stop . . . I don't want to administer any more [extremely excited] . . . I will gladly refund the check, but I will not harm this man . . . I'm sorry, I will not give him any more if he obviously wants to get out. There is no money in the world that will make me hurt another individual.
>   [*Subject 010X*]

And here is a transcript from an obedient subject. He began the experiment calmly, but became increasingly tense as the experiment proceeded. After administering the 150-volt shock, he began to address the experimenter in agitated tones:

> *150 volts delivered.* You want me to keep going?
> *165 volts delivered.* That guy is hollering in there. There's a lot of them here. He's liable to have a heart condition. You want me to go?
> *180 volts delivered.* He can't stand it! I'm not going to kill that man in there! You hear him hollering? He's hollering. He can't stand it. What if something happens to him? . . . I'm not going to get that man sick in there. He's hollering in there. You know what I mean? I mean I refuse to take responsibility. He's getting hurt in there. He's in there hollering. Too many left here. Geez, if he gets

them wrong. There's too many of them left. I mean who is going to take responsibility if anything happens to that gentleman?
[*The experimenter accepts responsibility.*] All right.
195 volts delivered. You see he's hollering. Hear that. Gee, I don't know.
[*The experimenter says: "The experiment requires that you go on."*] — I know it does, sir, but I mean — hugh — he don't know what he's in for. He's up to 195 volts.
210 volts delivered.
225 volts delivered.
240 volts delivered. Aw, no. You mean I've got to keep going up with the scale? No sir. I'm not going to kill that man! I'm not going to give him 450 volts!
[*The experimenter says: "The experiment requires that you go on."*] — I know it does, but that man is hollering there, sir . . .

Despite his numerous, agitated objections, which were constant accompaniments to his actions, the subject unfailingly obeyed the experimenter, proceeding to the highest shock level on the generator. He displayed a curious dissociation between word and action. Although at the verbal level he had resolved not to go on, his actions were fully in accord with the experimenter's commands. This subject did not want to shock the victim, and he found it an extremely disagreeable task, but he was unable to invent a response that would free him from *E*'s authority. Many subjects cannot find the specific verbal formula that would enable them to reject the role assigned to them by the experimenter. Perhaps our culture does not provide adequate models for disobedience.

One puzzling sign of tension was the regular occurrence of nervous laughing fits. In the first four conditions 71 of the 160 subjects showed definite signs of nervous laughter and smiling. The laughter seemed entirely out of place, even bizarre. Full-blown, uncontrollable seizures were observed for 15 of these subjects. On one occasion we observed a seizure so violently convulsive that it was necessary to call a halt to the experiment. In the post-experimental interviews subjects took pains to point out that they were not sadistic types and that the laughter did not mean they enjoyed shocking the victim.

In the interview following the experiment subjects were asked to indicate on a 14-point scale just how nervous or tense they felt at the point of maximum tension (Figure 2). The scale ranged from "not at all tense and nervous" to "extremely tense and nervous." Self-reports of this sort are of limited precision and at best provide only a rough indication of the subject's emotional response. Still, taking the reports for what they are worth, it can be seen that the distribution of responses spans the entire range of the scale, with the majority of subjects concentrated at the center and upper extreme. A further breakdown showed that obedient subjects reported themselves as having been slightly more tense and nervous than the defiant subjects at the point of maximum tension.

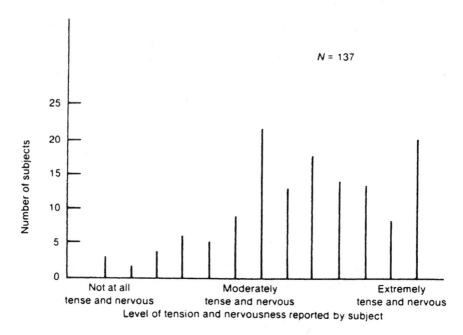

FIGURE 2 Level of tension and nervousness: the self-reports on "tension and nervousness" for 137 subjects on the Proximity experiments. Subjects were given a scale with 14 values ranging from "not at all tense and nervous" to "extremely tense and nervous." They were instructed: "Thinking back to that point in the experiment when you felt the most tense and nervous, indicate just how you felt by placing an X at the appropriate point on the scale." The results are shown in terms of midpoint values.

How is the occurrence of tension to be interpreted? First, it points to the presence of conflict. If a tendency to comply with authority were the only psychological force operating in the situation, all subjects would have continued to the end and there would have been no tension. Tension, it is assumed, results from the simultaneous presence of two or more incompatible response tendencies (Miller, 1944). If sympathetic concern for the victim were the exclusive force, all subjects would have calmly defied the experimenter. Instead, there were both obedient and defiant outcomes, frequently accompanied by extreme tension. A conflict develops between the deeply ingrained disposition not to harm others and the equally compelling tendency to obey others who are in authority. The subject is quickly drawn into a dilemma of a deeply dynamic character, and the presence of high tension points to the considerable strength of each of the antagonistic vectors.

Moreover, tension defines the strength of the aversive state from which the subject is unable to escape through disobedience. When a person is uncomfortable, tense, or stressed, he tries to take some action that will allow him to terminate this unpleasant state. Thus tension may serve as a drive that leads to escape behavior. But in the present situation, even where ten- 50 sion is extreme, many subjects are unable to perform the response that will bring about relief. Therefore there must be a competing drive, tendency, or inhibition that precludes activation of the disobedient response. The strength of this inhibiting factor must be of greater magnitude than the stress experienced, or else the terminating act would occur. Every evidence of extreme tension is at the same time an indication of the strength of the forces that keep the subject in the situation.

Finally, tension may be taken as evidence of the reality of the situations for the subjects. Normal subjects do not tremble and sweat unless they are implicated in a deep and genuinely felt predicament.

Background Authority

In psychophysics, animal learning, and other branches of psychology, the fact that measures are obtained at one institution rather than another is irrelevant to the interpretation of the findings, so long as the technical facilities for measurement are adequate and the operations are carried out with competence.

But it cannot be assumed that this holds true for the present study. The effectiveness of the experimenter's commands may depend in an important way on the larger institutional context in which they are issued. The experiments described thus far were conducted at Yale University, an organization which most subjects regarded with respect and sometimes awe. In post-experimental interviews several participants remarked that the locale and sponsorship of the study gave them confidence in the integrity, competence, and benign purposes of the personnel; many indicated that they would not have shocked the learner if the experiments had been done elsewhere.

This issue of background authority seemed to us important for an interpretation of the results that had been obtained thus far; moreover it is highly relevant to any comprehensive theory of human obedience. Consider, for example, how closely our compliance with the imperatives of others is tied to particular institutions and locales in our day-to-day activities. On request, we expose our throats to a man with a razor blade in the barber shop, but would not do so in a shoe store; in the latter setting we willingly follow the clerk's request to stand in our stockinged feet, but resist the command in a bank. In the laboratory of a great university, subjects may comply with a set of commands that would be resisted if given elsewhere. *One must always question the relationship of obedience to a person's sense of the context in which he is operating.*

To explore the problem we moved our apparatus to an office building in industrial Bridgeport and replicated experimental conditions, without any visible tie to the university.

Bridgeport subjects were invited to the experiment through a mail circular similar to the one used in the Yale study, with appropriate changes in letterhead, etc. As in the earlier study, subjects were paid $4.50 for coming to the laboratory. The same age and occupational distributions used at Yale and the identical personnel were employed.

The purpose in relocating in Bridgeport was to assure a complete dissociation from Yale, and in this regard we were fully successful. On the surface, the study appeared to be conducted by Research Associates of Bridgeport, an organization of unknown character (the title had been concocted exclusively for use in this study).

The experiments were conducted in a three-room office suite in a somewhat run-down commercial building located in the downtown shopping area. The laboratory was sparsely furnished, though clean, and marginally respectable in appearance. When subjects inquired about professional affiliations, they were informed only that we were a private firm conducting research for industry.

Some subjects displayed skepticism concerning the motives of the Bridgeport experimenter. One gentleman gave us a written account of the thoughts he experienced at the control board:

> . . . Should I quit this damn test? Maybe he passed out? What dopes we were not to check up on this deal. How do we know that these guys are legit? No furniture, bare walls, no telephone. We could of called the Police up or the Better Business Bureau. I learned a lesson tonight. How do I know that Mr. Williams [the experimenter] is telling the truth . . . I wish I knew how many volts a person could take before lapsing into unconsciousness . . .
>
> [*Subject 2414*]

Another subject stated:

> I questioned on my arrival my own judgment [about coming]. I had doubts as to the legitimacy of the operation and the consequences of participation. I felt it was a heartless way to conduct memory or learning processes on human beings and certainly dangerous without the presence of a medical doctor. [*Subject 2440V*]

There was no noticeable reduction in tension for the Bridgeport subjects. And the subjects' estimation of the amount of pain felt by the victim was slightly, though not significantly, higher than in the Yale study.

A failure to obtain complete obedience in Bridgeport would indicate that the extreme compliance found in New Haven subjects was tied closely to the background authority of Yale University; if a large proportion of the subjects remained fully obedient, very different conclusions would be called for.

As it turned out, the level of obedience in Bridgeport, although somewhat reduced, was not significantly lower than that obtained at Yale. A large proportion of the Bridgeport subjects were fully obedient to the experimenter's commands (48 percent of the Bridgeport subjects delivered the maximum shock versus 65 percent in the corresponding condition at Yale).

How are these findings to be interpreted? It is possible that if commands of a potentially harmful or destructive sort are to be perceived as legitimate they must occur within some sort of institutional structure. But it is clear from the study that it need not be a particularly reputable or distinguished institution. The Bridgeport experiments were conducted by an unimpressive firm lacking any credentials; the laboratory was set up in a respectable office building with a title listed in the building directory. Beyond that, there was no evidence of benevolence or competence. It is possible that the *category* of institution, judged according to its professed function, rather than its qualitative position within that category, wins our compliance. Persons deposit money in elegant, but also in seedy-looking banks, without giving much thought to the differences in security they offer. Similarly, our subjects may consider one laboratory to be as competent as another, so long as it is a scientific laboratory.

It would be valuable to study the subjects' performance in other contexts which go even further than the Bridgeport study in denying institutional support to the experimenter. It is possible that, beyond a certain point, obedience disappears completely. But that point had not been reached in the Bridgeport office: almost half the subjects obeyed the experimenter fully.

Further Experiments

We may mention briefly some additional experiments undertaken in   65
the Yale series. A considerable amount of obedience and defiance in everyday life occurs in connection with groups. And we had reason to feel in light of the many group studies already done in psychology that group forces would have a profound effect on reactions to authority. A series of experiments was run to examine these effects. In all cases only one naïve subject was studied per hour, but he performed in the midst of actors who, unknown to him, were employed by the experimenter. In one experiment (Groups for Disobedience) two actors broke off in the middle of the experiment. When this happened 90 percent of the subjects followed suit and defied the experimenter. In another condition the actors followed the orders obediently; this strengthened the experimenter's power only slightly. In still a third experiment the job of pushing the switch to shock the learner was given to one of the actors, while the naïve subject performed a subsidiary act. We wanted to see how the teacher would respond if he were involved in the situation but did not actually give the shocks. In this situation only three subjects out of forty broke off. In a final group experiment the subjects themselves determined the shock level they were going to use. Two actors suggested higher and higher shock levels; some subjects insisted,

despite group pressure, that the shock level be kept low; others followed along with the group.

Further experiments were completed using women as subjects, as well as a set dealing with the effects of dual, unsanctioned, and conflicting authority. A final experiment concerned the personal relationship between victim and subject. These will have to be described elsewhere, lest the present report be extended to monographic length.

It goes without saying that future research can proceed in many different directions. What kinds of response from the victim are most effective in causing disobedience in the subject? Perhaps passive resistance is more effective than vehement protest. What conditions of entry into an authority system lead to greater or lesser obedience? What is the effect of anonymity and masking on the subject's behavior? What conditions lead to the subject's perception of responsibility for his own actions? Each of these could be a major research topic in itself, and can readily be incorporated into the general experimental procedure described here.

Levels of Obedience and Defiance

One general finding that merits attention is the high level of obedience manifested in the experimental situation. Subjects often expressed deep disapproval of shocking a man in the face of his objections, and others denounced it as senseless and stupid. Yet many subjects complied even while they protested. The proportion of obedient subjects greatly exceeded the expectations of the experimenter and his colleagues. At the outset, we had conjectured that subjects would not, in general, go above the level of "Strong Shock." In practice, many subjects were willing to administer the most extreme shocks available when commanded by the experimenter. For some subjects the experiment provided an occasion for aggressive release. And for others it demonstrated the extent to which obedient dispositions are deeply ingrained and engaged, irrespective of their consequences for others. Yet this is not the whole story. Somehow, the subject becomes implicated in a situation from which he cannot disengage himself.

The departure of the experimental results from intelligent expectation, to some extent, has been formalized. The procedure was to describe the experimental situation in concrete detail to a group of competent persons, and to ask them to predict the performance of 100 hypothetical subjects. For purposes of indicating the distribution of break-off points, judges were provided with a diagram of the shock generator and recorded their predictions before being informed of the actual results. Judges typically underestimated the amount of obedience demonstrated by subjects.

In Figure 3, we compare the predictions of forty psychiatrists at a leading medical school with the actual performance of subjects in the experiment. The psychiatrists predicted that most subjects would not go beyond the tenth shock level (150 volts; at this point the victim makes his first explicit

70

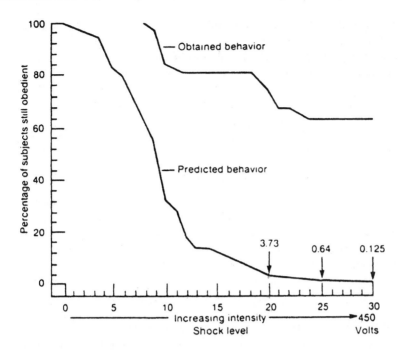

FIGURE 3 Predicted and obtained behavior in voice feedback.

demand to be freed). They further predicted that by the twentieth shock level (300 volts; the victim refuses to answer) 3.73 percent of the subjects would still be obedient; and that only a little over one-tenth of one percent of the subjects would administer the highest shock on the board. But, as the graph indicates, the obtained behavior was very different. Sixty-two percent of the subjects obeyed the experimenter's commands fully. Between expectation and occurrence there is a whopping discrepancy.

Why did the psychiatrists underestimate the level of obedience? Possibly, because their predictions were based on an inadequate conception of the determinants of human action, a conception that focuses on motives *in vacuo*. This orientation may be entirely adequate for the repair of bruised impulses as revealed on the psychiatrist's couch, but as soon as our interest turns to action in larger settings, attention must be paid to the situations in which motives are expressed. A situation exerts an important press on the individual. It exercises constraints and may provide push. In certain circumstances it is not so much the kind of person a man is, as the kind of situation in which he is placed, that determines his actions.

Many people, not knowing much about the experiment, claim that subjects who go to the end of the board are sadistic. Nothing could be more foolish than an overall characterization of these persons. It is like saying that a person thrown into a swift-flowing stream is necessarily a fast swimmer, or that he has great stamina because he moves so rapidly relative to the bank. The context of action must always be considered. The individual, upon entering the laboratory, becomes integrated into a situation that carries its own momentum. The subject's problem then is how to become disengaged from a situation which is moving in an altogether ugly direction.

The fact that disengagement is so difficult testifies to the potency of the forces that keep the subject at the control board. Are these forces to be conceptualized as individual motives and expressed in the language of personality dynamics, or are they to be seen as the effects of social structure and pressures arising from the situational field?

A full understanding of the subject's action will, I feel, require that both perspectives be adopted. The person brings to the laboratory enduring dispositions toward authority and aggression, and at the same time he becomes enmeshed in a social structure that is no less an objective fact of the case. From the standpoint of personality theory one may ask: What mechanisms of personality enable a person to transfer responsibility to authority? What are the motives underlying obedient and disobedient performance? Does orientation to authority lead to a short-circuiting of the shame-guilt system? What cognitive and emotional defenses are brought into play in the case of obedient and defiant subjects?

The present experiments are not, however, directed toward an exploration of the motives engaged when the subject obeys the experimenter's commands. Instead, they examine the situational variables responsible for the elicitation of obedience. Elsewhere, we have attempted to spell out some of the structural properties of the experimental situation that account for high obedience, and this analysis need not be repeated here (Milgram, 1963). The experimental variations themselves represent our attempt to probe that structure, by systematically changing it and noting the consequences for behavior. It is clear that some situations produce greater compliance with the experimenter's commands than others. However, this does not necessarily imply an increase or decrease in the strength of any single definable motive. Situations producing the greatest obedience could do so by triggering the most powerful, yet perhaps the most idiosyncratic, of motives in each subject confronted by the setting. Or they may simply recruit a greater number and variety of motives in their service. But whatever the motives involved — and it is far from certain that they can ever be known — action may be studied as a direct function of the situation in which it occurs. This has been the approach of the present study, where we sought to plot behavioral regularities against manipulated properties of the social field. Ultimately, social psychology would like to have a compelling *theory of situations* which will, first, present a language in terms of which situations can be defined; proceed to a typology of situations; and then point to the manner in which definable properties of situations are transformed into psychological forces in the individual.[12]

75

---

[12]My thanks to Professor Howard Leventhal of Yale for strengthening the writing in this paragraph.

Postscript

Almost a thousand adults were individually studied in the obedience research, and there were many specific conclusions regarding the variables that control obedience and disobedience to authority. Some of these have been discussed briefly in the preceding sections, and more detailed reports will be released subsequently.

There are now some other generalizations I should like to make, which do not derive in any strictly logical fashion from the experiments as carried out, but which, I feel, ought to be made. They are formulations of an intuitive sort that have been forced on me by observation of many subjects responding to the pressures of authority. The assertions represent a painful alteration in my own thinking; and since they were acquired only under the repeated impact of direct observation, I have no illusion that they will be generally accepted by persons who have not had the same experience.

With numbing regularity good people were seen to knuckle under the demands of authority and perform actions that were callous and severe. Men who are in everyday life responsible and decent were seduced by the trappings of authority, by the control of their perceptions, and by the uncritical acceptance of the experimenter's definition of the situation, into performing harsh acts.

What is the limit of such obedience? At many points we attempted to establish a boundary. Cries from the victim were inserted; not good enough. The victim claimed heart trouble; subjects still shocked him on command. The victim pleaded that he be let free, and his answers no longer registered on the signal box; subjects continued to shock him. At the outset we had not conceived that such drastic procedures would be needed to generate disobedience, and each step was added only as the ineffectiveness of the earlier techniques became clear. The final effort to establish a limit was the Touch-Proximity condition. But the very first subject in this condition subdued the victim on command, and proceeded to the highest shock level. A quarter of the subjects in this condition performed similarly.

The results, as seen and felt in the laboratory, are to this author disturbing. They raise the possibility that human nature or, more specifically, the kind of character produced in American democratic society cannot be counted on to insulate its citizens from brutality and inhumane treatment at the direction of malevolent authority. A substantial proportion of people do what they are told to do, irrespective of the content of the act and without limitations of conscience, so long as they perceive that the command comes from a legitimate authority. If in this study an anonymous experimenter could successfully command adults to subdue a fifty-year-old man and force on him painful electric shocks against his protests, one can only wonder what government, with its vastly greater authority and prestige, can command of its subjects. There is, of course, the extremely important question of whether malevolent political institutions could or would arise in American society. The present research contributes nothing to this issue.

In an article titled "The Danger of Obedience," Harold J. Laski wrote:

> . . . civilization means, above all, an unwillingness to inflict un-
> necessary pain. Within the ambit of that definition, those of us who
> heedlessly accept the commands of authority cannot yet claim to be
> civilized men.
>   . . . Our business, if we desire to live a life, not utterly devoid of
> meaning and significance, is to accept nothing which contradicts
> our basic experience merely because it comes to us from tradition or
> convention or authority. It may well be that we shall be wrong; but
> our self-expression is thwarted at the root unless the certainties we
> are asked to accept coincide with the certainties we experience.
> That is why the condition of freedom in any state is always a wide-
> spread and consistent skepticism of the canons upon which power
> insists.

References

Buss, Arnold H. 1961. *The Psychology of Aggression*. New York and London: John
    Wiley.
Kierkegaard, S. 1843. *Fear and Trembling*. English edition, Princeton: Princeton
    University Press, 1941.
Laski, Harold J. 1929. "The dangers of obedience." *Harper's Monthly Magazine*,
    15 June, 1–10.
Milgram, S. 1961. "Dynamics of obedience: experiments in social psychology."
    Mimeographed report, *National Science Foundation*, January 25.
——— 1963. "Behavioral study of obedience." *J. Abnorm. Soc. Psychol.* 67,
    371–378.
——— 1964. "Issues in the study of obedience: a reply to Baumrind." *Amer. Psy-
    chol.* 1, 848–852.
Miller, N. E. 1944. "Experimental studies of conflict." In J. McV. Hunt (ed.), *Per-
    sonality and the Behavior Disorders*. New York: Ronald Press.
Scott, J. P. 1958. *Aggression*. Chicago: University of Chicago Press.

QUESTIONS

1. What did Milgram want to determine by his experiment? What were
   his anticipated outcomes?
2. What conclusions did Milgram reach about the extent to which ordinary individuals would obey the orders of an authority figure? Under
   what conditions is this submission most probable? Under what conditions is defiance most likely?
3. Describe the general procedures of this experiment. Some people have
   questioned Milgram's methods. Do you think it is ethical to expose
   participants without warning to experiments that might have a lasting

effect on them? What effects might this experiment have had on its participants?

4. One characteristic of this article is Milgram's willingness to consider several possible explanations of the same phenomenon. Study the interpretations in paragraphs 28 through 35. What do you make of the range of interpretation there and elsewhere in the article? How does Milgram achieve such a range?

5. A report such as Milgram's is not structured in the same way as a conventional essay. His research is really a collection of separate but related experiments, each one of which requires its own interpretation. Describe the groups into which these experiments fall. Which results seemed most surprising to you? Which were easiest to anticipate?

6. In Milgram's experiment, people who are responsible and decent in everyday life were seduced, he says, by trappings of authority. Most of us, however, like to believe that we would neither engage in brutality on our own nor obey directions of this kind. Has Milgram succeeded in getting you to question your own behavior? Would you go so far as to say that he forces you to question your own human nature?

7. In paragraph 46, Milgram comments, "Perhaps our culture does not provide adequate models for disobedience." What do you think of this hypothesis? Are there such models? Ought there to be? Have such models appeared since the experiment was conducted? Explain your stand on Milgram's statement.

8. If research in social psychology takes place in your school today, a panel of some sort probably enforces guidelines on research with human participants. Locate that board, if it exists, and find out whether this experiment could take place today. Report to your class on the rules that currently guide researchers. Do you think that those rules are wise?

9. What, in your opinion, should be the guidelines for psychological research with human subjects? List the guidelines that you think are appropriate, and compare your list with the lists of your classmates. Would your guidelines have allowed Milgram's experiment?

10. Think of a situation in which you were faced with the moral and ethical dilemma of whether to obey a figure of authority. How did you behave? Did your behavior surprise you? Describe and explain that experience.

MAKING CONNECTIONS

1. One of the conditions of valid scientific research is the replicability of its experiments. When we are persuaded that results are replicable, we are inclined to believe that they are valid. What provisions for replicability does Milgram make in his experiments? Compare his stance to that of Oliver Sacks (p. 711), whose observations are not replicable but who is also concerned with writing authoritative science.

2. Think of other essays in this collection in which ethical matters are at issue, particularly the ethics of composing some kind of story. Consider Richard Selzer's "A Mask on the Face of Death" (p. 605). In it, human subjects seem to be manipulated for the sake of the writer's interests. Perhaps you would prefer to offer another example. Whatever study you choose, compare it to Milgram's, and discuss the two writers' sensitivity to their human subjects. Note also the last sentence of Milgram's first footnote. What choices do the writers have in the cases that interest you most?

ON THE FEAR OF DEATH

Elisabeth Kübler-Ross

Elisabeth Kübler-Ross (1926–2004), a Swiss American psychiatrist, was one of the leaders of the movement that may help change the way Americans think about death. Born in Zurich, she received her M.D. from the University of Zurich in 1957 and came to the United States as an intern the following year. Kübler-Ross began her work with terminally ill patients while teaching psychiatry at the University of Chicago Medical School. She founded the hospice care movement in the United States and ran Shanti Nilaya (Sanskrit for "home of peace"), an organization "dedicated to the promotion of physical, emotional, and spiritual health." She was the author of more than twenty books and the recipient of numerous awards and honors, including being named one of Time *magazine's 100 Most Important Thinkers of the Century in 1999. Her last book,* On Grief and Grieving, *cowritten with David Kessler, was published posthumously in 2005. This selection is taken from her first and most famous book,* On Death and Dying *(1969).*

> Let me not pray to be sheltered from
> dangers but to be fearless in facing them.
> Let me not beg for the stilling of my
> pain but for the heart to conquer it.
> Let me not look for allies in life's battle-
> field but to my own strength.
> Let me not crave in anxious fear to be
> saved but hope for the patience to win my
> freedom.
> Grant me that I may not be a coward,
> feeling your mercy in my success alone;
> but let me find the grasp of your hand in
> my failure.
> —RABINDRANATH TAGORE, *Fruit-Gathering*

Epidemics have taken a great toll of lives in past generations. Death in infancy and early childhood was frequent and there were few families who didn't lose a member of the family at an early age. Medicine has changed greatly in the last decades. Widespread vaccinations have practically eradicated many illnesses, at least in western Europe and the United States. The use of chemotherapy, especially the antibiotics, has contributed to an ever-decreasing number of fatalities in infectious diseases. Better child care and education have effected a low morbidity and mortality among children. The many diseases that have taken an impressive toll among the young and middle-aged have been conquered. The number of old people is on the rise, and with this fact come the number of people with malignancies and chronic diseases associated more with old age.

Pediatricians have less work with acute and life-threatening situations as they have an ever-increasing number of patients with psychosomatic disturbances and adjustment and behavior problems. Physicians have more people in their waiting rooms with emotional problems than they have ever had before, but they also have more elderly patients who not only try to live with their decreased physical abilities and limitations but who also face loneliness and isolation with all its pains and anguish. The majority of these people are not seen by a psychiatrist. Their needs have to be elicited and gratified by other professional people, for instance, chaplains and social workers. It is for them that I am trying to outline the changes that have taken place in the last few decades, changes that are ultimately responsible for the increased fear of death, the rising number of emotional problems, and the greater need for understanding of and coping with the problems of death and dying.

When we look back in time and study old cultures and people, we are impressed that death has always been distasteful to man and will probably always be. From a psychiatrist's point of view this is very understandable and can perhaps best be explained by our basic knowledge that, in our unconscious, death is never possible in regard to ourselves. It is inconceivable for our unconscious to imagine an actual ending of our own life here on earth, and if this life of ours has to end, the ending is always attributed to a malicious intervention from the outside by someone else. In simple terms, in our unconscious mind we can only be killed; it is inconceivable to die of a natural cause or of old age. Therefore death in itself is associated with a bad act, a frightening happening, something that in itself calls for retribution and punishment.

One is wise to remember these fundamental facts as they are essential in understanding some of the most important, otherwise unintelligible communications of our patients.

The second fact that we have to comprehend is that in our unconscious 5
mind we cannot distinguish between a wish and a deed. We are all aware of some of our illogical dreams in which two completely opposite statements can exist side by side — very acceptable in our dreams but unthinkable and illogical in our wakening state. Just as our unconscious mind cannot differentiate between the wish to kill somebody in anger and the act of having done so, the young child is unable to make this distinction. The child who angrily wishes his mother to drop dead for not having gratified his needs will be traumatized greatly by the actual death of his mother — even if this event is not linked closely in time with his destructive wishes. He will always take part or the whole blame for the loss of his mother. He will always say to himself — rarely to others — "I did it, I am responsible, I

was bad, therefore Mommy left me." It is well to remember that the child will react in the same manner if he loses a parent by divorce, separation, or desertion. Death is often seen by a child as an impermanent thing and has therefore little distinction from a divorce in which he may have an opportunity to see a parent again.

Many a parent will remember remarks of their children such as, "I will bury my doggy now and next spring when the flowers come up again, he will get up." Maybe it was the same wish that motivated the ancient Egyptians to supply their dead with food and goods to keep them happy and the old American Indians to bury their relatives with their belongings.

When we grow older and begin to realize that our omnipotence is really not so omnipotent, that our strongest wishes are not powerful enough to make the impossible possible, the fear that we have contributed to the death of a loved one diminishes — and with it the guilt. The fear remains diminished, however, only so long as it is not challenged too strongly. Its vestiges can be seen daily in hospital corridors and in people associated with the bereaved.

A husband and wife may have been fighting for years, but when the partner dies, the survivor will pull his hair, whine and cry louder and beat his chest in regret, fear and anguish, and will hence fear his own death more than before, still believing in the law of talion — an eye for an eye, a tooth for a tooth — "I am responsible for her death, I will have to die a pitiful death in retribution."

Maybe this knowledge will help us understand many of the old customs and rituals which have lasted over the centuries and whose purpose is to diminish the anger of the gods or the people as the case may be, thus decreasing the anticipated punishment. I am thinking of the ashes, the torn clothes, the veil, the *Klage Weiber* of the old days[1] — they are all means to ask you to take pity on them, the mourners, and are expressions of sorrow, grief, and shame. If someone grieves, beats his chest, tears his hair, or refuses to eat, it is an attempt at self-punishment to avoid or reduce the anticipated punishment for the blame that he takes on the death of a loved one.

This grief, shame, and guilt are not very far removed from feelings of 10 anger and rage. The process of grief always includes some qualities of anger. Since none of us likes to admit anger at a deceased person, these emotions are often disguised or repressed and prolong the period of grief or show up in other ways. It is well to remember that it is not up to us to judge such feelings as bad or shameful but to understand their true meaning and origin as something very human. In order to illustrate this I will again use the example of the child — and the child in us. The five-year-old who loses his mother is both blaming himself for her disappearance and being angry at her for having deserted him and for no longer gratifying his needs. The dead person then turns into something the child loves and wants very much but also hates with equal intensity for this severe deprivation.

---

[1]*Klage Weiber*: Wailing women (German). [Eds.]

The ancient Hebrews regarded the body of a dead person as something unclean and not to be touched. The early American Indians talked about the evil spirits and shot arrows in the air to drive the spirits away. Many other cultures have rituals to take care of the "bad" dead person, and they all originate in this feeling of anger which still exists in all of us, though we dislike admitting it. The tradition of the tombstone may originate in the wish to keep the bad spirits deep down in the ground, and the pebbles that many mourners put on the grave are leftover symbols of the same wish. Though we call the firing of guns at military funerals a last salute, it is the same symbolic ritual as the Indian used when he shot his spears and arrows into the skies.

I give these examples to emphasize that man has not basically changed. Death is still a fearful, frightening happening, and the fear of death is a universal fear even if we think we have mastered it on many levels.

What has changed is our way of coping and dealing with death and dying and our dying patients.

Having been raised in a country in Europe where science is not so advanced, where modern techniques have just started to find their way into medicine, and where people still live as they did in this country half a century ago, I may have had an opportunity to study a part of the evolution of mankind in a shorter period.

I remember as a child the death of a farmer. He fell from a tree and was not expected to live. He asked simply to die at home, a wish that was granted without question. He called his daughters into the bedroom and spoke with each one of them alone for a few moments. He arranged his affairs quietly, though he was in great pain, and distributed his belongings and his land, none of which was to be split until his wife should follow him in death. He also asked each of his children to share in the work, duties, and tasks that he had carried on until the time of the accident. He asked his friends to visit him once more, to bid goodbye to them. Although I was a small child at the time, he did not exclude me or my siblings. We were allowed to share in the preparations of the family just as we were permitted to grieve with them until he died. When he did die, he was left at home, in his own beloved home which he had built, and among his friends and neighbors who went to take a last look at him where he lay in the midst of flowers in the place he had lived in and loved so much. In that country today there is still no make-believe slumber room, no embalming, no false makeup to pretend sleep. Only the signs of very disfiguring illnesses are covered up with bandages and only infectious cases are removed from the home prior to the burial.

Why do I describe such "old-fashioned" customs? I think they are an indication of our acceptance of a fatal outcome, and they help the dying patient as well as his family to accept the loss of a loved one. If a patient is allowed to terminate his life in the familiar and beloved environment, it requires less adjustment for him. His own family knows him well enough to replace a sedative with a glass of his favorite wine; or the smell of a home-cooked soup may give him the appetite to sip a few spoons of fluid which, I think, is still more enjoyable than an infusion. I will not minimize the need for sedatives and infusions and realize full well from my own experience as

15

a country doctor that they are sometimes life-saving and often unavoidable. But I also know that patience and familiar people and foods could replace many a bottle of intravenous fluids given for the simple reason that it fulfills the physiological need without involving too many people and/or individual nursing care.

The fact that children are allowed to stay at home where a fatality has struck and are included in the talk, discussions, and fears gives them the feeling that they are not alone in their grief and gives them the comfort of shared responsibility and shared mourning. It prepares them gradually and helps them view death as part of life, an experience which may help them grow and mature.

This is in great contrast to a society in which death is viewed as taboo, discussion of it is regarded as morbid, and children are excluded with the presumption and pretext that it would be "too much" for them. They are then sent off to relatives, often accompanied by some unconvincing lies of "Mother has gone on a long trip" or other unbelievable stories. The child senses that something is wrong, and his distrust in adults will only multiply if other relatives add new variations of the story, avoid his questions or suspicions, shower him with gifts as a meager substitute for a loss he is not permitted to deal with. Sooner or later the child will become aware of the changed family situation and, depending on the age and personality of the child, will have an unresolved grief and regard this incident as a frightening, mysterious, in any case very traumatic experience with untrustworthy grownups, which he has no way to cope with.

It is equally unwise to tell a little child who lost her brother that God loved little boys so much that he took little Johnny to heaven. When this little girl grew up to be a woman she never solved her anger at God, which resulted in a psychotic depression when she lost her own little son three decades later.

We would think that our great emancipation, our knowledge of science 20
and of man, has given us better ways and means to prepare ourselves and our families for this inevitable happening. Instead the days are gone when a man was allowed to die in peace and dignity in his own home.

The more we are making advancements in science, the more we seem to fear and deny the reality of death. How is this possible?

We use euphemisms, we make the dead look as if they were asleep, we ship the children off to protect them from the anxiety and turmoil around the house if the patient is fortunate enough to die at home, we don't allow children to visit their dying parents in the hospitals, we have long and controversial discussions about whether patients should be told the truth — a question that rarely arises when the dying person is tended by the family physician who has known him from delivery to death and who knows the weaknesses and strengths of each member of the family.

I think there are many reasons for this flight away from facing death calmly. One of the most important facts is that dying nowadays is more gruesome in many ways, namely, more lonely, mechanical, and dehumanized; at times it is even difficult to determine technically when the time of death has occurred.

Dying becomes lonely and impersonal because the patient is often taken out of his familiar environment and rushed to an emergency room. Whoever has been very sick and has required rest and comfort especially may recall his experience of being put on a stretcher and enduring the noise of the ambulance siren and hectic rush until the hospital gates open. Only those who have lived through this may appreciate the discomfort and cold necessity of such transportation which is only the beginning of a long ordeal — hard to endure when you are well, difficult to express in words when noise, light, pumps, and voices are all too much to put up with. It may well be that we might consider more the patient under the sheets and blankets and perhaps stop our well-meant efficiency and rush in order to hold the patient's hand, to smile, or to listen to a question. I include the trip to the hospital as the first episode in dying, as it is for many. I am putting it exaggeratedly in contrast to the sick man who is left at home — not to say that lives should not be saved if they can be saved by a hospitalization but to keep the focus on the patient's experience, his needs and his reactions.

When a patient is severely ill, he is often treated like a person with no   25
right to an opinion. It is often someone else who makes the decision if and when and where a patient should be hospitalized. It would take so little to remember that the sick person too has feelings, has wishes and opinions, and has — most important of all — the right to be heard.

Well, our presumed patient has now reached the emergency room. He will be surrounded by busy nurses, orderlies, interns, residents, a lab technician perhaps who will take some blood, an electrocardiogram technician who takes the cardiogram. He may be moved to X-ray and he will overhear opinions of his condition and discussions and questions to members of the family. He slowly but surely is beginning to be treated like a thing. He is no longer a person. Decisions are made often without his opinion. If he tries to rebel he will be sedated, and after hours of waiting and wondering whether he has the strength, he will be wheeled into the operating room or intensive treatment unit and become an object of great concern and great financial investment.

He may cry for rest, peace, and dignity, but he will get infusions, transfusions, a heart machine, or tracheotomy if necessary. He may want one single person to stop for one single minute so that he can ask one single question — but he will get a dozen people around the clock, all busily preoccupied with his heart rate, pulse, electrocardiogram or pulmonary functions, his secretions or excretions but not with him as a human being. He may wish to fight it all but it is going to be a useless fight since all this is done in the fight for his life, and if they can save his life they can consider the person afterwards. Those who consider the person first may lose precious time to save his life! At least this seems to be the rationale or justification behind all this — or is it? Is the reason for this increasingly mechanical, depersonalized approach our own defensiveness? Is this approach our own way to cope with and repress the anxieties that a terminally or critically ill patient evokes in us? Is our concentration on equipment, on blood pressure, our desperate attempt to deny the impending death which is so frightening and discomforting to us that we displace all our knowledge onto machines, since they are less close to us than the suffering face of another human being which would remind us once more of our lack of omnipotence, our own limits and failures, and last but not least perhaps our own mortality?

Maybe the question has to be raised: Are we becoming less human or more human? . . . It is clear that whatever the answer may be, the patient is suffering more — not physically, perhaps, but emotionally. And his needs have not changed over the centuries, only our ability to gratify them.

QUESTIONS

1. Why does Kübler-Ross describe the death of a farmer? What point is she making in explaining "such 'old-fashioned' customs" (paragraph 16)?
2. To what extent is this essay explanatory? Summarize a particular explanation of hers that you find intriguing. Is it persuasive?
3. At what point in this essay does Kübler-Ross turn from explanation to argument? Do you think that she has taken a stand on her subject? How sympathetic are you to her position?
4. In paragraphs 2 and 10, Kübler-Ross indicates a specialized audience for her writing. Who is that audience, and how do you relate to it?
5. Think of the audience that you described in question 4 as a primary audience and of yourself as a member of a secondary audience. To what extent do the two audiences overlap? How thoroughly can you divide one from the other?
6. What experiences of death have you had so far? Write of a death that you know something about, even if your relation to it is distant, perhaps only through the media. Can you locate elements of fear and anger in your own behavior or in the behavior of other people involved? Does Kübler-Ross's interpretation of those reactions help you come to terms with the experience?
7. What kind of balance do you think is best between prolonging life and allowing a person to die with dignity? What does the phrase "dying with dignity" mean?
8. If you were told you had a limited time to live, how would that news change the way you are living? Or would it? Offer an explanation for your position.

MAKING CONNECTIONS

Kübler-Ross suggests that we have significant lessons to learn from the dying and warns that we avoid thinking about death only at our own peril. Read Francine du Plessix Gray's essay "The Work of Mourning" (p. 104), and imagine a conversation between Kübler-Ross and Gray.

NONVERBAL COURTSHIP PATTERNS IN WOMEN:
Context and Consequences

Monica M. Moore

Monica M. Moore (b. 1953) is a professor of psychology at Webster University in St. Louis, Missouri. Moore has conducted research on nonverbal courtship behavior in women since 1978, publishing articles in such journals as Semiotica *and the* Journal of Sex Research. *In this article, which originally appeared in the journal* Ethology and Sociobiology, *Moore applied the research methods of psychology to study the mating habits of the human female.*

[Abstract.] *There is a class of nonverbal facial expressions and gestures, exhibited by human females, that are commonly labeled "flirting behaviors." I observed more than 200 randomly selected adult female subjects in order to construct a catalog of these nonverbal solicitation behaviors. Pertinent behaviors were operationally defined through the use of consequential data; these behaviors elicited male attention. Fifty-two behaviors were described using this method. Validation of the catalog was provided through the use of contextual data. Observations were conducted on 40 randomly selected female subjects in one of four contexts: a singles' bar, a university snack bar, a university library, and at university Women's Center meetings. The results indicated that women in "mate relevant" contexts exhibited higher average frequencies of nonverbal displays directed at males. Additionally, women who signaled often were also those who were most often approached by a man; and this relationship was not context specific.*

I suggest that the observation of women in field situations may provide clues to criteria used by females in the initial selection of male partners. As much of the work surrounding human attraction has involved laboratory studies or data collected from couples in established relationships, the observation of nonverbal behavior in field settings may provide a fruitful avenue for the exploration of human female choice in the preliminary stages of male-female interaction.

Introduction

Biologically, one of the most important choices made by an organism is the selection of a mate. The evolution of traits that would assist in the identification of "superior mates" prior to the onset of mating is clearly advantageous. One legacy of anisogamy[1] is that errors in mate selection are generally more expensive to females than to males (Trivers 1972). Hence, the females of a wide variety of species may be expected to exhibit traits that would facilitate the assessment of the quality of potential suitors in respect to their inherited attributes and acquired resources. There are many examples of female selectivity in a variety of species, including elephant seals (LeBoeuf and Peterson 1969; Bertram 1975), mice (McClearn and Defries 1973), fish (Weber and Weber 1975), rats (Doty 1974), gorillas (Nadler 1975), monkeys (Beach 1976), birds (Selander 1972; Wiley 1973; Williams 1975), and a few ungulates[2] (Beuchner and Schloeth 1965; Leuthold 1966).

Very few studies in the area of human mate selection and attraction have focused on the issue of female choice. Fowler (1978) interviewed women to identify the parameters of male sexual attractiveness. The results showed that the male's value as a sexual partner correlated with the magnitude of emotional and material security he provided. Baber (1939) found that women emphasize qualities such as economic status, disposition, family religion, morals, health, and education in a prospective marriage partner, whereas men most frequently chose good looks, morals, and health as important qualities. More recent studies (Coombs and Kenkel 1966; Tavris 1977) also found women rating attributes such as physical attractiveness as less important than did men. Reiss (1960) believes that many more women than men choose "someone to look up to" and Hatkoff and Luswell (1977) presented data that indicated that women want the men with whom they fall in love to be persons whom they can respect and depend on. Daly and Wilson (1978) conclude from cross-cultural data that a male's financial status is an important determinant of his mating success.

Although these reports are valuable, it is clear that the mechanisms and expression of male assessment and female choice in humans have received little attention. In addition, much of the information available regarding human female choice is derived from interviews or questionnaires. Few studies have focused on initial choice situations in field observations. There are several difficulties with a field approach. A major problem surrounds the determination that a choice situation is being observed when verbal information is unavailable. I suggest that this problem may be solved through observations of nonverbal behavior. Indeed, there appears to be a repertoire of gestures and facial expressions that are used by humans as courtship signals (Birdwhistell 1970), much as there is signaling

5

---

[1]*anisogamy*: The union of unlike gametes — or mates, in this case. [Eds.]

[2]*ungulates*: Hoofed, herbivorous mammals, including camels, horses, and swine. [Eds.]

between members of the opposite sex in other species. Even in humans courtship and the choice of a mate have been characterized as largely non-verbal, with the cues being so persuasive that they can, as one observer put it, "turn a comment about the weather into a seductive invitation" (Davis 1971, p. 97).

The focus of much study in the area of nonverbal communication has been description (Scheflen 1965; Birdwhistell 1970; Mehrabian 1972). The primary aim of this research has been the categorization and analysis of nonverbal behaviors. By employing frame-by-frame analysis of films, Bird-whistell and his associates have been able to provide detailed descriptions of the facial expressions and movements or gestures of subjects in a variety of contexts. Observations conducted in this fashion as well as field studies have resulted in the labeling of many nonverbal behaviors as courtship signals. For example, Givens (1978) has described five phases of courtship between un-acquainted adults. Scheflen (1965) investigated flirting gestures in the context of psychotherapy, noting that both courtship behaviors and qualifiers of the courtship message were exhibited by therapists and clients. Eibl-Eibesfeldt (1971) used two approaches to describe flirting behavior in people from di-verse cultural backgrounds. Employing a camera fitted with right angle lenses to film people without their knowledge, he found that an eyebrow flash com-bined with a smile was a common courtship behavior. Through comments made to women, Eibl-Eibesfeldt has been able to elicit the "coy glance," an ex-pression combining a half-smile and lowered eyes. Kendon (1975) filmed a couple seated on a park bench in order to document the role of facial expres-sion during a kissing round. He discovered that it was the female's behavior, particularly her facial expressions that functioned as a regulator in modulat-ing the behavior of the male. Cary (1976) has shown that the female's behav-ior is important in initiating conversation between strangers. Both in laboratory settings and singles' bars conversation was initiated only after the female glanced at the male. These results are valuable in documenting the im-portance of nonverbal behavior in human courtship. But what is lacking is an ethogram[3] of female solicitation behavior.

The purpose of this study was to describe an ensemble of visual and tactile displays emitted by women during initial meetings with men. I shall argue here that these nonverbal displays are courtship signals; they serve as attractants and elicit the approach of males or ensure the continued at-tention of males. In order to establish the immediate function of the de-scribed behaviors as courtship displays, I employed two classes of evidence described by Hinde (1975) for use in the establishment of the immediate function of a behavior; contextual evidence and consequential evidence. The rationale behind the use of consequential data was that behavior has certain consequences and that if the consequence appears to be a "good

---

[3]*ethogram:* A pictorial catalog of behavior patterns shown by members of a species. [Eds.]

thing" it should have relevance for the immediate function of the behavior in question. It should be noted, however, that Eibl-Eibesfeldt (1970) has pointed out the danger in this approach because of interpretations of value on the part of the observer. Therefore, contextual information was provided as further documentation that the nonverbal behaviors in question were courtship signals. Hinde has noted that if certain behaviors are seen in some contexts but are absent in others their function must relate to those contexts in which they were observed. Together these two classes of information provide an indication of the immediate function of the behavior, in this case nonverbal behavior in women interacting with men. Thus, this study consisted of two parts: catalog compilation based on consequential information and validation of the catalog obtained through contextual data.

Development of the Catalog

Method

Subjects   For the initial study, more than 200 subjects were observed in order to obtain data to be used in the development of the catalog of nonverbal solicitation signals. Subjects were judged to be between the ages of 18 and 35 years. No systematic examination was made of background variables due to restrictions imposed by anonymity. All subjects were white and most were probably college students.

Procedure   Subjects were covertly observed in one social context where opportunities for male–female interaction were available, a singles' bar. Subjects were observed for 30 minutes by two trained observers. Focal subjects were randomly selected from the pool of possible subjects at the start of the observation period. We observed a woman only if she was surrounded by at least 25 other people (generally there were more than 50 others present) and if she was not accompanied by a male. In order to record all instances of the relevant behaviors, observers kept a continuous narrative account of all behaviors exhibited by a single subject and the observable consequences of those actions (Altmann 1974). The following criteria were used for identifying behaviors: a nonverbal solicitation behavior was defined as a movement of body part(s) or whole body that resulted in male attention, operationally defined, within 15 seconds following the behavior. Male attention consisted of the male performing one of the following behaviors: approaching the subject, talking to her, leaning toward her or moving closer to her, asking the subject to dance, touching her, or kissing her. Field notes were transcribed from concealed audio tape recorders. Estimates of interobserver reliability were calculated for 35 hours of observation using the formula:

$$\frac{\text{No. of agreements (A + B)}}{\text{No. of agreements (A + B) + No. seen by B only + No. seen by A only}}$$

(McGrew 1972). The range of interobserver reliability scores was 0.72–0.98, with the average score equaling .88. Low reliability scores were obtained only for behaviors difficult for an observer to catch in a darkened room, such as glancing behaviors.

Subsequently, five randomly selected subjects were observed for a pe-   10
riod of at least 1 hour. Again observers kept a continuous narrative account of all nonverbal behavior exhibited by the woman.

The behaviors observed in courting women can be conceptualized in various ways: distance categories (Crook 1972), directional versus nondirectional, or on the basis of body part and movement employed in the exhibition of the nonverbal pattern (McGrew 1972). The third framework was chosen because the displays were most discretely partitioned along these dimensions.

Results

Fifty-two different behaviors were exhibited by the subjects in the present study. Nonverbal solicitation behaviors and their frequencies are summarized in Table 1 according to category. These behaviors were highly visible and most appeared very similar in form in each subject. In other words, each behavior was discrete, or distinct from all other solicitation behaviors.

Descriptions of Nonverbal Solicitation Behaviors

FACIAL AND HEAD PATTERNS. A number of different facial and head patterns were seen in the women we observed. All women performed glancing behaviors, although the particular pattern varied among the individual subjects in the duration or length of time involved in eye to eye contact.

Type I glance (the room encompassing glance) was not restricted to an identifiable recipient. It was usually exhibited early in the evening and often was not seen later in the evening, particularly if the woman made contact with a man. The woman moved her head rapidly, orienting her face around the room. This movement was followed by another head movement that reoriented the woman's face to its original position. The total duration of the glance was brief, 5–10 seconds, with the woman not making eye contact with any specific individual. In some women this pattern of behavior was exaggerated: the woman stood up as her glance swept about the room.

The glancing behavior called the *type II glance (the short darting glance)*   15
was a solicitation behavior that appeared directed at a particular man. The woman directed her gaze at the man, then quickly away (within 3 seconds). The target axis of the horizontal rotation of the head was approximately 25–45 degrees. This behavior was usually repeated in bouts, with three glances the average number per bout.

In contrast, *type III glance (gaze fixate)* consisted of prolonged (more than 3 seconds) eye contact. The subject looked directly at the man; sometimes her glance was returned. Again, this behavior was seen several times in a period of minutes in some subjects.

TABLE 1
Catalog of Nonverbal Solicitation Behaviors

Facial and Head Patterns	Frequency	Gestures	Frequency	Posture Patterns	Frequency
Type I glance (room-encompassing glance)	253	Arm flexion	10	Lean	121
		Tap	8	Brush	28
		Palm	18	Breast touch	6
Type II glance (short darting glance)	222				
Type III glance (gaze fixate)	117				
Eyebrow flash	4	Gesticulation	62	Knee touch	25
Head toss	102	Hand hold	20	Thigh touch	23
Neck presentation	58	Primp	46	Foot to foot	14
Hair flip	139	Hike skirt	4	Placement	19
Head nod	66	Object caress	56	Shoulder hug	25
Lip lick	48	Caress (face/hair)	5	Hug	11
Lipstick application	1	Caress (leg)	32	Lateral body contact	1
Pout	27	Caress (arm)	23	Frontal body contact	7
Smile	511	Caress (torso)	8	Hang	2
Coy smile	20	Caress (back)	17	Parade	41
Laugh	249	Buttock pat	8	Approach	18
Giggle	61			Request dance	12
Kiss	6			Dance (acceptance)	59
Whisper	60			Solitary dance	253
Face to face	9			Point/permission grant	62
			9	Aid solicitation	34
				Play	31

Another movement involving the eye area was an *eyebrow flash*, which consisted of an exaggerated raising of the eyebrows of both eyes, followed by a rapid lowering to the normal position. The duration of the raised eyebrow portion of the movement was approximately 2 seconds. This behavior was often combined with a smile and eye contact.

Several behaviors involved the head and neck region. In *head tossing*, the head was flipped backwards so that the face was tilted upwards briefly (less than 5 seconds). The head was then lowered to its original position. The head toss was often combined with or seen before the *hair flip*. The hair flip consisted of the woman raising one hand and pushing her fingers through her hair or running her palm along the surface of her hair. Some women made only one hand movement, while in others there were bouts of hair stroking; the woman put her hand to her hair several times within a 30-second interval. The *head nod* was seen when the woman was only a short distance from the man. Usually exhibited during conversation, the head was moved forward and backward on the neck, which resulted in the face of the subject moving up and down. Another head pattern was called *face to face*. In this behavior pattern the head and face of the woman were brought directly opposite another person's face so that the noses almost touched, a distance of approximately 5 cm. A final behavior involving the head and neck was the *neck presentation*. The woman tilted her head sideways to an angle of approximately 45 degrees. This resulted in the ear almost touching the ipsilateral[4] shoulder, thereby exposing the opposite side of the neck. Occasionally the woman stroked the exposed neck area with her fingers.

There were a number of signals that involved the lips and mouth of the observed subjects. *Lipstick application* was a rare behavior. The woman directed her gaze so that she made eye contact with a particular man. She then slowly applied lipstick to her lips. She engaged in this behavior for some time (15 seconds), repeatedly circling her lips. In contrast, the *lip lick* was seen quite often, particularly in certain subjects. The woman opened her mouth slightly and drew her tongue over her lips. Some women used a single lip lick, wetting only the upper or the lower lip, while others ran the tongue around the entire lip area. The *lip pout* was another behavior involving the mouth. The lips were placed together and protruded. Generally, the lower lip was extended somewhat farther than the upper lip, so that it was fuller in appearance.

Smiling was among the most prevalent behaviors observed in the sampled women. The smile consisted of the corners of the mouth being turned upward. This resulted in partial or sometimes full exposure of the teeth. In some women the smile appeared fixed and was maintained for long periods of time. The *coy smile* differed from the smile in that the woman displaying a coy smile combined a half-smile (the teeth were often not displayed or only partially shown) with a downward gaze or eye contact

20

---

[4]*ipsilateral*: Situated on the same side of the body. [Eds.]

which was very brief (less than 3 seconds). In the latter case the woman's glance slid quickly away from an onlooker who had become aware that he was being looked at.

Laughing and giggling were generally responses to another person's comments or behavior and were very common. In some women the *laugh* was preceded by a head toss. *Giggling* was less intense laughter. The mouth of the woman was often closed and generally the sounds were softer.

Kissing was rather unusual in the bar context. The slightly protruded lips were brought into contact with another person's body by a forward head movement. Variations consisted of the area touched by the woman's lips. The most common targets were the lips, face, and neck of the man. The woman, however, sometimes puckered her lips and waited, as if "offering" them to the male.

Finally, the *whisper* was used by most of the subjects in the sample. The woman moved her mouth near another person's ear and soft vocalizations presumedly were produced. Sometimes body contact was made.

GESTURES. There were several nonverbal patterns that involved movement of the hands and arms. Most were directed at a particular person. Some involved touching another individual. Others functioned at a distance.

Arm flexion occurred when the arm was flexed at wrist and elbow and was moved toward the body. It was often repeated two or three times in a bout. This behavior was often followed by the approach of another individual toward whom the subject gazed. If the male was in close physical proximity, the female sometimes used *tapping* instead to get his attention. The elbow or wrist was flexed repeatedly so that the woman's finger was moved vertically on an object (usually another person's arm).

Women occasionally *palmed*. Palming occurred when the hand was extended or turned so that the palm faced another person for a brief period of time, less than 5 seconds. In this study, palming was also recorded when the woman coughed or touched herself with the palm up.

In several women rapid movements of the hands and arms were seen accompanying speech. This behavior was labeled *gesticulation*. Arms and hands, while held in front of the woman's torso, were waved or extended upwards in an exaggerated, conspicuous manner. This behavior was often followed by a lean forward on the part of the man.

A hand gesture sometimes initiated by a woman was the *hand hold*. The woman grasped the man's hand so that her palm was next to the man's palm. This occurred on the dance floor as well as when the man was seated at the table with the woman. Generally, this behavior had a long duration, more than 1 minute.

There were several behaviors that appeared related to each other because they involved inanimate objects. The first of these was the *primp*. In this gesture the clothing was patted or smoothed, although to the observer it appeared in no need of adjustment. A shirt was tucked in or a skirt was pulled down. On the other hand, the *skirt hike* was performed by raising

25

the hem of the skirt with a movement of the hand or arm so that more leg was exposed. This behavior was only performed by two women and was directed at a particular man. When another man looked the skirt was pushed rapidly into place. Instead of patting or smoothing clothing, subjects sometimes "played with" an object, called *object caress*. For example, keys or rings were often fondled. Glasses were caressed with the woman sliding her palm up and down the surface of the glass. A cigarette pack was another item frequently toyed with in an object caress.

Finally, many women touched other people in a caressing fashion. Each incidence of caressing was considered separately in terms of the part of the body that was touched, because the message, in each case, may have been quite different. In *caress (face/hair)* the woman moved her hand slowly up and down the man's face and neck area or tangled her hands in his hair. While the couple was seated, women have been observed stroking the man's thigh and inner leg, *caress (leg)*. The *buttock pat*, however, occurred while the couple was standing, often while dancing. In this gesture the woman moved her hand, palm side down, up and down the man's buttocks. Other items in this group included *caress (arm)*, *caress (torso)*, and *caress (back)*.

POSTURE PATTERNS. Compared to the two categories just presented, there were some behaviors which involved more of the body in movement. These I called posture patterns. Many of these behaviors could only be accomplished while the woman was standing or moving about the room.

Lean was a common solicitation pattern. Generally while seated, the woman moved her torso and upper body forward, which resulted in closer proximity to the man. This movement was sometimes followed by a *brush* or a *breast touch*. The brush occurred when brief body contact (less than 5 seconds) was initiated by the woman against another individual. This occurred when a woman was walking across the room; she bumped into a man. The result was often conversation between the man and the woman. The breast touch also appeared accidental; and it was difficult to tell, except by length of time of contact, whether or not the movement was purposeful. The upper torso was moved so the breast made contact with the man's body (usually his arm). Most often the contact was brief (less than 5 seconds), but sometimes women maintained this position for several minutes.

There were four other actions that were similar to the brush and breast touch in that the woman made bodily contact with the man. In the *knee touch* the legs were brought into contact with the man's legs so that the knees touched. Interactants were always facing one another while seated. If the man and woman were sitting side by side, the woman may have initiated a *thigh touch*. The leg was brought into contact with the man's upper leg. *Foot to foot* resulted in the woman moving her foot so that it rested on top of the man's foot. Finally, rather than make contact with some part of her own body, an observed woman sometimes took the man's hand and placed it on her body. I called this behavior *placement*. For example, on two occasions, a woman put a man's hand in her lap. Other targets were the thigh or arm.

There was another constellation of behaviors that appeared related to each other. All of these behaviors were variations of some contact made between the woman's upper body and her partner's upper body. These were generally behaviors of long duration, more than 1 minute. The most common of these behaviors was the *shoulder hug*. In this signal, the partially flexed arm was draped on and around another person's shoulder. In contrast, the *hug* occurred when both arms were moved forward from a widespread position and around the man, thereby encircling him. The duration of this behavior, however, was brief (less than 10 seconds). *Lateral body contact* was similar to shoulder hug except that the woman moved under the man's arm so that his arm was draped around her shoulders rather than vice versa. Similarly, *frontal body contact* occurred when the chest and thighs of the woman rested against the chest and thighs of the man. This behavior was like the hug except that there was no squeeze pressure and the arms did not necessarily encircle the other person. This posture pattern was often seen on the dance floor or when a couple was standing at the bar. *Hanging* was similar to frontal body contact except that the man was supporting the woman's weight. This behavior was initiated by the woman who placed her arms around the man's neck. She was then lifted off her feet while her torso and hips rested against the man's chest and hip. This was a behavior low in frequency and brief in duration, less than 5 seconds.

There were two behaviors that involved whole body movement. These were called *parade* and *approach*. Parade consisted of the woman walking across the room, perhaps on her way to the bar or the restroom. Yet rather than maintaining a relaxed attitude, the woman exaggerated the swaying motion of her hips. Her stomach was held in and her back was arched so that her breasts were pushed out; her head was held high. In general she was able to make herself "look good." The other behavior that involved walking was approach. The woman went up to the man and stood very close to him, within 2 feet. Usually verbal interaction ensued.

Some women followed an approach with a *request dance*. This was demonstrated nonverbally by the woman pointing and/or nodding in the direction of the dance floor. Two other categories involving dancing behavior were included in the catalog. *Dance (female acceptance)* was included because by accepting a dance with the man the woman maintained his attention. Another dancing behavior was one of the most frequently seen signals. It was called the *solitary dance* because, while seated or standing, the woman moved her body in time to the music. A typical male response was to request a dance.

Just as a woman, in agreeing to dance with a man, was telling him, nonverbally, that he was acceptable for the moment she also told him so when she allowed him to sit at her table with her. Thus, *point/permission*

35

grant was given a place in the catalog. The woman pulled out the chair for the man or pointed or nodded in the direction of the chair. There was generally a verbal component to the signal which could not be overheard.

Aid solicitation consisted of several behaviors that involved the request of help by the subject. For example, the woman handed her jacket to the man and allowed him to help her put it on. Other patterns in this category included indicating that a drink be refilled, waiting to be seated, or holding a cigarette for lighting.

The final category of solicitation behavior was also a variety of posture patterns. Called *play*, these behaviors consisted of the woman pinching the man, tickling him, sticking out her tongue at him, or approaching him from behind covering his eyes. Some women sat on the man's lap, and several women in the sample came up behind men and stole their hats. All of these behaviors were simply recorded as play behavior.

Validation of the Catalog

Method

Subjects.   Forty women were covertly observed for the second portion of   40
the study, validation of the catalog. Subjects were judged between the ages of 18 and 35. All subjects were white. Again no systematic examination of background variables was possible.

Procedure.   To justify the claim that the nonverbal behaviors described above were courtship signals, that is, carried a message of interest to the observing man, women were covertly observed in different social contexts. The four contexts selected for study were a singles' bar, a university snack bar, a university library, and university Women's Center meetings. These contexts were chosen in order to sample a variety of situations in which nonverbal solicitation might be expected to occur as well as situations in which it was unlikely to be exhibited. The selection of contexts was based on information collected through interviews and pilot observations. If nonverbal solicitation was found in situations where male–female interaction was likely but either was not found or occurred in lower frequencies where male–female interactions were impossible, then the immediate function of nonverbal solicitation can be said to be the enhancement of male–female relationships.

The methodology employed in this section was similar to that used in the development of the catalog. Focal individual sampling was the method of choice for the 40 subjects, 10 in each of the 4 contexts. Each subject was randomly selected from those individuals present at the beginning of the observation period. Sessions were scheduled to begin at 9:00 p.m. and end at 11:00 p.m. in the bar context. This time was optimal because crowd density was at its peak. Sessions in the Women's Center context always began at noon or at 7:00 p.m. because that was the time at which programs were scheduled. Observations were randomly made in both the library and the snack bar contexts; for each context, four sessions were conducted at 11:00 a.m., three at 2:00 p.m., and three at 7:00 p.m. Subjects were observed for a period of 1 hour. (Any subject who did not remain for 1 hour of observation was excluded from the analyses.) Observations were conducted using either a concealed audio recorder or, when appropriate, paper and pen. No subject evidenced awareness of being observed. Again, we observed a woman only if she was surrounded by at least 25 other people and if she was not accompanied by a male.

Data for each woman consisted of a frequency measure, the number of nonverbal solicitation behaviors, described above, that she exhibited during the hour of observation. Observers counted not only the total number of nonverbal solicitation behaviors, but also kept a tally of the specific behaviors that were used by each woman.

Results

Frequency and Categorization of Nonverbal Solicitation Behaviors. Data collected on 40 subjects and the respective frequencies of their solicitation displays are given in Table 2. The results show that the emission of the cataloged behaviors was context specific in respect to both the frequency of displays and the number of different categories of the repertoire. The subjects observed in the singles' bar emitted an average of 70.6 displays in the sampled interval, encompassing a mean number of 12.8 different categories of the catalog. In contrast, the corresponding data from the snack bar, library, and women's meetings were 18.6 and 7.5, 9.6 and 4.0, and 4.7 and 2.1, respectively. The asymmetry in display frequency was highly significant ($\chi^2 = 25.079$, df = 3, $p < 0.001$). In addition, the asymmetry in the number of categories utilized was also significant ($\chi^2 = 23.099$, df = 3, $p < 0.001$).

Rate of Display. The quartile display frequencies for the four contexts are given in Figure 1. As can be seen, the display frequency accelerated over time in the singles' bar context but was relatively invariant in the other three contexts.

Frequency of Approach. If subjects are pooled across contexts in which males are present and partitioned into high- and low-display categories, where the high display category is defined as more than 35 displays per hour, the data show that the high-display subjects elicited greater than 4 approaches per hour, whereas low display subjects elicited less than 0.48 approaches per hour. The number of approaches to subjects by a male in each context is presented in Table 2. Approaches were most frequent in the singles' bar where displays were also most frequent.

For the three contexts in which males were present (the singles' bar, the snack bar, and the library), the number of approaches to the subject was compared to the number of categories employed in solicitation displays.

Table 2
Social Context: Display Frequency and Number of Approaches[a]

	Singles' Bar	Snack Bar	Library	Women's Meetings
Number of subjects	10	10	10	10
Total number of displays	706	186	96	47
Mean number of displays	70.6	18.6	9.6	4.7
Mean number of catagories utilized	12.8	7.5	4.0	2.1
Number of approaches to the subject by a male	38	4	4	0
Number of approaches to a male by the subject	11	4	1	0

[a]The tabulated data are for a 60-minute observation interval. Asymmetry in display frequency: $\chi^2 = 25.079$, df = 3, $p < 0.001$; asymmetry in number of categories utilized: $\chi^2 = 23.099$, df = 3, $p < 0.001$.

Subjects were pooled across these contexts and divided into two groups — those who utilized less than ten categories and those who employed ten or more categories. The results were highly significant ($\chi^2 = 12.881$, df = 1, $p < 0.025$): regardless of when the woman utilized a high number of categories she was more likely to be approached by a male.

Also given in Table 2 are the figures for female-to-male approaches. In both cases (female to male, and male to female), approaches were much higher in the bar context. To show that the number of male approaches correlated with frequency of female solicitation, Spearman rank correlations[5] were determined for these measures. The correlation between number of male approaches and total number of solicitations, across all three contexts, equaled 0.89 ($p < 0.05$). Clearly, those women who signaled often were also those who were most often approached by a man; and this relationship was not context specific.

Discussion

The results of this study are in no way discoveries of "new" behaviors. The behaviors cataloged here have been described as courtship behaviors by others. But there has been little firm evidence to support this claim of their function, aside from references to context. This study was the first

---

[5]*Spearman rank correlations*: Measurements of associations between two variables. This method of measuring the strength of correlations when actual values are not available was first proposed by the English psychologist Charles Spearman in 1904. [Eds.]

attempt to bring all the behaviors together in catalog form and provide documentation of their function.

When we compare those behaviors contained in the catalog compiled   50
in this study to other descriptions of courtship in humans, we find many areas of congruence. Scheflen (1965) has outlined four categories of heterosexual courtship behavior: courtship readiness, preening behavior, positional cues, and actions of appeal or invitation. Many of the behaviors observed in courting women are similar to those seen by Scheflen during psychotherapy sessions. For example, Scheflen's category of courtship readiness bears resemblance to parade behavior. Preening behaviors, as described by Scheflen, are similar to the hair flip, primp, skirt hike, and object caress cataloged here. Positional cues are found in the catalog under leaning, brushing, and caressing or touching signals. Finally, Scheflen's actions of appeal or invitation are included as aid solicitation, point/permission grant, request dance, palm and solitary dance. What appears to be absent in courting women are the qualifiers of the courtship message observed by Scheflen during psychotherapy.

There is significant continuity between the expressions and gestures described in this study and those Givens (1978) believed to be important during the first four phases of courtship. According to Givens, the essence of the first stage, the attention phase, is ambivalence. Behaviors seen by Givens during this stage and observed in this study include primping, object caressing, and glancing at and then away from the male. During the recognition phase Givens has observed head cocking, pouting, primping, eyebrow flashing and smiling, all of which were seen by me. During the interaction stage, conversation is initiated and the participants appear highly animated. Indeed, women in this study, while talking to men, appeared excited, laughing, smiling, and gesticulating frequently. Givens has indicated that in the fourth stage, the sexual arousal phase, touching gestures are exchanged. Similarly, it was not unusual to see couples hold hands, caress, hug, or kiss after some period of interaction.

Givens' work has indicated that it is often the female who controls interaction in these early phases. The observations of Cary (1976) seem to bear this out and glancing behavior appears to be a significant part of the female role. In this study glancing often took place over a period of time prior to a male approach. As Crook (1972) has stated, males are generally hesitant to approach without some indication of interest from the partner, and repeated eye contact seems to demonstrate that interest. Rejection behaviors were not cataloged here, but it is entirely possible that one way women reject suitors is by failing to recognize their presence through eye contact.

Eibl-Eibesfeldt has also stressed importance of the eye area in two flirting gestures he has observed in several cultures. The first, a rapid raising and lowering of the eyebrows, accompanied by a smile and a nod, was seen rarely in this study. Raised eyebrows were sometimes seen in the bar context and when directed at a man with a quick glance to the dance floor were often followed by a request to dance. Raised eyebrows also sometimes followed comments by a man when he had joined a woman at her table. Eibl-Eibesfeldt (1970) has also presented pictures of women exhibiting what he calls the coy glance. Although the coy glance was sometimes seen in this study (here called the coy smile), it was more usual for a young American woman to use direct eye contact and a full smile. Yet the fact that these behaviors were observed is significant, and later cross-cultural studies may demonstrate that there are more behaviors that share the courtship message.

It appears then that although glancing behaviors were important in signaling interest, initially, other behaviors seemed to reaffirm the woman's interest later in the observation period. Behaviors such as nodding, leaning close to the man, smiling and laughing were seen in higher frequencies after the man had made contact with the woman and was dancing with her or was seated at her table. This accounts for the rise in frequency of solicitation near the end of the observation period in the bar context. Yet it is difficult to make any firm statements about a sequential pattern in the exhibition of solicitation behavior. Although these behaviors are distinct in form, variability among subjects with regard to timing was great. Neither was it possible to determine the potency of particular behaviors. Indeed, it often appeared as though behaviors had a cumulative effect; that is, the man waited to respond to the woman until after he had observed several solicitations.

However, it is clear that there is a constellation of nonverbal behaviors 55
associated with female solicitation that has been recognized by many investigators in several contexts and with similar results (Morris 1971; Kendon and Feber 1973; Nieremberg and Calero 1973; Clore et al. 1975; Key 1975; Knapp 1978; Lockard and Adams 1980). This is strong circumstantial evidence supporting the current results that these are "real" contextually valid movements, not random behaviors. Furthermore, these expressions and gestures appear to function as attractants and advertisers of female interest.

Traditionally, women have had more control in choosing men for relationships, being able to pace the course of sexual advances and having the prerogative to accept or decline proposals (Hatkoff and Luswell 1977). Nonverbal solicitation is only one of the first steps in the sequence of behaviors beginning with mate attraction and culminating with mate selection. However, these courtship gestures and expressions appear to aid the woman in her role as discriminating chooser. Females are able to determine when and where they wish to survey mate potential by exhibiting or withholding displays. They can elicit a high number of male approaches, allowing them to choose from a number of available men. Or they may direct solicitations at a particular male.

What happens after the approach of a man then becomes increasingly important. Much of the basis of actual choice must rest on what the man says to the woman in addition to his behavior toward her and others. It seems reasonable that females would enhance their fitness by making the most informed judgment possible. Yet before interaction is initiated some initial choice is made. These initial impressions and the selection of those men deemed interesting enough to warrant further attention by a woman have been virtually ignored. If, indeed, the woman is exercising her right to choose, what sort of filter system is she using? Which men are chosen for further interaction and which are rejected? Literature cited earlier indicates that behaviors that indicate status, wealth, and dependability are attributes that women may assess in initial encounters. At present data are not available to address these issues. But I believe that hypotheses regarding the particulars of human female choice can be tested through covert observation of female invitational behavior. Information obtained through observations in field settings can be added to verbal reports. The results of such a venture may present us with a more complete picture of the levels of selection involved in human female choice.

References

Altmann, J. Observational study of behavior: sampling methods. *Behavior* 49: 227–267 (1974).

Baber, R. E. *Marriage and Family.* New York: McGraw-Hill, 1939.

Beach, R. A. Sexual attractivity, proceptivity and receptivity in female mammals. *Hormones and Behavior* 7: 105–138 (1976).

Bertram, B. C. Social factors influencing reproduction in wild lions. *Journal of Zoology* 177: 463–482 (1975).

Beuchner, H. K., Schloeth, R. Ceremonial mating system in Uganda kob (*Adenota kob thomase* Neuman). *Zeitschrift fur Tierpsychologie* 22: 209–225 (1965).

Birdwhistell, R. L. *Kinesics and Context.* Philadelphia: University of Pennsylvania Press, 1970.

Cary, M. S. Talk? Do you want to talk? Negotiation for the initiation of conversation between the unacquainted. Ph.D. dissertation, University of Pennsylvania, 1976.

Clore, G. L., Wiggins, N. H., Itkin, I. Judging attraction from nonverbal behavior: the gain phenomenon. *Journal of Consulting and Clinical Pyschology* 43: 491–497 (1975).

Coombs, R. H., Kenkel, W. F. Sex differences in dating aspirations and satisfaction with computer selected partners. *Journal of Marriage and the Family* 28: 62–66 (1966).

Crook, J. H. Sexual selection, dimorphism, and social organization in primates. In *Sexual Selection and the Descent of Man 1871–1971*, B. Campbell (Ed.). Chicago: Aldine, 1972.

―――― The socio-ecology of primates. In *Social Behavior in Birds and Mammals: Essays on the Social Ethology of Animals and Man*, J. H. Crook (Ed.). London: Academic, 1972.

Daly, M., Wilson, M. *Sex, Evolution, and Behavior.* North Scituate, MA: Duxbury, 1978.

Davis, F. *Inside Intuition.* New York: McGraw-Hill, 1971.

Doty, R. L. A cry for the liberation of the female rodent: Courtship and copulation in Rodentia. *Psychological Bulletin* 81: 159–172 (1974).

Eibl-Eibesfeldt, I. *Ethology: The Biology of Behavior.* New York: Holt, Rinehart, and Winston, 1970.

―――― *Love and Hate.* New York: Holt, Rinehart and Winston, 1971.

Fowler, H. F. Female choice: An investigation into human breeding system strategy. Paper presented to Animal Behavior Society, Seattle, June 1978.

Givens, D. The nonverbal basis of attraction: Flirtation, courtship, and seduction. *Psychiatry* 41: 346–359 (1978).

Hatkoff, T. S., Luswell, T. E. Male–female similarities and differences in conceptualizing love. In *Love and Attraction*, M. Cook, G. Wilson (Eds.). Oxford: Pergamon, 1977.

Hinde, R. A. The concept of function. In *Function and Evolution in Behavior*, S. Bariends, C. Beer, and A. Manning (Eds.). Oxford: Clarendon, 1975.

Kendon, A. Some functions of the face in a kissing round. *Semiotica* 15: 299–334 (1975).

———, Ferber, A. A description of some human greetings. In *Comparative Ecology and Behavior of Primates*, R. P. Michael and J. H. Crook (Eds.). London: Academic, 1973.

Key, M. R. *Male/Female Language*. Metuchen, NJ: Scarecrow, 1975.

Knapp, M. L. *Nonverbal Communication in Human Interaction*. New York: Holt, Rinehart, and Winston, 1978.

LeBoeuf, B. J., Peterson, R. S. Social status and mating activity in elephant seals. *Science* 163: 91–93 (1969).

Leuthold, W. Variations in territorial behavior of Uganda kob *Adenota kob thomasi* (Neumann 1896). *Behaviour* 27: 215–258 (1966).

Lockard, J. S., Adams, R. M. Courtship behaviors in public: Different age/sex roles. *Ethology and Sociobiology* 1(3): 245–253 (1980).

McClearn, G. E., Defries, J. C. *Introduction to Behavioral Genetics*. San Francisco: Freeman, 1973.

McGrew, W. C. *An Ethological Study of Children's Behavior*. New York: Academic, 1972.

Mehrabian, A. *Nonverbal Communication*. Chicago: Aldine, 1972.

Morris, D. *Intimate Behavior*. New York: Random House, 1971.

Nadler, R. D. Sexual cyclicity in captive lowland gorillas. *Science* 189: 813–814 (1975).

Nieremberg, G. I., Calero, H. H. *How to Read a Person Like a Book*. New York: Hawthorne, 1973.

Reiss, I. L. Toward a sociology of the heterosexual love relationship. *Marriage and Family Living* 22: 139–145 (1960).

Scheflen, A. E. Quasi-courtship behavior in psychotherapy. *Psychiatry* 28: 245–257 (1965).

Selander, R. K. Sexual selection and dimorphism in birds. In *Sexual Selection and the Descent of Man 1871–1971*, B. Campbell (Ed.). Chicago: Aldine, 1972.

Tavris, C. Men and women report their views on masculinity. *Psychology Today* 10: 34–42 (1977).

Trivers, R. L. Parental investment and sexual selection. In *Sexual Selection and the Descent of Man 1871–1971*, B. Campbell (Ed.). Chicago: Aldine, 1972.

Weber, P. G., Weber, S. P. The effect of female color, size, dominance and early experience upon mate selection in male convict cichlids, *cichlosoma nigrofasciatum Gunther* (pisces, cichlidae). *Behaviour* 56: 116–135 (1975).

Wiley, R. H. Territoriality and nonrandom mating in sage grouse, *Centrocerus urophasiamis*. *Animal Behavior Monographs* 6: 85–169 (1973).

Williams, G. C. *Sex and Evolution*. Princeton, NJ: Princeton University Press, 1975.

QUESTIONS

1. Which of Moore's observations or conclusions do you find the most interesting or unusual? Explain.
2. The interest of this piece lies in its subject — flirting — which is frequently treated in popular how-to books and on talk shows. Based on your familiarity with these popular treatments and on your knowledge of the subject through your own observations, how accurate a report do you find Moore's article to be?
3. Moore suggests that different courtship behaviors may be exhibited in other cultures. If you have knowledge of another culture's courtship rituals, explain how they compare with Moore's findings.
4. Moore concludes by suggesting that further study should be made on women's "filter system," meaning how they choose a man for further interaction. She suggests that this can be done through additional "covert observation" (paragraph 57). Do you agree? What would one look for?
5. What does Moore mean when she writes, "It seems reasonable that females would enhance their fitness by making the most informed judgment possible" (paragraph 57)? What sort of "fitness" do you think Moore means?
6. Would it be possible to replicate this experiment by studying courtship behavior in males? Write an essay in which you suggest some of the categories of male courtship behavior that such a study might reveal.

MAKING CONNECTIONS

What similarities in method or substantive findings can you find between Moore's study and Jane van Lawick-Goodall's "First Observations" (p. 395)? Note that before the article was published, Moore presented portions of it at a meeting of the Animal Behavior Society.

ZENO AND THE DISTANCE BETWEEN US

Sharon Wahl

Sharon Wahl (b. 1956) was born in New York City, raised in New York State, and currently lives in Tucson, Arizona. She received her B.A. in music from Wesleyan University and then did graduate work in math at M.I.T., where she started writing fiction, but left the program before finishing her Ph.D. Wahl later received an M.F.A. in creative writing from Washington University in St. Louis. She is currently finishing her first book, a series of love stories based on classic philosophy texts, entitled I Also Dated Zarathustra and Other Philosophical Romances. *Of her writing style Wahl says, "I am interested in creating dramatic effects such as tension and resolution through the use of internal structures (and sometimes external forms) rather than through a more traditional use of plot. Many of my stories are also very internal; sometimes more happens in the imagination or memory of the character narrating the story than in the external situation." Her short stories and poems have appeared in* The Iowa Review *(Tim McGinnis Award),* Chicago Tribune *(Nelson Algren Award finalist),* Pleiades *(Editors' Prize in poetry),* Literal Latte *(Fiction Contest winner),* Harvard Review, *and other journals. One of her stories, "I Also Dated Zarathustra," is available online. Wahl has received two fellowships from the Arizona Commission for the Arts and a writer residency at Penn State University, among other awards. "Zeno and the Distance between Us" appeared in 1999 in* The Iowa Review.

How wide is the arm of a seat in a dark theater? We are both touching the wooden armrest, leaning into it from either side with our bony elbows and our thin naked arms. Our shoulders are so close that the loose sleeves of our tee shirts almost touch. How different it would be if my arm could pass right through. But it is only this solid piece of wood between us that allows us to get so close. The inanimate accepts touch, but can't return it; so simple things get rubbed smooth. Look how this armrest has been battered with attention, polished and popcorn-oiled by all the hands that have sat here with nothing else to hold.

Emerging past the armrest, side by side on our blue jean thighs, our flickering hands. We are blue in movie light, and the shadows of our finger-joints, our knuckles, our bony wrists, are both spooky and exquisite. We could be statues. Marble in moonlight.

Have I ever touched him? Once, as I walked behind him at a crowded party. I put my hand on his shoulder, lightly, just barely resting my fingers on the fabric of his shirt. He was talking and didn't notice. I did this only once, though we were there all night. The room was dim, and always people dancing and chatting and bumping each other as they passed with drinks. And I, just passing, could easily have reached out again to steady myself with a light hand on his tee shirt, pressing just enough this time to test how bony his shoulder was or feel the muscles along his spine.

His index finger curls and straightens. Mine does the same, as if to know what he is feeling is to feel him. Even this tiny movement reminds my finger of my knee, the knee of the finger, returns the texture of the cloth between them.

How wide is the arm of a seat in a dark theater? The philosopher Zeno   5
gave this paradox of motion: to reach him, I must cross half the distance between us. Then half the distance remaining; then half of that, and half again, and again, and again: I can only go halfway.

Proving, motion is impossible.

And yet.

That night at the party, for instance. He walked outside onto the porch, where it was quite dark, and looked up at the sky, maybe at the stars, recognizing a constellation, or maybe just in a vague way admiring the lights in so much dark. No one else was around. I had followed him at a little distance and stood leaning against the doorframe pretending to be part of the room inside, the dancing and drinking. But I was there with the sky and the crickets, watching him. And for minutes he stood with his beer on the porch railing. His back to me. His bony shoulder. Perfectly natural, it would have been perfectly natural for me to walk up, reach a hand to his shoulder, the hand of, Hey don't want to startle you what's up, and leave it there, just friendly, the dark, the drink, the music. A warm night, starting to cool with a little breeze but sweaty for dancing. Just out here for the breeze. Great party, isn't it? Perfectly natural for his arm to go around me, just loosely around my waist. And as we talked, friendly and hardly able to see each other in the dark, so it was hardly real, moving his hand lower to rub my hip.

Tonight we ran into each other checking videos from the library. We talked about an actress we both loved, who had a new movie. We both asked at the same time. Do you want to — ? That was easy. Now, for two hours, his hand will be in reach. His leg is in reach. My hand is on my thigh, like his, and my thigh is so close to his that moving the hand from mine to his, fitting my long fingers between his longer ones, would take less effort than shaking hands.

But look at him. In the first minutes of this movie, a woman, the beau-   10
tiful actress, has lost her husband and daughter in a car wreck. Look at his face, the worry in his eyes and brows, the way his lips, drawn together, seem bruised. Look how sad this movie has made him. Since the accident

his fingers have tensed and dented his thigh. Now the actress is walking through a walled garden. She looks distracted and hollow. She stops at a rose bush as if to smell it, and with no warning rakes her bare arm over the thorns. His fingers clutch into fists. He stares wide-eyed at the screen as tendrils of blood sprout across her arm.

His hand is still close to mine, really it's only five or six inches away. But covering a hand clenched into a fist would be a gesture of comfort, soothing him of some pain that perhaps I shared. And that isn't true. I'm dismayed. This movie is the wrong thing to be thinking about. When I touch him I want him to be aware of me as skin, to notice how the skin on the back of my hand is so tight it feels almost polished, while the palm is warmer, moister, plumper. If you take someone's hand in sympathy, you can't trace your fingers up and down his arm and give him goosebumps. You can't tease all his attention into the space between his first and second fingers.

As soon as his hand relaxes, I tell myself, I'll move my hand, and cover it. As soon as it comes back onto his thigh. I rub my palm on my cheek to test it: not damp and not dry, very soft. It smells just slightly of cucumber soap.

It seems so simple now. Once we were standing at the porch railing arm in arm, I could have said, so easily. Come on, let's look at the garden, let's see what the flowers do at night. And led him by the hand down the stairs, and stayed hand in hand as we told each other how good the roses and the lavender smelled, and wow, what was that? Along the fence, a vine that smells fantastic, oh, it's honeysuckle! isn't it? isn't that what honeysuckle looks like? And we would finally drop hands, so that he could break off a tendril of honeysuckle and loop it behind my ear. And I would pick a couple sprigs of lavender for him, and pretend that it was difficult to attach them, as he had no buttonholes, though I would pretend there were and try to poke through the tee shirt, or through his collarbone where there should be a collar button, or through his nose which wasn't pierced after all, my what a surprise, finally stuffing them into the front pocket of his shirt, crushing the little flowers to release more scent.

And here he is, just as close as in the garden. Instead of relaxing, one by one his hands have left his thighs to grip each other's arm at the elbow, to clench and comfort each other. His legs are pressed together at the knees. His shoulders are hunched from slumping lower and lower in the seat. But his eyes are still wide open, peering up at the screen in fascinated anticipation of the further pain he expects it to inflict.

I shift my elbow onto the armrest, so he won't be quite so far away. I   15
edge the elbow slowly, deliberately across and over the armrest, for the first time violating his unpatrolled chairspace. He is so skinny and so tightly huddled that it's still inches from the closest part of him. I watch him breathe, all locked up.

Watching him instead of the movie feels like stealing something. It is a little like watching someone sleep. We are in another world, and the expressions left behind on our faces are vulnerable. But why would I want to watch a movie, when he is here? It's such a luxury to look over and see him next to me. In my imagination his face always lacks detail. Here it is, all filled in. Here is his cheek shaved very smooth with an eyelash fallen onto it, and his nose without any bumps in it. Profiles take getting used to; they don't always look like the same face. Especially this close. The nose is larger, and the mouth is smaller, and there's a different chin.

He is so still. Only his eyes move; he blinks. I could put my hand on his leg. His leg is right here. It's just a leg. I look at it and feel fond of the way his knee has rubbed the jeans into thready patches. His thigh would feel hard and solid like mine. Harder, maybe. There's the familiar lump of keys in his right pocket, maybe tissues, stuff wadded up. Loose folds at the hip, such skinny hips.

All the time I've been watching him he hasn't once looked at me. It's a little insulting. At first I watched sideways, sneakily, but he didn't notice and now I'm just outright staring. I can't believe he doesn't see me. I imagine putting my hand on his thigh, wrapping my fingers into the inside of the thigh a little. What would he do? I imagine him pulling me onto the floor in a passion oblivious to sticky spills and dead popcorn kernels. I imagine my hand sitting on his thigh, squeezing it, my poor excited finally happy hand, and him staying still and staring up at the screen and just blinking.

The movie is already half over.

The scent of honeysuckle was so strong, he said he could find me just by 20 smelling. So I ran into the shadow of a tree and told him to close his eyes and try. No, I couldn't smell him in the dark under the tree, lavender is delicate. But that wasn't the point. There we were, giggling, in the dark. With my eyes closed I couldn't help but walk with arms stretched out, to take slow steps and grope the air. I heard him stepping on leaves, and he heard me, stepping and giggling, so of course we found each other, our stretched arms hit and withdrew from the species' monster-instinct, help, Something in the dark! Then reached again, is that a hand, yes, and what is this? Finding arms and pulling on them, finding a head and hair, textures and bumps, touching it all as though it was a thing to be identified, a new thing we hadn't expected to find. Really it was a strange thing in the dark, all the parts of us seeming to be unconnected and needing to be put together — the scoops and hollows, thicks and thins — until finally they all fit, my hands on his back pulling his chest to my breasts, and even our belt buckles cooperatively clicking.

I look over to see if he is wearing a belt. He isn't. Neither am I.

Some months have passed in the movie, and the grieving woman has decided to take a lover. Finally. Of course I'm hoping that watching a love scene with a woman he finds attractive might remind this man in the seat next to me of other, less distant, possibilities. But as soon as they are alone the actress undresses and commands her admirer to strip. This is a man who has loved her secretly for many years. She gives him thirty seconds. "No, the man next to me says. The word is forced out of him, in pain for the man this time.

"He should just leave," I say.

"Shhh," he says gently, as the woman onscreen is saying something else, something equally cruel, and he wouldn't want to miss it.

This is so annoying that I withdraw my elbow, in punishment. But all I   25
think about, after that, is how far apart we are, and how much I notice it, and how he doesn't notice it at all.

Under the tree, under his shirt, under my hands, his skinny back, wingtips, spine, his skinny ribs, ticklish if touched too lightly. Then we are kissing. A nuzzle of beardstubble, then his lips. The rest is easy. This is how it starts this time the party and the porch, the flowers, the tree. I have a copy of the Kama Sutra illustrated with Indian miniatures. My favorite of them shows a man being driven by horsecart between his lovers: a plump woman with a parrot who sits astride his lap; a slender pale woman who lies underneath him in a garden; a dark playful one who squats on top of him under a tree full of squirrels and white herons. They've spread a golden carpet under the tree, and the woman, while raising and lowering herself on the naked man, pets a small deer. That is me in the horsecart, on my way to try again, and all the women are him, each time in a different colored tee shirt, each setting a different missed seduction: the walk home after we met in a bookstore; in his car, the night he drove me home from a party and I asked him to drop the others off first; the theater: another dark, close, logical, suggestive place.

We always meet accidentally, and I'm always unprepared. Even when hoping desperately to see him, hanging around the bookstore or a cafe because those are places he might appear — even then, I try to make the meeting look accidental. The lovers in the Kama Sutra would never let this happen. They would have spent the day being oiled and perfumed and painted, laying golden carpets under the trees, choosing incense and ragas for their powers of aphrodesia, instructing the servants as to when they might appear with wine or trays of perfect fruit. Their intentions couldn't possibly be mistaken, or the women themselves, resisted. I, however, have not painted the palms of my hands with henna, nor taken a bath perfumed with sandalwood. I'm wearing a tee shirt and jeans. Nothing that suggests it wants to be touched, the way silk or lace would give out instructions on their own.

I roll up the sleeves of my tee shirt. That isn't much, but there is so little I can do here. I wish I had a tattoo, something that could be revealed. I take off my shoes, and my socks, and put my bare feet up on the seat in front of us. Look, something naked. Look at the toes, the high arches. The delicate anklebone.

His eyes never leave the screen. The movie is in French, which I don't understand, and I haven't been reading the subtitles, so by now I have no idea what is happening. The expressions that cross his face are completely incomprehensible.

I finally edge my elbow far enough across the armrest that it nudges his. All my attention is in this elbow, and it is feeling quite coquettish. It bumps

him again, rubbing against him suggestively, hey there, Mr. Elbow. "Oh, 30
sorry," he whispers, as though he is crowding me, as though he has accidentally jostled a complete stranger. He leans against the armrest on his
other side.

I leave quietly, thinking he won't notice. He is quiet too, so quiet I don't
realize he's followed me until he catches me right outside the theater, on the
sidewalk under the bright marquee.

"I was not in the mood for that," I say.

"Yeah, that was pretty intense," he says.

"Yup," I say. I sit down on the sidewalk to put on my socks and shoes,
right down on the flat cement, deliberately ungraceful. This confuses him:
did I carry my shoes into the theater? Wasn't I wearing them? Where did
they come from? Maybe he is seeing me for the first time.

He says it's hard to talk after something like that: Yeah, Yup. He says 35
he will walk me home. We leave the Loop for streets with the lights further
apart, with large trees shadowing the sidewalks, leaf-shaped shadows mixing with our leggy shadows which grow taller in one direction then shorter
in the other between the streetlights, Look at that, and treefrogs, which
hush when you get too close, he tells me, Listen, and crickets, which don't;
the night, still warm though it is late, and both of us are sleepy, and shy.

QUESTIONS

1. As her title and first paragraph make clear, Wahl's piece is about the distance between two people sitting side by side in a movie theater. In what
   ways are they distant from each other? In what ways are they close? In
   what ways does the distance increase or decrease from the beginning to
   the end of the piece?

2. Though the title suggests that the ancient Greek philosopher Zeno is relevant to understanding the distance between them, he is mentioned only
   once, in paragraph 5. Given what you learn about Zeno's ideas in that
   paragraph, how does it help explain the distance between them and the
   possibility of bridging it? In what ways might Zeno's thinking pertain to
   the remainder of the piece? Consult an encyclopedia or online reference
   source to learn more about Zeno's philosophy.

3. Who do you think is more responsible for the distance — the man
   watching the movie, or the narrator watching the man and imagining an
   encounter between them in the garden? Or do you think they are equally
   responsible, or perhaps are caught in a situation in which distance is inevitable and therefore neither is responsible?

4. Though the narrator does not explicitly discuss the broader implications of
   this movie-house episode, the narrator's firsthand impressions, thoughts,
   and fantasies are often predicated on widely held assumptions about
   human behavior. Note as many of these assumptions as you can find,

and consider how they add up to a psychological explanation of distance in this episode and similar situations.

5. Imagine that you were the man watching the movie and had just discovered this written account of that day at the theater. What would you think of it? How would you respond to it? Write a piece addressed to the narrator, telling what you think about that account of your behavior.

6. At some point in your life, you have probably been involved in a situation in which you suddenly felt a distance between yourself and someone with whom you had ordinarily been close. Write an essay or story telling about the episode, how it arose, who was responsible for the distance, how it was resolved, and what you learned from the experience.

Making Connections

Consider how useful it might be to analyze Wahl's story in terms of the methodology and categories that Monica M. Moore sets forth in "Nonverbal Courtship Patterns in Women" (p. 486), paying special attention to her sections on "Gestures" and "Posture Patterns."

INSIDE DOPE

Marcus Laffey

Marcus Laffey is the pseudonym of Edward C. Conlon, a New York City police officer who has written essays about policing for The New Yorker *since 1997. In 2004, he published* Blue Blood, *a book on the same subject, under his own name. The third generation of his family to join the force (both his father and grandfather were police officers), he is a 1987 graduate of Harvard and didn't expect to find himself in law enforcement. "It kind of took me by surprise," he told an interviewer. "I wanted to give it a shot." When the following essay was published in* The New Yorker *in 1999, the writer was a five-year veteran of the force.*

If there were ever a Super Bowl matchup of junkies versus crackheads, it would be hard to figure which team the odds would favor. Both sides would most likely disappear during halftime. The crackheads would believe that they had won, and the junkies wouldn't care. If they did manage to finish the game, the smartest money would invest in a pawnshop next to the stadium, and within hours the investors would own every Super Bowl ring, for pennies on the dollar. Winners and losers would again be indistinguishable.

The war on drugs is a game for me, no matter how urgent it is for poor neighborhoods or how grave the risks are for cops. We call dealers "players," and there are rules as in chess, percentages as in poker, and moves as in schoolyard ball. When I went from being a beat cop to working in narcotics, the change was refreshing. For one thing, you deal only with criminals. No more domestic disputes, barricaded schizophrenics, or D.O.A.s, the morass of negotiable and nonnegotiable difficulties people have with their neighbors or boyfriends or stepchildren. Patrol cops deal with the fluid whole of people's lives, but usually when the tide's going out: people who have the cops called on them aren't happy to see you; people who call the cops aren't calling when they're having a good time. Now all I do is catch sellers of crack and heroin, and catch their customers to show that they sold it. The parts of their lives unaffected by coca- or opium-based products are none of my business. Patrol is politics, but narcotics is pure technique.

My unit, which consists of half a dozen cops and a sergeant, makes arrests for "observation sales." One or two of us go to an observation post ("the OP," and if you're in it you're "doing OPs") on a rooftop or in a vacant apartment to watch a "set," or drug operation, and transmit information to the "catch car," the unmarked van used to pick up the perps. The set might be a lone teen-ager standing on a corner with one pocket full of crack and another full of cash. Or it might be an organization of such intricate subterfuge — with lookouts, managers, moneymen, steerers (to guide customers), and pitchers (for the hand-to-hand transactions) — that you'd think its purpose was to deliver Soviet microfilm to covert operatives instead of a ten-dollar bag of junk to a junkie. But we watch, and give descriptions of buyers for the catch team to pick up, a few blocks away. Sometimes the dealers send out phantom or dummy buyers — people who appear to have bought narcotics but haven't — to see if they're stopped; we wait until we have a handful of buyers, then move in on the set. Most of the spots that we hit are well established, visited by both customers and cops on a regular basis; others pop up and disappear. You might drive around to see who's out — the faces at the places, the traffic pattern of steady customers and usual suspects. Sometimes you feel like the man on the catwalks over the casino floor, scanning the tables for the sharps and card counters, looking out for luck that's too good to be true. Other times, you feel as if you were watching a nature program, some *National Geographic* special on the felony ecology of the streets.

You read the block, seeing who moves and who stands still, their reactions and relations to one another; you sift the players from the idlers, the buyers from the passersby. Most people occupy their environment blithely, with only a slack and occasional awareness of their surroundings. A store window or a noisy garbage truck might distract them in passing, and they might look around before crossing the street, but the ordinary pedestrian is a poster child for daydreams and tunnel vision. Not so in the narcotics trade, where the body language of buyer and seller alike signals a taut awareness of opportunity and threat. There are distinctive addict walks, such as that of the prowler, who might be new to the spot, or sussing out an operation that has shifted to a more favorable corner. He hovers, alert for the deal, floating like a flake of ash above a fire. The addict on a "mission walk" moves with double-quick footsteps, leaning forward, as if against a strong wind, so as not to waste an extra second of his already wasted life. A player, on the other hand, has a self-contained watchfulness, a false repose, like a cat sunning itself on a windowsill, eyes half-closed but ready to pounce.

Every street set operates through an odd combination of aggressive marketing and strategic defense, needing simultaneously to broadcast and to deny its function. The young man on the park bench should look like a high-school senior from thirty yards away but has to show he's a merchant at three yards, and he has to have the drugs near enough for convenience but far enough away to be out of his "custody and control" should he be stopped. If he's holding the drugs, he has to have an escape route — through a hole in a fence, say, or into an alley, or into the building where his grandmother lives. The man on the bench is just a man on a bench, after all, until his context proves him otherwise. But, as you watch, figures emerge from the flow of street life like coördinates on a grid, like pins on a drug map.

Say you're doing OPs from a rooftop, looking down on a street that has three young guys on the corner by the bodega, a couple with a baby in a carriage by the stoop, and a group of old men with brown-bagged brandy bottles by the vacant lot. A man on a bicycle moves in a slow, lazy slalom, up and down the street. The corner boys are the obvious pick, but I have to wait. When a buyer comes, he is easier to recognize, and his arrival on the set sends a signal, a vibration, like a fly landing in the web. The buyer is the bellwether and the bait: he draws the players out and makes them work, prompts them into visible display.

The buyer walks past the old men at the lot, the family on the stoop, to the corner boys, as expected. One corner boy takes the buyer aside and palms his cash, the second stands still, watching up and down the block, and the third goes to the family on the stoop and has a word with the woman with the baby. The woman steps inside the lobby for a few seconds — Thank God, I think, it's not in the carriage — and when she returns she hands something to the third boy, who meets up with the first corner boy and the buyer and hands off the product. The buyer walks away, retracing his route. The man on the bicycle follows him slowly.

I put the buyer over the air: "Hispanic male; red cap; Tommy Hilfiger jacket, blue; bluejeans. South on Third. Be advised, you got a lookout on a bike — white T-shirt, bluejeans, black bike — tailing him to see if he gets picked up. Let him run a couple of blocks, if you can."

Now I have a three-player set, with Mama and corner boys Nos. 1 and 3 down cold. The buyer should be taken, and No. 2 only observed for now. Mama's short time in the building tells me that the stash is not in an apartment but either on her person or right in the lobby, in an unlocked mailbox or a crack in the wall. Corner boy No. 2 is the one to watch, to see if he's the manager or a lookout, up a rank from the others or down. His position will become clear as I watch the group dynamic of the trio — the choreography of who stands where, who talks and who listens, who tells the jokes and who laughs, who's the one that runs to the bodega for the chips and soda. Until he participates in the exchanges, taking money or product, he's legally safe from arrest for an observation sale. If he's a manager, he's the one we want; if he's a smart manager, touching neither cash nor stash, he's the one we're least likely to get. In a sense, everybody wants the spot to get busy: the players grow careless as they get greedy, bringing out more product, paying more heed to the customer and less to us. The manager might have to step in and lend an incriminating hand. When the spot is slow, both groups — the cops and the players — have to be patient.

Even when nothing happens, there is much to interpret. Are they out of product, and will they re-up within ten minutes or an hour? Are they "raised" — afraid we're around — and, if so, is it because they saw our van (unmarked but patently obvious) or saw one of us peering over the roofline, or is it because a patrol car raced by, to a robbery three blocks away? Did

10

they turn away another customer because he wanted credit, or because they thought he was an undercover cop, and were they right? Is the next deal worth the wait?

The wait can be the most trying part of the operation. I've spent hours on tar rooftops, crouched down till my legs cramped, sweating, shivering, wiping the rain from my binoculars every ten seconds. There have been times when I've forgotten to look down before I knelt by the ledge, and settled in beside piles of shit, broken glass, or syringes. On one rooftop, there was an ornate Victorian birdcage, five feet tall, bell-shaped and made of brass, and chained to it, still on a rotten leather leash, was the skeleton of a pit bull. You walk up dirty stairs to a dirty roof to watch a dirty street. At night, even the light is dirty, the sodium-vapor street lights giving off a muddy yellow haze. But sometimes, when something finally does happen, you realize that your concentration is perfect: you feel the cool, neutral thrill of being completely submerged in your task. The objects of surveillance inhabit a living landscape, and you can be struck by the small, random graces of the scene even as you transmit a streak of facts over the radio: "Gray livery cab, buyer in back seat, passenger side, possible white with white sleeves, U-turning now to the left. . . ."

A soap bubble, then two, then dozens rise up in front of me, iridescent, shimmering in their uncertainty. There is a child two floors below me, as rapt with the view above as I am with the view below.

"Arright, we got one, he's beelining to the player, they just popped into the lobby. . . . Now he's out — that's fast, he must have the stash on him. Arright, buyer's walking off now — Hold on, he's just kind of idling across the street. It's not an I-got-my-rock walk. I don't think he got done. Stand by. . . ."

A man standing on another tenement roof whirls an orange flag, and makes it snap like a towel. His flock of pigeons takes flight from the coop with a whoosh like a gust of wind, spiralling out in broadening arcs — showing the smoky gray of their backs as they bank out, the silver-white of their bellies as they circle in — rising up all the while.

"Player's walking off, he sent the last two away, he's out, he's raised, I   15 don't know, but — Go! Go! Go! Hit the set!"

An incinerator chimney shoots out a lash of black smoke, which loops into a lariat before dissolving into the grimy sky.

At the other end of the OP is the catch car. You want a buyer's description, or "scrip," to have something distinctive about it — something beyond the "white T-shirt, bluejeans" of warm weather, "black jacket, bluejeans" of cold. You don't want "Male, walking three pit bulls." You're glad to hear about hot pink and lime green, or T-shirts with legible writing on them, or, even better, "Female in purple-and-yellow tracksuit, with a Cat-in-the-Hat hat, riding a tiny bicycle." For crackheads, as much as for any other species, protective coloration can be a successful evolutionary strategy.

Once you get the scrip and the buyer's direction of flight, you move in, allowing yourself some distance from the set, but not too much, or else the buyer will be home; in neighborhoods like this, people don't have to go far for hard drugs. Sometimes buyers run, and sometimes they fight, and sometimes they toss the drugs (though sometimes you can find those drugs later), and sometimes they eat them when they see you coming. There have been buyers who at the sight of me have reacted with a loss of bowel control, and control of the belly and the bladder as well. The truth is, I am the least of their problems: a night on a cell bench, with prison bologna sandwiches to eat, ranks fairly low amid the hazards of being at the bottom of the criminal food chain.

For crackheads, in particular, a stint as a model prisoner might be a career peak. While the street dealers at dope spots are often junkies themselves, crackheads can't be trusted with the stash — they can't even hold a job whose main requirements are to stand still and watch. The majority of them are figures from a famine: bone-thin and filthy. Months of that life take years from their lives, and thirty-year-olds can pass for fifty, burned out almost literally, with a red-hot core of desperation beneath a dead, charred surface. Junkies generally have a longer ride to the bottom, as the habit gradually slides from being a part of their lives to becoming the point of them. Heroin is purer now than it was in the past, and fewer than half the addicts I arrest have needles on them. They snort it instead of shooting it, which decreases the risk of disease and also seems to slow the forward momentum of addiction. But to me the terminal junkies are especially awful, because they have none of the trapped-rat frenzy of the crackhead; instead, they possess a fatal calm, as if they were keeping their eyes open while drowning. When you collar them, they can have a look of confirmed and somewhat contented self-hatred, as if the world were doing to them what they expect and deserve.

Addicts deserve pity, always, though often they inspire contempt. We 20 collared one crackhead, bumping into him by accident as he stood in a project lobby counting out a handful of vials. He was a street peddler who sold clothing, and had about eighty dollars in his pocket. He had the shrink-wrapped look that crackheads get, as if his skin were two sizes too small. He moaned and wept for his infant child, who would starve, he said, without his support. Yes, he acknowledged, the baby lived with its mother, but he was the provider. The mother and child were only about ten blocks away, at a playground, so we drove to meet them. The mother was a pretty, well-dressed woman, though her soccer-mom wholesomeness may have been artificially heightened by the presence of her handcuffed mate. We called her over, and her look of mild confusion became one of mild dismay as she saw our back-seat passenger. She didn't look surprised, and didn't ask questions. He took out his wad of cash, peeled off four dollars, and handed it to me to give to her. "You gotta be kidding me," I said. "You give me all this father-of-the-year shit, just to throw her four bucks?"

"C'mon," he said. "When you get out of Central Booking, you're hungry, you want some real McDonald's or something."

I gave him back the four dollars and took the wad for the mother. "The Number Two Special, two cheeseburgers and fries, is three-twenty-nine,"

I told him. "It's what I get, and it's all you can afford." For an addict, the priorities are never unclear.

After you've collared the buyers, it's time to move in on the dealers. When you hit a set, there is always a charge of adrenaline, arising from the jungle-war vagaries of opponent and terrain. There are elusive adversaries, explosive ones, and lots of sitting ducks. Some dealers opt for a businesslike capitulation, aware that it's the way to go through the process with the least fuss. Others, especially lobby dealers with access to an apartment upstairs, tend to make a mad dash for freedom. The bust could be a surrender as slow and dignified as Lee's at Appomattox or it could be bedlam — roiling bodies and airborne stash. When you can't count the evidence at the scene, you have to at least control it — the hundreds of dollars in small bills, the fistfuls of crack slabs, the loose decks, the bundles of dope — so you jam it in your pockets like a handful of ball bearings, and all the while there may be a crowd screaming, or perps for whom the fight-or-flight reflex is not a simple either-or proposition.

The smarter dealers carry nothing on them, but you await information from the OP, sometimes with a distaste that verges on dread:

"It's in his sock." 25

"It's in the cast on his right hand — "

"It's in his cheek — sorry, guy, the other cheek. I mean, check between 'em, you copy?"

Stash can be hidden under a bottle cap or in a potato-chip bag, or strewn among heaps of noncriminal trash; it can be wedged in a light fixture in a hall or tucked inside the bumper of a car; it can be in a magnetic key case stuck to the iron bolt beneath a park bench; or it can be on a string taped to the wall and dangling down the garbage-disposal chute. A thorough search can lead to unexpected threats and rewards. Once, when I was rooting through a janitor's closet in a housing project after hitting a heroin set, I found a machine gun in the bottom of a bag of clothes. We continued to search the building and found more than a thousand dollars' worth of heroin, two more guns — a 9-mm. handgun and a .45 revolver — and also ammunition for another machine gun, an AK-47: copper-jacketed bullets more than two inches long, coming to a sharp, conical point like a dunce cap. An AK-47 can discharge bullets at a speed of more than two thousand feet per second, which would allow them to pass through my vest with barely a pause.

In the movies, there are a lot of drug-dealer villains, but those characters usually have to slap their girlfriends or kill a lot of cops to heighten the dramatic point of their bad-guyness. Because the victims of drug sales line up and pay, so to speak, for the privilege, the perpetrators don't have the forthright menace of violent felons. But most of the players I collar have a rap sheet that shows a more diversified criminal career — of earlier forays into robbery or theft — before they settled on the more lucrative and "less illegal" world of drug sales. And although some drug spots operate in a fairly quiet, orderly manner, as if a man were selling newspapers on the street, or a couple were running a catalogue business out of their apartment, most are established and maintained by means of assault, murder, and many subtler thefts of human dignity.

In New York, heroin dealers stamp brand names on the little wax-paper 30
envelopes in which the drug is packaged. This practice gives a glimpse not
only of a corporate structure, when the same brands appear in different sites,
but also of a corporate imagination, showing what they believe their product
should mean to their customers. Some convey the blandly generic aspiration
of quality — "First Class," "President," "Original" — that you might find on
brands of cornflakes or of detergent in some discount supermarket. Others
go for a racier allure, but the gimmick is so hackneyed in conventional advertising that the genuinely illicit thrill of "Knockout" or "No Limit" suggests
the mock-illicit thrill of ads for perfume or fat-free ice cream. Topical references are common, from the flat-out copyright infringement of "DKNY" or
"Ford" to the movie tagline "Show Me the Money." But the best brand
names are the literal ones, which announce without apology the bad things to
come: "911," "25 to Life," "Undertaker," "Fuck You." There is a suicidal
candor to "Lethal Injection" and "Virus," a forthright finality to "O.D." — a
truth in advertising here that few products can match.

Recently, I had a talk with one of my informants, a junkie with AIDS
who sleeps in an alley. A few days before, I'd obtained a search warrant for
a spot he visits several times a day, and he fervently wished me luck with
the warrant's execution. That my success would cause him inconvenience in
supplying his own habit was a mild irony that did not trouble him. He said,
"I know you're a cop and I'm —" and there was a sliver of space before his
next word, enough for me to wonder what term he might use for a shorthand self-portrait. And, knowing that there would be a measure of harsh
truth in it, I was still surprised, and even felt sorry for him, when he said,
"And I'm a fucking scumbag." But he was equally firm in his opinion of
those who had benefitted from his self-destruction: "I done time, I'm no
hero, but these people are blood-suckers. Them and rapists are as bad as
people get. Those people are worse than rapists. Those dealers will suck
you dry. I hope you get every last one of them."

Every day, we go out and hunt people. When we do well — picking off
the customers with dispatch, swooping in on the dealers, taking trophies of
their product and profit — we feel skilled and lucky at once, at the top of our
game. We have shut down spots, reduced robberies and shootings, made
whole blocks cleaner, safer, saner places. But other spots withstand daily assaults from us with negligible losses, and I've driven home after a twenty-hour day only to recognize, with the hallucinatory clarity of the sleep-deprived, the same man, on the same mission walk, that I'd collared the
night before. Typically, buyers spend a night in jail and are sentenced to a
few days of community service. Players might get less, odd as that may seem,
if there weren't enough transactions in open view, or if no stash was recovered. We'll all meet again, soon enough. There are breaks and interruptions,
retirements and replacements, but, no matter how often the whistle blows,
the game is never over.

QUESTIONS

1. The conceptual metaphor that undergirds Laffey's essay is summed up in the first words of the second paragraph: "The war on drugs is a game for me." This idea of a *game* frames the essay's beginning and end and serves as an explanatory context for some of his incidental comments throughout. For instance, "the cool, neutral thrill of being completely submerged in your task" (paragraph 11) recalls the intensity of athletic performance. What other connections to a *game* can you find in the essay? Based on your reading of the essay, does this seem to be a valid comparison to make? Explain. What does the author gain? What is the purpose of positing such a vivid metaphor?

2. How does Laffey convey the repetitive quality of his work? Does calling it a *game* rather than a *war* convey a sense of futility? Explain.

3. At the beginning of paragraph 4, Laffey says that "You read the block." How exactly does his job resemble "reading"? In your own experience, what techniques of reading could be applied in such a pursuit?

4. At some points in the essay, the telling is interrupted by almost lyrical description — for example, when the "flock of pigeons takes flight from the coop with a whoosh like a gust of wind" (paragraph 14). What effect does this have on the reader? Have you ever used this kind of descriptive interruption in your own personal essays?

5. Why do you think Laffey frequently shifts between the impersonal, hypothetical "you" ("Say you're doing OPs from a rooftop," paragraph 6) and his autobiographical "I" ("I have to wait," paragraph 6)? Compose a paragraph about a typical classroom experience that begins by referring to "you" but then narrows its focus to "I" by the end.

6. Write an account of a job that you have held. Use the framework of a typical day to structure your essay. As the narrative proceeds, move beyond reporting what you do, and include moments of reflective explanation to clarify particular aspects of your job.

MAKING CONNECTIONS

Laffey offers his readers closely observed details of the narcotics beat. Look at the techniques other essayists use — Malcolm Gladwell (pp. 313 and 519) or George Orwell (p. 354), for instance — to understand how writers frame their interpretations from the evidence they present.

THE NAKED FACE

Malcolm Gladwell

Biographical information for Malcolm Gladwell can be found on page 313. The following article about facial expressions originally appeared in The New Yorker *in 2002.*

1.

Some years ago, John Yarbrough was working patrol for the Los Angeles County Sheriff's Department. It was about two in the morning. He and his partner were in the Willowbrook section of South Central Los Angeles, and they pulled over a sports car. "Dark, nighttime, average stop," Yarbrough recalls. "Patrol for me was like going hunting. At that time of night in the area I was working, there was a lot of criminal activity, and hardly anyone had a driver's license. Almost everyone had something intoxicating in the car. We stopped drunk drivers all the time. You're hunting for guns or lots of dope, or suspects wanted for major things. You look at someone and you get an instinctive reaction. And the longer you've been working the stronger that instinctive reaction is."

Yarbrough was driving, and in a two-man patrol car the procedure is for the driver to make the approach and the officer on the passenger side to provide backup. He opened the door and stepped out onto the street, walking toward the vehicle with his weapon drawn. Suddenly, a man jumped out of the passenger side and pointed a gun directly at him. The two of them froze, separated by no more than a few yards. "There was a tree behind him, to his right," Yarbrough recalls. "He was about seventeen. He had the gun in his right hand. He was on the curb side. I was on the other side, facing him. It was just a matter of who was going to shoot first. I remember it clear as day. But for some reason I didn't shoot him." Yarbrough is an ex-marine with close-cropped graying hair and a small mustache, and he speaks in measured tones. "Is he a danger? Sure. He's standing there with a gun, and what person in his right mind does that facing a uniformed armed policeman? If you looked at it logically, I should have shot him. But logic had nothing to do with it. Something just didn't feel right. It was a gut reaction not to shoot—a hunch that at that exact moment he was not an imminent threat to me." So Yarbrough stopped, and, sure enough, so did the kid. He pointed a gun at an armed policeman on a dark street in South Central L.A., and then backed down.

Yarbrough retired last year from the sheriff's department after almost thirty years, sixteen of which were in homicide. He now lives in western

Arizona, in a small, immaculate house overlooking the Colorado River, with pictures of John Wayne, Charles Bronson, Clint Eastwood, and Dale Earnhardt on the wall. He has a policeman's watchfulness: while he listens to you, his eyes alight on your face, and then they follow your hands, if you move them, and the areas to your immediate left and right — and then back again, in a steady cycle. He grew up in an affluent household in the San Fernando Valley, the son of two doctors, and he is intensely analytical: he is the sort to take a problem and break it down, working it over slowly and patiently in his mind, and the incident in Willowbrook is one of those problems. Policemen shoot people who point guns directly at them at two in the morning. But something he saw held him back, something that ninety-nine people out of a hundred wouldn't have seen.

Many years later, Yarbrough met with a team of psychologists who were conducting training sessions for law enforcement. They sat beside him in a darkened room and showed him a series of videotapes of people who were either lying or telling the truth. He had to say who was doing what. One tape showed people talking about their views on the death penalty and on smoking in public. Another featured a series of nurses who were all talking about a nature film they were supposedly watching, even though some of them were actually watching grisly documentary footage about burn victims and amputees. It may sound as if the tests should have been easy, because we all think we can tell whether someone is lying. But these were not the obvious fibs of a child, or the prevarications of people whose habits and tendencies we know well. These were strangers who were motivated to deceive, and the task of spotting the liars turns out to be fantastically difficult. There is just too much information — words, intonation, gestures, eyes, mouth — and it is impossible to know how the various cues should be weighted, or how to put them all together, and in any case it's all happening so quickly that you can't even follow what you think you ought to follow. The tests have been given to policemen, customs officers, judges, trial lawyers, and psychotherapists, as well as to officers from the F.B.I., the C.I.A., the D.E.A., and the Bureau of Alcohol, Tobacco, and Firearms — people one would have thought would be good at spotting lies. On average, they score fifty per cent, which is to say that they would have done just as well if they hadn't watched the tapes at all and just guessed. But every now and again — roughly one time in a thousand — someone scores off the charts. A Texas Ranger named David Maxwell did extremely well, for example, as did an ex-A.T.F. agent named J. J. Newberry, a few therapists, an arbitrator, a vice cop — and John Yarbrough, which suggests that what happened in Willowbrook may have been more than a fluke or a lucky guess. Something in our faces signals whether we're going to shoot, say, or whether we're lying about the film we just saw. Most of us aren't very good at spotting it. But a handful of people are virtuosos. What do they see that we miss?

2.

All of us, a thousand times a day, read faces. When someone says "I   5
love you," we look into that person's eyes to judge his or her sincerity.
When we meet someone new, we often pick up on subtle signals, so that,
even though he or she may have talked in a normal and friendly manner, afterward we say, "I don't think he liked me," or "I don't think she's very
happy." We easily parse complex distinctions in facial expression. If you
saw me grinning, for example, with my eyes twinkling, you'd say I was
amused. But that's not the only way we interpret a smile. If you saw me nod
and smile exaggeratedly, with the corners of my lips tightened, you would
take it that I had been teased and was responding sarcastically. If I made eye
contact with someone, gave a small smile and then looked down and
averted my gaze, you would think I was flirting. If I followed a remark with
an abrupt smile and then nodded, or tilted my head sideways, you might
conclude that I had just said something a little harsh, and wanted to take
the edge off it. You wouldn't need to hear anything I was saying in order to
reach these conclusions. The face is such an extraordinarily efficient instrument of communication that there must be rules that govern the way we interpret facial expressions. But what are those rules? And are they the same
for everyone?

In the nineteen-sixties, a young San Francisco psychologist named Paul
Ekman began to study facial expression, and he discovered that no one
knew the answers to those questions. Ekman went to see Margaret Mead,
climbing the stairs to her tower office at the American Museum of Natural
History. He had an idea. What if he travelled around the world to find out
whether people from different cultures agreed on the meaning of different
facial expressions? Mead, he recalls, "looked at me as if I were crazy." Like
most social scientists of her day, she believed that expression was culturally
determined—that we simply used our faces according to a set of learned
social conventions. Charles Darwin had discussed the face in his later writings; in his 1872 book, *The Expression of the Emotions in Man and Animals*, he argued that all mammals show emotion reliably in their faces. But
in the nineteen-sixties academic psychologists were more interested in motivation and cognition than in emotion or its expression. Ekman was un-
daunted; he began travelling to places like Japan, Brazil, and Argentina,
carrying photographs of men and women making a variety of distinctive
faces. Everywhere he went, people agreed on what those expressions
meant. But what if people in the developed world had all picked up the
same cultural rules from watching the same movies and television shows?
So Ekman set out again, this time making his way through the jungles of
Papua New Guinea, to the most remote villages, and he found that the
tribesmen there had no problem interpreting the expressions, either. This
may not sound like much of a breakthrough. But in the scientific climate of
the time it was a revelation. Ekman had established that expressions were

the universal products of evolution. There were fundamental lessons to be learned from the face, if you knew where to look.

Paul Ekman is now in his sixties. He is clean-shaven, with closely set eyes and thick, prominent eyebrows, and although he is of medium build, he seems much larger than he is: there is something stubborn and substantial in his demeanor. He grew up in Newark, the son of a pediatrician, and entered the University of Chicago at fifteen. He speaks deliberately: before he laughs, he pauses slightly, as if waiting for permission. He is the sort to make lists, and number his arguments. His academic writing has an orderly logic to it; by the end of an Ekman essay, each stray objection and problem has been gathered up and catalogued. In the mid-sixties, Ekman set up a lab in a ramshackle Victorian house at the University of California at San Francisco, where he holds a professorship. If the face was part of a physiological system, he reasoned, the system could be learned. He set out to teach himself. He treated the face as an adventurer would a foreign land, exploring its every crevice and contour. He assembled a videotape library of people's facial expressions, which soon filled three rooms in his lab, and studied them to the point where he could look at a face and pick up a flicker of emotion that might last no more than a fraction of a second. Ekman created the lying tests. He filmed the nurses talking about the movie they were watching and the movie they weren't watching. Working with Maureen O'Sullivan, a psychologist from the University of San Francisco, and other colleagues, he located people who had a reputation for being uncannily perceptive, and put them to the test, and that's how Yarbrough and the other high-scorers were identified. O'Sullivan and Ekman call this study of gifted face readers the Diogenes Project, after the Greek philosopher of antiquity who used to wander around Athens with a lantern, peering into people's faces as he searched for an honest man. Ekman has taken the most vaporous of sensations—the hunch you have about someone else — and sought to give them definition. Most of us don't trust our hunches, because we don't know where they came from. We think they can't be explained. But what if they can?

3.

Paul Ekman got his start in the face-reading business because of a man named Silvan Tomkins, and Silvan Tomkins may have been the best face reader there ever was. Tomkins was from Philadelphia, the son of a dentist from Russia. He was short, and slightly thick around the middle, with a wild mane of white hair and huge black plastic-rimmed glasses. He taught psychology at Princeton and Rutgers, and was the author of *Affect, Imagery, Consciousness*, a four-volume work so dense that its readers were evenly divided between those who understood it and thought it was brilliant and those who did not understand it and thought it was brilliant. He was a legendary talker. At the end of a cocktail party, fifteen people would sit, rapt, at Tomkins's feet, and someone would say, "One more question!" and they would all sit there for another hour and a half, as Tomkins held forth on, say, comic books, a television sitcom, the biology of emotion, his problem with Kant, and his enthusiasm for the latest fad diets, all enfolded into one extended riff. During the Depression, in the midst of his doctoral studies at Harvard, he worked as a handicapper for a horse-racing syndicate, and was so successful that he lived lavishly on Manhattan's Upper East Side. At the track, where he sat in the stands for hours, staring at the horses through binoculars, he was known as the Professor. "He had a system for predicting how a horse would do based on what horse was on either side of him, based on their emotional relationship," Ekman said. If a male horse, for instance, had lost to a mare in his first or second year, he would be ruined if he went to the gate with a mare next to him in the lineup. (Or something like that—no one really knew for certain.) Tomkins felt that emotion was the code to life, and that with enough attention to particulars the code could be cracked. He thought this about the horses, and, more important, he thought this about the human face.

Tomkins, it was said, could walk into a post office, go over to the "Wanted" posters, and, just by looking at mug shots, tell you what crimes the various fugitives had committed. "He would watch the show *To Tell the Truth*, and without fault he could always pick the person who was lying and who his confederates were," his son, Mark, recalls. "He actually wrote the producer at one point to say it was too easy, and the man invited him to come to New York, go backstage, and show his stuff." Virginia Demos, who teaches psychology at Harvard, recalls having long conversations with Tomkins. "We would sit and talk on the phone, and he would turn the sound down as Jesse Jackson was talking to Michael Dukakis, at the Democratic National Convention. And he would read the faces and give his predictions on what would happen. It was profound."

Ekman's most memorable encounter with Tomkins took place in the late sixties. Ekman had just tracked down a hundred thousand feet of film that had been shot by the virologist Carleton Gajdusek in the remote jungles of Papua New Guinea. Some of the footage was of a tribe called the South Fore, who were a peaceful and friendly people. The rest was of the Kukukuku, who were hostile and murderous and who had a homosexual ritual where pre-adolescent boys were required to serve as courtesans for the male elders of the tribe. Ekman was still working on the problem of whether human facial expressions were universal, and the Gajdusek film was invaluable. For six months, Ekman and his collaborator, Wallace Friesen, sorted through the footage. They cut extraneous scenes, focussing just on closeups of the faces of the tribesmen, and when the editing was finished Ekman called in Tomkins.

The two men, protégé and mentor, sat at the back of the room, as faces flickered across the screen. Ekman had told Tomkins nothing about the

10

tribes involved; all identifying context had been edited out. Tomkins looked on intently, peering through his glasses. At the end, he went up to the screen and pointed to the faces of the South Fore. "These are a sweet, gentle people, very indulgent, very peaceful," he said. Then he pointed to the faces of the Kukukuku. "This other group is violent, and there is lots of evidence to suggest homosexuality." Even today, a third of a century later, Ekman cannot get over what Tomkins did. "My God! I vividly remember saying, 'Silvan, how on earth are you doing that?' " Ekman recalls. "And he went up to the screen and, while we played the film backward, in slow motion, he pointed out the particular bulges and wrinkles in the face that he was using to make his judgment. That's when I realized, 'I've got to unpack the face.' It was a gold mine of information that everyone had ignored. This guy could see it, and if he could see it, maybe everyone else could, too."

Ekman and Friesen decided that they needed to create a taxonomy of facial expressions, so day after day they sat across from each other and began to make every conceivable face they could. Soon, though, they realized that their efforts weren't enough. "I met an anthropologist, Wade Seaford, told him what I was doing, and he said, 'Do you have this movement?' " — and here Ekman contracted what's called the triangularis, which is the muscle that depresses the corners of the lips, forming an arc of distaste — "and it wasn't in my system, because I had never seen it before. I had built a system not on what the face can do but on what I had seen. I was devastated. So I came back and said, 'I've got to learn the anatomy.' " Friesen and Ekman then combed through medical textbooks that outlined each of the facial muscles, and identified every distinct muscular movement that the face could make. There were forty-three such movements. Ekman and Friesen called them "action units." Then they sat across from each other again, and began manipulating each action unit in turn, first locating the muscle in their mind and then concentrating on isolating it, watching each other closely as they did, checking their movements in a mirror, making notes of how the wrinkle patterns on their faces would change with each muscle movement, and videotaping the movement for their records. On the few occasions when they couldn't make a particular movement, they went next door to the U.C.S.F. anatomy department, where a surgeon they knew would stick them with a needle and electrically stimulate the recalcitrant muscle. "That wasn't pleasant at all," Ekman recalls. When each of those action units had been mastered, Ekman and Friesen began working action units in combination, layering one movement on top of another. The entire process took seven years. "There are three hundred combinations of two muscles," Ekman says. "If you add in a third, you get over four thousand. We took it up to five muscles, which is over ten thousand visible facial configurations." Most of those ten thousand facial expressions don't mean anything, of course. They are the kind of nonsense faces that children make. But, by working through each action-unit combination, Ekman and Friesen identified about three thousand that did seem to mean something, until they had catalogued the essential repertoire of human emotion.

4.

On a recent afternoon, Ekman sat in his office at U.C.S.F., in what is known as the Human Interaction Laboratory, a standard academic's lair of books and files, with photographs of his two heroes, Tomkins and Darwin, on the wall. He leaned forward slightly, placing his hands on his knees, and began running through the action-unit configurations he had learned so long ago. "Everybody can do action unit four," he began. He lowered his brow, using his depressor glabellae, depressor supercilli, and corrugator. "Almost everyone can do A.U. nine." He wrinkled his nose, using his levator labii superioris, alaeque nasi. "Everybody can do five." He contracted his levator palpebrae superioris, raising his upper eyelid.

I was trying to follow along with him, and he looked up at me. "You've got a very good five," he said generously. "The more deeply set your eyes are, the harder it is to see the five. Then there's seven." He squinted. "Twelve." He flashed a smile, activating the zygomatic major. The inner parts of his eyebrows shot up. "That's A.U. one — distress, anguish." Then he used his frontalis, pars lateralis, to raise the outer half of his eyebrows. "That's A.U. two. It's also very hard, but it's worthless. It's not part of anything except Kabuki theatre. Twenty-three is one of my favorites. It's the narrowing of the red margin of the lips. Very reliable anger sign. It's very hard to do voluntarily." He narrowed his lips. "Moving one ear at a time is still the hardest thing to do. I have to really concentrate. It takes everything I've got." He laughed. "This is something my daughter always wanted me to do for her friends. Here we go." He wiggled his left ear, then his right ear. Ekman does not appear to have a particularly expressive face. He has the demeanor of a psychoanalyst, watchful and impassive, and his ability to transform his face so easily and quickly was astonishing. "There is one I can't do," he went on. "It's A.U. thirty-nine. Fortunately, one of my postdocs can do it. A.U. thirty-eight is dilating the nostrils. Thirty-nine is the opposite. It's the muscle that pulls them down." He shook his head and looked at me again. "Oooh! You've got a fantastic thirty-nine. That's one of the best I've ever seen. It's genetic. There should be other members of your family who have this heretofore unknown talent. You've got it, you've got it." He laughed again. "You're in a position to flash it at people. See, you should try that in a singles bar!"

Ekman then began to layer one action unit on top of another, in order to 15
compose the more complicated facial expressions that we generally recognize as emotions. Happiness, for instance, is essentially A.U. six and twelve — contracting the muscles that raise the cheek (orbicularis oculi, pars orbitalis) in combination with the zygomatic major, which pulls up the corners of the lips. Fear is A.U. one, two and four, or, more fully, one, two, four, five, and twenty, with or without action units twenty-five, twenty-six, or twenty-seven. That is: the inner brow raiser (frontalis, pars medialis) plus the outer brow raiser (frontalis, pars lateralis) plus the brow-lowering depressor supercilli plus the levator palpebrae superioris (which raises the upper lid), plus the

risorius (which stretches the lips), the parting of the lips (depressor labii), and the masseter (which drops the jaw). Disgust? That's mostly A.U. nine, the wrinkling of the nose (levator labii superioris, alaeque nasi), but it can sometimes be ten, and in either case may be combined with A.U. fifteen or sixteen or seventeen.

Ekman and Friesen ultimately assembled all these combinations — and the rules for reading and interpreting them — into the Facial Action Coding System, or FACS, and wrote them up in a five-hundred-page binder. It is a strangely riveting document, full of details like the possible movements of the lips (elongate, de-elongate, narrow, widen, flatten, protrude, tighten and stretch); the four different changes of the skin between the eyes and the cheeks (bulges, bags, pouches, and lines); or the critical distinctions between infraorbital furrows and the nasolabial furrow. Researchers have employed the system to study everything from schizophrenia to heart disease; it has even been put to use by computer animators at Pixar (*Toy Story*), and at DreamWorks (*Shrek*). FACS takes weeks to master in its entirety, and only five hundred people around the world have been certified to use it in research. But for those who have, the experience of looking at others is forever changed. They learn to read the face the way that people like John Yarbrough did intuitively. Ekman compares it to the way you start to hear a symphony once you've been trained to read music: an experience that used to wash over you becomes particularized and nuanced.

Ekman recalls the first time he saw Bill Clinton, during the 1992 Democratic primaries. "I was watching his facial expressions, and I said to my wife, 'This is Peck's Bad Boy,' " Ekman says. "This is a guy who wants to be caught with his hand in the cookie jar, and have us love him for it anyway. There was this expression that's one of his favorites. It's that hand-in-the-cookie-jar, love-me-Mommy-because-I'm-a-rascal look. It's A.U. twelve, fifteen, seventeen, and twenty-four, with an eye roll." Ekman paused, then reconstructed that particular sequence of expressions on his face. He contracted his zygomatic major, A.U. twelve, in a classic smile, then tugged the corners of his lips down with his triangularis, A.U. fifteen. He flexed the mentalis, A.U. seventeen, which raises the chin, slightly pressed his lips together in A.U. twenty-four, and finally rolled his eyes — and it was as if Slick Willie himself were suddenly in the room. "I knew someone who was on his communications staff. So I contacted him. I said, 'Look, Clinton's got this way of rolling his eyes along with a certain expression, and what it conveys is "I'm a bad boy." I don't think it's a good thing. I could teach him how not to do that in two to three hours.' And he said, 'Well, we can't take the risk that he's known to be seeing an expert on lying.' I think it's a great tragedy, because . . ." Ekman's voice trailed off. It was clear that he rather liked Clinton, and that he wanted Clinton's trademark expression to have been no more than a meaningless facial tic. Ekman shrugged. "Unfortunately, I guess, he needed to get caught — and he got caught."

5.

Early in his career, Paul Ekman filmed forty psychiatric patients, including a woman named Mary, a forty-two-year-old housewife. She had attempted suicide three times, and survived the last attempt — an overdose of pills — only because someone found her in time and rushed her to the hospital. Her children had left home and her husband was inattentive, and she was depressed. When she first went to the hospital, she simply sat and cried, but she seemed to respond well to therapy. After three weeks, she told her doctor that she was feeling much better and wanted a weekend pass to see her family. The doctor agreed, but just before Mary was to leave the hospital she confessed that the real reason she wanted to go on weekend leave was so that she could make another suicide attempt. Several years later, a group of young psychiatrists asked Ekman how they could tell when suicidal patients were lying. He didn't know, but, remembering Mary, he decided to try to find out. If the face really was a reliable guide to emotion, shouldn't he be able to look back on the film and tell that she was lying? Ekman and Friesen began to analyze the film for clues. They played it over and over for dozens of hours, examining in slow motion every gesture and expression. Finally, they saw it. As Mary's doctor asked her about her plans for the future, a look of utter despair flashed across her face so quickly that it was almost imperceptible.

Ekman calls that kind of fleeting look a "microexpression," and one cannot understand why John Yarbrough did what he did on that night in South Central without also understanding the particular role and significance of microexpressions. Many facial expressions can be made voluntarily. If I'm trying to look stern as I give you a tongue-lashing, I'll have no difficulty doing so, and you'll have no difficulty interpreting my glare. But our faces are also governed by a separate, involuntary system. We know this because stroke victims who suffer damage to what is known as the pyramidal neural system will laugh at a joke, but they cannot smile if you ask them to. At the same time, patients with damage to another part of the brain have the opposite problem. They can smile on demand, but if you tell them a joke they can't laugh. Similarly, few of us can voluntarily do A.U. one, the sadness sign. (A notable exception, Ekman points out, is Woody Allen, who uses his frontalis, pars medialis, to create his trademark look of comic distress.) Yet we raise our inner eyebrows all the time, without thinking, when we are unhappy. Watch a baby just as he or she starts to cry, and you'll often see the frontalis, pars medialis, shoot up, as if it were on a string.

Perhaps the most famous involuntary expression is what Ekman has dubbed the Duchenne smile, in honor of the nineteenth-century French neurologist Guillaume Duchenne, who first attempted to document the workings of the muscles of the face with the camera. If I ask you to smile, you'll flex your zygomatic major. By contrast, if you smile spontaneously, in the presence of genuine emotion, you'll not only flex your zygomatic but also tighten the orbicularis oculi, pars orbitalis, which is the muscle that encircles the eye. It is almost impossible to tighten the orbicularis oculi, pars lateralis, on demand, and it is equally difficult to stop it from tightening when we smile at something genuinely pleasurable. This kind of smile "does not obey the will," Duchenne wrote. "Its absence unmasks the false friend." When we experience a basic emotion, a corresponding message is automatically sent to the muscles of the face. That message may linger on the face for just a fraction of a second, or be detectable only if you attached electrical sensors to the face, but it's always there. Silvan Tomkins once began a lecture by bellowing, "The face is like the penis!" and this is what he meant—that the face has, to a large extent, a mind of its own. This doesn't mean we have no control over our faces. We can use our voluntary muscular system to try to suppress those involuntary responses. But, often, some little part of that suppressed emotion—the sense that I'm really unhappy, even though I deny it—leaks out. Our voluntary expressive system is the way we intentionally signal our emotions. But our involuntary expressive system is in many ways even more important: it is the way we have been equipped by evolution to signal our authentic feelings.

"You must have had the experience where somebody comments on your expression and you didn't know you were making it," Ekman says. "Somebody tells you, 'What are you getting upset about?' 'Why are you smirking?' You can hear your voice, but you can't see your face. If we knew what was on our face, we would be better at concealing it. But that wouldn't necessarily be a good thing. Imagine if there were a switch that all of us had, to turn off the expressions on our face at will. If babies had that switch, we wouldn't know what they were feeling. They'd be in trouble. You could make an argument, if you wanted to, that the system evolved so that parents would be able to take care of kids. Or imagine if you were married to someone with a switch? It would be impossible. I don't think mating and infatuation and friendships and closeness would occur if our faces didn't work that way."

Ekman slipped a tape taken from the O. J. Simpson trial into the VCR. It was of Kato Kaelin, Simpson's shaggy-haired house guest, being examined by Marcia Clark, one of the prosecutors in the case. Kaelin sits in the witness box, with his trademark vacant look. Clark asks a hostile question. Kaelin leans forward and answers softly. "Did you see that?" Ekman asked me. I saw nothing, just Kato being Kato—harmless and passive. Ekman stopped the tape, rewound it, and played it back in slow motion. On the screen, Kaelin moved forward to answer the question, and in that fraction of a second his face was utterly transformed. His nose wrinkled, as he flexed his levator labii superioris, alaeque nasi. His teeth were bared, his brows lowered. "It was almost totally A.U. nine," Ekman said. "It's disgust, with anger there as well, and the clue to that is that when your eyebrows go down, typically your eyes are not as open as they are here. The raised upper eyelid is a component of anger, not disgust. It's very quick." Ekman stopped the tape and played it again, peering at the screen. "You know, he looks like a snarling dog."

Ekman said that there was nothing magical about his ability to pick up an emotion that fleeting. It was simply a matter of practice. "I could show you forty examples, and you could pick it up. I have a training tape, and people love it. They start it, and they can't see any of these expressions. Thirty-five minutes later, they can see them all. What that says is that this is an accessible skill."

Ekman showed another clip, this one from a press conference given by Kim Philby in 1955. Philby had not yet been revealed as a Soviet spy, but two of his colleagues, Donald Maclean and Guy Burgess, had just defected to the Soviet Union. Philby is wearing a dark suit and a white shirt. His hair is straight and parted to the left. His face has the hauteur of privilege.

"Mr. Philby," he is asked. "Mr. Macmillan, the foreign secretary, said   25 there was no evidence that you were the so-called third man who allegedly tipped off Burgess and Maclean. Are you satisfied with that clearance that he gave you?"

Philby answers confidently, in the plummy tones of the English upper class. "Yes, I am."

"Well, if there was a third man, were you in fact the third man?"

"No," Philby says, just as forcefully. "I was not."

Ekman rewound the tape, and replayed it in slow motion. "Look at this," he said, pointing to the screen. "Twice, after being asked serious questions about whether he's committed treason, he's going to smirk. He looks like the cat who ate the canary." The expression was too brief to see normally. But at quarter speed it was painted on his face—the lips pressed together in a look of pure smugness. "He's enjoying himself, isn't he?" Ekman went on. "I call this—duping delight—the thrill you get from fooling other people." Ekman started the VCR up again. "There's another thing he does." On the screen, Philby was answering another question. "In the second place, the Burgess-Maclean affair has raised issues of great"— he pauses—"delicacy." Ekman went back to the pause, and froze the tape. "Here it is," he said. "A very subtle microexpression of distress or unhappiness. It's only in the eyebrows—in fact, just in one eyebrow." Sure enough, Philby's right inner eyebrow was raised in an unmistakable A.U. one. "It's very brief," Ekman said. "He's not doing it voluntarily. And it totally contradicts all his confidence and assertiveness. It comes when he's talking about Burgess and Maclean, whom he had tipped off. It's a hot spot that suggests, 'You shouldn't trust what you hear.'"

A decade ago, Ekman joined forces with J. J. Newberry—the ex-A.T.F.   30 agent who is one of the high-scorers in the Diogenes Project—to put together a program for educating law-enforcement officials around the world in the techniques of interviewing and lie detection. In recent months, they have flown to Washington, D.C., to assist the C.I.A. and the F.B.I. in counterterrorism training. At the same time, the Defense Advanced Research Projects Agency (DARPA) has asked Ekman and his former student Mark Frank, now at Rutgers, to develop experimental scenarios for studying deception that would be relevant to counter-terrorism. The objective is to teach people to look for discrepancies between what is said and what is signalled — to pick up on the difference between Philby's crisp denials and his fleeting anguish. It's a completely different approach from the shouting cop we see on TV and in the movies, who threatens the suspect and sweeps all of the papers and coffee cups off the battered desk. The Hollywood interrogation is an exercise in intimidation, and its point is to force the suspect to tell you what you need to know. It does not take much to see the limitations of this strategy. It depends for its success on the coöperation of the suspect — when, of course, the suspect's involuntary communication may be just as critical. And it privileges the voice over the face, when the voice and the face are equally significant channels in the same system.

Ekman received his most memorable lesson in this truth when he and Friesen first began working on expressions of anger and distress. "It was weeks before one of us finally admitted feeling terrible after a session where we'd been making one of those faces all day," Friesen says. "Then the other realized that he'd been feeling poorly, too, so we began to keep track." They then went back and began monitoring their body during particular facial movements. "Say you do A.U. one, raising the inner eyebrows, and six, raising the cheeks, and fifteen, the lowering of the corner of the lips," Ekman said, and then did all three. "What we discovered is that that expression alone is sufficient to create marked changes in the autonomic nervous system. When this first occurred, we were stunned. We weren't expecting this at all. And it happened to both of us. We felt *terrible*. What we were generating was sadness, anguish. And when I lower my brows, which is four, and raise the upper eyelid, which is five, and narrow the eyelids, which is seven, and press the lips together, which is twenty-four, I'm generating anger. My heartbeat will go up ten to twelve beats. My hands will get hot. As I do it, I can't disconnect from the system. It's very unpleasant, very unpleasant."

Ekman, Friesen, and another colleague, Robert Levenson, who teaches at Berkeley, published a study of this effect in *Science*. They monitored the bodily indices of anger, sadness, and fear — heart rate and body temperature — in two groups. The first group was instructed to remember and relive a particularly stressful experience. The other was told to simply produce a series of facial movements, as instructed by Ekman — to "assume the position," as they say in acting class. The second group, the people who were pretending, showed the same physiological responses as the first. A few years later, a German team of psychologists published a similar study. They had a group of subjects look at cartoons, either while holding a pen between their lips — an action that made it impossible to contract either of the two major smiling muscles, the risorius and the zygomatic major — or while holding a pen clenched between their teeth, which had the opposite effect and forced them to smile. The people with the pen between their teeth found the cartoons much funnier. Emotion doesn't just go from the inside out. It goes from the outside in. What's more, neither the subjects "assuming the position" nor the people with pens in their teeth knew they were making expressions of emotion. In the facial-feedback system, an expression you do not even know that you have can create an emotion you did not choose to feel.

It is hard to talk to anyone who knows FACS without this point coming up again and again. Face-reading depends not just on seeing facial expressions but also on taking them seriously. One reason most of us — like the TV cop — do not closely attend to the face is that we view its evidence as secondary, as an adjunct to what we believe to be *real* emotion. But there's nothing secondary about the face, and surely this realization is what set John Yarbrough apart on the night that the boy in the sports car came at him with a gun. It's not just that he saw a microexpression that the rest of us would have missed. It's that he took what he saw so seriously that he was able to overcome every self-protective instinct in his body, and hold his fire.

6.

Yarbrough has a friend in the L.A. County Sheriff's Department, Sergeant Bob Harms, who works in narcotics in Palmdale. Harms is a member of the Diogenes Project as well, but the two men come across very differently. Harms is bigger than Yarbrough, taller and broader in the chest, with soft brown eyes and dark, thick hair. Yarbrough is restoring a Corvette and wears Rush Limbaugh ties, and he says that if he hadn't been a cop he would have liked to stay in the Marines. Harms came out of college wanting to be a commercial artist; now he plans to open a bed-and-breakfast in Vermont with his wife when he retires. On the day we met, Harms was wearing a pair of jean shorts and a short-sleeved patterned shirt. His badge was hidden inside his shirt. He takes notes not on a yellow legal pad, which he considers unnecessarily intimidating to witnesses, but on a powder-blue one. "I always get teased because I'm the touchy-feely one," Harms said. "John Yarbrough is very analytical. He thinks before he speaks. There is a lot going on inside his head. He's constantly thinking four or five steps ahead, then formulating whatever his answers are going to be. That's not how I do my interviews. I have a conversation. It's not 'Where were you on Friday night?' Because that's the way we normally communicate. I never say, 'I'm Sergeant Harms.' I always start by saying, 'I'm Bob Harms, and I'm here to talk to you about your case,' and the first thing I do is smile."

The sensation of talking to the two men, however, is surprisingly similar. Normal conversation is like a game of tennis: you talk and I listen, you listen and I talk, and we feel scrutinized by our conversational partner only when the ball is in our court. But Yarbrough and Harms never stop watching, even when they're doing the talking. Yarbrough would comment on my conversational style, noting where I held my hands as I talked, or how long I would wait out a lull in the conversation. At one point, he stood up and soundlessly moved to the door — which he could have seen only in his peripheral vision — opening it just before a visitor rang the doorbell. Harms gave the impression that he was deeply interested in me. It wasn't empathy. It was a kind of powerful curiosity. "I remember once, when I was in prison custody, I used to shake prisoners' hands," Harms said. "The deputies thought I was crazy. But I wanted to see what happened, because that's what these men are starving for, some dignity and respect."

Some of what sets Yarbrough and Harms and the other face readers apart is no doubt innate. But the fact that people can be taught so easily to recognize microexpressions, and can learn FACS, suggests that we all have at least the potential capacity for this kind of perception. Among those who do very well at face-reading, tellingly, are some aphasics, such as stroke victims who have lost the ability to understand language. Collaborating with Ekman on a paper that was recently published in *Nature*, the psychologist Nancy Etcoff, of Massachusetts General Hospital, described how a group of aphasics trounced a group of undergraduates at M.I.T. on the nurses tape. Robbed of the power to understand speech, the stroke victims had apparently been forced to become far more sensitive to the information written on people's faces. "They are compensating for the loss in one channel through these other channels," Etcoff says. "We could hypothesize that there is some kind of rewiring in the brain, but I don't think we need that explanation. They simply exercise these skills much more than we do." Ekman has also done work showing that some abused children are particularly good at reading faces as well: like the aphasics in the study, they developed "interpretive strategies" — in their case, so they could predict the behavior of their volatile parents.

What appears to be a kind of magical, effortless intuition about faces, then, may not really be effortless and magical at all. This kind of intuition is a product of desire and effort. Silvan Tomkins took a sabbatical from Princeton when his son Mark was born, and stayed in his house on the Jersey Shore, staring into his son's face, long and hard, picking up the patterns of emotion — the cycles of interest, joy, sadness, and anger — that flash across an infant's face in the first few months of life. He taught himself the logic of the furrows and the wrinkles and the creases, the subtle differences between the pre-smile and the pre-cry face. Later, he put together a library of thousands of photographs of human faces, in every conceivable expression. He developed something called the Picture Arrangement Test, which was his version of the Rorschach blot: a patient would look at a series of pictures and be asked to arrange them in a sequence and then tell a story based on what he saw. The psychologist was supposed to interpret the meaning of the story, but Tomkins would watch a videotape of the patient with the sound off, and by studying the expressions on the patient's face teach himself to predict what the story was. Face-reading, for those who have mastered it, becomes a kind of compulsion; it becomes hard to be satisfied with the level and quality of information that most of us glean from normal social encounters. "Whenever we get together," Harms says of spending time with other face readers, "we debrief each other. We're constantly talking about cases, or some of these videotapes of Ekman's, and we say, 'I missed that, did you get that?' Maybe there's an emotion attached there. We're always trying to place things, and replaying interviews in our head."

This is surely why the majority of us don't do well at reading faces: we feel no need to make that extra effort. People fail at the nurses tape, Ekman says, because they end up just listening to the words. That's why, when Tomkins was starting out in his quest to understand the face, he always watched television with the sound turned off. "We are such creatures of language that what we hear takes precedence over what is supposed to be our primary channel of communication, the visual channel," he once said. "Even though the visual channel provides such enormous information, the fact is that the voice preëmpts the individual's attention, so that he cannot really see the face while he listens." We prefer that way of dealing with the world because it does not challenge the ordinary boundaries of human relationships. Ekman, in one of his essays, writes of what he learned from the legendary sociologist Erving Goffman. Goffman said that part of what it means to be civilized is not to "steal" information that is not freely given to us. When someone picks his nose or cleans his ears, out of unthinking habit, we look away. Ekman writes that for Goffman the spoken word is "the acknowledged information, the information for which the person who states it is willing to take responsibility," and he goes on:

> When the secretary who is miserable about a fight with her husband the previous night answers, "Just fine," when her boss asks, "How are you this morning?" — that false message may be the one relevant to the boss's interactions with her. It tells him that she is going to do her job. The true message — that she is miserable — he may not care to know about at all as long as she does not intend to let it impair her job performance.

What would the boss gain by reading the subtle and contradictory microexpressions on his secretary's face? It would be an invasion of her privacy and an act of disrespect. More than that, it would entail an obligation. He would be obliged to do something, or say something, or feel something that might otherwise be avoided entirely. To see what is intended to be hidden, or, at least, what is usually missed, opens up a world of uncomfortable possibilities. This is the hard part of being a face reader. People like that have more faith in their hunches than the rest of us do. But faith is not certainty. Sometimes, on a routine traffic stop late at night, you end up finding out that your hunch was right. But at other times you'll never know. And you can't even explain it properly, because what can you say? You did something the rest of us would never have done, based on something the rest of us would never have seen.

"I was working in West Hollywood once, in the nineteen-eighties," 40 Harms said. "I was with a partner, Scott. I was driving. I had just recently come off the prostitution team, and we spotted a man in drag. He was on Sunset, and I didn't recognize him. At that time, Sunset was normally for females. So it was kind of odd. It was a cold night in January. There was an all-night restaurant on Sunset called Ben Franks, so I asked my partner to roll down the window and ask the guy if he was going to Ben Franks — just to get a reaction. And the guy immediately keys on Scott, and he's got an overcoat on, and he's all bundled up, and he starts walking over to the car. It had been raining so much that the sewers in West Hollywood had backed up, and one of the manhole covers had been cordoned off because it was pumping out water. The guy comes over to the squad car, and he's walking right through that. He's fixated on Scott. So we asked him what he was doing. He says, 'I was out for a walk.' And then he says, 'I have something to show you.'"

Later, after the incident was over, Harms and his partner learned that the man had been going around Hollywood making serious threats, that he was unstable and had just attempted suicide, that he was in all likelihood about to erupt. A departmental inquiry into the incident would affirm that Harms and his partner had been in danger: the man was armed with a makeshift flamethrower, and what he had in mind, evidently, was to turn the inside of the squad car into an inferno. But at the time all Harms had was a hunch, a sense from the situation and the man's behavior and what he glimpsed inside the man's coat and on the man's face — something that was the opposite of whatever John Yarbrough saw in the face of the boy in Willowbrook. Harms pulled out his gun and shot the man through the open window. "Scott looked at me and was, like, 'What did you do?' because he didn't perceive any danger," Harms said. "But I did."

QUESTIONS

1. Gladwell tells the story of how emotions can be seen on the face. What does each character in his story add to his explanation of facial expressions? Why do you feel that the author chose to tell the story in this way?

2. Instead of just presenting the results of Ekman and Frisen's work, Gladwell tells the story of their work with emotions and the face from the very beginning — from their initial questions, to their making faces at each other, to their cataloging of the facial muscles that express emotions on the face. Why does Gladwell choose this approach? What is he showing us about the way that scientific inquiry works? How would the piece have been different had he not included the step-by-step evolution of their thoughts?

3. "Disgust? That's mostly A.U. nine, the wrinkling of the nose (levator labii superioris, alaeque nasi), but it can sometimes be ten, and in either case may be combined with A.U. fifteen or sixteen or seventeen" (paragraph 15). Gladwell explains some of the facial muscle patterns repre-

sented by these numbers, but he sometimes mentions only the emotion and the action unit numbers without explaining what muscles those numbers represent. Why do you think he does this? What effect does it have on the reader?

4. What is your reaction to Ekman's distillation of the display of emotion down to numbers and the Latin medical names of facial muscles? Gladwell writes that he "catalogued the essential repertoire of human emotion" (paragraph 12). How does knowing the exact muscle patterns of each emotional expression alter your perception of emotion?

5. "Emotion doesn't just go from the inside out. It goes from the outside in" (paragraph 32). What discovery allowed Ekman, Friesen, and Levenson to make this statement? What implications can you draw from the interactive nature of the facial muscles and the feelings of emotion — that is, that they are both causes and effects of each other?

6. Gladwell begins and ends his essay with stories of men whose keen perception of facial cues and behavior may have saved lives. For those of us who are not in law enforcement, how could enhanced awareness of the way that emotions are displayed on faces affect our lives? Could such awareness have negative consequences as well?

7. Closely observe the facial expressions of a friend or roommate, and write an essay explaining that person's pattern of expressions. What facial muscles seem to be most at work? Explain which emotion in particular is displayed the most often on his or her face, and describe the facial transformation that occurs. Instead of describing only the workings of their facial muscles, write a character sketch similar to Gladwell's treatment of Yarbrough, providing your reader with details about your subject's dress, appearance, mannerisms, and behavior.

MAKING CONNECTIONS

In their essays, Gladwell and Stephen W. Hawking (p. 724) present knowledge as a process instead of a product. Instead of summarizing the results of scientific research or personal thought, they explain to the reader how those results were achieved. Explain how each author makes the reader aware of the process behind the acquisition of knowledge. How are the reader's interest in and understanding of the material affected by this exploration of process rather than of product?

I'm Right, You're Wrong, Go to Hell

Bernard Lewis

Bernard Lewis has been called the foremost postwar historian of Islam and the Middle East — the culmination of a sixty-year career as a scholar and writer. Lewis was born in 1916 in London. He received his undergraduate and graduate degrees from the School of Oriental and African Studies at the University of London. After serving in World War II, Lewis taught at the University of London until 1974, when he began teaching at Princeton, where he was the Cleveland E. Dodge Professor of Near Eastern Studies until he retired in 1986. Lewis has written many articles and more than two dozen books. His work examines multiple facets of Islamic societies, from the Ottoman Empire to Islam's relationship with the West, from the medieval to the modern periods. After the 9/11 attacks, his work received renewed interest, especially his 1990 essay The Roots of Muslim Rage *and his book* What Went Wrong? Western Impact and Middle Eastern Response *(2002), which was written before the 9/11 attacks and has since become a best seller in the United States. In his recent books* The Crisis of Islam: Holy War and Unholy Terror *(2003) and* From Babel to Dragomans: Interpreting the Middle East *(2004), Lewis continues to visit common themes in his work, namely, how the historical indifference of the Muslim world toward other societies, coupled with a great veneration of Islamic history, contrasts markedly with Western views of the importance of history and of engagement with other societies. Lewis notes that many present-day Muslims are attracted to the modern idea of Western-style democratic freedoms. However, in the context of the relative absence of modernization in Islamic society, the resulting tension between traditional views and modern ones makes a clash of civilizations with the West inevitable. Lewis is also known for his literary debates with the late Professor Edward Said of Columbia University, who called Lewis an apologist for imperialism and Zionism. The following piece was published in* The Atlantic Monthly *in 2003.*

For a long time now it has been our practice in the modern Western world to define ourselves primarily by nationality, and to see other identities and allegiances — religious, political, and the like — as subdivisions of the larger and more important whole. The events of September 11 and after have made us aware of another perception — of a religion subdivided into nations rather than a nation subdivided into religions — and this has induced some of us to think of ourselves and of our relations with others in ways that had become unfamiliar. The confrontation with a force that defines itself as Islam has given a new relevance — indeed, urgency — to the theme of the "clash of civilizations."

At one time the general assumption of mankind was that "civilization" meant us, and the rest were uncivilized. This, as far as we know, was the view of the great civilizations of the past — in China, India, Greece, Rome, Persia, and the ancient Middle East. Not until a comparatively late stage did the idea emerge that there are different civilizations, that these civilizations meet and interact, and — even more interesting — that a civilization has a life-span: it is born, grows, matures, declines, and dies. One can perhaps trace that latter idea to the medieval Arab historian-philosopher Ibn Khaldun (1332–1406), who spoke in precisely those terms, though what he discussed was not civilizations but states — or, rather, regimes. The concept wasn't really adapted to civilizations until the twentieth century.

The first writer to make the connection was the German historian Oswald Spengler. Perhaps influenced by the horrors of World War I and the defeat of imperial Germany, he looked around him and saw civilization in decline. He built a philosophy on this perception, captured in the phrase "the decline of the West" — *Der Untergang des Abendlandes.* His two volumes under this title were published in 1918 and 1922. In these he discussed how different civilizations meet, interact, rise and decline, and fall. His approach was elaborated by Arnold Toynbee, who proceeded with a sort of wish list of civilizations — and, of course, also a hit list. Most recently Samuel Huntington, of Harvard University, has argued that the clash of civilizations, more than of countries or governments, is now the basic force of international relations. I think most of us would agree, and some of us have indeed said, that the clash of civilizations is an important aspect of modern international relations, though probably not many of us would go so far as to imply, as some have done, that civilizations have foreign policies and form alliances.

There have been a number of different civilizations in human history, and several are extant, though not all in the same condition. Mustafa Kemal, later known as Atatürk, dealt with the relative condition of civilizations in some of the speeches in which he urged the people of the newly established Turkish Republic to modernize. He put the issue with military directness and simplicity. People, he said, talked of this civilization and that civilization, and of interaction and influence between civilizations; but only one civilization was alive and well and advancing, and that was what he called modernity, the civilization "of our time." All the others were dying or dead, he said, and Turkey's choice was to join this civilization or be part of a dying world. The one civilization was, of course, the West.

Only two civilizations have been defined by religion. Others have had   5
religions but are identified primarily by region and ethnicity. Buddhism has

been a major religious force, and was the first to try to bring a universal message to all mankind. There is some evidence of Buddhist activities in the ancient Middle East, and the possibility has been suggested of Buddhist influence on Judaism and, therefore, on the rise of Christianity. But Buddhism has not expanded significantly for many centuries, and the countries where it flourishes — in South, Southeast, and East Asia — are defined, like their neighbors, by culture more than by creed. These other civilizations, with the brief and problematic exception of communism, have lacked the ideological capacity — and for the most part even the desire — for indefinite expansion.

Christianity and Islam are the two religions that define civilizations, and they have much in common, along with some differences. In English and in most of the other languages of the Christian world we have two words, "Christianity" and "Christendom." Christianity is a religion, a system of belief and worship with certain ecclesiastical institutions. Christendom is a civilization that incorporates elements that are non-Christian or even anti-Christian. Hitler and the Nazis, it may be recalled, are products of Christendom, but hardly of Christianity. When we talk of Islam, we use the same word for both the religion and the civilization, which can lead to misunderstanding. The late Marshall Hodgson, a distinguished historian of Islam at the University of Chicago, was, I think, the first to draw attention to this problem, and he invented the word "Islamdom." Unfortunately, "Islamdom" is awkward to pronounce and just didn't catch on, so the confusion remains. (In Turkish there is no confusion, because "Islam" means the civilization, and "Islamiyet" refers specifically to the religion.)

In looking at the history of civilization we talk, for example, of "Islamic art," meaning art produced in Muslim countries, not just religious art, whereas the term "Christian art" refers to religious or votive art, churches and pious sculpture and painting. We talk about "Islamic science," by which we mean physics, chemistry, mathematics, biology, and the rest under the aegis of Muslim civilization. If we say "Christian science," we mean something totally different and unrelated.

Does one talk about "Jewish science"? I don't think so. One may talk about Jewish scientists, but that's not the same thing. But then, of course, Judaism is not a civilization — it's a religion and a culture. Most of Jewish history since the Diaspora has taken place within either Christendom or Islam. There were Jews in India, there were Jews in China, but those communities didn't flourish. Their role was minimal, both in the history of the Jews and in the history of India and China. The term "Judeo-Christian" is a new name for an old reality, though in earlier times it would have been equally resented on both sides of the hyphen. One could use an equivalent term, "Judeo-Islamic," to designate another cultural symbiosis that flourished in the more recent past and ended with the dawn of modernity.

To what extent is a religiously defined civilization compatible with pluralism — tolerance of others within the same civilization but of different religions? This crucial question points to a major distinction between two types of religion. For some religions, just as "civilization" means us, and the rest are barbarians, so "religion" means ours, and the rest are infidels. Other religions, such as Judaism and most of the religions of Asia, concede that human beings may use different religions to speak to God, as they use different languages to speak to one another. God understands them all. I know in my heart that the English language is the finest instrument the human race has ever devised to express its thoughts and feelings, but I recognize in my mind that others may feel exactly the same way about their languages, and I have no problem with that. These two approaches to religion may conveniently be denoted by the terms their critics use to condemn them — "triumphalism" and "relativism" In one of his sermons the fifteenth-century Franciscan Saint John of Capistrano, immortalized on the map of California, denounced the Jews for trying to spread a "deceitful" notion among Christians: "The Jews say that everyone can be saved in his own faith, which is impossible." For once a charge of his against the Jews was justified. The Talmud does indeed say that the righteous of all faiths have a place in paradise. Polytheists and atheists are excluded, but monotheists of any persuasion who observe the basic moral laws are eligible. The relativist view was condemned and rejected by both Christians and Muslims, who shared the conviction that there was only one true faith, theirs, which it was their duty to bring to all humankind. The triumphalist view is increasingly under attack in Christendom, and is disavowed by significant numbers of Christian clerics. There is little sign as yet of a parallel development in Islam.

Tolerance is, of course, an extremely intolerant idea, because it means   10
"I am the boss: I will allow you some, though not all, of the rights I enjoy as long as you behave yourself according to standards that I shall determine." That, I think, is a fair definition of religious tolerance as it is normally understood and applied. In a letter to the Jewish community of Newport, Rhode Island, that George Washington wrote in 1790, he remarked, perhaps in an allusion to the famous "Patent of Tolerance" promulgated by the Austrian Emperor Joseph II a few years previously, "It is now no more that toleration is spoken of, as if it was by the indulgence of one class of people that another enjoyed the exercise of their inherent natural rights." At a meeting of Jews, Christians, and Muslims in Vienna some years ago the Cardinal Archbishop Franz Koenig spoke of tolerance, and I couldn't resist quoting Washington to him. He replied, "You are right. I shall no more speak of tolerance; I shall speak of mutual respect." There are still too few who share the attitude expressed in this truly magnificent response.

For those taking the relativist approach to religion (in effect, "I have my god, you have your god, and others have theirs"), there may be specific political or economic reasons for objecting to someone else's beliefs, but in principle there is no theological problem. For those taking the triumphalist approach (classically summed up in the formula "I'm right, you're wrong, go to hell"), tolerance is a problem. Because the triumphalist's is the only true and complete religion, all other religions are at best incomplete and more probably false and evil; and since he is the privileged recipient of

God's final message to humankind, it is surely his duty to bring it to others rather than keep it selfishly for himself.

Now, if one believes that, what does one do about it? And how does one relate to people of another religion? If we look at this question historically, one thing emerges very clearly: whether the other religion is previous or subsequent to one's own is extremely important. From a Christian point of view, for example, Judaism is previous and Islam is subsequent. From a Muslim point of view, both Judaism and Christianity are previous. From a Jewish point of view, both Christianity and Islam are subsequent — but since Judaism is not triumphalist, this is not a problem.

But it is a problem for Christians and Muslims — or perhaps I should say for traditional Christians and Muslims. From their perspective, a previous religion may be regarded as incomplete, as superseded, but it is not necessarily false if it comes in the proper sequence of revelation. So from a Muslim point of view, Judaism and Christianity were both true religions at the time of their revelation, but they were superseded by the final and complete revelation of Islam; although they are out-of-date — last year's model, so to speak — they are not inherently false. Therefore Muslim law, sharia, not only permits but requires that a certain degree of tolerance be accorded them.

It is, of course, a little more complicated: Jews and Christians are accused of falsifying their originally authentic scriptures and religions. Thus, from a Muslim point of view, the Christian doctrines of the Trinity and of the divinity of Jesus Christ are distortions. The point is made in several Koranic verses: "There is no God but God alone. He has no companion" and "He is God, one, eternal. He does not beget. He is not begotten, and He has no peer." These and similar verses appear frequently on early Islamic coins and in inscriptions, and are clearly polemical in intent. They are inscribed, notably, in the Dome of the Rock, in Jerusalem — a challenge to Christianity in its birthplace. Jews are accused of eliminating scriptural passages foretelling the advent of Muhammad. Anything subsequent to Muhammad, "the Seal of the Prophets," is, from the Muslim perspective, necessarily false. This explains the harsh treatment of post-Islamic religions, such as the Bahai faith and the Ahmadiya movement, in Islamic lands.

Muslims did not claim a special relationship to either of the predecessor religions, and if Jews and Christians chose not to accept Muhammad, that was their loss. Muslims were prepared to tolerate them in accordance with sharia, which lays down both the extent and the limits of the latitude to be granted those who follow a recognized religion: they must be monotheists and they must have a revealed scripture, which in practice often limited tolerance to Jews and Christians. The Koran names a third qualified group, the Sabians; there is some uncertainty as to who they were, and at times this uncertainty provided a convenient way of extending the tolerance of the Muslim state to Zoroastrians or other groups when it was thought expedient. On principle, no tolerance was extended to polytheists or idolaters, and this sometimes raised acute problems in Asian and African lands conquered by the Muslims.

Tolerance was a much more difficult question for Christians. For them, Judaism is a precursor of their religion, and Christianity is the fulfillment of the divine promises made to the Jews. The Jewish rejection of that fulfillment is therefore seen as impugning some of the central tenets of the Christian faith. Tolerance between different branches of Christianity would eventually become an even bigger problem. Of course, the outsider is more easily tolerated than the dissident insider. Heretics are a much greater danger than unbelievers. The English philosopher John Locke's famous *A Letter Concerning Toleration*, written toward the end of the seventeenth century, is a plea for religious tolerance, still a fairly new idea at that time. Locke wrote, "Neither pagan, nor Mahometan, nor Jew, ought to be excluded from the civil rights of the commonwealth, because of his religion." Someone is of course missing from that list: the Catholic. The difference is clear. For Locke and his contemporaries, the pagan, the Muslim, the Jew, were no threat to the Church of England, the Catholic was. The Catholic was trying to subvert Protestantism, to make England Catholic, and, as Protestant polemicists at the time put it, to make England subject to a foreign potentate — namely, the Pope in Rome.

Muslims were in general more tolerant of diversity within their own community, and even cited an early tradition to the effect that such diversity is a divine blessing. The concept of heresy — in the Christian sense of incorrect belief recognized and condemned as such by properly constituted religious authority — was unknown to classical Islam. Deviation and diversity, with rare exceptions, were persecuted only when they offered a serious threat to the existing order. The very notion of an authority empowered to rule on questions of belief was alien to traditional Islamic thought and practice. It has become less alien.

A consequence of the similarity between Christianity and Islam in background and approach is the long conflict between the two civilizations they defined. When two religions met in the Mediterranean area, each claiming to be the recipient of God's final revelation, conflict was inevitable. The conflict, in fact, was almost continuous: the first Arab-Islamic invasions took Islam by conquest to the then Christian lands of Syria, Palestine, Egypt, and North Africa, and, for a while, to Southern Europe; the Tatars took it into Russia and Eastern Europe; and the Turks took it into the Balkans. To each advance came a Christian rejoinder: the Reconquista in Spain, the Crusades in the Levant, the throwing off of what the Russians call the Tatar yoke in the history of their country, and, finally, the great European counterattack into the lands of Islam, which is usually called imperialism.

During this long period of conflict, of *jihad* and crusade, of conquest and reconquest, Christianity and Islam nevertheless maintained a level of communication, because the two are basically the same kind of religion. They could argue. They could hold disputations and debates. Even their screams of rage were mutually intelligible. When Christians and Muslims said to each other, "Thou are an infidel and you will burn in hell," each understood exactly what the other meant, because they both meant the same thing. (Their heavens are differently appointed, but their hells are much the same.) Such assertions and accusations would have conveyed little or no meaning to a Hindu, a Buddhist, or a Confucian.

Christians and Muslims looked at each other and studied each other in   20
strikingly different ways. This is owing in part, at least, to their different circumstances. Christian Europeans from the start had to learn foreign languages in order to read their scriptures and their classics and to communicate with one another. From the seventh century onward they had a further motive to look outward — their holy places, in the land where their faith was born, were under Muslim rule, and could be visited only with Muslim permission. Muslims had no comparable problems. Their holy places were in Arabia, under Arab rule; their scriptures were in Arabic, which across their civilization was the language also of literature, of science and scholarship, of government and commerce, and, increasingly, of everyday communication, as the conquered countries in Southwest Asia and North Africa were Arabized and forgot their ancient languages and scripts. In later times other Islamic languages emerged, notably Persian and Turkish; but in the early, formative centuries Arabic reigned alone.

This difference in the experiences and the needs of the two civilizations is reflected in their attitudes toward each other. From the earliest recorded times people in Europe tried to learn the languages of the Islamic world, starting with Arabic, the language of the most advanced civilization of the day. Later some, mostly for practical reasons, learned Persian and more especially Turkish, which in Ottoman times supplanted Arabic as the language of government and diplomacy. From the sixteenth century on there were chairs of Arabic at French and Dutch universities. Cambridge University had its first chair of Arabic in 1632, Oxford in 1636. Europeans no longer needed Arabic to gain access to the higher sciences. Now they learned it out of intellectual curiosity — the desire to know something about another civilization and its ways. By the eighteenth century Europe boasted a considerable body of scholarly literature regarding the Islamic world — editions of texts and translations of historical and literary and theological works, as well as histories of literature and religion and even general histories of Islamic countries, with descriptions of their people and their ways. Grammars and dictionaries of Arabic, Persian, and Turkish were available to European scholars from the sixteenth century onward. It is surely significant that far more attention was given to Arabic, the classical and scriptural language of Islam, than to Persian and Turkish, the languages of the current rulers of the world. In the course of the nineteenth century European and later also American scholars set to work to disinter, decipher, and interpret the buried and forgotten languages and writings of antiquity, and thus to recover an ancient and glorious chapter in history. These activities were greeted with incomprehension and then with suspicion by those who did not share and therefore could not understand this kind of curiosity.

The Islamic world, with no comparable incentives, displayed a total lack of interest in Christian civilization. An initially understandable, even justifiable, contempt for the barbarians beyond the frontier continued long after that characterization ceased to be accurate, and even into a time when it became preposterously inaccurate. It has sometimes been argued that the European interest in Arabic and other Eastern languages was an adjunct — or, given the time lag, a precursor — of imperialism. If that is so, we must acquit the Arabs and the Turks of any such predatory intent. The Arabs spent 800 years in Spain without showing much interest in Spanish or Latin. The Ottomans ruled much of southeastern Europe for half a millennium, but for most of that time they never bothered to learn Greek or any Balkan or European language — which might have been useful. When they needed interpreters, they used converts and others from these various countries. There was no Occidentalism until the expanding West forced itself on the attention of the rest of the world. We may find similar attitudes in present-day America.

Today we in the West are engaged in what we see as a war against terrorism, and what the terrorists present as a war against unbelief. Some on both sides see this struggle as one between civilizations or, as others would put it, between religions. If they are right, and there is much to support their view, then the clash between these two religiously defined civilizations results not only from their differences but also from their resemblances — and in these there may even be some hope for better future understanding.

QUESTIONS

1. Lewis reminds us of the difference embodied in the words "Christianity" and "Christendom," pointing out that an attempt to make the same distinction between "Islam" and "Islamdom" has not caught on. He sees this as a problem. Why?
2. Lewis also sees a problem in the word "tolerance." Why is "tolerance" a problem?
3. Lewis quotes a sentence on toleration from George Washington's letter to the Sephardic Jewish community in Newport, Rhode Island. What, exactly, does Washington seem to be saying in that sentence? (See "Making Connections," below, for a further question on this letter.)
4. From the Muslim point of view, what is wrong with Christianity — that is, what aspects of Christian faith are unacceptable to Muslims?
5. For Christians, Lewis asserts, "Heretics are a much greater danger than unbelievers" (paragraph 16). What does he mean by this? How does his quotation from John Locke (paragraph 16) support this assertion?
6. A major point of Lewis's discussion is that the conflict between Islam and Christianity has a lot to do with the similarity between them. What

similarity is he talking about? Why is this important? Does it offer any hope for the future? Take up these questions in a short essay in response to Lewis.

7. What is your own background and position on matters of religious faith? Write a personal essay in which you connect your own views with the issues raised by Lewis, amplifying, supporting, or contesting his explanation of the situation he discusses.

MAKING CONNECTIONS

The sentence from George Washington to the Jews of Newport (paragraph 10) was written about fifteen years after Thomas Jefferson drafted the U. S. Declaration of Independence (p. 554). The full text of the letter may be found at a number of sites on the Internet, including <http://bnaibrith.org/programs/ea/letter_touro.cfm>. What connections can you find between Washington's statement and Jefferson's Declaration?

ARGUING IN THE
Social Sciences and Public Affairs

A MODEST PROPOSAL

Jonathan Swift

Jonathan Swift (1667–1745) was born in Dublin, Ireland, of English parents and was educated in Irish schools. A graduate of Trinity College, Dublin, he received a master's degree from Oxford and was ordained as a priest in the Church of England in 1695. He was active in politics as well as religion, becoming an editor and pamphlet writer for the Tory party in 1710. After becoming Dean of St. Patrick's Cathedral, Dublin, in 1713, he settled in Ireland and began to take an interest in the English economic exploitation of Ireland, gradually becoming a fierce Irish patriot. By 1724, the English were offering a reward for the discovery of the writer of the Drapier's Letters, *a series of pamphlets that were secretly written by Swift and attacked the British for their treatment of Ireland. In 1726, Swift produced the first volume of a more universal satire, known to modern readers as* Gulliver's Travels, *which has kept his name alive for more than 250 years. "A Modest Proposal," his best-known essay on Irish affairs, appeared in 1729.*

A Modest Proposal
for Preventing the Children of Poor People in Ireland
from Being a Burden to Their Parents or Country,
and for Making Them Beneficial to the Public

It is a melancholy object to those who walk through this great town,[1] or travel in the country, when they see the streets, the roads and cabin-doors crowded with beggars of the female sex, followed by three, four, or six children, all in rags, and importuning every passenger for an alms. These mothers, instead of being able to work for their honest livelihood, are forced to employ all their time in strolling, to beg sustenance for their helpless infants, who, as they grow up, either turn thieves for want of work, or leave their dear native country to fight for the Pretender in Spain,[2] or sell themselves to the Barbadoes.[3]

I think it is agreed by all parties that this prodigious number of children, in the arms, or on the backs, or at the heels of their mothers, and frequently of their fathers, is in the present deplorable state of the kingdom a very great additional grievance; and therefore whoever could find out a fair, cheap, and easy method of making these children sound and useful members of the commonwealth would deserve so well of the public as to have his statue set up for a preserver of the nation.

But my intention is very far from being confined to provide only for the children of professed beggars; it is of a much greater extent, and shall take in the whole number of infants at a certain age who are born of parents in effect as little able to support them as those who demand our charity in the streets.

As to my own part, having turned my thoughts for many years upon this important subject, and maturely weighed the several schemes of other projectors, I have always found them grossly mistaken in their computation. It is true a child just dropped from its dam may be supported by her milk for a solar year with little other nourishment, at most not above the value of two shillings,[4] which the mother may certainly get, or the value in scraps, by her lawful occupation of begging, and it is exactly at one year old that I propose to provide for them, in such a manner as, instead of being a charge upon their parents, or the parish, or wanting food and raiment for the rest of their lives, they shall, on the contrary, contribute to the feeding and partly to the clothing of many thousands.

There is likewise another great advantage to my scheme, that it will   5
prevent those voluntary abortions, and that horrid practice of women murdering their bastard children, alas, too frequent among us, sacrificing the poor innocent babes, I doubt, more to avoid the expense than the shame, which would move tears and pity in the most savage and inhuman breast.

---

[1]*this great town*: Dublin. [Eds.]

[2]*Pretender in Spain*: A Catholic descendant of the British royal family of Stuart (James I, Charles I, Charles II, and James II). Exiled to France and Spain so that England could be governed by Protestant rulers, the Stuarts prepared various disastrous schemes for regaining the throne. [Eds.]

[3]*sell themselves to the Barbadoes*: Sell themselves as indentured servants, a sort of temporary slavery, to the sugar merchants of the British Caribbean islands. [Eds.]

[4]*shillings*: A shilling used to be worth about one day's labor. [Eds.]

The number of souls in Ireland being usually reckoned one million and a half, of these I calculate there may be about two hundred thousand couples whose wives are breeders, from which number I subtract thirty thousand couples who are able to maintain their own children, although I apprehend there cannot be so many under the present distresses of the kingdom, but this being granted, there will remain an hundred and seventy thousand breeders. I again subtract fifty thousand for those women who miscarry, or whose children die by accident or disease within the year. There only remain an hundred and twenty thousand children of poor parents annually born: the question therefore is, how this number shall be reared, and provided for, which as I have already said, under the present situation of affairs is utterly impossible by all the methods hitherto proposed, for we can neither employ them in handicraft or agriculture; we neither build houses (I mean in the country), nor cultivate land: they can very seldom pick up a livelihood by stealing until they arrive at six years old, except where they are of towardly parts, although I confess they learn the rudiments much earlier, during which time they can however be properly looked upon only as probationers, as I have been informed by a principal gentleman in the County of Cavan, who protested to me that he never knew above one or two instances under the age of six, even in a part of the kingdom so renowned for the quickest proficiency in that art.

I am assured by our merchants that a boy or girl before twelve years old, is no saleable commodity, and even when they come to this age, they will not yield above three pounds, or three pounds and half-a-crown at most on the Exchange, which cannot turn to account either to the parents or the kingdom, the charge of nutriment and rags having been at least four times that value.

I shall now therefore humbly propose my own thoughts, which I hope will not be liable to the least objection.

I have been assured by a very knowing American of my acquaintance in London, that a young healthy child well nursed is at a year old a most delicious, nourishing and wholesome food, whether stewed, roasted, baked, or boiled, and I make no doubt that it will equally serve in a fricassee, or a ragout.

I do therefore humbly offer it to public consideration, that of the hundred and twenty thousand children already computed, twenty thousand may be reserved for breed, whereof only one fourth part to be males, which is more than we allow to sheep, black-cattle, or swine, and my reason is that these children are seldom the fruits of marriage, a circumstance not much regarded by our savages, therefore one male will be sufficient to serve four females. That the remaining hundred thousand may at a year old be offered in sale to the persons of quality, and fortune, through the kingdom, always advising the mother to let them suck plentifully in the last month, so as to render them plump, and fat for a good table. A child will make two dishes at an entertainment for friends, and when the family dines alone, the fore or hind quarters will make a reasonable dish, and seasoned with a little pepper or salt will be very good boiled on the fourth day, especially in winter.

I have reckoned upon a medium, that a child just born will weigh twelve pounds, and in a solar year if tolerably nursed increaseth to twenty-eight pounds.

I grant this food will be somewhat dear, and therefore very proper for landlords, who, as they have already devoured most of the parents, seem to have the best title to the children.

Infant's flesh will be in season throughout the year, but more plentiful in March, and a little before and after, for we are told by a grave author, an eminent French physician,[5] that fish being a prolific diet, there are more children born in Roman Catholic countries about nine months after Lent than at any other season; therefore reckoning a year after Lent, the markets will be more glutted than usual, because the number of Popish infants is at least three to one in this kingdom, and therefore it will have one other collateral advantage by lessening the number of Papists among us.

I have already computed the charge of nursing a beggar's child (in which list I reckon all cottagers, laborers, and four-fifths of the farmers) to be about two shillings *per annum*, rags included, and I believe no gentleman would repine to give ten shillings for the carcass of a good fat child, which, as I have said, will make four dishes of excellent nutritive meat, when he hath only some particular friend of his own family to dine with him. Thus the Squire will learn to be a good landlord and grow popular among his tenants, the mother will have eight shillings net profit, and be fit for work until she produces another child.

Those who are more thrifty (as I must confess the times require) may   15
flay the carcass; the skin of which artificially dressed, will make admirable gloves for ladies, and summer boots for fine gentlemen.

As to our city of Dublin, shambles[6] may be appointed for this purpose, in the most convenient parts of it, and butchers we may be assured will not be wanting, although I rather recommend buying the children alive, and dressing them hot from the knife, as we do roasting pigs.

A very worthy person, a true lover of his country, and whose virtues I highly esteem was lately pleased, in discoursing on this matter to offer a refinement upon my scheme. He said that many gentlemen of this kingdom, having of late destroyed their deer, he conceived that the want of venison might be well supplied by the bodies of young lads and maidens, not exceeding fourteen years of age, nor under twelve, so great a number of both sexes in every county being now ready to starve, for want of work and service: and these to be disposed of by their parents if alive, or otherwise by their nearest relations. But with due deference to so excellent a friend, and so deserving a patriot, I cannot be altogether in his sentiments. For as to the

---

[5]*French physician:* François Rabelais (1494?–1553), a French physician and satirist who is known for his novel, *Gargantua and Pantagruel.* [Eds.]
[6]*shambles:* Slaughterhouses. [Eds.]

males, my American acquaintance assured me from frequent experience that their flesh was generally tough and lean, like that of our schoolboys, by continual exercise, and their taste disagreeable, and to fatten them would not answer the charge. Then as to the females, it would, I think with humble submission, be a loss to the public, because they soon would become breeders themselves: and besides, it is not improbable that some scrupulous people might be apt to censure such a practice (although indeed very unjustly) as a little bordering upon cruelty, which I confess, hath always been with me the strongest objection against any project, howsoever well intended.

But in order to justify my friend, he confessed that this expedient was put into his head by the famous Psalmanazar, a native of the island Formosa, who came from thence to London, above twenty years ago, and in conversation told my friend that in his country when any young person happened to be put to death, the executioner sold the carcass to persons of quality, as a prime dainty, and that, in his time, the body of a plump girl of fifteen, who was crucified for an attempt to poison the emperor, was sold to his Imperial Majesty's Prime Minister of State, and other great Mandarins of the Court, in joints from the gibbet, at four hundred crowns. Neither indeed can I deny that if the same use were made of several plump young girls in this town who, without one single groat to their fortunes, cannot stir abroad without a chair, and appear at the playhouse and assemblies in foreign fineries, which they never will pay for, the kingdom would not be the worse.

Some persons of a desponding spirit are in great concern about that vast number of poor people, who are aged, diseased, or maimed, and I have been desired to employ my thoughts what course may be taken to ease the nation of so grievous an encumbrance. But I am not in the least pain upon that matter, because it is very well known that they are every day dying, and rotting, by cold, and famine, and filth, and vermin, as fast as can be reasonably expected. And as to the younger laborers they are now in almost as hopeful a condition. They cannot get work, and consequently pine away from want of nourishment, to a degree that if at any time they are accidentally hired to common labor, they have not strength to perform it; and thus the country and themselves are in a fair way of being soon delivered from the evils to come.

I have too long digressed, and therefore shall return to my subject. I 20 think the advantages by the proposal which I have made are obvious and many, as well as of the highest importance.

For first, as I have already observed, it would greatly lessen the number of Papists, with whom we are yearly over-run, being the principal breeders of the nation, as well as our most dangerous enemies, and who stay at home on purpose with a design to deliver the kingdom to the Pretender, hoping to take their advantage by the absence of so many good Protestants, who have chosen rather to leave their country than stay at home and pay tithes against their conscience to an idolatrous Episcopal curate.

Secondly, the poorer tenants will have something valuable of their own, which by law may be made liable to distress, and help to pay their landlord's rent, their corn and cattle being already seized, and money a thing unknown.

Thirdly, whereas the maintenance of an hundred thousand children, from two years old, and upwards, cannot be computed at less than ten shillings a piece *per annum*, the nation's stock will be thereby increased fifty thousand pounds *per annum*, besides the profit of a new dish, introduced to the tables of all gentlemen of fortune in the kingdom, who have any refinement in taste, and the money will circulate among ourselves, the goods being entirely of our own growth and manufacture.

Fourthly, the constant breeders, besides the gain of eight shillings sterling *per annum*, by the sale of their children, will be rid of the charge of maintaining them after the first year.

Fifthly, this food would likewise bring great custom to taverns, where   25 the vintners will certainly be so prudent as to procure the best receipts for dressing it to perfection, and consequently have their houses frequented by all the fine gentlemen, who justly value themselves upon their knowledge in good eating; and a skillful cook, who understands how to oblige his guests, will contrive to make it as expensive as they please.

Sixthly, this would be a great inducement to marriage, which all wise nations have either encouraged by rewards, or enforced by laws and penalties. It would increase the care and tenderness of mothers towards their children, when they were sure of a settlement for life, to the poor babes, provided in some sort by the public to their annual profit instead of expense. We should soon see an honest emulation among the married women, which of them could bring the fattest child to the market. Men would become as fond of their wives, during the time of their pregnancy, as they are now of their mares in foal, their cows in calf, or sows when they are ready to farrow, nor offer to beat or kick them (as it is too frequent a practice) for fear of a miscarriage.

Many other advantages might be enumerated. For instance, the addition of some thousand carcasses in our exportation of barreled beef; the propagation of swine's flesh, and improvement in the art of making good bacon, so much wanted among us by the great destruction of pigs, too frequent at our tables, are no way comparable in taste or magnificence to a well-grown, fat yearling child, which roasted whole will make a considerable figure at a Lord Mayor's feast, or any other public entertainment. But this and many others I omit, being studious of brevity.

Supposing that one thousand families in this city would be constant customers for infants' flesh, besides others who might have it at merry meetings, particularly weddings and christenings; I compute that Dublin would take off annually about twenty thousand carcasses, and the rest of the kingdom (where probably they will be sold somewhat cheaper) the remaining eighty thousand.

I can think of no one objection that will possibly be raised against this proposal, unless it should be urged that the number of people will be thereby much lessened in the kingdom. This I freely own, and it was indeed one principal design in offering it to the world. I desire the reader will observe, that I calculate my remedy *for this one individual Kingdom of* Ireland, *and for no other that ever was, is, or, I think, ever can be upon earth.* Therefore let no man talk to me of other expedients: *Of taxing our absentees at five shillings a pound: Of using neither clothes, nor household furniture, except what is of our own growth and manufacture: Of utterly rejecting the materials and instruments that promote foreign luxury: Of curing the expensiveness of pride, vanity, idleness, and gaming in our women: Of introducing a vein of parsimony, prudence, and temperance: Of learning to love our country, wherein we differ even from* Laplanders, *and the inhabitants of* Topinamboo: *Of quitting our animosities and factions, nor act any longer like the* Jews, *who were murdering one another at the very moment their city was taken: Of being a little cautious not to sell our country and consciences for nothing: Of teaching landlords to have at least one degree of mercy towards their tenants.* Lastly, *of putting a spirit of honesty, industry, and skill into our shopkeepers, who, if a resolution could now be taken to buy only our native goods, would immediately unite to cheat and exact upon us in the price, the measure and the goodness, nor could ever yet be brought to make one fair proposal of just dealing, though often and earnestly invited to it.*

Therefore I repeat, let no man talk to me of these and the like expedients, till he hath at least a glimpse of hope that there will ever be some hearty and sincere attempt to put them in practice.

But as to myself, having been wearied out for many years with offering vain, idle, visionary thoughts, and at length utterly despairing of success, I fortunately fell upon this proposal, which as it is wholly new, so it hath something solid and real, of no expense and little trouble, full in our own power, and whereby we can incur no danger in disobliging England. For this kind of commodity will not bear exportation, the flesh being of too tender a consistence to admit a long continuance in salt, *although perhaps I could name a country which would be glad to eat up our whole nation without it.*

After all I am not so violently bent upon my own opinion as to reject any offer, proposed by wise men, which shall be found equally innocent, cheap, easy and effectual. But before some thing of that kind shall be advanced in contradiction to my scheme, and offering a better, I desire the author, or authors, will be pleased maturely to consider two points. First, as things now stand, how they will be able to find food and raiment for a hundred thousand useless mouths and backs? And secondly, there being a round million of creatures in human figure, throughout this kingdom, whose whole subsistence put into a common stock would leave them in debt two millions of pounds sterling; adding those who are beggars by profession, to the bulk of farmers, cottagers, and laborers with their wives and children, who are beggars in effect; I desire those politicians who dislike my overture, and may perhaps be so bold to attempt an answer, that they will first ask the parents of these mortals whether they would not at this day think it a great happiness to have been sold for food at a year old, in the manner I prescribe, and thereby have avoided such a perpetual scene of misfortunes as they have since gone through, by the oppression of landlords, the impossibility of paying rent without money or trade, the want of common sustenance, with neither house nor clothes to cover them from the inclemencies of weather, and the most inevitable prospect of entailing the like, or greater miseries upon their breed for ever.

I profess in the sincerity of my heart that I have not the least personal interest in endeavoring to promote this necessary work, having no other motive than the *public good of my country, by advancing our trade, providing for infants, relieving the poor, and giving some pleasure to the rich.* I have no children by which I can propose to get a single penny; the youngest being nine years old, and my wife past child-bearing.

QUESTIONS

1. A proposal always involves a proposer. What is the character of the proposer here? Do we perceive his character to be the same throughout the essay? Compare, for example, paragraphs 21, 26, and 33.
2. When does the proposer actually offer his proposal? What does he do before making his proposal? What does he do after making his proposal? How does the order in which he does things affect our impression of him and of his proposal?
3. What kinds of counterarguments to his own proposal does this proposer anticipate? How does he answer and refute proposals that might be considered alternatives to his?
4. In reading this essay, most people are certain that the author, Swift, does not endorse the proposer's idea. How do we distinguish between the author and the proposer? What details of style help us make this distinction?
5. Consider the proposer, the counterarguments that he acknowledges and refutes, and Swift himself, who presumably does not endorse the proposal. To what extent is Swift's position essentially the one that his proposer refutes? To what extent is it still a somewhat different position?
6. To what extent does an ironic essay like this depend on shared values that are held by both the author and the reader without question or reservation? Can you discover any such values explicitly or implicitly present in Swift's essay?
7. Use Swift's technique to write a "modest proposal" of your own about a contemporary situation. That is, use some outlandish proposal as a way of drawing attention to a situation that needs correcting. Consider carefully the character that you intend to project for your proposer and the way that you intend to make your own view distinguishable from hers or his.

MAKING CONNECTIONS

Pablo Picasso said that "art is a lie that makes us realize truth." Consider the way that this applies to Swift's essay. Is it a lie? What truth can it be said to make us realize? Consider some of the other works in this volume that might be called art, especially the poem by Robert Frost (p. 632) and the stories by Bruce Holland Rogers (p. 113), Douglas Trevor (p. 158), and James Alan McPherson (p. 176). What do they have in common with Swift's essay? Does Picasso's statement apply to all of them? In considering them, be as precise as possible about both the lie part and the truth part of the equation.

THE DECLARATION OF INDEPENDENCE

Thomas Jefferson

Thomas Jefferson (1743–1826) was born in Shadwell, Virginia, attended the College of William and Mary, and became a lawyer. He was elected to the Virginia House of Burgesses in 1769 and was a delegate to the Continental Congress in 1776. When the Congress voted in favor of Richard Henry Lee's resolution that the colonies "ought to be free and independent states," a committee of five members, including John Adams, Benjamin Franklin, and Jefferson, was appointed to draw up a declaration. Jefferson, because of his eloquence as a writer, was asked by this committee to draw up a first draft. Jefferson's text, with a few changes suggested by Franklin and Adams, was presented to the Congress. After a debate in which further changes were made, including striking out a passage condemning the slave trade, the Declaration was approved on July 4, 1776. Jefferson said of it, "Neither aiming at originality of principles or sentiments, nor yet copied from any particular and previous writing, it was intended to be an expression of the American mind."

In Congress, July 4, 1776
The unanimous Declaration of the
thirteen united States of America

When in the Course of human events it becomes necessary for one people to dissolve the political bands which have connected them with another, and to assume among the powers of the earth, the separate and equal station to which the Laws of Nature and of Nature's God entitle them, a decent respect to the opinions of mankind requires that they should declare the causes which impel them to the separation.

We hold these truths to be self-evident, that all men are created equal, that they are endowed by their Creator with certain unalienable Rights, that among these are Life, Liberty and the pursuit of Happiness. That to secure these rights, Governments are instituted among Men, deriving their just powers from the consent of the governed. That whenever any Form of Government becomes destructive of these ends, it is the Right of the People to alter or to abolish it, and to institute new Government, laying its foundation on such principles and organizing its powers in such form, as to them shall seem most likely to effect their Safety and Happiness. Prudence, indeed, will dictate that Governments long established should not be changed for light and transient causes; and accordingly all experience hath shewn that mankind are more disposed to suffer, while evils are sufferable, than to right themselves by abolishing the forms to which they are accustomed. But when a long train of abuses and usurpations, pursuing invariably the same Object evinces a design to reduce them under absolute Despotism, it is their right, it is their duty, to throw off such Government, and to provide new Guards for their future security. Such has been the patient sufferance of these Colonies; and such is now the necessity which constrains them to alter their former Systems of Government. The history of the present King of Great Britain is a history of repeated injuries and usurpations, all having in direct object the establishment of an absolute Tyranny over these States. To prove this, let Facts be submitted to a candid world.

He has refused his Assent to Laws, the most wholesome and necessary for the public good.

He has forbidden his Governors to pass laws of immediate and pressing importance, unless suspended in their operation till his Assent should be obtained; and when so suspended, he has utterly neglected to attend to them.

He has refused to pass other Laws for the accommodation of large dis- 5 tricts of people, unless those people would relinquish the right of Representation in the Legislature, a right inestimable to them and formidable to tyrants only.

He has called together legislative bodies at places unusual, uncomfortable, and distant from the depository of their Public Records, for the sole purpose of fatiguing them into compliance with his measures.

He has dissolved Representative Houses repeatedly, for opposing with manly firmness his invasions on the rights of the people.

He has refused for a long time, after such dissolutions, to cause others to be elected; whereby the Legislative Powers, incapable of Annihilation, have returned to the People at large for their exercise; the State remaining in the mean time exposed to all the dangers of invasion from without, and convulsions within.

He has endeavored to prevent the population of these States; for that purpose obstructing the Laws for Naturalization of Foreigners; refusing to pass others to encourage their migration hither, and raising the conditions of new Appropriations of Lands.

He has obstructed the Administration of Justice, by refusing his Assent 10 to Laws for Establishing Judiciary Powers.

He has made Judges dependent on his Will alone, for the tenure of their offices, and the amount and payment of their salaries.

He has erected a multitude of New Offices, and sent hither swarms of Officers to harass our people, and eat out their substance.

He has kept among us, in times of peace, Standing Armies without the Consent of our legislatures.

He has affected to render the Military independent of and superior to the Civil Power.

He has combined with others to subject us to a jurisdiction foreign to   15
our constitution, and unacknowledged by our laws; giving his Assent to the
Acts of pretended Legislation: For quartering large bodies of armed troops
among us: For protecting them, by a mock Trial, from punishment for any
Murders which they should commit on the Inhabitants of these States: For
cutting off our Trade with all parts of the world: For imposing Taxes on us
without our Consent: For depriving us in many cases, of the benefits of
Trial by Jury: For Transporting us beyond Seas to be tried for pretended of-
fenses: For abolishing the free System of English Laws in a neighboring
Province, establishing therein an Arbitrary government, and enlarging its
Boundaries so as to render it at once an example and fit instrument for introducing the same absolute rule into these Colonies: For taking away our
Charters, abolishing our most valuable Laws and altering fundamentally
the Forms of our Governments: For suspending our own Legislatures, and
declaring themselves invested with power to legislate for us in all cases
whatsoever.

He has abdicated Government here, by declaring us out of his Protection and waging War against us.

He has plundered our seas, ravaged our Coasts, burnt our towns, and
destroyed the lives of our people.

He is at this time transporting large Armies of foreign Mercenaries to
complete the works of death, desolation and tyranny, already begun with
circumstances of Cruelty & Perfidy scarcely paralleled in the most barbarous ages, and totally unworthy the Head of a civilized nation.

He has constrained our fellow Citizens taken Captive on the high Seas
to bear Arms against their Country, to become the executioners of their
friends and Brethren, or to fall themselves by their Hands.

He has excited domestic insurrections amongst us, and has endeavored   20
to bring on the inhabitants of our frontiers, the merciless Indian Savages,
whose known rule of warfare is an undistinguished destruction of all ages,
sexes, and conditions.

In every stage of these Oppressions We have Petitioned for Redress in
the most humble terms: Our repeated petitions have been answered only by
repeated injury. A Prince, whose character is thus marked by every act which
may define a Tyrant, is unfit to be the ruler of a free people.

Nor have we been wanting in attention to our British brethren. We
have warned them from time to time of attempts by their legislature to extend an unwarrantable jurisdiction over us. We have reminded them of the
circumstances of our emigration and settlement here. We have appealed to
their native justice and magnanimity, and we have conjured them by the ties
of our common kindred to disavow these usurpations, which would inevitably interrupt our connections and correspondence. They too have been
deaf to the voice of justice and of consanguinity. We must, therefore, acqui-

esce in the necessity, which denounces our Separation, and hold them, as we hold the rest of mankind, Enemies in War, in Peace Friends.

We, THEREFORE, the Representatives of the UNITED STATES OF AMERICA, in General Congress, Assembled, appealing to the Supreme Judge of the world for the rectitude of our intentions, do, in the Name, and by Authority of the good People of these Colonies, solemnly publish and declare, That these United Colonies are, and of Right ought to be FREE AND INDEPENDENT STATES; that they are Absolved from all Allegiance to the British Crown, and that all political connection between them and the State of Great Britain, is and ought to be totally dissolved; and that as Free and Independent States; they have full Power to levy War, conclude Peace, contract Alliances, establish Commerce, and to do all the Acts and Things which Independent States may of right do. And for the support of this Declaration, with a firm reliance on the protection of Divine Providence, we mutually pledge to each other our Lives, our Fortunes, and our sacred Honor.

QUESTIONS

1. The Declaration of Independence is frequently cited as a classic deductive argument. A deductive argument is based on a general statement, or premise, that is assumed to be true. What does this document assume that the American colonists are entitled to, and on what is this assumption based? Look at the reasoning in paragraph 2. What truths are considered self-evident? What does *self-evident* mean?

2. What accusations against the king of Great Britain are the Declaration's facts meant to substantiate? If you were the British king who was presented with this document, how might you reply to it? Would you attack its premise or reply to its accusations? Or would you do both? (How did George III respond?)

3. To what extent is the audience of the Declaration intended to be the king and people of Great Britain?

4. What other audiences were intended for this document? Define at least two other audiences, and describe how each might be expected to respond.

5. Although this declaration could have been expected to lead to war and all the horrors thereof, it is a civilized document, showing great respect throughout for certain standards of civility among people and among nations. Define the civilized standards that the Declaration assumes. Write an essay that identifies and characterizes the nature and variety of those expectations.

6. Write a declaration of your own, announcing your separation from some injurious situation (an incompatible roommate, a noisy sorority or fraternity house, an awful job, or whatever). Start with a premise, give reasons to substantiate it, provide facts that illustrate the injurious conditions, and conclude with a statement of what your new condition will mean to you and to other oppressed people.

MAKING CONNECTIONS

What if, rather than writing the Declaration of Independence, Jefferson had offered "a modest proposal" to the British king? What do you suppose he would have said? How would he have formulated his argument? Write your own "modest proposal" to the king, addressing him more or less in the manner of Jonathan Swift (p. 545) but drawing on the evidence that Jefferson provides in the Declaration.

LETTER FROM BIRMINGHAM JAIL

Martin Luther King Jr.

*The son of an Atlanta, Georgia, minister, civil rights leader Martin
Luther King Jr. (1929–1968) graduated from Morehouse College
and Crozier Theological Seminary before receiving a Ph.D. in
theology from Boston University in 1955. He became pastor of
Dexter Avenue Baptist Church in Montgomery, Alabama, in 1954
and the next year led a boycott of the city's segregated bus system
that brought him national attention when the system began to
be integrated in 1956. He organized the Southern Christian Leadership Conference to pursue civil rights gains through nonviolent
resistence, and his participation in nonviolent protests led to several
arrests. In 1963, King helped plan a massive march on Washington,
D.C., where he delivered his famous "I Have a Dream" speech,
calling for racial justice. The next year he was awarded the Nobel
Prize for peace. He was assassinated in Memphis, Tennessee, at the
age of thirty-nine. King wrote the following letter while serving
an eight-day jail sentence for participating in protests against segregated businesses in Birmingham, Alabama. In the introduction to
its published version, King noted, "This response to a published
statement by eight fellow clergymen from Alabama . . . was composed under somewhat constricting circumstance. Begun on the
margins of the newspaper in which the statement appeared while
I was in jail, the letter was continued on scraps of writing paper
supplied by a friendly Negro trusty, and concluded on a pad my
attorneys were eventually permitted to leave me. Although the text
remains in substance unaltered, I have indulged in the author's
prerogative of polishing it for publication."*

April 16, 1963

My Dear Fellow Clergymen:
   While confined here in the Birmingham city jail, I came across your recent statement calling my present activities "unwise and untimely." Seldom
do I pause to answer criticism of my work and ideas. If I sought to answer
all the criticisms that cross my desk, my secretaries would have little time
for anything other than such correspondence in the course of the day, and I
would have no time for constructive work. But since I feel that you are men
of genuine good will and that your criticisms are sincerely set forth, I want

to try to answer your statement in what I hope will be patient and reasonable terms.

I think I should indicate why I am here in Birmingham, since you have been influenced by the view which argues against "outsiders coming in." I have the honor of serving as president of the Southern Christian Leadership Conference, an organization operating in every southern state, with headquarters in Atlanta, Georgia. We have some eighty-five affiliated organizations across the South, and one of them is the Alabama Christian Movement for Human Rights. Frequently we share staff, educational, and financial resources with our affiliates. Several months ago the affiliate here in Birmingham asked us to be on call to engage in a nonviolent direct-action program if such were deemed necessary. We readily consented, and when the hour came we lived up to our promise. So I, along with several members of my staff, am here because I was invited here. I am here because I have organizational ties here.

But more basically, I am in Birmingham because injustice is here. Just as the prophets of the eighth century B.C. left their villages and carried their "thus saith the Lord" far beyond the boundaries of their home towns, and just as the Apostle Paul left his village of Tarsus and carried the gospel of Jesus Christ to the far corners of the Greco-Roman world, so am I compelled to carry the gospel of freedom beyond my own home town. Like Paul, I must constantly respond to the Macedonian call for aid.[1]

Moreover, I am cognizant of the interrelatedness of all communities and states. I cannot sit idly by in Atlanta and not be concerned about what happens in Birmingham. Injustice anywhere is a threat to justice everywhere. We are caught in an inescapable network of mutuality, tied in a single garment of destiny. Whatever affects one directly, affects all indirectly. Never again can we afford to live with the narrow, provincial, "outside agitator" idea. Anyone who lives inside the United States can never be considered an outsider anywhere within its bounds.

You deplore the demonstrations taking place in Birmingham. But your statement, I am sorry to say, fails to express a similar concern for the conditions that brought about the demonstrations. I am sure that none of you would want to rest content with the superficial kind of social analysis that deals merely with effects and does not grapple with underlying causes. It is unfortunate that demonstrations are taking place in Birmingham, but it is even more unfortunate that the city's white power structure left the Negro community with no alternative.

In any nonviolent campaign there are four basic steps: collection of the facts to determine whether injustices exist; negotiation; self-purification; and direct action. We have gone through all these steps in Birmingham. There can be no gainsaying the fact that racial injustice engulfs this community.

5

---

[1]*Macedonian call for aid*: A reference to Paul's vision of a Macedonian man requesting help (see Acts 16:9–10). [Eds.]

Birmingham is probably the most thoroughly segregated city in the United States. Its ugly record of brutality is widely known. Negroes have experienced grossly unjust treatment in the courts. There have been more unsolved bombings of Negro homes and churches in Birmingham than in any other city in the nation. These are the hard brutal facts of the case. On the basis of these conditions, Negro leaders sought to negotiate with the city fathers. But the latter consistently refused to engage in good-faith negotiation.

Then, last September, came the opportunity to talk with leaders of Birmingham's economic community. In the course of the negotiations, certain promises were made by the merchants — for example, to remove the stores' humiliating racial signs. On the basis of these promises, the Reverend Fred Shuttlesworth and the leaders of the Alabama Christian Movement for Human Rights agreed to a moratorium on all demonstrations. As the weeks and months went by, we realized that we were the victims of a broken promise. A few signs, briefly removed, returned; the others remained.

As in so many past experiences, our hopes had been blasted, and the shadow of deep disappointment settled upon us. We had no alternative except to prepare for direct action, whereby we would present our very bodies as a means of laying our case before the conscience of the local and the national community. Mindful of the difficulties involved, we decided to undertake a process of self-purification. We began a series of workshops on nonviolence, and we repeatedly asked ourselves: "Are you able to accept blows without retaliating?" "Are you able to endure the ordeal of jail?" We decided to schedule our direct-action program for the Easter season, realizing that except for Christmas, this is the main shopping period of the year. Knowing that a strong economic-withdrawal program would be the by-product of direct action, we felt that this would be the best time to bring pressure to bear on the merchants for the needed change.

Then it occurred to us that Birmingham's mayoral election was coming up in March, and we speedily decided to postpone action until after election day. When we discovered that the Commissioner of Public Safety, Eugene "Bull" Connor, had piled up enough votes to be in the run-off, we decided again to postpone action until the day after the run-off so that the demonstrations could not be used to cloud the issues. Like many others, we waited to see Mr. Connor defeated, and to this end we endured postponement after postponement. Having aided in this community need, we felt that our direct-action program could be delayed no longer.

You may well ask, "Why direct action? Why sit-ins, marches, and so   10
forth? Isn't negotiation a better path?" You are quite right in calling for negotiation. Indeed, this is the very purpose of direct action. Nonviolent direct action seeks to create such a crisis and foster such a tension that a community which has constantly refused to negotiate is forced to confront the issue. It seeks so to dramatize the issue that it can no longer be ignored. My citing the creation of tension as part of the work of the nonviolent resister may sound rather shocking. But I must confess that I am not afraid of the word "tension." I have earnestly opposed violent tension, but there is a type

of constructive, nonviolent tension which is necessary for growth. Just as Socrates felt that it was necessary to create a tension in the mind so that individuals could rise from the bondage of myths and half truths to the unfettered realm of creative analysis and objective appraisal, so must we see the need for nonviolent gadflies to create the kind of tension in society that will help men rise from the dark depths of prejudice and racism to the majestic heights of understanding and brotherhood.

The purpose of our direct-action program is to create a situation so crisis-packed that it will inevitably open the door to negotiation. I therefore concur with you in your call for negotiation. Too long has our beloved Southland been bogged down in a tragic effort to live in monologue rather than dialogue.

One of the basic points in your statement is that the action that I and my associates have taken in Birmingham is untimely. Some have asked: "Why didn't you give the new city administration time to act?" The only answer that I can give to this query is that the new Birmingham administration must be prodded about as much as the outgoing one, before it will act. We are sadly mistaken if we feel that the election of Albert Boutwell as mayor will bring the millennium[2] to Birmingham. While Mr. Boutwell is a much more gentle person than Mr. Connor, they are both segregationists, dedicated to maintenance of the status quo. I have hoped that Mr. Boutwell will be reasonable enough to see the futility of massive resistance to desegregation. But he will not see this without pressure from devotees of civil rights. My friends, I must say to you that we have not made a single gain in civil rights without determined legal and nonviolent pressure. Lamentably, it is an historical fact that privileged groups seldom give up their privileges voluntarily. Individuals may see the moral light and voluntarily give up their unjust posture; but, as Reinhold Niebuhr[3] has reminded us, groups tend to be more immoral than individuals.

We know through painful experience that freedom is never voluntarily given by the oppressor; it must be demanded by the oppressed. Frankly, I have yet to engage in a direct-action campaign that was "well timed" in the view of those who have not suffered unduly from the disease of segregation. For years now I have heard the word "Wait!" It rings in the ear of every Negro with piercing familiarity. This "Wait" has almost always meant "Never." We must come to see, with one of our distinguished jurists, that "justice too long delayed is justice denied."[4]

---

[2]*the millennium*: A reference to the Second Coming of Christ, which the Book of Revelation says will be followed by a thousand years of peace. [Eds.]

[3]*Reinhold Niebuhr* (1892–1971): A Protestant philosopher who urged church members to put their beliefs into action against social injustice. [Eds.]

[4]*"justice too long delayed is justice denied"*: A statement made by U.S. Supreme Court Chief Justice Earl Warren. It was inspired by English writer Walter Savage Landor's statement that "Justice delayed is justice denied." [Eds.]

We have waited for more than 340 years for our constitutional and God-given rights. The nations of Asia and Africa are moving with jet-like speed toward gaining political independence, but we still creep at horse-and-buggy pace toward gaining a cup of coffee at a lunch counter. Perhaps it is easy for those who have never felt the stinging darts of segregation to say, "Wait." But when you have seen vicious mobs lynch your mothers and fathers at will and drown your sisters and brothers at whim; when you have seen hate-filled policemen curse, kick, and even kill your black brothers and sisters; when you see the vast majority of your twenty million Negro brothers smothering in an airtight cage of poverty in the midst of an affluent society; when you suddenly find your tongue twisted and your speech stammering as you seek to explain to your six-year-old daughter why she can't go to the public amusement park that has just been advertised on television, and see tears welling up in her eyes when she is told that Funtown is closed to colored children, and see ominous clouds of inferiority beginning to form in her little mental sky, and see her beginning to distort her personality by developing an unconscious bitterness toward white people; when you have to concoct an answer for a five-year-old son who is asking, "Daddy, why do white people treat colored people so mean?"; when you take a cross-country drive and find it necessary to sleep night after night in the uncomfortable corners of your automobile because no motel will accept you; when you are humiliated day in and day out by nagging signs reading "white" and "colored"; when your first name becomes "nigger," your middle name becomes "boy" (however old you are) and your last name becomes "John," and your wife and mother are never given the respected title "Mrs."; when you are harried by day and haunted by night by the fact that you are a Negro, living constantly at tiptoe stance, never quite knowing what to expect next, and are plagued with inner fears and outer resentments; when you are forever fighting a degenerating sense of "nobodiness" — then you will understand why we find it difficult to wait. There comes a time when the cup of endurance runs over, and men are no longer willing to be plunged into the abyss of despair. I hope, sirs, you can understand our legitimate and unavoidable impatience.

You express a great deal of anxiety over our willingness to break laws.   15
This is certainly a legitimate concern. Since we so diligently urge people to obey the Supreme Court's decision of 1954 outlawing segregation in the public schools, at first glance it may seem rather paradoxical for us consciously to break laws. One may then ask: "How can you advocate breaking some laws and obeying others?" The answer lies in the fact that there are two types of laws: just and unjust. I would be the first to advocate obeying just laws. One has not only a legal but a moral responsibility to obey just laws. Conversely, one has a moral responsibility to disobey unjust laws. I would agree with St. Augustine that "an unjust law is no law at all."

Now, what is the difference between the two? How does one determine whether a law is just or unjust? A just law is a manmade code that squares with the moral law or the law of God. An unjust law is a code that is out of harmony with the moral law. To put it in the terms of St. Thomas Aquinas: An unjust law is a human law that is not rooted in eternal law and natural law. Any law that uplifts human personality is just. Any law that degrades human personality is unjust. All segregation statutes are unjust because segregation distorts the soul and damages the personality. It gives the segregator a false sense of superiority and the segregated a false sense of inferiority. Segregation, to use the terminology of the Jewish philosopher Martin Buber, substitutes an "I-it" relationship for an "I-thou" relationship and ends up relegating persons to the status of things. Hence segregation is not only politically, economically, and sociologically unsound, it is morally wrong and sinful. Paul Tillich has said that sin is separation. Is not segregation an existential expression of man's tragic separation, his awful estrangement, his terrible sinfulness? Thus it is that I can urge men to obey the 1954 decision of the Supreme Court, for it is morally right; and I can urge them to disobey segregation ordinances, for they are morally wrong.

Let us consider a more concrete example of just and unjust laws. An unjust law is a code that a numerical or power majority group compels a minority group to obey but does not make binding on itself. This is *difference* made legal. By the same token, a just law is a code that a majority compels a minority to follow and that it is willing to follow itself. This is *sameness* made legal.

Let me give another explanation. A law is unjust if it is inflicted on a minority that, as a result of being denied the right to vote, had no part in enacting or devising the law. Who can say that the legislature of Alabama which set up that state's segregation laws was democratically elected? Throughout Alabama all sorts of devious methods are used to prevent Negroes from becoming registered voters, and there are some counties in which, even though Negroes constitute a majority of the population, not a single Negro is registered. Can any law enacted under such circumstances be considered democratically structured?

Sometimes a law is just on its face and unjust in its application. For instance, I have been arrested on a charge of parading without a permit. Now, there is nothing wrong in having an ordinance which requires a permit for a parade. But such an ordinance becomes unjust when it is used to maintain segregation and to deny citizens the First Amendment privilege of peaceful assembly and protest.

I hope you are able to see the distinction I am trying to point out. In no   20
sense do I advocate evading or defying the law, as would the rabid segregationist. That would lead to anarchy. One who breaks an unjust law must do so openly, lovingly, and with a willingness to accept the penalty. I submit that an individual who breaks a law that conscience tells him is unjust, and who willingly accepts the penalty of imprisonment in order to arouse the conscience of the community over its injustice, is in reality expressing the highest respect for law.

Of course, there is nothing new about this kind of civil disobedience. It was evidenced subliminally in the refusal of Shadrach, Meshach, and Abednego to obey the laws of Nebuchadnezzar,[5] on the ground that a higher moral law was at stake. It was practiced superbly by the early Christians, who were willing to face hungry lions and the excruciating pain of chopping blocks rather than submit to certain unjust laws of the Roman Empire. To a degree, academic freedom is a reality today because Socrates practiced civil disobedience. In our own nation, the Boston Tea Party represented a massive act of civil disobedience.

We should never forget that everything Adolf Hitler did in Germany was "legal" and everything the Hungarian freedom fighters did in Hungary was "illegal." It was "illegal" to aid and comfort a Jew in Hitler's Germany. Even so, I am sure that, had I lived in Germany at the time, I would have aided and comforted my Jewish brothers. If today I lived in a Communist country where certain principles dear to the Christian faith are suppressed, I would openly advocate disobeying that country's antireligious laws.

I must make two honest confessions to you, my Christian and Jewish brothers. First, I must confess that over the past few years I have been gravely disappointed with the white moderate. I have almost reached the regrettable conclusion that the Negro's great stumbling block in his stride toward freedom is not the White Citizen's Counciler[6] or the Ku Klux Klanner, but the white moderate, who is more devoted to "order" than to justice; who prefers a negative peace which is the absence of tension to a positive peace which is the presence of justice; who constantly says, "I agree with you in the goal you seek, but I cannot agree with your methods of direct action"; who paternalistically believes he can set the timetable for another man's freedom; who lives by a mythical concept of time and who constantly advises the Negro to wait for a "more convenient season." Shallow understanding from people of good will is more frustrating than absolute misunderstanding from people of ill will. Lukewarm acceptance is much more bewildering than outright rejection.

I had hoped that the white moderate would understand that law and order exist for the purpose of establishing justice and that when they fail in this purpose they become the dangerously structured dams that block the flow of social progress. I had hoped that the white moderate would understand that the present tension in the South is a necessary phase of the

---

[5]"*the refusal of Shadrach . . . Nebuchadnezzar*": According to the Book of Daniel 1:7–3:30, Nebuchadnezzar (c. 630 BCE–c. 562 BCE), king of the Chaldean empire, ordered Shadrach, Meschach, and Abednego to worship a golden image. When they refused, they were cast into a fiery furnace but remained unharmed. [Eds.]

[6]*White Citizen's Counciler*: A member of an organization that was formed after the U.S. Supreme Court's 1954 *Brown v. Board of Education* decision. Its purpose was to maintain segregation. [Eds.]

transition from an obnoxious negative peace, in which the Negro passively accepted his unjust plight, to a substantive and positive peace, in which all men will respect the dignity and worth of human personality. Actually, we who engage in nonviolent direct action are not the creators of tension. We merely bring to the surface the hidden tension that is already alive. We bring it out in the open, where it can be seen and dealt with. Like a boil that can never be cured so long as it is covered up but must be opened with all its ugliness to the natural medicines of air and light, injustice must be exposed, with all the tension its exposure creates, to the light of human conscience and the air of national opinion, before it can be cured.

In your statement you assert that our actions, even though peaceful,   25 must be condemned because they precipitate violence. But is this a logical assertion? Isn't this like condemning a robbed man because his possession of money precipitated the evil act of robbery? Isn't this like condemning Socrates because his unswerving commitment to truth and his philosophical inquiries precipitated the act by the misguided populace in which they made him drink hemlock? Isn't this like condemning Jesus because his unique God-consciousness and never-ceasing devotion to God's will precipitated the evil act of crucifixion? We must come to see that, as the federal courts have consistently affirmed, it is wrong to urge an individual to cease his efforts to gain his basic constitutional rights because the quest may precipitate violence. Society must protect the robbed and punish the robber.

I had also hoped that the white moderate would reject the myth concerning time in relation to the struggle for freedom. I have just received a letter from a white brother in Texas. He writes: "All Christians know that the colored people will receive equal rights eventually, but it is possible that you are in too great a religious hurry. It has taken Christianity almost two thousand years to accomplish what it has. The teachings of Christ take time to come to earth." Such an attitude stems from a tragic misconception of time, from the strangely irrational notion that there is something in the very flow of time that will inevitably cure all ills. Actually, time itself is neutral; it can be used either destructively or constructively. More and more I feel that the people of ill will have used time much more effectively than have the people of good will. We will have to repent in this generation not merely for the hateful words and actions of the bad people, but for the appalling silence of the good people. Human progress never rolls in on wheels of inevitability; it comes through the tireless efforts of men willing to be co-workers with God, and without this hard work, time itself becomes an ally of the forces of social stagnation. We must use time creatively, in the knowledge that the time is always ripe to do right. Now is the time to make real the promise of democracy and transform our pending national elegy into a creative psalm of brotherhood. Now is the time to lift our national policy from the quicksand of racial injustice to the solid rock of human dignity.

You speak of our activity in Birmingham as extreme. At first I was rather disappointed that fellow clergymen would see my nonviolent efforts as those of an extremist. I began thinking about the fact that I stand in the middle of two opposing forces in the Negro community. One is a force of complacency, made up in part of Negroes who, as a result of long years of oppression, are so drained of self-respect and a sense of "somebodiness" that they have adjusted to segregation; and in part of a few middle-class Negroes who, because of a degree of academic and economic security and because in some ways they profit by segregation, have become insensitive to the problems of the masses. The other force is one of bitterness and hatred, and it comes perilously close to advocating violence. It is expressed in the various black nationalist groups that are springing up across the nation, the largest and best known being Elijah Muhammad's Muslim movement. Nourished by the Negro's frustration over the continued existence of racial discrimination, this movement is made up of people who have lost faith in America, who have absolutely repudiated Christianity, and who have concluded that the white man is an incorrigible "devil."

I have tried to stand between these two forces, saying that we need emulate neither the "do-nothingism" of the complacent nor the hatred and despair of the black nationalist. For there is the more excellent way of love and nonviolent protest. I am grateful to God that, through the influence of the Negro church, the way of nonviolence became an integral part of our struggle.

If this philosophy had not emerged, by now many streets of the South would, I am convinced, be flowing with blood. And I am further convinced that if our white brothers dismiss as "rabble-rousers" and "outside agitators" those of us who employ nonviolent direct action, and if they refuse to support our nonviolent efforts, millions of Negroes will, out of frustration and despair, seek solace and security in black nationalist ideologies — a development that would inevitably lead to a frightening racial nightmare.

Oppressed people cannot remain oppressed forever. The yearning for   30
freedom eventually manifests itself, and that is what has happened to the American Negro. Something within has reminded him of his birthright of freedom, and something without has reminded him that it can be gained. Consciously or unconsciously, he has been caught up by the *Zeitgeist*,[7] and with his black brothers of Africa and his brown and yellow brothers of Asia, South America, and the Caribbean, the United States Negro is moving with a sense of great urgency toward the promised land of racial justice. If one recognizes this vital urge that has engulfed the Negro community, one should readily understand why public demonstrations are taking place. The Negro has many pent-up resentments and latent frustrations, and he must release them. So let him march; let him make prayer pilgrimages to the city hall; let him go on freedom rides[8] — and try to understand why he must do so. If his repressed emotions are not released in nonviolent ways, they will

---

[7]*Zeitgeist*: The intellectual, moral, and cultural spirit of the times (German). [Eds.]

[8]*freedom rides*: The bus and train rides that black and white protesters took in the early 1960s to protest segregation. [Eds.]

seek expression through violence; this is not a threat but a fact of history. So I have not said to my people, "Get rid of your discontent." Rather, I have tried to say that this normal and healthy discontent can be channeled into the creative outlet of nonviolent direct action. And now this approach is being termed extremist.

But though I was initially disappointed at being categorized as an extremist, as I continued to think about the matter I gradually gained a measure of satisfaction from the label. Was not Jesus an extremist for love: "Love your enemies, bless them that curse you, do good to them that hate you, and pray for them which despitefully use you, and persecute you." Was not Amos an extremist for justice: "Let justice roll down like waters and righteousness like an everflowing stream." Was not Paul an extremist for the Christian gospel: "I bear in my body the marks of the Lord Jesus." Was not Martin Luther an extremist: "Here I stand; I cannot do otherwise, so help me God." And John Bunyan: "I will stay in jail to the end of my days before I make a butchery of my conscience." And Abraham Lincoln: "This nation cannot survive half slave and half free." And Thomas Jefferson: "We hold these truths to be self-evident, that all men are created equal . . ." So the question is not whether we will be extremists, but what kind of extremists we will be. Will we be extremists for hate or for love? Will we be extremists for the preservation of injustice or for the extension of justice? In that dramatic scene on Calvary's hill three men were crucified. We must never forget that all three were crucified for the same crime — the crime of extremism. Two were extremists for immorality, and thus fell below their environment. The other, Jesus Christ, was an extremist for love, truth, and goodness, and thereby rose above his environment. Perhaps the South, the nation, and the world are in dire need of creative extremists.

I had hoped that the white moderate would see this need. Perhaps I was too optimistic; perhaps I expected too much. I suppose I should have realized that few members of the oppressor race can understand the deep groans and passionate yearnings of the oppressed race, and still fewer have the vision, to see that injustice must be rooted out by strong, persistent, and determined action. I am thankful, however, that some of our white brothers in the South have grasped the meaning of this social revolution and committed themselves to it. They are still all too few in quantity, but they are big in quality. Some — such as Ralph McGill, Lillian Smith, Harry Golden, James McBride Dabbs, Ann Braden, and Sarah Patton Boyle — have written about our struggle in eloquent and prophetic terms. Others have marched with us down nameless streets of the South. They have languished in filthy, roach-infested jails, suffering the abuse and brutality of policemen who view them as "dirty nigger-lovers." Unlike so many of their moderate brothers and sisters, they have recognized the urgency of the moment and sensed the need for powerful "action" antidotes to combat the disease of segregation.

Let me take note of my other major disappointment. I have been so greatly disappointed with the white church and its leadership. Of course, there are some notable exceptions. I am not unmindful of the fact that each of you has taken some significant stands on this issue. I commend you, Reverend Stallings, for your Christian stand on this past Sunday, in welcoming Negroes to your worship service on a nonsegregated basis. I commend the Catholic leaders of this state for integrating Spring Hill College several years ago.

But despite these notable exceptions, I must honestly reiterate that I have been disappointed with the church. I do not say this as one of those negative critics who can always find something wrong with the church. I say this as a minister of the gospel, who loves the church; who was nurtured in its bosom; who has been sustained by its spiritual blessings and who will remain true to it as long as the cord of life shall lengthen.

When I was suddenly catapulted into the leadership of the bus protest in Montgomery, Alabama, a few years ago, I felt we would be supported by the white church. I felt that the white ministers, priests, and rabbis of the South would be among our strongest allies. Instead, some have been outright opponents, refusing to understand the freedom movement and misrepresenting its leaders; all too many others have been more cautious than courageous and have remained silent behind the anesthetizing security of stained-glass windows. 35

In spite of my shattered dreams, I came to Birmingham with the hope that the white religious leadership of this community would see the justice of our cause and, with deep moral concern, would serve as the channel through which our just grievances could reach the power structure. I had hoped that each of you would understand. But again I have been disappointed. . . .

There was a time when the church was very powerful — in the time when the early Christians rejoiced at being deemed worthy to suffer for what they believed. In those days the church was not merely a thermometer that recorded the ideas and principles of popular opinion; it was a thermostat that transformed the mores of society. Whenever the early Christians entered a town, the people in power became disturbed and immediately sought to convict the Christians for being "disturbers of the peace" and "outside agitators." But the Christians pressed on, in the conviction that they were "a colony of heaven," called to obey God rather than man. Small in number, they were big in commitment. They were too God-intoxicated to be "astronomically intimidated." By their effort and example they brought an end to such ancient evils as infanticide and gladiatorial contests.

Things are different now. So often the contemporary church is a weak, ineffectual voice with an uncertain sound. So often it is an archdefender of the status quo. Far from being disturbed by the presence of the church, the powerful structure of the average community is consoled by the church's silent — and often even vocal — sanction of things as they are.

But the judgment of God is upon the church as never before. If today's church does not recapture the sacrificial spirit of the early church, it will lose its authenticity, forfeit the loyalty of millions, and be dismissed as an irrelevant social club with no meaning for the twentieth century. Every day I meet young people whose disappointment with the church has turned into outright disgust.

Perhaps I have once again been too optimistic. Is organized religion too   40 inextricably bound to the status quo to save our nation and the world? Perhaps I must turn my faith to the inner spiritual church, the church within the church, as the true *ekklesia*[9] and the hope of the world. But again I am thankful to God that some noble souls from the ranks of organized religion have broken loose from the paralyzing chains of conformity and joined us as active partners in the struggle for freedom. They have left their secure congregations and walked the streets of Albany, Georgia, with us. They have gone down the highways of the South on torturous rides for freedom. Yes, they have gone to jail with us. Some have been dismissed from their churches, have lost the support of their bishops and fellow ministers. But they have acted in the faith that right defeated is stronger than evil triumphant. Their witness has been the spiritual salt that has preserved the true meaning of the gospel in these troubled times. They have carved a tunnel of hope through the dark mountain of disappointment.

I hope the church as a whole will meet the challenge of this decisive hour. But even if the church does not come to the aid of justice, I have no despair about the future. I have no fear about the outcome of our struggle in Birmingham, even if our motives are at present misunderstood. We will reach the goal of freedom in Birmingham and all over the nation, because the goal of America is freedom. Abused and scorned though we may be, our destiny is tied up with America's destiny. Before the pilgrims landed at Plymouth, we were here. Before the pen of Jefferson etched the majestic words of the Declaration of Independence across the pages of history, we were here. For more than two centuries our forebears labored in this country without wages; they made cotton king; they built the homes of their masters while suffering gross injustice and shameful humiliation — and yet out of a bottomless vitality they continued to thrive and develop. If the inexpressible cruelties of slavery could not stop us, the opposition we now face will surely fail. We will win our freedom because the sacred heritage of our nation and the eternal will of God are embodied in our echoing demands.

Before closing I feel impelled to mention one other point in your statement that has troubled me profoundly. You warmly commended the Birmingham police force for keeping "order" and "preventing violence." I doubt that you would have so warmly commended the police force if you had seen its dogs sinking their teeth into unarmed, nonviolent Negroes. I doubt that you would so quickly commend the policemen if you were to observe their ugly and inhumane treatment of Negroes here in the city jail; if you were to watch them push and curse old Negro women and young Negro girls; if you were to see them slap and kick old Negro men and young

---

[9]*ekklesia*: The church (Greek). It means the spirit of the church. [Eds].

boys; if you were to observe them, as they did on two occasions, refuse to give us food because we wanted to sing our grace together. I cannot join you in your praise of the Birmingham police department.

It is true that the police have exercised a degree of discipline in handling the demonstrators. In this sense they have conducted themselves rather "nonviolently" in public. But for what purpose? To preserve the evil system of segregation. Over the past few years I have consistently preached that nonviolence demands that the means we use must be as pure as the ends we seek. I have tried to make clear that it is wrong to use immoral means to attain moral ends. But now I must affirm that it is just as wrong, or perhaps even more so, to use moral means to preserve immoral ends. Perhaps Mr. Connor and his policemen have been rather nonviolent in public, as was Chief Pritchett in Albany, Georgia, but they have used the moral means of nonviolence to maintain the immoral end of racial injustice. As T. S. Eliot has said, "The last temptation is the greatest treason: To do the right deed for the wrong reason."

I wish you had commended the Negro sit-inners and demonstrators of Birmingham for their sublime courage, their willingness to suffer, and their amazing discipline in the midst of great provocation. One day the South will recognize its real heroes. They will be the James Merediths,[10] with the noble sense of purpose that enables them to face jeering and hostile mobs, and with the agonizing loneliness that characterizes the life of the pioneer. They will be old, oppressed, battered Negro women, symbolized in a seventy-two-year-old woman in Montgomery, Alabama, who rose up with a sense of dignity and with her people decided not to ride segregated buses and who responded with ungrammatical profundity to one who inquired about her weariness: "My feets is tired, but my soul is at rest." They will be the young high school and college students, the young ministers of the gospel and a host of their elders, courageously and nonviolently sitting in at lunch counters and willingly going to jail for conscience' sake. One day the South will know that when these disinherited children of God sat down at lunch counters, they were in reality standing up for what is best in the American dream and for the most sacred values in our Judaeo-Christian heritage, thereby bringing our nation back to those great wells of democracy which were dug deep by the founding fathers in their formulation of the Constitution and the Declaration of Independence.

Never before have I written so long a letter. I'm afraid it is much too   45
long to take your precious time. I can assure you that it would have been much shorter if I had been writing from a comfortable desk, but what else can one do when he is alone in a narrow jail cell, other than write long letters, think long thoughts, and pray long prayers?

---

[10]*James Meredith* (b. 1933): In 1962, the first African American to become a student at the University of Mississippi. [Eds.]

If I have said anything in this letter that overstates the truth and indicates an unreasonable impatience, I beg you to forgive me. If I have said anything that understates the truth and indicates my having a patience that allows me to settle for anything less than brotherhood, I beg God to forgive me.

I hope this letter finds you strong in the faith. I also hope that circumstances will soon make it possible for me to meet each of you, not as an integrationist or a civil rights leader but as a fellow clergyman and a Christian brother. Let us all hope that the dark clouds of racial prejudice will soon pass away and the deep fog of misunderstanding will be lifted from our fear-drenched communities, and in some not too distant tomorrow the radiant stars of love and brotherhood will shine over our great nation with all their scintillating beauty.

Yours in the cause of
Peace and Brotherhood,
Martin Luther King, Jr.

Questions

1. This justly famous argument is cast in the form of a letter. What advantages did King derive from using the letter format for his argument? Can principles of argumentation be learned from this format?
2. This large argument contains other arguments. The main argument is a justification of the specific actions that landed King in jail. A more general argument is about the injustice of segregation and the proper means to address that injustice. Within these two arguments that run throughout the letter are sections that argue specific subissues within the general topics. To understand how King constructed his essay, begin by locating these separate sections and their subarguments.
3. King is always aware of the positions against which he is arguing and the counterarguments that are offered by those who hold those positions. How does he represent those positions, and how does he deal with them? Base your response on specific instances in which he mentions such positions and responds to them.
4. What is the tone of King's essay? How does the tone relate to the position that he is arguing?
5. What kinds of authority does King invoke to support his right to speak on these issues and lend gravity to his words? How do his writing style and the texts and figures that he cites contribute to his argument?
6. At times, King's language verges on the poetical. His prose is full of images and metaphors. Locate some of these, and discuss their effects.
7. Imagine that you are one of the clergymen to whom this letter was addressed. Write your reply.

MAKING CONNECTIONS

King quotes Thomas Jefferson as the last person in his list of his fellow "extremists." The text of Jefferson's statement (the Declaration of Independence, p. 554) comes just before King's in this volume. Examine these two texts together. In what ways can they be said to be extreme? In what ways are they not extreme? Some would say that King was quoting Jefferson without regard for his intentions — namely, that Jefferson did not mean to include African Americans in his statement that "all men are created equal." This raises an important question about the interpretation of texts, which applies to documents like the Declaration of Independence and to literary texts. Are such texts to be interpreted only in the light of their authors' intentions, or do readers have the right to their own interpretations? Make an argument about that issue, using texts in this volume for your illustrative material, and apply your argument specifically to King's use of Jefferson. In your argument, consider how we might determine Jefferson's intention in this case. Your research into Jefferson's views on race may well take you beyond this volume. Try putting "Thomas Jefferson and race" into a major online search engine. You will find hundreds of thousands of hits, but remember to return to and focus on the issue of interpretation and the rights of author and reader in such matters.

SIFTING THE ASHES

Jonathan Franzen

Jonathan Franzen (b. 1959) grew up in a suburb of St. Louis, Missouri. A graduate of Swarthmore College, he studied in Germany as a Fulbright scholar and later worked in the seismology laboratory at Harvard's Department of Earth and Planetary Sciences. He published his first novel, The Twenty-Seventh City, *in 1988, followed by* Strong Motion *in 1992, both called "intellectual thrillers." It was his much anticipated* The Corrections (2001), *however, that catapulted him into the public spotlight, in part because of the critical acclaim that the novel received and in part because of Franzen's notorious reluctance to allow the book to be included as a choice for Oprah Winfrey's celebrated book club. Despite the controversy,* The Corrections *went on to win the National Book Award. Franzen's most recent book is the essay collection* How to Be Alone (2002). *The following essay first appeared in* The New Yorker *in 1996 with the subtitle "Confessions of a Conscientious Objector in the Cigarette Wars."*

Cigarettes are the last thing in the world I want to think about. I don't consider myself a smoker, don't identify with the forty-six million Americans who have the habit. I dislike the smell of smoke and the invasion of nasal privacy it represents. Bars and restaurants with a stylish profile — with a clientele whose exclusivity depends in part on the toxic clouds with which it shields itself — have started to disgust me. I've been gassed in hotel rooms where smokers stayed the night before and in public bathrooms where men use the nasty, body-odorish Winston as a laxative. ("Winston tastes bad/ Like the one I just had" runs the grammatically unimpeachable parody from my childhood.) Some days in New York it seems as if two-thirds of the people on the sidewalk, in the swirls of car exhaust, are carrying lighted cigarettes; I maneuver constantly to stay upwind. The first casino I ever went to, in Nevada, was a vision of damnation: row upon row of middle-aged women with foot-long faces puffing on foot-long Kents and compulsively feeding silver dollars to the slots. When someone tells me that cigarettes are sexy, I think of Nevada. When I see an actress or an actor drag deeply in a movie, I imagine the pyrenes and phenols ravaging the tender epithelial cells and hardworking cilia of their bronchi, the carbon monoxide and cyanide binding to their hemoglobin, the heaving and straining of their chemically panicked hearts. Cigarettes are a distillation of a more general paranoia that besets our culture, the awful knowledge of our bodies' fragility in a world of molecular hazards. They scare the hell out of me.

Because I'm capable of hating almost every attribute of cigarettes (let's not even talk about cigars), and because I smoked what I believed was my last cigarette five years ago and have never owned an ashtray, it's easy for me to think of myself as nicotine-free. But if the man who bears my name is not a smoker, then why is there again a box fan for exhaust purposes in his living-room window? Why at the end of every workday is there a small collection of cigarette butts in the saucer on the table by this fan?

Cigarettes were the ultimate taboo in the culturally conservative household I grew up in — more fraught, even, than sex or drugs. The year before I was born, my mother's father died of lung cancer. He'd taken up cigarettes as a soldier in the First World War and smoked heavily all his life. Everyone who met my grandfather seems to have loved him, and, much as I may sneer at our country's obsession with health — at the elevation of fitness to godliness and of sheer longevity to a mark of divine favor — the fact remains that if my grandfather hadn't smoked I might have had the chance to know him.

My mother still speaks of cigarettes with loathing. I secretly started smoking them myself in college, perhaps in part because she hated them, and as the years went by I developed a fear of exposure very similar, I'm convinced, to a gay man's fear of coming out to his parents. My mother had created my body out of hers, after all. What rejection of parentage could be more extreme than deliberately poisoning that body? To come out is to announce: this is who I am, this is my identity. The curious thing about "smoker" as a label of identity, though, is its mutability. I could decide tomorrow not to be one anymore. So why not pretend not to be one today? To take control of their lives, people tell themselves stories about the person they want to be. It's the special privilege of the smoker, who at times feels so strongly the resolve to quit that it's as if he'd quit already, to be given irrefutable evidence that these stories aren't necessarily true: here are the butts in the ashtray, here is the smell in the hair.

As a smoker, then, I've come to distrust not only my stories about myself but *all* narratives that pretend to unambiguous moral significance. And it happens that . . . Americans have been subjected to just such a narrative in the daily press, as "secret" documents shed light on the machinations of Big Tobacco, industry scientists step forward to indict their former employers, nine states and a consortium of sixty law firms launch massive liability suits, and the Food and Drug Administration undertakes to regulate cigarettes as nicotine-delivery devices. The prevailing liberal view that Big Tobacco is Evil with a capital "E" is summed up in the *Times'* review of Richard Kluger's excellent new history of the tobacco industry, *Ashes to Ashes*. Chiding Kluger for (of all things) his "objectivity" and "impartiality," Christopher Lehmann-Haupt suggests that the cigarette business is on a moral par with slavery and the Holocaust. Kluger himself, impartial or not, repeatedly links the word "angels" with anti-smoking activists. In the introduction to his book he offers a stark pair of options: either cigarette manufacturers are "businessmen basically like any other" or they're "moral lepers preying on the ignorant, the miserable, the emotionally vulnerable, and the genetically susceptible."

5

My discomfort with these dichotomies may reflect the fact that, unlike Lehmann-Haupt, I have yet to kick the habit. But in no national debate do I feel more out of synch with the mainstream. For all that I distrust American industry, and especially an industry that is vigorously engaged in buying congressmen, some part of me insists on rooting for tobacco. I flinch as I force myself to read the latest health news: SMOKERS MORE LIKELY TO BEAR RETARDED BABIES, STUDY SAYS. I pounce on particularly choice collisions of metaphor and melodrama, such as this one from the *Times*: "The affidavits are the latest in a string of blows that have undermined the air of invincibility that once cloaked the $45 billion tobacco industry, which faces a deluge of lawsuits." My sympathy with cohorts who smoke disproportionately — blue-collar workers, African-Americans, writers and artists, alienated teens, the mentally ill — expands to include the companies that supply them with cigarettes. I think, We're all underdogs now. Wartime is a time of lies, I tell myself, and the biggest lie of the cigarette wars is that the moral equation can be reduced to ones and zeroes. Or have I, too, been corrupted by the weed?

I took up smoking as a student in Germany in the dark years of the early eighties. Ronald Reagan had recently made his "evil empire" speech, and Jonathan Schell was publishing "The Fate of the Earth." The word in Berlin was that if you woke up to an undestroyed world on Saturday morning you were safe for another week; the assumption was that NATO was at its sleepiest late on Friday nights, that Warsaw Pact forces would choose those hours to come pouring through the Fulda Gap, and that NATO would have to go ballistic to repel them. Since I rated my chances of surviving the decade at fifty-fifty, the additional risk posed by smoking seemed negligible. Indeed, there was something invitingly apocalyptic about cigarettes. The nightmare of nuclear proliferation had a counterpart in the way cigarettes — anonymous, death-bearing, missilelike cylinders — proliferated in my life. Cigarettes are a fixture of modern warfare, the soldier's best friend, and, at a time when a likely theater of war was my own living room, smoking became a symbol of my helpless civilian participation in the Cold War.

Among the anxieties best suited to containment by cigarettes is, paradoxically, the fear of dying. What serious smoker hasn't felt the surge of panic at the thought of lung cancer and immediately lighted up to beat the panic down? (It's a Cold War logic: we're afraid of nuclear weapons, so let's build even more of them.) Death is a severing of the connection between self and world, and, since the self can't imagine not existing, perhaps what's really scary about the prospect of dying is not the extinguishment of my consciousness but the extinguishment of the world. The potential deadliness of cigarettes was comforting because it allowed me, in effect, to become familiar with apocalypse, to acquaint myself with the contours of its terrors, to make the world's potential death less strange and so a little less threatening. Time stops for the duration of a cigarette: when you're smoking, you're acutely present to yourself; you step outside the unconscious forward rush of life. This is why the condemned are allowed a final cigarette, this is why (or so the story goes) gentlemen in evening dress stood puffing at the rail as the Titanic went down: it's a lot easier to leave the world if you're certain you've really been in it. As Goethe[1] writes in *Faust*, "Presence is our duty, be it only a moment."

The cigarette is famously the herald of the modern, the boon companion of industrial capitalism and high-density urbanism. Crowds, hyperkinesis, mass production, numbingly boring labor, and social upheaval all have correlatives in the cigarette. The sheer number of individual units consumed surely dwarfs that of any other manufactured consumer product. "Short, snappy, easily attempted, easily completed or just as easily discarded before completion," the *Times* wrote in a 1925 editorial that Richard Kluger quotes, "the cigarette is the symbol of a machine age in which the ultimate cogs and wheels and levers are human nerves." Itself the product of a mechanical roller called the Bonsack machine, the cigarette served as an opiate for assembly-line workers, breaking up into manageable units long days of grinding sameness. For women, the *Atlantic Monthly* noted in 1916, the cigarette was "the symbol of emancipation, the temporary substitute for the ballot." Altogether, it's impossible to imagine the twentieth century without cigarettes. They show up with Zelig-like[2] ubiquity in old photographs and newsreels, so devoid of individuality as to be hardly noticeable and yet, once noticed, utterly strange.

Kluger's history of the cigarette business reads like a history of American business in general. An industry that in the early eighteen-eighties was splintered into hundreds of small, family-owned concerns had by the turn of the century come under the control of one man, James Buchanan Duke, who by pioneering the use of the Bonsack roller and reinvesting a huge portion of his revenues in advertising, and then by alternately employing the stick of price wars and the carrot of attractive buyout offers, built his American Tobacco Company into the equivalent of Standard Oil or Carnegie Steel. Like his fellow-monopolists, Duke eventually ran afoul of the trust-busters, and in 1911 the Supreme Court ordered the breakup of American. The resulting oligopoly immediately brought out new brands — Camel, Lucky Strike, and Chesterfield — that have vied for market share ever since. To American retailers, the cigarette was the perfect commodity, a staple that generated large profits on a small investment in shelf space and inventory; cigarettes, Kluger notes, "were lightweight and durably packed, rarely spoiled, were hard to steal since they were usually sold from behind the counter, underwent few price changes, and required almost no selling effort."

---

[1]*Johann Wolfgang Goethe* (1749–1832): A German author and scientist, author of the dramatic poem *Faust*. [Eds.]

[2]*Zelig*: The protagonist of Woody Allen's 1982 film *Zelig*, a pseudo-documentary film about Leonard Zelig, a man who has the ability to turn into the kind of people who are around him. [Eds.]

Since every brand tasted pretty much the same, tobacco companies learned early to situate themselves at the cutting edge of advertising. In the twenties, American Tobacco offered five free cartons of Lucky Strike ("it's toasted") to any doctor who would endorse it, and then launched a campaign that claimed, "20,679 Physicians Say Luckies Are Less Irritating"; American was also the first company to target weight-conscious women ("When tempted to over-indulge, reach for a Lucky instead"). The industry pioneered the celebrity endorsement (the tennis star Bill Tilden: "I've smoked Camels for years, and I never tire of their smooth, rich taste"), radio sponsorship (Arthur Godfrey: "I smoked two or three packs of these things [Chesterfields] every day—I feel pretty good"), assaultive outdoor advertising (the most famous was the "I'd Walk a Mile for a Camel" billboard in Times Square, which for twenty-five years blew giant smoke rings), and, finally, the sponsorship of television shows like "Candid Camera" and "I Love Lucy." The brilliant TV commercials made for Philip Morris—Benson & Hedges smokers whose hundred-millimeter cigarettes were crushed by elevator doors; faux-hand-cranked footage of chambermaids sneaking smokes to the tune of "You've got your own cigarette now, baby"—were vital entertainments of my childhood. I remember, too, the chanted words "Silva Thins, Silva Thins," the mantra for a short-lived American Tobacco product that wooed the female demographic with such appalling copy as "Cigarettes are like girls, the best ones are thin and rich."

The most successful campaign of all, of course, was for Marlboro, an upscale cigarette for ladies which Philip Morris reintroduced in 1954 in a filtered version for the mainstream. Like all modern products, the new Marlboro was designed with great care. The tobacco blend was strengthened so as to survive the muting of a filter, the "flip-top" box was introduced to the national vocabulary, the color red was chosen to signal strong flavor, and the graphics underwent endless tinkering before the final look, including a fake heraldic crest with the motto "*Veni, vidi, vici*,"[3] was settled on; there was even market-testing in four cities to decide the color of the filter. It was in Leo Burnett's ad campaign for Marlboro, however, that the real genius lay. The key to its success was its transparency. Place a lone ranch hand against a backdrop of buttes at sunset, and just about every positive association a cigarette can carry is in the picture: rugged individualism, masculine sexuality, escape from an urban modernity, strong flavors, the living of life intensely. The Marlboro marks our commercial culture's passage from an age of promises to an age of pleasant empty dreams.

It's no great surprise that a company smart enough to advertise as well as this ascended, in just three decades, to a position of hegemony in the industry. Kluger's account of the triumph of Philip Morris is the kind of thing that business schools have their students read for edification and inspiration:

---

[3] "*Veni, vidi, vici*": "I came, I saw, I conquered" (Latin). These are the words that Julius Caesar used to describe his swift conquest of Asia Minor in 48 BCE [Eds.]

to succeed as an American corporation, the lesson might be, do exactly what Philip Morris did. Concentrate on products with the highest profit margin. Design new products carefully, then get behind them and push *hard*. Use your excess cash to diversify into businesses that are structurally similar to your own. Be a meritocracy. Avoid crippling debt. Patiently build your overseas markets. Never scruple to gouge your customers when you see the opportunity. Let your lawyers attack your critics. Be classy — sponsor "The Mahabharata." Defy conventional morality. Never forget that your primary fealty is to your stockholders.

While its chief competitor, R. J. Reynolds, was growing logy and inbred down in Winston-Salem — sinking into the low-margin discount-cigarette business, diversifying disastrously, and nearly drowning in debt after its leveraged buyout by Kohlberg Kravis Roberts & Company — Philip Morris was becoming the global leader in the cigarette industry and one of the most profitable corporations in the world. By the early nineties, its share of the domestic nondiscount-cigarette market had risen to eighty percent. One share of Philip Morris stock bought in 1966 was worth a hundred and ninety-two shares in 1989 dollars. Healthy, wealthy, and wise the man who quit smoking in '64 and put his cigarette money into Philip Morris common.

The company's spectacular success is all the more remarkable for having occurred in the decades when the scientific case against cigarettes was becoming overwhelming. With the possible exception of the hydrogen bomb, nothing in modernity is more generative of paradox than cigarettes. Thus, in 1955, when the Federal Trade Commission sought to curb misleading advertising by banning the publication of tar and nicotine levels, the ruling proved to be a boon to the industry, by enabling it to advertise filter cigarettes for their implicit safety even as it raised the toxic yields to compensate for the filters. So it went with the 1965 law requiring warning labels on cigarette packs, which preempted potentially more stringent state and local regulations and provided a priceless shield against future liability suits. So it went, too, with the 1971 congressional ban on broadcast cigarette advertising, which saved the industry millions of dollars, effectively froze out potential new competitors by denying them the broadcast platform, and put an end to the devastating anti-smoking ads then being broadcast under the fairness doctrine. Even such left-handed regulation as the 1982 increase in the federal excise tax benefited the industry, which used the tax as a screen for a series of price increases, doubling the price per pack in a decade, and invested the windfall in diversification. Every forward step taken by government to regulate smoking — the broadcast ban, the ban on in-flight smoking, the welter of local bans on smoking in public places — has moved cigarettes a step further back from the consciousness of nonsmoking voters. The result, given the political power of tobacco-growing states, has been the specific exemption of cigarettes from the Fair Labeling and Packaging Act of 1966, the Controlled Substances Act of 1970, the Consumer Product Safety Act of 1972, and the Toxic Substances Act of 1976. In the industry's defense in liability suits, the paradox can be seen in its purest form: because no plaintiff can claim ignorance of tobacco's hazards — i.e., precisely *because* the cigarette is the most notoriously lethal product in America — its manufacturers cannot be held negligent for selling it. Small wonder that until the Liggett Group broke ranks . . . no cigarette maker had ever paid a penny in civil damages.

Now, however, the age of paradox may be coming to an end. As the nation dismantles its missiles, its attention turns to cigarettes. The wall of secrecy that protected the industry is coming down as surely as the Berlin Wall did. The Third Wave is upon us, threatening to extinguish all that is quintessentially modern. It hardly seems an accident that the United States, which is leading the way into the information age, is also in the forefront of the war on cigarettes. Unlike the nations of Europe, which have taken a more pragmatic approach to the smoking problem, taxing cigarettes at rates as high as five dollars a pack, the anti-smoking forces in this country bring to the battle a puritanical zeal. We need a new Evil Empire, and Big Tobacco fills the bill.

The argument for equating the tobacco industry with slave traders and the Third Reich goes like this: because nearly half a million Americans a year die prematurely as a direct consequence of smoking, the makers of cigarettes are guilty of mass murder. The obvious difficulty with the argument is that the tobacco industry has never physically forced anyone to smoke a cigarette. To speak of its "killing" people, therefore, one has to posit more subtle forms of coercion. These fall into three categories. First, by publicly denying a truth well known to its scientists, which was that smokers were in mortal peril, the industry conspired to perpetrate a vast and deadly fraud. Second, by luring impressionable children into a habit very difficult to break, the industry effectively "forced" its products on people before they had developed full adult powers of resistance. Finally, by making available and attractive a product that it knew to be addictive, and by manipulating nicotine levels, the industry willfully exposed the public to a force (addiction) with the power to kill.

A "shocking" collection of "secret" industry documents which was express-mailed by a disgruntled employee of Brown & Williamson to the anti-smoking crusader Stanton A. Glantz, and has now been published by the University of California Press as "The Cigarette Papers," makes it clear that Big Tobacco has known for decades that cigarettes are lethal and addictive and has done everything in its power to suppress and deny that knowledge. "The Cigarette Papers" and other recent disclosures have prompted the Justice Department to pursue perjury charges against various industry executives, and may provide the plaintiffs now suing the industry with positive proof of tortious fraud. In no way, though, are the disclosures shocking. How could anyone who noticed that different cigarette brands have different (but consistent) nicotine levels fail to conclude that the industry can and does control the dosage? What reasonable person could have believed that the industry's public avowals of "doubt" about the deadliness of its products were anything but obligatory, ceremonial lies? If researchers unearthed a secret document proving that Bill Clinton inhaled, would we be shocked? When industry spokesmen impugn the integrity of the Surgeon General and persist in denying the undeniable, they're guilty not so much of fraud as of sounding (to borrow the word of one executive quoted by Kluger) "Neanderthal."

"The simple truth," Kluger writes, "was that the cigarette makers were getting richer and richer as the scientific findings against them piled higher and higher, and before anyone fully grasped the situation, the choice seemed to have narrowed to abject confession and surrender to the health advocates or steadfast denial and rationalization." In the early fifties, when epidemiological studies first demonstrated the link between smoking and lung cancer, cigarette executives did indeed have the option of simply liquidating their businesses and finding other work. But many of these executives came from families that had been respectably trading in tobacco for decades, and most of them appear to have been heavy smokers themselves: unlike the typical heroin wholesaler, they willingly ran the same risks they imposed on their customers. Because they were corporate officers, moreover, their ultimate allegiance was to their stockholders. If having simply stayed in business constitutes guilt, then the circle of those who share this guilt must be expanded to include every individual who held stock in a tobacco company after 1964, either directly or through a pension fund, a mutual fund, or a university endowment. We might also toss in every drugstore and supermarket that sold cigarettes and every publication that carried ads for them, since the Surgeon General's warning, after all, was there for everyone to see.

Once the companies made the decision to stay in business, it was only a matter of time before the lawyers took over. Nothing emerges from *Ashes to Ashes* more clearly than the deforming influence of legal counsel on the actions of the industry. Many industry scientists and some executives appear to have genuinely wished both to produce a safer cigarette and to acknowledge frankly the known risks of smoking. But the industry's attempts to do good were no less paradoxically self-defeating than the government's attempts at regulation. When executives in R. & D. proposed that filtered cigarettes and reduced tar and nicotine yields be marketed as a potential benefit to public health, in-house lawyers objected that calling one brand "safe" or "safer" constituted an admission that other brands were hazardous and thus exposed the maker to liability claims. Likewise, after Liggett had spent millions of dollars developing a substantially less carcinogenic "palladium cigarette" in the seventies, it was treated like contagion by the company's lawyers. Marketing it was bad from a liability standpoint, and developing it and then not marketing it was even worse, because in that case the company could be sued for negligently failing to introduce it. Epic, as the new cigarette was called, was ultimately smothered in legal paper.

Kluger describes an industry in which lawyerly paranoia quickly metastasized into every vital organ. Lawyers coached the executives appearing before congressional committees, oversaw the woefully self-serving "independent" research that the industry sponsored, and made sure that all paperwork

20

connected with studies of addiction or cancer was funneled through outside counsel so that it could be protected under the attorney-client privilege. The result was a weird replication of the dual contradictory narratives with which I, as a smoker, explain my life: a true story submerged beneath a utilitarian fiction. One longtime Philip Morris executive quoted by Kluger sums it up like this:

> There was a conflict in the company between science and the law that's never been resolved . . . and so we go through this ritual dance — what's "proven" and what isn't, what's causal and what's just an association — and the lawyers' answer is, "Let's stonewall.". . . If Helmut Wakeham [head of R. & D.] had run things, I think there would have been some admissions. But he was outflanked by the lawyers . . . who . . . were saying, in effect, "My God, you can't make that admission" without risking liability actions against the company. So there was no cohesive plan — when critics of the industry speak of a "conspiracy," they give the companies far too much credit.

In the inverted moral universe of a tobacco-liability trial, every honest or anguished statement by an executive is used to prove the defendants' guilt, while every calculated dodge is used to support their innocence. There's something very wrong here; but absent a demonstration that Americans actually swallowed the industry's lies it's far from clear that this something qualifies as murder.

More damning are recent reports of the industry's recruitment of underage smokers. Lorillard representatives have been observed handing out free Newports to kids in Washington, D.C.; Philip J. Hilts, in his new book, *Smoke Screen*, presents evidence that R. J. Reynolds deliberately placed special promotional displays in stores and kiosks known to be high-school hangouts; and the cuddly, penis-faced Joe Camel must rank as one of the most disgusting apparitions ever to appear in our cultural landscape. Tobacco companies claim that they are merely vying for market share in the vital eighteen-to-twenty-four age group, but internal industry documents described by Hilts suggest that at least one Canadian company has in fact studied how to target entry-level smokers as young as twelve. (According to Hilts, studies have shown that eighty-nine percent of today's adult smokers picked up the habit before the age of nineteen.) In the opinion of anti-tobacco activists, cigarette advertising hooks young customers by proffering images of carefree, attractive adult smokers while failing to hint at the havoc that smoking wreaks. By the time young smokers are old enough to appreciate the fact of mortality, they're hopelessly addicted.

Although the idea that a manufacturer might willingly stress the downside of its products is absurd, I have no doubt that the industry aims its ads at young Americans. I do doubt, though, whether these ads cause an appreciable number of children to start smoking. The insecure or alienated teen who lights up for the first time is responding to peer pressure or to the example of grownup role models — movie villains, rock stars, supermodels. At most, the industry's ads function as an assurance that smoking is a socially acceptable grownup activity. For that reason alone, they should probably be banned or more tightly controlled, just as cigarette-vending machines should be outlawed. Most people who start smoking end up regretting it, so any policy that reduces the number of starters is laudable.

That cigarettes innately appeal to teen-agers, however, is hardly the fault of the manufacturers. In recent weeks, I've noticed several anti-tobacco newspaper ads that offer, evidently for its shock value, the image of a preadolescent girl holding a cigarette. The models are obviously not real smokers, yet, despite their phoniness, they're utterly sexualized by their cigarettes. The horror of underage smoking veils a horror of teen and preteen sexuality, and one of the biggest pleasant empty dreams being pushed these days by Madison Avenue is that a child is innocent until his or her eighteenth birthday. The truth is that without firm parental guidance teen-agers make all sorts of irrevocable decisions before they're old enough to appreciate the consequences — they drop out of school, they get pregnant, they major in sociology. What they want most of all is to sample the pleasures of adulthood, like sex or booze or cigarettes. To impute to cigarette advertising a "predatory" power is to admit that parents now have less control over the moral education of their children than the commercial culture has. Here, again, I suspect that the tobacco industry is being scapegoated — made to bear the brunt of a more general societal rage at the displacement of the family by the corporation.

The final argument for the moral culpability of Big Tobacco is that addiction is a form of coercion. Nicotine is a toxin whose ingestion causes the smoker's brain to change its chemistry in defense. Once those changes have occurred, the smoker must continue to consume nicotine on a regular schedule in order to maintain the new chemical balance. Tobacco companies are well aware of this, and an attorney cited by Kluger summarizes the legal case for coercion as follows: "You addicted me, and you knew it was addicting, and now you say it's my fault." As Kluger goes on to point out, though, the argument has many flaws. Older even than the common knowledge that smoking causes cancer, for example, is the knowledge that smoking is a tough habit to break. Human tolerance of nicotine varies widely, moreover, and the industry has long offered an array of brands with ultra-low doses. Finally, no addiction is unconquerable: millions of Americans quit every year. When a smoker says he wants to quit but can't, what he's really saying is "I want to quit, but I want even more not to suffer the agony of withdrawal." To argue otherwise is to jettison any lingering notion of personal responsibility.

If nicotine addiction were purely physical, quitting would be relatively easy, because the acute withdrawal symptoms, the physical cravings, rarely last more than a few weeks. At the time I myself quit, six years ago, I was able to stay nicotine-free for weeks at a time, and even when I was working

25

I seldom smoked more than a few ultralights a day. But on the day I decided that the cigarette I'd had the day before was my last, I was absolutely flattened. A month passed in which I was too agitated to read a book, too fuzzy-headed even to focus on a newspaper. If I'd had a job at the time, or a family to take care of, I might have hardly noticed the psychological withdrawal. But as it happened nothing much was going on in my life. "Do you smoke?" Lady Bracknell asks Jack Worthing in *The Importance of Being Earnest,* and when he admits that he does she replies, "I am glad to hear it. A man should always have an occupation of some kind."

There's no simple, universal reason that people smoke, but of one thing I'm convinced: they don't do it because they're slaves to nicotine. My best guess about my own attraction to the habit is that I belong to a class of people whose lives are insufficiently structured. The mentally ill and the indigent are also members of this class. We embrace a toxin as deadly as nicotine, suspended in an aerosol of hydrocarbons and nitrosamines, because we have not yet found pleasures or routines that can replace the comforting, structure-bringing rhythm of need and gratification that the cigarette habit offers. One word for this structuring might be "self-medication"; another might be "coping." But there are very few serious smokers over thirty, perhaps none at all, who don't feel guilty about the harm they inflict on themselves. Even Rose Cipollone, the New Jersey woman whose heirs in the early eighties nearly sustained a liability judgment against the industry, had to be recruited by an activist. The sixty law firms that have pooled their assets for a class-action suit on behalf of all American smokers do not seem to me substantially less predatory than the suit's corporate defendants. I've never met a smoker who blamed the habit on someone else.

The United States as a whole resembles an addicted individual, with the corporated id going about its dirty business while the conflicted political ego frets and dithers. What's clear is that the tobacco industry would not still be flourishing, thirty years after the first Surgeon General's report, if our legislatures weren't purchasable, if the concepts of honor and personal responsibility hadn't largely given way to the power of litigation and the dollar, and if the country didn't generally endorse the idea of corporations whose ultimate responsibility is not to society but to the bottom line. There's no doubt that some tobacco executives have behaved despicably, and for public-health advocates to hate these executives, as the nicotine addict comes eventually to hate his cigarettes, is natural. But to cast them as moral monsters — a point source of evil — is just another form of prime-time entertainment.

By selling its soul to its legal advisers, Big Tobacco long ago made clear   30
its expectation that the country's smoking problem would eventually be resolved in court. The industry may soon suffer such a devastating loss in a liability suit that thereafter only foreign cigarette makers will be able to afford to do business here. Or perhaps a federal court will undertake to legislate a solution to a problem that the political process has clearly

proved itself unequal to, and the Supreme Court will issue an opinion that does for the smoking issue what *Brown v. Board of Education* did for racial segregation and *Roe v. Wade* for abortion. "Businessmen are combatants, not healers," Kluger writes in *Ashes to Ashes*, "and when they press against or exceed the bounds of decency in their quest for gain, unhesitant to profit from the folly of others, should the exploited clientele and victimized society expect the perpetrators to restrain themselves out of some sudden divine visitation of conscience? Or must human nature be forcibly corrected when it goes awry?"

Liggett's recent defection notwithstanding, the Medicare suits filed by nine states seem unlikely to succeed as a forcible correction. Kluger notes that these cases arguably amount to "personal injury claims in disguise," and that the Supreme Court has ruled that federal cigarette-labeling laws are an effective shield against such claims. Logically, in other words, the states ought to be suing smokers, not cigarette makers. And perhaps smokers, in turn, ought to be suing Social Security and private pension funds for all the money they'll save by dying early. The best estimates of the nationwide dollar "cost" of smoking, including savings from premature death and income from excise taxes, are negative numbers. If the country's health is to be measured fiscally, an economist quoted by Kluger jokes, "cigarette smoking should be subsidized rather than taxed."

The giant class-action suit filed in New Orleans in March of 1994 represents a more serious threat to Big Tobacco. If a judge concludes that smoking constitutes a social ill on a par with racial segregation, he or she is unlikely to deny standing to the forty-six-million-member "class" represented by the consortium of law firms, and once plaintiffs in a class-action suit are granted standing they almost never lose. The case for regulation of tobacco by the F.D.A is likewise excellent. The modern cigarette is a heavily engineered product, bolstered with a long list of additives, and its nicotine content is manipulable at will. Tobacco companies insist that cigarettes, because no health claims are made for them by the companies, should not be considered a drug. But if nicotine is universally understood to be habit-forming — a central tenet of the industry's liability defense — then the absence of explicit health claims is meaningless. Whether Congress, in its various wafflings, intended cigarettes to be immune from F.D.A. regulation in the first place is, again, a matter that will be decided in court, but a demonstrable history of lies and distortion is sure to weaken the industry's defense.

Ultimately, the belief that the country's century-long love affair with the cigarette can be ended rationally and amicably seems as fond as the belief that there's a painless way to kick nicotine. The first time I quit, I stayed clean for nearly three years. I found I was able to work *more* productively without the distraction and cumulative unpleasantness of cigarettes, and I was happy finally to be the nonsmoker that my family had always taken me to be. Eventually, though, in a season of great personal loss, I came to resent having quit for other people rather than for myself. I was hanging out with smokers, and I drifted back into the habit. Smoking may not look sexy to me anymore, but it still *feels* sexy. The pleasure of carrying the drug, of surrendering to its imperatives and relaxing behind a veil of smoke, is thoroughly licentious. If longevity were the highest good that I could imagine, I might succeed now in scaring myself into quitting. But to the fatalist who values the present more than the future, the nagging voice of conscience — of society, of family — becomes just another factor in the mental equilibrium that sustains the habit. "Perhaps," Richard Klein writes in *Cigarettes Are Sublime*, "one stops smoking only when one starts to love cigarettes, becoming so enamored of their charms and so grateful for their benefits that one at last begins to grasp how much is lost by giving them up, how urgent it is to find substitutes for some of the seductions and powers that cigarettes so magnificently combine." To live with uncontaminated lungs and an unracing heart is a pleasure that I hope someday soon to prefer to the pleasure of a cigarette. For myself, then, I'm cautiously optimistic. For the body politic, rhetorically torn between shrill condemnation and Neanderthal denial, and habituated to the poison of tobacco money in its legal system, its legislatures, its financial markets, and its balance of foreign trade, I'm considerably less so.

A few weeks ago in Tribeca, in a Magritte-like twilight,[4] I saw a woman in a lighted window on a high floor of a loft apartment building. She was standing on a chair and lowering the window's upper sash. She tossed her hair and did something complicated with her arms which I recognized as the lighting of a cigarette. Then she leaned her elbow and her chin on the sash and blew smoke into the humid air outside. I fell in love at first sight as she stood there, both inside and outside, inhaling contradiction and breathing out ambivalence.

QUESTIONS

1. In publishing this essay with the subtitle "Confessions of a Conscientious Objector in the Cigarette Wars," *The New Yorker* sets it up as confessional, yet we have placed it in one of the "Arguing" sections of this book. How would you categorize this essay? Is Franzen confessing or arguing or both? Give examples to support your opinion.
2. How does Franzen answer the questions of why he started smoking, why he gave it up, and why he started again? Note how he uses the first question as a frame, returning to it in paragraph 28 to link his own addiction to a national addiction.
3. Consider the symbolic values given the cigarette and cigarette smoking. If giving up cigarettes means, as Richard Klein says, finding "substitutes

---

[4]*René Magritte* (1898–1967): A French surrealist artist whose twilight skies were sometimes full of hats or umbrellas. [Eds.]

for some of the seductions and powers that cigarettes so magnificently combine" (paragraph 33), what would you suggest as some possible substitutes?

4. The central section of Franzen's essay presents some of the evidence that has been gathered against "Big Tobacco" and its attempts to squelch evidence of how harmful cigarette smoking is. "The argument for equating the tobacco industry with slave traders and the Third Reich" starts in paragraph 17. What does Franzen mean by this comparison?

5. How strong is the evidence Franzen presents for his argument? In what order does he place his evidence? Why do you think he organizes his evidence in this way?

6. Since this article was published, the Food and Drug Administration has decided to regulate tobacco. Do some research on this issue, and report on the implications of such regulation, as well as the issues Franzen raises in paragraph 32.

MAKING CONNECTIONS

There is an argument in this text, about the guilt of the tobacco companies, but a lot more is going on here. Compare the use of personal experience and feelings in this piece with their use in one or more of the other texts in this book. You might consider Barbara Ehrenreich's "Nickel and Dimed" (p. 429), Robert Frost's "Design" (p. 632), or Micahel J. Sandel's "The Case against Perfection" (p. 793).

ISN'T MARRIAGE FOR PROCREATION?

Evan Wolfson

Evan Wolfson was born in 1957 in Brooklyn, raised in Pittsburgh, received degrees from Yale College and Harvard Law School, and spent two years in West Africa with the Peace Corps. He worked as a state prosecutor and special counsel in the Iran-Contra investigation and worked at Lambda Legal Defense & Education Fund before founding Freedom to Marry. Wolfson was cocounsel in the Hawaii marriage case Baehr v. Miike, *which launched the nationwide debate on gay marriage. Citing his national leadership on marriage equality and his appearance before the U.S. Supreme Court in* Boy Scouts of America v. James Dale, *the* National Law Journal *in 2000 named Wolfson one of "the 100 most influential lawyers in America." Wolfson was named one of* Time *magazine's 100 Most Influential People in 2004, the same year in which he published* Why Marriage Matters: America, Equality, and Gay People's Right to Marry. *Commenting on his target audience for the book, Wolfson says, "Why Marriage Matters is aimed at persuading not the die-hard anti-gay segment of the population, but the uncomfortable, the reachable-but-not-reached. I would not get hung up trying to persuade the most adamant of opponents. I would instead focus my energy and use the book as a tool to engage the fair-minded people who have some concerns but who are not blind with hatred or prejudice." The following piece appears as a chapter in* Why Marriage Matters.

Marriage is not about affirming somebody's love for somebody else. It's about uniting together to be open to children, to further civilization in our society.

U.S. Senator Rick Santorum (R-Pennsylvania)[1]

Our laws of civil marriage do not privilege procreative heterosexual intercourse between married people above every other form of adult intimacy and every other means of creating a family. . . . Even people who cannot stir from their deathbed may marry. While it is certainly true that many, perhaps most, married couples have children together (assisted or unassisted), it is the exclusive and permanent commitment of the marriage partners to one another, not the begetting of children, that is the sine qua non of civil marriage.

Massachusetts Supreme Judicial Court,
Goodridge v. Department of Public Health (2003)[2]

If you go to any of the hundreds of fundamentalist Web sites on the Internet today, you have a good chance of coming across a list of talking points against "same-sex marriage." One such script, put together by the Christian radio show *Point Of View*, gives thirteen reasons why listeners should be opposed to gay couples' freedom to marry. High on the list is a lesson in "basic biology." According to the *Point of View*'s script, anti-marriage-equality activists are supposed to say, "Homosexual relations deny the self-evident truth that male and female bodies complement each other. Human sexuality and procreation is based upon a man and a woman coming together as one flesh. Marriage between a man and a woman promotes procreation and makes intimate sexual activity orderly and socially accountable."[3]

Let's put aside for the time being the objections many of us, gay and non-gay alike, probably have to the totalitarian notion that intimate sexual activity should be "orderly and socially accountable." Focus, instead, on the rest of the scripted answer, which, if it were rephrased, might read like one of those analytical word problems on a college entrance exam: "If it's a given that the primary purpose of marriage is having children, and it's a given that only a man and a woman — together — can biologically have a child, shouldn't marriage be solely about the union of two different-sex people?"

At first glance, the "basic biology" argument seems to make some sense. After all, it doesn't take more than a fourth-grade health class education to know that men's and women's bodies in some sense "complement each other" and that when a man and a woman come "together as one flesh" it often leads to procreation.

In fact, the "basic biology" argument makes enough sense at first glance that it was used in each of this country's high-profile cases against the freedom to marry — first in Hawaii and then in Vermont and Massachusetts. In each case, attorneys for the state said the government's interest in basic biology, or in "promoting procreation," was a primary reason — if not the only justification — for prohibiting gay couples from getting married.

In 1994, Hawaii argued that the state's marriage law could be traced all the way back to an 1846 decree by King Kamehameha III, who, the state contended, meant for marriage to promote procreation between a man and a woman. (The state failed even to acknowledge Hawaii's older, pre-Christian tradition; of *aikane*, which involved taking a same-sex partner instead of — or sometimes along with — a wife. Kamehameha the Great who first unified the islands, himself had an *aikane* partner, a high chief named Kuakini.)[4] "There is a mystical bond between a mother, a father, and their child," the state instead told the court. "The purpose of the marriage law is to encourage procreation through male-female marriages. . . . No same-sex couples, as a couple, can have children."[5]

In 1998, lawyers for Vermont agreed with the plaintiffs that gay people have a fundamental right to marry, but they said the right extends only so far as to allow them to marry someone of the other sex, regardless of love.[6] "To say [otherwise] would be to say there's absolutely no connection between marriage and procreation," the states attorneys told the state supreme court. "It's a unique social institution based on the sexual communion of a man and a woman."[7]

And in 2003, lawyers for the Commonwealth of Massachusetts said the state can forbid gay couples from marrying because "limiting marriage to opposite-sex couples furthers the state's interest in fostering the link between marriage and procreation."[8]

Because the "basic biology" argument just seems so, well, basic, I understand why some people want to stop right there. But, as I'm sure many of you have already realized, the overstated link between procreation and marriage actually doesn't explain why we bar same-sex couples (and same-sex couples alone) from marriage as it now exists under law and in our society. In fact, once you scratch the surface of this argument — which is actually more of a gut feeling than a thought-out rationale — you can see that it's riddled with holes. And thankfully, these are holes that the justices in Hawaii, Vermont, and Massachusetts saw right through.

In Hawaii, Judge Kevin Chang returned to the analysis of marriage put forward by Justice Sandra Day O'Conner, writing for the unanimous U.S. Supreme Court in its 1987 ruling in *Turner v. Safley*. . . . The Supreme Court noted that prisoners, whose incarceration might keep them from having sex with a spouse (and thus, in turn, prevent them from having biological children), might have many other reasons for wanting to exercise their constitutional freedom to marry. Significantly, the Supreme Court did not include conceiving or raising children on its list of the "important attributes" of marriage under the law.

Twelve years later in the Hawaii freedom-to-marry case that Dan Foley   10
and I litigated, Judge Chang wrote:

> In Hawaii, and elsewhere, people marry for a variety of reasons including, but not limited to the following: (1) having or raising children; (2) stability and commitment; (3) emotional closeness; (4) intimacy and monogamy; (5) the establishment of a framework for a long-term relationship; (6) personal significance; (7) recognition by society; and (8) certain legal and economic protections, benefits and obligations.[9]

"Gay men and lesbian women," the judge found, "share this same *mix* of reasons for wanting to be able to marry," a mix that may include having, or caring for, one's kids, but often does not, and that for many couples turns on other important aspects of marriage.

In Vermont, Chief Justice Jeffrey Amestoy seemed to find it hard to take the state's "procreation" argument seriously. If Vermont truly based a couple's competency to marry on that couple's ability to procreate, he suggested, state officials might want to take a second look at some of the marriage licenses they have been issuing.

> It is . . . undisputed that many opposite-sex couples marry for reasons unrelated to procreation, that some of these couples never intend to have children, and that others are incapable of having children. Therefore, if the purpose of the statutory exclusion of same-sex couples is to "further the link between procreation and child rearing," it is significantly under-inclusive. The law extends the benefits and protections of marriage to many persons with no logical connection to the stated governmental goal.[10]

And in Massachusetts, Chief Justice Margaret Marshall didn't even wait to write the court's decision in the case before letting the state's attorneys know what she thought about their use of the "promotion of procreation" as Massachusetts' justification for excluding gay couples from marriage.

"I think it would be a stretch to say it was for procreation," she said to the state's lawyers during the oral argument. "The State is free to say, for example, after a heterosexual couple has been married for ten years and has produced no children, unless there is evidence that both are infertile, that they should be divorced so that they can be free to try and procreate with another couple?" Despite the asserted link between marriage and procreation put forward to justify excluding gay couples, the state refused to apply any such link to heterosexuals: "For the State to draw the line that way would be an impermissible intrusion into the private lives of the people involved," the assistant attorney general replied (giving no similar weight to the intrusiveness of denying gay people the right to marry and make their own parenting and personal choices like non-gay couples).

Chief Justice Marshall then pointed out that Massachusetts (like Vermont) not only allows nonprocreative couples to marry and stay married, but also permits gay parents to adopt, has many parents who conceived their children through alternative insemination and other means, and has a strong public policy of supporting kids, no matter who their parents are or what their family configuration is.[11] 15

Indeed, even U.S. Supreme Court Justice Antonin Scalia, hardly a proponent of equal rights for gay men and lesbians, wrote in his 2003 dissent to *Lawrence v. Texas* that the promotion of procreation is a very weak argument for maintaining bans on gay people's freedom to marry. "If moral disapprobation of homosexual conduct is 'no state interest' for purposes of proscribing [private adult sex]," Scalia wrote, "what justification could there possibly be for denying the benefits of marriage to homosexual couples? Surely not the encouragement of procreation, since the sterile and the elderly are allowed to marry."[12]

Actually, the Supreme Court's drawing of a distinction between marriage and procreation goes beyond *Lawrence v. Texas* in 2003 and *Turner v. Safley* in 1987. To hear the opponents of gay equality today, one would not know that for decades the law of the land (America that is, unlike more theocratic or women-subordinating societies) has been to recognize that marriage is not just about procreation — indeed, is not necessarily about procreation at all.

The Court recognized the right *not* to procreate in marriage, a personal choice protected in a free society under the Constitution, as early as *Eisenstadt v. Baird* in 1972 and *Griswold v. Connecticut* in 1965. In such cases, the justices ruled that government officials could not block a couple — married or unmarried — from making their own decisions about procreation, sex, and the use of contraception. "If the right to privacy means anything, the court ruled in *Eisenstadt*, "it is the right of the individual, married or single, to be free from unwarranted governmental intrusion into matters so fundamentally affecting a person as the decision whether to bear or beget a child."[13]

Given these legal precedents, are Senator Santorum and other opponents correct in saying that "[m]arriage is not about affirming somebody's love for somebody else"?[14] Or is that some other century's, some other country's idea of what the freedom to marry means?

But now let's put these constitutional, legal and historical understandings of marriage and love aside for a moment and instead focus on some of   20 the commonsense reasons why the procreation argument doesn't work to explain or justify the denial of gay people's freedom to marry. First there is the point raised by Vermont's Chief Justice Amestoy and by U.S. Supreme Court Justice Scalia: No state requires that non-gay couples prove that they can procreate — or promise that they will procreate — before issuing them a marriage licenses. Indeed, no state requires as a condition of a valid marriage that a couple promises to even engage in sexual intercourse, which would be required for traditional procreation.

And when states issue marriage licenses, none of them come with a "sunset provision" whereby a couple has two or three years to produce a child or the marriage expires. Just imagine how such a law could put millions of marriages in jeopardy. Bob and Elizabeth Dole, John and Teresa Heinz Kerry, and Pat and Shelley Buchanan are just a few of the married couples that would be forced to divorce by such a law. And certainly George Washington, the Father of Our Country, who never had any children with his wife, Martha, would have objected to such a procreation requirement — a requirement our opponents seem only to conjure up when they seek to deny marriage licenses to gay couples.

Every U.S. state routinely issues marriage licenses to elderly, sterile, and even impotent couples. No state requires them to procreate or to raise children; states recognize that these couples have many other reasons for wanting to marry, including, yes, love, adult companionship, mutual caring and support, and personal commitment.

Meanwhile, every state also recognizes that these and other couples can, and very often do, become parents through adoption or any of a number of other approaches to child-bearing, including donor insemination and surrogacy. The "basic biology" argument ignores that gay and lesbian couples do have, and will continue to have, children by these same means.

And many gay and lesbian parents are raising children they may have conceived during other relationships. Remember Antoinette Pregil, one of the Hawaii marriage plaintiffs? Together with her partner, Tammy Rodrigues, Toni raised her biological daughter, Leina'ala. Leina'ala was only four years old when her mothers met. Fourteen years later she graduated from high school with honors. "I honestly don't think there's a difference" between two different-sex parents or two same-sex parents, Tammy told the Associated Press after the state of Hawaii asserted that gay couples cannot procreate and are not the "optimal" parents. "You can have a mother and a father or you can have a child being brought up with all the love. To me, it's the love."[15]

And how about Hillary and Julie Goodridge? Plaintiffs in the Massachusetts freedom-to-marry case, they were a committed couple for several years when, in anticipation, of the birth of their daughter, Annie, they took the shared last name Goodridge to help bond their growing family and acknowledge their increased and shared family responsibilities. "We want to get married because we love each other and we want to make our family as strong as it could be," Julie told *People* magazine.[16]

And then there are Richard Linnell and Gary Chalmers, who joined Hillary and Julie as plaintiffs in Massachusetts. The men had been together fourteen years and are fathers to a teenage daughter, Paige, whom they adopted as an infant. "I shouldn't have to explain to [Paige] that her parents aren't married, but love each other very much and the three of us are a family," Gary said in a statement released by Gay & Lesbian Advocates & Defenders, the plaintiffs' stellar lawyers. "This shouldn't be a complicated conversation. We have the same concerns, the same routines as any other parents, and we should be recognized and treated in the same way."[17]

In short, while marriage may not be right or available for every parent, most people do choose to have children within the context of marriage. Raising their kids within marriage is precisely what many gay people are seeking to do, despite attacks on their families from the very groups that constantly claim to be "pro-family." Of the thirteen plaintiff couples in the freedom-to-marry cases in Hawaii, Vermont, and Massachusetts, six of them are parents, with seven children between them. Preventing these and other gay and lesbian couples from accessing the tangible and intangible protections and responsibilities of marriage does nothing to help these parents or their kids, nor does it facilitate or encourage procreation by any other group of people. Presumably, non-gay men and women will continue to procreate and marry, even once gay men and lesbians are treated equally.

That's why court after court has determined what common sense and a moment's honest reflection reveal: that "basic biology" is no reason to block gay and lesbian couples from marriage.

In fact, if we as a society care about kids — real kids, not just rhetorical children used as a weapon in a culture war — then we have to acknowledge that same-sex couples do have children and those children, it follows, have gay parents. In fact, at least eight thousand children in Massachusetts are being raised by parents in same-sex couples, reported one 2004 study,[18] and researchers analyzing census data have concluded that as many as one in five gay male couples, and one in three lesbian couples, are raising kids.[19]

Basic biology or not, those kids, too, deserve protection and security. It simply makes no sense to, on the one hand, say, "We care about children," and then, on the other hand, punish some kids for having the "wrong parents" by denying their families marriage and its many benefits.[20] . . .

[1] *Fox News Sunday*, News Network, August 3, 2003.

[2] *Goodridge v. Department of Public Health*, 440 Mass. 309 (Massachusetts Supreme Judicial Court, 2003).

[3] "Talking Points Against Same-Sex Marriage," *Point of View* radio talk show, *Christianity.com* http://www.pointofview.net/partner/Article_Display_Page/o_PTID320166%7CCHID644214%7CCIID1690590.00.html.

[4] Matthew Johnson, "Lily Pads/Pink Flowers: Gay Marriage, Hawaii Sovereignty, and Justice for All in Paradise," http://www.gwu.edu/~english/ccsc/2002%20Pages/Johnson.htm; see also Robert J. Morris, "Configuring the Bounds of Marriage: The Implications of Hawaiian Culture and Values for the Debate About Homogamy," *Yale Journal of Law and the Humanities* 8 (1996); 132–57.

[5] Closing argument by Hawaii Deputy State Attorney General Rick Eichor, *Baehr v. Miike* (Hawaii Supreme Court, September 1996).

[6] "Vermont Gay Couples Tell Court Why They Should Be Allowed to Marry," CNN.com, November 18, 1998, http://www.cnn.com/US/9811/18/gay.marriage.03.

[7] "Supreme Court Considers Gay Marriage Case," *Out in the Mountains*, December 1998, http://www.mountainpridemedia.org/dec98/court.htm.

[8] M. R. F. Buckley, "State's High Court Debates Gay Marriage," *The Boston Channel.com*, November 19, 2003, http://www.thebostonchannel.com/news/2645605/detail.htm.

[9] *Baehr v. Miike*, 994 P.2d 566 (Hawaii Supreme Court, 1999).

[10] *Baker v. Vermont*, 774 A.2d 864 (Vermont Supreme Court, 1999).

[11] Buckley, "States High Court Debates Gay Marriage."

[12] *Lawrence v. Texas*, No. 02-102 (U.S. Supreme Court, 2003) (Scalia, J., dissenting).

[13] *Eisenstadt v. Baird*, 405 U.S. 438 (U.S. Supreme Court, 1972).

[14] *Fox News Sunday*, Fox News Network, August 3, 2003.

[15] Bruce Dunford, "Absent Fireworks, Gay Marriage Trial Focuses on Parenting," Associated Press, September 15, 1996.

[16] Jerome Richard, "State of the Union," *People*, August 18, 2003, p. 100.

[17] Gay & Lesbian Advocates & Defenders, "GLAD — Marriage in Massachusetts," http://www.glad.org/marriage/goodridge_plaintiffs.shtml.

[18] University of Massachusetts at Amherst, "Umass Study of Census Data Shows that 8,000 Massachusetts Children with Same-Sex Parents Would Greatly

Benefit from Gay Marriage," news release, February 9, 2004, http://www
.umass.edu/newsoffice/archive/2004/020904iglss.html.
    [19]Urban Institute/Human Rights Campaign analysis, March 2004, http://
www.hrc.org.
    [20]Michael S. Wald, "Same-Sex Couples: Marriage, Families, and Chil-
dren," *BuddyBuddy.com*, December 1999, http://www.buddybuddy.com/
wald1.html.

QUESTIONS

1. The author of this piece is a lawyer, who is skilled in arguing. We
   can learn something from the way he constructs his argument,
   whether we agree with it or not. Begin, then, by making an outline
   of the main sections of the argument.
2. One of the features of a good argument is that it considers opposed positions with some care. One such position summarized
   here is what Wolfson calls the "basic biology" argument. What is
   that argument? Does Wolfson present it clearly and fairly?
3. In order to make his counterargument significant, Wolfson has to
   first demonstrate that the basic biology argument is important.
   How does he go about doing this? Does he succeed?
4. Within this argument are two main subarguments — one to the effect that marriage need not entail procreation, and the other to the
   effect that many homosexual couples are indeed raising children.
   Are these positions in conflict, or do they support each other in the
   general argument?
5. Are you persuaded by Wolfson's argument? If you are not, write
   your own counterargument in which you consider and refute his
   position. If you are persuaded, write an analytical essay in which
   you explain what makes his argument persuasive.

MAKING CONNECTIONS

Except for Jonathan Swift's "A Modest Proposal,"the essays in this
section make straightforward arguments, for the most part, dealing
with opposing positions and making the case for their own views.
Write an essay in which you consider as many of them as you can,
and explain what moves or gestures by a writer make for a strong argument. Or, if you wish to focus on two essays only, consider this one
and Martin Luther King Jr.'s "Letter from Birmingham Jail" (p. 559)
as examples of argument involving legal issues. What do King and
Wolfson have in common as constructors of arguments? How do their
arguments or ways of arguing differ?

FOOLS' PARADISE

Ronald Wright

*Ronald Wright (b. 1948) was born in England and in 1970 moved
to Canada, where he currently lives near Port Hope, Ontario. He
received his undergraduate and master's degrees from the University
of Cambridge, where he studied archaeology and anthropology.
He has contributed numerous articles and reviews to periodicals,
including the* New York Times Book Review, Canadian Forum,
Times Literary Supplement, Travel Review, *and* Washington Post.
He has written two novels, A Scientific Romance *(1998), which
won the Higham Prize for Fiction (U.K.) and was a New York
Times Notable Book of 1998, and* Henderson's Spear *(2002), and
a collection of travel pieces,* Home and Away *(1993). He has also
written several books that combine history, anthropology, and
social commentary. The best known of these books are the international best sellers and Trillium Book Award finalists* Time among
the Maya: Travels in Belize, Guatemala, and Mexico *(1989) and*
Stolen Continents: The Americas through Indian Eyes since 1492
*(1992). In these works, Wright describes the struggles of indigenous
societies to maintain their traditional ways of life when faced with
colonialism and discrimination brought by encroaching Western
culture. "Fools' Paradise" originally appeared in the* Times Literary
Supplement *in 2004.*

The greatest wonder of the ancient world is how recent it all is. No city
or monument is much more than 5,000 years old. Only about seventy: life-
times, of seventy years, have been lived end to end since civilization began.
Its entire run occupies a mere 0.2 per cent of the nearly 3 million years since
our first ancestor sharpened a stone. The progress of "man the hunter" during the Old Stone Age, or Palaeolithic — his perfection of weapons and
techniques — led directly to the end of hunting as a way of life. The big
game was all but exterminated, except in a few places where conditions favored the prey. Next came the discovery of farming — most likely by
women — during the New Stone Age, or Neolithic, in several parts of the
world. And from that grew the experiment of worldwide civilization, which
began as many independent enterprises but over the last few centuries has
coalesced, mainly by hostile takeover, into one big system that covers and
consumes the Earth.

Not all past civilizations fell because of plague or conquest; many
collapsed internally, victims of their own success, after wearing out their

welcome from the natural world. The wrecks of these failed experiments lie in deserts and jungles like fallen airliners whose flight reorders can tell us what went wrong. They are no longer of merely antiquarian interest. Civilization is now expanding at such a pace, and on such a scale, that we must understand its inherent patterns and dangers.

Archaeology is perhaps the best tool we have for doing so, for answering Gauguin's questions: what we are, where we have come from, and where we are likely to be going. Unlike written history, which is often highly edited, archaeology uncovers the deeds we have forgotten, or have chosen to forget. It also offers a much longer reading of the direction and momentum of the human course through time. A realistic understanding of the past is quite a new thing, a late fruit of the Enlightenment, although people of many times have felt the tug of what the Elizabethan antiquarian, William Camden, called the "back-looking curiousity." Antiquity, he wrote, "hath a certaine resemblance with eternity: [It] is a sweet food of the mind."

Not everyone's mind was so open in his day. An early Spanish viceroy of Peru who had just seen the Inca capital high in the Andes, with its walls of megaliths fitted like gems, wrote back to his king: "I have examined the fortress that [the Incas] built . . . which shows clearly the work of the Devil . . . for it does not seem possible that the strength and skill of men could have made it." Even today, some opt for the comforts of mystification, preferring to believe that the wonders of the ancient world were built by Atlanteans, gods, or space travellers, instead of by thousands toiling in the sun. Such thinking robs our forerunners of their due, and us of their experience. Because then one can believe whatever one likes about the past — without having to confront the bones, potsherds, and inscriptions which tell us that people all over the world, time and again, have made similar advances and mistakes.

About two centuries after the Spanish invasion of Peru, a Dutch fleet in the South Seas far to the west of Chile and below the Tropic of Capricorn came upon a sight hardly less awesome, and even more inexplicable, than the megalithic buildings of the Andes. On Easter Day 1722, the Dutchmen sighted an unknown island so treeless and eroded that they mistook its barren hills for dunes. They were amazed, as they drew near, to see hundreds of standing stone images as tall as Amsterdam houses. "We could not comprehend how it was possible that these people, who are devoid of heavy thick timber [or] strong ropes, nevertheless had been able to erect such images, which were fully thirty feet high."

Captain Cook later confirmed the island's desolation, finding: "no wood for fuel; nor any fresh water worth taking on board." He described the islanders' tiny canoes, made from scraps of driftwood stitched together like shoe-leather, as the worst in the Pacific. Nature, he concluded, had "been exceedingly sparing of her favours to this spot." The great mystery of Easter Island that struck all early visitors was not just that these colossal statues stood in such a tiny and remote corner of the world, but that the stones seemed to have been put there without tackle, as if set down from the sky. The Spaniard who attributed the marvels of Inca architecture to the Devil was merely unable to recognize another culture's achievements. But even scientific observers could not, at first, account for the megaliths of Easter Island. The figures stood there mockingly, defying common sense.

We now know the answer to the riddle, and it is a chilling one. *Pace* Captain Cook, nature had not been unusually stingy with her favors. Pollen studies of the island's crater lakes have shown that it was once well watered and green, with rich volcanic soil supporting thick woods of the Chilean wine palm, a fine timber that can grow as tall as an oak. No natural disaster had changed that: no eruption, drought, or disease. The catastrophe on Easter Island was man.

Rapa Nui, as Polynesians call the place, was settled during the fifth century AD by migrants from the Marquesas or the Gambiers, arriving in big catamarans stocked with their usual range of crops and animals: dogs, chickens, edible rats, sugar cane, bananas, sweet potatoes, and mulberry for making bark-cloth. (Thor Heyerdahl's theory that the island was peopled from South America has not been supported by recent work, though sporadic contact between Peru and Oceania probably did take place.) Easter Island proved too cold for breadfruit and coconut palms, but was rich in seafood: fish, seals, porpoises, turtles, and nesting seabirds. Within five or six centuries, the settlers multiplied to about 10,000 people — a lot for sixty-four square miles. They built villages with good houses on stone footings, and cleared all the best land for fields. Socially they split into clans and ranks — nobles, priests, commoners — and there may have been a paramount chief or "king."

Like Polynesians on some other islands, each clan began to honor its ancestry with impressive stone images. These were hewn from the yielding volcanic tuff of a crater and set up on platforms by the shore. As time went on, the statue cult became increasingly rivalrous and extravagant, reaching its apogee during Europe's high Middle Ages, while the Plantagenet kings ruled England. Each generation of images grew bigger than the last, demanding more timber, rope, and manpower for hauling to the ahu, or altars. Trees were cut down faster than they could grow, a problem worsened by the settlers' rats, who ate the seeds and saplings. By AD 1400, no more tree pollen is found in the annual strata of the crater lakes: the woods had been utterly destroyed by both the largest and the smallest mammal on the island.

We might think that in such a limited place where, from the height of Terevaka, islanders could survey their whole world at a glance, steps would have been taken to halt the cutting, to protect the saplings, to replant. We might think that as trees became scarce, the erection of statues would have been curtailed, and timber reserved for essential purposes such as boat-building and roofing. But that is not what happened. The people who felled the last tree could see it was the last, could know with complete certainty that there would never be another. And they felled it anyway.

All shade vanished from the land except the hard-edged shadows cast by the petrified ancestors, whom the people loved all the more because they made them feel less alone. For a generation or so there was enough old lumber to haul the great stones and still keep a few canoes seaworthy for deep water. But the day came when the last good boat was gone. The people then knew there would be little seafood and — worse — no way of escape. The word for wood, *rakau*, became the dearest in their language. Wars broke out over ancient planks and worm-eaten bits of jetsam. They ate all their dogs, and nearly all the nesting birds; and the unbearable stillness of the place deepened with animal silences. There was nothing left now but the *moai*, the stone giants who had devoured the land. And still these promised the return of plenty if only the people would keep faith and honor them with increase.

But how will we take you to the altars? asked the carvers, and the *moai* answered that when the time came they would walk there on their own. So the sound of hammering still rang from the quarries, and the crater walls came alive with hundreds of new giants, growing even bigger now they had no need of human transport. The tallest ever set on an altar is over 30 feet high and weighs 80 tons; the tallest ever carved is 65 feet and weighs more than *200* tons, comparable to the greatest stones worked by the Incas or Egyptians. Except, of course, that it never moved an inch.

By the end there were more than 1,000 *moai,* one for every ten islanders in their heyday. But the good days were gone — gone with the good earth, which had been carried away on the endless wind and washed by flash floods into the sea. The people had been seduced by a kind of progress that becomes a mania, an "ideological pathology" as some anthropologists call it. When Europeans arrived in the eighteenth century the worst was over; they found only one or two living souls per statue, a sorry remnant, "small, lean, timid and miserable," in Cook's words. Now without roof beams, many people were dwelling in caves their only buildings were stone hen-houses where they guarded this last non-human protein from each other day and night. The Europeans heard tales of how the warrior class had taken power, how the island had convulsed with burning villages, gory battles, and cannibal feasts. The one innovation of this end-period was to turn the use of obsidian (a razor-keen volcanic glass) from toolmaking to weapons. Daggers and spearheads became the commonest artifacts on the island, hoarded in pits like the grenades and assault rifles kept by modern-day survivalists. Even this was not quite the nadir. Between the Dutch visit of 1722 and Cook's fifty years later, the people again made war on each other and, for the first time, on the ancestors as well. Cook found *moai* toppled from their platforms, cracked and beheaded, the ruins littered with human bones.

There is no reliable account of how or why this happened. Perhaps it started as the ultimate atrocity between enemy clans, like European nations bombing cathedrals in the Second World War. Perhaps it began with the shattering of the island's solitude by strangers in floating castles of unimaginable wealth and menace. These possessors of wood were also bringers of death and disease. Scuffles with sailors often ended with natives gunned down on the beach.

We do not know exactly what promises had been made by the demand-   15
ing *moai* to the people, but it seems likely that the arrival of an outside world might have exposed certain illusions of the statue cult, replacing compulsive belief with equally compulsive disenchantment. Whatever its animus, the destruction on Rapa Nui raged for at least seventy years. Each foreign ship saw fewer upright statues, until not one giant was left standing on its altar. (Those standing today have been restored.) The work of demolition must have been extremely arduous for the few descendants of the builders. Its thoroughness and deliberation speak of something deeper than clan warfare: of a people angry at their reckless fathers, a revolt against the dead.

The lesson that Rapa Nui holds for our world has not gone unremarked. In the epilogue to their 1992 book, *Easter Island, Earth Island,* the archaeologists Paul Bahn and John Flenley are explicit. The islanders, they write,

> carried out for us the experiment of permitting unrestricted population growth, profligate use of resources, destruction of the environment and boundless confidence in their religion to take care of

the future. The result was an ecological disaster leading to a population crash. . . . Do we have to repeat the experiment on [a] grand scale? . . . Is the human personality always the same as that of the person, who felled the last tree?

QUESTIONS

1. This is an argument in the form of a narrative that ends with a question. Begin your analysis of this essay by summarizing the story and paraphrasing the question.
2. The article has a subtitle: "Easter Island's unlearned lesson." What lesson is this? And who has failed to learn it?
3. Make explicit the argument implied in this article. What is the conclusion? What evidence is used to support it?
4. Suppose a reader said, "Wright's article makes an argument that is not just about Easter Island and the past but about our modern world as well." What do you suppose that person means by such a statement? That is, what argument is being made about the modern world in Wright's article?
5. Do you find Wright's explanation about what happened on Easter Island persuasive? And what about what Wright calls "the lesson that Rapa Nui holds for our world" (paragraph 16)? Is that equally persuasive?
6. Are there parts of Wright's story or argument that you are reluctant to accept? Discuss the strengths and weaknesses of this argument — and of the use of stories as a form of argument in general.
7. We are asked in this piece to consider "the person who felled the last tree" (paragraph 16). Write a short piece in which you imagine that person and that event.

MAKING CONNECTIONS

Compare this essay with Jonathan Franzen's piece on smoking (p. 574), and think about not their arguments but rather their view of humanity. Do these two writers see human beings in the same way, or do they have different views of human nature? Are they optimistic about the future of the race and the planet, or pessimistic? Do you find yourself liking one writer more than the other? Explore and attempt to explain your own reaction to these essays. Try to persuade your readers that they should share your views.

SCIENCES AND TECHNOLOGIES

REFLECTING IN THE

Sciences and Technologies

A MASK ON THE FACE OF DEATH

Richard Selzer

Richard Selzer (b. 1928) is the son of a general practitioner father and a singer mother, both of whom wanted their son to follow in their footsteps. At ten he began sneaking into his father's office to look at his medical textbooks, where he discovered "the rich alliterative language of medicine — words such as cerebellum which, when said aloud, melt in the mouth and drip from the end of the tongue like chocolate." After his father's death, he decided to become a doctor and was for many years a professor of surgery at Yale Medical School. Only after working as a doctor for many decades did he begin to write. About the similarities between surgery and writing he says, "In surgery, it is the body that is being opened up and put back together. In writing it is the whole world that is taken in for repairs, then put back in working order piece by piece." His articles have appeared in Vanity Fair, Harper's, Esquire, *and the* New York Times Magazine. *His books include the short story collections* Rituals of Surgery *(1974) and* The Doctor Stories *(1998); the essay collections* Mortal Lessons *(1976),* Raising the Dead *(1994),* The Exact Location of the Soul *(2001), and* The Whistler's Room *(2004); and an autobiography,* Down from Troy *(1992). This essay appeared in* Life *in 1988.*

It is ten o'clock at night as we drive up to the Copacabana, a dilapidated brothel on the rue Dessalines in the red-light district of Port-au-Prince. My guide is a young Haitian, Jean-Bernard. Ten years before, J-B tells me, at the age of fourteen, "like every good Haitian boy" he had been brought here by his older cousins for his *rite de passage*. From the car to the entrance, we are accosted by a half dozen men and women for sex. We enter, go down a long hall that breaks upon a cavernous room with a stone floor. The cubicles of the prostitutes, I am told, are in an attached wing of the building. Save for a red-purple glow from small lights on the walls, the place is unlit. Dark shapes float by, each with a blindingly white stripe of teeth. Latin music is blaring. We take seats at the table farthest from the door. Just outside, there is the rhythmic lapping of the Caribbean Sea. About twenty men are seated at the tables or lean against the walls. Brightly dressed women, singly or in twos or threes, stroll about, now and then exchanging banter with the men. It is as though we have been deposited in act two of Bizet's *Carmen*. If this place isn't Lillas Pastia's tavern, what is it?

Within minutes, three light-skinned young women arrive at our table. They are very beautiful and young and lively. Let them be Carmen, Mercedes and Frasquita.

"I want the old one," says Frasquita, ruffling my hair. The women laugh uproariously.

"Don't bother looking any further," says Mercedes. "We are the prettiest ones."

"We only want to talk," I tell her.   5

"Aaah, aaah," she crows. "*Massissi*. You are *massissi*." It is the contemptuous Creole term for homosexual. If we want only to talk, we must be gay. Mercedes and Carmen are slender, each weighing one hundred pounds or less. Frasquita is tall and hefty. They are dressed for work: red taffeta, purple chiffon and black sequins. Among them a thousand gold bracelets and earrings multiply every speck of light. Their bare shoulders are like animated lamps gleaming in the shadowy room. Since there is as yet no business, the women agree to sit with us. J-B orders beer and cigarettes. We pay each woman $10.

"Where are you from?" I begin.

"We are Dominican."

"Do you miss your country?"

"Oh, yes, we do." Six eyes go muzzy with longing. "Our country is   10
the most beautiful in the world. No country is like the Dominican. And it doesn't stink like this one."

"Then why don't you work there? Why come to Haiti?"

"Santo Domingo has too many whores. All beautiful, like us. All light-skinned. The Haitian men like to sleep with light women."

"Why is that?"

"Because always, the whites have all the power and the money. The black men can imagine they do, too, when they have us in bed."

Eleven o'clock. I look around the room that is still sparsely peopled   15
with men.

"It isn't getting any busier," I say. Frasquita glances over her shoulder.
Her eyes drill the darkness.

"It is still early," she says.

"Could it be that the men are afraid of getting sick?" Frasquita is
offended.

"Sick! They do not get sick from us. We are healthy, strong. Every week
we go for a checkup. Besides, we know how to tell if we are getting sick."

"I mean sick with AIDS." The word sets off a hurricane of taffeta, chif-   20
fon and gold jewelry. They are all gesticulation and fury. It is Carmen who
speaks.

"AIDS!" Her lips curl about the syllable. "There is no such thing. It is a
false disease invented by the American government to take advantage of the
poor countries. The American President hates poor people, so now he makes
up AIDS to take away the little we have." The others nod vehemently.

"*Mira, mon cher.* Look, my dear," Carmen continues. "One day the
police came here. Believe me, they are worse than the *tonton macoutes* with
their submachine guns. They rounded up one hundred and five of us and
they took our blood. That was a year ago. None of us have died, you see?
We are all still here. *Mira*, we sleep with all the men and we are not sick."

"But aren't there some of you who have lost weight and have diarrhea?"

"One or two, maybe. But they don't eat. That is why they are weak."

"Only the men die," says Mercedes. "They stop eating, so they die. It is   25
hard to kill a woman."

"Do you eat well?"

"Oh, yes, don't worry, we do. We eat like poor people, but we eat."
There is a sudden scream from Frasquita. She points to a large rat that has
emerged from beneath our table.

"My God!" she exclaims. "It is big like a pig." They burst into laughter. For a moment the women fall silent. There is only the restlessness of
their many bracelets. I give them each another $10.

"Are many of the men here bisexual?"

"Too many. They do it for money. Afterward, they come to us."   30
Carmen lights a cigarette and looks down at the small lace handkerchief
she has been folding and unfolding with immense precision on the table. All
at once she turns it over as though it were the ace of spades.

"*Mira, blanc* . . . look, white man," she says in a voice suddenly full of
foreboding. Her skin seems to darken to coincide with the tone of her voice.

"*Mira*, soon many Dominican women will die in Haiti!"

"Die of what?"

She shrugs. "It is what they do to us."

"Carmen," I say, "if you knew that you had AIDS, that your blood was   35
bad, would you still sleep with men?" Abruptly, she throws back her head
and laughs. It is the same laughter with which Frasquita had greeted the rat
at our feet. She stands and the others follow.

"*Méchant*! You wicked man," she says. Then, with terrible solemnity, "You don't know anything."

"But you are killing the Haitian men," I say.

"As for that," she says, "everyone is killing everyone else." All at once, I want to know everything about these three—their childhood, their dreams, what they do in the afternoon, what they eat for lunch.

"Don't leave," I say. "Stay a little more." Again, I reach for my wallet. But they are gone, taking all the light in the room with them—Mercedes and Carmen to sit at another table where three men have been waiting. Frasquita is strolling about the room. Now and then, as if captured by the music, she breaks into a few dance steps, snapping her fingers, singing to herself.

Midnight. And the Copacabana is filling up. Now it is like any other   40
seedy nightclub where men and women go hunting. We get up to leave. In the center a couple are dancing a *méringue*. He is the most graceful dancer I have ever watched; she, the most voluptuous. Together they seem to be riding the back of the music as it gallops to a precisely sexual beat. Closer up, I see that the man is short of breath, sweating. All at once, he collapses into a chair. The woman bends over him, coaxing, teasing, but he is through. A young man with a long polished stick blocks my way.

"I come with you?" he asks. "Very good time. You say yes? Ten dollars? Five?"

I have been invited by Dr. Jean William Pape to attend the AIDS clinic of which he is the director. Nothing from the outside of the low whitewashed structure would suggest it as a medical facility. Inside, it is divided into many small cubicles and a labyrinth of corridors. At nine a.m. the hallways are already full of emaciated silent men and women, some sitting on the few benches, the rest leaning against the walls. The only sounds are subdued moans of discomfort interspersed with coughs. How they eat us with their eyes as we pass.

The room where Pape and I work is perhaps ten feet by ten. It contains a desk, two chairs and a narrow wooden table that is covered with a sheet that will not be changed during the day. The patients are called in one at a time, asked how they feel and whether there is any change in their symptoms, then examined on the table. If the patient is new to the clinic, he or she is questioned about sexual activities.

A twenty-seven-year-old man whose given name is Miracle enters. He is wobbly, panting, like a groggy boxer who has let down his arms and is waiting for the last punch. He is neatly dressed and wears, despite the heat, a heavy woolen cap. When he removes it, I see that his hair is thin, dull reddish and straight. It is one of the signs of AIDS in Haiti, Pape tells me. The man's skin is covered with a dry itchy rash. Throughout the interview and examination he scratches himself slowly, absentmindedly. The rash is called prurigo. It is another symptom of AIDS in Haiti. This man has had diarrhea for six months. The laboratory reports that the diarrhea is due to an organism called cryptosporidium, for which there is no treatment. The telltale rattling of the tuberculous moisture in his chest is audible without a stethoscope. He is like a leaky cistern that bubbles and froths. And, clearly, exhausted.

"Where do you live?" I ask.   45

"Kenscoff." A village in the hills above Port-au-Prince.

"How did you come here today?"

"I came on the *tap-tap*." It is the name given to the small buses that swarm the city, each one extravagantly decorated with religious slogans, icons, flowers, animals, all painted in psychedelic colors. I have never seen a *tap-tap* that was not covered with passengers as well, riding outside and hanging on. The vehicles are little masterpieces of contagion, if not of AIDS then of the multitude of germs which Haitian flesh is heir to. Miracle is given a prescription for a supply of Sera, which is something like Gatorade, and told to return in a month.

"*Mangé kou bêf*," says the doctor in farewell. "Eat like an ox." What can he mean? The man has no food or money to buy any. Even had he food, he has not the appetite to eat or the ability to retain it. To each departing patient the doctor will say the same words—"*Mangé kou bêf*." I see that it is his way of offering a hopeful goodbye.

"Will he live until his next appointment?" I ask.   50

"No." Miracle leaves to catch the *tap-tap* for Kenscoff.

Next is a woman of twenty-six who enters holding her right hand to her forehead in a kind of permanent salute. In fact, she is shielding her eye from view. This is her third visit to the clinic. I see that she is still quite well nourished.

"Now, you'll see something beautiful, tremendous," the doctor says. Once seated upon the table, she is told to lower her hand. When she does, I see that her right eye and its eyelid are replaced by a huge fungating ulcerated tumor, a side product of her AIDS. As she turns her head, the cluster of lymph glands in her neck to which the tumor has spread is thrown into relief. Two years ago she received a blood transfusion at a time when the country's main blood bank was grossly contaminated with AIDS. It has since been closed down. The only blood available in Haiti is a small supply procured from the Red Cross.

"Can you give me medicine?" the woman wails.

"No."   55

"Can you cut it away?"

"No."

"Is there radiation therapy?" I ask.

"No."

"Chemotherapy?" The doctor looks at me in what some might call   60
weary amusement. I see that there is nothing to do. She has come here because there is nowhere else to go.

"What will she do?"

"Tomorrow or the next day or the day after that she will climb up into the mountains to seek relief from the *houngan*, the voodoo priest, just as her slave ancestors did two hundred years ago."

Then comes a frail man in his thirties, with a strangely spiritualized face, like a child's. Pus runs from one ear onto his cheek, where it has dried and caked. He has trouble remembering, he tells us. In fact, he seems confused. It is from toxoplasmosis of the brain, an effect of his AIDS. This man is bisexual. Two years ago he engaged in oral sex with foreign men for money. As I palpate the swollen glands of his neck, a mosquito flies between our faces. I swat at it, miss. Just before coming to Haiti I had read that the AIDS virus had been isolated from a certain mosquito. The doctor senses my thought.

"Not to worry," he says. "So far as we know there has never been a case transmitted by insects."

"Yes," I say. "I see."   65

And so it goes until the last, the thirty-sixth AIDS patient has been seen. At the end of the day I am invited to wash my hands before leaving. I go down a long hall to a sink. I turn on the faucets but there is no water.

"But what about *you*?" I ask the doctor. "You are at great personal risk here — the tuberculosis, the other infections, no water to wash . . ." He shrugs, smiles faintly and lifts his hands palm upward.

We are driving up a serpiginous steep road into the barren mountains above Port-au-Prince. Even in the bright sunshine the countryside has the bloodless color of exhaustion and indifference. Our destination is the Baptist Mission Hospital, where many cases of AIDS have been reported. Along the road there are slow straggles of schoolchildren in blue uniforms who stretch out their hands as we pass and call out, "Give me something." Already a crowd of outpatients has gathered at the entrance to the mission compound. A tour of the premises reveals that in contrast to the aridity outside the gates, this is an enclave of productivity, lush with fruit trees and poinsettia.

The hospital is clean and smells of creosote. Of the forty beds, less than a third are occupied. In one male ward of twelve beds, there are two patients. The chief physician tells us that last year he saw ten cases of AIDS each week. Lately the number has decreased to four or five.

"Why is that?" we want to know.   70

"Because we do not admit them to the hospital, so they have learned not to come here."

"Why don't you admit them?"

"Because we would have nothing but AIDS here then. So we send them away."

"But I see that you have very few patients in bed."

"That is also true."   75

"Where do the AIDS patients go?"

"Some go to the clinic in Port-au-Prince or the general hospital in the city. Others go home to die or to the voodoo priest."

"Do the people with AIDS know what they have before they come here?"

"Oh, yes, they know very well, and they know there is nothing to be done for them."

Outside, the crowd of people is dispersing toward the gate. The clinic 80
has been canceled for the day. No one knows why. We are conducted to the
office of the reigning American pastor. He is a tall, handsome Midwesterner
with an ecclesiastical smile.

"It is voodoo that is the devil here." He warms to his subject. "It is a
demonic religion, a cancer on Haiti. Voodoo is worse than AIDS. And it is
one of the reasons for the epidemic. Did you know that in order for a man
to become a *houngan* he must perform anal sodomy on another man? No,
of course you didn't. And it doesn't stop there. The *houngans* tell the men
that in order to appease the spirits they too must do the same thing. So you
have ritualized homosexuality. That's what is spreading the AIDS." The
pastor tells us of a nun who witnessed two acts of sodomy in a provincial
hospital where she came upon a man sexually assaulting a houseboy and
another man mounting a male patient in his bed.

"Fornication," he says. "It is Sodom and Gomorrah all over again, so
what can you expect from these people?" Outside his office we are shown a
cage of terrified, cowering monkeys to whom he coos affectionately. It is
clear that he loves them. At the car, we shake hands.

"By the way," the pastor says, "what is your religion? Perhaps I am a
kinsman?"

"While I am in Haiti," I tell him, "it will be voodoo or it will be nothing at all."

Abruptly, the smile breaks. It is as though a crack had suddenly ap- 85
peared in the face of an idol.

From the mission we go to the general hospital. In the heart of Port-au-
Prince, it is the exact antithesis of the immaculate facility we have just
left — filthy, crowded, hectic and staffed entirely by young interns and residents. Though it is associated with a medical school, I do not see any members
of the faculty. We are shown around by Jocelyne, a young intern in a scrub
suit. Each bed in three large wards is occupied. On the floor about the beds,
hunkered in the posture of the innocent poor, are family members of the patients. In the corridor that constitutes the emergency room, someone lies on a
stretcher receiving an intravenous infusion. She is hardly more than a cadaver.

"Where are the doctors in charge?" I ask Jocelyne. She looks at me
questioningly.

"We are in charge."

"I mean your teachers, the faculty."

"They do not come here." 90

"What is wrong with that woman?"

"She has had diarrhea for three months. Now she is dehydrated." I ask
the woman to open her mouth. Her throat is covered with the white
plaques of thrush, a fungus infection associated with AIDS.

"How many AIDS patients do you see here?"

"Three or four a day. We send them home. Sometimes the families
abandon them, then we must admit them to the hospital. Every day, then, a

relative comes to see if the patient has died. They want to take the body. That is important to them. But they know very well that AIDS is contagious and they are afraid to keep them at home. Even so, once or twice a week the truck comes to take away the bodies. Many are children. They are buried in mass graves."

"Where do the wealthy patients go?"   95

"There is a private hospital called Canapé Vert. Or else they go to Miami. Most of them, rich and poor, do not go to the hospital. Most are never diagnosed."

"How do you know these people have AIDS?"

"We don't know sometimes. The blood test is inaccurate. There are many false positives and false negatives. Fifteen percent of those with the disease have negative blood tests. We go by their infections—tuberculosis, diarrhea, fungi, herpes, skin rashes. It is not hard to tell."

"Do they know what they have?"

"Yes. They understand at once and they are prepared to die."   100

"Do the patients know how AIDS is transmitted?"

"They know, but they do not like to talk about it. It is taboo. Their memories do not seem to reach back to the true origins of their disaster. It is understandable, is it not?"

"Whatever you write, don't hurt us any more than we have already been hurt." It is a young Haitian journalist with whom I am drinking a rum punch. He means that any further linkage of AIDS and Haiti in the media would complete the economic destruction of the country. The damage was done early in the epidemic when the Centers for Disease Control in Atlanta added Haitians to the three other high-risk groups—hemophiliacs, intravenous drug users and homosexual and bisexual men. In fact, Haitians are no more susceptible to AIDS than anyone else. Although the CDC removed Haitians from special scrutiny in 1985, the lucrative tourism on which so much of the country's economy was based was crippled. Along with tourism went much of the foreign business investment. Worst of all was the injury to the national pride. Suddenly Haiti was indicted as the source of AIDS in the western hemisphere.

What caused the misunderstanding was the discovery of a large number of Haitian men living in Miami with AIDS antibodies in their blood. They denied absolutely they were homosexuals. But the CDC investigators did not know that homosexuality is the strongest taboo in Haiti and that no man would ever admit to it. Bisexuality, however, is not uncommon. Many married men and heterosexually oriented males will occasionally seek out other men for sex. Further, many, if not most, Haitian men visit female prostitutes from time to time. It is not difficult to see that once the virus was set loose in Haiti, the spread would be swift through both genders.

Exactly how the virus of AIDS arrived is not known. Could it have been   105
brought home by the Cuban soldiers stationed in Angola and thence to Haiti, about fifty miles away? Could it have been passed on by the thousands of

Haitians living in exile in Zaire, who later returned home or immigrated to the United States? Could it have come from the American and Canadian homosexual tourists, and, yes, even some U.S. diplomats who have traveled to the island to have sex with impoverished Haitian men all too willing to sell themselves to feed their families? Throughout the international gay community Haiti was known as a good place to go for sex.

On a private tip from an official at the Ministry of Tourism, J-B and I drive to a town some fifty miles from Port-au-Prince. The hotel is owned by two Frenchmen who are out of the country, one of the staff tells us. He is a man of about thirty and clearly he is desperately ill. Tottering, short of breath, he shows us about the empty hotel. The furnishings are opulent and extreme — tiger skins on the wall, a live leopard in the garden, a bedroom containing a giant bathtub with gold faucets. Is it the heat of the day or the heat of my imagination that makes these walls echo with the painful cries of pederasty?

The hotel where we are staying is in Pétionville, the fashionable suburb of Port-au-Prince. It is the height of the season but there are no tourists, only a dozen or so French and American businessmen. The swimming pool is used once or twice a day by a single person. Otherwise, the water remains undisturbed until dusk, when the fruit bats come down to drink in midswoop. The hotel keeper is an American. He is eager to set me straight on Haiti.

"What did and should attract foreign investment is a combination of reliable weather, an honest and friendly populace, low wages and multilingual managers."

"What spoiled it?"

"Political instability and a bad American press about AIDS." He pauses, 110 then adds: "To which I hope you won't be contributing."

"What about just telling the truth?" I suggest.

"Look," he says, "there is no more danger of catching AIDS in Haiti than in New York or Santo Domingo. It is not where you are but what you do that counts." Agreeing, I ask if he had any idea that much of the tourism in Haiti during the past few decades was based on sex.

"No idea whatsoever. It was only recently that we discovered that that was the case."

"How is it that you hoteliers, restaurant owners and the Ministry of Tourism did not know what *tout*[1] Haiti knew?"

"Look. All I know is that this is a middle-class, family-oriented hotel. 115 We don't allow guests to bring women, or for that matter men, into their rooms. If they did, we'd ask them to leave immediately."

At five a.m. the next day the telephone rings in my room. A Creole-accented male voice.

---

[1] *tout*: All. [Eds.]

"Is the lady still with you, sir?"

"There is no lady here."

"In your room, sir, the lady I allowed to go up with a package?"

"There is no lady here, I tell you."   120

At seven a.m. I stop at the front desk. The clerk is a young man.

"Was it you who called my room at five o'clock?"

"Sorry," he says with a smile. "It was a mistake, sir. I meant to ring the room next door to yours." Still smiling, he holds up his shushing finger.

Next to Dr. Pape, director of the AIDS clinic, Bernard Liautaud, a dermatologist, is the most knowledgeable Haitian physician on the subject of the epidemic. Together, the two men have published a dozen articles on AIDS in international medical journals. In our meeting they present me with statistics:

- There are more than one thousand documented cases of AIDS in Haiti, and as many as one hundred thousand carriers of the virus.

- Eighty-seven percent of AIDS is now transmitted heterosexually. While it is true that the virus was introduced via the bisexual community, that route has decreased to 10 percent or less.

- Sixty percent of the wives or husbands of AIDS patients tested positive for the antibody.

- Fifty percent of the prostitutes tested in the Port-au-Prince area are infected.

- Eighty percent of the men with AIDS have had contact with prostitutes.

- The projected number of active cases in four years is ten thousand. (Since my last visit, the Haitian Medical Association broke its silence on the epidemic by warning that one million of the country's six million people could be carriers by 1992.)

The two doctors have more to tell. "The crossing over of the plague   125
from the homosexual to the heterosexual community will follow in the United States within two years. This, despite the hesitation to say so by those who fear to sow panic among your population. In Haiti, because bisexuality is more common, there was an early crossover into the general population. The trend, inevitably, is the same in the two countries."

"What is there to do, then?"

"Only education, just as in America. But here the Haitians reject the use of condoms. Only the men who are too sick to have sex are celibate."

"What is to be the end of it?"

"When enough heterosexuals of the middle and upper classes die, perhaps there will be the panic necessary for the people to change their sexual lifestyles."

This evening I leave Haiti. For two weeks I have fastened myself to this   130
lovely fragile land like an ear pressed to the ground. It is a country to break

a traveler's heart. It occurs to me that I have not seen a single jogger. Such a public expenditure of energy while everywhere else strength is ebbing — it would be obscene. In my final hours, I go to the Cathédrale of Sainte Trinité, the inner walls of which are covered with murals by Haiti's most renowned artists. Here are all the familiar Bible stories depicted in naïveté and piety, and all in such an exuberance of color as to tax the capacity of the retina to receive it, as though all the vitality of Haiti had been turned to paint and brushed upon these walls. How to explain this efflorescence at a time when all else is lassitude and inertia? Perhaps one day the plague will be rendered in poetry, music, painting, but not now. Not now.

Questions

1. Summarize the scene at the Copacabana. Which details are memorable? Why does Selzer spend so much time with Carmen, Mercedes, and Frasquita? Why are their attitudes toward AIDS so important?
2. Selzer writes at great length about his visit to the AIDS clinic directed by Dr. Jean William Pape. What does Selzer learn from observing patients at this clinic? What does Selzer learn about AIDS from the doctor at work?
3. A young Haitian journalist tells Selzer, "Whatever you write, don't hurt us any more than we have already been hurt" (paragraph 103). What is the significance of this request? After reading Selzer's essay, do you think Selzer has honored this request?
4. In the final paragraph of the essay, Selzer writes, "For two weeks I have fastened myself to this lovely fragile land like an ear pressed to the ground. It is a country to break a traveler's heart." What has Selzer learned about the politics of AIDS from his journey to Haiti?
5. Look at the various scenes and vignettes Selzer offers his readers. How does he connect these different scenes? How does this structure succeed in presenting his reflections?
6. What have you learned about the politics of AIDS from reading Selzer's essay? Write an essay reflecting on Selzer's essay.
7. Selzer offers his reflections as a way of justifying his strong feelings about AIDS. In other words, his reflections become a kind of argument. How would you make a more objective argument for his position?

Making Connections

Selzer and Serge Schmemann (p. 415) both write as spectators of, rather than as participants in, the events they report. Compare and contrast the ways they develop their reflections within such a perspective.

CLOSE ENCOUNTER
OF THE HUMAN KIND

Abraham Verghese

*Abraham Verghese was born in 1955 in Addis Ababa, Ethiopia,
the son of two physicists who were immigrants from India. He
attended medical school in Ethiopia and worked in hospitals in
the United States before completing his medical degree at Madras
University. In 1991, he received an M.F.A. from the University of
Iowa. His first book,* My Own Country: A Doctor's Story *(1994),
is a memoir about treating AIDS in Johnson City, Tennessee. The
book was a finalist for the National Book Critics Circle Award in
nonfiction, won the Lambda Literary Award for nonfiction, was
named one of the five best books of 1994 by* Time *magazine, and
was made into a Showtime original movie. In his second book,*
The Tennis Partner: A Story of Friendship and Loss *(1998), Verghese wrote about coming to terms with love and loss through the
death of his best friend and tennis partner. Verghese has contributed
many articles to medical journals and has published stories, articles,
and reviews in magazines and newspapers, including the* North
American Review, Sports Illustrated, The New Yorker, Granta,
and MD. *Verghese has noted of his two professions, "Writing has
many similarities to the practice of internal medicine. Both require
astute observation and a fondness for detail." He has also said, "I
suspect that the challenge for doctors in the next century will be to
rediscover why the profession was once called the 'ministry of healing.'. . . People who visit doctors are looking for more than a cure,
they are looking for 'healing' as well. To understand the distinction
between 'healing' and 'curing,' let me use an analogy: If you have
ever been robbed, and if the cops came back an hour later with
all the stuff taken from your home, you would be 'cured' but not
'healed' — your sense of spiritual violation would still remain. In
the same way, all illnesses have these two components: a physical
violation and a spiritual violation." The following article appeared
in the* New York Times Magazine *in 2005.*

With the first bus loads of Katrina refugees about to arrive in San Antonio, the call went out for physician volunteers, and I signed up for the
2 a.m. to 8 a.m. shift. On the way, riding down dark, deserted streets, I

thought of driving in for night shifts in the I.C.U. as an intern many years ago, and how I would try to steel myself, as if putting on armor.

Within a massive structure at Kelly U.S.A. (formerly Kelly Air Force Base), a brightly lighted processing area led to office cubicles, where after registering, new arrivals with medical needs came to see us. My first patient sat before me, haggard, pointing to what ailed her, as if speech no longer served her. I peeled her shoes from swollen feet, trying not to remove skin in the process. Cuts from submerged objects and immersion in standing water had caused the swelling, as well as infection of both feet. An antibiotic, a pair of slip-ons from the roomful of donated clothing, and a night with her feet elevated — that would help.

The ailments common among the refugees included diarrhea, bronchitis, sore throat, and voices hoarse or lost. And stress beyond belief. People didn't have their medications, and blood sugars and blood pressures were out of control.

I prayed, as I wrote prescriptions, that their memories of particular pills were accurate. For a man on methadone maintenance who was now cramping and sweating, I prescribed codeine to hold him. Another man, clutching a gym bag as if I might snatch it from him, admitted when I gently probed that he was hearing voices again. We sat together looking through the Physicians' Desk Reference. "That's it," he said, recognizing the pill he hadn't taken since the storm hit.

Hesitantly, I asked each patient, "Where did you spend the last five days?" I wanted to reconcile the person in front of me with the terrible locales on television. But as the night wore on, I understood that they *needed* me to ask; to not ask was to not honor their ordeal. Hard men wiped at their eyes and became animated in the telling. The first woman, the one who seemed mute from stress, began a recitation in a courtroom voice, as if preparing for future testimony.

It reminded me of my previous work in field clinics in India and Ethiopia, where, with so few medical resources at hand, the careful listening, the thorough exam, the laying of hands was the therapy. And I felt the same helplessness, knowing that the illness here was inextricably linked to the bigger problem of homelessness, disenfranchisement, and despair.

Near the end of my shift, a new group of patients arrived. A man in his 70's with gray hair and beard came in looking fit and vigorous. One eye was milky white and sightless, but the glint in his good eye was enough for two. His worldly belongings were in a garbage bag, but his manner was dignified.

He was out of medicine, and his blood sugar and blood pressure were high. He couldn't pay for his medication, so his doctor always gave him samples: "Whatever he have. Whatever he have." He had kept his shoes on for five days, he said, removing the battered, pickled, but elegant pair, a cross between bowling shoes and dancing shoes. His toes were carved ebony, the tendons on the back like cables, the joints gnarled but sturdy. All night I had seen many feet; in his bare feet I read resilience.

He told me that for two nights after the floods, he had perched on a ledge so narrow that his legs dangled in the water. At one point, he said, he saw Air Force One fly over, and his hopes soared. "I waited, I waited," he said, but no help came. Finally a boat got him to a packed bridge. There, again, he waited. He shook his head in disbelief, smiling though. "Doc, they treat refugees in other countries better than they treated us."

"I'm so sorry," I said. "So sorry."   10

He looked at me long and hard, cocking his head as if weighing my words, which sounded so weak, so inadequate. He rose, holding out his hand, his posture firm as he shouldered his garbage bag. "Thank you. Doc. I needed to hear that. All they got to say is sorry. All they got to say is sorry."

I was still troubled by him when I left, even though he seemed the hardiest of all. This encounter between two Americans, between doctor and patient, had been carried to all the fullness that was permitted, and yet it was incomplete, as if he had, as a result of this experience, set in place some new barriers that neither I nor anyone else would ever cross.

Driving home, I remembered my own metaphor of strapping on armor for the night shift. The years have shown that there is no armor. There never was. The willingness to be wounded may be all we have to offer.

QUESTIONS

1. The bulk of this piece is devoted to reporting, but, as in many such essays, it moves to reflection at a certain point. Exactly where is that move made in this essay?

2. When the reflection comes, it is more complex than the reporting — as is often the case. Try to put the gist of that reflection in your own words.

3. Does the reflection make sense to you? Do you agree with it? Do you find it comforting, or disturbing, or what?

4. The reporting section of this essay can be divided into a number of sections. Make an outline of them. At a certain point, the author is reminded of other experiences. Why are those particular connections made in this essay? That is, what do India and Ethiopia have to do with San Antonio and New Orleans?

5. There is one main anecdote in the reporting part of this piece. Summarize it, and analyze the result.

6. Have you had any experience of helping other people when they were in need? If so, report on it, and add your reflections on the meaning of your experience.

7. Take your response to question 3, and shape it into an essay in which you reflect on your response and on Verghese's essay as a whole.

MAKING CONNECTIONS

Examine two other pieces that report on disasters, Serge Schmemann's "U.S. Attacked" (p. 415), on the events of 9/11, and Peter Applebome, Christopher Drew, Jere Longman, and Andrew Revkin's "A Delicate Balance" (p. 638), also on Hurricane Katrina. What does the personal style of Verghese's piece allow him to do that the impersonal style of the other two pieces do not allow? Be sure to point to specific places in the texts where you can characterize the style. Verghese's piece appeared in a magazine, while the other two appeared in newspapers. How does that help account for the differences in the way the pieces are written? Under what circumstances might one style be more appropriate than the other? More effective? More accurate?

CAN WE KNOW THE UNIVERSE?
Reflections on a Grain of Salt

Carl Sagan

Carl Sagan (1934–1996) was renowned both as a scientist and as a writer. For his work with the National Aeronautics and Space Administration's Mariner, Viking, *and* Voyager *expeditions, he was awarded NASA's Medals for Exceptional Scientific Achievement and for Distinguished Public Service. Sagan produced the* Cosmos *television series for public television and received the Peabody Award in 1981. He received the Pulitzer Prize in literature, for his book* The Dragons of Eden *(1977). Among his later works are* Comet *(1985),* Contact *(1985, a novel with Ann Druyan),* Shadows of Forgotten Ancestors *(1992), and* Billions and Billions: Thoughts on Life and Death at the Brink of the Millennium *(1997). The following selection is from* Broca's Brain: Reflections on the Romance of Science *(1979).*

> Nothing is rich but the inexhaustible wealth
> of nature. She shows us only surfaces,
> but she is a million fathoms deep.
> —RALPH WALDO EMERSON

Science is a way of thinking much more than it is a body of knowledge. Its goal is to find out how the world works, to seek what regularities there may be, to penetrate to the connections of things — from subnuclear particles, which may be the constituents of all matter, to living organisms, the human social community, and thence to the cosmos as a whole. Our intuition is by no means an infallible guide. Our perceptions may be distorted by training and prejudice or merely because of the limitations of our sense organs, which, of course, perceive directly but a small fraction of the phenomena of the world. Even so straightforward a question as whether in the absence of friction a pound of lead falls faster than a gram of fluff was answered incorrectly by Aristotle and almost everyone else before the time of Galileo. Science is based on experiment, on a willingness to challenge old dogma, on an openness to see the universe as it really is. Accordingly, science sometimes requires courage — at the very least the courage to question the conventional wisdom.

Beyond this the main trick of science is to *really* think of something: the shape of clouds and their occasional sharp bottom edges at the same altitude everywhere in the sky; the formation of a dewdrop on a leaf; the origin of a name or a word — Shakespeare, say, or "philanthropic"; the reason for human social customs — the incest taboo, for example; how it is that a lens in sunlight can make paper burn; how a "walking stick" got to look so much like a twig; why the Moon seems to follow us as we walk; what prevents us from digging a hole down to the center of the Earth; what the definition is of "down" on a spherical Earth; how it is possible for the body to convert yesterday's lunch into today's muscle and sinew; or how far is up — does the universe go on forever, or if it does not, is there any meaning to the question of what lies on the other side? Some of these questions are pretty easy. Others, especially the last, are mysteries to which no one even today knows the answer. They are natural questions to ask. Every culture has posed such questions in one way or another. Almost always the proposed answers are in the nature of "Just So Stories," attempted explanations divorced from experiment, or even from careful comparative observations.

But the scientific cast of mind examines the world critically as if many alternative worlds might exist, as if other things might be here which are not. Then we are forced to ask why what we see is present and not something else. Why are the Sun and the Moon and the planets spheres? Why not pyramids, or cubes, or dodecahedra? Why not irregular, jumbly shapes? Why so symmetrical, worlds? If you spend any time spinning hypotheses, checking to see whether they make sense, whether they conform to what else we know, thinking of tests you can pose to substantiate or deflate your hypotheses, you will find yourself doing science. And as you come to practice this habit of thought more and more you will get better and better at it. To penetrate into the heart of the thing — even a little thing, a blade of grass, as Walt Whitman said — is to experience a kind of exhilaration that, it may be, only human beings of all the beings on this planet can feel. We are an intelligent species and the use of our intelligence quite properly gives us pleasure. In this respect the brain is like a muscle. When we think well, we feel good. Understanding is a kind of ecstasy.

But to what extent can we *really* know the universe around us? Sometimes this question is posed by people who hope the answer will be in the negative, who are fearful of a universe in which everything might one day be known. And sometimes we hear pronouncements from scientists who confidently state that everything worth knowing will soon be known — or even is already known — and who paint pictures of a Dionysian or Polynesian age in which the zest for intellectual discovery has withered, to be replaced by a kind of subdued languor, the lotus eaters drinking fermented coconut milk or some other mild hallucinogen. In addition to maligning both the Polynesians, who were intrepid explorers (and whose brief respite in paradise is now sadly ending), as well as the inducements to intellectual discovery provided by some hallucinogens, this contention turns out to be trivially mistaken.

Let us approach a much more modest question: not whether we can   5
know the universe or the Milky Way Galaxy or a star or a world. Can we

know, ultimately and in detail, a grain of salt? Consider one microgram of table salt, a speck just barely large enough for someone with keen eyesight to make out without a microscope. In that grain of salt there are about 10^{16} sodium and chlorine atoms. This is a 1 followed by 16 zeros, 10 million billion atoms. If we wish to know a grain of salt, we must know at least the three-dimensional positions of each of these atoms. (In fact, there is much more to be known — for example, the nature of the forces between the atoms — but we are making only a modest calculation.) Now, is this number more or less than the number of things which the brain can know?

How much *can* the brain know? There are perhaps 10^{11} neurons in the brain, the circuit elements and switches that are responsible in their electrical and chemical activity for the functioning of our minds. A typical brain neuron has perhaps a thousand little wires, called dendrites, which connect it with its fellows. If, as seems likely, every bit of information in the brain corresponds to one of these connections, the total number of things knowable by the brain is no more than 10^{14}, one hundred trillion. But this number is only one percent of the number of atoms in our speck of salt.

So in this sense the universe is intractable, astonishingly immune to any human attempt at full knowledge. We cannot on this level understand a grain of salt, much less the universe.

But let us look more deeply at our microgram of salt. Salt happens to be a crystal in which, except for defects in the structure of the crystal lattice, the position of every sodium and chlorine atom is predetermined. If we could shrink ourselves into this crystalline world, we could see rank upon rank of atoms in an ordered array, a regularly alternating structure — sodium, chlorine, sodium, chlorine, specifying the sheet of atoms we are standing on and all the sheets above us and below us. An absolutely pure crystal of salt could have the position of every atom specified by something like 10 bits of information.[1] This would not strain the information-carrying capacity of the brain.

If the universe had natural laws that governed its behavior to the same degree of regularity that determines a crystal of salt, then, of course, the universe would be knowable. Even if there were many such laws, each of considerable complexity, human beings might have the capacity to understand them all. Even if such knowledge exceeded the information-carrying capacity of the brain, we might store the additional information outside our bodies — in books, for example, or in computer memories — and still, in some sense, know the universe.

---

[1]Chlorine is a deadly poison gas employed on European battlefields in World War I. Sodium is a corrosive metal which burns upon contact with water. Together they make a placid and unpoisonous material, table salt. Why each of these substances has the properties it does is a subject called chemistry, which requires more than 10 bits of information to understand.

Human beings are, understandably, highly motivated to find regulari- 10
ties, natural laws. The search for rules, the only possible way to understand
such a vast and complex universe, is called science. The universe forces
those who live in it to understand it. Those creatures who find everyday experience a muddled jumble of events with no predictability, no regularity,
are in grave peril. The universe belongs to those who, at least to some degree, have figured it out.

It is an astonishing fact that there *are* laws of nature, rules that summarize conveniently — not just qualitatively but quantitatively — how the
world works. We might imagine a universe in which there are no such laws,
in which the 10^{80} elementary particles that make up a universe like our own
behave with utter and uncompromising abandon. To understand such a
universe we would need a brain at least as massive as the universe. It seems
unlikely that such a universe could have life and intelligence, because beings
and brains require some degree of internal stability and order. But even if in
a much more random universe there were such beings with an intelligence
much greater than our own, there could not be much knowledge, passion,
or joy.

Fortunately for us, we live in a universe that has at least important
parts that are knowable. Our common-sense experience and our evolutionary history have prepared us to understand something of the workaday
world. When we go into other realms, however, common sense and ordinary intuition turn out to be highly unreliable guides. It is stunning that as
we go close to the speed of light our mass increases indefinitely, we shrink
toward zero thickness in the direction of motion, and time for us comes as
near to stopping as we would like. Many people think that this is silly, and
every week or two I get a letter from someone who complains to me about
it. But it is a virtually certain consequence not just of experiment but also of
Albert Einstein's brilliant analysis of space and time called the Special Theory of Relativity. It does not matter that these effects seem unreasonable to
us. We are not in the habit of traveling close to the speed of light. The testimony of our common sense is suspect at high velocities.

Or consider an isolated molecule composed of two atoms shaped something like a dumbbell — a molecule of salt, it might be. Such a molecule ro-
tates about an axis through the line connecting the two atoms. But in the
world of quantum mechanics, the realm of the very small, not all orienta-
tions of our dumbbell molecule are possible. It might be that the molecule
could be oriented in a horizontal position, say, or in a vertical position, but
not at many angles in between. Some rotational positions are forbidden.
Forbidden by what? By the laws of nature. The universe is built in such a
way as to limit, or quantize, rotation. We do not experience this directly in
everyday life; we would find it startling as well as awkward in sitting-up exercises, to find arms outstretched from the sides or pointed up to the skies
permitted but many intermediate positions forbidden. We do not live in the
world of the small, on the scale of 10^{-13} centimeters, in the realm where

there are twelve zeros between the decimal place and the one. Our common-sense intuitions do not count. What does count is experiment — in this case observations from the far infrared spectra of molecules. They show molecular rotation to be quantized.

The idea that the world places restrictions on what humans might do is frustrating. Why *shouldn't* we be able to have intermediate rotational positions? Why *can't* we travel faster than the speed of light? But so far as we can tell, this is the way the universe is constructed. Such prohibitions not only press us toward a little humility; they also make the world more knowable. Every restriction corresponds to a law of nature, a regularization of the universe. The more restrictions there are on what matter and energy can do, the more knowledge human beings can attain. Whether in some sense the universe is ultimately knowable depends not only on how many natural laws there are that encompass widely divergent phenomena, but also on whether we have the openness and the intellectual capacity to understand such laws. Our formulations of the regularities of nature are surely dependent on how the brain is built, but also, and to a significant degree, on how the universe is built.

For myself, I like a universe that includes much that is unknown and,   15
at the same time, much that is knowable. A universe in which everything is known would be static and dull, as boring as the heaven of some weak-minded theologians. A universe that is unknowable is no fit place for a thinking being. The ideal universe for us is one very much like the universe we inhabit. And I would guess that this is not really much of a coincidence.

QUESTIONS

1. How are *science* and *scientific thinking* defined in the first three paragraphs? What is Sagan's purpose in defining these terms? What does this tell you about Sagan's conception of his audience?
2. Sagan's mode of reflection might be considered less personal than others in this section in that he is reflecting on an idea rather than on an event in his life. How does Sagan keep his tone from becoming abstract? What elements of the personal are present in this essay?
3. Sagan cites scientists who believe that "everything worth knowing will soon be known" (paragraph 4). How does the evidence in this essay challenge that assumption?
4. We might consider paragraph 15 to be Sagan's most personal statement in his reflections on the universe: he likes "a universe that includes much that is unknown and, at the same time, much that is knowable." Why is this balance important to Sagan? Do you agree with his closing statements? Explain.
5. Consider the statement, "The more restrictions there are on what matter and energy can do, the more knowledge human beings can attain" (para-

graph 14). Describe an example in your own experience (or another's) when you learned that rules or laws were helpful in ensuring your personal freedom.

6. In paragraph 3, Sagan concludes, "Understanding is a kind of ecstasy." Describe a time in your life when you understood something for the first time — when, as they say, the light went on in your head, shining on a difficult problem and bringing about a realization. Could your feelings at the time be considered ecstatic, or did you experience some other emotion?

7. What sort of universe would you consider ideal? What would you like to know about the universe that is now unknown to you? Explain.

MAKING CONNECTIONS

1. A number of the writers in the "Reflecting" sections offer their reflections to justify a belief or a strong feeling about a subject. In other words, their reflections become a kind of argument. Lucy Grealy (p. 62), Frederick Douglass (p. 74), Martin Luther King Jr. (p. 346), and George Orwell (p. 354) come to mind as well as Sagan. How convincing is the argument in each case? How has the writer used purely personal responses to make a persuasive case? How would you go about developing a more objective argument for one of their positions? What would be the difference in effect?

2. Does Sagan's concern for "passion" and "joy" (paragraph 11) surprise you? Where else, especially in the writings by scientists in this section, do you find evidence of the same concerns? Citing several examples from essayists you have read, write an essay on the role of passion and joy in the work of scientists and other writers.

MEMORIA EX MACHINA

Marshall Jon Fisher

Marshall Jon Fisher was born in 1963 in Ithaca, New York, and grew up in Miami. He graduated from Brandeis University in 1985 and worked as a sportswriter in Miami and a tennis pro in Munich before moving to New York City, where he received an M.A. in English at City College. Since 1990, he has been a freelance writer and editor. He has written on a wide range of topics for The Atlantic Monthly; *his work has also appeared in* Discover, DoubleTake, *other magazines, and* The Best American Essays 2003. *His book* The Ozone Layer *(1992) was selected by the New York Public Library as one of the best books for teenagers of 1993. With his father, David E. Fisher, he has written* Tube: The Invention of Television *(1996),* Strangers in the Night: A Brief History of Life on Other Worlds *(1998), which was selected by the New York Public Library as one of the 25 Books to Remember of 1998, and* Mysteries of Lost Empires *(2000). Fisher lives in the Berkshires of western Massachusetts. The following piece appeared in* DoubleTake *in 2002.*

It was a silver Seiko watch with a clasp that folded like a map and snapped shut. The stainless-steel casing was a three-dimensional octagon with distinct edges, too thick and ponderous, it seems now, for a thirteen-year-old. Four hands — hour, minute, second, and alarm — swept around a numberless metallic-blue face. I received it for my bar mitzvah, and a quarter-century later I can, in my mind, fingernail the button out just one click to set the alarm hand — not too far, or I'll change the time — and pull out the other, obliquely positioned, button to turn on the alarm. When the hour hand finally overcame the angle between itself and the alarm hand, a soft, deep mechanical buzzing would ensue — a pleasant hum long since obliterated by hordes of digital beeps. I haven't seen my watch for twenty years, but I can hear that buzz, feel its vibrations in my wrist.

What I cannot remember is the timbre or inflection of my sister's voice from that time. She flitted in and out of view, appearing between high school and club meetings and dates. I can't even recall her at the dinner table with my parents, my brother, and me, though she must have been there most of the time.

After she and my brother left for college, and I was in high school, I spent countless hours lying in bed listening to my clock radio. I can still see the burnt-amber numerals and the way their discrete line segments would metamorphose each minute. The tuning knob-on the right-hand side, and the way that it resisted torque as you approached either end of the dial, remain as clear to me as the remote controls of my new DVD player. I was listening in the dark to a Monday-night Miami Dolphins/New England Patriots game when the radio broadcast broke to Howard Cosell announcing that John Lennon had been shot. I heard Bruce Springsteen singing "Racing in the Street" for the first time on that radio, along with other songs I'd rather forget, like Queen's "We Are the Champions," dedicated one night to some local high-school basketball team. I remember the golden light from within illuminating the frequency band, and I remember tuning by sound for years after that light burned out.

Yet I can't remember what time I went to bed as an adolescent, or anything else about my nocturnal ritual. Did I say goodnight and then go off to my room, or did my parents come in to say goodnight after I was in bed? I don't know, but I do know, decades after it found oblivion, exactly how to set that radio to play for half an hour and then shut off.

The memory of my quotidian habits of those years has been washed away by a thousand new habits, just as my sister's teenage presence has given way to her succeeding selves. In his novel *Vertigo*, W. G. Sebald paraphrases Stendahl's advice "not to purchase engravings of fine views and prospects seen on one's travels, since before very long they will displace our memories completely, indeed one might say destroy them. For instance," Sebald continues, "[Stendahl] could no longer recall the wonderful Sistine Madonna he had seen in Dresden, try as he might, because Müller's engraving after it had become superimposed in his mind." In the same way, as the people in our lives grow older, their new faces, voices, and demeanours replace their former selves in our memory. Yet the new technology that continually replaces old machines in our lives fails to have the same effect, because these individuals — the radios, wristwatches, automobiles that inhabited our lives — never change. That chrome "sleep knob" on my clock radio still looks exactly the same, wherever it may now rest deep in some unknowable mountainous landfill.

"The past," wrote Proust, "is hidden somewhere outside the realm, beyond the reach of intellect, in some material object (in the sensation which that material object will give us) which we do not suspect . . ." And just as the taste of the famous "petite madeleine" awakens in his narrator an entire vanished world — the memories of his childhood vacations in Combray — the thought of my old Walkman resurrects my post-collegiate existence. It was a red and black 1985 model, and I've never seen one just like it. The tendency of Sony so frequently to bring out new designs lent an air of individuality to one's Walkman, but it also caused successful designs to get lost in the shuffle. Mine was a particularly pleasing construction — sleek, rounded, with an analog radio dial and push-buttons that made you feel like you were *doing* something — that should have survived the rush for new fashions. Unlike many other models, it also worked properly for

5

years; it provided the soundtrack to a decade of my life. I can summon the physical memory of squeezing the "play" button, the middle of three oblong pieces of silver metal, and suddenly I am back in Munich in 1986, listening to the new Bob Dylan album on a brown threadbare corduroy sofa in my Goethestrasse apartment. Or I'm driving eight hours down I-95 to visit a girlfriend, listening to tapes on the Walkman because my Rabbit's stereo has been stolen. Or I'm riding the Amtrak between New York and Boston, listening to Indigo Girls while the autumn leaves blow by the window. I can even tell you the album and track that unwound on the tape, visible through the tape player's window, in that particular recollection. I have no idea why that moment should survive in my mind, but the red-and-black Walkman is as much a part of it as the music itself, and the leaves, and the dark, sheltering train.

Another machine still lingering in the afterlife: the 1973 Datsun 1200 my dad handed down to me to run into the ground, which I eventually did. A bottom-of-the-line economy model, "the Green Machine," as my friends called it, looked like a vehicle out of Dr. Seuss, but it always started and got forty miles to the gallon — a cause for nostalgia indeed, in these simmering, gas-guzzling days. I can still see the schematic four-gear diagram on the head of the stick shift and feel the knob, and the worn transmission of the gears, in my right hand. The radio had five black cuboid push-buttons for preset stations: the two on the left sported "AM" in white indentations, and the other three said "FM." It took almost the entire ride to school for the anemic defogger to rid the windshield of its early-morning dew. One day that teary view was replaced, at forty miles an hour, by green. A rusted latch had finally given out, and the wind had opened the hood and slapped it all the way against the glass. Luckily, the glass didn't break, and I could see enough through the rust holes to avoid collision as I pulled over. Whenever the friend I drove to school wasn't ready to go, her father would come out and wait with me, looking the green machine up and down and shaking his head.

What does it mean that some of my fondest memories are of technology? Have we begun our slide towards the ineluctable merging of man and machine? Are Walkman headphones in the ears the first step towards a computer chip implanted in the brain? Or is it merely that inanimate objects, whether Citizen Kane's wooden "Rosebud" or my handheld electronic circuitry, by virtue of their obliviousness to the passage of time, seize our longing? As photographs do, these objects capture particular periods of our lives. The sense memory of turning that clock-radio knob, or shifting that gear stick, fixes the moment in time as well as any photograph. Just as we painstakingly fit photos into albums or, in the new age, organize them into computer folders and make digital copies for safekeeping, so I hang onto the impression of a stainless-steel wristwatch that once applied a familiar force of weight to my left wrist.

(Where have they gone, these mechanisms of my youth? The Datsun was hauled off for parts. The clock radio and the Walkman no doubt were tossed without a second thought when they no longer functioned properly. But the Seiko? Who would throw out a fine watch that, to my recollection, never broke? My mother swears she wouldn't have. Spring cleaning is not exactly my father's pastime. Could a watch, along with its deep blue case with the silvery embossed square border, vanish into time itself?)

Of course, my memory of these objects may be far from accurate. Were   10
I to come upon my old clock radio, wrapped in old T-shirts inside a thread-bare leather overnight bag in the attic, the sensation might be like that on entering a high-school reunion and being jolted by the discrepancy between the memory of old friends and their current reality. In this case the object has not aged, but the memory has. In his wonderful book-length essay *U and I*, Nicholson Baker practices what he calls "memory criticism": he records his impressions of John Updike's works without allowing himself to reread them. When he does go back to the texts to check himself, he finds that his memories of many passages, so emblazoned upon his mind, are imperfect. He fashions an argument around a remembered line from a poem, discovers that the actual poem doesn't support the argument, and finishes off the argument anyway. A story remembered fondly for its metaphor likening a character's sick stomach to "an unprepossessing tuber" turns out not to carry the treasured trope. Baker remembers Updike making a brilliant comparison between "a strange interruption in his act of signature, between the *p* and the *d*," and his verbal stuttering — comparison that had never in fact been made.

Even Nabokov, that grandmaster of recollection, with a self-ascribed "almost pathological keenness of the retrospective faculty," is fallible. In the first version of his autobiography, *Speak, Memory*, he describes his family coat of arms as featuring "two bears posing with a great chessboard propped up between them." Later, the chess-loving author is chagrined to discover that the bears are lions and that they support a knight's shield comprising "only one sixteenth of a checkerboard."

So perhaps the clock radio is better off in oblivion. Unearthed, it might strike me as simply a cheap JCPenney's item from the 1970s — hardly a golden age for design. Or, worse, holding the object in my hands might remind me of the bored loneliness of the years I spent steering its tuning knob, just as Baker feared being "disappointed by the immediate context of a phrase [of Updike's he] loved, when the context was now hazy and irrelevant."

Once, these humanly flawed recollections were all we had to reconstruct the past. And even though our selective memory may have been salubrious, we yearned to possess the past more completely. Now, for better or worse, we have created the technology to satisfy our longing. Only machines — tape recorders, cameras, video cameras — can accurately preserve the details of our former selves, our loved ones' younger faces, of our long-gone possessions. Nostalgia, even for machines, is bolstered by machines of nostalgia.

I am typing this on a Macintosh G4 Powerbook. Will the thought of this laptop someday conjure up such piquant memories? As much as the recollection of my first computer, a 1985 Kaypro I received for college graduation? It was the first "portable" computer — a thirty-pound metal box the size of a small suitcase, with a keyboard that detached from one end. I can still feel the power switch on the right side of the back, where I reached to flick it on thousands of times. The green glow of the characters on screen, the five-and-a-half-inch floppy disks that had to be inserted in order to boot up or run Wordstar, even the control-K commands that brought up various menus: they all seem like the markings of a bygone era while at the same time retaining an intimate immediacy.

Yet computers, while they have replaced the automobile and the television as the most dominating technological feature of many people's daily lives, seem to have reached a uniformity — as well as a dismayingly short lifespan — that may weaken their nostalgic potential. This laptop isn't very different from past laptops; I've gone through a succession of desktops with almost identical exteriors. I feel little nostalgia for my PCs of the early 1990s. It's hard to get choked up about the fact that a particular box packed only twenty megabytes.

Perhaps, though, this very act of typing is what will linger one day in my mind's reliquary. Voice-recognition software is pounding at the gates; videomail seems every day more feasible. How much longer will our computers even have keyboards? Typing may someday survive only as another sense memory. A writer, while composing with his voice, will still tap his fingers on his desk like an amputee scratching a wooden leg. Rather than the ghost of a particular machine, it will be this metacarpal tapdance, an apparition of the way we used to express language, that will haunt him.

QUESTIONS

1. This writer expects you to know some things — names of people, kinds of cars and computers, and so forth. Make a list of names mentioned, and discuss the list, filling in any gaps in your own information.
2. How is this essay organized? It's not exactly a story or an argument. If you list the topics taken up in the order in which they appear, does a structure for the piece emerge that you can describe?
3. Reflective pieces have a loose structure. So, how does a writer achieve closure — that is, give the reader the sense of an ending? How does Fisher do it in this piece?
4. Fisher gives reasons for his experiences of memory — why some kinds of things seem to be present in his mind and others are gone. Do these reasons make sense to you? How similar is your own experience of memory to this author's?

5. A reflective piece like this should be the occasion for some reflection of your own. Write a short essay on objects from your own past that are preserved in your memory. You may wish to start with a list such as the one you developed for Question 2. But even if you begin to write without first having created a list, such a list should be evident once you have finished.

MAKING CONNECTIONS

Fisher wonders, "Have we begun our slide towards the ineluctable merging of man and machine?" (paragraph 8). In what ways do his concerns mirror those of Michael J. Sandel (p. 793)? How might each writer comment on the way that technology changes our lives? What are their concerns? Are there similarities in their viewpoints? If so, what are they?

DESIGN

Robert Frost

Robert Frost (1874–1963) was born in San Francisco and lived there until he was eleven. When his father died, the family moved to Massachusetts, where Robert did well in school, especially in the classics, but eventually he dropped out of both Dartmouth College and Harvard University. He went unrecognized as a poet until 1913, when he was first published in England, where he had moved with his wife and four children. On returning to the United States, he quickly achieved success with more publications and became the most celebrated poet in mid-twentieth-century America. Over the years, he received an unprecedented number and range of literary, academic, and public honors. He held a teaching position at Amherst College and received many honorary degrees as well as an invitation to recite a poem at John F. Kennedy's inauguration. Although his work is principally associated with the life and landscape of New England, and although he was a poet of traditional verse forms and metrics, he is also a quintessentially modern poet in his adherence to language as it is actually spoken, in the psychological complexity of his portraits, and in the degree to which his work is infused with layers of ambiguity and irony.

Design

I found a dimpled spider, fat, and white,
On a white heal-all, holding up a moth
Like a white piece of rigid satin cloth —
Assorted characters of death and blight
Mixed ready to begin the morning right,   5
Like the ingredients of a witches' broth —
A snow-drop spider, a flower like a froth,
And dead wings carried like a paper kite.

What had the flower to do with being white,
The wayside blue and innocent heal-all?   10
What brought the kindred spider to that height,
Then steered the white moth thither in the night?
What but design of darkness to appall? —
If design govern in a thing so small.

QUESTIONS

1. First of all, forget that this is a poem. The first section (think of it as a paragraph) is a report on an event. Retell it in your own words.
2. The second section (paragraph) asks a question and offers an answer. What is the question?
3. What is the answer?
4. The answer seems to open the way to another question. Try to make explicit that implied question.
5. Frost's text was written long before the current debates on "intelligent design" — which tells us that these debates are not exactly new. If you consider this text as a contribution to these debates, however, what point does it make?
6. Now, remember that this is a poem, which means that extra care has been taken with the words. Consider the word "appall" in the next-to-last line. What is the meaning of this word? What does it have to do with whiteness and darkness? What can "design of darkness" mean, anyway?

MAKING CONNECTIONS

Connecting Frost's reflections to other discussions of evolution and intelligent design, such as those by Steven Weinberg (p. 778) and Daniel C. Dennett (p. 787), how do these thoughts fit in? Do they take a position in the debate? Or do they cut across it in some way?

Reporting in the
Sciences and Technologies

A Delicate Operation
Roy C. Selby Jr.

Roy C. Selby Jr. (1930–2001) graduated from Louisiana State University and the University of Arkansas Medical School, where he specialized in neurology and neurosurgery. He was the author of numerous professional articles on neurosurgery and a member of the American Association of Neurological Surgeons. "A Delicate Operation," which first appeared in Harper's magazine in 1975, reports for a more general audience the details of a difficult brain operation.

In the autumn of 1973 a woman in her early fifties noticed, upon closing one eye while reading, that she was unable to see clearly. Her eyesight grew slowly worse. Changing her eyeglasses did not help. She saw an ophthalmologist, who found that her vision was seriously impaired in both eyes. She then saw a neurologist, who confirmed the finding and obtained X rays of the skull and an EMI scan — a photograph of the patient's head. The latter revealed a tumor growing between the optic nerves at the base of the brain. The woman was admitted to the hospital by a neurosurgeon.

Further diagnosis, based on angiography, a detailed X-ray study of the circulatory system, showed the tumor to be about two inches in diameter and supplied by many small blood vessels. It rested beneath the brain, just above the pituitary gland, stretching the optic nerves to either side and intimately close to the major blood vessels supplying the brain. Removing it would pose many technical problems. Probably benign and slow-growing, it may have been present for several years. If left alone it would continue to grow and produce blindness and might become impossible to remove completely. Removing it, however, might not improve the patient's vision and could make it worse. A major blood vessel could be damaged, causing a stroke. Damage to the undersurface of the brain could cause impairment of memory and changes in mood and personality. The hypothalamus, a most important structure of the brain, could be injured, causing coma, high fever, bleeding from the stomach, and death.

The neurosurgeon met with the patient and her husband and discussed the various possibilities. The common decision was to operate.

The patient's hair was shampooed for two nights before surgery. She was given a cortisonelike drug to reduce the risk of damage to the brain during surgery. Five units of blood were cross-matched, as a contingency against hemorrhage. At 1:00 p.m. the operation began. After the patient was anesthetized her hair was completely clipped and shaved from the scalp. Her head was prepped with an organic iodine solution for ten minutes. Drapes were placed over her, leaving exposed only the forehead and crown of the skull. All the routine instruments were brought up — the electrocautery used to coagulate areas of bleeding, bipolar coagulation forceps to arrest bleeding from individual blood vessels without damaging adjacent tissues, and small suction tubes to remove blood and cerebrospinal fluid from the head, thus giving the surgeon a better view of the tumor and surrounding areas.

A curved incision was made behind the hairline so it would be concealed when the hair grew back. It extended almost from ear to ear. Plastic clips were applied to the cut edges of the scalp to arrest bleeding. The scalp was folded back to the level of the eyebrows. Incisions were made in the muscle of the right temple, and three sets of holes were drilled near the temple and the top of the head because the tumor had to be approached from directly in front. The drill, powered by nitrogen, was replaced with a fluted steel blade, and the holes were connected. The incised piece of skull was pried loose and held out of the way by a large sponge.

Beneath the bone is a yellowish leatherlike membrane, the dura, that surrounds the brain. Down the middle of the head the dura carries a large vein, but in the area near the nose the vein is small. At that point the vein and dura were cut, and clips made of tantalum, a hard metal, were applied to arrest and prevent bleeding. Sutures were put into the dura and tied to the scalp to keep the dura open and retracted. A malleable silver retractor, resembling the blade of a butter knife, was inserted between the brain and skull. The anesthesiologist began to administer a drug to relax the brain by removing some of its water, making it easier for the surgeon to manipulate the retractor, hold the brain back, and see the tumor. The nerve tracts for smell were cut on both sides to provide additional room. The tumor was seen approximately two-and-one-half inches behind the base of the nose. It was pink in color. On touching it, it proved to be very fibrous and tough. A special retractor was attached to the skull, enabling the other retractor blades to be held automatically and freeing the surgeon's hands. With further displacement of the frontal lobes of the brain, the tumor could be seen better, but no normal structures — the carotid arteries, their branches, and the optic nerves — were visible. The tumor obscured them.

A surgical microscope was placed above the wound. The surgeon had selected the lenses and focal length prior to the operation. Looking through the microscope, he could see some of the small vessels supplying the tumor and he coagulated them. He incised the tumor to attempt to remove its core and thus collapse it, but the substance of the tumor was too firm to be removed in this fashion. He then began to slowly dissect the tumor from the adjacent brain tissue and from where he believed the normal structures to be.

Using small squares of cotton, he began to separate the tumor from very loose fibrous bands connecting it to the brain and to the right side of the part of the skull where the pituitary gland lies. The right optic nerve and carotid artery came into view, both displaced considerably to the right. The optic nerve had a normal appearance. He protected these structures with cotton compresses placed between them and the tumor. He began to raise the tumor from the skull and slowly to reach the point of its origin and attachment — just in front of the pituitary gland and medial to the left optic nerve, which still could not be seen. The small blood vessels entering the tumor were cauterized. The upper portion of the tumor was gradually separated from the brain, and the branches of the carotid arteries and the branches to the tumor were coagulated. The tumor was slowly and gently lifted from its bed, and for the first time the left carotid artery and optic nerve could be seen. Part of the tumor adhered to this nerve. The bulk of the tumor was amputated, leaving a small bit attached to the nerve. Very slowly and carefully the tumor fragment was resected.

The tumor now removed, a most impressive sight came into view — the pituitary gland and its stalk of attachment to the hypothalamus, the hypothalamus itself, and the brainstem, which conveys nerve impulses between the body and the brain. As far as could be determined, no damage had been done to these structures or other vital centers, but the left optic nerve, from chronic pressure of the tumor, appeared gray and thin. Probably it would not completely recover its function.

After making certain there was no bleeding, the surgeon closed the   10
wounds and placed wire mesh over the holes in the skull to prevent dimpling of the scalp over the points that had been drilled. A gauze dressing was applied to the patient's head. She was awakened and sent to the recovery room.

Even with the microscope, damage might still have occurred to the cerebral cortex and hypothalamus. It would require at least a day to be reasonably certain there was none, and about seventy-two hours to monitor for the major postoperative dangers — swelling of the brain and blood clots forming over the surface of the brain. The surgeon explained this to the patient's husband, and both of them waited anxiously. The operation had required seven hours. A glass of orange juice had given the surgeon some additional energy during the closure of the wound. Though exhausted, he could not fall asleep until after two in the morning, momentarily expecting a call from the nurse in the intensive care unit announcing deterioration of the patient's condition.

At 8:00 a.m. the surgeon saw the patient in the intensive care unit. She was alert, oriented, and showed no sign of additional damage to the optic nerves or the brain. She appeared to be in better shape than the surgeon or her husband.

QUESTIONS

1. Why did Selby decide to operate? What could have happened if the patient chose not to have the operation? What effect does knowing this information have on the reader?
2. Although the essay is probably based on Selby's experience, it is reported in the third person. What effect does this have on the information reported? How would the report have come across if it had been written in the first person?
3. Selby uses different methods of reporting to create the drama of "A Delicate Operation." At what point in the essay does he provide background information? How much of the essay reports events before, during, and after the operation? At what points does the writer explain terms and procedures for the reader?
4. Which passages in this essay do you find especially powerful? How did Selby create this effect?
5. Write a report of a procedure with which you are familiar. Select a procedure that calls for some expertise or sensitivity because there is the chance that something could go wrong. Proceed step by step, giving the reader as much information as necessary to understand and follow the procedure. At appropriate points, also include the problems you face. Possible topics are trimming a Christmas tree, carrying out a chemistry experiment, getting a child off to school, or preparing a gourmet meal.

MAKING CONNECTIONS

1. Compare Selby's essay with Edward O. Wilson's "Life Is a Narrative" (p. 746). Whereas Selby writes in the third person, Wilson uses the first. How do those choices affect the resulting essays?
2. Rewrite several paragraphs of Selby's and Wilson's essays, changing Selby's piece from third person to first person and Wilson's piece from first person to third person. How do these changes alter the nature of the information presented and the effect of each report?

A Delicate Balance Is Undone in a Flash, and a Battered City Waits

*Peter Applebome, Christopher Drew,
Jere Longman, and Andrew Revkin*

Peter Applebome is a New York Times *journalist whose articles have also appeared in such periodicals as the* Wall Street Journal, Washington Monthly, New Republic, *and* Texas Observer. *He was born in New York and received degrees from Duke University and Northwestern University. Applebome has written* Dixie Rising: How the South Is Shaping American Values, Politics, and Culture *(1996),* The Grand Review: The Civil War Continues to Shape America *(2000; written with Georg R. Sheets, L. Douglas Wilder, and Charles Reagan Wilson), and* Scout's Honor: A Father's Unlikely Foray into the Woods *(2003). Christopher Drew is a* New York Times *journalist who has also worked for the* Chicago Tribune, *where he won two awards from the White House Correspondents' Association; the* Wall Street Journal; *and the* Times-Picayune *in New Orleans, where he was born and raised and graduated from Tulane University. With Annette Lawrence Drew and Sherry Sontag, Drew wrote* Blind Man's Bluff: The Untold Story of American Submarine Espionage *(1998), which received the Theodore and Franklin D. Roosevelt Naval History Prize and was named one of the best investigative books of 1998 by the national journalism group Investigative Reporters and Editors. Jere Longman is an award-winning* New York Times *sports writer. In the summer of 1999, Longman spent much of his time with the U.S. women's soccer team, resulting in his book* The Girls of Summer: The U.S. Women's Soccer Team and How It Changed the World *(2000). In the book, Longman presents profiles of the team's players and describes the background of legal, historical, social, and athletic developments in women's sports that provided the backdrop for the team's dramatic World Cup win. Andrew Revkin is a science writer for the* New York Times. *Revkin received degrees from Brown University and the Columbia School of Journalism and has taught environmental reporting at the School of Journalism. Revkin has won the National Academies Communication Award for print journalism, the Science Journalism Award of the American Association for the Advancement of Science (twice), and the Investigative Reporter and Editors Award, and he was part of the* New York Times'

Pulitzer Prize–winning Nation Challenged team. His first book, The
Burning Season *(1990), recounts the life of Chico Mendes, the slain
Amazon activist. A* New York Times *Notable Book of the Year, it
won the Sidney Hillman Foundation Book Prize and a Robert F.
Kennedy Book award and was the basis for an award-winning
HBO film of the same name. His second book,* Global Warming:
Understanding the Forecast *(1992), accompanied an exhibition on
global warming that was created by the American Museum of Natural History. Revkin also performs in a band and writes about
music, and his* New York Times *profile of a heavy-metal singer was
the basis for the 2001 movie* Rock Star. *The following piece appeared on September 4, 2005, in the* New York Times.

NEW ORLEANS, Sept. 2 — They waited, and they waited, and then
they waited some more in the 90 degree heat, as many as 5,000 people huddled at a highway underpass on Interstate 10, waiting for buses that never
arrived to take them away from the storm they could not escape.

Babies cried. The sick huddled in the shade in wheelchairs or rested on
cots. Dawn Ray, 40, was in tears, looking after an autistic niece who had
soiled herself and her son who is blind and has cerebral palsy. A few others,
less patient, simply started walking west with nowhere to go, like a man
pushing a bike in one hand and pulling a shopping cart in another. But
most just waited with resigned patience — sad, angry, incredulous, scared,
exhausted, people who seemed as discarded as the bottles of water and
food containers that littered the ground.

"Disease, germs," one woman, Claudette Paul, said, covering her mouth
with a cloth, her voice smoldering with anger. "We need help. We don't live
like this in America."

New Orleans has always existed in a delicate balance between land and
water, chaos and order, black and white, the very rich and the very poor. It
has been the lacy ironwork of French Quarter balconies, the magical shops
and galleries on Royal Street and the magisterial cuisine not just at Gala-
toire's or Mr. B's or Commander's Palace but at humble po-boy joints and
neighborhood restaurants in every part of town.

But it has also been a place of crushing poverty, of dreary housing proj-   5
ects and failing schools, where crime and violence have been an incessant
shadow in daily life, as much a part of the local sensibility as the damp,
smothering blanket of heat and humidity.

This week, bit by bit, that delicate balance came completely undone.
Water took over earth when levees broke, putting 80 percent of the city
under water. The mix of fatalism and bravado that allowed the city's biggest
fear — a killer hurricane — to become the national drink of Bourbon Street

Orlando Harrington holding his daughter, Deseris, 4, yesterday as they wait for
buses with other refugees under Interstate 10 in New Orleans. Spirits seemed to lift
on signs that they were finally moving to better conditions.

gave way to terror and despair and horrifying spasms of looting and violence. New Orleans became unrecognizable not just physically, but psychologically as well. Faced with a disaster of biblical proportions, everything
fell apart.

The flood control apparatus, which government officials and scientists
had long said was inadequate, failed as some predicted. The city's evacuation plan worked, except for thousands who were too poor or disabled to
find their own way out of the city before the storm. The radios and cellphones that officials and police officers use to communicate failed, erasing
any remaining semblance of authority in a city beset by chaos and crime.
And finally, a full federal response came only after the dialogue between
local and federal officials devolved into shouting.

Just two months ago new evidence emerged that the city and its levees
were sinking, increasing the risk of a catastrophic flood, even as federal
funds to protect the city were being cut. As flood waters rose on Tuesday,
Senator Mary L. Landrieu tried to impress upon colleagues in Washington
that this was America's tsunami, but she said the more she pleaded, the
more she felt she was not being heard. Most local officials who, were supposed to be running the city eventually left, mainly because they couldn't
communicate with the outside world, whose help they desperately needed.

New Orleans, Flannery O'Connor once wrote, is a place where the devil's existence is freely recognized.

But not this devil. Not the devil of bloated bodies floating in muddy   10
waters washing lazily over submerged pickups and campers, of corpses being eaten by rats as they decomposed on city streets, of people dying in wheelchairs outside the convention center as friends poured water over their heads, to try to keep them alive.

Not the devil who left Bill and Gail Orris sitting exhausted, dazed after escaping through the hole they poked through the roof of their home in nearby Chalmette, while their 20-year-old daughter, Lennie, unable to walk and mentally disabled, sucked her thumb and jerked spasmodically back and forth in her wheelchair in the hot sun.

Not the devil who left Catherine Weiss at 75, apologizing profusely for not having her teeth with her — she had left in a hurry, after all, when the water filled her house like a bathtub — and panicked about what had happened to her nephew, Michael Phillippello, who collapsed as a boat ferried them across the river to safety.

Not the man on talk radio, stranded in his house but begging people not to try to come back to see what they had left behind.

"It's like the five stages of accepting death," he said. "First, I was thinking if I had enough ice to save the good shrimp and tilapia, then it's whether

Fires burned in parts of New Orleans early yesterday, adding to the destruction. Much of the city was still under water.

I can save the house, now it's about my life. If I had two AK's I'd feel safe here. As it is someone could pop me off, and I could end up bloated, no one would check for bullet holes, and I'd just end up in some potter's field. You can feel human life kind of receding like the waters." It began as Tropical Depression 12, yet another swirl of tropical turbulence in the southeastern Bahamas. But each step of the way Hurricane Katrina seemed to overachieve. It hit Florida with more power than expected killing nine people and knocking out electricity for a million more. Then it crossed back into the Gulf of Mexico, intensifying into one of the strongest storms on record as, in a horrific bit of timing, it churned directly over the "loop current," a great, deep whorl of tropics-hot seawater that pulses in between the Yucatán and Cuba each year and then stays south of Louisiana into late summer. Often, storms weaken as they suck up cool water that lies stratified beneath the warm surface. But in the loop, even the depths are hot.

"We are facing a storm that most of us have long feared," said Mayor   15
C. Ray Nagin, who urged people on Saturday to leave town and then gave an evacuation order on Sunday, when it looked as if the Category 5 storm, with winds as high as 175 miles an hour, could be headed for New Orleans. "This is a once-in-a-lifetime event."

Many of the 1.3 million people in the metropolitan area did that, paralyzing traffic along major highways.

But, as always, many did not. This surprised exactly no one. In a 2003 poll conducted by Louisiana State University researchers, 31 percent of New Orleans residents said they would stay in the city even if a Category 4 hurricane struck.

Many stayed because they felt they had no choice, particularly the poor and the elderly.

The survey found that those who said they would stay tended to be poor, less educated, disabled, older, childless or isolated, or had lived in the city for a long period. Twenty-eight percent of the population of New Orleans lives below the poverty line, compared with 9 percent nationwide, according to census figures. Twenty-four percent of its adults are disabled, compared with 19 percent nationwide. An estimated 50,000 households in New Orleans do not have cars.

And there was another bit of bad timing: the hurricane came at the end   20
of the month, when those depending on public assistance are waiting for their next checks, typically mailed on the first of every month.

"They wouldn't have had any money to evacuate," said Councilwoman Cynthia Hedge-Morrell.

Experts disagreed on whether adequate plans were in place to evacuate the poor, the elderly, and the infirm.

Brian Wolshon, an L.S.U. civil engineering professor who served as a consultant on the state evacuation plan, said the city relied almost entirely in its planning on a "Good Samaritan scenario," in which residents would check on elderly and disabled neighbors and drive them out of the city if necessary.

"That was the thinking," Professor Wolshon said. "Maybe even the cornerstone of that plan."

Planning for their evacuation was stymied by a shortage of buses, he said. As many as 2,000 buses, far more than New Orleans possessed, would be needed to evacuate an estimated 100,000 elderly and disabled people.

But Chester Wilmot, an L.S.U. civil engineering professor who studies evacuation plans, said the city successfully improvised. He said witnesses described seeing city buses shuttle residents to the Superdome before Hurricane Katrina struck.

"What I've heard is that there were buses, but they weren't very well utilized," Professor Wilmot said. "They literally carried very few people."

The two professors agreed that the evacuation of New Orleans residents with cars went well. They said a new "contraflow plan," which used all lanes of I-10 for outbound traffic, relieved congestion that snarled traffic for hours during a voluntary evacuation of the city during Hurricane Ivan in 2001.

"What you're going to find is that everyone who wanted to get, got out," said Professor Wolshon "Except for the people who didn't have access to transportation."

But many others stayed because they wanted to stay. Because their friends were staying. Because they were worried about looters if they left. Because they felt they could protect their property by staying home. They stayed because they had elderly parents who were going to stay, because they thought they knew which parts of the city flooded and which did not. Or because they always had.

"Hard-headed, honey," said Mrs. Weiss, when asked why she rode out the storm in the same brick home where she has stayed for storms for 41 years. "From now on, I'm leaving for a tropical storm."

And then there were the tourists, many of whom came with only the haziest sense of what they were facing and not the slightest idea of what they should do. When Chris and Tammy Distefano, Kris and Mike Miller, and Chad and Michelle Toomey arrived from York, Pa., on Saturday morning for their first trip to New Orleans, they asked the limo driver, Joseph, what to expect. Not much, he answered. The storms always went somewhere else. He took them on a tour and dropped them off at their hotel. They dropped off their bags and walked over to Pat O'Brien's for a hurricane, the mix of dark rum, passion fruit, and other juices that people drink from plastic cups as they tour the French Quarter. They were scared to death as the storm rattled their hotel, shutting off the power, Sunday night and Monday morning.

But as Monday rolled into afternoon and the storm moved west, people peeked outside to find streets battered, trees down, roots torn up, but the city mostly dry. It looked like the N'awlins luck had held again.

Tuesday, Aug. 23	Wednesday, Aug. 24	Thursday, Aug. 25
The National Hurricane Center classifies an area over the Bahamas **Tropical Depression 12**, and anticipates "steady intensification."	The N.H.C. warns that **Tropical Storm Katrina** could cross Florida and "re-intensify over the eastern Gulf of Mexico" in the days ahead.	Rising to a **category 1 hurricane**, Katrina is forecast to be "a dangerous hurricane in the northeastern Gulf of Mexico in about three days."

❶ GOVERNMENT ACTION

		Gov. Jeb Bush declares a state of emergency in Florida.

❷ GOVERNMENT RELIEF EFFORTS

❸ PEOPLE HOUSED BY THE RED CROSS — 584 in 6 shelters

❹ NEW ORLEANS REFUGEES AND EVACUATIONS

❺ CUSTOMERS WITHOUT ELECTRICITY

❻ LEVEE BREACHES AND FLOODING

Monday, Aug. 29	Tuesday, Aug. 30	Wednesday, Aug. 31

Katrina drops to a **category 4 hurricane** before it makes landfall, and dissipates to a **tropical storm** as it moves inland.	The N.H.C. issues its final advisory on **Tropical Depression Katrina**, which "is primarily now a heavy rain event."	

❶
Thousands of National Guard troops are called up to assist in relief operations.	President Bush cuts short his vacation. The city government of New Orleans regroups in Baton Rouge.	Mayor Nagin calls for a total evacuation of the city. President Bush flies over the region on his way back to Washington and convenes a federal task force.

❷
FEMA search and rescue teams wait for the worst of the storm to pass before attempting to enter the disaster zone.	The Pentagon announces it will send five ships, though four are several days away.	By Wednesday, FEMA has deployed 39 medical teams to set up field hospitals under tents, and mobilized 1,700 trailer trucks.

❸ 37,091 in 239 shelters | 42,059 in 208 shelters | 52,719 in 259 shelters

❹ 708,010 across four states | 2,722,928 | 2,338,278

❺
Officials estimate 80 percent of New Orleans residents obeyed the order to evacuate. The Coast Guard rescues 1,200 people from the flood waters.	More than 12,000 people are in the **Superdome**. The international airport is reopened for relief flights.	Military transport planes carry seriously ill and injured patients to Houston; 1,400 police officers are ordered to cease rescue operations and control widespread looting.

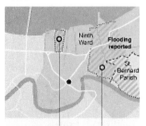	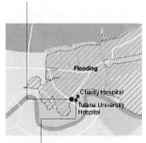	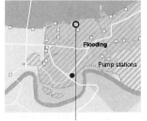

❻
17th Street Canal and **Industrial Canal** levees are breached, pouring lake water into the city.	**City hospitals** flood. Mayor Nagin estimates that 80 percent of the city is underwater.	Officials become aware of a breach at **London Avenue Canal**; pump stations are all offline.

Friday, Aug. 26	Saturday, Aug. 27	Sunday, Aug. 28
"Katrina is forecast to move directly over the warm loop current of the Gulf of Mexico . . . which is like adding high-octane fuel to the fire."	Now a **category 3 hurricane** on the Saffir-Simpson scale, Katrina is expected to make "landfall in southeastern Louisiana in 48–60 hours."	Now **category 5**, Katrina "is a large hurricane that will affect a large area. . . . Preparations should be rushed to completion."
	President Bush declares a state of emergency in Louisiana. Gov. Haley Barbour declares a state of emergency in Mississippi.	Mayor Lee Nagin of New Orleans orders a mandatory evacuation. From his Texas ranch, the president declares a state of emergency for Mississippi, Florida and Alabama.
		The Federal Emergency Management Agency sends water, food and other supplies to staging centers in Georgia and Texas.
252 in 3 shelters	845 in 13 shelters	1,084 in 78 shelters
1,221,500 in Florida	880,000 in Florida	550,930 in Florida
	Residents of New Orleans board up their homes. Voluntary evacuations are called in some parishes.	Lines form at gas stations and outside the **Superdome**, which takes in as many as 10,000 of the estimated 100,000 people who remain in the city.
		Based on the size and track of the storm, **computer models** predict flooding across parts of the city.

Thursday, Sept. 1	Friday, Sept. 2	Saturday, Sept. 3

Thursday, Sept. 1	Friday, Sept. 2	Saturday, Sept. 3
The governor of Louisiana says that deaths may be in the "thousands."	President Bush flies to Mobile, Ala., tours the disaster area and meets with survivors.	In his weekly radio address, President Bush says "We will not rest until we get this right and the job is done."
Senate and House officials prepare a $10 billion emergency aid package.	6,500 National Guard troops arrive in New Orleans; by day's end, nearly 20,000 troops are stationed in Louisiana and Mississippi.	10,000 additional National Guard troops are expected in the region within the next few days.
76, 453 in 275 shelters	94,308 in 308 shelters	
2,091,833	1,600,358	
As many as 45,000 refugees fill the **Superdome** and **Convention Center**, where conditions continue to deteriorate.	A large convoy of relief supplies arrives at the **Convention Center**. Commercial airlines begin flying people out of the city, and the **Superdome** begins to empty.	Fewer than 2,000 people remain at the **Superdome**, and state officials say evacuations may be finished by today.

Thursday, Sept. 1	Friday, Sept. 2	Saturday, Sept. 3
With flood levels stable, the Army Corps of Engineers continues to work on the breached levees.	An explosion at a **chemical storage facility** sends a column of acrid smoke into the sky.	**Pump stations** may be activated as early as tomorrow.

Thriving on Bluff

And why not? For generations — centuries, really — this city had thrived in part on the poker-hand bluff, on its sheer allure as much as its starker realities.

Eighteenth-century accounts sent back to France as the first settlers   35
carved into the Mississippi silt focused on the fantastical, not the real. said Craig E. Colten; a geographer at L.S.U. and the author of a new book on the city with the apt title "An Unnatural Metropolis."

"There were paintings of New Orleans with mountains in the background," Dr. Colten said, but few entrepreneurs seeking to sell the idea of building a town on this swampy island mention that as they dug into the earth, they came upon recently buried tree trunks — a sign that they were standing on land laid down by epic floods.

Not only were there no mountains, the city grew between the Mississippi River and the broad, shallow Lake Pontchartrain. As the city expanded, so too did efforts to ring it with earthen levees. But the very expansion of the city contributed to the rising flood-risk, Dr. Colten said. As swampier spots were drained, the drying soil compressed, causing reclaimed land to sink ever more.

In the twentieth century, more land was drained as the city's legendary system of pump stations and purging canals spread. But that made it sink all that much faster.

Hurricanes feeding on warmth from the gulf rumbled by most summers. Some potent ones smashed other Gulf Coast towns, like Galveston, Tex., in 1900, and storms in 1947 and 1965, struck New Orleans directly, but with survivable intensity. Hurricane Betsy, in September 1965, finally spurred a federal hurricane protection plan for Lake Pontchartrain and vicinity.

But the system that emerged was a compromise from the start, cut back   40
by competing Army Corps of Engineer projects, by pressure from local communities that had to pay part of the tab, and by the tendency to focus more on current costs than on future risks.

Officials settled on a system of levees sufficient to protect against another Hurricane Betsy — roughly akin to what is now called a Category 3 storm, the kind that statistics, estimate might strike New Orleans once in 200 years.

A lull in Atlantic hurricane frequency from around 1970 until 1995 probably contributed to complacency, said Bob Sheets, a former director of the National Hurricane Center. But more recently, a string of studies found that after 1995, a natural Atlantic cycle had switched from the pattern that stifles storms to one that nurtured them. Other studies pointed to an eventual increase in storm intensity from human-caused global warming.

Computer simulations showed ever more clearly how New Orleans could swamp like a low boat in high seas under the assault from certain hurricanes.

People walking along Interstate 10 near the Superdome on Wednesday after the storm. The stadium became a last point of refuge.

Still, the compromises over flood protection persisted. After a scare from Hurricane Georges in 1998, Congress authorized the Corps of Engineers to begin studying bolstering the city's defenses against a Category 5 storm. But money for that study, and simply for finishing the last components of the original plan to protect against a Category 3 storm, dribbled in to the New Orleans Army Corps district at a fraction of annual requests.

In 2004, with insufficient money to close contracts with the companies doing the work, Alfred Naomi, a senior district project manager, told the local East Jefferson Levee Authority, according to the New Orleans Times-Picayune: "The system is in great shape, but the levees are sinking. Everything is sinking, and if we don't get the money fast enough to raise them, then we can't stay ahead of the settlement."   45

This year, the New Orleans district was hit by a $71.2 million cut. Without more federal money, the district reported in May, the raising of various levees and other "pressing needs" would not be met. In June, at a meeting of emergency planners and hurricane experts, Roy Dokka, an L.S.U. engineer who has spent much of his career refining measurements of elevations around the gulf, presented findings that parts of the coast and New Orleans were sinking at rates 2 to 50 times faster than earlier estimates.

Many spots were two to four feet lower than anyone thought, recalled Stephen Baig, a National Hurricane Center meteorologist, a chilling hint that calculations of the flood potential of particular storms and the vulnerability of levees, might be significantly underestimated.

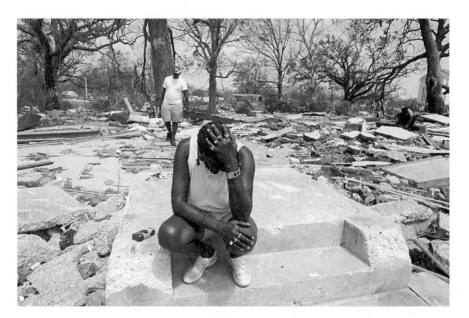

Glenda Thomas sits on the steps that once led to her home in Gulfport, Miss., one of the towns hit hardest by Hurricane Katrina. The number of destroyed homes and addresses has hampered search-and-rescue efforts.

"For levee heights, and for our models," Dr. Baig recalled, "that could mean the difference between overtopping and not overtopping."

On Monday, there was nothing dramatic when the levee failed, no sound of an explosion or a crash. At midday, as the storm was blowing out of the city, the Web site of The Times-Picayune quoted residents near the 17th Street canal saying that after experiencing only minor flooding from the storm, suddenly the water in their yards was rising from what seemed to be a breech in the canal. One man said later that afternoon that the water was rising one brick on his house every 20 minutes.

By 4:20 p.m. on Monday, the Web site reported that the water had al- 50 ready rolled through the nearby Lakeview neighborhood and on down to the center of the city. By then, the water in Lakeview had reached the second stories of many houses. The berms along Lake Pontchartrain had held. The problem was in canals that had been built to carry water pumped from city drains out to the lake. But on Monday, with the lake rising, the flow in the canals reversed.

A surge, probably 10 feet above normal, flowed in from the lake, rising until it began cascading over the top of the sleek, butter-colored walls that stood between the east side of the 17th Street Canal and the city's Bucktown neighborhood.

Greg Breerwood, a deputy district engineer for the Corps said it appeared that as the weight of the water pressed on the high part of the wall, the water pouring over the top hit the ground on the other side and ate away at the soil supporting its base.

A section of the wall pushed in and the rush of water turned that breach into a gash as broad as a football field is long: The lake and below-sea-level city were becoming one body of water.

"We heard about the flood wall failing," Mr. Breerwood said. "Then we realized there was an open corridor to the city."

Once the levee broke, most long-time New Orleanians knew that the   55 city could unravel quickly, with nothing to stop the lake from pouring into neighborhoods that were still dry and surging across a huge city park and into downtown.

Senator Mary L. Landrieu, a Democrat who grew up in New Orleans, whose father, Moon Landrieu, had been mayor, whose brother, Mitch, is now Louisiana's lieutenant governor, was at the federal and state command center in Baton Rouge when the first warnings about the break flashed on Monday afternoon. Ms. Landrieu knew how reluctant people could be to leave. This was the first time her own father had ever left during a hurricane. She said in an interview that she knew instantly that thousands who thought they had survived the storm would now be trapped in their houses, racing the rising floodwaters to their second floors, or to their attics or rooftops.

But she and other local officials suddenly faced a new problem: how to convince federal officials that just one break in one canal with such a mundane name could bring on a cataclysm that would require far more resources than had been needed to ward off the storm.

"I have been with Michael Brown since the minute he landed in this center," Ms. Landrieu said Friday in Baton Rouge, referring to the director of the Federal Emergency Management Agency, "and I have been telling him from the moment he arrived about the urgency of the situation."

But, she said, "I just have to tell you that he had a difficult time understanding the enormity of the task before us."

Natalie Rule, a spokeswoman for FEMA, disputed Ms Landrieu's ac-   60 count. "There was no doubt in our minds that a Category 3, 4, or, 5 headed for New Orleans was going to be dangerous," Ms. Rule said. She said agency officials told state and local leaders: "We will be there for you. You just go for it. We've got your back."

But if they did no one knew it. And as the flood control system broke down, so soon did everything else.

There was no immediate announcement that the levee had been breached or what it meant, but different people realized at different times that maybe the bullet had not been dodged, after all. The prestorm evacuation, as chaotic as it seemed to anyone stuck on the road, was still part of a plan. With the levee break, a whole new ad hoc stage began.

The tourists from York ventured out Monday to see gangs of youths, maybe four, then a dozen, then another four, breaking into the Canal Place Mall, home to high-dollar retailers like Saks and Gucci, Brooks Brothers and Ann Taylor. Worried that things were slipping out of control, they

Many New Orleanians fled the city last Sunday morning as the hurricane approached, but tens of thousands stayed behind.

managed to make a plane reservation at $637 a ticket to get out of town. A local family staying at the hotel drove them out for $100 a head, the best money they ever spent. There had been no plans, for what to do with stranded tourists, and before long the hotels were closing down.

With the Superdome overloaded and without food or air-conditioning, the hotels guided visitors to the Ernest N. Morial Convention Center, a huge rectangular building that stretches about a mile and is several hundred yards wide. It has been used for conventions with more than 70,000 people. But soon the situation there devolved into anarchy, too, to the point that officials, often circumspect and cagey with the news media, were just the opposite.

"The tourists are walking around there and as soon as these individuals   65
see them, they're being preyed upon. They are beating, they are raping them in the streets," said P. Edwin Compass III, superintendent of police. "We have 15 to 20,000 people in there that is trapped. We have individuals who are getting raped. We have individuals who are getting beaten."

The Flooded Ninth

Before dawn on Tuesday, Ms. Landrieu's brother, the lieutenant governor, and Sgt. Troy McConnell of the state police left Baton Rouge to assist

Damage to bridges like the one between Pass Christian and Bay St. Louis, Miss., has hurt rescue efforts in hard-hit areas.

in the rescue of flooded residents of the Ninth Ward in New Orleans. Mr. Landrieu knew the city intimately. But now he was navigating the Lower Ninth Ward not by car, but by boat. The four men on board would cut the engine and float in watery silence, listening for calls for help from inside houses or attics.

People yelled from rooftops or waved shirts or rags, as if they were flags, from vents in the attic. A few wooden houses floated like buoys.

It had become so hot inside the fetid houses that some residents shivered in the cold water as they swam to the rescue boat. One woman was so heavy and immobile that 12 men were needed to lift her off a gurney. They must have rescued 100 people, but by the end of the day the mood began to change to one of irritated impatience. "By dusk, people were getting agitated and upset," Sergeant McConnell said. "They had been in those houses for two days with nothing to eat or drink."

Soon there was a small army of evacuees, refugees with no place to go who were deposited on the island of dry land at the edge of I-10 in Metairie. During the long, hot afternoon and into the humid night, the crowd swelled to 2,000 hungry, flood-weary people, residents of the northern neighborhoods of New Orleans and of St. Bernard Parish to the northeast who had been plucked from their roofs and attics.

Barefoot women cradling naked, screaming babies limped from a 70
National Guard rescue truck, everything they owned on their backs after

36 hours of watching the floodwaters breach their doors, topple their refrigerators and drive them to the only high ground available — roofs, trees,
attics, and bridge spans. Behind them, elderly couples in nightgowns and
slippers leaned on each other for support as they walked slowly from the
helicopter that rescued them. Many clutched garbage bags holding all the
possessions they could salvage; many had no more than damp tank tops
and shorts clinging to their bodies. Most were hungry, thirsty, and alone.

Chermaine Daniels, 49, had left her flooded one-story house in the
Ninth Ward on Tuesday morning, gashing her ankle on a fence as she struggled to swim to a neighbor's two-story house. Later that day, Ms. Daniels
and several others were rescued by a uniformed officer in a boat and deposited at an I-10 encampment.

"What do we do now?" she asked the boat driver.

"You're on your own," the driver replied.

Increasingly, local officials also felt that they were on their own.

On Tuesday night, Mayor Nagin complained that while federal officials   75
had agreed that morning that stemming the flow from the breach was the
highest priority, "it didn't get done."

Ms. Landrieu said she had talked to Senator Bill Frist of Tennessee, the
majority leader, on Tuesday and said she told him: "'You remember when I
flew over the tsunami with you? This was worse than anything we saw.' He

National Guard troops examine the remains of the U.S. 90 bridge between Biloxi
and Ocean Springs, Miss.

said, 'No, you've got to be kidding.' I said, 'I know it's hard to grasp.' And he said, 'we're on it.'" Mr. Frist's office did not respond to requests for comment.

By Wednesday, with little visible response from the federal government, Ms. Landrieu said that she talked to FEMA officials. "I started to sense they were thinking I was a little overwrought, that maybe I was exaggerating a little bit," she said. When she pressed Mr. Brown on when he was going to finally get buses to pick up the people, who had been trapped at the Superdome, "he just mumbled," she said.

By then, the state leaders also had an array of other complaints. People were infuriated about the lack of National Guard troops to keep order and end the looting. How could the Corps of Engineers, which builds and takes care of the levees, have not had a contingency plan for dealing with a levee breach, especially in such a critical spot? And each time another federal agency offered to help, FEMA seemed to delay in providing guarantees that it would reimburse them later.

For instance, a defense agency had packages of communications gear ready to deploy and held them while awaiting FEMA's approval, according to two congressional aides.

Natalie Rule, a spokeswoman for FEMA, said the agency has a great   80
relationship with state and local officials and that FEMA officials told them: "We will be there for you. You just go for it. We've got your back."

Inside New Orleans, city officials were trying to keep some semblance of control over their city, and failing.

The most basic reason was a massive breakdown of the communications system. Cellphones failed and satellite phones did not arrive for several days, according to Representative Charlie Melancon, a Democrat who represents suburban New Orleans.

Ms. Landrieu said on Wednesday: "Our communications systems are not functioning adequately; they are compromised. Not Louisiana's communications system. The United States of America. We didn't have the right communications system for 9/11. We don't have the right communications system now. By that I mean the simplest things. A police chief in a city talking to a mayor in a city wasn't happening while this was going on because their cellphones were down and their radios didn't communicate."

The flooded city was also becoming lawless. There were acts of desperation and acts of depravity.

As water rose into his home on Tuesday, Louis Martin Sr., a 36-year-   85
old truck driver, said he commandeered a flatbed truck to rescue his family from the second floor of a neighboring home. He then made several trips, ferrying neighbors to the convention center at the instructions of a police officer. By now the crowd there had reached about 25,000.

On Wednesday, Mr. Martin said, armed youths appeared when evacuation buses didn't. "They had guns and they were looking for someone," he said. "I saw two boys running. There were shots."

Beverley Hayes and Erica Daniels, who are housekeepers at the Holiday Inn in Gulfport, washed linens on Thursday in the hotel pool.

At the Convention Center, food and water grew scarce. Dead bodies sagged in wheelchairs. Residents reported hearing bursts of sporadic gunfire. A number of city police officers walked of their jobs in despair.

By Wednesday, many city officials left for Baton Rouge, mainly because they could not communicate with the outside world and they needed to work with the federal and state leaders directing operations from the command center there, said Ms. Hedge-Morrell, the councilwoman In Baton Rouge, she said, "we could yell and scream and keep fussing at them." By Thursday, local officials were yelling and screaming in public.

Col. Terry Ebbert, director of homeland security for New Orleans, complained that the whole recovery operation had been "carried on the backs of the little guys for four goddamn days," and "the rest of the nation can't get us any resources for security." He added, "It's like FEMA has never been to a hurricane."

And Thursday night. Mayor Nagin issued a "desperate S O S" and blew   90 up in a radio interview over the delays in sending a large contingent of troops to the city.

"Don't tell me 40,000 people are coming here," he said. "They're not here. It's too doggone late. Now get off your asses and do something, and let's fix the biggest goddamn crisis in the history of this country."

Finally, Hope

Friday, for the first time, there was a brisk dose of hope.

President Bush's visit to New Orleans, where he met with Mayor Nagin, and to the rest of the tattered Gulf Coast region, helped calm some of the tensions. Referring to the federal emergency actions, Mr. Bush said: "What is not working right, we're going to make it right."

The first sizable contingent of troops rolled into town and restored a measure of order to the convention center. There was food and water. There was a sense that maybe, things at least would stop getting worse.

But at a time when the nation fears disaster as never before, there was a horrific view of how unprepared emergency preparedness can be. 95

Louisiana's other United States senator, David Vitter, called FEMA's response completely dysfunctional, completely overwhelmed. He said the death toll might reach 10,000 unless the rescue is speeded up. "Hopefully today is the turnaround, that is my prayer," Mr. Vitter, a Republican, told reporters traveling with Mr. Bush.

But this sense of expectancy dissipated at the causeway on I-10 where the crowd of refugees had swollen from about 2,500 to 5,000, according to Lt. Michael R. Field of the Louisiana State Police.

"It's worse today," he said. "There's no command structure that I can see."

Jerome Wise, 46, who said he retired with a disability as a postal worker, tripped as he climbed out of a helicopter and shattered the one possession he had taken from his flooded home: a framed family photograph. His wife and seven of his

A family photograph is seen among the debris scattered throughout Gulfport.

children were somewhere in Mississippi. His eighth child, Calvin Holmes, was with him. He had been born 19 years ago on this day, but there was not much to celebrate.

"Doesn't feel like a birthday," Mr. Holmes said. 100

QUESTIONS

1. The title of this report suggests that it deals with a single incident that took place "in a flash," but the piece actually covers a complex web of events that evolved over a twelve-day period. Make an outline of the

piece to see how the authors have organized their material in order to create a dramatic and informative report that provides a clear story of the unfolding plot without losing sight of the complex circumstances that contributed to the disaster.

2. Notice how the graphic illustrations contribute to the report. What did you learn from the graphics that you did not learn from the authors' written report? What did you learn from their writing that you did not learn from the graphics?

3. Paragraphs 34 through 48 do not constitute reportage of events that took place during the twelve-day period. In fact, one could completely eliminate those paragraphs without damaging the continuity, as you can see by jumping from the end of paragraph 33 to the beginning of paragraph 49. What, then, is the purpose of paragraphs 34 through 48? What do they contribute to the report that would be missing without them?

4. Although we have classified this work as a piece of reporting, it begins with such an emotionally evocative description in the first three paragraphs that one might think that the authors are trying to arouse and engage their readers to take sides in an argument. What evidence do you find in the rest of the piece that the authors might have structured their report so as to influence readers concerning the cause(s) of the disaster?

5. What happened in New Orleans during the days and weeks following this report? Consult daily online versions of the *New York Times* or the *New Orleans Times Picayune* for at least twelve days following this report—that is, from September 5, 2006, to at least September 16. Then, on the basis of your research, write a report covering twelve or more days following September 4. Use graphic illustrations as needed to supplement your report, and organize your material so as to give a clear-cut and dramatic understanding of the period that you chose to cover in your report.

6. Think about a twelve-day or two-week period in your life when things suddenly took a turn for the worse in ways that you were unable to remedy at the time. What happened during that period, what were the causes of the problem, how did you and others respond? How did you come to terms with the problem in the wake of that period? Write an essay telling your story in a way that will help show the complexity of its causes and aftermath.

MAKING CONNECTIONS

Compare this report of Hurricane Katrina with Douglas Trevor's story of the 1935 hurricane (p. 158). Notice, in particular, how each piece narrates the development, climax, and aftermath of the hurricane. Which is more vividly detailed, and which is more informative?

JOEY: A "MECHANICAL BOY"

Bruno Bettelheim

Austrian-born psychotherapist Bruno Bettelheim (1903–1990) received his Ph.D. from the University of Vienna and was strongly influenced by the work of Sigmund Freud. Imprisoned as a Jew in Nazi concentration camps between 1938 and 1939, he wrote about these experiences after his immigration to the United States in an article titled "Individual and Mass Behavior in Extreme Situations" (1943) and later in the book The Informed Heart *(1960). From 1944 to 1973, he was director of a Chicago-based school for the rehabilitation of emotionally disturbed children, a subject he addressed in numerous works on child psychology and child rearing, including* Love Is Not Enough *(1950) and* The Empty Fortress *(1967). He was also the author of the highly influential* The Uses of Enchantment *(1976), a study of children and fairy tales. Since his suicide at the age of eighty-seven, Bettelheim has been the subject of a number of sharp attacks regarding the veracity of some of his work, and a 1997 biography by Richard Pollak was particularly damning. Still, Bettelheim continues to have his defenders, including his most recent biographer, his friend and literary agent Theron Raines. The following essay was first published in* Scientific American *in 1959.*

Joey, when we began our work with him, was a mechanical boy. He functioned as if by remote control, run by machines of his own powerfully creative fantasy. Not only did he himself believe that he was a machine, but, more remarkably, he created this impression in others. Even while he performed actions that are intrinsically human, they never appeared to be other than machine-started and executed. On the other hand, when the machine was not working, we had to concentrate on recollecting his presence, for he seemed not to exist. A human body that functions as if it were a machine and a machine that duplicates human functions are equally fascinating and frightening. Perhaps they are so uncanny because they remind us that the human body can operate without a human spirit, that body can exist without soul. And Joey was a child who had been robbed of his humanity.

Not every child who possesses a fantasy world is possessed by it. Normal children may retreat into realms of imaginary glory or magic powers, but they are easily recalled from these excursions. Disturbed children are not always able to make the return trip; they remain withdrawn, prisoners of the inner

657

world of delusion and fantasy. In many ways Joey presented a classic example of this state of infantile autism.[1]

At the Sonia Shankman Orthogenic School of the University of Chicago, it is our function to provide a therapeutic environment in which such children may start life over again. I have previously described in this magazine[2] the rehabilitation of another of our patients. This time I shall concentrate upon the illness, rather than the treatment. In any age, when the individual has escaped into a delusional world, he has usually fashioned it from bits and pieces of the world at hand. Joey, in his time and world, chose the machine and froze himself in its image. His story has a general relevance to the understanding of emotional development in a machine age.

Joey's delusion is not uncommon among schizophrenic[3] children today. He wanted to be rid of his unbearable humanity, to become completely automatic. He so nearly succeeded in attaining this goal that he could almost convince others, as well as himself, of his mechanical character. The descriptions of autistic children in the literature take for their point of departure and comparison the normal or abnormal human being. To do justice to Joey, I would have to compare him simultaneously to a most inept infant and a highly complex piece of machinery. Often we had to force ourselves by a conscious act of will to realize that Joey was a child. Again and again his acting-out of his delusions froze our own ability to respond as human beings.

During Joey's first weeks with us, we would watch absorbedly as this at once fragile-looking and imperious nine-year-old went about his mechanical existence. Entering the dining room, for example, he would string an imaginary wire from his "energy source" — an imaginary electric outlet — to the table. There he "insulated" himself with paper napkins and finally plugged himself in. Only then could Joey eat, for he firmly believed that the "current" ran his ingestive apparatus. So skillful was the pantomime that one had to look twice to be sure there was neither wire nor outlet nor plug. Children and members of our staff spontaneously avoided stepping on the "wires" for fear of interrupting what seemed the source of his very life.   5

For long periods of time, when his "machinery" was idle, he would sit so quietly that he would disappear from the focus of the most conscientious observation. Yet in the next moment he might be "working" and the center of our captivated attention. Many times a day he would turn himself on and shift noisily through a sequence of higher and higher gears until he "exploded," screaming "Crash, crash!" and hurling items from his ever present

---

[1]*autism*: A complex developmental disability that affects an individual in the areas of social interaction and communication. [Eds.]

[2]*in this magazine*: Bruno Bettelheim, "Schizophrenic art: A case study," *Scientific American* (April 1952). [Eds.]

[3]*schizophrenic*: Relating to a severe mental disorder that is characterized by thought disorder, delusions, and hallucinations. [Eds.]

apparatus — radio tubes, light bulbs, even motors or, lacking these, any handy breakable object. (Joey had an astonishing knack for snatching bulbs and tubes unobserved.) As soon as the object thrown had shattered, he would cease his screaming and wild jumping and retire to mute, motionless nonexistence.

Our maids, inured to difficult children, were exceptionally attentive to Joey; they were apparently moved by his extreme infantile fragility, so strangely coupled with megalomaniacal superiority. Occasionally some of the apparatus he fixed to his bed to "live him" during his sleep would fall down in disarray. This machinery he contrived from masking tape, cardboard, wire, and other paraphernalia. Usually the maids would pick up such things and leave them on a table for the children to find, or disregard them entirely. But Joey's machine they carefully restored: "Joey must have the carburetor so he can breathe." Similarly they were on the alert to pick up and preserve the motors that ran him during the day and the exhaust pipes through which he exhaled.

How had Joey become a human machine? From intensive interviews with his parents we learned that the process had begun even before birth. Schizophrenia often results from parental rejection, sometimes combined ambivalently with love. Joey, on the other hand, had been completely ignored.

"I never knew I was pregnant," his mother said, meaning that she had already excluded Joey from her consciousness. His birth, she said, "did not make any difference." Joey's father, a rootless draftee in the wartime civilian army, was equally unready for parenthood. So, of course, are many young couples. Fortunately most such parents lose their indifference upon the baby's birth. But not Joey's parents. "I did not want to see or nurse him," his mother declared. "I had no feeling of actual dislike — I simply didn't want to take care of him." For the first three months of his life Joey "cried most of the time." A colicky baby, he was kept on a rigid four-hour feeding schedule, was not touched unless necessary and was never cuddled or played with. The mother, preoccupied with herself, usually left Joey alone in the crib or playpen during the day. The father discharged his frustration by punishing Joey when the child cried at night.

Soon the father left for overseas duty, and the mother took Joey, now a year and a half old, to live with her at her parents' home. On his arrival the grandparents noticed that ominous changes had occurred in the child. Strong and healthy at birth, he had become frail and irritable; a responsive baby, he had become remote and inaccessible. When he began to master speech, he talked only to himself. At an early date he became preoccupied with machinery, including an old electric fan which he could take apart and put together again with surprising deftness.

Joey's mother impressed us with a fey quality that expressed her insecurity, her detachment from the world, and her low physical vitality. We were struck especially by her total indifference as she talked about Joey. This seemed much more remarkable than the actual mistakes she made in handling him. Certainly he was left to cry for hours when hungry, because she

10

fed him on a rigid schedule; he was toilet-trained with great rigidity so that he would give no trouble. These things happen to many children. But Joey's existence never registered with his mother. In her recollections he was fused at one moment with one event or person; at another, with something or somebody else. When she told us about his birth and infancy, it was as if she were talking about some vague acquaintance, and soon her thoughts would wander off to another person or to herself.

When Joey was not yet four, his nursery school suggested that he enter a special school for disturbed children. At the new school his autism was immediately recognized. During his three years there he experienced a slow improvement. Unfortunately a subsequent two years in a parochial school destroyed this progress. He began to develop compulsive defenses, which he called his "preventions." He could not drink, for example, except through elaborate piping systems built of straws. Liquids had to be "pumped" into him, in his fantasy, or he could not suck. Eventually his behavior became so upsetting that he could not be kept in the parochial school. At home things did not improve. Three months before entering the Orthogenic School he made a serious attempt at suicide.

To us Joey's pathological behavior seemed the external expression of an overwhelming effort to remain almost nonexistent as a person. For weeks Joey's only reply when addressed was "Bam." Unless he thus neutralized whatever we said, there would be an explosion, for Joey plainly wished to close off every form of contact not mediated by machinery. Even when he was bathed he rocked back and forth with mute, engine-like regularity, flooding the bathroom. If he stopped rocking, he did this like a machine too; suddenly he went completely rigid. Only once, after months of being lifted from his bath and carried to bed, did a small expression of puzzled pleasure appear on his face as he said very softly: "They even carry you to your bed here."

For a long time after he began to talk, he would never refer to anyone by name, but only as "that person" or "the little person" or "the big person." He was unable to designate by its true name anything to which he attached feelings. Nor could he name his anxieties except through neologisms or word contaminations.[4] For a long time he spoke about "master paintings" and "a master painting room" (i.e., masturbating and masturbating room). One of his machines, the "criticizer," prevented him from "saying words which have unpleasant feelings." Yet he gave personal names to the tubes and motors in his collection of machinery. Moreover, these dead things had feelings; the tubes bled when hurt and sometimes got sick. He consistently maintained this reversal between animate and inanimate objects.

In Joey's machine world everything, on pain of instant destruction,   15
obeyed inhibitory laws much more stringent than those of physics. When

---

[4]*neologisms or word contaminations*: Words that Joey made up or words that he peculiarly altered. [Eds.]

  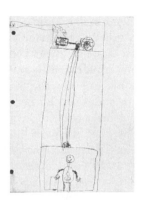

Growing self-esteem is shown in this sequence of drawings. At left Joey portrays himself as an electrical "papoose," completely enclosed, suspended in empty space and operated by wireless signals. In center drawing his figure is much larger, though still under wireless control. At right he is able to picture the machine which controls him, and he has acquired hands with which he can manipulate his immediate environment.

we came to know him better, it was plain that in his moments of silent withdrawal, with his machine switched off, Joey was absorbed in pondering the compulsive laws of his private universe. His preoccupation with machinery made it difficult to establish even practical contacts with him. If he wanted to do something with a counselor, such as play with a toy that had caught his vague attention, he could not do so: "I'd like this very much, but first I have to turn off the machine." But by the time he had fulfilled all the requirements of his preventions, he had lost interest. When a toy was offered to him, he could not touch it because his motors and his tubes did not leave him a hand free. Even certain colors were dangerous and had to be strictly avoided in toys and clothing, because "some colors turn off the current, and I can't touch them because I can't live without the current."

Joey was convinced that machines were better than people. Once when he bumped into one of the pipes on our jungle gym he kicked it so violently that his teacher had to restrain him to keep him from injuring himself. When she explained that the pipe was much harder than his foot, Joey replied: "That proves it. Machines are better than the body. They don't break; they're much harder and stronger." If he lost or forgot something, it merely proved that this brain ought to be thrown away and replaced by machinery. If he spilled something, his arm should be broken and twisted off because it did not work properly. When his head or arm failed to work as it should, he tried to punish it by hitting it. Even Joey's feelings were mechanical. Much later in his therapy, when he had formed a timid attachment to another child and had been rebuffed, Joey cried: "He broke my feelings."

Gradually we began to understand what had seemed to be contradictory in Joey's behavior — why he held on to the motors and tubes, then suddenly destroyed them in a fury, then set out immediately and urgently to equip himself with new and larger tubes. Joey had created these machines to run his body and mind because it was too painful to be human. But again and again he became dissatisfied with their failure to meet his need and rebellious at the way they frustrated his will. In a recurrent frenzy he "exploded" his light bulbs and tubes, and for a moment became a human being — for one crowning instant he came alive. But as soon as he had asserted his dominance through the self-created explosion, he felt his life ebbing away. To keep on existing he had immediately to restore his machines and replenish the electricity that supplied his life energy.

What deep-seated fears and needs underlay Joey's delusional system? We were long in finding out, for Joey's preventions effectively concealed the secret of his autistic behavior. In the meantime we dealt with his peripheral problems one by one.

During his first year with us Joey's most trying problem was toilet behavior. This surprised us, for Joey's personality was not "anal" in the Freudian sense; his original personality damage had antedated the period of his toilet-training. Rigid and early toilet-training, however, had certainly contributed to his anxieties. It was our effort to help Joey with this problem that led to his first recognition of us as human beings.

Going to the toilet, like everything else in Joey's life, was surrounded by   20 elaborate preventions. We had to accompany him; he had to take off all his clothes; he could only squat, not sit, on the toilet seat; he had to touch the wall with one hand, in which he also clutched frantically the vacuum tubes that powered his elimination. He was terrified lest his whole body be sucked down.

To counteract this fear we gave him a metal wastebasket in lieu of a toilet. Eventually, when eliminating into the wastebasket, he no longer needed to take off all his clothes, nor to hold on to the wall. He still needed the tubes and motors which, he believed, moved his bowels for him. But here again the all-important machinery was itself a source of new terrors. In Joey's world the gadgets had to move their bowels, too. He was terribly concerned that they should, but since they were so much more powerful than men, he was also terrified that if his tubes moved their bowels, their feces would fill all of space and leave him no room to live. He was thus always caught in some fearful contradiction.

Our readiness to accept his toilet habits, which obviously entailed some hardship for our counselors, gave Joey the confidence to express his obsessions in drawings. Drawing these fantasies was a first step toward letting us in, however distantly, to what concerned him most deeply. It was the first step in a yearlong process of externalizing his anal preoccupations. As a result he began seeing feces everywhere; the whole world became to him a mire of excrement. At the same time he began to eliminate freely wherever he happened to be. But with this release from his infantile imprisonment in compulsive rules, the toilet and the whole process of elimination became less dangerous. Thus far it had been beyond Joey's comprehension that anybody could possibly move his bowels without mechanical aid. Now Joey took a further step forward; defecation became the first physiological process he could perform without the help of vacuum tubes. It must not be thought that he was proud of this ability. Taking pride in an achievement presupposes that one accomplishes it of one's own free will. He still did not feel himself an autonomous person who could do things on his own. To Joey defecation still seemed enslaved to some incomprehensible but utterly binding cosmic law, perhaps the law his parents had imposed on him when he was being toilet-trained.

It was not simply that his parents had subjected him to rigid, early training. Many children are so trained. But in some cases the parents have a deep emotional investment in the child's performance. The child's response in turn makes training an occasion for interaction between them and for the building of genuine relationships. Joey's parents had no emotional investment in him. His obedience gave them no satisfaction and won him no affection or approval. As a toilet-trained child he saved his mother labor, just as household machines saved her labor. As a machine he was not loved for his performance, nor could he love himself.

So it had been with all other aspects of Joey's existence with his parents. Their reactions to his eating or noneating, sleeping or wakening, urinating or defecating, being dressed or undressed, washed or bathed did not flow from any unitary interest in him, deeply embedded in their personalities. By treating him mechanically his parents made him a machine. The various functions of life — even the parts of his body — bore no integrating relationship to one another or to any sense of self that was acknowledged and confirmed by others. Though he had acquired mastery over some functions, such as toilet-training and speech, he had acquired them separately and kept them isolated from each other. Toilet-training had thus not gained him a pleasant feeling of body mastery; speech had not led to communication of thought or feeling. On the contrary, each achievement only steered him away from self-mastery and integration. Toilet-training had enslaved him. Speech left him talking in neologisms that obstructed his and our ability to relate to each other. In Joey's development the normal process of growth had been made to run backward. Whatever he had learned put him not at the end of his infantile development toward integration but, on the contrary, farther behind than he was at its very beginning. Had we understood this sooner, his first years with us would have been less baffling.

It is unlikely that Joey's calamity could befall a child in any time and culture but our own. He suffered no physical deprivation; he starved for human contact. Just to be taken care of is not enough for relating. It is a necessary but not a sufficient condition. At the extreme where utter scarcity reigns, the forming of relationships is certainly hampered. But our society of mechanized plenty often makes for equal difficulties in a child's learning to relate. Where parents can provide the simple creature-comforts for their children only at the cost of significant effort, it is likely that they will feel

Elaborate sewage system in Joey's drawing of a house reflects his long preoccupation with excretion. His obsession with sewage reflected intense anxieties
produced by his early toilet-training, which was not only rigid but also completely
impersonal.

pleasure in being able to provide for them; it is this, the parents' pleasure,
that gives children a sense of personal worth and sets the process of relating
in motion. But if comfort is so readily available that the parents feel no particular pleasure in winning it for their children, then the children cannot develop the feeling of being worthwhile around the satisfaction of their basic
needs. Of course parent and children can and do develop relationships
around other situations. But matters are then no longer so simple and direct.
The child must be on the receiving end of care and concern given with pleasure and without the exaction of return if he is to feel loved and worthy of respect and consideration. This feeling gives him the ability to trust; he can en-
trust his well-being to persons to whom he is so important. Out of such trust
the child learns to form close and stable relationships.

For Joey relationship with his parents was empty of pleasure in comfort-
giving as in all other situations. His was an extreme instance of a plight that
sends many schizophrenic children to our clinics and hospitals. Many months
passed before he could relate to us; his despair that anybody could like him
made contact impossible.

When Joey could finally trust us enough to let himself become more infantile, he began to play at being a papoose. There was a corresponding
change in his fantasies. He drew endless pictures of himself as an electrical

Growing autonomy is shown in Joey's drawings of the imaginary "Carr" (car) family. Top drawing shows a machine which can move but is unoccupied. Machine in center is occupied, but by a passive figure. In bottom drawing figure has gained control of machine.

papoose. Totally enclosed, suspended in empty space, he is run by unknown, unseen powers through wireless electricity.

As we eventually came to understand, the heart of Joey's delusional system was the artificial, mechanical womb he had created and into which he had locked himself. In his papoose fantasies lay the wish to be entirely reborn in a womb. His new experiences in the school suggested that life, at all, might be worth living. Now he was searching for a way to be reborn in a better way. Since machines were better than men, what was more natural than to try rebirth through them? This was the deeper meaning of this electrical papoose.

As Joey made progress, his pictures of himself became more dominant in his drawings. Though still machine-operated, he has grown in self-importance. Another great step forward is represented in the picture above. . . . Now he has acquired hands that do something, and he has had the courage to make a picture of the machine that runs him. Later still the papoose became a person, rather than a robot encased in glass.

Eventually Joey began to create an imaginary family at the school: the   30
"Carr" family. Why the Carr family? In the car he was enclosed as he had been in his papoose, but at least the car was not stationary; it could move. More important, in a car one was not only driven but also could drive. The Carr family was Joey's way of exploring the possibility of leaving the school, of living with a good family in a safe, protecting car.

Gentle landscape painted by Joey after his recovery symbolizes the human emotions he had regained. At 12, having learned to express his feelings, he was no longer a machine.

Joey at last broke through his prison. In this brief account it has not been possible to trace the painfully slow process of his first true relations with other human beings. Suffice it to say that he ceased to be a mechanical boy and became a human child. This newborn child was, however, nearly 12 years old. To recover the lost time is a tremendous task. That work has occupied Joey and us ever since. Sometimes he sets to it with a will; at other times the difficulty of real life makes him regret that he ever came out of his shell. But he has never wanted to return to his mechanical life.

One last detail and this fragment of Joey's story has been told. When Joey was 12, he made a float for our Memorial Day parade. It carried the slogan: "Feelings are more important than anything under the sun." Feelings, Joey had learned, are what make for humanity; their absence, for a mechanical existence. With this knowledge Joey entered the human condition.

QUESTIONS

1. Bettelheim's task was to explain Joey's behavior as best he could. What did he and his colleagues do, what did they examine, and how did they behave as they developed their explanation of Joey?

2. Joey had come to some conclusions about himself and about the world he inhabited before Bettelheim encountered him. These explanations seem to have become fixed as interpretations, by which we mean simply that he had come to understand himself in terms of something else. In which passages does Bettelheim come closest to presenting Joey as his own interpreter? Summarize Joey's interpretation of himself — the structure or set of principles by which he understands himself.

3. To begin to be cured, Joey had to *reinterpret* his life. What were the major steps toward that reinterpretation? What changed for Joey?

4. Even to say *cured*, as we just did in question 3, involves an unexamined interpretation. What assumptions guide our use of that word? Do you find *cured* a satisfying explanation of what begins to happen to Joey?

5. The introduction to this section mentions this essay as an example of a case study — that is, a close examination of a unique person, event, or situation over time in a set of circumstances that are probably not replicable. Using this essay as your example, what else might characterize a case study? What makes a case study believable?

6. Quite a few people play roles or assume characterizations that deviate from what we think we know about them. Describe a person who does that. Offer your own limited case study. Try to indicate the extent to which the person's understanding of himself or herself is based on reality and the extent to which it isn't.

7. College can lead students to reinterpret themselves. In fact, reinterpretation traditionally has been a large part of the experience of going to

college. Write an explanation of yourself or of someone else you know well who is undergoing such a reinterpretation. What terms prevailed before college? What happened to call them into question? What kind of change has occurred, and what is at stake in this matter?

MAKING CONNECTIONS

1. If Bettelheim's essay is a kind of a case study, what other essays in this collection present something like it? What about one of the pieces in "Reflecting in the Arts and Humanities," such as essays by Maya Angelou (p. 43), Alice Walker (p. 54), or Frederick Douglass (p. 74)? Pick two or three pieces that seem close to being case studies, and describe how they are like and unlike this example by Bettelheim.

2. What does it mean to be human? Taking into account several essays besides Bettelheim's — essays by Stephen Jay Gould (p. 771), Jane van Lawick-Goodall (p. 395), and Alice Walker (p. 54) are all possibilities — take a stab at defining our essential human nature. What if anything seems invariable within a wealth of human possibilities? Is Joey's slogan (paragraph 32) a convincing expression of what is essentially human, or would you point to something else?

WHY MCDONALD'S FRIES TASTE SO GOOD

Eric Schlosser

Investigative journalist Eric Schlosser (b. 1960) graduated from Princeton University and later studied history at Oxford University in England. His journalism career began in college when he worked summers as a mailroom clerk at New York magazine and as a fact checker at Esquire. After pursuing a career as a playwright with little success, Schlosser returned to journalism. Since then, his work has appeared in major national magazines, including The Atlantic Monthly, Rolling Stone, *and* U.S. News & World Report, *and his 1994 series in* The Atlantic *about harsh prison terms for small-time marijuana users and dealers won the National Magazine Award for reporting. In 1995, Schlosser was a finalist for the same award for a report on the plight of migrant farmworkers in California. Of his work, Schlosser has said, "I did a graduate degree in history, and a lot of the stuff that I've done as a journalist is really similar to history. . . . I always start in the library. I always start with the source material. But ultimately, it's driven by, 'Oh, this is something people should know. I didn't know this either.'" Schlosser began investigating the fast-food industry for a two-part* Rolling Stone *article that appeared in 1998. The following essay is a chapter from his best-selling book on the subject,* Fast Food Nation: The Dark Side of the All-American Meal *(2001).*

The french fry was "almost sacrosanct for me," Ray Kroc, one of the founders of McDonald's, wrote in his autobiography, "its preparation a ritual to be followed religiously." During the chain's early years french fries were made from scratch every day. Russet Burbank potatoes were peeled, cut into shoestrings, and fried in McDonald's kitchens. As the chain expanded nationwide, in the mid-1960s, it sought to cut labor costs, reduce the number of suppliers, and ensure that its fries tasted the same at every restaurant. McDonald's began switching to frozen french fries in 1966 — and few customers noticed the difference. Nevertheless, the change had a profound effect on the nation's agriculture and diet. A familiar food had been transformed into a highly processed industrial commodity. McDonald's fries now come from huge manufacturing plants that can peel, slice, cook, and freeze 2 million pounds of potatoes a day. The rapid expansion of McDonald's and the popularity of its low-cost, mass-produced fries changed the way Americans eat. In

1960 Americans consumed an average of about eighty-one pounds of fresh potatoes and four pounds of frozen french fries. In 2000 they consumed an average of about fifty pounds of fresh potatoes and thirty pounds of frozen fries. Today McDonald's is the largest buyer of potatoes in the United States.

The taste of McDonald's french fries played a crucial role in the chain's success — fries are much more profitable than hamburgers — and was long praised by customers, competitors, and even food critics. James Beard[1] loved McDonald's fries. Their distinctive taste does not stem from the kind of potatoes that McDonald's buys, the technology that processes them, or the restaurant equipment that fries them: other chains use Russet Burbanks, buy their french fries from the same large processing companies, and have similar fryers in their restaurant kitchens. The taste of a french fry is largely determined by the cooking oil. For decades McDonald's cooked its french fries in a mixture of about 7 percent cottonseed oil and 93 percent beef tallow.[2] The mixture gave the fries their unique flavor — and more saturated beef fat per ounce than a McDonald's hamburger.

In 1990, amid a barrage of criticism over the amount of cholesterol in its fries, McDonald's switched to pure vegetable oil. This presented the company with a challenge: how to make fries that subtly taste like beef without cooking them in beef tallow. A look at the ingredients in McDonald's french fries suggests how the problem was solved. Toward the end of the list is a seemingly innocuous yet oddly mysterious phrase: "natural flavor." That ingredient helps to explain not only why the fries taste so good but also why most fast food — indeed, most of the food Americans eat today — tastes the way it does.

Open your refrigerator, your freezer, your kitchen cupboards, and look at the labels on your food. You'll find "natural flavor" or "artificial flavor" in just about every list of ingredients. The similarities between these two broad categories are far more significant than the differences. Both are manmade additives that give most processed food most of its taste. People usually buy a food item the first time because of its packaging or appearance. Taste usually determines whether they buy it again. About 90 percent of the money that Americans now spend on food goes to buy processed food. The canning, freezing, and dehydrating techniques used in processing destroy most of food's flavor — and so a vast industry has arisen in the United States to make processed food palatable. Without this flavor industry today's fast food would not exist. The names of the leading American fast-food chains and their best-selling menu items have become embedded in our popular culture and famous worldwide. But few people can name the companies that manufacture fast food's taste.

---

[1]*James Beard* (1903–1985): A chef, teacher, author, speaker, and television host who has been hailed as the "Father of American Cooking." [Eds.]

[2]*Beef tallow*: Solid fat obtained from the bodies of cattle. [Eds.]

The flavor industry is highly secretive. Its leading companies will not   5
divulge the precise formulas of flavor compounds or the identities of clients.
The secrecy is deemed essential for protecting the reputations of beloved
brands. The fast-food chains, understandably, would like the public to believe that the flavors of the food they sell somehow originate in their restaurant kitchens, not in distant factories run by other firms. A McDonald's
french fry is one of countless foods whose flavor is just a component in a
complex manufacturing process. The look and the taste of what we eat
now are frequently deceiving — by design.

The New Jersey Turnpike runs through the heart of the flavor industry, an
industrial corridor dotted with refineries and chemical plants. International
Flavors & Fragrances (IFF), the world's largest flavor company, has a manufacturing facility off Exit 8A in Dayton, New Jersey; Givaudan, the world's
second largest flavor company, has a plant in East Hanover. Haarmann &
Reimer, the largest German flavor company, has a plant in Teterboro, as does
Takasago, the largest Japanese flavor company. Flavor Dynamics has a plant
in South Plainfield; Frutarom is in North Bergen; Elan Chemical is in Newark.
Dozens of companies manufacture flavors in the corridor between Teaneck
and South Brunswick. Altogether the area produces about two thirds of the
flavor additives sold in the United States.

The IFF plant in Dayton is a huge pale-blue building with a modern office complex attached to the front. It sits in an industrial park, not far from
a BASF plastics factory, a Jolly French Toast factory, and a plant that manufactures Liz Claiborne cosmetics. Dozens of tractor-trailers were parked at
the IFF loading dock the afternoon I visited, and a thin cloud of steam
floated from a roof vent. Before entering the plant, I signed a nondisclosure
form, promising not to reveal the brand names of foods that contain IFF flavors. The place reminded me of Willy Wonka's chocolate factory.[3] Wonderful smells drifted through the hallways, men and women in neat white lab
coats cheerfully went about their work, and hundreds of little glass bottles
sat on laboratory tables and shelves. The bottles contained powerful but
fragile flavor chemicals, shielded from light by brown glass and round white
caps shut tight. The long chemical names on the little white labels were as
mystifying to me as medieval Latin. These odd-sounding things would be
mixed and poured and turned into new substances, like magic potions.

I was not invited into the manufacturing areas of the IFF plant, where,
it was thought, I might discover trade secrets. Instead I toured various laboratories and pilot kitchens, where the flavors of well-established brands
are tested or adjusted, and where whole new flavors are created. IFF's

---

[3] *Willy Wonka's chocolate factory*: The setting for the popular children's book
Charlie and the Chocolate Factory by Roald Dahl. It was made into a popular film,
retitled *Willy Wonka and the Chocolate Factory* (1971). [Eds.]

snack-and-savory lab is responsible for the flavors of potato chips, corn chips, breads, crackers, breakfast cereals, and pet food. The confectionery lab devises flavor for ice cream, cookies, candies, toothpastes, mouth-washes, and antacids. Everywhere I looked, I saw famous, widely adver-tised products sitting on laboratory desks and tables. The beverage lab was full of brightly colored liquids in clear bottles. It comes up with flavors for popular soft drinks, sports drinks, bottled teas, and wine coolers, for all-natural juice drinks, organic soy drinks, beers, and malt liquors. In one pilot kitchen I saw a dapper food technologist, a middle-aged man with an elegant tie beneath his crisp lab coat, carefully preparing a batch of cookies with white frosting and pink-and-white sprinkles. In another pilot kitchen I saw a pizza oven, a grill, a milkshake machine, and a french fryer identical to those I'd seen at innumerable fast-food restaurants.

In addition to being the world's largest flavor company, IFF manufac-tures the smells of six of the ten best-selling fine perfumes in the United States, including Estée Lauder's Beautiful, Clinique's Happy, Lancôme's Trésor, and Calvin Klein's Eternity. It also makes the smells of household products such as deodorant, dishwashing detergent, bath soap, shampoo, furniture polish, and floor wax. All these aromas are made through essen-tially the same process: the manipulation of volatile chemicals. The basic science behind the scent of shaving cream is the same as that governing the flavor of your TV dinner.

Scientists now believe that human beings acquired the sense of taste as   10 a way to avoid being poisoned. Edible plants generally taste sweet, harmful ones bitter. The taste buds on our tongues can detect the presence of half a dozen or so basic tastes, including sweet, sour, bitter, salty, astringent, and umami, a taste discovered by Japanese researchers — a rich and full sense of deliciousness triggered by amino acids in foods such as meat, shellfish, mushrooms, potatoes, and seaweed. Taste buds offer a limited means of de-tection, however, compared with the human olfactory system, which can perceive thousands of different chemical aromas. Indeed, "flavor" is prima-rily the smell of gases being released by the chemicals you've just put in your mouth. The aroma of a food can be responsible for as much as 90 per-cent of its taste.

The act of drinking, sucking, or chewing a substance releases its volatile gases. They flow out of your mouth and up your nostrils, or up the passage-way in the back of your mouth, to a thin layer of nerve cells called the olfac-tory epithelium, located at the base of your nose, right between your eyes. Your brain combines the complex smell signals from your olfactory epithe-lium with the simple taste signals from your tongue, assigns a flavor to what's in your mouth, and decides if it's something you want to eat.

A person's food preferences, like his or her personality, are formed dur-ing the first few years of life, through a process of socialization. Babies in-nately prefer sweet tastes and reject bitter ones; toddlers can learn to enjoy hot and spicy food, bland health food, or fast food, depending on what the people around them eat. The human sense of smell is still not fully understood. It is greatly affected by psychological factors and expectations. The mind focuses intently on some of the aromas that surround us and filters out the overwhelming majority. People can grow accustomed to bad smells or good smells; they stop noticing what once seemed overpowering. Aroma and memory are somehow inextricably linked. A smell can suddenly evoke a long-forgotten moment. The flavors of childhood foods seem to leave an indelible mark, and adults often return to them, without always knowing why. These "comfort foods" become a source of pleasure and reassurance — a fact that fast-food chains use to their advantage. Childhood memories of Happy Meals, which come with french fries, can translate into frequent adult visits to McDonald's. On average, Americans now eat about four servings of french fries every week.

The human craving for flavor has been a largely unacknowledged and unexamined force in history. For millennia royal empires have been built, unexplored lands traversed, and great religions and philosophies forever changed by the spice trade. In 1492 Christopher Columbus set sail to find seasoning. Today the influence of flavor in the world marketplace is no less decisive. The rise and fall of corporate empires — of soft-drink companies, snack-food companies, and fast-food chains — is often determined by how their products taste.

The flavor industry emerged in the mid-nineteenth century, as processed foods began to be manufactured on a large scale. Recognizing the need for flavor additives, early food processors turned to perfume companies that had long experience working with essential oils and volatile aromas. The great perfume houses of England, France, and the Netherlands produced many of the first flavor compounds. In the early part of the twentieth century Germany took the technological lead in flavor production, owing to its powerful chemical industry. Legend has it that a German scientist discovered methyl anthranilate, one of the first artificial flavors, by accident while mixing chemicals in the laboratory. Suddenly the lab was filled with the sweet smell of grapes. Methyl anthranilate later became the chief flavor compound in grape Kool-Aid. After World War II much of the perfume industry shifted from Europe to the United States, settling in New York City near the garment district and the fashion houses. The flavor industry came with it, later moving to New Jersey for greater plant capacity. Manmade flavor additives were used mostly in baked goods, candies, and sodas until the 1950s, when sales of processed food began to soar. The invention of gas chromatographs and mass spectrometers — machines capable of detecting volatile gases at low levels — vastly increased the number of flavors that could be synthesized. By the mid-1960s flavor companies were churning out compounds to supply the taste of Pop Tarts, Bac-Os, Tab, Tang, Filet-O-Fish sandwiches, and literally thousands of other new foods.

The American flavor industry now has annual revenues of about $1.4 billion. Approximately ten thousand new processed-food products are

15

introduced every year in the United States. Almost all of them require flavor additives. And about nine out of ten of these products fail. The latest flavor innovations and corporate realignments are heralded in publications such as *Chemical Market Reporter*, *Food Chemical News*, *Food Engineering*, and *Food Product Design*. The progress of IFF has mirrored that of the flavor industry as a whole. IFF was formed in 1958, through the merger of two small companies. Its annual revenues have grown almost fifteenfold since the early 1970s, and it currently has manufacturing facilities in twenty countries.

Today's sophisticated spectrometers, gas chromatographs, and headspace-vapor analyzers provide a detailed map of a food's flavor components, detecting chemical aromas present in amounts as low as one part per billion. The human nose, however, is even more sensitive. A nose can detect aromas present in quantities of a few parts per trillion — an amount equivalent to about 0.000000000003 percent. Complex aromas, such as those of coffee and roasted meat, are composed of volatile gases from nearly a thousand different chemicals. The smell of a strawberry arises from the interaction of about 350 chemicals that are present in minute amounts. The quality that people seek most of all in a food — flavor — is usually present in a quantity too infinitesimal to be measured in traditional culinary terms such as ounces or teaspoons. The chemical that provides the dominant flavor of bell pepper can be tasted in amounts as low as 0.02 parts per billion; one drop is sufficient to add flavor to five average-size swimming pools. The flavor additive usually comes next to last in a processed food's list of ingredients and often costs less than its packaging. Soft drinks contain a larger portion of flavor additives than most products. The flavor in a twelve-ounce can of Coke costs about half a cent.

The color additives in processed foods are usually present in even smaller amounts than the flavor compounds. Many of New Jersey's flavor companies also manufacture these color additives, which are used to make processed foods look fresh and appealing. Food coloring serves many of the same decorative purposes as lipstick, eye shadow, mascara — and is often made from the same pigments. Titanium dioxide, for example, has proved to be an especially versatile mineral. It gives many processed candies, frostings, and icings their bright white color; it is a common ingredient in women's cosmetics; and it is the pigment used in many white oil paints and house paints. At Burger King, Wendy's, and McDonald's coloring agents have been added to many of the soft drinks, salad dressings, cookies, condiments, chicken dishes, and sandwich buns.

Studies have found that the color of a food can greatly affect how its taste is perceived. Brightly colored foods frequently seem to taste better than bland-looking foods, even when the flavor compounds are identical. Foods that somehow look off color often seem to have off tastes. For thousands of years human beings have relied on visual cues to help determine what is edible. The color of fruit suggests whether it is ripe, the color of meat whether it is rancid. Flavor researchers sometimes use colored lights to modify the influence of visual cues during taste tests. During one experiment in the early 1970s people were served an oddly tinted meal of steak and french fries that appeared normal beneath colored lights. Everyone thought the meal tasted fine until the lighting was changed. Once it became apparent that the steak was actually blue and the fries were green, some people became ill.

The federal Food and Drug Administration does not require companies to disclose the ingredients of their color or flavor additives so long as all the chemicals in them are considered by the agency to be GRAS ("generally recognized as safe"). This enables companies to maintain the secrecy of their formulas. It also hides the fact that flavor compounds often contain more ingredients than the foods to which they give taste. The phrase "artificial strawberry flavor" gives little hint of the chemical wizardry and manufacturing skill that can make a highly processed food taste like strawberries.

A typical artificial strawberry flavor, like the kind found in a Burger   20
King strawberry milkshake, contains the following ingredients: amyl acetate, amyl butyrate, amyl valerate, anethol, anisyl formate, benzyl acetate, benzyl isobutyrate, butyric acid, cinnamyl isobutyrate, cinnamyl valerate, cognac essential oil, diacetyl, dipropyl ketone, ethyl acetate, ethyl amyl ketone, ethyl butyrate, ethyl cinnamate, ethyl heptanoate, ethyl heptylate, ethyl lactate, ethyl methylphenylglycidate, ethyl nitrate, ethyl propionate, ethyl valerate, heliotropin, hydroxyphenyl-2-butanone (10 percent solution in alcohol), α-ionone, isobutyl anthranilate, isobutyl butyrate, lemon essential oil, maltol, 4-methylacetophenone, methyl anthranilate, methyl benzoate, methyl cinnamate, methyl heptine carbonate, methyl naphthyl ketone, methyl salicylate, mint essential oil, neroli essential oil, nerolin, neryl isobutyrate, orris butter, phenethyl alcohol, rose, rum ether, γ-undecalactone, vanillin, and solvent.

Although flavors usually arise from a mixture of many different volatile chemicals, often a single compound supplies the dominant aroma. Smelled alone, that chemical provides an unmistakable sense of the food. Ethyl-2-methyl butyrate, for example, smells just like an apple. Many of today's highly processed foods offer a blank palette: whatever chemicals are added to them will give them specific tastes. Adding methyl-2-pyridyl ketone makes something taste like popcorn. Adding ethyl-3-hydroxy butanoate makes it taste like marshmallow. The possibilities are now almost limitless. Without affecting appearance or nutritional value, processed foods could be made with aroma chemicals such as hexanal (the smell of freshly cut grass) or 3-methyl butanoic acid (the smell of body odor).

The 1960s were the heyday of artificial flavors in the United States. The synthetic versions of flavor compounds were not subtle, but they did not have to be, given the nature of most processed food. For the past twenty years food processors have tried hard to use only "natural flavors" in their products. According to the FDA, these must be derived entirely from natural sources — from herbs, spices, fruits, vegetables, beef, chicken, yeast, bark, roots, and so forth. Consumers prefer to see natural flavors on a label, out of a belief that they are more healthful. Distinctions between artificial and natural flavors can be arbitrary and somewhat absurd, based more on how the flavor has been made than on what it actually contains.

"A natural flavor," says Terry Acree, a professor of food science at Cornell University, "is a flavor that's been derived with an out-of-date technology." Natural flavors and artificial flavors sometimes contain exactly the same chemicals, produced through different methods. Amyl acetate, for example, provides the dominant note of banana flavor. When it is distilled from bananas with a solvent, amyl acetate is a natural flavor. When it is produced by mixing vinegar with amyl alcohol and adding sulfuric acid as a catalyst, amyl acetate is an artificial flavor. Either way it smells and tastes the same. "Natural flavor" is now listed among the ingredients of everything from Health Valley Blueberry Granola Bars to Taco Bell Hot Taco Sauce.

A natural flavor is not necessarily more healthful or purer than an artificial one. When almond flavor — benzaldehyde — is derived from natural sources, such as peach and apricot pits, it contains traces of hydrogen cyanide, a deadly poison. Benzaldehyde derived by mixing oil of clove and amyl acetate does not contain any cyanide. Nevertheless, it is legally considered an artificial flavor and sells at a much lower price. Natural and artificial flavors are now manufactured at the same chemical plants, places that few people would associate with Mother Nature.

The small and elite group of scientists who create most of the flavor in   25
most of the food now consumed in the United States are called "flavorists." They draw on a number of disciplines in their work: biology, psychology, physiology, and organic chemistry. A flavorist is a chemist with a trained nose and a poetic sensibility. Flavors are created by blending scores of different chemicals in tiny amounts — a process governed by scientific principles but demanding a fair amount of art. In an age when delicate aromas and microwave ovens do not easily coexist, the job of the flavorist is to conjure illusions about processed food and, in the words of one flavor company's literature, to ensure "consumer likeability." The flavorists with whom I spoke were discreet, in keeping with the dictates of their trade. They were also charming, cosmopolitan, and ironic. They not only enjoyed fine wine but could identify the chemicals that give each grape its unique aroma. One flavorist compared his work to composing music. A well-made flavor compound will have a "top note" that is often followed by a "dry-down" and a "leveling-off," with different chemicals responsible for each stage. The taste of a food can be radically altered by minute changes in the flavoring combination. "A little odor goes a long way," one flavorist told me.

In order to give a processed food a taste that consumers will find appealing, a flavorist must always consider the food's "mouthfeel" — the unique combination of textures and chemical interactions that affect how the flavor is perceived. Mouthfeel can be adjusted through the use of various fats, gums, starches, emulsifiers, and stabilizers. The aroma chemicals in a food can be precisely analyzed, but the elements that make up mouthfeel are much harder to measure. How does one quantify a pretzel's hardness, a french fry's crispness? Food technologists are now conducting basic research in rheology, the branch of physics that examines the flow and deformation of materials. A number of companies sell sophisticated devices that attempt to measure mouthfeel. The TA.XT2i Texture Analyzer, produced by the Texture Technologies Corporation, of Scarsdale, New York, performs calculations based on data derived from as many as 250 separate probes. It is essentially a mechanical mouth. It gauges the most important rheological properties of a food — bounce, creep, breaking point, density, crunchiness, chewiness, gumminess, lumpiness, rubberiness, springiness, slipperiness, smoothness, softness, wetness, juiciness, spreadability, springback, and tackiness.

Some of the most important advances in flavor manufacturing are now occurring in the field of biotechnology. Complex flavors are being made using enzyme reactions, fermentation, and fungal and tissue cultures. All the flavors created by these methods — including the ones being synthesized by fungi — are considered natural flavors by the FDA. The new enzyme-based processes are responsible for extremely true-to-life dairy flavors. One company now offers not just butter flavor but also fresh creamy butter, cheesy butter, milky butter, savory melted butter, and super-concentrated butter flavor, in liquid or powder form. The development of new fermentation techniques, along with new techniques for heating mixtures of sugar and amino acids, have led to the creation of much more realistic meat flavors.

The McDonald's Corporation most likely drew on these advances when it eliminated beef tallow from its french fries. The company will not reveal the exact origin of the natural flavor added to its fries. In response to inquiries from *Vegetarian Journal*, however, McDonald's did acknowledge that its fries derive some of their characteristic flavor from "an animal source." Beef is the probable source, although other meats cannot be ruled out. In France, for example, fries are sometimes cooked in duck fat or horse tallow.

Other popular fast foods derive their flavor from unexpected ingredients. McDonald's Chicken McNuggets contain beef extracts, as does Wendy's Grilled Chicken Sandwich. Burger King's BK Broiler Chicken Breast Patty contains "natural smoke flavor." A firm called Red Arrow Products specializes in smoke flavor, which is added to barbecue sauces, snack foods, and processed meats. Red Arrow manufactures natural smoke flavor by charring sawdust and capturing the aroma chemicals released into the air. The smoke is captured in water and then bottled, so that other companies can sell food that seems to have been cooked over a fire.

The Vegetarian Legal Action Network recently petitioned the FDA to [30] issue new labeling requirements for foods that contain natural flavors. The group wants food processors to list the basic origins of their flavors on their labels. At the moment vegetarians often have no way of knowing whether a flavor additive contains beef, pork, poultry, or shellfish. One of the most widely used color additives — whose presence is often hidden by the phrase "color added" — violates a number of religious dietary restrictions, may cause allergic reactions in susceptible people, and comes from an unusual source. Cochineal extract (also known as carmine or carminic acid) is made from the desiccated bodies of female *Dactylopius coccus Costa*, a small insect harvested mainly in Peru and the Canary Islands. The bug feeds on red cactus berries, and color from the berries accumulates in the females and their un-hatched larvae. The insects are collected, dried, and ground into a pigment. It takes about seventy thousand of them to produce a pound of carmine, which is used to make processed foods look pink, red, or purple. Dannon strawberry yogurt gets its color from carmine, and so do many frozen fruit bars, candies, and fruit fillings, and Ocean Spray pink-grapefruit juice drink.

In a meeting room at IFF, Brian Grainger let me sample some of the company's flavors. It was an unusual taste test — there was no food to taste. Grainger is a senior flavorist at IFF, a soft-spoken chemist with graying hair, an English accent, and a fondness for understatement. He could easily be mistaken for a British diplomat or the owner of a West End brasserie with two Michelin stars.[4] Like many in the flavor industry, he has an Old World, old-fashioned sensibility. When I suggested that IFF's policy of secrecy and discretion was out of step with our mass-marketing, brand-conscious, self-promoting age and that the company should put its own logo on the countless products that bear its flavors, instead of allowing other companies to enjoy the consumer loyalty and affection inspired by those flavors, Grainger politely disagreed, assuring me that such a thing would never be done. In the absence of public credit or acclaim, the small and secretive fraternity of flavor chemists praise one another's work. By analyzing the flavor formula of a product, Grainger can often tell which of his counterparts at a rival firm devised it. Whenever he walks down a supermarket aisle, he takes a quiet pleasure in seeing the well-known foods that contain his flavors.

Grainger had brought a dozen small glass bottles from the lab. After he opened each bottle, I dipped a fragrance-testing filter into it — a long white strip of paper designed to absorb aroma chemicals without producing off notes. Before placing each strip of paper in front of my nose, I closed my eyes. Then I inhaled deeply, and one food after another was conjured from the glass bottles. I smelled fresh cherries, black olives, sautéed onions, and shrimp. Grainger's most remarkable creation took me by surprise. After closing my eyes, I suddenly smelled a grilled hamburger. The aroma was uncanny, almost miraculous — as if someone in the room were flipping burgers on a hot grill. But when I opened my eyes, I saw just a narrow strip of white paper and a flavorist with a grin.

---

[4] *West End brasserie with two Michelin stars:* The West End is London's theater district. A brasserie is a small restaurant. Michelin publishes guidebooks that describe and rate restaurants and hotels; two stars indicates "excellent cooking, worth a detour." [Eds.]

Questions

1. How would you describe the title of this piece? Attention-getting? Misleading? Ironic?
2. Much of this article presents scientific terms, but Schlosser is writing for a general audience rather than for scientists. How does he present those scientific terms and concepts for the general reader? What is his purpose in presenting the entire list of ingredients in strawberry flavor (paragraph 20)? How do you feel about strawberry flavor after reading the list of ingredients?
3. How does Schlosser arrange his material? His tour of the IFF plant and his experiences there structure much of his report, but how much background research is present?
4. Check the ingredients on a package of your favorite processed food. Does it contain any "natural" flavors? If so, what natural flavor? Does it contain any of the chemicals mentioned in the text?
5. Schlosser claims that about 90 percent of the food we buy is processed. How much processed food is in your home right now? How much fresh food? Make lists of each, and compare your lists with your classmates' lists. Categorize the foods and beverages, and write a report on the food preferences of the class. What are the percentages of processed and of unprocessed food consumed by your class?
6. If you had some money to invest, would you consider investing it in the flavor industry? Why or why not?
7. In paragraph 12, Schlosser talks about psychological factors connected with smells and flavors. Write a report on your favorite "comfort food" and the memories connected with it. Or take the opposite approach: describe the memories that are aroused by a smell or flavor that you detest.

Making Connections

Both Schlosser and Malcolm Gladwell, in "The Naked Face" (p. 519), deal with subjects that are so familiar as to be overlooked: Schlosser with the taste of food and Gladwell with the expression of emotions on a person's face. How does each writer create interest in such a commonplace topic? What are the similarities in their methods, and what are the differences? You might start by examining the first sentence of each piece. What does each sentence *do*? What expectations does each raise? You might also consider what kind of background material each writer provides to capture the reader's attention. How does each writer weave together description and background information?

FUN WITH PHYSICS

K. C. Cole

*K. C. Cole was born in 1946 in Detroit, spent some of her early
childhood in Rio de Janeiro, and received her bachelor's degree
from Barnard College. She started her career as a journalist writing
about eastern Europe and the Soviet Union. But after discovering
the Exploratorium, the interactive science museum in San Francisco, Cole became entranced with physics and began writing about
science. Since 1994, she has been a science writer for the* Los Angeles Times, *where for several years she wrote the column "Mind over
Matter." Her writing has been published in the* New York Times,
The New Yorker, Discover, Smithsonian, Omni, Glamour, Cosmopolitan, Ms., *and other publications. Cole has taught at UCLA,
Yale, and Wesleyan, and has been a fellow at the Mathematical Sciences Research Institute and the Exploratorium. Among other
awards, she has received the American Institute of Physics Science
Writing prize in 1995, the* Los Angeles Times *Pulitzer Prize nomi-
nation in 1998, and the* Los Angeles Times *award for best explanatory journalism in 1999. Cole is widely recognized and acclaimed
for writing about very complex subjects in a clear, concise, and
often lyrical way. Her many books, some on scientific topics and
some on women's issues, include* What Only a Mother Can Tell
You about Having a Baby *(1980),* The Universe and the Teacup:
The Mathematics of Truth and Beauty *(1998),* The Hole in the
Universe: How Scientists Peered over the Edge of Emptiness and
Found Everything *(2001), and* Mind over Matter: Conversations
with the Cosmos *(2003). The following piece appeared in 2003 in*
The New Yorker.*

Janet Conrad fell in love with the universe at 3 a.m. on a cold autumn
night in Wooster, Ohio. A teenager, she had no desire to get out of bed and
face the frigid air in order to help her father, a dairy scientist, spray warm
water on the prize dahlias they were growing together. But when she did go
out to the garden she saw, for the first time in her life, how a shower of electrically charged particles flung from a star ninety-three million miles away
can cover the sky in glowing pastel curtains: "I remember standing there
and looking at the northern lights, and it was so neat that something so
remote, so very far away, could be creating something so beautiful right
in front of my eyes," she says. Twenty-five years later, Conrad, who is now
thirty-nine and an associate professor of physics at Columbia University,

created her own universe — a spherical particle detector, forty feet in diameter, that she built under an igloo of dirt at the Fermi National Accelerator Laboratory (Fermilab), near Chicago. The particle detector is lined with a constellation of twelve hundred eight-inch-wide "eyes," or phototubes, and is filled with eight hundred tons of baby oil, which is used to detect the shock waves generated by particle interactions. Early last fall, the detector began an unblinking vigil for subatomic stealth particles known as "sterile" neutrinos.

A lot can go wrong in large-scale physics experiments. Conrad has been basted in foul-smelling oil. She has been squirted with sticky insulating goo. She has had giant helium balloons get away because the soccer nets she was using to hold them down came loose. And she watched in dismay as the pristine white tank for her current experiment acquired a tough yellow scum (which her mother helpfully advised her to remove with Arm & Hammer baking soda). Nothing that Conrad has done in the past, however, approaches the challenge of her current experiment, which involves some fifty scientists from twelve institutions — including the experiment's co-leader, Bill Louis, of the Los Alamos National Laboratory. Conrad's goal is to understand the character of neutrinos, mere wisps of matter that are more numerous, more elusive, and arguably more important than any other subatomic particle.

Neutrinos outnumber all ordinary particles by a billion to one — a thousand trillion of them occupy your body at every second, streaming down from the sky, up from the ground, and even from radioactive atoms inside you. But, for all their omnipresence, they might just as well be ghosts. As John Updike put it in his poem "Cosmic Gall":

> The earth is just a silly ball.
> To them, through which they simply pass,
> Like dustmaids down a drafty hall.

Neutrinos can slip through a hundred light-years' worth of lead without stirring up so much as a breeze, and yet they power the most violent events in the universe, making stars shine and, in the process, creating every element, every dust mote, every raindrop, and, ultimately every thought. They are the alchemists of the cosmos, the catalysts that make nuclear fusion possible, releasing the radiation that melts rock and makes the continents move. Because neutrinos can penetrate almost everything, they can take scientists to places they've never been before — into the cores of exploding stars, for instance, or back to the big bang. As the universe evolved, neutrinos, because they interact so rarely with other particles, were, in effect, left behind, frozen in time. They are still there (or here, if you will) today, imprinted with information about the state of the universe at its birth. Most important, neutrinos break the basic rules that govern other particles, thereby suggesting that the rules themselves are wrong. If Conrad's experiment

Janet Conrad holding a photo multiplier tube.

confirms her suspicions, she will show that a particle that was barely believed to exist can carry enough weight to determine the drape of galaxies.

When I met up with Conrad at a gathering of the group of Columbia
professors who work on high-energy physics, she was the only woman
there. Some of her fellow-physicists seemed not to know what to make of
her. In contrast to earlier generations of women physicists, she has managed
to remain unabashedly girlish. She uses words like "neat" and "cool," and
her talks are often embellished with whimsical drawings and analogies to
hair dye, shopping, or flowers. "She gets away with it because she knows
her stuff so well—nobody can attack her," Bonnie Fleming, a Fermilab
physicist, says. Rocky Kolb, a cosmologist at Fermilab, explains, "She obtains what she wants in a different way than most physicists. She can tell
you you're wrong without telling you you're stupid. That's unusual.This is
not a field for the faint of heart—its like herding cats. You have a hundred
physicists and deep down inside they all think they are smarter than you
are. Everyone else herds with a cattle prod. Janet does it with charm." Conrad's charisma has carried her to the top of a field that has traditionally had
few places for women, and has won her acclaim and honors such as the
prestigious Presidential Early Career Award and the New York City
Mayor's Award for Excellence in Science and Technology (During the presentation of the latter, she had to teach then Mayor Giuliani how to pronounce quantumchromodynamics.")

Next to her colleagues in khaki and oxford blue, Conrad, with shiny   5
auburn hair, a short cranberry-colored skirt, and matching heels, offered a

study in contrasts. She laughs a lot, and her speech comes in staccato bursts, with few transitions. "Conversations seem to jump around, but, if you probe, there's a logical connection," her mentor, the Columbia physicist Michael Shaevitz, says. "She has this wealth of information stored away in different areas, and she pulls it in like an octopus with tentacles." Conrad also gets angry easily. "I have a tendency to fight bitterly," she admits. "I'm so hotheaded that half the time I get myself into trouble." But, she adds, "A little bit of hotheadedness doesn't hurt you in this field." Conrad applied for tenure at Columbia at the first possible moment (and got it, at the age of thirty-six), because she simply couldn't stand the suspense of waiting. A lot of her energy seems to be fuelled by Diet Coke; empty cans line up wherever she goes, like bread crumbs marking her trail (She drinks so much of it that her mother bought her stock in the company.) It is this combination of charm and restlessness — as well as her ability to design clever and elegant experiments that has made Conrad successful enough to persuade Columbia to put up a million dollars to get her experiment going while she waited for grant money to arrive. It was an enormous sum for any young physicist to receive, let alone a woman.

Neutrinos have been eluding physicists ever since Wolfgang Pauli first hypothesized their existence, in 1930. In the physical universe, what goes in always equals what comes out, in one form or another. But physicists had noticed that when radioactive atoms spat out electrons and transformed into other kinds of atoms, some of the original energy appeared to be missing. Pauli proposed that it had been carried away by a virtually invisible particle. The thought was so preposterous, however, that even he seemed disinclined to take it seriously. I have hit upon a desperate remedy," he wrote to his colleagues. "But I don't feel secure enough to publish anything about this idea." He went on to express his embarrassment at his own heresy: "I have a done a terrible thing. I have postulated a particle that cannot be detected." In 1931, the physicist Enrico Fermi baptized the hypothetical parade "neutrino," or "little neutral one," but his paper was rejected by the journal Nature as too "speculative" and "remote from reality."

The first experiment actually to hunt for neutrinos was called, appropriately enough, Project Poltergeist. In 1956, the Los Alamos–based physicists Clyde Cowan and Fred Reines found a definite trace of neutrinos in the intense wash of radiation spewed forth from newly commissioned nuclear reactors. They wrote to Pauli, who reportedly shared a case of champagne with friends. But detecting neutrinos from a reactor was one thing, and detecting them in nature was another. The first neutrinos from the sun weren't discovered until twelve years later, in the Homestake gold mine, in South Dakota, where they created reactions in a tank filled with chlorinated cleaning fluid. To everyone's surprise, however, the Homestake experiment, led by Raymond Davis, Jr., also discovered that about two-thirds of the neutrinos that had been expected to arrive from the sun as a product of nuclear fusion were missing. A 1992 experiment designed to detect atmospheric neutrinos found a similar portion absent. Physicists came up with various theories to account for these disappearances, but in the past few years they have settled on one: neutrinos aren't really "missing"; they are simply altering themselves en route. "You start out with a race of house cats, and you find you have lions in the end," Conrad explains; the physicists set their traps for kittens, and lions ignore the bait.

Of course, it is misleading to think of fundamental particles as "clearly defined entities like cats. They are more like waves. You can imagine a particle, for example, as the sound wave, you make by plucking a guitar string. A neutrino, however, is not a single defined wave. It is a mixture of waves — messy yet fundamental, like a signature. Neutrinos are known to exist in three different forms, each associated with a member of the electron family — the electron neutrino, the muon neutrino, and the tau neutrino. Yet any neutrino can be part electron, part muon, and part tau neutrino, and it can change as its waves fall in and out of step with each other. The discovery that neutrinos oscillate between forms has huge consequences. The particles were originally thought to be weightless, but in order for the waves to fall in and out of synch they must have some mass. (Guitar strings with different masses produce different sounds because they vibrate at different frequencies; if neutrinos had no mass, there could be no oscillation.) Given their numbers, this means that neutrinos — even if their mass is minute — must weigh as much as all the stars in the sky.

Although physicists can easily tell how many neutrinos go "missing," they can't always tell what forms they have changed into. Most are transforming between the familiar electron, muon, and tau forms. But a highly controversial experiment, conducted at the Los Alamos National Laboratory in 1995, uncovered a fourth possibility: that a portion of the neutrinos were changing into a completely unknown species, not electron, muon, or tau, and perhaps substantially more massive than any of those — a species that was undetectable by any means except its gravitational pull. This hypothetical form is known as the sterile neutrino.

Most physicists were skeptical of the results, in large part because the numbers seemed out of line with those from previous experiments. And, when Conrad and Michael Shaevitz decided to design an experiment to prove or disprove the Los Alamos results, their colleagues were dumbfounded. They couldn't believe, according to Shaevitz, that such "well-respected physicists" would even bother. Conrad's friends asked her why she wanted to "waste her life." In 1998, however, combining her skills as an experimenter and a salesperson, Conrad presented her proposal to the advisory council at Fermilab. In contrast to the many larger experiments performed at the lab, hers was designed to give clear results quickly, relatively inexpensively, and with mostly recycled equipment. Even the project's name was chosen to stress its streamlined approach: Mini Booster Neutrino Experiment (or MiniBooNE). "The name was just weird enough that everyone remembered it," Conrad says — which is no small matter when it comes

10

to securing funding. It was the only time that anyone remembers applause at such a meeting. "We usually sit there and scowl," Andreas Kronfeld, a Fermilab physicist, says. "Then this sparkling young person gives a really good talk. It was a little sunshine in all that gray."

Fermilab was founded in 1967 by Robert Rathbun Wilson, a Berkeley-trained physicist who had worked on the Manhattan Project and then, after the bombing of Nagasaki, refused to take part in weapons research. Wilson was also a sculptor, and he planted his works everywhere on the sixty-eight-hundred-acre grounds. There is a Mobius strip in a pool on the roof of the auditorium, a staircase modelled on a double strand of DNA. Even the utility poles are shaped like the symbol for pi. Thousands of physicists come here now, mostly to conduct experiments with the world's highest-energy accelerator, a circular racetrack for particles called the Tevatron. Around its four-mile circumference, superconducting magnets steer protons travelling at almost the speed of light into head-on collisions, setting off fireworks of particles as the energy of speed congeals into matter. In effect, each collision creates a miniature big bang — creation all over again, thousands of times per second. Shopping-mall-size detectors (think of them as elaborate electronic eyes) are needed to keep track of just a tiny part of this activity.

The Tevatron ring is bordered, on the outside, by a river of cooling water, like a moat. Inside, Wilson and his successors have reverentially re-created twelve hundred acres of Illinois prairie. If Fermilab was to be the frontier of physics, Wilson reasoned, then it should have its roots in the literal frontier. The grasses grow up to ten feet tall, and much of the original wildlife has returned, including deer, foxes, salamanders, turtles, beavers, weasels, mink, and hundreds of species of birds. As a final touch, Wilson added a herd of buffalo. There is another poignancy at Fermilab these days, a palpable sense that billion-dollar particle accelerators and physics labs — the "cathedrals of contemporary science," as Wilson called them — have fallen from favor since the post–Second World War period, when physics produced not only the H-bomb but also such leaders in the disarmament effort as Einstein and Wilson himself. In many ways, this makes the results of small experiments such as MiniBooNE even more pivotal.

I attended a MiniBooNE meeting at Fermilab a few months before the experiment was due to be launched. The meeting took place in a glass-walled high-rise building that Wilson modelled on Beauvais Cathedral, in France. It was a difficult time for the project. The head contractor had been killed in a car accident the day before the meeting, and a building designed to house part of the experiment was still unfinished. A shipment of baby oil from Exxon had turned out to be unusable, and the company was struggling to replace it. "A million things that I never thought could happen have happened on this experiment," Conrad said. "You'd never dream that your contractor could die." Many of the researchers had gathered to bring one another up to date on the experiment's progress: the people who would generate the beam of muon neutrinos, which Conrad and her collaborators hoped to observe oscillating into "sterile" forms; the people building the detector; the people in charge of the oil and of the computer programs to keep track of it all; and the people working on the physics itself — the properties of neutrinos, and possible astrophysics applications. There was conversation about dump-chunks, QTsmear, spillsplitters, and Roefitters. Someone passed around a heavy ring, a custom-made flange. It was an odd pairing of mathematics and metal, of the ephemeral and the concrete. "That's one of the neat things about being an experimentalist," Conrad says. "You can actually see what you've accomplished."

Childhood in a small Ohio town was, it turns out, a surprisingly good preparation for a career in particle physics. Conrad learned many of her practical skills in the local 4-H Club. "Electronics really isn't that different from cooking or sewing," she says. "There's a certain set of rules that you follow, a certain set of patterns. You may want to try variations on the theme, but, once you know your patterns it's pretty easy." Conrad believes that she was probably born to be a scientist.

"I loved having conversations with my parents about how the world   15 works," she says. "They never treated me as someone who couldn't understand." Her uncle, Walter Lipscomb, a Nobel laureate in chemistry, challenged her whenever he came to visit, throwing out puzzles at the dinner table. I was a miniature adult as far as he was concerned, and he was happy to let me in on his world," Conrad says. After her sophomore year at Swarthmore, her uncle offered her his apartment in Cambridge, Massachusetts, for the summer, and suggested some people she might approach for jobs at Harvard. One of them was the late physicist Frank Pipkin, who was using the Harvard cyclotron to test parts of an experiment to be installed at Fermilab. Conrad worked with Pipkin that summer. The following summer, she went with him to Fermilab. As soon as she saw the detectors, she says, "I knew I wanted to play with them. It was big and dirty and it was just so me."

Dirt, it seems, is an important ingredient in particle-physics experiments. The otherwise flat topology of Fermilab is interrupted by big mounds of earth, long ridges that look as if some large, determined animal were burrowing beneath. The earth acts as an insulator, protecting the experiments below from stray cosmic rays, and the people above from radiation produced by the particle beams. The tank of baby oil that is the heart of MiniBooNE sits under a dirt hill that Conrad describes as "remarkably like a home for Teletubbies." Bill Louis, Conrad's partner, drove me to the site. We bounced over unpaved tracks until we came to something that looked like a huge yurt with prairie grasses sprouting from the top of it. A small antechamber inside was stacked with metal cabinets full of computers. Louis opened a square entry hatch and extended a rickety metal ladder, and we crawled down backward into the huge white tank, which was about to be sealed for good.

Building such an experiment can involve some difficult choices. The quarry you're chasing can't be seen directly, so you have to induce it to leave visible traces. The world's most famous neutrino experiment, Super-Kamiokande (or Super-K), in Japan, uses fifty thousand tons of purified water — watched over by twelve thousand phototubes — to catch the wakes produced by the traceable particles in neutrino interactions. Workers ride inside the vast cavern in a little rubber boat. MiniBooNE uses oil, which leaves slightly better wakes but precludes the possibility of boat travel ("If I fell out, I would sink to the bottom and die," Conrad says, laughing.) The wake is actually a shockwave made by an electrically charged particle travelling through the oil — something like a sonic boom — and the phototubes pick it up as a ring of light. A fuzzy ring signals that the incoming neutrino was an electron neutrino; a sharp one signals a muon neutrino. But it's not always that simple. Other kinds of reactions may be impossible to identify. "Until you've tried to work with a particle as elusive as a neutrino, you have no idea how hard this can actually be," Conrad says. There are so many decisions to be made: Do you watch for neutrinos to disappear or for puzzling appearances? And where, exactly, do you look? Say you start off with lions and they change into cats after two miles, then back into lions two miles later; if you placed your detector at the four-mile mark, you'd see only lions and could easily conclude that nothing had happened. "So often you pose a question, and you build a detector to look at it," Conrad says. "Then the detector answers some other question."

Conrad took me to a hangarlike area, where a critical part of the experiment was being tested. It was an enormous aluminum "horn" designed to focus pions, unstable particles that naturally disintegrate into neutrinos as they travel through a hundred and fifty feet of sewer pipe buried underground. A purified beam of neutrinos would then continue on, through ordinary ground, toward the detector full of oil. To anyone who has spent time in a physics lab, this seems peculiar: other sorts of particle beams are steered through pristine vacuum pipes to insure that they aren't bumped off their course by unintended collisions with air. Neutrinos, however, don't "see" air, any more than they see lead; everything is a vacuum to them. Conrad expects neutrinos from the beam to collide with molecules in the oil several times a minute. But, for every controlled neutrino encounter, a hundred thousand will be caused by cosmic rays from the atmosphere. To avoid these false signals, most neutrino experiments are performed at the bottom of deep mines. MiniBooNE, instead, will receive its beam of neutrinos in bursts, five every second. By comparing the timing of the bursts and of the signals, Conrad and her collaborators hope to sort the needles from the hay. Three hundred extra phototubes line an outer wall of the Mini-BooNE sphere, forming a "veto region" designed specifically to flag stray signals — a muon entering from the outside, say, rather than being created by a neutrino in the oil.

In Conrad's tenth-floor office at Fermilab, a field of fake gerbera daisies swayed on tall metal rods like orange and red lollipops. The bottom shelf of a bookcase held a small bottle of Tide detergent and a black light (to

demonstrate how scintillators glow), tuning forks (for explaining oscillating neutrinos), and little vials of oil. Conrad never passes up an opportunity
to discuss what she's doing. On planes, she draws other passengers into
conversations, inviting them to visit Fermilab. She recently completed a
radio series, "Earth and Sky," which aired on National Public Radio. And
she works with high-school teachers, and even students, whom she hires
to help her on experiments. When she won the Maria Goeppert-Mayer
Award — for outstanding achievement by a young woman physicist — in
2001, she began to turn her attention more directly to the problem of
bringing women into her field. She acknowledges that women tend to have
a different style of doing physics from men; they use more words relative to
equations, for instance, and this can count against them on exams. "You
can watch the guys look at this and say, 'Too many words. Must not know
what she's talking about,'" Conrad says. But, in response to those who
question whether the specialized equipment is intimidating to women, she
insists that it's a lot less complicated than what you find in an average well-
stocked kitchen. Conrad's presence has already made a big difference in the
Columbia physics department. When she first started teaching there, eight
years ago, a site report by the American Physical Society concluded starkly,
"Columbia is not a friendly place for women students and perhaps for students in general." By 2000, half of the undergraduates in the high-energy-
physics program were female, a shift that many people attribute to Conrad's aggressive attempts to draw young women into the department.

When colleagues at Columbia talk about what she has accomplished,   20
they often tell the story about the benches. In the fall of 1996, she noticed
that students were sitting on the dirty floor in the hallway, waiting for her
class to start. When she asked for benches to be installed, the administration
balked at the expense. Over the Thanksgiving break, she was visiting a former student's family and mentioned the problem. The next day, the student's
father, a Columbia alumnus, mailed her a check for a thousand dollars,
which she used to buy five plain benches. Other people in the department
liked the look of them, and started to add their own touches to the hallway —
posters and plants. Then, as Conrad tells it, "the university people came
back and said, 'Wow, this looks really nice, but these benches are not the top-
notch benches we would like to have here.' So they went and bought nice
benches and gave me back mine." "It's one of those things that really made a
difference," Steve Kahn, then the chair of the physics department, says.

After our day at Fermilab, Conrad took me to her house in nearby
Geneva, Illinois. She has two other homes as well — an apartment in Manhattan and a house in Las Cruces, New Mexico, where her husband, Vassili
Papavassiliou, teaches physics at New Mexico State University. Conrad and
Papavassiliou met while they were wiring two tiers of the same experiment
(one is reminded of Lady and the Tramp sharing that fateful strand of
spaghetti), but, like many academic couples, they couldn't find work in the

same city. They make do, often meeting at Chicago's O'Hare airport for dinner. "It's really bad when the waitress at the airport starts to know you," Conrad said.

A suitcase full of dirty laundry had waited by the door of Conrad's Geneva house for several days, but the night before she had prepared two Greek pies for our dinner, brushing thirty separate layers of phyllo dough with butter — after a full day's work and a friend's fortieth-birthday party. "That's why people don't like to be around me much," she said. "I wear them out." The previous weekend, she had planted three hundred tulip and daffodil bulbs. Spread out on the coffee table were photographs of her father's dahlias, which she was examining in order to choose roots for next year. She called them "bursts of light," and they did seem to explode, like red and pink and orange fireworks against the black backgrounds. "I look at these beautifully symmetric flowers, and yet I find that the one little flaw in them is the thing that makes the flower interesting," she said. "And that's true in high-energy physics, too. It's the little flaws that make it fascinating. And some of the little flaws are not so little."

Of course, it's hard to know whether a flaw is just a flaw, or whether it's a crack in the edifice of physics, a first glimpse into something entirely unexpected. Because data are always ambiguous, it can be years before physicists feel confident enough to publish potentially controversial results. On September 1, 2002, neutrinos began to trickle into the baby oil at Mini-BooNE. By the middle of this month, the detector's phototubes had already picked up a hundred thousand interactions. Conrad says that she won't know for at least two years whether the disparaged Los Alamos results were right after all. But it should be worth the wait. If MiniBooNE eventually proves the existence of the sterile neutrino, it will require physicists to rethink everything, from the details of the big bang to the formation of the elements. It could even help explain why there is matter in the universe at all. On the other hand, it will be just as important if MiniBooNE proves that there is no sterile neutrino. "Not finding the ether was a successful experiment," Rocky Kolb says, referring to an experiment that proved there was no medium for carrying light — a finding that helped to cement Einstein's theory of relativity. "A lot of people have too much ego to work on confirming experiments," he adds. "Janet is one of the world's leaders in neutrino physics, and, whatever the future of particle physics is, she'll play a major role."

As MiniBooNE began to take in data, a second experiment gearing up at Fermilab was preparing to send a beam of neutrinos four hundred and fifty miles to a deep mine in Minnesota. Another experiment aims to send neutrinos from Geneva, Switzerland, through the Alps to a lab under a mountain near Rome. An endeavor aptly named ICECUBE will turn a cubic kilometre of ice at the South Pole into a detector to observe neutrinos from the stars and cores of galaxies. Conrad, meanwhile, has taken a lead role in pushing for a National Underground Science Laboratory in the Homestake mine, where neutrinos from the sun were first observed to be missing. (Raymond Davis, who led the first Homestake discovery, won the 2002 Nobel Prize in Physics.) And last year Conrad completed her work on a select panel of physicists charged with deciding what kind of major particle accelerator should follow Fermilab's designated successor, now under construction in Europe. As usual, Conrad was one of the youngest people on the panel, and there were some difficult moments. Some people blamed her for orchestrating a protest against a few of the panel's recommendations, even though she claims she had nothing to do with it. "I believe I make things clot," she says. "You add me to a mixture, and all of a sudden big chunks of stuff will fall to the bottom."

Two days after I left Fermilab, one of the twelve thousand phototubes   25
in Super-K, the Japanese detector, collapsed while it was being refilled with water after routine maintenance. The shock wave from the collapse created a storm inside the tank. Seven thousand phototubes were shattered. "This is a real disaster," Conrad told me over lunch in Madison, Wisconsin. She'd driven up from Fermilab with Len Bugel, a physics teacher at Stratton Mountain School, in Vermont, with whom she'd worked for many years, and in the car she had persuaded Bugel to try to figure out how to duplicate the effect on a small scale — to see whether MiniBooNE's tubes would collapse under the same conditions. "Creative resource-getting is the No. 1 thing you have to learn," Conrad said. And, by the way, she asked, was I interested in spending the summer at Fermilab, helping out on her experiment? "We'll teach you what you need to know," she said.

QUESTIONS

1. Cole offers readers a portrait of Janet Conrad — the woman leading the hunt for nature's most elusive particles. What are the goals of Conrad's large-scale physics experiments?
2. What questions is Conrad asking about neutrinos? Why do these questions matter?
3. Conrad tells us, "So often you pose a question, and you build a detector to look at it. Then the detector answers some other question" (paragraph 17). What do you learn about the nature of science from Conrad's statement?
4. What is Conrad's explanation for why women are underrepresented in physics? What hypotheses might you develop to explain the underrepresentation of women in science? Explain your hypotheses.
5. Cole's essay was written in 2003. Do some research to find out the current status of Conrad's research. What has changed? Why does Conrad's research continue to matter in the world of physics?
6. Interview a woman scientist at your college. See what you can uncover about the nature of research and about the challenges for women in science. Using Cole's essay about Janet Conrad as a model, write a profile of the scientist you have interviewed.

MAKING CONNECTIONS

In this piece, Cole creates a portrait of scientist Janet Conrad. Select another essay that creates a human portrait. You might consider essays by Bruno Bettelheim (p. 657), Amanda Coyne (p. 141), John Hersey (p. 133), or Oliver Sacks (p. 711). What techniques do Cole and your chosen writer use to provide a well-rounded view of their subject? Is there any information included that surprises you? What information is left out that you would be interested in knowing about the subject?

THE OTHER STEM-CELL DEBATE

Jamie Shreeve

Jamie Shreeve received his B.A. in English from Brown University in 1973 and graduated from the Iowa Writers Workshop in 1979. He contributed fiction to a number of literary magazines before turning to science writing. From 1983 to 1985, he was the director of public information at the Marine Biological Laboratory in Woods Hole, Massachusetts. While there, Shreeve founded and edited MBL Science, *a magazine for general readers, and created the MBL Science Writing Fellowship Program. He has written for* Discover, National Geographic, Science, Smithsonian, The Atlantic Monthly, *and the* New York Times. *He has been a fellow of the Alfred P. Sloan Foundation and the Alicia Patterson Foundation. His books, under the name James Shreeve, include* Nature: The Other Earthlings *(1987), a companion book to the public television series;* Lucy's Child: The Discovery of a Human Ancestor *(1989), written with Donald Johanson, the paleontologist who discovered the fossil remains of "Lucy";* The Neandertal Enigma: Solving the Mystery of Modern Human Origins *(1995); and* The Genome War: How Craig Venter Tried to Capture the Code of Life and Save the World *(2004), an account of the two competing attempts to sequence the human genome. The following article appeared in the* New York Times Magazine *in 2005.*

Except for the three million human brain cells injected into his cranium, XO47 is just an average green vervet monkey. He weighs about 12 pounds and measures 34 inches from the tip of his tail to the sutured incision on the top of his head. His fur is a melange of black, yellow, and olive, with white underparts and a coal-black face. Until his operation, two days before I met him, he was skittering about an open-air enclosure on the grounds of a biomedical facility on the Caribbean island of St. Kitts. Afterward, he was caged in a hut shared with half a dozen other experimental monkeys, all of whom bore identical incisions in their scalps. Judging from the results of previous experiments, the human neural stem cells inserted into their brains would soon take hold and begin to grow, their fibers reaching out to shake hands with their monkey counterparts. The green vervets' behavior was, and will remain, all monkey. To a vervet, eye contact signals aggression, and when I peered into XO47's cage he took umbrage, vigorously bobbing his head in a stereotypical threat display. Still, it was hard not to stare.

By virtue of the human material added to his brain, XO47 is a chimera — that is, an organism assembled out of living parts taken from more than one biological species. The word comes from the monstrous creature of Greek mythology — part lion, part serpent, and part goat — that is slain by the hero Bellerophon. Less fearsome chimeras occur naturally — lichen, for instance, is a mix of fungus and algae. Most, however, are created in the laboratory by scientists like Dr. Eugene Redmond of Yale University, the soft-spoken 65-year-old psychiatrist and neurosurgeon who operated on XO47. He set up the St. Kitts Biomedical Foundation on this island because that is where the monkeys are — an overabundant feral population of them, ideally suited for research. Redmond has transplanted immature human brain cells into a region of XO47's brain that produces dopamine, a neurochemical that is depleted in the brains of people with Parkinson's disease. If the human cells can take hold and differentiate and bolster the monkey's own dopamine-producing machinery, a similar operation on a Parkinson's patient, the reasoning goes, should have an even greater chance of success.

Redmond is of the opinion that the insertion of a few human cells into a monkey brain is no big deal, and most biologists would agree. But many bioethicists and policy makers are alarmed by recent research developments that have made chimeric experiments more common and increasingly capable of producing human-animal amalgamations that are more ambitious, more "unnatural" — and thus more troubling — than Redmond's vervets.

Driving the surge in chimeric experimentation is the enormous but still untested promise of human stem cells. In theory, stem cells isolated from an early human embryo can transform themselves into virtually any kind of cell in the body, kindling hope that one day they may be transplanted into human patients to provide new tissue wherever it is needed — heart muscle for cardiac patients, insulin-producing cells for diabetics, nerve cells to repair crushed spinal cords, and so on. But there are serious hurdles to overcome before this dream can be realized, including figuring out what controls the differentiation of stem cells and combating their tendency to form tumors. Clearly it is unethical to study the unknown actions of stem cells in human subjects. One obvious solution is to insert the cells into animals and watch how they develop. Depending on what kind of stem cells are used and where they are put in the animal, it may also be possible to pluck some particular human biological feature or disease trait out of its natural context and recreate it in an animal model, where it can be examined and manipulated at will.

While the objections to stem-cell research have largely revolved around 5 the ethics of using human embryos, there is another debate bubbling to the surface: how "human" are chimeric creatures made from human stem cells? Fueling the anxiety has been the lack of coherent regulations in the United Slates governing the creation of chimeras. The President's Council on Bioethics has twice taken up the issue in recent weeks, and Senator Sam Brownback, the Kansas Republican and outspoken social conservative, has introduced legislation to restrict chimeric experiments. Meanwhile, the National Academy of Sciences is expected to issue guidelines later this month as part of a widely anticipated report on the proper use of human stem cells. While the academy's recommendations will carry considerable clout, compliance will be voluntary.

Few people argue that all experiments mixing human and animal material should be banned outright. But where should the lines be drawn? "Some scientists are completely upset with even a single human cell in a monkey brain," says Evan Snyder, a neurobiologist who has conducted chimeric experiments with Redmond. "I don't have problems with putting in a large percentage of cells — 10 or 20 percent — if I felt it could help a patient. It comes down to what percentage of human cells starts making you squirm."

Françoise Baylis, a bioethicist at Dalhousie University in Halifax, Nova Scotia, and a co-author of Canada's stem-cell guidelines, squirms not at a percentage of human cells but at the place where awareness begins. "We have to be sure we are not creating beings with consciousness," she says. The very existence of biologically ambiguous creatures could lead to "inexorable moral confusion" in a society with two ancient and irreconcilable codes of conduct governing the treatment of humans and animals. That said, all modern genetic research, including the sequencing of the human genome itself, underscores how trivial the biological difference really is between a human being and the rest of life. Ninety-nine percent of our genome is shared with chimpanzees. Thirty-one percent of our genes are interchangeable with those of yeast. Does the nearness of our kinship with the rest of nature make the prospect of a quasi-human chimera among us less of a threat to our collective psyche or more of one?

Chimeras have been with us for some time. In 1988, Dr. Irving Weissman and his colleagues at Stanford University created a lab model for AIDS by endowing a mouse with an entirely human immune system. Since then, scientists have tailored mice and other animals with human kidneys, blood, skin, muscles, and various other components. Baboon and chimp hearts have been transplanted into human chest cavities, pig cells into the brains of Parkinson's disease patients and, more routinely, pig heart valves into people with heart disease, including Jesse Helms, the former U.S. senator.

For most of us, a senator with a partly porcine heart or a mouse with a human immune system is not sufficient to provoke the kind of instinctive queasiness known among ethicists as "the yuck factor." The man most identified with that term, Dr. Leon Kass, the bioethicist and current chairman of the President's Council on Bioethics, is of the opinion that widespread feelings of repugnance may be an alarm that something is morally wrong, even if you are not able to articulate precisely why. The mouse and the senator may not trigger a yuck because they look just like a rodent and a person. But what about a normal-looking mouse with a headful of human brain cells or a human-animal embryo that is only briefly alive and never seen?

If you want to get a peek at a real live chimera, drive about five miles   10
east from downtown Reno, Nev., until you come to a farm that looks pretty
much like any other farm. The gate will be locked, but from the road you
can see some pens holding sheep that look pretty much like any other
sheep. Pound for pound, however, these may be the most thoroughly humanized animals on the planet. They are the work of Esmail Zanjani, a
hematologist in the College of Agriculture, Biotechnology, and Natural Resources at the University of Nevada at Reno. Several years ago, Zanjani
and his colleagues began injecting fetal lambs with human stem cells,
mostly ones derived from human bone marrow. He said he hoped that the
cells would transform into blood cells so that he could use the sheep to
study the human blood system. According to Zanjani, when he examined
the sheep he discovered that the human cells had traveled with their lym-
phatic system throughout the sheep's body, developing into blood, bone,
liver, heart, and assorted other cells, including some in the brain. While
some scientists are skeptical of his findings, Zanjani told me that some have
livers that are as much as 40 percent humanized, with distinct human structural units pumping out uniquely human proteins.

While the idea of partly humanized sheep might make some people a
little uncomfortable, it isn't easy to see where they trespass across some unambiguous ethical line. But according to Dr. William Hurlbut, a physician
and consulting professor in human biology at Stanford, who serves with
Kass on the President's Council for Bioethics, the seeing is exactly the point.
What if, instead of internal human organs, Zanjani's sheep sported recog-
nizably human parts on the outside — human limbs or genitals, for instance, ready for transplant should the need arise? Hurlbut maintains that
this is scientifically plausible. But it would be wrong. Every living thing has
a natural trajectory through its life beginning at conception, and in Hurlbut's view, a visible chimera would veer dangerously off course.

"It has to do with the relationship between signs and their meaning,"
he told me. "Human appearance is something we should reserve for humans. Anything else that looks human debases the coinage of truth."

Understanding the world as divided into distinct categories is a fundamental organizing principle of civilization. We conceive of the living aspect
of that world as separated into species, with boundaries around them that
should not be purposively muddled. The underlying validity of our categorical constructs is not as important as how we use them to make sense of the
world. Our minds have evolved to be hypersensitive to the borders between
species, just as we see a rainbow as composed of six or seven distinct colors
when it is really a continuum of wavelengths of light. "When we start to
blend the edges of things, we're uneasy," Hurlbut says. "That's why chimeric creatures are monsters in mythology in the first place."

It is easy to marshal rational arguments to counter this thinking. The
limitations of a typological concept of species, which goes back to Aristotle,
are well known. Some species interbreed with closely related ones on the
borders of their habitats. Evolutionary biologists cannot agree on how to

define what a species really is in the first place, so it is hard to see how the boundaries between them can be absolute. Even if species boundaries do have a natural integrity, how alarming is it to find that those walls can be perforated by artificial means? We have been engaging in unnatural acts upon nature for centuries, grafting plants onto one another or breeding dogs in visible shapes and sizes that diverge wildly from their natural state—let alone performing heart transplants and in vitro fertilizations. I'm not sure I would undergo a crisis of truth at the sight of a sheep with a human arm, especially if it were the best means available for replacing a lost one. But everyone has a squirm threshold. What would you make of a sheep with a human face?

The reason Zanjani's chimeras look like perfectly ordinary sheep is that   15
he injected them with stem cells in a late stage of their fetal development, when their body plans were already laid down. The reason he was allowed to conduct the experiment at all is that he works in the United States, as opposed to Canada or Great Britain where such chimeric research is restricted. Older fetuses are not as impressionable as younger ones, and embryos are the most vulnerable of all. And the younger the human stem cell you insert, the more powerful an influence it can have on the body and brain of the host animal. The way to produce the most homogenous blend of human and animal would thus be to inject fully potent human embryonic stem cells into the very early embryo of, say, a mouse. This is the experiment that policies in those countries are most keen to prevent.

It is also the one that Ali Brivanlou is poised to begin. For several years, Brivanlou, a 45-year-old developmental biologist at Rockefeller University in New York, has been arguing that one of the best ways to understand the usefulness of stem cells for regenerative medicine is to first insert them in an animal embryo and see how they divide and differentiate in a living system. The experiment is explicitly prohibited by the institutions that supply the stem-cell lines approved by the Bush administration, so he is using private funds to develop his own lines. He plans to insert them into 3-to-5-day-old mouse embryos, which he will then implant in the wombs of female mice. Brivanlou is anxiously awaiting the publication of the National Academy of Sciences guidelines before proceeding, but he says he doubts that they will prove an impediment. In his view, showing the potency of stem cells only in a petri dish is like testing the power of a new car by revving its engine in the garage. He wants to take the car out on the track and see how it might perform some day on the open road.

"This experiment must be done," he says. "We can't go directly from culture to a patient. That would be extremely dangerous."

But his experiment is one that most are very reluctant to undertake, even in the private sector. When I inquired at Geron Corporation, a biotechnology company in California, whether scientists there were considering such work, I received a terse e-mail reply that "the company is not, has not and will not pursue inter-species stem-cell chimeras."

Robert Lanza, vice president for medical and scientific development at Advanced Cell Technology, in Worcester, Mass., says much the same thing. "I personally don't want to engage in those kinds of experiments, and I won't have any of my scientists do that work," he says. "Sure, we could reach our endpoints quicker that way. But it takes you into very murky water."

Why all the shuddering? For starters, there is the gonad quandary. If   20
the experiment really works, the human cells should differentiate into all of the embryo's cell lineages, including the one that eventually forms the animal's reproductive cells. If the mouse were male, some of its sperm might thus be human, and if it were female, some of its eggs might be human eggs. If two such creatures were to mate there would be a chance that a human embryo could be conceived and begin to grow in a mouse uterus — a sort of Stuart Little scenario, but in reverse and not so cute.

"Literally nobody wants to see an experiment where two mice that have eggs and sperm of human origin have the opportunity to mate and produce human offspring," says Dr. Norman Post, professor of pediatrics and director of the bioethics program at the University of Wisconsin and a member of the National Academy of Sciences committee reviewing stem-cell research policies. "That's beyond anybody's wildest nightmare."

Is the concern over the reproductive issue overblown? It is, of course, biologically impossible for a human fetus to be delivered from a rodent uterus. Moreover, for a human embryo to be conceived, the chimeras would have to be born first in order to mate, and Brivanlou says he has no intention of allowing them to come to term. He plans to terminate them and examine the fate of the human cells after a week. Still, there remains the question of what kind of being would be present during those seven days. Nobody knows. Does even the fleeting, prenatal existence of a chimera of unknown aspect cross a moral line — not because of what it might look like or become but simply for what it is?

Brivanlou is not troubled by that question. He sees the other methods of testing the stem cells' power — in vitro or in the body of an older fetus or of a fully developed animal — as inadequate, and he says he wants the science to be allowed to follow its natural course. "One thing that is important to remember — we've been here before," he says. "In the 70's, there was a huge debate around whether recombinant DNA should be allowed. Now they do it in high-school labs. For any new technology that emerges, the first reaction is fear. Time will take care of that. When people take the time to think, it becomes routine."

During my visit to St. Kitts, I watched as Gene Redmond, dressed in blue surgical scrubs in the operating room, drilled into the skull of a vervet monkey. Once he penetrated the skull, Redmond positioned a four-inch hypodermic needle on a mount over the hole and ever so slowly lowered it into the monkey's cerebral cortex, down through structures associated with emotion and on until it reached its target in the basal ganglia at the base of the brain. He let the brain settle around the needle for a while and then injected a solution of donor cells into the target.

If he were performing this operation on a human patient, the procedure would be more or less the same. But he would need a much longer needle. If it is not some categorical essentialism that draws a bright line between us and the rest of the animals, surely it is the size and power of our brains. They are the physical address of everything we think of as uniquely human — our rational thinking, intelligence, language, complex emotions and unparalleled ability to imagine a future and remember the past. Not surprisingly, chimeric experiments that seed the brain of an animal with a little neural matter of our own are uniquely suspect, especially those that meddle with the sites of higher function in the cortex.

"If you create stem-cell lines that might produce dopamine and want to put them in an animal first to see if they retained their stability, that's not problematic," Norman Fost maintains. "But what if you want to study brain cortex? You'd want to create a stem-cell line that looks and acts like cortex and put this in an animal. In the toughest case, you'd want to put it in a very early stage of development. This is extremely hypothetical, but suppose these cells completely took over the brain of the animal? A goat or a pig with a purely human brain. Unlikely, but imaginable. That would certainly raise questions about what experiences that animal was having. Is it a very smart pig? Or something having human experiences? These are interesting questions that no one has thought about before because they haven't had to."

The scientist most responsible for making people think about those questions — and squirm and fume — is Irving Weissman. Several years ago, Weissman and his colleagues at Stanford and at StemCells Inc., a private company he helped to found, transplanted human neural stem cells into the brains of newborn mice. The human cells spread throughout the mouse brain, piggybacking on the host's developmental pathways to eventually make up as much as 1 percent of some parts of the host's neural tissue. Once again, the ultimate purpose of the chimera was to create a research model for human brain function and disease. While somewhat successful in this regard, Weissman said he felt his model was hampered by the 99 percent of it that was still mouse. So he came up with an ingenious idea: why not make a mouse with a brain composed entirely of human neurons? In theory, at least, this could be achieved by transplanting human neural stem cells into the fetal brain of a strain of mouse whose own neurons happen to die off just before birth. If the human stem cells took up the slack and differentiated along the same lines as in the earlier experiment, you might just end up with a living newborn mouse controlled by a functioning brain that just happened to be composed of human cells.

Before proceeding with this experiment, Weissman said he thought it might be a good idea to solicit some ethical input. He contacted Hank Greely, a bioethicist at Stanford's law school, who put together a committee to review the benefits and risks involved. The members agreed that the human neuronal mouse could be an extremely beneficial tool to study the effects of pathogens and disease in the human brain and the action of new drugs. They identified several areas of risk. The most difficult one to articulate, as Greely told the National Academy of Sciences panel reviewing the use of human stem cells, was the "nontrivial chance of conferring significant aspects of humanness on the nonhuman organism."

"Though exceedingly remote, we thought this possibility was reason for caution and concern," Greely told me recently. His committee, which has yet to publish its report, did not find that risk alone was sufficient grounds for canceling the experiment. Instead, the members suggested that Weissman incorporate into the experimental protocol a series of "stopping points." Some of the fetal mice should be terminated and examined before birth, and if there should appear any "disquieting or disturbing results," the experiment should be suspended pending further ethical review. Results deemed troubling would include any evidence that the transplant was shaping the architecture of the mouse's neural edifice, as opposed to just contributing the bricks. Mice have sensory structures in their brains called "whisker barrels," for instance, which we lack, while we have a far more complicated visual cortex. Shrunken whisker barrels or swollen visual cortex in the fetal mice brains would be a red flag. If everything appeared normal, the remaining animals could be brought to term and monitored for the appearance of any odd, and especially humanlike, behavior, which would again warrant stopping the experiment and seeking additional input from the ethical community.

Weissman is still months or even years away from actually trying his human neuron mouse experiment, and it has already drawn "This shall not Stand" rhetoric from Jeremy Rifkin, the anti-biotech activist, Bill O'Reilly, and numerous religious commentators and bloggers.   30

The real problem with Weissman's proposed mouse, however, may turn out to be not that it is too human but that it is not human enough. The basic structure of our nerve cells is not all that different from those of any other mammal, including a mouse's. But because our brains are so much bigger, the cells that compose them reach across greater distances, and the timing of their development is much longer. How likely is it that human nerve cells will develop into a whole functioning brain in the tiny arena of a fetal mouse's skull? Weissman concedes that his proposed chimeric experiment may not succeed. But, hypothetically speaking, what if you could conduct the analogous experiment in an animal with a brain more like our own, like a monkey or a chimpanzee? Strictly from a biomedical perspective, a human–ape chimera could be the ultimate research model for human biology and disease — one that is completely human in everything but its humanity.

"If someone were to try Irv's mouse experiment with a great ape or even a monkey, I'd get real worried," Greely says. "I'd want to make sure people thought long and hard about that."

The danger, of course, is in how difficult it would be to know when you've slipped over the edge. While Greely's committee has been brooding over Weissman's mouse and the National Academy has been pondering its recommendations for the use of embryonic stem cells, another ethics group has been meeting at the Phoebe R. Berman Bioethics Institute at Johns Hopkins University to grapple with the especially dicey issue of human–primate chimeras. Could the introduction of human cells into nonhuman primate brains cause changes that would make them more humanlike? How would one tell? Would it be morally problematic to create a chimera with a significant degree of humanlike consciousness, cognition, or emotion? Should such experimentation be banned? If such chimeras were to be created, what legal rights and protections should they have, distinct from other animals?

The report of the Working Group on Interspecific Chimeric Brains is expected to be published later this spring in a scientific journal. While the group's recommendations remain confidential until then, a rough idea of the boundary they might draw between allowable and prohibited research is suggested by two experiments that have already been conducted. One was carried out in 2001 by Evan Snyder, then at Harvard University and now director of the stem-cell program at the Burnham Institute in La Jolla, Calif. Snyder and his colleagues implanted human neural stem cells into the brains of 12-week-old fetal bonnet monkeys, aborted them four weeks later, and found that the human cells had migrated and differentiated into both cerebral hemispheres, including into regions of the developing monkey cortex. Like Redmond, Snyder discounts any possibility that had the monkeys been brought to term the relatively small number of human cells in their brain would have had any effect on their normal cognition and behavior.

"Even if I were to make a monkey with a hippocampus composed entirely of human cells, it's not going to stand up and quote Shakespeare," Snyder says. "Those sophisticated in human functioning know that it's more than the cellular components that make a human brain. It's the connections, the blood vessels that feed them; it's the various surfaces on which they migrate, the timing by which various synaptic molecules are released and impact other things, like molecules from the bloodstream and from the bone."

It's quite likely that the members of the Johns Hopkins committee (it includes distinguished philosophers, bioethicists, neuroscientists, primatologists, and stem-cell researchers) will conclude that an experiment like Snyder's is ethically safe. A relatively small scattering of human cells could be introduced into a primate brain, late in its development when there would be no chance the human cells could influence its fundamental architecture. But a result of another experiment, performed in the late 1980's by Evan Balaban, who is now at McGill University in Montreal, might give the group pause about mixing human and primate tissue in a very early fetus. Balaban removed a section from the midbrain of a chick embryo, grafting in its place the corresponding piece of proto-brain from an embryonic quail. While many of the embryos failed to develop, a few matured and eventually hatched. The newborn chicks were normal in most respects — except they crowed like quails.

35

"One could imagine that if you took a human embryonic midbrain and spliced it into a developing chimpanzee, you could get a chimp with many of our automatic vocalizations," says Terrence Deacon, a biological anthropologist at the University of California at Berkeley and a member of the Johns Hopkins committee. "It wouldn't be able to talk. But it might laugh or sob, instead of pant-hoot."

Of course, Deacon adds quickly, such an experiment would be highly unethical. The notion of a chimpanzee normal except for its human sobbing would probably exceed the squirm threshold of the other members of the Johns Hopkins group. Perhaps it is not what a human–animal chimera would be that violates some fundamental categorical construct in our minds, or what it would look like, as William Hurlbut maintains, as much as what it could *do*—whether it would have a brain that makes it act in a way that is uncomfortably familiar. "Humanness" surely resides in the emergent layers building the vastly complex architecture of the human brain.

But is there a clear biological distinction between us and the rest of creation, one that should never be confounded by the scuffling of strange new feet in laboratory basements? Deacon has devoted a great deal of thought and research to such questions. While his is hardly the only view, after a career spent comparing the brains of living primates and the skulls of fossilized hominids, he says that there is little evidence for the sudden appearance of some new thing"—a uniquely human gene, a completely novel brain structure in the hominid lineage—that sets us distinctly apart. Obviously, there has been an overall increase in brain size. But the telling difference is in more subtle shifts in proportion and connections between regions of the brain, "a gerrymandering of the system" that corresponds to a growing reliance on the use of language and other symbolic behavior as a means of survival. This shift, which Deacon believes began as long as two and a half million years ago, is reflected most prominently in the swollen human prefrontal cortex.

"We humans have been shaped by the use of symbols," he says. "We 40 are embedded in a world of human creation, where demands for success and reproduction are all powerfully dependent on how well we swim through our symbolic niche."

This raises some fascinating questions, not just about the chimeras we might create with our scalpels and stem cells but also about the ones we may already have fashioned by coaxing humanlike behaviors from animals who have the latent capacity to express them. In the wild, chimpanzees and other apes do not engage in any symbolic behavior remotely comparable to what humans have evolved. But in the laboratory they can learn to communicate with sign language and other means on a par with the skills of a toddler. The difference is that the toddler's symbolic behavior becomes increasingly enriched, while the chimpanzee hits a wall. How much further could a bioengineered chimera go? Could it swim in our symbolic niche well enough to communicate what is going on inside its hybrid mind? What could it teach us about animals? What could it teach us about us? And what is the price of the knowing?

QUESTIONS

1. Who is XO47, and why is he a chimera?
2. Why, according to Shreeve, have chimeric experiments become more common? Explain one of the chimeric experiments that Shreeve describes.
3. Why do biologically ambiguous creatures change the stem-cell debate? Why do they, according to Shreeve, lead to moral confusion?
4. Shreeve writes that "everyone has a squirm threshold" (paragraph 14) when it comes to biologically ambiguous creatures. What is your "squirm threshold"? Explain your position.
5. The danger of chimeric experiments, according to Shreeve, is the difficulty of "know[ing] when you've slipped over the edge" (paragraph 33). Why does it matter to find the "edge" in the stem-cell debate? What moral questions are raised by chimeric experiments?
6. Take a stand. Do you think chimeric experimentation should be encouraged or banned? Write a position paper to defend your point of view.
7. What scientific, moral, and religious questions does Shreeve's essay raise for you? Exchange questions and viewpoints with your classmates. Ask classmates to pose questions and positions that counter your point of view.

MAKING CONNECTIONS

Both Shreeve and Peter Singer, an ethicist described in Harriet McBryde Johnson's "Unspeakable Conversations" (p. 86), consider the question of what makes us human. In what ways do the positions put forth by the scientists in "The Other Stem-Cell Debate" mesh with or oppose Singer's? Whose arguments do you find most compelling? Why?

EXPLAINING IN THE

Sciences and Technologies

WHY THE SKY IS BLUE

James Jeans

*Sir James Jeans (1877–1946) was a British physicist and astrono-
mer. Educated at Trinity College, Cambridge, he lectured there and
was a professor of applied mathematics at Princeton University
from 1905 to 1909. He later did research at Mount Wilson Obser-
vatory in California. Jeans won many honors for his work and
wrote a number of scholarly and popular scientific books. The following selection is from* The Stars in Their Courses (1931), *a written version of what began as a series of radio talks for an audience
assumed to have no special knowledge of science.*

Imagine that we stand on any ordinary seaside pier, and watch the
waves rolling in and striking against the iron columns of the pier. Large
waves pay very little attention to the columns — they divide right and left and
re-unite after passing each column, much as a regiment of soldiers would if a
tree stood in their road; it is almost as though the columns had not been
there. But the short waves and ripples find the columns of the pier a much
more formidable obstacle. When the short waves impinge on the columns,
they are reflected back and spread as new ripples in all directions. To use the
technical term, they are "scattered." The obstacle provided by the iron
columns hardly affects the long waves at all, but scatters the short ripples.

We have been watching a sort of working model of the way in which
sunlight struggles through the earth's atmosphere. Between us on earth and
outer space the atmosphere interposes innumerable obstacles in the form of

molecules of air, tiny droplets of water, and small particles of dust. These are represented by the columns of the pier.

The waves of the sea represent the sunlight. We know that sunlight is a blend of lights of many colors — as we can prove for ourselves by passing it through a prism, or even through a jug of water, or as Nature demonstrates to us when she passes it through the raindrops of a summer shower and produces a rainbow. We also know that light consists of waves, and that the different colors of light are produced by waves of different lengths, red light by long waves and blue light by short waves. The mixture of waves which constitutes sunlight has to struggle through the obstacles it meets in the atmosphere, just as the mixture of waves at the seaside has to struggle past the columns of the pier. And these obstacles treat the light-waves much as the columns of the pier treat the sea-waves. The long waves which constitute red light are hardly affected, but the short waves which constitute blue light are scattered in all directions.

Thus, the different constituents of sunlight are treated in different ways as they struggle through the earth's atmosphere. A wave of blue light may be scattered by a dust particle, and turned out of its course. After a time a second dust particle again turns it out of its course, and so on, until finally it enters our eyes by a path as zigzag as that of a flash of lightning. Consequently the blue waves of the sunlight enter our eyes from all directions. And that is why the sky looks blue.

QUESTIONS

1. Analogy, the comparison of something familiar with something less familiar, occurs frequently in scientific explanation. Jeans introduces an analogy in his first paragraph. How does he develop that analogy as he develops his explanation?
2. The analogy Jeans provides enables him to explain the process by which the blue light-waves scatter throughout the sky. Hence he gives us a brief process analysis of that phenomenon. Summarize that process in your own words.
3. Try rewriting this essay without the analogy. Remove paragraph 1 and all the references to ocean waves and pier columns in paragraphs 2 and 3. How clear an explanation is left?
4. Besides the sea-waves, what other familiar examples does Jeans use in his explanation?
5. This piece opens with "Imagine that we stand. . . ." Suppose that every *we* was replaced with a *you*. How would the tone of the essay change?
6. While analogy can be effective in helping to explain difficult scientific concepts, it can be equally useful in explaining and interpreting familiar things by juxtaposing them in new ways. Suppose, for example, that you wish to explain to a friend why you dislike a course you are taking.

Select one of the following ideas for an analogy (or find a better one) —
a forced-labor camp, a three-ring circus, squirrels on a treadmill, a tea
party, a group-therapy session. Think through the analogy to your course,
and write a few paragraphs of explanation. Let Jeans's essay guide you
in organizing your own.

MAKING CONNECTIONS

1. Jeans's essay is a clear explanation of a complex phenomenon, yet it is
   quite short. Where else in this volume have you found clear explanations? A number of short passages in the essays by Stephen W. Hawking
   (p. 724) and Diane Ackerman (p. 706) could provide examples. Choose
   a descriptive passage that you find clear in the work of one of these writers, and compare it to Jeans's. Is an analogy central to the passage you
   selected? If not, what are the differences in the authors' explanations?
2. Describe the audience that Jeans seems to have in mind for his explanation. How does that sense of audience differ for Stanley Milgram (p. 453)
   or Malcolm Gladwell (p. 519)? Compare one of those essays with Jeans's
   account of "Why the Sky Is Blue," and discuss how the task of explaining shifts according to the writer's assumptions about an audience.

WHY LEAVES TURN COLOR IN THE FALL

Diane Ackerman

*Poet, essayist, and naturalist Diane Ackerman was born in
Waukegan, Illinois, in 1948 and received her M.F.A and Ph.D in
English from Cornell University. Her earliest works, published
when she was still a doctoral student, were the poetry collections*
The Planets *(1976) and* Wife of Life *(1978); since then she has produced several further volumes, most recently* I Praise My Destroyer
(1998) and Origami Bridges *(2002). Ackerman's first book of prose
was* Twilight of the Tenderfoot *(1980), about her experiences working on a cattle ranch in New Mexico. Her subsequent prose works
have focused on a range of subjects, as suggested by some of their
titles:* The Moon by Whale Light: And Other Adventures among
Bats, Crocodilians, Penguins, and Whales *(1990),* The Rarest of the
Rare: Vanishing Animals, Timeless Worlds *(1995),* A Natural History of Love *(1994),* Cultivating Delight: A Natural History of My
Garden *(2001), and* An Alchemy of Mind *(2004). All, however, are
characterized by Ackerman's deeply insightful observations of the
natural world, as evidenced perhaps most fully in her most popular
book and the source of a highly rated public television series,* A
Natural History of the Senses *(1990), where the following selection
appeared. Admitting that her work is difficult to categorize, Ackerman has said, "I write about nature and human nature. And most
often about that twilight zone where the two meet and have something they can teach each other."*

The stealth of autumn catches one unaware. Was that a goldfinch
perching in the early September woods, or just the first turning leaf? A red-
winged blackbird or a sugar maple closing up shop for the winter? Keen-
eyed as leopards, we stand still and squint hard, looking for signs of movement. Early-morning frost sits heavily on the grass, and turns barbed wire
into a string of stars. On a distant hill, a small square of yellow appears to
be a lighted stage. At last the truth dawns on us: Fall is staggering in, right
on schedule, with its baggage of chilly nights, macabre holidays, and spectacular, heart-stoppingly beautiful leaves. Soon the leaves will start cringing
on the trees, and roll up in clenched fists before they actually fall off. Dry
seedpods will rattle like tiny gourds. But first there will be weeks of gushing
color so bright, so pastel, so confettilike, that people will travel up and
down the East Coast just to stare at it — a whole season of leaves.

Where do the colors come from? Sunlight rules most living things with its golden edicts. When the days begin to shorten, soon after the summer solstice on June 21, a tree reconsiders its leaves. All summer it feeds them so they can process sunlight, but in the dog days of summer the tree begins pulling nutrients back into its trunk and roots, pares down, and gradually chokes off its leaves. A corky layer of cells forms at the leaves' slender petioles, then scars over. Undernourished, the leaves stop producing the pigment chlorophyll, and photosynthesis ceases. Animals can migrate, hibernate, or store food to prepare for winter. But where can a tree go? It survives by dropping its leaves, and by the end of autumn only a few fragile threads of fluid-carrying xylem hold leaves to their stems.

A turning leaf stays partly green at first, then reveals splotches of yellow and red as the chlorophyll gradually breaks down. Dark green seems to stay longest in the veins, outlining and defining them. During the summer, chlorophyll dissolves in the heat and light, but it is also being steadily replaced. In the fall, on the other hand, no new pigment is produced, and so we notice the other colors that were always there, right in the leaf, although chlorophyll's shocking green hid them from view. With their camouflage gone, we see these colors for the first time all year, and marvel, but they were always there, hidden like a vivid secret beneath the hot glowing greens of summer.

The most spectacular range of fall foliage occurs in the northeastern United States and in eastern China, where the leaves are robustly colored, thanks in part to a rich climate. European maples don't achieve the same flaming reds as their American relatives, which thrive on cold nights and sunny days. In Europe, the warm, humid weather turns the leaves brown or mildly yellow. Anthocyanin, the pigment that gives apples their red and turns leaves red or red-violet, is produced by sugars that remain in the leaf after the supply of nutrients dwindles. Unlike the carotenoids, which color carrots, squash, and corn, and turn leaves orange and yellow, anthocyanin varies from year to year, depending on the temperature and amount of sunlight. The fiercest colors occur in years when the fall sunlight is strongest and the nights are cool and dry (a state of grace scientists find vexing to forecast). This is also why leaves appear dizzyingly bright and clear on a sunny fall day: The anthocyanin flashes like a marquee.

Not all leaves turn the same colors. Elms, weeping willows, and the ancient ginkgo all grow radiant yellow, along with hickories, aspens, bottlebrush buckeyes, cottonweeds, and tall, keening poplars. Basswood turns bronze, birches bright gold. Water-loving maples put on a symphonic display of scarlets. Sumacs turn red, too, as do flowering dogwoods, black gums, and sweet gums. Though some oaks yellow, most turn a pinkish brown. The farmlands also change color, as tepees of cornstalks and bales of shredded-wheat-textured hay stand drying in the fields. In some spots, one slope of a hill may be green and the other already in bright color, because the hillside facing south gets more sun and heat than the northern one.

An odd feature of the colors is that they don't seem to have any special purpose. We are predisposed to respond to their beauty, of course. They shimmer with the colors of sunset, spring flowers, the tawny buff of a colt's pretty rump, the shuddering pink of a blush. Animals and flowers color for a reason — adaptation to their environment — but there is no adaptive reason for leaves to color so beautifully in the fall any more than there is for the sky or ocean to be blue. It's just one of the haphazard marvels the planet bestows every year. We find the sizzling colors thrilling, and in a sense they dupe us. Colored like living things, they signal death and disintegration. In time, they will become fragile and, like the body, return to dust. They are as we hope our own fate will be when we die: Not to vanish, just to sublime from one beautiful state into another. Though leaves lose their green life, they bloom with urgent colors, as the woods grow mummified day by day, and Nature becomes more carnal, mute, and radiant.

We call the season "fall," from the Old English *feallan*, to fall, which leads back through time to the Indo-European *phol*, which also means to fall. So the word and the idea are both extremely ancient, and haven't really changed since the first of our kind needed a name for fall's leafy abundance. As we say the word, we're reminded of that other Fall, in the garden of Eden, when fig leaves never withered and scales fell from our eyes. Fall is the time when leaves fall from the trees, just as spring is when flowers spring up, summer is when we simmer, and winter is when we whine from the cold.

Children love to play in piles of leaves, hurling them into the air like confetti, leaping into soft unruly mattresses of them. For children, leaf fall is just one of the odder figments of Nature, like hailstones or snowflakes. Walk down a lane overhung with trees in the never-never land of autumn, and you will forget about time and death, lost in the sheer delicious spill of color. Adam and Eve concealed their nakedness with leaves, remember? Leaves have always hidden our awkward secrets.

But how do the colored leaves fall? As a leaf ages, the growth hormone, auxin, fades, and cells at the base of the petiole divide. Two or three rows of small cells, lying at right angles to the axis of the petiole, react with water, then come apart, leaving the petioles hanging on by only a few threads of xylem. A light breeze, and the leaves are airborne. They glide and swoop, rocking in invisible cradles. They are all wing and may flutter from yard to yard on small whirlwinds or updrafts, swiveling as they go. Firmly tethered to earth, we love to see things rise up and fly — soap bubbles, balloons, birds, fall leaves. They remind us that the end of a season is capricious, as is the end of life. We especially like the way leaves rock, careen, and swoop as they fall. Everyone knows the motion. Pilots sometimes do a maneuver called a "falling leaf," in which the plane loses altitude quickly and on purpose, by slipping first to the right, then to the left. The machine weighs a ton or more, but in one pilot's mind it is a weightless thing, a falling leaf. She has seen the motion before, in the Vermont woods where she played as a child. Below her the trees radiate gold, copper, and red. Leaves are falling, although she can't see them fall, as she falls, swooping down for a closer view.

At last the leaves leave. But first they turn color and thrill us for weeks 10 on end. Then they crunch and crackle underfoot. They *shush*, as children drag their small feet through leaves heaped along the curb. Dark, slimy mats of leaves cling to one's heels after a rain. A damp, stuccolike mortar of semidecayed leaves protects the tender shoots with a roof until spring, and makes a rich humus. An occasional bulge or ripple in the leafy mounds signals a shrew or a field mouse tunneling out of sight. Sometimes one finds in fossil stones the imprint of a leaf, long since disintegrated, whose outlines remind us how detailed, vibrant, and alive are the things of this earth that perish.

QUESTIONS

1. Where, specifically, in the essay does Ackerman explain the natural process that leaves undergo in changing colors and eventually dropping from their trees' branches? Do you find this explanation clear and enlightening? Now, what makes up the remainder of the essay? Based on this analysis, how would you describe Ackerman's purpose (or purposes) here?

2. In paragraph 6, Ackerman writes that we are "predisposed" to respond favorably to the coloring of autumn leaves. What does she mean? Do you tend to agree with her? Why or why not?

3. In paragraphs 6, 9, and 10, Ackerman makes a connection between autumn leaves and the concept of death more generally. How would you summarize the point she is making here? What does this idea suggest about her view of death?

4. In paragraph 7 and at the beginning of paragraph 10, Ackerman engages in some rather whimsical wordplay. Does this wordplay seem to you in keeping with the overall tone of the essay? Why do you respond as you do?

5. The structure of "Why Leaves Turn Color in the Fall" is fairly loose, even seemingly digressive in places. Look, in particular, at the seeming digressions in paragraphs 8 and 9. Considering that this essay comes from a book titled *A Natural History of the Senses*, how might you relate them to Ackerman's larger point?

6. Think of other natural phenomena that can be considered beautiful in the way that colorful autumn leaves are for many: the formation of clouds that scud across a clear sky, for example, or waves rolling over the edge of a beach or a rosebud forming, maturing, and blooming — anything that you yourself regard as, in Ackerman's word, "spectacular." Choose one such phenomenon, and do some research to learn about the biological, geological, or other natural process that produces it. Then write an

essay in which, like Ackerman, you explain the technical aspects of the natural process while also describing the beauty of the phenomenon and perhaps exploring some of the reasons humans might respond to it as they do.

MAKING CONNECTIONS

The title of James Jeans's essay "Why the Sky Is Blue" (p. 703) sets up expectations similar to those that Ackerman's title does: that what follows will provide an explanation of a natural process. In fact, how similar — and how different — are the two essays? Do you feel that one provides a clearer or more effective explanation than the other does? Why or why not? Which do you respond to more favorably?

The Man Who Mistook His Wife for a Hat

Oliver Sacks

Oliver Sacks was born in London, England, in 1933 and educated in London and Oxford before coming to the United States to complete his education in California and New York. At present he is clinical professor of neurology at Albert Einstein College of Medicine. He is best known, however, for his extraordinary writing on matters related to his medical studies, in such books as Awakenings *(1974),* Seeing Voices: A Journey into the World of the Deaf *(1989),* An Anthropologist on Mars *(1995),* The Island of the Colorblind *(1997), and his national best seller,* The Man Who Mistook His Wife for a Hat *(1986), from which the following selection was adapted. Interested in the art of storytelling as well as in clinical neurology, Sacks subtitled the book in which this essay appeared, "and Other Clinical Tales." He insists that his essays are not just case studies, though they are that, but also tales or fables of "heroes, victims, martyrs, warriors." In his writing, he says, "the scientific and romantic . . . come together at the intersection of fact and fable." Sacks's prose style is lyrical as well as accurate; his explanation of prosopagnosia (perception without recognition) seeks to engage our interest and emotions while it defines and illustrates a syndrome unfamiliar to many readers.*

Dr. P. was a musician of distinction, well known for many years as a singer, and then, at the local School of Music, as a teacher. It was here, in relation to his students, that certain strange problems were first observed. Sometimes a student would present himself, and Dr. P. would not recognize him; or, specifically, would not recognize his face. The moment the student spoke, he would be recognized by his voice. Such incidents multiplied, causing embarrassment, perplexity, fear — and, sometimes, comedy. For not only did Dr. P. increasingly fail to see faces, but he saw faces when there were no faces to see: genially, Magoo-like, when in the street he might pat the heads of water hydrants and parking meters, taking these to be the heads of children; he would amiably address carved knobs on the furniture and be astounded when they did not reply. At first these odd mistakes were laughed off as jokes, not least by Dr. P. himself. Had he not always had a quirky sense of humor and been given to Zen-like paradoxes and jests? His musical powers were as dazzling as ever; he did not feel ill — he had never felt better; and the mistakes were so ludicrous — and so ingenious — that they could hardly be serious or betoken anything serious. The notion of there being "something the matter" did not emerge until some three years later, when diabetes developed. Well aware that diabetes could affect his eyes, Dr. P. consulted an ophthalmologist, who took a careful history and examined his eyes closely. "There's nothing the matter with your eyes," the doctor concluded. "But there is trouble with the visual parts of your brain. You don't need my help, you must see a neurologist." And so, as a result of this referral, Dr. P. came to me.

It was obvious within a few seconds of meeting him that there was no trace of dementia in the ordinary sense. He was a man of great cultivation and charm who talked well and fluently, with imagination and humor. I couldn't think why he had been referred to our clinic.

And yet there *was* something a bit odd. He faced me as he spoke, was oriented towards me, and yet there was something the matter — it was difficult to formulate. He faced me with his *ears*, I came to think, but not with his eyes. These, instead of looking, gazing, at me, "taking me in," in the normal way, made sudden strange fixations — on my nose, on my right ear, down to my chin, up to my right eye — as if noting (even studying) these individual features, but not seeing my whole face, its changing expressions, "me," as a whole. I am not sure that I fully realized this at the time — there was just a teasing strangeness, some failure in the normal interplay of gaze and expression. He saw me, he *scanned* me, and yet . . .

"What seems to be the matter?" I asked him at length.

"Nothing that I know of," he replied with a smile, "but people seem to   5
think there's something wrong with my eyes."

"But *you* don't recognize any visual problems?"

"No, not directly, but I occasionally make mistakes."

I left the room briefly to talk to his wife. When I came back, Dr. P. was sitting placidly by the window, attentive, listening rather than looking out. "Traffic," he said, "street sounds, distant trains — they make a sort of symphony, do they not? You know Honegger's[1] *Pacific 234?*"

What a lovely man, I thought to myself. How can there be anything seriously the matter? Would he permit me to examine him?

"Yes, of course, Dr. Sacks."   10

I stilled my disquiet, his perhaps, too, in the soothing routine of a neurological exam — muscle strength, coordination, reflexes, tone. . . . It was while examining his reflexes — a trifle abnormal on the left side — that the first bizarre experience occurred. I had taken off his left shoe and scratched the sole of his foot with a key — a frivolous-seeming but essential test of a reflex — and then, excusing myself to screw my ophthalmoscope together, left him to put on the shoe himself. To my surprise, a minute later, he had not done this.

"Can I help?" I asked.

---

[1]*Arthur Honegger* (1892–1955): French composer. [Eds.]

"Help what? Help whom?"

"Help you put on your shoe."

"Ach," he said, "I had forgotten the shoe," adding, *sotto voce*, "The   15
shoe? The shoe?" He seemed baffled.

"Your shoe," I repeated. "Perhaps you'd put it on."

He continued to look downwards, though not at the shoe, with an intense but misplaced concentration. Finally his gaze settled on his foot:
"That is my shoe, yes?"

Did I mis-hear? Did he mis-see?

"My eyes," he explained, and put a hand to his foot. "*This* is my shoe,
no?"

"No, it is not. That is your foot. *There* is your shoe."   20

"Ah! I thought that was my foot."

Was he joking? Was he mad? Was he blind? If this was one of his
"strange mistakes," it was the strangest mistake I had ever come across.

I helped him on with his shoe (his foot), to avoid further complication.
Dr. P. himself seemed untroubled, indifferent, maybe amused. I resumed my
examination. His visual acuity was good: he had no difficulty seeing a pin
on the floor, though sometimes he missed it if it was placed to his left.

He saw all right, but what did he see? I opened out a copy of the *National Geographic Magazine* and asked him to describe some pictures in it.

His responses here were very curious. His eyes would dart from one   25
thing to another, picking up tiny features, individual features, as they had
done with my face. A striking brightness, a color, a shape would arrest his
attention and elicit comment — but in no case did he get the scene-as-a-
whole. He failed to see the whole, seeing only details, which he spotted like
blips on a radar screen. He never entered into relation with the picture as a
whole — never faced, so to speak, *its* physiognomy. He had no sense whatever of a landscape or scene.

I showed him the cover, an unbroken expanse of Sahara dunes.

"What do you see here?" I asked.

"I see a river," he said. "And a little guest-house with its terrace on the
water. People are dining out on the terrace. I see colored parasols here and
there." He was looking, if it was "looking," right off the cover into mid-air
and confabulating nonexistent features, as if the absence of features in the
actual picture had driven him to imagine the river and the terrace and the
colored parasols.

I must have looked aghast, but he seemed to think he had done rather
well. There was a hint of a smile on his face. He also appeared to have decided that the examination was over and started to look around for his hat.
He reached out his hand and took hold of his wife's head, tried to lift it off,
to put it on. He had apparently mistaken his wife for a hat! His wife looked
as if she was used to such things.

I could make no sense of what had occurred in terms of conventional   30
neurology (or neuropsychology). In some ways he seemed perfectly preserved, and in others absolutely, incomprehensibly devastated. How could

he, on the one hand, mistake his wife for a hat and, on the other, function, as apparently he still did, as a teacher at the Music School?

I had to think, to see him again — and to see him in his own familiar habitat, at home.

A few days later I called on Dr. P. and his wife at home, with the score of the *Dichterliebe* in my briefcase (I knew he liked Schumann),[2] and a variety of odd objects for the testing of perception. Mrs. P. showed me into a lofty apartment, which recalled fin-de-siècle Berlin. A magnificent old Bösendorfer stood in state in the center of the room, and all around it were music stands, instruments, scores. . . . There were books, there were paintings, but the music was central. Dr. P. came in, a little bowed, and, distracted, advanced with outstretched hands to the grandfather clock, but, hearing my voice, corrected himself, and shook hands with me. We exchanged greetings and chatted a little of current concerts and performances. Diffidently, I asked him if he would sing.

"The *Dichterliebe*!" he exclaimed. "But I can no longer read music. You will play them, yes?"

I said I would try. On that wonderful old piano even my playing sounded right, and Dr. P. was an aged but infinitely mellow Fischer-Dieskau,[3] combining a perfect ear and voice with the most incisive musical intelligence. It was clear that the Music School was not keeping him on out of charity.

Dr. P.'s temporal lobes were obviously intact: he had a wonderful musi-   35
cal cortex. What, I wondered, was going on in his parietal and occipital lobes, especially in those areas where visual processing occurred? I carry the Platonic solids in my neurological kit and decided to start with these.

"What is this?" I asked, drawing out the first one.

"A cube, of course."

"Now this?" I asked, brandishing another.

He asked if he might examine it, which he did swiftly and systematically: "A dodecahedron, of course. And don't bother with the others — I'll get the icosahedron, too."

Abstract shapes clearly presented no problems. What about faces? I   40
took out a pack of cards. All of these he identified instantly, including the jacks, queens, kings, and the joker. But these, after all, are stylized designs, and it was impossible to tell whether he saw faces or merely patterns. I decided I would show him a volume of cartoons which I had in my briefcase. Here, again, for the most part, he did well. Churchill's cigar, Schnozzle's nose: as soon as he had picked out a key feature he could identify the face. But cartoons, again, are formal and schematic. It remained to be seen how he would do with real faces, realistically represented.

---

[2]*Robert Schumann* (1810–1856): German romantic composer. [Eds.]

[3]*Dietrich Fischer-Dieskau* (b. 1925): German baritone, noted for his interpretations of Schumann's vocal music. [Eds.]

I turned on the television, keeping the sound off, and found an early Bette Davis film. A love scene was in progress. Dr. P. failed to identify the actress — but this could have been because she had never entered his world. What was more striking was that he failed to identify the expressions on her face or her partner's, though in the course of a single torrid scene these passed from sultry yearning through passion, surprise, disgust, and fury to a melting reconciliation. Dr. P. could make nothing of any of this. He was very unclear as to what was going on, or who was who or even what sex they were. His comments on the scene were positively Martian.

It was just possible that some of his difficulties were associated with the unreality of a celluloid, Hollywood world; and it occurred to me that he might be more successful in identifying faces from his own life. On the walls of the apartment there were photographs of his family, his colleagues, his pupils, himself. I gathered a pile of these together and, with some misgivings, presented them to him. What had been funny, or farcical, in relation to the movie, was tragic in relation to real life. By and large, he recognized nobody: neither his family, nor his colleagues, nor his pupils, nor himself. He recognized a portrait of Einstein because he picked up the characteristic hair and mustache; and the same thing happened with one or two other people. "Ach, Paul!" he said, when shown a portrait of his brother. "That square jaw, those big teeth — I would know Paul anywhere!" But was it Paul he recognized, or one or two of his features, on the basis of which he could make a reasonable guess as to the subject's identity? In the absence of obvious "markers," he was utterly lost. But it was not merely the cognition, the gnosis, at fault; there was something radically wrong with the whole way he proceeded. For he approached these faces — even of those near and dear — as if they were abstract puzzles or tests. He did not relate to them, he did not behold. No face was familiar to him, seen as a "thou," being just identified as a set of features, an "it." Thus, there was formal, but no trace of personal, gnosis. And with this went his indifference, or blindness, to expression. A face, to us, is a person looking out — we see, as it were, the person through his *persona*, his face. But for Dr. P. there was no *persona* in this sense — no outward *persona*, and no person within.

I had stopped at a florist on my way to his apartment and bought myself an extravagant red rose for my buttonhole. Now I removed this and handed it to him. He took it like a botanist or morphologist given a specimen, not like a person given a flower.

"About six inches in length," he commented. "A convoluted red form with a linear green attachment."

"Yes," I said encouragingly, "and what do you think it *is*, Dr. P.?"   45

"Not easy to say." He seemed perplexed. "It lacks the simple symmetry of the Platonic solids, although it may have a higher symmetry of its own. . . . I think this could be an inflorescence or flower."

"Could be?" I queried.

"Could be," he confirmed.

"Smell it," I suggested, and he again looked somewhat puzzled, as if I had asked him to smell a higher symmetry. But he complied courteously, and took it to his nose. Now, suddenly, he came to life.

"Beautiful!" he exclaimed. "An early rose. What a heavenly smell!" He 50 started to hum "*Die Rose, die Lillie . . .*" Reality, it seemed, might be conveyed by smell, not by sight.

I tried one final test. It was still a cold day, in early spring, and I had thrown my coat and gloves on the sofa.

"What is this?" I asked, holding up a glove.

"May I examine it?" he asked, and, taking it from me, he proceeded to examine it as he had examined the geometrical shapes.

"A continuous surface," he announced at last, "infolded on itself. It appears to have" — he hesitated — "five outpouchings, if this is the word."

"Yes," I said cautiously. "You have given me a description. Now tell 55 me what it is."

"A container of some sort?"

"Yes," I said, "and what would it contain?"

"It would contain its contents!" said Dr. P., with a laugh. "There are many possibilities. It could be a change purse, for example, for coins of five sizes. It could . . ."

I interrupted the barmy flow. "Does it not look familiar? Do you think it might contain, might fit, a part of your body?"

No light of recognition dawned on his face.[4]   60

No child would have the power to see and speak of "a continuous surface . . . infolded on itself," but any child, any infant, would immediately know a glove as a glove, see it as familiar, as going with a hand. Dr. P. didn't. He saw nothing as familiar. Visually, he was lost in a world of lifeless abstractions. Indeed, he did not have a real visual world, as he did not have a real visual self. He could speak about things, but did not see them face-to-face. Hughlings Jackson, discussing patients with aphasia and left-hemisphere lesions, says they have lost "abstract" and "propositional" thought — and compares them with dogs (or, rather, he compares dogs to patients with aphasia). Dr. P., on the other hand, functioned precisely as a machine functions. It wasn't merely that he displayed the same indifference to the visual world as a computer but — even more strikingly — he construed the world as a computer construes it, by means of key features and schematic relationships. The scheme might be identified — in an "identi-kit" way — without the reality being grasped at all.

The testing I had done so far told me nothing about Dr. P.'s inner world. Was it possible that his visual memory and imagination were still intact? I asked him to imagine entering one of our local squares from the

---

[4]Later, by accident, he got it on, and exclaimed, "My God, it's a glove!" This was reminiscent of Kurt Goldstein's patient "Lanuti," who could only recognize objects by trying to use them in action.

north side, to walk through it, in imagination or in memory, and tell me the buildings he might pass as he walked. He listed the buildings on his right side, but none of those on his left. I then asked him to imagine entering the square from the south. Again he mentioned only those buildings that were on the right side, although these were the very buildings he had omitted before. Those he had "seen" internally before were not mentioned now; presumably, they were no longer "seen." It was evident that his difficulties with leftness, his visual field deficits, were as much internal as external, bisecting his visual memory and imagination.

What, at a higher level, of his internal visualization? Thinking of the almost hallucinatory intensity with which Tolstoy visualizes and animates his characters, I questioned Dr. P. about *Anna Karenina*. He could remember incidents without difficulty, had an undiminished grasp of the plot, but completely omitted visual characteristics, visual narrative, and scenes. He remembered the words of the characters but not their faces; and though, when asked, he could quote, with his remarkable and almost verbatim memory, the original visual descriptions, these were, it became apparent, quite empty for him and lacked sensorial, imaginal, or emotional reality. Thus, there was an internal agnosia as well.[5]

But this was only the case, it became clear, with certain sorts of visualization. The visualization of faces and scenes, of visual narrative and drama — this was profoundly impaired, almost absent. But the visualization of *schemata* was preserved, perhaps enhanced. Thus, when I engaged him in a game of mental chess, he had no difficulty visualizing the chessboard or the moves — indeed, no difficulty in beating me soundly.

Luria[6] said of Zazetsky that he had entirely lost his capacity to play   65
games but that his "vivid imagination" was unimpaired. Zazetsky and Dr. P. lived in worlds which were mirror images of each other. But the saddest difference between them was that Zazetsky, as Luria said, "fought to regain his lost faculties with the indomitable tenacity of the damned," whereas Dr. P. was not fighting, did not know what was lost, did not indeed know that anything was lost. But who was more tragic, or who was more damned — the man who knew it, or the man who did not?

---

[5]I have often wondered about Helen Keller's visual descriptions, whether these, for all their eloquence, are somehow empty as well? Or whether, by the transference of images from the tactile to the visual, or, yet more extraordinarily, from the verbal and the metaphorical to the sensorial and the visual, she *did* achieve a power of visual imagery, even though her visual cortex had never been stimulated, directly, by the eyes? But in Dr. P.'s case it is precisely the cortex that was damaged, the organic prerequisite of all pictorial imagery. Interestingly and typically he no longer dreamed pictorially — the "message" of the dream being conveyed in nonvisual terms.

[6]*Alexander Luria* (1902–1977): Russian neuropsychologist who developed theories of brain function that were based, in part, on his work with people with traumatic head injuries. [Eds.]

When the examination was over, Mrs. P. called us to the table, where there was coffee and a delicious spread of little cakes. Hungrily, hummingly, Dr. P. started on the cakes. Swiftly, fluently, unthinkingly, melodiously, he pulled the plates towards him and took this and that in a great gurgling stream, an edible song of food, until, suddenly, there came an interruption: a loud, peremptory rat-tat-tat at the door. Startled, taken aback, arrested by the interruption, Dr. P. stopped eating and sat frozen, motionless, at the table, with an indifferent, blind bewilderment on his face. He saw, but no longer saw, the table; no longer perceived it as a table laden with cakes. His wife poured him some coffee: the smell titillated his nose and brought him back to reality. The melody of eating resumed.

How does he do anything? I wondered to myself. What happens when he's dressing, goes to the lavatory, has a bath? I followed his wife into the kitchen and asked her how, for instance, he managed to dress himself. "It's just like the eating," she explained. "I put his usual clothes out, in all the usual places, and he dresses without difficulty, singing to himself. He does everything singing to himself. But if he is interrupted and loses the thread, he comes to a complete stop, doesn't know his clothes — or his own body. He sings all the time — eating songs, dressing songs, bathing songs, everything. He can't do anything unless he makes it a song."

While we were talking my attention was caught by the pictures on the walls.

"Yes," Mrs. P. said, "he was a gifted painter as well as a singer. The School exhibited his pictures every year."

I strolled past them curiously — they were in chronological order. All his earlier work was naturalistic and realistic, with vivid mood and atmosphere, but finely detailed and concrete. Then, years later, they became less vivid, less concrete, less realistic and naturalistic, but far more abstract, even geometrical and cubist. Finally, in the last paintings, the canvases became nonsense, or nonsense to me — mere chaotic lines and blotches of paint. I commented on this to Mrs. P.   70

"Ach, you doctors, you're such Philistines!"[7] she exclaimed. "Can you not see *artistic development* — how he renounced the realism of his earlier years, and advanced into abstract, nonrepresentational art?"

"No, that's not it," I said to myself (but forbore to say it to poor Mrs. P.). He had indeed moved from realism to nonrepresentation to the abstract, yet this was not the artist, but the pathology, advancing — advancing towards a profound visual agnosia, in which all powers of representation and imagery, all sense of the concrete, all sense of reality, were being destroyed. This wall of paintings was a tragic pathological exhibit, which belonged to neurology, not art.

---

[7]*Philistines*: Uncultured, materialistic people. According to the Bible, the Philistines were enemies of the Israelites. [Eds.]

And yet, I wondered, was she not partly right? For there is often a struggle, and sometimes, even more interestingly, a collusion between the powers of pathology and creation. Perhaps, in his cubist period, there might have been both artistic and pathological development, colluding to engender an original form; for as he lost the concrete, so he might have gained in the abstract, developing a greater sensitivity to all the structural elements of line, boundary, contour — an almost Picasso-like power to see, and equally depict, those abstract organizations embedded in, and normally lost in, the concrete. . . . Though in the final pictures, I feared, there was only chaos and agnosia.

We returned to the great music room, with the Bösendorfer in the center, and Dr. P. humming the last torte.

"Well, Dr. Sacks," he said to me. "You find me an interesting case, I   75
perceive. Can you tell me what you find wrong, make recommendations?"

"I can't tell you what I find wrong," I replied, "but I'll say what I find right. You are a wonderful musician, and music is your life. What I would prescribe, in a case such as yours, is a life which consists entirely of music. Music has been the center, now make it the whole, of your life."

This was four years ago — I never saw him again, but I often wondered about how he apprehended the world, given his strange loss of image, visuality, and the perfect preservation of a great musicality. I think that music, for him, had taken the place of image. He had no body-image, he had body-music: this is why he could move and act as fluently as he did, but came to a total confused stop if the "inner music" stopped. And equally with the outside, the world. . . .[8]

In *The World as Representation and Will*, Schopenhauer[9] speaks of music as "pure will." How fascinated he would have been by Dr. P., a man who had wholly lost the world as representation, but wholly preserved it as music or will.

And this, mercifully, held to the end — for despite the gradual advance of his disease (a massive tumor or degenerative process in the visual parts of his brain) Dr. P. lived and taught music to the last days of his life.

Postscript

How should one interpret Dr. P.'s peculiar inability to interpret, to   80
judge, a glove as a glove? Manifestly, here, he could not make a cognitive judgment, though he was prolific in the production of cognitive hypotheses.

---

[8]Thus, as I learned later from his wife, though he could not recognize his students if they sat still, if they were merely "images," he might suddenly recognize them if they *moved*. "That's Karl," he would cry. "I know his movements, his body-music."

[9]*Arthur Schopenhauer* (1788–1860): German philosopher whose work included a theory to explain the life and work of the artist. [Eds.]

A judgment is intuitive, personal, comprehensive, and concrete — we "see" how things stand, in relation to one another and oneself. It was precisely this setting, this relating, that Dr. P. lacked (though his judging, in all other spheres, was prompt and normal). Was this due to lack of visual information, or faulty processing of visual information? (This would be the explanation given by a classical, schematic neurology.) Or was there something amiss in Dr. P.'s attitude, so that he could not relate what he saw to himself?

These explanations, or modes of explanation, are not mutually exclusive — being in different modes they could coexist and both be true. And this is acknowledged, implicitly or explicitly, in classical neurology: implicitly, by Macrae, when he finds the explanation of defective schemata, or defective visual processing and integration, inadequate; explicitly, by Goldstein, when he speaks of "abstract attitude." But abstract attitude, which allows "categorization," also misses the mark with Dr. P. — and, perhaps, with the concept of "judgment" in general. For Dr. P. *had* abstract attitude — indeed, nothing else. And it was precisely this, his absurd abstractness of attitude — absurd because unleavened with anything else — which rendered him incapable of perceiving identity, or particulars, rendered him incapable of judgment.

Neurology and psychology, curiously, though they talk of everything else, almost never talk of "judgment" — and yet it is precisely the downfall of judgment . . . which constitutes the essence of so many neuropsychological disorders. Judgment and identity may be casualties — but neuropsychology never speaks of them.

And yet, whether in a philosophic sense (Kant's sense),[10] or an empirical and evolutionary sense, judgment is the most important faculty we have. An animal, or a man, may get on very well without "abstract attitude" but will speedily perish if deprived of judgment. Judgment must be the *first* faculty of higher life or mind — yet it is ignored, or misinterpreted, by classical (computational) neurology. And if we wonder how such an absurdity can arise, we find it in the assumptions, or the evolution, of neurology itself. For classical neurology (like classical physics) has always been mechanical — from Hughlings Jackson's mechanical analogies to the computer analogies of today.

Of course, the brain is a machine and a computer — everything in classical neurology is correct. But our mental processes, which constitute our being and life, are not just abstract and mechanical, but personal, as well — and, as such, involve not just classifying and categorizing, but continual judging and feeling also. If this is missing, we become computer-like, as Dr. P. was. And, by the same token, if we delete feeling and judging, the personal, from the cognitive sciences, we reduce them to something as defective as Dr. P. — and we reduce our apprehension of the concrete and real.

---

[10]*Immanuel Kant* (1724–1804): German philosopher; some of his work concerned ethics and moral judgment. [Eds.]

By a sort of comic and awful analogy, our current cognitive neurology   85
and psychology resemble nothing so much as poor Dr. P.! We need the concrete and real, as he did; and we fail to see this, as he failed to see it. Our
cognitive sciences are themselves suffering from an agnosia essentially similar to Dr. P.'s. Dr. P. may therefore serve as a warning and parable — of
what happens to a science which eschews the judgmental, the particular, the
personal, and becomes entirely abstract and computational.

It was always a matter of great regret to me that, owing to circumstances beyond my control, I was not able to follow his case further, either
in the sort of observations and investigations described, or in ascertaining
the actual disease pathology.

One always fears that a case is "unique," especially if it has such extraordinary features as those of Dr. P. It was, therefore, with a sense of great
interest and delight, not unmixed with relief, that I found, quite by
chance — looking through the periodical *Brain* for 1956 — a detailed description of an almost comically similar case, similar (indeed identical) neu-
ropsychologically and phenomenologically, though the underlying pathology (an acute head injury) and all personal circumstances were wholly
different. The authors speak of their case as "unique in the documented history of this disorder" — and evidently experienced, as I did, amazement at
their own findings.[11] The interested reader is referred to the original paper,
Macrae and Trolle (1956), of which I here subjoin a brief paraphrase, with
quotations from the original.

Their patient was a young man of 32, who, following a severe automobile accident, with unconsciousness for three weeks, " . . . complained, exclusively, of an inability to recognize faces, even those of his wife and children." Not a single face was "familiar" to him, but there were three he
could identify; these were workmates: one with an eye-blinking tic, one
with a large mole on his cheek, and a third "because he was so tall and thin
that no one else was like him." Each of these, Macrae and Trolle bring out,
was "recognized solely by the single prominent feature mentioned." In general (like Dr. P.) he recognized familiars only by their voices.

---

[11]Only since the completion of this book have I found that there is, in fact, a
rather extensive literature on visual agnosia in general, and prosopagnosia in particular. In particular I had the great pleasure recently of meeting Dr. Andrew Kertesz,
who has himself published some extremely detailed studies of patients with such agnosias (see, for example, his paper on visual agnosia, Kertesz 1979). Dr. Kertesz
mentioned to me a case known to him of a farmer who had developed prosopagnosia and in consequence could no longer distinguish (the faces of) his *cows*, and of
another such patient, an attendant in a Natural History Museum, who mistook his
own reflection for the diorama of an *ape*. As with Dr. P., and as with Macrae and
Trolle's patient, it is especially the animate which is so absurdly misperceived. The
most important studies of such agnosias, and of visual processing in general, are
now being undertaken by A. R. and H. Damasio.

He had difficulty even recognizing himself in a mirror, as Macrae and Trolle describe in detail: "In the early convalescent phase he frequently, especially when shaving, questioned whether the face gazing at him was really his own, and even though he knew it could physically be none other, on several occasions grimaced or stuck out his tongue 'just to make sure.' By carefully studying his face in the mirror he slowly began to recognize it, but 'not in a flash' as in the past—he relied on the hair and facial outline, and on two small moles on his left cheek."

In general he could not recognize objects "at a glance," but would have   90
to seek out, and guess from, one or two features—occasionally his guesses were absurdly wrong. In particular, the authors note, there was difficulty with the *animate*.

On the other hand, simple schematic objects—scissors, watch, key, etc.—presented no difficulties. Macrae and Trolle also note that: "His *topographical memory* was strange: the seeming paradox existed that he could find his way from home to hospital and around the hospital, but yet could not name streets *en route* [unlike Dr. P., he also had some aphasia] or appear to visualize the topography."

It was also evident that visual memories of people, even from long before the accident, were severely impaired—there was memory of conduct, or perhaps a mannerism, but not of visual appearance or face. Similarly, it appeared, when he was questioned closely, that he no longer had visual images in his *dreams*. Thus, as with Dr. P., it was not just visual perception, but visual imagination and memory, the fundamental powers of visual representation, which were essentially damaged in this patient—at least those powers insofar as they pertained to the personal, the familiar, the concrete.

A final, humorous point. Where Dr. P. might mistake his wife for a hat, Macrae's patient, also unable to recognize his wife, needed her to identify herself by a visual *marker*, by ". . . a conspicuous article of clothing, such as a large hat."

QUESTIONS

1. Summarize as clearly as you can the nature of Dr. P.'s problem. What are the symptoms? What seems to have caused them?
2. What conclusions can be drawn from the case of Dr. P. about the way our visual systems work? Using what Sacks himself says and whatever additional conclusions you yourself can draw, what does the case of Dr. P. tell us about how we see things and what it means to recognize what we see?
3. Sacks has a way of drawing readers into his case studies, of making them concerned about the individuals whose cases he presents. How does he do this? That is, considering him as a writer rather than as a doctor, what aspects of his writing arouse interest and concern? Look at the opening paragraphs of the essay in particular.

4. Is this essay to any degree a story with a plot? Most people find Sacks a compelling writer. What about his way of writing causes this response? How does he keep readers reading?

5. This essay is not only a single case history and an explanation of some curious behavior. It also contains an argument about the nature of the cognitive sciences — how they should and should not proceed. What is that argument? Do you agree or disagree with the view of cognitive science that Sacks is advocating? Write an essay in which you present his position, and develop one of your own on this matter.

6. Write an essay in which you discuss Sacks as a writer and a scientist. Consider such matters as his style of writing, his interest in the arts, his clinical procedures, and the values that he expresses or implies in his work. If your instructor wishes, you may look further into his work to write this essay.

MAKING CONNECTIONS

Compare Sacks's essay with the reports of John Hersey, "Hatsuyo Naka-mura" (p. 133), and Roy C. Selby Jr., "A Delicate Operation" (p. 634). What elements of a case study do these reports contain? Are they also tales or fables similar to Sacks's essay?

OUR PICTURE OF THE UNIVERSE

Stephen W. Hawking

Stephen W. Hawking (b. 1942), the Lucasian Professor of Mathematics at Cambridge University, is one of the world's leading theoretical physicists. Carl Sagan described the moment in 1974 when he observed "an ancient rite, the investiture of new fellows into the Royal Society, one of the most ancient scholarly organizations on the planet. In the front row a young man in a wheelchair was, very slowly, signing his name in a book that bore on its earliest pages the signature of Isaac Newton. When at last he finished, there was a stirring ovation. Stephen Hawking was a legend even then." Hawking's extraordinary achievements have drawn broad popular admiration in part because he suffers from the serious physical disabilities associated with Lou Gehrig's disease. Hawking is known especially for his work on "black holes" and their implications for a unified theory of physical phenomena. His best-selling book A Brief History of Time *(1988) made his thinking available to the general reader, with over a million copies in print. (In 1992, filmmaker Erroll Morris released a fascinating documentary portrait of Hawking under the same title.) The essay reprinted below is the first chapter of that book, unchanged except for the removal of references to the book as a whole.*

A well-known scientist (some say it was Bertrand Russell) once gave a public lecture on astronomy. He described how the earth orbits around the sun and how the sun, in turn, orbits around the center of a vast collection of stars called our galaxy. At the end of the lecture, a little old lady at the back of the room got up and said: "What you have told us is rubbish. The world is really a flat plate supported on the back of a giant tortoise." The scientist gave a superior smile before replying, "What is the tortoise standing on?" "You're very clever, young man, very clever," said the old lady. "But it's turtles all the way down!"

Most people would find the picture of our universe as an infinite tower of tortoises rather ridiculous, but why do we think we know better? What do we know about the universe, and how do we know it? Where did the universe come from, and where is it going? Did the universe have a beginning, and if so, what happened *before* then? What is the nature of time? Will it ever come to an end? Recent breakthroughs in physics, made possible in part by fantastic new technologies, suggest answers to some of these longstanding questions. Someday these answers may seem as obvious to us as the earth orbiting the sun — or perhaps as ridiculous as a tower of tortoises. Only time (whatever that may be) will tell.

As long ago as 340 B.C. the Greek philosopher Aristotle, in his book *On the Heavens*, was able to put forward two good arguments for believing that the earth was a round sphere rather than a flat plate. First, he realized that eclipses of the moon were caused by the earth coming between the sun and the moon. The earth's shadow on the moon was always round, which would be true only if the earth was spherical. If the earth had been a flat disk, the shadow would have been elongated and elliptical, unless the eclipse always occurred at a time when the sun was directly under the center of the disk. Second, the Greeks knew from their travels that the North Star appeared lower in the sky when viewed in the south than it did in more northerly regions. (Since the North Star lies over the North Pole, it appears to be directly above an observer at the North Pole, but to someone looking from the equator, it appears to lie just at the horizon.) From the difference in the apparent position of the North Star in Egypt and Greece, Aristotle even quoted an estimate that the distance around the earth was 400,000 stadia. It is not known exactly what length a stadium was, but it may have been about 200 yards, which would make Aristotle's estimate about twice the currently accepted figure. The Greeks even had a third argument that the earth must be round, for why else does one first see the sails of a ship coming over the horizon, and only later see the hull?

Aristotle thought that the earth was stationary and that the sun, the moon, the planets, and the stars moved in circular orbits about the earth. He believed this because he felt, for mystical reasons, that the earth was the center of the universe, and that circular motion was the most perfect. This idea was elaborated by Ptolemy in the second century A.D. into a complete cosmological model. The earth stood at the center, surrounded by eight spheres that carried the moon, the sun, the stars, and the five planets known at the time, Mercury, Venus, Mars, Jupiter, and Saturn (Figure 1). The planets themselves moved on smaller circles attached to their respective spheres in order to account for their rather complicated observed paths in the sky. The outermost sphere carried the so-called fixed stars, which always stay in the same positions relative to each other but which rotate together across the sky. What lay beyond the last sphere was never made very clear, but it certainly was not part of mankind's observable universe.

Ptolemy's model provided a reasonably accurate system for predicting the positions of heavenly bodies in the sky. But in order to predict these positions correctly, Ptolemy had to make an assumption that the moon followed a path that sometimes brought it twice as close to the earth as at other times. And that meant that the moon ought sometimes to appear twice as big as at other times! Ptolemy recognized this flaw, but nevertheless his model was generally, although not universally, accepted. It was adopted by the Christian church as the picture of the universe that was in accordance

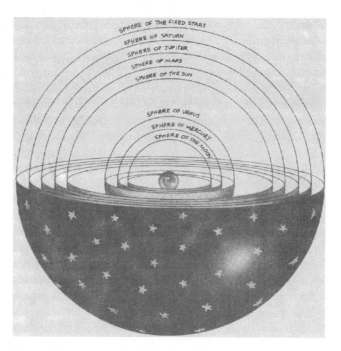

FIGURE 1

with Scripture, for it had the great advantage that it left lots of room outside the sphere of fixed stars for heaven and hell.

A simpler model, however, was proposed in 1514 by a Polish priest,
Nicholas Copernicus. (At first, perhaps for fear of being branded a heretic
by his church, Copernicus circulated his model anonymously.) His idea was
that the sun was stationary at the center and that the earth and the planets
moved in circular orbits around the sun. Nearly a century passed before
this idea was taken seriously. Then two astronomers—the German, Johannes Kepler, and the Italian, Galileo Galilei—started publicly to support
the Copernican theory, despite the fact that the orbits it predicted did not
quite match the ones observed. The death blow to the Aristotelian/ Ptole-
maic theory came in 1609. In that year, Galileo started observing the night
sky with a telescope, which had just been invented. When he looked at the
planet Jupiter, Galileo found that it was accompanied by several small satel-
lites or moons that orbited around it. This implied that everything did
not have to orbit directly around the earth, as Aristotle and Ptolemy had
thought. (It was, of course, still possible to believe that the earth was stationary at the center of the universe and that the moons of Jupiter moved
on extremely complicated paths around the earth, giving the *appearance*
that they orbited Jupiter. However, Copernicus's theory was much simpler.)
At the same time, Johannes Kepler had modified Copernicus's theory, sug-

gesting that the planets moved not in circles but in ellipses (an ellipse is an elongated circle). The predictions now finally matched the observations.

As far as Kepler was concerned, elliptical orbits were merely an ad hoc hypothesis, and a rather repugnant one at that, because ellipses were clearly less perfect than circles. Having discovered almost by accident that elliptical orbits fit the observations well, he could not reconcile them with his idea that the planets were made to orbit the sun by magnetic forces. An explanation was provided only much later, in 1687, when Sir Isaac Newton published his *Philosophiae Naturalis Principia Mathematica*, probably the most important single work ever published in the physical sciences. In it Newton not only put forward a theory of how bodies move in space and time, but he also developed the complicated mathematics needed to analyse those motions. In addition, Newton postulated a law of universal gravitation according to which each body in the universe was attracted toward every other body by a force that was stronger the more massive the bodies and the closer they were to each other. It was this same force that caused objects to fall to the ground. (The story that Newton was inspired by an apple hitting his head is almost certainly apocryphal. All Newton himself ever said was that the idea of gravity came to him as he sat "in a contemplative mood" and "was occasioned by the fall of an apple.") Newton went on to show that, according to his law, gravity causes the moon to move in an elliptical orbit around the earth and causes the earth and the planets to follow elliptical paths around the sun.

The Copernican model got rid of Ptolemy's celestial spheres, and with them, the idea that the universe had a natural boundary. Since "fixed stars" did not appear to change their positions apart from a rotation across the sky caused by the earth spinning on its axis, it became natural to suppose that the fixed stars were objects like our sun but very much farther away.

Newton realized that, according to his theory of gravity, the stars should attract each other, so it seemed they could not remain essentially motionless. Would they not fall together at some point? In a letter in 1691 to Richard Bentley, another leading thinker of his day, Newton argued that this would indeed happen if there were only a finite number of stars distributed over a finite region of space. But he reasoned that if, on the other hand, there were an infinite number of stars, distributed more or less uniformly over infinite space, this would not happen, because there would not be any central point for them to fall to.

This argument is an instance of the pitfalls that you can encounter in 10 talking about infinity. In an infinite universe, every point can be regarded as the center, because every point has an infinite number of stars on each side of it. The correct approach, it was realized only much later, is to consider the finite situation, in which the stars all fall in on each other, and then to ask how things change if one adds more stars roughly uniformly distributed outside this region. According to Newton's law, the extra stars would make no difference at all to the original ones on average, so the stars would fall in just as fast. We can add as many stars as we like, but they will still always collapse in on themselves. We now know it is impossible to have an infinite static model of the universe in which gravity is always attractive.

It is an interesting reflection on the general climate of thought before the twentieth century that no one had suggested that the universe was expanding or contracting. It was generally accepted that either the universe had existed forever in an unchanging state, or that it had been created at a finite time in the past more or less as we observe it today. In part this may have been due to people's tendency to believe in eternal truths, as well as the comfort they found in the thought that even though they may grow old and die, the universe is eternal and unchanging.

Even those who realized that Newton's theory of gravity showed that the universe could not be static did not think to suggest that it might be expanding. Instead, they attempted to modify the theory by making the gravitational force repulsive at very large distances. This did not significantly affect their predictions of the motions of the planets, but it allowed an infinite distribution of stars to remain in equilibrium—with the attractive forces between nearby stars balanced by the repulsive forces from those that were farther away. However, we now believe such an equilibrium would be unstable: if the stars in some region got only slightly nearer each other, the attractive forces between them would become stronger and dominate over the repulsive forces so that the stars would continue to fall toward each other. On the other hand, if the stars got a bit farther away from each other, the repulsive forces would dominate and drive them farther apart.

Another objection to an infinite static universe is normally ascribed to the German philosopher Heinrich Olbers, who wrote about this theory in 1823. In fact, various contemporaries of Newton had raised the problem, and the Olbers article was not even the first to contain plausible arguments against it. It was, however, the first to be widely noted. The difficulty is that in an infinite static universe nearly every line of sight would end on the surface of a star. Thus one would expect that the whole sky would be as bright as the sun, even at night. Olbers's counterargument was that the light from distant stars would be dimmed by absorption by intervening matter. However, if that happened the intervening matter would eventually heat up until it glowed as brightly as the stars. The only way of avoiding the conclusion that the whole of the night sky should be as bright as the surface of the sun would be to assume that the stars had not been shining forever but had turned on at some finite time in the past. In that case the absorbing matter might not have heated up yet or the light from distant stars might not yet have reached us. And that brings us to the question of what could have caused the stars to have turned on in the first place.

The beginning of the universe had, of course, been discussed long before this. According to a number of early cosmologies and the Jewish/Christian/Muslim tradition, the universe started at a finite, and not very distant, time in the past. One argument for such a beginning was the feeling that it was necessary to have "First Cause" to explain the existence of the universe. (Within the universe, you always explained one event as being caused by some earlier event, but the existence of the universe itself could be explained in this way only if it had some beginning.) Another argument was put forward by St. Augustine in his book *The City of God*. He pointed out that civilization is progressing and we remember who performed this deed or developed that technique. Thus man, and so also perhaps the universe, could not have been around all that long. St. Augustine accepted a date of about 5000 B.C. for the Creation of the universe according to the book of Genesis. (It is interesting that this is not so far from the end of the last Ice Age, about 10,000 B.C. which is when archaeologists tell us that civilization really began.)

Aristotle, and most of the other Greek philosophers, on the other hand, did not like the idea of a creation because it smacked too much of divine intervention. They believed, therefore, that the human race and the world around it had existed, and would exist, forever. The ancients had already considered the argument about progress described above, and answered it by saying that there had been periodic floods or other disasters that repeatedly set the human race right back to the beginning of civilization.

The questions of whether the universe had a beginning in time and whether it is limited in space were later extensively examined by the philosopher Immanuel Kant in his monumental (and very obscure) work, *Critique of Pure Reason*, published in 1781. He called these questions antinomies (that is, contradictions) of pure reason because he felt that there were equally compelling arguments for believing the thesis, that the universe had a beginning, and the antithesis, that it had existed forever. His argument for the thesis was that if the universe did not have a beginning, there would be an infinite period of time before any event, which he considered absurd. The argument for the antithesis was that if the universe had a beginning, there would be an infinite period of time before it, so why should the universe begin at any one particular time? In fact, his cases for both the thesis and the antithesis are really the same argument. They are both based on his unspoken assumption that time continues back forever, whether or not the universe had existed forever. As we shall see, the concept of time has no meaning before the beginning of the universe. This was first pointed out by St. Augustine. When asked: What did God do before he created the universe? Augustine didn't reply: He was preparing Hell for people who asked such questions. Instead, he said that time was a property of the universe that God created, and that time did not exist before the beginning of the universe.

When most people believed in an essentially static and unchanging universe, the question of whether or not it had a beginning was really one of metaphysics or theology. One could account for what was observed equally well on the theory that the universe had existed forever or on the theory that it was set in motion at some finite time in such a manner as to look as though it had existed forever. But in 1929, Edwin Hubble made the landmark observation that wherever you look, distant galaxies are moving rapidly away from us. In other words, the universe is expanding. This means that at earlier times objects would have been closer together. In fact, it seemed that there was a time, about ten or twenty thousand million years ago, when they were all at exactly the same place and when, therefore, the density of the universe was infinite. This discovery finally brought the question of the beginning of the universe into the realm of science.

Hubble's observations suggested that there was a time, called the big bang, when the universe was infinitesimally small and infinitely dense. Under such conditions all the laws of science, and therefore all ability to predict the future, would break down. If there were events earlier than this time, then they could not affect what happens at the present time. Their existence can be ignored because it would have no observational consequences. One may say that time had a beginning at the big bang, in the sense that earlier times simply would not be defined. It should be emphasized that this beginning in time is very different from those that had been considered previously. In an unchanging universe a beginning in time is something that has to be imposed by some being outside the universe; there is no physical necessity for a beginning. One can imagine that God created the universe at literally any time in the past. On the other hand, if the universe is expanding, there may be physical reasons why there had to be a beginning. One could still imagine that God created the universe at the instant of the big bang, or even afterwards in just such a way as to make it look as though there had been a big bang, but it would be meaningless to suppose that it was created *before* the big bang. An expanding universe does not preclude a creator, but it does place limits on when he might have carried out his job!

In order to talk about the nature of the universe and to discuss questions such as whether it has a beginning or an end, you have to be clear about what a scientific theory is. I shall take the simpleminded view that a theory is just a model of the universe, or a restricted part of it, and a set of rules that relate quantities in the model to observations that we make. It exists only in our minds and does not have any other reality (whatever that might mean). A theory is a good theory if it satisfies two requirements: It must accurately describe a large class of observations on the basis of a model that contains only a few arbitrary elements, and it must make definite predictions about the results of future observations. For example, Aristotle's theory that everything was made out of four elements, earth, air, fire, and water, was simple enough to qualify, but it did not make any definite predictions. On the other hand, Newton's theory of gravity was based on an even simpler model, in which bodies attracted each other with a force that was proportional to a quantity called their mass and inversely proportional to the square of the distance between them. Yet it predicts the motions of the sun, the moon, and the planets to a high degree of accuracy.

Any physical theory is always provisional, in the sense that it is only a   20
hypothesis: you can never prove it. No matter how many times the results of experiments agree with some theory, you can never be sure that the next time the result will not contradict the theory. On the other hand, you can disprove a theory by finding even a single observation that disagrees with

the predictions of the theory. As philosopher of science Karl Popper has emphasized, a good theory is characterized by the fact that it makes a number of predictions that could in principle be disproved or falsified by observation. Each time new experiments are observed to agree with the predictions the theory survives, and our confidence in it is increased; but if ever a new observation is found to disagree, we have to abandon or modify the theory. At least that is what is supposed to happen, but you can always question the competence of the person who carried out the observation.

In practice, what often happens is that a new theory is devised that is really an extension of the previous theory. For example, very accurate observations of the planet Mercury revealed a small difference between its motion and the predictions of Newton's theory of gravity. Einstein's general theory of relativity predicted a slightly different motion from Newton's theory. The fact that Einstein's predictions matched what was seen, while Newton's did not, was one of the crucial confirmations of the new theory. However, we still use Newton's theory for all practical purposes because the difference between its predictions and those of general relativity is very small in the situations that we normally deal with. (Newton's theory also has the great advantage that it is much simpler to work with than Einstein's!)

The eventual goal of science is to provide a single theory that describes the whole universe. However, the approach most scientists actually follow is to separate the problem into two parts. First, there are the laws that tell us how the universe changes with time. (If we know what the universe is like at any one time, these physical laws tell us how it will look at any later time.) Second, there is the question of the initial state of the universe. Some people feel that science should be concerned with only the first part; they regard the question of the initial situation as a matter for metaphysics or religion. They would say that God, being omnipotent, could have started the universe off any way he wanted. That may be so, but in that case he also could have made it develop in a completely arbitrary way. Yet it appears that he chose to make it evolve in a very regular way according to certain laws. It therefore seems equally reasonable to suppose that there are also laws governing the initial state.

It turns out to be very difficult to devise a theory to describe the universe all in one go. Instead, we break the problem up into bits and invent a number of partial theories. Each of these partial theories describes and predicts a certain limited class of observations, neglecting the effects of other quantities, or representing them by simple sets of numbers. It may be that this approach is completely wrong. If everything in the universe depends on everything else in a fundamental way, it might be impossible to get close to a full solution by investigating parts of the problem in isolation. Nevertheless, it is certainly the way that we have made progress in the past. The classic example again is the Newtonian theory of gravity, which tells us that the gravitational force between two bodies depends only on one number associated with each body, its mass, but is otherwise independent of what the bodies are made of. Thus one does not need to have a theory of the structure and constitution of the sun and the planets in order to calculate their orbits.

Today scientists describe the universe in terms of two basic partial theories—the general theory of relativity and quantum mechanics. They are the great intellectual achievements of the first half of this century. The general theory of relativity describes the force of gravity and the large-scale structure of the universe, that is, the structure on scales from only a few miles to as large as a million million million million (1 with twenty-four zeros after it) miles, the size of the observable universe. Quantum mechanics, on the other hand, deals with phenomena on extremely small scales, such as a millionth of a millionth of an inch. Unfortunately, however, these two theories are known to be inconsistent with each other—they cannot both be correct. One of the major endeavors in physics today . . . is the search for a new theory that will incorporate them both—a quantum theory of gravity. We do not yet have such a theory, and we may still be a long way from having one, but we do already know many of the properties that it must have. And . . . we already know a fair amount about the predictions a quantum theory of gravity must make.

Now, if you believe that the universe is not arbitrary, but is governed by   25
definite laws, you ultimately have to combine the partial theories into a complete unified theory that will describe everything in the universe. But there is a fundamental paradox in the search for such a complete unified theory. The ideas about scientific theories outlined above assume we are rational beings who are free to observe the universe as we want and to draw logical deductions from what we see. In such a scheme it is reasonable to suppose that we might progress even closer toward the laws that govern our universe. Yet if there really is a complete unified theory, it would also presumably determine our actions. And so the theory itself would determine the outcome of our search for it! And why should it determine that we come to the right conclusions from the evidence? Might it not equally well determine that we draw the wrong conclusion? Or no conclusion at all?

The only answer that I can give to this problem is based on Darwin's principle of natural selection. The idea is that in any population of self-reproducing organisms, there will be variations in the genetic material and upbringing that different individuals have. These differences will mean that some individuals are better able than others to draw the right conclusions about the world around them and to act accordingly. These individuals will be more likely to survive and reproduce and so their pattern of behavior and thought will come to dominate. It has certainly been true in the past that what we call intelligence and scientific discovery has conveyed a survival advantage. It is not so clear that this is still the case: our scientific discoveries may well destroy us all, and even if they don't, a complete unified theory may not make much difference to our chances of survival. However, provided the universe has evolved in a regular way, we might expect that the reasoning abilities that natural selection has given us would be valid also in our search for a complete unified theory, and so would not lead us to the wrong conclusions.

Because the partial theories that we already have are sufficient to make accurate predictions in all but the most extreme situations, the search for the ultimate theory of the universe seems difficult to justify on practical grounds. (It is worth noting, though, that similar arguments could have been used against both relativity and quantum mechanics, and these theories have given us both nuclear energy and the microelectronics revolution!) The discovery of a complete unified theory, therefore, may not aid the survival of our species. It may not even affect our life-style. But ever since the dawn of civilization, people have not been content to see events as unconnected and inexplicable. They have craved an understanding of the underlying order in the world. Today we still yearn to know why we are here and where we came from. Humanity's deepest desire for knowledge is justification enough for our continuing quest. And our goal is nothing less than a complete description of the universe we live in.

QUESTIONS

1. The essay has a break after paragraph 18, indicated by extra space between paragraphs. If you had to provide a subtitle for each of the two sections demarcated by that break, what would these subtitles be?
2. What is the function of the anecdote in paragraph 1? Why do you suppose Hawking begins with that story?
3. What is the function of paragraph 2? What kind of sentence structure predominates in this paragraph? Why?
4. The first date mentioned in the essay comes in paragraph 3. Make a list of all the other exact dates that are given, noting the paragraphs in which they appear. Discuss any patterns (or violations of pattern) that you note. What does this list tell you about the organization of the essay?
5. Hawking uses the word God with some frequency. How would you describe the notion of God generated by his text? Is it different from your own views? How important is God to Hawking's view of the universe?
6. What is the notion of science that can be derived from Hawking's use of that word? That is, with what definition or concept of science is he working? Is it the same as your own? Discuss.
7. In the latter part of his essay, Hawking takes up the philosophical question of how we can know that we know what we know. Describe and discuss the view that he presents, bringing in any other theories of knowledge that you have encountered in your studies or reading on the subject.

MAKING CONNECTIONS

Read Carl Sagan's essay, "Can We Know the Universe? Reflections on a Grain of Salt" (p. 620). Are Sagan and Hawking talking about the same universe? Note Sagan's strongest beliefs as expressed in his final paragraphs. Are Sagan and Hawking thinking along the same lines? To what extent does Hawking seem to be answering the challenge that Sagan makes?

NATURAL-BORN LIARS

David Livingstone Smith

David Livingstone Smith (b. 1954) grew up in southern Florida and received his master's degree from Antioch University and his Ph.D. from the University of London. He currently lives in Maine, where he is the director of the New England Institute for Cognitive Science and Evolutionary Psychology at the University of New England. He has directed the graduate program in psychotherapy and counseling at Regent's College in London, worked as a consultant to the national governments of Austria and the United Kingdom, and directed the clinical arm of a nonprofit organization that provides psychological support for inner-city children. Of his switch from these pursuits to getting a doctorate in philosophy, Smith says, "Philosophy gave me a way to integrate my childhood love of biology with my adult interest in the human mind by focusing on the deeper significance of evolutionary biology and how it can help us understand human nature." Smith says that because human nature is so complex, it must be approached from many perspectives and studied through many disciplines, from philosophy to evolutionary biology and cognitive science. He has written five books, most recently Why We Lie: The Evolutionary Roots of Deception and the Unconscious Mind *(2004). The following article appeared in a 2005 issue of* Scientific American Mind.

Deception runs like a red thread throughout all of human history. It sustains literature, from Homer's wily Odysseus to the biggest pop novels of today. Go to a movie, and odds are that the plot will revolve around deceit in some shape or form. Perhaps we find such stories so enthralling because lying pervades human life. Lying is a skill that wells up from deep within us, and we use it with abandon. As the great American observer Mark Twain wrote more than a century ago: "Everybody lies . . . every day, every hour, awake, asleep, in his dreams, in his joy, in his mourning. If he keeps his tongue still his hands, his feet, his eyes, his attitude will convey deception." Deceit is fundamental to the human condition.

Research supports Twain's conviction. One good example was a study conducted in 2002 by psychologist Robert S. Feldman of the University of Massachusetts Amherst. Feldman secretly videotaped students who were asked to talk with a stranger. He later had the students analyze their tapes and tally the number of lies they had told. A whopping 60 percent admitted to lying at least once during 10 minutes of conversation, and the group averaged 2.9 untruths in that time period. The transgressions ranged from intentional exaggeration to flat-out fibs. Interestingly, men and women lied with equal frequency; however, Feldman found that women were more likely to lie to make the stranger feel good, whereas men lied most often to make themselves look better.

In another study a decade earlier by David Knox and Caroline Schacht, both now at East Carolina University, 92 percent of college students confessed that they had lied to a current or previous sexual partner, which left the husband-and-wife research team wondering whether the remaining 8 percent were lying. And whereas it has long been known that men are prone to lie about the number of their sexual conquests, recent research shows that women tend to underrepresent their degree of sexual experience. When asked to fill out questionnaires on personal sexual behavior and attitudes, women wired to a dummy polygraph machine reported having had twice as many lovers as those who were not, showing that the women who were not wired were less honest. It's all too ironic that the investigators had to deceive subjects to get them to tell the truth about their lies.

These references are just a few of the many examples of lying that pepper the scientific record. And yet research on deception is almost always focused on lying in the narrowest sense — literally saying things that aren't true. But our fetish extends far beyond verbal falsification. We lie by omission and through the subtleties of spin. We engage in myriad forms of nonverbal deception, too: we use makeup, hairpieces, cosmetic surgery, clothing, and other forms of adornment to disguise our true appearance, and we apply artificial fragrances to misrepresent our body odors. We cry crocodile tears, fake orgasms, and flash phony "have a nice day" smiles. Out-and-out verbal lies are just a small part of the vast tapestry of human deceit.

The obvious question raised by all of this accounting is: Why do we   5
lie so readily? The answer: because it works. The *Homo sapiens* who are best able to lie have an edge over their counterparts in a relentless struggle for the reproductive success that drives the engine of evolution. As humans, we must fit into a close-knit social system to succeed, yet our primary aim is still to look out for ourselves above all others. Lying helps. And lying to ourselves — a talent built into our brains — helps us accept our fraudulent behavior.

Passport to Success

If this bald truth makes any one of us feel uncomfortable, we can take some solace in knowing we are not the only species to exploit the lie. Plants and animals communicate with one another by sounds, ritualistic displays, colors, airborne chemicals, and other methods, and biologists once naively assumed that the sole function of these communication systems was to transmit accurate information. But the more we have learned, the more

The Padded Résumé
Lying goes far beyond spoken words; we exaggerate, falsify,
flatter, and manipulate in many ways.

obvious it has become that nonhuman species put a lot of effort into sending *inaccurate* messages.

The mirror orchid, for example, displays beautiful blue blossoms that
are dead ringers for female wasps. The flower also manufactures a chemical
cocktail that simulates the pheromones released by females to attract
mates. These visual and olfactory cues keep hapless male wasps on the
flower long enough to ensure that a hefty load of pollen is clinging to their
bodies by the time they fly off to try their luck with another orchid in disguise. Of course, the orchid does not "intend" to deceive the wasp. Its fak-
ery is built into its physical design, because over the course of history plants
that had this capability were more readily able to pass on their genes than
those that did not. Other creatures deploy equally deceptive strategies.
When approached by an erstwhile predator, the harmless hog-nosed snake
flattens its head, spreads out a cobralike hood, and, hissing menacingly,
pretends to strike with maniacal aggression, all the while keeping its mouth
discreetly closed.

These cases and others show that nature favors deception because it
provides survival advantages. The tricks become increasingly sophisticated
the closer we get to *Homo sapiens* on the evolutionary chain. Consider an
incident between Mel and Paul:

Mel dug furiously with her bare hands to extract the large succu-
lent corm from the rock-hard Ethiopian ground. It was the dry season and food was scarce. Corms are edible bulbs somewhat like

onions and are a staple during these long, hard months. Little Paul sat nearby and surreptitiously observed Mel's labors. Paul's mother was out of sight; she had left him to play in the grass, but he knew she would remain within earshot in case he needed her. Just as Mel managed, with a final pull, to yank her prize out of the earth, Paul let out an ear-splitting cry that shattered the peace of the savannah. His mother rushed to him. Heart pounding and adrenaline pumping, she burst upon the scene and quickly sized up the situation: Mel had obviously harassed her darling child. Shrieking, she stormed after the bewildered Mel, who dropped the corm and fled. Paul's scheme was complete. After a furtive glance to make sure nobody was looking, he scurried over to the corm, picked up his prize, and began to eat. The trick worked so well that he used it several more times before anyone wised up.

The actors in this real-life drama were not people. They were Chacma baboons, described in a 1987 article by primatologists Richard W. Byrne and Andrew Whiten of the University of St. Andrews in Scotland for *New Scientist* magazine and later recounted in Byrne's 1995 book *The Thinking Ape* (Oxford University Press). In 1983 Byrne and Whiten began noticing

---

THE LIE OF HAPPINESS

Lying to ourselves may be one way of maintaining our mental health. Several classic studies indicate that moderately depressed people actually deceive themselves less than so-called normal folks. Lauren B. Alloy of Temple University and Lyn Y. Abramson of the University of Wisconsin–Madison unveiled this trend by clandestinely manipulating the outcome of a series of games. Healthy subjects who participated in the games were inclined to take credit when they won the rigged games and also typically underestimated their contributions to the outcome when they did poorly.

Depressed subjects, however, evaluated their contributions much more accurately. In another study, psychologist Peter M. Lewinsohn, professor emeritus at the University of Oregon, showed that depressives judge other people's attitudes toward them far more accurately than nondepressed subjects. Furthermore, this ability actually degenerates as the psychological symptoms of depression lift in response to treatment.

Perhaps mental health rests on self-deception, and becoming depressed is based on an impairment of the ability to deceive oneself. After all, we are all going to die, all of our loved ones are going to die, and a great deal of the world lives in abject misery. These are hardly reasons to be happy!

— *D. L. S.*

The Fake Smile
(Appearance: That was a funny story, boss.)
(Agenda: Give us that raise.)

deceptive tactics among the mountain baboons in Drakensberg, South Africa. Catarrhine primates, the group that includes the Old World monkeys, apes, and ourselves, are all able to tactically dupe members of their own species. The deceptiveness is not built into their appearance, as with the mirror orchid, nor is it encapsulated in rigid behavioral routines like those of the hog-nosed snake. The primates' repertoires are calculated, flexible, and exquisitely sensitive to shifting social contexts.

Byrne and Whiten catalogued many such observations, and these became the basis for their celebrated Machiavellian intelligence hypothesis, which states that the extraordinary explosion of intelligence in primate evolution was prompted by the need to master ever more sophisticated forms of social trickery and manipulation. Primates had to get smart to keep up with the snowballing development of social gamesmanship. 10

The Machiavellian intelligence hypothesis suggests that social complexity propelled our ancestors to become progressively more intelligent and increasingly adept at wheeling, dealing, bluffing, and conniving. That means human beings are natural-born liars. And in line with other evolutionary trends, our talent for dissembling dwarfs that of our nearest relatives by several orders of magnitude.

The complex choreography of social gamesmanship remains central to our lives today. The best deceivers continue to reap advantages denied to their more honest or less competent peers. Lying helps us facilitate social interactions, manipulate others, and make friends.

The Thumbs-Up
(Appearance: Great to see you. You're the best.)
(Agenda: Pick me for that VP job.)

There is even a correlation between social popularity and deceptive skill. We falsify our résumés to get jobs, plagiarize essays to boost grade-point averages, and pull the wool over the eyes of potential sexual partners to lure them into bed. Research shows that liars are often better able to get jobs and attract members of the opposite sex into relationships. Several years later Feldman demonstrated that the adolescents who are most popular in their schools are also better at fooling their peers. Lying continues to work. Although it would be self-defeating to lie all the time (remember the fate of the boy who cried, "Wolf"), lying often and well remains a passport to social, professional, and economic success.

Fooling Ourselves

Ironically, the primary reasons we are so good at lying to others is that we are good at lying to ourselves. There is a strange asymmetry in how we apportion dishonesty. Although we are often ready to accuse others of deceiving us, we are astonishingly oblivious to our own duplicity. Experiences of being a victim of deception are burned indelibly info our memories, but our own prevarications slip off our tongues so that we often do not notice them for what they are.

The strange phenomenon of self-deception has perplexed philosophers   15
and psychologists for more than 2,000 years. On the face of it, the idea that

a person can con oneself seems as nonsensical as cheating at solitaire or embezzling from one's own bank account. But the paradoxical character of self-deception flows from the idea, formalized by French polymath René Descartes in the seventeenth century, that human minds are transparent to their owners and that introspection yields an accurate understanding of our own mental life. As natural as this perspective is to most of us, it turns out to be deeply misguided.

If we hope to understand self-deception, we need to draw on a more scientifically sound conception of how the mind works. The brain comprises a number of functional systems. The system responsible for cognition—the thinking part brain—is somewhat distinct from the system that produces conscious experiences. The relation between the two systems can be thought similar to the relation between the processor and monitor of a personal computer. The work takes place in the processor; the monitor does nothing but display information the processor transfers to it. By the same token, the brain's five systems do the thinking, whereas consciousness displays the information that it has received. Consciousness plays a less important role in cognition than previously expected.

This general picture is supported by a great deal of experimental evidence. Some of the most remarkable and widely discussed studies were conducted several decades ago by neuroscientist Benjamin Libet, now professor emeritus at the University of California at San Diego. In one experiment, Libet placed subjects in front of a button and a rapidly moving clock and asked them to press the button whenever they wished and to note the time, as displayed on the clock, the moment they felt an impulse to press the button. Libet also attached electrodes over the motor cortex, which controls movement, in each of his subjects to monitor the electrical tension that mounts as the brain prepares to initiate an action. He found that our brains begin to prepare action just over a third of a second *before we consciously decide to act*. In other words, despite appearances, it is not the conscious

---

BIG-BRAINED BAMBOOZLERS

Homo sapiens have big brains. So do our relatives, the monkeys and apes. Normally, brain size among species rises with increasing body size and metabolic intake, but according to this formula, monkeys and apes have the brain volume of creatures twice as large. Most of the enlargement comes from massive development of the neocortex. A 2004 study by Richard W. Byrne and Nadia Corp of the University of St. Andrews in Scotland shows that the use of deception by primate species rises with neocortical volume. That is, the members of species with the beefiest brains are the most inclined to deceive one another. Human brain size, of course, outranks all other on the body-size chart.   — D. L. S.

mind that decides to perform an action: the decision is made unconsciously. Although our consciousness likes to take the credit (so to speak), it is merely informed of unconscious decisions after the fact. This study and others like it suggest that we are systematically deluded about the role consciousness plays in our lives. Strange as it may seem, consciousness may not do anything except display the results of unconscious cognition.

This general model of the mind, supported by various experiments beyond Libet's, gives us exactly what we need to resolve the paradox of self-deception — at least in theory. We are able to deceive ourselves by invoking the equivalent of a cognitive filter between unconscious cognition and conscious awareness. The filter preempts information before it reaches consciousness, preventing selected thoughts from proliferating along the neural pathways to awareness.

Solving the Pinocchio Problem

But why would we filter information? Considered from a biological perspective, this notion presents a problem. The idea that we have an evolved tendency to *deprive* ourselves of information sounds wildly implausible, self-defeating, and biologically disadvantageous. But once again we can find a clue from Mark Twain, who bequeathed to us an amazingly insightful explanation. "When a person cannot deceive himself," he wrote, "the chances are against his being able to deceive other people." Self-deception is advantageous because it helps us lie to others more convincingly. Concealing the truth from ourselves conceals it from others.

In the early 1970s biologist Robert L. Trivers, now at Rutgers University, put scientific flesh on Twain's insight. Trivers made the case that our flair for self-deception might be a solution to an adaptive problem that repeatedly faced ancestral humans when they attempted to deceive one another. Deception can be a risky business. In the tribal, hunter-gatherer bands that were presumably the standard social environment in which our hominid ancestors lived, being caught red-handed in an act of deception could result in social ostracism or banishment from the community, to become hyena bait. Because our ancestors were socially savvy, highly intelligent primates, there came a point when they became aware of these dangers and learned to be self-conscious liars.

This awareness created a brand-new problem. Uncomfortable, jittery liars are bad liars. Like Pinocchio, they give themselves away by involuntary, nonverbal behaviors. A good deal of experimental evidence indicates that humans are remarkably adept at making inferences about one another's mental states on the basis of even minimal exposure to nonverbal information. As Freud once commented, "No mortal can keep a secret. If his lips are silent, he chatters with his fingertips; betrayal oozes out of him at every pore." In an effort, to quell our rising anxiety, we may automatically raise the pitch of our voice, blush, break out into the proverbial cold sweat,

The Come-On
"You're the sexiest woman at this party."
(Agenda: Come home with me tonight.)

scratch our nose, or make small movements with our feet as though barely squelching an impulse to flee.

Alternatively, we may attempt to rigidly control the tone of our voice and, in an effort to suppress telltale stray movements, raise suspicion by our stiff, wooden bearing. In any case, we sabotage our own efforts to deceive. Nowadays a used-car salesman can hide his shifty eyes behind dark sunglasses, but this cover was not available during the Pleistocene epoch. Some other solution was required.

Natural selection appears to have cracked the Pinocchio problem by endowing us with the ability to lie to ourselves. Fooling ourselves allows us to selfishly manipulate others around us while remaining conveniently innocent of our own shady agendas.

If this is right, self-deception took root in the human mind as a tool for social manipulation. As Trivers noted, biologists propose that the overriding function of self-deception is the more fluid acceptance of others. Self-deception helps us ensnare other people more effectively. It enables us to lie sincerely, to lie without knowing that we are lying. There is no longer any need to put on an act, to pretend that we are telling the truth. Indeed, a self-deceived person is actually telling the truth to the best of his or her knowledge, and believing one's own story makes it all the more persuasive.

Although Trivers's thesis is difficult to test, it has gained wide currency   25
as the only biologically realistic explanation of self-deception as an adap-

tive feature of the human mind. The view also fits very well with a good deal of work on the evolutionary roots of social behavior that has been supported empirically.

Of course, self-deception is not always so absolute. We are sometimes aware that we are willing dupes in our own con game, stubbornly refusing to explicitly articulate to ourselves just what we are up to. We know that the stories we tell ourselves do not jibe with our behavior, or they fail to mesh with physical signs such as a thumping heart or sweaty palms that betray our emotional states. For example, the students described earlier, who admitted their lies when watching themselves on videotape, knew they were lying at times, and most likely they did not stop themselves because they were not disturbed by this behavior.

BETTER POLYGRAPHS

Although advocates of the polygraph claim an accuracy rate around 90 percent, many critics say that despite its "lie detector" moniker, the machine does not really spot falsehoods. It's electrodes, arranged in various places on a subject's body, measure physiological signs of stress, such as elevated heart rate and blood pressure. These do often accompany lying, but if a person can lie calmly he or she stands a good chance of beating the polygraph. Conversely, a truth-telling individual who is anxious about the procedure can elicit a false positive reading.

Scientists are working on a new breed of lie detectors that zeros in on lying itself. For example, neuroscientist Lawrence A Farwell of Brain Fingerprinting Laboratories has developed a method of the same name. A subject wears a helmet of electrodes that produces an electroencephalogram (EEG) — a record of electrical changes in the brain. By monitoring neural activity this way, Farwell claims he can detect dishonesty with nearly 100 percent accuracy. The method relies on telltale signs of visual recognition in the brain. For example, a suspect who is shown a murder weapon may say that he has never seen it before, but his brain, Farwell maintains, will generate a wave called P300 that automatically occurs when we recognize an object.

Another approach is being pioneered by psychologist Stephen M. Kosslyn of Harvard University. Kosslyn uses imaging technologies to study what the brain does when we lie. His findings indicate that lying is associated with greater brain activity than truth telling and that activity in certain areas of the brain is associated with distinct kinds of lies.

Although these methods and others remain controversial, it is most likely that the next decade will give investigators unprecedented access to the secret recesses of tour minds — for good or for ill.   —*D.L.S.*

The Forced Cry
(Appearance: You hurt my feelings.)
(Agenda: Take me out for a lavish evening,
and I might forgive you.)

At other times, however, we are happily unaware that we are pulling the wool over our own eyes. A biological perspective helps us understand why the cognitive gears of self-deception engage so smoothly and silently. They cleverly and imperceptibly embroil us in performances that are so skillfully crafted that the act gives every indication of complete sincerity, even to the actors themselves.

Further Reading

- "On the Decay of the Art of Lying." Mark Twain in *The Stolen White Elephant, Etc.* James R. Osgood and Company, 1882.

- "The Thinking Primate's Guide to Deception." Richard W. Byrne and Andrew A. Whiten in *New Scientist*, No. 1589, pages 54–57; December 3, 1987.

- "Who Lies?" Deborah A. Kashy and Bella M. DePaulo in *Journal of Personality and Social Psychology*, Vol. 70, No. 5, pages 1037–1051; 1996.

- *Natural Selection and Social Theory: Selected Papers of Robert Trivers.* Robert Trivers. Oxford University Press, 2002.

QUESTIONS

1. Why, according to Smith, do we lie? Do you agree with Smith's claim that "[d]eceit is fundamental to the human condition (paragraph 1)?"
2. Smith claims that "nature favors deception" (paragraph 8). What evidence does he provide to support this claim? Do you find his evidence persuasive?
3. Why, according to Smith, is self-deception advantageous? Why does self-deception help us lie?
4. How does a biological perspective help us understand self-deception as an adaptive feature of the human mind?
5. Interview ten friends about the type of lies they tell. What patterns do you uncover about the type of lies your friends tell? What hypotheses might you develop to explain these lies? Write a report in which you present the findings of your research.
6. "[T]he primary reason we are so good at lying to others is that we are good at lying to ourselves," writes Smith in paragraph 14. Do you agree or disagree with this statement? What questions do this statement and Smith's article raise for you? Write a response to Smith.

MAKING CONNECTIONS

Both Smith and Malcolm Gladwell, in "The Naked Face" (p. 519), deal with the ways we determine the intentions of others based on our observations of them. What conclusions do Smith and Gladwell agree on? In what ways do their conclusions differ?

LIFE IS A NARRATIVE

Edward O. Wilson

Edward O. Wilson was born in Birmingham, Alabama, in 1929. He received his undergraduate and master's degrees from the University of Alabama and his doctorate from Harvard University, where he has taught since 1956 and is now Pellegrino University Professor Emeritus and Honorary Curator in Entomology at the Museum of Comparative Zoology. Among his many awards are a 1977 National Medal of Science and two Pulitzer Prizes, for On Human Nature *(1978) and* The Ants *(1990). Wilson unwittingly touched off a major controversy with his book* Sociobiology: The New Synthesis *(1975), in which he argued that human behavior is profoundly affected by genetics. On the basis of that argument, his critics, including some well-known colleagues at Harvard, accused him of propounding genetic determinism and racism. However, Wilson refuted that claim, and the development of evolutionary psychology in the 1990s has largely borne out his basic theory. In* The Diversity of Life *(1992), Wilson strongly urges us to conserve the biodiversity of our ecosystems. And in his book* Consilience: The Unity of Knowledge *(1998), Wilson suggests that a small number of natural laws underlie seemingly disparate disciplines, from the arts and religion to biology, anthropology, and psychology, and that all can be organized in one coherent scientific system. The writer Ian McEwan calls Wilson "a scientific materialist who warmly embraces the diversity of human achievement — including religion and art, which he sees in evolutionary terms. He is fundamentally a rational optimist who shows us the beauty of the narrative of life on earth." The following piece appeared as the introduction to* The Best American Science and Nature Writing: 2001, *which Wilson edited.*

Let me tell you a story. It is about two ants. In the early 1960s, when I was a young professor of zoology at Harvard University, one of the vexing mysteries of evolution was the origin of ants. That was far from a trivial problem in science. Ants are the most abundant of insects, the most effective predators of other insects, and the busiest scavengers of small dead animals. They transport the seeds of thousands of plant species, and they turn and enrich more soil than earthworms. In totality (they number roughly in the million billions and weigh about as much as all of humanity), they are among the key players of Earth's terrestrial environment. Of equal general interest, they have attained their dominion by means of the most advanced social organization known among animals.

I had chosen these insects for the focus of my research. It was the culmination of a fascination that dated back to childhood. Now, I spent a lot of time thinking about how they came to be. At first the problem seemed insoluble, because the oldest known ants, found in fossil deposits up to 57 million years old, were already advanced anatomically. In fact, they were quite similar to the modem forms all about us. And just as today, these ancient ants were among the most diverse and abundant of insects. It was as though an opaque curtain had been lowered to block our view of everything that occurred before. All we had to work with was the tail end of evolution.

Somewhere in the world the Ur-ants awaited discovery. I had many conversations with William L. Brown, a friend and fellow myrmecologist, about where the missing links might turn up and what traits they possess that could reveal their ancestry among the nonsocial wasps. We guessed that they first appeared in the late Mesozoic era, 65 million or more years ago, far back enough to have stung and otherwise annoyed the last of the dinosaurs. We were not willing to accept the alternative hypothesis favored by some biblical creationists, that ants did not evolve at all but appeared on Earth full-blown.

Because well-preserved fossils had already been collected by the tens of thousands from all around the northern hemisphere over a period of two centuries without any trace of the Ur-species, I was afraid I would never see one in my lifetime. Then, as so often happens in science, a chance event changed everything. One Sunday morning in 1967, a middle-aged couple, Mr. and Mrs. Edmund Frey, were strolling along the base of the seaside bluffs at Cliftwood Beach, New Jersey, collecting bits of fossilized wood and amber from a thin layer of clay freshly exposed by a storm the day before. They were especially interested in the amber, which are jewel-like fragments of fossil tree sap. In one lump they rescued, clear as yellow glass, were two beautifully preserved ants. At first, that might have seemed nothing unusual: museums, including the one at Harvard, are awash in amber ants. What made these specimens important, however, was their age: about 90 million years, from the middle of the Cretaceous period, Mesozoic era, in the Age of Dinosaurs.

The Freys were willing to share their find, and soon the two specimens found their way to me for examination. There they came close to disaster. As I nervously fumbled the amber piece out of its mailing box I dropped it to the floor, where it broke into two halves. Luck stayed with me, however. The break was as clean as though made by a jeweler, and each piece contained an undamaged specimen. Within minutes I determined that the ants were the long-sought Holy Grail of ant paleontology, or at least very close to it. Brown and I later formally placed them in a new genus, Sphecomyrma freyi (literally, "Frey's wasp ant"). They were more primitive than all other known ants, living and fossil. Moreover, in a dramatic confirmation of evolution as

5

a predictive theory, they possessed most of the intermediate traits that according to our earlier deductions should connect modern ants to the nonsocial wasps.

As a result of the discovery, other entomologists intensified their search, and many more ant fossils of Mesozoic age were soon found. Originating from deposits in New Jersey, Canada, Siberia, and Brazil, they compose a mix of primitive and more advanced species. Bit by bit, they have illuminated the history of ants from near the point of origin over 100 million years ago to the start of the great radiative spread that created the modern fauna.

Science consists of millions of stories like the finding of New Jersey's dawn ants. These accounts, some electrifying, most pedestrian, become science when they can be tested and woven into cause-and-effect explanations to become part of humanity's material worldview. Science, like the rest of culture, is based on the manufacture of narrative. That is entirely natural, and in a profound sense it is a Darwinian necessity. We all live by narrative, every day and every minute of our lives. Narrative is the human way of working through a chaotic and unforgiving world bent on reducing our bodies to malodorous catabolic molecules. It delays the surrender of our personal atoms and compounds back to the environment for the assembly of more humans, and ants.

By narrative we take the best stock we can of the world and our predicament in it. What we see and recreate is seldom the blinding literal truth. Instead, we perceive and respond to our surroundings in narrow ways that most benefit our organismic selves. The narrative genius of Homo sapiens is an accommodation to the inherent inability of the three pounds of our sensory system and brain to process more than a minute fraction of the information the environment pours into them. In order to keep the organism alive, that fraction must be intensely and accurately selective. The stories we tell ourselves and others are our survival manuals.

With new tools and models, neuroscientists are drawing close to an understanding of the conscious mind as narrative generator. They view it as an adaptive flood of scenarios created continuously by the working brain. Whether set in the past, present, or future, whether fictive or reality based, the free-running constructions are our only simulacrum of the world outside the brain. They are everything we will ever possess as individuals. And, minute by minute, they determine whether we live or die.

The present in particular is constructed from sensations very far in excess of what can be put into the simulacrum. Working at a frantic pace, the brain summons memories — past scenarios — to help screen and organize the incoming chaos. It simultaneously creates imaginary scenarios to create fields of competing options, the process we call decision-making, Only a tiny fraction of the narrative fragments — the focus — is selected for higher-order processing in the prefrontal cortex. That segment constitutes the theater of running symbolic imagery we call the conscious mind. During the story-building process, the past is reworked and returned to memory stor-

10

age. Through repeated cycles of recall and supplementation the brain holds on to shrinking segments of the former conscious states. Across generations the most important among these fragments are communicated widely and converted into history, literature, and oral tradition. If altered enough, they become legend and myth. The rest disappear. The story I have just told you about Mesozoic ants is all true as best I can reconstruct it from my memory and notes. But it is only a little bit of the whole truth, most of which is beyond my retrieval no matter how hard I might try.

This brings me to the relation between science and literature. Science is not a subculture separate from that of literature. Its knowledge is the totality of what humanity can verify about the real world, testable by repeated experiment or factual observation, bound to related information by general principles, and — this is the part most often missed — ultimately subject to cause-and-effect explanations consilient across the full range of disciplines. The most democratic of human mental activity, it comprises the nonfiction stories you can take to the bank.

Everyone can understand the process of science, and, once familiar with a modest amount of factual information and the elementary terminology of particular disciplines, he or she can grasp the intuitive essence of at least some scientific knowledge. But the scientific method is not natural to the human mind. The phenomena it explicates are by and large unfamiliar to ordinary experience. New scientific facts and workable theories, the silver and gold of the scientific enterprise, come slow and hard, less like nuggets lying on a streambed than ore dug from mines. To enjoy them while maintaining an effective critical attitude requires mental discipline. The reason, again, is the innate constraints of the human brain. Gossip and music flow easily through the human mind, because the brain is genetically predisposed to receive them. Theirs is a Paleolithic cogency. Calculus and reagent chemistry, in contrast, come hard, like ballet on pointe. They have become relevant only in modern, postevolutionary times. Of the hundreds of fellow scientists I have known for more than fifty years, from graduate students to Nobelists, all generally prefer at random moments of their lives to listen to gossip and music rather than to scientific lectures. Trust me: physics is hard even for physicists. Somewhere on a distant planet, there may exist a species that hereditarily despises gossip and thrives on calculus. But I doubt it.

The central task of science writing for a broad audience is, in consequence, how to make science human and enjoyable without betraying nature. The best writers achieve that end by two means. They present the phenomena as a narrative, whether historical, evolutionary, or phenomenological, and they treat the scientists as protagonists in a story that contains, at least in muted form, the mythic elements of challenge and triumph.

To wring honest journalism and literature from honest science, the writer must overcome formidable difficulties. First is the immensity and exponential growth of the primary material itself, which has experienced a phenomenally short doubling time of fifteen years for over three hundred years, all the while coupled with a similarly advancing technology. It has spread its reach into every conceivable aspect of material existence, from the origin of the universe to the creative process of the mind itself. Its relentless pursuit of detail and theory long ago outstripped the minds of individual scientists themselves to hold it. So fragmented are the disciplines and specialized the language resulting from the growth that experts in one subject often cannot grasp the technical reports of experts in closely similar specialties. Insect neuroendocrinologists, for example, have a hard time understanding mammalian neuroendocrinologists, and the reverse. To see this change in science graphically you need only place opened issues of a premier journal such as *Nature* or *Science* from fifty years ago side by side with issues of the same journal today. The science writer must somehow thread his way into this polyglot activity, move to a promising sector of the front, and, then, accepting a responsibility the research scientists themselves typically avoid, turn the truth of it into a story interesting to a broad public.

A second obstacle to converting science into literature is the standard   15
format of research reportage in the technical journals. Scientific results are by necessity couched in specialized language, trimmed for brevity, and delivered raw. Metaphor is unwelcome except in small homeopathic doses. Hyperbole, no matter how brilliant, spells death to a scientific reputation. Understatement and modesty, even false modesty, are preferred, because in science discovery counts for everything and personal style next to nothing. In pure literature, metaphor and personal style are, in polar contrast, everything. The creative writer, unlike the scientist, seeks channels of cognitional and emotional expression already deeply carved by instinct and culture. The most successful innovator in literature is an honest illusionist. His product, as Picasso said of visual art, is the lie that helps us to see the truth. Imagery, phrasing, and analogy in pure literature are not crafted to report empirical facts. They are instead the vehicles by which the writer transfers his own feelings directly into the minds of his readers in order to evoke the same emotional response.

The central role of pure literature is the transmission of the details of human experience by artifice that directs aesthetic reaction. Originality and power of metaphor, not new facts and theory, are coin of the realm in creative writing. Their source is an intuitive understanding of human nature as opposed to an accurate knowledge of the material world, at least in the literal, quantifiable form required for science. Metaphor in the best writing strikes the mind in an idiosyncratic manner. Its effect ripples out in a hypertext of culture-bound meaning, yet it triggers emotions that transcend culture. Technical scientific reporting tries to achieve exactly the reverse: it narrows meaning and avoids metaphor in order to preserve literalness and repeatability. It saves emotional resonance for another day and venue.

To illustrate the difference, I've contrived the following imaginary examples of the two forms of writing applied to the same subject, the search for life in a deep cave:

SCIENCE. The central shaft of the cavern descends from the vege-
tated rim to the oblique slope of fallen rock at the bottom, reaching
a maximum depth of 86 meters before giving way to a lateral channel. On the floor of this latter passageway we found a small assemblage of troglobitic invertebrates, including two previously unde-
scribed eyeless species of the carabid subfamily Bembidini (see also
Harrison, in press).

LETTERS. After an hour's rappel through the Hadean darkness we at
last reached the floor of the shaft almost 300 feet below the fern-
lined rim. From there we worked our way downward across a
screelike rubble to the very bottom. Our headlamps picked out the
lateral cavern exactly where Romero's 1926 map claimed it to
be. Rick pushed ahead and within minutes shouted back that he
had found blind, white cave inhabitants. When we caught up, he
pointed to scurrying insects he said were springtails and, to round
out the day, at least two species of ground beetles new to science.

In drawing these distinctions in the rules of play, I do not mean to depict
scientists as stony Pecksniffs. Quite the contrary. They vary enormously in
temperament, probably to the same degree as a random sample from the
nonscientific population. Their conferences and seminars are indistinguishable in hubbub from business conventions. Nothing so resembles an ecstatic prospector as a scientist with an important discovery to report to colleagues, to family, to grant officers, to anyone who will listen.

A scientist who has made an important discovery is as much inclined to
show off and celebrate as anyone else. Actually, this can be accomplished in
a technical article, if done cautiously. The heart of such a report is always
the Methods and Materials, followed by Results, all of which must read
like your annual tax report. But up front there is also the Introduction,
where the author briefly explains the significance of the topic, what was
known about it previously, who made the previous principal advances, and
what aspect of the whole the author's own findings are meant to address. A
smidgen of excitement, maybe even a chaste metaphor or two, is allowed in
the Introduction. Still more latitude is permitted for the Discussion, which
follows the Results. Here the writer is expected to expatiate on the data and
hypotheses as inclination demands. He or she may also push the envelope
and make cautious guesses about what lies ahead for future researchers.
However, there must be no outbursts such as, "I was excited to find . . ." or
"This is certain to be a major advance."

Science writers are in the difficult position of locating themselves somewhere between the two stylistic poles of literature and science. They risk
appearing both as journalists to the literati and as amateurs to the scientists. But these judgments, if made, are ignorant and unfair. Enormous
room for original thought and expression exists in science writing. Its potential is nothing less than the establishment of what Sir Charles Snow

called the third culture, a concept also recently promoted by the author and
literary agent John Brockman.

The position nearest the literary pole is that broadly classified as nature   20
writing. With roots going back to nineteenth-century romanticism, it culti-
vates the facts and theories of science but relies heavily on personal narrative and aesthetic expression. Thanks to writers of the first rank such
as Annie Dillard, Barry Lopez, Peter Matthiessen, Bill McKibben, David
Quammen, and Jonathan Weimer (a representative but far from exclusive
list!), nature writing has become a distinctive American art form.

The pole nearest science is occupied primarily by scientists who choose
to deliver their dispatches from the front to a broader public. Ranging from
memoirs to philosophical accounts of entire disciplines, their writing res-
onates with a certain firsthand authority but is constrained to modesty in
emotional expression by the conventions of their principal trade. Writing
scientists also frequently struggle with the handicap imposed by the lack of
connection of their subject to ordinary human experience: few tingles of the
spine come from bacterial genetics, and generally the only tears over physical chemistry come as a result of trying to learn it. Despite the inherent difficulties, science writing is bound to grow in influence, because it is the best
way to bridge the two cultures into which civilization is still split. Most educated people who are not professionals in the field do not understand science and technology, despite the profound effect of these juggernauts of
modernity on every aspect of their lives. Symmetrically, most scientists are
semiliterate journeymen with respect to the humanities. They are thus correspondingly removed from the heart and spirit of our species. How to
solve this problem is more than just a puzzle for creative writers. It is, if you
will permit a scientist a strong narrative-laden metaphor, the central challenge of education in the twenty-first century.

QUESTIONS

1. Wilson begins his essay with these opening lines: "Let me tell you a
   story. It is about two ants." What story does Wilson tell about ants?
   What story does he tell about science?
2. Why did Wilson choose ants as the focus of his research?
3. Wilson writes, "Then, as so often happens in science, a chance event
   changed everything" (paragraph 4).What was this chance event that
   Wilson describes? What was the significance of this event for Wilson?
   For science?
4. In paragraph 8, Wilson writes, "The stories we tell ourselves and others
   are our survival manuals." What, according to Wilson, is the role of narrative in life and in science?
5. Why, according to Wilson, is "the scientific method . . . not natural to
   the human mind" (paragraph 12)?

6. Wilson describes the central task of science writing this way — "to make science human and enjoyable without betraying nature" (paragraph 13). Find a piece of science writing that you enjoy. How has the writer appealed to a broad audience without "betraying nature"?

7. In paragraph 14, Wilson urges readers to place a premier journal such as *Nature* or *Science* "from fifty years ago side by side with issues of the same journal today" to understand the enormous changes in science. Go to the library and compare a current issue of a scientific magazine with one from fifty years ago. What do you learn about the nature of science from such a comparison? What has changed? Write a report.

8. Wilson ends his essay with a strong claim that "most scientists are semi-literate journeymen with respect to the humanities . . . correspondingly removed from the heart and spirit of our species." Do you agree or disagree with this claim? Write a response to Wilson's essay.

MAKING CONNECTIONS

1. Wilson makes the claim that stories are a key way to present science. Choose one of the stories in this book, and test Wilson's assertion about the importance of narrative and its ability to help us "take the best stock we can of the world and our predicament in it" (paragraph 8). You might consider choosing a story by Bruce Holland Rogers (p. 113), Douglas Trevor (p. 158), James Alan McPherson (p. 176), Susan Choi (p. 198), Richard Harding Davis (p. 405), or Sharon Wahl (p. 504). What does a narrative structure allow your chosen writer to do that another form — such as an argument, or a comparison and contrast, or a series of examples — does not permit?

2. Select an essay by one of the following authors: Stephen W. Hawking (p. 724), Oliver Sacks (p. 711), Emily Martin (p. 754), or Bruno Bettelheim (p. 657). Does your chosen piece of science writing tell a story? If so, what is that story? In what ways does your chosen piece support or refute Wilson's assertion that good science writing for a general audience is fundamentally narrative in structure, that it *must* tell a story in order to be effective?

Arguing in the
Sciences and Technologies

The Egg and the Sperm:
How Science Has Constructed a Romance Based on Stereotypical Male-Female Roles

Emily Martin

Emily Martin (b. 1944) is a professor of anthropology at New York University. She has written The Woman in the Body: A Cultural Analysis of Reproduction *(1987) and* Flexible Bodies: Tracking Immunity in American Culture — From the Days of Polio to the Age of AIDS *(1994). In the following article, which originally appeared in the journal* Signs *(1991), Martin's intent is to expose the cultural stereotypes operative in the so-called scientific language surrounding human reproduction.*

Portions of this article were presented as the 1987 Becker Lecture, Cornell University. I am grateful for the many suggestions and ideas I received on this occasion. For especially pertinent help with my arguments and data I thank Richard Cone, Kevin Whaley, Sharon Stephens, Barbara Duden, Susanne Kuechler, Lorna Rhodes, and Scott Gilbert. The article was strengthened and clarified by the comments of the anonymous *Signs* reviewers as well as the superb editorial skills of Amy Gage.

The theory of the human body is always a part of a world-picture. . . .
The theory of the human body is always a part of a fantasy.
— [JAMES HILLMAN, *The Myth of Analysis*][1]

As an anthropologist, I am intrigued by the possibility that culture shapes how biological scientists describe what they discover about the natural world. If this were so, we would be learning about more than the natural world in high school biology class; we would be learning about cultural beliefs and practices as if they were part of nature. In the course of my research I realized that the picture of egg and sperm drawn in popular as well as scientific accounts of reproductive biology relies on stereotypes central to our cultural definitions of male and female. The stereotypes imply not only that female biological processes are less worthy than their male counterparts but also that women are less worthy than men. Part of my goal in writing this article is to shine a bright light on the gender stereotypes hidden within the scientific language of biology. Exposed in such a light, I hope they will lose much of their power to harm us.

Egg and Sperm: A Scientific Fairy Tale

At a fundamental level, all major scientific textbooks depict male and female reproductive organs as systems for the production of valuable substances, such as eggs and sperm.[2] In the case of women, the monthly cycle is described as being designed to produce eggs and prepare a suitable place for them to be fertilized and grown — all to the end of making babies. But the enthusiasm ends there. By extolling the female cycle as a productive enterprise, menstruation must necessarily be viewed as a failure. Medical texts describe menstruation as the "debris" of the uterine lining, the result of necrosis, or death of tissue. The descriptions imply that a system has gone awry, making products of no use, not to specification, unsalable, wasted, scrap. An illustration in a widely used medical text shows menstruation as a chaotic disintegration of form, complementing the many texts that describe it as "ceasing," "dying," "losing," "denuding," "expelling."[3]

Male reproductive physiology is evaluated quite differently. One of the texts that sees menstruation as failed production employs a sort of breathless

---

[1]James Hillman, *The Myth of Analysis* (Evanston, Ill.: Northwestern University Press, 1972), 220.

[2]The textbooks I consulted are the main ones used in classes for undergraduate premedical students or medical students (or those held on reserve in the library for these classes) during the past few years at Johns Hopkins University. These texts are widely used at other universities in the country as well.

[3]Arthur C. Guyton, *Physiology of the Human Body*, 6th ed. (Philadelphia: Saunders College Publishing, 1984), 624.

prose when it describes the maturation of sperm: "The mechanisms which guide the remarkable cellular transformation from spermatid to mature sperm remain uncertain. . . . Perhaps the most amazing characteristic of spermatogenesis is its sheer magnitude: the normal human male may manufacture several hundred million sperm per day."[4] In the classic text *Medical Physiology*, edited by Vernon Mountcastle, the male/female, productive/destructive comparison is more explicit: "Whereas the female *sheds* only a single gamete each month, the seminiferous tubules *produce* hundreds of millions of sperm each day" (emphasis mine).[5] The female author of another text marvels at the length of the microscopic seminiferous tubules, which, if uncoiled and placed end to end, "would span almost one-third of a mile!" She writes, "In an adult male these structures produce millions of sperm cells each day." Later she asks, "How is this feat accomplished?"[6] None of these texts expresses such intense enthusiasm for any female processes. It is surely no accident that the "remarkable" process of making sperm involves precisely what, in the medical view, menstruation does not: production of something deemed valuable.[7]

One could argue that menstruation and spermatogenesis are not analogous processes and, therefore, should not be expected to elicit the same kind of response. The proper female analogy to spermatogenesis, biologically, is ovulation. Yet ovulation does not merit enthusiasm in these texts either. Textbook descriptions stress that all of the ovarian follicles containing ova are already present at birth. Far from being *produced*, as sperm are, they merely sit on the shelf, slowly degenerating and aging like overstocked inventory: "At birth, normal human ovaries contain an estimated one million follicles [each], and no new ones appear after birth. Thus, in marked contrast to the male, the newborn female already has all the germ cells she will ever have. Only a few, perhaps 400, are destined to reach full maturity during her active productive life. All the others degenerate at some point in their development so that few, if any, remain by the time she reaches menopause at approximately 50 years of age."[8] Note the "marked contrast" that this description sets up between male and female: the male, who

---

[4]Arthur J. Vander, James H. Sherman, and Dorothy S. Luciano, *Human Physiology: The Mechanisms of Body Function*, 3d ed. (New York: McGraw Hill, 1980), 483–84.

[5]Vernon B. Mountcastle, *Medical Physiology*, 14th ed. (London: Mosby, 1980), 2:1624.

[6]Eldra Pearl Solomon, *Human Anatomy and Physiology* (New York: CBS College Publishing, 1983), 678.

[7]For elaboration, see Emily Martin, *The Woman in the Body: A Cultural Analysis of Reproduction* (Boston: Beacon, 1987), 27–53.

[8]Vander, Sherman, and Luciano, 568.

continuously produces fresh germ cells, and the female, who has stockpiled germ cells by birth and is faced with their degeneration.

Nor are the female organs spared such vivid descriptions. One scientist writes in a newspaper article that a woman's ovaries become old and worn out from ripening eggs every month, even though the woman herself is still relatively young: "When you look through a laparoscope . . . at an ovary that has been through hundreds of cycles, even in a superbly healthy American female, you see a scarred, battered organ."[9]

To avoid the negative connotations that some people associate with the female reproductive system, scientists could begin to describe male and female processes as homologous. They might credit females with "producing" mature ova one at a time, as they're needed each month, and describe males as having to face problems of degenerating germ cells. This degeneration would occur throughout life among spermatogonia, the undifferentiated germ cells in the testes that are the long-lived, dormant precursors of sperm.

But the texts have an almost dogged insistence on casting female processes in a negative light. The texts celebrate sperm production because it is continuous from puberty to senescence, while they portray egg production as inferior because it is finished at birth. This makes the female seem unproductive, but some texts will also insist that it is she who is wasteful.[10] In a section heading for *Molecular Biology of the Cell*, a best-selling text, we are told that "Oogenesis is wasteful." The text goes on to emphasize that of the seven million oogonia, or egg germ cells, in the female embryo, most degenerate in the ovary. Of those that do go on to become oocytes, or eggs, many also degenerate, so that at birth only two million eggs remain in the ovaries. Degeneration continues throughout a woman's life: by puberty 300,000 eggs remain, and only a few are present by menopause. "During the 40 or so years of a woman's reproductive life, only 400 to 500 eggs will have been released," the authors write. "All the rest will have degenerated. It is still a mystery why so many eggs are formed only to die in the ovaries."[11]

---

[9]Melvin Konner, "Childbearing and Age," *New York Times Magazine* (December 27, 1987), 22–23, esp. 22.

[10]I have found but one exception to the opinion that the female is wasteful: "Smallpox being the nasty disease it is, one might expect nature to have designed antibody molecules with combining sites that specifically recognize the epitopes on smallpox virus. Nature differs from technology, however: it thinks nothing of wastefulness. (For example, rather than improving the chance that a spermatozoon will meet an egg cell, nature finds it easier to produce millions of spermatozoa.)" (Niels Kaj Jerne, "The Immune System," *Scientific American* 229, no. 1 [July 1973]: 53.) Thanks to a *Signs* reviewer for bringing this reference to my attention.

[11]Bruce Alberts et al., *Molecular Biology of the Cell* (New York: Garland, 1983), 795.

The real mystery is why the male's vast production of sperm is not seen as wasteful.[12] Assuming that a man "produces" 100 million (10^8) sperm per day (a conservative estimate) during an average reproductive life of sixty years, he would produce well over two trillion sperm in his lifetime. Assuming that a woman "ripens" one egg per lunar month, or thirteen per year, over the course of her forty-year reproductive life, she would total five hundred eggs in her lifetime. But the word "waste" implies an excess, too much produced. Assuming two or three offspring, for every baby a woman produces, she wastes only around two hundred eggs. For every baby a man produces, he wastes more than one trillion (10^{12}) sperm.

How is it that positive images are denied to the bodies of women? A look at language — in this case, scientific language — provides the first clue. Take the egg and the sperm.[13] It is remarkable how "femininely" the egg behaves and how "masculinely" the sperm.[14] The egg is seen as large and passive.[15] It does not *move* or *journey*, but passively "is transported," "is swept,"[16] or even "drifts"[17] along the fallopian tube. In utter contrast, sperm are small,

---

[12]In her essay "Have Only Men Evolved?" (in *Discovering Reality: Feminist Perspectives on Epistemology, Metaphysics, Methodology, and Philosophy of Science*, ed. Sandra Harding and Merrill B. Hintikka [Dordrecht, The Netherlands: Reidel, 1983], 45–69, esp. 60–61), Ruth Hubbard points out that sociobiologists have said the female invests more energy than the male in the production of her large gametes, claiming that this explains why the female provides parental care. Hubbard questions whether it "really takes more 'energy' to generate the one or relatively few eggs than the large excess of sperms required to achieve fertilization." For further critique of how the greater size of eggs is interpreted in sociobiology, see Donna Haraway, "Investment Strategies for the Evolving Portfolio of Primate Females," in *Body/Politics*, ed. Mary Jacobus, Evelyn Fox Keller, and Sally Shuttleworth (New York: Routledge, 1990), 155–56.

[13]The sources I used for this article provide compelling information on interactions among sperm. Lack of space prevents me from taking up this theme here, but the elements include competition, hierarchy, and sacrifice. For a newspaper report, see Malcolm W. Browne, "Some Thoughts on Self Sacrifice," *New York Times* (July 5, 1988), C6. For a literary rendition, see John Barth, "Night-Sea Journey," in his *Lost in the Funhouse* (Garden City, N.Y.: Doubleday, 1968), 3–13.

[14]See Carol Delaney, "The Meaning of Paternity and the Virgin Birth Debate," *Man* 21, no. 3 (September 1986): 494–513. She discusses the difference between this scientific view that women contribute genetic material to the fetus and the claim of long-standing Western folk theories that the origin and identity of the fetus comes from the male, as in the metaphor of planting a seed in soil.

[15]For a suggested direct link between human behavior and purportedly passive eggs and active sperm, see Erik H. Erikson, "Inner and Outer Space: Reflections on Womanhood," *Daedalus* 93, no. 2 (Spring 1964): 582–606, esp. 591.

[16]Guyton (n. 3), 619; and Mountcastle (n. 5), 1609.

[17]Jonathan Miller and David Pelham, *The Facts of Life* (New York: Viking Penguin, 1984), 5.

"streamlined,"[18] and invariably active. They "deliver" their genes to the egg, "activate the developmental program of the egg,"[19] and have a "velocity" that is often remarked upon.[20] Their tails are "strong" and efficiently powered.[21] Together with the forces of ejaculation, they can "propel the semen into the deepest recesses of the vagina."[22] For this they need "energy," "fuel,"[23] so that with a "whiplashlike motion and strong lurches"[24] they can "burrow through the egg coat"[25] and "penetrate" it.[26]

At its extreme, the age-old relationship of the egg and the sperm takes on a royal or religious patina. The egg coat, its protective barrier, is sometimes called its "vestments," a term usually reserved for sacred, religious dress. The egg is said to have a "corona,"[27] a crown, and to be accompanied by "attendant cells."[28] It is holy, set apart and above, the queen to the sperm's king. The egg is also passive, which means it must depend on sperm for rescue. Gerald Schatten and Helen Schatten liken the egg's role to that of Sleeping Beauty: "a dormant bride awaiting her mate's magic kiss, which instills the spirit that brings her to life."[29] Sperm, by contrast, have a "mission,"[30] which is to "move through the female genital tract in quest of the ovum."[31] One popular account has it that the sperm carry out a "perilous journey" into the "warm darkness," where some fall away "exhausted." "Survivors" "assault" the egg, the successful candidates "surrounding the prize."[32] Part of the urgency of this journey, in more scientific terms, is that "once released from the supportive environment of the ovary, an egg will die within hours unless rescued by a sperm."[33] The wording stresses the fragility and dependency of the egg, even though the same text acknowledges elsewhere that sperm also live for only a few hours.[34]

10

---

[18]Alberts et al., 796.

[19]Ibid., 796.

[20]See, e.g., William F. Ganong, *Review of Medical Physiology*, 7th ed. (Los Altos, Calif.: Lange Medical Publications, 1975), 322.

[21]Alberts et al. (n. 11), 796.

[22]Guyton, 615.

[23]Solomon (n. 6), 683.

[24]Vander, Sherman, and Luciano (n. 4), 4th ed. (1985), 580.

[25]Alberts et al., 796.

[26]All biology texts quoted use the word "penetrate."

[27]Solomon, 700.

[28]A. Beldecos et al., "The Importance of Feminist Critique for Contemporary Cell Biology," *Hypatia* 3, no. 1 (Spring 1988): 61–76.

[29]Gerald Schatten and Helen Schatten, "The Energetic Egg," *Medical World News* 23 (January 23, 1984): 51–53, esp. 51.

[30]Alberts et al., 796.

[31]Guyton (n. 3), 613.

[32]Miller and Pelham (n. 17), 7.

[33]Alberts et al. (n. 11), 804.

[34]Ibid., 801.

In 1948, in a book remarkable for its early insights into these matters, Ruth Herschberger argued that female reproductive organs are seen as biologically interdependent, while male organs are viewed as autonomous, operating independently and in isolation:

> At present the functional is stressed only in connection with women: it is in them that ovaries, tubes, uterus, and vagina have endless interdependence. In the male, reproduction would seem to involve "organs" only.
>
> Yet the sperm, just as much as the egg, is dependent on a great many related processes. There are secretions which mitigate the urine in the urethra before ejaculation, to protect the sperm. There is the reflex shutting off of the bladder connection, the provision of prostatic secretions, and various types of muscular propulsion. The sperm is no more independent of its milieu than the egg, and yet from a wish that it were, biologists have lent their support to the notion that the human female, beginning with the egg, is congenitally more dependent than the male.[35]

Bringing out another aspect of the sperm's autonomy, an article in the journal *Cell* has the sperm making an "existential decision" to penetrate the egg: "Sperm are cells with a limited behavioral repertoire, one that is directed toward fertilizing eggs. To execute the decision to abandon the haploid state, sperm swim to an egg and there acquire the ability to effect membrane fusion."[36] Is this a corporate manager's version of the sperm's activities — "executing decisions" while fraught with dismay over difficult options that bring with them very high risk?

There is another way that sperm, despite their small size, can be made to loom in importance over the egg. In a collection of scientific papers, an electron micrograph of an enormous egg and tiny sperm is titled "A Portrait of the Sperm."[37] This is a little like showing a photo of a dog and calling it a picture of the fleas. Granted, microscopic sperm are harder to photograph than eggs, which are just large enough to see with the naked eye. But surely the use of the term "portrait," a word associated with the powerful and wealthy, is significant. Eggs have only micrographs or pictures, not portraits.

One depiction of sperm as weak and timid, instead of strong and powerful — the only such representation in Western civilization, so far as I know — occurs in Woody Allen's movie *Everything You Always Wanted to*

---

[35]Ruth Herschberger, *Adam's Rib* (New York: Pelligrini & Cudaby, 1948), esp. 84. I am indebted to Ruth Hubbard for telling me about Herschberger's work, although at a point when this paper was already in draft form.

[36]Bennett M. Shapiro, "The Existential Decision of a Sperm," *Cell* 49, no. 3 (May 1987): 293–94, esp. 293.

[37]Lennart Nilsson, "A Portrait of the Sperm," in *The Functional Anatomy of the Spermatozoan*, ed. Bjorn A. Afzelius (New York: Pergamon, 1975), 79–82.

Know about Sex But Were Afraid to Ask. Allen, playing the part of an apprehensive sperm inside a man's testicles, is scared of the man's approaching orgasm. He is reluctant to launch himself into the darkness, afraid of contraceptive devices, afraid of winding up on the ceiling if the man masturbates.

The more common picture — egg as damsel in distress, shielded only by   15
her sacred garments; sperm as heroic warrior to the rescue — cannot be proved to be dictated by the biology of these events. While the "facts" of biology may not *always* be constructed in cultural terms, I would argue that in this case they are. The degree of metaphorical content in these descriptions, the extent to which differences between egg and sperm are emphasized, and the parallels between cultural stereotypes of male and female behavior and the character of egg and sperm all point to this conclusion.

New Research, Old Imagery

As new understandings of egg and sperm emerge, textbook gender imagery is being revised. But the new research, far from escaping the stereotypical representations of egg and sperm, simply replicates elements of textbook gender imagery in a different form. The persistence of this imagery calls to mind what Ludwik Fleck termed "the self-contained" nature of scientific thought. As he described it, "the interaction between what is already known, what remains to be learned, and those who are to apprehend it, go to ensure harmony within the system. But at the same time they also preserve the harmony of illusions, which is quite secure within the confines of a given thought style."[38] We need to understand the way in which the cultural content in scientific descriptions changes as biological discoveries unfold, and whether that cultural content is solidly entrenched or easily changed.

In all of the texts quoted above, sperm are described as penetrating the egg, and specific substances on a sperm's head are described as binding to the egg. Recently, this description of events was rewritten in a biophysics lab at Johns Hopkins University — transforming the egg from the passive to the active party.[39]

Prior to this research, it was thought that the zona, the inner vestments of the egg, formed an impenetrable barrier. Sperm overcame the barrier by mechanically burrowing through, thrashing their tails and slowly working their way along. Later research showed that the sperm released digestive enzymes that chemically broke down the zona; thus, scientists presumed that the sperm used mechanical *and* chemical means to get through to the egg.

In this recent investigation, the researchers began to ask questions

---

[38]Ludwik Fleck, *Genesis and Development of a Scientific Fact*, ed. Thaddeus J. Trenn and Robert K. Merton (Chicago: University of Chicago Press, 1979), 38.

[39]Jay M. Baltz carried out the research I describe when he was a graduate student in the Thomas C. Jenkins Department of Biophysics at Johns Hopkins University.

about the mechanical force of the sperm's tail. (The lab's goal was to develop a contraceptive that worked topically on sperm.) They discovered, to their great surprise, that the forward thrust of sperm is extremely weak, which contradicts the assumption that sperm are forceful penetrators.[40] Rather than thrusting forward, the sperm's head was now seen to move mostly back and forth. The sideways motion of the sperm's tail makes the head move sideways with a force that is ten times stronger than its forward movement. So even if the overall force of the sperm were strong enough to mechanically break the zona, most of its force would be directed sideways rather than forward. In fact, its strongest tendency, by tenfold, is to escape by attempting to pry itself off the egg. Sperm, then, must be exceptionally efficient at *escaping* from any cell surface they contact. And the surface of the egg must be designed to trap the sperm and prevent their escape. Otherwise, few if any sperm would reach the egg.

The researchers at Johns Hopkins concluded that the sperm and egg   20
stick together because of adhesive molecules on the surfaces of each. The egg traps the sperm and adheres to it so tightly that the sperm's head is forced to lie flat against the surface of the zona, a little bit, they told me, "like Br'er Rabbit getting more and more stuck to tar baby the more he wriggles." The trapped sperm continues to wiggle ineffectually side to side. The mechanical force of its tail is so weak that a sperm cannot break even one chemical bond. This is where the digestive enzymes released by the sperm come in. If they start to soften the zona just at the tip of the sperm and the sides remain stuck, then the weak, flailing sperm can get oriented in the right direction and make it through the zona — provided that its bonds to the zona dissolve as it moves in.

Although this new version of the saga of the egg and the sperm broke through cultural expectations, the researchers who made the discovery continued to write papers and abstracts as if the sperm were the active party who attacks, binds, penetrates, and enters the egg. The only difference was that sperm were now seen as performing these actions weakly.[41] Not until August 1987, more than three years after the findings described above, did these researchers reconceptualize the process to give the egg a more active role. They began to describe the zona as an aggressive sperm catcher, cov-

---

[40]Far less is known about the physiology of sperm than comparable female substances, which some feminists claim is no accident. Greater scientific scrutiny of female reproduction has long enabled the burden of birth control to be placed on women. In this case, the researchers' discovery did not depend on development of any new technology. The experiments made use of glass pipettes, a manometer, and a simple microscope, all of which have been available for more than one hundred years.

[41]Jay Baltz and Richard A. Cone, "What Force Is Needed to Tether a Sperm?" (abstract for Society for the Study of Reproduction, 1985), and "Flagellar Torque on the Head Determines the Force Needed to Tether a Sperm" (abstract for Biophysical Society, 1986).

ered with adhesive molecules that can capture a sperm with a single bond and clasp it to the zona's surface.[42] In the words of their published account: "The innermost vestment, the *zona pellucida*, is a glyco-protein shell, which captures and tethers the sperm before they penetrate it. . . . The sperm is captured at the initial contact between the sperm tip and the *zona*. . . . Since the thrust [of the sperm] is much smaller than the force needed to break a single affinity bond, the first bond made upon the tip-first meeting of the sperm and *zona* can result in the capture of the sperm."[43]

Experiments in another lab reveal similar patterns of data interpretation. Gerald Schatten and Helen Schatten set out to show that, contrary to conventional wisdom, the "egg is not merely a large, yolk-filled sphere into which the sperm burrows to endow new life. Rather, recent research suggests the almost heretical view that sperm and egg are mutually active partners."[44] This sounds like a departure from the stereotypical textbook view, but further reading reveals Schatten and Schatten's conformity to the aggressive-sperm metaphor. They describe how "the sperm and egg first touch when, from the tip of the sperm's triangular head, a long, thin filament shoots out and harpoons the egg." Then we learn that "remarkably, the harpoon is not so much fired as assembled at great speed, molecule by molecule, from a pool of protein stored in a specialized region called the acrosome. The filament may grow as much as twenty times longer than the sperm head itself before its tip reaches the egg and sticks."[45] Why not call this "making a bridge" or "throwing out a line" rather than firing a harpoon? Harpoons pierce prey and injure or kill them, while this filament only sticks. And why not focus, as the Hopkins lab did, on the stickiness of the egg, rather than the stickiness of the sperm?[46] Later in the article, the Schattens replicate the common view of the sperm's perilous journey into the warm darkness of the vagina, this time for the purpose of explaining its journey into the egg itself: "[The sperm]

---

[42]Jay M. Baltz, David F. Katz, and Richard A. Cone, "The Mechanics of the Sperm-Egg Interaction at the Zona Pellucida," *Biophysical Journal* 54, no. 4 (October 1988): 643–54. Lab members were somewhat familiar with work on metaphors in the biology of female reproduction. Richard Cone, who runs the lab, is my husband, and he talked with them about my earlier research on the subject from time to time. Even though my current research focuses on biological imagery and I heard about the lab's work from my husband every day, I myself did not recognize the rôle of imagery in the sperm research until many weeks after the period of research and writing I describe. Therefore, I assume that any awareness the lab members may have had about how underlying metaphor might be guiding this particular research was fairly inchoate.

[43]Ibid., 643, 650.

[44]Schatten and Schatten (n. 29), 51.

[45]Ibid., 52.

[46]Surprisingly, in an article intended for a general audience, the authors do not point out that these are sea urchin sperm and note that human sperm do not shoot out filaments at all.

still has an arduous journey ahead. It must penetrate farther into the egg's huge sphere of cytoplasm and somehow locate the nucleus, so that the two cells' chromosomes can fuse. The sperm dives down into the cytoplasm, its tail beating. But it is soon interrupted by the sudden and swift migration of the egg nucleus, which rushes toward the sperm with a velocity triple that of the movement of chromosomes during cell division, crossing the entire egg in about a minute."[47]

Like Schatten and Schatten and the biophysicists at Johns Hopkins, another researcher has recently made discoveries that seem to point to a more interactive view of the relationship of egg and sperm. This work, which Paul Wassarman conducted on the sperm and eggs of mice, focuses on identifying the specific molecules in the egg coat (the zona pellucida) that are involved in egg-sperm interaction. At first glance, his descriptions seem to fit the model of an egalitarian relationship. Male and female gametes "recognize one another," and "interactions . . . take place between sperm and egg."[48] But the article in *Scientific American* in which those descriptions appear begins with a vignette that presages the dominant motif of their presentation: "It has been more than a century since Hermann Fol, a Swiss zoologist, peered into his microscope and became the first person to see a sperm penetrate an egg, fertilize it and form the first cell of a new embryo."[49] This portrayal of the sperm as the active party — the one that *penetrates* and *fertilizes* the egg and *produces* the embryo — is not cited as an example of an earlier, now outmoded view. In fact, the author reiterates the point later in the article: "Many sperm can bind to and penetrate the zona pellucida, or outer coat, of an unfertilized mouse egg, but only one sperm will eventually fuse with the thin plasma membrane surrounding the egg proper (*inner sphere*), fertilizing the egg and giving rise to a new embryo."[50]

The imagery of sperm as aggressor is particularly startling in this case: the main discovery being reported is isolation of a particular molecule *on the egg coat* that plays an important role in fertilization! Wassarman's choice of language sustains the picture. He calls the molecule that has been isolated, ZP3, a "sperm receptor." By allocating the passive, waiting role to the egg, Wassarman can continue to describe the sperm as the actor, the one that makes it all happen: "The basic process begins when many sperm first attach loosely and then bind tenaciously to receptors on the surface of the egg's thick outer coat, the zona pellucida. Each sperm, which has a large number of egg-binding proteins on its surface, binds to many sperm receptors on the egg. More specifically, a site on each of the egg-binding proteins fits a complementary site on a sperm receptor, much as a key fits a lock."[51]

[47]Schatten and Schatten, 53.

[48]Paul M. Wassarman, "Fertilization in Mammals," *Scientific American* 259, no. 6 (December 1988): 78–84, esp. 78, 84.

[49]Ibid., 78.

[50]Ibid., 79.

[51]Ibid., 78.

With the sperm designated as the "key" and the egg the "lock," it is obvious which one acts and which one is acted upon. Could this imagery not be reversed, letting the sperm (the lock) wait until the egg produces the key? Or could we speak of two halves of a locket matching, and regard the matching itself as the action that initiates the fertilization?

It is as if Wassarman were determined to make the egg the receiving   25
partner. Usually in biological research, the *protein* member of the pair of binding molecules is called the receptor, and physically it has a pocket in it rather like a lock. As the diagrams that illustrate Wassarman's article show, the molecules on the sperm are proteins and have "pockets." The small, mobile molecules that fit into these pockets are called ligands. As shown in the diagrams, ZP3 on the egg is a polymer of "keys"; many small knobs stick out. Typically, molecules on the sperm would be called receptors and molecules on the egg would be called ligands. But Wassarman chose to name ZP3 on the egg the receptor and to create a new term, "the egg-binding protein," for the molecule on the sperm that otherwise would have been called the receptor.[52]

Wassarman does credit the egg coat with having more functions than those of a sperm receptor. While he notes that "the zona pellucida has at times been viewed by investigators as a nuisance, a barrier to sperm and hence an impediment to fertilization," his new research reveals that the egg coat "serves as a sophisticated biological security system that screens incoming sperm, selects only those compatible with fertilization and development, prepares sperm for fusion with the egg and later protects the resulting embryo from polyspermy [a lethal condition caused by fusion of more than one sperm with a single egg]."[53] Although this description gives the egg an active role, that role is drawn in stereotypically feminine terms. The egg *selects* an appropriate mate, *prepares* him for fusion, and then *protects* the resulting offspring from harm. This is courtship and mating behavior as seen through the eyes of a sociobiologist: woman as the hard-to-get prize, who, following union with the chosen one, becomes woman as servant and mother.

And Wassarman does not quit there. In a review article for *Science*, he outlines the "chronology of fertilization."[54] Near the end of the article are two subject headings. One is "Sperm Penetration," in which Wassarman describes how the chemical dissolving of the zona pellucida combines with the "substantial propulsive force generated by sperm." The next heading is "Sperm-Egg Fusion." This section details what happens inside the zona

---

[52]Since receptor molecules are relatively immotile and the ligands that bind to them relatively motile, one might imagine the egg being called the receptor and the sperm the ligand. But the molecules in question on egg and sperm are immotile molecules. It is the sperm as a cell that has motility, and the egg as a cell that has relative immotility.

[53]Wassarman, 78–79.

[54]Paul M. Wassarman, "The Biology and Chemistry of Fertilization," *Science* 235, no. 4788 (January 30, 1987): 553–60, esp. 554.

after a sperm "penetrates" it. Sperm "can make contact with, adhere to, and fuse with (that is, fertilize) an egg."[55] Wassarman's word choice, again, is astonishingly skewed in favor of the sperm's activity, for in the next breath he says that sperm *lose* all motility upon fusion with the egg's surface. In mouse and sea urchin eggs, the sperm enters at the *egg's* volition, according to Wassarman's description: "Once fused with egg plasma membrane [the surface of the egg], how does a sperm enter the egg? The surface of both mouse and sea urchin eggs is covered with thousands of plasma membrane-bound projections, called microvilli [tiny "hairs"]. Evidence in sea urchins suggests that, after membrane fusion, a group of elongated microvilli cluster tightly around and interdigitate over the sperm head. As these microvilli are resorbed, the sperm is drawn into the egg. Therefore, sperm motility, which ceases at the time of fusion in both sea urchins and mice, is not required for sperm entry."[56] The section called "Sperm Penetration" more logically would be followed by a section called "The Egg Envelops," rather than "Sperm-Egg Fusion." This would give a parallel — and more accurate — sense that both the egg and the sperm initiate action.

Another way that Wassarman makes less of the egg's activity is by describing components of the egg but referring to the sperm as a whole entity. Deborah Gordon has described such an approach as "atomism" ("the part is independent of and primordial to the whole") and identified it as one of the "tenacious assumptions" of Western science and medicine.[57] Wassarman employs atomism to his advantage. When he refers to processing going on within sperm, he consistently returns to descriptions that remind us from whence these activities came: they are part of sperm that penetrate an egg or generate propulsive force. When he refers to processes going on within eggs, he stops there. As a result, any active role he grants them appears to be assigned to the parts of the egg, and not to the egg itself. In the quote above, it is the microvilli that actively cluster around the sperm. In another example, "the driving force for engulfment of a fused sperm comes from a region of cytoplasm just beneath an egg's plasma membrane."[58]

Social Implications: Thinking Beyond

All three of these revisionist accounts of egg and sperm cannot seem to escape the hierarchical imagery of older accounts. Even though each new account gives the egg a larger and more active role, taken together they bring into play another cultural stereotype: woman as a dangerous and ag-

---

[55]Ibid., 557.

[56]Ibid., 557–58. This finding throws into question Schatten and Schatten's description (n. 29 above) of the sperm, its tail beating, diving down into the egg.

[57]Deborah R. Gordon, "Tenacious Assumptions in Western Medicine," in *Biomedicine Examined*, ed. Margaret Lock and Deborah Gordon (Dordrecht, The Netherlands: Kluwer, 1988), 19–56, esp. 26.

[58]Wassarman, "The Biology and Chemistry of Fertilization," 558.

gressive threat. In the Johns Hopkins lab's revised model, the egg ends up as the female aggressor who "captures and tethers" the sperm with her sticky zona, rather like a spider lying in wait in her web.[59] The Schatten lab has the egg's nucleus "interrupt" the sperm's dive with a "sudden and swift" rush by which she "clasps the sperm and guides its nucleus to the center."[60] Wassarman's description of the surface of the egg "covered with thousands of plasma membrane-bound projections, called microvilli" that reach out and clasp the sperm adds to the spiderlike imagery.[61]

These images grant the egg an active role but at the cost of appearing   30
disturbingly aggressive. Images of woman as dangerous and aggressive, the femme fatale who victimizes men, are widespread in Western literature and culture.[62] More specific is the connection of spider imagery with the idea of an engulfing, devouring mother.[63] New data did not lead scientists to eliminate gender stereotypes in their descriptions of egg and sperm. Instead, scientists simply began to describe egg and sperm in different, but no less damaging, terms.

Can we envision a less stereotypical view? Biology itself provides another model that could be applied to the egg and the sperm. The cybernetic model — with its feedback loops, flexible adaptation to change, coordination of the parts within a whole, evolution over time, and changing response to the environment — is common in genetics, endocrinology, and ecology and has a growing influence in medicine in general.[64] This model has the potential to shift our imagery from the negative, in which the female reproductive system is castigated both for not producing eggs after birth and for producing (and thus wasting) too many eggs overall, to something more positive. The female reproductive system could be seen as responding to the environment (pregnancy or menopause), adjusting to monthly changes (menstruation), and flexibly changing from reproductivity after puberty to nonreproductivity later in life. The sperm and egg's interaction could also be described in cybernetic terms. J. F. Hartman's research in reproductive biology demonstrated fifteen years ago that if an egg is killed by being pricked with a needle, live sperm cannot get through the zona.[65]

---

[59]Baltz, Katz, and Cone (n. 42 above), 643, 650.

[60]Schatten and Schatten, 53.

[61]Wassarman, "The Biology and Chemistry of Fertilization," 557.

[62]Mary Ellman, *Thinking about Women* (New York: Harcourt Brace Jovanovich, 1968), 140; Nina Auerbach, *Woman and the Demon* (Cambridge, Mass.: Harvard University Press, 1982), esp. 186.

[63]Kenneth Alan Adams, "Arachnophobia: Love American Style," *Journal of Psychoanalytic Anthropology* 4, no. 2 (1981): 157–97.

[64]William Ray Arney and Bernard Bergen, *Medicine and the Management of Living* (Chicago: University of Chicago Press, 1984).

[65]J. F. Hartman, R. B. Gwatkin, and C. F. Hutchison, "Early Contact Interactions between Mammalian Gametes *In Vitro*," *Proceedings of the National Academy of Sciences (U.S.)* 69, no. 10 (1972): 2767–69.

Clearly, this evidence shows that the egg and sperm *do* interact on more mutual terms, making biology's refusal to portray them that way all the more disturbing.

We would do well to be aware, however, that cybernetic imagery is hardly neutral. In the past, cybernetic models have played an important part in the imposition of social control. These models inherently provide a way of thinking about a "field" of interacting components. Once the field can be seen, it can become the object of new forms of knowledge, which in turn can allow new forms of social control to be exerted over the components of the field. During the 1950s, for example, medicine began to recognize the psychosocial *environment* of the patient: the patient's family and its psychodynamics. Professions such as social work began to focus on this new environment, and the resulting knowledge became one way to further control the patient. Patients began to be seen not as isolated, individual bodies, but as psychosocial entities located in an "ecological" system: management of "the patient's psychology was a new entrée to patient control."[66]

The models that biologists use to describe their data can have important social effects. During the nineteenth century, the social and natural sciences strongly influenced each other: the social ideas of Malthus about how to avoid the natural increase of the poor inspired Darwin's *Origin of Species*.[67] Once the *Origin* stood as a description of the natural world, complete with competition and market struggles, it could be reimported into social science as social Darwinism, in order to justify the social order of the time. What we are seeing now is similar: the importation of cultural ideas about passive females and heroic males into the "personalities" of gametes. This amounts to the "implanting of social imagery on representations of nature so as to lay a firm basis for reimporting exactly that same imagery as natural explanations of social phenomena."[68]

Further research would show us exactly what social effects are being wrought from the biological imagery of egg and sperm. At the very least, the imagery keeps alive some of the hoariest old stereotypes about weak damsels in distress and their strong male rescuers. That these stereotypes are now being written in at the level of the *cell* constitutes a powerful move to make them seem so natural as to be beyond alteration.

The stereotypical imagery might also encourage people to imagine that   35
what results from the interaction of egg and sperm — a fertilized egg — is the result of deliberate "human" action at the cellular level. Whatever the intentions of the human couple, in this microscope "culture" a cellular "bride" (or femme fatale) and a cellular "groom" (her victim) make a cellular baby. Rosalind Petchesky points out that through visual representations such as sonograms, we are given "*images* of younger and younger, and tinier and tinier, fetuses being 'saved.'" This leads to "the point of viability

---

[66]Arney and Bergen, 68.
[67]Ruth Hubbard, "Have Only Men Evolved?" (n. 12 above), 51–52.
[68]David Harvey, personal communication, November 1989.

being 'pushed back' *indefinitely.*"[69] Endowing egg and sperm with intentional action, a key aspect of personhood in our culture, lays the foundation for the point of viability being pushed back to the moment of fertilization. This will likely lead to greater acceptance of technological developments and new forms of scrutiny and manipulation, for the benefit of these inner "persons": court-ordered restrictions on a pregnant woman's activities in order to protect her fetus, fetal surgery, amniocentesis, and rescinding of abortion rights, to name but a few examples.[70]

Even if we succeed in substituting more egalitarian, interactive metaphors to describe the activities of egg and sperm, and manage to avoid the pitfalls of cybernetic models, we would still be guilty of endowing cellular entities with personhood. More crucial, then, than what *kinds* of personalities we bestow on cells is the very fact that we are doing it at all. This process could ultimately have the most disturbing social consequences.

One clear feminist challenge is to wake up sleeping metaphors in science, particularly those involved in descriptions of the egg and the sperm. Although the literary convention is to call such metaphors "dead," they are not so much dead as sleeping, hidden within the scientific content of texts — and all the more powerful for it.[71] Waking up such metaphors, by becoming aware of when we are projecting cultural imagery onto what we study, will improve our ability to investigate and understand nature. Waking up such metaphors, by becoming aware of their implications, will rob them of their power to naturalize our social conventions about gender.

QUESTIONS

1. Summarize Martin's argument. How has she structured it?
2. The first subheading in the essay is "Egg and Sperm: A Scientific Fairy Tale." The implications are that the actions of the egg and sperm constitute a story written by scientists. Why does Martin call it a fairy tale? What fairy tales does it resemble? In the process of your sexual education, what stories were you told?

---

[69]Rosalind Petchesky, "Fetal Images: The Power of Visual Culture in the Politics of Reproduction," *Feminist Studies* 13, no. 2 (Summer 1987): 263–92, esp. 272.

[70]Rita Arditti, Renate Klein, and Shelley Minden, *Test-Tube Women* (London: Pandora, 1984); Ellen Goodman, "Whose Right to Life?" *Baltimore Sun* (November 17, 1987); Tamar Lewin, "Courts Acting to Force Care of the Unborn," *New York Times* (November 23, 1987), A1 and B10; Susan Irwin and Brigitte Jordan, "Knowledge, Practice, and Power: Court Ordered Cesarean Sections," *Medical Anthropology Quarterly* 1, no. 3 (September 1987): 319–34.

[71]Thanks to Elizabeth Fee and David Spain, who in February 1989 and April 1989, respectively, made points related to this.

3. Martin's argument raises the issue of scientific objectivity. Do you think there can be such a thing as a "pure" fact? Or can we only say that one fact is less encumbered by cultural baggage than another fact? What does Martin suggest as the best approach in presenting reproductive facts?

4. Look at some biology textbooks. How is reproduction presented? Are the same or similar "sleeping metaphors" that Martin discusses present in the discussion? What about other bodily processes and functions? Is the male body used as the sole example in discussions of the heart, blood pressure, digestion, or AIDS, for instance?

5. Using the biological information in Martin's essay, write a nonsexist description of the reproductive functions. In your conclusion, reflect on any difficulties you encountered in keeping your cellular entities free of personhood. Switch papers with a classmate to check each other for "sleeping metaphors."

6. Look at a sampling of sex education texts and materials designed for elementary or secondary school students to see if the cultural stereotypes that Martin warns against are present. What analogies and metaphors do you find being used? Write up your discussion as an argument either for or against the revision of those texts.

MAKING CONNECTIONS

Martin warns us to be on the alert for "sleeping metaphors." Consider the way that metaphors are used in some of the essays in the "Arguing" sections. If we assume that sleeping metaphors are used without the full awareness of the writer, then they may be a good place to begin a counterargument. Can you find essays that work by waking the sleeping metaphors of others? Can you find sleeping metaphors in one of these essays and use them for an argument of your own? Write an essay in which you do one or both of these things.

WOMEN'S BRAINS

Stephen Jay Gould

*Stephen Jay Gould (1941–2002) was a professor of biology, geol-
ogy, and the history of science at Harvard University for more than
thirty years. He was also a baseball fan and a prolific essayist. In
1974, he began writing "This View of Life," a monthly column for*
Natural History, *where he not only explained and defended Darwinian ideas of evolution but also exposed abuses and misunder-
standings of scientific concepts and methods. Some of the most
recent of his more than twenty books are* Crossing Over: Where
Art and Science Meet *(2000),* The Structure of Evolutionary Theory
(2002), Triumph and Tragedy in Mudville: A Lifelong Passion for
Baseball *(2003), and* The Hedgehog, the Fox, and the Magister's
Pox *(2003). The following essay appeared in* Natural History
in 1992.

In the prelude to *Middlemarch*, George Eliot[1] lamented the unfulfilled
lives of talented women:

> Some have felt that these blundering lives are due to the inconve-
> nient indefiniteness with which the Supreme Power has fashioned
> the natures of women: if there were one level of feminine incompe-
> tence as strict as the ability to count three and no more, the social
> lot of women might be treated with scientific certitude.

Eliot goes on to discount the idea of innate limitation, but while she
wrote in 1872, the leaders of European anthropometry were trying to measure "with scientific certitude" the inferiority of women. Anthropometry,
or measurement of the human body, is not so fashionable a field these days,
but it dominated the human sciences for much of the nineteenth century
and remained popular until intelligence testing replaced skull measurement
as a favored device for making invidious comparisons among races, classes,
and sexes. Craniometry, or measurement of the skull, commanded the most
attention and respect. Its unquestioned leader, Paul Broca (1824–80), professor of clinical surgery at the Faculty of Medicine in Paris, gathered a
school of disciples and imitators around himself. Their work, so meticulous

---

[1]*George Eliot*: The pen name of Marianne Evans (1819–1880), British novelist.
Middlemarch (1871–1872) is considered her greatest work. [Eds.]

and apparently irrefutable, exerted great influence and won high esteem as a jewel of nineteenth-century science.

Broca's work seemed particularly invulnerable to refutation. Had he not measured with the most scrupulous care and accuracy? (Indeed, he had. I have the greatest respect for Broca's meticulous procedure. His numbers are sound. But science is an inferential exercise, not a catalog of facts. Numbers, by themselves, specify nothing. All depends upon what you do with them.) Broca depicted himself as an apostle of objectivity, a man who bowed before facts and cast aside superstition and sentimentality. He declared that "there is no faith, however respectable, no interest, however legitimate, which must not accommodate itself to the progress of human knowledge and bend before truth." Women, like it or not, had smaller brains than men and, therefore, could not equal them in intelligence. This fact, Broca argued, may reinforce a common prejudice in male society, but it is also a scientific truth. L. Manouvrier, a black sheep in Broca's fold, rejected the inferiority of women and wrote with feeling about the burden imposed upon them by Broca's numbers:

> Women displayed their talents and their diplomas. They also invoked philosophical authorities. But they were opposed by *numbers* unknown to Condorcet[2] or to John Stuart Mill.[3] These numbers fell upon poor women like a sledge hammer, and they were accompanied by commentaries and sarcasms more ferocious than the most misogynist imprecations of certain church fathers. The theologians had asked if women had a soul. Several centuries later, some scientists were ready to refuse them a human intelligence.

Broca's argument rested upon two sets of data: the larger brains of men in modern societies, and a supposed increase in male superiority through time. His most extensive data came from autopsies performed personally in four Parisian hospitals. For 292 male brains, he calculated an average weight of 1,325 grams; 140 female brains averaged 1,144 grams for a difference of 181 grams, or 14 percent of the male weight. Broca understood, of course, that part of this difference could be attributed to the greater height of males. Yet he made no attempt to measure the effect of size alone and actually stated that it cannot account for the entire difference because we know, a priori, that women are not as intelligent as men (a premise that the data were supposed to test, not rest upon):

---

[2]*Marquis de Condorcet* (1743–1794): A French mathematician and revolutionary. [Eds.]

[3]*John Stuart Mill* (1806–1873): A British economist and philosopher. [Eds.]

We might ask if the small size of the female brain depends exclusively upon the small size of her body. Tiedemann has proposed this explanation. But we must not forget that women are, on the average, a little less intelligent than men, a difference which we should not exaggerate but which is, nonetheless, real. We are therefore permitted to suppose that the relatively small size of the female brain depends in part upon her physical inferiority and in part upon her intellectual inferiority.

In 1873, the year after Eliot published *Middlemarch*, Broca measured the cranial capacities of prehistoric skulls from L'Homme Mort cave. Here he found a difference of only 99.5 cubic centimeters between males and females, while modern populations range from 129.5 to 220.7. Topinard, Broca's chief disciple, explained the increasing discrepancy through time as a result of differing evolutionary pressures upon dominant men and passive women:

> The man who fights for two or more in the struggle for existence, who has all the responsibility and the cares of tomorrow, who is constantly active in combating the environment and human rivals, needs more brain than the woman whom he must protect and nourish, the sedentary woman, lacking any interior occupations, whose role is to raise children, love, and be passive.

In 1879, Gustave Le Bon, chief misogynist of Broca's school, used these data to publish what must be the most vicious attack upon women in modern scientific literature (no one can top Aristotle). I do not claim his views were representative of Broca's school, but they were published in France's most respected anthropological journal. Le Bon concluded:

> In the most intelligent races, as among the Parisians, there are a large number of women whose brains are closer in size to those of gorillas than to the most developed male brains. This inferiority is so obvious that no one can contest it for a moment; only its degree is worth discussion. All psychologists who have studied the intelligence of women, as well as poets and novelists, recognize today that they represent the most inferior forms of human evolution and that they are closer to children and savages than to an adult, civilized man. They excel in fickleness, inconstancy, absence of thought and logic, and incapacity to reason. Without doubt there exist some distinguished women, very superior to the average man, but they are as exceptional as the birth of any monstrosity, as, for example, of a gorilla with two heads; consequently, we may neglect them entirely.

Nor did Le Bon shrink from the social implications of his views. He was horrified by the proposal of some American reformers to grant women higher education on the same basis as men:

A desire to give them the same education, and, as a consequence, to propose the same goals for them, is a dangerous chimera. . . . The day when, misunderstanding the inferior occupations which nature has given her, women leave the home and take part in our battles; on this day a social revolution will begin, and everything that maintains the sacred ties of the family will disappear.

Sound familiar?[4]

I have reexamined Broca's data, the basis for all this derivative pronouncement, and I find his numbers sound but his interpretation ill-founded, to say the least. The data supporting his claim for increased difference through time can be easily dismissed. Broca based his contention on the samples from L'Homme Mort alone — only seven male and six female skulls in all. Never have so little data yielded such far ranging conclusions.

In 1988, Topinard published Broca's more extensive data on the Parisian hospitals. Since Broca recorded height and age as well as brain size, we may use modern statistics to remove their effect. Brain weight decreases with age, and Broca's women were, on average, considerably older than his men. Brain weight increases with height, and his average man was almost half a foot taller than his average woman. I used multiple regression, a technique that allowed me to assess simultaneously the influence of height and age upon brain size. In an analysis of the data for women, I found that, at average male height and age, a woman's brain would weigh 1,212 grams. Correction for height and age reduces Broca's measured difference of 181 grams by more than a third, to 113 grams.

I don't know what to make of this remaining difference because I cannot assess other factors known to influence brain size in a major way. Cause of death has an important effect: degenerative disease often entails a substantial diminution of brain size. (This effect is separate from the decrease attributed to age alone.) Eugene Schreider, also working with Broca's data, found that men killed in accidents had brains weighing, on average, 60 grams more than men dying of infectious diseases. The best modern data I can find (from American hospitals) records a full 100-gram difference between death by degenerative arteriosclerosis and by violence or accident. Since so many of Broca's subjects were elderly women, we may assume that lengthy degenerative disease was more common among them than among the men.

More importantly, modern students of brain size still have not agreed on a proper measure for eliminating the powerful effect of body size. Height is partly adequate, but men and women of the same height do not share the same body build. Weight is even worse than height, because most

10

---

[4]When I wrote this essay, I assumed that Le Bon was a marginal, if colorful, figure. I have since learned that he was a leading scientist, one of the founders of social psychology, and best known for a seminal study on crowd behavior, still cited today (*La psychologie des foules*, 1895), and for his work on unconscious motivation.

of its variation reflects nutrition rather than intrinsic size — fat versus skinny exerts little influence upon the brain. Manouvrier took up this subject in the 1880s and argued that muscular mass and force should be used. He tried to measure this elusive property in various ways and found a marked difference in favor of men, even in men and women of the same height. When he corrected for what he called "sexual mass," women actually came out slightly ahead in brain size.

Thus, the corrected 113-gram difference is surely too large; the true figure is probably close to zero and may as well favor women as men. And 113 grams, by the way, is exactly the average difference between a 5 foot 4 inch and a 6 foot 4 inch male in Broca's data. We would not (especially us short folks) want to ascribe greater intelligence to tall men. In short, who knows what to do with Broca's data? They certainly don't permit any confident claim that men have bigger brains than women.

To appreciate the social role of Broca and his school, we must recognize that his statements about the brains of women do not reflect an isolated prejudice toward a single disadvantaged group. They must be weighed in the context of a general theory that supported contemporary social distinctions as biologically ordained. Women, blacks, and poor people suffered the same disparagement, but women bore the brunt of Broca's argument because he had easier access to data on women's brains. Women were singularly denigrated but they also stood as surrogates for other disenfranchised groups. As one of Broca's disciples wrote in 1881: "Men of the black races have a brain scarcely heavier than that of white women." This juxtaposition extended into many other realms of anthropological argument, particularly to claims that, anatomically and emotionally, both women and blacks were like white children — and that white children, by the theory of recapitulation, represented an ancestral (primitive) adult stage of human evolution. I do not regard as empty rhetoric the claim that women's battles are for all of us.

Maria Montessori did not confine her activities to educational reform for young children. She lectured on anthropology for several years at the University of Rome, and wrote an influential book entitled *Pedagogical Anthropology* (English edition, 1913). Montessori was no egalitarian. She supported most of Broca's work and the theory of innate criminality proposed by her compatriot Cesare Lombroso. She measured the circumference of children's heads in her schools and inferred that the best prospects had bigger brains. But she had no use for Broca's conclusions about women. She discussed Manouvrier's work at length and made much of his tentative claim that women, after proper correction of the data, had slightly larger brains than men. Women, she concluded, were intellectually superior, but men had prevailed heretofore by dint of physical force. Since technology has abolished force as an instrument of power, the era of women may soon be upon us: "In such an epoch there will really be superior human beings, there will really be men strong in morality and in sentiment. Perhaps in this way the reign of women is approaching, when the enigma of her anthropological superiority will be deciphered. Woman was always the custodian of human sentiment, morality and honor."

This represents one possible antidote to "scientific" claims for the con- 15 stitutional inferiority of certain groups. One may affirm the validity of bio-logical distinctions but argue that the data have been misinterpreted by prejudiced men with a stake in the outcome, and that disadvantaged groups are truly superior. In recent years, Elaine Morgan has followed this strategy in her *Descent of Woman*, a speculative reconstruction of human prehis-tory from the woman's point of view—and as farcical as more famous tall tales by and for men.

I prefer another strategy. Montessori and Morgan followed Broca's philosophy to reach a more congenial conclusion. I would rather label the whole enterprise of setting a biological value upon groups for what it is: ir-relevant and highly injurious. George Eliot well appreciated the special tragedy that biological labeling imposed upon members of disadvantaged groups. She expressed it for people like herself—women of extraordinary talent. I would apply it more widely—not only to those whose dreams are flouted but also to those who never realize that they may dream—but I cannot match her prose. In conclusion, then, the rest of Eliot's prelude to *Middlemarch*:

> The limits of variation are really much wider than anyone would imagine from the sameness of women's coiffure and the favorite love stories in prose and verse. Here and there a cygnet is reared uneasily among the ducklings in the brown pond, and never finds the living stream in fellowship with its own oary-footed kind. Here and there is born a Saint Theresa, foundress of nothing, whose lov-ing heartbeats and sobs after an unattained goodness tremble off and are dispersed among hindrances instead of centering in some long-recognizable deed.

Questions

1. In paragraph 3, Gould claims, "Numbers, by themselves, specify noth-ing. All depends upon what you do with them." What exactly does Gould do with numbers?
2. How does Gould's use of numbers differ from what Broca and his fol-lowers did with numbers? Specifically, what distinguishes Gould's and Broca's methods of calculating and interpreting the facts about women's brains?
3. It might also be said, "Quotations, by themselves, specify nothing. All depends upon what you do with them." What does Gould do with quo-tations in this essay?
4. Why do you suppose Gould begins and ends his piece with passages by George Eliot?

5. Why does Gould quote so extensively from Broca and his followers, particularly from Le Bon? What purpose do all of these quotations serve in connection with the points that Gould is trying to make about women's brains and "biological labeling"?
6. Using Gould's essay as a model, write an essay on a subject with which you are familiar, showing how different ways of gathering, calculating, and interpreting numbers have produced significantly different understandings of the subject in question.

MAKING CONNECTIONS

Compare the stereotyping of women's reproductive functions, as presented by Emily Martin in "The Egg and the Sperm: How Science Has Constructed a Romance Based on Stereotypical Male-Female Roles" (p. 754), with the stereotyping that Gould presents in this essay. What similarities do you find?

A DESIGNER UNIVERSE?

Steven Weinberg

Steven Weinberg was born in 1933 in New York. He received his undergraduate degree from Cornell University, did graduate work in Copenhagen, and received his doctorate from Princeton University. He has taught at Columbia University, the University of California at Berkeley, MIT, Harvard University, and the University of Texas at Austin, where he currently holds the Josey Regental Chair in Science. Weinberg has won numerous awards, including the Nobel Prize in physics in 1979 and the National Medal of Science in 1991. He also received the Lewis Thomas Prize, awarded to the researcher who best embodies "the scientist as poet." Weinberg has contributed more than two hundred articles to periodicals and scientific journals, including Scientific American, Science, New York Times Book Review, *and* Daedalus, *and is the author, coauthor, and coeditor of more than a dozen books, including his best-selling study of the Big Bang,* The First Three Minutes: A Modern View of the Origin of the Universe *(1977; updated 1993), which has been translated into more than twenty languages; a much anticipated three-volume set of textbooks that present a modern approach to quantum field theory,* The Quantum Theory of Fields *(1995, 1996, 2003), and* Facing Up: Science and Its Cultural Adversaries *(2001). Weinberg asserts that the objective reality of science is unaffected by the cultural background of the scientist, and he is an outspoken critic of religion. The following piece appeared in the* New York Review of Books *and is based on a talk given in 1999 at the Conference on Cosmic Design of the American Association for the Advancement of Science.*

I have been asked to comment on whether the universe shows signs of having been designed. I don't see how it's possible to talk about this without having at least some vague idea of what a designer would be like. Any possible universe could be explained as the work of some sort of designer. Even a universe that is completely chaotic, without any laws or regularities at all, could be supposed to have been designed by an idiot.

The question that seems to me to be worth answering, and perhaps not impossible to answer, is whether the universe shows signs of having been designed by a deity more or less like those of traditional monotheistic religions — not necessarily a figure from the ceiling of the Sistine Chapel, but at least some sort of personality, some intelligence, who created the universe and has some special concern with life, in particular with human life. I expect that this is not the idea of a designer held by many here. You may tell me that you are thinking of something much more abstract, some cosmic spirit of order and harmony, as Einstein did. You are certainly free to think that way, but then I don't know why you use words like "designer" and "God," except perhaps as a form of protective coloration.

It used to be obvious that the world was designed by some sort of intelligence. What else could account for fire and rain and lightning and earthquakes? Above all, the wonderful abilities of living things seemed to point to a creator who had a special interest in life. Today we understand most of these things in terms of physical forces acting under impersonal laws. We don't yet know the most fundamental laws, and we can't work out all the consequences of the laws we do know. The human mind remains extraordinarily difficult to understand, but so is the weather. We can't predict whether it will rain one month from today, but we do know the rules that govern the rain, even though we can't always calculate their consequences. I see nothing about the human mind any more than about the weather that stands out as beyond the hope of understanding as a consequence of impersonal laws acting over billions of years.

There do not seem to be any exceptions to this natural order, any miracles. I have the impression that these days most theologians are embarrassed by talk of miracles, but the great monotheistic faiths are founded on miracle stories — the burning bush, the empty tomb, an angel dictating the Koran to Mohammed — and some of these faiths teach that miracles continue at the present day. The evidence for all these miracles seems to me to be considerably weaker than the evidence for cold fusion, and I don't believe in cold fusion. Above all, today we understand that even human beings are the result of natural selection acting over millions of years of breeding and eating.

I'd guess that if we were to see the hand of the designer anywhere, it   5 would be in the fundamental principles, the final laws of nature, the book of rules that govern all natural phenomena. We don't know the final laws yet, but as far as we have been able to see, they are utterly impersonal and quite without any special role for life. There is no life force. As Richard Feynman has said, when you look at the universe and understand its laws, "the theory that it is all arranged as a stage for God to watch man's struggle for good and evil seems inadequate."

True, when quantum mechanics was new, some physicists thought that it put humans back into the picture, because the principles of quantum mechanics tell us how to calculate the probabilities of various results that might be found by a human observer. But starting with the work of Hugh Everett forty years ago, the tendency of physicists who think deeply about these things has been to reformulate quantum mechanics in an entirely objective way, with observers treated just like everything else. I don't know if this program has been completely successful yet, but I think it will be.

I have to admit that even when physicists have gone as far as they can go, when we have a final theory, we will not have a completely satisfying picture of the world, because we will still be left with the question "Why?" Why this theory rather than some other theory? For example, why is the world described by quantum mechanics? Quantum mechanics is the one part of our present physics that is likely to survive intact in any future theory, but there is nothing logically inevitable about quantum mechanics; I can imagine a universe governed by Newtonian mechanics instead. So there seems to be an irreducible mystery that science will not eliminate.

But religious theories of design have the same problem. Either you mean something definite by a God, a designer, or you don't. If you don't, then what are we talking about? If you do mean something definite by "God" or "design"—if, for instance, you believe in a God who is jealous, or loving, or intelligent, or whimsical—then you still must confront the question "Why?" A religion may assert that the universe is governed by that sort of God rather than some other sort of God, and it may offer evidence for this belief, but it cannot explain why this should be so.

In this respect, it seems to me that physics is in a better position to give us a partly satisfying explanation of the world than religion can ever be, because although physicists won't be able to explain why the laws of nature are what they are and not something completely different, at least we may be able to explain why they are not *slightly* different. For instance, no one has been able to think of a logically consistent alternative to quantum mechanics that is only slightly different. Once you start trying to make small changes in quantum mechanics, you get into theories with negative probabilities or other logical absurdities. When you combine quantum mechanics with relativity, you increase its logical fragility. You find that unless you arrange the theory in just the right way, you get nonsense, like effects preceding causes or infinite probabilities. Religious theories, on the other hand, seem to be infinitely flexible, with nothing to prevent the invention of deities of any conceivable sort.

Now, it doesn't settle the matter for me to say that we cannot see the   10
hand of a designer in what we know about the fundamental principles of science. It might be that although these principles do not refer explicitly to life, much less human life, they are nevertheless craftily designed to bring it about.

Some physicists have argued that certain constants of nature have values that seem to have been mysteriously fine-tuned to just the values that allow for the possibility of life, in a way that could only be explained by the intervention of a designer with some special concern for life. I am not impressed with these supposed instances of fine-tuning. For instance, one of the most frequently quoted examples of fine-tuning has to do with a property of the nucleus of the carbon atom. The matter left over from the first few minutes of the universe was almost entirely hydrogen and helium, with virtually none of the heavier elements like carbon, nitrogen, and oxygen that seem to be necessary for life. The heavy elements that we find on earth were built up hundreds of millions of years later in a first generation of stars, and then spewed out into the interstellar gas out of which our solar system eventually formed.

The first step in the sequence of nuclear reactions that created the heavy elements in early stars is usually the formation of a carbon nucleus out of three helium nuclei. There is a negligible chance of producing a carbon nucleus in its normal state (the state of lowest energy) in collisions of three helium nuclei, but it would be possible to produce appreciable amounts of carbon in stars if the carbon nucleus could exist in a radioactive state with an energy roughly 7 million electron volts (MeV) above the energy of the normal state, matching the energy of three helium nuclei, but (for reasons I'll come to presently) not more than 7.7 MeV above the normal state.

This radioactive state of a carbon nucleus could be easily formed in stars from three helium nuclei. After that, there would be no problem in producing ordinary carbon; the carbon nucleus in its radioactive state would spontaneously emit light and turn into carbon in its normal nonradioactive state, the state found on earth. The critical point in producing carbon is the existence of a radioactive state that can be produced in collisions of three helium nuclei.

In fact, the carbon nucleus is known experimentally to have just such a radioactive state, with an energy 7.65 MeV above the normal state. At first sight this may seem like a pretty close call; the energy of this radioactive state of carbon misses being too high to allow the formation of carbon (and hence of us) by only 0.05 MeV, which is less than one percent of 7.65 MeV. It may appear that the constants of nature on which the properties of all nuclei depend have been carefully fine-tuned to make life possible.

Looked at more closely, the fine-tuning of the constants of nature here does not seem so fine. We have to consider the reason why the formation of carbon in stars requires the existence of a radioactive state of carbon with an energy not more than 7.7 MeV above the energy of the normal state. The reason is that the carbon nuclei in this state are actually formed in a two-step process: first, two helium nuclei combine to form the unstable nucleus of a beryllium isotope, beryllium 8, which occasionally, before it falls apart, captures another helium nucleus, forming a carbon nucleus in its radioactive state, which then decays into normal carbon. The total energy of the beryllium 8 nucleus and a helium nucleus at rest is 7.4 MeV above the energy of the normal state of the carbon nucleus, so if the energy of the radioactive state of carbon were more than 7.7 MeV, it could only be formed in a collision of a helium nucleus and a beryllium 8 nucleus if the energy of motion of these two nuclei were at least 0.3 MeV — an energy that is extremely unlikely at the temperatures found in stars.

Thus the crucial thing that affects the production of carbon in stars is not the 7.65 MeV energy of the radioactive state of carbon above its normal state, but the 0.25 MeV energy of the radioactive state, an unstable composite of a beryllium 8 nucleus and a nucleus, above the energy of those nuclei at rest.[1] This energy misses being too high for the production of carbon by a fractional amount of 0.05 MeV/0.25 MeV, or 20 percent, which is not such a close call after all.

This conclusion about the lessons to be learned from carbon synthesis is somewhat controversial. In any case, there *is* one constant whose value does seem remarkably well adjusted in our favor. It is the energy density of empty space, also known as the cosmological constant. It could have any value, but from first principles one would guess that this constant should be very large, and could be positive or negative. If large and positive, the cosmological constant would act as a repulsive force that increases with distance, a force that would prevent matter from clumping together in the early universe, the process that was the first step in forming galaxies and stars and planets and people. If large and negative, the cosmological constant would act as an attractive force increasing with distance, a force that would almost immediately reverse the expansion of the universe and cause it to recollapse, leaving no time for the evolution of life. In fact, astronomical observations show that the cosmological constant is quite small, very much smaller than would have been guessed from first principles.

It is still too early to tell whether there is some fundamental principle that can explain why the cosmological constant must be this small. But even if there is no such principle, recent developments in cosmology offer the possibility of an explanation of why the measured values of the cosmological constant and other physical constants are favorable for the appearance of intelligent life. According to the "chaotic inflation" theories of André Linde and others, the expanding cloud of billions of galaxies that we call the big bang may be just one fragment of a much larger universe in which big bangs go off all the time, each one with different values for the fundamental constants.

In any such picture, in which the universe contains many parts with different values for what we call the constants of nature, there would be no difficulty in understanding why these constants take values favorable to intelligent life. There would be a vast number of big bangs in which the constants of nature take values unfavorable for life, and many fewer where life is possible. You don't have to invoke a benevolent designer to explain why we are in one of the parts of the universe where life is possible: in all the

---

[1]This was pointed out in a 1989 paper by M. Uvio, D. Hollowell, A. Weiss, and J. W. Truran, "The anthropic significance of the existence of an excited state of ^{12}C," *Nature* 340, no. 6231 (July 27, 1989). They did the calculation quoted here of the 7.7 MeV maximum energy of the radioactive state of carbon, above which little carbon is formed in stars.

other parts of the universe there is no one to raise the question.[2] If any theory of this general type turns out to be correct, then to conclude that the constants of nature have been fine-tuned by a benevolent designer would be like saying, "Isn't it wonderful that God put us here on earth, where there's water and air and the surface gravity and temperature are so comfortable, rather than some horrid place like Mercury or Pluto?" Where else in the solar system other than on earth could we have evolved?

Reasoning like this is called "anthropic." Sometimes it just amounts to an assertion that the laws of nature are what they are so that we can exist, without further explanation. This seems to me to be little more than mystical mumbo-jumbo. On the other hand, if there really is a large number of worlds in which some constants take different values, then the anthropic explanation of why in our world they take values favorable for life is just common sense, like explaining why we live on the earth rather than Mercury or Pluto. The actual value of the cosmological constant, recently measured by observations of the motion of distant supernovas, is about what you would expect from this sort of argument: it is just about small enough so that it does not interfere much with the formation of galaxies. But we don't yet know enough about physics to tell whether there are different parts of the universe in which what are usually called the constants of physics really do take different values. This is not a hopeless question; we will be able to answer it when we know more about the quantum theory of gravitation than we do now.

It would be evidence for a benevolent designer if life were better than could be expected on other grounds. To judge this, we should keep in mind that a certain capacity for pleasure would readily have evolved through natural selection, as an incentive to animals who need to eat and breed in order to pass on their genes. It may not be likely that natural selection on any one planet would produce animals who are fortunate enough to have the leisure and the ability to do science and think abstractly, but our sample of what is produced by evolution is very biased, by the fact that it is only in these fortunate cases that there is anyone thinking about cosmic design. Astronomers call this a selection effect.

The universe is very large, and perhaps infinite, so it should be no surprise that among the enormous number of planets that may support only

---

[2]The same conclusion may be reached in a subtler way when quantum mechanics is applied to the whole universe. Through a reinterpretation of earlier work by Stephen Hawking, Sidney Coleman has shown how quantum mechanical effects can lead to a split of the history of the universe (more precisely, in what is called the wave function of the universe) into a huge number of separate possibilities each one corresponding to a different set of fundamental constants. See Sidney Coleman, "Black holes as red herrings: Topological fluctuations and the loss of quantum coherence," *Nuclear Physics* B307(1988): 867.

unintelligent life and the still vaster number that cannot support life at all, there is some tiny fraction on which there are living beings who are capable of thinking about the universe, as we are doing here. A journalist who has been assigned to interview lottery winners may come to feel that some special providence has been at work on their behalf, but he should keep in mind the much larger number of lottery players whom he is not interviewing because they haven't won anything. Thus, to judge whether our lives show evidence for a benevolent designer, we not only have to ask whether life is better than would be expected in any case from what we know about natural selection, but we need also to take into account the bias introduced by the fact that it is we who are thinking about the problem.

This is a question that you all will have to answer for yourselves. Being a physicist is no help with questions like this, so I have to speak from my own experience. My life has been remarkably happy, perhaps in the upper 99.99 percentile of human happiness, but even so, I have seen a mother die painfully of cancer, a father's personality destroyed by Alzheimer's disease, and scores of second and third cousins murdered in the Holocaust. Signs of a benevolent designer are pretty well hidden.

The prevalence of evil and misery has always bothered those who believe in a benevolent and omnipotent God. Sometimes God is excused by pointing to the need for free will. Milton gives God this argument in *Paradise Lost*:

> I formed them free, and free they must remain
> Till they enthrall themselves: I else must change
> Their nature, and revoke the high decree
> Unchangeable, eternal, which ordained
> Their freedom; they themselves ordained their fall.

It seems a bit unfair to my relatives to be murdered in order to provide an opportunity for free will for Germans, but even putting that aside, how does free will account for cancer? Is it an opportunity of free will for tumors?

I don't need to argue here that the evil in the world proves that the universe is not designed, but only that there are no signs of benevolence that might have shown the hand of a designer. But in fact the perception that God cannot be benevolent is very old. Plays by Aeschylus and Euripides make a quite explicit statement that the gods are selfish and cruel, though they expect better behavior from humans. God in the Old Testament tells us to bash the heads of infidels and demands of us that we be willing to sacrifice our children's lives at his orders, and the God of traditional Christianity and Islam damns us for eternity if we do not worship him in the right manner. Is this a nice way to behave? I know, I know, we are not supposed to judge God according to human standards, but you see the problem here: if we are not yet convinced of his existence and are looking for signs of his benevolence, then what other standards *can* we use?

The issues that I have been asked to address here will seem to many to be terribly old-fashioned. The "argument from design" made by the English theologian William Paley is not on most people's minds these days. The prestige of religion seems today to derive from what people take to be its moral influence, rather than from what they may think has been its success in accounting for what we see in nature. Conversely, I have to admit that although I really don't believe in a cosmic designer, the reason I am taking the trouble to argue about it is that I think on balance the moral influence of religion has been awful.

This is much too big a question to be settled here. On one side, I could point out endless examples of the harm done by religious enthusiasm, through a long history of pogroms, crusades, and jihads. In our own century it was a Muslim zealot who killed Sadat, a Jewish zealot who killed Rabin, and a Hindu zealot who killed Gandhi. No one would say that Hitler was a Christian zealot, but it is hard to imagine Nazism taking the form it did without the foundation provided by centuries of Christian anti-Semitism. On the other side, many admirers of religion would set countless examples of the good done by religion. For instance, in his recent book *Imagined Worlds*, the distinguished physicist Freeman Dyson has emphasized the role of religious belief in the suppression of slavery. I'd like to comment briefly on this point, not to try to prove anything with one example but just to illustrate what I think about the moral influence of religion.

It is certainly true that the campaign against slavery and the slave trade was greatly strengthened by devout Christians, including the Evangelical layman William Wilberforce in England and the Unitarian minister William Ellery Channing in America. But Christianity, like other great world religions, lived comfortably with slavery for many centuries, and slavery was endorsed in the New Testament. So what was different for antislavery Christians like Wilberforce and Channing? There had been no discovery of new sacred scriptures, and neither Wilberforce nor Channing claimed to have received any supernatural revelations. Rather, the eighteenth century had seen a widespread increase in rationality and humanitarianism, which led others — for instance, Adam Smith, Jeremy Bentham, and Richard Brinsley Sheridan — also to oppose slavery, on grounds having nothing to do with religion. Lord Mansfield, the author of the decision in Somersett's Case, which ended slavery in England (though not its colonies), was no more than conventionally religious, and his decision did not mention religious arguments. Although Wilberforce was the instigator of the campaign against the slave trade in the 1700s, this movement had essential support from many in Parliament like Fox and Pitt, who were not known for their piety. As far as I can tell, the moral tone of religion benefited more from the spirit of the times than the spirit of the times benefited from religion.

Where religion did make a difference, it was more in support of slavery than in opposition to it. Arguments from scripture were used in Parliament to defend the slave trade. Frederick Douglass told in his *Narrative* how his condition as a slave became worse when his master underwent a religious conversion that allowed him to justify slavery as the punishment of the children of Ham. Mark Twain described his mother as a genuinely good person whose soft heart pitied even Satan but who had no doubt about the legitimacy of slavery, because in years of living in antebellum Missouri, she had never heard any sermon opposing slavery but only countless sermons preaching that slavery was God's will. With or without religion, good people can behave well and bad people can do evil; but for good people to do evil — that takes religion.

In an e-mail message from the American Association for the Advance-   30
ment of Science, I learned that the aim of this conference is to have a constructive dialogue between science and religion. I am all in favor of a dialogue between science and religion, but not a constructive dialogue. One of the great achievements of science has been, if not to make it impossible for intelligent people to be religious, then at least to make it possible for them not to be religious. We should not retreat from this accomplishment.

QUESTIONS

1. What question is Weinberg asking in his essay? Why, according to Weinberg, is this question worth answering?
2. According to Weinberg, what are the limitations of scientific and religious theories of design?
3. Outline Weinberg's argument. What evidence does he offer to support his argument? How does he acknowledge positions counter to his argument?
4. Imagine a conversation between Weinberg and a proponent of intelligent design. On what points would they agree and disagree? Pick one such point, and write a brief exchange to illustrate the differences in points of view.
5. Do you agree with, disagree with, or want to qualify Weinberg's argument? Write a response to Weinberg.
6. Develop a series of questions, and interview ten friends or family members about intelligent design. What do you learn about intelligent design from your interviews? Share your research with your classmates. Write a paper summarizing your research.

MAKING CONNECTIONS

What are the similarities in the questions that Weinberg and Daniel C. Dennett (p. 787) ask? What are the differences? How might each writer go about answering the questions posed by the other?

SHOW ME THE SCIENCE

Daniel C. Dennett

Daniel C. Dennett was born in 1942 in Boston. He earned degrees at Harvard University and Oxford University and currently teaches at Tufts University. He has received many awards and honors, including two Guggenheim Fellowships, a Fulbright Fellowship, and membership in the American Academy of Arts and Sciences. He has published more than one hundred scholarly articles in philosophy journals, including Artificial Intelligence, Behavioral and Brain Sciences, *and* Poetics Today *and has written numerous books, including* Content and Consciousness *(1969),* Consciousness Explained *(1991),* Darwin's Dangerous Idea: Evolution and the Meanings of Life *(1995), and* Breaking the Spell: Religion as a Natural Phenomenon *(2006). Dennett is known for his vivid examples and engaging writing style, which earns him praise even from critics of his philosophical theories. In* Consciousness Explained, *Dennett's belief that evolution can explain some of the content-producing features of consciousness is developed. In* Darwin's Dangerous Idea, *Dennett maintains that even developments that do not appear to follow Darwin's concept of natural selection are in fact outgrowths of this process, although he does not believe that human moral behavior has a purely genetic grounding. The following piece appeared in 2005 in the* New York Times.

President Bush, announcing this month that he was in favor of teaching about "intelligent design" in the schools, said, "I think that part of education is to expose people to different schools of thought." A couple of weeks later, Senator Bill Frist of Tennessee, the Republican leader, made the same point. Teaching both intelligent design and evolution "doesn't force any particular theory on anyone," Mr. Frist said. "I think in a pluralistic society that is the fairest way to go about education and training people for the future."

Is "intelligent design" a legitimate school of scientific thought? Is there something to it, or have these people been taken in by one of the most ingenious hoaxes in the history of science? Wouldn't such a hoax be impossible? No. Here's how it has been done.

First, imagine how easy it would be for a determined band of naysayers to shake the world's confidence in quantum physics — how weird it is! — or Einsteinian relativity. In spite of a century of instruction and popularization by physicists, few people ever really get their heads around the concepts involved. Most people eventually cobble together a justification for accepting the assurances of the experts: "Well, they pretty much agree with one another, and they claim that it is their understanding of these strange topics that allows them to harness atomic energy, and to make transistors and lasers, which certainly do work . . ."

Fortunately for physicists, there is no powerful motivation for such a band of mischief-makers to form. They don't have to spend much time persuading people that quantum physics and Einsteinian relativity really have been established beyond all reasonable doubt.

With evolution, however, it is different. The fundamental scientific idea　　5
of evolution by natural selection is not just mind-boggling; natural selection, by executing God's traditional task of designing and creating all creatures great and small, also seems to deny one of the best reasons we have for believing in God. So there is plenty of motivation for resisting the assurances of the biologists. Nobody is immune to wishful thinking. It takes scientific discipline to protect ourselves from our own credulity, but we've also found ingenious ways to fool ourselves and others. Some of the methods used to exploit these urges are easy to analyze; others take a little more unpacking.

A creationist pamphlet sent to me some years ago had an amusing page in it, purporting to be part of a simple questionnaire:

Test Two
Do you know of any building that didn't have a builder? [YES] [NO]
Do you know of any painting that didn't have a painter? [YES] [NO]
Do you know of any car that didn't have a maker? [YES] [NO]
If you answered YES for any of the above, give details:

Take that, you Darwinians! The presumed embarrassment of the test-taker when faced with this task perfectly expresses the incredulity many people feel when they confront Darwin's great idea. It seems obvious, doesn't it, that there couldn't be any designs without designers, any such creations without a creator.

Well, yes — until you look at what contemporary biology has demonstrated beyond all reasonable doubt: that natural selection — the process in which reproducing entities must compete for finite resources and thereby engage in a tournament of blind trial and error from which improvements automatically emerge — has the power to generate breathtakingly ingenious designs.

Take the development of the eye, which has been one of the favorite challenges of creationists. How on earth, they ask, could that engineering marvel be produced by a series of small, unplanned steps? Only an intelligent designer could have created such a brilliant arrangement of a shape-shifting lens, an aperture-adjusting iris, a light-sensitive image surface of exquisite sensitivity, all housed in a sphere that can shift its aim in a hundredth of a second and send megabytes of information to the visual cortex every second for years on end.

But as we learn more and more about the history of the genes involved,　　10
and how they work — all the way back to their predecessor genes in the

sightless bacteria from which multicelled animals evolved more than a half-billion years ago—we can begin to tell the story of how photosensitive spots gradually turned into light-sensitive craters that could detect the rough direction from which light came, and then gradually acquired their lenses, improving their information-gathering capacities all the while.

We can't yet say what all the details of this process were, but real eyes representative of all the intermediate stages can be found, dotted around the animal kingdom, and we have detailed computer models to demonstrate that the creative process works just as the theory says.

All it takes is a rare accident that gives one lucky animal a mutation that improves its vision over that of its siblings; if this helps it have more off-spring than its rivals, this gives evolution an opportunity to raise the bar and ratchet up the design of the eye by one mindless step. And since these lucky improvements accumulate—this was Darwin's insight—eyes can automatically get better and better and better, without any intelligent designer.

Brilliant as the design of the eye is, it betrays its origin with a tell-tale flaw: the retina is inside out. The nerve fibers that carry the signals from the eye's rods and cones (which sense light and color) lie on top of them, and have to plunge through a large hole in the retina to get to the brain, creating the blind spot. No intelligent designer would put such a clumsy arrangement in a camcorder, and this is just one of hundreds of accidents frozen in evolutionary history that confirm the mindlessness of the historical process.

If you still find Test Two compelling, a sort of cognitive illusion that you can feel even as you discount it, you are like just about everybody else in the world; the idea that natural selection has the power to generate such sophisticated designs is deeply counterintuitive. Francis Crick, one of the discoverers of DNA, once jokingly credited his colleague Leslie Orgel with "Orgel's Second Rule": Evolution is cleverer than you are. Evolutionary biologists are often startled by the power of natural selection to "discover" an "ingenious" solution to a design problem posed in the lab.

This observation lets us address a slightly more sophisticated version of   15
the cognitive illusion presented by Test Two. When evolutionists like Crick marvel at the cleverness of the process of natural selection they are not acknowledging intelligent design. The designs found in nature are nothing short of brilliant, but the process of design that generates them is utterly lacking in intelligence of its own.

Intelligent design advocates, however, exploit the ambiguity between process and product that is built into the word "design." For them, the presence of a finished product (a fully evolved eye, for instance) is evidence of an intelligent design process. But this tempting conclusion is just what evolutionary biology has shown to be mistaken.

Yes, eyes are for seeing, but these and all the other purposes in the natural world can be generated by processes that are themselves without purposes and without intelligence. This is hard to understand, but so is the idea that colored objects in the world are composed of atoms that are not themselves colored, and that heat is not made of tiny hot things.

The focus of intelligent design has, paradoxically, obscured something else: genuine scientific controversies about evolution that abound. In just about every field there are challenges to one established theory or another. The legitimate way to stir up such a storm is to come up with an alternative theory that makes a prediction that is crisply denied by the reigning theory — but that turns out to be true, or that explains something that has been baffling defenders of the status quo, or that unifies two distant theories at the cost of some element of the currently accepted view.

To date, the proponents of intelligent design have not produced anything like that. No experiments with results that challenge any mainstream biological understanding. No observations from the fossil record or genomics or biogeography or comparative anatomy that undermine standard evolutionary thinking.

Instead, the proponents of intelligent design use a ploy that works   20
something like this. First you misuse or misdescribe some scientist's work. Then you get an angry rebuttal. Then, instead of dealing forthrightly with the charges leveled, you cite the rebuttal as evidence that there is a "controversy" to teach.

Note that the trick is content-free. You can use it on any topic. "Smith's work in geology supports my argument that the earth is flat," you say, misrepresenting Smith's work. When Smith responds with a denunciation of your misuse of her work, you respond, saying something like: "See what a controversy we have here? Professor Smith and I are locked in a titanic scientific debate. We should teach the controversy in the classrooms." And here is the delicious part: you can often exploit the very technicality of the issues to your own advantage, counting on most of us to miss the point in all the difficult details.

William Dembski, one of the most vocal supporters of intelligent design, notes that he provoked Thomas Schneider, a biologist, into a response that Dr. Dembski characterizes as "some hair-splitting that could only look ridiculous to outsider observers." What looks to scientists — and is — a knockout objection by Dr. Schneider is portrayed to most everyone else as ridiculous hair-splitting.

In short, no science. Indeed, no intelligent design hypothesis has even been ventured as a rival explanation of any biological phenomenon. This might seem surprising to people who think that intelligent design competes directly with the hypothesis of non-intelligent design by natural selection. But saying, as intelligent design proponents do, "You haven't explained everything yet," is not a competing hypothesis. Evolutionary biology certainly hasn't explained everything that perplexes biologists. But intelligent design hasn't yet tried to explain anything.

To formulate a competing hypothesis, you have to get down in the trenches and offer details that have testable implications. So far, intelligent design proponents have conveniently sidestepped that requirement, claiming that they have no specifics in mind about who or what the intelligent designer might be.

To see this shortcoming in relief, consider an imaginary hypothesis of   25
intelligent design that could explain the emergence of human beings on this
planet:

> About six million years ago, intelligent genetic engineers from
> another galaxy visited Earth and decided that it would be a more
> interesting planet if there was a language-using, religion-forming
> species on it, so they sequestered some primates and genetically re-
> engineered them to give them the language instinct, and enlarged
> frontal lobes for planning and reflection. It worked.

If some version of this hypothesis were true, it could explain how and
why human beings differ from their nearest relatives, and it would discon-
firm the competing evolutionary hypotheses that are being pursued.

We'd still have the problem of how these intelligent genetic engineers
came to exist on their home planet, but we can safely ignore that complication for the time being, since there is not the slightest shred of evidence in
favor of this hypothesis.

But here is something the intelligent design community is reluctant to
discuss: no other intelligent-design hypothesis has anything more going for
it. In fact, my farfetched hypothesis has the advantage of being testable in
principle: we could compare the human and chimpanzee genomes, looking
for unmistakable signs of tampering by these genetic engineers from another
galaxy. Finding some sort of user's manual neatly embedded in the apparently functionless "junk DNA" that makes up most of the human genome
would be a Nobel Prize–winning coup for the intelligent design gang, but if
they are looking at all, they haven't come up with anything to report.

It's worth pointing out that there are plenty of substantive scientific
controversies in biology that are not yet in the textbooks or the classrooms.
The scientific participants in these arguments vie for acceptance among the
relevant expert communities in peer-reviewed journals, and the writers and
editors of textbooks grapple with judgment, about which findings have
risen to the level of acceptance — not yet truth — to make them worth serious consideration by undergraduates and high school students.

So get in line, intelligent designers. Get in line behind the hypothesis   30
that life started on Mars and was blown here by a cosmic impact. Get in
line behind the aquatic ape hypothesis, the gestural origin of language hypothesis, and the theory that singing came before language, to mention just
a few of the enticing hypotheses that are actively defended but still insufficiently supported by hard facts.

The Discovery Institute, the conservative organization that has helped
to put intelligent design on the map, complains that its members face hostility from the established scientific journals. But establishment hostility is not
the real hurdle to intelligent design. If intelligent design were a scientific idea
whose time had come, young scientists would be dashing around their labs,
vying to win the Nobel Prizes that surely are in store for anybody who can
overturn any significant proposition of contemporary evolutionary biology.

Remember cold fusion? The establishment was incredibly hostile to that hypothesis, but scientists around the world rushed to their labs in the effort to explore the idea, in hopes of sharing in the glory if it turned out to be true.

Instead of spending more than $1 million a year on publishing books and articles for non-scientists and on other public relations efforts, the Discovery Institute should finance its own peer-reviewed electronic journal. This way, the organization could live up to its self-professed image: the doughty defenders of brave iconoclasts bucking the establishment. For now, though, the theory they are promoting is exactly what George Gilder, a long-time affiliate of the Discovery Institute, has said it is: "Intelligent design itself does not have any content."

Since there is no content, there is no "controversy" to teach about in biology class. But here is a good topic for a high school course on current events and politics: Is intelligent design a hoax? And if so, how was it perpetrated?

QUESTIONS

1. Dennett poses the question: Is intelligent design a legitimate school of thought? What is Dennett's answer to his own question?
2. Dennett offers an extended example of the development of the eye. What, according to Dennett, does this example explain? What alternative theory would intelligent-design advocates offer to explain the development of the eye?
3. In paragraph 16, Dennett argues that intelligent-design advocates "exploit the ambiguity between process and product that is built into the word 'design.'" How would an intelligent-design advocate respond to this claim?
4. According to Dennett, the nature of science is to formulate competing hypotheses. In an effort to discredit intelligent design, Dennett offers an imaginary hypothesis. What does this imaginary hypothesis explain? Why does he propose an imaginary hypothesis, not a real one?
5. How would an intelligent-design advocate counter Dennett's argument? Imagine the conversation between Dennett and such an advocate.
6. Do you believe that intelligent design should be taught in biology courses? Defend your position.

MAKING CONNECTIONS

Characterize the kinds of evidence presented by Dennett and Steven Weinberg (p. 778), and then compare them. How are the kinds of evidence similar, and how are they different? What kinds of evidence in the pieces do you find most persuasive? Least persuasive?

THE CASE AGAINST PERFECTION

Michael J. Sandel

Michael J. Sandel was born in 1953 and received his undergraduate degree from Brandeis University and his doctorate from Oxford University, where he was a Rhodes scholar. He lives in Brookline, Massachusetts, and is the Anne T. and Robert M. Bass Professor of Government at Harvard University, where he has taught political philosophy since 1980. His publications include Liberalism and the Limits of Justice *(1982), which was translated into seven languages;* Liberalism and Its Critics *(1984);* Democracy's Discontent: America in Search of a Public Philosophy *(1996), a book that touched off widespread discussion about American politics, philosophy, and law; and* Public Philosophy: Essays on Morality in Politics *(2005), in which Sandel examines the role of morality and justice in American political life. He has also published articles in law reviews, scholarly journals, and general periodicals such as* The Atlantic Monthly, The New Republic, *and the* New York Times. *Sandel teaches courses in contemporary political philosophy, and his undergraduate course,* Justice, *has enrolled more than 10,000 students over a twenty-year period, making it one of the most popular courses in Harvard's history. He was awarded the Harvard-Radcliffe Phi Beta Kappa Teaching Prize and in 1999 was named a Harvard College Professor. From 2002 to 2005, Sandel served on the President's Council on Bioethics, for which his paper* "What's Wrong with Enhancement" *(2002) explored themes similar to those found in the following essay, which appeared in* The Atlantic Monthly *in 2004.*

Breakthroughs in genetics present us with a promise and a predicament. The promise is that we may soon be able to treat and prevent a host of debilitating diseases. The predicament is that our newfound genetic knowledge may also enable us to manipulate our own nature — to enhance our muscles, memories, and moods; to choose the sex, height, and other genetic traits of our children; to make ourselves "better than well." When science moves faster than moral understanding, as it does today, men and women struggle to articulate their unease. In liberal societies they reach first for the language of autonomy, fairness, and individual rights. But this part of our moral vocabulary is ill equipped to address the hardest questions posed by genetic engineering. The genomic revolution has induced a kind of moral vertigo.

Consider cloning. The birth of Dolly the cloned sheep, in 1997, brought a torrent of concern about the prospect of cloned human beings. There are good medical reasons to worry. Most scientists agree that cloning is unsafe, likely to produce offspring with serious abnormalities. (Dolly recently died a premature death.) But suppose technology improved to the point where clones were at no greater risk than naturally conceived offspring. Would human cloning still be objectionable? Should our hesitation be moral as well as medical? What, exactly, is wrong with creating a child who is a genetic twin of one parent, or of an older sibling who has tragically died — or, for that matter, of an admired scientist, sports star, or celebrity?

Some say cloning is wrong because it violates the right to autonomy: by choosing a child's genetic makeup in advance, parents deny the child's right to an open future. A similar objection can be raised against any form of bioengineering that allows parents to select or reject genetic characteristics. According to this argument, genetic enhancements for musical talent, say, or athletic prowess, would point children toward particular choices, and so designer children would never be fully free.

At first glance the autonomy argument seems to capture what is troubling about human cloning and other forms of genetic engineering. It is not persuasive, for two reasons. First, it wrongly implies that absent a designing parent, children are free to choose their characteristics for themselves. But none of us chooses his genetic inheritance. The alternative to a cloned or genetically enhanced child is not one whose future is unbound by particular talents but one at the mercy of the genetic lottery.

Second, even if a concern for autonomy explains some of our worries   5
about made-to-order children, it cannot explain our moral hesitation about people who seek genetic remedies or enhancements for themselves. Gene therapy on somatic (that is, nonreproductive) cells, such as muscle cells and brain cells, repairs or replaces defective genes. The moral quandary arises when people use such therapy not to cure a disease but to reach beyond health, to enhance their physical or cognitive capacities, to lift themselves above the norm.

Like cosmetic surgery, genetic enhancement employs medical means for nonmedical ends — ends unrelated to curing or preventing disease or repairing injury. But unlike cosmetic surgery, genetic enhancement is more than skin-deep. If we are ambivalent about surgery or Botox injections for sagging chins and furrowed brows, we are all the more troubled by genetic engineering for stronger bodies, sharper memories, greater intelligence, and happier moods. The question is whether we are right to be troubled, and if so, on what grounds.

In order to grapple with the ethics of enhancement, we need to confront questions largely lost from view — questions about the moral status of nature, and about the proper stance of human beings toward the given world. Since these questions verge on theology, modern philosophers and political theorists tend to shrink from them. But our new powers of biotechnology make them unavoidable. To see why this is so, consider four examples already on the horizon: muscle enhancement, memory enhancement, growth-hormone treatment, and reproductive technologies that enable parents to choose the sex and some genetic traits of their children. In each case what began as an attempt to treat a disease or prevent a genetic disorder now beckons as an instrument of improvement and consumer choice.

Muscles

Everyone would welcome a gene therapy to alleviate muscular dystropy and to reverse the debilitating muscle loss that comes with old age. But what if the same therapy were used to improve athletic performance? Researchers have developed a synthetic gene that, when injected into the muscle cells of mice, prevents and even reverses natural muscle deterioration. The gene not only repairs wasted or injured muscles but also strengthens healthy ones. This success bodes well for human application. H. Lee Sweeney, of the University of Pennsylvania, who leads the research, hopes his discovery will cure the immobility that afflicts the elderly. But Sweeney's bulked-up mice have already attracted the attention of athletes seeking a competitive edge. Although the therapy is not yet approved for human use, the prospect of genetically enhanced weight lifters, home-run sluggers, linebackers, and sprinters is easy to imagine. The widespread use of steroids and other performance-improving drugs in professional sports suggests that many athletes will be eager to avail themselves of genetic enhancement.

Suppose for the sake of argument that muscle-enhancing gene therapy, unlike steroids, turned out to be safe — or at least no riskier than a rigorous weight-training regimen. Would there be a reason to ban its use in sports? These is something unsettling about the image of genetically altered athletes lifting SUVs or hitting 650-foot home runs or running a three-minute mile. But what, exactly, is troubling about it? Is it simply that we find such superhuman spectacles too bizarre to contemplate? Or does our unease point to something of ethical significance?

It might be argued that a genetically enhanced athlete, like a drug- 10 enhanced athlete, would have an unfair advantage over his unenhaneed competitors. But the fairness argument against enhancement has a fatal flaw: it has always been the case that some athletes are better endowed genetically than others, and yet we do not consider this to undermine the fairness of competitive sports. From the standpoint of fairness, enhanced genetic differences would be no worse than natural ones, assuming they were safe and made available to all. If genetic enhancement in sports is morally objectionable, it must be for reasons other than fairness.

Memory

Genetic enhancement is possible for brains as well as brawn. In the mid-1990s scientists managed to manipulate a memory-linked gene in fruit flies, creating flies with photographic memories. More recently researchers have produced smart mice by inserting extra copies of a memory-related gene into mouse embryos. The altered mice learn more quickly and remember things longer than normal mice. The extra copies were programmed to remain active even in old age, and the improvement was passed on to offspring.

Human memory is more complicated, but biotech companies, including Memory Pharmaceuticals, are in hot pursuit of memory-enhancing drugs, or "cognition enhancers," for human beings. The obvious market for such drugs consists of those who suffer from Alzheimer's and other serious memory disorders. The companies also have their sights on a bigger market: the 81 million Americans over fifty, who are beginning to encounter the memory loss that comes naturally with age. A drug that reversed age-related memory loss would be a bonanza for the pharmaceutical industry: a Viagra for the brain. Such use would straddle the line between remedy and enhancement. Unlike a treatment for Alzheimer's, it would cure no disease; but insofar as it restored capacities a person once possessed, it would have a remedial aspect. It could also have purely nonmedical uses: for example, by a lawyer cramming to memorize facts for an upcoming trial, or by a business executive eager to learn Mandarin on the eve of his departure for Shanghai.

Some who worry about the ethics of cognitive enhancement point to the danger of creating two classes of human beings: those with access to enhancement technologies, and those who must make do with their natural capacities. And if the enhancements could be passed down the generations, the two classes might eventually become subspecies — the enhanced and the merely natural. But worry about access ignores the moral status of enhancement itself. Is the scenario troubling because the unenhanced poor would be denied the benefits of bioengineering, or because the enhanced affluent would somehow be dehumanized? As with muscles, so with memory: the fundamental question is not how to ensure equal access to enhancement but whether we should aspire to it in the first place.

Height

Pediatricians already struggle with the ethics of enhancement when confronted by parents who want to make their children taller. Since the 1980s human growth hormone has been approved for children with a hormone deficiency that makes them much shorter than average. But the treatment also increases the height of healthy children.

Some parents of healthy children who are unhappy with their stature   15
(typically boys) ask why it should make a difference whether a child is short

because of a hormone deficiency or because his parents happen to be short. Whatever the cause, the consequences are the same.

In the face of this argument some doctors began prescribing hormone treatments for children whose short stature was unrelated to any medical problem. By 1996 such "off-label" use accounted for 40 percent of human-growth-hormone prescriptions. Although it is legal to prescribe drugs for purposes not approved by the Food and Drug Administration, pharmaceutical companies cannot promote such use. Seeking to expand its market, Eli Lilly & Co. recently persuaded the FDA to approve its human growth hormone for healthy children whose projected adult height is in the bottom one percentile — under five feet three inches for boys and four feet eleven inches for girls. This concession raises a large question about the ethics of enhancement: If hormone treatments need not be limited to those with hormone deficiencies, why should they be available only to very short children? Why shouldn't all shorter-than-average children be able to seek treatment? And what about a child of average height who wants to be taller so that he can make the basketball team?

Some oppose height enhancement on the grounds that it is collectively self-defeating; as some become taller, others become shorter relative to the norm. Except in Lake Wobegon, not every child can be above average. As the unenhanced began to feel shorter, they, too, might seek treatment, leading to a hormonal arms race that left everyone worse off, especially those who couldn't afford to buy their way up from shortness.

But the arms-race objection is not decisive on its own. Like the fairness objection to bioengineered muscles and memory, it leaves unexamined the attitudes and dispositions that prompt the drive for enhancement. If we were bothered only by the injustice of adding shortness to the problems of the poor, we could remedy that unfairness by publicly subsidizing height enhancements. As for the relative height deprivation suffered by innocent bystanders, we could compensate them by taxing those who buy their way to greater height. The real question is whether we want to live in a society where parents feel compelled to spend a fortune to make perfectly healthy kids a few inches taller.

Sex Selection

Perhaps the most inevitable nonmedical use of bioengineering is sex selection. For centuries parents have been trying to choose the sex of their children. Today biotech succeeds where folk remedies failed.

One technique for sex selection arose with prenatal tests using amnio- 20 centesis and ultrasound. These medical technologies were developed to detect genetic abnormalities such as spina bifida and Down syndrome. But they can also reveal the sex of the fetus — allowing for the abortion of a fetus of an undesired sex. Even among those who favor abortion rights, few advocate abortion simply because the parents do not want a girl. Nevertheless, in traditional societies with a powerful cultural preference for boys, this practice has become widespread.

Sex selection need not involve abortion, however. For couples undergoing *in vitro* fertilization (IVF), it is possible to choose the sex of the child before the fertilized egg is implanted in the womb. One method makes use of pre-implantation genetic diagnosis (PGD), a procedure developed to screen for genetic diseases. Several eggs are fertilized in a petri dish and grown to the eight-cell stage (about three days). At that point the embryos are tested to determine their sex. Those of the desired sex are implanted; the others are typically discarded. Although few couples are likely to undergo the difficulty and expense of IVF simply to choose the sex of their child, embryo screening is a highly reliable means of sex selection. And as our genetic knowledge increases, it may be possible to use PGD to cull embryos carrying undesired genes, such as those associated with obesity, height, and skin color. The science-fiction movie *Gattaca* depicts a future in which parents routinely screen embryos for sex, height, immunity to disease, and even IQ. There is something troubling about the *Gattaca* scenario, but it is not easy to identify what exactly is wrong with screening embryos to choose the sex of our children.

One line of objection draws on arguments familiar from the abortion debate. Those who believe that an embryo is a person reject embryo screening for the same reasons they reject abortion. If an eight-cell embryo growing in a petri dish is morally equivalent to a fully developed human being, then discarding it is no better than aborting a fetus, and both practices are equivalent to infanticide. Whatever its merits, however, this "pro-life" objection is not an argument against sex selection as such.

The latest technology poses the question of sex selection unclouded by the matter of an embryo's moral status. The Genetics & IVF Institute, a for-profit infertility clinic in Fairfax, Virginia, now offers a sperm-sorting technique that makes it possible to choose the sex of one's child before it is conceived. X-bearing sperm, which produce girls, carry more DNA than Y-bearing sperm, which produce boys; a device called a flow cytometer can separate them. The process, called MicroSort, has a high rate of success.

If sex selection by sperm sorting is objectionable, it must be for reasons that go beyond the debate about the moral status of the embryo. One such reason is that sex selection is an instrument of sex discrimination — typically against girls, as illustrated by the chilling sex ratios in India and China. Some speculate that societies with substantially more men than women will be less stable, more violent, and more prone to crime or war. These are legitimate worries — but the sperm-sorting company has a clever way of addressing them. It offers MicroSort only to couples who want to choose the sex of a child for purposes of "family balancing." Those with more sons than daughters may choose a girl, and vice versa. But customers may not use the technology to stock up on children of the same sex, or even to choose the sex of their firstborn child. (So far the majority of MicroSort clients have chosen girls.) Under restrictions of this kind, do any ethical issues remain that should give us pause?

The case of MicroSort helps us isolate the moral objections that would persist if muscle-enhancement, memory-enhancement, and height-enhancement technologies were safe and available to all.

It is commonly said that generic enhancements undermine our humanity by threatening our capacity to act freely, to succeed by our own efforts, and to consider ourselves responsible — worthy of praise or blame — for the things we do and for the way we are. It is one thing to hit seventy home runs as the result of disciplined training and effort, and something else, something less, to hit them with the help of steroids or genetically enhanced muscles. Of course, the roles of effort and enhancement will be a matter of degree. But as the role of enhancement increases, our admiration for the achievement fades — or, rather, our admiration for the achievement shifts from the player to his pharmacist. This suggests that our moral response to enhancement is a response to the diminished agency of the person whose achievement is enhanced.

Though there is much to be said for this argument, I do not think the main problem with enhancement and genetic engineering is that they undermine effort and erode human agency. The deeper danger is that they represent a kind of hyperagency — a Promethean aspiration to remake nature, including human nature, to serve our purposes and satisfy our desires. The problem is not the drift to mechanism but the drive to mastery. And what the drive to mastery misses and may even destroy is an appreciation of the gifted character of human powers and achievements.

To acknowledge the giftedness of life is to recognize that our talents and powers are not wholly our own doing, despite the effort we expend to develop and to exercise them. It is also to recognize that not everything in the world is open to whatever use we may desire or devise. Appreciating the gifted quality of life constrains the Promethean project and conduces to a certain humility. It is in part a religious sensibility. But its resonance reaches beyond religion.

It is difficult to account for what we admire about human activity and achievement without drawing upon some version of this idea. Consider two types of athletic achievement. We appreciate players like Pete Rose, who are not blessed with great natural gifts but who manage, through striving, grit, and determination, to excel in their sport. But we also admire players like Joe DiMaggio, who display natural gifts with grace and effortlessness. Now, suppose we learned that both players took performance-enhancing drugs. Whose turn to drugs would we find more deeply disillusioning? Which aspect of the athletic ideal — effort or gift — would be more deeply offended?

Some might say effort: the problem with drugs is that they provide a shortcut, a way to win without striving. But striving is not the point of sports; excellence is. And excellence consists at least partly in the display of natural talents and gifts that are no doing of the athlete who possesses them. This is an uncomfortable fact for democratic societies. We want to believe that success, in sports and in life, is something we earn, not something we inherit. Natural gifts, and the admiration they inspire, embarrass the meritocratic faith; they cast doubt on the conviction that praise and rewards flow from effort alone. In the face of this embarrassment we inflate the moral significance of striving, and depreciate giftedness. This distortion can be seen, for example, in network-television coverage of the Olympics, which focuses less on the feats the athletes perform than on heartrending stories of the hardships they have overcome and the struggles they have waged to triumph over an injury or a difficult upbringing or political turmoil in their native land.

But effort isn't everything. No one believes that a mediocre basketball player who works and trains even harder than Michael Jordan deserves greater acclaim or a bigger contract. The real problem with genetically altered athletes is that they corrupt athletic competition as a human activity that honors the cultivation and display of natural talents. From this standpoint, enhancement can be seen as the ultimate expression of the ethic of effort and willfulness — a kind of high-tech striving. The ethic of willfulness and the biotechnological powers it now enlists are arrayed against the claims of giftedness.

The ethic of giftedness, under siege in sports, persists in the practice of parenting. But here, too, bioengineering and genetic enhancement threaten to dislodge it. To appreciate children as gifts is to accept them as they come, not as objects of our design or products of our will or instruments of our ambition. Parental love is not contingent on the talents and attributes a child happens to have. We choose our friends and spouses at least partly on the basis of qualities we find attractive. But we do not choose our children. Their qualities are unpredictable, and even the most conscientious parents cannot be held wholly responsible for the kind of children they have. That is why parenthood, more than other human relationships, teaches what the theologian William F. May calls an "openness to the unbidden."

May's resonant phrase helps us see that the deepest moral objection to enhancement lies less in the perfection it seeks than in the human disposition it expresses and promotes. The problem is not that parents usurp the autonomy of a child they design. The problem lies in the hubris of the designing parents, in their drive to master the mystery of birth. Even if this disposition did not make parents tyrants to their children, it would disfigure the relation between parent and child, and deprive the parent of the humility and enlarged human sympathies that an openness to the unbidden can cultivate.

To appreciate children as gifts or blessings is not, of course, to be passive in the face of illness or disease. Medical intervention to cure or prevent illness or restore the injured to health does not desecrate nature but honors it. Healing sickness or injury does not override a child's natural capacities but permits them to flourish.

Nor does the sense of life as a gift mean that parents must shrink from   35
shaping and directing the development of their child. Just as athletes and
artists have an obligation to cultivate their talents, so parents have an obligation to cultivate their children, to help them discover and develop their
talents and gifts. As May points out, parents give their children two kinds
of love: accepting love and transforming love. Accepting love affirms the
being of the child, whereas transforming love seeks the well-being of the
child. Each aspect corrects the excesses of the other, he writes: "Attachment
becomes too quietistic if it slackens into mere acceptance of the child as he
is." Parents have a duty to promote their children's excellence.

These days, however, overly ambitious parents are prone to get carried
away with transforming love — promoting and demanding all manner of
accomplishments from their children, seeking perfection. "Parents find it
difficult to maintain an equilibrium between the two sides of love," May observes. "Accepting love, without transforming love, slides into indulgence
and finally neglect. Transforming love, without accepting love, badgers and
finally rejects." May finds in these competing impulses a parallel with modern science: it, too, engages us in beholding the given world, studying and
savoring it, and also in molding the world, transforming and perfecting it.

The mandate to mold our children, to cultivate and improve them,
complicates the case against enhancement. We usually admire parents who
seek the best for their children, who spare no effort to help them achieve
happiness and success. Some parents confer advantages on their children by
enrolling them in expensive schools, hiring private tutors, sending them to
tennis camp, providing them with piano lessons, ballet lessons, swimming
lessons, SAT-prep courses, and so on. If it is permissible and even admirable
for parents to help their children in these ways, why isn't it equally admirable for parents to use whatever genetic technologies may emerge (provided they are safe) to enhance their children's intelligence, musical ability,
or athletic prowess?

The defenders of enhancement are right to this extent: improving children through genetic engineering is similar in spirit to the heavily managed,
high-pressure child-rearing that is now common. But this similarity does
not vindicate genetic enhancement. On the contrary, it highlights a problem
with the trend toward hyperparenting. One conspicuous example of this
trend is sports-crazed parents bent on making champions of their children.
Another is the frenzied drive of overbearing parents to mold and manage
their children's academic careers.

As the pressure for performance increases, so does the need to help dis-
tractible children concentrate on the task at hand. This may be why diag-
noses of attention deficit and hyperactivity disorder have increased so
sharply. Lawrence Diller, a pediatrician and the author of *Running on Ritalin*, estimates that five to six percent of American children under eighteen
(a total of four to five million kids) are currently prescribed Ritalin, Adderall, and other stimulants, the treatment of choice for ADHD. (Stimulants
counteract hyperactivity by making it easier to focus and sustain attention.)

The number of Ritalin prescriptions for children and adolescents has tripled over the past decade, but not all users suffer from attention disorders or hyperactivity. High school and college students have learned that prescription stimulants improve concentration for those with normal attention spans, and some buy or borrow their classmates' drugs to enhance their performance on the SAT or other exams. Since stimulants work for both medical and nonmedical purposes, they raise the same moral questions posed by other technologies of enhancement.

However those questions are resolved, the debate reveals the cultural   40
distance we have traveled since the debate over marijuana, LSD, and other drugs a generation ago. Unlike the drugs of the 1960s and 1970s, Ritalin and Adderall are not for checking out but for buckling down, not for beholding the world and taking it in but for molding the world and fitting in. We used to speak of nonmedical drug use as "recreational." That term no longer applies. The steroids and stimulants that figure in the enhancement debate are not a source of recreation but a bid for compliance — a way of answering a competitive society's demand to improve our performance and perfect our nature. This demand for performance and perfection animates the impulse to rail against the given. It is the deepest source of the moral trouble with enhancement.

Some see a clear line between genetic enhancement and other ways that people seek improvement in their children and themselves. Genetic manipulation seems somehow worse — more intrusive, more sinister — than other ways of enhancing performance and seeking success. But morally speaking, the difference is less significant than it seems. Bioengineering gives us reason to question the low-tech, high-pressure child-rearing practices we commonly accept. The hyperparenting familiar in our time represents an anxious excess of mastery and dominion that misses the sense of life as a gift. This draws it disturbingly dose to eugenics.

The shadow of eugenics hangs over today's debates about genetic engineering and enhancement. Critics of genetic engineering argue that human cloning, enhancement, and the quest for designer children are nothing more than "privatized" or "free-market" eugenics. Defenders of enhancement reply that genetic choices freely made are not really eugenic — at least not in the pejorative sense. "To remove the coercion, they argue, is to remove the very thing that makes eugenic policies repugnant.

Sorting out the lesson of eugenics is another way of wrestling with the ethics of enhancement. The Nazis gave eugenics a bad name. But what, precisely, was wrong with it? Was the old eugenics objectionable only insofar as it was coercive? Or is there something inherently wrong with the resolve to deliberately design our progeny's traits?

James "Watson, the biologist who, with Francis Crick, discovered the structure of DNA, sees nothing wrong with genetic engineering and enhancement, provided they are freely chosen rather than state-imposed. And yet Watson's language contains more than a whiff of the old eugenic sensibility. "If you really are stupid, I would call that a disease," he recently told *The Times* of London. "The lower 10 percent who really have difficulty, even in elementary school. What's the cause of it? A lot of people would like to say, "Well, poverty, things like that.' It probably isn't. So I'd like to get rid of that, to help the lower 10 percent." A few years ago "Watson stirred controversy by saying that if a gene for homosexuality were discovered, a woman should be free to abort a fetus that carried it. When his remark provoked an uproar, he replied that he was not singling out gays but asserting a principle: women should be free to abort fetuses for any reason of genetic preference — for example, if the child would be dyslexic, or lacking musical talent or too short to play basketball.

Watson's scenarios are clearly objectionable to those for whom all   45 abortion is an unspeakable crime. But for those who do not subscribe to the pro-life position, these scenarios raise a hard question: If it is morally troubling to contemplate abortion to avoid a gay child or a dyslexic one, doesn't this suggest that something is wrong with acting on any eugenic preference, even when no state coercion is involved?

Consider the market in eggs and sperm. The advent of artificial insemination allows prospective parents to shop for gametes with the genetic traits they desire in their offspring. It is a less predictable way to design children than cloning or pre-implantation genetic screening, but it offers a good example of a procreative practice in which the old eugenics meets the new consumerism. A few years ago some Ivy League newspapers ran an ad seeking an egg from a woman who was at least five feet ten inches tall and atthletic, had no major family medical problems, and had a combined SAT score of 1400 or above. The ad offered $50,000 for an egg from a donor with these traits. More recently a Web site was launched claiming to auction eggs from fashion models whose photos appeared on the site, at starting bids of $15,000 to $150,000.

On what grounds, if any, is the egg market morally objectionable? Since no one is forced to buy or sell, it cannot be wrong for reasons of coercion. Some might worry that hefty prices would exploit poor women by presenting them with an offer they couldn't refuse. But the designer eggs that fetch the highest prices are likely to be sought from the privileged, not the poor. If the market for premium eggs gives us moral qualms, this, too, shows that concerns about eugenics are not put to rest by freedom of choice.

A tale of two sperm banks helps explain why. The Repository for Germinal Choice, one of America's first sperm banks, was not a commercial enterprise. It was opened in 1980 by Robert Graham, a philanthropist dedicated to improving the wortd's "germ plasm" and counteracting the rise of "retrograde humans." His plan was to collect the sperm of Nobel Prize–winning scientists and make it available to women of high intelligence, in hopes of breeding super-smart babies. But Graham had trouble persuading Nobel laureates to donate their sperm for his bizarre scheme, and so settled for sperm from young scientists of high promise. His sperm bank closed in 1999.

In contrast, California Cryobank, one of the world's leading sperm banks, is a for-profit company with no overt eugenic mission. Cappy Rothman, M.D., a co-founder of the firm, has nothing but disdain for Graham's eugenics, although the standards Cryobank imposes on the sperm it recruits are exacting. Cryobank has offices in Cambridge, Massachusetts, between Harvard and MIT and in Palo Alto, California, near Stanford. It advertises for donors in campus newspapers (compensation up to $900 a month), and accepts less than five percent of the men who apply. Cryobank's marketing materials play up the prestigious source of its sperm. Its catalogue provides detailed information about the physical characteristics of each donor, along with his ethnic origin and college major. For an extra fee prospective customers can buy the results of a test that assesses the donor's temperament and character type. Rothman reports that Cryobank's ideal sperm donor is six feet tall, with brown eyes, blond hair, and dimples, and has a college degree — not because the company wants to propagate those traits, but because those are the traits his customers want: "If our customers wanted high school dropouts, we would give them high school dropouts."

Not everyone objects to marketing sperm. But anyone who is troubled   50
by the eugenic aspect of the Nobel Prize sperm bank should be equally troubled by Cryobank, consumer-driven though it be. What, after all, is the moral difference between designing children according to an explicit eugenic purpose and designing children according to the dictates of the market? Whether the aim is to improve humanity's "germ plasm" or to cater to consumer preferences, both practices are eugenic insofar as both make children into products of deliberate design.

A number of political philosophers call for a new "liberal eugenics." They argue that a moral distinction can be drawn between the old eugenic policies and genetic enhancements that do not restrict the autonomy of the child. "While old-fashioned authoritarian eugenicists sought to produce citizens out of a single centrally designed mould," writes Nicholas Agar, "the distinguishing mark of the new liberal eugenics is state neutrality" Government may not tell parents what sort of children to design, and parents may engineer in their children only those traits that improve their capacities without biasing their choice of life plans. A recent text on genetics and justice, written by the bioethicists Allen Buchanan, Dan W. Brock, Norman Daniels, and Daniel Wikler, offers a similar view. The "bad reputation of eugenics," they write, is due to practices that "might be avoidable in a future eugenic program." The problem with the old eugenics was that its burdens fell disproportionately on the weak and the poor, who were unjustly sterilized and segregated. But provided that the benefits and burdens of genetic improvement are fairly distributed, these bioethicists argue, eugenic measures are unobjectionable and may even be morally required.

The libertarian philosopher Robert Nozick proposed a "genedc supermarket" that would enable parents to order children by design without imposing a single design on the society as a whole: "This supermarket system has the great virtue that it involves no centralized decision fixing the future human type(s)."

Even the leading philosopher of American liberalism, John Rawls, in his classic *A Theory of Justice* (1971), offered a brief endorsement of non-coercive eugenics. Even in a society that agrees to share the benefits and burdens of the genetic lottery, it is "in the interest of each to have greater natural assets," Rawls wrote. "This enables him to pursue a preferred plan of life." The parties to the social contract "want to insure for their descendants the best genetic endowment (assuming their own to be fixed)." Eugenic policies are therefore not only permissible but required as a matter of justice. "Thus over time a society is to take steps at least to preserve the general level of natural abilities and to prevent the diffusion of serious defects."

But removing the coercion does not vindicate eugenics. The problem with eugenics and genetic engineering is that they represent the one-sided triumph of willfulness over giftedness, of dominion over reverence, of molding over beholding. Why, we may wonder, should we worry about this triumph? Why not shake off our unease about genetic enhancement as so much superstition? What would be lost if biotechnology dissolved our sense of giftedness?

From a religious standpoint the answer is clear: To believe that our talents and powers are wholly our own doing is to misunderstand our place in creation, to confuse our role with God's. Religion is not the only source of reasons to care about giftedness, however. The moral stakes can also be described in secular terms. If bioengineering made the myth of the "self-made man" come true, it would be difficult to view our talents as gifts for which we are indebted, rather than as achievements for which we are responsible. This would transform three key features of our moral landscape: humility, responsibility, and solidarity.

In a social world that prizes mastery and control, parenthood is a school for humility. That we care deeply about our children and yet cannot choose the kind we want teaches parents to be open to the unbidden. Such openness is a disposition worth affirming, not only within families but in the wider world as well. It invites us to abide the unexpected, to live with dissonance, to rein in the impulse to control. A *Gattaca*-like world in which parents became accustomed to specifying the sex and generic traits of their children would be a world inhospitable to the unbidden, a gated community writ large. The awareness that our talents and abilities are not wholly our own doing restrains our tendency toward hubris.

Though some maintain that generic enhancement erodes human agency by overriding effort, the real problem is the explosion, not the erosion, of responsibility. As humility gives way, responsibility expands to daunting proportions. We attribute less to chance and more to choice. Parents become responsible for choosing, or failing to choose, the right traits for their children. Athletes become responsible for acquiring, or failing to acquire, the talents that will help their teams win.

One of the blessings of seeing ourselves as creatures of nature, God, or fortune is that we are not wholly responsible for the way we are. The more we become masters of our genetic endowments, the greater the burden we bear for the talents we have and the way we perform. Today when a basketball player misses a rebound, his coach can blame him for being out of position. Tomorrow the coach may blame him for being too short. Even now the use of performance-enhancing drugs in professional sports is subtly transforming the expectations players have for one another; on some teams players who take the field free from amphetamines or other stimulants are criticized for "playing naked."

The more alive we are to the chanced nature of our lot, the more reason we have to share our fate with others. Consider insurance. Since people do not know whether or when various ills will befall them, they pool their risk by buying health insurance and life insurance. As life plays itself out, the healthy wind up subsidizing the unhealthy, and those who live to a ripe old age wind up subsidizing the families of those who die before their time. Even without a sense of mutual obligation, people pool their risks and resources and share one another's fate.

But insurance markets mimic solidarity only insofar as people do not   60
know or control their own risk factors. Suppose genetic testing advanced to the point where it could reliably predict each person's medical future and life expectancy. Those confident of good health and long life would opt out of the pool, causing other people's premiums to skyrocket. The solidarity of insurance would disappear as those with good genes fled the actuarial company of those with bad ones.

The fear that insurance companies would use genetic data to assess risks and set premiums recently led the Senate to vote to prohibit genetic discrimination in health insurance. But the bigger danger, admittedly more speculative, is that genetic enhancement, if routinely practiced, would make it harder to foster the moral sentiments that social solidarity requires.

Why, after all, do the successful owe anything to the least-advantaged members of society? The best answer to this question leans heavily on the notion of giftedness. The natural talents that enable the successful to flourish are not their own doing but, rather, their good fortune — a result of the genetic lottery. If our genetic endowments are gifts, rather than achievements for which we can claim credit, it is a mistake and a conceit to assume that we are entitled to the full measure of the bounty they reap in a market economy. We therefore have an obligation to share this bounty with those who, through no fault of their own, lack comparable gifts.

A lively sense of the contingency of our gifts — a consciousness that none of us is wholly responsible for his or her success — saves a meritocratic society from sliding into the smug assumption that the rich are rich because they are more deserving than the poor. Without this, the successful would become even more likely than they are now to view themselves as self-made and self-sufficient, and hence wholly responsible for their success. Those at the bottom of society would be viewed not as disadvantaged, and thus worthy of a measure of compensation, but as simply unfit, and thus worthy of eugenic repair. The meritocracy, less chastened by chance, would become harder, less forgiving. As perfect genetic knowledge would end the simulacrum of solidarity in insurance markets, so perfect generic control would erode the actual solidarity that arises when men and women reflect on the contingency of their talents and fortunes.

Thirty-five years ago Robert L. Sinsheimer, a molecular biologist at the California Institute of Technology, glimpsed the shape of things to come. In an article titled "The Prospect of Designed Genetic Change" he argued that freedom of choice would vindicate the new genetics, and set it apart from the discredited eugenics of old.

> To implement the older eugenics . . . would have required a massive social programme carried out over many generations. Such a programme could not have been initiated without the consent and co-operation of a major fraction of the population, and would have been continuously subject to social control. In contrast, the new eugenics could, at least in principle, be implemented on a quite individual basis, in one generation, and subject to no existing restrictions.

According to Sinsheimer, the new eugenics would be voluntary rather than coerced, and also more humane. Rather than segregating and eliminating the unfit, it would improve them. "The old eugenics would have required a continual selection for breeding of the fit, and a culling of the unfit," he wrote. "His new eugenics would permit in principle the conversion of all the unfit to the highest genetic level."

Sinsheimer's paean to genetic engineering caught the heady, Promethean self-image of the age. He wrote hopefully of rescuing "the losers in that chromosomal lottery that so firmly channels our human destinies," including not only those born with genetic defects but also "the 50,000,000 'normal' Americans with an IQ of less than 90." But he also saw that something bigger than improving on nature's "mindless, age-old throw of dice" was at stake. Implicit in technologies of genetic intervention was a more exalted place for human beings in the cosmos. "As we enlarge man's freedom, we diminish his constraints and that which he must accept as given," he wrote. Copernicus and Darwin had "demoted man from his bright glory at the focal point of the universe," but the new biology would restore his central role. In the mirror of our genetic knowledge we would see ourselves as more than a link in the chain of evolution: "We can be the agent of transition to a whole new pitch of evolution. This is a cosmic event."

There is something appealing, even intoxicating, about a vision of human freedom unfettered by the given. It may even be the case that the allure of that vision played a part in summoning the genomic age into being. It is often assumed that the powers of enhancement we now possess arose as an inadvertent by-product of biomedical progress — the genetic revolution came, so to speak, to cure disease, and stayed to tempt us with the prospect of enhancing our performance, designing our children, and perfecting our nature. That may have the story backwards. It is more plausible to view genetic engineering as the ultimate expression of our resolve to see ourselves astride the world, the masters of our nature. But that promise of mastery is flawed. It threatens to banish our appreciation of life as a gift, and to leave us with nothing to affirm or behold outside our own will.

QUESTIONS

1. According to Sandel, what is the promise and the predicament of genetic breakthroughs?
2. Look carefully at the structure of Sandel's argument. How does he identify debates? Synthesize competing positions? Notice questions and implications that arise from this synthesis? Offer counterarguments? Propose solutions?
3. Sandel poses the question: Should parents be able to use whatever genetic technologies are available to enhance their children's intelligence, musical ability, or athletic prowess? What is Sandel's answer to his own question? How does he illustrate the complications of both his question and his answer?
4. Sandel describes an advertisement that offered $50,000 for an egg donor. Do you find such an ad morally objectionable? Develop an argument to explain your position.
5. Sandel asks his readers if we are right to be troubled by the promise and the predicament of genetic breakthroughs. What is your position on this topic?
6. Sandel writes, "When science moves faster than moral understanding, as it does today, men and women struggle to articulate their unease" (paragraph 1). Interview your classmates about their moral comfort or unease about genetic breakthroughs. What do they think is wrong (or right) with designer children, bionic athletes, and genetic engineering? What do you learn from these interviews? Write a report.

MAKING CONNECTIONS

Create an imaginary conversation between Sandel and Jamie Shreeve (p. 692) on the implications of genetic manipulation. Structure it in the form of a dialogue or an interview. What kinds of questions might each ask of the other? What kinds of answers might each provide? Then insert yourself into the conversation. What might you contribute? What are your positions on the issues raised?

Acknowledgments

Diane Ackerman. "Why Leaves Turn Color in the Fall." From *A Natural History of the Senses*. Copyright © 1990 by Diane Ackerman. Reprinted with the permission of Random House, Inc.

Joan Acocella. "Blocked." From *The New Yorker*, June 14/21, 2004. Copyright © 2004 by Joan Acocella. Reprinted with the permission of the author.

Maya Angelou. "Graduation" [editors' title]. From *I Know Why the Caged Bird Sings*. Copyright © 1969 and renewed © 1997 by Maya Angelou. Reprinted with the permission of Random House, Inc.

Peter Applebome, Christopher Drew, Jere Longman, and Andrew Revkin. "A Delicate Balance Is Undone in a Flash, and a Battered City Waits." From *The New York Times*, September 4, 2005. Copyright © 2005 by The New York Times Company. Reprinted with permission.

James Baldwin. "If Black English Isn't a Language, Then Tell Me, What Is?" From *The New York Times*, July 29, 1979, Op-Ed. Copyright © 1979 by James Baldwin. Reprinted by arrangement with the James Baldwin Estate.

John Berger. "Hiroshima." From *The Sense of Sight*. Copyright © 1985 by John Berger. Reprinted with the permission of Pantheon Books, a division of Random House, Inc.

Bruno Bettelheim. "Joey: A 'Mechanical Boy.'" From *Scientific American* Vol. 200 (1959). Copyright © 1959 by Scientific American, Inc. All rights reserved.

Christina Boufis. "Teaching Literature at the County Jail." From *The Common Review* 1, no. 1. Copyright © 2001. Reprinted with the permission of the author.

Jan Harold Brunvand. "Urban Legends: The Boyfriend's Death." From *The Vanishing Hitchhiker: American Urban Legends and Their Meaning*. Copyright © 1981 by Jan Harold Brunvand. Reprinted with the permission of W. W. Norton & Company, Inc.

Susan Choi. "Memorywork." From *Hard Choices: An Iowa Review Reader,* edited by David Hamilton. Originally published in The Iowa Review 23, Spring/Summer 1993. Copyright © 1993. Reprinted with the permission of the author.

Judith Ortiz Cofer. "The Story of My Body." From *The Latin Deli: Prose and Poetry*. Copyright © 1993 by Judith Ortiz Cofer. Reprinted with the permission of The University of Georgia Press.

K. C. Cole. "Fun with Physics: The Woman Leading the Hunt for Nature's Most Elusive Particles." From *The New Yorker*, June 2, 2003. Copyright © 2003 by K. C. Cole. Reprinted with the permission of the author. This piece includes an excerpt from John Updike, "Cosmic Gall," From *Telephone Poles and Other Poems*. Copyright © 1960 by John Updike. Reprinted with the permission of Alfred A. Knopf, a division of Random House, Inc.

Amanda Coyne. "The Long Goodbye: Mother's Day in Federal Prison." From *Harper's*, May 1997. Copyright © 1997 by Harper's Magazine. Reprinted with the permission of *Harper's*. All rights reserved.

Daniel C. Dennett. "Show Me the Science." From *The New York Times*, August 28, 2005. Copyright © 2005 by The New York Times Company. Reprinted with permission.

Joan Didion. "On Keeping a Notebook." From *Slouching Towards Bethlehem*. Copyright © 1966, 1968 by Joan Didion. Reprinted with the permission of Farrar, Straus & Giroux, LLC.

Barbara Ehrenreich. excerpt from *Nickel and Dimed: On (Not) Getting By in America*. Copyright © 1999 by Barbara Ehrenreich. Reprinted with the permission of International Creative Management, Inc.

Marshall Jon Fisher. "Memoria ex Machina." From *Doubletake*, Summer 2002. Copyright © 2002 by Marshall Jon Fisher. Reprinted with the permission of the author.

Anne Frank. "At Home, At School, In Hiding." From *The Diary of a Young Girl: The Definitive Edition*, edited by Otto M. Frank and Mirjam Pressler, translated by Susan Massotty. Translation copyright © 1995 by Doubleday, a division of Random House, Inc. Reprinted with the permission of Doubleday, a division of Random House, Inc.

Elisabeth Kübler-Ross. "On the Fear of Death." From *On Death and Dying.* Copyright © 1969 by Elisabeth Kübler-Ross. Reprinted with the permission of Scribner, an imprint of Simon & Schuster Adult Publishing

Marcus Laffey. "Inside Dope." From *Blue Blood.* Copyright © 1999 by Edward Conlon. Originally published in The New Yorker, February 1, 1999. Reprinted with the permission of Riverhead Books, an imprint of Penguin Group (USA) Inc.

William L. Lawrence. "Atomic Bombing of Nagasaki Told by a Flight Member." From *The New York Times*, September 9, 1945. Copyright © 1945 by The New York Times Company. Reprinted with permission.

Bernard Lewis. "I'm Right, You're Wrong, Go to Hell." From *The Atlantic Monthly*, May 2003. Copyright © 2003 by Bernard Lewis. Reprinted with the permission of the author.

Emily Martin. "The Egg and the Sperm: How Science Has Constructed a Romance Based on Stereotypical Male-Female Roles." From *Signs: Journal of Women in Culture and Society* 16, no. 3. Copyright © 1991 by The University of Chicago Press. Reprinted with the permission of the publisher and the author.

James Alan McPherson. "Problems of Art." From *Elbow Room*, Boston: Little, Brown, 1977. Copyright © 1977 by James Alan McPherson. Reprinted with the permission of the Faith Childs Literary Agency, on behalf of the author.

Stanley Milgram. "Some Conditions of Obedience and Disobedience to Authority." From *Human Relations* 18, no. 1 (1965). Copyright © 1972 by Stanley Milgram. Reprinted with permission. All rights controlled by Alexandra Milgram, Literary Executor.

N. Scott Momaday. "The Way to Rainy Mountain." From *The Way to Rainy Mountain.* Originally published in *The Reporter*, January 26, 1967. Copyright © 1969 by N. Scott Momaday. Reprinted with the permission of The University of New Mexico Press.

Monica M. Moore. "Nonverbal Courtship in Women: Context and Consequences." From *Ethology and Sociobiology* 6, no. 4 (1995). Copyright © 1995 by Monica M. Moore. Reprinted with the permission of the author.

George Orwell. "Politics and the English Language" and "Shooting an Elephant." From *Shooting an Elephant and Other Stories.* Copyright 1950 by Sonia Brownell Orwell and renewed © 1978 by Sonia Pitt-Rivers. Reprinted with the permission of Harcourt, Inc.

Bruce Holland Rogers. "Don Ysidro." From *Polyphony* 3, October 2003. Copyright © 2003 by Bruce Holland Rogers. Reprinted with the permission of the author.

Phyllis Rose. "Tools of Torture: An Essay on Beauty and Pain." From *The Atlantic Monthly*, October 1986. Copyright © 1986 by Phyllis Rose. Reprinted with the permission of The Wylie Agency, Inc.

Oliver Sacks. "The Man Who Mistook His Wife for a Hat." From *The Man Who Mistook His Wife for a Hat and Other Clinical Tales.* Copyright © 1970, 1981, 1983, 1984, 1985 by Oliver Sacks. Reprinted with the permission of Simon & Schuster Adult Publishing Group.

Carl Sagan. "Can We Know the Universe? Reflections on a Grain of Salt." From *Broca's Brain: Reflections on the Romance of Science.* Copyright © 1979 by Carl Sagan. Reprinted with the permission of the Estate of Carl Sagan.

Michael J. Sandel. "The Case against Perfection." From *The Atlantic Monthly* 293, No. 3, April 2004. Copyright © 2004 by Michael J. Sandel. Reprinted with the permission of the author.

Eric Schlosser. "Why McDonald's Fries Taste So Good." From *Fast Food Nation: The Dark Side of the All-American Meal.* Originally published in *The Atlantic Monthly*, January 2001. Reprinted with the permission of Houghton Mifflin Company. All rights reserved.

Serge Schmemann. "U.S. Attacked; Hijacked Jets Destroy Twin Towers and Hit Pentagon in Day of Terror: President Vows to Exact Punishment for Evil." From *The New York Times*, September 12, 2001, p. A1. Copyright © 2001 by The New York Times. Reprinted with permission.

Roy C. Selby Jr. "A Delicate Operation." From *Harper's*, December 1975. Copyright © 1975 by Harper's Magazine. Reprinted with permission. All rights reserved.

Richard Selzer. "A Mask in the Face of Death." From *Life* (1988). Copyright © 1987 by Richard Selzer. Reprinted with the permission of Georges Borchardt, Inc.

Picture Credits

Page 87: © John Madere

Page 91: James Estrin/Copyright © The New York Times Company

Page 142: © Tim Zielenbach/Contact Press Images

Page 243: From *The Great Dialogues of Plato* by Plato, translated by W. H. D. Rouse, copyright © 1956, renewed © 1984 by J. C. G. Rouse. Used by permission of Dutton Signet, a division of Penguin Group (USA) Inc.

Pages 270–271: From *Unforgettable Fire: Pictures Drawn by Atomic Bomb Survivors*, edited by The Japan Broadcasting Association, Copyright © 1977 by NHK. Used by permission of Pantheon Books, a division of Random House, Inc. Photo: General Research Division, The New York Public Library. Courtesy Hiroshima Peace Memorial Museum.

Page 332: Illustration by Al Momaday from *The Way to Rainy Mountain* by N. Scott Momaday, University of New Mexico Press, 1969. © N. Scott Momaday. Photo: General Research Division, The New York Public Library.

Page 377: Alinari/Art Resource, NY

Page 379: Bridgeman-Giraudon/Art Resource, NY

Page 392: AP/Wide World Photos

Pages 396, 397, 402: Photographs and line drawing from *In the Shadow of Man* by Jane Goodall, photographs by Hugo van Lawick. Copyright © 1971 by Hugo and Jane van Lawick-Goodall. Reprinted by permission of Houghton Mifflin Company. All rights reserved.

Page 416: Copyright © 2001 by The New York Times Company

Page 599: Adalberto Rios Szalay/Sexto Sol/Getty Images

Page 640: Tyler Hicks/Copyright © The New York Times Company

Page 641: Vincent Laforet/Copyright © The New York Times Company

Page 647: Irwin Thompson/© Copyright The Dallas Morning News

Page 648: Ross Taylor/© Getty Images

Page 650: Bill Haber/AP/Wide World Photos

Pages 651 and 654: © Erik S. Lesser

Page 652: Stephen Crowley/Copyright © The New York Times Company

Page 655: Robert Sullivan/AFP/Getty Images

Pages 661, 664, 665, 666: Copyright © 1967 by Bruno Bettelheim, by permission of Raines & Raines. First published in *Scientific American*, March 1959, © Scientific American. Drawings on pages 661, 664, 665, and 666 were subsequently reprinted with permission in *The Empty Fortress* by Bruno Bettelheim, The Free Press, NY, 1967. Photos: General Research Division, The New York Public Library. Drawing on page 666 from *Scientific American*, March 1959. Photos: Science, Industry, & Business Library, The New York Public Library.

Page 682: Photo of Janet Conrad courtesy of Fermilab Visual Media Services/Photographer: Reidar Hahn

Page 726: "Interior illustration" by Ron Miller, copyright © 1988 by Ron Miller, from *A Brief History of Time* by Stephen W. Hawking. Used by permission of Bantam Books, a division of Random House, Inc. Photo: General Research Division, The New York Public Library.

Page 736: Chabruken/Taxi/Getty Images

Page 738: Ranald Mackechnie/Photonica/Getty Images

Page 739: Chabruken/Taxi/Getty Images

Page 742: Erik Dreyer/Stone/Getty Images

Page 744: Manfred Baumann/ age fotostock

Rhetorical Index

Author and Title Index